Pearson Arab World Editions—Business & Economics

The Arab world's location between three continents ensures its place at the center of an increasingly integrated global economy, as distinctive as any business culture. We think learning should be as dynamic, relevant, and engaging as the business environment. Our new Arab World Editions for Business & Economics provide this uniquely Arab perspective for students in and of the Arab world.

Each Arab World Edition integrates cases, companies, research, people, and discussions representing the diverse economic, political, and cultural situations across the nations that span the Arab world, whilst retaining the quality, research, and relevant global perspectives of the world's leading business thinkers.

We hope that you find this edition a valuable contribution to your teaching or business studies. We aim to set a new benchmark for contextualized learning with our adapted and new titles, and hope that they will prove a valuable contribution in the success of students and teachers along each step of their business program.

Supplementary support includes PowerPoint slides, instructor manuals, test bank generators, and MyLab online tutorial and homework systems.

Titles span a range of subjects and disciplines, including:

- Management—Robbins & Coulter
- Principles of Marketing—Kotler & Armstrong
- Economics—Hubbard & O'Brien
- Statistics for Business—Benghezal
- Principles of Managerial Finance—Gitman
- Marketing Management—Kotler & Keller
- Organizational Behavior—Robbins & Judge
- Human Resource Management—Dessler
- Strategic Management—David
- Introductory Mathematical Analysis for Business, Economics, and Life and Social Sciences—Haeussler
- Marketing Research—Malhotra
- Operations Management—Heizer
- Auditing and Assurance Services—Arens

To find out more, go to www.pearson.com/middleeast/awe

ALWAYS LEARNING

PEARSON

AUDITING AND ASSURANCE SERVICES

AN INTEGRATED APPROACH

Arab World Edition

ALVIN A. ARENS

PricewaterhouseCoopers
Emeritus Professor
Michigan State University

RANDAL J. ELDER

Syracuse University

MARK S. BEASLEY

North Carolina State University
Deloitte Professor of Enterprise Risk Management

MOHAMED A. HEGAZY

Crowe Horwath Egypt
The American University in Cairo
Cairo University

Acquisitions Editor: Rasheed Roussan
Project Editor: Stephanie Dias
Editor: Fay Gibbons
Copy Editor: Val Rice
Proofreaders: Tammi Merrell, Barbara Eastman, Paul Stirner
Permissions Editor: Rachel Thorne
Marketing Manager: Sue Mainy
Design Manager: Sarah Fach
Picture Researcher: Zohir Naciri
Cover Design: Sarah Fach
Cover Image: Alamy
Indexer: Indexing Specialists (UK) Ltd
Typesetter: Integra
Typeface: 11/12.5 Minion Regular
Printed in the United Kingdom by Ashford Colour Press Ltd.

Pearson Education Limited
Edinburgh Gate
Harlow
Essex CM20 2JE
England

and Associated Companies throughout the world

20 19
IMP 10 9 8 7 6 5 4 3

ISBN-13: 978-1-4082-7241-1
ISBN-10: 1-4082-7241-5

ABOUT THE AUTHORS

Al Arens was the PricewaterhouseCoopers Professor of Accounting Emeritus at Michigan State University. In addition to writing books on auditing, he was a coauthor of computerized accounting supplements and was actively involved in the continuing education of practitioners with local and regional CPA firms. Al was a past president of the American Accounting Association and a former member of the AICPA Auditing Standards Board. He practiced public accounting with both a local CPA firm and the predecessor firm to Ernst & Young. He received many awards including the AAA Auditing Section Outstanding Educator award, the AICPA Outstanding Educator award, the national Beta Alpha Psi Professor of the Year award and many teaching and other awards at Michigan State.

Randy Elder is a Professor of Accounting at Syracuse University. He teaches undergraduate and graduate auditing courses, and has received several teaching awards. His research focuses on audit quality and current audit firm practices. He has extensive public accounting experience with a large regional CPA firm, frequently teaches continuing education for a large international CPA firm, and is a member of the AICPA and Michigan Association of CPAs.

Mark S. Beasley is the Deloitte Professor of Enterprise Risk Management and Professor of Accounting at North Carolina State University. He teaches undergraduate and graduate auditing courses, and has received several teaching awards including membership in NC State's Academy of Outstanding Teachers. He has extensive professional audit experience with the predecessor firm to Ernst & Young and has extensive standards setting experience working with the Auditing Standards Board as a Technical Manager in the Audit and Assurance Division of the AICPA. He served on the ASB's Fraud Standard Task Force responsible for developing SAS 99, the ASB's Antifraud Programs and Controls Task Force, and the Advisory Council overseeing COSO's Enterprise Risk Management Framework project. He is now a member of the COSO Board, representing the AAA.

Mohamed Hegazy is a Professor of Auditing at the School of Business, the American University in Cairo and Cairo University, where he has taught both undergraduate and postgraduate courses, and supervised a number of MSc and PhD theses in accounting and auditing, as well as a number of undergraduate independent projects. He is a member of the Egyptian Society of Accountants and Auditors (ESAA) and partner at Crowe Dr. A.M. Hegazy & Co. He provides assurance services to financial institutions, manufacturing and service companies, hotels and tourism, and insurance companies and is a co-founder and chairman of the Financial Consultancies Company for Marketable Securities. Professor Hegazy has also published several articles in international journals, as well as chapters in international books in the areas of accounting, auditing, and taxation.

BRIEF CONTENTS

CONTENTS

AUDIT REPORTS

CHAPTER 3

LEGAL LIABILITY

CHAPTER 4

PROFESSIONAL ETHICS

CHAPTER 5

PART 2 THE AUDIT PROCESS

CHAPTER 6 AUDIT RESPONSIBILITIES AND OBJECTIVES

CHAPTER 7 AUDIT EVIDENCE

AUDIT PLANNING AND ANALYTICAL PROCEDURES

CHAPTER
8

MATERIALITY AND RISK

CHAPTER
9

INTERNAL CONTROL AND CONTROL RISK

CHAPTER
10

CHAPTER 11

FRAUD AUDITING

CHAPTER 12

THE IMPACT OF INFORMATION TECHNOLOGY ON THE AUDIT PROCESS

CHAPTER 13

THE OVERALL AUDIT PLAN AND AUDIT PROGRAM

APPLICATION OF THE AUDIT PROCESS TO THE SALES AND COLLECTION CYCLE

PART **3**

AUDIT OF THE SALES AND COLLECTION CYCLE: TESTS OF CONTROLS AND SUBSTANTIVE TESTS OF TRANSACTIONS

CHAPTER **14**

AUDIT SAMPLING FOR TESTS OF CONTROLS AND SUBSTANTIVE TESTS OF TRANSACTIONS

CHAPTER **15**

CHAPTER 16

COMPLETING THE TESTS IN THE SALES AND COLLECTION CYCLE: ACCOUNTS RECEIVABLE

CHAPTER 17

AUDIT SAMPLING FOR TESTS OF DETAILS OF BALANCES

APPLICATION OF THE AUDIT PROCESS TO OTHER CYCLES

PART 4

AUDIT OF THE ACQUISITION AND PAYMENT CYCLE: TESTS OF CONTROLS, SUBSTANTIVE TESTS OF TRANSACTIONS, AND ACCOUNTS PAYABLE

CHAPTER 18

COMPLETING THE TESTS IN THE ACQUISITION AND PAYMENT CYCLE: VERIFICATION OF SELECTED ACCOUNTS

CHAPTER 19

AUDIT OF THE PAYROLL AND PERSONNEL CYCLE

CHAPTER 20

PREFACE

INTEGRATED APPROACH FOR RISK ASSESSMENT AND AUDIT DECISION MAKING

Auditing and Assurance Services: Arab World Edition is an introduction to auditing and other assurance services aimed specifically at students studying in the region. It is intended for either a one-quarter or one-semester course at the undergraduate or graduate level. This book is also appropriate for introductory professional development courses for CPA firms, internal auditors, and government auditors.

The primary emphasis in this text is on the auditor's decision-making process during an audit of financial statements. We believe that the most fundamental concepts in auditing concern determining the nature and amount of evidence the auditor should gather after considering the unique circumstances of each engagement. If students of auditing understand the objectives to be accomplished in a given audit area, the risks related to the engagement, and the decisions to be made, they should be able to determine the appropriate evidence to gather and how to evaluate the evidence obtained.

Our objective is to provide up-to-date coverage of auditing concepts with practical examples about the implementation of those concepts in real-world settings—both internationally and within the Arab world. The collective experience of the author team in the practice of auditing is extensive. All four authors have worked in the auditing profession, in large international audit firms as well as regional firms. All four authors have frequently taught continuing education for either large international or small CPA firms and one has extensive practice and experience within the Arab world. Three of the authors have been involved in standards-setting activities of the Auditing Standards Board and the Public Company Accounting Oversight Board (PCAOB), and one currently serves as a board member on the Committee of Sponsoring Organizations of the Treadway Commission (COSO). These experiences provide unique perspectives about the integration of auditing concepts in real-world settings.

Our purpose is to integrate the most important concepts of auditing in a logical manner to assist students in understanding audit decision making and evidence accumulation in today's complex, global auditing environment. For example, the risk assessment standards issued by the International Auditing and Assurance Standards Board are integrated into all of the planning chapters, as well as each chapter dealing with a particular transaction cycle and related accounts. Internal control is related to tests of controls and substantive tests of transactions that are performed in an audit of financial statements. Tests of controls and substantive tests of transactions are, in turn, related to the tests of details of financial statement balances for the area. Audit sampling is applied to the evaluation of audit evidence rather than treated as a separate topic. Risk assessment, technology, fraud, and auditing of internal control issues are integrated throughout the chapters. Similarly, developments related to international auditing and issues affecting auditing in a global environment are described throughout the book, with specific examples of how these can be applied to the Arab world.

KEY FEATURES IN THE ARAB WORLD EDITION

New to the Arab World Edition

This new edition includes many Arab world-specific features that will enable students to connect auditing theory with real Arab world companies and examples that they can relate to:

* New opening case studies from the Arab world that enable students to see how material in the chapter is used in real-life auditing situations.
* A list at the beginning of every chapter of the International Standards on Auditing, related to issues discussed in the chapter and to the audit process and its application in the Arab region.
* Examples from leading Arab and international companies such as Nuqul, Orascom, Media Production Company, Xerox, Zarooni, Mizin, Agility, Istithmar World, Dubai Islamic Bank, Etisalat, Microsoft, Apple, Hawkamah, Anwal/Omar Effendi, Linkdotnet, and many others.
* Over 100 international, pan-Arab, and local examples, problems, and case studies featuring real data from the Arab world.
* Integrated Arab auditing examples providing students with cultural and social insights.
* Extracts from CPA firm management letters showing audit findings in the Arab world.
* Revised language, making it easier for non-native English speakers to comprehend.
* Marginal key-term definitions for students' quick reference whilst reading.
* New end-of-chapter cases from the Arab world.
* An English–Arabic glossary at the end of the book.

Emphasis on International and Arab World Issues

The Arab World Edition contains integrated coverage of developments related to international standards on auditing and emphasizes issues affecting audits of multinational entities. Examples are provided throughout the book of how international standards on auditing have been applied by companies in many Arab world countries, showing the specific culture and economic environment in this important part of the world. Chapter 1 introduces the importance of considering international standards on auditing developments, followed by discussion in Chapter 2 about the role of the International Auditing and Assurance Standards Board (IAASB) in the issuance of international auditing standards. Chapter 2 also discusses Islamic accounting standards issued by the Accounting and Auditing Organization for Islamic Financial Institutions (AAOIFI) and the Islamic Financial Services Board (IFSB). Chapter 3 highlights implications for auditor reports on companies reporting under International Financial Reporting Standards (IFRS) and describes the Securities and Exchange Commission's (SEC's) current roadmap proposal for embracing the use of IFRS for financial reporting by U.S. public companies. Several chapters throughout the book include text or mid-chapter vignette coverage of international issues and their application in the Arab world. International and Arab world issues are also addressed in homework problems, including internet problems.

ACL Problems

CPA firms are increasingly using audit software to perform audit testing including tests for fraud. We have included selected problems using ACL in several chapters in the text. These problems are related to the topic of the chapter so that students can see how audit software is used to perform specific types of audit tests. Additional guidance for students on the use of ACL is included both in the MyLab and as an appendix to this text. The educational version of ACL software is included with every new copy of this edition.

Coverage of the Sarbanes–Oxley Act and Section 404 Reporting

The requirements of the Sarbanes–Oxley Act, including Section 404 and PCAOB Auditing Standard 5, are integrated throughout the text. We provide extensive coverage of internal controls to help provide students with the understanding of controls necessary to perform a 404 audit, as well as meet the requirements of the risk assessment standards. Although the adherence to the Sarbanes–Oxley Act is required only in the U.S., this topic is important for students studying principles of auditing in the Arab world as many capital market authorities in Arab countries are currently taking the necessary steps to establish a model similar to the PCAOB to assess the quality of the audit provided for listed companies.

Arabian Hardware Annual Report

The annual report for the Arabian Hardware Company is included as a four-color insert to the text. Financial statements and other information included in the annual report are used in examples throughout the text to illustrate chapter concepts. The annual report also includes management's report on internal control required by Section 404 and the auditor's report consistent with PCAOB Auditing Standard 5.

ORGANIZATION

The text is divided into six parts. The chapters are relatively brief and designed to be easily read and comprehended by students.

Part 1, The Auditing Profession (Chapters 1–5) The book begins with an opening vignette, featuring the Enron fraud, to help students begin to see the connection between recent frauds and the new responsibilities for auditing internal control and other requirements of the Sarbanes–Oxley Act. Chapter 1 introduces key provisions of the Act, including the creation of the PCAOB and Section 404 internal control reporting requirements. Chapter 2 covers the CPA profession, with particular emphasis on the standards-setting responsibilities of the PCAOB and how those responsibilities differ from those of the Auditing Standards Board (ASB) of the American Institute of Certified Public Accountants (AICPA). This chapter also introduces the International Auditing and Assurance Standards Board (IAASB) with application in the Arab world. Chapter 3 provides a detailed discussion of audit reports, including a separate section on the report on internal control over financial reporting for a public company. The chapter also emphasizes conditions affecting the type of report the auditor must issue and the type of audit report applicable to each condition under varying levels of materiality. Chapter 4 investigates auditors' legal liability. Chapter 5 ends this part with an explanation of ethical dilemmas, professional ethics, independence, and the IFAC *Code of Ethics for Professional Accountants*.

Part 2, The Audit Process (Chapters 6–13) The first two of these chapters deal with auditor and management responsibilities, audit objectives, general concepts of evidence accumulation, and audit documentation, including the management assertions and evidence concepts in the risk assessment standards. Chapter 8 deals with planning the engagement, including understanding the company's business and its industry as part of risk assessment procedures, and using analytical procedures as an audit tool. Chapter 9 introduces materiality and risk and how the auditor responds to risks of significant misstatement with further audit procedures. Chapter 10 shows how effective internal controls can reduce planned audit evidence in the audit of financial statements. Most of the chapter describes how auditors integrate evidence related to understanding, testing, and assessing internal control to provide a basis for their assessment of control risk in the financial statement audit. Fraud auditing is the focus of Chapter 11 and describes the auditor's responsibility for assessing fraud risk and detecting fraud. The chapter also includes specific examples of fraud and discusses warning signs and procedures to detect fraud. Chapter 12 addresses the most important effects of information technology on internal controls in businesses, risks the auditor must consider, and audit evidence changes. Chapter 13 summarizes Chapters 6 through 12 and integrates them with the remainder of the text.

Part 3, Application of the Audit Process to the Sales and Collection Cycle (Chapters 14–17) These chapters apply the concepts from Part 2 to the audit of sales, cash receipts, and the related income statement and balance sheet accounts. The appropriate audit procedures for accounts in the sales and collection cycle are related to internal control and audit objectives for tests of controls, substantive tests of transactions, and tests of details of balances in the context of the audit of financial statements.

Students also learn to apply audit sampling to the audit of sales, cash receipts, and accounts receivable. Chapter 15 begins with a general discussion of audit sampling for tests of controls and substantive tests of transactions. Similarly, Chapter 17 begins with general sampling concepts for tests of details of balances. The next topic in each chapter is extensive coverage of nonstatistical sampling. The last part of each chapter covers statistical sampling techniques.

Part 4, Application of the Audit Process to Other Cycles (Chapters 18–23) Each of these chapters deals with a specific transaction cycle or part of a transaction cycle in much the same manner as Chapters 14 through 17 cover the sales and collection cycle. Each chapter in Part 4 demonstrates the relationship of internal controls, tests of controls, and substantive tests of transactions for each broad category of transactions to the related balance sheet and income statement accounts. We integrate discussion of implications related to the audit of internal control throughout all these transaction cycle chapters. Cash in the bank is studied late in the text to demonstrate how the audit of cash balances is related to most other audit areas.

Part 5, Completing the Audit (Chapter 24) This part includes only one chapter, which deals with performing additional tests to address presentation and disclosure objectives, summarizing all audit tests, reviewing audit documentation, obtaining management representations in an integrated audit of financial statements and internal control, communicating with those charged with governance, and all other aspects of completing an audit.

Part 6, Other Assurance and Nonassurance Services (Chapters 25 and 26) The last two chapters deal with various types of engagements and reports, other than the audit of financial statements. Topics covered include assurance services, review and compilation services, agreed-upon procedures engagements, attestation engagements, other audit engagements, internal financial auditing, and operational auditing.

SUPPLEMENTS

Resources for instructors can be accessed via our website www.pearsonmiddleeastawe.com/arens.

Instructor's Resource Manual Suggestions for each chapter include homework problems, how learning objectives correlate with chapter problem material, and transparency masters. Chapters have been designed so that their arrangement and selection provides maximum flexibility in course design. Sample syllabi and suggested term projects are provided.

Solutions Manual Included are detailed solutions to all the end-of-chapter exercises, problems, and cases. Guidelines for responses to review questions and discussion questions are offered.

Test Item File & TestGen The printed *Test Item File* includes multiple choice exercises, true/false responses, essay questions, and questions related to the chapter vignettes. To assist the instructor in selecting questions for use in examinations and quizzes, each question has been assigned one of three difficulty ratings—easy, medium, or challenging.

In addition, questions that uniquely relate to the integrated audits of public companies or to the provisions of the Sarbanes–Oxley Act and Section 404 have been separately labeled for easy identification by the instructor. TestGen testing software is an easy-to-use computerized testing program. It can create exams, evaluate, and track student results. All Test Item File questions are available in the TestGen format.

PowerPoint Slides PowerPoint presentations are available for each chapter of the text. Instructors have the flexibility to add slides and/or modify the existing slides to meet course needs.

MyAccountingLab Pearson has created a MyAccountingLab specifically for users of this Arab World Edition. This resource provides resources for both students and faculty, including:

- *Internet Problems:* End-of-chapter assignments for many chapters, requiring students to utilize the internet to conduct research in order to develop a solution.
- *Pinnacle Manufacturing Integrated Case:* A six-part, integrated case based on a large, multi-division company called Pinnacle Manufacturing. Each part of the case is designed to give students hands-on experience, and is connected to the other parts so that students will gain a better understanding of how the parts of the audit are integrated by the audit process.
- *Links to other resources:* Such as instructor resources.
- *Online Study Guide:* Provides students with immediate feedback on quizzes, including total score, an explanation provided for each incorrect answer, and the ability to e-mail the results to a faculty member. All questions are created specifically for this Study Guide. This is included with the price of the text.

ACKNOWLEDGMENTS

I gratefully acknowledge the American Institute of Certified Public Accountants for permission to quote extensively from Statements on Auditing Standards, Uniform CPA Examinations, and other publications. The willingness of this major accounting organization to permit the use of its materials has proved a significant contribution to the book.

I would like to acknowledge and thank the contributions of the following instructors for their constructive and helpful review comments during the preparation of this Arab World Edition:

Modar Abdullatif, Middle East University, Amman, Jordan
Jeremy Cripps, American University of Kuwait, Kuwait
Yasser Fallatah, King Fahd University of Petroleum and Minerals, Saudi Arabia
Esam E. Moustafa Hussein, United Arab Emirates University, Abu Dhabi
Gagan Kukreja, Ahlia University, Bahrain
Yousef M. Sa'adeh, Applied Science University, Amman, Jordan
Mohamed Salem, University of Sharjah, U.A.E.
Hatem M. EL-Shishini, Tanta University, Egypt

This text would also not have been possible without the many contributions of reviewers and contributors in previous editions of *Auditing and Assurance Services*.

Finally, special thanks also go to research assistant Amira Nadim for her dedication, patience, and significant efforts in verifying and editing the text and for her moral support throughout the preparation of the Arab World Edition. Also a special recognition goes to Marwa Nabil for her assistance in production and moral support. Her concern for quality is highly appreciated and recognized.

Mohamed Hegazy

THE AUDITING PROFESSION

These first five chapters provide background for performing financial audits, which is our primary focus. This background will help you understand why auditors perform audits the way they do.

This book begins with a description of assurance services, including auditing, and the role of licensed accountants or certified public accounting (CPA) firms (the auditor) and other organizations in doing audits. The chapters in Part I emphasize the regulation and control of auditing firms through legal responsibilities of auditors as well as auditing and ethical standards. We also present a detailed discussion of audit reports, which are the final products of audits.

CHAPTER 1

AUDIT AND ASSURANCE SERVICES

Where Were The Auditors?

In August 2000, the shareholders of Enron Holdings were riding high. Andy thought so anyway. He had invested in Enron at the beginning and poured a great majority of his life savings into the promising company. Every week he invested 10 percent of his pay check into Enron stock. Enron was the next Microsoft, they all said. Enron was named America's Most Innovative Company by *Fortune* magazine for six consecutive years, from 1996 to 2001. During the 1997–2000 period, Enron's share price quadrupled as investors saw remarkable revenue growth. Enron's price was up to US$90 per share, the company was profitable, and the investment seemed solid. Management was promising share prices of US$130 per share in the near future. With such a solid record and blue chip status, thousands of other investors and pension management funds had holdings in the company as well. Andy was well on his way to purchasing his first house and setting himself up for retirement one day.

Then, on November 28, 2001, Enron's stocks tumbled to just pennies per share when news of the losses went public. Andy's savings disappeared. All of his hard earned money used to purchase these shares had simply vanished. Now, instead of purchasing that new house, Andy had lost everything. "What are we going to do?" he asked Martha, his wife. "I don't know," she said. "I guess we start over."

Andy wasn't alone; Bill had lost his entire retirement fund. He was set to retire in two years. Now it looked like he wouldn't retire at all. There were thousands of stories like this.

In the weeks after, Bill and Andy followed the developments online with each accusation as unbelievable as the next. Enron had created fake offshore entities, which allowed Enron to sell its own assets that it couldn't sell elsewhere to itself at an inflated price, hiding untold losses. Loans were made to look like profit from sales, sales of contracts were secretly repurchased but not reported, and transactions were made to look like swaps but were actually loans. Overseas companies were also affected; Enron had spent millions investing in global companies like gas pipelines in South America, and clean energy plants in Indonesia and India. The list goes on and on.

What's worse is that outside parties like banks and law firms had a hand in the deception all for their own personal gain. With the help of banks, Enron sold phony assets at an overvalued price—assets which never even changed hands. With the help of law firms, Enron structured favorable transactions and prepared false submissions to the Security and Exchange Commission (SEC). SEC is the body responsible to oversee investors' welfare in U.S. capital markets. Securities analysts made false, rosy assessments of Enron's condition to entice investors. Underwriters approved incomplete and incorrect financial statements when approving the sale of US$2 billion in securities to investors.

All in all, losses to investors are estimated at US$25 billion. "What had happened? Aren't there people out there who are supposed to catch this kind of thing?" Andy and the other investors asked in disbelief. The answer to their question is yes, and one of those people was the auditing firm, Arthur Andersen. An auditor's ultimate responsibility is to the *users of the financial statements*, which in this case were the investors—investors who were sorely let down by the auditors and so many other parties.

Sources: Guma, Greg. 'Toward Freedom—Enron's Global Game.' Toward Freedom; Dec, 2001. http://www.towardfreedom.com/home/content/view/80/69/

Each chapter's opening story illustrates important auditing principles based on realistic situations. Some of these stories are based on public information about the audits of real companies, whereas others are fictitious. Any resemblance in the latter stories to real firms, companies, or individuals is unintended and purely coincidental.

The opening story illustrates the importance of the role of auditors and their responsibility to the users of the financial statements not only in the U.S. but all over the world. It is important that regulators, academics, and practitioners study the Enron case and identify measures which will prevent such fraud cases from occurring—especially in those countries in the Arab world with limited financial resources, except perhaps the Gulf States. In the aftermath of Enron and other major financial reporting frauds, U.S. Congress passed the **Sarbanes–Oxley Act**, called by many the most significant securities legislation since the 1933 and 1934 Securities Acts. The provisions of the Act apply to publicly held companies and their audit firms, and include the requirement in Section 404 that the external auditor report on the effectiveness of the company's internal control over financial reporting. Such measures have yet to be introduced in most of the Arab countries as financial oversight boards, or audit bureaus, which protect investors' interests, are currently developing a professional unit to assess the performance of the auditors and ensure their full compliance with international standards on auditing and securities laws. The audit of the internal controls in Arab countries is made while the auditors are forming their opinion about the company's financial statements. Reports on internal control and other provisions of the Act are discussed throughout the text.

This chapter introduces **auditing** and other assurance services provided by auditors, as well as the role of auditors in the Arab world. Students are required to understand the concepts and techniques of audit so they can apply them when they join auditing firms. The audit and other assurance services provide value by offering assurance on financial statements, the effectiveness of internal control, and other information. There is also a discussion of the types of audits and auditors, including the requirements for becoming a certified public accountant (CPA).

Sarbanes–Oxley Act

A U.S. federal securities law passed in 2002 that provides for additional regulation of public companies and their auditors; the Act established the Public Company Accounting Oversight Board and also requires auditors to audit the effectiveness of internal control over financial reporting.

Auditing

The accumulation and evaluation of evidence about information to determine and report on the degree of correspondence between the information and established criteria.

Relevant International Standards on Auditing	
IAASB	International Framework for Assurance Engagements
ISA 200	Overall Objectives of the Independent Auditor and the Conduct of an Audit in Accordance with International Standards on Auditing
ISA 210	Agreeing the Terms of Audit Engagements
ISA 260	Communication with Those Charged with Governance
ISA 300	Planning an Audit of Financial Statements
ISAEs 3000	Assurance Engagements Other than Audits or Review of Historical Financial Information

NATURE OF AUDITING

> Auditing is the systematic process of objectively accumulating and evaluating evidence about information to determine and report on the degree of correspondence between the information and established criteria. Auditing should be done by a competent, independent person.

OBJECTIVE I-I

Describe auditing.

The definition includes several key words and phrases. For ease of understanding, we'll discuss the terms in a different order than they occur in the description.

Information and Established Criteria

To do an audit, there must be information in a *verifiable form* and some standards (*criteria*) by which the auditor can evaluate the information. Information can and does take many forms. Auditors routinely perform audits of quantifiable information, including companies' financial statements and individuals' and corporate income tax returns. Auditors also audit more subjective information, such as the effectiveness of computer systems and the efficiency of manufacturing operations.

The criteria for evaluating information also vary depending on the information being audited. In the audit of historical financial statements by auditing firms, the criteria is generally accepted accounting principles (GAAP) originally developed in the U.S., or International Financial Reporting Standards (IFRS) or other particular local accounting standards. This means that in an audit of the financial statements of Egyptair, Kuwait Airways or any of the Gulf airlines, the CPA firm will determine whether these financial statements have been prepared in accordance with Egyptian Accounting Standards (EAS) or IFRS applied in those Arab countries. In the U.S. for an audit of internal control over financial reporting, the criteria will be a recognized framework for establishing internal control, such as *Internal Control - Integrated Framework* issued by the Committee of Sponsoring Organizations of the Treadway Commission. It is important to mention that the above internal control framework is also used to assess internal controls when auditing firms in the Arab countries form their opinion about companies' financial statements.

For the audit of tax returns by the local tax authority (LTA), the criteria are found in the local tax law. For example, in the Egyptian Tax Authority audit of the Egyptair tax return, the tax inspectors use the tax law as well as the EAS as the criteria for correctness. The tax inspectors examine details included in the company's tax return in light of the requirements for accepting expenses, revenues, and other related transactions included in the Egyptian tax law. Similar requirements are found in Kuwait, Lebanon, Jordan, and most of the Gulf States.

For more subjective information, it is more difficult to establish criteria. Typically, auditors and the entities being audited agree on the criteria well before the audit starts. For example, in an audit of the effectiveness of specific aspects of computer operations, the criteria might include the allowable level of input or output errors. Also, auditors may discuss with management the criteria for the efficient collection of the entity's receivables, including the number of days allowable for customers to pay in light of the credit facilities received from the suppliers and other creditors.

Accumulating and Evaluating Evidence

Audit evidence is any information used by the auditor to determine whether the information being audited is stated in accordance with the established criteria. Evidence takes many different forms, including:

- Electronic and documentary data about transactions
- Written communication with outsiders

Audit evidence

Any information used by the auditor to determine whether the information being audited is stated in accordance with established criteria.

• Observations by the auditor
• Oral testimony of the auditee (client)

To satisfy the purpose of the audit, auditors must obtain a sufficient quality and volume of evidence. Auditors must determine the types and amount of evidence necessary and evaluate whether the information corresponds to the established criteria. This is a critical part of every audit and the primary subject of this book.

Competent, Independent Person

The auditor must be qualified to understand the criteria used and must be *competent* to know the types and amount of evidence to accumulate to reach the proper conclusion after examining the evidence. The auditor must also have an *independent mental attitude*. The competence of those performing the audit is of little value if they are biased in the accumulation and evaluation of evidence.

Auditors strive to maintain a high level of independence to keep the confidence of users relying on their reports. Auditors reporting on company financial statements are often called **independent auditors**. Even though such auditors are paid fees by the company, they are normally sufficiently independent to conduct audits that can be relied on by users. Even internal auditors—those employed by the companies they audit—usually report directly to top management and the **board of directors**, keeping the auditors independent of the operating units they audit.

Reporting

The final stage in the auditing process is preparing the **audit report**, which communicates the auditor's findings to users. Reports differ in nature, but all must inform readers of the degree of correspondence between information and established criteria. Reports also differ in form and can vary from the highly technical type usually associated with financial statement audits to a simple oral report in the case of an operational audit of a small department's effectiveness.

The key parts in the description of auditing are illustrated in Figure 1-1 using a tax authority inspector audit of an individual's tax return as an example. To determine whether the tax return was prepared in a manner consistent with the requirements of the tax law, the inspector examines supporting records provided by the taxpayer and from other sources, such as the taxpayer's employer. After completing the audit, the

Independent auditors

Certified public accountants or accounting firms that perform audits of commercial and non-commercial financial entities.

Board of directors

Persons elected by the entity's shareholders to manage, direct, and monitor the affairs of the company.

Audit report

The communication of audit findings to users.

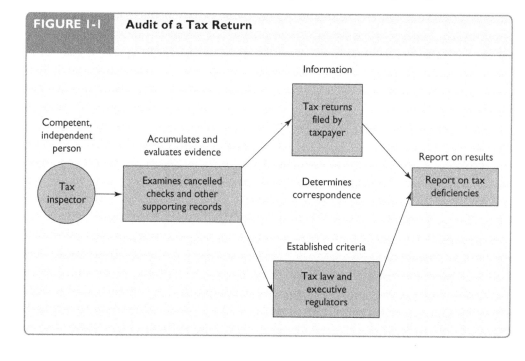

FIGURE 1-1   Audit of a Tax Return

tax inspector issues a report to the taxpayer assessing additional taxes, advising that a refund is due, which is seldom the case in the Arab world, or stating that there is no change in the status of the tax return.

DISTINCTION BETWEEN AUDITING AND ACCOUNTING

Many financial statement users and the general public confuse auditing with accounting. The confusion may arise from the title 'certified public accountant' given to many individuals who perform audits.

Accounting is the recording, classifying, and summarizing of economic events in a logical manner for the purpose of providing financial information for decision making. To provide relevant information, accountants must have a thorough understanding of the principles and rules that provide the basis for preparing the accounting information. In addition, accountants must develop a system to make sure that the entity's economic events are properly recorded on a timely basis and at a reasonable cost.

When auditing accounting data, auditors focus on determining whether recorded information properly reflects the economic events that occurred during the accounting period. Because U.S. or international accounting standards, or local accounting standards in some countries, provide the criteria for evaluating whether the accounting information is properly recorded, auditors must thoroughly understand those accounting standards.

In addition to understanding accounting, the auditor must possess expertise in the accumulation and interpretation of audit evidence. It is this expertise that distinguishes auditors from accountants. Determining the proper audit procedures, deciding the number and types of items to test, and evaluating the results are unique to the auditor.

> **OBJECTIVE 1-2**
>
> Distinguish between auditing and accounting.

> **Accounting**
>
> The recording, classifying, and summarizing of economic events in a logical manner for the purpose of providing financial information for decision making.

ECONOMIC DEMAND FOR AUDITING

To illustrate the need for auditing, consider the decision of the management of a telecommunications company to list its shares on the stock exchange. The reason behind the management decision to list the company's shares is to finance future growth of the company by increasing the capital and using the financed funds to extend the services of the company. In order to give confidence to investors in the stock market management must provide audited financial statements. The management appointed Pricewaterhouse Coopers, one of the Big Four international auditing firms, to audit the company's financial statements. This demonstrates the importance of the audit function to listed companies. Auditing helps ensure that information included in the financial statements is understandable, relevant, reliable, and timely. Also, consider the decision of a bank officer in making a loan to a business. This decision will be based on such factors as previous financial relationships with the business and the financial condition of the business as reflected by its financial statements. If the bank makes the loan, it will charge a rate of interest determined primarily by three factors:

> **OBJECTIVE 1-3**
>
> Explain the importance of auditing in reducing information risk.

1. *Risk-free interest rate.* This is approximately the rate the bank could earn by investing in government treasury notes for the same length of time as the business loan.
2. *Business risk for the customer.* This risk reflects the possibility that the business will not be able to repay its loan because of economic or business conditions, such as a recession, poor management decisions, or unexpected competition in the industry.
3. *Information risk.* **Information risk** reflects the possibility that the information upon which the business risk decision was made was inaccurate. A likely cause of the information risk is the possibility of inaccurate financial statements.

Auditing has no effect on either the risk-free interest rate or business risk, but it can have a significant effect on information risk. If the bank officer is satisfied that there

> **Information risk**
>
> The risk that information upon which a business decision is made is inaccurate.

is minimal information risk because a borrower's financial statements are audited by competent and independent auditors, the bank's risk is substantially reduced and the overall interest rate to the borrower can be reduced. The reduction of information risk can have a significant effect on the borrower's ability to obtain capital at a reasonable cost. For example, assume a large company has total interest-bearing debt of approximately US$10 billion. If the interest rate on that debt is reduced by only one percent, the annual amount of interest saved is US$100 million.

Causes of Information Risk

As society becomes more complex, decision makers are more likely to receive unreliable information. There are several reasons for this: remoteness of information, biases and motives of the provider, voluminous data, and the existence of complex exchange transactions.

Remoteness of Information In a global economy, it is nearly impossible for a decision maker to have much firsthand knowledge about the organization with which they do business. For example, Etisalat or Dubai Media City have a large number of shareholders. It is not practical for each stockholder to visit the company head office or branches to read the accounting records for information. Therefore, information provided by the management of the business must be relied upon. When information is obtained from others, the likelihood of it being intentionally or unintentionally misstated increases. Thus, someone qualified and independent (i.e. the auditor) is needed to check the accuracy of such information.

Biases and Motives of the Provider If information is provided by someone (i.e. a manager) whose goals are inconsistent with those of the decision maker (i.e. a shareholder), the information may be biased in favor of the provider. The reason can be honest optimism about future events or an intentional emphasis designed to influence users. In either case, the result is a misstatement of information. For example, when a borrower provides financial statements to a lender, there is considerable likelihood that the borrower will bias the statements by overstating the company's assets and profits to increase the chance of obtaining a loan. The misstatement could be incorrect dollar amounts or inadequate or incomplete disclosures of information.

Voluminous Data As organizations become larger, so does the volume of their exchange transactions. This increases the likelihood that improperly recorded information is included in the records—perhaps buried in a large amount of other information. For example, if a large manufacturing company overpays a supplier's invoice by US$2,000, it is unlikely to be uncovered unless the company has instituted reasonably complex procedures to find this type of misstatement. If many minor misstatements remain undiscovered, the combined total can be significant.

FOUR-WHEEL DRIVES AND CORRUPTION OF MORE THAN US$5 MILLION

A corruption case was revealed in a media company where officials in the security department violated the acceptable uses of the company's assets leading to the loss of US$5.185 million. They authorized the purchase of top of the range four-wheel drive vehicles as benefits for the heads of sectors as well as paying pecuniary rewards to employees in their offices. The documents uncovered by the company auditor revealed that the head of the security department spent US$5.185 million on 11 vehicles, claiming that they would be used as wireless stations to connect the external areas with the television company's head office and branches, while in reality they were intended for personal use by the heads of a number of sectors within the company. Other documents uncovered by the auditor of the company revealed that the head of the security department paid US$1 million over six months as bonuses for officials in the sector for their efforts in doing extra jobs, without any evidence that they actually did the work.

Complex Exchange Transactions In the past few decades, exchange transactions between organizations have become increasingly complex and therefore more difficult to record properly. For example, the correct accounting treatment of the acquisition of one entity by another poses relatively difficult accounting problems. Other examples include properly combining and disclosing the results of operations of subsidiaries in different industries and properly disclosing derivative financial instruments under IFRS 32 and 38.

Reducing Information Risk

After comparing costs and benefits, business managers and financial statement users may conclude that the best way to deal with information risk is simply to have it remain reasonably high. A small company may find it less expensive to pay higher interest costs than to increase the costs of reducing information risk. For larger businesses, it is usually practical to incur costs to reduce information risk.

Audited Financial Statements Provided The most common way for users to obtain reliable information is to have an independent audit. Decision makers can then use the audited information on the assumption that it is reasonably complete, accurate, and unbiased.

Typically, the management of a private company or the audit committee of a public company engages the auditor to provide assurances to users that the financial statements are reliable. If the financial statements are ultimately determined to be incorrect, the auditor can be sued by both the users and management. Auditors obviously have considerable legal responsibility for their work. Auditors, thus, play an important role in the so called principal–agent relationship.

The relationship between an owner (principal) and manager (the agent) often results in **information asymmetry**. Information asymmetry explains that the manager generally has more information about the true financial position and results of operations of the business than does the absentee owner. There is always a conflict of interest between the manager and the absentee owner. Each party may seek to maximize their own interests; the manager therefore may not always act in the best interests of the owner. Managers may spend funds on assets such as vehicles and furniture and make risky financial investments at the expense of stockholders' benefits. Also, management may manipulate reported income of the business in order to inflate the price of the business share in order to receive larger bonuses, remuneration and sell their own shares at high prices. Auditors help to reduce the effects of information asymmetry by examining the information in the financial statements and related books and records to ensure its reliability. Auditors help to promote the notion of holding management accountable to the owner. Auditing plays an important role in monitoring the contractual relationships between the business and its stakeholders including shareholders, managers, employees, and creditors.

Information asymmetry

The concept that the manager generally has more information about the true financial position, results of operations, and cash flow of the company than the absentee owner.

SHAREHOLDERS REACTED TO IMPROPER DISCLOSURE

Arab businesses are becoming more and more aware of the importance of transparency and disclosure of information to shareholders. During the annual general meeting of a Gulf bank, a joint venture bank owned by one of the Gulf Kingdoms and other private businessmen and 30 percent by members of the public, shareholders forced the management of the bank to change its current auditor. Shareholders claimed that the current auditor did not properly comply with the IFRS in relation to full disclosure of the provision formed for the bank loan portfolio. There was also a lack of detail concerning the number of companies at which the bank had investments including publicly listed corporations such as the Industrial Development Company, XYZ for Electricity, and National Company for Food Manufacturing, in addition to a number of brokerage firms. Shareholders also criticized the management for agreeing to lease the bank buildings even though some of these buildings are considered part of the architectural heritage of the Arab Kingdom.

ASSURANCE SERVICES

Assurance service

An independent professional service that improves the quality of information for decision makers.

An **assurance service** is an independent professional service that improves the quality of information for decision makers. A more detailed definition is provided by IFAC[1] (2010).

> Assurance engagement means an engagement in which a practitioner expresses a conclusion designed to enhance the degree of confidence of the intended users other than the responsible party about the outcome of the evaluation or measurement of a subject matter against a criteria.

For example, an auditor (i.e. a practitioner) expresses an opinion (i.e. conclusion) that the financial statements of a client (i.e. subject matter) are prepared in accordance with IFRS (i.e. criteria). Another example is when an auditor gives an opinion that the company's internal control is operating according to established company policies. Such services are valued because the assurance provider is independent and perceived as being unbiased with respect to the information examined.

Individuals who are responsible for making business decisions seek assurance services to help improve the reliability and relevance of the information used as the basis for their decisions. Assurance services, however, rarely involve the authentication of documents, nor is the practitioner trained as or expected to be an expert in such authentication. The practitioner must consider the reliability of the information used as evidence such as photocopies, facsimiles, filmed, digitized, or other electronic documents and controls over their preparation and maintenance.

The need for assurance is not new. Auditors have provided many assurance services for years, particularly assurances about historical financial statement information. Audit firms have also performed assurance services related to lotteries and contests to provide assurance that winners were determined in an unbiased fashion in accordance with contest rules. More recently, audit firms have expanded the types of assurance services they perform to include forward-looking and other types of information, such as company financial forecasts and website controls. For example, businesses and consumers using the internet to conduct business need independent assurances about the reliability and security of electronic information. The demand for assurance services continues to grow as the demand for information increases and as more real-time information becomes available through the internet. However, the development of the use of assurance services for information technology (IT) usages in the Arab world are still in progress and more efforts are required from both audit firms and other IT companies to ensure the reliability of information provided to users of the internet in this area of the world.

Attestation Services

Attestation service

A type of assurance service in which the CPA firm issues a report about the reliability of an assertion that is the responsibility of another party.

One category of assurance services provided by audit firms is attestation services. An **attestation service** is a type of assurance service in which the audit firm issues a report about the reliability of an assertion that is made by another party. Attestation services fall into five categories:

1. Audit of historical financial statements
2. Audit of internal control over financial reporting
3. Review of historical financial statements
4. Attestation services on information technology
5. Other attestation services that may be applied to a broad range of subject matter

Audit of Historical Financial Statements In an **audit of historical financial statements**, management asserts that the statements are fairly stated in accordance with applicable international accounting standards. An audit of these statements is a form of attestation service in which the auditor issues a written report expressing an opinion about whether the financial statements are fairly stated in accordance with the applicable accounting standards. These audits are the most common assurance service provided by audit firms.

Publicly traded companies in Arab countries are required to have audits under the Capital or Stock Market Acts. Auditor reports can be found in all public companies' annual financial reports. Most public companies' audited financial statements can be accessed over the internet directly from each company's website. Many privately held companies also have their annual financial statement audited to obtain financing from banks and other financial institutions. Government and not-for-profit entities often have audits to meet the requirements of lenders or funding sources.

External users such as stockholders and lenders who rely on those financial statements to make business decisions look to the auditor's report as an indication of the statements' reliability. They value the auditor's assurance because of the auditor's independence from the client and knowledge of financial statement reporting matters. Figure 1-2 illustrates the relationships among the auditor, client, and financial statement users.

Audit of Internal Control Over Financial Reporting For an audit of **internal control over financial reporting**, management asserts that internal controls have been developed and implemented following well established criteria. In the U.S., Section 404 of the Sarbanes–Oxley Act requires public companies to report management's assessment of the effectiveness of internal control. The Act also requires auditors to attest to the effectiveness of internal control over financial reporting. This evaluation, which is integrated with the audit of the financial statements, increases user confidence about future financial reporting, because effective internal controls reduce the likelihood of future misstatements in the financial statements.

In the Arab world, there are no specific requirements, other than those included in the International Standards on Auditing numbers 220 and 265 or local auditing standards, that the audit of the company's internal controls must be carried out separately from the audit of the financial statements.

Review of Historical Financial Statements Investors need updated financial information at regular intervals during the accounting period. Quarterly and semi-annual financial statements must be prepared by listed companies for presentation

Audit of historical financial statements

A form of attestation service in which the auditor issues a written report stating whether the financial statements are in material conformity with accounting standards.

Internal control over financial reporting

An engagement in which the auditor reports on the effectiveness of internal control over financial reporting; such reports are required for public companies under Section 404 of the Sarbanes–Oxley Act in the U.S.

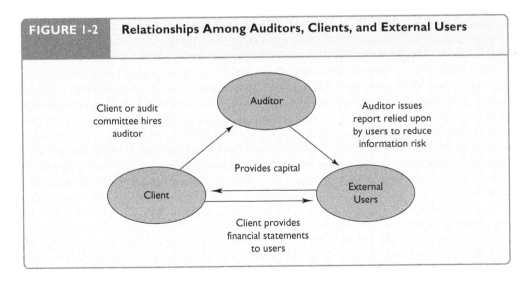

FIGURE 1-2   Relationships Among Auditors, Clients, and External Users

Review of historical financial statements

A form of attestation in which a CPA firm issues a written report that provides less assurance than an audit as to whether the financial statements are in material conformity with generally accepted accounting principles, International Financial Reporting Standards or local standards.

to investors and other stakeholders. For a **review of historical financial statements**, management asserts that the quarterly or semi-annual statements are fairly stated in accordance with accounting standards. The auditor provides only a moderate level of assurance for reviews of financial statements compared to a high level for audits, therefore less evidence is needed. A review is often adequate to meet users' needs and can be provided by the audit firm for a much lower fee than an audit because less evidence is needed. Many non-public companies who are keen to achieve a high element of monitoring and control and who look for future Initial Public Offering (IPO) use this attestation option to provide moderate assurance on their financial statements without incurring the cost of an audit.

Attestation Services on Information Technology For attestations on information technology, management makes various assertions about the reliability and security of electronic information. Many business functions, such as ordering and making payments, are conducted over the internet or directly between computers using electronic data interchange (EDI). As transactions and information are shared online and in real time, businesspeople demand even greater assurances about information, transactions, and the security protecting them. *WebTrust* and *SysTrust* are examples of attestation services developed to address these assurance needs.

> *WebTrust*: The AICPA and the Canadian Institute of Chartered Accountants (CICA) jointly created the *WebTrust* attestation service. Auditing firms that are licensed by the AICPA to perform this service provide assurance to users of websites through the CPA's electronic *WebTrust* seal displayed on the website. This seal assures the user that the website owner has met established criteria related to business practices, transaction integrity, and information processes. The *WebTrust* seal is a symbolic representation of the auditor's report on management's assertions about its disclosure of electronic commerce practices.

> *SysTrust*: The AICPA and CICA jointly created the *SysTrust* attestation service to evaluate and test system reliability in areas such as security and data integrity. Whereas the *WebTrust* assurance service is primarily designed to provide assurance to third-party users of a website, *SysTrust* services might be used by auditors to provide assurance to management, the board of directors, or third parties about the reliability of information systems used to generate real-time information.

The AICPA and CICA have developed five principles related to online privacy, security, processing integrity, availability, and confidentiality to be used in performing services such as *WebTrust* and *SysTrust*. These principles are also being applied by some companies operating in the Arab world taking into consideration that many multinational companies have subsidiaries and associated companies providing their services to users in the Arab countries. These subsidiaries and associated companies have the resources and technical capabilities to develop their Arab *WebTrust* and *SysTrust* systems. However, local businesses lack expertise and resources to apply such techniques for their online information provided to users in the Arab world. *WebTrust* and *SysTrust* services and their principles for application are discussed further in Chapter 25.

Other Attestation Services Auditing firms provide numerous other attestation services. Many of these services are natural extensions of the audit of historical financial statements, as users seek independent assurances about other types of information. In each case, the organization being audited must provide an assertion before the auditor can provide the attestation. For example, when a bank lends money to a company, the loan agreement may require the company to engage an auditor to provide assurance about the company's compliance with the financial provisions of the loan. The company requesting the loan must assert the loan provisions to be attested to before the auditor can accumulate the evidence needed to issue the attestation report. Auditors can also, for example, attest to the information in a client's forecasted financial statements, which are often used to obtain financing. We discuss attestation services further in Chapter 25.

Other Assurance Services

Most of the other assurance services that audit firms provide do not meet the definition of attestation services, but the auditor must still be independent and must provide assurance about information used by decision makers. These assurance services differ from attestation services in that the auditor is not required to issue a written report, and the assurance does not have to be about the reliability of another party's assertion about compliance with specified criteria. These other assurance service engagements focus on improving the quality of information for decision makers. For example, an auditor may provide assurances on a company's use of personal data provided by customers by setting up procedures for checking the accuracy of this personal data in order to determine their credit facilities.

Audit firms face severe competition in the market for other assurance services. Audits and some types of attestation services are limited by regulation to licensed auditors, but the market for other forms of assurance is open to competitors who are not auditors. For example, audit firms compete with market research firms to assist clients in the preparation of customer surveys and in the evaluation of the reliability and relevance of survey information. However, audit firms have the competitive advantage of their reputation for competence and independence.

The types of assurance services that auditors can provide are almost limitless. A survey of large audit firms identified more than 200 assurance services that are currently being provided. Table 1-1 lists some of the other assurance service opportunities for audit firms. Additional information on the performance of assurance services is included in Chapter 25.

In the Arab world, most assurance services relate to the audit of financial statements, reviews of quarterly financial statements, a few cases of fraud investigation mainly from government units, different ISO certificates, evaluation of risks associated

TABLE I-I	Other Assurance Services
Other Assurance Services	**Service Activities**
Controls over and risks related to investments, including policies related to derivatives	Assess the processes in a company's investment practices to identify risks and to determine the effectiveness of those processes
Mystery shopping	Perform anonymous shopping to assess sales personnel dealings with customers and procedures they follow
Assess risks of accumulation, distribution, and storage of digital information	Assess security risks and related controls over electronic data, including the adequacy of backup and off-site storage
Fraud and illegal acts risk assessment	Develop fraud risk profiles, and assess the adequacy of company systems and policies in preventing and detecting fraud and illegal acts
Compliance with trading policies and procedures	Examine transactions between trading partners to ensure that transactions comply with agreements; identify risks in the agreements
Compliance with entertainment royalty agreements	Assess whether royalties paid to artists, authors, and others comply with royalty agreements
ISO 9000 certifications	Certify a company's compliance with ISO 9000 quality control standards, which help ensure company products are of high quality
Environmental audit	Assess whether company policies and practices ensure the company's compliance with environmental standards and laws

Source: Adapted from AICPA Special Committee on Assurance Services.

with investments, lending assurance for computerized accounting systems, and limited assignments in the area of environmental audits.

Nonassurance Services Provided by Audit Firms

Audit firms perform numerous other services that generally fall outside the scope of assurance services. Three specific examples are:

1. Accounting and bookkeeping services
2. Tax services
3. Management consulting services

Most accounting and bookkeeping services, tax services, and management consulting services fall outside the scope of assurance services, although there is some common area of overlap between consulting and assurance services. While the primary purpose of an assurance service is to improve the quality of information, the primary purpose of a management consulting engagement is to generate a recommendation to management for good decision making.

Although the quality of information is often an important criterion in management consulting, this goal is normally not the primary purpose. For example, an audit firm may be engaged to design and install a new information technology system for a client as a consulting engagement. The purpose of that engagement is to install the new system, with the goal of improved information being a by-product of that engagement. Another example is where an audit firm is hired to assess the financial feasibility of a project to ensure an adequate rate of return for such a project and an appropriate period for collecting investors' capital invested.

Figure 1-3 reflects the relationship between assurance and nonassurance services. Audits, reviews, reports on the effectiveness of internal control over financial reporting, attestation services on information technology, and other attestation services are all examples of attestation services, which fall under the scope of assurance services. Some assurance services, such as *WebTrust* and *SysTrust*, also meet the criteria of attestation services.

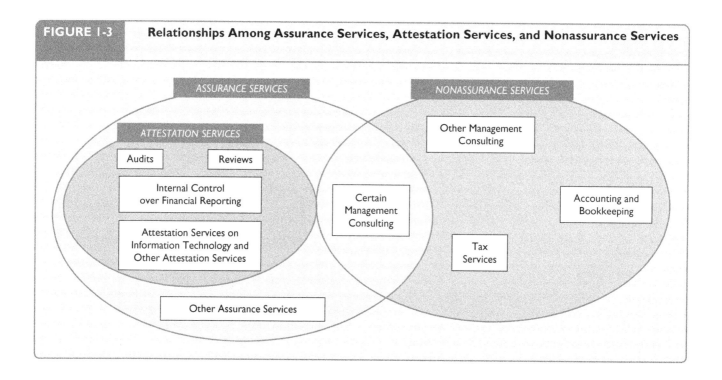

FIGURE 1-3   **Relationships Among Assurance Services, Attestation Services, and Nonassurance Services**

TYPES OF AUDITS

Auditors or CPAs perform four primary types of audits, as illustrated with examples in Table 1-2:

1. Operational audit
2. Compliance audit
3. Financial statement audit
4. Forensic audit

Operational Audits

An **operational audit** evaluates the *efficiency* and *effectiveness* of any part of an organization's operating procedures and methods. At the completion of an operational audit, management normally expects recommendations for improving operations. For example, auditors might evaluate the efficiency and accuracy of processing payroll transactions in a newly installed computer system. Another example, where most accountants feel less qualified, is evaluating the efficiency, accuracy, and customer satisfaction in processing the distribution of letters and packages by a company such as Federal Express. The complexity of the process of distribution of such letters and packages makes it difficult for ordinary accountants to identify deficiencies leading to delays or loss of letters and packages.

In operational auditing, the reviews are not limited to accounting. They can include the evaluation of organizational structure, computer operations, production methods, marketing, and any other area in which the auditor is qualified. Because of the many different areas in which operational effectiveness can be evaluated, it is impossible to characterize the conduct of a typical operational audit. In one organization, the auditor might evaluate the relevancy and sufficiency of the information used by management in making decisions to acquire new fixed assets. In a different organization, the auditor might evaluate the efficiency of the information flow in processing sales.

Operational audit

A review of any part of an organization's operating procedures and methods for the purpose of evaluating efficiency and effectiveness.

TABLE 1-2	Examples of the Four Types of Audit			
Type of Audit	**Example**	**Information**	**Established Criteria**	**Available Evidence**
Operational audit	Evaluate whether the computerized payroll processing for subsidiary H is operating efficiently and effectively	Number of payroll records processed in a month, costs of the department, and number of errors made	Company standards for efficiency and effectiveness in payroll department	Error reports, payroll records, and payroll processing costs
Compliance audit	Determine whether bank requirements for loan continuation have been met	Company records	Loan agreement provisions	Financial statements and calculations by the auditor
Financial statement audit	Annual audit of Egyptair's financial statements	Egyptair's financial statements	Egyptian Accounting Standards	Documents, records, and outside sources of evidence
Forensic audit	Investigate the causes of fraud in the Enron Case	Financial statements and company records	International Standards on Auditing and other guidelines for fraud detection	Documents, records, and outside sources of evidence

It is more difficult to objectively evaluate whether the efficiency and effectiveness of operations meet established criteria than it is for compliance and financial statement audits. Also, establishing criteria for evaluating the information in an operational audit is extremely subjective. In this sense, operational auditing is more like management consulting than what is usually considered auditing. For example, a company may hire an auditor with the purpose of assessing the effectiveness of management in collecting the company's receivables. The criteria to be used by the auditor may differ from one company to another company. The auditor may assess the effectiveness of collection of receivables based on the company's own policies for cash and credit sales or he may use industry indicators or other competitors' collection credit terms. Operational auditing is discussed in greater depth in Chapter 26.

Compliance Audits

Compliance audit

(1) A review of an organization's financial records performed to determine whether the organization is following specific procedures, rules, or regulations set by some higher authority; (2) an audit performed to determine whether an entity that receives financial assistance from the federal government has complied with specific laws and regulations.

A **compliance audit** is conducted to determine whether the auditee is following specific procedures, rules, or regulations set by the company itself or some higher authority. Following are examples of compliance audits for a private business.

- Determine whether accounting personnel are following the procedures prescribed by the company manuals and job descriptions and supervised by the controller.
- Review wage rates for compliance with minimum wage laws.
- Examine contractual agreements with bankers and other lenders to be sure the company is complying with legal requirements.
- Review tax returns prepared by the company's management for compliance with tax laws.

Governmental units, such as public sector companies, ministries, hospitals and school districts are subject to considerable compliance auditing because of extensive government regulation. Also, compliance audits for government funded grant programs are often done by audit firms. Many private and not-for-profit organizations have prescribed policies, contractual agreements, and legal requirements that may require compliance auditing.

Results of compliance audits are typically reported to management, rather than outside users, because management is the primary group concerned with the extent of compliance with prescribed procedures and regulations.

Financial Statement Audits

Financial statement audit

An audit conducted to determine whether the overall financial statements of an entity are stated in accordance with specified criteria (usually U.S., international accounting standards or local accounting standards).

A **financial statement audit** is conducted to determine whether the financial statements (the information being verified) are stated in accordance with specified criteria. Normally, the criteria are international accounting standards or local accounting standards, although auditors may conduct audits of financial statements prepared using the cash basis or some other basis of accounting appropriate for the organization. For example, Gezira, Heliopolis, and Shooting sporting clubs in Cairo each has more than 40,000 members and they record members' annual subscriptions on a cash received basis even though they record all their expenses on an accrual basis. As the number of members is significant, the management of the clubs ensure that only collected subscriptions are included in the statement of revenue and expenditure so that there is no overstatement of such revenue. In determining whether financial statements are fairly stated in accordance with accounting standards, the auditor gathers evidence to determine whether the statements contain material errors or other misstatements. The primary focus of this book is on financial statement audits.

As businesses increase in complexity, it is no longer sufficient for auditors to focus only on accounting transactions. An integrated approach to auditing considers both the risk of misstatements and operating controls intended to prevent misstatements. The auditor must also have a thorough understanding of the entity and its environment. This understanding includes knowledge of the client's industry and its regulatory and operating environment, including external relationships, such as with suppliers, customers, and creditors. The auditor also considers the client's business strategies and processes and critical success factors related to those strategies. This analysis helps the auditor identify risks associated with the client's strategies that may affect whether the financial statements are fairly stated.

Forensic Audit

Forensic audit is the process of investigating cases of fraud in the company's financial statements, accounting books and records, and any other documents used in the company's operations that may be used in white-collar crime. In other words, forensic audit helps the detection and deterrence of fraudulent activities. The **forensic auditor** understands, and is responsible for, testing and assessing the company's internal control system to ensure its effectiveness in preventing and detecting instances of fraud. Examples of situations where forensic audit can be performed are misappropriation of assets and fraudulent financial reporting, white-collar crime, shareholders and partnership disputes, and business economic and market losses. Figure 1-4 shows elements of forensic accounting and fraud detection.

Forensic auditor

The process of investigating cases of fraud in the company's financial statements, accounting books and records, and any other documents used in the company's operations that may be used in white-collar crime.

FIGURE 1-4   Forensic Accounting and Fraud Detection

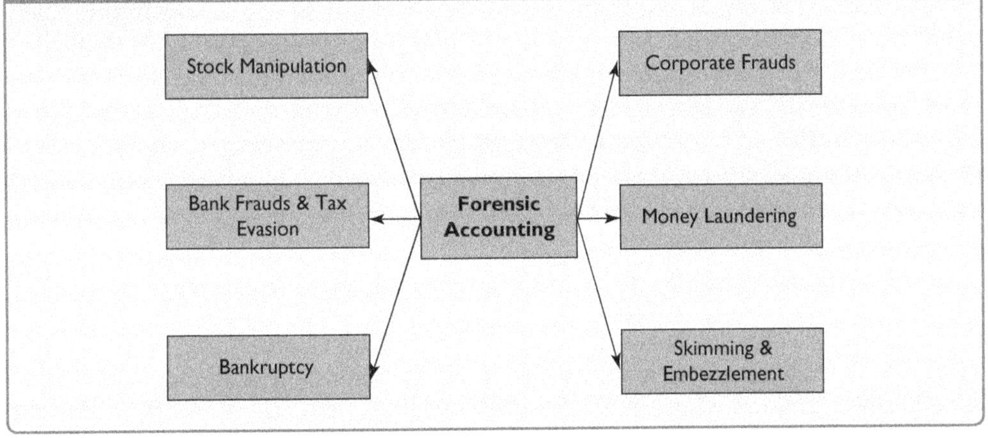

TYPES OF AUDITORS

Several types of auditors are in practice today. The most common are certified public accounting firms (i.e. audit firms), government accountability office auditors, tax inspectors, internal auditors, and forensic auditors.

OBJECTIVE 1-7

Identify the primary types of auditors.

Certified Public Accounting Firms

Certified public accounting firms are responsible for auditing the published historical financial statements of all publicly traded companies, most other reasonably large companies, and many smaller companies and noncommercial organizations. Because of the widespread use of audited financial statements in many of the Arab countries, as well as businesspersons' and other users' familiarity with these statements, it is common to use the terms *auditor, licensed accountants*, and *CPA firm* synonymously, even though several different types of auditors exist. The title *certified public accounting firm* reflects the fact that auditors who express audit opinions on financial statements must be licensed as CPAs or licensed accountants. Audit firms are often called *external auditors* or *independent auditors* to distinguish them from internal auditors.

Government Accountability Office Auditors

A **government accountability office auditor** is an auditor working for the local government accountability office (GAO). A government accountability office usually performs the four types of audit. Different terminologies are used for such government auditors in the Arab world. In Egypt, they are called the Central Audit Organization (CAO) and in the United Arab Emirates there is the Abu Dhabi Accountability Authority (ADAA); in Saudi Arabia the General Auditing Bureau (GAB); in Kuwait it is known as the State Audit Bureau (SAB); and in Lebanon it is called the Audit Bureau (AB).

The Audit Bureau in Lebanon has a special characteristic as it is considered an administrative court with the responsibility to achieve the financial mission to ensure the protection of public funds. The main objectives of the bureau are to:

1. monitor the use of public funds and the applicability of its use according to laws and regulations
2. decide on the validity and legal transactions and accounts, and
3. prosecute those responsible for violation of the laws and regulations relating thereto (Article 1 of Legislative Decree No. 82 for 1983 amended by Decree Law No. 5 for 1985 and Act No. 132 for 1992)

Headed by the comptroller general, the GAO reports to and is responsible solely to either the Congress in the U.S. or to the various parliaments in the Arab countries.

The GAO's primary responsibility is to perform the audit function for the people represented by the parliament, and it has many of the same audit responsibilities as an audit firm. The GAO audits much of the financial information prepared by various government units before it is submitted to the parliaments. Because the authority for expenditures and receipts of governmental units is defined by law, there is considerable emphasis on compliance in these audits.

An increasing portion of the GAO's audit efforts is devoted to evaluating the operational efficiency and effectiveness of various government programs. Also, because of the immense size of many government units, especially in countries like Egypt, Tunisia, Morocco, and Lebanon and the similarity of their operations, the GAO has made significant advances in developing better methods of auditing through the widespread use of highly sophisticated statistical sampling and computer risk assessment techniques. The use of IDEA and ACL as audit tools is increasing in both the private and public audit practices.

In many Arab countries experience as a GAO auditor fulfills the experience requirement for becoming a licensed accountant or CPA. In those countries, if an individual passes the professional examination to become a licensed accountant and fulfills the experience stipulations by becoming a GAO auditor, he or she may then obtain an auditor certificate.

As a result of their great responsibility for auditing the expenditures of the government, their use of advanced auditing concepts, their eligibility to be licensed accountants, and their opportunities for performing operational audits, GAO auditors are highly regarded in the auditing profession. They are regarded as the safeguarders of the public funds. Because they are government auditors, they are recognized as being highly independent, thus increasing their ability to report all deficiencies in both the organization's internal control as well as its financial statements.

Tax Inspectors

Tax inspectors, under the direction of the head of the tax directorate, are responsible for enforcing the *government tax laws* as they have been defined by parliament and interpreted by the courts. The major responsibility of the tax authority is to audit taxpayers' returns to determine whether they have complied with the tax laws. These audits are solely compliance audits carried out by auditors called **tax inspectors**.

It might seem that the audit of returns for compliance with the tax laws is simple and straightforward, but nothing is further from the truth. Tax laws are highly complicated, and there are hundreds of volumes of interpretations for articles included in the main body of the laws in addition to the executive regulations. The tax returns being audited vary from the simple returns of individuals who work for only one employer and pay standard tax deductions to the highly complex returns of multinational corporations. Taxation problems may involve individual income taxes, stamp taxes, estate taxes, corporate taxes, sales or value added tax, and so on. An auditor involved in any of these areas must have considerable tax knowledge and auditing skills to conduct effective audits.

Tax inspectors

Auditors who work for the tax authority and conduct examinations of taxpayers' returns.

Internal Auditors

Internal auditors are employed by companies to audit for management, much as the GAO does for parliament. Internal auditors' responsibilities vary considerably, depending on the employer. Some internal audit staffs consist of only one or two employees doing routine compliance auditing. Other internal audit staffs may have more than 20 employees who have diverse responsibilities, including many outside the accounting area. Many internal auditors are involved in operational auditing or have expertise in evaluating computer systems.

To maintain independence from other business functions, the internal audit group typically reports directly to the chairman of the board of directors, another high executive officer, or the audit committee of the board of directors. However, internal auditors cannot be entirely independent of the entity as long as an employer–employee relationship exists. Users from outside the entity are unlikely to want to rely on information verified solely by internal auditors because of their lack of independence. This lack of independence is the major difference between internal auditors and external auditors.

In many Arab countries, internal audit experience can be used to fulfill the experience requirement for becoming a licensed accountant. Many internal auditors pursue certification as a certified internal auditor (CIA), and some internal auditors pursue both the certified public accountants and certified internal auditor designations.

Internal auditors

Auditors employed by a company to audit and report directly to the company's board of directors and management.

Forensic Auditor

Forensic auditors are appointed by companies, government authorities, audit firms, and other consulting businesses. Because forensic auditors are trained in detecting, investigating, and deterring fraud and white-collar crime, they are appointed widely by companies to ensure systems are well designed or modified to prevent and detect fraud and white-collar crime. Forensic auditors perform similar functions to ordinary auditors as they gather evidence, collect statements, prepare reports, and help investigate different types of fraud. Examples of events and incidents where forensic auditors can play an important role are:

- Investigating and documenting embezzlement and negotiating settlement of insurance disputes related to fraud and white-collar crime.
- Reconstructing incidents of cash transactions related to money-laundering activities.
- Reconstructing incomplete accounting records to settle receivables theft, inventory valuation, suppliers' payments, etc.
- Assessing deficiencies in internal control systems and providing recommendations for making such systems more effective in preventing and detecting fraud.

The organization providing guidelines and licenses for forensic auditors is the Association of Certified Fraud Examiners (ACFE). The ACFE is composed of more than 40,000 members and provides technical training and exams for certified fraud examiners (CFE) who are responsible for detecting, investigating, and preventing fraud and white-collar crime. Individuals such as auditors, accountants, lawyers, educators, and other fraud investigators interested in becoming a CFE must pass the Uniform CFE Examination. The examinations test candidates' knowledge of accounting, laws, auditing, and other subjects associated with fraud and white-collar crime.

FORENSIC ACCOUNTING: HOT ON THE TRAIL AROUND THE WORLD

"Forensic accountants are really financial detectives," says Alex Brown of the forensic group in the Institute of Chartered Accountants in England and Wales. Brown has worked on cases involving Caribbean money laundering, Eastern European smuggling, and major commercial disputes. Forensic accountants use rigorous accounting skills and a flair for investigation to sniff out fraud, uncover money laundering, and trace missing assets.

The day-to-day work of a forensic accountant involves interviewing key people, studying accounts and, increasingly, examining electronic documents. The ever-growing volume of such documentation means that there is now a new branch of forensic accounting. Specialist computing forensic experts usually have a background in IT and receive accounting training on the job.

Forensic accounting is booming: the number of cases handled by the forensics team at one Big Four firm in the United Kingdom has tripled in the last two years. The increase reflects less tolerance for suspected fraud, as well as an increased ability to spot fraudulent activity using computer-assisted auditing techniques. New money-laundering and anti-terrorism measures have also increased demand for skilled forensic accountants.

"I was attracted to forensic accountancy because, like science, you need to have investigative skills," says forensic trainee Amy Hawkins. "I really like the sleuthing side of the job, where you're finding out whodunit and where the money went." Forensic accountant Simon Bevan adds, "When you find that killer document it's a real reward for all your hard work."

The need for forensic auditors has increased in the Arab world due to severe fraud and corruption cases occurring in many private, public, and government entities. The Big Four CPA firms are leading the way for the employment of forensic auditors who investigate fraud cases and provide recommendations for strengthening the internal controls and ensuring compliance with laws and regulations.

Source: Adapted from Amy McClellan, 'Forensic Accountancy: Hot on the Trail of the Fraudsters,' *The Independent* (April 26, 2006).

CERTIFIED PUBLIC ACCOUNTANT (CPA)

OBJECTIVE 1-8

Describe the requirements for becoming a CPA.

Certified public accountant

A person who has met the country's regulatory requirements, including passing the Uniform CPA Examination, and has thus been certified; a CPA may have as his or her primary responsibility the performance of the audit function on published historical financial statements of commercial and non commercial financial entities.

In the U.S., the use of the title **certified public accountant (CPA)** is regulated by state law through the licensing departments of each state. Within any state, the regulations usually differ for becoming a CPA and retaining a license to practice after the designation has been initially achieved. To become a CPA, three requirements must be met. These are summarized in Figure 1-5.

For a person planning to become a CPA, it is essential to know the requirements in the state where he or she plans to obtain and maintain the CPA designation. The best source of that information is the State Board of Accountancy for the state in which the person plans to be certified. The National Association of State Boards of Accountancy (NASBA) website (www.nasba.org) provides information on licensure requirements and links to the website of each state board. It is possible to transfer the CPA designation from one state to another, but additional requirements often must be met for formal education, practice experience, or continuing education.

In the Arab world, similar requirements are established by either the local Association of Accountants and Auditors (i.e. the professional body organizing the accounting and audit profession) or the Ministry of Finance or Commerce. For

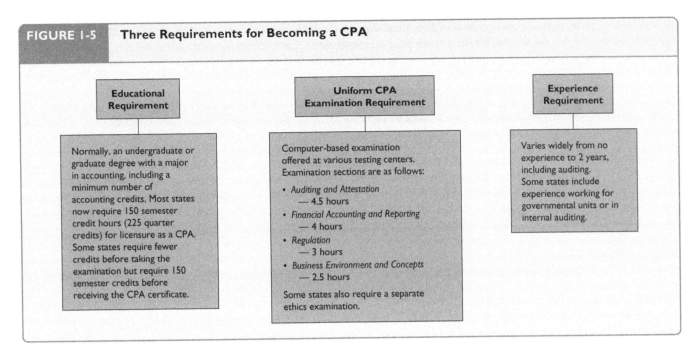

FIGURE I-5   Three Requirements for Becoming a CPA

Educational Requirement

Normally, an undergraduate or graduate degree with a major in accounting, including a minimum number of accounting credits. Most states now require 150 semester credit hours (225 quarter credits) for licensure as a CPA. Some states require fewer credits before taking the examination but require 150 semester credits before receiving the CPA certificate.

Uniform CPA Examination Requirement

Computer-based examination offered at various testing centers. Examination sections are as follows:

- *Auditing and Attestation*
  — 4.5 hours
- *Financial Accounting and Reporting*
  — 4 hours
- *Regulation*
  — 3 hours
- *Business Environment and Concepts*
  — 2.5 hours

Some states also require a separate ethics examination.

Experience Requirement

Varies widely from no experience to 2 years, including auditing. Some states include experience working for governmental units or in internal auditing.

example, in Lebanon as well as in Kuwait an accountant becomes a licensed accountant or a CPA if he or she complies with the following requirements:

a. Must be a national of the state with a minimum age of 25 for Kuwaitis and 21 for Lebanese.
b. Holder of a bachelor's degree in accounting or its equivalent from a recognized university. A technical certificate in accounting is accepted also in Lebanon.
c. Five to seven years of work experience in audit firm or accounting and auditing function of private or public company or government ministry after graduation.
d. Pass the CPA exams or their equivalents set by the local audit professional association or a holder of the United Kingdom audit professional certificates such as Chartered Accountant (CA) or Association of Chartered Certified Accountants (ACCA).

Most young professionals who want to become licensed accountants or CPAs start their careers working for an audit firm. After they become CPAs, many leave the firm to work in industry, government, or education. These people may continue to be CPAs but often give up their right to practice as independent auditors. To maintain the right to practice as independent auditors, CPAs must meet defined continuing education and licensing requirements. Therefore, it is common for accountants to be CPAs who do not practice as independent auditors.

Information about the CPA examination can be found in the *Uniform CPA Examination Candidate Bulletin Information for Applicants* and the *Uniform CPA Examination Content Specifications*, both of which can be downloaded from the CPA Exam website (www.cpa-exam.org). The AICPA also publishes selected examination questions with unofficial answers indexed to the content specification outlines of the examinations. Website addresses are as follows:

- The Arab Society of Certified Accountants (ASCA) (www.ascasociety.org)
- Egyptian Society of Accountants and Auditors (www.esaaegypt.com)
- Kuwait Association of Accountants and Auditors (www.kwaaa.org)
- Accountants & Auditors Association in United Arab Emirates (www.aaa4uae.com)
- Jordan Association of Certified Public Accountants (www.jacpa.org.jo)
- Lebanese Association of Certified Public Accountants (www.lacpa.org.lb)

Some of the questions and problems at the end of the chapters in this book have been taken from past U.S. and Arab CPA examinations. They are designated 'AICPA' or 'AICPA adapted or Arab Association Examinations.'

SUMMARY

This chapter defined auditing and distinguished auditing from accounting. Audits are valuable because they reduce information risk, which lowers the cost of obtaining capital. The chapter also described attestation and assurance services, including reports on the effectiveness of internal control over financial reporting, and described the relationships among audits, attestation services, and assurance services. The chapter also described different types of audits and auditors and requirements for becoming a CPA in the U.S. and in the Arab world.

ESSENTIAL TERMS

Accounting   p. 7

Assurance service   p. 10

Attestation service   p. 10

Audit evidence   p. 5

Audit of historical financial statements   p. 11

Audit report   p. 6

Auditing   p. 4

Board of directors   p. 6

Certified public accountant   p. 20

Compliance audit   p. 16

Financial statement audit   p. 16

Forensic auditor   p. 17

Government accountability office auditor   p. 18

Independent auditors   p. 6

Information asymmetry   p. 9

Information risk   p. 7

Internal auditors   p. 19

Internal control over financial reporting   p. 11

Operational audit   p. 15

Review of historical financial statements   p. 12

Sarbanes–Oxley Act   p. 4

Tax inspectors   p. 19

REVIEW QUESTIONS

1-1 (Objective 1-5) Explain the relationships among audit services, attestation services, and assurance services, and give examples of each.

1-2 (Objective 1-3) Discuss the major factors in today's society that have made the need for independent audits much greater than it was 50 years ago.

1-3 (Objective 1-3) Distinguish among the following three risks: risk-free interest rate, business risk, and information risk. Which one or ones does the auditor reduce by performing an audit?

1-4 (Objective 1-4) Identify the major causes of information risk and identify why external audit can reduce such risk.

1-5 (Objective 1-1) Explain what is meant by determining the degree of correspondence between information and established criteria. What are the information and established criteria for the audit of Techno Company's tax return by a tax inspector? What are they for the audit of Techno Company's financial statements by a CPA firm?

1-6 (Objectives 1-1, 1-7) Describe the nature of the evidence the tax inspector will use in the audit of Techno Company's tax return.

1-7 (Objective 1-2) In the conduct of audits of financial statements, it would be a serious breach of responsibility if the auditor did not thoroughly understand accounting. However, many competent accountants do not have an understanding of the auditing process. What causes this difference?

1-8 (Objective 1-6) What are the differences and similarities in audits of financial statements, compliance audits, forensic audits, and operational audits?

1-9 (Objectives 1-6, 1-7) List three examples of specific operational audits that can be conducted by an internal auditor in a manufacturing company.

1-10 (Objectives 1-5, 1-6) What knowledge does the auditor need about the client's business in an audit of historical financial statements? Explain how this knowledge may be useful in performing other assurance or consulting services for the client.

1-11 (Objective 1-7) What are the major differences in the scope of the audit responsibilities for CPAs, GAO auditors, tax authority inspectors (TAI), and internal auditors?

1-12 (Objective 1-8) Identify the four parts of the Uniform CPA Examination and explain how they are different from examinations set by the Arab Association of Certified Public Accountants. (Look at examination details for Kuwait and Lebanese Associations of Certified Public Accountants.)

1-13 (Objective 1-8) Identify the main differences between requirements for becoming a CPA in the U.S. and in some Arab countries.

1-14 (Objective 1-5) Explain why CPAs need to be knowledgeable about e-commerce technologies.

MULTIPLE CHOICE QUESTIONS FROM CPA EXAMINATIONS

1-15 (Objectives 1-1, 1-3, 1-5) The following questions deal with audits by audit firms. Choose the best response.

   a. Which of the following best describes why an independent auditor is asked to express an opinion on the fair presentation of financial statements?
   (1) It is difficult to prepare financial statements that fairly present a company's financial position, operations, and cash flows without the expertise of an independent auditor.
   (2) It is management's responsibility to seek available independent aid in the appraisal of the financial information shown in its financial statements.
   (3) The opinion of an independent party is needed because a company may not be objective with respect to its own financial statements.
   (4) It is a customary courtesy that all stockholders of a company receive an independent report on management's stewardship of the affairs of the business.
   b. Independent auditing can best be described as:
   (1) a branch of accounting.
   (2) a discipline that attests to the results of accounting and other functional operations and data.
   (3) a professional activity that measures and communicates financial and business data.
   (4) a regulatory function that prevents the issuance of improper financial information.
   c. Which of the following professional services is an attestation engagement?
   (1) A consulting service engagement to provide computer-processing advice to a client.
   (2) An engagement to report on compliance with statutory requirements.
   (3) An income tax engagement to prepare tax returns.
   (4) The compilation of financial statements from a client's financial records.

    d. In performing an attestation engagement, an auditor typically:
      (1) supplies litigation support services.
      (2) assesses control risk at a low level.
      (3) expresses a conclusion about an assertion.
      (4) provides management consulting advice.

1-16 (Objectives 1-6, 1-7) The following questions deal with types of audits and auditors. Choose the best response.

    a. Operational audits generally have been conducted by internal auditors and government accountability office auditors but may be performed by certified public accountants. A primary purpose of an operational audit is to provide:
      (1) a means of assurance that internal accounting controls are functioning as planned.
      (2) a measure of management performance in meeting organizational goals.
      (3) the results of internal examinations of financial and accounting matters to a company's top-level management.
      (4) aid to the independent auditor, who is conducting the audit of the financial statements.

    b. In comparison to the external auditor, an internal auditor is more likely to be concerned with:
      (1) internal administrative control.
      (2) cost accounting procedures.
      (3) operational auditing.
      (4) internal control.

    c. Which of the following best describes the operational audit?
      (1) It requires the constant review by internal auditors of the administrative controls as they relate to the operations of the company.
      (2) It concentrates on implementing financial and accounting control in a newly organized company.
      (3) It attempts and is designed to verify the fair presentation of a company's results of operations.
      (4) It concentrates on seeking aspects of operations in which waste could be reduced by the introduction of controls.

    d. Compliance auditing often extends beyond audits leading to the expression of opinions on the fairness of financial presentation and includes audits of efficiency, economy, and effectiveness, as well as:
      (1) accuracy.
      (2) evaluation.
      (3) adherence to specific rules or procedures.
      (4) internal control.

DISCUSSION QUESTIONS AND PROBLEMS

1-17 (Objective 1-5) The list below indicates various audit, attestation, and assurance engagements involving auditors.

    1. A report indicating whether a governmental entity has complied with certain government regulations.
    2. A report on the effectiveness of internal control over financial reporting as required by Section 404 of the Sarbanes–Oxley Act.
    3. A report on compliance with a royalty agreement.
    4. An evaluation of the effectiveness of key measures used to assess an entity's success in achieving specific targets linked to an entity's strategic plan and vision.
    5. An auditor's report on whether the financial statements are fairly presented in accordance with International Financial Reporting Standards (IFRS).
    6. A report on the examination of a financial forecast.

7. An electronic seal indicating that an electronic seller observes certain practices.
8. A review report that provides moderate assurance about whether financial statements are fairly stated in accordance with local accounting standards.
9. A report about management's assertion on the effectiveness of controls over the availability, reliability, integrity, and maintainability of its accounting information system.

Required

    a. For each of the services listed above, indicate the type of service from the list that follows.
       (1) An audit of historical financial statements.
       (2) An attestation service other than an audit service.
       (3) An assurance service that is not an attestation service.
    b. For each of the services listed above, indicate the type of auditor or other experts who may be hired to provide such service.

1-18 (Objective 1-3) The Pyramids Company has an existing loan in the amount of US$4.5 million with an annual interest rate of 5.5 percent. The company provides an internal company-prepared financial statement to the bank under the loan agreement. Two competing banks have offered to replace Pyramids' existing loan agreement with a new one. Egyptian National Bank has offered to loan Pyramids US$4.5 million at a rate of 4.5 percent but requires Pyramids to provide financial statements that have been reviewed by an audit firm. Cairo Bank has offered to loan Pyramids US$4.5 million at a rate of 3.5 percent but requires Pyramids to provide financial statements that have been audited by an audit firm. The controller of Pyramids Company approached a CPA firm and was given an estimated cost of US$20,000 to perform a review and US$45,000 to perform an audit.

Required

a. Explain why the interest rate for the loan that requires a review report is lower than that for the loan that did not require a review. Explain why the interest rate for the loan that requires an audit report is lower than the interest rate for the other two loans.
b. Calculate Pyramids' annual costs under each loan agreement, including interest and costs for the auditing firm's services. Indicate whether Pyramids should keep its existing loan, accept the offer from Egyptian National Bank, or accept the offer from Cairo Bank.
c. Assume that Egyptian National Bank has offered the loan at a rate of 4.0 percent with a review, and the cost of the audit has increased to US$55,000 due to new auditing standards requirements. Indicate whether Pyramids should keep its existing loan, accept the offer from Egyptian National Bank, or accept the offer from Cairo Bank.
d. Discuss why Pyramids may desire to have an audit, ignoring the potential reduction in interest costs.
e. Explain how a strategic understanding of the client's business may increase the value of the audit service.

1-19 (Objective 1-7) A group of accounting students in the American University in Beirut (AUB) is discussing their future plans as part of an activity at an Employment day sponsored by the school. Karim dreams of becoming an auditor for the audit bureau because he believes that this career will provide excellent experience in risk assessment and management techniques. Sherif mentions that he is interested in income taxes and believes a career working for a tax revenues and customs authority would best fulfill his interest. Edward is considering working for an audit firm for the next five years. He believes the variety of experience in auditing might provide a wide range of opportunities and allow for personal growth. However, he does not want to plan beyond five years, because he is not sure that he wants to make it a permanent career. Yasmine is planning for a career in internal auditing within an Arab international company such as Al-Waseet or Showtime Arabia because she is drawn by the many different aspects of the organization with which internal auditors become involved. Jordan knows that he wants to pursue some aspect of auditing as a career, but tells the group that he has not yet decided on the type of organization he wants to enter. He desires an opportunity for professional development, and he also believes his employment should be interesting and meaningful.

a. What are the major advantages and disadvantages of each of the types of auditing careers mentioned by the students?

b. What other types of auditing careers might the students pursue?

1-20 (Objective 1-1) Adel Bassam works at the National Bank of Kuwait. According to the bank's records, there is currently an outstanding loan of US$380,000 to Nosco Transportation Services, a company that schedules truck trips between Kuwait City and Baghdad. The company recently missed a loan payment, and Adel is becoming concerned about whether Nosco will be able to repay the full amount of the loan. According to the documents held by the bank, the collateral on the loan consists of 20 large trucks. Each truck has an average estimated value of US$25,000. As part of his investigation of the company, Adel wants to make sure that these trucks still exist.

Adel decides that the best way to handle the situation would be to hire an auditor to count the trucks. Adel therefore engages the services of Talal abou Taha, CPA, who Adel knows has an extensive background in auditing automobile, bus, and trucking companies. Adel gives Talal the trucks' registration information, which was provided to the bank when the original loan documents were signed. He then asks him to investigate the company and write a report that includes the following information:

1. Which of the 20 registered trucks is parked in Nosco's parking lot on the night of August 31, 2011.
2. If Nosco Transportation Services actually owns or is responsible for maintaining the trucks.
3. The physical condition of each truck, using the guidelines poor, good, and excellent.

The fair market value of each truck is based on Sabour Engineering Office Valuation, which estimates the approximate wholesale prices of all used truck models, using the poor, good, and excellent conditions guidelines established in Part 3.

a. For each of the following parts of the definition of auditing, state which part of the preceding narrative fits the definition:
   (1) Information
   (2) Established criteria
   (3) Accumulating and evaluating evidence
   (4) Competent, independent person
   (5) Reporting results

b. What difficulties might Talal encounter when performing this audit?

1-21 (Objectives 1-6, 1-7) In the normal course of performing their responsibilities, auditors often conduct audits or reviews of the following:

1. Computer operations of a corporation to evaluate whether the computer center is being operated as efficiently as possible.
2. Operations of the tax authority to determine whether the tax inspectors are using their time efficiently in conducting audits.
3. Financial statements of a branch of the government to make sure that the statements present fairly the actual disbursements made during a period of time.
4. Financial statement fraud to be investigated for reporting purposes to stockholders.
5. The computer operations of a large corporation to evaluate whether the internal controls are likely to prevent misstatements in accounting and operating data.
6. Individual income tax return of an officer of the corporation to determine whether he or she has included all taxable income in his or her return.
7. Annual statements for the use of management.
8. Disbursements of a branch of the government for a special research project to determine whether it would have been possible to accomplish the same research results at a lower cost to the taxpayers.
9. Statements for bankers and other creditors when the client is too small to have an audit staff.
10. Corporate income tax returns of a corporation to determine whether the tax laws have been followed.

11. Disbursements of a branch of the government for a special research project to determine whether the expenditures were consistent with the legislative bill that authorized the project.
12. A bond indenture agreement to make sure a company is following all requirements of the contract.

   a. For these 12 examples, state the most likely type of auditor (CPA, GAO or audit bureau, internal auditors, or forensic auditor) to perform each.

   Required

   b. In each example, state the type of audit (financial statement audit, operational audit, compliance audit, or forensic audit).

CASE

1-22 (Objectives 1-3, 1-4, 1-5) As a manager responsible for the expected new audit clients, you visited Al Abor Company which is a limited liability company that manufactures the supplies of many specialized materials in the construction industry. Mr. Mounir, the executive manager and the holder of the majority stocks, asked your office to audit the company and provide the company with financial consultancy. During your first meeting you realized that:

- The sales figure increased from US$4 million to US$7 million in the last two years and the company was profitable. In addition there is expected growth as Mr. Mounir has the following plans:
  1. Increase the company's customers through making certain materials available for the public through the trade of the construction materials.
  2. Expand the products base through building a factory overseas to manufacture the components of Carbonates Silicon. Mr. Mounir directly negotiated the prices with each of the suppliers and customers.

- An accounting office was assigned in the beginning of this year to help to monitor the credit and to state more formal accounting systems and procedures, and that the computer will provide the essential information about sales, customers, inventory, and salaries.

- Mr. Mounir's stepbrother wrote the computer program to satisfy the company's requirements. Some purchases require the conversion of foreign currency and this has to be recorded manually. At the end of each month there are small differences but the accounts to monitor the customers and suppliers are not adjusted.

- The annual budget estimates the actual revenues and the actual expenses less than necessary, because the increasing growth is more than expected, and the management's accounts are prepared infrequently on an irregular basis.

- For the managerial accounting purposes the sales cost is calculated as a percentage of the sales value of the products' different categories. Historically this method proved that it is reasonably reliable when compared with the year-end evaluation of the annual inventory's physical examination.

- The production lines profit margin became increasingly variable at the current time, also Al Abor Company faces a high level of spoiled products, and these materials are returned to the warehouses as they cannot be sold for cash with a discount.

- Mr. Mounir is negotiating a bank loan to fund the costs of planned new buildings, and the contracts with the contractors and the work has started. The bank waits for the profits forecasts before the final approval on a loan amounting to US$6 million.

- Al Abor Company tends increasingly to skip the facilitation of the agreed upon bank's overdraft. Mr. Mounir said that large receivables from one of the customers are expected at the end of this month which will be used to pay the tax liability and pay an amount of US$90,000 in the loan's account.

- Recently Mr. Mounir was married and he bought an expensive apartment and a new car. He is satisfied with the accounting organization that currently audit the annual financial statements, and he said that the failure of adjusting the general ledgers is due to that, also he claimed that the organization was incapable of suggesting how to increase his rewards against his personal needs.

Required

a. Identify and describe the major activity risks associated with Al Abor Company.

b. Identify and comment on the factors that should affect the auditor's decisions if the audit office should present a proposal to audit this company.

c. Justify the appropriate audit strategy of the first audit of Al Abor Company.

d. Suggest two types of procedures that Al Abor Company should directly implement to improve its accounting procedures and financial monitoring.

MYLAB ACTIVITY

Visit MyAccountingLab and complete the following activity:

→ Internet Problem 1-1: Sarbanes–Oxley Act Internal Control Reporting Requirements.

THE PUBLIC ACCOUNTING PROFESSION

Good Auditing Includes Good Client Service

Sherif has just graduated from the School of Business, Future University, and joined one of the Big Four CPA firms. Ahmed, the audit manager, assigned him to an important but simple audit client, All-In-One Sporting Club. This sporting and social club has a simple accounting system and limited numbers of activities including tennis, squash and a number of restaurants. Ibrahim, the audit supervisor, has explained to Sherif the various audit tests that have to be carried out. Sherif needs to understand and test the club organization chart, job descriptions, and the procedures used to perform the club activities. The objective is to assess whether employees at the club are complying with such procedures or not. Also, Sherif is asked to evaluate the jobs carried out by the club employees to see whether redundancies may be possible as the club has not made a surplus over expenses for the last three years. The report prepared by Sherif with the assistance of Ibrahim and Ahmed provided several recommendations to the club management about ways in which the operating costs could be reduced to enhance revenues and minimize expenses.

LEARNING OBJECTIVES

After studying this chapter, you should be able to

2-1 Describe the nature of auditing firms, what they do, and their structure.

2-2 Understand the role of the Associations of Accountants and Auditors and other related bodies in Arab countries.

2-3 Understand the role of the Securities and Exchange Commission and the Public Company Accounting Oversight Board and the effects of the Sarbanes–Oxley Act on the CPA profession in the U.S.

2-4 Describe the key functions performed by the AICPA.

2-5 Discuss the nature of U.S. auditing standards and international standards on auditing and their applications in Arab countries.

2-6 Use generally accepted auditing standards as a basis for further study.

2-7 Identify quality control standards and practices within the accounting profession.

We learned in the first chapter that auditing plays an important role in society by reducing information risk and facilitating access to capital, and that audit firms provide additional, value-added service to their clients. As the opening story to this chapter demonstrates, audit professionals at all experience levels serve as valued advisors to their clients. This chapter describes the organization of auditing firms and the types of services they provide. We also discuss the role played by the various Associations of Accountants and Auditors in the Arab countries and the application of International Financial Reporting Standards (IFRS) in the preparation of the companies' financial statements in those countries. It also considers the effects of auditing under the Sarbanes–Oxley Act and the Public Company Accounting Oversight Board (PCAOB), as well as other standards and regulatory agencies that influence auditor performance.

Relevant International Standards on Auditing	
ISA 200	Overall Objectives of the Independent Auditor and the Conduct of an Audit in Accordance with International Standards on Auditing
ISA 220	Quality Control for an Audit of Financial Statements
ISQC1	International Standard on Quality Control (ISQC) requires firms to establish and record quality control policies and procedures regarding audit and assurance work

CERTIFIED PUBLIC ACCOUNTING FIRMS

OBJECTIVE 2-1

Describe the nature of auditing firms, what they do, and their structure.

Except for certain governmental organizations, the audits of all general use financial statements in the U.S. are done by certified public accountant (CPA) firms. The legal right to perform audits is granted to such auditing firms by regulation in each state. Auditing firms also provide many other services to their clients, such as tax and advisory services. The same applies to many Arab countries where licensed auditors perform the audit for listed and unlisted companies in those countries' stock exchanges and in the private business market.

More than 45,000 auditing firms exist in the U.S., ranging in size from one person to 20,000 partners and staff. *Accounting Today* publishes an annual list of the 100 largest accounting or auditing firms. Table 2-1 shows data for international and regional auditing firms, although the list also includes a few companies such as H&R Block Tax Services. Four size categories are used to describe CPA firms: Big Four international firms, national firms, regional and large local firms, and small local firms.

- *Big Four international firms.* The four largest auditing firms worldwide are called the 'Big Four' international auditing firms. They are the first four firms listed in Table 2-1. These four firms have offices throughout the world. All Big Four auditing firms are represented in every country in the Arab world. The Big Four firms audit nearly all of the largest companies both in the U.S. and worldwide and many smaller companies as well.
- *Regional and large local firms.* There are fewer than 200 CPA firms with professional staffs of more than 100 people. Some have only one office and serve clients primarily within commuting distance. Others have several offices in a state or region and serve a larger radius of clients. For example, Table 2-1 shows that the largest regional firms are not dramatically smaller than three of the national firms. Regional and large local firms compete for clients with other CPA firms, including national and Big Four firms.
- *Small local firms.* More than 95 percent of all auditing firms have fewer than 25 professionals in a single-office firm. They perform audits and related services

TABLE 2-1	CPA firms in the U.S.

2010 Size by Revenue	Firm	Net Revenue U.S. only (in US$ millions)	Partners	Professionals	U.S. Offices	Percentage of Total Revenue from Accounting and Auditing/Taxes/ Management Consulting and Other
BIG FOUR						
1	Deloitte & Touche	10,722.0	2,968	30,637	102	37/24/39
2	Ernst & Young	7,620.0	2,500	17,500	80	41/33/26
3	PricewaterhouseCoopers	7,369.4	2,235	22,729	76	54/31/15
4	KPMG	5,076.0	1,847	15,803	88	48/27/25
NATIONAL						
5	RSM McGladrey/McGladrey & Pullen[1]	1,460.7	751	5,331	93	44/35/21
6	Grant Thornton	1,147.8	535	3,700	52	47/26/27
7	BDO Seidman	620.0	273	1,849	37	60/25/15
8	CBiz/Mayer Hoffman McCann[2]	6600.7	465	2,085	180	23/27/50
REGIONAL[3]						
9	Crowe Horwath	508.0	240	1,636	25	65/22/13
10	BKD	393.0	258	1,256	31	52/30/18
11	Moss Adams	323.0	240	1,130	18	49/34/17
12	Plante & Moran	301.2	221	1,108	18	50/32/18
50	Holthouse Carlin & Van Tright	58.0	27	164	7	22/67/11
75	LeMaster & Daniels	41.7	27	193	12	28/51/21

[1] RSM McGladrey and McGladrey & Pullen have an alternative practice structure in which each is a separate and independent legal entity. The firm now operates under the single name McGladrey.

[2] CBiz and Mayer Hoffman and McCann are affiliated through an alternative practice structure.

[3] Only the six largest regional firms are listed.

Source: *Accounting Today* (www.webcpa.com).

primarily for smaller businesses and not-for-profit entities, although some have one or two clients with public ownership. Many small local firms do not perform audits and primarily provide accounting and tax services to their clients.

In the Arab world, a similar structure of CPA firms exists. The Big Four are well represented in most Arab countries. Local qualified and experienced partners manage and direct the services provided by such audit firms. There is joint partnership between the International CPA networks and local accountant(s) in every Arab country where the International CPA networks provide the technical knowledge in relation to assurance, audit, and other advisory services while the local accountants provide the offices and personnel needed to perform the above services. In a number of situations, some international CPA networks provide financial support for the activities of the joint partnerships to ensure recruitment of highly qualified and experienced personnel in addition to helping in the provision of highly technical audit and consultancy assignments. Audit manuals and other technical software and bulletins are provided by the head offices of the Big Four to partners and employees at those firms as guidelines for providing high quality services. The technical manuals and other supporting materials ensure consistency in the provision of services among all members of the Big Four CPA firms. Firms other than the Big Four, called the remaining top 10 CPA firms, are also represented in most Arab countries providing audit and other management advisory services. In Arab countries, there are local auditing firms with offices all over the country. Some of these auditing firms have international affiliation and others do not. Due to the traditions and culture current in the Arab countries, most of these local auditing firms are owned and managed by reputable academics, former businessmen, previous key figures in the government, and those who retired early from either the tax authorities or audit bureaus in these countries. More small local firms are found in countries such as Egypt, Tunisia, and Lebanon where one individual CPA or very few CPAs provide their services to individual smaller businesses, not-for-profit entities, or limited liability companies.

ACTIVITIES OF CPA FIRMS

As discussed in Chapter 1, CPA firms provide audit services, as well as other attestation and assurance services. Additional services commonly provided by auditing firms include accounting and bookkeeping services, tax services, and management consulting services. Auditing firms continue to develop new products and services, such as financial planning, business valuation, forensic accounting, and information technology advisory services.

- *Accounting and bookkeeping services.* Many small clients with limited accounting staff rely on auditing firms to prepare their financial statements. Some small clients lack the personnel or expertise to use accounting software to maintain their own accounting records. Thus, auditing firms perform a variety of accounting and bookkeeping services to meet the needs of these small clients. In many cases for publicly listed companies in which the financial statements are to be given to a third party, a review or even an audit is also performed. When neither of these is done, the financial statements are accompanied by a type of report by the auditing firm called a compilation report, which provides no assurance to third parties. As Table 2-1 shows, attestation services and accounting and bookkeeping services are the major source of revenue for most large auditing firms.
- *Tax services.* Auditing firms prepare corporate and individual tax returns for both audit and non-audit clients. Almost every audit firm performs tax services, which may include estate tax, stamp tax, tax planning, and other aspects of tax services. For many small firms, such services are far more important to their practice than auditing, as most of their revenue may be generated from tax services.
- *Management consulting services.* Most auditing firms provide certain services that enable their clients to operate their businesses more effectively. These services are called management consulting or management advisory services. These services range from simple suggestions for improving the client's accounting system to advice in risk management, information technology and e-commerce system design, mergers and acquisitions, due diligence, business valuations, and actuarial benefit consulting. Many large auditing firms have departments involved exclusively in management consulting services with little interaction with the audit or tax staff.

Although the Sarbanes–Oxley Act and Securities and Exchange Commission (SEC) in the U.S. and other local capital market laws and decrees in most Arab countries restrict auditors from providing many consulting services to public company audit clients, some services are allowed, and audit firms are not restricted from providing consulting to private companies and public companies that are not audit clients. Management consulting and other services continue to be a significant source of revenue for Deloitte & Touche, the only Big Four firm that has not disposed of all or most of its consulting practice. Consulting also continues to be an important source of revenue for other accounting firms. Unfortunately, information about the size of these management advisory services provided by many audit firms in Arab countries is not available because Arab culture and tradition does not allow such information to be made public.

Additional Value-Added Services

Moreover, auditors provide a number of value-added services to their clients other than accounting and bookkeeping, tax, and consultancy. These important services to clients include financial and administrative restructuring, IT consultancy, assessing business risk, and important strategic planning and recommendations for proper internal and external reporting activities. Auditors are successful in providing the above additional services due to their experience with various industry clients. Opportunities for additional value-added services should be considered by the auditor and his team to ensure client satisfaction and reduce costs and information risk to their clients.

STRUCTURE OF CPA FIRMS

CPA firms vary in the nature and range of services offered, which affects the organization and structure of the firms. Three main factors influence the organizational structure of all firms:

1. *The need for independence from clients.* Independence permits auditors to remain unbiased in drawing conclusions about the financial statements.
2. *The importance of a structure to encourage competence.* Competence permits auditors to conduct audits and perform other services efficiently and effectively. This structure means that similar types of services must be grouped into separate sections using specialization in the provisions of services to clients.
    i. The number of qualified partners and their ability to require audit and other consultancy services. The more partners there are in a CPA, the more specialized are the services provided to such clients whether audit or other consultancy.
    ii. The nature of the audit firms and their affiliation with the international CPA network. Local audit firms with international affiliation tend to classify their services in similar ways to other large member firms within the network.
    iii. The availability of funds to invest in CPA staff. The smaller the size of the audit firm with its limited funds, the smaller the number of staff and the less specialization in a CPA structure.
3. *The increased litigation risk faced by auditors.* Audit firms continue to experience increases in litigation-related costs. Some organizational structures afford a degree of protection to individual firm members by allowing limited liability status for audit firms.

Organizational Structures

A number of organizational structures are available to auditing firms. Except for the proprietorship, each structure results in an entity separate from the CPA personally, which helps promote auditor independence.

Proprietorship   Only CPA firms with one owner can operate in this form. Traditionally, all one-owner CPA firms were organized as proprietorships, but in recent years, most of them have changed to organizational forms with more limited liability because of litigation risks. Most CPA firms in the Arab world are similar to this with some ranging from firms consisting of one single auditor to firms with more than 100 auditors.

General Partnership This form of organization is the same as a proprietorship, except that there are multiple owners. This organizational structure is less popular as other types of ownership that offer some legal liability protection become authorized under various laws. Several CPA firms operating in the Arab world are composed of more than one partner forming a general partnership, with each partner sharing in the provision of services and assuming part of the financial resources needed to run the activities of the audit firm.

General Corporation The advantage of a corporation is that shareholders are liable only to the extent of their investment in the corporation. However, CPA firms in most countries in the Arab world are prohibited by law from becoming general corporations. The increased number of fraud and corruption cases in many Arab countries has prevented legislatures from allowing the formation of a CPA firm with limited liability.

Hierarchy of a Typical CPA Firm

The organizational hierarchy in a typical CPA firm includes partners or shareholders, managers, supervisors, seniors or in-charge auditors, and assistants. A new employee usually starts as an assistant and spends two or three years at each level before achieving partner status. The titles of the positions vary from firm to firm, but the structure is similar in all. When we refer in this text to the auditor, we mean the person performing some aspect of an audit. It is common to have one or more auditors from each level on larger engagements.

Table 2-2 summarizes the experience and responsibilities of each classification level within CPA firms. Advancement in CPA firms is fairly rapid, with evolving duties and responsibilities. In addition, audit staff members usually gain diverse experience across client engagements. Because of advances in computer and audit technology, junior staff on the audit are rapidly being given greater responsibility and challenges. They are required to grasp all new technology and apply it in testing the documents and records of CPA clients. Moreover, assistants must learn to use the intranet to communicate and get advice while performing the audit work.

The hierarchical nature of CPA firms helps promote competence. Individuals at each level of the audit supervise and review the work of others at the level just below them in the organizational structure. A new staff assistant is supervised directly by the senior or in-charge auditor. The staff assistant's work is then reviewed by the in-charge auditor as well as by the manager and partner.

TABLE 2-2	**Staff Levels and Responsibilities**	
Staff Level	Average Experience	Typical Responsibilities
Staff assistant	0–2 years	Performs most of the detailed audit work.
Senior or in-charge auditor	2–5 years	Coordinates and is responsible for the audit field work, including supervising and reviewing staff work.
Manager	5–10 years	Helps the in-charge auditor plan and manage the audit, reviews the in-charge auditor's work, and manages relations with the client. A manager may be responsible for more than one engagement at the same time.
Partner	10+ years	Reviews the overall audit work and is involved in significant audit decisions. A partner is an owner of the firm and therefore has the ultimate responsibility for conducting the audit and serving the client.

THE ASSOCIATIONS OF ACCOUNTANTS AND AUDITORS AND OTHER RELATED BODIES IN THE ARAB WORLD

In order to organize a particular profession, experts in the field of such a profession form an association to help promote the activities of the profession and provide licenses for those interested to practice in light of certain rules and requirements. The professional association represents its members with third parties including government authorities. Associations may publish magazines and newsletters and provide training seminars to improve the skills and knowledge of its members. In the auditing profession in every Arab country there are a number of associations organizing the performance of the audit and related activities.

> **OBJECTIVE 2-2**
>
> Understand the role of the Associations of Accountants and Auditors and other related bodies in Arab countries.

- In Kuwait, the Kuwait Association of Accountants and Auditors (KAAA) organizes and supervises the accounting and auditing profession.
- In Lebanon, the Lebanese Association of Certified Public Accountants (LACPA) identifies the requirements for accountants to become licensed auditors.
- In Saudi Arabia and United Arab Emirates, the Saudi Organization for Certified Public Accountants (SOCPA) and United Arab Emirates Accountants and Auditors Association (UAE-AAA) are the bodies responsible for determining the minimum years of experience for an accountant to become a licensed auditor.
- In Egypt, the Egyptian Society of Accountants and Auditors (ESAA) was established by a royal decree dated April 24, 1946 with the following objectives:
  1. Work for the improvement of the scientific and practical levels of practitioners in the accounting and auditing fields and to maintain the good reputation of the profession on an international level.
  2. Organize training programs and seminars for accountants wishing to join the society and sit for its membership required exams.
  3. Organize lectures, seminars, and other discussions related to all topics of the accounting and auditing profession.
  4. Exchange ideas and experience with local, Arab, and other international societies in order to ensure high quality services of accounting and auditing.
  5. Enhance and promote the preparation of researches and academic dissertation in all areas serving the profession.

To be a member of the ESAA, accountants must pass two levels of examination. For the intermediate level the candidate must pass all five courses represented in financial accounting, auditing, taxation, cost accounting, and accounting information systems. This candidate must have spent one and a half years in a CPA firm before he or she is allowed to sit this intermediate level exam. After passing the intermediate level, the candidate must continue acquiring audit experience in a CPA firm for another one and a half years before sitting the final level exams in four subjects, namely advance financial accounting, auditing, advanced taxation, and managerial accounting.

The Situation in the U.A.E.

Similarly, the UAE-AAA, established by the decision of the Ministry of Labour and Social Affairs No. 227 for 1997, aims to develop and consolidate the rules and standards for the practice of the profession of accounting and auditing in the country. The statute of the AAA includes the following objectives:[2]

1. To prepare and study the accounting and auditing standards and to submit proposals for their development to the concerned authorities in the country for ratification and issuance.
2. To propose ways and means to organize the profession and enhance its professional performance.
3. To propose the establishment of the appropriate organization for field control to ensure the implementation of accounting and auditing standards.

U.A.E. practitioners must be registered in one of the three registers maintained by the Ministry of Economy and Commerce based on the Federal Law No. 22 for 1995:

1. Register for practicing auditors
2. Register for audit trainees
3. Register for non-practicing auditors

Accountants are not allowed to work as auditors unless their names are listed in the register of practicing auditors. To be listed in the above registers, accountants must fulfill the following requirements:

1. The person must be a U.A.E. national.
2. Must maintain good behavior and conduct.
3. Must enjoy the full civil eligibility.
4. Must hold a university degree in accounting or the equivalent, or a high diploma after secondary school or he must be duly licensed by the Ministry of Economy and Commerce.
5. Must be working in the field of accounting and auditing.
6. Must accept the terms of the statute of the Accounting and Auditors Association and its related instructions.
7. To obtain approval from the Board of Directors.

Accountants move from the register for trainees to practicing auditors based on their years of experience and other qualifications. The training period is one year for those holding a fellowship degree from one of the certified accountants institutes or societies, as determined by a decision from the minister, two years for those holding a membership in such institutes or societies and those receiving a PhD in accounting and three continuous years for those holding a university degree in accounting.

Naturalized persons who wish to be included in the schedule of practicing auditors must have passed the training period, or have previously worked, after obtaining their educational qualification, for a period as specified in Article 6 of Federal Law No. 22 in one of the following fields:[3]

a. Practicing accountancy, audit, or inspection of accounts in one of the ministries, institutions, or public corporations.
b. Teaching accountancy or auditing in one of the public colleges or educational institutes.

Article 10 of Law No. 22 of 1995 allows the establishment of a company as a CPA firm on the following conditions:

- That at least one of the partners in charge must be a U.A.E. national and registered on the schedule of practicing auditors.
- The company articles of association must be drafted in Arabic, and duly attested by the concerned authorities.
- All partners should be natural persons entered in the schedule of practicing auditors, and if one of the partners was a legal entity incorporated outside the state, it must hold a license to practice the profession in the country in which it is incorporated.

Moreover, the law also requires that an auditor whose application for entry in the schedule of practicing auditors is approved must, prior to commencing his practice, take the following oath:

> "I swear to God Almighty that I undertake to perform my work with the utmost honesty, to respect the laws of the state, to safeguard the integrity of the profession, to respect its traditions and ethics, to adhere to accounting and audit standards and not to reveal the secrets of my clients, or any information entrusted to me through my work, except within the limits stipulated in the prevailing laws and regulations."

The oath shall be taken before the Undersecretary of the Ministry or his representative, and recorded in a report to be deposited with the competent administration in the Ministry.

Similar requirements exist in other countries in the Middle East and the Arab world with differences in the number of years of experience and qualifications needed for listing in the register for trainee auditors.

A Summary of the Situation in Other Countries

In Lebanon, in order for a candidate to become a CPA he should have practical experience of not less than five years, have passed the CPA exams or must be a holder of CPA or Association of Chartered Certified Accountants (ACCA) certificates.

In Saudi Arabia the candidate must have practical experience in the field of accounting after graduation with any of the following: CPA offices approved by SOCPA, or government bodies, companies or sole proprietorships.

Finally, in Kuwait a person, after graduation in auditing, must have five to seven years' experience of working in banks, insurance, other financial companies or other CPA firms, or working in the accounting or audit function of private or public companies or government ministries.

THE ACCOUNTING AND AUDITING ORGANIZATION FOR ISLAMIC INSTITUTIONS

The Accounting and Auditing Organization for Islamic Financial Institutions (AAOIFI) is an Islamic international autonomous non-profit standard setting body based in Bahrain. The organization prepares accounting, auditing, governance, ethics, and Shari'a standards for Islamic financial institutions and industry.

Islamic accounting is an accounting process which provides appropriate information (not necessarily limited to financial data) to stakeholders of an entity which will enable them to ensure that it is continuously operating within the boundaries of Shari'a and delivering on its socioeconomic objectives.

AAOIFI was established in accordance with the Agreement of Association which was signed by Islamic financial institutions in 1990 and then registered in Bahrain in 1991. As an independent international organization, AAOIFI is supported by institutional members (200 members from 40 countries as of 2011) including central banks, Islamic financial institutions, and other participants from the international Islamic banking and finance industry worldwide.

Islamic accounting

An accounting process which provides appropriate information (not necessarily limited to financial data) to stakeholders of an entity which will enable them to ensure that it is continuously operating within the boundaries of Shari'a and delivering on its socioeconomic objectives.

AAOIFI has gained support for the implementation of its standards and these are now adopted by the leading Islamic financial institutions in the Middle East, Asia, Africa, Europe, and North America.

AAOIFI Objectives

AAOIFI aims to 'develop accounting, auditing, governance and ethical thought relating to the activities of Islamic financial institutions'. In doing so, it seeks to build on those international standards and practices that comply with Islamic Shari'a rules. The organization seeks to harmonize the accounting policies adopted by Islamic financial institutions and to improve the quality and uniformity of auditing and governance practices. It supports the work of the Shari'a supervisory boards of these institutions by providing educational and training programs, including supporting professional development in accounting, auditing, ethics, governance, Shari'a, and other related areas. It promotes good practice within the Islamic financial industry by preparing and disseminating codes of ethics. AAOIFI also encourages any other financial institution that offers Islamic financial products to adopt its standards and guidelines. A full list of AAOIFI's objectives can be found on the organization's website.[4]

Islamic Shari'a is followed when carrying out these objectives as it presents a blueprint for all aspects of Islamic life and the environment in which Islamic financial institutions have developed. This means that users of the financial statements of Islamic financial institutions can have confidence in the information presented to them so that they will be encouraged to invest in or deposit their funds in such financial institutions and use other services provided by them.

The Islamic Financial Services Board

Based in Kuala Lumper, The Islamic Financial Services Board (IFSB) was established in 2002 and began operating in March 2003. The IFSB is the international standard-setting body for all regulatory and supervisory agencies, and aims to ensure that the Islamic financial services industry (which includes banking, capital markets, and insurance) is operating effectively and transparently. This is achieved by introducing, and encouraging the adoption of, new international standards that have been adapted to ensure consistency with Shari'a principles.

As of March 2012, the IFSB has 187 members throughout 43 jurisdictions. These include regulatory and supervisory authorities, international inter-governmental organizations, and more than 120 firms, industry associations, and other market players.

The IFSB has published a number of Standards and Guiding principles for the Islamic financial services industry (see Table 2-3), as well as a number of Guidance and Technical Notes.

SARBANES–OXLEY ACT AND PUBLIC COMPANY ACCOUNTING OVERSIGHT BOARD

OBJECTIVE 2-3

Understand the role of the Securities and Exchange Commission and the Public Company Accounting Oversight Board and the effects of the Sarbanes–Oxley Act on the CPA profession in the U.S.

Triggered by the bankruptcies and alleged audit failures involving such companies as Enron and WorldCom, the Sarbanes–Oxley Act is considered by many to be the most important legislation affecting the auditing profession since the 1933 and 1934 Securities Acts. The provisions of the Act dramatically changed the relationship between publicly held companies in the U.S. and their audit firms.

TABLE 2-3	Standards issued by IFSB
IFSB-1:	Guiding Principles of Risk Management for Institutions (other than Insurance Institutions) offering only Islamic Financial Services (IFS)
IFSB-2:	Capital Adequacy Standard for Institutions (other than Insurance Institutions) offering only Islamic Financial Services (IFS)
IFSB-3:	Guiding Principles on Corporate Governance for Institutions offering only Islamic Financial Services (excluding Islamic Insurance (*Takaful*) Institutions and Islamic Mutual Funds)
IFSB-4:	Disclosures to Promote Transparency and Market Discipline for Institutions offering Islamic Financial Services (excluding Islamic Insurance (*Takaful*) Institutions and Islamic Mutual Funds)
IFSB-5:	Guidance on Key Elements in the Supervisory Review Process of Institutions offering Islamic Financial Services (excluding Islamic Insurance (*Takaful*) Institutions and Islamic Mutual Funds)
IFSB-6:	Guiding Principles on Governance for Islamic Collective Investment Schemes
IFSB-7:	Capital Adequacy Requirements for *Sukuk*, Securitizations and Real Estate investment
IFSB-8:	Guiding Principles on Governance for *Takaful* (Islamic Insurance) Undertakings
IFSB-9:	Guiding Principles on Conduct of Business for Institutions offering Islamic Financial Services
IFSB-10:	Guiding Principles on *Shari'a* Governance Systems for Institutions offering Islamic Financial Services
IFSB-11:	Standard on Solvency Requirements for *Takaful* (Islamic Insurance) Undertakings
IFSB-12:	Guiding Principles on Liquidity Risk Management for Institutions offering Islamic Financial Services
IFSB-13:	Guiding Principles on Stress Testing for Institutions offering Islamic Financial Services

Source: IFSB website, http://www.ifsb.org/published.php (accessed July 3, 2012)

The Sarbanes–Oxley Act established the **Public Company Accounting Oversight Board (PCAOB)**, appointed and overseen by the SEC. The PCAOB provides oversight for auditors of public companies, establishes auditing and quality control standards for public company audits, and performs inspections of the quality controls at audit firms performing those audits.

The PCAOB conducts inspections of registered accounting firms to assess their compliance with the rules of the PCAOB and SEC, professional standards, and each firm's own quality control policies. The PCAOB requires annual inspections of accounting firms that audit more than 100 issuers and inspections of other registered firms at least once every three years. Any violations could result in disciplinary action by the PCAOB and be reported to the SEC and state accountancy boards.

Public Company Accounting Oversight Board (PCAOB)

Board created by the Sarbanes–Oxley Act to oversee auditors of public companies, including establishing auditing and quality control standards and performing inspections of registered accounting CPA firms.

SECURITIES AND EXCHANGE COMMISSION (SEC)

The **Securities and Exchange Commission (SEC)**, an agency of the U.S. federal government, assists in providing investors with reliable information upon which to make investment decisions. The U.S. Securities Act of 1933 requires most companies planning to issue *new securities* to the public to submit a registration statement to the SEC for approval. The U.S. Securities Exchange Act of 1934 provides additional protection by requiring public companies and others to file detailed annual reports with the commission. The commission examines these statements for completeness and adequacy before permitting the company to sell its securities through the securities exchanges.

Although the SEC requires considerable information that is not of direct interest to CPAs, the Securities Acts of 1933 and 1934 require financial statements, accompanied by the opinion of an independent public accountant, as part of a registration statement and subsequent reports.

Securities and Exchange Commission (SEC)

A U.S federal agency that oversees the orderly conduct of the securities markets; the SEC assists in providing investors in public corporations with reliable information upon which to make investment decisions.

Of special interest to auditors are several specific reports that are subject to the reporting provisions of the securities acts. The most important of these are as follows:

- *Form S-1.* S forms apply to the Securities Act of 1933 and must be completed and registered with the SEC when a company plans to issue new securities to the public. The S-1 form is the general form used when there is no specifically prescribed form. The others are specialized forms. For example, S-11 is for registration of securities of certain real estate companies.
- *Form 8-K.* This report is filed to report significant events that are of interest to public investors. Such events include the acquisition or sale of a subsidiary, a change in officers or directors, an addition of a new product line, or a change in auditors.
- *Form 10-K.* This report must be filed annually within 60 to 90 days after the close of each fiscal year, depending on the size of the company. Extensive detailed financial information, including audited financial statements, is contained in this report.
- *Form 10-Q.* This report must be filed quarterly for all publicly held companies. It contains certain financial information and requires timely auditor reviews of the financial statements before filing with the commission.

Because large CPA firms usually have clients that must file one or more of these reports each year, and the rules and regulations affecting filings with the SEC are extremely complex, most CPA firms have specialists who spend a large portion of their time ensuring that their clients satisfy all SEC requirements.

The SEC has considerable influence in setting generally accepted accounting principles (GAAP) and disclosure requirements for financial statements as a result of its authority for specifying reporting requirements considered necessary for fair disclosure to investors. The SEC has power to establish rules for any CPA associated with audited financial statements submitted to the commission. The SEC's attitude is generally considered in any major change proposed by the Financial Accounting Standards Board (FASB), the independent organization that establishes U.S. GAAP.

The SEC requirements of greatest interest to CPAs are set forth in the commission's Regulation S-X, Accounting Series Releases, and Accounting and Auditing Enforcement Releases. These publications constitute important regulations, as well as decisions and opinions on accounting and auditing issues affecting any CPA dealing with publicly held companies.

AMERICAN INSTITUTE OF CERTIFIED PUBLIC ACCOUNTANTS (AICPA)

In the U.S., CPAs are licensed by the state in which they practice, but a significant influence on CPAs is exerted by their national professional organization, the American Institute of Certified Public Accountants (**AICPA**). Membership in the AICPA is restricted to CPAs, but not all members are practicing as independent auditors. Many members formerly worked for CPA firms but are currently working in government, industry, and education. AICPA membership is voluntary, so not all CPAs join. With over 350,000 CPAs, the AICPA is the largest professional association for CPAs in the U.S. Many graduates in the Arab countries are motivated to sit the AICPA exams, as a license to practice from this prestigious professional body would enable them to join any of the Big Four CPA firms anywhere in the world. There is some competition between the AICPA and the British professional associations including the Institute of Chartered Accountants in England and Wales (ICAEW) and the ACCA for the provision of chartered accountants' (CA) certificates and many Arab graduates are attracted to join one of these bodies. A decision was made recently that AICPA could hold its examinations in Dubai, Lebanon, and Kuwait. The AICPA decision was made in light of the decision made by ACCA that all its exams could be held in every country in the Arab world.

The AICPA sets professional requirements for CPAs, conducts research, and publishes materials on many different subjects related to accounting, auditing, attestation and assurance services, management consulting services, and taxes. The AICPA also promotes the accounting profession through organizing national advertising campaigns, promoting new assurance services, and developing specialist certificates to help market and ensure the quality of services in specialized practice areas. For example, the association currently offers specialty designations in business valuation, financial planning, information technology, and financial forensics. Similar requirements and activities are provided by both the ICAEW and ACCA in the UK.

OBJECTIVE 2-4

Describe the key functions performed by the AICPA.

AICPA

American Institute of Certified Public Accountants, a voluntary organization of CPAs that sets professional requirements, conducts research, and publishes materials relevant to accounting, auditing, management consulting services, and taxes.

Establishing Standards and Rules

The AICPA sets standards and rules that all members and other practicing CPAs must follow. Four major areas in which the AICPA has authority to set standards and make rules are as follows:

1. *Auditing standards.* The Auditing Standards Board (ASB) is responsible for issuing pronouncements on auditing matters for all entities other than publicly traded companies. ASB pronouncements are called **Statements on Auditing Standards (SASs)**. They are further discussed later in this chapter and throughout the text.
2. *Compilation and review standards.* The Accounting and Review Services Committee is responsible for issuing pronouncements of the CPA's responsibilities for review and compilation services when a CPA is associated with financial statements of privately owned companies that are not audited. They are called Statements on Standards for Accounting and Review Services (SSARS), and they provide guidance for performing compilation and review services. In a compilation service, the accountant helps the client prepare financial statements without providing any assurance. In a review service, the accountant performs inquiry and analytical procedures that provide a reasonable basis for expressing limited assurance on the financial statements.

Statements on Auditing Standards (SASs)

Pronouncements issued by the AICPA to interpret generally accepted auditing standards.

3. *Other attestation standards.* Statements on Standards for Attestation Engagements provide a framework for the development of standards for attestation engagements. Detailed standards have been developed for specific types of attestation services, such as reports on prospective financial information in forecasts and projections. Assurance standards are studied in Chapter 25.
4. *Code of Professional Conduct.* The AICPA Committee on Professional Ethics sets rules of conduct that CPAs are required to meet. The rules and their relationships to ethical conduct are the subject of Chapter 5.

Other AICPA Functions

In addition to writing and grading the CPA examination, the AICPA performs many educational and other functions for CPAs. The association supports research by its own research staff and provides grants to others. It also publishes a variety of materials, including journals such as the *Journal of Accountancy*, industry audit guides for several industries, periodic updates of the *Codification of Statements on Auditing Standards*, and the *Code of Professional Conduct.*

CPAs must meet continuing education requirements to maintain their licenses to practice and to stay current on the extensive and ever-changing body of knowledge in accounting, auditing, attestation and assurance services, management consulting services, and taxes. The AICPA provides a considerable number of seminars and educational aids in a variety of subjects, such as online continuing education opportunities and reference materials in its *CPExpress* online learning library.

U.S. AND INTERNATIONAL STANDARDS ON AUDITING

OBJECTIVE 2-5

Discuss the nature of U.S. auditing standards and international standards on auditing and their applications in the Arab countries.

Auditing standards are general guidelines to aid auditors in fulfilling their professional responsibilities in the audit of historical financial statements. They include consideration of professional qualities such as competence and independence, reporting requirements, and evidence. The three main sets of auditing standards are International Standards on Auditing, U.S. generally accepted auditing standards, and PCAOB auditing standards.

International Standards on Auditing

International Standards on Auditing (ISAs)

Statements issued by the International Auditing and Assurance Standards Board of the International Federation of Accountants to promote international acceptance of auditing standards.

International Standards on Auditing (ISAs) are issued by the International Auditing and Assurance Standards Board (IAASB) of the International Federation of Accountants (IFAC). IFAC is the worldwide organization for the accountancy profession, with 157 member organizations in 123 countries, representing more than 2.5 million accountants throughout the world. The IAASB works to improve the uniformity of auditing practices and related services throughout the world by issuing pronouncements on a variety of audit and attest functions and by promoting their acceptance worldwide.

The IAASB publishes international standards including International Standards on Quality Control (ISQCs), ISAs, International Standards on Review Engagements (ISREs), International Standards on Assurance Engagements (ISAEs), and International Standards on Related Services (ISRSs). All the above standards are called the IAASB's *Engagement Standards*. A detailed list of all International Standards on Auditing issued up to 2010 is shown in Table 2-4.

TABLE 2-4	International Standards on Auditing

200–299	**General Principles and Responsibilities**
ISA 200	Objectives of the Independent Auditor and the Conduct of an Audit in Accordance with International Standards on Auditing
ISA 210	Agreeing the Terms of Audit Engagements
ISA 220	Quality Control for an Audit of Financial Statements
ISA 230	Audit Documentation
ISA 240	The Auditor's Responsibilities Relating to Fraud in an Audit of Financial Statements
ISA 250	Considerations of Laws and Regulations in an Audit of Financial Statements
ISA 260	Communication with Those Charged with Governance
ISA 265	Communicating Deficiencies in Internal Control to Those Charged with Governance and Management
300–499	**Risk Assessment and Response to Assessed Risks**
ISA 300	Planning an Audit of Financial Statements
ISA 315	Identifying and Assessing the Risks of Material Misstatement through Understanding the Entity and its Environment
ISA 320	Materiality in Planning and Performing an Audit
ISA 330	The Auditor's Responses to Assessed Risks
ISA 402	Audit Considerations Relating to an Entity using a Service Organization
ISA 450	Evaluation of Misstatements Identified during the Audit
500–599	**Audit Evidence**
ISA 500	Audit Evidence
ISA 501	Audit Evidence – Specific Considerations for Selected Items
ISA 505	External Confirmations
ISA 510	Initial Audit Engagements – Opening Balances
ISA 520	Analytical Procedures
ISA 530	Audit Sampling
ISA 540	Auditing Accounting Estimates, including Fair Value Accounting Estimates and Related Disclosures
ISA 550	Related Parties
ISA 560	Subsequent Events
ISA 570	Going Concern
ISA 580	Written Representation
600–699	**Using the Work of Others**
ISA 600	Special Considerations – Audits of Group Financial Statements (including The Work of Component Auditors)
ISA 610	Using the Work of Internal Auditors
ISA 620	Using the Work of an Auditor's Expert
700–799	**Audit Conclusions and Reporting**
ISA 700	Forming an Opinion and Reporting on Financial Statements
ISA 705	Modifications to the Opinion in the Independent Auditor's Report
ISA 706	Emphasis of Matter Paragraphs and Other Matter Paragraphs in the Independent Auditor's Report
ISA 710	Comparative Information – Corresponding Figures and Comparative Financial Statements
ISA 720	The Auditor's Responsibilities Relating to other Information in Documents containing Audited Financial Statements
800–899	**Specialized Areas**
ISA 800	Special Considerations – Audits of Financial Statements Prepared in Accordance with Special Purpose Frameworks
ISA 805	Special Considerations – Audits of Single Financial Statements and Specific Elements, Accounts or Items of a Financial Statement
ISA 810	Engagements to Report on Summary Financial Statements

Source: As listed on IFAC website: http://www.ifac.org/auditing-assurance/clarity-center/clarified-standards

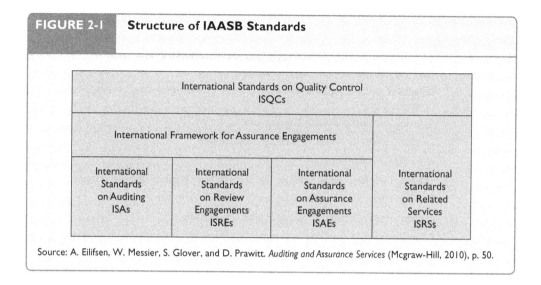

FIGURE 2-1   Structure of IAASB Standards

International Standards on Quality Control ISQCs			
International Framework for Assurance Engagements			
International Standards on Auditing ISAs	International Standards on Review Engagements ISREs	International Standards on Assurance Engagements ISAEs	International Standards on Related Services ISRSs

Source: A. Eilifsen, W. Messier, S. Glover, and D. Prawitt. *Auditing and Assurance Services* (Mcgraw-Hill, 2010), p. 50.

The Public Interest Oversight Board (PIOB) oversees the auditing and assurance, ethics, and education standard-setting activities of the IAASB, the International Ethics Standards Board for Accountants (IESBA), and the International Accounting Education Standards Board (IAESB). The PIOB must approve all exposure drafts of proposed auditing standards before they are considered official pronouncements. The PIOB assesses whether the standard setting has met the needs of stakeholders including investors, regulators, and other users of financial statements. A consultative advisory group (CAG) for each board responsible for standard setting provides additional public interest feedback into the standard-setting process.

ISAs do not override a country's regulations governing the audit of financial or other information, as each country generally has its own regulations governing audit practices. These regulations may be either government statutes or statements issued by regulatory or professional bodies. Most countries base their auditing standards on ISAs, modified as appropriate for each country's regulatory environment and statutory requirements. In Europe, the European Commission (EC) decided that the performance of the statutory audit in the European Union shall comply fully with the ISAs according to the newly issued 8th Directive on Statutory Audit. The directive determines principles for public oversight, criteria for external quality assurance programs (structure and systems), and requirements for auditors' and CPA firms' independence.

Similar steps have been taken in many Arab countries to ensure compliance with auditing standards by companies whether listed or unlisted. In Egypt, for example, the General Supervisory Financial Authority (GSFA) in cooperation with the Egyptian Society of Accountants and Auditors (ESAA) issued the Egyptian Standards on Auditing (ESA) reflecting a translated set of ISAs. In Kuwait, Lebanon, and the United Arab Emirates practitioners apply the ISAs whenever they provide audit services for listed and non-listed companies. In Saudi Arabia, the convergence of the national standards with ISAs is one of the objectives of the SOCPA.

U.S. Generally Accepted Auditing Standards

Auditing standards for private entities in the United States are established by the ASB. These generally accepted auditing standards (GAAS) are similar to the ISAs, although there are some differences. If an auditor in the United States is auditing historical financial statements in accordance with ISAs, the auditor must meet any ISA requirements that extend beyond GAAS. Major differences must be determined between U.S. GAAS and ISAs, and auditors are required to comply fully with additional requirements embedded in ISAs.

Prior to passage of the Sarbanes–Oxley Act, the ASB established auditing standards for private and public companies. The PCAOB now has responsibility for auditing standards for public companies, while the ASB continues to provide auditing standards for private companies.

PCAOB Auditing Standards

The PCAOB adopted existing auditing standards established by the ASB as interim audit standards. As a result, auditing standards for U.S. public and private companies are mostly similar and are primarily based on standards previously established by the ASB. The PCAOB is now issuing its own auditing standards, including establishing standards for audits of the effectiveness of internal control over financial reporting. These standards are referred to as PCAOB auditing standards in the audit reports of public companies and when referenced in the text, and apply only to the audits of public companies. Statements on auditing standards issued by the ASB after the establishment of the PCAOB do not have to be followed in the audit of public companies. However, when reference is made to a Statement on Auditing Standards (SAS) issued by the ASB, it is assumed that the standard applies to both public and private companies unless noted otherwise.

Figure 2-2 summarizes the relations among international auditing standards, generally accepted auditing standards, and PCAOB auditing standards. International auditing standards as adopted by standard-setting bodies in individual countries apply to audits of entities in the majority of countries all over the world. Generally accepted auditing standards are similar to international auditing standards and apply to the audits of private companies and other entities in the United States. PCAOB auditing standards apply to audits of U.S. public companies and other SEC registrants.

The overlapping ovals illustrate that there are more similarities than differences in the three sets of standards. The auditing concepts illustrated throughout this book are generally applicable to all audits. When we refer to 'auditing standards,' the term refers to the ISAs.

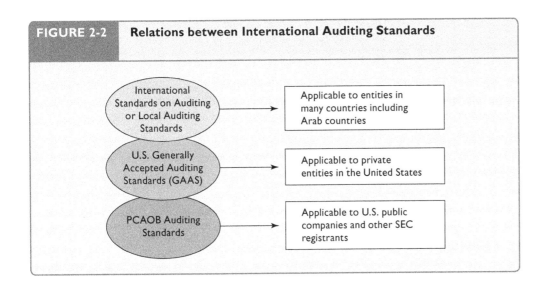

FIGURE 2-2   Relations between International Auditing Standards

GENERALLY ACCEPTED AUDITING STANDARDS

OBJECTIVE 2-6

Use generally accepted auditing standards as a basis for further study.

Generally accepted auditing standards (GAAS)

Ten auditing standards, developed by the AICPA, consisting of general standards, standards of field work, and standards of reporting, along with interpretations; often called auditing standards.

The broadest guidelines available to auditors in the U.S. are the ten **generally accepted auditing standards (GAAS)**, which were developed by the AICPA and most recently updated by SAS 105 and SAS 113. These standards, detailed in Table 2-5, are not sufficiently specific to provide any meaningful guide to practitioners, but they do represent a framework upon which the AICPA can provide interpretations.

As illustrated in Figure 2-3, the 10 generally accepted auditing standards fall into three categories:

- General standards
- Standards of field work
- Reporting standards

TABLE 2-5	**Generally Accepted Auditing Standards**

General Standards

1. The auditor must have adequate technical training and proficiency to perform the audit.
2. The auditor must maintain independence in mental attitude in all matters relating to the audit.
3. The auditor must exercise due professional care in the performance of the audit and the preparation of the report.

Standards of Field Work

1. The auditor must adequately plan the work and must properly supervise any assistants.
2. The auditor must obtain a sufficient understanding of the entity and its environment, including its internal control, to assess the risk of material misstatement of the financial statements whether due to error or fraud, and to design the nature, timing, and extent of further audit procedures.
3. The auditor must obtain sufficient appropriate audit evidence by performing audit procedures to afford a reasonable basis for an opinion regarding the financial statements under audit.

Standards of Reporting

1. The auditor must state in the auditor's report whether the financial statements are presented in accordance with generally accepted accounting principles (GAAP).
2. The auditor must identify in the auditor's report those circumstances in which such principles have not been consistently observed in the current period in relation to the preceding period.
3. When the auditor determines that informative disclosures are not reasonably adequate, the auditor must so state in the auditor's report.
4. The auditor must either express an opinion regarding the financial statements, taken as a whole, or state that an opinion cannot be expressed, in the auditor's report. When the auditor cannot express an overall opinion, the auditor should state the reasons therefore in the auditor's report. In all cases where an auditor's name is associated with financial statements, the auditor should clearly indicate the character of the auditor's work, if any, and the degree of responsibility the auditor is taking, in the auditor's report.

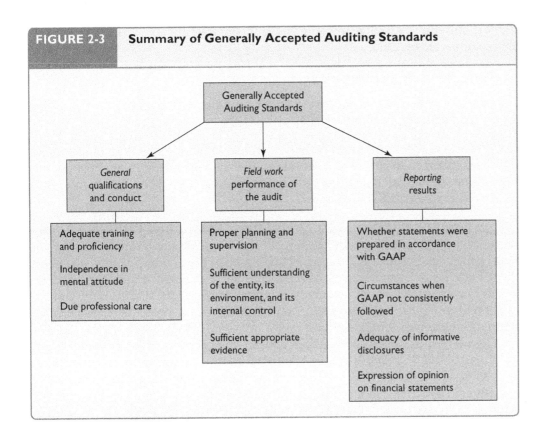

FIGURE 2-3   **Summary of Generally Accepted Auditing Standards**

General Standards

The general standards stress the important personal qualities that the auditor should possess.

Adequate Technical Training and Proficiency   The first general standard is normally interpreted as requiring the auditor to have formal education in auditing and accounting, adequate practical experience for the work being performed, and continuing professional education. Recent court cases clearly demonstrate that auditors must be technically qualified and experienced in those industries in which their audit clients are engaged.

In any case in which the CPA or the CPA's assistants are not qualified to perform the work, a professional obligation exists to acquire the requisite knowledge and skills, suggest someone else who is qualified to perform the work, or decline the engagement.

Independence in Mental Attitude   The importance of independence was emphasized in Chapter 1 under the definition of auditing. The *Code of Professional Conduct* and ISAs stress the need for independence. CPA firms are required to follow several practices to increase the likelihood of independence of all personnel. Auditors are prohibited from providing audit services for companies where a close relative holds a significant executive position or is a member of that company's board of directors. Specific methods to ensure that auditors maintain their independence are studied in Chapter 5.

Due Professional Care   The third general standard involves due care in the performance of all aspects of auditing. Simply stated, this means that auditors are professionals responsible for fulfilling their duties diligently and carefully. Due care includes consideration of the completeness of the audit documentation, the sufficiency of the audit evidence, and the appropriateness of the audit report. As professionals, auditors must not act negligently or in bad faith, but they are not expected to be infallible or suspected of fraud.

Standards of Field Work

The standards of field work concern evidence accumulation and other activities during the actual conduct of the audit.

Adequate Planning and Supervision The first standard requires that the audit be sufficiently planned to ensure an adequate audit and proper supervision of assistants. Supervision is essential in auditing because a considerable portion of the field work is done by less experienced staff members.

Understand the Entity and its Environment, Including Internal Control
To adequately perform an audit, the auditor must have an understanding of the client's business and industry. This understanding helps the auditor identify significant **client business risks** and the risk of significant misstatements in the financial statements. For example, to audit a bank, an auditor must understand the nature of the bank's operations, banking and central bank regulations, and risks affecting significant accounts such as loan loss reserves.

> **Client business risk**
>
> The risk that the client will fail to achieve its objectives related to (1) reliability of financial reporting, (2) effectiveness and efficiency of operations, and (3) compliance with laws and regulations.

One of the most widely accepted concepts in the theory and practice of auditing is the importance of the client's system of internal control for mitigating client business risks, safeguarding assets and records, and generating reliable financial information. If the auditor is convinced that the client has an excellent system of internal control, one that includes adequate internal controls for providing reliable data, the amount of audit evidence to be accumulated can be significantly less than when controls are not adequate. In some instances, internal control may be so inadequate as to preclude conducting an effective audit.

Sufficient Appropriate Evidence Decisions about how much and what types of evidence to accumulate for a given set of circumstances require professional judgment. A major portion of this book is concerned with the study of evidence accumulation and the circumstances affecting the amount and types needed.

Standards of Reporting

The four reporting standards require the auditor to prepare a report on the financial statements taken as a whole, including informative disclosures. The reporting standards also require that the report state whether the statements are presented in accordance with GAAP and also identify any circumstances in which GAAP have not been consistently applied in the current year compared with the previous one.

STATEMENTS ON AUDITING STANDARDS

The ten GASS are too general to provide meaningful guidance, so auditors turn to the SASs issued by the ASB for more specific guidance. These statements interpret the ten GASS and have the status of GAAS and are often referred to as auditing standards or GAAS, even though they are not part of the ten GASS. GASS and SASs are regarded as *authoritative* literature, and every member who performs audits of historical financial statements in the U.S. is required to follow them under the AICPA *Code of Professional Conduct*. The ASB issues new statements when an auditing problem arises of sufficient importance to warrant an official interpretation.

Classification of Statements on Auditing Standards

All SASs are given two classification numbers: an SAS number and an AU number that indicates location in the *Codification of Auditing Standards*. Both classification systems are used in practice. For example, the Statement on Auditing Standards, *The Relationship of Generally Accepted Auditing Standards to Quality Control Standards*, is SAS 25 and AU 161. The SAS number identifies the order in which it was issued in relation to other SASs; the AU number identifies its location in the AICPA codification of all SASs. AUs beginning with a '2' are always interpretations of the general standards. Those beginning with a '3' are related to field work standards, and those beginning with a '4,' '5,' or '6' deal with reporting standards.

GAAS and Standards of Performance

Although GAAS, SASs, and ISAs are the authoritative auditing guidelines for members of the profession in the U.S. and in other countries including the Arab world, they provide less direction to auditors than might be assumed. Almost no specific audit procedures are required by the standards, and there are no specific requirements for auditors' decisions, such as determining sample size, selecting sample items from the population for testing, or evaluating results. Many practitioners believe that the standards should provide more clearly defined guidelines for determining the extent of evidence to be accumulated. Such specificity would eliminate some difficult audit decisions and provide a line of defense for a CPA firm charged with conducting an inadequate audit. However, highly specific requirements could turn auditing into mechanistic evidence gathering, devoid of professional judgment. From the point of view of both the profession and the users of auditing services, there is probably greater harm in defining authoritative guidelines too specifically than too broadly.

GAAS, SASs, and ISAs should be looked on by practitioners as *minimum standards* of performance rather than as maximum standards or ideals. At the same time, the existence of auditing standards does not mean the auditor must always follow them blindly. If an auditor believes that the requirement of a standard is impractical or impossible to perform, the auditor is justified in following an alternative course of action. Similarly, if the issue in question is immaterial in amount, it is also unnecessary to follow the standard. However, the burden of justifying departures from the standards falls on the auditor.

When auditors desire more specific guidelines, they must turn to less authoritative sources, including textbooks, journals, and technical publications. Materials published by the AICPA, such as the *Journal of Accountancy* and industry audit guides, provide assistance on specific questions.

The same applies to countries in the Arab world. For example, in Kuwait, a similar magazine is distributed to members of the KAAA.

QUALITY CONTROL

For a CPA firm, **quality control** comprises the methods used to ensure that the firm meets its professional responsibilities to clients and others. These methods include the organizational structure of the audit firm and the procedures the firm establishes. For example, an audit firm might have an organizational structure that ensures the technical review of every engagement by a partner who has expertise in the client's industry.

The International Standard on Quality Control (ISQC) discusses a firm's responsibilities for its system of quality control for audits and reviews of financial statements,

> **OBJECTIVE 2-7**
>
> Identify quality control standards and practices within the accounting profession.

Quality control

Methods used by a CPA firm to ensure that the firm meets its professional responsibilities to clients and others.

and other assurance and related services engagements. ISA 220 deals with quality control procedures for audit of financial statements. The standard states that the objective of the firm is to establish and maintain a system of quality control in order to provide it with reasonable assurance that:

a. the firm and its employees comply with professional standards and applicable legal and regulatory requirements; and

b. the reports issued by the firm reflecting the results of its services are appropriate in the circumstances.

Auditing standards require each audit firm to establish quality control policies and procedures. The standards recognize that a quality control system can provide only reasonable assurance, not a guarantee, that auditing standards are followed.

Quality control is closely related to but distinct from auditing standards. To ensure that GAAS are followed on every audit, an audit firm follows specific quality control procedures that help it meet those standards consistently on every engagement. Quality controls are therefore established for the entire audit firm, whereas GAAS are applicable to individual engagements.

Elements of Quality Control

Each firm should document its quality control policies and procedures. Procedures should depend on such things as the size of the firm including the number of partners and employees, the organizational structure of the firm, the number of practice offices, and the nature of the practice. The quality control procedures of a 150-office international firm with many complex multinational clients should differ considerably from those of a five-person firm specializing in small audits in one or two industries.

The system of quality control should include policies and procedures that address six elements. These are listed in Table 2-6 with brief descriptions and procedural examples that firms might use to satisfy the requirement.

TABLE 2-6	Elements of Quality Control	
Element	**Summary of Requirements**	**Example of a Procedure**
Leadership responsibilities for quality within the firm ('tone at the top')	The firm should promote a culture that quality is essential in performing engagements and should establish policies and procedures that support that culture.	The firm's training programs emphasize the importance of quality work, and this is reinforced in performance evaluation and compensation decisions.
Relevant ethical requirements	All personnel on engagements should maintain independence in mind and in appearance, perform all professional responsibilities with integrity, and maintain objectivity in performing their professional responsibilities.	Each partner and employee must answer an 'independence questionnaire' annually, dealing with such things as stock ownership and membership on boards of directors.
Acceptance and continuation of clients and engagements	Policies and procedures should be established for deciding whether to accept or continue a client relationship. These policies and procedures should minimize the risk of associating with a client whose management lacks integrity. The firm should also only undertake engagements that can be completed with professional competence.	A client evaluation form, dealing with such matters as predecessor auditor comments and evaluation of management, must be prepared for every new client before acceptance.

(Table 2-6 continued on next page)

TABLE 2-6	Elements of Quality Control (*Cont.*)	
Element	**Summary of Requirements**	**Example of a Procedure**
Human resources	Policies and procedures should be established to provide the firm with reasonable assurance that • All new personnel should be qualified to perform their work competently. • Work is assigned to personnel who have adequate technical training and proficiency. • All personnel should participate in continuing professional education and professional development activities that enable them to fulfil their assigned responsibilities. • Personnel selected for advancement have the qualifications necessary for the fulfillment of their assigned responsibilities.	Each professional must be evaluated on every engagement using the firm's individual engagement evaluation report.
Engagement performance	Policies and procedures should exist to ensure that the work performed by engagement personnel meets applicable professional standards, regulatory requirements, and the firm's standards of quality.	The firm's director of accounting and auditing is available for consultation and must approve all engagements before their completion.
Monitoring	Policies and procedures should exist to ensure that the other quality control elements are being effectively applied.	The quality control partner must test the quality control procedures at least annually to ensure the firm is in compliance.

Peer Review

In the U.S., public accounting firms must be enrolled in an AICPA approved practice-monitoring program for members in the firm to be eligible for membership in the AICPA. Practice-monitoring, also known as **peer review**, is the review, by CPAs, of a CPA firm's compliance with its quality control system. The purpose of a peer review is to determine and report whether the audit firm being reviewed has developed adequate quality control policies and procedures and follows them in practice. Unless a firm has a peer review, all members of the audit firm lose their eligibility for AICPA membership.

Peer review
The review by CPAs of a CPA firm's compliance with its quality control system.

The two AICPA-approved practice-monitoring programs are the Center for Public Company Audit Firms Peer Review Program and the AICPA Peer Review Program. Firms required to be registered with and inspected by the PCAOB must be enrolled in the Center for Public Company Audit Firms Peer Review Program, which is designed to review and evaluate the non-SEC portion of the firm's accounting and auditing practice that is not inspected by the PCAOB.

The AICPA Peer Review Program is administered by the state CPA societies under the overall direction of the AICPA peer review board. Reviews are conducted every three years, and are normally performed by a CPA firm selected by the firm being reviewed, although the firm can request that it be assigned a reviewer through the administering state society. However, the state CPA societies can object to the selection of a CPA firm. After the review is completed, the reviewers issue a report stating their conclusions and recommendations. Results of the peer review are included in a public file by the AICPA.

Peer review benefits individual firms by helping them meet quality control standards, which, in turn, benefits the profession through improved practitioner performance and higher-quality audits. A firm having a peer review can further benefit if the review improves the firm's practice, and thereby enhances its reputation and effectiveness, and reduces the likelihood of lawsuits. Of course, peer reviews are expensive to conduct, so the benefits come at a cost.

In the Arab world, the review of the quality of the audit provided by auditing firms is undertaken by the international CPA networks. Each CPA network carries out an interim review of its members' quality of services using standard practices applied within the network. The head office of the CPA network assigns the assessment of a member performance to one or more partners and managers of other member firms within the network. They must be located in the same geographical area where there are common features relating to the accounting and auditing profession as well as possible similarities in the languages used in the audit and preparation of the financial statements and the provision of management advisory services. It is the responsibility of the assigned partner to examine and evaluate the internal system of the member including the firm's working papers and audit manual, to ensure strict adherence to quality control standards applied by the member firm and the network. Moreover, in most of the Arab countries, organizations supervising capital markets have established units to assess the quality of the audit services provided by audit firms to listed companies. The need to protect investors and other users of listed companies' financial statements forced some Arab countries to establish a smaller model of the U.S. PCAOB. It is expected that the established units for assessing the quality of auditors' performance will hire retired professional auditors to undertake the inspection of the audit firm working papers and report their findings to the board of such units to ensure adherence to auditing standards.

Audit Practice and Quality Centers

In the U.S. the AICPA has established audit practice and quality centers as resource centers to improve audit practice quality. The Center for Audit Quality is an autonomous public policy organization affiliated with the AICPA serving investors, public company auditors, and the capital markets. The Center's mission is to foster confidence in the audit process and to make public company audits even more reliable and relevant for investors. The Private Companies Practice Section (PCPS) provides practice management information to firms of all sizes.

In addition to these firm resources, the AICPA has established audit quality centers for governmental audits and employee benefit plan audits. Figure 2-4 summarizes the relationships among GAAS, quality control, the audit practice and quality centers, and peer review in ensuring audit quality.

QUALITY CONTROL MEASURES IN THE ARAB WORLD

Only in Saudi Arabia and Egypt are there a number of government bodies established to ensure compliance with quality control procedures and policies applied by audit firms. In July 2009, the Capital Market Authority (CMA) in Egypt established a unit responsible for monitoring the quality of services provided by registered audit firms with CMA. The unit issued a set of quality control guidelines which must be followed by registered audit firms. The unit intends to carry out inspections of the working papers of selected listed clients of those audit firms. In Saudi Arabia, standards for quality control are being issued by the SOCPA. The standards include independence, assigning personnel to engagements, consultation, supervision, acceptance of clients, etc. Two approaches are used to select subjects for quality assurance review: the cycle approach and the risk-based approach with a maximum number of three years for both

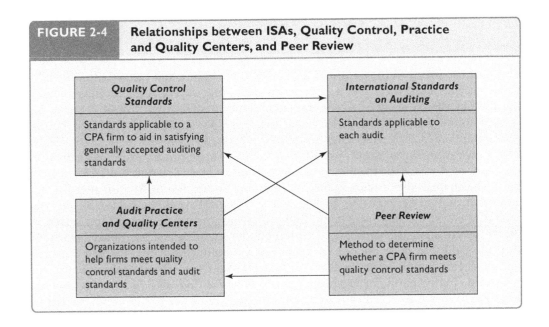

FIGURE 2-4   Relationships between ISAs, Quality Control, Practice and Quality Centers, and Peer Review

partner and the audit firm. Risk factors used to determine which firms or partners are reviewed include: number of listed entity clients; number of entities considered to be of public interest; past results of quality assurance reviews; failure to meet continuing professional development requirements; independence violations; and previously identified deficiencies in the design of, or compliance with, the firm's system of quality control. Elsewhere, systems of quality control vary. For example, there is no quality assurance review program for members of the professional body in Kuwait. Also, no supervisory body has yet been established in Lebanon for monitoring reporting practices and ensuring consistency in the application of ISAs.

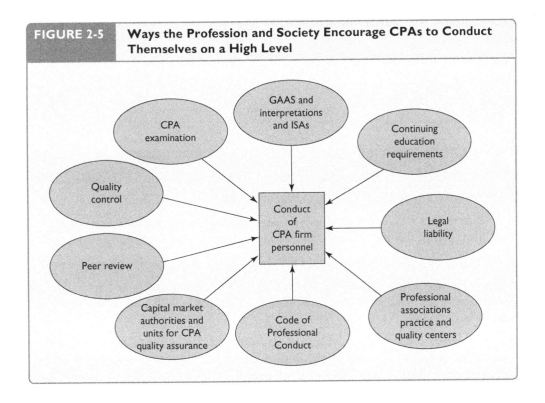

FIGURE 2-5   Ways the Profession and Society Encourage CPAs to Conduct Themselves on a High Level

SUMMARY

This chapter discussed the nature of the auditing profession and the activities of audit firms. Because audit firms play an important social role, several organizations, including the Egyptian Society of Accountants and Auditors (ESAA), Kuwait Association of Accountants and Auditors (KAAA), Lebanese Association of Certified Public Accountants (LACPA), Saudi Organization for Certified Public Accountants (SOCPA), and United Arab Emirates Accountants and Auditors Association (UAE-AAA), provide oversight to increase the likelihood of appropriate audit quality and professional conduct. The chapter also discussed the International Federation of Accountants (IFAC) and other major organizations such as AICPA, PCAOB, and SEC and explains how they affected the accounting and auditing profession worldwide. The chapter reviewed the process of standard-setting of the International Auditing and Assurance Standards Board (IAASB). In 2010, the IAASB completed a comprehensive revision and clarification of all International Standards on Auditing (ISAs) used in most of the countries in the world. The potential for legal liability as well as the *Code of Ethics for Professional Accountants* are also significant influences on auditor conduct and are discussed in Chapters 4 and 5.

ESSENTIAL TERMS

AICPA   p. 41

Client business risk   p. 48

Generally accepted auditing standards (GAAS)   p. 46

International Standards on Auditing (ISAs)   p. 42

Islamic accounting   p. 37

Peer review   p. 51

Public Company Accounting Oversight Board (PCAOB)   p. 39

Quality control   p. 50

Securities and Exchange Commission (SEC)   p. 39

Statements on Auditing Standards (SASs)   p. 41

REVIEW QUESTIONS

2-1 (Objective 2-1) State the four major types of services CPAs perform, and explain each.

2-2 (Objectives 2-1, 2-7) What major characteristics of the organization and conduct of audit firms permit them to fulfill their social function competently and independently?

2-3 (Objective 2-3) What is the role of the Public Company Accounting Oversight Board?

2-4 (Objectives 2-2, 2-3) Describe the role of the SEC in the U.S. and Capital Market Authorities in the Arab countries. Discuss their relationship with, and influence on, the practice of auditing.

2-5 (Objectives 2-2, 2-4) What roles are played by the American Institute of Certified Public Accountants for its members? Are there any differences between AICPA roles and those at some of the similar associations in the Arab countries?

2-6 (Objective 2-4) What are the purposes of the AICPA *Statements on Standards for Attestation Engagements*?

2-7 (Objectives 2-2, 2-4, 2-5)

a. Who is responsible for establishing auditing standards for audits of public companies in the U.S. and in your own country? Who is responsible for establishing auditing standards for private companies in the U.S. and in your own country? Explain.

b. Are there any major differences between ISAs and the local auditing standards applicable in some Arab countries?

2-8 (Objective 2-6) Distinguish between generally accepted auditing standards and generally accepted accounting principles, and give two examples of each.

2-9 (Objective 2-6) The first standard of field work requires the performance of the audit by a person or persons having adequate technical training and proficiency as an auditor. What are the various ways in which auditors can fulfill the requirement of the standard? Is there any relationship between GAAS and statements on Auditing standards (U.S.) and International Standards on Auditing (worldwide)?

2-10 (Objective 2-6) International Standards on Auditing as well as local auditing standards have been criticized by different sources for failing to provide useful guidelines for conducting an audit. The critics believe the standards should be more specific to enable practitioners to improve the quality of their performance. As the standards are now stated, some critics believe that they provide little more than an excuse to conduct inadequate audits. Evaluate this criticism of the International Standards on Auditing.

2-11 (Objective 2-5) Describe the role of International Standards on Auditing. Discuss whether an auditor who conducts an audit in accordance with generally accepted auditing standards simultaneously complies with International Standards on Auditing.

2-12 (Objective 2-7) What is meant by the term *quality control* as it relates to an audit firm?

2-13 (Objective 2-7) The following is an example of an audit firm's quality control procedure requirement: "Any person being considered for employment by the firm must have completed a basic auditing course and have been interviewed and approved by an audit partner of the firm before he or she can be hired for the audit staff." Which element of quality control does this procedure affect and what is the purpose of the requirement?

2-14 (Objective 2-7) State what is meant by the term *peer review*. What are the implications of peer review for the profession?

2-15 (Objective 2-7) What are the two AICPA resource centers to which CPA firms may belong? What are the primary purposes of the two centers? Are there similar resource centers to which auditing firms may belong in the Arab World?

MULTIPLE CHOICE QUESTIONS FROM CPA EXAMINATIONS

2-16 (Objective 2-6) The following questions deal with generally accepted auditing standards. Choose the best response.

a. The first general standard, which states in part that the audit must be performed by a person or persons having adequate technical training, requires that an auditor have
   (1) education and experience in the field of auditing.
   (2) ability in the planning and supervision of the audit work.
   (3) proficiency in business and financial matters.
   (4) knowledge in the areas of financial accounting.

b. Which of the following best describes what is meant by generally accepted auditing standards?
   (1) Acts to be performed by the auditor.
   (2) Measures of the quality of the auditor's performance.

(3) Procedures to be used to gather evidence to support financial statements.

(4) Audit objectives generally determined on audit engagements.

c. The general group of the generally accepted auditing standards includes a requirement that:

(1) field work be adequately planned and supervised.

(2) the auditor's report states whether or not the financial statements conform to generally accepted accounting principles.

(3) due professional care be exercised by the auditor.

(4) informative disclosures in the financial statements are reasonably adequate.

d. What is the general character of the three generally accepted auditing standards classified as standards of field work?

(1) The competence, independence, and professional care of persons performing the audit.

(2) Criteria for the content of the auditor's report on financial statements and related footnote disclosures.

(3) The criteria of audit planning and evidence gathering.

(4) The need to maintain independence in mental attitude in all matters pertaining to the audit.

2-17 (Objective 2-7) The following questions concern quality control standards. Choose the best response.

a. A CPA firm is reasonably assured of meeting its responsibility to provide services that conform with professional standards by:

(1) adhering to generally accepted auditing standards or ISAs.

(2) having an appropriate system of quality control.

(3) joining professional societies that enforce ethical conduct.

(4) maintaining an attitude of independence in its engagements.

b. The nature and extent of a CPA firm's quality control policies and procedures depend on:

	The CPA Firm's Size	The Nature of the CPA Firm's Practice	Cost–benefit Considerations
(1)	Yes	Yes	Yes
(2)	Yes	Yes	No
(3)	Yes	No	Yes
(4)	No	Yes	Yes

c. Which of the following are elements of a CPA firm's quality control that should be considered in establishing its quality control policies and procedures?

	Human Resources	Monitoring	Engagement Performance
(1)	Yes	Yes	No
(2)	Yes	Yes	Yes
(3)	No	Yes	Yes
(4)	Yes	No	Yes

d. Which of the following is an element of a CPA firm's quality control system that should be considered in establishing its quality control policies and procedures?

(1) Complying with laws and regulations.

(2) Using statistical sampling techniques.

(3) Managing personnel.

(4) Considering audit risk and materiality.

DISCUSSION QUESTIONS AND PROBLEMS

2-18 (Objective 2-7) For each of the following procedures taken from the quality control manual of an audit firm, identify the applicable element of quality control.

a. Appropriate accounting and auditing research requires adequate technical reference materials. Each professional has online password access through the firm's internet website to electronic reference materials on accounting, auditing, tax, and other technical information, including industry data.

b. Each audit engagement of the firm is directed by a partner and, in most instances, a manager of the firm. On every engagement, an attempt is made to maintain continuity of at least a portion of the personnel.

c. Audit engagement team members enter their electronic signatures in the firm's engagement management software to indicate the completion of specific audit program steps. At the end of the audit engagement, the engagement management software will not allow archiving of the engagement file until all audit program steps have been electronically signed.

d. At all stages of any engagement, an effort is made to involve professional staff at appropriate levels in the accounting and auditing decisions. Various approvals of the manager or senior accountant are obtained throughout the audit.

e. No employee will have any direct or indirect financial interest, association, or relationship (for example, a close relative serving a client in a decision-making capacity) not otherwise disclosed that might be adverse to the firm's best interest.

f. Each office of the firm shall be visited at least annually by review persons selected by the director of accounting and auditing. Procedures to be undertaken by the reviewers are illustrated by the office review program.

g. Existing clients of the firm are reviewed on a continuing basis by the engagement partner. Termination may result if circumstances indicate that there is reason to question the integrity of management or our independence, or if accounting and auditing differences of opinion cannot be reconciled. Doubts concerning whether the client–auditor relationship should be continued must be promptly discussed with the director of accounting and auditing.

h. Individual partners submit the nominations of those persons whom they wish to be considered for partner. To become a partner, an individual must have exhibited a high degree of technical competence; must possess integrity, motivation, and judgment; and must have a desire to help the firm progress through the efficient dispatch of the job responsibilities to which he or she is assigned.

i. Through our continuing employee evaluation and counselling program and through the quality control review procedures as established by the firm, educational needs are reviewed and formal staff training programs modified to accommodate changing needs. At the conclusion of practice office reviews, apparent accounting and auditing deficiencies are summarized and reported to the firm's director of personnel.

j. The firm's mission statement indicates its commitment to quality, and this commitment is emphasized in all staff training programs.

2-19 (Objective 2-6) Ibrahim, the owner of a small company, asked Sara, a CPA, to conduct an audit of the company's records. Ibrahim told Sara that an audit was to be completed in time to submit audited financial statements to a bank as part of a loan application. Sara immediately accepted the engagement and agreed to provide an auditor's report within three weeks. Ibrahim agreed to pay Sara a fixed fee plus a bonus if the loan was granted.

Sara hired two accounting students to conduct the audit and spent several hours telling them exactly what to do. Sara told the students not to spend time reviewing the controls but instead to concentrate on proving the mathematical accuracy of the ledger accounts and summarizing the data in the accounting records that support Ibrahim's financial statements. The students followed Sara's instructions and after two weeks gave Sara the financial statements, which did not include footnotes. Sara reviewed the statements and prepared an unmodified auditor's report. The report did not refer to generally accepted accounting principles or to the consistent application of such principles.

Required Briefly describe each of the ten generally accepted auditing standards and indicate how the action(s) of Sara resulted in a failure to comply with each standard.

Organize your answer as follows:[5]

Brief Description of GAAS	Sara's Actions Resulting in Failure to Comply with GAAS

CHAPTER 3

AUDIT REPORTS

Is The Audit Report Important For Investors And Other Users Of Reports Of Listed Companies?

Vodafone, a telecommunications company traded on the Egyptian Stock Exchange, provides telecommunication services to millions of users in Egypt and the Arab world. Vodafone has a number of segments, each reflecting an aspect of its activities. There is a segment selling mobile phones and other telecommunications devices to customers. Other segments include provision of communication lines, technical support, and other activities. The capital of the company is equal to US$200 million with total investments amounting to more than US$2 billion. There are thousands of shareholders who buy and sell the company shares almost on a daily basis. None of those stockholders has the right to inspect the company's books and records to assess the fair presentation of the company's individual transactions. Shareholders have access to only one document: the annual report including the auditor's report, which provides those shareholders and other users with information pertaining to the fair presentation of the company's financial position, results of operations, and its cash flow.

LEARNING OBJECTIVES

After studying this chapter, you should be able to

3-1 Describe the parts of the standard unmodified audit report.

3-2 Specify the conditions required to issue the standard unmodified audit report.

3-3 Understand reporting on financial statements and internal control over financial reporting in the U.S. under Section 404 of the Sarbanes–Oxley Act.

3-4 Describe the circumstances when an unmodified report with an emphasis of a matter or other matter paragraph is appropriate.

3-5 Identify the types of audit reports that can be issued when an unmodified opinion is not justified.

3-6 Explain how materiality affects audit reporting decisions.

3-7 Draft appropriately modified audit reports under a variety of circumstances.

3-8 Determine the appropriate audit report for a given audit situation.

3-9 Understand the need for uniformity between U.S. accounting and auditing standards and international accounting and auditing standards.

3-10 Understand situations for special reporting matters.

Reports are essential to audit and assurance engagements because they communicate the auditor's findings. Users of financial statements rely on the auditor's report to provide assurance on the company's financial statements.

The audit report is the final step in the entire audit process. The reason for studying it now is to permit reference to different audit reports as evidence accumulation is studied throughout this text. These evidence concepts are more meaningful after you understand the form and content of the final product of the audit. We begin by describing the content of the standard auditor's report.

Relevant International Standards on Auditing	
ISA 260	Communication with Those Charged with Governance
ISA 315	Identifying and Assessing the Risks of Material Misstatement through Understanding the Entity and its Environment
ISA 320	Materiality in Planning and Performing an Audit
ISA 330	The Auditor's Responses to Assessed Risks
ISA 450	Evaluation of Misstatements Identified during the Audit
ISA 500	Audit Evidence
ISA 550	Related Parties
ISA 560	Subsequent Events
ISA 570	Going Concern
ISA 700	Forming an Opinion and Reporting on Financial Statements
ISA 705	Modifications to the Opinion in the Independent Auditor's Report
ISA 706	Emphasis of Matter Paragraphs and Other Matter Paragraphs in the Independent Auditor's Report
ISA 710	Comparative Information—Corresponding Figures and Comparative Financial Statements
ISA 720	The Auditor's Responsibilities Relating to Other Information in Documents Containing Audited Financial Statements

STANDARD UNMODIFIED AUDIT REPORT

OBJECTIVE 3-1

Describe the parts of the standard unmodified audit report.

Standard unmodified audit report

The report a CPA issues when all auditing conditions have been met, no significant misstatements have been discovered and left uncorrected, and it is the auditor's opinion that the financial statements are fairly stated in accordance with IFRS.

To allow users to understand audit reports, International Auditing and Assurance Standards Board (IAASB) professional standards provide uniform wording for the auditor's report, as illustrated in the auditor's standard unmodified audit report in Figure 3-1. The standard form of the audit report prevents misunderstanding and confusion in the communication of the auditor's opinion to the various users of the financial statements. A written report encompasses reports prepared in hard copy format and those using an electronic medium to reach users of the financial statements. Different auditors may alter the wording or presentation slightly, but the meaning will be the same.

Parts of Standard Unmodified Audit Report

The auditor's **standard unmodified audit report** contains ten distinct parts as stated by ISA 700 and 706, and these are labeled in bold letters in the margin beside Figure 3-1.

FIGURE 3-1	Example of a Standard Unmodified Auditor's Report

INDEPENDENT AUDITOR'S REPORT

Report Title

To the Shareholders of Egyptian Oil Company.

Audit Report Address

Report on the Financial Statements

Introductory Paragraph

We have audited the accompanying financial statements of Egyptian Oil Company, which comprise the balance sheet as at December 31, 2011, and the income statement, statement of changes in equity and cash flow statement for the year then ended, and a summary of significant accounting policies and other explanatory notes.

Management's Responsibility for the Financial Statements

Management Responsibility

Management is responsible for the preparation and fair presentation of these financial statements in accordance with Egyptian Accounting Standards and the applicable Egyptian laws. This responsibility includes: designing, implementing, and maintaining internal control relevant to the preparation and fair presentation of financial statements that are free from material misstatement, whether due to fraud or error; selecting and applying appropriate accounting policies; and making accounting estimates that are reasonable in the circumstances.

Auditor's Responsibility

The Auditor's Responsibility

Our responsibility is to express an opinion on these financial statements based on our audit. We conducted our audit in accordance with Egyptian Auditing Standards and the applicable Egyptian laws. Those standards require that we comply with ethical requirements and plan and perform the audit to obtain reasonable assurance whether the financial statements are free from material misstatement.

An audit involves performing procedures to obtain audit evidence about the amounts and disclosures in the financial statements. The procedures selected depend on the auditor's judgment, including the assessment of the risks of material misstatement of the financial statements, whether due to fraud or error. In making those risk assessments, the auditor considers internal control relevant to the entity's preparation and fair presentation of the financial statements in order to design audit procedures that are appropriate in the circumstances, but not for the purpose of expressing an opinion on the effectiveness of the entity's internal control. An audit also includes evaluating the appropriateness of accounting policies used and the reasonableness of accounting estimates made by management, as well as evaluating the overall presentation of the financial statements.

We believe that the audit evidence we have obtained is sufficient and appropriate to provide a basis for our audit opinion.

Opinion

Opinion Paragraph

In our opinion, the financial statements give a true and fair view of the financial position of Egyptian Oil Company, as of December 31, 2011, and of its financial performance and its cash flows for the year then ended in accordance with Egyptian Accounting Standards and the applicable Egyptian laws and regulations.

Report on Other Legal and Regulatory Requirements

Other Reporting Responsibilities

The company maintains proper books of accounts, which include all that is required by the law and the accompanying financial statements agree therewith.

The financial data stated in the board of directors' annual report, in accordance with Law number 159 for 1981 and its executive regulations, is in conformity with those stated in the company's books.

Sherif Seghir

Sherif Seghir

Names and Signatures of the Auditors

Karim Seghir & Co, Saleh Road, Alexandria

Auditor's Address

Alexandria, February 24, 2012.

Date of the Auditor's Report

1. *Report title.* Auditing standards require that the report be titled and that the title include the word "independent," for example, "independent auditor's report," or "report of an independent auditor." This requirement conveys to users that the audit was unbiased in all aspects.

2. *Audit report address.* The report is usually addressed to those for whom the report is prepared being the company, its stockholders, the board of directors, or those charged with governance (i.e. audit committee). In recent years, it has become customary to address the report to the shareholders to indicate that the auditor is independent of the company.

3. *Introductory paragraph.* The first paragraph of the report does four things. First, it makes the simple statement that the audit firm has done an audit. This is intended to distinguish the report from a compilation or review report.

   Second, it identifies the entity whose financial statements have been audited listing such statements as the balance sheet and the income statement, statement of cash flow, and statement of changes in shareholders' equity. The wording of the financial statements in the report should be identical to those used by management on the financial statements.

   Third, the introductory paragraph also refers to the summary of the significant accounting policies and other explanatory information. This part of the report confirms that such a summary forms an integral part of the financial statements.

   Fourth, the introductory paragraph also specifies the date or period covered by each financial statement comprising the financial statements.

4. *Management's responsibility for the financial statements.* The purpose of this statement is to communicate that management is responsible for the preparation of the financial statements in accordance with the applicable financial reporting framework and for such internal control as it determines is necessary to ensure the financial statements are free from **material misstatement**, whether due to fraud or error. The purpose of these statements is to communicate that management is responsible for selecting the appropriate accounting standards and making the measurement decisions and disclosures in applying those standards.

5. *Auditor's responsibility.* The auditor's report shall indicate that the responsibility of the auditor is to form an opinion on the financial statements based on the audit. The report will also clarify that the audit was conducted in accordance with applicable auditing standards whether International Standards on Auditing or local auditing standards. Paragraph 30 of ISA 700 requires that the auditor comply with ethical requirements and that the auditor plans and performs the audit to obtain **reasonable assurance** about whether the financial statements are free from material misstatements.

   The inclusion of the word *material* conveys that auditors are responsible only to search for significant misstatements, not minor misstatements that do not affect users' decisions. The use of the term *reasonable assurance* is intended to indicate that an audit cannot be expected to completely eliminate the possibility that a material misstatement will exist in the financial statements. In other words, an audit provides a high level of assurance, but it is not a guarantee.

   The remainder of the auditor's responsibility paragraph discusses the audit evidence accumulated and states that the auditor believes that the evidence accumulated was appropriate for the circumstances to express the opinion presented. The words *test basis* indicates that sampling was used rather than an audit of every transaction and amount on the statements. Also, ISA 700 states that the audit procedures selected depend on the auditor's judgment, including the assessment of the risks of material misstatement of the financial statements. In making those risk assessments, the auditor is required to assess internal control pertaining to the entity's preparation of the financial statements in order to design audit procedures that are appropriate in the circumstances, but not for the purpose of expressing an opinion on the effectiveness of the entity's internal control.

Material misstatement

A misstatement in the financial statements, knowledge of which would affect a decision of a reasonable user of the statements.

Reasonable assurance

The concept that audit function is not a guarantee for complete accuracy of the financial statements after being audited as the auditor performs the audit on a test basis and provides a high but not an absolute level of assurance.

Whereas the management's responsibilities paragraph of the report states that management is responsible for the preparation and content of the financial statements, the auditor's responsibility paragraph states that the auditor evaluates the appropriateness of those accounting principles, estimates, and financial statement disclosures and presentations given.

6. *Opinion paragraph.* The final paragraph in the standard report states the auditor's conclusions based on the results of the audit. This part of the report is so important that often the entire audit report is referred to simply as the *auditor's opinion.* The opinion paragraph is stated as an opinion rather than as a statement of absolute fact or a guarantee. The intent is to indicate that the conclusions are based on professional judgment. The phrase *in our opinion* indicates that there may be some information risk associated with the financial statements, even though the statements have been audited.

   The auditor is required to state an opinion about the financial statements taken as a whole, including a conclusion about whether the company followed the International Financial Reporting Standards (IFRS) issued by the International Accounting Standards Board (IASB) or local accounting standards issued by a government or professional body.

   One of the controversial parts of the auditor's report is the meaning of the term *present fairly.* Does this mean that if IFRS or local accounting standards are followed, the financial statements are presented fairly, or something more? Occasionally, the courts have concluded that auditors are responsible for looking beyond the accounting standards to determine whether users might be misled, even if those standards are followed. Most auditors believe that financial statements are 'presented fairly' when the statements are in accordance with IFRS or local accounting standards, but that it is also necessary to examine the substance of transactions and balances for possible misinformation.

7. *Other reporting responsibilities.* Under the heading "report on other legal and regulatory requirements" the auditor may include specific requirements embedded in local laws or regulations for the audit of the company's financial statements. For example, in Jordan the Companies' Act 22 for 1997 requires that auditors report about how effective the cost accounting systems are for manufacturing companies as well as that information in the board of directors' report comply with information in the company's financial statements. Also, the Central Bank of Jordan explicitly requires auditors to indicate whether management of banks operating in Jordan adhere to the regulations in the banking law. In some jurisdiction, law or regulation may specifically refer to a responsibility for the adequacy of accounting books and records, or accounting systems. However, as books, records, and systems are an integral part of internal control (as defined in ISA 315), auditors are not required to make specific reference to them.

8. *Name and signature of the auditor.* The name identifies the auditing firm or practitioner who performed the audit. Typically, the name of the auditor as well as the firm's name is used because the entire audit firm has the legal and professional responsibility to ensure that the quality of the audit meets professional standards.

9. *Auditor's address.* The auditor's report shall name the location in the jurisdiction where the auditor practices. It is always preferable that the auditor include the location at which the audit is provided to its client not the head office of the audit firm or any of its branches.

10. *Date of the auditor's report.* The appropriate date for the report is the one on which the auditor completed the auditing procedures in the field. This date is important to users because it indicates the last day of the auditor's responsibility for the review of significant events that occurred after the date of

the financial statements. In the audit report in Figure 3-1, the balance sheet is dated December 31, 2011, and the audit report is dated February 24, 2012. This indicates that the auditor has searched for material unrecorded transactions and events that occurred up to February 24, 2012.

Conditions for Standard Unmodified Audit Report

The standard unmodified audit report is issued when the following conditions have been met:

1. Sufficient appropriate evidence has been accumulated, and the auditor has conducted the engagement in a manner that enables him or her to conclude that auditing standards have been met.
2. The financial statements are presented in accordance with IFRS or applicable local accounting standards. This also means that adequate disclosures have been included in the footnotes and other parts of the financial statements.
3. There are no circumstances requiring the addition of an **emphasis of a matter** or **other matter paragraph** in the report.
4. There are no circumstances which indicate that the auditor is not independent.

Emphasis of a matter paragraph

An unmodified report in which the financial statements are fairly presented, but the auditor believes it is important, or is required, to refer to a matter other than those presented or disclosed in the financial statements that, in the auditor's judgment, is relevant to users' understanding of the audit, the auditor's responsibilities or the auditor's report.

Other matter paragraph

An unmodified report in which the financial statements are fairly presented, but the auditor believes it is important, or is required, to refer to a matter other than those presented or disclosed in the financial statements that, in the auditor's judgment, is relevant to users' understanding of the audit, the auditor's responsibilities, or the auditor's report.

When these conditions are met, the standard unmodified audit report, as shown in Figure 3-1, is issued. The standard unmodified audit report is sometimes called a clean opinion because there are no circumstances requiring a modification of the auditor's opinion. The standard unmodified report is the most common audit opinion. Sometimes circumstances beyond the client's or auditor's control prevent the issuance of a clean opinion. However, in most cases, companies make the appropriate changes to their accounting records to avoid a modification by the auditor.

If any of the four requirements for the standard unmodified audit report are not met, the standard unmodified report cannot be issued. Figure 3-2 indicates the categories of audit reports that can be issued by the auditor. The departures from a standard unmodified report are considered increasingly severe as one moves down the figure. Financial statement users are normally much more concerned about a disclaimer or

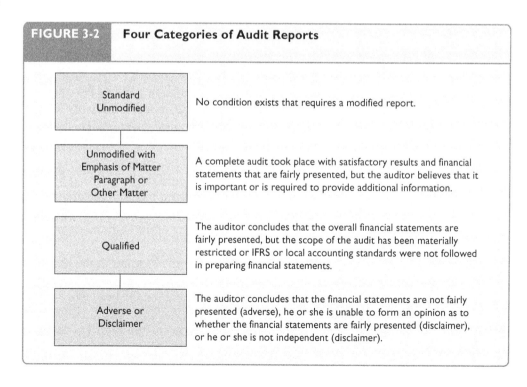

FIGURE 3-2   Four Categories of Audit Reports

Standard Unmodified	No condition exists that requires a modified report.
Unmodified with Emphasis of Matter Paragraph or Other Matter	A complete audit took place with satisfactory results and financial statements that are fairly presented, but the auditor believes that it is important or is required to provide additional information.
Qualified	The auditor concludes that the overall financial statements are fairly presented, but the scope of the audit has been materially restricted or IFRS or local accounting standards were not followed in preparing financial statements.
Adverse or Disclaimer	The auditor concludes that the financial statements are not fairly presented (adverse), he or she is unable to form an opinion as to whether the financial statements are fairly presented (disclaimer), or he or she is not independent (disclaimer).

adverse opinion than an unmodified report with an emphasis of a matter or other matter. These other categories of audit reports are discussed in the following sections.

REPORT ON INTERNAL CONTROL OVER FINANCIAL REPORTING IN THE U.S. UNDER SECTION 404 OF THE SARBANES–OXLEY ACT

As discussed in Chapter 1, Section 404 of the Sarbanes–Oxley Act in the U.S. requires the auditor of a public company to attest to management's report on the effectiveness of internal control over financial reporting. PCAOB Auditing Standard 5 requires the audit of internal control to be integrated with the audit of the financial statements. However, the auditor may choose to issue separate reports, such as the *separate report on internal control over financial reporting* shown in Figure 3-3, or in a combined report. The *combined report on financial statements and internal control over financial reporting* addresses both the financial statements and management's report on internal control over financial reporting. While the combined report is permitted, the separate report on internal control over financial reporting is more common and includes these elements:

> **OBJECTIVE 3-3**
>
> Understand reporting on financial statements and internal control over financial reporting in the U.S. under Section 404 of the Sarbanes–Oxley Act.

- The introductory, scope, and opinion paragraphs describe that the scope of the auditor's work and opinion is on internal control over financial reporting, and the introductory paragraph highlights management's responsibility for and its separate assessment of internal control over financial reporting.
- The introductory and opinion paragraphs also refer to the framework used to evaluate internal control.
- The report includes a paragraph after the scope paragraph defining internal control over financial reporting.
- The report also includes an additional paragraph before the opinion that addresses the inherent limitations of internal control.
- Although the audit opinion on the financial statements addresses multiple reporting periods, the auditor's opinion about the effectiveness of internal control is as of the end of the most recent fiscal year.
- The last paragraph of the report includes a cross-reference to the auditor's separate report on the financial statements.

The separate report in Figure 3-3 is an unqualified opinion (the word unqualified is used in U.S. auditing standards instead of unmodified in the International Standards on Auditing) on the effectiveness of internal control over financial reporting. The auditor may issue a qualified opinion, adverse opinion, or disclaimer of opinion on the operating effectiveness of internal control over financial reporting.

FIGURE 3-3	**Separate Report on Internal Control over Financial Reporting**

REPORT OF INDEPENDENT REGISTERED PUBLIC ACCOUNTING FIRM To the Board of Directors and Shareholders of Westbrook Company, Inc.: We have audited Westbrook Company, Inc.'s internal control over financial reporting as of December 31, 2011, based on criteria established in Internal Control - Integrated Framework issued by the Committee of Sponsoring Organizations of the Treadway Commission (the COSO criteria). Westbrook Company, Inc.'s management is responsible for maintaining effective internal control over financial reporting, and for its assessment of the effectiveness of internal control over financial reporting included in the accompanying Management Report on Internal Control Over Financial Reporting. Our responsibility is to express an opinion on the company's internal control over financial reporting based on our audit.	**Introductory Paragraph**

(Figure 3-3 continued on next page)

FIGURE 3-3	Separate Report on Internal Control over Financial Reporting (*Cont.*)

Scope Paragraph	We conducted our audit in accordance with the standards of the Public Company Accounting Oversight Board (United States). Those standards require that we plan and perform the audit to obtain reasonable assurance about whether effective internal control over financial reporting was maintained in all material respects. Our audit included obtaining an understanding of internal control over financial reporting, assessing the risk that a material weakness exists, testing and evaluating the design and operating effectiveness of internal control based on the assessed risk, and performing such other procedures as we considered necessary in the circumstances. We believe that our audit provides a reasonable basis for our opinion.
Definition Paragraph	A company's internal control over financial reporting is a process designed to provide reasonable assurance regarding the reliability of financial reporting and the preparation of financial statements for external purposes in accordance with generally accepted accounting principles. A company's internal control over financial reporting includes those policies and procedures that (1) pertain to the maintenance of records that, in reasonable detail, accurately and fairly reflect the transactions and dispositions of the assets of the company; (2) provide reasonable assurance that transactions are recorded as necessary to permit preparation of financial statements in accordance with generally accepted accounting principles, and that receipts and expenditures of the company are being made only in accordance with authorizations of management and directors of the company; and (3) provide reasonable assurance regarding prevention or timely detection of unauthorized acquisition, use, or disposition of the company's assets that could have a material effect on the financial statements.
Inherent Limitations Paragraph	Because of its inherent limitations, internal control over financial reporting may not prevent or detect misstatements. Also, projections of any evaluation of effectiveness to future periods are subject to the risk that controls may become inadequate because of changes in conditions, or that the degree of compliance with the policies or procedures may deteriorate.
Opinion Paragraph	In our opinion, Westbrook Company, Inc. maintained, in all material respects, effective internal control over financial reporting as of December 31, 2011, based on the COSO criteria.
Cross-Reference Paragraph	We also have audited, in accordance with the standards of the Public Company Accounting Oversight Board (United States), the consolidated balance sheets of Westbrook Company, Inc. as of December 31, 2011 and 2010, and the related consolidated statements of income, shareholders' equity, and cash flows for each of the three years in the period ended December 31, 2011 of Westbrook Company, Inc. and our report dated February 11, 2012 expressed an unqualified opinion thereon.

UNMODIFIED AUDIT REPORT WITH EMPHASIS OF A MATTER OR OTHER MATTER PARAGRAPH

OBJECTIVE 3-4

Describe the circumstances when an unmodified report with an emphasis of a matter or other matter paragraph is appropriate.

Unmodified audit report with emphasis of a matter or other matter

An unmodified report in which the financial statements are fairly presented, but the auditor believes it is important, or is required, to provide additional information for a matter appropriately presented or disclosed in the financial statements that, in the auditor's judgment, is of such importance that it is fundamental to users' understanding of the financial statements.

The remainder of this chapter deals with reports, other than standard unmodified reports, on the audit of financial statements. In certain situations, an unmodified audit report on the financial statements is issued, but the wording deviates from the standard unmodified report. The **unmodified audit report with emphasis of a matter or other matter** meets the criteria of a complete audit with satisfactory results and financial statements that are fairly presented, but the auditor believes it is important or is required to provide additional information. In a qualified, adverse, or disclaimer report, the auditor either has not performed a satisfactory audit, is not satisfied that the financial statements are fairly presented, or is not independent.

ISA 706 titled "Emphasis of Matter Paragraphs and Other Matter Paragraphs in the Independent Auditor's Report" discusses types of communication in the auditor's report when the auditor considers it necessary to:

a. Draw users' attention to a matter or matters presented or disclosed in the financial statements that are of such importance that they are fundamental to users' understanding of the financial statements; or
b. Draw users' attention to any matter or matters other than those presented or disclosed in the financial statements that are relevant to users' understanding of the audit, the auditor's responsibilities, or the auditor's report (ISA 706, para 1).

The emphasis of a matter paragraph should be included in a separate section immediately after the opinion paragraph in the auditor's report. The auditor is required to include a clear reference to the matter being emphasized and to the relevant disclosure in the footnotes of the financial statements that fully describes such matter. The auditor is also required to indicate that his opinion is not modified in respect of the matter emphasized. Examples of circumstances requiring the emphasis of a matter paragraph in the auditor's report may include:

a. An uncertainty relating to the future outcome of exceptional litigation or regulatory action.
b. Substantial doubt about the company's **going concern** assumption (ISA 570).
c. The existence of significant related party transactions.
d. Important events occurring subsequent to the balance sheet date.
e. Early application of a new international financial reporting standards or a local accounting standard that may have a highly material effect on the financial statements in advance of its effective date.
f. A major catastrophe that has had, or continues to have, a significant effect on the entity's financial position, results of its operations, or its cash flow.
g. The description of accounting matters affecting the comparability of the financial statements with those of the preceding year.
h. Material uncertainties disclosed in the footnotes.

Going concern

The assumption under which a business is established and reflects the financial viability of the business enterprise.

Auditors are advised not to overuse the emphasis of a matter paragraph as it may diminish the effectiveness of the auditor's communication of such matters (ISA 706). Auditors are requested to limit the use of an emphasis of matter paragraph to matters presented or disclosed in the financial statements. Figures 3-4, 3-5, and 3-6 provide examples of unmodified audit reports with an emphasis of matter paragraph.

a. The auditor may report in a separate paragraph titled "Other Matter" those procedures that he performed for a specific assignment or express an opinion on specific matters.
b. The auditor may indicate in the other matter paragraph that the auditor's report is intended solely for the intended users for a specific assignment, and should not be distributed to or used by other parties.
c. The auditor may include an other matter paragraph if an entity prepares one set of financial statements in accordance with two acceptable financial reporting frameworks and engages the auditor to report on both sets of financial statements.

FIGURE 3-4	Example 1 of an Auditor's Report with Emphasis of Matter Paragraph

INDEPENDENT AUDITOR'S REPORT	
(Same introductory, management responsibility, auditor's responsibility, and opinion paragraphs as the standard report.)	
Emphasis of Matter	**Fourth Paragraph—Emphasis of Matter Paragraph**
The Arab Republic of Egypt has suffered from events that significantly affected the tourism sector in general and consequently the rates of hotel occupancy in particular, resulting in a significant drop in hotel revenues starting from January 2011. This decline in revenues resulting from a significant drop in hotel occupancy will not be compensated by a corresponding decrease in expenditure, considering that there is a fixed burden sustained by the hotel regardless of occupancy rates. It is therefore possible that the events referred to will have a substantial impact on the elements of the assets and liabilities and their redemption value, as well as the business results during the upcoming periods. It is currently impractical to determine the size of this effect on the assets and liabilities listed in the current financial statements of the company.	

FIGURE 3-5	Example 2 of an Auditor's Report with Emphasis of Matter Paragraph

	INDEPENDENT AUDITOR'S REPORT
	(Same introductory, management responsibility, auditor's responsibility, and opinion paragraphs as the standard report.)
Fourth Paragraph— Emphasis of Matter Paragraph	**Emphasis of Matter** The accompanying financial statements have been prepared assuming that Fairfax Company will continue as a going concern. As discussed in Note 11 to the financial statements, Fairfax Company has suffered recurring losses from operations and has a net capital deficiency that raises substantial doubts about the company's ability to continue as a going concern. Management's plans in regard to these matters are also described in Note 11. The financial statements do not include any adjustments that might result from the outcome of this uncertainty.

FIGURE 3-6	Example 3 of an Auditor's Report with Emphasis of Matter Paragraph

	INDEPENDENT AUDITOR'S REPORT
	(Same introductory, management responsibility, auditor's responsibility, and opinion paragraphs as the standard report.)
Fourth Paragraph— Emphasis of Matter Paragraph	**Emphasis of Matter** Without considering the following as a qualification, the company transferred its right in the amount of US$11,408,799 to Kuwait National Bank (in settlement of dues owed to the bank) and owed from the Kuwaiti General Authority for Land Reclamation to the company for the land seized for public benefits by the Authority for constructing a motorway to link the capital of Kuwait with a new airport to be built in nearby area as explained in detail in note no (12).

FIGURE 3-7	Audit Report with Other Matter Paragraph for Prior Corresponding Figures Audited by a Predecessor Auditor

	INDEPENDENT AUDITOR'S REPORT
	(Standard wording for the introductory, management's responsibility, auditor's responsibility, and opinion paragraphs.)
Emphasis of Matter Paragraph	The financial statements of Kappa Company for the year ended December 31, 2011, were audited by another auditor who expressed an unmodified opinion on those statements on March 31, 2012.

It is important to note that an other matter paragraph should not include information that is required to be provided by management in the normal circumstances related to the preparation of the company's financial statements or management undertaken in their day-to-day normal responsibilities. In general, the other matter paragraph is included immediately after the opinion paragraph and any emphasis of matter paragraph. However, if an other matter paragraph is included to draw users' attention to a matter relating to other reporting responsibilities addressed in the auditor's report, the paragraph may be included in the section sub-titled "Report on Other Legal and Regulatory Requirements."

The auditor is required to communicate the proposed emphasis of a matter or an other matter paragraph in his audit report to those charged with governance and the management of the company providing reasons for such reporting.

Substantial Doubt About Going Concern

Even though the purpose of an audit is not to evaluate the financial health of the business, the auditor has a responsibility to evaluate whether the company is likely to continue as a going concern. For example, the existence of one or more of the following factors causes uncertainty about the ability of a company to continue as a going concern:

1. Significant recurring operating losses or working capital deficiencies.
2. Inability of the company to pay its obligations as they come due.
3. Loss of major customers, the occurrence of uninsured catastrophes such as an earthquake or flood, or unusual labor difficulties.
4. Legal proceedings, legislation, or similar matters that have occurred that might jeopardize the entity's ability to operate.

The auditor's concern in such situations is the possibility that the client may not be able to continue its operations or meet its obligations for a reasonable period. For this purpose, a reasonable period is considered not to exceed one year from the date of the financial statements being audited.

When the auditor concludes that there is substantial doubt about the entity's ability to continue as a going concern, an unmodified opinion with an emphasis of a matter paragraph is required, regardless of the disclosures made by management in the financial statements about such matter. Figure 3-8 provides an example in which there is substantial doubt about going concern.

Auditing standards permit but do not require a disclaimer of opinion when there is substantial doubt about going concern. The criteria for issuing a disclaimer of opinion instead of adding an emphasis of a matter paragraph are not stated in the standards, and this type of opinion is rarely issued in practice. An example for which a disclaimer might be issued is when a regulatory government body, such as the Environmental Protection Authority, is considering a severe sanction against a company and, if the proceedings result in an unfavorable outcome, the company will be forced to liquidate.

Reports Involving Other Auditors

When an auditor relies on a different audit firm to perform part of the audit, which is common when the client has several widespread branches or subdivisions, the principal audit firm has three alternatives. Only the second is a clean report with modified wording.

1. Make No Reference in the Audit Report When no reference is made to the other auditor, a standard unmodified opinion is given unless other circumstances require a departure. This approach is typically followed when the other auditor audited an immaterial portion of the statements, the other auditor is well known or closely supervised by the principal auditor, or the principal auditor has thoroughly reviewed the other auditor's work. The other auditor is still responsible for his or her own report and work in the event of a lawsuit or Capital Market Authority action.

FIGURE 3-8	Unmodified Audit Report with Emphasis of a Matter Paragraph for Going Concern Issue
INDEPENDENT AUDITOR'S REPORT (Same introductory, management responsibility, auditor's responsibility, and opinion paragraphs as the standard report.) Without qualifying our opinion, we draw attention to Note 7 in the financial statements which indicates that the company incurred a net loss of US$10 million during the year ended December 31, 2011, and, as of that date, the company's current liabilities exceeded its total assets by US$50 million. These conditions, along with other matters as set forth in Note 11, indicate the existence of a material uncertainly that may cast significant doubt about the company's ability to continue as a going concern.	**Fourth Paragraph— Emphasis of Matter Paragraph**

2. Make Reference in the Report (Modified Wording Report) This type of report is called a shared opinion or report. A shared unmodified report is appropriate when it is impractical to review the work of the other auditor or when the portion of the financial statements audited by the other auditor is material in relation to the whole. An example of an unmodified shared report is shown in Figure 3-9. Notice that the report does not include a separate paragraph that discusses the shared responsibility, but does so in the introductory paragraph and refers to the other auditor in the auditor's responsibility and opinion paragraphs. The portions of the financial statements audited by the other auditor can be stated as percentages or absolute amounts.

3. Qualify the Opinion A qualified opinion or disclaimer, depending on materiality, is required if the principal auditor is not willing to assume any responsibility for the work of the other auditor. The principal auditor may also decide that a qualification is required in the overall report if the other auditor qualified his or her portion of the audit. Qualified opinions and disclaimers are discussed in a later section.

FIGURE 3-9	Example of an Auditor's Report with Modified Wording

INDEPENDENT AUDITOR'S REPORT

Shareholders and Board of Directors
Palestine Dairy Co.

Report on Financial Statements & Management Responsibility

We have audited the accompanying consolidated balance sheets of Palestine Dairy Co. as of July 31, 2012 and 2011, and the related consolidated statements of income, retained earnings, and cash flows for the years then ended. These financial statements are the responsibility of the company's management. Our responsibility is to express an opinion on these financial statements based on our audits. We did not audit the financial statements of El-Fatah Dairy, a consolidated subsidiary in which the company had an equity interest of 84% as of July 31, 2012, which statements reflect total assets of US$2,420,000 and US$2,237,000 as of July 31, 2012 and 2011, respectively were audited by other auditors whose report has been furnished to us, and our opinion, insofar as it relates to the amounts included for El-Fatah Dairy, is based solely on the report of the other auditors.

Auditor's Responsibilities

Our responsibility is to express an opinion on these financial statements based on our audit. We conducted our audit in accordance with International Standards on Auditing and the applicable laws. Those standards require that we comply with ethical requirements and plan and perform the audit to obtain reasonable assurance whether the financial statements are free from material misstatement.

An audit involves performing procedures to obtain audit evidence about the amounts and disclosures in the financial statements. The procedures selected depend on the auditor's judgment, including the assessment of the risks of material misstatement of the financial statements, whether due to fraud or error. In making those risk assessments, the auditor considers internal control relevant to the entity's preparation and fair presentation of the financial statements in order to design audit procedures that are appropriate in the circumstances, but not for the purpose of expressing an opinion on the effectiveness of the entity's internal control. An audit also includes evaluating the appropriateness of accounting policies used and the reasonableness of accounting estimates made by management, as well as evaluating the overall presentation of the financial statements.

We believe that the audit evidence we have obtained is sufficient and appropriate to provide a basis for our audit opinion.

Opinion Paragraph— Modified Wording

In our opinion, based on our audits and the report of other auditors, the consolidated financial statements referred to above present fairly, in all material respects, the financial position of Palestine Dairy as of July 31, 2011 and 2010, and the results of its operations and its cash flows for the years then ended in conformity with International Financial Reporting Standards and the applicable laws.

September 16, 2012
Sawalha & Co.
Certified Public Accountant
Amman, Jordan

DEPARTURES FROM AN UNMODIFIED AUDIT REPORT

It is essential that auditors and readers of audit reports understand the circumstances when an unmodified report is inappropriate and the type of audit report to be issued in each circumstance. In the study of audit reports that depart from an unmodified report, there are three closely related topics: the conditions requiring a departure from an unmodified opinion, the types of opinions other than unmodified, and materiality.

First, the three conditions requiring a departure are briefly summarized. Each is discussed in greater depth later in the chapter.

OBJECTIVE 3-5

Identify the types of audit reports that can be issued when an unmodified opinion is not justified.

1. The Scope of the Audit Has Been Restricted (Scope Limitation) When the auditor has not accumulated sufficient appropriate evidence to conclude whether financial statements are stated in accordance with IFRS, a **scope limitation** exists. There are two major causes of scope restrictions: restrictions imposed by the client and those caused by circumstances beyond either the client's or auditor's control. An example of a client restriction is management's refusal to permit the auditor to confirm material receivables or to physically examine inventory (ISA 501). An example of a restriction caused by circumstances is when the engagement is not agreed on until after the client's year-end. It may not be possible to physically observe inventories, confirm receivables, or perform other important procedures after the balance sheet date. Also, a fire may destroy accounting records preventing the auditor from performing substantive tests on various financial statements accounts balances.

Scope limitation

A situation where the auditor is unable to obtain sufficient competent evidence that may prevent the auditor from expressing an unmodified opinion.

2. The Financial Statements Have Not Been Prepared in Accordance with IFRS or Local Accounting Standards (IFRS Departure) For example, if the client insists on using replacement costs for fixed assets or values inventory at selling price rather than the lower of cost or net realizable value as required by IFRS, a departure from the unmodified report is required. Whenever IFRS are referred to in this context, consideration of the adequacy of all informative disclosures, including footnotes, is especially important.

3. The Auditor is Not Independent Independence ordinarily is determined by the rules of the *Code of Ethics for Professional Accountants*. Auditor independence requirements and the *Code of Ethics for Professional Accountants* are further discussed in Chapter 5.

When any of the three conditions requiring a departure from an unmodified report exists and is material, a report other than an unmodified report must be issued. Three main types of audit reports are issued under these conditions: qualified opinion, adverse opinion, and disclaimer of opinion.

Qualified Opinion

A **qualified opinion** report can result from a limitation on the scope of the audit or failure to follow IFRS or local accounting standards. A qualified opinion report can be used *only when the auditor concludes that material parts of the overall financial statements are not fairly stated*. A disclaimer or an adverse report must be used if the auditor believes that the condition being reported on is highly material making the overall financial statements misleading (i.e. adverse opinion) or auditor's inability to collect sufficient evidence resulting in his inability to form his opinion (a disclaimer). Therefore, the qualified opinion is considered the least severe type of departure from an unmodified report.

Qualified opinion

A report issued when the auditor believes that the overall financial statements are fairly stated but that either the scope of the audit was limited or the financial data indicated a failure to follow IFRS.

A qualified report can take the form of a *qualification of both the scope and the opinion* or of the *opinion alone*. A scope and opinion qualification can be issued only when the auditor has been unable to accumulate all of the evidence required by International Standards on Auditing. Therefore, this type of qualification is used when the auditor's scope has been restricted by the client or when circumstances exist that prevent the auditor from conducting a complete audit. The use of a qualification of the opinion alone is restricted to situations in which the financial statements are not stated in accordance with IFRS or local accounting standards.

When an auditor issues a qualified report, he or she must use the term *except for* in the opinion paragraph. The implication is that the auditor is satisfied that the overall financial statements are correctly stated "except for" a specific aspect of them. Examples of this qualification are given later in this chapter. It is unacceptable to use the phrase *except for* with any other type of audit opinion. Figures 3-10, 3-11, and 3-12 present examples of the qualified reports for scope limitation, departure from accounting standards, and inadequate disclosure.

Adverse Opinion

Adverse opinion

A report issued when the auditor believes the financial statements are so materially misstated or misleading as a whole that they do not present fairly the entity's financial position or the results of its operations and cash flows in conformity with IFRS.

An **adverse opinion** is used only when the auditor believes that the overall financial statements are so *materially misstated or misleading* that they do not present fairly the financial position or results of operations and cash flows in conformity with IFRS or local accounting standards. The adverse opinion report can arise only when the auditor has knowledge, after an adequate investigation, of the absence of conformity. This is uncommon in the U.S., European Union, and the Arab world and thus the adverse opinion is rarely used. Figure 3-13 presents an example of adverse opinion.

Disclaimer of Opinion

Disclaimer of opinion

A report issued when the auditor is not able to become satisfied that the overall financial statements are fairly presented or the auditor is not independent.

A **disclaimer of opinion** is issued when the auditor has been *unable to satisfy himself or herself* that the overall financial statements are fairly presented. The necessity

---

FIGURE 3-10	Audit Report with a Qualified Opinion: Scope Limitation
	INDEPENDENT AUDITOR'S REPORT
	(Standard wording for the introductory and management's responsibility paragraphs.)
	(Same wording as for the standard auditor's responsibility paragraph, except for last sentence.)
Auditor's Responsibility	We believe that the audit evidence we have obtained is sufficient and appropriate to provide a basis for our qualified audit opinion.
Basis for Qualified Opinion	Alfa Company's investment in Beta Company, a foreign associate acquired during the year and accounted for by the equity method, is carried at €12,500,000 (approximately US$16.8 million) on the balance sheet as at December 31, 2009 and Alfa's share of Beta's net income of €1,200,000 (approximately US$1.6 million) is included in Alfa's income for the year ended. We were unable to obtain sufficient appropriate audit evidence about the carrying amount of Alfa's investment in Beta as at December 31, 2009 and Alfa's share of Beta's net income for the year because we were denied access to the financial information, management, and the auditors of Beta. Consequently, we were unable to determine whether any adjustments to these amounts were necessary.
Qualified Opinion	In our opinion, except for the possible effects of the matter described in the Basis for Qualified Opinion paragraph, the financial statements present fairly […] (same wording as for the remainder of the standard opinion paragraph).
	Source: Adapted from ISA 705 modifications to the opinion in the Independent Auditor's Report, IAASB (2010).

FIGURE 3-11	Audit Report with a Qualified Opinion: Departure from the Financial Reporting Framework

INDEPENDENT AUDITOR'S REPORT

(Standard wording for the introductory and management's responsibility paragraphs.)

(Same wording as for the standard auditor's responsibility paragraph, except for last sentence.)

We believe that the evidence we have obtained is sufficient and appropriate to provide a basis for our qualified audit opinion.
Auditor's Responsibility

The company's short-term marketable securities are carried in the balance sheet at €47,570,000 (approximately US$64 million). Management has not marked these securities to market but has instead stated them at cost which constitutes a departure from International Financial Reporting Standards. The company's records indicate that had management marked the marketable securities to market the company would have recognized an unrealized loss of €15,460 (approximately US$21,000) in the income statement for the year. The carrying amount of the securities in the balance sheet and shareholders' equity at December 31, 2009 would have been reduced by the same amount.
Basis for Qualified Opinion

In our opinion, except for the effects of the matter described in the basis for Qualified Opinion paragraph, the financial statements present fairly [...] (same wording as for the remainder of the standard opinion paragraph).
Qualified Opinion

We draw attention on Note 17 to the financial statements which describes the uncertainty related to the outcome of the lawsuit filed against the company by Gamma Company. Our opinion is not qualified in respect of this matter.
Emphasis of Matter

Source: Adapted from ISA 706 Emphasis of Matters Paragraphs and Other Matters Paragraphs in the Independent Auditor's Report, IAASB (2010).

FIGURE 3-12	Audit Report with a Qualified Opinion: Inadequate Disclosure

INDEPENDENT AUDITOR'S REPORT

(Standard wording for the introductory and management's responsibility paragraphs.)

(Same wording as for the standard auditor's responsibility paragraph, except for last sentence.)

We believe that the audit evidence we have obtained is sufficient and appropriate to provide a basis for our qualified audit opinion.
Auditor's Responsibility

The company declined to present a cash flow statement for the year ended December 31, 2009. The omission constitutes a departure from International Financial Reporting Standards.
Basis for Qualified Opinion

In our opinion, except for the omission of cash flow statement described in the Basis for Qualified Opinion paragraph, the financial statements present fairly, in all material respects, the financial position of the Zeta Company as at December 31, 2009 and their financial performance then ended in accordance with International Financial Reporting Standards.
Qualified Opinion

for disclaiming an opinion may arise because of a *severe limitation on the scope* of the auditor or a *non-independent relationship* under the *Code of Ethics for Professional Accountants* between the auditor and the client. Either of these situations prevents the auditor from expressing an opinion on the financial statements as a whole. The auditor also has the option to issue a disclaimer of opinion for a going concern problem.

The disclaimer is distinguished from an adverse opinion in that it can arise only from a *lack of knowledge* by the auditor, whereas to express an adverse opinion, the auditor must have knowledge that the financial statements are not fairly stated. Both disclaimers and adverse opinions are used only when the condition is highly material. Figure 3-14 presents an example of a disclaimer of opinion.

FIGURE 3-13	**Audit Report with an Adverse Opinion: Departure from the Financial Reporting Framework**

INDEPENDENT AUDITOR'S REPORT

(Standard wording for the introductory and management's responsibility paragraphs.)

(Same wording as for the standard auditor's responsibility paragraph except for last sentence.)

Auditor's Responsibility

We believe that the audit evidence we have obtained is sufficient and appropriate to provide a basis for our adverse audit opinion.

Basis for Adverse Opinion

As explained in Note 7, the Delta Company has not consolidated the financial statements of subsidiary Epsilon Company it acquired during 2009 because it has not yet been able to ascertain the fair values of certain of the subsidiary's material assets and liabilities at the acquisition date. This investment is therefore accounted for on a cost basis. Under International Financial Reporting Standards, the subsidiary should have been consolidated because it is controlled by the company. Had Epsilon Company been consolidated, many elements in the accompanying financial statements would have been materially affected. The effects on the financial statements of the failure to consolidate have been determined.

Adverse Opinion

In our opinion, because of the significance of the matter discussed in the Basis for Adverse Opinion paragraph, the consolidated financial statements do not present fairly the financial position of Delta Company and its subsidiaries as at December 31, 2009 and their financial performance and cash flows for the year then ended in accordance with International Financial Reporting Standards.

Source: Adapted from ISA 705 modifications to the opinion in the Independent Auditor's Report, IAASB (2010).

FIGURE 3-14	**Audit Report with a Disclaimer of Audit Opinion: Scope Limitation**

INDEPENDENT AUDITOR'S REPORT

We were engaged to audit the accompanying financial statements of Kosar Company, which comprise the balance sheet as at December 31, 2009, and the income statement, statement of changes in equity and cash flow statement for the year then ended, and a summary of significant accounting policies and other explanatory information.

(Standard wording for the management's responsibility paragraph.)

Auditor's Responsibility

Our responsibility is to express an opinion on these financial statements based on conducting the audit in accordance with International Standards on Auditing. Because of the matters described in the basis for disclaimer of opinion paragraph, however, we were not able to obtain sufficient appropriate audit evidence to provide a basis for an audit opinion.

Basis for Disclaimer of Opinion

We were not appointed as auditors of the company until after December 31, 2009 and thus did not observe the counting of physical inventories at the beginning and end of the year. We were unable to satisfy ourselves by alternative means concerning the inventory quantities held at December 31, 2008 and 2009 which are stated in the balance sheet at €4,250,000 (approximately US$5.7 million) and €4,575,000 (approximately US$6 million), respectively. As a result, we were unable to determine whether any adjustments might have been found necessary in respect of recorded or unrecorded inventories, and the elements making up the income statement and the statement of changes in equity and cash flow statement.

Disclaimer of Opinion

Because of the significance of the matters described in the Basis for Disclaimer of Opinion paragraph, we have not been able to obtain sufficient appropriate audit evidence to provide a basis for an audit opinion; accordingly, we do not express an opinion on the financial statements.

Source: Adapted from ISA 705 modifications to the opinion in the Independent Auditor's Report, IAASB (2010).

MATERIALITY

OBJECTIVE 3-6

Explain how materiality affects audit reporting decisions.

Materiality is an essential consideration in determining the appropriate type of report for a given set of circumstances. For example, if a misstatement is immaterial relative to the financial statements of the entity for the current period, it is appropriate to issue an unmodified report. A common instance is the immediate expensing of office supplies rather than carrying the unused portion in inventory because the amount is insignificant.

The situation is totally different when the amounts are of such significance that the financial statements are materially affected as a whole. In these circumstances, it is necessary to issue a disclaimer of opinion or an adverse opinion, depending on whether an IFRS departure or scope limitation is involved. In situations of lesser materiality, a qualified opinion is appropriate.

Levels of Materiality

The common definition of materiality as it applies to accounting and therefore to audit reporting is as follows:

> A misstatement in the financial statements can be considered material if knowledge of the misstatement will affect a decision of a reasonable user of the statements.

In applying this definition, three levels of materiality are used for determining the type of opinion to issue. (Figure 3-15 presents the level of materiality and their effects on the type of auditor's report.)

Amounts are Immaterial When a misstatement in the financial statements exists but is unlikely to affect the decisions of a reasonable user, it is considered to be immaterial. An unmodified opinion is therefore appropriate. For example, assume that management recorded prepaid insurance as an asset in the previous year and decides to expense it in the current year to reduce record-keeping costs. Management has failed to follow IFRS, but if the amounts are small, the misstatement is immaterial and a standard unmodified audit report is appropriate.

Amounts are Material but Do Not Overshadow the Financial Statements as a Whole The second level of materiality exists when a misstatement in the financial statements would affect a user's decision, but the overall statements are still fairly stated and therefore useful. For example, knowledge of a large misstatement in fixed assets might affect a user's willingness to loan money to a company if the assets were the collateral. A misstatement of inventory does not mean that cash, accounts receivable, and other elements of the financial statements, or the financial statements as a whole, are materially incorrect.

To make materiality decisions when a condition requiring a departure from an unmodified report exists, the auditor must evaluate all effects on the financial statements. Assume that the auditor is unable to satisfy himself or herself whether inventory is fairly stated in deciding on the appropriate type of opinion. Because of the effect of a misstatement in inventory on other accounts and on totals in the statements, the auditor needs to consider the materiality of the combined effect on inventory, total current assets, total working capital, total assets, income taxes, income taxes payable, total current liabilities, cost of goods sold, net income before taxes, and net income after taxes.

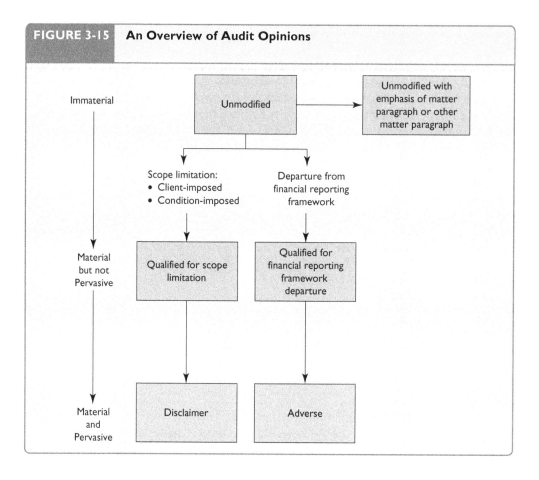

FIGURE 3-15   An Overview of Audit Opinions

When the auditor concludes that a misstatement is material but does not over-shadow the financial statements as a whole, a qualified opinion (using "except for") is appropriate.

Amounts are So Material or So Pervasive That Overall Fairness of the Statements is in Question The highest level of materiality exists when users are likely to make incorrect decisions if they rely on the overall financial statements. Auditing standards (ISA 705) define **pervasive** and pervasive effects on the financial statements as follows:

"A term used, in the context of misstatements, to describe the effects on the financial statements of misstatements or the possible effects on the financial statements of misstatements, if any, that are undetected due to an inability to obtain sufficient appropriate audit evidence." Pervasive effects on the financial statements are those that, in the auditor's judgment:

a. Are not confined to specific elements, accounts, or items of the financial statements;

b. If so confined, represent or could represent a substantial proportion of the financial statements; or

c. In relation to disclosures, are fundamental to users' understanding of the financial statements.

To return to the previous example, if inventory is the largest balance on the financial statements (such as 30 to 50 percent of the total assets of the company), a large misstatement would probably be so material that the auditor's report should indicate the financial statements taken as a whole cannot be considered fairly stated. When the highest level of materiality exists, the auditor must issue either a disclaimer of opinion or an adverse opinion, depending on which conditions exist.

Pervasive

A misstatement or misstatements contained in the audited financial statements that are considered highly material in its effect on users' decisions concerning such statements.

When determining whether an exception is highly material, the extent to which the exception affects different parts of the financial statements must be considered. This is called pervasiveness. A misclassification between cash and accounts receivable affects only those two accounts and is therefore not pervasive. On the other hand, failure to record a material sale is highly pervasive because it affects sales, accounts receivable, income tax expense, accrued income taxes, and retained earnings, which in turn affect current assets, total assets, current liabilities, total liabilities, owners' equity, gross margin, and operating income.

As misstatements become more pervasive, the likelihood of issuing an adverse opinion rather than a qualified opinion increases. For example, suppose the auditor decides a misclassification between cash and accounts receivable should result in a qualified opinion because it is material; the failure to record a sale of the same dollar amount may result in an adverse opinion because of pervasiveness.

Regardless of the amount involved, a disclaimer of opinion must be issued if the auditor is determined to lack independence under the rules of the *Code of Ethics for Professional Accountants*. This strict requirement reflects the importance of independence to auditors. Any deviation from the independence rule is therefore considered highly material. Table 3-1 summarizes the relationship between materiality and the type of opinion to be issued.

Materiality Decisions

In concept, the effect of materiality on the type of opinion to issue is straightforward. In application, deciding on actual materiality in a given situation is a difficult judgment. There are no simple, well-defined guidelines that enable auditors to decide when something is immaterial, material, or highly material. The evaluation of materiality also depends on whether the situation involves a failure to follow IFRS or a scope limitation.

Materiality Decisions—Non-IFRS Condition When a client has failed to follow IFRS or local standards, the audit report will be unmodified, qualified opinion only, or adverse, depending on the materiality of the departure. Several aspects of materiality must be considered.

Dollar Amounts Compared with a Base The primary concern in measuring materiality when a client has failed to follow IFRS is usually the total amount/value of the misstatement in the accounts involved, compared with some base. A US$10,000 misstatement might be material for a small company but not for a larger one. Therefore, misstatements must be compared with some measurement base before a decision can be made about the materiality of the failure to follow IFRS. Common bases include net income, total assets, current assets, and working capital.

For example, assume that the auditor believes there is a US$100,000 overstatement of inventory because of the client's failure to follow IFRS. Also assume recorded

TABLE 3-1	Relationship of Materiality to Type of Opinion	
Materiality Level	Significance in Terms of Reasonable Users' Decisions	Type of Opinion
Immaterial	Users' decisions are unlikely to be affected.	Unmodified
Material	Users' decisions are likely to be affected only if the information in question is important to the specific decisions being made. The overall financial statements are presented fairly.	Qualified
Highly material	Most or all users' decisions based on the financial statements are likely to be significantly affected.	Disclaimer or Adverse

Note: Lack of independence requires a disclaimer regardless of materiality.

inventory of US$1 million, current assets of US$3 million, and net income before taxes of US$2 million. In this case, the auditor must evaluate the materiality of a misstatement of inventory of 10 percent, current assets of 3.3 percent, and net income before taxes of 5 percent.

To evaluate overall materiality, the auditor must also combine all unadjusted misstatements and judge whether there may be individually immaterial misstatements that, when combined, significantly affect the statements. In the inventory example just given, assume the auditor believes there is also an overstatement of US$150,000 in accounts receivable. The total effect on current assets is now 8.3 percent (US$250,000 divided by US$3 million) and 12.5 percent on net income before taxes (US$250,000 divided by US$2 million).

When comparing potential misstatements with a base, the auditor must carefully consider all accounts affected by a misstatement (pervasiveness). For example, it is important not to overlook the effect of an understatement of inventory on cost of goods sold, income before taxes, income tax expense, and accrued income taxes payable.

Measurability The dollar amount of some misstatements cannot be accurately measured. For example, a client's unwillingness to disclose an existing lawsuit or the acquisition of a new company subsequent to the balance sheet date is difficult if not impossible to measure in terms of dollar amounts. The materiality question the auditor must evaluate in such situations is the effect on statement users of the failure to make the disclosure.

Nature of the Item The decision of a user may also be affected by the kind of misstatement. The following may affect a user's decision and therefore the auditor's opinion in a different way (i.e. issue a disclaimer or adverse opinion) than most misstatements:

1. Transactions are illegal or fraudulent.
2. An item may materially affect some future period, even though it is immaterial when only the current period is considered.
3. An item has a 'psychic' effect (for example, the item changes a small loss to a small profit, maintains a trend of increasing earnings, or allows earnings to exceed analysts' expectations).
4. An item may be important in terms of possible consequences arising from contractual obligations (for example, the effect of failure to comply with a debt restriction may result in a material loan being called).

Materiality Decisions—Scope Limitations Condition When there is a scope limitation in an audit, the audit report will be unmodified, qualified, or disclaimer, depending on the materiality of the scope limitation. The auditor will consider the same three factors included in the previous discussion about materiality decisions for failure to follow IFRS, but they will be considered differently. The size of *potential* misstatements, rather than known misstatements, is important in determining whether an unmodified report, a qualified report, or a disclaimer of opinion is appropriate for a scope limitation. For example, if recorded accounts payable of US$400,000 was not audited, the auditor must evaluate the potential misstatement in accounts payable and decide how materially the financial statements could be affected. The pervasiveness of these potential misstatements must also be considered.

It is typically more difficult to evaluate the materiality of potential misstatements resulting from a scope limitation than for failure to follow IFRS or local accounting standards. Misstatements resulting from failure to follow IFRS or local accounting standards are known. Those resulting from scope limitations must usually be subjectively measured in terms of potential or likely misstatements. For example, a recorded accounts payable of US$400,000 might be understated by more than US$1 million, which may affect several totals, including gross margin, net earnings, and total assets.

DISCUSSION OF CONDITIONS REQUIRING A DEPARTURE

You should now understand the relationships among the conditions requiring a departure from an unmodified report, the major types of reports other than unmodified, and the three levels of materiality. This part of the chapter examines the conditions requiring a departure from an unmodified report in greater detail and shows examples of reports.

> **OBJECTIVE 3-7**
>
> Draft appropriately modified audit reports under a variety of circumstances.

Auditor's Scope Has Been Restricted

The most common case in which conditions beyond the client's and auditor's control represent a scope restriction is when an engagement was agreed on after the client's balance sheet date and the auditor is unable to perform the requisite audit tests. The confirmation of accounts receivable, physical examination of inventory, and other important procedures may be impossible under those circumstances. When the auditor cannot perform procedures he or she considers desirable but can be satisfied with alternative procedures that the information being verified is fairly stated, an unmodified report is appropriate. If alternative procedures cannot be performed, a qualified scope and opinion or disclaimer of opinion is necessary, depending on materiality.

A restriction on the scope of the auditor's examination requires a qualifying paragraph preceding the opinion to describe the restriction. In the case of a disclaimer, the entire scope paragraph is excluded from the report.

For example, the reports in Figures 3-16 and 3-17 are appropriate for an audit in which the amounts were material but not pervasive and the auditor could not obtain audited financial statements supporting an investment in a foreign affiliate and could not satisfy himself or herself by alternate procedures.

When the amounts are so material that a disclaimer of opinion rather than a qualified opinion is required, the auditor uses only three paragraphs. The first (Report on the Financial Statements) paragraph is modified slightly to say "We were engaged to audit…". The second paragraph is the same as the third paragraph in Figure 3-14. The Auditor's Responsibility paragraph is summarized to include only auditor's responsibility to express an opinion in accordance with International Standards on Auditing and the inability to obtain sufficient evidence to provide a basis for an audit opinion. The final (opinion) paragraph is changed to a disclaimer. The reason for deleting the details of the scope of the audit from the Auditor's Responsibility paragraph is to avoid

---

FIGURE 3-16	**Example 1 of the Qualified Auditor's Report: Scope Restrictions**

INDEPENDENT AUDITOR'S REPORT

(Same introductory paragraph, management responsibility, and auditor's responsibility as standard report.)

We were unable to obtain audited financial statements supporting the company's investment in a foreign affiliate stated at US$475,000 or its equity in earnings of that affiliate of US$365,000, which is included in net income, as described in Note X to the financial statements. Because of the nature of the company's record, we were unable to satisfy ourselves as to the carrying value of the investment or the equity in its earnings by means of other auditing procedures.	**Basis for Qualified Opinion**
In our opinion, except for the effects of such adjustments, if any, as might have been determined to be necessary had we been able to examine evidence regarding the foreign affiliate investment and earnings, the financial statements referred to above present fairly, in all material respects, the financial position of Beirut Corporation for Metal Industries as of December 31, 2010 and the results of its operations and its cash flows for the year then ended in conformity with International Financial Reporting Standards (IFRS).	**Qualified Opinion Paragraph**

FIGURE 3-17	Example 2 of the Qualified Auditor's Report: Scope Restrictions

INDEPENDENT AUDITOR'S REPORT

(Same introductory, management responsibility, and auditor's responsibility paragraphs.)

Basis for Qualified Opinion	ABC Company's investment in XYZ Company, a foreign associate acquired during the year and accounted for by the equity method, is carried at xxx on the statement of financial position as at December 31, 2012, and ABC's share of XYZ's net income of xxx is included in ABC's income for the year then ended. We were unable to obtain sufficient appropriate audit evidence about the carrying amount of ABC's investment in XYZ as at December 31, 2012 and ABX's share of XYZ's net income for the year because we were denied access to the financial information, management, and the auditors of XYZ. Consequently, we were unable to determine whether any adjustments to these amounts were necessary.
Qualified Opinion Paragraph	In our opinion, except for the possible effects of the matter described in the Basis for Qualified Opinion paragraph, the financial statements present fairly, in all material respects, (*or give a true and fair view of*) the financial position of ABC Company as at December 31, 2012, and (*of*) its financial performance and its cash flows for the year then ended in accordance with International Financial Reporting Standards.

stating anything that might lead readers to believe that other parts of the financial statements were audited and therefore might be fairly stated. Figure 3-18 shows the audit report assuming the auditor had concluded that the facts in Figure 3-19 required a disclaimer rather than a qualified opinion.

Statements Are Not in Conformity with IFRS or Local Accounting Standards When the auditor knows that the financial statements may be misleading because they were not prepared in conformity with IFRS or local accounting standards, and the client is unable or unwilling to correct the misstatement, he or she must issue a qualified or an adverse opinion, depending on the materiality of the item in question. The opinion must clearly state the nature of the departure from accepted standards and the amount of the misstatement, if it is known. Figure 3-20 shows an example of a qualified opinion when a client did not capitalize leases as required by

FIGURE 3-18	Example 1 of Disclaimer Opinion

INDEPENDENT AUDITOR'S REPORT

(Same report on the financial statements, and management responsibilities paragraphs.)

Auditor's Responsibility Paragraph	Our responsibility is to express an opinion on these financial statements based on conducting the audit in accordance with International Standards on Auditing. Because of the matter described in the Basis for Disclaimer of Opinion paragraph, however, we were not able to obtain sufficient appropriate audit evidence to provide a basis for an audit opinion.
Basis for Disclaimer of Opinion Paragraph	The company's investment in its joint venture XYZ (Country X) Company is carried at US$10,000,000 on the company's statement of financial position, which represents over 90% of the company's net assets as at December 31, 2010. We were not allowed access to the management and the auditors of XYZ, including XYZ's auditor's audit documentation. As a result, we were unable to determine whether any adjustments were necessary in respect of the company's proportional share of XYZ's assets that it controls jointly, its proportional share of XYZ's liabilities for which it is jointly responsible, its proportional share of XYZ's income and expenses for the year, and the elements making up the statement of changes in equity and cash flows statement.
Disclaimer of Opinion Paragraph	Because of the significance of the matter described in the Basis for Disclaimer of Opinion paragraph, we have not been able to obtain sufficient appropriate audit evidence to provide a basis for an audit opinion. Accordingly, we do not express an opinion on the financial statements.

FIGURE 3-19   **Example 2 of Disclaimer Opinion**

INDEPENDENT AUDITOR'S REPORT

(Same report on the financial statements, and management responsibilities paragraphs.)

Our responsibility is to express an opinion on these financial statements based on conducting the audit in accordance with International Standards on Auditing. Because of the matter described in the Basis for Disclaimer of Opinion paragraph, however, we were not able to obtain sufficient appropriate audit evidence to provide a basis for an audit opinion.

Auditor's Responsibility Paragraph

We were not appointed as auditors of the company until after December 31, 2010 and thus did not observe the counting of physical inventories at the beginning and end of the year. We were unable to satisfy ourselves by alternative means concerning the inventory quantities held at December 31, 2010. In addition, the introduction of a new computerized accounts receivable. As of the date of our audit report, management was still in the process of rectifying the system deficiencies and correcting the errors. We were unable to confirm or verify by alternative means accounts receivable included in the statement of financial position at a total amount of US$6,000,000 as at December 31, 2010. As a result of these matters, we were unable to determine whether any adjustments might have been found necessary in respect of recorded or unrecorded inventories and accounts receivable, and the elements making up the statement of comprehensive income, statement of changes in equity, and statement of cash flows.

Basis for Disclaimer of Opinion Paragraph

Because of the significance of the matter described in the Basis for Disclaimer of Opinion paragraph, we have not been able to obtain sufficient appropriate audit evidence to provide a basis for an audit opinion. Accordingly, we do not express an opinion on the financial statements.

Disclaimer of Opinion Paragraph

FIGURE 3-20   **Example 1 of Qualified Auditor's Report: Departure from Accounting Standards**

INDEPENDENT AUDITOR'S REPORT

(Same report on the financial statements, and management and auditor's responsibilities.)

The company has excluded from property and debt in the accompanying balance sheet certain lease obligations that, in our opinion, should be capitalized to conform with International Financial Reporting Standards. If these lease obligations were capitalized, property would be increased by US$4,600,000, long-term debt by US$4,200,000, and retained earnings by US$400,000 as of December 31, 2009, and net income and earnings per share would be increased by US$400,000 and US$1.75, respectively, for the year then ended.

Basis for Qualified Opinion

In our opinion, except for the effects of not capitalizing lease obligations, as discussed in the preceding paragraph, the financial statements referred to above present fairly, in all material respects, the financial position of Future Company as of December 31, 2010, and the results of its operations and its cash flows for the year then ended in conformity with International Financial Reporting Standards.

Qualified Opinion Paragraph

---

the accounting standards. Figure 3-21 shows another example where management did not comply with measurement basis for inventory.

When the amounts are so material or pervasive that an adverse opinion is required, the scope is still unmodified and the qualifying paragraph can remain the same, but the opinion paragraph might be as shown in Figure 3-22.

When the client fails to include information that is necessary for the fair presentation of financial statements in the body of the statements or in the related footnotes, it is the auditor's responsibility to present the information in the audit report and to issue a qualified or an adverse opinion. It is common to put this type of qualification in an added paragraph preceding the opinion and to refer to the added paragraph in the opinion paragraph. Figure 3-23 shows an example of an audit report in which the auditor considered the financial statement disclosure inadequate.

FIGURE 3-21 — Example 2 of Qualified Auditor's Report: Departure from Accounting Standards

INDEPENDENT AUDITOR'S REPORT

(Same report on the financial statements, and management and auditor's responsibilities as the standard report.)

Basis for Qualified Opinion Paragraph

The company's inventories are carried in the statement of financial position at December 31, 2010. Management has not stated the inventories at the lower of cost and net realizable value but has stated them solely at cost, which constitutes a departure from International Financial Reporting Standards. The company's records indicate that had management stated the inventories at the lower of cost and net realizable value, an amount of US$1,900,000 would have been required to write the inventories down to their net realizable value. Accordingly, cost of sales would have been increased by US$1,900,000 and income tax, net income, and shareholders' equity would have been reduced, respectively.

Qualified Opinion Paragraph

In our opinion, except for the effects of the matter described in the Basis for Qualified Opinion paragraph, the financial statements present fairly, in all material respects, the financial position of ABC Company as at December 31, 2010, and its financial performance and its cash flows for the year then ended in accordance with International Financial Reporting Standards.

FIGURE 3-22 — Example of an Adverse Audit Report

INDEPENDENT AUDITOR'S REPORT

(Same report on the financial statements, and management responsibilities as the standard report except adding the word consolidated before financial statements.)

Basis for Adverse Opinion

As explained in Note X, the company has not consolidated the financial statements of subsidiary XYZ Company it acquired during 2010 because it has not yet been able to ascertain the fair values of certain of the subsidiary's material assets and liabilities at the acquisition date. This investment is therefore accounted for on a cost basis. Under International Financial Reporting Standards, the subsidiary should have been consolidated because it is controlled by the company. Had XYZ Company been consolidated, many elements in the accompanying financial statements would have been materially affected. The effects on the financial statements of the failure to consolidate have been determined.

Adverse Opinion

In our opinion, because of the significance of the matter discussed in the Basis for Adverse Opinion paragraph, the consolidated financial statements do not present fairly the financial position of ABC company and its subsidiaries as at December 31, 2010 and their financial performance and their cash flows for the year then ended in accordance with the International Financial Reporting Standards.

FIGURE 3-23 — Example of a Qualified Auditor's Report: Inadequate Disclosure

INDEPENDENT AUDITOR'S REPORT

(Same report on the financial statements, management responsibilities, and auditor's responsibility as the standard report.)

Basis for Qualified Opinion Paragraph

On January 15, 2010, the company issued debentures in the amount of US$3,600,000 for the purpose of financing plant expansion. The debenture agreement restricts the payment of future cash dividends to earnings after December 31, 2010. In our opinion, disclosure of this information is required to conform with accounting principles generally accepted in the United States of America.

Qualified Opinion Paragraph

In our opinion, except for the omission of the information discussed in the preceding paragraph, the financial statements referred to above present fairly...(remainder is the same as the opinion in the standard report).

Auditor is Not Independent

If the auditor is not independent as specified by the *Code of Ethics for Professional Accountants*, a disclaimer of opinion is required even though all the audit procedures considered necessary in the circumstances were performed. The wording in Figure 3-24 is recommended when the auditor is not independent.

The lack of independence overrides any other scope limitations. Therefore, no other reason for disclaiming an opinion should be cited. There should be no mention in the report of the performance of any audit procedures. As a result, it is a one-paragraph audit report.

FIGURE 3-24	**Example of an Auditor's Report: Auditor is Not Independent**

INDEPENDENT AUDITOR'S REPORT	
(Same report on the financial statements, and management responsibilities as the standard report.)	
We are not independent with respect to Home Decors.com, Inc., and the accompanying balance sheet as of December 31, 2009, and the related statements of income, retained earnings, and cash flows for the year then ended were not audited by us. Accordingly, we do not express an opinion on them.	**Disclaimer of Opinion due to Non-Independence Paragraph**

AUDITOR'S DECISION PROCESS FOR AUDIT REPORTS

Auditors use a well-defined process for deciding the appropriate audit report in a given set of circumstances. The auditor must first assess whether any conditions exist requiring a departure from a standard unmodified report. If any condition exists, the auditor must then assess the materiality of the condition and determine the appropriate type of report.

OBJECTIVE 3-8

Determine the appropriate audit report for a given audit situation.

Determine Whether Any Condition Exists Requiring a Departure from a Standard Unmodified Report Auditors identify conditions requiring reports or unmodified with an emphasis of a matter or other matter paragraphs as they perform the audit and include information about any condition in the audit files as discussion items for audit reporting. If none of these conditions exist, which is the case in most audits, the auditor issues a standard unmodified audit report.

Decide the Materiality for Each Condition When a condition requiring a departure from a standard unmodified opinion exists, the auditor evaluates the potential effect on the financial statements. For departures from IFRS or scope restrictions, the auditor must decide among immaterial, material, and highly material. All other conditions, except for lack of auditor independence, require only a distinction between immaterial and material. The materiality decision is a difficult one, requiring considerable judgment. For example, assume that there is a scope limitation in auditing inventory. It is difficult to assess the potential misstatement of an account that the auditor does not audit.

Decide the Appropriate Type of Report for the Condition Given the Materiality Level After making the first two decisions, it is easy to decide the appropriate type of opinion by using a decision aid. For example, assume that the auditor concludes that there is a departure from IFRS or a local accounting standard and it is material, but not highly material. The appropriate audit report is a qualified opinion.

Write the Audit Report Most auditing firms have computer templates that include precise wording for different circumstances to help the auditor write the audit report. Also, one or more partners in most auditing firms have special expertise in writing audit reports. These partners typically write or review all audit reports before they are issued.

More Than One Condition Requiring a Departure or Modification

Auditors often encounter situations involving more than one of the conditions requiring a departure from an unmodified report or modification of the standard unmodified report. In these circumstances, the auditor should modify his or her opinion for each condition unless one has the effect of neutralizing the others. For example, if there is a scope limitation and a situation in which the auditor is not independent, the scope limitation should not be revealed. The following situations are examples when more than one modification should be included in the report:

- The auditor is not independent and the auditor knows that the company has not followed International Financial Reporting Standards.
- There is a scope limitation and there is substantial doubt about the company's ability to continue as a going concern.
- There is a substantial doubt about the company's ability to continue as a going concern and information about the causes of the uncertainties is not adequately disclosed in a footnote.
- There is a deviation in the statements' preparation in accordance with IFRS and another accounting standard was applied on a basis that was not consistent with that of the preceding year.

Figure 3-25 shows an auditor report containing both a qualified paragraph and an emphasis of a matter.

FIGURE 3-25	Example of Auditor's Report with both Emphasis of Matter and Qualified Opinion
	INDEPENDENT AUDITOR'S REPORT
	To shareholders of ABC
	(Same report on the financial statements, management responsibility, and auditor's responsibilities.)
Basis for Qualified Opinion Paragraph	The company's short-term marketable securities are carried in the statement of financial position at US$50,000,000. Management has not marked these securities to market but has instead stated them at cost, which constitutes a departure from International Financial Reporting Standards. The company's records indicate that had management marked the marketable securities to market, the company would have recognized an unrealized loss of US$12,000,000 in the statement of comprehensive income for the year. The carrying amount of the securities in the statement of financial position would have been reduced by the same amount at December 31, 2010 and income tax, net income, and shareholders' equity would have been reduced.
Qualified Opinion Paragraph	In our opinion, except for the effects of the matter described in the Basis for Qualified Opinion paragraph, the financial statements present fairly, in all material respects, the financial position of ABC Company as at December 31, 2010, and its financial performance and its cash flows for the year then ended in accordance with International Financial Reporting Standards.
Emphasis of Matter Paragraph	We draw attention to Note (12) to the financial statements which describes the uncertainty related to the outcome of the lawsuit filed against the company by ABC Company. Our opinion is not qualified in respect of this matter.

INTERNATIONAL ACCOUNTING AND AUDITING STANDARDS

The increasing globalization of the world's capital markets and the expanding presence of business operations in multiple countries are leading to calls for the establishment of a single set of accounting standards to be used around the world. IFRS is increasingly accepted worldwide as the basis of accounting used to prepare financial statements in most countries.

The Securities and Exchange Commission (SEC) in the U.S. has proposed a roadmap that could lead to the use of IFRS by U.S. public companies beginning in 2014. Currently, U.S. public companies are required to prepare financial statements that are filed with the SEC in accordance with generally accepted accounting principles in the United States. Under the proposal, the SEC made a decision in 2011 allowing the adoption of IFRS by listed companies in U.S stock markets. Such a decision was made in the public interest and beneficial to investors of U.S. based companies.

As discussed in Chapter 2, the IAASB issues International Standards on Auditing (ISAs). Auditing standards in the United States now allow an auditor to perform an audit of financial statements of a U.S. entity in accordance with both generally accepted auditing standards in the U.S. and the ISAs. The auditor's responsibility paragraph is modified to indicate that the audit was conducted in accordance with auditing standards generally accepted in the United States of America and in accordance with International Standards on Auditing.

> **OBJECTIVE 3-9**
>
> Understand the need for uniformity between U.S. accounting and auditing standards and International Accounting and Auditing Standards.

Other information

Information that could be financial or non-financial (other than the client's financial statements and the auditor's report thereon) which is required to be included with the audited financial statements and the auditor's report either by law, regulation, or custom.

SPECIAL REPORTING MATTERS

The previous sections discussed various types of the auditor's reports in the normal course of the auditor performing his examinations of the clients' financial statements. However, auditors may face a number of situations where they must issue special reports on audited financial statements. Three important and practical issues are discussed in the following section:

a. Reports on comparative information.
b. **Other information** in documents accompanying audited financial statements.
c. Reporting on **summary financial statements**.

Reports On Comparative Information

It is the auditor's responsibility to obtain sufficient and appropriate audit evidence about whether the comparative information included in the audited financial statements presents a fair picture of the financial position, results of operations, and cash flows for the period being reported and examined by the auditor.

There are two types of comparative information. The first is called **comparative financial statements** which are considered separate financial statements and are included with the current year figures for comparison purposes. The level of information to be included in comparative financial statements should be comparable with that of the financial statements of the current period. When preparing his report, the auditor must refer to each period for which the financial statements are presented. The second type,

> **OBJECTIVE 3-10**
>
> Understand situations for special reporting matters.

Summary financial statements

A summary of the original historical financial statements which contains less detail than such statements, while still providing sufficient information to users to enable them to make their investment decisions.

Comparative financial statements

Comparative information including amounts and other disclosures related to the prior period and used for comparison with the financial statements of the current period.

Corresponding figures

Comparative information including amounts and other disclosures related to prior period and used as an integral part of the current period financial statements, and are intended to be read only in relation to the amounts and disclosures relating to the current period.

corresponding figures, is comparative information where amounts and disclosures related to prior periods are considered an integral part of the current period's financial statements, and are intended to be read only in relation to current period figures.

Figure 3-26 shows an audit report with a qualified opinion due to the fact that the audit report on the prior period included a qualified opinion for a matter which was unresolved until the current period.

Figure 3-26 describes the opinion of the auditor of XYZ company on the current period's financial statements because the effects of unresolved matter on the current period's figures are material. However, when the management of the company modifies the financial statements to resolve the matter of qualification, the current period audit report does not normally refer to the previous modification.

Finally, the auditor is required to express his opinion separately on the financial statements of each period when the comparative information is presented as comparative financial statements. The comparative financial statements are individually identified in the introductory and opinion paragraph of the audit report. (See Figure 3-27.)

FIGURE 3-26	Corresponding Figures: Audit Report with a Qualified Opinion

	INDEPENDENT AUDITOR'S REPORT
	We have audited the accompanying financial statements of XYZ Company, which comprise the balance sheet as at December 31, 2011, and the income statement, statement of changes in equity, and cash flow statement for the year then ended, and a summary of significant accounting policies and other explanatory information.
	(Standard wording for the management's responsibility paragraph.)
Auditor's Responsibility	(Same wording as for the standard auditor's responsibility paragraph, except for last sentence.)
	We believe that the audit evidence we have obtained is sufficient and appropriate to provide a basis for our qualified audit opinion.
Basis for Qualified Opinion	As discussed in Note 5 to the financial statements, no impairment has been calculated in the financial statements for accounts receivable balances, which constitutes a departure from International Financial Reporting Standards (IFRS). We qualified our report for the prior year due to the decision made by the management of the company not to perform impairment test for receivables which was calculated by us to require the decrease in the value of such receivables by US$1,500,000 in 2010 and US$2,300,000 in 2011.
Qualified Opinion	Except for the effect of the above matter described in the Basis for Qualified Opinion paragraph, the financial statements present fairly, in all material respects, the financial position of the XYZ Company as at December 31, 2011, and its financial performance and its cash flows for the year then ended in accordance with International Financial Reporting Standards.

FIGURE 3-27	Comparative Financial Statements: Audit Report with an Unmodified Opinion

	INDEPENDENT AUDITOR'S REPORT
	We have audited the accompanying financial statements of the BBNC Company, which comprise the balance sheets as at December 31, 2011 and 2010, and the income statements, statements of changes in equity, and cash flow statements for the year ended, and a summary of significant accounting policies and other explanatory information.
	(Standard wording for the management's responsibility and auditor's responsibility paragraphs.)
Opinion	In our opinion, the financial statements present fairly, in all material respects, the financial position of the BBNC Company as of December 31, 2011 and 2010, and of its financial performance and its cash flows for the years then ended in accordance with International Financial Reporting Standards.

It is worth noting that the auditor will express two different opinions for the comparative financial statements whenever the circumstances indicate a need to modify the auditor's opinion for the prior period due to material facts uncovered during the current period. The auditor is required by ISA to disclose reasons for the different opinion in an other matter paragraph. Similar disclosure requirements in an other matter paragraph should be considered when the comparative financial statements were audited by another auditor.

Other Information in Documents Accompanying Audited Financial Statements

The **annual report** prepared by the management of the company and presented to the shareholders at the annual general meetings held at the end of each financial period includes:

- board of directors' report or the chairman's report
- financial summaries or highlights
- financial ratios
- names of directors and officers and other management statistics concerning the performance of the company during the audited accounting period in addition to the auditor's report and the financial statements.

The information in the above documents other than the audited financial statements must be examined by the auditor for consistency with the information contained in the audited financial statements due to legal requirements in some jurisdictions. For example, under the Egyptian Companies Act auditors are responsible for auditing information contained in the report of the board of directors or management together with the audited financial statements published in the annual report. Auditors inspect the report of the board to ensure consistency between information contained in such report and audited financial statements.

ISA 720 provides detailed guidance concerning the auditor's responsibility for other information in documents contained with audited financial statements. Auditors should read the other information and identify any material inconsistency with the audited financial statements. For example, the report of the directors may discuss the number of employees and their salaries, growth or decline percentage of sales and administrative expenses. The auditor is required to determine whether the report of the board or the financial statements would need to be revised by management. If management refuses to revise the other information, then the auditor is required to include an other matter paragraph in the auditor's report explaining the material inconsistency between other information and the audited financial statements. It is important to note that a material **misstatement of fact** may affect the credibility of the document included with audited financial statements.

Figure 3-28 describes the use of an other matter paragraph for a material inconsistency related to information included in the chairman's report in the annual report.

Reporting on Summary Financial Statements

Because the cost of publishing the annual report of the companies including the financial statements and the auditor's report in daily newspapers and magazines is expensive, ISA 810 provides guidance on auditor's reporting on summary financial statements. The summary financial statements may contain aggregated information and limited disclosure, with less detail than the financial statements. The auditor's professional judgment is important for setting the criteria for the preparation of summary financial statements taking into consideration guidelines provided by auditing standards, professional associations, management practice, laws, and regulations. When the auditor's report presents an opinion other than an unmodified report, the auditor

Annual report

The document prepared by the management of the company on an annual basis, to be presented to shareholders at the annual general meeting and includes the auditor's report, the audited financial statements and board of directors' or chairman's report.

Misstatement of fact

Information contained in documents related to audited financial statements that is not related to matters appearing in the audited financial statements, and is incorrectly measured, presented, or disclosed.

FIGURE 3-28	Audit Report with Other Matter Paragraph for Material Inconsistency
Other Matter	**INDEPENDENT AUDITOR'S REPORT** (Standard wording for the introductory, management's responsibility, auditor's responsibility, and opinion paragraphs.) In the Chairman's Report contained in the Annual Report, it is stated that the company has realized a relative increase in profitability this year over that of the prior year. While this statement is consistent with regard to earnings before interest, taxes, depreciation and amortization (EBITDA), it is inconsistent with regard to profit for the year, which has decreased from last year. Source: Adapted from (proposed) ISA 706 Emphasis of Matter Paragraphs and Other Matter Paragraphs in the Independent Auditor's Report, IAASB (2010).

FIGURE 3-29	Auditor's Report on Summary Financial Statements
REPORT OF THE INDEPENDENT AUDITOR ON THE SUMMARY FINANCIAL STATEMENTS	The accompanying summary financial statements, which comprise the summary balance sheet as at December 31, 2010, the summary income statement, summary statement of changes in equity, and summary cash flow statement for the year then ended, and related notes, are derived from the audited financial statements of XYZ Company for the year ended December 31, 2010. We expressed an unmodified audit opinion on those financial statements in our report dated February 10, 2011. The summary financial statements do not contain all the disclosures required by the International Financial Reporting Standards. Reading the summary financial statements, therefore, is not a substitute for reading the audited financial statements of XYZ Company.
Management's Responsibility for the Summary Financial Statements	Management is responsible for the preparation of a summary of the audited financial statements on the basis described in Note 2.
Auditor's Responsibility	Our responsibility is to express an opinion on the summary financial statements based on our procedures, which were conducted in accordance with International Standard on Auditing (ISA) 810, "Engagements to Report on Summary Financial Statements."
Opinion	In our opinion, the summary financial statements derived from the audited financial statements of XYZ Company for the year ended December 31, 2009 are consistent, in all material respects, with those financial statements, on the basis described in Note 2. Source: Adapted with modifications from ISA 810 Engagements to Report on Summary Financial Statements, IAASB (2010).

states this fact in the report of the summary financial statements and provides reasons supporting such opinion. However, whenever the summary financial statements are not consistent with the audited financial statements, the auditor should express an adverse opinion on the summary financial statements.

Figure 3-29 provides an example of the auditor's report on summary financial statements.

SUMMARY

This chapter describes the auditor's standard unmodified audit report, as well as reports for circumstances where there is a departure from IFRS or local accounting standards or a scope limitation exists on the auditor's ability to accumulate sufficient evidence to provide his audit opinion or lack of independence. The four categories of audit reports and the auditor's decision process in choosing the appropriate audit report to issue were then discussed. In some circumstances, an emphasis of a matter or other matter paragraph is required. When there is a material departure from IFRS or local accounting standards or a material limitation on the scope of the audit, an unmodified report cannot be issued.

The appropriate report to issue in these circumstances depends on whether the situation involves an IFRS or local accounting standard departure or a scope limitation, as well as the level of materiality. Finally, the chapter discussed the auditor's reporting responsibility related to special reporting issues. The auditor's responsibility relating to comparative information including other corresponding information and comparative figures were discussed in detail giving examples of their application in practice. The information included in documents other than audited financial statements were described showing the auditor's responsibility to ensure consistency with financial statements and the auditor's reporting on summary financial statements.

ESSENTIAL TERMS

Adverse opinion   p. 72

Annual report   p. 87

Comparative financial statements   p. 85

Corresponding figures   p. 86

Disclaimer of opinion   p. 72

Emphasis of a matter paragraph   p. 64

Going concern   p. 67

Material misstatement   p. 62

Misstatement of fact   p. 87

Other information   p. 85

Pervasive   p. 76

Qualified opinion   p. 71

Reasonable assurance   p. 62

Scope limitation   p. 71

Standard unmodified audit report   p. 60

Summary financial statements   p. 85

Unmodified audit report with emphasis of a matter or other matter   p. 67

REVIEW QUESTIONS

3-1 (Objective 3-1) Explain why auditors' reports are important to users of financial statements and why it is desirable to have standard wording.

3-2 (Objective 3-1) List the ten parts of a standard unmodified audit report and explain the meaning of each part. How do the parts compare with those found in a qualified report?

3-3 (Objective 3-1) What are the purposes of the auditor's responsibility paragraph in the auditor's report? Identify the most important information included in the auditor's responsibility paragraph.

3-4 (Objective 3-1) What are the purposes of the opinion paragraph in the auditor's report? Identify the most important information included in the opinion paragraph.

3-5 (Objectives 3-1, 3-2) What conditions are required for a standard unmodified report to be issued?

3-6 (Objectives 3-4, 3-8) What type of opinion should an auditor issue when the financial statements are not in accordance with IFRS or local accounting standards because such adherence would result in misleading statements?

3-7 (Objectives 3-4, 3-5) Distinguish between an unmodified report with an emphasis of a matter or other matter and a qualified report. Give examples when an emphasis of a matter or other matter paragraphs should be used in an unmodified opinion.

3-8 (Objective 3-4) Describe what is meant by reports involving the use of other auditors. What are the three options available to the principal auditor and when should each be used?

3-9 (Objective 3-4) The client has restated the prior year statements because of a change from last in, first out (LIFO) to first in, first out (FIFO). How should this be reflected in the auditor's report?

3-10 (Objectives 3-4, 3-5) List the three conditions that require a departure from an unmodified opinion and give one specific example of each of those conditions.

3-11 (Objective 3-5) Distinguish between a qualified opinion, an adverse opinion, and a disclaimer of opinion, and explain the circumstances under which each is appropriate.

3-12 (Objective 3-6) Define materiality as it is used in audit reporting. What conditions will affect the auditor's determination of materiality?

3-13 (Objective 3-6) Explain how materiality differs for failure to follow IFRS or local accounting standards and for lack of independence.

3-14 (Objective 3-8) How does the auditor's opinion differ between scope limitations caused by client restrictions and limitations resulting from conditions beyond the client's control? Under which of these two will the auditor be most likely to issue a disclaimer of opinion? Explain.

3-15 (Objective 3-5) Distinguish between a report qualified as to opinion only and one with both a scope and opinion qualification.

3-16 (Objectives 3-7, 3-8) Identify the three alternative opinions that may be appropriate when the client's financial statements are not in accordance with IFRS or local accounting standards. Under what circumstance is each appropriate?

3-17 (Objectives 3-6, 3-8) When an auditor discovers more than one condition that requires departure from or modification of the standard unmodified report, what should the auditor's report include?

MULTIPLE CHOICE QUESTIONS FROM CPA EXAMINATIONS

3-18 (Objectives 3-1, 3-2, 3-4) The following questions concern unmodified audit reports. Choose the best response.

a. The date of the auditor's opinion on the financial statements of the client should be the date of the:
   (1) closing of the client's books.
   (2) receipt of the client's letter of representation.
   (3) completion of all important audit procedures.
   (4) submission of the report to the client.

b. If a principal auditor decides to refer in his or her report to the audit of another auditor, he or she is required to disclose the
   (1) name of the other auditor.
   (2) nature of the inquiry into the other auditor's professional standing and extent of the review of the other auditor's work.
   (3) portion of the financial statements audited by the other auditor.
   (4) reasons for being unwilling to assume responsibility for the other auditor's work.

3-19 (Objectives 3-4, 3-8) The following questions concern unmodified audit reports with an emphasis of a matter or other matter. Choose the best response.

a. An entity changed from the straight-line method to the declining-balance method of depreciation for all newly acquired assets. This change has no material effect on the current year's financial statements but is reasonably certain to have a substantial effect in later years. If the change is disclosed in the notes to the financial statements, the auditor should issue a report with a(an):
   (1) qualified opinion.
   (2) unmodified opinion with emphasis of a matter paragraph.
   (3) unmodified opinion.
   (4) adverse opinion.

b. When the financial statements are fairly stated but the auditor concludes there is substantial doubt whether the client can continue in existence, the auditor should issue a (an):
   (1) adverse opinion.
   (2) qualified opinion only.
   (3) unmodified opinion.
   (4) unmodified opinion with emphasis of a matter.

c. The report on the financial statements paragraph of an auditor's report contains the following: "We did not audit the financial statements of EZ Inc., a wholly owned subsidiary, which statements reflect total assets and revenues constituting 27 percent and 29 percent, respectively, of the consolidated totals. Those statements were audited by other auditors whose report has been furnished to us, and our opinion, insofar as it relates to the amounts included for EZ Inc., is based solely on the report of the other auditors." These sentences:
   (1) indicate a division of responsibility.
   (2) assume responsibility for the other auditor.
   (3) require a departure from an unmodified opinion.
   (4) are an improper form of reporting.

3-20 (Objectives 3-5, 3-8) The following questions concern audit reports other than unmodified audit reports with standard wording. Choose the best response.

a. An auditor will issue an adverse auditor's opinion if
   (1) the scope of the audit is limited by the client.
   (2) the exception to the fairness of presentation is so material that an "except for" opinion is not justified.
   (3) the auditor did not perform sufficient auditing procedures to form an opinion on the financial statements taken as a whole.
   (4) major uncertainties exist concerning the company's future.

b. An auditor will most likely disclaim an opinion because of
   (1) the client's failure to present a cash flow statement as required by IFRS.
   (2) inadequate disclosure of material information.
   (3) a client-imposed scope limitation.
   (4) the qualification of an opinion by the other auditor of a subsidiary when responsibility has been divided.

c. The opinion paragraph of an auditor's report states: "In our opinion, except for the effects of not capitalizing certain lease obligations, as discussed in the preceding paragraph, the financial statements present fairly, in all material respects, . . .". This paragraph expresses a(an):
   (1) unmodified opinion.
   (2) unmodified opinion with emphasis of a matter paragraph.
   (3) qualified opinion.
   (4) adverse opinion.

DISCUSSION QUESTIONS AND PROBLEMS

3-21 (Objectives 3-1, 3-2, 3-4, 3-6, 3-8) Khaled, CPA, has completed the audit of the financial statements of Optima Global Corporation for Marketable Securities located in Dubai as of and for the year ended December 31, 2011. Khaled also audited and reported on the Optima financial statements for the prior year. Khaled drafted the following report for 2011.

We have audited the balance sheet and statements of income and retained earnings of Optima Global Corporation as of December 31, 2011. We conducted our audit in accordance with International Financial Reporting Standards. Those standards require that we plan and perform the audit to obtain reasonable assurance about whether the financial statements are free of misstatement.

We believe that our audits provide a reasonable basis for our opinion.

In our opinion, the financial statements referred to above present fairly the financial position of Optima Global Corporation as of December 31, 2011, and the results of its operations for the year then ended in conformity with International Standards on Auditing, applied on a basis consistent with those of the preceding year.

Khaled, CPA
(Signed)

Other Information

- Optima is presenting comparative financial statements.
- Optima does not wish to present a statement of cash flows for either year.
- During 2011, Optima changed its method of accounting for Available for Sale Investments and properly reflected the effect of the change in the current year's financial statements and restated the prior year's statements. Khaled is satisfied with Optima's justification for making the change. The change is discussed in footnote 12.
- Khaled was unable to perform normal accounts receivable confirmation procedures, but alternative procedures were used to satisfy Khaled as to the existence of the receivables.
- Optima Corporation is the defendant in a litigation, the outcome of which is highly uncertain. If the case is settled in favour of the plaintiff, Optima will be required to pay a substantial amount of cash, which might require the sale of certain fixed assets. The litigation and the possible effects have been properly disclosed in footnote 11.
- Optima issued debentures on January 31, 2010, in the amount of US$10 million. The funds obtained from the issuance were used to finance the expansion of branches in various governorates. The debenture agreement restricts the payment of future cash dividends to earnings after December 31, 2014. Optima declined to disclose this essential data in the footnotes to the financial statements.

Required

a. Identify and explain any items included in "Other Information" that need not be part of the auditor's report.

b. Explain the deficiencies in Khaled's report as drafted.

3-22 (Objective 3-1) A careful reading of an unmodified report indicates several important phrases. Explain why each of the following phrases or clauses is used rather than the alternative provided:

a. "The financial statements referred to above present fairly in all material respects the financial position" rather than "The financial statements mentioned above are correctly stated."

b. "In conformity with International Financial Reporting Standards" rather than "are properly stated to represent the true economic conditions."

c. "In our opinion, the financial statements present fairly" rather than "The financial statements present fairly."

d. "Ashraf & Khuffash, CPAs (firm name)," rather than "Ashraf Khuffash, CPA (individual partner's name)."

e. "We conducted our audit in accordance with International Standards on Auditing" rather than "Our audit was performed to detect material misstatements in the financial statements."

3-23 (Objectives 3-4, 3-5, 3-6, 3-7, 3-8) For the following independent situations, assume that you are the audit partner on the engagement:

1. El Fatah's Used Cars, a client of yours, recently changed its depreciation method from straight-line to declining method. The effect of the change on the current year's income is not material, but in future years, you suspect the effect will become material. The facts are adequately disclosed in footnotes.

2. Jordan Minerals recently decided to change its direction and spent the last eight months developing business in the potash mining business. There are significant potential rewards, but the company's management recognizes that there are significant risks in the business that could jeopardize the success of its existing mining business. Since starting the new venture, the company has had no successes and some decline in profits. The facts are adequately disclosed in footnotes.

3. You recently noticed that Millennium Technology Solutions routinely excludes their statement of cash flows in the company's annual financial statements. Their reasoning, as explained to you, is that the statements are confusing to their readers, so they prefer to leave the information out.

4. A group of long-time friends decided to try their hand at online art auctions and online trade in antiquities. Although their venture started out well enough, a market-wide downturn in e-commerce sales abruptly plunged the start-up into the red. The future of the company looks bleak; both sales and cash position have declined substantially. If the market does not turn around soon, you think the company may not be able to continue to operate.

5. The controller of a company you're auditing will not allow you to confirm the receivable balances from any of its customers. However, the amounts of the receivables are material in relation to the company's financial statements. You cannot use any other methods to check the receivable balances.

6. Your firm has been unusually busy, so you asked another audit firm to do about 30 percent of the audit for Abdoun's Arts, Inc. After a thorough review of their working papers, you are convinced that they did an excellent job on their portion of the audit. However, you are reluctant to take complete responsibility for their work.

For each situation, do the following:

a. Identify which of the conditions requiring a modification of or a deviation from an unmodified report is applicable.   **Required**

b. State the level of materiality as immaterial, material, or highly material. If you cannot decide the level of materiality from the given information, state the additional information that you would need to make a decision.

c. Given your answers to parts a and b, state the appropriate audit report from the following alternatives (if you have not decided on one level of materiality in part b, state the appropriate report for each alternative materiality level):
   (1) Unmodified—standard wording
   (2) Unmodified—emphasis of a matter
   (3) Unmodified—other matter
   (4) Qualified opinion
   (5) Disclaimer
   (6) Adverse

d. Based on your answer to part c, indicate which paragraphs, if any, should be modified in the standard audit report. Be sure to indicate whether an additional paragraph in the form of an emphasis of a matter or other matter is necessary and, if so, where it should be located in the report.

3-24 (Objectives 3-4, 3-5, 3-6, 3-7, 3-8) For the following independent situations, assume that you are the audit partner on the engagement:

1. During your audit of Dubai.com, Inc., you conclude that there is a possibility that inventory is materially overstated. The client refuses to allow you to expand the scope of your audit sufficiently to verify whether the balance is actually misstated.

2. Four weeks after the year-end date, a major customer of Prince Construction Co. declared bankruptcy. Because the customer had confirmed the balance due to Prince at the balance sheet date, management refuses to charge off the account or otherwise disclose the information. The receivable represents approximately 10 percent of accounts receivable and 20 percent of net earnings before taxes.

3. You complete the audit of Johnson Department Store, and in your opinion, the financial statements are fairly presented. On the last day of the audit, you discover that one of your supervisors assigned to the audit has a material investment in Johnson.

4. El Watanyia Company has a fleet of several delivery trucks. In the past, El Watanayia had followed the policy of purchasing all equipment. In the current year, they decided to lease the trucks. The method of accounting for the trucks is therefore changed to lease capitalization. This change in policy is fully disclosed in footnotes.

5. You are auditing Middle East Linen Services for the first time. Middle East has been in business for several years but has never had an audit before. After the audit is completed, you conclude that the current year balance sheet is stated correctly in accordance with IFRS. The client did not authorize you to do test work for any of the previous years.

6. You were engaged to audit the El Azz Steel Company's financial statements after the close of the corporation's fiscal year. Because you were not engaged until after the balance sheet date, you were not able to physically observe inventory, which is highly material. On the completion of your audit, you are satisfied that El Azz's financial statements are presented fairly, including inventory about which you were able to satisfy yourself by the use of alternative audit procedures.

Required   For each situation, do the following:

a. Identify which of the conditions requiring a modification of or a deviation from an unmodified standard report is applicable.

b. State the level of materiality as immaterial, material, or highly material. If you cannot decide the level of materiality, state the additional information needed to make a decision.

c. Given your answers in parts a and b, state the type of audit report that should be issued. If you have not decided on one level of materiality in part b, state the appropriate report for each alternative materiality level.

3-25 (Objectives 3-1, 3-2, 3-4) The following tentative auditor's report was drafted by a staff accountant and submitted to a partner in the accounting firm of Kayed & Basel, CPAs:

AUDIT REPORT

To the Audit Committee of El Tameer Communication Company, Inc.

We have examined the consolidated balance sheets of El Tameer Inc. and subsidiaries as of December 31, 2011 and 2010, and the related consolidated statements of income, retained earnings, and cash flow for the years then ended. These financial statements are the responsibility of the company's management. Our responsibility is to express an opinion on these financial statements based on our audits.

Our audits were made in accordance with International Standards on Auditing as we considered necessary in the circumstances. Other auditors audited the financial statements of certain subsidiaries and have furnished us with reports thereon containing no exceptions. Our opinion expressed herein, insofar as it relates to the amounts included for those subsidiaries, is based solely upon the reports of the other auditors.

As fully discussed in Note 7 to the financial statements, in 2011, the company extended the use of the last-in, first-out (LIFO) method of accounting to include all inventories. In examining inventories, we engaged Dr. Mahdy to test check the technical requirements and specifications of certain items of equipment manufactured by the company.

In our opinion, the financial statements referred to above present fairly the financial position of El Tameer Company, Inc. as of December 31, 2011, and the results of operations for the years then ended, in conformity with International Financial Reporting Standards.

To be signed by
Kayed & Basel, CPAs
March 1, 2012

Identify deficiencies in the staff accountant's tentative report that constitute departures from the International Standards on Auditing reporting conventions.

Required

3-26 (Objectives 3-1, 3-8) The following is an auditor's report prepared in accordance with International Standards on Auditing (ISAs) issued by the International Auditing and Assurance Standards Board (IAASB):

INDEPENDENT AUDITOR'S REPORT

To the Shareholders of Zaatar w Zeit Restaurants, Inc.

We have audited the accompanying financial statements of Zaatar w Zeit Restaurants Inc., which comprise the balance sheet as of December 31, 2011, and the income statement, statement of changes in equity, and cash flow statement for the year then ended, and a summary of significant accounting policies and other explanatory notes.

Management's Responsibility for the Financial Statements

Management is responsible for the preparation and fair presentation of these financial statements in accordance with International Financial Reporting Standards. This responsibility includes: designing, implementing, and maintaining internal control relevant to the preparation and fair presentation of financial statements that are free from material misstatement, whether due to fraud or error; selecting and applying appropriate accounting policies; and making accounting estimates that are reasonable in the circumstances.

Auditor's Responsibility

Our responsibility is to express an opinion on these financial statements based on our audit. We conducted our audit in accordance with International Standards on Auditing. Those standards require that we comply with ethical requirements and plan and perform the audit to obtain reasonable assurance that the financial statements are free from material misstatement.

An audit involves performing procedures to obtain audit evidence about the amounts and disclosures in the financial statements. The procedures selected depend on the auditor's judgment, including the assessment of the risks of material misstatement of the financial statements, whether due to fraud or error. In making those risk assessments, the auditor considers internal control relevant to the entity's preparation and fair presentation of the financial statements in order to design audit procedures that are appropriate in the circumstances, but not for the purpose of expressing an opinion on the effectiveness of the entity's internal control. An audit also includes evaluating the appropriateness of accounting policies used and the reasonableness of accounting estimates made by management, as well as evaluating the overall presentation of the financial statements.

We believe that the audit evidence we have obtained is sufficient and appropriate to provide a basis for our audit opinion.

Opinion

In our opinion, the financial statements give a true and fair view of the financial position of Zaatar w Zeit Restaurants, Inc. as of December 31, 2011, and of its financial performance and cash flows for the year then ended in accordance with International Financial Reporting Standards.

Shukri & Halaby, CPAs
February 20, 2012
Damascus, Syria

Describe elements in the audit report based on International Standards on Auditing that are more extensive than an audit report based on U.S. auditing standards.

Required

CASES

3-37 (Objectives 3-4, 3-5, 3-6, 3-8, 3-9) Some situations concerning the clients of the audit office in Jordan you work for were discovered as shown below.

1. During the audit of El Aquaba Company (registered in the stock market) and in the audit of the investments, the financial manager gave you a copy of the bank letter assuring the company's ownership of stock certificates. You discover through direct inquiry with the bank that this letter is forged. The financial manager admitted that he transferred the stocks as a guarantee for a personal loan, knowing that the stocks' value is insignificant according to the financial statements.

2. El Nogom Company is a big company manufacturing children's toys. The minutes of the board of directors indicate that the most recent company product which achieved high sales does not conform with the legal safety standards. You then discover that the company concealed the technical data related to this product from the government inspectors, and that the financial manager refused to make a provision for the consequences of the product's failure and its withdrawal from the markets, because he maintains that violation of the laws was technical and does not affect the product's safety.

3. Lion Ltd., a company working in the television production field, is paying benefits to the scenario writers according to previously agreed percentages from the sales revenues. The audit procedures performed discovered that the paid benefits' value had decreased from their actual value. The financial manager maintains that any payments that were less than the actual value were unintentional. The financial manager also stated that the scenario writers had the right to review the way of calculating the payments and as they did not do that then the company is not responsible.

4. The audit of the payroll records showed that a salary has been paid to a fake worker for many years, knowing that the paid amounts are insignificant according to the financial statements.

Required   After reading each situation, write your comments on the resultant impacts on the audit, discuss the additional procedures that the auditor should perform in each situation, and state whether you are going to issue a qualified report and why.

LEGAL LIABILITY

Effects Of Courts Decisions Charging Auditors With Negligence Or Fraud On The Auditors' Continuity To Practice The Profession

Mostafa Shawki & Co—a member firm of Mazars International—one of the top ten international CPA networks in the world audited Capiks Holding Company during the period 2003–2008. Ahmed Mostafa Shawki—a principal partner in the firm—was fined EGP 10,000 (US$1,600) for issuing an erroneous audit report which did not include a disclosure that Capiks Holding Company purchased treasury stocks amounting to EGP 5,873,850 (US$1 million) from a number of shareholders during the period 2003–2005. The company chairman purchased such stocks and transferred shares equal to EGP 3,600,000 (US$600,000) to his name without disclosing such capital transactions in the financial statements of the company during the period 2005–2006. A number of shareholders sued the auditor, Ahmed Shawki, and the chairman for issuing a falsi-fied auditor's report and financial statements which did not include the information that the company had treasury stocks and that the chair-man had purchased some of these treasury stocks without proper disclo-sure or appropriate legal procedures for the transfer of Capiks' shares. Shareholders claimed that the auditor knew about such transactions and that he did not ask the management to restate the financial statements for the above years to include the value of the treasury stocks and the sale of some treasury stocks to the chairman. Shareholders also claimed that the auditor colluded with the management to mislead them and other users of the financial statements. Shareholders asked the Ministry of Finance to cancel Ahmed Shawki's name from the register of practicing auditors after the court ruled that he was guilty and fined him EGP 10,000 (US$1,600). The committee responsible for registering auditors in the Ministry of Finance refused to cancel the name of Ahmed Shawki from its register claiming that the fine paid by him was the only penalty against the auditor and it would be an injustice if another verdict was made against Ahmed Shawki for the same unethical act.

Source: Based on www.alwafd.org/index.php?option=com_content&view=article&id=22854%3A%D8%AA%D8%BA

LEARNING OBJECTIVES

After studying this chapter, you should be able to

4-1 Understand the litigious environment in which CPAs practice.

4-2 Explain why the failure of financial statement users to differentiate among business failure, audit fail-ure, and audit risk has resulted in lawsuits.

4-3 Use the primary legal concepts and terms concerning accountants' liability as a basis for studying legal liability of auditors.

4-4 Describe accountants' liability to clients and related defenses.

4-5 Describe accountants' liability to third parties under common law and related defenses.

4-6 Describe accountants' civil liability under statutory laws and related defenses.

4-7 Specify what constitutes criminal liability for accountants.

4-8 Describe what the profession and the individual auditor can do and what is being done to reduce the threat of litigation.

As the auditor at Mostafa Shawki & Co learned the hard way, legal liability and its consequences are significant. Although audit firms have insurance to help alleviate the impact of assessed damages, the premiums are high and the policies available to the firms require large excesses. The amount of this excess is such that large firms are essentially self-insured for losses of many millions of dollars.

This chapter on **legal liability** and the following one on professional ethics highlight the environment in which auditors fulfill their responsibilities according to International Standards on Auditing (ISAs) and the *Code of Ethics for Professional Accountants* operate. These chapters provide an overview of the importance of protecting the profession's reputation of high ethical standards, highlight consequences accountants face when others believe they have failed to live up to those standards, and show how auditors can be held legally liable for the professional services they provide.

In this chapter we focus on legal liability for auditors both on a conceptual level and in terms of specific legal suits that have been filed against CPAs. We also discuss actions available to the profession and individual practitioners to minimize liability while, at the same time, maintaining high ethical and professional standards and meeting the needs of society.

Legal liability

The professional's obligation under the law to provide a reasonable level of care while performing work for those served.

Relevant International Standards on Auditing	
IAASB	International Framework for Assurance Engagements
ISA 200	Overall Objectives of the Independent Auditor and the Conduct of an Audit in Accordance with International Standards on Auditing
ISA 240	The Auditor's Responsibilities Relating to Fraud in an Audit of Financial Statements
ISA 315	Identifying and Assessing the Risks of Material Misstatement through Understanding the Entity and Its Environment
ISA 500	Audit Evidence

CHANGED LEGAL ENVIRONMENT

OBJECTIVE 4-1

Understand the litigious environment in which CPAs practice.

Professionals have always been required to provide a reasonable level of care while performing work for those they serve. Under common law, audit professionals have a responsibility to fulfill implied or expressed contracts with clients. Should auditors fail to provide the services or not exercise due care in their performance, they are liable to their clients for negligence and/or breach of contract, and, in certain circumstances, to parties other than their clients.

Although the criteria for legal actions against auditors by third parties vary from one country to another depending on capital market law requirements, the auditor generally owes a duty of care to third parties who are part of a limited group of persons whose reliance is 'foreseen' by the auditor. For example, auditors expect investors to study and analyze the annual report including audited financial statements, therefore auditors are liable to investors for the reliability of information provided in these statements. In addition to common law liability, auditors may be held liable to third parties under statutory law in the Arab world. For example, in Kuwait and Saudi Arabia the law organizing the audit profession identified the types of misconduct when the auditors would be liable to both client and third parties. These include criminal acts, acts likely to bring the profession into disrepute, breaches of professional or ethical standards, and gross negligence. In Lebanon, there is an explicit requirement for the auditor's liability in the case of performing any work which contradicts the *Code of Professional Conduct*. In the United Arab Emirates, the types of misconduct where the auditor would be liable include engaging in trade activities, contravening professional behavior, or violating the integrity of the professional standards.

In the U.S., despite efforts by the profession to address legal liability of CPAs, both the number of lawsuits and sizes of awards to plaintiffs remain high, including suits involving third parties under both common law and the Companies Acts, and Securities Acts. No simple reasons explain this trend, but the following factors are major contributors:

- Growing awareness of the responsibilities of public accountants by users of financial statements.
- An increased consciousness on the part of the capital markets authorities (CMAs) for their responsibility for protecting investors' interests
- The complexity of auditing and accounting functions caused by the increasing size of businesses, the globalization of business, and the complexities of business operations.
- The use of sampling in the audit makes it quite difficult for the auditor to defend himself in lawsuits filed against him, increasing the probability of the plaintiffs winning cases against auditors and receiving large sums in compensation.
- The tendency of society to accept lawsuits by injured parties against anyone who might be able to provide compensation, regardless of who was at fault, coupled with the joint and several liability doctrine (often called the deep-pocket concept of liability). Large civil court judgments against audit firms awarded in a few cases, encouraging attorneys to provide legal services on a contingent-fee basis, which offers the injured party a potential gain when the suit is successful, but minimal losses when it is not.
- Many auditing firms being willing to settle legal problems out of court in an attempt to avoid costly legal fees and adverse publicity, rather than pursuing resolution through the judicial process.
- The difficulty judges and jurors have in understanding and interpreting technical accounting and auditing matters.

INTERNATIONAL AFFILIATIONS BRING LEGAL EXPOSURE

In the wake of a major accounting fraud in 2003 that exceeded US$9 billion at Italian dairy giant Parmalat, CPA firms are reviewing the structure of their international affiliations to protect themselves from legal exposure for the actions of their international affiliates. Italy's Grant Thornton, a small member firm of Grant Thornton International, was the accounting firm most directly associated with the accounting scandal. The Italian member firm of Deloitte International was also involved in the audit of Parmalat. Following disclosure of the fraud and alleged audit deficiencies, Grant Thornton International expelled its Italian affiliate. Grant Thornton also declared that the fraud occurred only within the Italian affiliate, and that it should not be legally liable for Grant Thornton actions. However, Grant Thornton and Deloitte International, as well as their U.S. member firms, have been forced to defend themselves in lawsuits related to Parmalat.

The legal concept that makes one party potentially responsible for the conduct of another is known as 'vicarious liability.' In response, both the International Federation of Accountants (IFAC) and American Institute of Certified Public Accountants (AICPA) have taken actions to more clearly set out to define a 'network' compared to an 'association' as it relates to accounting firms. An association ensures strict independence among the member firms, and does not have a common naming structure or operating manuals. In contrast, a network structure includes common ownership or control, and does allow for common naming and operating procedures.

Sources: Adapted from 1. Richard I. Miller, 'Liability for Someone Else's Sins: The Risks of Accounting Firm Alliances,' *Journal of Accountancy* (December 2006) pp. 30–32; 2. Kevin Mead, 'Find the Membership Group that's Right for Your Firm,' *Accounting Today* (July 21, 2008) (www.webcpa.com)

However, the matter is different in the Arab world as cases of negligence and fraud against auditors in the region are seldom published because the system for documenting and making available the details of such cases is inadequate. Also, the Arab culture in which friendships and the inability of those charged with governance to ensure the strict application of laws and regulations against auditors has resulted in the non-publication of details of many fraud cases. Moreover, those charged with governance in some situations believe that the publication of such cases affects not only the reputation of the charged auditor but also the name of the whole family. It is expected that this tendency to maintain confidentiality of penalties taken against auditors will be changed soon to accommodate the proper and real application of the international *Code of Ethics for Professional Accountants* issued by the IFAC.

Litigation costs for accountants are a concern because they are borne by all members of society. In recent years, legislative efforts have attempted to control litigation costs by discouraging no meritorious lawsuits and by bringing damages more in line with relative fault. Nevertheless, accountants' liability remains burdensome and is a major consideration in the conduct of an audit firm's professional practice.

DISTINGUISHING BUSINESS FAILURE, AUDIT FAILURE, AND AUDIT RISK

OBJECTIVE 4-2

Explain why the failure of financial statement users to differentiate among business failure, audit failure, and audit risk has resulted in lawsuits.

Business failure

The situation when a business is unable to repay its lenders or meet the expectations of its investors because of economic or business conditions.

Audit failure

A situation in which the auditor issues an incorrect audit opinion as the result of an underlying failure to comply with the requirements of auditing standards.

Audit risk

The risk that the auditor will conclude after conducting an adequate audit that the financial statements are fairly stated and an unqualified opinion can therefore be issued when, in fact, they are materially misstated.

Many accounting and legal professionals believe that a major cause of lawsuits against audit firms is financial statement users' lack of understanding of two concepts:

1. The difference between a business failure and an audit failure.
2. The difference between an audit failure and audit risk.

A **business failure** occurs when a business is unable to repay its lenders or meet the expectations of its investors because of economic or business conditions, such as a recession, poor management decisions, or unexpected competition in the industry. **Audit failure** occurs when the auditor issues an incorrect audit opinion because it failed to comply with the requirements of auditing standards. An example is a firm assigning unqualified assistants to perform certain audit tasks where they failed to notice material misstatements in the client's records that a qualified auditor would have found. **Audit risk** represents the possibility that the auditor concludes after conducting an adequate audit that the financial statements were fairly stated when, in fact, they were materially misstated. Audit risk is unavoidable, because auditors gather evidence only on a test basis and because well-concealed frauds are extremely difficult to detect. An auditor may fully comply with auditing standards and still fail to uncover a material misstatement due to fraud.

Accounting professionals tend to agree that in most cases, when an audit has failed to uncover material misstatements and the wrong type of audit opinion is issued, it is appropriate to question whether the auditor exercised due care in performing the audit. In cases of audit failure, the law often allows parties who suffered losses to recover some or all of the losses caused by the audit failure. In practice, because of the complexity of auditing, it is difficult to determine when the auditor has failed to use due care. Also, legal precedent makes it difficult to determine who has the right to expect the benefit of an audit and recover losses in the event of an audit failure. Nevertheless, an auditor's failure to follow due care often results in liability and, when appropriate, damages against the auditor and his audit firm.

It is important to note that difficulties often arise when a business failure, not an audit failure, occurs. For example, when a company files for bankruptcy protection or cannot pay its debts, statement users commonly claim that an audit failure has occurred, especially when the most recently issued auditor's report indicates that the financial statements were fairly stated. Even worse, if a business failure happens and the financial statements are later determined to have been misstated, users may claim the auditor was negligent even if the audit was conducted in accordance with auditing standards. This conflict between statement users and auditors often arises because of an 'expectation gap' between users and auditors. Most auditors believe that the conduct of the audit in accordance with auditing standards is all that can be expected of auditors. However, many users believe that auditors guarantee the accuracy of financial statements, and some users even believe that the auditor guarantees the financial viability of the business. Fortunately for the profession, courts continue to support the auditor's view. Nonetheless, the expectation gap often results in unwarranted lawsuits. Perhaps in the future, the profession will take on a greater responsibility for educating statement users about the role of auditors and the differences between business failure, audit failure, and audit risk. For now, however, auditors must recognize that, in part, the claims of audit failure may also result from the hope of those who suffer a business loss to recover from any source, regardless of who is at fault.

LEGAL CONCEPTS AFFECTING LIABILITY

An auditor is responsible for every aspect of his or her public accounting work, including auditing, taxes, management advisory services, and accounting and bookkeeping services. If an auditor fails to correctly prepare and file a client's tax return, he or she can be held liable for any penalties and interest that the client was required to pay plus the tax preparation fee charged.

Most of the major lawsuits against audit firms have dealt with audited or unaudited financial statements. In the Arab countries, the few cases discussed in courts have dealt only with audited financial statements or acts of fraud affecting the company's transactions and records. The discussion in this chapter is restricted primarily to those two aspects of public accounting. First, we examine several legal concepts pertinent to lawsuits involving auditors.

OBJECTIVE 4-3

Use the primary legal concepts and terms concerning accountants' liability as a basis for studying legal liability of auditors.

Prudent Person Concept

There is agreement within the profession and the courts that the auditor is not a guarantor or insurer of financial statements. The auditor is expected only to conduct the audit with due care, and is not expected to be perfect. This standard of due care is often called the **prudent person concept**. It is expressed in the case of *Cooley on Torts* as follows:

Prudent person concept

The legal concept that a person has a duty to exercise reasonable care and diligence in the performance of obligations to another.

- Every man who offers his service to another and is employed assumes the duty to exercise in the employment such skill as he possesses with reasonable care and diligence. In all these employments where peculiar skill is prerequisite, if one offers his service, he is understood as holding himself out to the public as possessing the degree of skill commonly possessed by others in the same employment, and, if his pretensions are unfounded, he commits a species of fraud upon every man who employs him in reliance on his public profession. But no man, whether skilled or unskilled, undertakes that the task he assumes shall be performed successfully, and without fault or error. *He undertakes for good faith and integrity, but not for infallibility*, and he is liable to his employer for negligence, bad faith, or dishonesty, but not for losses consequent upon pure errors of judgment.

Referring to the Mazars fraud case at the beginning of this chapter, Ahmed Shawki, the principal partner and his subordinates, were found guilty by the court because they did not exercise due professional care when they *falsified* the auditor's report and financial statements in relation to treasury stock. The acts of the partner and his subordinates are a good example of *violation of the prudent person concept*.

Liability for the Acts of Others

In the U.S., generally, the partners, or shareholders in the case of a professional corporation, are jointly liable for the civil actions against any owner. Similar legal requirements exist in many of the Arab countries where the auditor practices under proprietorship and partnership and he or she or the partners are jointly responsible for compensating the third parties for any harm caused.

The partners may also be liable for the work of others on whom they rely under the laws of agency. Under such laws, the auditors are considered representative of their subordinates and other specialists whom they rely on to perform some tasks related to the audit assignment. The three groups an auditor is most likely to rely on are *employees*, *other CPA firms* engaged to do part of the work, and *specialists* called upon to provide technical information. If an employee performs improperly in doing an audit, the partners can be held liable for the employee's performance. Legal requirements in many of the Arab countries also make auditors liable for their employees' acts.

Referring to the Mazars case, the partner in charge and his subordinates were ordered by the court of law to compensate shareholders for the damage and harm caused to them through falsifying the audited financial statements in relation to treasury stock. The Mazars firm paid US$4,600 for the partner's unethical act.

Lack of Privileged Communication

Under common law, CPAs do not have the right to withhold information from the courts on the grounds that the information is privileged. Confidential discussions between the client and auditor cannot be withheld from the courts. (See Chapter 5 on how auditor's documentation can be subpoenaed by a court.)

Generally speaking, many Arab countries (including Egypt, Kuwait, and U.A.E.) have statutes that permit privileged communication between the client and auditor. Even then, the intent at the time of the communication must have been for the communication to remain confidential. However, it is quite difficult in an Arab country for an auditor to refuse to testify in a court of law, or in a committee formed under a professional body or the ministry responsible for organizing the profession, by claiming privileged communications statutes. Auditors should not be allowed to hide information or documents related to acts of negligence or fraud committed by them or the management of the company.

Legal Terms Affecting CPAs' Liability

Before proceeding in the discussion of legal liability, we examine several common legal terms that affect CPAs' liability. These terms are defined in Table 4-1. Take a moment to review these definitions. Be sure to note the distinction between joint and several liability and separate and proportionate liability, because the amounts assessed will likely vary greatly between these two approaches when courts assess damages. Generally, these damage approaches only apply in cases of liability to third parties under common law and under the statutory laws. In the Arab countries, the notion of joint and several liability are more common for application of the legal liability concepts where every auditor is responsible for the work performed in addition to the responsibility of their subordinates and other specialists.

A client or a third party in the Arab world can select one of the auditors to sue and claim compensation for unethical acts, gross negligence, or fraud. Courts in the Arab world allow the notion of joint liability but it can take years for the court to make their ruling so people tend to change auditors in cases of negligence rather than taking legal actions against them. Also, the amount of compensation as evidenced in the Mazars case is always small so from the client's and third party's points of view it is not beneficial to those parties to assume the legal and financial burdens related to legal claims.

TABLE 4-1	Legal Terms Affecting CPAs' Liability

Legal Term	Description
Terms Related to Negligence and Fraud	
Ordinary negligence	Absence of reasonable care that can be expected of a person in a set of circumstances. For auditors, it is in terms of what other competent auditors would have done in the same situation.
Gross negligence	Existence of extreme or unusual negligence made by a person even though there was no intent to deceive or do harm. Gross negligence is also termed recklessness. Recklessness in the case of an audit is present if the auditor knew an adequate audit was not done but still issued an opinion, even though there was no intention of deceiving statement users.
Fraud	Occurs when a misstatement is made and there is both the knowledge of its falsity and the intent to deceive.
Terms Related to Contract Law	
Breach of contract	Failure of one or both parties in a contract to fulfill the requirements of the contract. An example is the failure of a CPA firm to deliver a tax return on the agreed-upon date. Parties who have a relationship that is established by a contract are said to have privity of contract.
Third-party beneficiary	A third party who does not have privity of contract (i.e. a party with contractual relationship with the auditor) but is known to the contracting parties and is intended to have certain rights and benefits under the contract. A common example is a bank that has a large loan outstanding at the balance sheet date and requires an audit as a part of its loan agreement.
Other Terms	
Common law	Laws that have been developed through court decisions rather than through government statutes.
Statutory law	Laws that have been passed by the country's parliament or U.S. Congress and other governmental units. For example, in Kuwait, Law No. 5 for 1981 organizes the audit profession and auditors' legal liability. In the United Arab Emirates, Federal Law Organizing the Auditing Profession No. 22 for 1995 includes explicit requirements for auditors' legal liability. In Egypt, the Companies Act 159 for 1981, Tax Law No. 9 for 2005 and Capital Market Law No. 95 for 1992 discuss the legal liability of auditors. In the U.S., the Securities Acts of 1933 and 1934 and Sarbanes–Oxley Act of 2002 are important statutory laws affecting auditors.
Joint and several liability	The assessment against a defendant of the full loss suffered by a plaintiff, regardless of the extent to which other parties shared in the wrongdoing. For example, if management intentionally misstates financial statements, an auditor can be assessed the entire loss to shareholders if the company is bankrupt and management is unable to pay.
Separate and proportionate liability	The assessment against a defendant of that portion of the damage caused by the defendant's negligence. For example, if the courts determine that an auditor's negligence in conducting an audit was the cause of 30 percent of a loss to a defendant, only 30 percent of the aggregate damage will be assessed to the CPA firm.

Sources of Legal Liability

The remainder of this chapter addresses the four sources of auditor's legal liability:

1. Liability to clients
2. Liability to third parties under common law
3. Civil liability under the statutory laws
4. Criminal liability

Figure 4-1 provides examples of each of these classifications of liability. Let's examine each of these liability classifications in more detail.

FIGURE 4-1	Four Major Sources of Auditors' Legal Liability
Source of Liability	**Example of Potential Claim**
Liability to clients	Client sues auditor for not discovering a material fraud during the audit.
Liability to third parties under common law	Bank sues auditor for not discovering that a borrower's financial statements are materially misstated.
Civil liability under statutory laws	Combined group of stockholders sues auditor for not discovering materially misstated financial statements.
Criminal liability	Government prosecutes auditor for knowingly issuing an incorrect audit report.

LIABILITY TO CLIENTS

OBJECTIVE 4-4

Describe accountants' liability to clients and related defenses.

The most common source of lawsuits against auditors is from clients. The suits vary widely, including such claims as failure to complete a non-audit engagement on the agreed-upon date, inappropriate withdrawal from an audit, failure to discover an embezzlement (theft of assets), and breach of the confidentiality requirements of auditors. Typically, the amount of these lawsuits is relatively small, and they do not receive the publicity often given to other types of suits.

An example of inappropriate withdrawal is when the auditor does not properly perform the audit tasks and in order to protect himself, decides to withdraw from the engagement leaving responsibility for misstatements to the management of the company. In such case, shareholders as well as third parties are advised to take legal action against the auditor for not taking responsibility for his work.

Another typical lawsuit brought by a client involves a claim that the auditor did not discover an employee theft as a result of negligence in the conduct of the audit. The lawsuit can be for breach of contract, a tort action for negligence, or both. Tort actions are more common because the amounts recoverable under them are normally larger than under breach of contract. Tort actions can be based on ordinary negligence, gross negligence, or fraud. Refer to Table 4-1 for distinctions among these three levels of negligent actions.

The principal issue in cases involving alleged negligence is usually the level of care required. Although it is generally agreed that no one's perfect, not even a professional, in most instances, any significant error or mistake in judgment creates at least a presumption of negligence that the professional will have to rebut. In audits, failure to meet auditing standards is often conclusive evidence of negligence. Let's examine a typical case that raised the question of negligent performance by a CPA firm: *Cenco Incorporated* v. *Seidman & Seidman*. The case, which is described in more detail in Figure 4-2, involved alleged negligence by the auditor in failing to find fraud. In the legal suit by Cenco's management, the auditor was able to successfully argue that it was not negligent and that the previous management team's deceitful actions had prevented the auditor from uncovering the fraud.

The question of level of care becomes more difficult in the environment of a review or a compilation of financial statements in which there are fewer accepted standards to evaluate performance. Figure 4-3 summarizes a widely known example of a lawsuit in the U.S. dealing with the failure to uncover fraud in unaudited financial statements. Although the CPA was never engaged to conduct an audit for the 1136 Tenants Corporation, the CPA was found liable for failing to detect an embezzlement scheme conducted by one of the client's managers. One of the reasons for this outcome was the lack of a clear understanding between the client and the CPA as to the exact nature of the services to be performed by the CPA. As noted in Figure 4-3, *engagement letters*

FIGURE 4-2	Cenco Incorporated v. Seidman & Seidman (1982)—Liability to Clients

Between 1970 and 1975 Cenco's managerial employees, ultimately including top management, were involved in a massive fraud to inflate the value of the company's inventory. This in turn enabled the company to borrow money at a lower interest rate and to obtain higher fire insurance settlements than were proper. After the fraud was discovered by an employee of Cenco and reported to the SEC, a class action suit was filed by stockholders against Cenco, its management, and its auditors. The audit firm settled out of court on the class action suit by paying US$3.5 million.

By now, new management was operating Cenco. They brought a second suit against the audit firm on behalf of Cenco for breach of contract, professional negligence, and fraud. The primary defense used by the audit firm was that a diligent attempt was made on the part of the auditors to follow up any indications of fraud, but the combined efforts of a large number of Cenco's management prevented them from uncovering the fraud. The audit firm argued that the wrongdoings of management were a valid defense against the charges.

The Seventh Circuit Court of Appeals concluded that the audit firm was not responsible in this case. The wrongdoings of Cenco's management were considered an appropriate defense against the charges of breach of contract, negligence, and fraud, even though the management no longer worked for the company. Considering management's involvement, the audit firm was not deemed negligent.

FIGURE 4-3	1136 Tenants v. Max Rothenberg and Company (1967)—Liability to Clients

The *1136 Tenants* case was a civil case concerning an auditor's failure to uncover fraud as a part of unaudited financial statements. The tenants recovered approximately US$235,000.

An audit firm was engaged by a real estate management agent for US$600 per year to prepare financial statements, a tax return, and a schedule showing the apportionment of real estate taxes for the 1136 Tenants Corporation, a cooperative apartment house. The statements were sent periodically to the tenants. The statements included the words *unaudited,* and there was a cover letter stating that "the statement was prepared from the books and records of the cooperative and no independent verifications were taken thereon."

During the period of the engagement, from 1963 to 1965, the manager of the management firm embezzled significant funds from the tenants of the cooperative. The tenants sued the audit firm for negligence and breach of contract for failure to find the fraud.

There were two central issues in the case. Was the audit firm engaged to do an audit instead of only accounting, and was there negligence on the part of the audit firm? The court answered yes on both counts. The reasoning for the court's conclusion that an audit had taken place was the performance of "some audit procedures" by the audit firm, including the preparation of a worksheet entitled "missing invoices." Had the auditor followed up on these, the fraud would likely have been uncovered. Most important, the court concluded that even if the engagement had not been considered an audit, the auditor had a duty to follow up on any potential significant exceptions uncovered during an engagement.

Two developments resulted from the *1136 Tenants* case and similar lawsuits concerning unaudited financial statements:

- Engagement letters between the auditor and client were strongly recommended for all engagements, but especially for unaudited engagements. The letter should clearly define the intent of the engagement, the auditor's responsibilities, and any restrictions imposed on the auditor.
- The Accounting and Review Services Committee was formed as a major committee of the AICPA to set forth guidelines for unaudited financial statements of nonpublic companies.

between the client and the CPA firm developed as a result of this case. Now, CPA firms and clients typically sign engagement letters, which are required for audits, to formalize their agreements about the services to be provided, fees, and timing. *Privity of contract* (see breach of contract in Table 4-1) can exist without a written agreement, but an engagement letter defines the contract more clearly.

In the Arab world, laws and ministerial decrees determine the legal liability of the auditors toward the client and possibly third parties as well. For example, in Saudi Arabia, the Saudi Organization for Certified Public Accountants (SOCPA) through Certified Public Accountants Regulations, Royal Decree No. M/12 for 1991 imposed sanctions for misconduct of auditors such as loss or restriction of practice rights, fines or loss of professional title and exclusion from the organization's membership. In Kuwait, the Kuwait Association of Accountants and Auditors (KAAA) shares the responsibility with the Ministry of Commerce and Industry (MOCI) for investigating and disciplining auditors for misconduct and breaches of professional standards and rules by its individual members. However, the KAAA establishes in its constitution the rules, provisions, and processes for investigating and disciplining the members. Article No. 32 of the Law No. 5 for 1981 determines that a CPA shall be punishable by imprisonment for a period not exceeding one year (in United Arab Emirates the period would not exceed 6 months—Article 45 of Federal Law No. 22 for 1995) and be liable for a financial penalty not exceeding 1,000 Dinar. In the United Arab Emirates the fine ranges from 10,000 to 20,000 dirhams if:

a. Any person performed the audit without his name being registered in the register of auditors at MOCI.
b. Any person continues to perform an audit even though his name was excluded from the register of auditors.
c. Any person whose name is not registered in the register of auditors uses an advertisement to mislead members of the public that he is registered as an auditor.
d. Any person recorded his name in the register of auditors by providing incorrect information or certificates related to his actual status.

All the above penalties will be doubled if the defendant commits similar acts within a period not exceeding five years from the date of the previous judgment. The law also requires publication of the judgment in two local Arabic daily newspapers at the expense of the sentenced person. All these sanctions provide forms of protection to clients and other users of the audited financial statements.

Moreover, in Kuwait, Article 21 of Law No. 5 for 1981 determines that the Undersecretary of the Ministry of Commerce and Industry has the right to refer an auditor to a disciplinary committee or public prosecution if infringement of provisions hereof or principles of the profession or committing gross negligence or an act breaching dignity and faith or a crime are attributed to him. Sanctions which may be imposed include: a warning, loss or restriction of practice rights for a period of three years, loss of professional title (designation), and exclusion from membership. The member cannot be reinstated until five years from the date of his or her exclusion from membership.

Auditor's Defenses Against Client Suits

The audit firm normally uses one or a combination of four defenses when there are legal claims by clients: lack of duty to perform the service, non-negligent performance, contributory negligence, and absence of causal connection.

Lack of duty to perform

An auditor's legal defense under which the auditor claims that no contract existed with the client; therefore, no duty existed to perform the disputed service.

Lack of Duty The **lack of duty to perform** the service means that the audit firm claims that there was no implied or expressed contract. For example, the audit firm might claim that misstatements were not uncovered because the firm did a review service, not an audit. The audit firm's use of an engagement letter provides a basis to demonstrate a lack of duty to perform. Many litigation experts believe that a well-written engagement letter significantly reduces the likelihood of adverse legal actions. However, this type of defense is considered a weak defense as most of the audit assignments have a written engagement letter or formal approval for the appointment of the auditors by the client's annual general meeting (AGM). In the Arab world, the minutes of the company's AGM is strong evidence that the audit firm is assigned to examine the client's financial statements in accordance with ISA.

Non-negligent Performance For **non-negligent performance** in an audit, the audit firm claims that the audit was performed in accordance with auditing standards. Even if there were undiscovered misstatements, the auditor is not responsible if the audit was conducted properly. The prudent person concept establishes in law that the audit firm is not expected to be infallible. Similarly, ISA No. 200 makes it clear that an audit in accordance with ISAs is subject to limitations and cannot be relied on for complete assurance that all misstatements will be found. Requiring auditors to discover all material misstatements would, in essence, make them insurers or guarantors of the accuracy of the financial statements. The courts do not require that.

In order for auditors to succeed in using a non-negligence defense audit firms must maintain: an effective system of quality control which provides for proper recruitment of auditors at all levels within the firm; adequate and complete working papers for all client's audit assignments; proper supervision over audit teams from audit seniors and partners; partner rotation and reviews on an interim basis; and finally some form of external monitoring from either professionals in the network or Public Company Accounting Oversight Board (PCAOB) model within the Arab countries.

Non-negligent performance

An auditor's legal defense under which the auditor claims that the audit was performed in accordance with auditing standards.

Contributory Negligence A defense of **contributory negligence** exists when the auditor claims the client's own actions either resulted in the loss that is the basis for damages or interfered with the conduct of the audit in such a way that prevented the auditor from discovering the cause of the loss. Suppose a client claims that an audit firm was negligent in not uncovering an employee's theft of cash. If the audit firm had notified the client (preferably in writing) of a weakness in internal control that would have prevented the theft but management did not correct it, the audit firm would have a defense of contributory negligence. Similarly, an auditor can claim contributory negligence if the credit manager gave him false documents when assessing collectability of receivables.

In the Mazars case, it would have been difficult for the audit partner to claim that the management of the company did not disclose information about treasury stock as it is the responsibility of the auditors to check evidence supporting the names and percentage of ownership of shareholders in the company's financial statements.

Contributory negligence

An auditor's legal defense under which the auditor claims that the client failed to perform certain obligations and that it is the client's failure to perform those obligations that brought about the claimed damages.

Absence of Causal Connection To succeed in an action against the auditor, the client must be able to show that there is a close causal connection between the auditor's failure to follow auditing standards and the damages suffered by the client. Assume that an auditor failed to complete an audit on the agreed-upon date. The client alleges that this caused a bank not to renew an outstanding loan, which caused damages. A potential auditor defense is that the bank refused to renew the loan for other reasons, such as the weakening financial condition of the client. This defense is called an **absence of causal connection**.

Absence of causal connection

An auditor's legal defense under which the auditor contends that the damages claimed by the client were not brought about by any act of the auditor.

LIABILITY TO THIRD PARTIES UNDER COMMON LAW

In addition to being sued by clients, auditors may be liable to third parties under common law. Third parties include actual and potential stockholders, vendors, bankers and other creditors, employees, and customers. An audit firm may be liable to third parties if a loss was incurred by the claimant due to reliance on misleading financial statements. A typical suit occurs when a bank is unable to collect a major loan from an insolvent customer and the bank then claims that misleading audited financial statements were relied on in making the loan and that the audit firm should be held responsible because it failed to perform the audit with due care. In the following sections the

OBJECTIVE 4-5

Describe accountants' liability to third parties under common law and related defenses.

development of the legal liability toward third parties in the U.S. will be presented showing whether the current legal liability toward third parties exists in similar forms in the Arab countries or not.

Ultramares Doctrine The leading precedent-setting auditing case in third-party liability was *Ultramares Corporation* v. *Touche* (1931), which established the **Ultramares doctrine.** Take a moment to read the summary of the case in Figure 4-4.

In this case, the court held that although the accountants were negligent, they were not liable to the creditors because the creditors were not a *primary beneficiary*. In this context, a primary beneficiary is one about whom the auditor was informed before conducting the audit (a *known third party*). This case established a precedent, commonly called the *Ultramares* doctrine, that ordinary negligence is insufficient for liability to third parties because of the lack of *privity of contract* between the third party and the auditor, unless the third party is a *primary beneficiary*. However, in a subsequent trial of the *Ultramares* case, the court pointed out that had there been fraud or gross negligence on the part of the auditor, the auditor could have been held liable to more general third parties. This final court decision is considered in line with the statutory requirements shaping the legal liability of the auditors toward third parties as will be explained later in the chapter.

Another example showing the importance of a primary beneficiary in the Arab world is found in the case brought by the Egyptian Financial Supervisory Authority when it removed an auditor's name from the register of auditors allowed to audit listed corporations. This was based on evidence pertaining to charges of gross negligence and audit failure and non-compliance with the Egyptian Standards on Auditing which were brought by shareholders. The charges made against the auditor included the following:

- The auditor issued an audit report on the financial statements of his client company (a marketable securities company) for the financial year ending December 31, 2008 without having received an engagement letter appointing him as the auditor of the client for that period.
- The auditor did not comply with the Egyptian Standard on Auditing No. 500 concerning the accumulation of appropriate evidence to help him form his opinion on the company's financial statements. As a result, when he was only three months away from issuing his report on the 2008 financial statements he requested that the company's AGM be postponed so that he could gather further audit evidence.
- The auditor did not comply with the Egyptian Standard on Auditing No. 720 as he did not read and study the content of the report from the client's board of directors to ensure that the information contained in the report complied with the information included in the company's financial statements. Also, the auditor, not the company's management, prepared the client's financial statements

---

Ultramares doctrine

A common-law approach to third-party liability, established in 1931 in the case of Ultramares Corporation v. Touche, in which ordinary negligence is insufficient for liability to third parties because of the lack of privity of contract between the third party and the auditor, unless the third party is a primary beneficiary.

FIGURE 4-4   Ultramares Corporation v. Touche (1931)—Liability to Third Parties

The auditors of an insolvent corporation (Ultramares) relied on the audited financials and subsequently sued the accountants, alleging that they were guilty of negligence and fraudulent misrepresentation. The accounts receivable had been falsified by adding to approximately US$650,000 in accounts receivable another item of over US$700,000. The creditors alleged that careful investigation would have shown the US$700,000 to be fraudulent. The accounts payable contained similar discrepancies.

The court held that the accountants had been negligent but ruled that accountants would not be liable to third parties for honest blunders beyond the bounds of the original contract unless they were primary beneficiaries. The court held that only one who enters into a contract with an accountant for services can sue if those services are rendered negligently.

as well as performing the audit function, a matter which is considered in violation of the Egyptian Standard on Auditing No. 200.

- The auditor did not comply with the Egyptian Standard on Auditing No. 240 as he had information that the company had issued another set of financial statements and, instead of attending the AGM to inform the shareholders about such a fraudulent act by the company's management, asked for the meeting to be postponed and then decided to withdraw from the engagement without informing the shareholders or even the management of his reasons.

- The auditor did not comply with the requirement of Egyptian Standard on Auditing No. 700 as he stated that he had audited the cash flow statement even though the company did not prepare such a statement. Also, the auditor issued an unmodified report on the financial statements even though the statements did include misstatements such as reporting the capital of the company at US$840,000 although the paid capital was only US$500,000. The financial statements did not include both the cash flow statements and the statement of changes in shareholders' equity. The financial statements contained the following errors: the improper classification of the financial position as investments in a subsidiary were classified as a short-term rather than a long-term investment; the improper inclusion of shareholders' other credit balances in owners' equity rather than as a current liability; incomplete disclosure in the footnotes about the accounting policies used in preparing the statements—mainly those related to impairment of assets, revenue recognition, deferred tax assets and liabilities, and financial instruments. Finally, the income statement reported a profit figure different from that included in the balance sheet.[6]

Foreseen Users

In recent years, courts in the U.S. have broadened the *Ultramares* doctrine to allow recovery by third parties in more circumstances by introducing the concept of **foreseen users**, who are members of a limited class of users that the auditor knows will rely on the financial statements. For example, a bank that has loans outstanding to a client at the balance sheet date may be a foreseen user. Under this concept, a foreseen user is treated the same as a known third party.

> **Foreseen users**
> Members of a limited class of users whom the auditor is aware will rely on the financial statements.

Although the concept of foreseen users may appear straightforward, courts in the United States have generated several different interpretations. At present, the three leading approaches that have emerged are described as follows:

Credit Alliance In *Credit Alliance* v. *Arthur Andersen & Co.* (1986) in New York, a lender brought suit against the auditor of one of its borrowers, claiming that it relied on the financial statements of the borrower, who was in default, in granting the loan. The New York State Court of Appeals upheld the basic concept of privity established by *Ultramares* and stated that to be liable (1) an auditor must know and intend that the work product would be used by the third party for a specific purpose, and (2) the knowledge and intent must be evidenced by the auditor's conduct.

Restatement of Torts The approach followed by most states is to apply the rule cited in the *Restatement of Torts*, an authoritative set of legal principles. The *Restatement Rule* is that foreseen users must be members of a *reasonably limited and identifiable group of users* that have relied on the CPA's work, such as creditors, even though those persons were not specifically known to the CPA at the time the work was done. A leading case supporting the application of this rule is *Rusch Factors* v. *Levin*, as presented in Figure 4-5.

> | **FIGURE 4-5** | **Rusch Factors v. Levin (1968)—Liability to Third Parties** |
>
> The plaintiff, Rusch Factors, a lender, asked the defendant auditor to audit the financial statements of a company seeking a loan. The auditor, Levin, issued an unqualified opinion on the financial statements, indicating that the company was solvent when, in fact, it was insolvent. The plaintiff loaned the company money, suffered a subsequent loss, and sued the auditor for recovery.
>
> The auditor's defense in the case was based on the absence of privity on the part of Rusch Factors. The court found in favor of this plaintiff. Although the court could have found in favor of Rusch Factors under Ultramares in that it was a primary beneficiary, it chose to rely on the Restatement of Torts, stating that the auditor should be liable for ordinary negligence in audits where the financial statements are relied on by *actually foreseen and limited classes of persons*.

Foreseeable users

An unlimited class of users that the auditor should have reasonably been able to foresee as being likely users of financial statements.

Foreseeable User The broadest interpretation of the rights of third-party beneficiaries is to use the concept of **foreseeable users**. Under this concept, any users that the auditor should have reasonably been able to foresee as likely users of the client's financial statements have the same rights as those with privity of contract. These users are often called an unlimited class. Although a significant number of states in the U.S. followed this approach in the past, it is now used in only two states.

In the Arab world, most of courts of law would accept the legal liability of auditors against parties for whom damage or harm was caused by the acts or conduct of the auditors. This concept of legal liability would represent an auditor's liability towards management, shareholders, investors, creditors, employees, etc. who are considered foreseen users.

Auditor Defenses Against Third-Party Suits

Three of the four defenses available to auditors in suits by clients are also available in third-party lawsuits: lack of duty to perform the service, non-negligent performance, and absence of causal connection. Contributory negligence is ordinarily not available because a third party is not in a position to contribute to misstated financial statements.

A lack of duty defense in third-party suits contends lack of privity of contract. The extent to which privity of contract is an appropriate defense and the nature of the defense depend heavily on the judge's interpretation of the facts of the case and the nature of the law requirements. It is not considered sufficient evidence for an auditor to indicate that there is no agreement between him and the third party for the service provided by him or his firm. The facts of the case may provide evidence that he did not foresee the party which was harmed due to his misconduct or improper performance of his services.

If the auditor is unsuccessful in using the lack of duty defense to have a case dismissed, the preferred defense in third-party suits is non-negligent performance. If the auditor conducted the audit in accordance with auditing standards, that eliminates the need for the other defenses. Unfortunately, non-negligent performance can be difficult to demonstrate to a court because auditors apply the test basis and audit management estimates where no complete assurance can be provided for such audit situations.

In the Arab world, this type of defense for the auditor is very weak as investors and other foreseen third parties have rights of protection under capital market laws for the provision of honest and reliable information in audited financial statements.

At the same time, absence of causal connection in third-party suits often means no reliance on the financial statements by the user. Assume that the auditor can demonstrate that a lender relied on an ongoing banking relationship with a customer, rather than the financial statements, in making a loan. In that situation, auditor negligence in the conduct of the audit is not relevant.

CIVIL LIABILITY UNDER STATUTORY LAWS

OBJECTIVE 4-6

Describe accountants' civil liability under the statutory laws and related defenses.

Although there has been some growth in actions brought against accountants by their clients and third parties under common law, the greatest growth in auditors or CPAs liability litigation has been under the statutory laws, mainly securities laws. Litigants commonly seek statutory remedies because of the availability of class-action litigation and the relative ease of obtaining massive recovery from defendants.

Statutory Laws in Arab Countries

In Arab countries, securities laws provide explicit requirements for investors to sue auditors in case of fraudulent financial reporting. Such requirements, however, must be investigated by the appropriate authority whether it is a ministry or an oversight board, and professional associations of accountants and auditors play a significant role in assessing the reality of the fraud or illegal acts committed by the auditors. For example, in the United Arab Emirates, Article 32 of the Federal Law No. 22 for 1995 requires the auditor to be held responsible for his audit and the correctness of the data contained in his report. The article explicitly holds the auditor liable for any damages sustained by the client or third parties as a result of his professional negligence or dereliction performance of his profession. In the case that there is more than one auditor, they shall be held jointly responsible, unless damages are attributed to negligence or dereliction on the part of any one of them. The said article also states that if the audit was conducted by a professional firm, all the partners in the firm will be held jointly liable for any damages incurred by third parties due to professional errors or negligence. As to the possible sanctions for auditor's negligence or fraud, Article 36 of the Federal Law No. 22 for 1995 requires any auditor who fails to comply with his professional obligations, acts in a degrading manner, or violates common professional ethics and acceptable accounting standards, will be liable to the following disciplinary actions:

1. A warning letter addressed to the auditor drawing his attention to his malpractice and asking him not to repeat such an act in the future.
2. Suspension from practicing for a period not exceeding two years.
3. Striking his name off the relevant register.

Finally, Article 37 of this law permits the Ministry of Economy and Commerce (MEC) in U.A.E., based on a request submitted by the competent authority or a complaint submitted to it, to conduct an investigation with the auditor regarding what is attributed to him from the matters stipulated in Article 36 of the law. If it is revealed to the ministry that the incident attributed to the auditor amounts to a criminal offense, it shall refer the matter for public prosecution. If it constitutes a disciplinary violation, the ministry shall then institute the disciplinary action and instigate the relevant procedures.

The Egyptian Companies Act 159, 1981, and its executive regulations include explicit articles allowing client and third parties to sue the auditors and the management for fraudulent financial reporting and obtain proper compensation for all damages. Also, the article states that one year must elapse before the civil responsibility of the auditor ends and no more claims can be raised by the client or third parties. Auditors may be imprisoned for a period of not less than two years and a penalty of not less than US$340 and up to US$1,600 imposed if he or one of his subordinates presents an incorrect report about the results of his audit or deliberately conceals important facts from inclusion in his report to affect the company reported results (Article 162 of Law No. 159). In addition, Article No. 131 of the Executive Regulations of the Egyptian Tax Law No. 91 for 2005 states that any registered auditor who certifies fictitious tax returns, documents, or reports supporting such returns is punishable by imprisonment and a penalty of not less than EGP 10,000 (approximately US$1,600) and not exceeding EGP 100,000 (approximately US$16,000). Finally, Capital Market Law No. 95 for 1992 confirmed the legal liability of the auditor toward the client and third parties as Article 63 states that imprisonment for a period not more than five years and a penalty of not less than EGP 50,000 (approximately US$8,000) and not exceeding EGP 100,000 (approximately US$16,000), shall be applied in the case of auditors providing falsified information in initial public offerings (IPOs) or documents for formation of companies. The same imprisonment terms and penalties apply to any person who falsifies information in a company's records and documents.

SEC and Capital Market Authorities Sanctions

Closely related to auditors' liability is the SEC's and capital market authorities' authority to impose sanctions. In the U.S., the SEC has the power in certain circumstances to sanction or suspend practitioners from doing audits for SEC companies. The SEC's *Rules of Practice* permit it to temporarily or permanently deny a CPA or CPA firm from being associated with financial statements of public companies, either because of a lack of appropriate qualifications or having engaged in unethical or improper professional conduct.

In recent years, the SEC has temporarily suspended a number of individual CPAs from doing any audits of SEC clients. It has similarly prohibited a number of CPA firms from accepting any new SEC clients for a period, such as six months. In some cases, the SEC has required an extensive review of a major CPA firm's practices by another CPA firm, or made CPA firms make changes in their practices. Individual CPAs and their firms have also been required to participate in continuing education programs. Sanctions such as these are published by the SEC and are often reported in the business press, making them a significant embarrassment to those involved.

In the Arab world, similar sanctions can be imposed by capital market authorities or sometimes financial supervisory authorities. These supervisory bodies can prohibit auditors from accepting any new listed clients for a specific period, such as one year. For example, Eisa Refai, a partner in Mazars & Co, Egypt, was prohibited from accepting new clients for a period of one year and the office was warned for not providing quality audit, with a recommendation for the enhancement of the qualifications and experience of the employees of the firm. No similar cases were published in other Arab countries in relation to sanctions against either individual auditors or audit firms. However, such lack of transparency is not expected to continue with government and professional associations and organizations working towards full compliance with the *Code of Ethics for Professional Accountants* issued by IFAC (sometimes with some modifications to consider exceptional requirements governing the accounting and auditing profession) currently applicable in most of the Arab countries.

CRIMINAL LIABILITY

OBJECTIVE 4-7

Specify what constitutes criminal liability for accountants.

Criminal liability for accountants

Defrauding a person through knowing involvement with false financial statements.

A fourth way auditors can be held liable is under **criminal liability for accountants**. Auditors can be found guilty for criminal action under criminal and other related local laws. Under such laws, the most likely statutes to be enforced are the Securities Acts. In the U.S., the more relevant federal laws affecting auditors are the 1933 and 1934 Securities Acts, as well as the Federal Mail Fraud Statute and the Federal False Statements Statute. All make it a criminal offense to defraud another person through *knowingly being involved* with false financial statements. In addition, the Sarbanes–Oxley Act of 2002 made it a felony to destroy or create documents to impede or obstruct a federal investigation. Under Sarbanes–Oxley, a person may face fines and imprisonment of up to 20 years for altering or destroying documents. These provisions were

FIGURE 4-6 **United States v. Andersen (2002)—Criminal Liability**

In this case, the government charged Andersen with destruction of documents related to the firm's audit of Enron. During the period between October 19, 2001, when Enron alerted Andersen that the SEC had begun an inquiry into Enron's accounting for certain special purpose entities, and November, 8, 2001, when the SEC served Andersen with a subpoena in connection with its work for Enron, Andersen personnel shredded extensive amounts of physical documentation and deleted computer files related to Enron.

The firm was ultimately convicted of one count of obstruction of justice. The conviction was not based on the document shredding, but it was based on the alteration of a memo related to Enron's characterization of charges as nonrecurring in its third quarter 2001 earnings release, in which the company announced a loss of US$618 million.

As a result of the conviction, Andersen was no longer able to audit publicly traded U.S. companies. The conviction was overturned by the U.S. Supreme Court in 2005 because the instructions provided to the jury were too broad. The victory was largely symbolic since the firm effectively ceased operations after the original conviction.

adopted following the *United States* v. *Andersen* (2002) case described in Figure 4-6, in which the government charged Andersen with obstruction of justice for the destruction and alteration of documents related to its audit of Enron.

Unfortunately, in recent years several notorious criminal cases have involved CPAs. Although these are not great in absolute number, they have damaged the integrity of the profession. On the positive side, these criminal actions have encouraged practitioners to use extreme care and exercise good faith in their activities.

Historically, one of the leading cases of criminal action against CPAs is *United States* v. *Simon*, which occurred in 1969. In this case, three auditors were prosecuted for filing false financial statements of a client with the government, and all three were held criminally liable. Three major criminal cases followed Simon:

- In *United States* v. *Natelli* (1975), two auditors were convicted of criminal liability under the 1934 act for certifying financial statements of National Student Marketing Corporation that contained inadequate disclosures pertaining to accounts receivable.
- In *United States* v. *Weiner* (1975), three auditors were convicted of securities fraud in connection with their audit of Equity Funding Corporation of America. Equity Funding engaged in fraud that was so extensive and the audit work so poor that the court concluded that the auditors must have been aware of the fraud and were therefore guilty of knowing complicity.
- In *ESM Government Securities* v. *Alexander Grant & Co.* (1986), management revealed to the partner in charge of the audit of ESM that the previous year's audited financial statements contained a material misstatement. Rather

LESSONS LEARNED FROM AUDITOR LITIGATION

As we consider the advisability of legislation for the reform of accountants' liability, it is useful to review actual experiences with past accountants' litigation. Accordingly, a review was conducted of 23 cases of alleged audit failure with which I have been involved as a litigation consultant and expert witness. Of these 23 cases, six were clearly without merit and should not have been brought on equitable grounds. Of the 17 that were with merit, 13 did, in fact, represent a real audit failure. Considering the nature of the failure in each case, the evidence that would lead the auditor to identify the misstatement was usually present. In other words, the problem was not any inadequacy in the audit process as presented by professional standards; it was a *lack of professional skepticism* on the part of the auditor. The auditor had evidence in his or her possession that indicated the problem, but did not see it as such.

Source: Presentation by James K. Loebbecke at the Forum on Responsibilities and Liabilities of Accountants and Auditors, United Nations Conference on Trade and Development, March 16, 1995.

than complying with professional and firm standards, the partner agreed to say nothing in the hope that management would work its way out of the problem during the current year. Instead, the situation worsened until company losses exceeded US$300 million. For his role in sustaining the fraud, the partner was convicted of criminal charges and was sentenced to a 12-year prison term.

These cases teach several critical lessons:

- An investigation of the integrity of management is an important part of deciding on the acceptability of clients and the extent of work to perform. Auditing guidance for auditors in investigating new clients will be discussed in Chapter 8.
- Auditors can be found criminally guilty in the conduct of an audit even if their background indicates integrity in personal and professional life. Criminal liability can extend to partners and staff.
- As discussed in Chapter 5, independence in appearance and in mind by all individuals on the engagement is essential, especially in a defense involving criminal actions.
- Transactions with related parties require special scrutiny because of the potential for misstatement. Auditing requirements for related-party transactions are discussed in Chapter 8.
- Accounting standards cannot be relied on exclusively in deciding whether financial statements are fairly presented. The substance of the statements, considering all facts, is required.
- Good documentation may be just as important in the auditor's defense of criminal charges as in a civil suit.
- The potential consequences of the auditor knowingly committing a wrongful act are so severe that it is unlikely that the potential benefits can ever justify the actions.

Turning to the situation in Arab countries, several securities laws in those countries include specific requirements that in cases of fraudulent financial reporting affecting investors' investments the auditor should be imprisoned. For example, in Saudi Arabia the prosecution department of the Capital Market Authority (CMA) prosecutes cases of violation and exploitation in the Saudi capital market for financial reporting and audit malpractices. Sanctions to be imposed include freezing of assets including bank and investment accounts of violators, travel ban, financial penalties, ban from trading, imprisonment, etc. Also, SOCPA is obligated under local laws to report possible involvement in serious crimes and offenses by its individual members or member firms to the appropriate public authority and disclose related information to that authority. In Kuwait, the Ministry of Commerce and Industry (MOCI) can refer any cases of criminal acts to the Kuwait general prosecutor for the offender to be put to trial under Kuwait criminal law. Similar requirements exist in the United Arab Emirates where the Ministry of Economy and Commerce (MEC) can refer an auditor to the public prosecutor if the incident attributed to him represents a criminal offense. On the other hand, the Beirut Stock Exchange (BSE) has the power to suspend trading or delist noncompliant companies in relation to audit of financial statements according to auditing standards. However, the BSE lacks the necessary authority to penalize or blacklist financial statements preparers and auditors. The only body which can impose criminal sentences for violations in financial reporting and other fraud acts is the Audit Bureau according to Legislative Decree No. 82 for 1983 which is considered an administrative court to protect public funds and prosecute those responsible for violation of laws and regulations.

THE PROFESSION'S RESPONSE TO LEGAL LIABILITY

The AICPA, professional accountants' associations governing the auditing profession in the Arab countries, and the profession in general can do a number of things to reduce practitioners' exposure to lawsuits:

OBJECTIVE 4-8

Describe what the profession and the individual auditor can do and what is being done to reduce the threat of litigation.

1. Seek protection from no meritorious litigation
2. Improve auditing to better meet users' needs
3. Educate users about the limits of auditing

Let's discuss some specific activities briefly:

- *Standard and rule setting.* The professional organizations in Arab countries and their counterparts in the U.S. (i.e. AICPA and PCAOB) and at the international level (i.e. IAASB), must constantly set standards and revise them to meet the changing needs of auditing. For example, changes in auditing standards on the auditor's responsibility to detect fraud were issued to address users' needs and expectations as to auditor performance.

- *Oppose lawsuits.* Auditing firms must continue to oppose unwarranted lawsuits even if, in the short run, the costs of winning are greater than the costs of settling.

- *Education of users.* The AICPA and other professional associations, leaders of auditing firms, and educators should educate investors and others who read financial statements as to the exact meaning of an auditor's opinion and to the extent and nature of the auditor's work. In addition, users need to understand that auditors do not test 100 percent of all records and do not guarantee the accuracy of the financial records or the future prosperity of an audited company. People outside of the profession need to understand that accounting and auditing are arts, not sciences. Perfection and precision are simply not achievable.

- *Sanction members for improper conduct and performance.* A profession must police its own membership. The AICPA as well as local professional institutions has made progress in dealing with the problems of inadequate CPA performance, but more rigorous review of alleged failures is still needed.

- *Forum of Firms.* The establishment of the Forum of Firms with its quality control measures for international CPA networks can play a significant role in ensuring CPAs adherence to requirements of auditing standards. All international CPA networks are represented in most Arab countries and member firms located in the region are required to provide information about the quality of their audit to the head office of the network for submission by the head offices of the CPAs networks to the Forum of Firms.

PROTECTING INDIVIDUAL CPAs FROM LEGAL LIABILITY

Practicing auditors may also take specific action to minimize their liability. Some of the more common actions are as follows:

- *Deal only with clients possessing integrity.* There is an increased likelihood of having legal problems when a client lacks integrity in dealing with customers, employees, units of government, and others. An audit firm needs procedures to evaluate the integrity of clients and should dissociate itself from clients found lacking integrity.

- *Maintain independence.* Independence is more than merely financial. Independence, in fact, requires an attitude of responsibility separate from the client's interest. Much litigation has arisen from a too-willing acceptance by an auditor of a client's representation or of a client's pressures. The auditor must maintain an attitude of healthy skepticism.
- *Understand the client's business.* The lack of knowledge of industry practices and client operations has been a major factor in auditors failing to uncover misstatements in several cases. The audit team needs to be educated in these areas.
- *Perform quality audits.* Quality audits require that auditors obtain appropriate evidence and make appropriate judgments about the evidence. It is essential, for example, that the auditor understands the client's internal controls and modifies the evidence to reflect the findings. Improved auditing reduces the likelihood of failing to detect misstatements and the likelihood of lawsuits.
- *Document the work properly.* The preparation of good audit documentation helps the auditor organize and perform quality audits. Quality audit documentation is essential if an auditor has to defend an audit in court, including an *engagement letter* and a *representation letter* that define the respective obligations of the client and the auditor.
- *Exercise professional skepticism.* Auditors are often liable when they are presented with information indicating a problem that they fail to recognize. Auditors need to strive to maintain a healthy level of skepticism, one that keeps them alert to potential misstatements, so that they can recognize misstatements when they exist.

It is also important for auditors to carry adequate insurance and choose a form of organization that provides some form of legal liability protection to owners. In the event of actual or threatened litigation, an auditor should consult with experienced legal counsel.

SUMMARY

This chapter provides insight into the environment in which auditors operate by highlighting the significance of the legal liability facing the CPA profession. No reasonable auditor wants to eliminate the profession's legal responsibility for fraudulent or incompetent performance. It is certainly in the profession's best interest to maintain public trust in the competent performance of the auditing profession, while avoiding liability for cases involving strictly business failure and not audit failure. To more effectively avoid legal liability, auditors need to have an understanding of how they can be held liable to their clients or third parties. Knowledge about how auditors are liable to clients under common law, to third parties under common law, to third parties under statutory laws, and for criminal liability, provides auditors with an awareness of issues that may subject them to greater liability. A detailed comparison between the legal liability of auditors in the U.S. and in many Arab countries was presented. Also, the role of professional associations in many Arab countries was highlighted, giving sanctions expected to be imposed for misconduct or malpractice by auditors. CPAs can protect themselves from legal liability in numerous ways, and the profession has worked diligently to identify ways to help CPAs reduce the profession's potential exposure. It is necessary for the profession and society to determine a reasonable trade-off between the degree of responsibility the auditor should take for fair presentation and the audit cost to society. CPAs, parliaments, the SEC, capital market authorities in many Arab countries, and the courts will all continue to have a major influence in shaping the final solution.

ESSENTIAL TERMS

Absence of causal connection   p. 107

Audit failure   p. 100

Audit risk   p. 100

Business failure   p. 100

Contributory negligence   p. 107

Criminal liability for accountants   p. 112

Foreseeable users   p. 110

Foreseen users   p. 109

Lack of duty to perform   p. 106

Legal liability   p. 98

Non-negligent performance   p. 107

Prudent person concept   p. 101

Ultramares doctrine   p. 108

REVIEW QUESTIONS

4-1 (Objective 4-1) State several factors that have affected the incidence of lawsuits against CPAs in recent years.

4-2 (Objective 4-1) Lawsuits against CPA firms continue to increase. State your opinion of the positive and negative effects of the increased litigation on CPAs and on society as a whole.

4-3 (Objective 4-2) Distinguish between business failure and audit risk. Why is business failure a concern to auditors?

4-4 (Objective 4-3) How does the prudent person concept affect the liability of the auditor?

4-5 (Objective 4-3) Distinguish between 'fraud' and 'gross negligence.'

4-6 (Objectives 4-1, 4-8) Discuss why many CPA firms have willingly settled lawsuits out of court. What are the implications to the profession?

4-7 (Objective 4-4) A common type of lawsuit against CPAs is for the failure to detect a fraud. State the auditor's responsibility for such discovery. Give authoritative support for your answer.

4-8 (Objectives 4-3, 4-4) What is meant by contributory negligence? Under what conditions will this likely be a successful defense?

4-9 (Objective 4-4) Explain how an engagement letter might affect an auditor's liability to clients under common law.

4-10 (Objectives 4-4, 4-5) Compare and contrast traditional auditors' legal responsibilities to clients and third-party users under common law. How has that law changed in recent years?

4-11 (Objective 4-5) Is the auditor's liability affected if the third party was unknown rather than known? Explain.

4-12 (Objective 4-6) Contrast the auditor's liability under the Securities Act of 1933 with that under the Securities Exchange Act of 1934. Compare auditor's liability under statutory laws in Arab countries with that of the U.S.

4-13 (Objectives 4-4, 4-5, 4-6, 4-7) Distinguish between the auditor's potential liability to the client, liability to third parties under common law, civil liability under the statutory laws, and criminal liability. Describe one situation for each type of liability in which the auditor can be held legally responsible.

4-14 (Objective 4-6) What potential sanctions does the SEC have against a CPA firm? Will those sanctions differ if the auditor is liable under statutory law in an Arab country?

4-15 (Objective 4-8) In what ways can the profession positively respond to and reduce liability in auditing?

MULTIPLE CHOICE QUESTIONS FROM CPA EXAMINATIONS

4-16 (Objectives 4-4, 4-5) The following questions concern CPA firms' liability under common law. Choose the best response.

a. Michel, CPA, was engaged by Rasheed & Co, a partnership, to give an opinion on the financial statements that were to be submitted to several prospective partners as part of a planned expansion of the firm. Michel's fee was fixed on a per diem basis. After a period of intensive work, Michel completed about half of the necessary field work. Then, because of unanticipated demands on his time by other clients, Michel was forced to abandon the work. The planned expansion of the firm failed to materialize because the prospective partners lost interest when the audit report was not promptly available. Michel offered to complete the task at a later date. This offer was refused. Rasheed & Co suffered damages of US$400,000 as a result. Under the circumstances, what is the probable outcome of a lawsuit between Michel and Rasheed & Co?
   (1) Michel will be compensated for the reasonable value of the services actually performed.
   (2) Rasheed & Co will recover damages for breach of contract.
   (3) Rasheed & Co will recover both punitive damages and damages for breach of contract.
   (4) Neither Michel nor Rasheed & Co will recover against the other.

b. In a common law action against an accountant, lack of privity is a viable defense if the plaintiff
   (1) is the client's creditor who sues the accountant for negligence.
   (2) can prove the presence of gross negligence that amounts to a reckless disregard for the truth.
   (3) is the accountant's client.
   (4) bases the action upon fraud.

c. If a CPA firm is being sued for common-law fraud by a third party based on materially false financial statements, which of the following is the best defense the accountants can assert?
   (1) Lack of privity.
   (2) Non-negligent performance.
   (3) A disclaimer contained in the engagement letter.
   (4) Contributory negligence on the part of the client.

d. The *1136 Tenants* case was important chiefly because of its emphasis on the legal liability of the CPA when associated with
   (1) an SEC engagement.
   (2) unaudited financial statements.
   (3) an audit resulting in a disclaimer of opinion.
   (4) letters for underwriters.

4-17 (Objective 4-6) The following questions deal with liability under Securities Acts. Choose the best response.

a. Hazem Salama & Co., CPAs, are the auditors of Arabia Technologies. In connection with the public offering of US$10 million of Arabia securities, Hazem Salama expressed an unmodified opinion as to the financial statements. Subsequent to the offering, certain misstatements were revealed. Hazem Salama has been sued by the purchasers of the stock offered pursuant to the registration statement that included the financial statements audited by Hazem. In the ensuing lawsuit by the Arabia investors, Hazem will be able to avoid liability if

(1) the misstatements were caused primarily by Arabia Technologies.

(2) it can be shown that at least some of the investors did *not* actually read the audited financial statements.

(3) it can prove due diligence in the audit of the financial statements of Arabia Technologies.

(4) Arabia Technologies had expressly assumed any liability in connection with the public offering.

b. Under the 1933 Securities Act, which of the following must be proven by the purchaser of the security?

	Reliance on the Financial Statements	Fraud by the CPA
1	Yes	Yes
2	Yes	No
3	No	Yes
4	No	No

c. Donalds & Company, CPAs, audited the financial statements included in the annual report submitted by Markum Securities, Inc. to the SEC. The audit was improper in several respects. Markum is now insolvent and unable to satisfy the claims of its customers. The customers have instituted legal action against Donalds based on Section 10b and Rule 10b-5 of the Securities Exchange Act of 1934. Which of the following is likely to be Donalds' best defense?

(1) They did *not* intentionally certify false financial statements.

(2) Section 10b does *not* apply to them.

(3) They were *not* in privity of contract with the creditors.

(4) Their engagement letter specifically disclaimed any liability to any party that resulted from Markum's fraudulent conduct.

DISCUSSION QUESTIONS AND PROBLEMS

4-18 (Objectives 4-4, 4-5) Habiba & Karim Co., a medium-sized CPA firm, was engaged to audit El Gouna Supply Company. Several staff were involved in the audit, all of whom had attended the firm's in-house training program on effective auditing methods. Throughout the audit, Karim spent most of his time in the field planning the audit, supervising the staff, and reviewing their work.

A significant part of the audit entailed verifying the physical count, cost, and summarization of inventory. Inventory was highly significant to the financial statements, and Karim knew the inventory was pledged as collateral for a large loan to Ahli United Bank. In reviewing El Gouna's inventory count procedures, Karim told the president he believed the method of counting inventory at different locations on different days was highly undesirable. The president stated that it was impractical to count all inventory on the same day because of personnel shortages and customer preference. After considerable discussion, Karim agreed to permit the practice if the president would sign a statement that no other method was practical. The CPA firm had at least one person at each site to audit the inventory count procedures and actual count. There were more than 40 locations.

Eighteen months later, Karim found out that the worst had happened. Management below the president's level had conspired to materially overstate inventory as a means of covering up obsolete inventory and inventory losses resulting from mismanagement. The misstatement occurred by physically transporting inventory at night to other locations after it had been counted in a given location. The accounting records were inadequate to uncover these illegal transfers.

Both El Gouna Supply Company and Ahli United Bank sued Habiba & Karim Co.

Required

Answer the following questions, setting forth reasons for any conclusions stated:

    a. What defense should Habiba & Karim Co. use in the suit by El Gouna?

    b. What defense should Habiba & Karim Co. use in the suit by Ahli United Bank?

    c. Is Karim likely to be successful in his defenses?

    d. Would the issues or outcome be significantly different if the suit was brought under the Capital Market Law, Companies Act or criminal law in United Arab Emirates or Kuwait?

4-19 (Objectives 4-3, 4-4, 4-5) In confirming accounts receivable on December 31, 2011, the auditor found 15 discrepancies between the customers' records and the recorded amounts in the accounts receivable master file. A copy of all confirmations that had exceptions was turned over to the company controller to investigate the reason for the difference. He, in turn, had the bookkeeper perform the analysis. The bookkeeper analyzed each exception, determined its cause, and prepared an elaborate spreadsheet explaining each difference. Most of the differences in the bookkeeper's report indicated that the exceptions were caused by timing differences in the client's and customer's records. The auditor reviewed the spreadsheet and concluded that there were no material exceptions in accounts receivable.

Two years subsequent to the audit, it was determined that the bookkeeper had stolen thousands of dollars in the past three years by taking cash and overstating accounts receivable. In a lawsuit by the client against the CPA, an examination of the auditor's December 31, 2011, accounts receivable working papers, which were subpoenaed by the court, indicated that one of the explanations in the bookkeeper's analysis of the exceptions was fictitious. The analysis stated the exception was caused by a sales allowance granted to the customer for defective merchandise the day before the end of the year. The difference was actually caused by the bookkeeper's theft.

Required

    a. What are the legal issues involved in this situation? What should the auditor use as a defense in the event that he is sued?

    b. What was the CPA's deficiency in conducting the audit of accounts receivable?

4-20 (Objectives 4-4, 4-5, 4-7) Hazem, CPA, is the auditor for Ahmonsito Manufacturing Corporation, a privately owned company that has a June 30 fiscal year. Ahmonsito arranged for a substantial bank loan that was dependent on the bank's receiving, by September 30, audited financial statements that showed a current ratio of at least 2 to 1. On September 25, just before the audit report was to be issued, Hazem received an anonymous letter on Ahmonsito's stationery indicating that a five-year lease by Ahmonsito, as lessee, of a factory building accounted for in the financial statements as an operating lease was, in fact, a capital lease. The letter stated that there was a secret written agreement with the lessor modifying the lease and creating a capital lease.

Hazem confronted the president of Ahmonsito, who admitted that a secret agreement existed but said it was necessary to treat the lease as an operating lease to meet the current ratio requirement of the pending loan and that nobody would ever discover the secret agreement with the lessor. The president said that if Hazem did not issue his report by September 30, Ahmonsito would sue Hazem for substantial damages that would result from not getting the loan. Under this pressure and because the audit files contained a copy of the five-year lease agreement that supported the operating lease treatment, Hazem issued his report with an unmodified opinion on September 29.

Despite the fact that the loan was received, Ahmonsito went bankrupt within two years. The bank is suing Hazem to recover its losses on the loan, and the lessor is suing Hazem to recover uncollected rents.

Answer the following questions, setting forth reasons for any conclusions stated: Required

  a. Is Hazem liable to the bank?

  b. Is Hazem liable to the lessor?

  c. Is there potential for criminal action against Hazem?[7]

4-21 (Objective 4-4) Rasim & Sartawi, CPAs, were the auditors of Nakheel Real Estate, Inc., a real estate company that owned several shopping centers. It was Nakheel's practice to let each shopping center manager negotiate that center's leases; they thought that such an arrangement resulted in much better leases because a local person did the negotiating.

Two of the center managers were killed in a plane accident returning home from a company meeting at the head office in Dubai. In both cases, the new managers appointed to take their places discovered kickback schemes in operation; the managers had negotiated lower rents than normal in return for kickbacks from the tenants.

Nakheel brought in a new audit firm, Tabazo & Co., to investigate the extent of the fraud at those two locations and the possibility of similar frauds at other centers. Tabazo & Co. completed their investigation and found that four locations were involved quite independently of each other and that the total loss over five years was more than US$1 million. Nakheel sued Rasim & Sartawi for negligence for US$1 million plus interest.

What defense will Rasim & Sartawi use? What will they have to prove? Required

4-22 (Objective 4-6) Gordon & Groton, CPAs, were the auditors of Bank & Company, a brokerage firm and member of a national stock exchange. Gordon & Groton audited and reported on the financial statements of Bank, which were filed with the Securities and Exchange Commission.

Several of Bank's customers were swindled by a fraudulent scheme perpetrated by Bank's president, who owned 90 percent of the voting stock of the company. The facts establish that Gordon & Groton were negligent but not reckless or grossly negligent in the conduct of the audit, and neither participated in the fraudulent scheme nor knew of its existence.

The customers are suing Gordon & Groton under the antifraud provisions of Section 10b and Rule 10b-5 of the Securities Exchange Act of 1934 for aiding and abetting the fraudulent scheme of the president. The customers' suit for fraud is predicated exclusively on the nonfeasance of the auditors in failing to conduct a proper audit, thereby failing to discover the fraudulent scheme.

Answer the following questions, setting forth reasons for any conclusions stated: Required

  a. What is the probable outcome of the lawsuit?

  b. What other theory of liability might the customers have asserted?[8]

4-23 (Objective 4-5) Sarah Robertson, CPA, had been the auditor of Majestic Co. for several years. As she and her staff prepared for the audit for the year ended December 31, 2011, Herb Majestic told her that he needed a large bank loan to "tide him over" until sales picked up as expected in late 2012.

In the course of the audit, Robertson discovered that the financial situation at Majestic was worse than Majestic had revealed and that the company was technically bankrupt. She discussed the situation with Majestic, who pointed out that the bank loan will "be his solution"—he was sure he will get it as long as the financial statements don't look too bad.

Robertson stated that she believed the statements will have to include a going concern emphasis of a matter paragraph. Majestic said that this wasn't needed because the bank loan was so certain and that inclusion of the going concern paragraph will certainly cause the management of the bank to change its mind about the loan.

Robertson finally concurred and the audited statements were issued without a going concern paragraph. The company received the loan, but things did not improve as Majestic thought they would and the company filed for bankruptcy in August 2011.

The bank sued Sarah Robertson for fraud.

Indicate whether or not you think the bank will succeed. Support your answer. Required

CASE

4-24 (Objectives 4-5, 4-6) *Part 1.* Optima Holding Company is a brokerage firm registered under statutory law in the United Arab Emirates (U.A.E.). The law requires such a brokerage firm to file audited financial statements with the capital market authority (CMA) annually. El Gasam & Marzouk, CPAs, performed the annual audit for the year ended December 31, 2011, and rendered an unmodified opinion, which was filed with the CMA in U.A.E. along with Optima's financial statements. During 2011, El-Boushy, the president of Optima, engaged in a huge embezzlement scheme that eventually bankrupted the firm. As a result, substantial losses were suffered by customers and shareholders of the company, including Mountain Ali Real Estate Company, who had recently purchased several shares of stock of Optima Company after reviewing the company's 2011 audit report. El Gasam & Marzouk's audit was deficient; if they had complied with auditing standards, the embezzlement would have been discovered. However, the auditors had no knowledge of the embezzlement, nor can their conduct be categorized as reckless.

Required

Answer the following questions, setting forth reasons for any conclusions stated:

a. What liability to Mountain Ali Company, if any, does El Gasam & Marzouk have under the statutory law in U.A.E.? Will such liability be different if the auditors were listed with the PCAOB and the company is registered with SEC in the U.S.?

b. What theory or theories of liability, if any, are available to Optima Company's customers and shareholders under common law?

Part 2. Wafaa is a sophisticated investor. As such, she was initially a member of a small group that was going to participate in a private placement of US$1 million of common stock of El-Wasiat Corporation. Numerous meetings were held between management and the investor group. Detailed financial and other information was supplied to the participants. Upon the eve of completion of the placement, it was aborted when one major investor withdrew. El-Wasiat then decided to offer US$2.5 million of El-Wasiat common stock to the public pursuant to the registration requirements of the statutory law in the U.A.E. Wafaa subscribed to US$300,000 of the El-Wasiat public stock offering. Nine months later, El-Wasiat's earnings dropped significantly, and as a result, the stock dropped 20 percent beneath the offering price. In addition, the U.A.E. Stock Market Industrial Average was down 10 percent from the time of the offering.

Wafaa sold her shares at a loss of US$60,000 and seeks to hold all parties liable who participated in the public offering, including El-Wasiat's CPA firm of Al-Fatah & Co. Although the audit was performed in conformity with auditing standards, there were some relatively minor misstatements. The financial statements of El-Wasiat Corporation, which were part of the registration statement, contained minor misleading facts. It is believed by El-Wasiat and Al-Fatah & Co. that Wafaa's asserted claim is without merit.

Required

Answer the following questions, setting forth reasons for any conclusions stated:

a. If Wafaa sues under the statutory law in U.A.E., what will be the basis of her claim? Will the liability of the Al-Fatah & Co. be different if El-Wasiat is a public listed company in the U.S.?

b. What are the probable defenses that might be asserted by Al-Fatah & Co. in light of these facts?[9]

CHAPTER 5

PROFESSIONAL ETHICS

The Value Of The Audit Depends On Auditor Independence

Gasem Gaafar works on the audit of Jordanian Communication Networks, an audit client in his firm's Amman office. Gasem has watched the stock of Communication Networks soar for the past six months. Communication Networks is gaining market share, and he knows that their sales will continue to soar with the new technology they are developing. Finally, he can't resist any longer. He calls his stockbroker, Randa Mohamed, and places an order for 200 shares of Communication Networks' stock. "Are you sure this is okay?" asked Randa. "I thought Communication Networks was your client." Randa knows about professional responsibilities because she worked with Gasem at the audit firm before becoming a stockbroker, and they remain friends. "Why don't you check it out and get back to me?" Randa added.

The next morning, Gasem is glad that he has Randa Mohamed for a stockbroker. The Amman Stock Exchange just announced that it had uncovered numerous independence violations at another audit firm. The firm had to recall several audit reports, and a few partners and audit staff were terminated for making stock investments similar to the investment that Gasem had contemplated the day before. Gasem would certainly have violated the independence requirements included in the *Code of Ethics for Professional Accountants* by buying the Communication Networks stocks. There is a conflict of interest between Gasem as an auditor aiming at forming an opinion about the reliability of information in the company's financial statements and his interest in maximizing dividends distributed because he is a shareholder of the company. As he thinks about the requirement that he should not own stock in an audit client, he still concludes, "There must be other good investments out there. The financial interests behind investments in such companies is highly beneficial."

In preceding chapters, audit reports and the demand for audit and other assurance services were discussed. The value of the audit report and the demand for audit services depend on public confidence in the independence and integrity of auditors. This chapter discusses ethics and the independence and other ethical requirements for auditors under the International Federation of Accountants (IFAC) *Code of Ethics for Professional Accountants*. Then a quick overview of the AICPA *Code of Professional Conduct* is undertaken. However, we begin the chapter with a discussion of general ethical principles and their application to the auditing profession.

Relevant International Standards on Auditing and Pronouncements	
IESBA	Code of Ethics for Professional Accountants
ISA 200	Overall Objectives of the Independent Auditor and the Conduct of an Audit in Accordance with International Standards on Auditing
ISA 210	Agreeing the Terms of Audit Engagements
ISA 230	Audit Documentation
ISA 250	Consideration of Laws and Regulations in an Audit of Financial Statements
ISA 260	Communication with Those Charged with Governance

WHAT ARE ETHICS?

OBJECTIVE 5-1

Distinguish ethical from unethical behavior in personal and professional contexts.

Ethics

An integrated structure of code of professional conduct and set of best practices established from moral duties and responsibilities which show how a professional should behave in given circumstances.

Ethics can be defined broadly as a set of moral principles or values. Each of us has such a set of values, although we may or may not have considered them explicitly. Religious organizations, philosophers, and other groups have defined in various ways ideal sets of moral principles or values. Examples of prescribed sets of moral principles or values include Qur'an, church doctrine, laws and regulations, codes of business ethics for professional groups such as professional accountants or lawyers, medical doctors, and codes of conduct within organizations. An example of a prescribed set of principles is included in Figure 5-1.

It is common for people to differ in their moral principles and values and the relative importance they attach to these principles. These differences reflect life experiences, successes and failures, as well as the influences of parents, teachers, and friends.

FIGURE 5-1	Illustrative Prescribed Ethical Principles

The following are the six core ethical values that the Josephson Institute associates with ethical behavior:

Trustworthiness includes honesty, integrity, reliability, and loyalty. Honesty requires a good faith intent to convey the truth. Integrity means that the person acts according to conscience, regardless of the situation. Reliability means making all reasonable efforts to fulfill commitments. Loyalty is a responsibility to promote and protect the interests of certain people and organizations.

Respect includes notions such as civility, courtesy, decency, dignity, autonomy, tolerance, and acceptance. A respectful person treats others with consideration and accepts individual differences and beliefs without prejudice.

Responsibility means being accountable for one's actions and exercising restraint. Responsibility also means pursuing excellence, self-restraint, and leading by example, including perseverance and engaging in continuous improvement.

Fairness and justice include issues of equality, impartiality, proportionality, openness, and due process. Fair treatment means that similar situations are handled consistently.

Caring means being genuinely concerned for the welfare of others and includes acting altruistically and showing benevolence.

Citizenship includes obeying laws and performing one's fair share to make society work, including such activities as voting, serving on juries, conserving resources, and giving more than one takes.

Need for Ethics

Ethical behavior is necessary for a society to function in an orderly manner. It can be argued that ethics is the glue that holds a society together. Imagine, for example, what would happen if we couldn't depend on the people we deal with to be honest. If parents, teachers, employers, siblings, coworkers, and friends all consistently lied, it would be almost impossible to have effective communication. The need for ethics in society is sufficiently important that many commonly held ethical values are incorporated into laws.

Why People Act Unethically

Most people define *unethical behavior* as conduct that differs from what they believe is appropriate given the circumstances. Each of us decides for ourselves what we consider unethical behavior, both for ourselves and others. It is important to understand what causes people to act in a manner that we decide is unethical.

There are two primary reasons why people act unethically: the person's ethical standards are different from those of society as a whole, or the person chooses to act selfishly. Frequently, both reasons exist.

Person's Ethical Standards Differ from General Society
Extreme examples of people whose behavior violates almost everyone's ethical standards are drug dealers, bank robbers, and larcenists. Most people who commit such acts feel no remorse when they are apprehended because their ethical standards differ from those of society as a whole.

There are also many far less extreme examples when others violate our ethical values. When people cheat on their tax returns, treat other people with hostility, lie on employment applications, or perform below their competence level as employees, most of us regard that as unethical behavior. If the other person has decided that this behavior is ethical and acceptable, there is a conflict of ethical values that is unlikely to be resolved.

The Person Chooses to Act Selfishly
The following example illustrates the difference between ethical standards that differ from general society's and acting selfishly. Person A finds a briefcase in an airport containing important papers and US$1,000. He throws away the briefcase and keeps the money. He brags to his family and friends about his good fortune. Person A's values probably differ from most of society's. Person B faces the same situation but responds differently. He keeps the money but leaves the briefcase in a conspicuous place. He tells nobody and spends the money on a new wardrobe. It is likely that Person B has violated his own ethical standards, but he decided that the money was too important to pass up. He has chosen to act selfishly.

A considerable portion of unethical behavior results from selfish behavior. Political scandals result from the desire for political power; cheating on tax returns and expense reports is motivated by financial greed; performing below one's competence and cheating on tests typically arise from laziness. In each case, the person knows that the behavior is inappropriate but chooses to do it anyway because of the personal sacrifice needed to act ethically.

ETHICAL DILEMMAS

An **ethical dilemma** is a situation a person faces in which a decision must be made about the appropriate behavior. A simple example of an ethical dilemma is finding a diamond ring, which necessitates deciding whether to attempt to find the owner or to keep it.

Auditors, accountants, and other businesspeople face many ethical dilemmas in their business careers. Dealing with a client who threatens to seek a new auditor unless an unmodified opinion is issued presents an ethical dilemma if an unmodified opinion is

OBJECTIVE 5-2

Resolve ethical dilemmas using an ethical framework.

Ethical dilemma

A situation in which a decision must be made about the appropriate behavior.

inappropriate. Deciding whether to confront a supervisor who has materially overstated departmental revenues as a means of receiving a larger bonus is an ethical dilemma. Continuing to be a part of the management of a company that harasses and mistreats employees or treats customers dishonestly is an ethical dilemma, especially if the person has a family to support and the job market is tight.

Rationalizing Unethical Behavior

There are alternative ways to resolve ethical dilemmas, but care must be taken to avoid methods that are rationalizations of unethical behavior. The following are rationalization methods commonly employed that can easily result in unethical conduct:

Everybody Does It The argument that it is acceptable behavior to falsify tax returns, cheat in exams, or sell defective products is commonly based on the rationalization that everyone else is doing it and therefore it is acceptable.

If it's Legal, it's Ethical Using the argument that all legal behavior is ethical relies heavily on the perfection of laws. Under this philosophy, one would have no obligation to return a lost object unless the other person could prove that it was his or hers.

Likelihood of Discovery and Consequences This philosophy relies on evaluating the likelihood that someone else will discover the behavior. Typically, the person also assesses the severity of the penalty (consequences) if there is a discovery. An example is deciding whether to correct an unintentional overbilling to a customer when the customer has already paid the full amount. If the seller believes that the customer will detect the error and respond by not buying in the future, the seller will inform the customer now; otherwise, the seller will wait to see if the customer complains.

SOME ETHICAL VIOLATIONS ARE MORE SEVERE THAN OTHERS

Amira Ezz Eldin's ethical dilemma involves a situation in which she is asked to work without recording the time, which is sometimes called kitchen-tabling or eating time. One of the concerns with kitchen-tabling is that it can lead to a more severe problem known as premature signoff, in which a staff person signs off as having completed work without performing the necessary procedures.

Ayman Taleb has far too busy a social life to work overtime. To make certain that his work does not interfere with his social life, he tests only part of the assigned sample. For example, if he is asked to test 25 cash disbursement transactions, he tests the first 15 but indicates that he has tested all 25.

A supervisor, curious about Ayman's amazing ability to beat the time budget, decides to carefully review Ayman's work. When the firm discovers that Ayman is signing off procedures without completing them, he is dismissed that day—no counseling out, no two weeks' notice.

SPECIAL NEED FOR ETHICAL CONDUCT IN PROFESSIONS

OBJECTIVE 5-3

Explain the importance of ethical conduct for the accounting profession.

Our society has attached a special meaning to the term *professional*. Professionals are expected to conduct themselves at a higher level than most other members of society. For example, when the press reports that a physician, lawyer, or CPA or auditor has been indicted for a crime, most people feel more disappointment than when the same thing happens to people who are not labeled as professionals.

The term *professional* means a responsibility for conduct that extends beyond satisfying individual responsibilities and beyond the requirements of our society's laws and regulations. An auditor, as a professional, recognizes a responsibility to the public, to the client, and to fellow practitioners, including honorable behavior, even if that means personal sacrifice.

The reason for an expectation of a high level of professional conduct by any profession is the need for *public confidence* in the quality of service by the profession, regardless of the individual providing it. For the auditor, it is essential that the client and external financial statements' users have confidence in the quality of audits and other services. If users of services do not have confidence in physicians, judges, or auditors, the ability of those professionals to serve clients and the public effectively is diminished.

It is not practical for most customers to evaluate the quality of the performance of professional services because of their *complexity*. A patient cannot be expected to evaluate whether an operation was properly performed. A financial statements' user cannot be expected to evaluate audit performance. Most users have neither the competence nor the time for such an evaluation. Therefore, public confidence in the quality of professional services is enhanced when the profession encourages high standards of performance and conduct on the part of all practitioners.

Difference between Audit Firms and Other Professionals

Audit firms have a different relationship with users of financial statements than most other professionals have with their customers. Attorneys, for example, are typically engaged and paid by a client and have primary responsibility to be an advocate for that client. Audit firms are engaged by management for private companies and the **audit committee** for public companies, and are paid by the company issuing the financial statements, but the primary beneficiaries of the audit are financial statements' users. Often, the auditor does not know or have contact with the financial statements' users but has frequent meetings and ongoing relationships with client personnel.

It is essential that users regard audit firms as competent and unbiased. If users believe that audit firms do not perform a valuable service (reduce information risk), the value of the firms' audit and other attestation reports is reduced and the demand for these services will thereby also be reduced. Therefore, there is considerable incentive for audit firms to conduct themselves at a high professional level.

Audit firm

A sole practitioner, partnership, or corporation of professional accountants; an entity that controls such parties, through ownership, management, or other means; and an entity controlled by such parties, through ownership, management, or other means.

Audit committee

Selected members of a client's board of directors whose responsibilities include helping auditors to remain independent of management.

Ways CPAs are Encouraged to Conduct Themselves Professionally

The IFAC has issued and updated the *Code of Ethics for Professional Accountants* (International Ethics Standards Board of Accountants (IESBA) Code). The code establishes ethical requirements for professional accountants. The code states: "A member body of IFAC or firm shall not apply less stringent standards than those stated in this code (IESBA code). However, if a member body or firm is prohibited from complying with certain parts of this code by law or regulation, they shall comply with all other parts of this code" (IESBA, 2010). The code discusses important ethical elements for professional accountants such as integrity, objectivity, professional competence and due care, confidentiality, and professional behavior. Figure 5-2 shows Principles 'X1' applied by the management of a leading industrial company in Jordan.

Auditors providing audit services in most Arab countries are required to comply with the *Code of Ethics* issued by IESBA. While CPAs in the U.S. must follow the AICPA code, the AICPA's Professional Ethics Executive Committee closely monitors IESBA activities to converge the U.S. guidance, where appropriate, to guidance in the IESBA's code.

The remainder of this chapter addresses the IESBA's code, AICPA code and related PCAOB and SEC requirements and finally the application of the code *of Ethics* in the Arab countries.

FIGURE 5-2   **XI (Inspiring Star the future is here)**

The "We Meet" Principles

WE RESPECT
Start and end on time/short meetings (30/40/55 minutes)

WE TRUST
Confidentiality of session

WE SHARE
Right to speak and be heard

WE FOCUS
One conversation at a time/one topic per meeting

WE TEAM
Build on each other's ideas/meeting leads facilitates

WE HONOR
Mobiles off/texting out

Source: Nuqul Group Jordan.

IFAC CODE OF ETHICS FOR PROFESSIONAL ACCOUNTANTS

OBJECTIVE 5-4

Describe the purpose and content of the IFAC *Code of Ethics for Professional Accountants* and its conceptual framework.

Professional accountant

An individual who is a member of an IFAC member body.

Professional accountant in business

A professional accountant employed or engaged in an executive or non-executive capacity in such areas as commerce, industry, service, the public sector, education, the not-for-profit sector, regulatory bodies or professional bodies, or a professional accountant contracted by such entities.

CPAs or professional accountants are governed and managed by ethical standards which they must adhere to. In general, auditors have a direct responsibility to the shareholders of the company for which they provide their audit service. Auditors are required to act in the public interest. The *Code of Ethics for Professional Accountants* has been prescribed by the IESBA. The code describes the requirements for professional accountants, who perform audit or other non assurance services. Member bodies of IFAC must not apply any less stringent standards than those stated in the IESBA code. In some countries, there could be ethical requirements which differ from the IESBA code. Professional accountants must be aware of the differences and must comply with the more stringent requirements and guidance unless a law or regulation prohibits such compliance.

The *Code of Ethics for Professional Accountants* is divided into three parts:

- Part A establishes the fundamental principles of professional ethics for accountants, providing a professional framework for applying those principles.
- Part B applies to professional accountants who work in practice.
- Part C applies to professional accountants who work in business.

Parts B and C provide examples of safeguards that may be appropriate to address threats to compliance with the fundamental principles.

Before we discuss the details of the *Code of Ethics for Professional Accountants*, it is important to highlight some important related definitions.

- *Professional accountant*. An individual who is a member of an IFAC member body.
- *Professional accountant in business*. A professional accountant employed or engaged in an executive or non-executive capacity in such areas as commerce, industry, service, the public sector, education, the not-for-profit sector, regulatory bodies or professional bodies, or a professional accountant contracted by such entities.
- *Professional accountant in public practice*. A professional accountant, irrespective of functional classification (e.g. audit, tax, or consulting) in a firm that provides professional services.

TABLE 5-1	Elements of the Code of Ethics for Professional Accountants
Part A:	**General Application of the Code**
Section 100:	Introduction and Fundamental Principles
Section 110:	Integrity
Section 120:	Objectivity
Section 130:	Professional Competence and Due Care
Section 140:	Confidentiality
Section 150:	Professional Behavior
Part B:	**Professional Accountants in Public Practice**
Section 200:	Introduction
Section 210:	Professional Appointment
Section 220:	Conflicts of Interest
Section 230:	Second Opinions
Section 240:	Fees and Other Types of Remuneration
Section 250:	Marketing Professional Services
Section 260:	Gifts and Hospitality
Section 270:	Custody of Clients Assets
Section 280:	Objectivity–All Services
Section 290:	Independence–Audit and Review Engagements
Section 291:	Independence–Other Assurance Engagements
Part C:	**Professional Accountants in Business**
Section 300:	Introduction
Section 310:	Potential Conflicts
Section 320:	Preparation and Reporting of Information
Section 330:	Acting with Sufficient Expertise
Section 340:	Financial Interests
Section 350:	Inducements

Source: *Code of Ethics for Professional Accountants*, IESBA, 2010 revision.

- *Professional services*. Services requiring accountancy or related skills performed by a professional accountant including accounting, auditing, taxation, management consulting, and financial management services.

Table 5-1 lists the contents of the IESBA code.

Fundamental Principles of Ethics for Professional Accountants

A professional accountant is required to observe compliance with five fundamental principles: integrity; objectivity; professional competence and due care; confidentiality; and professional behavior. Table 5-2 summarizes the requirements of the code in relation to those fundamental principles.

Each of the fundamental principles is discussed in detail in the following sections.

Integrity At all times during the course of their service professional accountants must be honest and straightforward in all professional and business relationships. In order to observe the fundamental principle of integrity, the professional accountant

Professional services

Services requiring accountancy or related skills performed by a professional accountant, including accounting, auditing, taxation, management consulting, and financial management services.

TABLE 5-2	Fundamental Principles

A professional accountant shall comply with the following fundamental principles:

a. Integrity	to be straightforward and honest in all professional and business relationships.
b. Objectivity	do not allow bias, conflict of interest, or undue influence of others to override professional or business judgments.
c. Professional Competence and Due Care	to maintain professional knowledge and skill at the level required to ensure that a client or employer receives competent professional services based on current developments in practice, legislation, and techniques and act diligently and in accordance with applicable technical and professional standards.
d. Confidentiality	to respect the confidentiality of information acquired as a result of professional and business relationships and, therefore, not disclose any such information to third parties without proper and specific authority, unless there is a legal or professional right or duty to disclose, nor use the information for the personal advantages of the professional accountant or third parties.
e. Professional Behavior	to comply with relevant laws and regulations and avoid any action that discredits the profession.

Source: *Code of Ethics for Professional Accountants*, IESBA, 2010 revision, section 100.5.

should not allow his name to be associated with reports, returns, or other forms of communication where the professional accountant believes that the information:

a. contains a material false or misleading statement;
b. contains statements or information obtained recklessly; or
c. omits or obscures information required to be included where such omission or obscurity would be misleading.

In terms of auditing, it could be the case that an auditor's opinion is modified because the financial statements which have been subject to audit do not present fairly in all material aspects the financial positions and results of the company's operations. In these circumstances, where the auditor's opinion is modified, his action will not be considered in violation of the situations presented in (a) to (c) above.

For example, if the professional accountant issues an unmodified opinion while the financial statements of his audit client contain material misstatements concerning the valuation of inventory, he is in violation of the principle of integrity.

Objectivity A professional accountant should not allow bias, conflict of interest, or undue influence of others to override his professional judgments. In some circumstances, the auditor may be exposed to situations that may affect his objectivity. The auditor should, in all cases, ensure that objectivity is not affected by implementing safeguards to maintain independence and objectivity. For example, the auditor should have the courage to issue the appropriate audit opinion even

---

FICTITIOUS SALES FIGURES AND CLEAN REPORT

Sammy Abdel Rahim, an audit manager, found that one of his clients overstated the sales figures for the year ending December 31, 2011 by recording sales invoices actually issued in 2012 in 2011 so that the management of the client achieved its target total revenues figures for 2011. Sammy asked the audit partner to discuss the issue with the chief financial officer (CFO) of the client confirming that the amount of sales overstated represented 15 percent of actual sales figures for 2011. The CFO informed the audit partner that the

company stock price dropped by almost 5 percent during the last month due to a significant decline in the demand for the company's products. The CFO politely informed the audit partner that the company is always in support of the audit firm as it uses the firm for other services equivalent to 100 percent of the annual audit fees.

If you were the audit partner, what would be your decision if the CFO did not agree to restate the income statement to reflect the actual sales for the year ending 2011?

if he receives significant fees from consultancy provided to his audit clients. He should maintain his objectivity by maintaining always his unbiased professional judgments.

Professional Competence and Due Care A professional accountant must maintain professional knowledge and skill at the level required to provide his client with a competent and professional service. Audit firms must not, therefore, accept appointment as auditor unless they are competent and possess the skills and expertise in addition to sufficient resources available to undertake the audit work.

Professional accountants also have an obligation to act diligently in accordance with appropriate professional standards when providing professional services. Professional competence can be divided into two levels:

- Attainment of professional competence.
- Maintenance of professional competence.

In order to maintain professional competence, professional accountants must be up to date with technical developments including updates related to accounting and auditing standards. Continuing professional development (CPD) or education (CPE) will guarantee maintenance of professional competence.

Confidentiality Confidentiality is of paramount importance and Section 140 of the IESBA *Code of Ethics* describes the responsibilities of a professional accountant to maintain confidentiality as well as establishing the circumstances where the professional accountant can depart from this fundamental principle.

Professional accountants are prohibited from disclosing information acquired as a result of professional services without the consent of the client or if there is a legal or professional obligation. Disclosure is required by law if it is ordered in the course of legal proceedings or is required to advise the appropriate public authorities of infringements of the law.

Also, professional accountants should not use information acquired from the client for their personal benefit or to third party advantage. For example, an auditor should not use information collected about the profitability of a listed company to buy shares or stocks in his name or in the name of a member of his family or friends and to make capital gain from selling the stocks in the future. This business decision would violate the principle of confidentiality.

The code also confirms the notion that professional accountants must not, inadvertently or otherwise, disclose information in a social environment. For example, if the auditor is having a social gathering he is not allowed to discuss his audit client affairs or results so that a third party attending such a gathering would benefit from any information disclosed about the client. If the auditor inappropriately discusses his audit client's affairs or results he is violating the confidentiality principle. Professional accountants, **partners**, and audit managers should ensure that their subordinates also respect the duty of confidentiality as well as experts assisting the accountants.

Professional Behavior At all times, professional accountants must comply with relevant laws and regulations and avoid any action which would discredit the profession. Accountants need to behave in a professional manner in relation to marketing or advertising. Professional accountants must not mislead clients by presenting incorrect information that they have professional qualifications, when that is not true. They should not accept work which they are not professionally competent to undertake. Professional accountants also have a responsibility to ensure that they do not make erroneous references or unsubstantiated comparisons to the work of others.

For example, auditors are not allowed to attach the word CPA to their firm's name unless all partners are CPAs, and they should not use recruitment and advertising

Partner
Any individual with authority to bind the firm with respect to the performance of a professional services engagement.

to market their audit firm services by presenting detailed information about the firm's human resource capabilities, salaries and remunerations, and numbers of its qualified personnel unless the information is required to achieve the main objective of the advertisement.

Threats to Ethical Principles

The IESBA *Code of Ethics for Professional Accountants* states that it is impossible to define every situation that creates threats to compliance with the fundamental principles and specify the appropriate action. The difference in the nature of engagements may result in different threats requiring the application of different safeguards.

At all times during the auditing process, the auditor must remain independent to ensure the audit objective is maintained. Varying degrees of circumstances or relationships can create threats which in turn may affect more than one fundamental ethical principle. When the auditor identifies a threat then he is required to employ safeguards to ensure the threat is reduced to an acceptable level.

Auditing includes different types of threats:

* Self-interest threat.
* Self-review threat.
* Advocacy threat.
* Familiarity threat.
* Intimidation threat.

Table 5-3 summarizes the nature of the various threats discussed in the IESBA code.

Parts B and C of the IESBA code explain how these categories of threats may be created for professional accountants in public practice and professional accountants in business, respectively. Professional accountants in public practice may also find part C relevant to their particular circumstances.

Contingent fee

A fee calculated on a predetermined basis relating to the outcome of a transaction or the result of the services performed by the firm. A fee that is established by a court or other public authority is not a contingent fee.

Example of self-interest threats are when the auditor holds shares in an audit client or where the audit firm has significant dependence on the fees from an audit client or is concerned about the possibility of losing an important client. Also, when an auditor enters into a **contingent fee** arrangement relating to an assurance service it is considered a self-interest threat.

A self-review threat occurs when an auditor prepares a set of financial statements for an audit client and then audits the same financial statements. Also, a self-review

TABLE 5-3	Types of Threat
a. Self-interest threat	the threat that a financial or other interest will inappropriately influence the professional accountant's judgment or behavior.
b. Self-review threat	the threat that a professional accountant will not appropriately evaluate the results of a previous judgment made or service performed by the professional accountant, or by another individual within the professional accountant's firm or employing organization, on which the accountant will rely when forming a judgment as part of providing a current service.
c. Advocacy threat	the threat that a professional accountant will promote a client's or employer's position to the point that the professional accountant's objectivity is compromised.
d. Familiarity threat	the threat that due to a long or close relationship with a client or employer, a professional accountant will be too sympathetic to their interests or too accepting of their work.
e. Intimidation threat	the threat that a professional accountant will be deterred from acting objectively because of actual or perceived pressures, including attempts to exercise undue influence over the professional accountant.

Source: Adapted from *Code of Ethics for Professional Accountants*, IESBA, 2010 revision, Section 100.12.

THE AUDITOR PREVENTS THE ISSUANCE OF AUDITED FINANCIAL STATEMENTS	Nassef Halim, an audit manager in an Arab CPA firm, was jailed for three years because he was found guilty of allowing the management of a land reclamation company to delay the issue of the audited financial statements for the years 2006–2008 until 2010. In return for a bribe of US$50,000, Nassef colluded with the management of the company to prepare letters confirming the inability of the management to issue the financial statements, attributing this to a lack of accounting staff to record the company's	transactions as well as a problem with the information technology system. During that period, management used the fact that the shareholders had delegated the responsibility for agreeing the management's remuneration to the board and collected remuneration exceeding US$1 million. The matter was uncovered when the audit manager, Nassef, was replaced and a new manager uncovered the conspiracy through information provided by one of the company's internal auditors.

threat may occur when an employee of an audit client joins the audit team of the same audit client and actively participates in the audit examination. In addition, a self-review threat exists when an audit firm prepared the original data used to generate records that are the subject of an assurance engagement including audit work. There may also be a self-review threat when a member of the assurance team is or has recently been a director or officer of the client.

Advocacy threat occurs when the professional accountant or the auditor represents a client in legal proceedings. Another example is when the audit firm promotes shares of an audit client.

A familiarity threat arises when an auditor becomes disproportionately close or familiar with the client to the extent that he may be too sympathetic to their interests. Moreover, when a member of the engagement team has a close or **immediate family** member who is a director or officer of the client or when he accepts gifts or preferential treatment from a client, it is considered a familiarity threat. All the above discussed situations affect the auditors' independence.

Immediate family
A spouse or dependent.

Finally, an intimidation threat would exist in situations when the professional accountant or the auditor receives significant fees for services other than the audit and is under pressure to issue an erroneous audit report in order not to sacrifice these additional fees. An intimidation threat also exists when an auditor is pressured to materially reduce the value of work performed in order to reduce fees.

Safeguards for Ethical Threats

Safeguards are actions by the professional accountant or the auditor in an attempt to either completely eliminate the threats or reduce those threats to an acceptable level. The safeguards fall into two categories:

- Safeguards created by the profession, legislation or regulation; and
- Safeguards in the actual working environment.

Safeguards created by the profession include compliance with professional standards, including those issued by professional bodies. There are also other safeguards which include:

- Training and development
- Corporate governance regulations
- Regulatory monitoring by professional bodies
- External reviews by a legally empowered third party of reports, returns, communications or information prepared by professional accountants.

Training and development includes training and experience requirements for entry into the profession and the maintenance of these skills by undertaking CPD or CPE.

Regulatory monitoring includes reviews of professional accountants' or auditors' work by professional bodies, such as the Kuwait Association of Accountants and Auditors or the Association of Chartered Certified Accountants (ACCA), to ensure that professional standards, independence, and objectivity are maintained at all times.

External reviews can take various forms, but in terms of auditing are usually split into two types of review:

- Hot file review
- Cold file review.

A 'hot' file review is undertaken by an external file reviewer prior to the auditor's report being issued. Such reviews look at the audit work undertaken and whether the audit evidence is sufficient and appropriate enough to support the proposed opinion in the auditor's report, or modifications are required to the opinion proposed. This review is usually undertaken by another partner in the firm or a senior audit manager.

A 'cold' file review is undertaken by the external file reviewer after the auditor's report has been issued. Such reviews are mandatorily required by various professional bodies, or they can be undertaken as part of a regulatory monitoring visit. In addition, a cold file review can be done on a periodic basis by the firm or the CPA network as part of their quality assurance procedures.

An audit firm should maintain written safeguards to ensure that the firm complies, in all respects, with the fundamental principles and be satisfied that their staff act, at all times, in the interests of the public.

In Arab countries, most of the Big Four CPA firms have a peer review policy where a competent, qualified, and experienced partner(s) visits the offices of other firms to review and assess working papers and internal organizational structure to ensure consistency in the application of the quality control measures throughout the profession. Other audit firms implement measures to ensure proper monitoring of the activities of the firm including recruitment of university graduates, good command of the English language, motivation to sit for local professional organization or CPA exams, and applicants' intention to become senior managers within the audit firm.

Moreover, procedures which firms can adopt to ensure adequate safeguards are in place to deal with threats include:

- Published policies to identify various threats and the procedures to be adopted in evaluating the significance of those threats. In instances where the threats cannot be mitigated to an acceptable level, then the firm should resign or decline the engagement.
- Engaging different partners on audit and non-audit engagements.
- Engaging different staff on audit engagements where non-audit services have been provided to an audit client.
- Discussing difficult matters occurring during the course of an audit with senior and well trained staff. For example, difficult taxation matters should be referred to a firm's tax department or tax partner.
- Ensuring staff are kept technically up to date through the use of CPD or CPE.
- Formulating a disciplinary mechanism to promote a firm's policies and procedures.
- Ensuring regular, independent, file reviews are undertaken to make sure the firm's audit work is in compliance with auditing standards.
- Rotating partners and other member of staff on an interim basis.
- Promoting the notion of discussing important matters with those charged with governance.

PROFESSIONAL ETHICS IN PUBLIC PRACTICE

Part B of the *Code of Ethics* discusses several issues related to the application of the code to practitioners—see Table 5-1. Part B covers application of the conceptual framework to the following situations:

OBJECTIVE 5-5

Understand professional ethics for professional accountants in public practice.

- Professional Appointment (Accepting an audit client)
- Conflicts of Interest
- Fees and Other Types of Remuneration
- Marketing Professional Services
- Gifts and Hospitality
- Custody of the Clients Assets
- Family and close relationships
- Objectivity—All Services (Non-audit services provided to the client)
- Independence—Audit and Review Engagements
- Independence—Other Assurance Engagements.

The above are examples of situations that could be faced by a practitioner that may result in threats to compliance with fundamental principles included in the IESBA *Code of Ethics*. There are a number of threats which differ from one situation to another. The significance of the threats will depend on the nature of such threats and the type of service or engagement provided by the practitioner, whether the audit client is a public interest company, an assurance client that is not an audit client, or a non-assurance client.

Examples of Situations that May Create Threats to Fundamental Principles

Self-interest threats

- Partner or member of the audit team has a direct financial interest with the audit client.
- Member of the audit team is an employee of the audit client.
- An audit firm total audit fees depends significantly on fees received from one or a few audit clients.
- An audit firm quotes a low fee to an audit client affecting the quality of audit services provided to that client.
- Member of the assurance team has a close business relationship with an assurance client.
- Member of the audit team is negotiating employment with the audit client.

Self-review threats

- Member of the audit team carries out or shares in recruiting services to an audit client.
- Member of an audit team undertakes accounting and bookkeeping services to an audit client.
- Member of an audit team becomes a director of an assurance client.
- The audit firm performs internal audit services for an audit client.

Advocacy threats

- An audit firm marketing and promoting shares for an audit client.
- A practitioner assigned as an advocate to an audit client in litigation with third parties.

Familiarity threats

- Member of an assurance team having an immediate family member as a director of the assurance client or in a position having a significant influence over the issue(s) of the assignment.
- A director or senior employee of the audit client serving as the current partner responsible for the engagement with such audit client.
- A partner or member of the audit team accepting gifts or preferential treatment from a client.

Intimidation threats

- An audit firm being threatened with dismissal from a client engagement.
- Disclosure in public about a gift or preferential treatment being given to a practitioner who accepted the gift or preferential treatment and such fact is known to the public.
- Audit client relating the granting of nonassurance services to an audit client if it stops disagreeing with the client's accounting treatment for a particular transaction.
- A practitioner agreeing with the decision of a client manager or senior employee because the above management has more expertise on the matter related with the above decision.

Professional Appointment (Accepting an Audit Client)

Auditors or professional accountants are required to ensure that they are technically and professionally competent to undertake the work of a potential client. Auditors must also assess whether they have the necessary resources available to provide the client with quality service. A professional accountant, before accepting an assignment, should consider whether the acceptance of the client would result in threats to compliance with fundamental principles. For example, the professional accountant should consider whether the client is involved in illegal activities (i.e. money laundering, dishonest or questionable financial reporting practices).

A professional accountant should assess whether such threats can be reduced to an acceptable level, otherwise he must decline the engagement. Before accepting the engagement, he or she should obtain knowledge about and understand the client, its owners, managers, and those responsible for its governance and business activities. He or she should assess the level of complexity of the entity's operations and develop an understanding of the nature and scope of the work to be performed.

In Arab countries, the acceptance of the audit client differs in the criteria used for such a decision between an audit firm with international affiliation, and other local firms. In audit firms with international affiliation, partners accept audit clients in different industries due to their ability to provide assurance and nonassurance services, availability of financial resources to provide high quality of audit, sufficiency of competent and experienced staff and a large number of either CPAs or licensed accountants. These firms assess the nature and reputation of the audit client according to ISA with special attention given to the client's ability to pay the audit fees when the audit assignment is completed. Local audit firms do not necessarily identify these criteria when accepting clients as most of the audit work relates to tax and accounting services without any form of assurance.

Factors which a professional accountant needs to consider in order to assess the work of an expert include reputation, expertise, resources available, and applicable professional and ethical standards.

Also, the professional accountant needs to ensure that both his firm and his client have a realistic time frame to undertake the relevant work. The professional accountant should consider any deadlines imposed on its audit client. For example, in Arab countries, audited financial statements should be presented to shareholders within 90 days from the balance sheet date. The professional accountants should ensure they are able to meet these deadlines.

Conflicts of Interests

A professional accountant has a duty, at all times, to identify any circumstances which might give rise to a conflict of interest. The firm should also ensure that they have procedures in place to deal with any such conflicts of interest. For example, the professional accountant's objectivity may be affected when he competes directly with a client or has a joint venture or similar arrangement with a major competitor of a client. Another example of threats to objectivity and confidentiality is when a professional accountant performs services for clients whose interests conflict or are in dispute with each other in relation to the matters being studied or examined.

Where a conflict of interest arises, then safeguards must be employed. Such safeguards could be the use of separate engagement teams (also known as 'Chinese walls'). When the use of separate engagement teams is employed, then each team must observe confidentiality. This objective confidentiality can be achieved if confidentiality agreements are signed by employees and partners of the firm.

In most Arab countries auditors comply with the confidentiality principle as legal penalties are imposed if client confidentiality is breached. Also, the reputation of audit firms may be significantly affected if it is discovered that a particular client's information has been disclosed to a third party without client consent. However, there are circumstances where client information could be disclosed if it is ordered by a court of law or professional disciplinary committee.

Fees and Other Types of Remuneration

Professional accountants have the flexibility to quote whatever fee is deemed appropriate for the level of work involved. However, professional accountants need to be careful to avoid 'low-balling'—i.e. where a professional accountant quotes a fee that is so low (in order to undercut another firm) that it may become difficult to provide a quality service. This creates a self-interest threat if professional accountants think about their own benefit and disregard the quality of the services provided, thus affecting the reputation of the profession as a whole.

Professional accountants have a duty to ensure that the fees they quote to a client are appropriate taking into consideration the skills of the members of the team assigned to the engagement. Professional accountants should contract with their clients agreeing on the terms of the engagement and the fees agreed upon. This is usually achieved by way of a written engagement letter including terms of engagement and basis of fees.

Low-balling is a concept widely applied by audit firms in many Arab countries, where auditors compete for clients by offering significant reductions in their audit fees to win audit assignments. This certainly results in poor quality of audit services provided by some audit firms, especially those without international affiliation, as they consider reducing their fees as an effective means to attract clients. Professional organizations should take measures to help reduce low-balling by tightening the regulations allowing graduates to become certified public accountants and preventing accountants from practicing without passing either the international CPA certificate or examinations set by the local professional organizations.

Professional accountants may receive a referral fee or commission in relation to a service provided by another professional accountant. This creates a self-interest threat to objectivity and professional competence and due care. The professional accountant referring the client to another professional accountant should ensure that they have relevant safeguards in place to deal with such a threat such as:

- Disclosure of the commission or referral fee to another professional accountant for the work referred to them.
- Disclosure of the commission or referral fee to the client concerned and obtain their permission to receive such a fee.

No information is available concerning how referral fees are used in many Arab countries, especially in the light of low-balling, and the continuous reduction in audit fees and inability of audit firms to pay additional amounts for such referrals.

Marketing Professional Services

In cases when the professional accountant solicits services through advertising or other forms of marketing, there may be a threat to compliance with the fundamental principles. A self-interest threat to compliance with the principle of professional behavior occurs if the advertisement about the accountant's achievements, products, and services are marketed in a way that does not conform with that principle. Section 250 of the IESBA code requires that the professional accountant in public practice shall be honest and truthful, and should not make exaggerated claims for services offered, qualifications possessed, or experience gained.

Gifts and Hospitality

Some clients may offer gifts and/or hospitality to professional accountants. The IESBA code (Section 260) states that whether or not this may be termed a threat would depend on the nature, value, and overall intent by the client of the offer of gifts and hospitality. A self-interest or familiarity threat to objectivity may be created if the client gives a gift to the professional accountant when the client's financial statements include significant misstatements.

Another example, that of a client inviting a professional accountant to lunch after completion of a long and difficult assignment, might be construed by the professional accountant as being trivial. However, where the professional accountant concludes that threats to fundamental principles (objectivity) cannot be completely eradicated or reduced to an acceptable level, then the professional accountant must not accept the gift or hospitality.

Custody of the Client's Assets

A professional accountant in public practice shall not assume custody of client's assets unless permitted to do so by law and, if so, in compliance with any additional legal duties imposed on the professional accountant. For example, a professional accountant may decide to retain the books and original copies of a client's certified financial statements without affecting the responsibility of the client toward third parties until the audit fees are paid. A professional accountant has a duty to ensure that any threats to the fundamental principles caused by retaining client assets are reduced in totality or reduced to an acceptable level.

THE AUDITOR ASSUMED THE ROLE OF THE BANKER

George Amin is an audit manager in Hosam and Hassan, a CPA firm. Hosam and Hassan is responsible for the audit of ABC Bank. George performed the bank's audit during the period 2005–2010 and complied with the ISA requirements. The audit firm applied its policy for rotating partners in charge of the audit every five years. George was replaced with another audit manager as well as the audit partner. The new manager, Karim Harfoush, met with the chief accountant of the bank who informed him that George and his assistant, Mervat Awadallah, had applied for a loan through the bank. Because of their responsibility for the audit management they had been charged the same interest rate as the employees of the bank. Karim knew that such a decision was in violation of the *Code of Ethics for Professional Accountants* and he informed the audit partner who dismissed George and Mervat from the audit firm instantly without giving them any notice of termination.

Whenever the firm has custody of client assets, e.g. by holding client money, then they should ensure that the self-interest threat that arises in such circumstances is reduced to an acceptable level. This can be achieved by:

- Maintaining client assets separately from the firm's assets.
- Using such assets for the purposes only intended by the client.
- Being able to readily account for such assets.
- Complying with all relevant laws and regulations in respect of holding such assets.

Family and Close Relationships

Where family or close relationships exist between a member of the audit team and a director, officer, or employee of the audit client, then this will create a self-interest, familiarity, or intimidation threat.

When an immediate family member or a member of the audit team is (a) a director or officer of the audit client, or (b) an employee that is able to exert influence over the preparation of the client's accounting records or the financial statements on which the firm will express an opinion, the individual concerned must be removed from the audit team. No other safeguards can be implemented because the threat arising from the closeness of such a relationship cannot be reduced to an acceptable level unless the individual concerned is removed from the audit team.

There are also situations whereby a former member of the audit team may have taken up employment with the audit client. In such circumstances, independence is likely to be threatened to such an extent that it might not be possible to reduce the threat to an acceptable level. Independence would also be deemed to be compromised if a former member of the audit team or the audit partner joins the audit client as a director or officer, or as an employee with the ability to exert influence over the accounting records and financial statements on which the audit firm will express an opinion. Examples of safeguards which can be implemented to minimize the above threat could be to modify the audit plan and assign individuals to the audit who have the same experience as the individual who has joined the client. The audit firm may also have the work of the former member of the audit client reviewed by another professional accountant.

Objectivity—All Services (Non-Audit Services Provided to the Client)

It is extremely common for audit firms to undertake non-audit services on behalf of an audit client. For example, audit firms may provide taxation-related services to an audit client. The threat here is in relation to a 'self-review' threat. In terms of auditing, the self-review threat must be reduced to an acceptable level, for example, by having a 'hot' file review or employing the use of 'Chinese walls.' If the threat to independence cannot be mitigated to an acceptable level, the audit firm should either cease to act in the capacity of auditors, or decline the engagement.

INDEPENDENCE: AUDIT AND REVIEW ENGAGEMENTS

The value of auditing depends heavily on the public's perception of the independence of auditors. The reason that many diverse users are willing to rely on auditor's reports is their expectation of an unbiased viewpoint. Not only must auditors be independent of mind, but they must also be independent in appearance. **Independence of mind** exists when the auditor is actually able to maintain an unbiased attitude throughout the audit. Independence of mind should allow the auditor to express conclusion without being affected by influences that compromise professional judgment. This state of mind should permit an individual to act with integrity, and exercise objectivity and professional skepticism.

OBJECTIVE 5-6

Discuss independence issues for audit and review engagements

Independence of mind

The auditor's ability to take an unbiased viewpoint in the performance of professional services.

Independence in appearance

The auditor's ability to maintain an unbiased viewpoint in the eyes of others.

On the other hand, **independence in appearance** is the result of others' interpretations of this independence. This means that no significant facts or circumstances exist that would likely make third parties assess that a firm's or a member of the audit team's integrity, objectivity, or professional skepticism has been compromised. If auditors are independent of mind but users believe them to be advocates for the client, most of the value of the audit function is lost.

The IESBA code indicates that many different circumstances, or combinations of circumstances, may be relevant in assessing threats to independence. In practice, it is almost impossible to define every situation that creates threats to independence and to determine the appropriate action. Thus, the IESBA code states that the conceptual framework approach assists professional accountants in public practice in complying with the ethical requirements in this code especially in relation to independence. The conceptual framework approach to be applied by professional accountants involves a three-step process for assessing whether independence is impaired:

1. *Identify circumstances that might threaten independence.* For example, a CPA firm's reliance on revenue from a single audit client may be significant, posing a potential threat to the firm's independence from that client.
2. *Evaluate the significance of threats identified and determine whether safeguards are already in place or can be implemented that eliminate or sufficiently mitigate the threat.* In making this judgment, the auditor considers whether the circumstance would lead a reasonable person aware of all the relevant facts to conclude that there is an unacceptable threat to the auditor's independence.
3. *Apply safeguards when necessary to eliminate the threats or reduce them to an acceptable level.* For example, to address the threat associated with the excessive reliance on revenues from a single audit client, the audit firm establishes policies to closely monitor the firm's reliance on a single client's revenue and those policies include specific actions that prevent excessive reliance.

Auditors are advised to use their professional judgment in applying this framework.

Financial Interest

Financial interest

An interest in an equity or other security, debenture, loan, or other debt instrument of an entity, including rights and obligations to acquire such an interest and derivatives directly related to such interest.

Direct financial interest

The ownership of stock or other equity shares by members or their immediate family.

Indirect financial interest

A financial interest beneficially owned through a collective investment vehicle, estate, trust, or other intermediary over which the individual or entity has no control or ability to influence investment decisions. A close, but not direct, ownership relationship between the auditor and the client; an example is the ownership of stock by a member's grandparent.

The *Code of Ethics* (Section 290) states that a professional accountant holding a **financial interest** in an audit client may create a self-interest threat. The significance of any threat created and its effect on the professional accountant independence depends on:

a. The role of the person having the financial interest in the audit firm
b. The nature of the financial interest; whether it is considered direct (i.e. spouse or dependent) or indirect (grandfather and other member of auditor's family)
c. The materiality of the financial interest.

Direct Versus Indirect Financial Interest The ownership of stock or other equity shares by members or their immediate family is called a **direct financial interest.** For example, if either a partner in the office in which an audit is conducted or the partner's spouse has a financial interest in a company, the audit firm is prohibited from expressing an opinion on the financial statements of that company.

An **indirect financial interest** exists when there is a close, but not a direct, ownership relationship between the auditor and the client. An example of an indirect ownership interest is the auditor's ownership of a mutual fund that has an investment in a client.

Material or Immaterial *Materiality* affects independence of an auditor only for *indirect* ownership. Materiality must be considered in relation to the member person's wealth and income. For example, if an auditor has a significant amount of his or her personal wealth invested in a mutual fund and that fund has a large ownership position in a client

DID CONSULTING FEES JEOPARDIZE INDEPENDENCE?

In the aftermath of Enron, the Sarbanes–Oxley Act and SEC regulations further restrict the types of consulting services that auditors may provide to public company audit clients. Concerns about the potential effects of consulting services on auditor independence were raised as early as the late 1970s. In 2000, the SEC contemplated banning auditors from providing any consulting services to public company audit clients. Instead, the SEC approved additional restrictions on non-audit services and required the disclosure of audit and non-audit fees.

Many observers of the Enron case were not surprised that the company's auditors earned more in non-audit fees than audit fees. For the year 2000, Enron paid Andersen US$25 million in audit fees and US$27 million for non-audit services. There were many other companies where non-audit fees exceeded audit fees by a greater amount than at Enron. Did the non-audit services compromise auditor independence at Enron or at other companies with apparent audit failures? Lack of independence is difficult, if not impossible, to prove. Confidence in the profession depends on the appearance of independence, rather than auditors being independent in fact. What matters most is that the SEC, as well as many investors and other interested parties, believed that non-audit services compromised independence.

Similarly, in one of the Arab countries, the auditor of an Islamic mutual fund, which in the late 1980s used to receive cash from members of the public and pay them fixed interest, falsified the fund financial statements and was imprisoned for a few months because he was found guilty of receiving significant amounts for consulting services provided to the management of the fund.

company, a violation of the code is likely to exist. Independence is also not impaired if the auditor is not aware of a close relative's ownership interest in the client firm.

Similar requirements apply to other individuals in a position to influence the audit engagement or partners in the audit-engagement office. However, in these cases, the ownership interest does not impair independence unless the ownership interest is material to the close relative and allows the close relative to exercise significant influence over the audit client.

The IESBA code prohibits members, a member of the member's immediate family, or an audit firm from having a direct financial interest or a material indirect financial interest in the audit client. Under the above circumstances, the self-interest threat created would be so significant that no safeguards would reduce the threat to an acceptable level. For example, the auditor member is prohibited from owning any stock or other direct investment in audit clients because it is potentially damaging to actual audit independence (independence of mind), and it is certainly likely to affect users' perceptions of the auditors' independence (independence in appearance).

Related Financial Interest Issues

Financial Interests and Employment of Immediate and Close Family Members The financial interests of immediate family members, defined as a spouse or dependent, are ordinarily treated as if they were the financial interest of the professional accountant or the auditor. For example, if the spouse of a professional accountant on the audit engagement team owns any stock in the client, a self-interest threat is created. Independence is also impaired if an immediate family member holds a key position such as financial officer or chief executive officer with the client that allows them to influence accounting functions, preparation of financial statements, or the contents of the financial statements.

Ownership interests of **close family** members, defined as a parent, sibling, or nondependent child, do not normally impair independence unless the ownership interest is material to the close relative. Imagine the potential difficulty in maintaining independence and objectivity if the firm is asked to audit a client where the parent of the audit partner is chief executive officer and has a significant ownership interest in the client. For individuals on the engagement team, independence is impaired if a close

Close family
Any parent, child, or sibling who is not a dependent. (See immediate family.)

relative has a key position with the client or has a financial interest that is material to the close relative or enables the relative to exercise significant influence over the client. Immaterial ownership interests of close family members, defined as a parent, sibling, or nondependent child, do not normally impair independence.

Financial interest may be held through an intermediary (e.g. an investment vehicle, member of the member's not immediate family, estate, or trust). The code determines that the financial interest may be direct or indirect depending on whether the beneficial owner has control over the investment vehicle or the ability to influence its investment decisions. When the above control over investment exists, the IESBA code defines such financial interest to be a direct financial interest. Thus, indirect investments, such as ownership of stock which does not allow control over the client's company's operations and decisions by an auditor's grandfather, are not prohibited by the code.

At the same time, when a member of the audit team has a close family member who the audit team member knows has a direct financial interest or a material indirect financial interest in the audit client, a self-interest threat is created. The code identifies a number of safeguards which may be applied to eliminate or reduce the threat to an acceptable level such as:

- The close family member disposes all the financial interest or part of the indirect financial interest so the remaining interest is no longer material.
- Asking a professional accountant or a partner to review the work of the member of the audit team.
- Replacing the member of the audit team with another member of the audit firm.

It is important to note that a member of an audit team could own stock in a client corporation and not violate the code if the staff member is not involved in the engagement. However, if the staff member is assigned to the engagement or becomes a partner in the office of the partner responsible for the engagement, he or she would have to dispose of the stock or the firm would no longer be independent of that client. Some audit firms do not permit any ownership by staff of a client's stock regardless of which office serves the client. These firms have decided to have higher requirements than the minimum set by the code.

The code also states that if an auditor or professional accountant holds a retirement benefit plan (i.e. end of services bonuses) of a direct or material indirect financial interest in an audit client, this creates a self-interest threat. Also, if other partners in the office in which the engagement partner practices in connection with the audit engagement, or their immediate family members, hold a direct financial interest or a material indirect financial interest in that audit client, the code describes such interest as creating a highly significant self-interest threat and that no safeguards could reduce the threat to an acceptable level. It is recommended that neither such partners nor their immediate family members shall hold any financial interests in such an audit client.

The same applies whenever other partners and managerial employees who provide non-audit services to the audit client or immediate family members hold a direct financial interest or a material indirect financial interest in the audit client. This means that in the above case, the self-interest threat created would be so significant that no safeguards could reduce the threat to an acceptable level. An exception to such threat if other partners and managerial employees when providing non-audit services to the audit client their involvement is minimal even if these have direct financial interest or a material indirect financial interest.

Moreover, a self-interest threat is created and no safeguards would reduce it when the CPA firm or a member of the audit team, or a member of that individual's immediate family has a material financial interest in an entity and an audit client also has a material financial interest in that entity and can exercise significant influence over the entity's operations. The code states that the auditor's independence is not compromised if these interests are immaterial and the audit client cannot exercise significant influence over the entity. In all cases, the disposition of the interest or a sufficient amount of the interest so that the remaining interest is no longer material may be considered means by which such self-interest threat is minimized.

Finally, the code indicates that wherever a member of the audit team, or a member of that individual's immediate family, or the firm, has a financial interest in an entity and a director, officer, or controlling owner of the audit client is also known to have a financial interest in that entity, a self-interest, familiarity or intimidation threat is created. Factors affecting the existence and significance of such threat will depend on

- The role of auditor on the audit team
- The nature of the ownership of the entity and whether it is closely or widely held
- The nature of the interest and whether it gives the owner the ability to control or significantly influence the investee
- The materiality of the financial interest.

Examples of safeguards, to minimize or eliminate the above types of threats, include removing the member of the audit team with the financial interest or having another senior employee review the work of the member of the audit team. Similar requirements apply wherever an audit firm, a partner or employee of the firm or a member of that individual's immediate family receives financial interest by way of an inheritance, gift, or as a result of a merger.

Director, Officer, Manager, or Employee of a Company If an auditor is a member of the board of directors or an officer of a client company, his or her ability to make independent evaluations of the fair presentation of financial statements is affected. Even if holding one of these positions did not actually affect the auditor's independence, the frequent involvement with management and the decisions it makes is likely to affect how statement users perceive the auditor's independence. To eliminate this possibility, the code prohibits partners, senior auditors, and professional staff in the office of the partner responsible for the attest engagement from being a director or officer of an audit client company. Similarly, the auditor cannot be an underwriter, voting trustee, promoter, or trustee of a client's pension fund, or act in any other capacity of management, or be an employee of the company.

Moreover, family and personal relationships between a member of the audit team and a director, officer, or other employees (depending on their role in the company) of the audit client may result in a self-interest, familiarity, or intimidation threat. Also, threats to independence exist if an immediate family member of a member of the audit team is a director or officer of the audit client or an employee in a position to exert significant influence over the preparation of the client's financial statements and accounting records. The IESBA code (Section 290.128) states that the closeness of the relationship is such that no other safeguards could reduce the threat to an acceptable level and the individual must be removed from the audit team. Auditors or professional accountants, however, can do audits and be *honorary* directors or trustees for not-for-profit organizations, such as charitable and religious organizations, as long as the position is purely honorary. The auditor cannot vote or participate in any management functions.

Joint Investor or Investee Relationship with Client Assume, for example, that an auditor owns stock in a non-audit client, ABC Company. XYZ Company, which is an audit client, also owns stock in ABC Company. This may be a violation of IESBA *Code of Ethics*. Situations violating the code include where the client is either an investor or investee for a nonclient in which the auditor has an ownership interest.

1. *Client investor.* If the client's investment in the nonclient is material, any direct or material indirect investment by the auditor in the nonclient investee impairs independence. If the client's investment is not material, independence is impaired only if the auditor's investment is material.

2. *Client investee.* If investment in a client is material to a nonclient investor, any direct or material indirect investment by the auditor in the nonclient impairs independence. If the nonclient's investment in the client is not material, independence is not impaired unless the auditor's investment in the nonclient allows the auditor to exercise significant influence over the nonclient.

Former Practitioners In most situations, the code permits former partners or shareholders who left the firm, due to such things as retirement or the sale of their ownership interest, to have relationships with clients of the firm, without affecting a firm's independence. A violation of the code would occur if the former partner was held out as an associate of the firm or took part in activities that are likely to cause other parties to believe the person is still active in the firm.

The active status of the member with the firm would include exerting significant influence over the preparation of the client's accounting records or the financial statements on which the firm will express an opinion unless the individual is not entitled to any benefits or payments from the firm. Modifying the audit plan to assign other members of the firm or having an experienced member review the work of the former member are accepted safeguards.

Normal Lending Procedures and Other Products or Services Provider Generally, loans between an audit firm or member of the firm and an audit client are prohibited because it is a financial relationship. Accordingly, neither a member of the audit team, a member of that individual's immediate family, nor the audit firm shall accept such a loan or guarantee. However, the code states that if the loan or guarantee is made under normal lending procedures, terms and conditions, a self-interest threat does not exist. Thus, a loan, or a guarantee of a loan from an audit client that is a bank or similar institution to a member of an audit team, or a member of that individual's immediate family, does not create a threat to independence if the loan or guarantee is made under normal lending procedures, terms and conditions. Examples include automobile loans, loans fully collateralized by cash deposits at the same financial institution, and unpaid credit card balances and bank overdrafts. It is also acceptable to accept a financial institution as a client, even if members of the audit firm have existing home mortgages, other fully collateralized secured loans, and immaterial loans with the institution. All the above requirements are reasonable ones, considering the trade-off between independence and the need to permit the auditors to function as business-people and individuals.

Similarly, the purchase of goods and services from an audit client by the firm, a member of the audit team, or a member of that individual's immediate family, does not generally create a threat to independence if the transaction is in the normal course of business and at arm's length. If the above transactions are not made at arm's length, the threat exists and safeguards may include eliminating or reducing the magnitude of the transaction, or removing the member from the audit team.

Long-Association This refers to long association of senior personnel (including partner rotation) with an audit client. The IESBA code (Section 290.151) requires that an individual shall not be a **key audit partner** for more than seven years in respect of an audit of a **public interest entity**. After the elapse of such period of time, the individual shall not be a member of the engagement team or be a key audit partner for the client for two years. No participation in the audit of an entity, provision of quality control for the engagement, or consultation with the engagement team or the client regarding technical or industry-specific issues should be carried out by the individual during this two-year cooling off period.

Consulting and Other Non-Audit Services Audit firms offer many other services to attest clients that may potentially impair independence. Such activities are permissible as long as the member does not perform management functions or make

Key audit partner

The engagement partner, the individual responsible for the engagement quality control review, and other audit partners, if any, on the engagement team who make key decisions or judgments on significant matters with respect to the audit of the financial statements on which the firm will express an opinion. Depending upon the circumstances and the role of the individuals on the audit, 'other audit partners' may include, for example, audit partners responsible for significant subsidiaries or divisions.

Public interest entity

A listed entity, and an entity defined by regulation or legislation as a public interest entity or for which the audit is required by regulation or legislation to be conducted in compliance with the same independence requirements that apply to the audit of listed entities.

management decisions. Examples of activities that would generally be considered as a management responsibility include:

- Identifying policies and strategic decisions
- Directing and assessing responsibility for the actions of the entity's employees
- Taking responsibility to authorize transactions
- Making decisions related to the company's operations and activities
- Preparing the financial statements in accordance with acceptable accounting framework
- Being responsible for the design, and implementing and maintaining internal control.

For example, an audit firm may assist in the installation of a client's information system as long as the client makes the necessary management decisions about the system. Subject to some restrictions, audit firms may also provide internal auditing and other extended auditing services to their clients.

The audit firm must assess the client's willingness and ability to perform all management functions related to the engagement and must document the understanding with the client. The understanding should include a description of the services, the engagement objectives, any limitations on the engagement, the member's responsibilities, and the client's agreement to accept its responsibilities.

In the U.S., more restrictive SEC independence rules concerning provision of non-audit services apply to AICPA members when providing services to public company audit clients. However, the firm may provide services related to the preparation of financial statements and accounting records to an audit client that is not a public entity. Examples of such services may include:

- Assisting the company with payroll services
- Providing bookkeeping services including posting transactions by the client to general ledger.

As a result, providing non-audit services that are prohibited by the SEC to a public company audit client would be a violation of AICPA rules as well as PCAOB and SEC rules.

The IESBA code requires that a firm must not provide valuation services to an audit client that is a public entity if the valuations would have a material effect, separately or in aggregate, on the financial statements on which the firm will express an opinion. This is the situation applying to many Arab countries where auditors are prohibited to provide valuation studies for their audit clients.

Fees

Relative Size and Unpaid Fees IESBA *Code of Ethics* (Section 290.220) explicitly states that whenever the total fees from an audit client represent a significant percentage of the total fees of the firm expressing an audit opinion, such matter creates a self-interest or intimidation threat. The code (Section 290.222) further considers that in the case of an audit client and related entities which are public interest entities that pay total fees for two consecutive years representing more than 15 percent of the total fees received by an audit firm, the audit firm must disclose such facts to those charged with governance and apply one or more safeguards to reduce independence threat. The code also states that whenever the total fees significantly exceed 15 percent, the audit firm should determine whether the significance of the threat is such that a post-issuance review would not reduce the threat to an acceptable level and a pre-issuance review is required.

Independence is considered impaired if billed or unbilled fees remain unpaid for professional services provided more than one year before the date of the report. Such unpaid fees are considered a loan from the auditor to the client and the firm should consider whether it is appropriate for it to be reappointed or continue the audit engagement. However, unpaid fees from a client in bankruptcy do not violate the requirements of the code.

Contingent Fees

Section 290.224 of the IESBA Code 2010

Contingent fees are fees calculated on a predetermined basis relating to the outcome of a transaction or the result of the services performed by the firm… A fee is not regarded as being contingent if established by a court or other public authority.

Source: Adapted from *Code of Ethics for Professional Accountants*, IESBA, 2010 revision.

To help auditors maintain objectivity in conducting audits or other attestation services, basing fees on the outcome of engagements is prohibited. It is important for auditors to read rule 302 of the AICPA code for contingent fees as it helps to clarify requirements related to contingent fees received by an auditor from an audit client.

Rule 302 of the AICPA Code—Contingent Fees

A member in public practice shall not

(1) Perform for a contingent fee any professional services for, or receive such a fee from, a client for whom the member or member's firm performs:
   (a) an audit or review of a financial statement; or
   (b) a compilation of a financial statement when the member expects, or reasonably might expect, that a third party will use the financial statement and the member's compilation report does not disclose a lack of independence; or
   (c) an examination of prospective financial information;

   or

(2) Prepare an original or amended tax return or claim for a tax refund for a contingent fee for any client.
   The prohibition in (1) above applies during the period in which the member or the member's firm is engaged to perform any of the services listed above and the period covered by any historical financial statements involved in any such listed services.
   Except as stated in the next sentence, a contingent fee is a fee established for the performance of any service pursuant to an arrangement in which no fee will be charged unless a specified finding or result is attained, or in which the amount of the fee is otherwise dependent upon the finding or result of such service. Solely for purposes of this rule, fees are not regarded as being contingent if fixed by courts or other public authorities, or, in tax matters, if determined based on the results of judicial proceedings or the findings of governmental agencies.
   A member's fees may vary depending, for example, on the complexity of services rendered.

Source: Adapted from *Code of Ethics for Professional Accountants*, IESBA, 2010 revision.

To illustrate the requirement of the IESBA code on contingent fees, suppose an audit firm was permitted to charge a fee of US$50,000 if an unmodified opinion was provided but only US$25,000 if the opinion was modified. Such an agreement may tempt a practitioner to issue the wrong opinion violating the *Code of Ethics* (Section 290.224). It is also a violation of the code for members to prepare an original or amended tax return or a claim for tax refunds for a contingent fee.

Audit firms are permitted to charge contingent fees *for nonattestation services, unless the audit firm is also performing attestation services* for the same client. For example, it is *not* a violation for an auditor to charge fees as an expert witness determined by the amount awarded to the plaintiff or to base consulting fees on a percentage of a bond issue *if the audit firm does not also do an audit or other attestation for the same client.*

Prohibiting contingent fees for attestation services and tax return preparation is important because of the importance of independence and objectivity. Because auditors or professional accountants compete when providing other nonattestation services with other professions who do not have contingent fee restrictions, it would be unfair to prohibit the provision of these services on the same basis. When these nonattestation services are provided for a client receiving attestation services, the need for independence and objectivity prevails and the auditor is not allowed to provide the services on a contingent fee basis.

Litigation Between Audit Firm and Client

When there is a lawsuit or intent to start a lawsuit between an audit firm or one of the members of the audit team and its client, the ability of the audit firm and client to remain objective is questionable and self-interest and intimidation threats are created. For example, if management sues an audit firm claiming a deficiency in the previous audit, the audit firm is not considered independent for the current year's audit. Similarly, if the audit firm sues management for fraudulent financial reporting or deceit, independence is lost. The audit firm and client company or management may be defendants in a suit brought by a third party, such as in a securities class action. This litigation in itself does not affect independence. However, independence may be affected if cross-claims between the auditor and client are filed that have a significant risk of a material loss to the audit firm or client.

> **Review engagement**
> An assurance engagement that enables an auditor to state whether, on the basis of procedures which do not provide all the evidence that would be required in an audit, anything has come to the auditor's attention that causes the auditor to believe that the financial statements are not prepared, in all material respects, in accordance with an applicable financial reporting framework.

Litigation by the client related to tax or other non-audit services, or litigation against both the client and the audit firm by another party, does not usually impair independence. The key consideration in all such suits is the likely effect on the ability of client, management, and audit firm personnel to remain objective and comment freely. Also, the significance of the threats created will depend on such factors as the materiality of the litigation, and whether the litigation relates to a prior audit engagement. It is worth noting that the independence requirements in Section 290 of the IESBA *Code of Ethics* apply to all audit and **review engagements**.

INDEPENDENCE REQUIREMENTS FOR PROVISION OF NONASSURANCE SERVICES

> **OBJECTIVE 5-7**
> Explain independence requirements for the provision of nonassurance services

International audit firms and local firms with international affiliation are capable of providing a number of non assurance services to their audit clients as well as other companies. The provision of nonassurance services may create threats to independence, especially self-review, self-interest, and advocacy threats. In the case that the audit client is a public interest company, threats are considered more significant. Practitioners are advised to identify safeguards to eliminate or minimize the threats to an acceptable minimum level. The IESBA *Code of Ethics* discusses specific nonassurance services and their related circumstances which may affect the independent status of the auditor or the professional accountant:

- Accounting and bookkeeping services
- Valuation services and other corporate finance services
- Taxation services
- Internal audit services
- Litigation and other legal services
- Recruiting services
- Fees: relative size of fees, unpaid fees, and contingent fees
- Gifts and hospitality.

In the following sections, the nonassurance services will be discussed except for fees and gifts and hospitality as threats and safeguards for such elements are similar to those explained in previous sections.

Accounting and Bookkeeping Services

If an auditor records transactions in the journals for the client, posts monthly totals to the general ledger, makes adjusting entries, and subsequently does an audit, there is some question as to whether the practitioner can be independent in the audit role. The code *permits an audit firm to do both bookkeeping and auditing for a private company audit client.* There are important requirements that the auditor must satisfy before it is acceptable to do bookkeeping and auditing for the client:

1. The client must accept full responsibility for the financial statements. The client must be sufficiently knowledgeable about the enterprise's activities and financial condition and the applicable accounting principles so that the client can reasonably accept such responsibility, including the fairness of valuation and presentation and the adequacy of disclosure. When necessary, the practitioner must discuss accounting matters with the client to be sure that the client has the required degree of understanding.

2. The practitioner must not assume the role of employee or of management conducting the operations of an enterprise. For example, the practitioner cannot consummate transactions, have custody of assets, or exercise authority on behalf of the client. The client must prepare the source documents on all transactions in sufficient detail to identify clearly the nature and amount of such transactions and maintain accounting control over data processed by the practitioner such as control totals and document counts.

However, practitioners are permitted to perform activities considered a normal part of the audit process that generally do not threaten independence. Examples of such activities considered part of the audit process include the application of accounting policies and standards, and suggesting adjusting journal entries. Also, practitioners may assist an audit client in resolving account reconciliation problems or gathering appropriate information for regulatory reporting when the client is in the process of preparing the financial statements. For smaller audit clients, it is difficult for practitioners to avoid assuming management responsibility for recording transactions and preparing financial statements for an owner who may have little knowledge of or interest in accounting or processing transactions.

In general, the code states that firms may provide such services to an audit client that is not a public interest company if any self-review threats are reduced to an acceptable level. An example of a safeguard for the above threat is when the firm arranges for such a service to be performed by an individual who is not a member of the audit team. The code also confirms that practitioners should not provide accounting and bookkeeping services including payroll services, or prepare financial statements or financial information which forms the basis of financial statements for an audit client that is a public interest entity.

Valuation and Corporate Finance Services

Valuation services encompass using a number of valuation techniques under certain assumptions with the aim of calculating a value or values for the assets and liabilities of a business enterprise. A self-review threat may be created due to the use of subjective judgment concerning the development of the valuation assumptions and techniques used to compute the value or values of a business entity. Examples of safeguards needed to eliminate the threat or minimize it to a minimum acceptable level include having an individual(s) prepare the valuation who is not a member of the audit team or having a professional accountant who is not a member of the audit team review the audit or the valuation tasks. The code explicitly states that the audit firm should not provide a valuation service (or may decide to withdraw from the audit assignment) if the valuation service has a material effect on the financial statements and the valuation is based on a significant degree of subjectivity.

<table>
<tr><td>

OMAR
EFFENDI
CASE

</td><td>

Omar Effendi was one of the largest trading companies in Egypt where it had more than 85 branches, all of which sell all types of household appliances and other merchandise at various prices. The company was sold on November 6, 2006 to Anwal Holding Company for EGP 590 million (US$90 million) by its holding company, the Trading Holding Company which is owned by the Egyptian Government. There was an important dispute among the members of the valuation committee concerning the price at which this giant department stores company should be sold. While the replacement cost approach showed the fair value of the company at more than EGP 1.2 billion (US$200 million), the discounted cash flow method showed the value of the company at around EGP 490 million (US$82 million). After detailed discussions with the official at the Ministry of Investment, the company was sold at EGP 590 million (US$90 million) to Anwal Holding Company. The new management of the company spent millions of pounds on restructuring the company, sold five percent to the International Finance Corporation (IFC) and borrowed more than EGP 300 million (US$50 million) from various banks in Egypt and US$40 million from the World Bank to finance the sale. After five years, the Administrative Court in Egypt decided to cancel

</td><td>

the contract for selling 90 percent of the Trading Holding Company's shares to Anwal. The following reasons were given:

- The Trading Holding Company sold the company with all its owned land in violation of the Ministerial Decree for Privatization of Public Sector Corporations which only permits the long-term leasing of such land.
- The management provided the assets of more than 16 branches as collateral for loans amounting to more than EGP 460 million (US$77 million) while making net losses for the last three years of more than EGP 500 million (US$84 million). The loans reached almost the same amount paid by Anwal Holding Company to purchase Omar Effendi. It was therefore evident that the valuation study prepared by the independent consultant was unreliable and did not include the fair value of Omar Effendi.
- The inability of the company to pay salaries and wages to employees for a period exceeding six months resulted in the inability of the company to realize any profits and increased the share of losses sustained by the Trading Holding Company.

Source: Translated and adapted from *El-Ahram Newspapers* (May 7, 2011) p. 6.

</td></tr>
</table>

At the same time, corporate finance services include audit firms who provide technical assistance in mergers and acquisitions activities, advise on disposals of assets and business enterprises, develop corporate financial strategies, and arrange finance for businesses. The IESBA code relates the provision of the above services to advocacy and self-review threats. A possible safeguard is the use of a professional who is not a member of the audit team to provide the services. The code also prohibits the provision of certain corporate finance services such as promoting, dealing in or underwriting an audit client's shares if they depend in their provision on particular accounting treatment or presentation in the financial statements where:

a. The audit team is in doubt as to the adequacy of the related accounting treatment or presentation under the IFRS or local accounting framework; and
b. The results of the corporate finance advice will have a material effect on the financial statements.

Taxation Services

Audit firms are considered experts in the area of tax services. The code outlines four types of taxation services: tax return preparation, tax calculations for the purpose of preparing the company's accounting entries including deferred tax assets or liabilities, tax planning and other tax advisory services, and, finally, helping the client with reports, information, and documents to resolve any tax disputes with tax authorities.

The above tax services may create self-review threats if the services provided in this respect are presented in the company's financial statements. Moreover, advocacy threats may also be created when the firm represents an audit client in a tax dispute. The IESBA code states that for public interest audit clients the firm shall normally not prepare such tax returns and tax calculations of entries that are material to the financial statements. For other entities, safeguards such as having an individual who is not a member of the audit team perform the tax calculations should be applied to reduce threats to an acceptable level. Similar requirements apply to the firm when it provides tax planning and other tax advisory services.

Internal Audit Services

Internal audit services involve helping the audit client achieve the objectives of its internal audit function. The audit firm may provide internal audit outsourcing if it does not assume management responsibilities. Examples of activities associated with internal audit function as they relate to management include setting internal audit policies, recruiting internal auditors, and designing, implementing, and maintaining internal control. The IESBA code indicates that the provision of internal audit services creates a self-review threat to independence if the audit firm uses the results of the internal audit service for the performance of external audit. Factors affecting the significance of the threat include the degree of use of the results of the internal audit service and the materiality of the amounts in the financial statements tested by the internal auditors. The IESBA code confirms that audit firms should not provide internal audit services for public interest audit clients which relate to a significant part of the internal control over financial reporting or amounts or disclosures that are material to the financial statements.

Litigation and Other Legal Services

Litigation services include activities performed by the audit firm such as acting as an expert witness, calculating estimated damages or other amounts that might become receivable or payable, and assisting management to prepare documents supporting such services. The above services may create a self-review or advocacy threat. The IESBA code requires audit firms to apply similar safeguards to minimize the threats to independence by applying safeguards similar to those used for valuation services.

Recruiting Services

Audit firms review applications presented by candidates for employment with the client and assess their competence and level of experience. As long as the audit firm does not assume management responsibilities related to hiring those candidates, the firm can provide such services. However, the code states that the provision of such services by an audit firm may create self-interest, familiarity, or intimidation threats. The significance of these threats may be affected by the nature of the assistance provided by the audit firm and the role of the person to be recruited. Audit firms may use safeguards to reduce the threats to an acceptable level. Examples of such safeguards are to assign a high level manager at the client to review suggestions made by the audit firm and to ask the firm to suggest more than one competent candidate for the post.

CODE OF ETHICS FOR PROFESSIONAL ACCOUNTANTS IN BUSINESS

OBJECTIVE 5-8

Overview of ethical requirements for professional accountants in business.

Part C of the IESBA *Code of Ethics* requires professional accountants in business to comply with the fundamental principles and apply the conceptual framework when threats to those principles occur. The code discusses situations that may create threats and advises on possible safeguards. For example, an intimidation threat may occur in the case of threat of dismissal of the practitioner over a disagreement about the application of an accounting principle.

The IESBA code concentrates on a number of specific situations that may create threats to comply with the fundamental principles. These are:

1. Potential conflicts which may affect the ability of the employee to perform his duties with due care and diligence.
2. Preparation and reporting of information in the company's financial statements.
3. Acting with sufficient expertise to avoid errors and misstatements affecting the company's financial statements.
4. Financial interests may result in both self-interest threats to objectivity or confidentiality.
5. Inducements represented in gifts and preferential treatment creating self-interest threats to accountants.

For more details about the requirements of IESBA code, students should refer to the original content of the code at www.ifac.org/ethics.

CODES OF ETHICS FOR PROFESSIONAL ACCOUNTANTS IN THE ARAB WORLD

OBJECTIVE 5-9

Understand the application of codes of ethics in Arab countries.

As we mentioned earlier in the chapter, the IESBA *Code of Ethics* issued by the IFAC applies in most Arab countries. For example, in Saudi Arabia, the Saudi Organization for Certified Public Accountants (SOCPA) establishes ethical requirements (Islamic law prior to 2004) and a process of convergence to the IFAC approach to ethics as its objective. Although there is no established threats and safeguards framework in the national ethical requirements, ethical conflict resolution requirements and guidance have been adopted, similar to the IESBA code. This is in addition to compliance with provisions of Section 290 of the IESBA code regarding independence in audit and review engagements. There have been ongoing efforts by the SOCPA aimed at the full adoption of the IESBA code *of Ethics*. The IESBA code is not translated into Arabic but instead distributed among members in English.

Similarly, in Kuwait, the Kuwait Association of Accountants and Auditors (KAAA) establishes ethical requirements (e.g. *Code of Ethics,* code of conduct, ethics rules, member regulations, etc.) to ensure compliance by all its members. KAAA adopts the IESBA *Code of Ethics* but with modifications including Shari'a law and other cultural practices. But it considers the convergence with the IESBA code as its objective. And just like all the countries applying the IESBA code, in Kuwait professional accountants are required to comply with its fundamental principles (i.e. integrity, objectivity, professional competence and due care, confidentiality and professional behavior). The professional body has a threats and safeguards framework in place.

On the contrary, in Lebanon and Egypt, the Lebanese Association of Certified Public Accountants (LACPA) and the Egyptian Society of Accountants and Auditors (ESAA) adopt the IESBA *Code of Ethics* as issued, without modifications. Members of these Arab professional associations have started to apply the requirements of the IESBA code but no cases of violations of the code have yet emerged and any disciplinary decisions made against the members will be treated as confidential information. The change in the political environment in some Arab countries will certainly have an effect on the disclosure and transparency of acts of corruptions and fraud which will require the implementation of the fundamental principles of the *Code of Ethics*.

SUMMARY

The demand for audit and other assurance services provided by audit firms depends on public confidence in the profession. This chapter discussed the role of ethics in society and the unique ethical responsibilities of auditors and professional accountants.

Professional ethics are important to the accountancy and auditing profession and auditors must ensure they comply, at all times, with professional ethics. The fundamental principles of the IESBA *Code of Ethics* include: integrity, objectivity, professional competence and due care, confidentiality, and professional behavior. Where threats to independence are identified, these must be reduced to an acceptable level. Safeguards must be applied to help reduce threats to an acceptable level or eliminate them all together if it is possible. Most Arab countries apply the IESBA code with some modifications to consider the unique features of the laws and regulations, Shari'a, and other culture and political characteristics of the Arab world.

In the U.S., the professional activities of auditors are governed by the AICPA *Code of Professional Conduct*, and auditors of public companies are also subject to oversight by the PCAOB and SEC.

Foremost of all ethical responsibilities of auditors is the need for independence. The *Code of Ethics* provides guidance on permissible financial and other interests to help auditors maintain independence. It is also designed to maintain public confidence in the profession.

ESSENTIAL TERMS

Audit committee   p. 127

Audit firm   p. 127

Close family   p. 141

Contingent fee   p. 132

Direct financial interest   p. 140

Ethical dilemma   p. 125

Ethics   p. 124

Financial interest   p. 140

Immediate family   p. 133

Independence in appearance   p. 140

Independence of mind   p. 139

Indirect financial interest   p. 140

Key audit partner   p. 144

Partner   p. 131

Professional accountant   p. 128

Professional accountant in business   p. 128

Professional services   p. 129

Public interest entity   p. 144

Review engagement   p. 147

REVIEW QUESTIONS

5-1 (Objective 5-1) What are the main sources of ethical values?

5-2 (Objective 5-2) Describe an ethical dilemma.

5-3 (Objective 5-3) Why is there a special need for ethical behavior by professionals? Why do the ethical requirements of the audit profession differ from those of other professions?

5-4 (Objectives 5-4, 5-9) Describe the fundamental principles of ethics in the IESBA *Code of Ethics for Professional Accountants*.

5-5 (Objective 5-6) Distinguish between independence of mind and independence in appearance. State three activities that may not affect independence of mind but are likely to affect independence in appearance.

5-6 (Objective 5-6) Why is an auditor's independence so essential?

5-7 (Objective 5-5) What consulting or non-audit services are prohibited for auditors of public companies? What other restrictions and requirements apply to auditors when providing non-audit services to public companies?

5-8 (Objective 5-6) Explain how the rules concerning stock ownership apply to partners and professional staff. Give an example of when stock ownership would be prohibited for each.

5-9 (Objective 5-6) Many people believe that an auditor or professional accountant cannot be truly independent when payment of fees is dependent on the management of the client. Explain how one can reduce this appearance of lack of independence.

5-10 (Objective 5-5) After accepting an engagement, an auditor discovers that the client's industry is more technical than he realized and that he is not competent in certain areas of the operation. What are the auditor's options?

5-11 (Objective 5-6) Assume that an auditor makes an agreement with a client that the audit fee will be contingent upon the number of days required to complete the engagement. Is this a violation of the fundamental principles of the *Code of Ethics for Professional Accountants* issued by IESBA?

5-12 (Objective 5-4) The auditor's audit files usually can be provided to someone else only with the permission of the client. Give the exceptions associated with the *Code of Ethics* allowing the provision of audit files to third parties.

5-13 (Objective 5-5) Identify and explain factors that should keep the quality of audits high even though advertising and competitive bidding are allowed.

5-14 (Objective 5-5) Summarize the restrictions on advertising by audit firms in the fundamental principles of the IESBA *Code of Ethics*.

MULTIPLE CHOICE QUESTIONS FROM CPA EXAMINATIONS

5-15 (Objective 5-6) The following questions concern independence and the IESBA *Code of Ethics*. Choose the best response.

a. What is the meaning of the auditing standard that requires the auditor be independent?
   (1) The auditor must be without bias with respect to the client under audit.
   (2) The auditor must adopt a critical attitude during the audit.
   (3) The auditor's sole obligation is to third parties.
   (4) The auditor may have a direct ownership interest in the client's business if it is not material.

b. The independent audit is important to readers of financial statements because it
   (1) determines the future stewardship of the management of the company whose financial statements are audited.
   (2) measures and communicates financial and business data included in financial statements.
   (3) involves the objective examination of and reporting on management-prepared statements.
   (4) reports on the accuracy of all information in the financial statements.

c. An auditor strives to achieve independence in appearance to
   (1) maintain public confidence in the profession.
   (2) become independent in mind.
   (3) comply with the auditing standards requiring independence of the auditor.
   (4) maintain an unbiased mental attitude.

5-16 (Objectives 5-4, 5-5, 5-6) The following questions concern possible violations of the IESBA *Code of Ethics*. Choose the best response.

   a. In which one of the following situations would a professional accountant be in violation of the IESBA *Code of Ethics* in determining the audit fee?
      (1) A fee based on whether the auditor's report on the client's financial statements results in the approval of a bank loan.
      (2) A fee based on the outcome of a bankruptcy proceeding.
      (3) A fee based on the nature of the service rendered and the auditor's expertise instead of the actual time spent on the engagement.
      (4) A fee based on the fee charged by the prior auditor.

   b. The IESBA *Code of Ethics* states that a professional accountant shall not disclose any confidential information obtained in the course of a professional engagement except with the consent of the client. In which one of the following situations would disclosure by a professional accountant be in violation of the code?
      (1) Disclosing confidential information in order to properly discharge the professional accountant's responsibilities in accordance with the profession's standards.
      (2) Disclosing confidential information in compliance with a subpoena issued by a court.
      (3) Disclosing confidential information to another accountant interested in purchasing the professional accountant's practice.
      (4) Disclosing confidential information during an authorized peer review.

DISCUSSION QUESTIONS AND PROBLEMS

5-17 (Objective 5-7) The following situations involve the provision of non audit services. Indicate whether providing the service is a violation of IESBA *Code of Ethics* and Sarbanes–Oxley requirements on independence. Explain your answer as necessary.

   a. Providing bookkeeping services to a public company. The services were preapproved by the audit committee of the company.

   b. Providing internal audit services to a public company that is not an audit client.

   c. Designing and implementing a financial information system for a private company.

   d. Recommending a tax shelter to a client that is publicly held. The services were preapproved by the audit committee.

   e. Providing internal audit services to a public company audit client with the preapproval of the audit committee.

   f. Providing bookkeeping services to an audit client that is a private company.

5-18 (Objectives 5-5, 5-6) Each of the following situations involves a possible violation of the IESBA's *Code of Ethics*. For each situation, state the fundamental principle related to the situation and whether it is a violation.

   a. Fadl Shaker is a CPA, but not a partner, with three years of professional experience with Shaker & Shaker, CPAs. He owns 25 shares of stock in an audit client of the firm, but he does not take part in the audit of the client, and the amount of stock is not material in relation to his total wealth.

   b. A non-audit client requests assistance of Medhat Fahmy, CPA, in the installation of a local area network. Medhat had no experience in this type of work and no knowledge of the client's computer system, so he obtained assistance from a computer consultant. The consultant is not in the practice of public accounting, but Medhat is confident of his professional skills. Because of the highly technical nature of the work, Medhat is not able to review the consultant's work.

   c. In preparing the personal tax returns for a client, Samir Wakeel, CPA, observed that the deductions for contributions and interest were unusually large. When he asked the client for backup information to support the deductions, he was told, "Ask me no questions, and I will tell you no lies." Wakeel completed the return on the basis of the information acquired from the client.

d. Sally Moftah, licensed auditor, serves as controller of a Tunisia-based company that has a significant portion of its operations in several Middle Eastern countries. Certain government provisions in selected countries require the company to file financial statements based on international standards. Sally oversees the issuance of the company's financial statements and asserts that the statements are based on international financial accounting standards; however the standards she uses are not those issued by the International Accounting Standards Board.

e. Nermeen Fouad, licensed auditor, set up a casualty and fire insurance agency to complement her auditing and tax services. She does not use her own name on anything pertaining to the insurance agency and has a highly competent manager, Samar Habib, who runs it. Nermeen often requests Samar to review the adequacy of a client's insurance with management if it seems underinsured. She believes that she provides a valuable service to clients by informing them when they are underinsured.

f. Five small U.A.E. auditing firms have become involved in an information project by taking part in an inter-firm working paper review program. Under the program, each firm designates two partners to review the audit files, including the tax returns and the financial statements of another audit firm taking part in the program. At the end of each review, the auditors who prepared the working papers and the reviewers have a conference to discuss the strengths and weaknesses of the audit. They do not obtain authorization from the audit client before the review takes place.

g. Karim Gaber, licensed auditor, provides tax services, management advisory services, and bookkeeping services and conducts audits for the same nonpublic client. Because the firm is small, the same person often provides all the services.

5-19 (Objectives 5-6, 5-7) The following relate to auditors' independence:

a. Why is independence so essential for auditors?   **Required**

b. Compare the importance of independence of auditors with that of other professionals, such as attorneys.

c. Explain the difference between independence in appearance and of mind.

d. Assume that a partner of an audit firm owns two shares of stock of a large audit client on which he serves as the engagement partner. The ownership is an insignificant part of his total wealth.
   (1) Has he violated the *Code of Ethics*?
   (2) Explain whether the ownership is likely to affect the partner's independence of mind.

e. Discuss how each of the following could affect independence of mind and independence in appearance, and evaluate the social consequence of prohibiting auditors from doing each one:
   (1) Owning stock in a client company
   (2) Having bookkeeping services for an audit client performed by the same person who does the audit
   (3) Having the annual audit performed by the same audit team, except for assistants, for five years in a row
   (4) Having the annual audit performed by the same audit firm for ten years in a row
   (5) Having management select the audit firm
   (6) Recommending adjusting entries to the client's financial statements and preparing financial statements, including footnotes, for the client
   (7) Having management services for an audit client performed by individuals in a department that is separate from the audit department.

f. Which of (1) through (7) are prohibited by the IESBA *Code of Ethics* and the Sarbanes–Oxley Act or the SEC?

5-20 (Objective 5-7) Iman Radwan serves on the audit committee of Eagle Communications, Inc., a telecommunications start-up company. The company is currently a private company. One of the audit committee's responsibilities is to evaluate the external auditor's independence in performing the audit of the company's financial statements. In conducting this year's evaluation, Iman learned that Eagle Communications' external auditor also performed the following IT and e-commerce services for the company:

1. Installed Eagle Communications' information system hardware and software selected by Eagle management.
2. Supervised Eagle Communications' personnel in the daily operation of the newly installed information system.
3. Customized a prepackaged payroll software application, based on options and specifications selected by management.
4. Trained Eagle Communications' employees on the use of the newly installed information system.
5. Determined which Eagle Communications' products would be offered for sale on the company's internet website.
6. Operated Eagle Communications' local area network for several months while the company searched for a replacement after the previous network manager left the company.

Required   Consider each of the preceding services separately. Evaluate whether the performance of each service violates the IESBA *Code of Ethics*.

5-21 (Objectives 5-6, 5-7) Zeina El Magd encounters the following situations in doing the audit of a large auto dealership. Zeina is not a partner.

1. The sales manager tells her that there is a sale (at a substantial discount) on new cars that is limited to long-established customers of the dealership. Because her firm has been doing the audit for several years, the sales manager has decided that Zeina should also be eligible for the discount.
2. The auto dealership has an executive lunchroom that is available free to employees above a certain level. The controller informs Zeina that she can also eat there any time.
3. Zeina is invited to and attends the company's annual party. When presents are handed out, she is surprised to find her name included. The present has a value of approximately US$200.

Required   a. Describe how each of the situations might threaten Zeina's independence from the auto dealership.

b. Identify a safeguard that Zeina's firm could impose that would eliminate or mitigate the threat of each situation to Zeina's independence.

c. Assuming no safeguards are in place and Zeina accepts the offer or gift in each situation, discuss whether she has violated the IESBA *Code of Ethics*.

d. Discuss what Zeina should do in each situation.

CASES

5-22 (Objectives 5-4, 5-5, 5-6, 5-7, 5-8) The following are situations that may violate the IESBA *Code of Ethics*. Assume, in each case, that the CPA is a partner.

1. Jasmine, CPA, has set up a small financial services company that specializes in health plans for small businesses. However, Jasmine takes her CPA work with her when she is at the financial services company and has two other CPAs helping her with the financial company.
2. Elmyra, CPA, advertises her practice online, citing several prominent clients she has worked with. She has provided links to their websites and included quotes from her happy clients.
3. Upon reviewing a new client's financial statements, Hamza, CPA, approaches the company's president. He noticed that several of the company's checks have been canceled

and then rewritten at a later date, but there are two cashed checks for the same amount of money. The company's bookkeeper quit two months prior to the audit.

4. Samir, CPA, is hired to do the audit of Al-Sharif Transportation Co. Samir owns a substantial limited partnership interest in a construction company. Zubair Al-Sharif is a 100 percent owner in Al-Sharif Transportation Co. Al-Sharif also owns a substantial limited partnership in the same construction company as Samir.

5. After the auditor of a construction company suddenly quit, Basil, CPA, was hired to do the accounting for the company. The audits are due within two weeks, and there are several discrepancies between bank statements and the general ledger. He spoke to his supervisor, who told him to reconcile the two books as quickly as possible.

6. Jamal, CPA, works for Gilgamesh Practices. As part of his job, he is in charge of the audit, tax return, bookkeeping, and management services work for the Uthman Decorating Company. Makin Uthman relies on Jamal's advice before making any business decisions that could significantly affect the taxes or financial statements of his company. Jamal also attends all meetings of the company's board of directors. Because he doesn't know too much about the industry, Jamal attends some professional development courses in interior decorating. Recently, it was announced that Uthman's vice president will be retiring soon, and Uthman has hinted that he would like Jamal to join his company with a higher pay than he is currently receiving at Gilgamesh.

Required Which of the preceding situations indicates violations of the IESBA *Code of Ethics*? Which fundamental principles does the situation violate, and what is the nature of the violation(s)?

5-23 (Objectives 5-2, 5-7) Hala Zaki had great expectations about her future as she sat in her graduation ceremony in May 2011. She was about to receive her Master of Accountancy degree, and next week she would begin her career on the audit staff of Ahmed, Farid & Co., CPAs.

Things looked a little different to Hala in February 2012. She was working on the audit of Samaha Fabrics, a textile manufacturer with a calendar year-end. The pressure was enormous. Everyone on the audit team was putting in 70-hour weeks, and it still looked as if the audit wouldn't be done on time. Hala was doing work in the property area, vouching additions for the year. The audit program indicated that a sample of all items over US$20,000 should be selected, plus a judgmental sample of smaller items. When Hala went to take the sample, Khaled Moharam, the senior, had left the client's office and couldn't answer her questions about the appropriate size of the judgmental sample. Hala forged ahead with her own judgment and selected 50 smaller items. Her basis for doing this was that there were about 250 such items, so 50 was a reasonably good proportion of such additions.

Hala audited the additions with the following results: the items over US$20,000 contained no misstatements; however, the 50 small items contained a large number of misstatements. In fact, when Hala projected them to all such additions, the amount seemed quite significant.

A couple of days later, Khaled Moharam returned to the client's office. Hala brought her work to Khaled in order to apprise him of the problems she found and got the following response:

"Goodness, Hala, why did you do this? You were only supposed to look at the items over US$20,000 plus five or ten little ones. You've wasted a whole day on that work, and we can't afford to spend any more time on it. I want you to throw away the schedules where you tested the last 40 small items and forget you ever did them."

When Hala asked about the possible audit adjustment regarding the small items, none of which arose from the first ten items, Khaled responded, "Don't worry, it's not material anyway. You just forget it. It's my concern, not yours."

Required
a. In what way is this an ethical dilemma for Hala?
b. Use the six-step approach discussed in the book to resolve the ethical dilemma.

MYLAB ACTIVITY

Visit MyAccountingLab and complete the following activities:

→ Internet Problem 5-1: PCAOB Disciplinary Actions

PART

2

THE AUDIT PROCESS

Part 2 presents the audit process in a manner that will enable you to apply the concepts developed in these chapters to any audit area. Because the planning concepts covered in these chapters will be used extensively throughout the rest of the book, it is essential for you to master this material and fully understand the importance of audit planning.

- Chapters 6 and 7 deal with auditors' and managements' responsibilities, audit objectives, and general concepts of evidence accumulation.
- Chapters 8–12 study various aspects of audit planning in-depth, including risk assessment and auditors' responsibility for detecting fraud.
- Chapter 13 summarizes and integrates audit planning and audit evidence.

Throughout the remainder of the book, many of the concepts are illustrated with examples based on the Arabian Hardware Company. The financial statements and other information from the company's annual report are included in the full color insert material to the textbook.

CHAPTER 6

AUDIT RESPONSIBILITIES AND OBJECTIVES

Looking Closely at the Loans

As a means to encourage growth and trade, the United States offers interest-free loans to businesses in developing countries around the world. These humanitarian and financial efforts are funded by the United States Agency for International Development (USAID). Egypt is one of the top countries where USAID promotes business; the country received over US$30 billion in the past 30 years, providing Egyptian companies with financial help to succeed in the global market.

LinkdotNet, part of Egypt's largest cellular phone services Orascom, received such help in the form of a loan. The company was required to use the funds they received to buy electronic equipment from a U.S. company. They would then repay the loan to the Egyptian government in Egyptian pounds, which would further promote the financial sector in Egypt by using the money to buy products from other USAID programs. LinkdotNet's loan was for about US$2 million.

However, an audit of the company revealed that business was not going according to plan, and that the loan money was being spent in a way that went against the contract's terms. Instead of purchasing their communications equipment from a U.S. company, they used some of the money to pay off debts for previous purchases of office equipment and supplies. In addition to paying debts, LinkdotNet bought its new equipment from an Egyptian IT company for only US$800,000. The bids that the president and CEO, Khaled Bishara, had submitted to USAID when applying for the loan were unauthorized, and one of the prospective U.S. companies did not have a valid address.

LinkdotNet's Khaled Bishara was arrested in the United States for defrauding USAID. He pleaded not guilty to the charges, and Orascom stated that they backed him up completely. The parent company said that the matter had been discussed and settled with USAID over a year prior to the accusations. In October 2008, Bishara was still the successful CEO and chairman of the company. However, this case is a good example of how careful auditing and fact-checking can find errors that could lead to troubles for any company.

Sources: 1. Vivian Salama, 'LinkdotNet CEO struck in US on Fraud Charges,' *Business Today*, September 2004, http://www.businesstodayegypt.com/article .aspx?ArticleID=1317; 2. Jason Ingraham, 'Khaled Bichara faces charges in a New York federal court that he defrauded USAID of more than $1 million to pay off an old debt,' *Business Today*, September 2004, http://www.businesstodayegypt .com/article.aspx?ArticleID=1456; 3. Associated Press, 'Egypt firm's chief faces fraud charge in US,' *Khalegi Times Online*, August 19, 2004, http://www.khaleejtimes .com/DisplayArticle.asp?xfile=data/business/2004/August/business_August333 .xml&section=business&col=; 4. Reem Nafie, 'LinkdotNet in US dock,' *Al-Ahram Weekly Online*, September 24, 2004, http://weekly.ahram.org.eg/2004/705/eg5 .htm; 5. USAID, 'Egypt Stories,' *United States Agency of International Development,* http:// www.usaid.gov/our_work/features/egypt/, accessed September 18, 2008.

LEARNING OBJECTIVES

After studying this chapter, you should be able to

6-1 Explain the objective of conducting an audit of financial statements and an audit of internal controls.

6-2 Distinguish management's responsibility for the financial statements and internal control from the auditor's responsibility for verifying the financial statements and effectiveness of internal control.

6-3 Explain the auditor's responsibility in the audit of financial statements.

6-4 Classify transactions and account balances into financial statement cycles and identify benefits of a cycle approach to segmenting the audit.

6-5 Describe why the auditor obtains a combination of assurance by auditing classes of transactions and ending balances in accounts, including presentation and disclosure.

6-6 Distinguish among the three categories of management assertions about financial information.

6-7 Link the seven general transaction-related audit objectives to management assertions for classes of transactions.

6-8 Link the eight general balance-related audit objectives to management assertions for account balances.

6-9 Link the three presentation and disclosure-related audit objectives to management assertions for presentation and disclosure.

6-10 Explain the relationship between audit objectives and the accumulation of audit evidence.

The LinkdotNet story illustrates the success by the auditors to achieve the objectives of the audit of the company's financial statements. This chapter describes the overall objectives of the audit, the auditor's responsibilities in conducting the audit, and the specific objectives the auditor tries to accomplish. Without an understanding of these topics, planning and accumulating audit evidence during the audit has no relevance. Figure 6-1 summarizes the five topics that provide keys to understanding evidence accumulation. These are the steps used to develop specific audit objectives.

Relevant International Standards on Auditing	
ISA 200	Overall Objectives of the Independent Auditor and the Conduct of an Audit in Accordance with International Standards on Auditing
ISA 230	Audit Documentation
ISA 240	The Auditor's Responsibilities Relating to Fraud in an Audit of Financial Statements
ISA 250	Consideration of Laws and Regulations in an Audit of Financial Statements
ISA 260	Communication with Those Charged with Governance
ISA 620	Using the Work of an Auditor's Expert

OBJECTIVE OF CONDUCTING AN AUDIT OF FINANCIAL STATEMENTS

OBJECTIVE 6-1

Explain the objective of conducting an audit of financial statements and an audit of internal controls.

The International Standards on Auditing (ISA) state

> The objective of the ordinary audit of financial statements by the independent auditor is the expression of an opinion on the fairness with which they present, in all material respects, financial position, results of operations, and cash flows in conformity with International Financial Reporting Standards or local accounting standards.

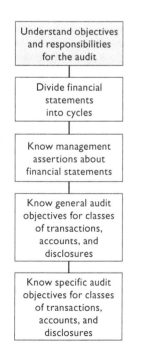

FIGURE 6-1   **Steps to Develop Audit Objectives**

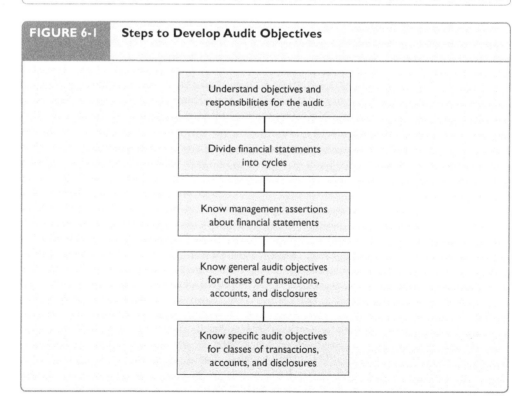

In the U.S., for public companies, the auditor issues a report on both the audit of financial statements and internal control over financial reporting. Auditors accumulate evidence in order to reach conclusions about whether the financial statements are fairly stated and to determine the effectiveness of internal control, after which they issue the appropriate audit report. In the Arab countries, auditors issue their opinion about the financial statements. The assessment of the company's internal control is made as a part of the audit of the companies' financial statements.

If the auditor believes that the statements are not fairly presented or is unable to reach a conclusion because of insufficient evidence, the auditor has the responsibility of notifying users through the auditor's report. Subsequent to their issuance, if facts indicate that the statements were not fairly presented, the auditor will probably have to demonstrate to the courts or supervisory authorities such as the Ministry of Finance, the Ministry of Commerce and Industry, or the Professional Association of Auditors that he or she conducted the audit in a proper manner and drew reasonable conclusions.

MANAGEMENT'S RESPONSIBILITIES

The responsibility for adopting sound accounting policies, maintaining adequate internal control, and making fair representations in the financial statements *rests with management* rather than with the auditor. Because they operate the business daily, a company's management knows more about the company's transactions and related assets, liabilities, and equity than the auditor. In contrast, the auditor's knowledge of these matters and internal control is limited to that acquired during the audit. The auditor should use his or her knowledge about the company's business and internal controls to assess the reliability of information included in the financial statements.

The annual reports of many publicly listed companies include a statement about management's responsibilities and relationship with the CPA firm. Figures 6-2 and 6-3 present the responsibilities of management section in the standard audit report issued by an Arab International Securities Brokerage and another example of a report prepared by management for the Boeing Company as a part of its annual report. The management responsibility in the brokerage firm standard audit report is required by ISA and Boeing's report is required under U.S. standards and laws. Read the reports carefully to determine what management states about its responsibilities.

Management's responsibility for the integrity and fairness of the representations (assertions) in the financial statements carries with it the privilege of determining which presentations and disclosures it considers necessary. If management insists on financial statement disclosure that the auditor finds unacceptable, the auditor can either issue an adverse or qualified opinion or withdraw from the engagement.

> **OBJECTIVE 6-2**
>
> Distinguish management's responsibility for the financial statements and internal control from the auditor's responsibility for verifying the financial statements and effectiveness of internal control.

FIGURE 6-2   **Arab International Securities Brokerage (S.A.E)**

MANAGEMENT'S RESPONSIBILITY FOR THE FINANCIAL STATEMENTS

These financial statements of the company are the responsibility of the Company's management. Management is responsible for the preparation and fair presentation of these financial statements in accordance with the International Financial Reporting Standards and in the light of the prevailing laws. Management responsibility includes designing, implementing and maintaining internal control relevant to the preparation and fair presentation of financial statements that are free from material misstatement, whether due to fraud or error. Management responsibility also includes selecting and applying appropriate accounting policies, and making accounting estimates that are reasonable in the circumstances.

FIGURE 6-3	The Boeing Company's Report of Management

BOEING

2007 Annual Report

REPORT OF MANAGEMENT

To the shareholders of the Boeing Company

The accompanying consolidated financial statements of The Boeing Company and subsidiaries have been prepared by management who are responsible for their integrity and objectivity. The statements have been prepared in conformity with accounting principles generally accepted in the United States of America and include amounts based on management's best estimates and judgments. Financial information elsewhere in this Annual Report is consistent with that in the financial statements.

Management has established and maintains a system of internal control designed to provide reasonable assurance regarding the reliability of financial reporting and the presentation of financial statements in accordance with accounting principles generally accepted in the United States of America, and has concluded that this system of internal control was effective as of December 31, 2007. In addition, management also has established and maintains a system of disclosure controls designed to provide reasonable assurance that information required to be disclosed is accumulated and reported in an accurate and timely manner. The system of internal control and disclosure control include widely communicated statements of policies and businesses practices which are designed to require all employees to maintain high ethical and business practices which are designed to require all employees to maintain high ethical standards in the conduct of Company affairs. The internal controls and disclosure controls are augmented by organizational arrangements that provide for appropriate delegation of authority and division of responsibility and by a program of internal audit with management follow-up.

The Audit Committee of the Board of Directors, composed entirely of outside directors, meets periodically with the independent certified public accountants, management and internal auditors to review accounting, auditing, internal accounting controls, litigation and financial reporting matters. The independent certified public accountants and the internal auditors have free access to this committee without management present.

James A. Bell
Executive Vice President,
Finance and Chief Financial Officer

W. James McNerney, Jr.
Chairman, President and
Chief Executive Officer

In the U.S., there are more restricted requirements for management and auditors' reporting on internal control under the Sarbanes–Oxley Act which increases management's responsibility for the financial statements by requiring the chief executive officer (CEO) and the chief financial officer (CFO) of public companies to certify the quarterly and annual financial statements submitted to the SEC. The U.S. requirements are not explicitly stated in ISA and many laws and regulations of many Arab countries. However, capital market authorities in many Arab countries are modifying their current structures to include in the near future requirements for assessing the quality of auditors' work to ensure effective application of corporate governance measures for the protection of investors' funds.

AUDITOR'S RESPONSIBILITIES

OBJECTIVE 6-3

Explain the auditor's responsibility in the audit of financial statements.

ISA 500 describes the auditor's responsibility as follows

The auditor's responsibility is to design and perform audit procedures to obtain sufficient appropriate audit evidence to be able to draw reasonable conclusions on which to base the auditor's opinion.

Auditors are required to form their opinion about their clients' financial statements. To achieve such an objective, auditors are responsible for detecting material misstatements in the financial statements. In the U.S., when the auditor also reports on the effectiveness of internal control over financial reporting, the auditor is also responsible for identifying material weaknesses in internal control over financial reporting. The auditor's responsibilities for audits of internal control are discussed in Chapter 10.

This paragraph and the related discussion in the standards about the auditor's responsibility to form an opinion about the financial statements including the detection of material misstatements include several important terms and phrases.

Material Versus Immaterial Misstatements Misstatements are usually considered material if the combined uncorrected errors and fraud in the financial statements would likely have changed or influenced the decisions of a reasonable person using the statements. Although it is difficult to quantify a measure of materiality, auditors are responsible for obtaining reasonable assurance that this materiality threshold has been satisfied. It would be extremely costly (and probably impossible) for auditors to have responsibility for finding all immaterial errors and fraud.

Reasonable Assurance or Conclusion Assurance is a measure of the level of certainty that the auditor has obtained at the completion of the audit. Auditing standards indicate reasonable assurance is a high, but not absolute, level of assurance that the financial statements are free of material misstatements. The concept of reasonable, but not absolute, assurance indicates that the auditor is not an insurer or guarantor of the correctness of the financial statements. Thus, an audit that is conducted in accordance with auditing standards may fail to detect a material misstatement.

The auditor is responsible for reasonable, but not absolute, assurance for several reasons:

1. Most audit evidence results from testing a sample of a population such as accounts receivable or inventory. Sampling inevitably includes some risk of not uncovering a material misstatement.
2. Accounting presentations contain complex estimates, such as the impairment of assets, the computations of fair values, the computations of provisions, the estimation of utility bills at end of financial year, warranty expenses, salvage value for property, plant and equipment, and depreciation rates which inherently involve uncertainty and can be affected by future events. As a result, the auditor has to rely on evidence that is persuasive, but not convincing.
3. Fraudulently prepared financial statements are often extremely difficult, if not impossible, for the auditor to detect, especially when there is collusion among management.

If auditors were responsible for making certain that all the assertions in the statements were correct, the types and amounts of evidence required and the resulting cost of the audit function would increase to such an extent that audits would not be economically practical. Auditors would be required to audit 100 percent of the business's transactions and balances. Even then, auditors would be unlikely to uncover all material misstatements in every audit due to misjudgment and other human errors. The auditor's best defense when material misstatements are not uncovered is to have conducted the audit in accordance with auditing standards.

Errors Versus Fraud ISA 240 distinguishes between two types of misstatements in the financial statements: errors and fraud. Either type of misstatement can be material or immaterial. An **error** is an *unintentional* misstatement of the financial statements, whereas **fraud** is *intentional*. Two examples of errors are a mistake in extending prices times quantity on a sales invoice and overlooking older raw materials in determining the lower of cost or market for inventory.

Error

An unintentional misstatement of the financial statements.

Fraud

An intentional misstatement of the financial statements.

Misappropriation of assets

A fraud involving the theft of an entity's assets.

Fraudulent financial reporting

Intentional misstatements or omissions of amounts or disclosures in financial statements to deceive users.

For fraud, there is a distinction between **misappropriation of assets**, often called defalcation or employee fraud, and **fraudulent financial reporting**, often called management fraud. An example of misappropriation of assets is a clerk taking cash at the time a sale is made and not entering the sale in the cash register. An example of fraudulent financial reporting is the intentional overstatement of sales near the balance sheet date to increase reported earnings.

ISA 240 states that the primary responsibility for the prevention and detection of fraud rests with those charged with governance of the entity such as the audit committee and management. Management must create a culture of honesty and ethical behavior which can be reinforced by an active oversight by those charged with governance. Auditors, on the other hand, should obtain reasonable assurance that the financial statements taken as a whole are free from material misstatement, whether caused by fraud or error. The risk of not detecting fraud is higher compared with errors due to sophisticated and carefully organized schemes designed to conceal such fraud as forgery, deliberate failure to record transactions, or intentional misrepresentations being made to the auditor. The concealment may be even more difficult to detect when accompanied by collusion between management and employees.

Professional Skepticism Auditing standards require that an audit be designed to provide reasonable assurance of detecting *both* material errors and fraud in the financial statements. To accomplish this, the audit must be planned and performed with an *attitude of professional skepticism* in all aspects of the engagement. Professional skepticism is an attitude that includes a questioning mind and a critical assessment of audit evidence. Auditors should not assume that management is dishonest, but the possibility of dishonesty must be considered. At the same time, auditors also should not assume that management is unquestionably honest.

Auditing standards indicate that unless auditors have reason to believe the contrary, the auditor may accept records and documents as genuine. However, where responses to inquiries of management or those charged with governance are inconsistent, the auditor should extend his investigations of such inconsistencies.

For example, auditors should assess the collectability of accounts receivables assuming that clients are expected to pay their debt but the possibility of uncollectability of some clients' debts must be considered. Auditors should examine the aged debtors schedule prepared by the management to assess the extent of receivables impairment and the adequacy of the allowance formed for doubtful debts. Also, auditors should check that clients' obligations are actual and real. Auditors should ensure that management sent letters to suppliers and other creditors to ensure that the obligations to them are real.

Auditor's Responsibilities for Detecting Material Errors

Auditors spend a great portion of their time planning and performing audits to detect unintentional mistakes made by management and employees. Auditors find a variety of errors resulting from such things as mistakes in calculations, omissions, misunderstanding and misapplication of accounting standards, and incorrect summarizations and descriptions. Throughout the rest of this book, we consider how the auditor plans and performs audits for detecting both errors and fraud.

Auditor's Responsibilities for Detecting Material Fraud

Auditing standards make no distinction between the auditor's responsibilities for searching for errors and fraud. In either case, the auditor must obtain reasonable assurance about whether the statements are free of material misstatements. The standards also recognize that fraud is often more difficult to detect because management or the employees perpetrating the fraud *attempt to conceal the fraud*. Still, the difficulty of detection does not change the auditor's responsibility to properly plan and perform the audit to detect material misstatements, whether caused by error or fraud.

Fraud Resulting from Fraudulent Financial Reporting Versus Misappropriation of Assets Both fraudulent financial reporting and misappropriation of assets are potentially harmful to financial statement users, but there is an important difference between them. Fraudulent financial reporting harms users by providing them with incorrect financial statement information for their decision making. For example, investors in the Kuwait stock market may face the risk of losing substantial funds if they invest in stocks of listed companies whose financial statements are manipulated by those charged with governance or management. When assets are misappropriated, stockholders, creditors, and others are harmed because assets are no longer available to their rightful owners. For example, a cashier may continuously steal cash related to sales transactions depriving the company from the use of such funds in addition to understating sales and cash balances in the financial statements.

Typically, fraudulent financial reporting is committed by management, sometimes without the knowledge of employees. Management is in a position to make accounting and reporting decisions without employees' knowledge. An example is the decision to omit an important footnote about pending litigation.

Usually, but not always, theft of assets is perpetrated by employees and not by management, and the amounts are often immaterial. However, there are well-known examples of extremely material misappropriation of assets by employees and management, similar to the Adelphia fraud described below.

For example, the criminal court in an Arab country issued its decisions for the imprisonment of the chairman of a logistics company for seven years and ordered him to pay US$2 million on two charges of misusing his company's funds and assets. The court accused the chairman of taraboh (illegally benefiting from the company's activities) and devaluing the company's assets and defrauding shareholders by allocating six vehicles for his personal use, including three Mercedes and other well-known makes such as BMW, Porsche, and Lexus—total value US$1.2 million—in addition to allocating more than 20 vehicles to branch managers—value US$1.6 million—while the company was in debt to banks and defaulting on payment of its loans. This act of corruption was carried out with the full knowledge of the board of directors.

CABLE MOGULS ARRESTED FOR CORPORATE LOOTING

Sometimes, misappropriation of assets involves significant amounts and occurs at the very top of the organization. In 2002 in the U.S., the SEC charged former Adelphia CEO John Rigas and other Rigas family members with "rampant self dealing" at Adelphia Communications Corp. in what has been called one of the most extensive financial frauds ever to take place at a public company. According to the SEC complaint, the Rigas family used Adelphia funds to finance open market purchases of stock, pay off margin loans and other family debts, purchase timber rights, construct a golf club, and purchase luxury condominiums in Colorado, Mexico, and New York City.

In the criminal complaint, prosecutors charged that the Rigas family "looted Adelphia on a massive scale, using the company as the Rigas family's per-sonal piggy bank, at the expense of public investors and creditors." After details of the misappropriations and fraudulent reporting in the company's financial statements became public, Adelphia filed for bankruptcy, and its stock collapsed from a price of US$20 per share to less than US$1 per share. John Rigas was convicted and sentenced to 15 years in prison; his son Timothy, the company's former CFO, was sentenced to 20 years in prison.

Sources: 1. SEC press release 2002-110 (www.sec.gov/news/press/2002-110.htm); 2. 'Rigas and sons arrested' (money.cnn.com/2002/07/24/news/rigas/); 3. 'Adelphia founder sentenced to 15 years' (money.cnn.com/2005/06/20/news/newsmakers/rigas_sentencing/).

There is an important distinction between the theft of assets and misstatements arising from the theft of assets. Consider the following three situations:

1. Assets were taken and the theft was covered by misstating assets. For example, cash collected from a customer was stolen before it was recorded as a cash receipt, and the account receivable for the customer's account was not credited. The misstatement has not been discovered.
2. Assets were taken and the theft was covered by understating revenues or overstating expenses. For example, cash from a cash sale was stolen, and the transaction was not recorded. Or, an unauthorized disbursement to an employee was recorded as a miscellaneous expense. The misstatement has not been discovered.
3. Assets were taken, but the misappropriation was discovered. The income statement and related footnotes clearly describe the misappropriation.

In all three situations, there was a misappropriation of assets, but the financial statements are misstated only in situations 1 and 2. In situation 1, the balance sheet is misstated, whereas in situation 2 revenues or expenses are misstated.

Auditor's Responsibilities for Discovering Illegal Acts

Illegal acts

Violations of laws or government regulations other than fraud.

Illegal acts are explained in auditing standards (ISA 250) as violations of laws or government regulations *other than fraud*. Examples of illegal acts are a violation of corporate tax laws and a violation of the Companies Act or environmental protection laws. Noncompliance with laws and regulations may result in fines, litigations, or other consequences for the entity, the costs of which may need to be provided for in the financial statements, but are not considered to have a direct effect on the financial statements. Auditing standards state that there are inherent limitations on the auditor's ability to detect illegal acts due to such reasons:

1. There are many laws and regulations relating to the operating activities of an entity that may not affect the financial statements and are not captured by the entity information systems relevant to financial reporting. Noncompliance by those charged with governance or management involves conduct designed to conceal such illegal acts through forgery, collusion, deliberate failure to record transactions, management override of controls, or intentional misrepresentations being made to the entity's auditor at a later date.
2. Whether an act constitutes noncompliance is ultimately a matter to be determined by a court of law. The auditor may not possess the ability and skills needed to identify whether a particular fact is considered an illegal act.

Direct-Effect Illegal Acts Certain violations of laws and regulations have a direct financial effect on specific account balances in the financial statements. For example, a violation of corporate tax laws directly affects income tax expense and income taxes payable. The auditor's responsibility for these direct-effect illegal acts is the same as for errors and fraud. On each audit, therefore, the auditor normally evaluates whether or not there is evidence available to indicate material violations of corporate tax laws. To do this evaluation, the auditor might hold discussions with client personnel and examine reports issued by the Tax Authorities after completion of an examination of the client's tax return.

In addition, management may violate the requirements embedded in the Companies Act for the distribution of profit. Management may decide to distribute dividends to shareholders, employees, and management without deducting the adequate allowances for either doubtful debts or pending litigations and the legal reserve according to the percentage stated in the Companies Act in many Arab countries. Moreover, management may reduce the financial burden related to the company's share for social insurance of

THE FORMER MINISTER OF FINANCE SENT TO PRISON FOR 15 YEARS	The criminal court north of Cairo sentenced the former Minister of Finance to 15 years in prison for unlawfully using the printing facilities of the Ministry of Finance to print costly flyers for his parliamentary election campaign in the six months before the election. The Minister not only ordered the printing of the flyers but also moved printers owned by the	Ministry of Finance to his election campaign headquarters so that they could be used for this printing. The former Minister of Finance left the country to avoid serving the 15 years imprisonment. Source: Based on *El-Akhbar*, (June 5, 2011) p. 7, (May 6, 2011) p. 6.

employees by minimizing amounts paid for such purpose. Auditors are responsible to uncover such illegal acts which violate requirement of social insurance laws in most Arab countries.

Indirect-Effect Illegal Acts Most illegal acts affect the financial statements only indirectly. For example, if the company violates environmental protection laws, financial statements are affected only if there is a fine or sanction. Potential material fines and sanctions indirectly affect financial statements by creating the need to disclose a contingent liability for the potential amount that might ultimately be paid. This is called an indirect-effect illegal act. Other examples of illegal acts that are likely to have only an indirect effect are violations of insider securities trading regulations, civil rights laws, and employee safety requirements. Auditing standards state that the auditor provides *no assurance* that indirect-effect illegal acts will be detected. Auditors lack legal expertise, and the frequent indirect relationship between illegal acts and the financial statements makes it impractical for auditors to assume responsibility for discovering those illegal acts.

Auditors have three levels of responsibility for finding and reporting illegal acts:

Evidence Accumulation When There is No Reason to Believe Indirect-Effect Illegal Acts Exist Many audit procedures normally performed on audits to search for errors and fraud may also uncover illegal acts. Examples include reading the minutes of the board of directors and inquiring of the client's attorneys about litigation. The auditor should also inquire of management about policies they have established to prevent illegal acts and whether management knows of any laws or regulations that the company has violated. Other than these procedures, the auditor should not search for indirect-effect illegal acts unless there is reason to believe they may exist.

Evidence Accumulation and Other Actions When There is Reason to Believe Direct- or Indirect-Effect Illegal Acts May Exist The auditor may find indications of possible illegal acts in a variety of ways. For example, the minutes may indicate that an investigation by a government authority is in process or the auditor may have identified unusually large payments to consultants or government officials.

ISA 250 lists a number of matters that if they exist may be an indication of noncompliance with laws and regulations:

1. Investigations by regulatory organizations and government departments or payment of fines or penalties.
2. Payments of unspecified services or loans to consultants, related parties, employees, or government employees.
3. Sales commissions or agent's fees that appear excessive in relation to the entity's normal business transactions.
4. Purchasing at prices significantly above or below market price.
5. Unusual payments in cash, purchases in the form of cashiers' checks payable to bearer, or transfers to numbered bank accounts.

6. Payments for goods and services made other than to the country from which the goods or services originated.
7. Payments without proper exchange control documentation.
8. Unauthorized transactions or improperly recorded transactions.

When the auditor believes that an illegal act may have occurred, several actions are necessary to determine whether the suspected illegal act actually exists:

1. The auditor should first inquire of those charged with governance or management at a level above those likely to be involved in the potential illegal act about such illegal acts and the entity's policies and procedures designed to prevent and detect such acts and other litigation claims.
2. The auditor should inspect correspondence, if any, with the relevant licensing or regulatory authorities.
3. The auditor should consult with the in-house, the external legal counsel, or other specialist who is knowledgeable about the potential illegal act concerning litigation, claims, and assessments.
4. The auditor should consider accumulating additional evidence and performing substantive tests of details of transactions, account balances, or disclosures to determine whether there actually is an illegal act and request a written representation letter from management confirming the non-existence of such acts.

Actions When the Auditor Knows of an Illegal Act The first course of action when an illegal act has been identified is to consider the effects on the financial statements, including the need to modify the financial statements and the adequacy of disclosures. These effects may be complex and difficult to resolve. For example, if management violates payroll tax requirements and deducts inappropriate tax amounts, the financial statements need to be adjusted to ensure proper recording of tax expense and tax payable for salaries and remuneration. Also, a violation of civil rights laws could involve significant fines, but it could also result in the loss of customers or key employees, which could materially affect future revenues and expenses. If the auditor concludes that the disclosures relative to an illegal act are inadequate, the auditor should modify the audit report accordingly.

Auditing standards state that if the auditor concludes that the noncompliance has a material effect on the financial statements, and has not been appropriately reflected in the financial statements, he shall, according to ISA 705, express a qualified opinion or an adverse opinion on the financial statements. If the auditor is precluded by management or those charged with governance from obtaining sufficient appropriate evidence to assess the likelihood of illegal acts and their effects on the financial statements, the auditor shall express a qualified opinion or disclaim an opinion on the financial statements.

The auditor should also consider the effect of such illegal acts on the audit firm's relationship with management. If management knew of the illegal act and failed to inform the auditor, it is questionable whether management can be believed in other discussions.

The auditor should communicate with the audit committee or others of equivalent authority to make sure that they know of the illegal act. The communication can be oral or written. If it is oral, the nature of the communication and discussion should be documented in the audit files. If the client either refuses to accept the auditor's modified report or fails to take appropriate remedial action concerning the illegal act, the auditor may find it necessary to withdraw from the engagement. If the client is publicly held, the auditor must also report the matter directly to those charged with governance and the appropriate supervisory authorities such as the country's Ministry of Finance, the Ministry of Commerce and Industry, the National Association of Accountants and Auditors, and the authorities that oversee and organize capital markets. Such decisions are complex and normally involve consultation by the auditor with the auditor's legal counsel.

ISA 250 provides examples of the types of policies and procedures an entity may implement to assist in the prevention and detection of noncompliance with laws and regulations.

a. Monitoring legal requirements relating to the entity's operations and ensuring that operating procedures are designed to meet these requirements.
b. Instituting and operating appropriate systems of internal control.
c. Developing, publicizing, and following a code of conduct.
d. Ensuring employees are properly trained and understand the code of conduct.
e. Monitoring compliance with the code of conduct and acting appropriately to discipline employees who fail to comply with it.
f. Requesting the assistance of legal advisors to help monitor legal requirements.
g. Maintaining a register or a list of significant laws and regulations with which the entity has to comply within its industry, and a record of complaints.

The auditing standards highlight the role of an internal audit function, an audit committee, and a compliance function in ensuring compliance with the above policies and procedures especially in larger entities.

Cycle approach

A method of dividing an audit by keeping closely related types of transactions and account balances in the same segment.

FINANCIAL STATEMENT CYCLES

Audits are performed by dividing the financial statements into smaller segments or components. The division makes the audit more manageable and aids in the assignment of tasks to different members of the audit team. For example, most auditors treat fixed assets and notes payable as different segments. Each segment is audited separately but not on a completely independent basis. (For example, the audit of fixed assets may reveal an unrecorded note payable.) After the audit of each segment is completed, including interrelationships with other segments, the results are combined. A conclusion can then be reached about the financial statements taken as a whole.

There are different ways of segmenting an audit. One approach is to treat every account balance on the statements as a separate segment. Segmenting that way is usually inefficient. It would result in the independent audit of such closely related accounts as inventory and cost of goods sold. Also, it would require a large number of auditors in the audit team which would be more costly than the original estimate and the audit would take significantly longer than planned.

OBJECTIVE 6-4

Classify transactions and account balances into financial statement cycles and identify benefits of a cycle approach to segmenting the audit.

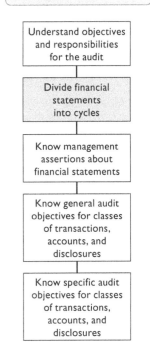

Understand objectives and responsibilities for the audit

Divide financial statements into cycles

Know management assertions about financial statements

Know general audit objectives for classes of transactions, accounts, and disclosures

Know specific audit objectives for classes of transactions, accounts, and disclosures

Cycle Approach to Segmenting an Audit

A common way to divide an audit is to keep closely related types (or classes) of transactions and account balances in the same segment. This is called the **cycle approach**. For example, sales (revenues), sales returns, cash receipts, and charge-offs of uncollectible accounts are the four classes of transactions that cause accounts receivable to increase and decrease. Therefore, they are all parts of the sales (revenues) and collection cycle. Similarly, payroll transactions and accrued payroll are parts of the payroll and personnel cycle.

The logic of using the cycle approach is that it ties to the way transactions are recorded in journals and summarized in the general ledger and financial statements. Figure 6-4 shows that flow. To the extent that it is practical, the cycle approach combines transactions recorded in different journals with the general ledger balances that result from those transactions.

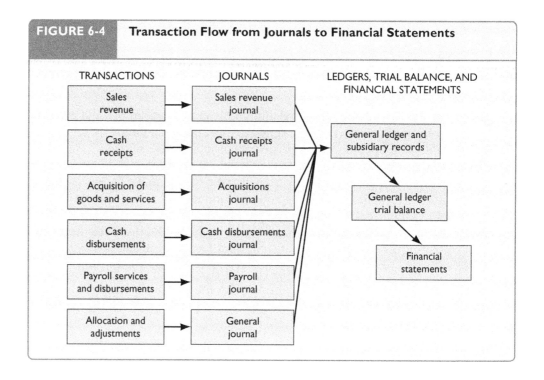

FIGURE 6-4   Transaction Flow from Journals to Financial Statements

The cycles used in this text are listed below and are then explained in detail. Note that each of these cycles is so important that one or more later chapters address the audit of each cycle:

- Sales (Revenues) and collection cycle
- Acquisition and payment cycle
- Payroll and personnel cycle
- Inventory and warehousing cycle
- Capital acquisition and repayment cycle

Figure 6-5 illustrates the application of cycles to audits using the December 31, 2012, trial balance for Arabian Hardware Company. (The financial statements prepared from this trial balance are included in the glossy insert to the textbook.) A trial balance is used to prepare financial statements and is a primary focus of every audit. Prior year account balances are usually included for comparative purposes, but are excluded from Figure 6-5 in order to focus on transaction cycles. The letter representing a cycle is shown for each account in the left column beside the account name. Observe that each account has at least one cycle associated with it, and only cash and inventory are a part of two or more cycles.

The accounts for Arabian Hardware Co. are summarized in Table 6-1 by cycle, and include the related journals and financial statements in which the accounts appear. The following observations expand on the information contained in Table 6-1.

- All general ledger accounts and journals for Arabian Hardware Co. are included at least once. For a different company, the number and titles of journals and general ledger accounts will differ, but all will be included.
- Some journals and general ledger accounts are included in more than one cycle. When that occurs, it means that the journal is used to record transactions from more than one cycle and indicates a tie-in between the cycles. The most important general ledger account included in and affecting several cycles is general cash (cash in bank). General cash connects most cycles.
- The sales and collection cycle is the first cycle listed and is a primary focus on most audits. Collections on trade accounts receivable in the cash receipts journal is the primary operating inflow to cash in the bank.

2012 Annual Report

Arabian Hardware Company 2012 Annual Report

CONTENTS

Rasheed Akram, President and Chief Operating Officer

DEAR SHAREHOLDERS

March 29, 2013

We are proud to announce another year of noticeable improvement.

In last year's letter we stated, "We are committed to increasing the efficiency and effectiveness of operations through cost savings and productivity improvements, in light of current economic conditions. In addition, we intend to maintain and further develop our customer base through recently implemented post-sale service programs." The operating results in this report demonstrate that our objectives have been achieved, resulting in a net income increase of US$740,000 from 2011 to 2012. This amounts to 15 cents per share, a 23.2% increase from last year. Our goal in the current year is to further improve the results of operations and create value for shareholders. In doing so, we will focus primarily on the following three strategic components of our business plan:

1. Post-sale service arrangements designed to further develop and maintain our customer base.
2. Aggressive advertising campaigns that allow us to penetrate markets dominated by regional wholesale hardware store chains.
3. Implementation of new warehouse technology designed to increase productivity and reduce stocking and distribution costs.

We will report our progress throughout the year.

Falih Al-Habib

Chief Executive Officer

Rasheed Akram

President and Chief Operating Officer

History

Arabian Stores Inc. began operations in 1982 in Jeddah, Saudi Arabia as a retail hardware store chain. On September 25, 1988, Arabian merged with Haddad Hardware and Lumber Company, which established the concept of selling high-quality hardware through wholesale distribution outlets, to form Haddad Arabian, Inc., a Cairo corporation. On June 5, 1992, after spinning off all of its lumber-related assets to Haddad Corporation, the company changed its name to Arabian Hardware, Inc. On October 22, 1994, the company reincorporated from Cairo to Riyadh and changed its name to Arabian Hardware Company (hereafter referred to as "the Company"), which trades on btflive.net under the symbol "ARBN."

Overview

Arabian Hardware Company is a wholesale distributor of hardware equipment to a variety of independent, high-quality hardware stores across the Arab world. The primary products are power and hand tools, landscaping equipment, electrical equipment, residential and commercial construction equipment, and a wide selection of paint products.

More than 90% of the Company's products are purchased from manufacturers and shipped either directly to customers or to the main warehouse in Jeddah, Saudi Arabia, where shipments are combined to minimize the costs of freight and handling.

Hardware retailers, now more than ever, find it advantageous to purchase from us rather than directly from manufacturers. We make it possible for smaller, independent retailers to purchase on an as-needed basis, rather than in bulk. Moreover, we offer our customers a range of high-quality products that cannot be found at most national chains.

We also offer far more post-sale services to customers than are offered by manufacturers and other regional distributors. We simplify the purchasing process by assigning each customer a permanent salesperson. Each salesperson becomes involved in the sales process, and also acts as a liaison between the customer and post-sale service areas. For example, when customers experience technical problems with recently purchased hardware, their salesperson has the responsibility to coordinate both exchanges and warranty repairs with the manufacturer. This process adds value for customers and makes post-sales service more efficient and less problematic. Low turnover and extensive training of our salespeople enhance this service.

To further encourage customer loyalty, each customer is given access to our internal database system—ONHAND (Online Niche-Hardware Availability Notification Database). The ONHAND system lets customers check the availability of hard-to-find products instantly over the internet. Moreover, the system includes data such as expected restock dates for items that are currently sold out and expected availability dates for items that will soon be introduced to the market.

Because of the two aforementioned processes, we have managed to maintain a repeat-customer base. Nearly 75% of all first-time customers make at least one additional purchase within one year of their first purchase.

Recently, there have been major consolidations in the wholesale hardware industry. We believe this consolidation trend is advantageous to our operations as a distributor of hard-to-find, high-quality hardware equipment. The recent consolidation of Builder's Plus Hardware, Inc., one of the top ten largest regional hardware store chains, is a case in point. One month after the consolidation, Builder's Plus decided not to carry high-end construction and landscaping equipment in order to focus on what it called the "typical hardware customer."

Products

To more effectively manage inventory, we carefully monitor the composition of net sales by category of items sold. The following chart indicates the percentage of net sales by class of merchandise sold during the years 2012, 2011, and 2010:

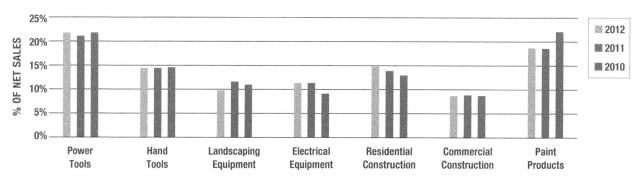

Competitors

National wholesale hardware store chains dominate the industry. Most of our competitors are not only larger, but have greater financial resources than our company. Ten regional chains exist in the geographic area in which Arabian Hardware Co. operates. Of the ten national chains, Mahran Hardware, Al Madina Tools & Paint, and Construction City account for a significant portion of the wholesale hardware market share and also carry the hard-to-find and high-quality items we provide. The success of our business depends on our ability to keep distribution costs to a minimum and our customers satisfied through superior customer service.

The chart below is a breakdown of market share in the wholesale hardware market by competitor category, including the 2% market share held by the Company. The chart illustrates that we have considerable opportunity for sales growth.

Marketing Program

This year, the Company made a significant investment in a new advertising campaign. Various internet, radio, newspaper, magazine, and television advertisements were purchased at the local and regional levels using the Company's new catchphrase, "Hardware for Hard Workers." The new jingle has been partially responsible for the fiscal 2012 increase in sales of 9%.

Customers

The majority of our customers are located in Saudi Arabia, the U.A.E., Egypt, and Lebanon. Our current customer base consists of more than 400 independently owned hardware stores. Approximately 25% of our customers make up more than 80% of total sales revenue. To promote long-standing relationships with customers, we offer an array of incentive and customer appreciation programs. Since these programs were implemented in 2002, customer satisfaction ratings have improved steadily in each subsequent year.

Suppliers

We purchase hardware and other products from more than 300 manufacturers in the United States. No single vendor accounted for more than 5% of our purchases during fiscal 2012, but our 25 largest vendors accounted for nearly 35%. We currently have long-term supply agreements with two vendors: Mechanical Tools and Painter's Paradise. These agreements are in effect until the end of fiscal year 2013. The combined dollar amount of each contract is not expected to exceed 5% of total purchases for the year.

Employees

Arabian Hardware currently employs 319 individuals. The majority of our employees are involved in day-to-day sales. Because of our marketing and customer relations strategy, we make significant investments in ongoing training and professional development activities. Each year employees are required to attend 75 hours of professional training. Each employee receives a performance evaluation at least four times per year, usually once each quarter. Our turnover is among the lowest in the industry because of our compensation, training, and evaluation programs. We regard our employees as our most valuable asset.

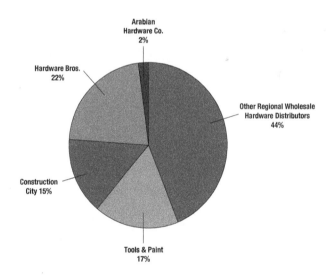

Properties

The Company owns and operates its main warehouse and an administrative office. The main warehouse and administrative office are in the same 475,000 square-foot building. We also rent a second warehouse for which rental fees are US$312,000 annually. The building, located in Beirut, Lebanon, serves as an off-site storage facility.

Legal Proceedings

On September 3, 2010, a suit was filed in Jeddah, Saudi Arabia against the Company. The product liability suit, *"Dirar Hassan v. Arabian Hardware Co."* is related to injuries that resulted from an alleged defective design of a tractor manufactured by Silo-Tractor, an Arab corporation. The suit is currently in pre-trial proceedings. In the opinion of our legal counsel the suit is without merit. We intend to vigorously defend our position.

The Company does not believe any other legal issues materially affect its finances.

Executive Officers

The following list provides names, ages, and present positions of the Company's officers:

NAME	AGE	POSITION
Jalil Soliman	55	Chairman of the Board
Falih Al-Habib	47	Chief Executive Officer (b)
Rasheed Akram	54	President and Chief Operating Officer (a)
Aila Al Nagshabandi	44	Chief Financial Officer
Bader Mohammed	51	Vice President Sales and Marketing
Maryam El Morshidy	36	Vice President Merchandising
Elham Nakhle	53	Vice President Operations (c)
George Ghoneim	64	Vice President Quality Assurance (d)

(a) Mr. Akram has been President and Chief Operating Officer of the Company for ten years, since November 2002. Mr. Akram was Chairman of the Board from 2005 to 2006.
(b) Mr. Zamil has been Chief Executive Officer of the Company since September 2002. Prior to his role as CEO, Mr. Zamil was employed from 1993–2001 by Tamimi Enterprises, an industrial distributor.
(c) Ms. Nakhle has been employed by the Company since its inception in 1995. She has held her current position since 2001 and served as an operations manager from 1995-2001.
(d) Mr. Ghoneim was Chief Operating Officer and President of Hardware Bros., one of the ten largest wholesale hardware chains in the region, from 1999–2004.

"We offer our customers a range of high-quality products that cannot be found at most regional chains."

Controls and Procedures

Pursuant to Section 404 of the Sarbanes–Oxley Act of 2002 and related Exchange Act Rules, we have carefully evaluated the design and operating effectiveness of our internal control over financial reporting. After careful review of all key controls over financial reporting, our Chief Executive Officer and Chief Financial Officer implemented new controls over the internal verification and timely recording of sales transactions. In compliance with Section 404 and related Exchange requirements, management has issued its report that internal controls over financial reporting are operating effectively as of December 31, 2012 based on criteria established in the COSO *Internal Control - Integrated Framework.*

Information Regarding Common Equity

Arabian Hardware Company's common stock currently trades on the btflive.net under the symbol "ARBN." The following chart shows the high and low prices of the Company's common stock by quarter for the years 2012 and 2011:

	2012		2011	
	HIGH	**LOW**	**HIGH**	**LOW**
Quarter 1	22.50	19.05	23.30	20.00
Quarter 2	22.55	20.10	22.75	20.25
Quarter 3	22.30	20.99	24.10	19.75
Quarter 4	22.40	17.95	21.50	18.20

On March 23, 2013, there were 1,250 shareholders of our common stock.

Dividend Policy

Dividend payments on common stock are authorized annually by the Board of Directors. For 2012, dividend payments totaled US$1.9 million, which is US$.38 per share.

REPORT OF INDEPENDENT REGISTERED ACCOUNTING FIRM

Board of Directors and Stockholders
Arabian Hardware Company

We have audited the accompanying balance sheets of Arabian Hardware Company as of December 31, 2012 and 2011, and the related statements of income, stockholders' equity and comprehensive income, and cash flows for each of the years in the three-year period ended December 31, 2012. We have also audited Arabian Hardware Company, Inc.'s internal control over financial reporting as of December 31, 2012, based on criteria established in *Internal Control - Integrated Framework* issued by the Committee of Sponsoring Organizations of the Treadway Commission (COSO). Arabian Hardware Company's management is responsible for these financial statements, for maintaining effective internal control over financial reporting, and for its assessment of the effectiveness of internal control over financial reporting, included in the accompanying report, Management's Responsibility for the Financial Statements. Our responsibility is to express an opinion on these financial statements and an opinion on the Company's internal control over financial reporting based on our audits.

We conducted our audits in accordance with the International Standards on Auditing. Those standards require that we plan and perform the audits to obtain reasonable assurance about whether the financial statements are free of material misstatement and whether effective internal control over financial reporting was maintained in all material respects. Our audit of financial statements included examining, on a test basis, evidence supporting the amounts and disclosures in the financial statements, assessing the accounting principles used and significant estimates made by management, and evaluating the overall financial statement presentation. Our audit of internal control over financial reporting included obtaining an understanding of internal control over financial reporting, assessing the risk that a material weakness exists, and testing and evaluating the design and operating effectiveness of internal control based on the assessed risk. Our audits also included performing such other procedures as we considered necessary in the circumstances. We believe that our audits provide a reasonable basis for our opinions.

A company's internal control over financial reporting is a process designed to provide reasonable assurance regarding the reliability of financial reporting and the preparation of financial statements for external purposes in accordance with generally accepted accounting principles. A company's internal control over financial reporting includes those policies and procedures that (1) pertain to the maintenance of records that, in reasonable detail, accurately and fairly reflect the transactions and dispositions of the assets of the company; (2) provide reasonable assurance that transactions are recorded as necessary to permit preparation of financial statements in accordance with generally accepted accounting principles, and that receipts and expenditures of the Company are being made only in accordance with authorizations of management and directors of the Company; and (3) provide reasonable assurance regarding the prevention or timely detection of unauthorized acquisition, use, or disposition of the Company's assets that could have a material effect on the financial statements.

Because of its inherent limitations, internal control over financial reporting may not prevent or detect misstatements. Also, projections of any evaluation of effectiveness to future periods are subject to the risk that controls may become inadequate because of changes in conditions, or that the degree of compliance with the policies or procedures may deteriorate.

In our opinion, the financial statements referred to above present fairly, in all material respects, the financial position of Arabian Hardware Company, Inc. as of December 31, 2012 and 2011, and the results of its operations and its cash flows for each of the years in the three-year period ended December 31, 2012 in conformity with accounting principles generally accepted in the Arab world. Also in our opinion, Arabian Hardware Company maintained, in all material respects, effective internal control over financial reporting as of December 31, 2012, based on criteria established in *Internal Control - Integrated Framework* issued by the Committee of Sponsoring Organizations of the Treadway Commission (COSO).

Faisal & Harb, LLP

Faisal and Harb, LLP
March 21, 2013

Management's Responsibility for the Financial Statements
To Our Shareholders:

The accompanying financial statements of Arabian Hardware Company have been prepared by management, which is responsible for their integrity and objectivity. The statements have been prepared in conformity with generally accepted accounting principles and include amounts based on management's best estimates and judgments. Management has also prepared information elsewhere in this Annual Report that is consistent with data in the financial statements. The Company's financial statements have been audited by Faisal and Harb, independent Certified Public Accountants. Our auditors were given unrestricted access to all financial records and related data, including minutes of the meetings of the Board of Directors. We believe all representations made to Faisal and Harb were legitimate and appropriate.

The management of Arabian Hardware Company is responsible for establishing and maintaining adequate internal control over financial reporting. Arabian Hardware Company's internal control system was designed to provide reasonable assurance to the Company's management and Board of Directors regarding the preparation and fair presentation of published financial statements.

Arabian Hardware Company management assessed the effectiveness of the Company's internal control over financial reporting as of December 31, 2012. In making this assessment, it used the criteria set forth by the Committee of Sponsoring Organizations of the Treadway Commission (COSO) in *Internal Control - Integrated Framework*. Based on our assessment we believe that, as of December 31, 2012, the Company's internal control over financial reporting is effective based on those criteria.

Arabian Hardware Company's independent auditors have issued an audit report on our financial statements and internal control over financial reporting. This report appears on the preceding page.

Jalil Soliman
Chairman of the Board

Falih Al Habib
Chief Executive Officer

Aila Al Nagshabandi
Chief Financial Officer

Arabian Hardware Company
Balance Sheets (in thousands)

		December 31	
ASSETS		**2012**	**2011**
Current assets			
Cash and cash equivalents		US$ 828	US$ 743
Trade receivables (net of allowances of $1,240 and $1,311)		18,957	16,210
Other receivables		945	915
Merchandise inventory		29,865	31,600
Prepaid expenses		432	427
Total current assets		51,027	49,895
Property and equipment			
Land		3,456	3,456
Buildings		32,500	32,000
Equipment, furniture, and fixtures		6,304	8,660
Less: accumulated depreciation		(31,920)	(33,220)
Total property and equipment (net)		10,340	10,896
Total assets		**US$ 61,367**	**US$ 60,791**
LIABILITIES AND STOCKHOLDERS' EQUITY			
Current liabilities			
Trade accounts payable		US$ 4,720	US$ 4,432
Notes payable		4,180	4,589
Accrued payroll		1,350	715
Accrued payroll tax		120	116
Accrued interest and dividends payable		2,050	1,975
Accrued income tax		796	523
Total current liabilities		13,216	12,350
Long-term notes payable		24,120	26,520
Deferred income taxes		738	722
Other long-term payables		830	770
STOCKHOLDERS' EQUITY			
Capital stock (US$1 par value; 5,000,000 shares issued)		5,000	5,000
Capital in excess of par value		3,500	3,500
Retained earnings		13,963	11,929
Total stockholders' equity:		**22,463**	**20,429**
Total liabilities and stockholders' equity		**US$ 61,367**	**US$ 60,791**

See Notes to Financial Statements.

Arabian Hardware Company
Statement of Operations (in thousands)

Year Ended December 31

	2012	2011	2010
Net sales	US$143,086	US$131,226	US$122,685
Cost of sales	103,241	94,876	88,724
Gross profit	39,845	36,350	33,961
Selling, general and administrative expenses	32,475	29,656	28,437
Operating income	7,370	6,694	5,524
Other income and expense			
Interest expense	2,409	2,035	2,173
Gain on sale of assets	(720)	—	—
Total other income/expense (net)	1,689	2,035	2,173
Earnings before income taxes	5,681	4,659	3,351
Provision for income taxes	1,747	1,465	1,072
Net income	US$ 3,934	US$ 3,194	US$ 2,279
Earnings per share	US$ 0.79	US$ 0.64	US$ 0.46

See Notes to Financial Statements.

Arabian Hardware Company
Statement of Stockholders' Equity (in thousands)

	Common Stock		Paid-in Capital	Retained Earnings	Total Stockholders' Equity
	Shares	Par value			
Balance as of December 31, 2009	5,000	US$ 5,000	US$ 3,500	US$ 10,256	US$ 18,756
Net income				2,279	2,279
Dividends paid				(1,900)	(1,900)
Balance as of December 31, 2010	5,000	US$ 5,000	US$ 3,500	US$ 10,635	US$ 19,135
Net income				3,194	3,194
Dividends paid				(1,900)	(1,900)
Balance as of December 31, 2011	5,000	US$ 5,000	US$ 3,500	US$ 11,929	US$ 20,429
Net income				3,934	3,934
Dividends paid				(1,900)	(1,900)
Balance as of December 31, 2012	5,000	US$ 5,000	US$ 3,500	US$ 13,963	US$ 22,463

See Notes to Financial Statements.

Cash Flows

Arabian Hardware Company
Statement of Cash Flows (in thousands)

	Year Ended December 31		
OPERATING ACTIVITIES	**2012**	**2011**	**2010**
Net income	US$ 3,934	US$ 3,194	US$ 2,279
Adjustments to reconcile net income to net cash provided by (used in) operating activities:			
Depreciation and amortization	1,452	1,443	1,505
(Gain) or Loss on sale of assets	(720)	–	–
Deferred income taxes increase (decrease)	16	(8)	43
Changes in assets and liabilities:			
Trade and other receivables	(2,777)	(393)	(918)
Merchandise inventory	1,735	(295)	(430)
Prepaid expenses	(5)	(27)	(55)
Accounts payable	288	132	76
Accrued liabilities	714	77	142
Income taxes payable	273	23	13
Net cash provided by operating activities	4,910	4,146	2,655
INVESTING ACTIVITIES			
Capital expenditures	(10,500)	(1,800)	(2,292)
Sale of equipment	10,324	–	–
Net cash used in investing activities	(176)	(1,800)	(2,292)
FINANCING ACTIVITIES			
Dividend payment	(1,900)	(1,900)	(1,900)
Proceeds (repayments) from borrowings (net)	(2,749)	(423)	1,602
Net cash used in financing activities	(4,649)	(2,323)	(298)
Net increase in cash and cash equivalents	85	23	65
Cash and cash equivalents at beginning of year	743	720	655
Cash and cash equivalents at end of year	US$ 828	US$ 743	US$ 720

See Notes to Financial Statements.

1. Description of Significant Accounting Policies and Business

We are a wholesale distributor of high-quality power tools, hand tools, electrical equipment, landscaping equipment, residential and commercial construction equipment, and paint products. The majority of our customers are smaller, independent hardware stores located in Saudi Arabia, the U.A.E., Egypt, and Lebanon.

Allowance for Doubtful Accounts: Our allowance for doubtful accounts is maintained to account for expected credit losses. Estimates of bad debts are based on individual customer risks and historical collection trends. Allowances are evaluated and updated when conditions occur that give rise to collection issues.

Merchandise Inventory: Merchandise inventory is presented at the lower of average cost or market. To present accurately the estimated net realizable value of the accounts, we adjust inventory balances when current and expected future market conditions, as well as recent and historical turnover trends, indicate adjustments are necessary.

Property, Plant and Equipment: Land, buildings, computers and other equipment, and furniture and fixtures are stated at historical cost. Depreciation is calculated on a straight-line basis over estimated useful lives of the assets. Estimated useful lives are 20 to 35 years for buildings and 2 to 10 years for equipment and furniture and fixtures.

Revenue Recognition: Revenues are recognized when goods are shipped, title has passed, the sales price is fixed, and collectibility is reasonably assured. A sales returns and allowance account is maintained to reflect estimated future returns and allowances. Adjustments to the sales returns and allowance account are made in the same period as the related sales are recorded and are based on historical trends, as well as analyses of other relevant factors. Sales are recorded net of returns and allowances in the statements referred to in this report.

Income Taxes: The deferred income tax account includes temporary differences between book (financial accounting) income and taxable income (for IRS reporting purposes). The account consists largely of temporary differences related to (1) the valuation of inventory, (2) depreciation, and (3) other accruals.

2. Other Receivables

The other receivables balance consists largely of vendor allowances and vendor rebates. When vendor allowances and vendor rebates are recognized (all activities required by the supplier are completed, the amount is determinable, and collectibility is reasonably certain), they are recorded as reductions of costs of goods sold.

3. Notes Payable

Notes payable for the year ended December 31, 2012, consists of three notes payable to the bank. Each note carries a fixed interest rate of 8.5%. One note for US$4,180,000 matures in June 2013 and the other two mature on December 31, 2015. During 2012, there was an additional note outstanding in the amount of US$4,400,000, which was paid off during October 2012.

4. Commitments

The Company is currently committed to an operating lease that expires in 2016. Rental payments for the remainder of the contract are set at US$312,000 per annum.

5. Segment Reporting

The Company operates in one segment. The breakdown of revenues (in thousands) from different products is listed in the chart below:

SEGMENT REPORTING

	2012	2011	2010
Power Tools	US$ 31,479	US$ 27,557	US$ 26,991
Hand Tools	21,463	19,684	18,403
Landscaping Equipment	14,309	15,645	13,494
Electrical Goods	17,170	15,849	11,042
Residential Construction Equipment	21,463	18,372	15,949
Commercial Construction Equipment	11,447	10,498	9,815
Paint Products	25,755	23,621	26,991
	US$143,086	**US$131,226**	**US$122,685**

6. Earnings Per Share

Earnings per share calculations for 2012, 2011, and 2010 were computed as follows:

Numerators
(net income in thousands): US$3,934, US$3,194, and US$2,279

Denominators
(shares of common stock): 5,000,000
(unchanged for all years)

Diluted earnings per share was the same as basic earnings per share for all years.

Management's Discussion and Analysis of Financial Condition and Results of Operations

The following discussion and analysis of the results of our operations and our financial condition are based on the financial statements and related notes included in this report. When preparing the financial statements, we are frequently required to use our best estimates and judgments. These estimates and judgments affect certain asset, liability, revenue, and expense account balances. Therefore, estimates are evaluated constantly based on our analyses of historical trends and our understanding of the general business environment in which we operate. There are times, however, when different circumstances and assumptions cause actual results to differ from those expected when judgments were originally made. The accounting policies referred to in Note 1 to the financial statements, in our opinion, influence the judgments and estimates we use to prepare our financial statements.

Results of Operations

For the year ended December 31, 2012, gross profit increased by 9.6% or US$3,495,000 from 2011. This increase in gross profit more than offsets the increase in operating expenses from 2011 to 2012 of US$2,819,000 or 9.5%. The increase in gross margin largely explains the operating income increase of $676,000.

For the year ended December 31, 2011, gross profit increased by US$2,389,000 or 7% from 2010. Total operating expenses increased by US$1,219,000 or approximately 4.3% from 2010. The increase in gross profit offset the total operating expense increase, and the net result was a US$1,170,000 increase in operating income.

Net Sales: From 2011 to 2012 net sales increased by US$11,860,000 or 9%. The increase in net sales can be explained largely by an aggressive advertising campaign that the Company organized during the second half of 2012. Net sales for 2011 increased by US$8,541,000 or 7.0% from 2010, which is consistent with industrywide average revenue growth of 7% from 2010 to 2011.

Gross Profit: Gross profit as a percentage of net sales stayed relatively stable at 27.68% and 27.70% in 2010 and 2011, respectively, but increased to 27.85% in 2012. The 2012 increase is mostly due to improved vendor incentive programs, our focus on cost containment, and increases in the resale values of certain commodities such as PVC piping material and certain types of metal wiring. While gross profit percentages in the industry have declined somewhat, our position as a niche provider in the overall hardware market allows us to charge premium prices without losing customers.

Selling, General and Administrative Expenses: Selling expenses increased by US$1,911,000 or 14.8% from 2011 to 2012 and by US$805,000 or 6.7% from 2010 to 2011. As a percentage of net sales, selling expenses increased by 0.52% since 2011 and decreased by 0.03% from 2010 to 2011. The increase in selling expenses as a percentage of net sales from 2011 to 2012 is due to our new advertising campaign and increased expenditures on sales meetings and training.

General and administrative expenses increased by US$908,000 or 5.4% from 2011 to 2012 and by US$414,000 or 2.5% from 2010 to 2011. As a percentage of net sales, general and administrative expenses decreased by 0.42% since 2011 and decreased by 0.55% from 2010 to 2011. The overall increase from 2011 to 2012 was caused mostly by unexpected repairs needed to reattach and replace damaged shelving units in our main warehouse building.

Interest Expense: In 2012, interest expense increased by $374,000, or approximately 18.4%, compared to 2011. The increase was due to an overall interest rate increase and the restructuring of debt covenants that are less restrictive but demand higher interest rates. In 2011 interest expense decreased by US$138,000 or 6.4% compared to 2010. The 2011 decrease was mainly due to the Company's decision to decrease the level of long-term debt. The average interest rates on short- and long-term debt during 2012 were approximately 10.5% and 8.5% respectively.

Liquidity

During 2012, our working capital requirements were primarily financed through our line of credit, under which we are permitted to borrow up to the lesser of US$7,000,000 or 75% of accounts receivable outstanding less than 30 days. The average interest rate on these short-term borrowings in 2012 was approximately 10.5%.

Cash provided by operating activities for 2012 and 2011 was US$4,910,000 and US$4,146,000 respectively. The change from 2011 to 2012 is primarily due to the increase in net income. Increases in receivables were largely offset by decreases in inventories and increases in payables and other current liabilities. The increase in cash provided from operating activities of US$1,491,000 from 2010 to 2011 is largely the result of the increase in net income and smaller increases in receivables and merchandise inventory in 2011 compared to 2010. We believe that cash flow from operations and the available short-term line of credit will continue to allow us to finance operations throughout the current year.

Statement of Condition

Merchandise inventory and trade accounts receivable together accounted for over 95% of current assets in both 2012 and 2011. Merchandise inventory turned over approximately 3.4 times in 2012 and 3.0 times in 2011. Average days to sell inventory were 108.6 and 120.9 in 2012 and 2011 respectively. Net trade receivables turned over approximately 7.6 times in 2012 and in 2011. Days to collect accounts receivable computations were 48.1 and 48.0 in 2012 and 2011 respectively. Both inventory and accounts receivable turnover are lower than industry averages. We plan for this difference to satisfy the market in which we operate. Our market consists of smaller, independent hardware stores that need more favorable receivable collection terms and immediate delivery of inventory. Because we hold large amounts of inventory, we are able to fill orders quicker than most of our competitors even during the busiest times of the year.

Outlook

During 2012 we experienced another year of noticeable improvement, despite the economic downturn. The Company's financial performance can largely be attributed to (1) a continued focus on cost containment, (2) productivity improvements, (3) aggressive advertising, and (4) the implementation of programs designed to enhance customer satisfaction.

During 2013, we will continue to apply the same strategic efforts that improved 2012 performance. We are also implementing a new warehouse information system designed to increase productivity and reduce stocking and distribution costs. Management believes that earnings growth will be primarily driven by (1) continued focus on customer satisfaction, (2) penetration into markets currently dominated by national wholesale hardware store chains, and (3) the use of technology to attract additional customers and promote more efficient operations.

Information Concerning Forward-Looking Statements

This report contains certain forward-looking statements (referenced by such terms as "expects" or "believes") that are subject to the effects of various factors including (1) changes in wholesale hardware prices, (2) changes in the general business environment, (3) the intensity of the competitive arena, (4) new national wholesale hardware chain openings, and (5) certain other matters influencing the Company's ability to react to changing market conditions. Therefore, management wishes to make readers aware that the aforementioned factors could cause the actual results of our operations to differ considerably from those indicated by any forward-looking statements included in this report.

Arabian Hardware Company
Summary of Financial Statements (in thousands)

BALANCE SHEET DATA:	2012	2011	2010	2009	2008
Current assets	US$ 51,027	US$ 49,895	US$ 49,157	US$ 47,689	US$ 46,504
Total assets	61,367	60,791	59,696	57,441	51,580
Current liabilities	13,216	12,350	12,173	12,166	9,628
Long-term notes payable	24,120	26,520	26,938	25,432	25,223
Total stockholders' equity	22,463	20,429	19,135	18,756	15,764

INCOME STATEMENT DATA:	2012	2011	2010	2009	2008
Net sales	US$ 143,086	US$ 131,226	US$ 122,685	US$ 120,221	US$ 117,115
Cost of sales	103,241	94,876	88,724	88,112	85,663
Gross profit	39,845	36,350	33,961	32,109	31,452
Earnings before income taxes	5,681	4,659	3,351	3,124	1,450
Net income	3,934	3,194	2,279	2,142	994
Cash provided by operating activities	4,910	4,146	2,655	1,811	1,232
Per common share data:					
Net income	US$ 0.79	US$ 0.64	US$ 0.46	US$ 0.43	US$ 0.22
Cash dividends per share	US$ 0.38	US$ 0.38	US$ 0.38	US$ —	US$ —
Common shares outstanding	5,000	5,000	5,000	5,000	4,500

KEY OPERATING RESULTS AND FINANCIAL POSITION RATIOS:	2012	2011	2010	2009	2008
Gross profit (%)	27.85%	27.70%	27.68%	26.71%	26.86%
Return on assets (%)	9.30%	7.73%	5.72%	5.73%	2.86%
Return on common equity (%)	26.49%	23.55%	17.69%	18.10%	9.50%

FIGURE 6-5	Arabian Hardware Co. Adjusted Trial Balance

ARABIAN HARDWARE CO.
TRIAL BALANCE
December 31, 2012

		Debit	Credit
S,A,P,C	Cash in bank	US$ 827,568	
S	Trade accounts receivable	20,196,800	
S	Allowance for uncollectible accounts		US$ 1,240,000
S	Other accounts receivable	945,020	
A,I	Inventories	29,864,621	
A	Prepaid expenses	431,558	
A	Land	3,456,420	
A	Buildings	32,500,000	
A	Computer and other equipment	3,758,347	
A	Furniture and fixtures	2,546,421	
A	Accumulated depreciation		31,920,126
A	Trade accounts payable		4,719,989
C	Notes payable		4,179,620
P	Accrued payroll		1,349,800
P	Accrued payroll taxes		119,663
C	Accrued interest		149,560
C	Dividends payable		1,900,000
A	Accrued income tax		795,442
C	Long-term notes payable		24,120,000
A	Deferred tax		738,240
A	Other accrued payables		829,989
C	Capital stock		5,000,000
C	Capital in excess of par value		3,500,000
C	Retained earnings		11,929,075
S	Sales		144,327,789
S	Sales returns and allowances	1,241,663	
I	Cost of goods sold	103,240,768	
P	Salaries and commissions	7,738,900	
P	Sales payroll taxes	1,422,100	
A	Travel and entertainment—selling	1,110,347	
A	Advertising	2,611,263	
A	Sales and promotional literature	321,620	
A	Sales meetings and training	924,480	
A	Miscellaneous sales expense	681,041	
P	Executive and office salaries	5,523,960	
P	Administrative payroll taxes	682,315	
A	Travel and entertainment—administrative	561,680	
A	Computer maintenance and supplies	860,260	
A	Stationery and supplies	762,568	
A	Postage	244,420	
A	Telephone and fax	722,315	
A	Rent	312,140	
A	Legal fees and retainers	383,060	
A	Auditing and related services	302,840	
A	Depreciation	1,452,080	
S	Bad debt expense	3,323,084	
A	Insurance	722,684	
A	Office repairs and maintenance	843,926	
A	Miscellaneous office expense	643,680	
A	Miscellaneous general expense	323,842	
A	Gain on sale of assets		719,740
A	Income taxes	1,746,600	
C	Interest expense	2,408,642	
C	Dividends	1,900,000	
		US$237,539,033	US$237,539,033

Note: The letters in the left-hand column refer to the following transaction cycles:
S = Sales and collection; I = Inventory and warehousing; A = Acquisition and payment; C = Capital acquisition and repayment; P = Payroll and personnel.

- The capital acquisition and repayment cycle is closely related to the acquisition and payment cycle. Transactions in the acquisition and payment cycle include the purchase of inventory, supplies, and other goods and services related to operations. Transactions in the capital acquisition and repayment cycle are related to financing the business, such as issuing stock or debt, paying dividends, and repaying debt.

Although the same journals are used for transactions in the acquisition and payment and capital acquisition and repayment cycles, it is useful to separate capital acquisition and repayment cycle transactions into a separate transaction cycle. First, capital acquisitions and repayments relate to financing the business, rather than operations. Second,

TABLE 6-1	Cycles Applied to Arabian Hardware Co.		
		General Ledger Accounts Included in the Cycle (See Figure 6-5)	
Cycle	Journals Included in the Cycle (See Figure 6-4)	Balance Sheet	Income Statement
Sales and collection	Sales journal Cash receipts journal General journal	Cash in bank Trade accounts receivable Other accounts receivable Allowance for uncollectible accounts	Sales Sales returns and allowances Bad debt expense
Acquisition and payment	Acquisitions journal Cash disbursements journal General journal	Cash in bank Inventories Prepaid expenses Land Buildings Computer and other equipment Furniture and fixtures Accumulated depreciation Trade accounts payable Other accrued payables Accrued income tax Deferred tax	Advertising[S] Travel and entertainment[S] Sales meetings and training[S] Sales and promotional literature[S] Miscellaneous sales expense[S] Travel and entertainment[A] Stationery and supplies[A] Postage[A] Telephone and fax[A] Computer maintenance and supplies[A] Depreciation[A] Rent[A] Legal fees and retainers[A] Auditing and related services[A] Insurance[A] Office repairs and maintenance[A] Miscellaneous office expense[A] Miscellaneous general expense[A] Gain on sale of assets Income taxes
Payroll and personnel	Payroll journal General journal	Cash in bank Accrued payroll Accrued payroll taxes	Salaries and commissions[S] Sales payroll taxes[S] Executive and office salaries[A] Administrative payroll taxes[A]
Inventory and warehousing	Acquisitions journal Sales journal General journal	Inventories	Cost of goods sold
Capital acquisition and repayment	Acquisitions journal Cash disbursements journal General journal	Cash in bank Notes payable Long-term notes payable Accrued interest Capital stock Capital in excess of par value Retained earnings Dividends Dividends payable	Interest expense

S = Selling expense; A = general and administrative expense.

most capital acquisition and repayment cycle accounts involve few transactions, but each is often highly material and therefore should be audited extensively. Considering both reasons, it is more convenient to separate the two cycles.

- The inventory and warehousing cycle is closely related to all other cycles. The cost of inventory includes raw materials (acquisition and payment cycle), direct labor (payroll and personnel cycle), and other overheads (acquisition and payment and payroll and personnel cycles). The provision of services or sale of goods involves the sales (revenues) and collection cycle. Because assets including inventory are material for most manufacturing companies, it is common to borrow money using assets including inventory as security. Inventory is included as a separate cycle both because it is related to other cycles and because for most manufacturing and retail companies inventory is usually highly material, there are unique systems and controls for inventory, and inventory is often complex to audit.

Relationships Among Cycles

Figure 6-6 illustrates the relationships of the five cycles and general cash. Note that cycles have no beginning or end except at the origin and final disposition of a company. A company begins by obtaining capital, usually in the form of cash. In a manufacturing company, cash is used to acquire raw materials, fixed assets, and related goods and services to produce inventory (acquisition and payment cycle). Similarly, in a service company cash is used to acquire fixed assets and related inventory needed to provide the services (acquisition and payment cycle). Cash is also used to acquire labor for the same reason (payroll and personnel cycle). Acquisition and payment, and payroll and personnel are similar in nature, but the functions are sufficiently different to justify separate cycles. The combined result of these two cycles is inventory (inventory and warehousing cycle). At a subsequent point, the inventory is sold or the services are provided and billings and collections result (sales (revenues) and collection cycle). The cash generated is used to pay dividends and interest or finance capital expansion and to start the cycles again. The cycles interrelate in much the same way in a service company, where there will be billings and collections, although there will be no material inventory's balance.

Transaction cycles are an important way to organize audits. For the most part, auditors treat each cycle separately during the audit. Although auditors need to consider the interrelationships between cycles, they typically treat cycles independently as much as possible to manage complex audits effectively.

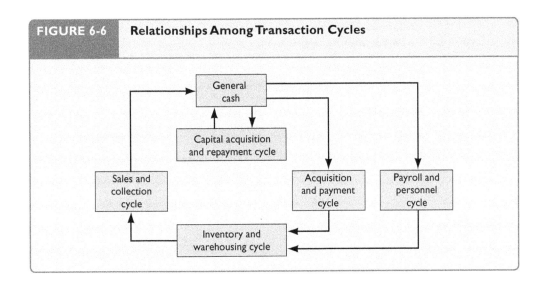

FIGURE 6-6   Relationships Among Transaction Cycles

SETTING AUDIT OBJECTIVES

OBJECTIVE 6-5

Describe why the auditor obtains a combination of assurance by auditing classes of transactions and ending balances in accounts, including presentation and disclosure.

Transaction-related audit objectives

Seven audit objectives that must be met before the auditor can conclude that the total for any given class of transactions is fairly stated; the general transaction-related audit objectives are occurrence, completeness, accuracy, posting and summarization, classification, timing, and rights and obligations.

Balance-related audit objectives

Eight audit objectives that must be met before the auditor can conclude that any given account balance is fairly stated; the general balance-related audit objectives are existence, completeness, accuracy, classification, cutoff, detail tie-in, realizable value, and rights and obligations.

Presentation and disclosure-related audit objectives

Three audit objectives that must be met before the auditor can conclude that presentation and disclosures are fairly stated; the three presentation and disclosure-related audit objectives are completeness, valuation and accuracy, and classification and understandability.

Auditors conduct financial statement audits using the cycle approach by performing audit tests of the transactions making up ending balances and also by performing audit tests of the account balances and related disclosures. Figure 6-7 illustrates this concept by showing the four classes of transactions that determine the ending balance in accounts receivable for Arabian Hardware Company. Assume that the beginning balance of US$17,521,000 was audited in the prior year and is therefore considered fairly stated. If the auditor could be completely sure that each of the four classes of transactions was correctly stated, the auditor could also be sure that the ending balance of US$20,197,000 was correctly stated. But it is almost always impractical for the auditor to obtain complete assurance about the correctness of each class of transactions, resulting in less than complete assurance about the ending balance in accounts receivable. In almost all audits, overall assurance can be increased by also auditing the ending balance of accounts receivable. Auditors have found that, generally, the most efficient and effective way to conduct audits is to *obtain some combination of assurance for each class of transactions and for the ending balance in the related accounts.*

For any given class of transactions, several audit objectives must be met before the auditor can conclude that the transactions are properly recorded. These are called **transaction-related audit objectives** in the remainder of this book. For example, there are specific sales (revenues) transaction-related audit objectives and specific sales returns and allowances transaction-related audit objectives.

Similarly, several audit objectives must be met for each account balance. These are called **balance-related audit objectives**. For example, there are specific accounts receivable balance-related audit objectives and specific accounts payable balance-related audit objectives. We show later in this chapter that the transaction-related and balance-related audit objectives are somewhat different but closely related.

The third category of audit objectives relates to the presentation and disclosure of information in the financial statements. These are called **presentation and disclosure-related audit objectives**. For example, there are specific presentation and disclosure-related audit objectives for accounts receivable and notes payable.

Throughout this text, the term *audit objectives* refers to transaction-related, balance-related, and presentation and disclosure-related audit objectives. Before examining audit objectives in more detail, we first deal with management assertions.

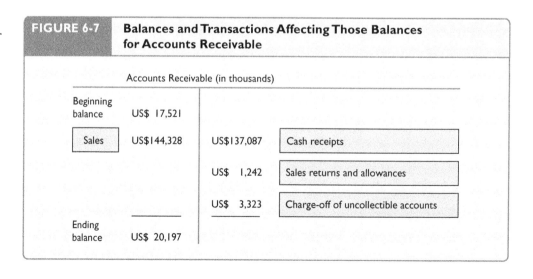

FIGURE 6-7   Balances and Transactions Affecting Those Balances for Accounts Receivable

MANAGEMENT ASSERTIONS

Management assertions are implied or expressed representations by management about classes of transactions and the related accounts and disclosures in the financial statements. In most cases they are implied. Examine Figure 6-5 on page 171. Management of Arabian Hardware Co. asserts that cash of US$827,568 was present in the company's bank accounts as of the balance sheet date. Unless otherwise disclosed in the financial statements, management also asserts that the cash was unrestricted and available for normal use. Management also asserts that all required disclosures related to cash are accurate and are understandable. This requires the proper presentation of cash in the balance sheet, cash flow statements, and footnotes. Similar assertions exist for each asset, liability, owners' equity, revenue, and expense item in the financial statements. These assertions apply to classes of transactions, account balances, and presentation and disclosures.

Management assertions are directly related to accounting standards as they are part of the *criteria that management uses to record and disclose accounting information in financial statements*. The definition of auditing in Chapter 1, in part, states that auditing is a comparison of information (financial statements) to established criteria (assertions established according to GAAP, IFRS or local accounting standards). Auditors must therefore understand the assertions to do adequate audits.

Assertions may be classified into three categories:

1. Assertions about classes of transactions and events for the period under audit
2. Assertions about account balances at period end
3. Assertions about presentation and disclosure.

The specific assertions included in each category are included in Table 6-2. The assertions are grouped so that assertions related across categories of assertions are included on the same table row.

> **OBJECTIVE 6-6**
>
> Distinguish among the three categories of management assertions about financial information.

Management assertions

Implied or expressed representations by management about classes of transactions, related account balances, and presentation and disclosures in the financial statements.

TABLE 6-2	**Management Assertions for Each Category of Assertions**	
Assertions About Classes of Transactions and Events	**Assertions About Account Balances**	**Assertions About Presentation and Disclosure**
Occurrence—Transactions and events that have been recorded have occurred and pertain to the entity.	*Existence*—Assets, liabilities, and equity interests exist.	
Completeness—All transactions and events that should have been recorded have been recorded.	*Completeness*—All assets, liabilities, and equity interests that should have been recorded have been recorded.	*Completeness*—All disclosures that should have been included in the financial statements have been included.
Accuracy—Amounts and other data relating to recorded transactions and events have been recorded appropriately.	*Valuation and allocation*—Assets, liabilities, and equity interests are included in the financial statements at appropriate amounts and any resulting valuation adjustments are appropriately recorded.	*Accuracy and valuation*—Financial and other information are disclosed appropriately and at appropriate amounts.
Classification—Transactions and events have been recorded in the proper accounts.		*Classification and understandability*—Financial and other information is appropriately presented and described and disclosures are clearly expressed.
Cutoff—Transactions and events have been recorded in the correct accounting period.		
Rights and obligations—The entity has title (i.e. ownership) of individual assets and obligations are actual for specific transactions.	*Rights and obligations*—The entity holds or controls the rights to assets and liabilities are the actual obligation of the entity.	

Assertions About Classes of Transactions and Events

Management makes several assertions about transactions. These assertions also apply to other events that are reflected in the accounting records, such as recording depreciation and recognizing pension obligations.

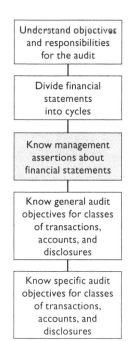

Understand objectives and responsibilities for the audit

Divide financial statements into cycles

Know management assertions about financial statements

Know general audit objectives for classes of transactions, accounts, and disclosures

Know specific audit objectives for classes of transactions, accounts, and disclosures

Occurrence The occurrence assertion concerns whether recorded transactions included in the financial statements actually occurred during the accounting period. For example, management asserts that recorded sales transactions represent exchanges of goods or services that actually took place.

Completeness This assertion addresses whether all transactions that should be included in the financial statements are in fact included. For example, management asserts that all sales of goods and services are recorded and included in the financial statements.

The completeness assertion addresses matters opposite from the occurrence assertion. The completeness assertion is concerned with the possibility of omitting transactions that should have been recorded, whereas the occurrence assertion is concerned with inclusion of transactions that should not have been recorded. Thus, violations of the occurrence assertion relate to account overstatements, whereas violations of the completeness assertion relate to account understatements. The recording of a sale that did not take place is a violation of the occurrence assertion, whereas the failure to record a sale that did occur is a violation of the completeness assertion.

Accuracy The accuracy assertion addresses whether transactions have been recorded at correct amounts. Using the wrong price to record a sales transaction and an error in calculating the extensions of price times quantity are examples of violations of the accuracy assertion.

Classification The classification assertion addresses whether transactions are recorded in the appropriate accounts. Recording administrative salaries in cost of sales is one example of a violation of the classification assertion.

Cutoff The cutoff assertion addresses whether transactions are recorded in the proper accounting period. Auditors must ensure that transactions occurring near the end of the financial period are recorded in the proper period. Recording a sales transaction in December when the goods were not shipped until January violates the cutoff assertion.

Rights and Obligations This assertion addresses whether the company has rights of title (i.e. ownership) of the asset and whether liabilities are the actual obligations of the entity at a given date. For example, management asserts that assets are owned by the company or that amounts capitalized for leases in the balance sheet represent the cost of the entity's rights to leased property and that the corresponding lease's liability represents an obligation of the entity.

Auditors should understand and test how internal control affects assertions included in the financial statements. Authorization of transactions is an important aspect of the design and effectiveness of the company's internal control that may relate to a number of financial statement assertions such as occurrence, completeness, and accuracy.

Assertions About Account Balances

Assertions about account balances at year-end address existence, completeness, valuation and allocation, and rights and obligations.

Existence The existence assertion deals with whether assets, liabilities, and equity interests included in the balance sheet actually existed on the balance sheet date. For example, management asserts that merchandise inventory included in the balance sheet exists and is available for sale at the balance sheet date.

Completeness This assertion addresses whether all accounts and amounts that should be presented in the financial statements are in fact included. For example, management asserts that notes payable in the balance sheet include all such obligations of the entity.

The completeness assertion addresses matters opposite from the existence assertion. Inclusion of a receivable for a customer that does not exist violates the existence assertion, whereas the failure to include a receivable from a customer violates the completeness assertion.

Valuation and Allocation The valuation and allocation assertion deals with whether assets, liabilities, and equity interests have been included in the financial statements at appropriate amounts, including any valuation adjustments to reflect asset amounts at net realizable value. For example, management asserts that property is recorded at historical cost and that such cost is systematically allocated to appropriate accounting periods through depreciation. Similarly, management asserts that trade accounts receivable included in the balance sheet are stated at net realizable value.

Rights and Obligations This assertion addresses whether assets are the rights of the entity and whether liabilities are the obligations of the entity at a given date. For example, management asserts that assets are owned by the company or that amounts capitalized for leases in the balance sheet represent the cost of the entity's rights to leased property and that the corresponding lease liability represents an obligation of the entity.

Assertions About Presentation and Disclosure

With increases in the complexity of transactions and the need for expanded disclosures about these transactions, assertions about presentation and disclosure have increased in importance. These assertions include completeness, accuracy and valuation, and classification and understandability.

Completeness This assertion deals with whether all required disclosures have been included in the financial statements. As an example, management asserts that all material transactions with related parties have been disclosed in the financial statements.

Accuracy and Valuation The accuracy and valuation assertion deals with whether financial information is disclosed fairly and at appropriate amounts. Management's disclosure of the amount of unfunded pension obligations and the assumptions underlying these amounts is an example of this assertion.

Classification and Understandability This assertion relates to whether amounts are appropriately classified in the financial statements and footnotes, and whether the balance descriptions and related disclosures are understandable. For example, management asserts that the classification of inventories as finished goods, work-in-process, and raw materials is appropriate, and the disclosures of the methods used to value inventories are understandable.

Auditors may use different terms to express the management assertions as long as all the aspects included in Table 6-2 are addressed. The auditor should consider the relevance of each assertion for each significant class of transactions, account balance, and presentation and disclosure. **Relevant assertions** have a meaningful bearing on whether the account is fairly stated and are used to assess the risk of material misstatement and the design and performance of audit procedures. For example, valuation is likely to be a relevant assertion for accounts receivable, but not for cash. After the relevant assertions have been identified, the auditor can then develop audit objectives for each category of assertions.

Relevant assertions

Assertions that have a meaningful bearing on whether an account is fairly stated and used to assess the risk of material misstatement and the design and performance of audit procedures.

TRANSACTION-RELATED AUDIT OBJECTIVES

The auditor's transaction-related audit objectives follow and are closely related to management assertions. That is not surprising because the auditor's primary responsibility is to determine whether management assertions about financial statements are justified.

These transaction-related audit objectives are intended to provide a *framework* to help the auditor accumulate sufficient appropriate evidence and decide the proper evidence to accumulate for classes of transactions given the circumstances of the engagement. The objectives remain the same from audit to audit, but the evidence varies, depending on the circumstances.

There is a difference between general transaction-related audit objectives and specific transaction-related audit objectives for each class of transactions. The seven general transaction-related audit objectives discussed here are applicable to every class of transactions and are stated in broad terms. Specific transaction-related audit objectives are also applied to each class of transactions but are stated in terms tailored to a specific class of transactions, such as sales transactions. Once the auditor establishes general transaction-related audit objectives, they can be used to develop specific transaction-related audit objectives for each class of transactions being audited.

General Transaction-Related Audit Objectives

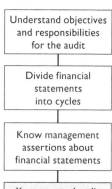

Understand objectives and responsibilities for the audit

Divide financial statements into cycles

Know management assertions about financial statements

Know general audit objectives for classes of transactions, accounts, and disclosures

Know specific audit objectives for classes of transactions, accounts, and disclosures

Occurrence—Recorded Transactions Exist This objective deals with whether recorded transactions have actually occurred. Inclusion of a sale in the sales journal when no sale occurred violates the occurrence objective. This objective is the auditor's counterpart to the management assertion of occurrence for classes of transactions.

Completeness—Existing Transactions are Recorded This objective deals with whether all transactions that should be included in the journals have actually been included. Failure to include a sale in the sales journal and general ledger when a sale occurred violates the completeness objective. This objective is the counterpart to the management assertion of completeness for classes of transactions.

The occurrence and completeness objectives emphasize opposite audit concerns. Occurrence deals with potential overstatement; completeness with unrecorded transactions (understatement).

Accuracy—Recorded Transactions are Stated at the Correct Amounts This objective addresses the accuracy of information for accounting transactions and is one part of the accuracy assertion for classes of transactions. For sales transactions, this objective is violated if the quantity of goods shipped was different from the quantity billed, the wrong selling price was used for billing, extension or adding errors occurred in billing, or the wrong amount was included in the sales journal.

It is important to distinguish between accuracy and occurrence or completeness. For example, if a recorded sales transaction should not have been recorded because the shipment was on consignment, the occurrence objective has been violated, even if the amount of the invoice was accurately calculated. If the recorded sale was for a valid shipment but the amount was calculated incorrectly, there is a violation of the accuracy objective but not of occurrence. The same relationship exists between completeness and accuracy.

Posting and Summarization—Recorded Transactions are Properly Included in the Master Files and are Correctly Summarized This objective deals with the accuracy of the transfer of information from recorded transactions in journals to subsidiary records and the general ledger. It is part of the accuracy assertion for classes of transactions. For example, if a sales transaction is recorded in the wrong customer's record or at the wrong amount in the master file or the sum of all sales transactions posted from the sales journal to the general ledger is inaccurate, this objective is violated. Because the posting of transactions from journals to subsidiary records, the general ledger, and other related master files is typically accomplished automatically by computerized accounting systems, the risk of random human error in posting is minimal. Once the auditor can establish that the computer is functioning properly, there is a reduced concern about posting process errors.

Classification—Transactions Included in the Client's Journals are Properly Classified This objective addresses whether transactions are included in the appropriate accounts, and is the auditor's counterpart to management's classification assertion for classes of transactions. Examples of misclassifications for sales are including cash sales as credit sales, recording a sale of operating fixed assets as revenue, and misclassifying commercial sales as residential sales, and normal maintenance expense for machinery as capitalized expense to be added to machinery account.

Timing—Transactions are Recorded on the Correct Dates The timing objective for transactions is the auditor's counterpart to management's cutoff assertion. A timing error occurs if a transaction is not recorded on the day it took place. A sales transaction, for example, should be recorded on the date of shipment.

Rights and Obligations Auditors must check that assets are owned before it is acceptable to include them in the financial statements. Similarly, liabilities must belong to the entity. Rights are always associated with assets and obligations with liabilities. Auditors are required to examine purchase invoices or contracts to ensure that the company owns equipment and machinery. At the same time suppliers' invoices and materials receiving reports would provide evidence that there is an obligation to pay the value of such materials delivered to the company.

Specific Transaction-Related Audit Objectives After the general transaction-related audit objectives are determined, specific transaction-related audit objectives for each material class of transactions can be developed. Such classes of transactions typically include sales or revenues, cash receipts, acquisitions of goods and services, payroll, and so on. At least one specific transaction-related audit objective should be included for each general transaction-related audit objective unless the auditor believes that the general transaction-related audit objective is not relevant or is unimportant in the circumstances.

Relationships Among Management Assertions and Transaction-Related Audit Objectives

Table 6-3 illustrates the relationships among management assertions, the general transaction-related audit objectives, and specific transaction-related audit objectives as applied to sales (revenues) for Arabian Hardware Company. Notice that there is a one-to-one relationship between assertions and objectives, except for the accuracy assertion. The accuracy assertion has two objectives because of the need to provide auditors with guidance in testing transaction accuracy.

TABLE 6-3	Arabian Hardware Co.: Management Assertions and Transaction-Related Audit Objectives Applied to Sales Transactions	

Management Assertions About Classes of Transactions and Events	General Transaction-Related Audit Objectives	Specific Sales Transaction-Related Audit Objectives
Completeness	Completeness	Existing sales transactions are recorded.
Accuracy	Accuracy	Recorded sales are for the amount of goods shipped and are correctly billed and recorded.
	Posting and summarization	Sales transactions are properly included in the master file and are correctly summarized.
Classification	Classification	Sales transactions are properly classified.
Cutoff	Timing	Sales transactions are recorded on the correct dates.
Occurrence	Occurrence	Sales transactions actually took place.
Rights and obligations	Rights and obligations	Entity has rights for sales transactions recorded.

BALANCE-RELATED AUDIT OBJECTIVES

OBJECTIVE 6-8

Link the eight general balance-related audit objectives to management assertions for account balances.

Balance-related audit objectives are similar to the transaction-related audit objectives just discussed. They also follow from management assertions and they provide a framework to help the auditor accumulate sufficient appropriate evidence related to account balances. There are also both general and specific balance-related audit objectives.

There are two differences between balance-related and transaction-related audit objectives. First, as the terms imply, balance-related audit objectives are applied to account balances such as accounts receivable and inventory rather than classes of transactions such as sales transactions and purchases of inventory. Second, there are eight balance-related audit objectives compared to seven transaction-related audit objectives.

Because of the way audits are performed, balance-related audit objectives are almost *always* applied to the ending balance in balance sheet accounts, such as accounts receivable, inventory, and notes payable. However, some balance-related audit objectives are applied to certain income statement accounts. These usually involve non-routine transactions and unpredictable expenses, such as legal expense or repairs and maintenance. Other income statement accounts are closely related to balance sheet accounts and are tested simultaneously, such as depreciation expense with accumulated depreciation and interest expense with notes payable.

When using the balance-related audit objectives to audit account balances, the auditor accumulates evidence to verify detail that supports the account balance, rather than verifying the account balance itself. For example, in auditing accounts receivable, the auditor obtains a listing of the accounts receivable master file that agrees to the general ledger balance. The accounts receivable balance-related audit objectives are applied to the customer accounts in that listing.

General Balance-Related Audit Objectives

Throughout the following discussion of the eight balance-related audit objectives, we make references to a supporting schedule, by which we mean a client-provided schedule or electronic file, such as the list of accounts receivable just discussed.

Existence—Amounts Included Exist This objective deals with whether the amounts included in the financial statements should actually be included. For example, inclusion of an account receivable from a customer in the accounts receivable trial balance when there is no receivable from that customer violates the existence objective. This objective is the auditor's counterpart to the management assertion of existence for account balances.

Completeness—Existing Amounts are Included This objective deals with whether all amounts that should be included have actually been included. Failure to include an account receivable from a customer in the accounts receivable trial balance when a receivable exists violates the completeness objective. This objective is the counterpart to the management assertion of completeness for account balances.

The existence and completeness objectives emphasize opposite audit concerns. Existence deals with potential overstatement; completeness deals with unrecorded amounts (understatement).

Accuracy—Amounts Included are Stated at the Correct Amounts The accuracy objective refers to amounts being included at the correct arithmetic amount. An inventory item on a client's inventory listing can be wrong because the number of units of inventory on hand was misstated, the unit price was wrong, or the total was incorrectly extended. Each of these violates the accuracy objective. Accuracy is one part of the management's valuation and allocation assertion for account balances.

Classification—Amounts Included in the Client's Listing are Properly Classified Classification involves determining whether items included on a client's listing are included in the correct general ledger accounts. For example, on the accounts receivable listing, receivables must be separated into short-term and long-term, and amounts due from affiliates, officers, and directors must be classified separately from amounts due from customers. Classification is also part of the valuation and allocation assertion. The classification balance-related audit objective is closely related to the presentation and disclosure-related audit objectives, but relates to how balances are classified in general ledger accounts so they can be appropriately presented and disclosed in the financial statements.

Cutoff—Transactions Near the Balance Sheet Date are Recorded in the Proper Period In testing for cutoff of account balances, the auditor's objective is to determine whether transactions are recorded and included in account balances in the proper period. An account balance is likely to be misstated by those transactions recorded near the end of the accounting period. For an annual audit this is as of the balance sheet date. Cutoff tests can be thought of as a part of verifying either the balance sheet accounts or the related transactions as they include testing transactions at the balance sheet date and after that date to confirm the accuracy of the end of the year balance. For this reason, we also include cutoff as a balance-related audit objective related to the valuation and allocation assertion for account balances. The timing objective for transactions deals with the proper timing of recording transactions throughout the year, whereas the cutoff objective for balance-related audit objectives relates only to transactions near year-end. For example, in a December 31 year-end audit, a sales transaction recorded in March for a February shipment is a transaction-related audit objective error, but not a balance-related audit objective error.

Detail Tie-in—Details in the Account Balance Agree with Related Master File Amounts, Foot to the Total in the Account Balance, and Agree with the Total in the General Ledger Account balances on financial statements are supported by details in master files and schedules prepared by clients. The detail tie-in objective is concerned that the details on lists are accurately prepared, correctly added, and agree with the general ledger. For example, individual accounts receivable on a listing of accounts receivable should be the same in the accounts receivable master file, and the total should equal the general ledger control account. Detail tie-in is also a part of the valuation and allocation assertion for account balances.

Realizable Value—Assets are Included at the Amounts Estimated to Be Realized This objective concerns whether an account balance has been reduced for declines from historical cost to net realizable value or when accounting standards require fair market value accounting treatment. Examples when the objective applies are considering the adequacy of the allowance for uncollectible accounts receivable and write-downs of inventory for obsolescence. The objective applies only to asset accounts and is also a part of the valuation and allocation assertion for account balances.

Rights and Obligations In addition to existence, most assets must be owned before it is acceptable to include them in the financial statements. Similarly, liabilities must belong to the entity. Rights are always associated with assets and obligations with liabilities. This objective is the auditor's counterpart to the management assertion of rights and obligations for accounts balances.

Specific Balance-Related Audit Objectives

The same as for transaction related-audit objectives, after the general balance-related audit objectives are determined, specific balance-related audit objectives for each account balance on the financial statements can be developed. At least one specific balance-related audit objective should be included for each general balance-related audit objective unless the auditor believes that the general balance-related audit objective is not relevant or is unimportant for the account balance being considered. There may be more than one specific balance-related audit objective for a general balance-related audit objective. For example, specific balance-related audit objectives for rights and obligations of the accounts receivable of Arabian Hardware Co. could include (1) the company has the right to collect all receivables recorded and (2) accounts receivable are not pledged as collateral for a loan unless such fact is disclosed.

Relationships Among Management Assertions and Balance-Related Audit Objectives

Table 6-4 illustrates the relationships among management assertions, the general balance-related audit objectives, and specific balance-related audit objectives as applied to accounts receivable for Arabian Hardware Co. Notice that there is a one-to-one relationship between assertions and objectives, except for the valuation and allocation assertion. The valuation and allocation assertion has multiple objectives because of the complexity of valuation issues and the need to provide auditors with additional guidance for testing valuation.

TABLE 6-4	Arabian Hardware Co.: Management Assertions and Balance-Related Audit Objectives Applied to Accounts Receivable	
Management Assertions About Account Balances	**General Balance-Related Audit Objectives**	**Specific Balance-Related Audit Objectives Applied to Accounts Receivable**
Existence	Existence	All recorded accounts receivables exist at the balance sheet date.
Completeness	Completeness	All existing receivables have been included in the receivable master file.
Valuation and allocation	Accuracy	Receivables details agree with those included in confirmations. Amounts of receivables are materially correct.
	Classification	Receivables are properly classified as short-term and long-term.
	Cutoff	Recording of receivables cutoff at year-end is proper. Sales cutoff at year-end is proper.
	Detail tie-in	Total of receivables items agrees with general ledger.
	Realizable value	Receivables have been written down where net realizable value is impaired.
Rights and obligations	Rights and obligations	The company has rights to all receivables items listed. Receivables are not pledged as collateral.

PRESENTATION AND DISCLOSURE-RELATED AUDIT OBJECTIVES

The presentation and disclosure-related audit objectives are identical to the management assertions for presentation and disclosure discussed previously. The same concepts that apply to balance-related audit objectives apply equally to presentation and disclosure audit objectives. Table 6-5 includes the management assertions about presentation and disclosure, related general presentation and disclosure-related audit objectives, and specific audit objectives for notes payable for Arabian Hardware Co.

OBJECTIVE 6-9

Link the three presentation and disclosure-related audit objectives to management assertions for presentation and disclosure.

TABLE 6-5	Arabian Hardware Co.: Management Assertions and Presentation and Disclosure-Related Audit Objectives Applied to Notes Payable	
Management Assertions About Presentation and Disclosure	General Presentation and Disclosure-Related Audit Objectives	Specific Presentation and Disclosure-Related Audit Objectives Applied to Notes Payable
Completeness	Completeness	All required disclosures related to notes payable are included in the financial statement footnotes.
Valuation and allocation	Valuation and accuracy	Footnote disclosures related to notes payable are accurate.
Classification and understandability	Classification and understandability	Notes payable are appropriately classified as to short-term and long-term obligations and related financial statement disclosures are understandable.

HOW AUDIT OBJECTIVES ARE MET

The auditor must obtain sufficient appropriate audit evidence to support all management assertions in the financial statements. This is done by accumulating evidence in support of some appropriate combination of transaction-related audit objectives and balance-related audit objectives. A comparison of Tables 6-3 and 6-4 illustrates the significant overlap between the transaction-related and balance-related audit objectives. Presentation and disclosure-related audit objectives are closely related to the balance-related audit objectives. Auditors often consider presentation and disclosure audit objectives when addressing the balance-related audit objectives.

The auditor must decide the appropriate audit objectives and the evidence to accumulate to meet those objectives on every audit. To do this, auditors follow an audit process, which is a well-defined methodology for organizing an audit to ensure that the evidence gathered is both sufficient and appropriate and that all required audit objectives are both specified and met. The audit process, as described in this text, has four specific phases, as shown in Figure 6-8. The rest of this chapter provides a brief introduction to each of the four **phases of the audit process**.

OBJECTIVE 6-10

Explain the relationship between audit objectives and the accumulation of audit evidence.

Phases of the audit process

The four aspects of a complete audit: (1) plan and design an audit approach, (2) perform tests of controls and substantive tests of transactions, (3) perform analytical procedures and tests of details of balances, and (4) complete the audit and issue an audit report.

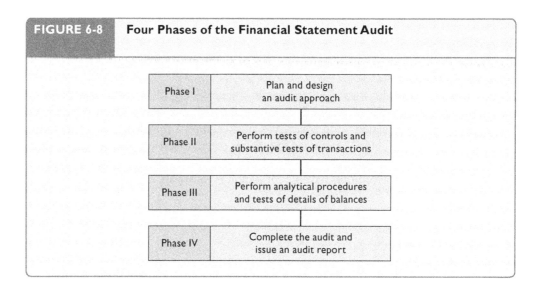

FIGURE 6-8   Four Phases of the Financial Statement Audit

Phase I	Plan and design an audit approach
Phase II	Perform tests of controls and substantive tests of transactions
Phase III	Perform analytical procedures and tests of details of balances
Phase IV	Complete the audit and issue an audit report

Plan and Design an Audit Approach (Phase I)

For any given audit, there are many ways in which an auditor can accumulate evidence to meet the overall audit objective of providing an opinion on the financial statements. Two overriding considerations affect the approach the auditor selects:

1. Sufficient appropriate evidence must be accumulated to meet the auditor's professional responsibility.
2. The cost of accumulating the evidence should be minimized.

The first consideration is the most important, but cost minimization is necessary if audit firms are to be competitive and profitable. If there were no concern for controlling costs, evidence decision making would be easy. Auditors would keep adding evidence, without concern for efficiency, until they were sufficiently certain that there were no material misstatements.

Concern for sufficient appropriate evidence and cost control necessitates planning the engagement. The plan should result in an effective audit approach at a reasonable cost. Planning and designing an audit approach can be broken down into several parts. Three key aspects are introduced here and are discussed in subsequent chapters.

Obtain An Understanding of the Entity and its Environment To adequately assess the risk of misstatements in the financial statements and to interpret information obtained throughout the audit, the auditor must have a thorough understanding of the client's business and related environment, including knowledge of strategies and processes. The auditor should study the client's business model, perform analytical procedures and make comparisons to competitors. The auditor must also understand any unique accounting requirements of the client's industry. For example, when auditing an insurance company, the auditor must understand how loss reserves are calculated. For banks and financial institutions, the regulations and requirements issued by the central banks and the organizations controlling capital markets must be understood and properly applied.

Understand Internal Control and Assess Control Risk The risk of misstatement in the financial statements is reduced if the client has effective controls over computer operations and transaction processing. Internal controls help to generate reliable financial information and safeguard assets and records. The auditor identifies internal controls and evaluates their effectiveness, a process called *assessing control risk*. If internal controls are considered effective, planned assessed control risk can be reduced and the amount of audit evidence to be accumulated can be significantly less than when internal controls are not adequate.

Assess Risk of Material Misstatement The auditor uses the understanding of the client's industry and business strategies, as well as the effectiveness of controls, to assess the risk of misstatements in the financial statements. This assessment will then impact the audit plan and the nature, timing, and extent of audit procedures. For example, if the client is expanding sales by taking on new customers with poor credit ratings, the auditor will assess a higher risk of misstatement for net realizable value of accounts receivable and plan to expand testing in this area.

Perform Tests of Controls and Substantive Tests of Transactions (Phase II)

Before auditors can justify reducing planned assessed control risk when internal controls are believed to be effective, they must first test the effectiveness of the controls. The procedures for this type of testing are commonly referred to as **tests of controls**. For example, assume a client's internal controls require the verification by an independent clerk of all unit selling prices on sales before sales invoices are mailed to customers. This control is directly related to the accuracy transaction-related audit objective for sales. The auditor might test the effectiveness of this control by examining a sample of duplicate sales invoices for the clerk's initials indicating that the unit selling price was verified.

Auditors also evaluate the client's recording of transactions by verifying the monetary amounts of transactions, a process called **substantive tests of transactions**. For example, the auditor might compare the unit selling price on a duplicate sales invoice with the approved price list as a test of the accuracy objective for sales transactions. Like the test of control in the preceding paragraph, this test satisfies the accuracy transaction-related audit objective for sales. For the sake of efficiency, auditors often perform tests of controls and substantive tests of transactions at the same time.

Perform Analytical Procedures and Tests of Details of Balances (Phase III)

There are two general categories of phase III procedures. **Analytical procedures** use comparisons and relationships to assess whether account balances or other data appear reasonable. For example, to provide some assurance for the accuracy objective for both sales transactions (transaction-related audit objective) and accounts receivable (balance-related audit objective), the auditor might examine sales transactions in the sales journal for unusually large amounts and also compare total monthly sales with prior years. If a company is consistently using incorrect sales prices or improperly recording sales, significant differences are likely.

Tests of details of balances are specific procedures intended to test for monetary misstatements in the balances in the financial statements. An example related to the accuracy objective for accounts receivable (balance-related audit objective) is direct written communication with the client's customers to identify incorrect amounts. Tests of details of ending balances are essential to the conduct of the audit because most of the evidence is obtained from a source independent of the client and therefore is considered to be of high quality.

Complete the Audit and Issue an Audit Report (Phase IV)

After the auditor has completed all procedures for each audit objective and for each financial statement account and related disclosures, it is necessary to combine the information obtained to reach an *overall conclusion* as to whether the financial statements are fairly presented. This highly subjective process relies heavily on the auditor's professional judgment. When the audit is completed, the auditor must issue an audit report to accompany the client's published financial statements. These reports were discussed in Chapter 3.

Tests of controls

Audit procedures to test the effectiveness of controls in support of a reduced assessed control risk.

Substantive tests of transactions

Audit procedures testing for monetary misstatements to determine whether the seven transaction-related audit objectives have been satisfied for each class of transactions.

Analytical procedures

Use of comparisons and relationships to assess whether account balances or other data appear reasonable.

Tests of details of balances

Audit procedures testing for monetary misstatements to determine whether the eight balance-related audit objectives have been satisfied for each significant account balance.

SUMMARY

This chapter described management's responsibility for the financial statements and internal control and the auditor's responsibility to audit the financial statements and the effectiveness of internal control over financial reporting. This chapter also discussed management assertions and the related objectives of the audit and the way the auditor subdivides an audit to result in specific audit objectives. The auditor then accumulates evidence to obtain assurance that each audit objective has been satisfied. The illustration on meeting the accuracy objectives for sales transactions and accounts receivable shows that the auditor can obtain assurance by accumulating evidence using tests of controls, substantive tests of transactions, analytical procedures, and tests of details of balances. In some audits, there is more emphasis on certain tests such as analytical procedures and tests of controls, whereas in others, there is emphasis on substantive tests of transactions and tests of details of balances.

ESSENTIAL TERMS

Analytical procedures   p. 185

Balance-related audit objectives   p. 174

Cycle approach   p. 169

Error   p. 163

Fraud   p. 163

Fraudulent financial reporting   p. 164

Illegal acts   p. 166

Management assertions   p. 175

Misappropriation of assets   p. 164

Phases of the audit process   p. 183

Presentation and disclosure-related audit objectives   p. 174

Relevant assertions   p. 177

Substantive tests of transactions   p. 185

Tests of controls   p. 185

Tests of details of balances   p. 185

Transaction-related audit objectives   p. 174

REVIEW QUESTIONS

6-1 (Objective 6-1) State the objective of the audit of financial statements. In general terms, how do auditors meet that objective?

6-2 (Objectives 6-2, 6-3) Distinguish between management's and the auditor's responsibility for the financial statements being audited.

6-3 (Objective 6-3) Distinguish between the terms *errors* and *fraud*. What is the auditor's responsibility for finding each?

6-4 (Objective 6-3) Distinguish between fraudulent financial reporting and misappropriation of assets. Discuss the likely difference between these two types of fraud on the fair presentation of financial statements.

6-5 (Objective 6-3) Because management operates the business on a daily basis, they know more about the company's transactions and related assets, liabilities, and equity than the auditor. For example, it is extremely difficult, if not impossible, for the auditor to evaluate the obsolescence of inventory as well as management can in a highly complex business. Given these observations, evaluate the auditor's responsibility for detecting material misrepresentations in the financial statements by management.

6-6 (Objective 6-3) List two major characteristics that are useful in predicting the likelihood of fraudulent financial reporting in an audit. For each of the characteristics, state two things that the auditor can do to evaluate its significance in the engagement.

6-7 (Objective 6-4) Describe what is meant by the cycle approach to auditing. What are the advantages of dividing the audit into different cycles?

6-8 (Objective 6-4) Identify the cycle to which each of the following general ledger accounts will ordinarily be assigned: sales, accounts payable, retained earnings, accounts receivable, inventory, and repairs and maintenance.

6-9 (Objectives 6-4, 6-5) Why are sales, sales returns and allowances, bad debts, cash discounts, accounts receivable, and allowance for uncollectible accounts all included in the same cycle?

6-10 (Objective 6-6) Define what is meant by a management assertion about financial statements. Identify the three broad categories of management assertions.

6-11 (Objectives 6-5, 6-6) Distinguish between the general audit objectives and management assertions. Why are the general audit objectives more useful to auditors?

6-12 (Objective 6-7) An acquisition of a fixed-asset repair by a construction company is recorded on the wrong date. Which transaction-related audit objective has been violated? Which transaction-related audit objective has been violated if the acquisition had been capitalized as a fixed asset rather than expensed?

6-13 (Objective 6-8) Distinguish between the existence and completeness balance-related audit objectives. State the effect on the financial statements (overstatement or understatement) of a violation of each in the audit of accounts receivable.

6-14 (Objectives 6-7, 6-8, 6-9) What are specific audit objectives? Explain their relationship to the general audit objectives.

6-15 (Objectives 6-6, 6-8) Identify the management assertion and general balance-related audit objective for the specific balance-related audit objective: all recorded fixed assets exist at the balance sheet date.

6-16 (Objectives 6-6, 6-8) Explain how management assertions, general balance-related audit objectives, and specific balance-related audit objectives are developed for an account balance such as accounts receivable.

6-17 (Objectives 6-6, 6-9) Identify the management assertion and presentation and disclosure-related audit objective for the specific presentation and disclosure-related audit objective: read the fixed asset footnote disclosure to determine that the types of fixed assets, depreciation methods, and useful lives are clearly disclosed.

6-18 (Objective 6-10) Identify the four phases of the audit. What is the relationship of the four phases to the objective of the audit of financial statements?

MULTIPLE CHOICE QUESTIONS FROM CPA EXAMINATIONS

6-19 (Objective 6-1) The following questions concern the reasons auditors do audits. Choose the best response.

a. Which of the following best describes the reason why an independent auditor reports on financial statements?
   (1) A misappropriation of assets may exist, and it is more likely to be detected by independent auditors.
   (2) Different interests may exist between the company preparing the statements and the persons using the statements.
   (3) A misstatement of account balances may exist and is generally corrected as the result of the independent auditor's work.
   (4) Poorly designed internal controls may be in existence.

b. An independent audit aids in the communication of economic data because the audit
   (1) confirms the accuracy of management's financial representations.
   (2) lends credibility to the financial statements.
   (3) guarantees that financial data are fairly presented.
   (4) assures the readers of financial statements that any fraudulent activity has been corrected.

c. The major reason an independent auditor gathers audit evidence is to
   (1) form an opinion on the financial statements.
   (2) detect fraud.
   (3) evaluate management.
   (4) assess control risk.

6-20 (Objective 6-3) The following questions deal with errors and fraud. Choose the best response.

a. An independent auditor has the responsibility to design the audit to provide reasonable assurance of detecting errors and fraud that might have a material effect on the financial statements. Which of the following, if material, is a fraud as defined in auditing standards?
   (1) Misappropriation of an asset or groups of assets.
   (2) Clerical mistakes in the accounting data underlying the financial statements.
   (3) Mistakes in the application of accounting principles.
   (4) Misinterpretation of facts that existed when the financial statements were prepared.

b. What assurance does the auditor provide that errors, fraud, and direct-effect illegal acts that are material to the financial statements will be detected?

	Errors	Fraud	Direct-Effect Illegal Acts
(1)	Limited	Negative	Limited
(2)	Reasonable	Reasonable	Reasonable
(3)	Limited	Limited	Reasonable
(4)	Reasonable	Limited	Limited

c. Which of the following statements describes why a properly designed and executed audit may not detect a material misstatement in the financial statements resulting from fraud?
   (1) Audit procedures that are effective for detecting unintentional misstatements may be ineffective for an intentional misstatement that is concealed through collusion.
   (2) An audit is designed to provide reasonable assurance of detecting material errors, but there is no similar responsibility concerning fraud.
   (3) The factors considered in assessing control risk indicated an increased risk of intentional misstatements, but only a low risk of unintentional misstatements.
   (4) The auditor did not consider factors influencing audit risk for account balances that have effects pervasive to the financial statements taken as a whole.

DISCUSSION QUESTIONS AND PROBLEMS

6-21 (Objective 6-4) The following are the classes of transactions and the titles of the journals used for Ghabour Retail Co.

Classes of Transactions	Titles of Journals
Cost of goods sold	Cash receipts journal
Sales	Cash disbursements journal
Charge-off of uncollectible accounts	Acquisitions journal
Acquisition of goods and services (except payroll)	Sales journal
Sales allowances	Payroll journal
Adjusting entries (for payroll)	Adjustments journal
Payroll service and payments	
Cash disbursements (except payroll)	
Cash receipts	
Sales returns	

a. Identify one financial statement balance that is likely to be affected by each of the ten classes of transactions.

b. For each class of transactions, identify the journal that is likely to be used to record the transactions.

c. Identify the transaction cycle that is likely to be affected by each of the ten classes of transactions.

d. Explain how total sales, as cited on the financial statements of Ghabour Retail Co., is accumulated in journals and is summarized on the financial statements.

6-22 (Objective 6-4) The following general ledger accounts are included in the trial balance for an audit client, Prince Stationery Store.

Income tax expense	Allowance for doubtful accounts
Income tax payable	Inventory
Accounts receivable	Property tax expense
Advertising expense	Interest expense
Travel expense	Depreciation expense—furniture and equipment
Accounts payable	Retained earnings
Bonds payable	Sales
Common stock	Salaries, office and general
Unexpired insurance	Telephone and fax expense
Furniture and equipment	Bad debt expense
Cash	Insurance expense
Notes receivable—trade	Interest receivable
Purchases	Interest income
Sales salaries expense	Accrued sales salaries
Accumulated depreciation of furniture and equipment	Rent expense
	Prepaid interest expense
Notes payable	Property tax payable

a. Identify the accounts in the trial balance that are likely to be included in each transaction cycle. Some accounts will be included in more than one cycle. Use the format that follows.

Cycle	Balance Sheet Accounts	Income Statement Accounts
Sales (revenues) and collection		
Acquisition and payment		
Payroll and personnel		
Inventory and warehousing		
Capital acquisition and repayment		

b. How will the general ledger accounts in the trial balance most likely differ if the company were a retail store rather than a wholesale company? How will they differ for a hospital or a not-for-profit organization?

6-23 (Objective 6-6) The following are various management assertions (1 through 13) related to sales and accounts receivable.

Management Assertion

1. All sales transactions have been recorded.

2. Receivables are appropriately classified as to trade and other receivables in the financial statements and are clearly described.

3. Accounts receivable are recorded at the correct amounts.

4. Sales transactions have been recorded in the proper period.

5. Sales transactions have been recorded in the appropriate accounts.

6. All required disclosures about sales and receivables have been made.

7. All accounts receivable have been recorded.

8. There are no liens or other restrictions on accounts receivable.

9. Disclosures related to receivables are at the correct amounts.

10. Recorded sales transactions have occurred.

11. Recorded accounts receivable exist.

12. Sales transactions have been recorded at the correct amounts.

13. Disclosures related to sales and receivables relate to the entity.

Required

a. Explain the differences among management assertions about classes of transactions and events, management assertions about account balances, and management assertions about presentation and disclosure.

b. For each assertion, indicate whether it is an assertion about classes of transactions and events, an assertion about account balances, or an assertion about presentation and disclosure.

c. Indicate the name of the assertion made by management. (*Hint*: See Table 6-2.)

6-24 (Objectives 6-6, 6-9) The followings are specific presentation and disclosure-related audit objectives applied to presentation and disclosure for fixed assets (a through c) and management assertions (1 through 3).

Specific Presentation and Disclosure-Related Audit Objective

a. All required disclosures regarding fixed assets have been made.

b. Footnote disclosures related to fixed assets are clear and understandable.

c. Methods and useful lives disclosed for each category of fixed asset are accurate.

Management Assertion about Presentation and Disclosure
1. Completeness
2. Valuation and accuracy
3. Classification and understandability

Required

For each specific presentation and disclosure-related audit objective, identify the appropriate management assertion. (*Hint*: See Table 6-5.)

6-25 (Objective 6-8) The following (1 through 19) are the balance-related, transaction-related, and presentation and disclosure-related audit objectives.

Balance-Related Audit Objectives	Transaction-Related Audit Objectives	Presentation and Disclosure-Related Audit Objectives
1. Existence	9. Occurrence	16. Completeness
2. Completeness	10. Completeness	17. Valuation and accuracy
3. Accuracy	11. Accuracy	18. Classification and understandability
4. Classification	12. Classification	
5. Cutoff	13. Timing	
6. Detail tie-in	14. Posting and summarization	
7. Realizable value		
8. Rights and obligations	15. Rights and obligations	

Required

Identify the specific audit objective (1 through 18) that each of the following specific audit procedures (a. through h.) satisfies in the audit of sales, accounts receivable, and cash receipts for fiscal year ended December 31, 2011.

a. Examine a sample of duplicate sales invoices to determine whether each one has a shipping document attached.

b. Add all customer balances in the accounts receivable trial balance and agree the amount to the general ledger.

c. For a sample of sales transactions selected from the sales journal, verify that the amount of the transaction has been recorded in the correct customer account in the accounts receivable sub ledger.

d. Inquire of the client whether any accounts receivable balances have been pledged as collateral on long-term debt and determine whether all required information is included in the footnote description for long-term debt.

e. For a sample of shipping documents selected from shipping records, trace each shipping document to a transaction recorded in the sales journal.

f. Discuss with credit department personnel the likelihood of collection of all accounts as of December 31, 2011 with a balance greater than US$100,000 and greater than 90 days old as of year-end.

g. Examine sales invoices for the last five sales transactions recorded in the sales journal in 2011 and examine shipping documents to determine they are recorded in the correct period.

h. For a sample of customer accounts receivable balances for December 31, 2011, examine subsequent cash receipts in January 2012 to determine whether the customer paid the balance due.

CASE

6-26 (Objectives 6-1, 6-3) Hakim Mubarak opened a small cotton and textiles store in 1985 with money he had saved working as a Tayseer Mardini store manager. He named it Mubarak Baladi. Because of the excellent location and his fine management skills, Mubarak Baladi grew to three locations by 1991. By that time, he needed additional capital. He obtained financing through a local bank at 3 percent above prime, under the condition that he submits quarterly financial statements reviewed by an audit firm approved by the bank. After interviewing several firms, he decided to use the firm of El-Gazzar & Al-Zu'bi CPAs, after obtaining approval from the bank.

In 1994, the company expanded to five stores, and Hakim developed a business plan to add another ten stores over the course of six years. Mubarak Baladi's capital needs had also grown, so Hakim decided to add two business partners who both had considerable capital and some expertise in textile stores. After further discussions with the bank and continued conversations with future business partners, he decided to have an annual audit and quarterly reviews done by Abdullah & Elhakeem, even though the additional cost was almost US$50,000 annually. The bank agreed to reduce the interest rate on the US$10 million of loans to 2 percent above prime.

By 1999, things were going smoothly, with the two business partners heavily involved in day-to-day operations and the company adding two new stores each year. The company was growing steadily and was more profitable than they had expected. By the end of 2000, one of the business partners, Malik Zaater, had taken over responsibility for accounting and finance operations, as well as some marketing. Annually Abdullah & Elhakeem did an in-depth review of the accounting system, including internal controls, and reported their conclusions and recommendations to the board of directors. Specialists in the firm provided tax and other advice. The other partner, Fatina El Sayid, managed most of the stores and was primarily responsible for building new stores. Hakim was president and managed four stores.

The company went public in 2005. The partners hoped that this would enable them to add more stores and update their original buildings. The public offering was a major success, resulting in US$75 million in new capital and nearly 1,500 shareholders. Mubarak Baladi added stores rapidly under the three managers, and the company remained highly profitable under the leadership of Mubarak, Zaater, and El Sayid.

Hakim retired in 2007 after a highly successful career. During the retirement celebration, he thanked his business partners, employees, and customers. He also added a special thanks to the bank management for their outstanding service and to Abdullah & Elhakeem for being partners in the best and most professional sense of the word. He mentioned their integrity, commitment, high-quality service in performing their audits and reviews, and considerable tax and business advice for more than two decades.

Required

a. Why did the bank impose a requirement of a quarterly review of the financial statements as a condition of obtaining the loan at 3 percent above prime? Also explain why the bank didn't require an audit and why the bank demanded the right to approve which audit firm was engaged.

b. Why did Mubarak Baladi agree to have an audit performed rather than a review, considering the additional cost of US$50,000?

c. What did Hakim mean when he referred to Abdullah & Elhakeem as partners? Does the audit firm have an independence problem?

d. What benefit does Abdullah & Elhakeem provide to stockholders, creditors, and management in performing the audit and related services?

e. What are the responsibilities of the audit firm to stockholders, creditors, management, and other users in this situation?

AUDIT EVIDENCE

Evidence Is The Heart Of The Reliability Of Information Presented To Users

TechKitch is an international trade name for a Spanish company which manufactures home appliances. TechKitch provided its trade name to a number of companies in various Arab countries including Jordan, Lebanon, U.A.E., and Egypt. TechKitch allowed an Egyptian joint stock company to sell home appliances in the Egyptian market in return for royalty fees to be paid upon the calculation of the actual quantities of home appliances sold under the name of TechKitch. Similar requirements are also followed in Jordan, Lebanon, and U.A.E. TechKitch Spain requires, at the end of every annual financial year, that TechKitch Egypt provides a certificate confirming the quantities of home appliances products sold and the calculation of the royalty fees accordingly.

To ensure the reliability and accuracy of the information about the quantities of home appliances and the royalty fees, TechKitch Spain needed this certificate to be verified and stamped by the auditor of the Egyptian company. The auditor of the Egyptian business examines the schedule of sales made by the company during the previous year with all supporting documents such as delivery notes and other shipping vouchers in addition to the price list of all home appliances sold under TechKitch before stamping the certificate to be submitted to TechKitch Spain.

The foundation of any audit is the evidence gathered and evaluated by the auditor. The auditor must have the knowledge and skill to accumulate sufficient appropriate evidence on every audit to meet the standards of the profession. As described in this opening story, TechKitch Spain required the auditor of the Egyptian business to examine evidence associated with the sale of TechKitch home appliances before accepting the amount of royalty fees calculated for the use of the TechKitch trade name. This chapter deals with the types of evidence decisions auditors make, the evidence available to auditors, and the use of that evidence in performing audits and documenting the results.

Relevant International Standards on Auditing	
IAPS 1013	Electronic Commerce—Effect on the Audit of Financial Statements
ISA 230	Audit Documentation
ISA 320	Materiality in Planning and Performing an Audit
ISA 500	Audit Evidence
ISA 505	External Confirmations
ISA 510	Initial Audit Engagements—Opening Balances
ISA 520	Analytical Procedures
ISA 550	Related Parties
ISA 560	Subsequent Events
ISA 580	Written Representations

NATURE OF EVIDENCE

OBJECTIVE 7-1

Contrast audit evidence with evidence used by other professions.

Evidence was defined in Chapter 1 as any *information used by the auditor* to determine whether the information being audited is stated in accordance with the established criteria. ISA 500 defines audit evidence as information used by the auditor in arriving at the conclusions on which the auditors' opinion is based. Audit evidence includes both information contained in the accounting records underlying the financial statements and other information. Accounting records include documents and records of initial entries and other supporting records, such as invoices, checks, contracts, electronic transfers, general and subsidiary ledger, spreadsheets supporting cost allocations, all computations, reconciliations, and disclosures. Other information used by the auditor as audit evidence includes activities manuals, minutes of meetings, benchmarking, analysts' reports, and confirmations from third parties. Evidence includes information that is highly persuasive, such as the auditor's count of marketable securities, and less persuasive information, such as responses to questions to client employees. When using information prepared by the entity, the auditor is required under ISA 500 to ensure the accuracy and completeness of the information and that the information is sufficiently precise and detailed for the auditor's purposes. Some entities may use electronic forms for their accounting records. Source documents such as checks, invoices, and shipping documents are replaced with electronic messages or images. The electronic data interchange (EDI) and image processing systems (IPS) are used for such electronic documents. Clients may process sales transactions electronically using EDI. Clients may contact suppliers electronically whenever the inventory runs out. The suppliers will ship the required materials and send the invoice electronically. Upon receiving the supplier's invoice the client will instruct its bank to settle the invoice electronically. In IPS, transactions documents are scanned and converted to electronic images which are stored for auditor and other users' reference. Using the IPS, electronic evidence may exist at only a certain point of time and may not be retrievable at a later date. Auditors are advised to select a sample of items a number of times during the year rather than at year-end.

Audit Evidence Contrasted with Legal and Scientific Evidence

The use of evidence is not unique to auditors. Evidence is also used extensively by scientists, lawyers, and historians. For example, most people are familiar with legal dramas on television in which evidence is collected and used to argue for the guilt or innocence of a party charged with a crime. In legal cases, there are well-defined rules of evidence enforced by the judge for the protection of the innocent. In scientific experiments, researchers obtain evidence to test hypotheses using controlled experiments, such as a drug trial to test the effectiveness of a new medical treatment. Similarly, gathering evidence is a large part of what auditors do. Although these professionals rely on different types of evidence, and use evidence in different settings and in different ways, lawyers, scientists, and auditors all use evidence to help them draw conclusions.

AUDIT EVIDENCE DECISIONS

A major decision facing every auditor is determining the *appropriate types and amounts* of evidence needed to be satisfied that the client's financial statements are fairly stated, including the assessment of the client maintaining effective internal control. There are four decisions about what evidence to gather and how much of it to accumulate:

OBJECTIVE 7-2

Identify the four audit evidence decisions that are needed to create an audit program.

1. Which audit procedures to use
2. What sample size to select for a given procedure
3. Which items to select from the population
4. When to perform the procedures

Audit Procedures

An **audit procedure** is the detailed instructions given to the auditor in order to accumulate evidence to determine whether specific assertions are being met. Auditors may perform audit procedures to:

- Obtain an understanding of the entity and its environment.
- Test the entity's internal control systems used to prevent and detect fraud and errors.
- Undertake substantive procedures including tests of details of transactions and tests of details of balances.

For example, an example of an audit procedure for the verification of cash disbursements might be to obtain the cash disbursements journal and compare the payee name, amount, and date on the cancelled check with the cash disbursements journal.

Audit procedure

Specific acts performed by the auditor in gathering evidence to determine if specific assertions are being met; or detailed instruction for the collection of a type of audit evidence.

Sample Size

Once an audit procedure is selected, auditors can vary the sample size from one to all the items in the population being tested. In an audit procedure to verify cash disbursements, suppose 6,600 checks are recorded in the cash disbursements journal. The auditor might select a sample size of 50 checks for comparison with the cash disbursements journal.

The decision of how many items to test must be made by the auditor for each audit procedure. The sample size for any given procedure is likely to vary from audit to audit.

Items to Select

After determining the sample size for an audit procedure, the auditor must decide which items in the population to test. If the auditor decides, for example, to select 50 cancelled checks from a population of 6,600 for comparison with the cash disbursements journal, several different methods can be used to select the specific checks to be examined. The auditor can (1) select a week and examine the first 50 checks, (2) select the 50 checks with the largest amounts, (3) select the checks randomly, or (4) select those checks that the auditor thinks are most likely to be in error. Or, a combination of these methods can be used.

Timing

An audit of financial statements usually covers a period such as a year. Normally an audit is not completed until several weeks or months after the end of the period. The timing of audit procedures can therefore vary from early in the accounting period to long after it has ended. In part, the timing decision is affected by when the client needs the audit to be completed. In the audit of financial statements, the client normally wants the audit completed one to three months after year-end. The capital market authorities in many Arab countries as well as the SEC in the U.S. currently require that all public companies file audited financial statements within 90 days of the company's fiscal year-end. However, timing is also influenced by when the auditor believes the audit evidence will be most effective and when audit staff is available. For example, auditors often prefer to do counts of inventory as close to the balance sheet date as possible.

Audit procedures often incorporate sample size, items to select, and timing. The following is a modification of the audit procedure previously used to include all four audit evidence decisions. (Italics identify the timing, items to select, and sample size decisions.)

- Obtain, for example, the *October* cash disbursements journal and compare the payee name, amount, and date on the *cancelled check* with the cash disbursements journal for a *randomly selected sample of 40* check numbers.

Audit Program

Audit program

List of audit procedures for an audit area or an entire audit; the audit program always includes audit procedures and may also include sample sizes, items to select, and timing of the tests.

The list of audit procedures for an audit area or an entire audit is called an **audit program**. The audit program always includes a list of the audit procedures, the sample sizes, items to select, and the timing of the tests. Normally, there is an audit program, including several audit procedures, for each component of the audit. Therefore, there will be an audit program for accounts receivable, one for sales, and so on. A simple example of an audit program discussing audit procedures and timing of the audit is shown in Table 7-1.

To see an example of an audit program that includes audit procedures, sample size, items to select, and timing, turn to page 446 and see Table 13-4. The right side of the audit program also includes the balance-related audit objectives for each procedure, which were discussed in Chapter 6. Note that this table gives useful topics for a discussion about management assertions, the appropriate transaction/balance-related audit objectives for each procedure, sample likely to be selected given different balances for tangible and intangible assets, and timing for testing.

Most auditors use computers to facilitate the preparation of audit programs. The simplest computer application involves typing the audit program on a word

TABLE 7-1	Simple Audit Program for Tangible Fixed Assets			

Primary objective	Initials	Reference	Date
The amount at which fixed assets are stated in the financial statements represents all existing fixed assets which are the property of the company and are properly described, valued, and classified consistently with prior years.			

Detailed objective and audit work

All existing fixed assets are recorded as such in the financial statements and no material items, which should be capitalized, have been charged to revenues.

Review repair and maintenance accounts for items of capital expenditure.

All items have shown, as fixed assets are, the property of the company, used for the purpose of its business, and adequately safeguarded.

In respect of additions during the year check with supporting documentation (e.g. suppliers invoices, architects certificates, completion statements, etc.)

For approval ownership and for the correct allocation to nominal ledger accounts.

If the item selected represents land or buildings, verify the title by inspecting documents of title (e.g. title deeds, land register certificates, etc.)

Review overall changes in fixed assets and consider reasonableness in respect of other factors.

Items removed from fixed assets records are valid disposals, approved, and properly accounted for as per Lebanese General Accounting Plan.

Check that depreciation charges and provisions are adequate but not excessive, and have been calculated on an accepted and consistent basis with regard to useful lives and disposal values (rates should be compliant with income tax law).

All significant charges and commitments are properly reflected or disclosed in the financial statement.

processor and saving it from one year to the next to facilitate changes and updating. A more sophisticated application involves the use of a specialized program designed to help the auditor address risks and other audit planning considerations and select appropriate procedures using audit program generator software. Examples of audit software packages which help auditors design audit programs and perform audit tests are ACL (www.acl.com), ActiveData for Excel (www.informationactive.com), Excel (www.microsoft.com), IDEA (www.audimation.com) and Top CAATs (www.topcaats.com).

PERSUASIVENESS OF EVIDENCE

ISA 500 states that the objective of the auditor is to design and perform audit procedures in such a way as to enable the auditor to *obtain sufficient appropriate audit evidence to support the opinion issued*. Because of the nature of audit evidence and the cost considerations of doing an audit, it is unlikely that the auditor will be completely convinced that the opinion is correct. However, the auditor must be persuaded that the opinion is correct with a high level of assurance. By combining all evidence from the entire audit, the auditor is able to decide when he or she is persuaded to issue an audit report.

The two determinants of the **persuasiveness of evidence** are *appropriateness* and *sufficiency*, which are taken directly from ISA 500.

OBJECTIVE 7-3

Specify the characteristics that determine the persuasiveness of evidence.

Persuasiveness of evidence

The degree to which the auditor is convinced that the evidence supports the audit opinion; the two determinants of persuasiveness are the appropriateness and sufficiency of the evidence.

Appropriateness

Appropriateness of evidence is a measure of the quality of evidence, meaning its relevance and reliability in meeting audit objectives for classes of transactions, account balances, and related disclosures. If evidence is considered highly appropriate, it is a great help in persuading the auditor that financial statements are fairly stated.

Note that appropriateness of evidence deals only with the audit procedures selected. Appropriateness cannot be improved by selecting a larger sample size or different population items. It can be improved only by selecting audit procedures that are more relevant or provide more reliable evidence.

Relevance of Evidence Evidence must *pertain to or be relevant to the audit objective* that the auditor is testing before it can be appropriate. ISA 500 relates to **relevance of evidence**, indicating that relevance deals with the logical connection with, or bearing upon, the purpose of the audit procedure. The relevance of information to be used as audit evidence may be affected by the direction of testing. For example, assume that the auditor is concerned that a client is failing to bill customers for shipments (completeness transaction objective). If the auditor selects a sample of duplicate sales invoices and traces each to related shipping documents, the evidence is *not relevant* for the completeness objective and therefore is not appropriate evidence for that objective. A relevant procedure is to trace a sample of shipping documents to related duplicate sales invoices to determine whether each shipment was billed. The second audit procedure is relevant because the shipment of goods is the normal criterion used for determining whether a sale has occurred and should have been billed. By tracing from shipping documents to duplicate sales invoices, the auditor can determine whether shipments have been billed to customers. In the first procedure, when the auditor traces from duplicate sales invoices to shipping documents, it is impossible to find unbilled shipments. However, such procedure is considered appropriate to determine whether each sales transaction represents an actual delivery of merchandise (i.e. shipping documents). The audit objective in this case would be the occurrence of the sales transaction not completeness.

Another example is, when the auditor tests the overstatement in the existence or valuation of accounts payable, testing the recorded accounts payable may be a relevant audit procedure. On the other hand, the auditor would test information related to subsequent disbursements, unpaid invoices, suppliers' statements, and unmatched receiving reports to test for understatement in the existence or valuation of accounts payable.

Relevance can be considered only in terms of specific audit objectives, because evidence may be relevant for one audit objective but not for a different one. In the previous shipping example, when the auditor traced from the duplicate sales invoices to related shipping documents, the evidence was relevant for the occurrence transaction objective. Most evidence is relevant for more than one, but not all, audit objectives. For example, **inspection** of documents related to the collection of receivables after the end of the financial year may provide evidence regarding existence and valuation audit objectives, but not necessarily relevant for the cutoff objective.

Reliability of Evidence **Reliability of evidence** refers to the degree to which evidence can be believable or worthy of trust. Like relevance, if evidence is considered reliable it is a great help in persuading the auditor that financial statements are fairly stated. For example, if an auditor counts inventory, that evidence is more reliable than if management gives the auditor its own count amounts. ISA 500 states that audit evidence in documentary form, whether paper, electronic, or other medium, is more reliable than evidence obtained orally. For example, examining minutes of meetings of the board of directors is more reliable than oral representations of possible litigations against the entity. Also, audit evidence provided by original documents is more reliable than evidence provided by photocopies or facsimiles, or documents that have been filmed, digitized, or otherwise transformed into electronic form.

Reliability, and therefore appropriateness, depends on the following six characteristics of reliable evidence:

1. *Independence of provider.* Evidence obtained from a source outside the entity is more reliable than that obtained from within. Communications from banks, attorneys, or customers is generally considered more reliable than answers obtained from inquiries of the client. Similarly, documents that originate from outside the client's organization, such as an insurance policy, are considered more reliable than those that originate within the company and have never left the client's organization, such as a purchase requisition.

2. *Effectiveness of client's internal controls.* When a client's internal controls are effective, evidence obtained is more reliable than when they are weak. For example, if internal controls over sales and billing are effective, the auditor can obtain more reliable evidence from sales invoices and shipping documents than if the controls were inadequate.

3. *Auditor's direct knowledge.* Evidence obtained directly by the auditor through physical examination, observation, recalculation, and inspection is more reliable than information obtained indirectly. For example, if the auditor calculates the gross margin as a percentage of sales and compares it with previous periods, the evidence is more reliable than if the auditor relies on the calculations of the controller.

4. *Qualifications of individuals providing the information.* ISA 500 defines 'management's expert' as an individual or organization possessing expertise in a field other than accounting or auditing, whose work in that field is used to assist the entity in preparing the financial statements. Examples are those experts preparing actuarial calculations, valuations, or engineering data. An individual may have expertise in designing and applying models to estimate the fair value of securities for which there is no observable market. Although the source of information is independent, the evidence will not be reliable unless the individual providing it is qualified to do so. Therefore, communications from attorneys and bank confirmations are typically more highly regarded than accounts receivable confirmations received from persons not familiar with the nature of the business world. Also, evidence obtained directly by the auditor may not be reliable if the auditor lacks the qualifications to evaluate the evidence. For example, examining an inventory of diamonds by an auditor not trained to distinguish between diamonds and glass is not reliable evidence for the existence of diamonds.

5. *Degree of objectivity.* Objective evidence is more reliable than evidence that requires considerable judgment to determine whether it is correct. Examples of objective evidence include confirmation of accounts receivable and bank balances, the physical count of securities and cash, and adding (footing) a list of accounts payable to determine whether it agrees with the balance in the general ledger. Examples of subjective evidence include a letter written by a client's attorney discussing the likely outcome of outstanding lawsuits against the client, observation of obsolescence of inventory during physical examination, and inquiries of the credit manager about the collectability of noncurrent accounts receivable. When the reliability of subjective evidence is being evaluated, it is essential for auditors to assess the qualifications of the person providing the evidence.

6. *Timeliness.* The timeliness of audit evidence can refer either to when it is accumulated or to the period covered by the audit. Evidence is usually more reliable for balance sheet accounts when it is obtained as close to the balance sheet date as possible. This is due to evidence being highly related to the figures at the balance sheet date. For example, the auditor's count of marketable securities on the balance sheet date is more reliable than a count two months earlier. For

income statement accounts, evidence is more reliable if there is a sample from the entire period under audit, such as a random sample of sales transactions for the entire year, rather than from only a part of the period, such as a sample limited to only the first six months. The evidence collected from the entire period reflects appropriately the population being examined.

Sufficiency

Sufficiency of evidence

The quantity of evidence; proper sample size.

The *quantity* of evidence obtained determines its sufficiency. **Sufficiency of evidence** is measured primarily by the sample size the auditor selects. For a given audit procedure, the evidence obtained from a sample of 100 is ordinarily more sufficient than from a sample of 50.

Several factors determine the appropriate sample size in audits. The two most important ones are the auditor's expectation of misstatements and the effectiveness of the client's internal controls. Thus, the greater the risk of misstatement, the more audit evidence is likely to be required to meet the audit objective being tested. Also, the higher the quality of the evidence, the less the amount of evidence that is needed by the auditor to meet the audit test. To illustrate, assume in the audit of Microtech for Information Development Co., which sells El Motamem and infinity software in several Arab countries including Saudi Arabia, Jordan, Egypt, and U.A.E., that the auditor concludes that there is a high likelihood of obsolete inventory because of the nature of the client's industry. The auditor will sample more inventory items for obsolescence in this audit than one where the likelihood of obsolescence is low.

In addition to sample size, the individual items tested affect the sufficiency of evidence. Samples containing population items with large dollar values, items with a high likelihood of misstatement, and items that are representative of the population are usually considered sufficient. In contrast, most auditors usually consider samples insufficient that contain only the largest dollar items from the population unless these items make up a large portion of the total population amount.

Combined Effect

The persuasiveness of evidence can be evaluated only after considering the combination of appropriateness and sufficiency, including the effects of the factors influencing appropriateness and sufficiency. A large sample of evidence provided by an independent party is not persuasive unless it is relevant to the audit objective being tested. A large sample of evidence that is relevant but not objective is also not persuasive. Similarly, a small sample of only one or two pieces of highly appropriate evidence also typically lacks persuasiveness. When determining the persuasiveness of evidence, the auditor must evaluate the degree to which both appropriateness and sufficiency, including all factors influencing them, have been met.

Direct relationships among the four evidence decisions and the two qualities that determine the persuasiveness of evidence are shown in Table 7-2. To illustrate these relationships, assume an auditor is verifying inventory that is a major item in the financial statements. Auditing standards require that the auditor be reasonably persuaded that inventory is not materially misstated. The auditor must therefore obtain a sufficient amount of relevant and reliable evidence about inventory. This means deciding which procedures to use for auditing inventory, as well as determining the sample size and items to select from the population to satisfy the sufficiency requirement. The combination of these four evidence decisions must result in sufficiently persuasive evidence to satisfy the auditor that inventory is materially correct. The audit program section for inventory will reflect these decisions. In practice, the auditor applies the four evidence decisions to specific audit objectives in deciding sufficient appropriate evidence.

TABLE 7-2	Relationships Among Evidence Decisions and Persuasiveness
Audit Evidence Decisions	**Qualities Affecting Persuasiveness of Evidence**
Audit procedures and timing	Appropriateness
	Relevance
	Reliability
	Independence of provider
	Effectiveness of internal controls
	Auditor's direct knowledge
	Qualifications of provider
	Objectivity of evidence
	Timeliness
	When procedures are performed
	Portion of period being audited
Sample size and items to select	Sufficiency
	Adequate sample size
	Selection of proper population items

DRAFT vs. FINAL: A BIG DIFFERENCE

Star Technology, Inc., a manufacturer of scientific computers in the U.S., entered into a joint venture arrangement to loan funds to Glen Culler & Associates, a supercomputer developer, for the development of a new computer called the Culler 8. The loan repayment terms restricted Glen Culler's use of the funds to research and development on the Culler 8.

Star Technology reported its advance of funds to Glen Culler as a note receivable on its balance sheet. Star Technology's auditors obtained a draft of the loan agreement and used that as the primary audit evidence to support the accounting treatment. The auditors, however, failed to obtain the final executed loan agreement. Unfortunately, there were big differences between the draft and final versions of the agreement that materially impacted the substance of the transaction. Instead of supporting the inclusion of the advanced funds as a receivable on Star Technology's balance sheet, the terms of the final executed agreement supported treatment of the loaned funds as research and development expense to be reported on the income statement.

The audit firm learned about its oversight when its national office received an anonymous memo alleging the audit failure. The audit firm's follow-up on the matter ultimately led to an SEC investigation. The SEC eventually charged the audit firm partner for failure to obtain sufficient appropriate evidence and for failing to exercise due professional care. As a result of the partner's negligence, the SEC barred him from working in any capacity with a public company for a period of five years, among other penalties imposed by the SEC and the audit firm.

Source: *Accounting and Auditing Enforcement Release No. 455, Commerce Clearing House, Inc., Chicago, U.S.*

Persuasiveness and Cost

In making decisions about evidence for a given audit, both persuasiveness and cost must be considered. It is rare when only one type of evidence is available for verifying information. The persuasiveness and cost of all alternatives should be considered before selecting the best type or types of evidence. The auditor's goal is to obtain a sufficient amount of appropriate evidence at the lowest possible total cost. However, cost is never an adequate justification for omitting a necessary procedure or not gathering an adequate sample size.

TYPES OF AUDIT EVIDENCE

OBJECTIVE 7-4

Identify and apply the eight types of evidence used in auditing.

In deciding which audit procedures to use, the auditor can choose from eight broad categories of evidence, which are called *types of evidence*. Every audit procedure obtains one or more of the following types of evidence:

1. Physical examination
2. Observation
3. Confirmation
4. Inspection
5. Analytical procedures
6. Inquiries of the client
7. Recalculation
8. Reperformance

Figure 7-1 shows the relationship among auditing standards, four evidence decisions, and the types of audit evidence.

Remember that the standards are general, whereas audit procedures are specific.

Physical Examination

Physical examination

The auditor's inspection or count of a tangible asset.

Physical examination is the inspection or count by the auditor of a *tangible asset*. This type of evidence is most often associated with inventory and cash, but it is also applicable to the verification of securities, notes receivable, and tangible fixed assets. There is a distinction in auditing between the physical examination of assets, such as marketable

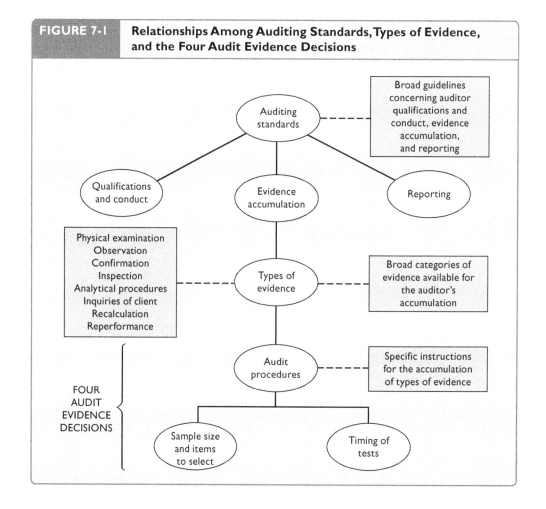

FIGURE 7-1   Relationships Among Auditing Standards, Types of Evidence, and the Four Audit Evidence Decisions

securities and cash, and the examination of documents, such as cancelled checks and sales documents. If the object being examined, such as a sales invoice, has no inherent value, the evidence is called inspection of documents. For example, before a check is signed, it is a document; after it is signed, it becomes an asset; and when it is cancelled, it becomes a document again. For correct auditing terminology, physical examination of the check can occur only while the check is an asset.

Physical examination is a direct means of verifying that an asset actually exists (existence objective), and to a lesser extent whether existing assets are recorded (completeness objective). It is considered one of the most reliable and useful types of audit evidence. Generally, physical examination is an objective means of ascertaining both the quantity and the description of the asset. In some cases, it is also a useful method for evaluating an asset's condition or quality. However, physical examination is not sufficient evidence to verify that existing assets are owned by the client (rights and obligations objective), and in many cases the auditor is not qualified to judge qualitative factors such as obsolescence or authenticity (realizable value objective). Also, proper valuation for financial statement purposes usually cannot be determined by physical examination (accuracy objective).

Observation

Observation is the use of the senses to assess client activities. Throughout the engagement with a client, auditors have many opportunities to use their senses—sight, hearing, touch, and smell—to evaluate a wide range of items. For example, the auditor's observation of inventory counting by the appropriate management committee or implementation of some control activities at a specific date or a period of time. Observation may provide evidence on valuation by identifying items that are obsolete or slow-moving. Observation consists of looking at a process or procedure being performed by employees, management, or others. Observation provides audit evidence about the performance of a process or procedures at a certain point of time at which the observation took place. The auditor may also tour the plant to obtain a general impression of the client's facilities, or watch individuals perform accounting tasks to determine whether the person assigned a responsibility is performing it properly. Observation is rarely sufficient by itself because of the risk of client personnel changing their behavior because of the auditor's presence. They may perform their responsibilities in accordance with company policy but resume normal activities not in line with company policy once the auditor is not in sight. Therefore, it is necessary to follow up initial impressions with other kinds of corroborative evidence. Corroborative evidence is additional evidence to support the original evidence. Nevertheless, observation is useful in most parts of the audit.

Observation
The use of the senses to assess client activities.

Confirmation

Confirmation describes the *receipt* of a *written or oral response* from an *independent third party* verifying the accuracy of information that was *requested by the auditor*. The request is made to the client, and the client asks the independent third party to respond directly to the auditor. Because confirmations come from sources independent of the client, they are a highly regarded and often-used type of evidence. Confirmations received directly by the auditor from confirming parties are more reliable than evidence generated internally by the entity. However, confirmations are relatively costly to obtain and may cause some inconvenience to those asked to supply them. Therefore, they are not used in every instance in which they are applicable. Because of the high reliability of confirmations, auditors typically obtain written responses whether in paper or electronic forms, or using other media, rather than oral ones when it is practical. Written confirmations are easier for supervisors to review, and they provide better support if it is necessary to demonstrate that a confirmation was received. Figure 7-2 shows an example of a bank confirmation.

Confirmation
The auditor's receipt of a written or oral response from an independent third party verifying the accuracy of information requested.

FIGURE 7-2	Example of a Bank Confirmation

Bank Trust Company   CABLE:
Church Street Station   SWIFT:
New York, New York, U.S.   TELEPHONE:

Date: January 6, 2012

Name of the external auditor
and his address

NAME OF CUSTOMER: ARAB INVESTMENT INTERNATIONAL BANK

Sir/Madam:
In connection with your examination of the books of the customer named above, we have inspected our records and, on the basis therefore, we believe that the following information is an accurate report of this customer's relationship with us, in our individual capacity indicated as of the close of business: December 31, 2011.

Balance in customer's account:

04039594	US$717,847.15

1. Customer's liability with respect to loans and discounts made directly with us by the customer: N/A
2. Customer's liability with respect to future exchange contacts, and drafts purchased by us from customer: N/A
3. Letters of credit issued by us for customer's account, or for account of another in reliance on customer's guarantee: N/A
4. Securities held in safekeeping for customer. In order for us to confirm securities we need amount, issue date, maturity date, etc.: N/A

Your attention is directed to the fact that this report covers only relations carried in our records at this office. This report does not include items received for exchange, transfer, redemption, collection, or delivery. Unless indicated above, it does not include any relationship recorded by Commercial Finance Division. We will be glad to confirm such items if you will furnish us with a list as shown on your customer's record.

If your investigation discloses any additions to or changes in the above, we would appreciate your advising the undersigned.

Very truly yours,
Authorized Signature

The information provided herein is based upon records maintained by the bank for its own business purposes and not for the purpose of responding to auditor inquiries concerning the bank's customers. No special internal inquiries have been made in connection with the response. We believe the information to be accurate and complete but cannot give any assurance to that effect. We have not included information with response to your client's support of its consolidated subsidiaries and affiliates, if any. Bank Trust Company has provided the information required in the instances when the customer has provided an account number. If no account is provided by the customer, the bank has not conducted any additional searches.

Auditors decide whether or not to use confirmations depending on the reliability needs of the situation as well as the alternative evidence available. Traditionally, confirmations are seldom used in the audit of fixed asset additions because these can be verified adequately by inspection and physical examination. Similarly, confirmations are ordinarily not used to verify individual transactions between organizations, such as sales transactions, because the auditor can use documents for that purpose. Naturally, there are exceptions. Assume the auditor determines that there are two extraordinarily large sales transactions recorded three days before year-end. Confirmation of these two transactions may be appropriate.

When practical and reasonable, auditing standards allow the confirmation of a sample of accounts receivable. This flexibility in performing an audit exists because accounts receivable usually represent a significant balance on the financial statements, and confirmations are a highly reliable type of evidence. Confirmation of accounts receivable is discussed further in Chapter 16. The major types of information that are often confirmed, along with the source of the confirmation, are indicated in Table 7-3.

To be considered reliable evidence, confirmations must be controlled by the auditor from the time they are prepared until they are returned. If the client controls the preparation of the confirmation, does the mailing, or receives the responses, the auditor has lost control and with it independence, thus reducing the reliability of the evidence. Auditors often attempt to authenticate the identity of the confirmation respondent, especially for facsimile or electronic confirmation responses. Confirmations are considered reliable audit evidence which help the auditor to respond to significant risks of material misstatement whether due to fraud or error. For example, using confirmation for accounts receivable and payable may flag up inaccuracies in the balances of such accounts. Further investigations by the auditors may lead to possible detection of fraud and errors.

ISA 505 identifies two types of confirmation: positive and negative confirmations. Positive confirmation is considered the most reliable when a request is made by the company that the confirming party respond directly to the auditor indicating whether the confirming party agrees or disagrees with the information in the request. A positive confirmation request asks the confirming party to reply to the auditor in all cases, either by indicating the confirming party's agreement with the given information, or by asking the confirming party to provide information about the matter of the audit. A negative confirmation consists of a request that the confirming party respond directly to the auditor only if the confirming party disagrees with the information provided in the request.

Under ISA 505 auditors are required to assess both the non-response situation as well as responses with exceptions. Auditors should consider the effect of a failure of the confirming party to respond to a positive confirmation request or a confirmation request returned undelivered. Auditors should inquire about the reasons behind such non-response to requested confirmation and may send an additional confirmation request when no response has been received within a reasonable period of time.

TABLE 7-3	Information Often Confirmed
Information	**Source**
Assets	
Cash in bank	Bank
Marketable securities	Investment custodian
Accounts receivable	Customer
Notes receivable	Maker
Owned inventory out on consignment	Consignee
Inventory held in public warehouses	Public warehouse
Cash surrender value of life insurance	Insurance company
Liabilities	
Accounts payable	Creditor
Notes payable	Lender
Advances from customers	Customer
Mortgages payable	Mortgagor
Bonds payable	Bondholder
Owners' Equity	
Shares outstanding	Registrar and transfer agent
Other Information	
Insurance coverage	Insurance company
Contingent liabilities	Bank, lender, and client's legal counsel
Bond indenture agreements	Bondholder
Collateral held by creditors	Creditor

Auditors may perform alternative audit procedures to obtain relevant and reliable audit evidence. For example, auditors may examine specific subsequent cash receipts, shipping documentation, and sales near the end of the period to attest to accounts receivable balances. They can also examine subsequent cash disbursements or correspondence from third parties, and other records, such as goods received notes.

Also, the auditors should discuss with management a response that indicates a difference between information requested to be confirmed, or contained in the entity records, and information provided by the confirming party. In cases where the auditor concludes that management's refusal to allow the auditor to send a confirmation request is unreasonable or the auditor is unable to accumulate relevant and reliable audit evidence from alternative audit procedures, the auditor before modifying his audit report should communicate such facts to those charged with governance.

Auditing standards identified some factors that may indicate doubts about the reliability of a response including the auditor receiving the response indirectly (i.e. the confirming party incorrectly addressed it to the entity rather than the auditor) or the response appearing not to come from the originally intended confirming party. Auditors are advised to assess the risk associated with receiving confirmation electronically, especially the risks as to reliability because proof of origin and authority of the respondent may be difficult to establish. Auditors are permitted to make direct contact using phone calls or any other means of communication with the confirming party to verify the source and contents of a response.

Finally, auditors should not confine external confirmations to account balances only. The auditor may request confirmation of the terms of agreement or transactions an entity has made with third parties. The confirmation request may be designed to ask if any modifications were made to the current agreement and, if so, what are the relevant details made to such agreement.

Inspection

Inspection of records and documents

Examination of internal and external documents and records whether they are in paper form, electronic form, or other media.

Inspection of records and documents is the auditor's examination of the client's internal or external documents and records to substantiate the information that is, or should be, included in the financial statements. Inspection can be used as a test of controls when the auditor examines records for evidence of an authorization. The documents examined by the auditor are the records used by the client to provide information for conducting its business in an organized manner, and may be in paper form, electronic form, or other media. Because each transaction in the client's organization is normally supported by at least one document, a large volume of this type of evidence is usually available. For example, the client often retains a journal voucher, customer order, a shipping document, and a duplicate sales invoice for each sales transaction. Figure 7-3 gives an example of the first document, a journal voucher, to be inspected to verify the accuracy of the accounting records.

Internal document

A document, such as an employee time report, that is prepared and used within the client's organization.

External document

A document, such as a vendor's invoice, that has been used by an outside party to the transaction being documented and that the client now has or can easily obtain.

Documents can be conveniently classified as internal and external. An **internal document** has been prepared and used within the client's organization and is retained without ever going to an outside party. Internal documents include journal vouchers, duplicate sales invoices, employees' time reports, inventory receiving reports, materials requisition forms, work sheets for cost allocation, minutes of board, committees and shareholders' meetings, and management representation. An **external document** has been handled by someone outside the client's organization who is a party to the transaction being documented. They are either currently held by the client or readily accessible. In some cases, external documents originate outside the client's organization and end up in the hands of the client. Examples of external documents include vendors' invoices, remittance advices returned with cash receipts from customer payment, bank statements, cancelled notes payable, confirmation from third parties, analysts' reports, insurance policies, and comparable data about competitors (benchmarking data). Some documents, such as cancelled checks, originate with the client, go to an outsider,

FIGURE 7-3	Journal Voucher

To: Accounting Department
    XYZ Company

Check Reason for Journal Voucher and Provide Explanation

[X] Transfer or correct previous revenue or expense transaction   [ ] For services rendered   [ ] Other

Instructions for completing this form are in Section 40 of the Manual of Business Procedures. Explain adjustments in detail—provide date, period covered, type of expenditure or revenue, references (CHK No., JVE No., etc.). Include in your explanation the reason for making the entry. An incomplete explanation will result in the return of the voucher for additional information. Corrections to previous transactions should be submitted within 90 days of their initial date, and should not cross fiscal years.

Explanation

Provide Department Name, Account Number, Object Code and Amount for Each Entry
(Shaded areas for Accounting use only)

		Acctg. T.C.	Account Number	Obj. Code	Amount	X
Debit	Accounts Receivable					
	Q Company		201		10,000,000	
	L Company		202			
	2 Company		203			
Credit	Sales					
	Q Company		401		10,000,000	
	L Company		402		2,000,000	
	2 Company		403		1,500,000	

Description to be put on ledger

_____   _____   _____
    Date   Authorized Signature (please sign in blue ink)   Phone

Routing:
1. Refer to Section 40 of the Manual of Business Procedures.
2. Obtain authorized signature(s).
3. Retain a copy for your records and send a copy to all departments impacted by the JVE.
4. Send original to Accounting, Room 360 Administration Building.

and are finally returned to the client. Figure 7-4 presents an example of an external document: a cash deposit slip.

The primary determinant of the auditor's willingness to accept a document as reliable evidence is whether it is internal or external and, when internal, whether it was created and processed under conditions of good internal control. Internal documents created and processed under conditions of weak internal control may not constitute reliable evidence. Original documents are considered more reliable than photocopies or facsimiles. Although auditors should consider the reliability of documentation, they rarely verify the authenticity of documentation. Auditors are not expected to be trained or be experts in document authentication.

Because external documents have been in the hands of both the client and another party to the transaction, there is some indication that both members are

FIGURE 7-4	An Example of a Cash Deposit Slip

ABC				ABC Bank	
Branch:		Cash Deposit		Date:	
Account Number		A/C Currency	For Bank Use Only		
Account Name		Deposit Currency	F.X. Rate	Valid Checked	
ID Details	Customer Signature(s) and/ or Stamp(s)	Amount			
	S.V				
Amount in Words					
Narrative			Deal No.		

in agreement about the information and the conditions stated on the document. Therefore, external documents are considered more reliable evidence than internal ones. Some external documents, such as title to land, insurance policies, indenture agreements, and contracts, have exceptional reliability because they are almost always prepared with considerable care and often have been reviewed by attorneys or other qualified experts.

When auditors use documentation to support recorded transactions or amounts, the process is often called **vouching**. To vouch recorded acquisition transactions, the auditor might, for example, verify entries in the acquisitions journal by examining supporting vendors' invoices and receiving reports and thereby satisfy the occurrence objective. If the auditor traces from receiving reports to the acquisitions journal to satisfy the completeness objective, however, it is not appropriate to call it vouching. This latter process is called 'tracing.'

Vouching

The use of documentation to support recorded transactions or amounts.

Analytical Procedures

Analytical procedures consist of evaluations of financial information through analysis of plausible relationships among both financial and non-financial data. Analytical procedures also investigate fluctuations or relationships that are considered inconsistent with other relevant information or that differ from expected values by a significant amount.

Analytical procedures use comparisons and relationships to assess whether account balances or other data appear reasonable compared to the auditor's expectations. For example, an auditor may compare the gross margin percent in the current year with the preceding year.

Analytical procedures are used extensively in practice, and are *required during the planning and completion phases on all audits*. We introduce the purposes of analytical procedures here and discuss the different types of analytical procedures more extensively in Chapter 8.

Understand the Client's Industry and Business
Auditors must obtain knowledge about a client's industry and business as a part of planning an audit. By conducting analytical procedures in which the current year's unaudited information is compared with prior years' audited information or industry data, changes are highlighted. These changes can represent important trends or specific events, all of which will influence audit planning. For example, a decline in gross margin percentages over time may indicate increasing competition in the company's market

SATYAM FRAUD CHECK SWITCHES TO PwC

As India's financial world struggles to digest revelations of the US$1.5 billion fraud in major software company, Satyam Computer Services, by the company's founder and chairman, Ramalinga Raju, accountants in the financial capital of Mumbai expressed bafflement at how the fraud was not exposed earlier.

"The accounting discrepancies should have been easily detected in the Satyam case," a senior accountant, Feroz Contractor, told *Asia Times Online*. "It appears from information available in the public domain that basic accounting procedures were not followed."

In a letter to Satyam's board of directors Raju, 53, confessed to inflating profits for years with "fictitious" assets and non-existent cash. Raju said that about US$1.04 billion, or 94 percent of the cash listed in assets at the end of the company's second quarter in September, was fictitious.

Debate in Mumbai is focused on whether Satyam, India's fourth largest computer software company, or its multinational auditors, PricewaterhouseCoopers (PwC), was more to blame for what is possibly corporate India's worst scandal. The case is similar to those involving Western companies after financial frauds, most notably Enron (2002) and the US$9 billion Worldcom accounting fraud the same year. The general verdict of accountants in Mumbai is that Satyam's auditors blew it big time, costing investors US$2 billion. The local unit of one of the Big Four audit firms, PwC, said in a statement that Satyam's accounts were supported by "appropriate audit evidence," according to Bloomberg. "Collusion" was a common term used by the accountant community. "My first reaction when I heard about the Satyam fraud was how had their auditors kept quiet about it," said Ramesh Kumar, an accountant with 19 years of experience in various companies. "Auditors not knowing about a fraud this size (US$1.5 billion) does not seem possible, particularly with the confession that Satyam has been doing it for years."

Audit procedures which should have been applied for specific accounts are:

- Bank balances: certificates from banks confirming the amount balance as shown in the company account books
- Cash in hand: the auditor has to physically check the client's cash reserves in sudden surprise inspections. Satyam reported a cash/bank balance of US$1.09 billion, while it actually only had about US$65 million as of September 30, 2008
- Outstanding debts: Satyam auditors seemingly have failed to spot faked outstanding debts worth US$99 million for the financial quarter ending September 2008, as no confirmations were sent to debtors thereby showing fake profits and duping investors.

Satyam's auditors have not apparently undertaken what traditionally would have been the minimum independent verification of the client's accounts as a chartered accountant firm is supposed to do.

The Institute of Chartered Accountants of India (ICAI) has said it is investigating the role of PwC in the scandal. "We are examining it on a high priority and strict action will be taken against auditors if found guilty," ICAI president Ved Jain told the media. "If found guilty of professional misconduct, the auditors stand to lose their practice licenses."

Source: Adapted from R. Murthy, 'Satyam fraud check switches to PwC', *Asia Times Online* (January 10, 2009) www.atimes.com.

---

area and the need to consider inventory pricing more carefully during the audit. Similarly, an increase in the balance in fixed assets may indicate a significant acquisition that must be reviewed.

Assess the Entity's Ability to Continue as a Going Concern Analytical procedures are often a useful indicator for determining whether the client company has financial problems. Certain analytical procedures can help the auditor assess the likelihood of failure. For example, if a higher-than-normal ratio of long-term debt to net worth is combined with a lower-than-average ratio of profits to total assets, a relatively high risk of financial failure may be indicated. Not only will such conditions affect the audit plan, they may indicate that substantial doubt exists about the entity's ability to continue as a going concern, which, as discussed in Chapter 3, requires a report modification.

Unusual fluctuations

Significant unexpected differences indicated by analytical procedures between the current year's unaudited financial data and other data used in comparisons.

Indicate the Presence of Possible Misstatements in the Financial Statements Significant unexpected differences between the current year's unaudited financial data and other data used in comparisons are commonly called **unusual fluctuations**. Unusual fluctuations occur when significant differences are not expected but do exist, or when significant differences are expected but do not exist. In either case, the presence of an accounting misstatement is one possible reason for the unusual fluctuation. If the unusual fluctuation is large, the auditor must determine the reason and be satisfied that the cause is a valid economic event and not a misstatement. For example, in comparing the ratio of the allowance for uncollectible accounts receivable to gross accounts receivable with that of the previous year, suppose that the ratio has decreased while, at the same time, accounts receivable turnover also decreased. The combination of these two pieces of information indicates a possible understatement of the allowance. This aspect of analytical procedures is often called 'attention directing' because it results in more detailed procedures in the specific audit areas where misstatements might be found.

Reduce Detailed Audit Tests When an analytical procedure reveals no unusual fluctuations, this implies the possibility of a material misstatement is minimized. In such cases, the analytical procedure constitutes substantive evidence in support of the fair statement of the related account balances, and it is possible to perform fewer detailed tests in connection with those accounts. In other cases, certain audit procedures can be eliminated, sample sizes can be reduced, or the timing of the procedures can be moved farther away from the balance sheet date.

Inquiries of the Client

Inquiry

The obtaining of written or oral information from the client in response to specific questions during the audit.

Inquiry is the obtaining of *written* or *oral* information from the client in response to questions from the auditor. Although considerable evidence is obtained from the client through inquiry, it usually cannot be regarded as conclusive because it is not from an independent source and may be biased in the client's favor. Therefore, when the auditor obtains evidence through inquiry, it is normally necessary to obtain corroborating evidence through other procedures. As an illustration, when the auditor wants to obtain information about the client's method of recording and controlling accounting transactions, the auditor usually begins by asking the client how the internal controls operate. Later, the auditor performs audit tests using inspection and observation to determine whether the transactions are recorded (completeness objective) and authorized (occurrence objective) in the manner stated. In certain circumstances, the auditor may consider it necessary to obtain written representation from management and, where appropriate, those charged with governance to confirm responses to oral inquiries. This is normally achieved as the last corroborating evidence just before the auditor issues his audit or review report.

Guidelines for auditors to conduct and assess inquiries may include:

- Consider the knowledge, objectivity, qualifications, and experience of the employee responding to inquiry.
- Ask clear, concise, and relevant questions.
- Listen actively and effectively to employees responses.
- Study the reactions and evaluate the responses of the employees and ask follow-up questions.
- Use open and closed questions appropriately.

Recalculation

Recalculation involves rechecking mathematical accuracy of documents or records. Recalculation includes extending sales invoices and inventory, adding journals and subsidiary records, and checking the calculation of depreciation expense and prepaid expenses. Recalculation may be performed manually or electronically. Nowadays, a large portion of auditors' recalculation is done using computer-assisted audit techniques (CAATs) to check the accuracy of the summarization of a particular electronic file.

Reperformance

Reperformance is the auditor's independent tests of client accounting procedures or controls that were originally done as part of the entity's accounting and internal control system. Whereas recalculation involves rechecking a computation, reperformance involves checking other procedures. For example, the auditor may compare the price on an invoice to an approved price list, or may reperform the aging of accounts receivable. Because the auditor creates this type of evidence, it is normally viewed as highly reliable. Another type of reperformance is for the auditor to recheck transfers of information by tracing information included in more than one place to verify that it is recorded at the same amount each time. For example, the auditor normally makes limited tests to ascertain that the information in the sales journal has been included for the proper customer and at the correct amount in the subsidiary accounts receivable records and is accurately summarized in the general ledger.

Appropriateness of Types of Evidence

As discussed earlier in this chapter, the characteristics for determining the appropriateness of evidence are relevance and reliability. Table 7-4 includes the eight types of evidence related to five of the six criteria that determine the reliability of evidence. Note that two of the characteristics that determine the appropriateness of evidence—relevance and

TABLE 7-4	Appropriateness of Types of Evidence				
	Criteria to Determine Appropriateness				
Type of Evidence	Independence of Provider	Effectiveness of Client's Internal Controls	Auditor's Direct Knowledge	Qualifications of Provider	Objectivity of Evidence
Physical examination	High (auditor does)	Varies	High	Normally high (auditor does)	High
Observation	High (auditor does)	Varies	High	Normally high (auditor does)	Medium
Confirmation	High	Not applicable	Low	Varies—usually high	High
Inspection	Varies—external documents more independent than internal	Varies	Low	Varies	High
Analytical procedures	High/low (auditor does/ client responds)	Varies	Low	Normally high (auditor does/ client responds)	Varies—usually low
Inquiries of client	Low (client provides)	Not applicable	Low	Varies	Varies—low to high
Recalculation	High (auditor does)	Varies	High	High (auditor does)	High
Reperformance	High (auditor does)	Varies	High	High (auditor does)	High

timeliness—are not included in Table 7-4. Each of the eight types of evidence included in the table has the potential to be both relevant and timely, depending on its source and when the evidence is obtained. Several other observations are apparent from studying Table 7-4.

- First, the effectiveness of a client's internal controls has significant influence on the reliability of most types of evidence. Obviously, internal documentation from a company with effective internal control is more reliable because the documents are more likely to be accurate. Conversely, analytical procedures will not be reliable evidence if the controls that produced the data provide inaccurate information.
- Second, both physical examination and recalculation are likely to be highly reliable if the internal controls are effective, but their use differs considerably. This effectively illustrates that two completely different types of evidence can be equally reliable.
- Third, a specific type of evidence is rarely sufficient by itself to provide appropriate evidence to satisfy any audit objective.

Cost of Types of Evidence

The two most expensive types of evidence are physical examination and confirmation. Physical examination is costly because it normally requires the auditor's presence when the client is counting the asset, often on the balance sheet date. For example, physical examination of inventory can result in several auditors traveling to scattered geographical locations. Confirmation is costly because the auditor must follow careful procedures in the confirmation preparation, mailing, and receipt, and in the follow-up of no responses and exceptions.

Inspection, analytical procedures, and reperformance are moderately costly. If client personnel locate documents for the auditor and organize them for convenient use, inspection usually has a fairly low cost. When auditors must find those documents themselves, however, inspection can be extremely costly. Even under ideal circumstances, information and data on documents are sometimes complex and require interpretation and analysis. It is usually time-consuming for an auditor to read and evaluate a client's contracts, lease agreements, and minutes of the board of directors' meetings. Because analytical procedures are considerably less expensive than confirmations and physical examination, most auditors prefer to replace tests of details with analytical procedures when possible. For example, it may be far less expensive to calculate and review sales and accounts receivable ratios than to confirm accounts receivable. If it is possible to reduce the use of confirmations by performing analytical procedures, considerable cost savings can be achieved. But analytical procedures require the auditor to decide which analytical procedures to use, make the calculations, and evaluate the results. Doing so often takes considerable time. The cost of reperformance tests depends on the nature of the procedure being tested. Comparatively simple tests such as reperforming the comparison of invoices to price lists are likely to take minimal time. However, reperforming procedures such as the client's bank reconciliation are likely to take considerable time.

The three least-expensive types of evidence are observation, inquiries of the client, and recalculation. Observation is normally done concurrently with other audit procedures. Auditors can easily observe whether client personnel are following appropriate inventory counting procedures at the same time they count a sample of inventory (physical examination). Inquiries of clients are done extensively on every audit and normally have a low cost, although certain inquiries may be costly, such as obtaining written statements from the client documenting discussions throughout the audit. Recalculation is usually low cost because it involves simple calculations and tracing that can be done at the auditor's convenience. Often, the auditor's computer software is used to perform many of these tests.

Application of Types of Evidence to the Four Evidence Decisions

Table 7-5 shows an application of three types of evidence to the four evidence decisions for one balance-related audit objective—inventory quantities on the client's perpetual records agree with items physically on hand. Take a moment to turn back to Table 6-4 and examine column 3. These are the balance-related audit objectives for the audit of inventory for Arabian Hardware Co. The overall objective is to obtain persuasive evidence at minimum cost to verify that inventory is materially correct. The auditor must therefore decide:

- Which audit procedures to use to satisfy each balance-related audit objective
- What the sample size should be for each procedure
- Which items from the population to include in the sample
- When to perform each procedure

For the objective 'inventory quantities on the client's perpetual records agree with items physically on hand,' the auditor selected the three types of evidence included in Table 7-5. The auditor decided that the other types of evidence studied in this chapter were not relevant or necessary for this objective. Only one audit procedure is included for each type of evidence, and illustrative decisions for sample size, items to select, and timing are shown for each procedure.

Terms Used in Audit Procedures

As stated earlier, audit procedures are the detailed steps, usually written in the form of instructions, for the accumulation of the eight types of audit evidence. They should be sufficiently clear to enable all members of the audit team to understand what is to be done.

Several terms commonly used to describe audit procedures are defined in Table 7-6. To illustrate each term, an audit procedure and associated type of evidence are also shown.

TABLE 7-5	Types of Evidence and Four Evidence Decisions for a Balance-Related Audit Objective for Inventory*			
		Evidence Decisions		
Type of Evidence	Audit Procedure	Sample Size	Items to Select	Timing
Observation	Observe client's personnel counting inventory to determine whether they are properly following instructions	All count teams	Not applicable	Balance sheet date
Physical examination	Count a sample of inventory and compare quantity and description to client's counts	120 items	40 items with large dollar value, plus 80 randomly selected	Balance sheet date
Inspection	Compare quantity on client's perpetual records to quantity on client's counts	70 items	30 items with large dollar value, plus 40 randomly selected	Balance sheet date

*Balance-related audit objective: Inventory quantities on the client's perpetual records agree with items physically on hand.

TABLE 7-6	Terms, Audit Procedures, and Types of Evidence	

Term and Definition	Illustrative Audit Procedure	Type of Evidence
Examine—A reasonably detailed study of a document or record to determine specific facts about it.	*Examine* a sample of vendors' invoices to determine whether the goods or services received are reasonable and of the type normally used by the client's business.	Inspection
Scan—A less-detailed examination of a document or record to determine whether there is something unusual warranting further investigation.	*Scan* the sales journal, looking for large and unusual transactions.	Analytical procedures
Read—An examination of written information to determine facts pertinent to the audit.	*Read* the minutes of a board of directors' meeting and summarize all information that is pertinent to the financial statements in an audit file.	Inspection
Compute—A calculation done by the auditor independent of the client.	*Compute* inventory turnover ratios and compare with those of previous years as a test of inventory obsolescence.	Analytical procedures
Recompute—A calculation done to determine whether a client's calculation is correct.	*Recompute* the unit sales price times the number of units for a sample of duplicate sales invoices and compare the totals with the calculations.	Recalculation
Foot—Addition of a column of numbers to determine whether the total is the same as the client's.	*Foot* the sales journal for a one-month period and compare all totals with the general ledger.	Recalculation
Trace—An instruction normally associated with inspection or reperformance. The instruction should state what the auditor is tracing and where it is being traced from and to. Often, an audit procedure that includes the term *trace* will also include a second instruction, such as *compare* or *recalculate*.	*Trace* a sample of sales transactions from sales invoices to the sales journal, and *compare* customer name, date, and the total dollar value of the sale.	Inspection
	Trace postings from the sales journal to the general ledger accounts.	Reperformance
Compare—A comparison of information in two different locations. The instruction should state which information is being compared in as much detail as practical.	Select a sample of sales invoices and *compare* the unit selling price as stated on the invoice to the list of unit selling prices authorized by management.	Inspection
Count—A determination of assets on hand at a given time. This term should be associated only with the type of evidence defined as physical examination.	*Count* a sample of 100 inventory items and compare quantity and description to client's counts.	Physical examination
Observe—The act of observation should be associated with the type of evidence defined as observation.	*Observe* whether the two inventory count teams independently count and record inventory counts.	Observation
Inquire—The act of inquiry should be associated with the type of evidence defined as inquiry.	*Inquire* of management whether there is any obsolete inventory on hand at the balance sheet date.	Inquiries of client
Vouch—The use of documents to verify recorded transactions or amounts.	*Vouch* a sample of recorded acquisition transactions to vendors' invoices and receiving reports.	Inspection

AUDIT DOCUMENTATION

Auditing standards state that **audit documentation** is the *principal record of auditing procedures applied, evidence obtained, and conclusions reached by the auditor in the engagement.* Audit documentation should include all the information the auditor considers necessary to adequately conduct the audit and to provide support for the audit report. Audit documentation may also be referred to as working papers, although, increasingly, audit documentation is maintained in computerized files.

OBJECTIVE 7-5

Understand the purposes of audit documentation.

Audit documentation

The principal record of auditing procedures applied, evidence obtained, and conclusions reached by the auditor in the engagement.

Purposes of Audit Documentation

The overall objective of audit documentation is to aid the auditor in providing reasonable assurance that an adequate audit was conducted in accordance with auditing standards. ISA 230 (para. 6a) states that:

> *Preparing sufficient and appropriate audit documentation on a timely basis helps to enhance the quality of the audit and facilitates the effective review and evaluation of the audit evidence obtained and conclusions reached before the auditor's report is finalized. Audit documentation prepared after the audit work has been performed is likely to be less accurate than documentation prepared at the time such work is performed.*

More specifically, audit documentation, as it pertains to the current year's audit, serves the following purposes.

A Basis for Planning the Audit If the auditor is to plan an audit adequately, the necessary reference information must be available in the **audit files**. The files may include such diverse planning information as descriptive information about internal control, various analyses and issues memoranda, checklists, a time budget for individual audit areas, the audit program, correspondence (including e-mail) concerning important issues and the results of the preceding year's audit. The auditor may also maintain abstracts or copies of the client's records such as significant and specific contracts and agreements and board and other committees' meetings. However, the auditor should not consider such audit documentation as a substitute for the client's accounting records.

Audit file

One or more folders or any other storage media whether in physical or electronic form, containing all records forming the audit documentation for a specific engagement.

A Record of the Evidence Accumulated and the Results of the Tests Audit documentation is the primary means of documenting that an adequate audit was conducted in accordance with auditing standards. If the need arises, the auditor must be able to demonstrate to regulatory authorities and courts that the audit was well planned and adequately supervised; the evidence accumulated was appropriate and sufficient; and the audit report was proper, considering the results of the audit. Such audit evidence must be in line with both auditing standards and applicable legal requirements.

When audit procedures involve sampling of transactions or balances, the audit documentation should identify the items tested. The audit files should also document significant audit findings or issues, actions taken to address them, and the basis for the conclusions reached. For example, the auditor should document specific transactions at year-end to determine whether transactions were recorded in the proper period. If misstatements are detected during these cutoff tests, the auditor should document the additional procedures performed to determine the extent of cutoff misstatements, the conclusion as to whether the account balances affected are fairly stated, and whether any audit adjustments should be proposed.

The documentation of the audit should also identify staff who performed the audit work, those who reviewed such work and the date the work was completed. Auditors must also document discussions of important issues with management, those charged with governance, and other parties responsible for the preparation and assessment of the client's financial statements. The auditor should pay attention to inconsistency in the application of accounting principles and document how he addressed such inconsistency.

Data for Determining the Proper Type of Audit Report Audit documentation provides an important source of information to assist the auditor in deciding whether sufficient appropriate evidence was accumulated to justify the audit report in a given set of circumstances. The data in the files are equally useful for evaluating whether the financial statements are fairly stated, given the audit evidence.

A Basis for Review by Supervisors and Partners The audit files are the primary frame of reference used by supervisory personnel to review the work of assistants. The careful review by supervisors also provides evidence that the audit was properly supervised.

In addition to the purposes directly related to the audit report, the audit files often serve as the basis for preparing tax returns, filings with the financial supervisory boards, and other reports. They are also a source of information for issuing communications to management and those charged with governance, such as the audit committee, concerning various matters such as internal control deficiencies or operational recommendations. Audit files are also a useful frame of reference for training personnel and as an aid in planning and coordinating subsequent audits.

Ownership of Audit Files

Audit documentation prepared during the engagement, including schedules prepared by the client for the auditor, is the *property of the auditor*. The only time anyone else, including the client, has a legal right to examine the files is when they are subpoenaed by a court as legal evidence. At the completion of the engagement, audit files are retained on the audit firm's premises for future reference and to comply with auditing standards related to document retention.

Confidentiality of Audit Files

According to the IFAC *Code of Ethics for Professional Accountants*, the auditor shall not disclose any confidential information obtained in the course of providing professional engagement unless an explicit consent is made by the client. Auditors may provide information obtained through their audit if they receive an order from a court of law or other financial supervisory board.

During the course of the audit, auditors obtain a considerable amount of information of a confidential nature, including officers' salaries, product pricing and advertising plans, and product cost data. If auditors divulged this information to outsiders or to client employees who have been denied access, their relationship with management would be seriously strained. Furthermore, having access to the audit files would give employees an opportunity to alter the files. For these reasons, care must be taken to safeguard the audit files at all times.

In most Arab countries, the Companies Acts explicitly prohibit auditors from disclosing clients information unless they are ordered to do so by a court of law or by a disciplinary committee of a professional association. Auditors would be liable to compensate their clients for any damages resulting from disclosing information without clients' consent. Also, clients can replace auditors who disclose information without their consent or legal requirement. Moreover, commercial laws and statutes of professional accountancy associations in countries such as Kuwait, Saudi Arabia, and the U.A.E. prohibit auditors from disclosing confidential information acquired during their audit and placing penalties for violations of such requirements.

Requirements for Retention of Audit Documentation

The International Standard on Quality Control (ISQC 1) mandates firms to establish policies and procedures for the timely completion of the audit working papers, ordinarily not more than 60 days after the date of the auditor's report (ISQC 1, Para 52 and A50). Any change to the working papers must be made during this final assembly period unless they are administrative in nature. Examples of administrative activities include cross referencing working papers and deleting or discarding draft documentation. Auditors are not allowed to delete or discard audit documentation of any nature before the end of the retention period.

In Kuwait, Article No. 16 of the Law No. 5 of 1981 requires that every auditor must maintain a file for every client company containing documents and copies of documents and correspondence related with his services to the client. Also, the above law requires auditors to maintain a register to record all matters related to their clients' services showing details of the work performed, time undertaken to complete the work, and names of all subordinates and other experts assigned to the service. The law requires that records for the work performed should be retained for a period of ten years.

In the United Arab Emirates, Article No. 33 of the Law No. 22 of 1995 states that the auditor should maintain the records, files, and data regarding his clients for a period of not less than five years, starting from the end of the last financial year in which he handled their accounts. The auditor's retirement will not relieve him of the obligation to maintain the files, records, and data referred to in the previous paragraph.

On the other hand, in Saudi Arabia, Article No. 12 of the Royal Decree No. M/12 of 1991 states that a certified public accountant, under all circumstances, shall maintain documents received from clients, audit working papers, and copies of financial statements pertaining to his clients for a minimum period of ten years from the date of issue of the audit report covering each financial year that is duly audited. In other Arab countries, similar requirements exist when auditors are required to maintain their working papers for a period of not less than 5 up to 15 years under civil laws. Instructors are advised to ask their students to investigate period of retention of auditors' working papers under various laws in their countries.

Auditing standards require that records for audits of private companies be retained for a minimum of five years. The Sarbanes–Oxley Act in the U.S. requires auditors of public companies to prepare and maintain audit files and other information related to any audit report in sufficient detail to support the auditor's conclusions, for a period of not less than seven years. The law makes the knowing and willful destruction of audit documentation within the seven-year period a criminal offense subject to financial fines and imprisonment up to ten years. No explicit requirements yet exist in laws in Arab countries for destruction of documents before the end of the period for retention of the auditor's working papers.

The destruction of documents and the indictment of Arthur Andersen in the Enron fraud case showed the importance of the practice of archiving and retaining audit documentation. The Andersen federal indictment and convictions on obstruction of justice charges for the deletion and alterations of audit documentation related to the Enron fraud case are explained next. The conviction of Arthur Andersen for such destruction of the audit evidence led to the failure of this giant CPA firm.

SEC rules in the U.S. require public company auditors to maintain the following documentation:

- Working papers or other documents that form the basis for the audit of the company's annual financial statements or review of the company's quarterly financial statements
- Memos, correspondence, communications, other documents, and records, including electronic records, related to the audit or review.

These rules significantly increase the audit documentation that must be retained for audits of public companies. For example, auditors of public companies are required to retain e-mail correspondence that contains information meeting the preceding criteria. On the other hand, ISA 230 does not provide specific requirements for audit documentation or provide examples of the types of documents the auditor can acquire to support the audit findings.

CONTENTS AND ORGANIZATION

OBJECTIVE 7-6

Prepare organized audit documentation.

Each audit firm establishes its own approach to preparing and organizing audit files, and the auditor must adopt the firm's approach. This section emphasizes general concepts common to all audit documentation.

Figure 7-5 illustrates the contents and organization of a typical set of audit files. They contain virtually everything involved in the audit. There is logic to the type of audit documentation prepared for an audit and the way it is arranged in the files, though different firms may follow somewhat different approaches. In the figure, the audit files start with general information, such as corporate data in the permanent files, and end with the financial statements and audit report. In between are the audit files supporting the auditor's tests.

FIGURE 7-5	Audit File Contents and Organization

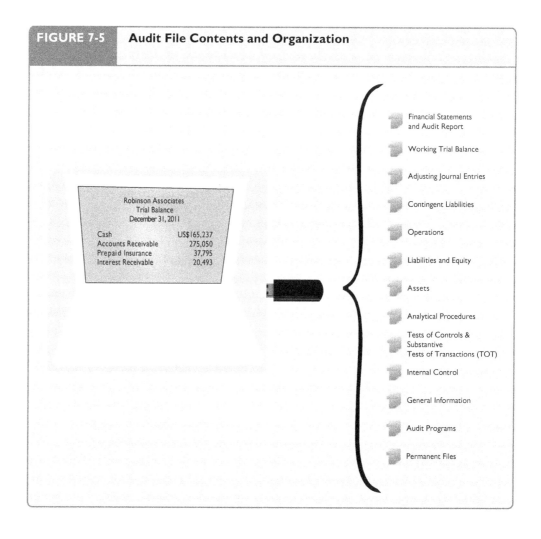

Permanent Files

Permanent files contain data of a *historical or continuing nature* pertinent to the current audit. These files provide a convenient source of information about the audit that is of continuing interest from year to year. The permanent files typically include the following:

- *Extracts or copies of such company documents of continuing importance as the articles of incorporation (or association), bylaws, bond indentures, and contracts.* The contracts may include pension plans, leases, stock options, and so on. Each of these documents is significant to the auditor for as many years as it is in effect.
- *Analyses from previous years of accounts that have continuing importance to the auditor.* These include accounts such as long-term debt, shareholders' equity accounts, goodwill, and fixed assets. Having this information in the permanent files enables the auditor to concentrate on analyzing only the changes in the current year's balance while retaining the results of previous years' audits in a form accessible for review.
- *Information related to understanding internal control and assessing control risk.* This includes organization charts, flowcharts, questionnaires, and other internal control information, including identification of controls and weaknesses in the system. These records are used as a starting point for documenting the auditor's understanding of the control system, since aspects of the systems are often unchanged from year to year.
- *The results of analytical procedures from previous years' audits.* Among these data are ratios and percentages computed by the auditor and the total balance or the balance by month for selected accounts. This information is useful in helping the auditor decide whether there are unusual changes in the current year's account balances that should be investigated more extensively.

Documenting analytical procedures, understanding of internal control, and assessing control risk are included in the current period audit files rather than in the permanent files by many CPA firms.

Current Files

The **current files** include all audit documentation applicable to the year under audit. There is one set of permanent files for the client and a set of current files for each year's audit. The following are types of information often included in the current file:

Audit Program   Auditing standards require a written audit program for every audit. The audit program is ordinarily maintained in a separate file to improve the coordination and integration of all parts of the audit, although some firms also include a copy of the audit program for each audit section with that section's audit documentation. As the audit progresses, each auditor initials or electronically signs the program for the audit procedures performed and indicates the date of completion. The inclusion in the audit files of a well-designed audit program completed in a conscientious manner is evidence of a high-quality audit.

General Information   Some audit files include current period information of a general nature rather than evidence designed to support specific financial statement amounts. This includes such items as audit planning memos, abstracts or copies of minutes of the board of directors' meetings, abstracts of contracts or agreements not included in the permanent files, notes on discussions with the client, supervisors' review comments, and general conclusions.

Working Trial Balance   Because the basis for preparing the financial statements is the general ledger, the amounts included in that record are the focal point of the audit.

Working trial balance

A listing of the general ledger accounts and their year-end balances.

Lead schedule

An audit schedule that contains the detailed accounts from the general ledger making up a line item total in the working trial balance.

As early as possible after the balance sheet date, the auditor obtains or prepares a listing of the general ledger accounts and their year-end balances. This schedule is the **working trial balance**. Software programs enable the auditor to download the client's ending general ledger balances into a working trial balance file.

The technique used by many firms is to have the auditor's working trial balance in the same format as the financial statements. Each line item on the trial balance is supported by a **lead schedule**, containing the detailed accounts from the general ledger making up the line item total. Each detailed account on the lead schedule is, in turn, supported by proper schedules supporting the audit work performed and the conclusions reached. For example, the relationship between cash as it is stated on the financial statements, the working trial balance, the lead schedule for cash, and the supporting audit documentation is presented in Figure 7-6. As indicated, cash on the financial statements is the same as on the working trial balance and the total of the detail on the cash lead schedule. Initially, amounts for the lead schedule were taken from the general ledger. The audit work performed resulted in an adjustment to cash that will be shown in the detail schedules and is reflected on the lead schedule, the working trial balance, and the financial statements.

Adjusting and Reclassification Entries When the auditor discovers material misstatements in the accounting records, the financial statements must be corrected. For example, if the client failed to properly reduce inventory for obsolete raw materials, the auditor can propose an adjusting entry to reflect the realizable value of the inventory. Even though adjusting entries discovered in the audit are often prepared by the auditor, they must be approved by the client because management has primary responsibility for the fair presentation of the statements. Figure 7-6 illustrates an adjustment of the general cash account for US$90.

Reclassification entries are frequently made in the statements to present accounting information properly, even when the general ledger balances are correct. A common example is the reclassification for financial statement purposes of material credit balances in accounts receivable to accounts payable. Because the balance in accounts receivable in the general ledger reflects the accounts receivable properly from the point of view of operating the company on a day-to-day basis, the reclassification entry is not included in the client's general ledger.

Only those adjusting and reclassification entries that significantly affect the fair presentation of financial statements must be recorded. Auditors decide when a misstatement should be adjusted based on materiality. At the same time, auditors must keep in mind that several immaterial misstatements that are not adjusted could, when combined, result in a material overall misstatement. It is common for auditors to summarize all entries that have not been recorded in a separate audit schedule as a means of assessing their cumulative effect.

Supporting schedules

Detailed schedules prepared by the client or the auditor in support of specific amounts on the financial statements.

Supporting Schedules The largest portion of audit documentation includes the detailed **supporting schedules** prepared by the client or the auditors in support of specific amounts on the financial statements. Auditors must choose the proper type of schedule for a given aspect of the audit in order to document the adequacy of the audit and to fulfill the other objectives of audit documentation. Here are the major types of supporting schedules:

- *Analysis.* An analysis is designed to show the *activity in a general ledger* account during the entire period under audit, tying together the beginning and ending balances. This type of schedule is normally used for accounts such as marketable securities; notes receivable; allowance for doubtful accounts; property, plant, and equipment; long-term debt; and all equity accounts. The common characteristic of these accounts is the significance of the activity in the account during the year. In most cases, the analysis has cross-references to other audit files.

FIGURE 7-6   Relationships of Audit Documentation to Financial Statements

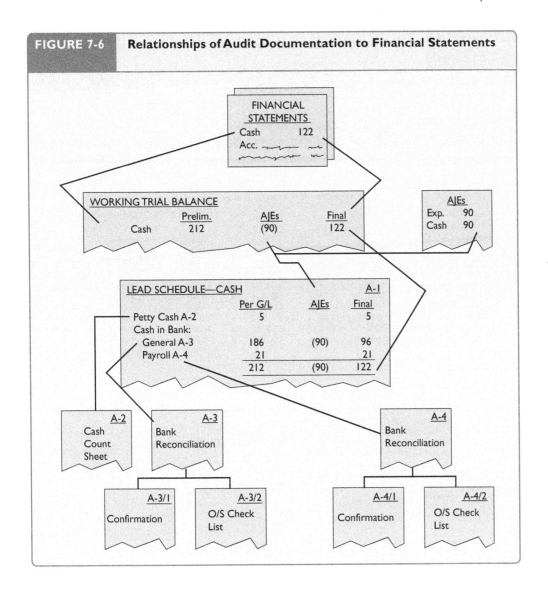

- *Trial balance or list.* This type of schedule consists of the *details that make up a year-end balance* of a general ledger account. It differs from an analysis in that it includes only those items making up the end-of-the-period balance. Common examples include trial balances or lists in support of trade accounts receivable, trade accounts payable, repair and maintenance expense, legal expense, and miscellaneous income. An example is included in Figure 7-7.
- *Reconciliation of amounts.* A reconciliation *supports a specific amount* and is normally expected to tie the amount recorded in the client's records to another source of information. Examples include the reconciliation of cash balances with bank statements, the reconciliation of subsidiary accounts receivable balances with confirmations from customers, and the reconciliation of accounts payable balances with vendors' statements. See the bank reconciliation example on page 753.
- *Tests of reasonableness.* A test of reasonableness schedule, as the name implies, contains information that enables the auditor to evaluate whether the client's balance appears to include a misstatement considering the circumstances in the engagement. Frequently, auditors test depreciation expense, the provision for income taxes, and the allowance for doubtful accounts using tests of reasonableness. These tests are primarily analytical procedures.
- *Summary of procedures.* Another type of schedule *summarizes the results* of a specific audit procedure. A summary schedule documents the extent of testing,

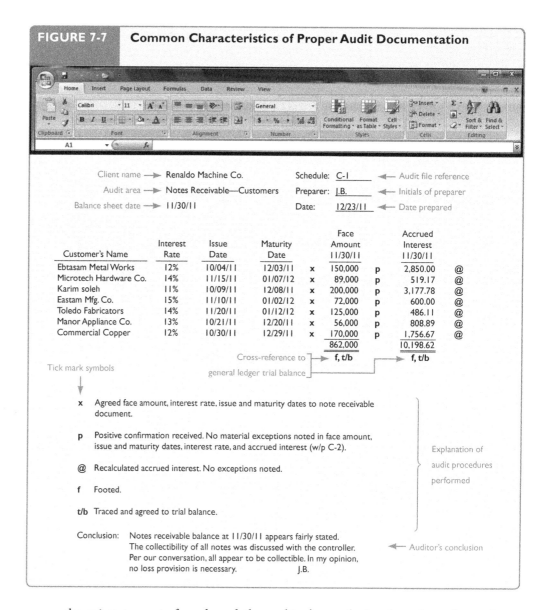

FIGURE 7-7 Common Characteristics of Proper Audit Documentation

the misstatements found, and the auditor's conclusion based on the testing. Examples are the summary of the results of accounts receivable confirmations and the summary of inventory observations.

- *Examination of supporting documents.* A number of special-purpose schedules are designed to *show detailed tests performed*, such documents examined during tests of controls and substantive tests of transactions. These schedules show no totals, and they do not tie in to the general ledger because their purpose is to document the tests performed and the results found. However, the schedules must state a positive or negative conclusion about the objective of the test.

- *Informational.* This type of schedule contains information as opposed to audit evidence. These schedules include information for tax returns and forms submitted to financial oversight boards organizing capital markets and data such as time budgets and the client's working hours, which are helpful in administration of the engagement.

- *Outside documentation.* Much of the content of the audit files consists of outside documentation gathered by auditors, such as confirmation replies and copies of client agreements. Although not 'schedules' in the usual sense, they are indexed and filed. Audit procedures are indicated on them in the same manner as on other schedules.

Preparation of Audit Documentation

The documentation should be prepared in sufficient detail to provide an experienced auditor with no connection to the audit a clear understanding of the work performed, the evidence obtained and its source, and the conclusions reached. Although the design depends on the objectives involved, audit documentation should possess certain characteristics:

- Each audit file should be properly identified with such information as the client's name, the period covered, a description of the contents, the initials of the preparer, the date of preparation, and an index code.
- Audit documentation should be indexed and cross-referenced to aid in organizing and filing. One type of indexing is illustrated in Figure 7-6. The lead schedule for cash has been indexed as A-1, and the individual general ledger accounts making up the total cash on the financial statements are indexed as A-2 through A-4. The final indexing is for the schedules supporting A-3 and A-4.
- Completed audit documentation must clearly indicate the audit work performed. This is accomplished in three ways: by a written statement in the form of a memorandum, by initialing the audit procedures in the audit program, and by notations directly on the schedules. Notations on schedules are accomplished by the use of **tick marks**, which are symbols adjacent to the detail on the body of the schedule. These notations must be clearly explained at the bottom of the schedule.
- Audit documentation should include sufficient information to fulfill the objectives for which it was designed. To properly prepare audit documentation, the auditor must know his or her goals. For example, if a schedule is designed to list the detail and show the verification of support of a balance sheet account, such as prepaid insurance, it is essential that the detail on the schedule reconciles with the trial balance.
- The conclusions that were reached about the segment of the audit under consideration should be plainly stated.

Tick marks

Symbols used on an audit schedule that provide additional information or details of audit procedures performed.

EFFECT OF TECHNOLOGY ON AUDIT EVIDENCE AND AUDIT DOCUMENTATION

Audit evidence is increasingly presented and stored in electronic form, and auditors must evaluate how electronic information affects their ability to gather sufficient, appropriate evidence. In certain instances, electronic evidence may exist only at a point in time. That evidence may not be retrievable later if files are changed and if the client lacks backup files. Therefore, auditors must consider the availability of electronic evidence early in the audit and plan their evidence gathering accordingly.

When evidence can be examined only in machine-readable form, auditors use computers to read and examine evidence. Commercial audit software programs, such as ACL Software and Interactive Data Extraction and Analysis (IDEA) software, are designed specifically for use by auditors. These programs are typically Windows-based and can easily be operated on the auditor's desktop or notebook computer. The auditor obtains copies of client databases or master files in machine-readable form and uses the software to perform a variety of tests of the client's electronic data. These audit software packages are relatively easy to use, even by auditors with little IT training, and can be applied to a wide variety of clients with minimal customization. Auditors also use spreadsheet software to perform audit tests.

A new electronic language XBRL (eXtensible Business Reporting Language) is now being used by listed companies to produce their financial statements on a quarterly and

OBJECTIVE 7-7

Describe how technology affects audit evidence and audit documentation.

annual basis to the SEC in the U.S. Auditors should be aware of the features of such language and be able to examine statements produced using this new IT language.

In the Arab countries, a number of financial oversight boards have taken steps to introduce XBRL as a tool to be used by listed companies to submit their interim and annual financial statements to such boards. The availability of adequate financial resources will help the successful implementation of the above IT tool for financial reporting purposes.

Auditors also use technology to convert traditional paper-based documentation into electronic files in order to organize and analyze audit documentation. Some firms develop their own software, while others buy commercial audit documentation software. Using audit management software, an auditor can prepare a trial balance, lead schedules, supporting audit documentation, and financial statements, as well as perform ratio analysis. Tick marks and other explanations, such as reviewer notes, can be entered directly into computerized files. In addition, data can be imported and exported to other applications, so auditors may download a client's general ledger or export tax information to a commercial tax preparation package. Auditors also use local area networks and group share software programs to access audit documentation simultaneously from remote locations.

SUMMARY

An important part of every audit is determining the proper types and amounts of audit evidence to gather. Auditors use eight types of evidence in an audit. The persuasiveness of the evidence depends on both its appropriateness and sufficiency. The appropriateness of audit evidence is determined by its relevance in meeting audit objectives and its reliability.

Audit documentation is an essential part of every audit for effectively planning the audit, providing a record of the evidence accumulated and the results of the tests, deciding the proper type of audit report, and reviewing the work of assistants. Auditing firms establish their own policies and approaches to audit documentation to make sure that these objectives are met. High-quality audit firms make sure that audit documentation is properly prepared and is sufficient for the circumstances in the audit.

ESSENTIAL TERMS

Appropriateness of evidence   p. 198

Audit documentation   p. 215

Audit file   p. 215

Audit procedure   p. 195

Audit program   p. 196

Confirmation   p. 203

Current files   p. 219

External document   p. 206

Inquiry   p. 210

Inspection   p. 198

Inspection of records and documents   p. 206

Internal document   p. 206

Lead schedule   p. 220

Observation   p. 203

Permanent files   p. 219

Persuasiveness of evidence   p. 197

Physical examination   p. 202

Recalculation   p. 211

Relevance of evidence   p. 198

Reliability of evidence   p. 198

Reperformance   p. 211

Sufficiency of evidence   p. 200

Supporting schedules   p. 220

Tick marks   p. 223

Unusual fluctuations   p. 210

Vouching   p. 208

Working trial balance   p. 220

REVIEW QUESTIONS

7-1 (Objective 7-1) Discuss the similarities and differences between evidence in a legal case and evidence in an audit of financial statements.

7-2 (Objective 7-2) List the four major evidence decisions that must be made on every audit.

7-3 (Objective 7-2) Describe what is meant by an audit procedure. Why is it important for audit procedures to be carefully worded?

7-4 (Objective 7-2) Describe what is meant by an audit program for accounts receivable. What four things should be included in an audit program?

7-5 (Objective 7-3) Explain why the auditor can be persuaded only with a reasonable level of assurance, rather than convinced, that the financial statements are correct.

7-6 (Objective 7-3) Identify the two factors that determine the persuasiveness of evidence. How are these two factors related to audit procedures, sample size, items to select, and timing?

7-7 (Objective 7-3) Identify the six characteristics that determine the reliability of evidence. For each characteristic, provide one example of a type of evidence that is likely to be reliable.

7-8 (Objective 7-4) List the eight types of audit evidence included in this chapter and give two examples of each.

7-9 (Objective 7-4) What are the four characteristics of the definition of a confirmation? Distinguish between a confirmation and external documentation.

7-10 (Objective 7-4) Distinguish between internal documentation and external documentation as audit evidence and give three examples of each.

7-11 (Objective 7-4) Explain the importance of analytical procedures as evidence in determining the fair presentation of the financial statements.

7-12 (Objective 7-4) Identify the most important reasons for performing analytical procedures.

7-13 (Objective 7-4) Your client, Hallab Oriental Sweets Company, has a contractual commitment as a part of a bond indenture to maintain a current ratio of 2.0. If the ratio falls below that level on the balance sheet date, the entire bond becomes payable immediately. In the current year, the client's financial statements show that the ratio has dropped from 2.6 to 2.05 over the past year. How should this situation affect your audit plan?

7-14 (Objective 7-4) Distinguish between attention-directing analytical procedures and those intended to eliminate or reduce detailed substantive procedures.

7-15 (Objective 7-5) List the purposes of audit documentation and explain why each purpose is important.

7-16 (Objectives 7-5, 7-6) What are the two criteria that auditors of public companies consider when determining whether memos, correspondence, and other documents must be maintained in the audit files?

7-17 (Objectives 7-5, 7-6) For how long does the auditing standards require auditors of public companies to retain audit documentation? Does the Sarbanes–Oxley Act have a different period to retain audit documentation? Does the period needed to retain audit documentation differ in your country?

7-18 (Objective 7-6) Explain why it is important for audit documentation to include each of the following: identification of the name of the client, period covered, description of the contents, initials of the preparer, date of the preparation, and an index code.

7-19 (Objective 7-6) Define what is meant by a permanent file, and list several types of information typically included. Why does the auditor not include the contents of the permanent file with the current year's audit file?

7-20 (Objective 7-6) Distinguish between the following types of current period supporting schedules and state the purpose of each: analysis, trial balance, and tests of reasonableness.

7-21 (Objective 7-6) Why is it essential that the auditor not leave questions or exceptions in the audit documentation without an adequate explanation?

7-22 (Objective 7-6) Define what is meant by a tick mark. What is its purpose?

7-23 (Objective 7-5) Who owns the audit files? Under what circumstances can they be used by other people?

7-24 (Objective 7-7) How does the auditor read and evaluate information that is available only in machine-readable form? What is XBRL and how can auditors benefit from its use?

7-25 (Objective 7-7) Explain the purposes and benefits of audit documentation software.

MULTIPLE CHOICE QUESTIONS FROM CPA EXAMINATIONS

7-26 (Objectives 7-3, 7-4) The following questions concern persuasiveness of evidence. Choose the best response.
  a. Which of the following types of documentary evidence should the auditor consider to be the most reliable?
    (1) A sales invoice issued by the client and supported by a delivery receipt from an outside delivery company.
    (2) Confirmation of an account payable balance mailed by and returned directly to the auditor.
    (3) A check, issued by the company and bearing the payee's endorsement, that is included with the bank statements mailed directly to the auditor.
    (4) An audit schedule prepared by the client's controller and reviewed by the client's treasurer.
  b. The most reliable type of audit evidence that an auditor can obtain is
    (1) physical examination by the auditor.
    (2) calculations by the auditor from company records.
    (3) confirmations received directly from third parties.
    (4) external documents.
  c. Audit evidence can come in different forms with different degrees of persuasiveness. Which of the following is the least persuasive type of evidence?
    (1) Vendor's invoice
    (2) Bank statement obtained from the client
    (3) Computations made by the auditor
    (4) Pre-numbered sales invoices
  d. Which of the following presumptions is correct about the reliability of audit evidence?
    (1) Information obtained indirectly from outside sources is the most reliable audit evidence.
    (2) To be reliable, audit evidence should be convincing rather than merely persuasive.
    (3) Reliability of audit evidence refers to the amount of corroborative evidence obtained.
    (4) Effective internal control provides more assurance about the reliability of audit evidence.

7-27 (Objectives 7-5, 7-6) The following questions concern audit documentation. Choose the best response.

a. Which of the following is *not* a primary purpose of audit documentation?
    (1) To coordinate the audit.
    (2) To assist in preparation of the audit report.
    (3) To support the financial statements.
    (4) To provide evidence of the audit work performed.

b. During an audit engagement, pertinent data are compiled and included in the audit files. The audit files primarily are considered to be
    (1) a client-owned record of conclusions reached by the auditors who performed the engagement.
    (2) evidence supporting financial statements.
    (3) support for the auditor's representations as to compliance with auditing standards.
    (4) a record to be used as a basis for the following year's engagement.

c. Although the quantity, type, and content of audit documentation will vary with the circumstances, audit documentation generally will include the
    (1) copies of those client records examined by the auditor during the course of the engagement.
    (2) evaluation of the efficiency and competence of the audit staff assistants by the partner responsible for the audit.
    (3) auditor's comments concerning the efficiency and competence of client management personnel.
    (4) auditing procedures followed and the testing performed in obtaining evidential matter.

d. The permanent file of an auditor's working papers most likely would include copies of the
    (1) lead schedule.
    (2) attorney's letters.
    (3) bank statements.
    (4) debt agreements.

DISCUSSION QUESTIONS AND PROBLEMS

7-28 (Objective 7-4) The following are examples of documentation typically obtained by auditors:

1. Vendors' invoices
2. General ledgers
3. Bank statements
4. Cancelled payroll checks
5. Payroll time cards
6. Purchase requisitions
7. Receiving reports (documents prepared when merchandise is received)
8. Minutes of the board of directors
9. Remittance advices
10. Signed lease agreements
11. Duplicate copies of bills of lading
12. Subsidiary accounts receivable records
13. Cancelled notes payable
14. Duplicate sales invoices
15. Articles of association or incorporation
16. Title insurance policies for real estate
17. Notes receivable

a. Classify each of the preceding items according to type of documentation: (1) internal or (2) external.   **Required**

b. Explain why external evidence is more reliable than internal evidence.

7-29 (Objective 7-4) List two examples of audit evidence the auditor can use in support of each of the following:

a. Recorded amount of entries in the acquisitions journal

b. Physical existence of inventory

c. Accuracy of accounts receivable

d. Ownership of fixed assets

e. Liability for accounts payable

f. Obsolescence of inventory

g. Existence of petty cash

7-30 (Objective 7-4) The following are examples of audit procedures:

1. Review the accounts receivable with the credit manager to evaluate their collectability.
2. Stand by the payroll time clock to determine whether any employee 'punches in' more than one time.
3. Count inventory items and record the amount in the audit files.
4. Obtain a letter from the client's attorney or lawyer addressed to the audit firm stating that the attorney or the lawyer is not aware of any existing lawsuits.
5. Extend the cost of inventory times the quantity on an inventory listing to test whether it is accurate.
6. Obtain a letter from an insurance company to the CPA firm stating the amount of the fire insurance coverage on buildings and equipment.
7. Examine an insurance policy stating the amount of the fire insurance coverage on buildings and equipment.
8. Calculate the ratio of cost of goods sold to sales as a test of overall reasonableness of gross margin relative to the preceding year.
9. Obtain information about internal control by requesting the client to fill out a questionnaire.
10. Trace the total on the cash disbursements journal to the general ledger.
11. Watch employees count inventory to determine whether company procedures are being followed.
12. Examine a piece of equipment to make sure that a major acquisition was actually received and is in operation.
13. Calculate the ratio of sales commission expense to sales as a test of sales commissions.
14. Examine corporate minutes to determine the authorization of the issue of bonds.
15. Obtain a letter from management stating that there are no unrecorded liabilities.
16. Review the total of repairs and maintenance for each month to determine whether any month's total was unusually large.
17. Compare a duplicate sales invoice with the sales journal for customer name and amount.
18. Add the sales journal entries to determine whether they were correctly totaled.
19. Make a petty cash count to make sure that the amount of the petty cash fund is intact.
20. Obtain a written statement from a bank stating that the client has US$15,671 on deposit and liabilities of US$500,000 on a demand note.

Required   Classify each of the preceding items according to the eight types of audit evidence:

1. Physical examination
2. Observation
3. Confirmation
4. Inspection
5. Analytical procedures

6. Inquiries of the client
7. Recalculation
8. Reperformance

7-31 (Objective 7-4) Eight different types of evidence were discussed. The following questions concern the reliability of that evidence:

Required

a. Explain why confirmations are normally more reliable evidence than inquiries of the client.

b. Describe a situation in which confirmation will be considered highly reliable and another in which it will not be reliable.

c. Under what circumstances is the physical observation of inventory considered relatively unreliable evidence?

d. Explain why recalculation tests are highly reliable but of relatively limited use.

e. Give three examples of relatively reliable documentation and three examples of less reliable documentation. What characteristics distinguish the two?

f. Give several examples in which the qualifications of the respondent or the qualifications of the auditor affect the reliability of the evidence.

g. Explain why analytical procedures are important evidence even though they are relatively unreliable by themselves.

7-32 (Objectives 7-3, 7-4) The following are nine situations, each containing two means of accumulating evidence:

1. Confirm receivables with consumers versus confirming accounts receivable with business organizations.
2. Physically examine 3 cm steel plates versus examining electronic parts.
3. Examine duplicate sales invoices when several competent people are checking each other's work versus examining documents prepared by a competent person on a one-person staff.
4. Physically examine inventory of parts for the number of units on hand versus examining them for the likelihood of inventory being obsolete.
5. Discuss the likelihood and amount of loss in a lawsuit against the client with client's in-house legal consultant versus discussion with the audit firm's own legal consultant.
6. Confirm the oil and gas reserves with a geologist specializing in oil and gas versus confirming a bank balance.
7. Confirm a bank balance versus examining the client's bank statements.
8. Physically count the client's inventory held by an independent party versus confirming the count with an independent party.
9. Obtain a physical inventory count from the company president versus physically counting the client's inventory.

Required

a. Identify the six factors that determine the reliability of evidence.

b. For each of the nine situations, state whether the first or second type of evidence is more reliable.

c. For each situation, state which of the six factors affected the reliability of the evidence.

7-33 (Objective 7-4) As auditor of the Star Manufacturing Company, you have obtained a trial balance taken from the books of Star one month before year-end. There are no inventories consigned either in or out. All notes receivable are due from outsiders and held by Star.

	Dr. (Cr.)
Cash in bank	US$ 87,000
Trade accounts receivable	345,000
Notes receivable	125,000
Inventories	317,000
Land	66,000
Buildings, net	350,000
Furniture, fixtures, and equipment, net	325,000
Trade accounts payable	(235,000)
Mortgages payable	(400,000)
Capital stock	(300,000)
Retained earnings	(510,000)
Sales	(3,130,000)
Cost of sales	2,300,000
General and administrative expenses	622,000
Legal and professional fees	3,000
Interest expense	35,000

Required   Which accounts should be confirmed with outside sources? Briefly describe from whom they should be confirmed and the information that should be confirmed. Organize your answer in the following format:

Account Name	From Whom Confirmed	Information to Be Confirmed

7-34 (Objective 7-4) The following audit procedures were performed in the audit of inventory to satisfy specific balance-related audit objectives as discussed in Chapter 6. The audit procedures assume that the auditor has obtained the inventory count sheets that list the client's inventory. The general balance-related audit objectives from Chapter 6 are also included.

Audit Procedures

1. Test extend unit prices times quantity on the inventory list, test foot the list, and compare the total to the general ledger.
2. Trace selected quantities from the inventory list to the physical inventory to make sure that it exists and the quantities are the same.
3. Question operating personnel about the possibility of obsolete or slow-moving inventory.
4. Select a sample of quantities of inventory in the factory warehouse and trace each item to the inventory count sheets to determine if it has been included and if the quantity and description are correct.
5. Compare the quantities on hand and unit prices on this year's inventory count sheets with those in the preceding year as a test for large differences.
6. Examine sales invoices and contracts with customers to determine whether any goods are out on consignment with customers. Similarly, examine vendors' invoices and contracts with vendors to determine whether any goods on the inventory listing are owned by vendors.
7. Send letters directly to third parties who hold the client's inventory and request that they respond directly to the auditors.

General Balance-Related Audit Objectives

Existence	Cutoff
Completeness	Detail tie-in
Accuracy	Realizable value
Classification	Rights and obligations

a. Identify the type of audit evidence used for each audit procedure.

b. Identify the general balance-related audit objective or objectives satisfied by each audit procedure.

CASE

7-35 (Objective 7-4) Nefret Stores is a large discount cosmetic department store chain. The company has recently expanded from 5 to 15 stores by borrowing from several large financial institutions and from a public offering of common stock. A recent investigation has disclosed that Nefret materially overstated net income. The company understated their accounts payable and recorded fictitious supplier credits that further reduced accounts payable. As a result, an Income and Sales Tax Department investigation was critical of the evidence gathered by Nefret's audit firm, Abdul & El-Emir, in testing accounts payable and the supplier credits.

1. Kashir Advertising Credits—Nefret had arrangements with some vendors to share the cost of advertising the vendor's product. The arrangements were usually agreed to in advance by the vendor and supported by evidence of the placing of the ad. Nefret created a 250-page list of approximately 1,000 vendors, supporting advertising credits of US$500,000. Nefret's auditors selected a sample of eight of the 2,500 items for direct confirmation. One item was confirmed by telephone, one traced to cash receipts, one to a vendor's credit memo for part of the amount and cash receipts for the rest, and one to a vendor's credit memo. Two of the amounts confirmed differed from the amount on the list, but the auditors did not seek an explanation for the differences because the amounts were not material.

   The rest of the credits were tested by selecting 30 items (several from each page of the list). Fourteen of the items were supported by examining the ads placed, and 16 were supported by Nefret debit memos charging the vendors for the promotional allowances.

2. Nashwa Credits—Nefret created 28 fictitious credit memos totaling US$363,000 from Nashwa Distributions, the main supplier of health and beauty aids to Nefret. Nefret's controller initially told the auditor that the credits were for returned goods, then said they were a volume discount, and finally stated that they were a payment so that Nefret would continue to use Nashwa as a supplier. However, an Abdul & El-Emir staff auditor noticed the amount and concluded that a US$257,000 payment to retain Nefret's business was too large to make economic sense.

   The credit memos indicated that the credits were for damaged merchandise, volume rebates, and advertising allowances. The audit firm requested a confirmation of the credits. In response, Ramses Abdullah, the president of Nefret Stores, placed a call to Saria Wasir, the president of Nashwa, and handed the phone to the staff auditor. In fact, the call had been placed to an officer of Nefret. The Nefret officer, posing as Wasir, orally confirmed the credits. Nefret refused to allow Abdul & El-Emir to obtain written confirmation supporting the credits. Although the staff auditor doubted the validity of the credits, the audit partner, Mufti Hussein, accepted the credits based on the credit memoranda, telephone confirmation of the credits, and oral representation of Nefret officers.

3. Zaki Credits—US$130,000 in credits based on 35 credit memoranda from Zaki, Inc., were purportedly for the return of overstocked goods from several Nefret stores. An Abdul & El-Emir staff auditor noted the size of the credit and that the credit memos were dated subsequent to year-end. He further noticed that a sentence on the credit memos from Zaki had been obliterated by a felt-tip marker. When held to the light, the accountant could read that the marked-out sentence read, "Do not post until merchandise received." The staff auditor thereafter called Omar Zaki, treasurer of Zaki, Inc., and was informed that the US$130,000 in goods had not been returned and the money was not owed to Nefret by Zaki. Abdullah, president of Nefret,

advised Hussein, the audit partner, not to have anyone call Zaki to verify the amount because of pending litigation between Nefret and Zaki, Inc.

4. Accounts Payable Accrual—Abdul & El-Emir assigned a senior with experience in the retail area to audit accounts payable. Although Nefret had poor internal controls, Abdul & El-Emir selected a sample of 50 for confirmation of the several thousand vendors who did business with Nefret. Twenty-seven responses were received, and 21 were reconciled to Nefret's records. These tests indicated an unrecorded liability of approximately US$290,000 when projected to the population of accounts payable. However, the investigation disclosed that Nefret's president made telephone calls to some suppliers who had received confirmation requests from Abdul & El-Emir and told them how to respond to the request.

Abdul & El-Emir also performed a purchase cutoff test by vouching accounts payable invoices received for nine weeks after year-end. The purpose of this test was to identify invoices received after year-end that should have been recorded in accounts payable. Thirty percent of the sample (US$150,000) was found to relate to the prior year, indicating a potential unrecorded liability of approximately US$500,000. The audit firm and Nefret eventually agreed on adjustment to increase accounts payable by US$260,000.

Required   Identify deficiencies in the sufficiency and appropriateness of the evidence gathered in the audit of accounts payable of Nefret Stores.

ACL PROBLEM

7-36 (Objective 7-4) This problem requires the use of ACL software, which is included in MyAccountingLab. Information about installing and using ACL and solving this problem can be found in the Appendix, pages 855–859. You should read all of the reference material preceding instructions about 'Quick Sort' before locating the appropriate command to answer questions a–f. For this problem, use the file labeled 'Payroll' in the 'Payroll_Analysis' subfolder under tables in 'Sample_Project.' The suggested command or other source of information needed to solve the problem requirement is included at the end of each question.

Required
a. Determine the number of payroll transactions in the file. (Read the bottom of the Payroll file screen.)

b. Determine the largest and smallest payroll transaction (gross pay) for the month of September. (Quick Sort)

c. Determine gross pay for September. (Total)

d. Determine and print gross pay by department. (Summarize)

e. Recalculate net pay for each payroll transaction for September and compare it to the amount included in the file. (Filter)

f. Determine if there are any gaps or duplicates in the check (cheque) numbers. If there are gaps or duplicates, what is your concern? (Gaps and Duplicates)

AUDIT PLANNING AND ANALYTICAL PROCEDURES

The Fall Of Enron: Did Anyone Understand Their Business?

The bankruptcy of Enron Corporation, at one time the largest energy whole-saling company in the U.S., represents the biggest corporate collapse in American history. Despite being listed as No. 7 on the Fortune 500 list with a market capitalization of US$75 billion before its collapse, the meltdown of Enron was rapid. The fall began in October 2001 when Enron officials reported a shocking US$618 million quarterly loss related to allegedly mysterious and hidden related party partnerships with company insiders. Then, in early November 2001, company officials were forced to admit that they had falsely claimed almost US$600 million in earnings dating back to 1997, requiring the restatement of four years of audited financial statements. By the end of 2001, the company was in bankruptcy.

Enron was created in 1985 out of a merger of two gas pipelines, and was a pioneer in trading natural gas and electricity in the newly deregulated utilities markets. In its earlier years, Enron made its money from hard assets like pipelines. However, by the end of the 1990s, 80% of Enron's earnings came from a more vague business known as "wholesale energy operations and services." Enron had built new markets, such as trading of weather securities. In early 2001, speculation about Enron's business dealings began to surface. One highly regarded investment banker publicly stated that no one could explain how Enron actually made money.

In the wake of the collapse, many wonder how these issues could go undetected for so long. Many point to Enron having an incredibly complicated business structure and related vague and confusing financial statements. "What we are looking at here is an example of superbly complex financial reports. They didn't have to lie. All they had to do was to obfuscate it with sheer complexity," noted John Dingell, U.S. Congressman from Michigan. Others even allege that the men running the company never even understood their business concept because it was too complicated.

Apparently, the complexity and uncertainty surrounding Enron's business and financial statements fooled their auditors, too. Enron's auditor faced a flurry of attacks, class action lawsuits, and a criminal indictment that ultimately led to the firm's demise. In a December 2001 congressional testimony, the audit firm's CEO admitted that the firm's professional judgment "turned out to be wrong" and that they mistakenly let Enron keep the related entities separate when they should have been consolidated.

The Enron disaster continues to provide many lessons for the auditing profession. One to be underscored for auditors is the paramount importance of understanding the company's business and industry to identify significant business risks that increase the risk of material misstatements in the financial statements. Without that understanding, it will be almost impossible to identify the next Enron.

Source: Adapted from Bethany McLean, 'Why Enron Went Bust,' *Fortune* (December 24, 2001), pp. 58–68.

LEARNING OBJECTIVES

After studying this chapter, you should be able to

8-1 Discuss why adequate audit planning is essential.

8-2 Make client acceptance decisions and perform initial audit planning.

8-3 Gain an understanding of the client's business and industry.

8-4 Assess client business risk.

8-5 Perform preliminary analytical procedures.

8-6 State the purposes of analytical procedures and the timing of each purpose.

8-7 Select the most appropriate analytical procedure from among the five major types.

8-8 Compute common financial ratios.

As the above story illustrates, Enron's complex and confusing business structure helped disguise material misstatements in Enron financial statements for several years. Gaining an understanding of the client's business and industry is one of the most important steps in audit planning. This chapter explains audit planning in detail with emphasis on the Arab world business and industry characteristics, including gaining an understanding of the client's business and industry, assessing client business risk, and performing preliminary analytical procedures.

Relevant International Standards on Auditing	
ISA 210	Agreeing the Terms of Audit Engagements
ISA 230	Audit Documentation
ISA 250	Consideration of Laws and Regulations in an Audit of Financial Statements
ISA 300	Planning an Audit of Financial Statements
ISA 315	Identifying and Assessing the Risks of Material Misstatement through Understanding the Entity and its Environment
ISA 320	Materiality in Planning and Performing an Audit
ISA 330	The Auditor's Responses to Assessed Risks
ISA 510	Initial Audit Engagement—Opening Balances
ISA 520	Analytical Procedures
ISA 550	Related Parties
ISA 610	Using the Work of Internal Auditors
ISA 620	Using the Work of an Auditor's Expert

PLANNING

OBJECTIVE 8-1

Discuss why adequate audit planning is essential.

The objective of planning the audit engagement is defined under ISA 300 as:

> To plan the audit so that it will be performed in an effective manner.

Overall audit strategy

The auditor's general plan for the proposed performance of the audit. The plan identifies the scope, timing, staffing, and direction of the audit and is the first step to prepare a detailed audit plan to ensure a quality audit.

Audit plan

A detailed direction on how to perform the audit, including the nature, timing, and extent of audit procedures to be undertaken by the auditor and his subordinates.

Auditors should establish an **overall audit strategy** which determines the scope, timing, and direction of the audit that guides the development of the **audit plan**. It is important to note that if the audit is not well planned, the results of the audit may not be achieved and the auditor may issue an erroneous audit report. The auditor usually summarizes the overall audit strategy in the form of memorandum that contains key decisions related to the overall scope, timing, and conduct of the audit. In Arab countries, auditors identify key elements of the company including the names and qualifications of the company's board of directors and whether any member is a government official; the reputation of the company in the market; the structure of the company's accounting systems; the results of the company and its ability to continue as a going concern; main competitors, etc. The nature and extent of planning activities will be modified according to the size and degree of complexity of the entity, the key engagement team members' previous experience with the entity, and changes in the circumstances that occur during the performance of the audit engagement.

There are four main reasons why the auditor should properly plan engagements: to help auditors consider factors that in their professional judgment help them select accounts and transactions needing most attention, to enable the auditor to obtain sufficient appropriate evidence for the circumstances, to help keep audit costs reasonable, and to avoid misunderstandings with the client. Obtaining sufficient appropriate evidence is essential if the audit firm is to minimize legal liability and maintain a good reputation in the business community. Keeping costs reasonable helps the firm remain competitive. Avoiding misunderstandings with the client is necessary for good client relations and for facilitating high-quality work at reasonable cost. Suppose that the auditor informs the client that the audit will be completed before June 30 but is unable to finish it until August because of inadequate scheduling of staff. The client is likely to be upset with the audit firm and may even sue for breach of contract.

Figure 8-1 presents the eight major parts of audit planning. Each of the first seven parts is intended to help the auditor develop the last part, an effective and efficient overall audit plan and audit program. The first four parts of the planning phase of an audit are studied in this chapter. The last four are studied separately in later chapters.

Before beginning our discussion, we briefly introduce two risk terms: *acceptable audit risk* and *inherent risk*. These two risks significantly influence the conduct and cost of audits. Much of the early planning of audits deals with obtaining information to help auditors assess these risks.

Acceptable audit risk is a measure of how willing the auditor is to accept that the financial statements may be materially misstated after the audit is completed and an unmodified opinion has been issued. When the auditor decides on a lower acceptable audit risk, it means that the auditor wants to be more certain that the financial statements are *not* materially misstated. Zero risk is certainty, and a 100 percent risk is complete uncertainty. There is an inverse relationship between this risk and audit evidence gathered. If the

Acceptable audit risk

A measure of how willing the auditor is to accept that the financial statements may be materially misstated after the audit is completed and an unmodified audit opinion has been issued; see also audit assurance.

FIGURE 8-1   Planning an Audit and Designing an Audit Approach

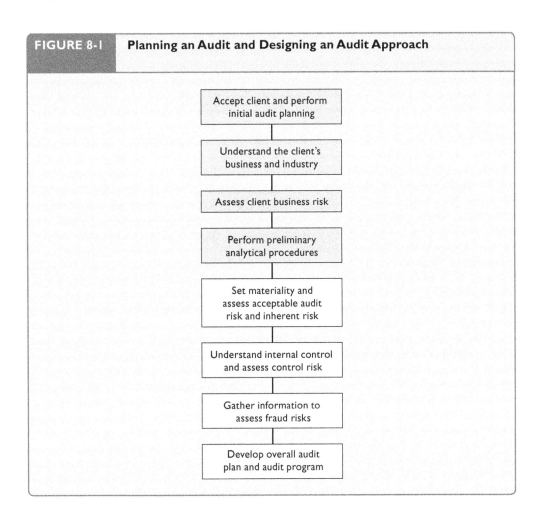

Accept client and perform initial audit planning

Understand the client's business and industry

Assess client business risk

Perform preliminary analytical procedures

Set materiality and assess acceptable audit risk and inherent risk

Understand internal control and assess control risk

Gather information to assess fraud risks

Develop overall audit plan and audit program

auditor's calculation is to minimize the above risk, he needs to accumulate more evidence. Accumulating sufficient audit evidence will enable the auditor to give his reasonable assurance about the reliability of the company's financial statements.

Inherent risk

A measure of the auditor's assessment of the likelihood that there are material misstatements in a segment before considering the effectiveness of internal control.

Inherent risk is a measure of the auditor's assessment of the likelihood that there are material misstatements in an account balance before considering the effectiveness of internal control. If, for example, the auditor concludes that there is a high likelihood of material misstatement in accounts receivable due to changing economic conditions, the auditor concludes that inherent risk for accounts receivable is high. There is a direct relationship between the auditor's assessment of this risk and the level of evidence gathered. The higher the inherent risk, the larger will be the sample size of accounts receivable transactions and balances selected for audit.

Assessing acceptable audit risk and inherent risk is an important part of audit planning because it helps determine the size of evidence that will need to be accumulated and staff assigned to the engagement. For example, if inherent risk for inventory is high because of complex valuation issues, more evidence will be accumulated in the audit of inventory, and more experienced staff will be assigned to perform testing in this area.

Internal audit function

An evaluation activity performed by qualified and experienced internal auditors who are responsible to examine, assess, and monitor the effectiveness of the internal control to prevent and detect fraud and tests daily transactions of the company.

In the Arab world, auditors gather as much evidence as possible in order to assess the acceptable audit risk as low. The reason behind such a decision lies in the deficiencies embedded in many internal controls for small and medium-sized companies, the inability to implement corporate governance measures due to a yet undeveloped self-monitoring culture within business enterprises, and widespread *wasta* in recruitment of personnel without relevant qualifications and experience. Another reason is the nonexistence of an **internal audit function** as well as deficiencies in its role, if it does exist in business enterprises, thus putting pressure on external auditors to increase evidence to check the reliability of the business's financial statements. Planning the audit engagement is therefore considered an important step toward achieving the audit objectives.

ACCEPT CLIENT AND PERFORM INITIAL AUDIT PLANNING

OBJECTIVE 8-2

Make client acceptance decisions and perform initial audit planning.

Initial audit planning involves four things, all of which should be done early in the audit:

1. The auditor decides whether to accept a new client or continue serving an existing one. This determination is typically made by an experienced auditor who is in a position to make important decisions. The auditor wants to make this decision early, before incurring any significant costs that cannot be recovered. The auditor must also determine the appropriate audit fee which will cover all cost of work to be provided.
2. The auditor identifies why the client wants or needs an audit. This information is likely to affect the remaining parts of the planning process.
3. To avoid misunderstandings, the auditor obtains an understanding with the client about the terms of the engagement.
4. The auditor develops an overall strategy for the audit, including engagement staffing and any required audit specialists.

Initial audit planning

Involves deciding whether to accept or continue doing the audit for the client, identifying the client's reasons for the audit, obtaining an engagement letter, and developing an audit strategy.

Client Acceptance and Continuance

Even though obtaining and retaining clients is not easy in a competitive profession such as public accounting, an audit firm must use care in deciding which clients are acceptable. The firm's legal and professional responsibilities are such that clients who lack integrity or argue constantly about the proper conduct of the audit and fees can cause more problems than they are worth. Some audit firms now refuse any clients in certain high-risk industries, such as software technology companies, health, and casualty insurance companies, and may even discontinue auditing existing companies in those industries. Some smaller audit firms will not do audits of publicly held clients because of the risk of litigation or because of costs associated with registering the audit firm with the appropriate professional body or government professional authority. Stated in terms of acceptable audit risk, an auditor is unlikely to accept a new client or continue serving an existing client if acceptable audit risk is below the risk threshold the firm is willing to accept. For example, the auditor may refuse an audit engagement if preliminary information about this prospective client indicates that there are a large number of legal disputes between the company, its suppliers, and various tax authorities. Auditors are expected to increase the size of their tests for such litigations and tax obligations. So the auditor may be willing to sacrifice the benefits associated with this client to protect his reputation and ensure a high quality of audit services.

In the Arab world, the situation is different as audit firms accept many audit engagements without due consideration for the integrity of the client, the adequacy of audit fees, and the level of risk of litigations. Small and medium-sized audit firms face severe competition for new audit clients, a matter which affects their decisions to undertake a complete investigation about those prospective clients. Audit fees are considered a key element in accepting a new client where low balling (i.e. each audit firm attempts to reduce its fees to gain either a prospective client or a client which has an existing auditor) is part of marketing the firm's activities.

New Client Investigation   Before accepting a new client, most audit firms investigate the company to determine its acceptability. They do this by examining, to the extent possible, the prospective client's standing in the business community, financial stability, and relations with its previous audit firm(s). For example, many audit firms use considerable caution in accepting new clients in newly formed, rapidly growing businesses. Many of these businesses fail financially and expose the audit firm to significant potential liability. According to the requirements of auditing standards, the audit firm examines the client's articles of association, annual reports, interim financial statements, analysts' reports, memoranda about their accounting and management systems, and income tax returns. The audit firm is permitted to inquire of third parties about the integrity of the management of the prospective client including their bankers, lawyers, credit agencies, and other members of the business community. The audit firm must also determine that it has the competency, such as industry knowledge, to accept the engagement and that the firm can satisfy all independence requirements.

For prospective clients that have previously been audited by another audit firm, the new (successor) auditor is *required* by auditing standards (ISA 300) *to communicate with the predecessor auditor*. The purpose of the requirement is to help the successor auditor evaluate whether to accept the engagement. The communication may, for example, inform the successor auditor that the client lacks integrity or that there have been disputes over accounting principles, audit procedures, or fees. Also, the successor auditor may inquire about the relationship between the predecessor auditor and those charged with governance and how effective and cooperative were discussions and decisions made by both the audit committees and the client's board of directors.

The burden of initiating the communication rests with the successor auditor, but the predecessor auditor is required to respond to the request for information. However, the confidentiality requirement in the *Code of Ethics for Professional Accountants* requires that the predecessor auditor obtain permission from the client before the communication can be made. In the event of unusual circumstances such as legal problems or disputes between the client and the predecessor, the predecessor's response can be limited to stating that no information will be provided. If a client will not permit the communication or the predecessor will not provide a comprehensive

Accept client and perform initial audit planning

Understand the client's business and industry

Assess client business risk

Perform preliminary analytical procedures

Set materiality and assess acceptable audit risk and inherent risk

Understand internal control and assess control risk

Gather information to assess fraud risks

Develop overall audit plan and audit program

response, the successor should seriously consider the desirability of accepting a prospective engagement, without considerable other investigation.

Even when a prospective client has been audited by another audit firm, a successor may make other investigations by gathering information from local attorneys, other CPAs, banks, and other businesses.

In the Arab world, auditors carry out a simple investigation of a new client. Auditors study the client's financial statements to assess the size of the client, investigate the financial position of the client in the market, the qualifications and reputations of the members of the board of directors or top management and, most importantly, the ability of the client to pay the audit fees. Auditors do not consider the risk of litigation when accepting a new client because of the long process associated with legal proceedings in most Arab countries and the fact that clients tend to replace auditors wherever they are not satisfied with their performance rather than considering taking legal action against them.

Continuing Clients Many audit firms evaluate existing clients annually to determine whether there are reasons for not continuing to do the audit. Previous conflicts over the appropriate scope of the audit, the type of opinion to issue, fees, or other matters may cause the auditor to discontinue association. The auditor may also drop a client after determining the client lacks integrity. Under the IESBA *Code of Ethics for Professional Accountants* on independence, if the client files a lawsuit against a CPA firm or vice versa, the firm cannot perform the audit. Similarly, if there are unpaid fees for services performed more than one year previously, the CPA firm cannot do the current year audit.

Even if none of the previously discussed conditions exist, the audit firm may decide not to continue doing audits for a client because of excessive risk. For example, an audit firm might decide that considerable risk of a regulatory conflict exists between a governmental body and a client, which could result in financial failure of the client and ultimately lawsuits against the audit firm. Even if the engagement is profitable, the long-term risk may exceed the short-term benefits of doing the audit.

Investigating new clients and reevaluating existing ones is an essential part of deciding acceptable audit risk. For example, assume a potential client operates in a reasonably risky industry, that its management has a reputation of integrity, but is also known to take aggressive financial risks. If the audit firm decides that acceptable audit risk is extremely low requiring costly audit procedures exceeding the audit fees proposed, it may choose not to accept the engagement. If the audit firm concludes that acceptable audit risk is low but the client is still acceptable, the firm may accept the engagement but increase the fee proposed to the client. Audits with a low acceptable audit risk will normally result in higher audit costs, which should be reflected in higher audit fees.

In the Arab world there is a different culture and an audit firm may prefer to maintain a good business relationship with the shareholders of the company, often a family-owned business, even if the company is in default of payment of the audit fee.

Identify Client's Reasons for Audit

Two major factors affecting acceptable audit risk are the likely statement users and their intended uses of the statements. The auditor is likely to accumulate more evidence when the statements are to be used extensively, as is often the case for publicly held companies, those with extensive indebtedness, and companies that are to be sold in the near future.

The most likely uses of the statements can be determined from previous experience with the client and discussions with management. Throughout the engagement, the auditor may get additional information about why the client is having an audit and the likely uses of the financial statements. This information may affect the auditor's acceptable audit risk.

Obtain an Understanding with the Client

A clear understanding of the terms of the engagement should exist between the client and the audit firm. Auditing standards (ISA 210) require that auditors document their understanding with the client in an **engagement letter**, including the engagement's objectives, the responsibilities of the auditor and management, and the engagement's limitations. For public companies, the audit committee or the board of directors is responsible for proposing the hiring of the auditor to the shareholders at the annual general meeting. The engagement letter formally records the arrangements made between the auditor and the client. It serves as the contract, specifying in clear terms the responsibilities of both parties and may prevent any future misunderstandings between the parties. Additional terms may be included in the engagement letter covering specific circumstances and conditions of the assignment such as the use of experts and the party responsible for their remuneration, any limitation of the liability of the auditor or the client, agreement concerning communication with the predecessor auditor and terms of confidentiality, and arrangements for the provision of other management advisory services (e.g. assurance, compilation, tax, and other consulting engagements). The engagement letter is typically signed by management for private companies. An example of an engagement letter for the audit of a private company is provided in Figure 8-2.

> **Engagement letter**
> An agreement between the CPA firm and the client as to the terms of the engagement for the conduct of the audit and related services.

The engagement letter may also include an agreement to provide other services such as tax returns or management consulting allowed under the *Code of Ethics for Professional Accountants* and regulatory requirements. It should also state any restrictions to be imposed on the auditor's work, deadlines for completing the audit, assistance to be provided by the client's personnel in obtaining records and documents, and schedules to be prepared for the auditor. It often includes an agreement on fees. The engagement letter also serves the purpose of informing the client that the auditor cannot guarantee that all acts of fraud will be discovered.

Engagement letter information is important in planning the audit principally because it affects the timing of the tests and the total amount of time the audit and other services will take. For example, if the deadline for submitting the audit report is soon after the balance sheet date, a significant portion of the audit must be done before the end of the year. If unexpected circumstances arise or if client assistance is not available, arrangements must be made to extend the amount of time for the engagement. Client-imposed restrictions on the audit can affect the procedures performed and possibly even the type of audit opinion issued.

Develop Overall Audit Strategy

After understanding the client's reasons for the audit, the auditor should develop a preliminary **audit strategy**. This strategy considers the nature of the client's business and industry, including areas where there is greater risk of significant misstatements. The auditor also considers other factors such as the number of client locations and the past effectiveness of client controls in developing a preliminary approach to the audit. The planned strategy helps the auditor determine the resources required for the engagement, including engagement staffing.

> **Audit strategy**
> Overall approach to the audit that considers the nature of the client, risk of significant misstatements, and other factors such as the number of client locations and past effectiveness of client controls.

Select Staff for Engagement   The auditor must assign the appropriate staff to the engagement to meet auditing standards and to promote audit efficiency. ISA 300 requires that the engagement partner and other key members of the engagement team must be involved in planning and performing the audit.

> Members of the audit team must have acquired the needed qualifications and experience to perform the audit.

| FIGURE 8-2 | An Engagement Letter for a Private Company |

Crowe Horwath Egypt
Cairo, Egypt

June 14, 2011

Mohamed Hashish
International Trade Company
El-Messaha St. – Dokki – Cairo – Egypt

Dear Mr. Mohamed:

This will confirm our understanding of the arrangements for our audit of the financial statements of International Trade Company for the year ending December 31, 2011.

We will audit the company's financial statements for the year ending December 31, 2011, for the purpose of expressing an opinion on the fairness with which they present, in all material respects, the financial position, results of operations, and cash flows in conformity with generally accepted accounting principles.

We will conduct our audit in accordance with International Standards on Auditing. Those standards require that we obtain reasonable, rather than absolute, assurance that the financial statements are free of material misstatement, whether caused by error or fraud. Accordingly, a material misstatement may remain undetected. Also, an audit is not designed to detect error or fraud that is immaterial to the financial statements; therefore, the audit will not necessarily detect misstatements less than this materiality level that might exist because of error, fraudulent financial reporting, or misappropriation of assets. If, for any reason, we are unable to complete the audit or are unable to form or have not formed an opinion, we may decline to express an opinion or decline to issue a report as a result of the engagement.

Although an audit includes obtaining an understanding of internal control sufficient to plan the audit and to determine the nature, timing, and extent of audit procedures to be performed, it is not designed to provide assurance on internal control or to identify significant deficiencies. However, we are responsible for ensuring that the audit committee is aware of any significant deficiencies that come to our attention.

The financial statements are the responsibility of the company's management. Management is also responsible for (1) establishing and maintaining effective internal control over financial reports, (2) identifying and ensuring the company complies with the laws and regulations applicable to its activities, (3) making all financial records and related information available to us, and (4) providing to us at the conclusion of the engagement a representation letter that, among other things, will confirm management's responsibility for the preparation of the financial statements in conformity with International Financial Reporting Standards, the availability of financial records and related data, the completeness and availability of all minutes of the board and committee meetings, and to the best of its knowledge and belief, the absence of fraud involving management or those employees who have a significant role in the entity's internal control.

The timing of our audit and the assistance to be supplied by your personnel, including the preparation of schedules and analyses of accounts, are described on a separate attachment. Timely completion of this work will facilitate the completion of our audit.

As part of our engagement for the year ending December 31, 2011, we will also prepare the income tax returns for International Trade Company.

Our fees will be billed as work progresses and are based on the amount of time required at various levels of responsibility, plus actual out-of-pocket expenses. Invoices are payable upon presentation. We will notify you immediately of any circumstances we encounter that could significantly affect our initial estimate of total fees of EGP 100,000.

If this letter correctly expresses your understanding, please sign the enclosed copy and return it to us. We appreciate the opportunity to serve you.

Accepted: Yours very truly:

By: Mohamed Hashish   Karim Abdel Aziz
Date: 21-6-2011   Partner

Appropriate resources must be deployed for specific audit areas including the use of the appropriate number of experienced team members for high risk areas and securing the assistance of experts on complex matters—for example, the number of the audit team members assigned to observe the inventory count at material locations, the extent of review of other auditors' work in the case of group auditors, or the audit budget in hours to allocate to high risk areas.

Staff must therefore be assigned based on their experience and qualifications and the nature of the audit engagement. Also, staff assigned to the engagement must be knowledgeable about the client's industry. Larger audit engagements are likely to require one or more partners and staff at several experience levels. Individuals in multiple offices of the firm may be included, including offices other than the head office of the audit firm, if the client has operations in numerous locations within the country or around the world. Specialists in such technical areas as statistical sampling, business valuation, and computer risk assessment may also be assigned. On smaller audits, only one or two staff members may be needed.

A major consideration of staffing is the need for continuity from year to year. Continuity helps the audit firm maintain familiarity with the technical requirements and closer interpersonal relations with client personnel. An inexperienced staff assistant is likely to become the most experienced non-partner on the engagement within a few years.

Consider a computer manufacturing client with an extensive inventory of computers and computer parts where inherent risk for inventory has been assessed as high. It is essential for the staff person doing the inventory portion of the audit to be experienced in auditing inventory. The auditor should also have a good understanding of the computer manufacturing industry. The audit firm may decide to engage a specialist if no one within the firm is qualified to evaluate whether the inventory is obsolete.

In the Arab world, auditors tend to concentrate on helping the audit clients with their tax issues. Due to bureaucracy and the nature of government operations in many Arab countries other than Saudi Arabia and the Gulf states, tax authorities attempt to collect as much in taxes as possible to cover yearly budget deficits and clients require their auditors to work closely with them to minimize the amount of tax expected to be paid during each financial period. Auditors are required to assess in detail the tax position of their audit clients in planning the audit to assess their effect on the client's financial statements.

Evaluate Need for Outside Specialists or Experts If the audit requires specialized knowledge, it may be necessary to consult a specialist. Auditing standards (ISA 620) establish the requirements for selecting specialists and reviewing their work. Examples include using a diamond expert to evaluate the replacement cost of diamonds; an actuary for determining the appropriateness of the recorded value of insurance loss reserves; an information technology expert to test the security and integrity of the client's IT systems; a legal expert to interpret a covenant agreement; an expert to calculate pension plans; and an engineer to assess the replacement cost of a machine or to value other financial instruments. Attorneys may also be consulted on the legal interpretation of contracts and titles or business valuation experts may be consulted regarding fair value accounting treatments.

The auditor must have a sufficient understanding of the client's business to recognize whether a specialist or an expert is needed. The auditor needs to evaluate the specialist's professional qualifications and understand the objectives and scope of the specialist's

---

NEED AN EXPERT TO VALUE A COMPANY'S SHARES

The prosecutor in one of the Gulf States held liable a chairman and managing director for their responsibility of the sale of one of the holding company's subsidiaries for an amount less than its actual fair value resulting in significant loss to the holdings' total wealth. The investigation revealed that the suspects sold the company for only US$13.5 million while its real and actual value was about US$30 million according to the company's documents. The subsidiary was considered one of the top companies specializing in export and import of food to many Arab countries especially to other Gulf States.

The purchaser of the subsidiary paid only 50 percent of the price of the company promising to pay the remainder within one year from the date of purchase. The chairman and managing director both were negligent as the remaining 50 percent of the company value was not paid until the issue became public and was investigated by the appropriate authority. The facts of this case show the importance of having a qualified and competent expert in valuing a company's shares. Auditors are required to get the help of an expert whenever the issue being examined is beyond the audit firm's technical capabilities.

work. The auditor should also consider the specialist's relationship to the client, including circumstances that might impair the specialist's objectivity. ISA 620 (para. 11(d)) states that it is necessary for the confidentiality provisions of relevant ethical requirements to be applied to the auditor as well as the auditor's expert. The use of a specialist does not affect the auditor's responsibility for the audit and the audit report should not refer to the specialist unless the specialist's report results in a modification of the audit opinion.

Assess the Function of the Internal Audit

If the client has an internal audit department, the auditor should assess the likelihood of using the work of the internal auditor. The auditor should understand the responsibilities of the internal audit department and its function within the client's organizational structure. The competence and integrity of the internal auditors must be carefully evaluated to determine the degree of reliance on their work (see Table 8-1). External auditors may rely on the tests performed by the internal auditors, if they are found to be competent and objective, about their company's internal control system to determine the nature, extent, and time of external auditors' substantive tests.

In the Arab world, not all businesses, even listed companies, have internal audit departments. The codes of corporate governance were recently introduced in most Arab countries so the establishment of effective and independent internal audit departments is being developed by management, audit firms, and the professional associations. Currently, auditors of private companies do not rely on the work of internal auditors in performing their examination of the companies' financial statements. At the same time, auditors of listed companies cooperate with the heads of the internal audit department (wherever such departments exist) in identifying areas of concern for detailed examination by the external auditors. Also, external auditors study the content of the internal auditor's report when preparing their audit strategy to fulfill their audit responsibilities.

TABLE 8-1	Elements for Evaluating the Competence and Integrity of Internal Auditors

Competence

- The level of education and professional expertise including years of experience.
- The existence of any professional certification and practitioners' continued education.
- The internal audit manual and how audit programs and timetables for audit tests are designed and implemented.
- The level of detail of the department examination of the company's internal control system, tests of transactions performed, and whether they cover all the company's activities.
- The nature of supervision and review of their audit activities.
- The adequacy and quality of the documentation of results of the audit.

Integrity

- The existence of proper follow-up procedures for implementing internal auditors' recommendations.
- The organization status of the internal audit department, the internal audit manager and internal auditors, their level of authority and their effective participation in the audit committee meetings.
- The degree of freedom given to internal auditors to examine important areas of the company's activities.

UNDERSTAND THE CLIENT'S BUSINESS AND INDUSTRY

OBJECTIVE 8-3

Gain an understanding of the client's business and industry.

A thorough understanding of the client's business and industry and knowledge about the company's operations are essential for the auditor to conduct an adequate audit. ISA 500 states:

> The objectives of the auditor are to design and perform audit procedures in such a way as to enable the auditor to obtain sufficient appropriate audit evidence to be able to draw conclusions on which to base the auditor's opinion.

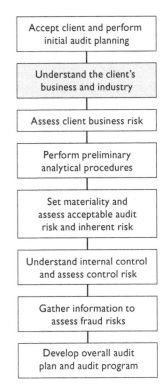

In order to achieve the above objective, the auditor must understand the nature of the client's business and industry. The nature of the client's business and industry affects client business risk and the risk of material misstatements in the financial statements. (Client business risk is the risk that the client will fail to meet its objectives. It is discussed further later in the chapter.) In recent years, several factors have increased the importance of understanding the client's business and industry:

- Recent significant declines in economic conditions around the world are likely to significantly increase a client's business risks. Auditors need to understand the nature of the client's business to understand the impact of major economic downturns on the client's financial statements and ability to continue as a going concern.
- Information technology connects client companies with major customers and suppliers. As a result, auditors need greater knowledge about major customers and suppliers and related risks.
- Clients have expanded operations globally, often through joint ventures or strategic alliances.
- Information technology affects internal client processes, improving the quality and timeliness of accounting information.
- The increased importance of human capital and other intangible assets has increased accounting complexity and the importance of management judgments and estimates.
- Many clients may have invested in complex financial instruments, such as collateralized debt obligations or unusual mortgage backed securities, which have little value and require complex accounting treatments.

Auditors consider these factors using a strategic systems approach to understanding the client's business. Figure 8-3 provides an overview of the approach to understanding the client's business and industry. Next, we will discuss several aspects of this approach.

Industry and External Environment

The three primary reasons for obtaining a good understanding of the client's industry and external environment are:

1. Risks associated with specific industries may affect the auditor's assessment of client business risk and acceptable audit risk—and may even influence auditors against accepting engagements in riskier industries, such as the financial services and health insurance industries.
2. Certain inherent risks are typically common to all clients in certain industries. Familiarity with those risks aids the auditor in assessing their relevance to the client. Examples include potential inventory obsolescence in the fashion clothing industry, and accounts receivable collection inherent risk in the consumer loan industry.
3. Many industries have unique accounting requirements that the auditor must understand to evaluate whether the client's financial statements are in accordance with International Financial Reporting Standards. For example, if the auditor is doing an audit of a public sector company or a government unit, the auditor must understand governmental accounting and auditing requirements. Unique accounting requirements exist for construction companies, railways, not-for-profit organizations, financial institutions, and many other organizations.

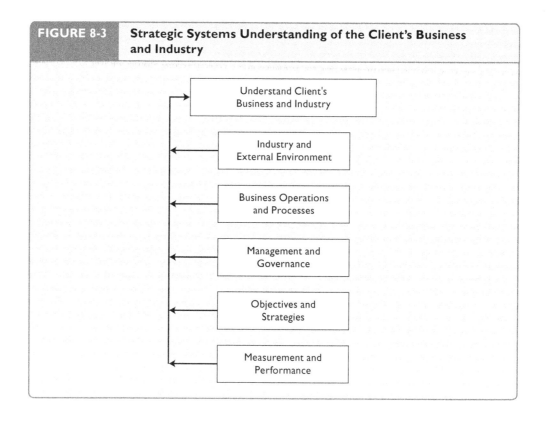

FIGURE 8-3   **Strategic Systems Understanding of the Client's Business and Industry**

Many auditor litigation cases (like those described in Chapter 4) result from the auditor's failure to fully understand the nature of transactions in the client's industry. For example, in the U.S. several major accounting firms paid large settlements to the federal government related to audits of failed savings and loans. In some of these audits, the auditors failed to understand the nature of significant real estate transactions. However, it is more difficult for auditors to uncover fraud cases even if they understand properly the nature of their clients' business transactions.

The auditor must also understand the client's external environment, including such things as wide volatility in economic conditions, extent of competition, and regulatory requirements. For example, auditors of insurance and financial companies need more than an understanding of the industry's unique regulatory accounting requirements. They must also know how recent deregulation in such industries has increased competition and how fluctuations in insurance and financial contracts pricing impact firm operations. To develop effective audit plans, auditors of all companies must have the expertise to assess external environment risks.

Business Operations and Processes

The auditor should understand factors such as major sources of revenue, key customers and suppliers, sources of financing, and information about related parties that may indicate areas of increased client business risk. For example, many technology firms are dependent on one or a few products that may become obsolete due to new technologies or stronger competitors. Dependence on a few major customers may result in material losses from bad debts or obsolete inventory.

Tour Client Facilities and Operations A tour of the client's facilities is helpful in obtaining a better understanding of the client's business operations because it provides an opportunity to observe operations firsthand and to meet key personnel. By viewing the physical facilities, the auditor can assess physical safeguards over assets and interpret accounting data related to assets such as inventory in process and factory equipment. With such first-hand knowledge, the auditor is better able to identify inherent risks, such as unused equipment or potentially unsalable inventory. Discussions with non-accounting employees during the tour and throughout the audit also help the auditor learn more about the client's business to aid in assessing inherent risk.

Identify Related Parties Transactions with related parties are important to auditors because International Financial Reporting Standards require that they be *disclosed in the financial statements* if they are material. A **related party** is defined in auditing standards (ISA 550) as an affiliated company, a principal owner of the client company, or any other party with which the client deals, where one of the parties can directly or indirectly influence the management or operating policies of the other. A **related party transaction** is any transaction between the client and a related party. Common examples include sales or purchase transactions between a parent company and its subsidiary, exchanges of equipment between two companies owned by the same person, and loans to officers. A less common example is the exercise of significant management influence on an audit client by its most important customer.

A transaction with a related party is not an arm's-length transaction. Therefore, there is a risk that they may not be valued at the same amount as a transaction with an independent third party. For example, a company may be able to purchase inventory from a related company at more favorable terms than from an outside vendor. Most auditors assess inherent risk as high for related parties and related party transactions, both because of the accounting disclosure requirements and the lack of independence between the parties involved in the transactions.

Information systems may also be ineffective at identifying or summarizing transactions and outstanding balances between the company and its related parties. Auditors need to obtain an understanding of the entity and any related party relationships and transactions to recognize fraud risk factors arising from related party relationships and transactions and to ensure fair presentation of the financial statements and that they are not misleading. Auditors must apply the concept of professional skepticism as required by ISA 200 in examining transactions made with related parties.

Because material related party transactions must be disclosed, all related parties need to be *identified and included in the auditor's permanent files* early in the engagement. (The disclosure requirements include the nature of the related party relationship; a description of transactions, including the size of the amounts; and amounts due from and to related parties.) Having all related parties included in the permanent audit files, and making sure all auditors on the team know who the related parties are, helps auditors identify undisclosed related party transactions as they do the audit. Common ways of identifying related parties include inquiry of management, review of board of directors' minutes for related party transactions, internal auditors' reports, contracts and agreements made with key management or/and those charged with governance, material contracts and agreements not in the company's ordinary activities, and examining stockholders' listings to identify principal stockholders.

Because of the lack of independence between related parties, the Sarbanes–Oxley Act in the U.S. prohibits related party transactions that involve personal loans to any director or executive officer of a public company. Similar restrictions are embedded in many of the Companies Acts or commercial laws governing companies operating in many Arab countries. However, U.S. banks and other financial institutions are permitted to make normal loans, such as residential mortgages, to their directors and officers using market rates.

Management and Governance

Because management establishes a company's strategies and business processes, an auditor should assess management's philosophy and operating style and its ability to identify and respond to risk, as these significantly influence the risk of material misstatements in the financial statements. For example, in one of the major financial

Related party

Affiliated company, principal owner of the client company, or any other party with which the client deals, where one of the parties can directly or indirectly influence the management or operating policies of the other.

Related party transaction

Any transaction between the client and a related party.

accounting scandals of the late 1990s, the significant annual increase in sales and earnings reported by the Sunbeam Corporation during the period 1996–1998 in a famous fraud case was ultimately determined to be based on various improper accounting techniques encouraged by the CEO and the CFO who, between them, orchestrated a fraudulent scheme to create the illusion of a successful restructuring of Sunbeam and facilitate the sale of the company at an inflated price. The CFO promised investors that, as a result of restructuring, Sunbeam would meet very aggressive revenue and earnings targets. The CFO deceived investors with a fictitious share price increase which was uncovered and both he and the CEO were charged with fraud.

A firm's governance includes its organizational structure, as well as the activities of the board of directors and the audit committee. An effective board of directors helps ensure that the company takes only appropriate risks, while the audit committee, through oversight of financial reporting, can reduce the likelihood of overly aggressive accounting. To gain an understanding of the client's governance system, the auditor should understand the corporate charter and bylaws, consider the company's code of ethics, and read the corporate minutes.

Code of Ethics Companies frequently communicate the entity's values and ethical standards through policy statements and codes of conduct. In the U.S., public companies are required to disclose whether they have adopted a code of ethics that applies to senior management, including the CEO, CFO, and principal accounting officer or controller. A company that has not adopted such a code must disclose this fact and explain why it has not done so. The SEC also requires companies to promptly disclose amendments and waivers to the code of ethics for any of their officers. Auditors should gain knowledge of the company's code of ethics and examine any changes and waivers of the code of conduct that have implications about the governance system and related integrity and ethical values of senior management.

In the Arab world, the matter is different. The codes of corporate governance in many Arab countries require the establishment of internal audit departments, and audit and remuneration committees, in addition to other elements of governance within the business organization. The codes of corporate governance are more flexible in relation to requirements for a code of ethics to be applied in publicly listed companies.

Minutes of Meetings The **corporate minutes** are the official record of the meetings of the board of directors and stockholders. They include key authorizations and summaries of the most important topics discussed at these meetings and the decisions made by the directors and shareholders. Common authorizations in the minutes include compensation of officers, new contracts and agreements, and acquisitions of property, loans, and dividend payments. Examples of other information relevant to the audit include discussions about litigation, a pending issue of stock, or a potential merger.

The auditor should read the minutes to obtain authorizations and other information that is relevant to performing the audit. This information should be included in the audit files by making an abstract of the minutes or by obtaining a copy and underlining significant portions. Before the audit is completed, the auditor must follow up on this information to be sure that management has complied with actions taken by the stockholders and the board of directors. As an illustration, the authorized compensation of officers should be traced to each individual officer's payroll record as a test of whether the correct total compensation was paid. Similarly, the auditor should compare the authorizations of loans with notes payable to make certain that these liabilities are recorded and key terms disclosed. Litigation, pending stock issues, and merger information may need to be included in footnotes.

Corporate minutes

The official record of the meetings of a corporation's board of directors and stockholders, in which corporate issues, such as the declaration of dividends and the approval of contracts, are documented.

Understand Client's Business and Industry

Industry and External Environment

Business Operations and Processes

Management and Governance

Objectives and Strategies

Measurement and Performance

Client Objectives and Strategies

Strategies are approaches followed by the entity to achieve organizational objectives. Auditors should understand client objectives related to:

1. Reliability of financial reporting
2. Effectiveness and efficiency of operations
3. Compliance with laws and regulations

Despite management's best efforts, business risks arise that threaten management's ability to achieve its objectives. As a result, knowledge of client objectives and strategies helps the auditor to assess client business risk and inherent risk in the financial statements. For example, product quality can have a significant impact on the financial statements through lost sales and through warranty and product liability claims. In the U.S., the toy manufacturer, Mattel, Inc., had to make a charge of over US$40 million against income in one quarter for toy recalls due to lead paint contamination in its international production process. In one of the Arab countries, a businessman was charged with US$5 million for improper disclosure of information about the composition of his company's ownership.

As part of understanding the client's objectives related to compliance with laws and regulations, the auditor should become familiar with the terms of client contracts and other legal obligations. These can include such diverse items as long-term notes and bonds payable, stock options, pension plans, contracts with vendors for future delivery of supplies, government contracts for completion and delivery of manufactured products, royalty agreements, union contracts, and leases. Most contracts are of primary interest in individual parts of the audit and, in practice, receive special attention during the different phases of the detailed tests. For example, the provisions of insurance or end of services bonus plans will receive substantial emphasis as a part of the audit of the unfunded liability for insurance and end of services bonuses. The auditor should review and abstract the documents early in the engagement to gain a better perspective of the organization and to better assess inherent risks. Later, these documents can be examined more carefully as a part of the tests of individual audit areas.

Measurement and Performance

A client's performance measurement system includes key performance indicators that management uses to measure progress toward its objectives. These indicators go beyond financial statement figures, such as sales and net income, to include measures tailored to the client and its objectives. Such key performance indicators may include market share, sales per employee, unit sales growth, unique visitors to a website, same-store sales, sales by country, and sales per square foot for a retailer.

Inherent risk of financial statement misstatements may be increased if the client has set unreasonable objectives or if the performance measurement system encourages aggressive accounting. For example, a company's objective may be to obtain the leading market share of industry sales. If management and salespeople are compensated based on achieving this goal, there is increased incentive to record sales before they have been earned or record sales for nonexistent transactions. In such a situation, the auditor is likely to increase assessed inherent risk and the extent of testing for the occurrence transaction-related audit objective for sales.

Performance measurement includes ratio analysis and benchmarking against key competitors. As part of understanding the client's business, the auditor should perform ratio analysis or review the client's calculations of key performance ratios. Performing preliminary analytical procedures is the fourth step in the planning process and is discussed later in this chapter.

ASSESS CLIENT BUSINESS RISK

Accept client and perform initial audit planning

Understand the client's business and industry

Assess client business risk

Perform preliminary analytical procedures

Set materiality and assess acceptable audit risk and inherent risk

Understand internal control and assess control risk

Gather information to assess fraud risks

Develop overall audit plan and audit program

The auditor uses knowledge gained from the understanding of the client's business and industry to assess client business risk, the risk that the client will fail to achieve its objectives. Client business risk can arise from any of the factors affecting the client and its environment, such as significant declines in the economy that threaten the client's cash flows, new technology eroding a client's competitive advantage, or a client failing to execute its strategies as well as its competitors.

The auditor's primary concern is the risk of material misstatements in the financial statements due to client business risk. For example, companies often make strategic acquisitions or mergers that depend on successfully combining the operations of two or more companies. If the planned synergies do not develop, the fixed assets and goodwill recorded in the acquisition may be impaired, affecting the fair presentation in the financial statements.

Figure 8-4 summarizes the relationship among the client's business and industry, client business risk, and the auditor's assessment of the risk of material financial statement misstatements. The auditor's assessment of client business risk considers the client's industry and other external factors, as well as the client's business strategies, processes, and other internal factors. The auditor also considers management controls that may mitigate business risk, such as effective risk assessment practices and corporate governance. Remaining risk after considering the effectiveness of top management controls is sometimes called residual risk. After evaluating client business risk, the auditor can then assess the risk of material misstatement in the financial statements, and then apply the audit risk model to determine the appropriate extent of audit evidence. Use of the audit risk model is discussed in Chapter 9.

Management is a primary source for identifying client business risks. In public companies, management should conduct thorough evaluations of relevant client business risks that affect financial reporting to be able to certify quarterly and annual financial statements, and to evaluate the effectiveness of disclosure controls and procedures. Boards of directors and senior executives are implementing an enterprise wide approach to risk management as described in Figure 8-4 on this page.

In the U.S., Sarbanes–Oxley requires management to certify that it has designed disclosure controls and procedures to ensure that material information about business risks are communicated to management and disclosed to external stakeholders, such as

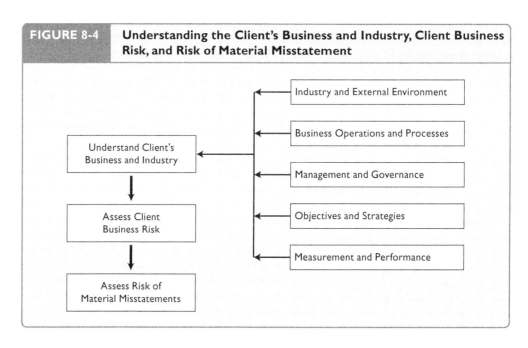

| FIGURE 8-4 | Understanding the Client's Business and Industry, Client Business Risk, and Risk of Material Misstatement |

investors. These procedures cover a broader range of information than is covered by an issuer's internal controls for financial reporting. The procedures should capture information that is relevant to assess the need to disclose developments and risks that pertain to the company's business. Inquiries of management about client business risks, in advance of certifying quarterly and annual financial statements, may provide a significant source of information for auditors about client business risks affecting financial reporting.

In the Arab world, auditors should assess the unique features of many Arab companies related to client's business risk. The economic and financial instability of some Arab governments has significant effects on the ability of business enterprises to maintain their successful operations. Auditors should be alert for management manipulations of some of the accounts to achieve budget targets or inflate share prices. High turnover of managers, employees, default in payment of loans, financial difficulties and liquidity problems, inability to secure appropriate percentage of market share, etc. are examples of factors which the auditors in the Arab countries are required to investigate and assess when they analyze their clients' business risk.

In the U.S., the Sarbanes–Oxley Act also requires management to certify that it has informed the auditor and audit committee of any significant deficiencies in internal control, including material weaknesses. Such information enables auditors to better evaluate how internal controls may affect the likelihood of material misstatements in financial statements. Moreover, ISA 315 discusses similar procedures which can be performed by auditors to identify and assess the risks of material misstatements through understanding the entity and its environment. ISAs are applied in the majority of countries in the Middle East.

PERFORM PRELIMINARY ANALYTICAL PROCEDURES

Analytical procedures are defined as consisting of evaluations of financial information through analysis of plausible relationships among both financial and non-financial data (ISA 520). Auditing standards require that the auditor applies analytical procedures at the planning phase for all audits. The objectives of preliminary analytical procedures at this phase of the audit are: (1) to understand the client's business and all related transactions; and (2) to identify the accounts in the client's financial statements that are likely to include misstatements. By identifying where errors are likely, the auditor can allocate more resources to investigate those accounts.

Auditors perform preliminary analytical procedures to better understand the client's business and to assess client business risk. One such procedure compares client ratios to industry or competitor benchmarks to provide an indication of the company's performance. Such preliminary tests can reveal unusual changes in ratios compared to prior years, or to industry averages, and help the auditor identify areas with increased risk of misstatements that require further attention during the audit.

The Arabian Hardware Co. example is used to illustrate the use of preliminary analytical procedures as part of audit planning. This is followed by a summary of the audit planning process, and further discussion of the use of analytical procedures throughout the audit.

Table 8-2 presents key financial ratios for Arabian Hardware Co., along with comparative industry information that auditors might consider during audit planning. These ratios are based on the Arabian Hardware Co. financial statements. (See the glossy insert in this textbook.) Arabian's annual report to shareholders describes the company as a wholesale distributor of hardware equipment to independent, high-quality hardware stores across the Arab world. The company is a niche provider in the overall hardware industry, which is dominated by national chains like Mahran Hardware and Construction City. Arabian's auditors identified potential increased competition from national chains as a specific client business risk. Arabian's market consists

---

OBJECTIVE 8-5

Perform preliminary analytical procedures.

- Accept client and perform initial audit planning
- Understand the client's business and industry
- Assess client business risk
- Perform preliminary analytical procedures
- Set materiality and assess acceptable audit risk and inherent risk
- Understand internal control and assess control risk
- Gather information to assess fraud risks
- Develop overall audit plan and audit program

TABLE 8-2	Key Financial Ratios for Arabian Hardware Co.			
Selected Ratios	Arabian Dec 31, 2012	Industry Dec 31, 2012	Arabian Dec 31, 2011	Industry Dec 31, 2011
Short-Term Debt-Paying Ability				
Cash ratio	0.06	0.22	0.06	0.20
Quick ratio	1.57	3.10	1.45	3.00
Current ratio	3.86	5.20	4.04	5.10
Liquidity Activity Ratios				
Accounts receivable turnover	7.59	12.15	7.61	12.25
Days to collect accounts receivable	48.09	30.04	47.96	29.80
Inventory turnover	3.36	5.20	3.02	4.90
Days to sell inventory	108.63	70.19	120.86	74.49
Ability to Meet Long-Term Obligations				
Debt to equity	1.73	2.51	1.98	2.53
Times interest earned	3.06	5.50	3.29	5.60
Profitability Ratios				
Gross profit percent	27.85	31.00	27.70	32.00
Profit margin	0.05	0.07	0.05	0.08
Return on assets	0.09	0.09	0.08	0.09
Return on common equity	0.26	0.37	0.24	0.35

of smaller, independent hardware stores. Increased competition could affect the sales and profitability of these customers, likely affecting Arabian's sales and the value of assets such as accounts receivable and inventory. An auditor might use ratio information to identify areas where Arabian faces increased risk of material misstatements.

The profitability measures indicate that Arabian is performing fairly well, despite the increased competition from larger national chains. Although lower than the industry averages, the liquidity measures indicate that the company is in good financial condition, and the leverage ratios indicate additional borrowing capacity. Because Arabian's market consists of smaller, independent stores, the company takes longer to collect receivables than the industry average.

In identifying areas of specific risk, the auditor is likely to focus on the liquidity activity ratios. Inventory turnover has improved but is still lower than the industry average. Accounts receivable turnover has declined slightly and is lower than the industry average. The collectability of accounts receivable and inventory obsolescence are likely to be assessed as high inherent risks and will therefore likely warrant additional attention in the current year's audit. These areas likely received additional attention during the prior year's audit as well.

SUMMARY OF THE PARTS OF AUDIT PLANNING

A major purpose of audit planning is to gain an understanding of the client's business and industry, which is used to assess acceptable audit risk, client business risk, and the risk of material misstatements in the financial statements. Figure 8-5 summarizes the four major parts of audit planning discussed in this section and the key components of each part, with a brief illustration of how a CPA firm applied each component to a continuing client, Arabian Hardware Co.

FIGURE 8-5   **Key Parts of Planning: Accept Client and Perform Initial Planning, Understand the Client's Business and Industry, Assess Client Business Risk, and Perform Preliminary Analytical Procedures Applied to Arabian Hardware Co.**

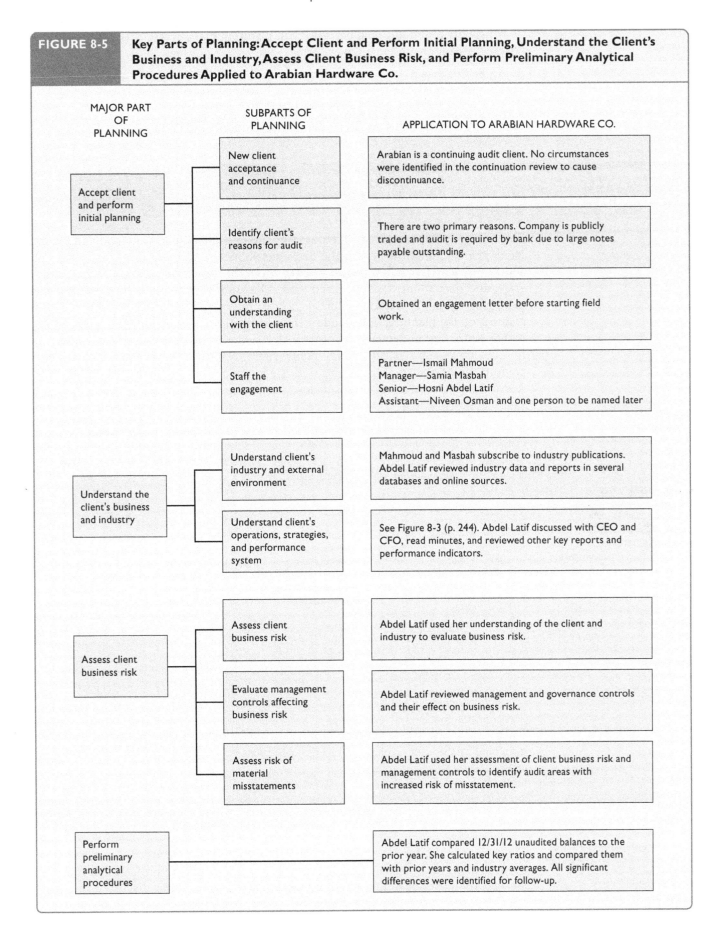

MAJOR PART OF PLANNING	SUBPARTS OF PLANNING	APPLICATION TO ARABIAN HARDWARE CO.
Accept client and perform initial planning	New client acceptance and continuance	Arabian is a continuing audit client. No circumstances were identified in the continuation review to cause discontinuance.
	Identify client's reasons for audit	There are two primary reasons. Company is publicly traded and audit is required by bank due to large notes payable outstanding.
	Obtain an understanding with the client	Obtained an engagement letter before starting field work.
	Staff the engagement	Partner—Ismail Mahmoud Manager—Samia Masbah Senior—Hosni Abdel Latif Assistant—Niveen Osman and one person to be named later
Understand the client's business and industry	Understand client's industry and external environment	Mahmoud and Masbah subscribe to industry publications. Abdel Latif reviewed industry data and reports in several databases and online sources.
	Understand client's operations, strategies, and performance system	See Figure 8-3 (p. 244). Abdel Latif discussed with CEO and CFO, read minutes, and reviewed other key reports and performance indicators.
Assess client business risk	Assess client business risk	Abdel Latif used her understanding of the client and industry to evaluate business risk.
	Evaluate management controls affecting business risk	Abdel Latif reviewed management and governance controls and their effect on business risk.
	Assess risk of material misstatements	Abdel Latif used her assessment of client business risk and management controls to identify audit areas with increased risk of misstatement.
Perform preliminary analytical procedures		Abdel Latif compared 12/31/12 unaudited balances to the prior year. She calculated key ratios and compared them with prior years and industry averages. All significant differences were identified for follow-up.

There are four additional parts of audit planning that are discussed in subsequent chapters. The four subsequent parts are:

- Set materiality and assess acceptable audit risk and inherent risk (Chapter 9)
- Understand internal control and assess control risk (Chapter 10)
- Gather information to assess fraud risks (Chapter 11)
- Develop an overall audit plan and audit program (Chapter 13)

OVERALL AUDIT STRATEGY AND AUDIT PLAN DOCUMENTATION

The auditor is responsible for documenting the overall audit strategy and audit plan. He or she is required to record the decisions about the nature, timing and extent of audit tests, as well as his or her knowledge about the client's business objectives, strategies, and related business and audit risks. The auditor documents how the client is managing its risk (i.e. through internal control processes) and the effect of the risks and controls on the planning of the audit evidence. Auditors should address the risks they identified in their understanding of the risk assessment process from the client's business objectives and strategy to audit plans. There are various ways of documenting the planning of the audit and they depend on the internal system applied by the audit firm. A simple illustration using a website developer company might look as follows:

Business Objectives and Strategy	Business Risks	Account(s)/ (Assertions)	Audit Risks	Controls	Effect on Audit Plan
Increase market share through sales at new locations (e.g. during the current year websites were developed for ten more countries)	Restrictive trade laws may affect sales tactics. Strong consumer protection in several European countries	Revenue: accuracy and valuation	Overstated due to pricing issues	The Co. has installed a special group to track compliance with local and international laws	Observe and test group's policies and procedures (see work paper R-11)
	Political uncertainty in less developed countries	Reserve for returns: completeness	Understated due to failure to properly track returns in new locations	The Co. has placed more frequent review of returns in new locations	Extend audit work on the Co.'s return tracking with emphasis on new locations
	Currency risks	Gains/losses from currency hedging valuation and accuracy	Gains/losses not properly calculated or accrued on hedging activity	Co. has strong controls in the Treasury Department to account for hedging activities	Increase the number of hedging contracts tested with particular emphasis on contracts in unstable currencies

The overall audit strategy and audit plan should be documented in a written plan as indicated by ISA 300. Table 8-3 presents some elements of an audit plan for substantive tests of accounts receivable.

ANALYTICAL PROCEDURES

Analytical procedures are one of the eight types of evidence introduced in Chapter 7. Because of the increased emphasis on analytical procedures in professional practice, this section moves beyond the preliminary analytical procedures discussed earlier in this chapter to discuss the uses of analytical procedures throughout the audit.

TABLE 8-3	Audit Plan for Substantive Procedures Testing of Accounts Receivable

Audit Procedures	W/P Ref	Completed	Date
1. Obtain the December 31, 2011, aged accounts receivable trial balances and			
a. Foot the trial balance and agree total to accounts receivable control account	_____	_____	_____
b. Randomly select 50 accounts from the aged trial balance; agree the information per the aged trial balance to the original sales invoice and determine if the invoice was included in the appropriate ageing category	_____	_____	_____
2. Confirm accounts receivable using a monetary-unit sampling plan. Set the desired confidence level = 95%, tolerable misstatement = US$70,000, and expected misstatement = US$35,000	_____	_____	_____
a. For all responses with exceptions, follow up on the cause of the error	_____	_____	_____
b. For all non-responses, examine subsequent cash receipts and/or supporting documents	_____	_____	_____
c. Summarize the sampling test results	_____	_____	_____
d. Summarize the confirmation results	_____	_____	_____
3. Test sales cutoff by identifying the last shipping advice for the year and examining five large sales for three days before and after year end	_____	_____	_____
4. Test the reasonableness of the allowance for doubtful accounts by the following:			
a. Test the reasonableness using past percentages on bad debts	_____	_____	_____
b. For any large account in the aged trial balance greater than 120 days old, test for subsequent cash receipts	_____	_____	_____
c. For the following financial ratios, compare the current year to the trend of the prior three years results and internal budgets:	_____	_____	_____
• Number of days outstanding in receivable	_____	_____	_____
• Aging of receivables	_____	_____	_____
• Write-offs as a percentage of sales	_____	_____	_____
• Bad debt expense as a percentage of sales	_____	_____	_____
5. Prepare a memo summarizing the tests, results, and conclusions	_____	_____	_____

Analytical procedures are defined by auditing standards (ISA 520) as *evaluations of financial information through analysis of plausible relationships among both financial and nonfinancial data.* Analytical procedures use comparisons and relationships to assess whether account balances or other data appear reasonable relative to the auditor's expectations.

The emphasis in the explanation of the nature of analytical procedures is on expectations developed by the auditor. For example, the auditor might compare current-year recorded commission expense to total recorded sales multiplied by the average commission rate as a test of the overall reasonableness of recorded commissions. For this analytical procedure to be relevant and reliable, the auditor has likely concluded that recorded sales are correctly stated, all sales earn a commission, and that the average actual commission rate is readily determinable.

Analytical procedures may be performed at any of three times during an engagement:

1. Analytical procedures are required in the *planning phase* to assist in determining the nature, extent, and timing of audit procedures. This helps the auditor identify significant matters requiring special consideration later in the engagement. For example, the calculation of inventory turnover before inventory price tests are done may indicate the need for special care during those tests. Analytical procedures done in the planning phase typically use data aggregated at a high level, and the sophistication, extent, and timing of the procedures vary among clients. For some clients, the comparison of prior-year and current-year account balances using the unaudited trial balance may be sufficient. For other clients, the procedures may involve extensive analysis of quarterly financial statements based on the auditor's judgment.

2. Analytical procedures are often done *during the testing phase* of the audit as a substantive test in support of account balances. These tests are often done in conjunction with other audit procedures. For example, the prepaid portion of each insurance policy might be compared with the same policy for the previous year as a part of doing tests of prepaid insurance. The assurance provided by analytical procedures depends on the predictability of the relationship, as well as the precision of the expectation and the reliability of the data used to develop the expectation.

3. Analytical procedures are also required *during the completion phase* of the audit. Such tests serve as a final review for material misstatements or financial problems and help the auditor take a final 'objective look' at the audited financial statements. Typically, a senior partner with extensive knowledge of the client's business conducts the analytical procedures during the final review of the audit files and financial statements to identify possible oversights in an audit.

Analytical procedures may decrease the cost and the need for using an auditor to perform detailed substantive tests. For example, analytical procedures involving the prediction of total rental revenue on a building divided into apartments, taking the rental rates, the number of apartments and apartment's vacancy rates into consideration, may provide the auditor with persuasive evidence and may reduce the need for additional examination of details for such account balance. However, this may not be true where the auditor calculates and compares gross margin percentages as a means to confirm a revenue figure as it may provide less persuasive evidence. The auditor can also minimize the cost of the audit and time spent by audit staff if he applies analytical procedures to an aging of customers' accounts in addition to performing tests of details on subsequent cash receipts to determine the collectability of receivables.

ISA 520 identified a number of factors which must exist in order for the auditor to benefit from the use of the analytical procedures as follows:

a. Source of the information is available and preferably from independent sources outside the company.

b. Comparability of the information available as broad industry data may need to be supplemented to be comparable to that of an entity that produces and sells specialized products.

c. Controls over the preparation of the information that are designed to ensure its completeness, accuracy, and validity such as controls over the preparation, review, and maintenance of **budgets**.

Budgets
Written records of the client's expectations for the period; a comparison of budgets with actual results may indicate whether or not misstatements are likely.

Figure 8-6 shows the purposes of analytical procedures during each of the three phases. The shaded boxes indicate when a purpose is applicable in each phase. More than one purpose may be indicated. Notice how analytical procedures are done during

FIGURE 8-6	Timing and Purposes of Analytical Procedures		
	Phase		
Purpose	(Required) Planning Phase	Testing Phase	(Required) Completion Phase
Understand the client's business and industry	Primary purpose		
Assess going concern	Secondary purpose		Secondary purpose
Indicate possible misstatements (attention directing)	Primary purpose	Secondary purpose	Primary purpose
Reduce detailed tests	Secondary purpose	Primary purpose	

the planning phase for all four purposes, while procedures during the other two phases are used primarily to determine appropriate audit evidence and to reach conclusions about the fair presentation of financial statements.

FIVE TYPES OF ANALYTICAL PROCEDURES

The usefulness of analytical procedures as audit evidence depends significantly on the auditor developing an *expectation* of what a recorded account balance or ratio *should be*, regardless of the type of analytical procedures used. Auditors develop an expectation of an account balance or ratio by considering information from prior periods, industry trends, client-prepared budgeted expectations, and nonfinancial information. The auditor typically compares the client's balances and ratios with expected balances and ratios using one or more of the following types of analytical procedures. In each case, auditors compare client data with:

> **OBJECTIVE 8-7**
>
> Select the most appropriate analytical procedure from among the five major types.

1. Industry data
2. Similar prior-period data
3. Client-determined expected results
4. Auditor-determined expected results
5. Expected results using nonfinancial data

Compare Client and Industry Data

Suppose that you are doing an audit and obtain the following information about the client and the average company in the client's industry:

	Client		Industry	
	2011	2010	2011	2010
Inventory turnover	3.4	3.5	3.9	3.4
Gross margin percent	26.3%	26.4%	27.3%	26.2%

If we look only at client information for the two ratios shown, the company appears to be stable with no apparent indication of difficulties. However, if we use industry data to develop expectations about the two ratios for 2011, we should expect both ratios for the client to increase. Although these two ratios by themselves may not indicate significant problems, this data illustrates how developing expectations using industry data may provide useful information about the client's performance and potential misstatements. Perhaps the company has lost market share, its pricing has not been competitive, it has incurred abnormal costs, or perhaps it has obsolete items in inventory or made errors in recording purchases. The auditor needs to determine if either of the last two occurred to have reasonable assurance that the financial statements are not misstated.

Another example to illustrate using analytical procedures with industry data, suppose an auditor computes a client's inventory turnover ratio for the last five years as follows:

$$\text{Inventory turnover} = \frac{\text{Cost of goods sold}}{\text{Inventory}}$$

The following analyses show a certain trend, which is compared to industry data:

	2007	2008	2009	2010	2011
Client	8.9	8.8	8.5	8.0	7.9
Industry	8.8	8.7	8.8	8.6	8.6

The client's inventory turnover ratio in this case has declined steadily over the five-year period, while the industry turnover ratio shows only a minor decline over the same period. The auditor might suspect that the client's inventory contains slow-moving or obsolete inventory. The auditor would then plan additional testing for selecting assertions such as valuation, completeness, and existence.

Dun & Bradstreet, Standard & Poor's, and other analysts, most of whom also provide their services within the Arab world, accumulate financial information for thousands of companies and compile the data for different lines of business. Many audit firms purchase this industry information for use as a basis for developing expectations about financial ratios in their audits.

The most important benefits of industry comparisons are to aid in understanding the client's business and as an indication of the likelihood of financial failure. They are less likely to help auditors identify potential misstatements. Financial information collected by the Risk Management Association or similar Central Agency for Public Mobilization and Statistics in the Arab world, for example, is primarily of a type that bankers and other credit analysts use in evaluating whether a company will be able to repay a loan. That same information is useful to auditors in assessing the relative strength of the client's capital structure, its borrowing capacity, and the likelihood of financial failure.

However, a major weakness in using industry ratios for auditing is the difference between the nature of the client's financial information and that of the firms making up the industry totals. Because the industry data are broad averages, the comparisons may not be meaningful. Often, the client's line of business is not the same as the industry standards. In addition, different companies follow different accounting methods, and this affects the comparability of data. For example, if most companies in the industry use FIFO inventory valuation and straight-line depreciation and the audit client uses LIFO and double-declining-balance depreciation, comparisons may not be meaningful. This does not mean that industry comparisons should be avoided. Rather, it is an indication of the need for care in using industry data to develop expectations about financial relationships and in interpreting the results. One approach to overcome the limitations of industry averages is to compare the client to one or more benchmark firms in the industry. Such one to one comparison may consider similarities between the nature of operations, the size of the firm, the style of management, and the number of employees between the company being analyzed and the benchmark company.

Compare Client Data with Similar Prior-Period Data

Suppose that the gross margin percentage for a company has been between 26 and 27 percent for each of the past four years but has dropped to 23 percent in the current year. This decline in gross margin should be a concern to the auditor if a decline is not expected. The cause of the decline could be a change in economic conditions. But, it could also be caused by misstatements in the financial statements, such as sales or purchase cutoff errors, unrecorded sales, overstated accounts payable, or inventory costing errors. The decline in gross margin is likely to result in an increase in evidence in one or more of the accounts that affect gross margin. The auditor needs to determine the cause of the decline to be confident that the financial statements are not materially misstated.

A wide variety of analytical procedures allow auditors to compare client data with similar data from one or more prior periods. Here are some common examples:

Compare the Current Year's Balance with that of the Preceding Year One of the easiest ways to perform this test is to include the preceding year's adjusted trial balance results in a separate column of the current year's trial balance spreadsheet. The auditor can easily compare the current year's balance and previous year's balance to decide, early in the audit, whether an account should receive more than the normal amount of attention because of a significant change in the balance. For example, if the auditor observes a substantial increase in supplies expense, the auditor should determine whether the cause was an increased use of supplies, an error in the account due to a misclassification, or a misstatement of supplies inventory. Also, if the auditor identifies a significant decrease in sales commissions, the auditor may analyze such decrease as a decline in the sales revenues, decrease in salespersons' commissions or a misstatement in sales commission account balance.

Compare the Detail of a Total Balance with Similar Detail for the Preceding Year If there have been no significant changes in the client's operations in the current year, much of the detail making up the totals in the financial statements should also remain unchanged. By briefly comparing the detail of the current period with similar detail of the preceding period, auditors often isolate information that needs further examination. Comparison of details may take the form of details over time, such as comparing the monthly totals for the current year and preceding year for sales, repairs, and other accounts, or details at a point in time, such as comparing the details of loans payable at the end of the current year with the detail at the end of the preceding year. In each of these examples, the auditor should first develop an expectation of a change or lack thereof based on the auditor's previous experience of the audit results, the operating style of the management and whether they are risk take or risk averse, and expected conditions of the market at which the company operates, before making the comparison.

Compute Ratios and Percent Relationships for Comparison with Previous Years Comparing totals or details with previous years has two shortcomings. First, it fails to consider growth or decline in business activity as the comparison relies only on absolute figures. Second, relationships of data to other data, such as sales to cost of goods sold, are ignored. Ratio and percent relationships overcome both shortcomings. For example, the gross margin is a common percent relationship used by auditors to identify whether there are abnormal discrepancies between the current year figures and prior years in relation to important accounts sales and cost of goods sold.

Table 8-4 includes a few ratios and internal comparisons to show the widespread use of ratio analysis. In all these cases, the comparisons should be made with calculations made in previous years for the same client. Many of the ratios and percents used for comparison with previous years are the same ones used for comparison with industry data. For example, auditors often compare current year gross margin with industry averages, as well as margins for previous years.

Numerous potential comparisons of current- and prior-period data extend beyond those normally available from industry data. For example, the percent of each expense category to total sales can be compared with that of previous years. Similarly, in a multiunit operation such as a retail chain, internal data comparisons for each unit can be made with previous periods.

Auditors often prepare *common-size* financial statements for one or more years that display all items as a percent of a common base, such as service revenues or sales.

TABLE 8-4	Internal Comparisons and Relationships
Ratio or Comparison	**Possible Misstatement**
Raw material turnover for a manufacturing company	Misstatement of inventory or cost of goods sold or obsolescence of raw material inventory
Sales commissions divided by net sales	Misstatement of sales commissions
Sales returns and allowances divided by gross sales	Misclassified sales returns and allowances or unrecorded returns and allowances subsequent to year-end
Cash surrender value of life insurance (current year) divided by cash surrender value of life insurance (preceding year)	Failure to record the change in cash surrender value or an error in recording the change
Each of the individual manufacturing expenses as a percent of total manufacturing expense	Significant misstatement of individual expenses within a total

Common-size financial statements allow for comparison between companies or for the same company over different time periods, revealing trends and providing insight into how different companies compare. Common-size income statement data for the past three years for Arabian Hardware are included in Figure 8-7. The auditor should calculate income statement account balances as a percent of sales when the level of service revenues has changed from the prior year—a likely occurrence in many businesses. Arabian's services revenues have *increased* significantly over the prior year. Note that accounts such as cost of service operations, sales salaries, and commissions have also *increased significantly* but are fairly consistent as a percent of service revenues, which we expect for these accounts.

The auditor is likely to require further explanation and corroborating evidence for the changes in advertising, bad debt expense, and office repairs and maintenance.

- Note that advertising expense has *increased* as a percent of service revenues. One possible explanation is the development of a new advertising campaign.
- The amount of *bad debt expense* has not changed significantly but has decreased as a percent of sales. The auditor needs to gather additional evidence to determine whether bad debt expense and the allowance for doubtful accounts are understated.
- Repairs and maintenance expense has also *increased*. Fluctuations in this account are not unusual if the client has incurred unexpected repairs. The auditor should investigate major expenditures in this account to determine whether they include any amounts that should be capitalized as a fixed asset.

Compare Client Data with Client-Determined Expected Results

Most companies prepare budgets for various aspects of their operations and financial results. Because budgets represent the client's expectations for the period, auditors should investigate the most significant differences between budgeted and actual results, as these areas may contain potential misstatements. The absence of differences may indicate that misstatements are unlikely. For example, audits of local and governmental units commonly use this type of analytical procedure.

When client data are compared with budgets, there are two special concerns. First, the auditor must evaluate whether the budgets were realistic plans. In some organizations, budgets are prepared with little thought or care and therefore are not realistic expectations. Such information has little value as audit evidence. A discussion of budget procedures with client personnel can provide insights about this concern. The second concern is the possibility that current financial information was changed by client personnel to conform to the budget. If that has occurred, the auditor will find no differences in comparing actual data with budgeted data, even if there are misstatements in the financial statements. Assessing control risk and detailed audit tests of actual data are usually done to minimize this concern.

Compare Client Data with Auditor-Determined Expected Results

Another common comparison of client data with expected results occurs when the *auditor calculates the expected balance for comparison with the actual balance*. In this type of analytical procedure, the auditor makes an estimate of what an account balance should be by relating it to some other balance sheet or income statement account or accounts, or by making a projection based on some historical trend. Here are two examples:

1. The auditor may make an independent calculation of interest expense on long-term notes payable by multiplying the ending monthly balance in notes payable by the average monthly interest rate (see Figure 8-8). This independent estimate based on the relationship between interest expense and notes payable is used to test the reasonableness of recorded interest expense.

FIGURE 8-7	Arabian Hardware Company Common-Size Income Statement

ARABIAN HARDWARE CO.
COMMON-SIZE INCOME STATEMENT
Three Years Ending December 31, 2012

	2012		2011		2010	
	(000) Preliminary	% of Net Sales	(000) Audited	% of Net Sales	(000) Audited	% of Net Sales
Sales	US$144,328	100.87	US$132,421	100.91	US$123,737	100.86
Less: Returns and allowances	1,242	0.87	1,195	0.91	1,052	0.86
Net sales	143,086	100.00	131,226	100.00	122,685	100.00
Cost of goods sold	103,241	72.15	94,876	72.30	88,724	72.32
Gross profit	39,845	27.85	36,350	27.70	33,961	27.68
Selling expense						
Salaries and commissions	7,739	5.41	7,044	5.37	6,598	5.38
Sales payroll taxes	1,422	0.99	1,298	0.99	1,198	0.98
Travel and entertainment	1,110	0.78	925	0.70	797	0.65
Advertising	2,611	1.82	1,920	1.46	1,790	1.46
Sales and promotional literature	322	0.22	425	0.32	488	0.40
Sales meetings and training	925	0.65	781	0.60	767	0.62
Miscellaneous sales expense	681	0.48	506	0.39	456	0.37
Total selling expense	14,810	10.35	12,899	9.83	12,094	9.86
Administration expense						
Executive and office salaries	5,524	3.86	5,221	3.98	5,103	4.16
Administrative payroll taxes	682	0.48	655	0.50	633	0.52
Travel and entertainment	562	0.39	595	0.45	542	0.44
Computer maintenance and supplies	860	0.60	832	0.63	799	0.65
Stationery and supplies	763	0.53	658	0.50	695	0.57
Postage	244	0.17	251	0.19	236	0.19
Telephone and fax	722	0.51	626	0.48	637	0.52
Rent	312	0.22	312	0.24	312	0.25
Legal fees and retainers	383	0.27	321	0.25	283	0.23
Auditing and related services	303	0.21	288	0.22	265	0.22
Depreciation	1,452	1.01	1,443	1.10	1,505	1.23
Bad debt expense	3,323	2.32	3,394	2.59	3,162	2.58
Insurance	723	0.51	760	0.58	785	0.64
Office repairs and maintenance	844	0.59	538	0.41	458	0.37
Miscellaneous office expense	644	0.45	621	0.47	653	0.53
Miscellaneous general expense	324	0.23	242	0.18	275	0.22
Total administrative expenses	17,665	12.35	16,757	12.77	16,343	13.32
Total selling and administrative expenses	32,475	22.70	29,656	22.60	28,437	23.18
Earnings from operations	7,370	5.15	6,694	5.10	5,524	4.50
Other income and expense						
Interest expense	2,409	1.68	2,035	1.55	2,173	1.77
Gain on sale of assets	(720)	(0.50)	0	0.00	0	0.00
Earnings before income taxes	5,681	3.97	4,659	3.55	3,351	2.73
Income taxes	1,747	1.22	1,465	1.12	1,072	0.87
Net income	US$ 3,934	2.75	US$ 3,194	2.43	US$ 2,279	1.86

2. The auditor may calculate the moving average of the allowance for uncollectible accounts receivable as a percent of gross accounts receivable, and then apply it to the balance of gross accounts receivable at the end of the audit year. By using such historical trends, the auditor can determine an expected value for the current allowance.

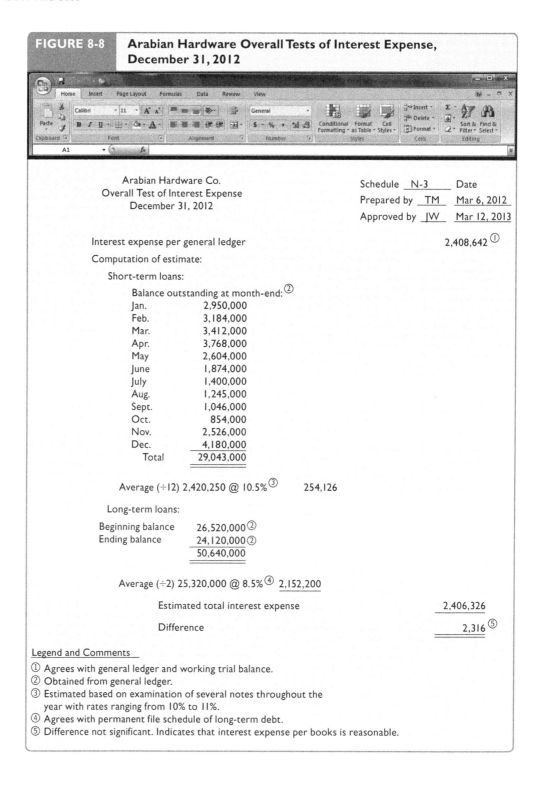

FIGURE 8-8 Arabian Hardware Overall Tests of Interest Expense, December 31, 2012

Arabian Hardware Co.
Overall Test of Interest Expense
December 31, 2012

Schedule N-3 Date
Prepared by TM Mar 6, 2012
Approved by JW Mar 12, 2013

Interest expense per general ledger   2,408,642 ①

Computation of estimate:

Short-term loans:

Balance outstanding at month-end: ②

Jan.	2,950,000
Feb.	3,184,000
Mar.	3,412,000
Apr.	3,768,000
May	2,604,000
June	1,874,000
July	1,400,000
Aug.	1,245,000
Sept.	1,046,000
Oct.	854,000
Nov.	2,526,000
Dec.	4,180,000
Total	29,043,000

Average (÷12) 2,420,250 @ 10.5% ③   254,126

Long-term loans:

Beginning balance   26,520,000 ②
Ending balance   24,120,000 ②
                     50,640,000

Average (÷2) 25,320,000 @ 8.5% ④ 2,152,200

Estimated total interest expense   2,406,326

Difference   2,316 ⑤

Legend and Comments

① Agrees with general ledger and working trial balance.
② Obtained from general ledger.
③ Estimated based on examination of several notes throughout the
   year with rates ranging from 10% to 11%.
④ Agrees with permanent file schedule of long-term debt.
⑤ Difference not significant. Indicates that interest expense per books is reasonable.

Compare Client Data with Expected Results Using Nonfinancial Data

Suppose that you are auditing a hotel. You may develop an expectation for total revenue from rooms by multiplying the number of rooms, the average daily rate for each room, and the average occupancy rate. You can then compare your estimate with recorded revenue as a test of the reasonableness of recorded revenue. The same approach can be applied to create estimates in other situations, such as tuition revenue at universities (average tuition multiplied by enrollment), factory payroll (total hours worked times the wage rate), and cost of materials sold (units sold times materials cost per unit).

The major concern in using nonfinancial data, however, is the accuracy of the data. In the hotel example, you should not use an estimated calculation of hotel revenue as audit evidence unless you are satisfied with the reasonableness of the count of the number of rooms, average room rate, and average occupancy rate. Obviously, the accuracy of the occupancy rate is more difficult to evaluate than the other two items.

COMMON FINANCIAL RATIOS

Auditors' analytical procedures often include the use of general financial ratios during planning and final review of the audited financial statements. These are useful for understanding recent events and the financial status of the business and for viewing the statements from the perspective of a user. The general financial analysis may be effective for identifying possible problem areas, where the auditor may do additional analysis and audit testing, as well as business problem areas in which the auditor can provide other assistance. When using these ratios, auditors must be sure to make appropriate comparisons. The most important comparisons are to those of previous years for the company and to industry averages or similar companies for the same year.

OBJECTIVE 8-8

Compute common financial ratios.

Ratios and other analytical procedures are normally calculated using spreadsheets and other types of audit software, in which several years of client and industry data can be maintained for comparative purposes. Ratios can be linked to the trial balance so that calculations are automatically updated as adjusting entries are made to the client's statements. For example, an adjustment to inventory and cost of goods sold affects a large number of ratios, including inventory turnover, the current ratio, gross margin, and other profitability measures.

We next examine some widely used financial ratios. The following computations are based on the 2012 financial statements of Arabian Hardware Co., which appear in the glossy insert to the textbook. These ratios were prepared from the trial balance in Figure 8-8.

Short-Term Debt-Paying Ability

$$\text{Cash ratio} = \frac{\text{cash} + \text{marketable securities}}{\text{current liabilities}} \qquad \frac{828}{13,216} = 0.06$$

$$\text{Quick ratio} = \frac{\text{cash} + \text{marketable securities} + \text{net accounts receivable}}{\text{current liabilities}} \qquad \frac{828 + 18,957 + 945}{13,216} = 1.57$$

$$\text{Current ratio} = \frac{\text{current assets}}{\text{current liabilities}} \qquad \frac{51,027}{13,216} = 3.86$$

Companies need a reasonable level of liquidity to pay their debts as they come due, and these three ratios measure liquidity. It is apparent by examining the three ratios that the cash ratio may be useful to evaluate the ability to pay debts immediately, whereas the current ratio requires the conversion of assets such as inventory and accounts receivable to cash before debts can be paid. The most important difference between the quick and current ratios is the inclusion of inventory in current assets for the current ratio.

Liquidity Activity Ratios

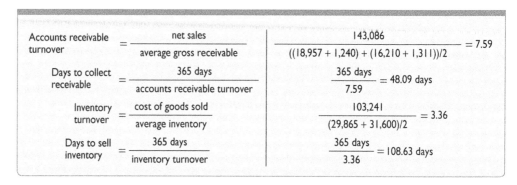

$$\text{Accounts receivable turnover} = \frac{\text{net sales}}{\text{average gross receivable}} \qquad \frac{143{,}086}{((18{,}957 + 1{,}240) + (16{,}210 + 1{,}311))/2} = 7.59$$

$$\text{Days to collect receivable} = \frac{365 \text{ days}}{\text{accounts receivable turnover}} \qquad \frac{365 \text{ days}}{7.59} = 48.09 \text{ days}$$

$$\text{Inventory turnover} = \frac{\text{cost of goods sold}}{\text{average inventory}} \qquad \frac{103{,}241}{(29{,}865 + 31{,}600)/2} = 3.36$$

$$\text{Days to sell inventory} = \frac{365 \text{ days}}{\text{inventory turnover}} \qquad \frac{365 \text{ days}}{3.36} = 108.63 \text{ days}$$

If a company does not have sufficient cash and cash-like items to meet its obligations, the key to its debt-paying ability is the time it takes the company to convert less liquid current assets into cash. This is measured by the liquidity activity ratios.

The activity ratios for accounts receivable and inventory are especially useful to auditors, who often use trends in the accounts receivable turnover ratio to assess the reasonableness of the allowance for uncollectible accounts. Auditors use trends in the inventory turnover ratio to identify potential inventory obsolescence. Average days to collect are a different way of looking at the average accounts receivable turnover data. The same is true of average days to sell compared to average inventory turnover.

Ability to Meet Long-Term Debt Obligations

$$\text{Debt to equity} = \frac{\text{total liabilities}}{\text{total equity}} \qquad \frac{13{,}216 + 25{,}688}{22{,}463} = 1.73$$

$$\text{Times interest earned} = \frac{\text{operating income}}{\text{interest expense}} \qquad \frac{7{,}370}{2{,}409} = 3.06$$

A company's long-run solvency depends on the success of its operations and on its ability to raise capital for expansion, as well as its ability to make principal and interest payments. Two ratios are key measures creditors and investors use to assess a company's ability to pay its debts.

The debt-to-equity ratio shows the extent of the use of debt in financing a company. If the debt-to-equity ratio is too high, it may indicate that the company has used up its borrowing capacity and has no cushion for additional debt. If it is too low, it may mean that available leverage is not being used to the owners' benefit.

The ability to make interest payments depends on the company's ability to generate positive cash flow from operations. The times interest earned ratio shows whether the company can comfortably make its interest payments, assuming that earnings trends are stable.

Profitability Ratios

A company's ability to generate cash for payment of obligations, expansion, and dividends is heavily dependent on profitability. The most widely used profitability ratio is earnings per share. Auditors calculate additional ratios to provide further insights into operations.

Gross profit percent shows the portion of sales available to cover all expenses and profit after deducting the cost of the product. Auditors find this ratio especially useful for assessing misstatements in sales, cost of goods sold, accounts receivable, and inventory.

Profit margin is similar to gross profit margin but subtracts both cost of goods sold and operating expenses in making the calculations. This ratio enables auditors to assess potential misstatements in operating expenses and related balance sheet accounts.

$$\text{Earnings per share} = \frac{\text{net income}}{\text{average common shares outstanding}} \qquad \frac{3,934}{5,000} = 0.79$$

$$\text{Gross profit percent} = \frac{\text{net sales} - \text{cost of goods sold}}{\text{net sales}} \qquad \frac{143,086 - 103,241}{143,086} = 27.85\%$$

$$\text{Profit margin} = \frac{\text{operating income}}{\text{net sales}} \qquad \frac{7,370}{143,086} = 0.056$$

$$\text{Return on assets} = \frac{\text{income before taxes}}{\text{average total assets}} \qquad \frac{5,681}{(61,367 + 60,791)/2} = 0.09$$

$$\text{Return on common equity} = \frac{\text{income before taxes} - \text{preferred dividends}}{\text{average stockholders' equity}} \qquad \frac{5,681 - 0}{(22,463 + 20,429)/2} = 0.26$$

Return on assets and return on common equity are measures of overall profitability of a company. These ratios show a company's ability to generate profit for each amount of assets and equity.

SUMMARY

The first part of this chapter discussed audit planning, including understanding the client's business and industry and performing preliminary analytical procedures to assess client business risk and the risk of material misstatements in the financial statements. Also, the chapter discussed how auditors in the Arab world assess the client's industry and business risk given their unique economic, culture, and regulatory business environment. Analytical procedures are the evaluation of recorded accounting information by computing ratios and developing other plausible relationships for comparison to expectations developed by the auditor. These analytical procedures are used in planning to understand the client's business and industry and throughout the audit to identify possible misstatements, reduce detailed tests, and to assess going-concern issues. The use of analytical procedures has increased because of their effectiveness at identifying possible misstatements at a low cost, and they are required in the planning and completion phases of the audit.

ESSENTIAL TERMS

Acceptable audit risk   p. 235

Audit plan   p. 234

Audit strategy   p. 239

Budgets   p. 254

Corporate minutes   p. 246

Engagement letter   p. 239

Inherent risk   p. 236

Initial audit planning   p. 236

Internal audit function   p. 236

Overall audit strategy   p. 234

Related party   p. 245

Related party transaction   p. 245

REVIEW QUESTIONS

8-1 (Objective 8-1) What are the benefits derived from planning audits?

8-2 (Objective 8-1) Identify the eight major steps in planning audits.

8-3 (Objective 8-2) What are the responsibilities of the successor and predecessor auditors when a company is changing auditors?

8-4 (Objective 8-2) What factors should an auditor consider prior to accepting an engagement? Explain. Are there special decisions to be made by auditors in the Arab countries before accepting a new client?

8-5 (Objective 8-2) What is the purpose of an engagement letter? What subjects should be covered in such a letter?

8-6 (Objective 8-2) What differences exist between accepting a new publicly listed company compared with new private companies in the Arab world?

8-7 (Objective 8-2) Which services must be preapproved by the audit committee of a public listed company?

8-8 (Objective 8-3) Explain why auditors need an understanding of the client's industry. What information sources are commonly used by auditors to learn about the client's industry?

8-9 (Objective 8-3) When an auditor has accepted an engagement from a new client who is a manufacturer, it is customary for the auditors to tour the client's plant facilities. Discuss the ways in which the auditor's observations made during the course of the plant tour will be of help in planning and conducting the audit. Do you think that auditors in your country will be allowed to tour plants at their clients' premises? If your answer is no provide justification for your answer.

8-10 (Objective 8-3) An auditor often tries to acquire background knowledge of the client's industry as an aid to audit work. How does the acquisition of this knowledge aid the auditor in distinguishing between obsolete and current inventory?

8-11 (Objective 8-3) Define what is meant by a related party. What are the auditor's responsibilities for related parties and related party transactions?

8-12 (Objective 8-3) Which types of loans to executives are permitted by the Sarbanes–Oxley Act in the U.S.? What are the procedures for executives to get loans in your country?

8-13 (Objective 8-3) In recent years the stock market experienced significant declines, unprecedented since the Great Depression. Why might it be important for you to consider current economic events as part of planning your audit? How might the economic instability in your country affect auditors' decisions for extent of testing, sample selection, and timing of the audit?

8-14 (Objective 8-3) For the audit of Salem Manufacturing Company, the audit partner asks you to carefully read the new mortgage contract with the Abu Dhabi National Bank and abstract all pertinent information. List the information in a mortgage that is likely to be relevant to the auditor.

8-15 (Objective 8-3) Identify two types of information in the client's minutes of the board of directors' meetings that are likely to be relevant to the auditor. Explain why it is important to read the minutes early in the engagement. (*Hint*: access websites for publicly listed companies in your country and look for information disclosed in board minutes.)

8-16 (Objective 8-3) Identify the three categories of client objectives. Indicate how each objective may affect the auditor's assessment of inherent risk and need for evidence accumulation.

8-17 (Objective 8-3) What is the purpose of the client's performance measurement system? How might that system be useful to the auditor? Give examples of key performance indicators for the following businesses: (1) a chain of retail clothing stores; (2) an internet portal; (3) a hotel chain.

8-18 (Objective 8-4) Define client business risk and describe several sources of client business risk. What is the auditor's primary concern when evaluating client business risk?

8-19 (Objective 8-4) Describe top management controls and their relation to client business risk. Give examples of effective management and governance controls. How might such controls be different in your country and describe their effects on auditors assessing client's business risk.

8-20 (Objectives 8-5, 8-6) What are the purposes of preliminary analytical procedures? What types of comparisons are useful when performing preliminary analytical procedures?

8-21 (Objective 8-6) When are analytical procedures required on an audit? What is the primary purpose of analytical procedures during the completion phase of the audit?

8-22 (Objective 8-7) Sherif Saad, CPA, has found ratio and trend analysis relatively useless as a tool in conducting audits. For several engagements, he computed the industry ratios included in publications by Standard and Poor's and compared them with industry standards. For most engagements, the client's business was significantly different from the industry data in the publication and the client automatically explained away any discrepancies by attributing them to the unique nature of its operations. In cases in which the client had more than one branch in different industries, Saad found the ratio analysis no help at all. How can Saad improve the quality of his analytical procedures?

8-23 (Objective 8-7) At the completion of every audit, Aya Mokhtar, CPA, calculates a large number of ratios and trends for comparison with industry averages and prior year calculations. She believes the calculations are worth the relatively small cost of doing them because they provide her with an excellent overview of the client's operations. If the ratios are out of line, Aya discusses the reasons with the client and often makes suggestions on how to bring the ratio back in line in the future. In some cases, these discussions with management have been the basis for management consulting engagements. Discuss the major strengths and shortcomings in Aya's use of ratio and trend analysis.

8-24 (Objective 8-8) Name the four categories of financial ratios and give an example of a ratio in each category. What is the primary information provided by each financial ratio category?

MULTIPLE CHOICE QUESTIONS FROM CPA EXAMINATIONS

8-25 (Objectives 8-1, 8-3) The following questions concern the planning of the engagement. Select the best response.

 a. Which of the following is an effective audit planning procedure that helps prevent misunderstandings and inefficient use of audit personnel?
   (1) Arrange to make copies, for inclusion in the audit files, of those client supporting documents examined by the auditor.
   (2) Arrange to provide the client with copies of the audit programs to be used during the audit.
   (3) Arrange a preliminary conference with the client to discuss audit objectives, fees, timing, and other information.
   (4) Arrange to have the auditor prepare and post any necessary adjusting or reclassification entries prior to final closing.
 b. When auditing related party transactions, an auditor places primary emphasis on
   (1) confirming the existence of the related parties.
   (2) verifying the valuation of related party transactions.

(3) evaluating the disclosure of the related party transactions.

(4) ascertaining the rights and obligations of the related parties.

c. Which of the following will most likely indicate the existence of related parties?

(1) Writing down obsolete inventory prior to year-end.

(2) Failing to correct weaknesses in the client's internal control.

(3) An unexplained increase in gross margin.

(4) Borrowing money at a rate significantly below the market rate.

d. When using the work of a specialist, the auditor may identify and refer to the specialist in the auditor's report if the

(1) auditor expresses a qualified opinion as a result of the specialist's findings.

(2) specialist is not independent of the client.

(3) auditor wishes to indicate a division of responsibility.

(4) specialist's work provides the auditor greater assurance of reliability.

8-26 (Objective 8-2) The following questions pertain to client acceptance. Choose the best response.

a. In assessing whether to accept a client for an audit engagement, a CPA should consider:

	Client Business Risk	Acceptable Audit Risk
(1)	Yes	Yes
(2)	Yes	No
(3)	No	Yes
(4)	No	No

b. When approached to perform an audit for the first time, the auditor should make inquiries of the predecessor auditor. This is a necessary procedure because the predecessor may be able to provide the successor with information that will assist the successor in determining whether

(1) the predecessor's work should be used.

(2) the company follows the policy of rotating its auditors.

(3) in the predecessor's opinion internal control of the company has been satisfactory.

(4) the engagement should be accepted.

c. A successor would most likely make specific inquiries of the predecessor auditor regarding

(1) specialized accounting principles of the client's industry.

(2) the competency of the client's internal audit staff.

(3) the uncertainty inherent in applying sampling procedures.

(4) disagreements with management as to auditing procedures.

8-27 (Objectives 8-5, 8-6, 8-7, 8-8) The following questions concern the use of analytical procedures during the planning phase of an audit. Select the best response.

a. Analytical procedures used in planning an audit should focus on identifying

(1) material weaknesses of internal control.

(2) the predictability of financial data from individual transactions.

(3) the various assertions that are embodied in the financial statements.

(4) areas that may represent specific risks relevant to the audit.

b. For all audits of financial statements made in accordance with International Financial Reporting Standards, the use of analytical procedures is required to some extent.

	In the Planning Stage	As a Substantive Test	In the Completion Stage
(1)	Yes	No	Yes
(2)	No	Yes	No
(3)	No	Yes	Yes
(4)	Yes	No	No

c. Which of the following is least likely to be comparable between similar corporations in the same industry line of business?

(1) Accounts receivable turnover
(2) Earnings per share
(3) Gross profit percent
(4) Return on assets before interest and taxes

d. Which of the following situations has the best chance of being detected when a CPA compares 2009 revenues and expenses with the prior year and investigates all changes exceeding a fixed percent?

(1) An increase in property tax rates has not been recognized in the company's 2009 accrual.
(2) The cashier began lapping accounts receivable in 2009.
(3) Because of worsening economic conditions, the 2009 provision for uncollectible accounts was inadequate.
(4) The company changed its capitalization policy for small tools in 2009.

DISCUSSION QUESTIONS AND PROBLEMS

8-28 (Objectives 8-2, 8-3, 8-4, 8-5) The following are various activities an auditor does during audit planning.

1. Send an engagement letter to the client.
2. Tour the client's plant and offices.
3. Compare key ratios for the company to industry competitors.
4. Review management's risk management controls and procedures.
5. Identify potential related parties that may require disclosure.
6. Identify whether any specialists are required for the engagement.
7. Review accounting principles unique to the client's industry.
8. Determine the likely users of the financial statements.

For each procedure, indicate which of the first four parts of audit planning the procedure primarily relates to: (1) accept client and perform initial audit planning; (2) understand the client's business and industry; (3) assess client business risk; (4) perform preliminary analytical procedures.   **Required**

8-29 (Objectives 8-5, 8-7, 8-8) You are auditing payroll for the Ghandour Confectionery Company for the year ended September 30, 2011. Included next are amounts from the client's trial balance, along with comparative audited information for the prior year.

	Audited Balance Sept 30, 2010	Preliminary Balance Sept 30, 2011
Sales	US$51,316,234	US$57,474,182
Executive salaries	546,940	615,970
Factory hourly payroll	10,038,877	11,476,319
Factory supervisors' salaries	785,825	810,588
Office salaries	1,990,296	2,055,302
Sales commissions	2,018,149	2,367,962

You have obtained the following information to help you perform preliminary analytical procedures for the payroll account balances.

1. There has been a significant increase in the demand for Ghandour Confectionery's products. The increase in sales was due to both an increase in the average selling price of 4 percent and an increase in units sold that resulted from the increased demand and an increased marketing effort.
2. Even though sales volume increased there was no addition of executives, factory supervisors, or office personnel.
3. All employees including executives, but excluding commission salespeople, received a 3 percent salary increase starting October 1, 2011. Commission salespeople receive their increased compensation through the increase in sales.
4. The increased number of factory hourly employees was accomplished by recalling employees that had been laid off. They receive the same wage rate as existing employees. Ghandour does not permit overtime.

5. Commission salespeople receive a 5 percent commission on all sales on which a commission is given. Approximately 75 percent of sales earn sales commission. The other 25 percent are 'call ins,' for which no commission is given. Commissions are paid in the month following the month they are earned.

Required
    a. Use the final balances for the prior year and the information in items 1 through 5 to develop an expected value for each account included above, except sales.

    b. Calculate the difference between your expectation and the client's recorded amount as a percentage using the formula (expected value − recorded amount)/expected value.

8-30 (Objectives 8-3, 8-7, 8-8) You've been asked to review the gross margin percent for El-Fagr Bookshop for the years 2009 through 2012. You find there's been a significant decline during this time. Here are the numbers:

	2012	2011	2010	2009
Sales (thousands)	US$47,175	US$44,039	US$37,073	US$35,035
CGS (thousands)	30,314	27,998	23,431	22,072
Gross margin	US$16,861	US$16,041	US$13,642	US$12,963
Percent	35.7	36.4	36.8	37.0

Your discussion with Mohamed Lotfy, the controller, brings to light two possible explanations. He informs you that the industry gross profit percent in the retail book industry declined fairly steadily for three years as more people purchase books online, which accounts for part of the decline. He also believes that online shopping and discount bookstores prevent the company from rapidly expanding its non-book items, such as magazines, candy, music, DVDs, and many other items sold. Lotfy feels strongly that these two factors are the cause of the decline.

The following additional information is obtained from independent sources and the client's records as a means of investigating the controller's explanations:

	El-Fagr Bookshop (US$ in thousands)				Industry Gross and Profit Percent for Retailers of Books Related Products
Year	Book Sales	Non-Book Sales	Book Cost of Goods Sold	Non-Book Cost of Goods Sold	
2012	US$21,500	US$25,675	US$13,169	US$17,145	39.8
2011	20,472	23,567	12,197	15,801	39.9
2010	17,851	19,222	10,543	12,888	40.0
2009	16,995	18,040	9,961	12,111	40.4

Required
    a. Evaluate the explanation provided by Lotfy. Show calculations to support your conclusions.

    b. Which specific aspects of the client's financial statements require intensive investigation in this audit?

8-31 (Objectives 8-7, 8-8) In the audit of the Worldwide Wholesale Company, you did extensive ratio and trend analysis. No material exceptions were discovered except for the following:

1. Commission expense as a percent of sales has stayed constant for several years but has increased significantly in the current year. Commission rates have not changed.
2. The rate of inventory turnover has steadily decreased for four years.
3. Inventory as a percent of current assets has steadily increased for four years.
4. The number of days' sales in accounts receivable has steadily increased for three years.
5. Allowance for uncollectible accounts as a percent of accounts receivable has steadily decreased for three years.
6. The absolute amounts of depreciation expense and depreciation expense as a percent of gross fixed assets are significantly smaller than in the preceding year.

Required
    a. Evaluate the potential significance of each of the exceptions just listed for the fair presentation of financial statements.

    b. State the follow-up procedures you would use to determine the possibility of material misstatements.

8-32 (Objectives 8-3, 8-5, 8-7) Following are the auditor's calculations of several key ratios for Taybat Zaman Products Co. The primary purpose of this information is to understand the client's business and assess the risk of financial failure, but any other relevant conclusions are also desirable.

Ratio	2011	2010	2009	2008	2007
1 Current ratio	2.08	2.26	2.51	2.43	2.50
2 Quick ratio	.97	1.34	1.82	1.76	1.64
3 Times interest earned	3.50	3.20	4.10	5.30	7.10
4 Accounts receivable turnover	4.20	5.50	4.10	5.40	5.60
5 Days to collect receivables	86.90	66.36	89.02	67.59	65.18
6 Inventory turnover	2.03	1.84	2.68	3.34	3.36
7 Days to sell inventory	179.80	198.37	136.19	109.28	108.63
8 Net sales divided by tangible assets	.68	.64	.73	.69	.67
9 Profit margin	.13	.14	.16	.15	.14
10 Return on assets	.09	.09	.12	.10	.09
11 Return on equity	.05	.06	.10	.10	.11
12 Earnings per share	US$4.30	US$4.26	US$4.49	US$4.26	US$4.14

a. What major conclusions can be drawn from this information about the company's future? **Required**

b. What additional information would be helpful in your assessment of this company's financial condition?

c. Based on the preceding ratios, which aspects of the company do you believe should receive special emphasis in the audit?

8-33 (Objectives 8-3, 8-5) As part of the analytical procedures of Mahogany Products Co., you perform calculations of the following ratios:

	Industry Averages		Mahogany Products	
Ratio	2011	2010	2011	2010
1 Current ratio	3.30	3.80	2.20	2.60
2 Days to collect receivables	87.00	93.00	67.00	60.00
3 Days to sell inventory	126.00	121.00	93.00	89.00
4 Purchases divided by accounts payable	11.70	11.60	8.50	8.60
5 Inventory divided by current assets	.56	.51	.49	.48
6 Operating income divided by tangible assets	.08	.06	.14	.12
7 Operating income divided by net sales	.06	.06	.04	.04
8 Gross profit percent	.21	.27	.21	.19
9 Earnings per share	US$14.27	US$13.91	US$2.09	US$1.93

For each of the preceding ratios: **Required**

a. State whether there is a need to investigate the results further and, if so, the reason for further investigation.

b. State the approach you would use in the investigation.

c. Explain how the operations of Mahogany Products appear to differ from those of the industry.

CASE

8-34 (Objectives 8-3, 8-4, 8-7) Arabia Air Parts Manufacturing is a highly successful, closely held Amman company that manufactures and assembles specialty parts that are sold by aircraft parts distributors. Sales and profits have expanded rapidly in the past few years, and the prospects for future years are every bit as encouraging. Business is so good that the Arabia Air Parts is considering either selling out to a large company or going public to obtain additional capital.

The company originated in 1990 when Salah El-Din Ayoubi decided to manufacture automobile parts. In 2000, the company changed over to the small training aircraft business. Although its facilities have been spacious enough for past projects, an increased number of projects are creating a severe space problem. To continue growth, expanded facilities will need to be built. However, land costs in Amman are currently highly inflated.

Arabia Air Parts has always relied on you for your help because the treasurer is sales-oriented and has little background in the controllership function. Salaries of all officers have been fairly modest in order to reinvest earnings in future growth. In fact, the company is oriented toward long-run wealth of the Ayoubi family more than short-run profit. The Ayoubi family has all of their personal wealth invested in the firm.

A major reason for the success of the Ayoubi family in running Arabia Air Parts has been its small but excellent sales force. The sales policy is to sell to small aircraft parts distributors at high prices. This policy is responsible for fairly high credit losses, but the profit margin is high and results have been highly successful. The firm has every intention of continuing this policy in the future.

Your firm has been auditing Arabia Air Parts since 1990, and you have been on the job for the past three years. The client has excellent internal controls and has always been cooperative. In recent years, the client has attempted to keep net income at a high level because of borrowing needs and future sellout possibilities. Overall, the client has always been pleasant to deal with and willing to help in any way possible. There have never been any major audit adjustments, and an unmodified opinion has always been issued.

In the current year, you've completed the tests of the sales and collection area. The tests of controls and substantive tests of transactions for sales and returns and allowances were excellent, and extensive confirmations yielded no material misstatements. You have carefully reviewed the cutoff for sales and for sales returns and allowances and find these to be excellent. All recorded bad debts appear reasonable, and a review of the aged trial balance indicates that conditions seem about the same as in past years.

Required

a. Evaluate the financial information below to provide assistance to management for improved operation of its business. You can prepare the supporting analysis using an electronic spreadsheet program.

b. Do you agree that sales, accounts receivable, and allowance for doubtful accounts are probably correctly stated? Show calculations to support your conclusion.

	Dec 31, 2011 (Current Year)	Dec 31, 2010	Dec 31, 2009	Dec 31, 2008
Balance Sheet	US$	US$	US$	US$
Cash	49,615	39,453	51,811	48,291
Accounts receivable	2,366,938	2,094,052	1,756,321	1,351,470
Allowance for doubtful accounts	(250,000)	(240,000)	(220,000)	(200,000)
Inventory	2,771,833	2,585,820	2,146,389	1,650,959
Current assets	4,938,386	4,479,325	3,734,521	2,850,720
Fixed assets	3,760,531	3,744,590	3,498,930	3,132,133
Total assets	8,698,917	8,223,915	7,233,451	5,982,853
Current liabilities	2,253,422	2,286,433	1,951,830	1,625,811
Long-term liabilities	4,711,073	4,525,310	4,191,699	3,550,481
Owners' equity	1,734,422	1,412,172	1,089,922	806,561
Total liabilities and owners' equity	8,698,917	8,223,915	7,233,451	5,982,853
Income Statement Information				
Sales	6,740,652	6,165,411	5,313,752	4,251,837
Sales returns and allowances	(207,831)	(186,354)	(158,367)	(121,821)
Sales discounts allowed	(74,147)	(63,655)	(52,183)	(42,451)
Bad debts	(248,839)	(245,625)	(216,151)	(196,521)
Net sales	6,209,835	5,669,777	4,887,051	3,891,044
Gross margin	1,415,926	1,360,911	1,230,640	1,062,543
Net income after taxes	335,166	322,250	283,361	257,829
Aged Accounts Receivable				
0–30 days	942,086	881,232	808,569	674,014
31–60 days	792,742	697,308	561,429	407,271
61–120 days	452,258	368,929	280,962	202,634
>120 days	179,852	146,583	105,361	67,551
Total	US$2,366,938	US$2,094,052	US$1,756,321	US$1,351,470

ACL PROBLEM

8-35 (Objectives 8-5, 8-7) This problem requires the use of ACL software, which is included in MyAccountingLab. Information about installing and using ACL and solving this problem can be found in the Appendix, pages 855–859. You should read all of the reference material preceding instructions about 'Quick Sort' before locating the appropriate command to answer questions a–c. For this problem use the 'Inventory' file in the 'Inventory Review' subfolder under tables in Sample_Project. The suggested command or other source of information needed to solve the problem requirement is included at the end of each question.

Required

a. Obtain and print statistical information for both Inventory Value at Cost and Market Value. Determine how many inventory items have positive, negative, and zero values for both Inventory Value at Cost and Market Values. (Statistics)

b. Use Quick Sort Ascending and Descending for both Inventory Value at Cost and Market Value. (Quick Sort) Use this information and the information from part a to identify any concerns you have in the audit of inventory.

c. Calculate the ratio of Inventory Value at Cost to Market Value and sort the result from low to high. (Computed Fields and Quick Sort) Identify concerns about inventory valuation, if any.

MYLAB ACTIVITIES

Visit MyAccountingLab and complete the following activities:

→ Integrated Case Application: Pinnacle Manufacturing: Part I

→ Internet Problem 8-1: Obtain Client Background Information.

MATERIALITY AND RISK

A Moving Target

Sherif El Sabah, a new staff auditor, arrives onsite during the middle of a whirlwind audit of Delicious Sweets Co., an entrepreneurial startup company with a new hot product that is flying off the shelves just in time for the celebration of Prophet Muhammad's (Peace Be Upon Him) birthday. Delicious Sweets also make other products, but they don't sell nearly as well as the primary product. This creates an inherent risk for the financials of this company, since all of the prophet-day celebration sweets are in one figurative basket.

Sherif will be joining another senior auditor and staff auditor who have been on this audit for months. Since Sherif is arriving mid-audit, many of the audit planning procedures have already been started. Initially, Sherif's firm planned to complete the audit with just these two auditors in the field, but the plan has changed—more people are needed. Once Sherif gets there and dives into the numbers, he can see why.

For the audit of the inventory section to which Sherif has been assigned, there are thousands, if not tens of thousands of transactions for the year. Sherif scans the papers documenting the original materiality assessment and plans substantive tests for the inventory area. He finds that the firm initially assigned a medium risk to this area and therefore was not planning to do extensive testing; instead, they planned to sample only a small part of the population. However, once testing actually started, numerous exceptions were found within other audit areas. As a result, the team decided to revise the risk assessment and the materiality assessment, expand testing and bring on more staff auditors to assist with the extra testing.

From his review of the unaudited financial statements, Sherif sees that the company has just obtained an additional US$10 million in private equity financing, by far the second largest amount on the balance sheet next to inventory. "Wow," Sherif whispers to himself. When Sherif arrives on site, he finds that all of the samples for review have been selected and set aside prior to his arrival. Once he is sitting in front of the enormous stack of paperwork, thinking of how much easier the sampling would have been, Sherif jokes to the partner on the audit, "How many vendor invoices can one staff auditor review?" to which the partner responds, "Let's put it this way: if it were your US$10 million, how many invoices would you look at?"

LEARNING OBJECTIVES

After studying this chapter, you should be able to

9-1 Apply the concept of materiality to the audit.

9-2 Make a preliminary judgment about what amounts to consider material.

9-3 Allocate preliminary materiality to segments of the audit during planning.

9-4 Use materiality to evaluate audit findings.

9-5 Define risk in auditing.

9-6 Describe the audit risk model and its components.

9-7 Consider the impact of business risk on acceptable audit risk.

9-8 Consider the impact of engagement risk on acceptable audit risk.

9-9 Consider the impact of several factors on the assessment of inherent risk.

9-10 Discuss the relationship of risks to audit evidence.

9-11 Discuss how materiality and risk are related and integrated into the audit process.

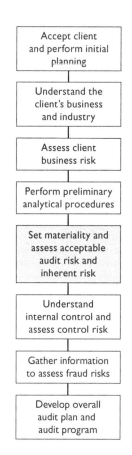

Accept client and perform initial planning

Understand the client's business and industry

Assess client business risk

Perform preliminary analytical procedures

Set materiality and assess acceptable audit risk and inherent risk

Understand internal control and assess control risk

Gather information to assess fraud risks

Develop overall audit plan and audit program

The auditor's report includes two important phrases (italicized below) that are directly related to materiality and risk.

"We conducted our audits in accordance with International Standards on Auditing. Those standards require that we plan and perform the audit to *obtain reasonable assurance* about whether the financial statements are *free of material misstatement.*"

The phrase *obtain reasonable assurance* is intended to inform users that auditors do not guarantee or ensure the fair presentation of the financial statements. Some risk that the financial statements are not fairly stated exists, even when the opinion is unmodified.

This risk is due to the inherent limitations in an audit of financial statements because of

- The use of testing and sampling during the audit
- The inherent limitations of internal control
- The possibility of misrepresentation for fraudulent purposes

The phrase *free of material misstatement* is intended to inform users that the auditor's responsibility is limited to material financial information. Materiality is important because it is impractical for auditors to provide assurances on immaterial amounts.

Materiality and risk are fundamental to planning the audit and designing an audit approach. In this chapter, we will show how these concepts fit into the planning phase of the audit. Note that the topic of this chapter is closely related to earlier discussions of auditor's responsibilities, transaction cycles, audit objectives (Chapter 6), and planning the audit (Chapter 8).

In this chapter, we apply both materiality and risk to the concepts studied in Chapter 6. We introduce the fifth step in planning the audit, which is a follow-up on the first four steps that were covered in Chapter 8. When auditors decide materiality and assess risks, they use a considerable amount of the information acquired and documented during the first four parts of audit planning.

Relevant International Standards on Auditing	
ISA 240	The Auditor's Responsibilities Relating to Fraud in an Audit of Financial Statements
ISA 250	Consideration of Laws and Regulations in an Audit of Financial Statements
ISA 300	Planning an Audit of Financial Statements
ISA 315	Identifying and Assessing the Risks of Material Misstatement through Understanding the Entity and Its Environment
ISA 320	Materiality in Planning and Performing an Audit
ISA 330	The Auditor's Responses to Assessed Risks
ISA 450	Evaluation of Misstatements Identified during the Audit
ISA 500	Audit Evidence

MATERIALITY

OBJECTIVE 9-1

Apply the concept of materiality to the audit.

ISA 320 describes the auditor's responsibilities in relation to the concept of materiality. Auditors must also refer to ISA 450 Evaluation of Misstatements Identified during the Audit which presents the auditor's responsibilities in evaluating the effect of identified misstatements on the audit and of uncorrected misstatements.

> ### ISA 320
> *Misstatements, including omissions, are considered to be material if they individually or in the aggregate, could reasonably be expected to influence the economic decisions of users taken on the basis of the financial statements. Judgments about materiality are made in light of surrounding circumstances, and are affected by the size or nature of a misstatement, or a combination of both.*

The Financial Accounting Standards Board (FASB 2) provides a similar definition for materiality:

> The magnitude of an omission or misstatement of accounting information that, in the light of surrounding circumstances, makes it *probable* that the judgment of a reasonable person relying on the information would have been changed or influenced by the omission or misstatement. [italics added]

Materiality is based on judgments which are made by auditors in relation to the specific circumstances surrounding both the audit and the company under audit. Materiality judgments are affected by the size, complexity, and objectives of the company being audited. Auditors must exercise professional judgment when assessing materiality. Auditors evaluate the level of materiality based on how misstatements can influence the decisions of users of financial statements. An account balance or transaction is material if the omission or misstatement could influence the decisions of users in relation to financial reporting. Auditors should be able to provide reasonable assurances that the company's financial statements are free from material misstatement, as well as ensuring that they conform to International Financial Reporting Standards or other acceptable frameworks for financial reporting.

The concepts of materiality discussed in this chapter are directly related to those we introduced in Chapter 3.

Because auditors are responsible for determining whether financial statements are materially misstated, they must, upon discovering a material misstatement, bring it to the client's attention so that a correction can be made. If the client refuses to correct the statements, the auditor must issue a qualified or an adverse opinion, depending on how material the misstatement is. To make such determinations, auditors depend on a thorough knowledge of the application of materiality.

A careful reading of both ISA 320 and the FASB definitions reveals the difficulty that auditors have in applying materiality in practice. While the definition emphasizes reasonable users who rely on the statements to make decisions, auditors must have knowledge of the likely users of the client's statements and the decisions that are being made. For example, if an auditor knows that financial statements will be relied on in a buy–sell agreement for the entire business, the amount that the auditor considers material may be smaller than that for an otherwise similar audit of a particular account balance such as inventory, receivables, or paid-in capital. In practice, of course, auditors may not know who all the users are or what decisions they may make based on the financial statements.

Auditors follow five closely related steps in applying materiality, as shown in Figure 9-1. The auditor first sets a preliminary judgment about materiality and then allocates this estimate to the segments of the audit, as shown in the first bracket of the figure. These two steps, which are part of planning, are our primary focus for the discussion of materiality in this chapter. Step 3 occurs throughout the engagement, where auditors estimate the amount of misstatements in each segment as they evaluate audit evidence. Near the end of the audit, during the engagement completion

> **Materiality**
> The magnitude of an omission or misstatement of accounting information that, in the light of surrounding circumstances, makes it probable that the judgment of a reasonable person relying on the information would have been changed or influenced by the omission or misstatement.

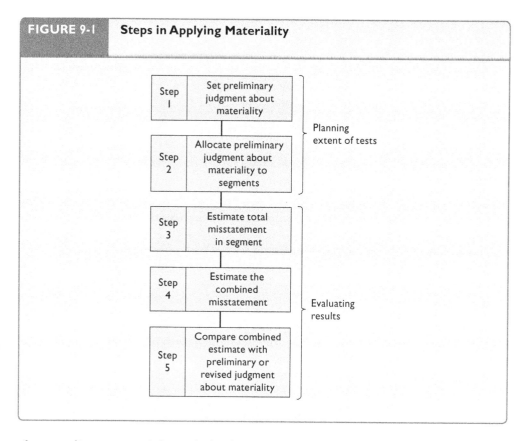

FIGURE 9-1   Steps in Applying Materiality

Step 1 — Set preliminary judgment about materiality

Step 2 — Allocate preliminary judgment about materiality to segments

} Planning extent of tests

Step 3 — Estimate total misstatement in segment

Step 4 — Estimate the combined misstatement

Step 5 — Compare combined estimate with preliminary or revised judgment about materiality

} Evaluating results

phase, auditors proceed through the final two steps. These latter three steps, as shown in the second bracket in Figure 9-1, are part of evaluating the results of audit tests.

SET PRELIMINARY JUDGMENT ABOUT MATERIALITY

Preliminary judgment about materiality

The maximum amount by which the auditor believes that the statements could be misstated and still not affect the decisions of reasonable users; used in audit planning.

Auditing standards require auditors to decide on the combined amount of misstatements in the financial statements that they would consider material early in the audit as they are developing the overall strategy for the audit. We refer to this as the **preliminary judgment about materiality**. It is called a preliminary judgment about materiality because, although a professional opinion, it may change during the engagement. This judgment must be documented in the audit files.

The preliminary judgment about materiality (Step 1 in Figure 9-1) is the maximum amount by which the auditor believes the statements could be misstated and still *not* affect the decisions of reasonable users. This judgment is one of the most important decisions the auditor makes, and it requires considerable professional wisdom.

Auditors set a preliminary judgment about materiality to help plan the appropriate evidence to accumulate. The lower the dollar amount of the preliminary judgment, the more evidence required. The logic behind this inverse relationship is that auditors are motivated to satisfy management needs by issuing unmodified audit reports without forgetting the quality of audit performed and results reported. This requires the gathering and assessing of sufficient appropriate evidence. If the auditor sets his materiality at a lower level he will gather a greater volume of evidence to form his opinion about the financial statements. On the other hand, if the auditor is satisfied that the company's internal control system is effective and the previous years' audit results indicate no significant misstatements, he or she can set materiality as high and reduce the amount of audit evidence. Materiality, however, is affected by the size of the company under audit. For example, US$10,000 might be considered by a user as highly material for a small partnership or limited liability company, but this amount would be considered immaterial for a transnational or multinational company.

During the audit, auditors often change the preliminary judgment about materiality. We refer to this as the **revised judgment about materiality**. Auditors are likely to make the revision because of changes in one of the factors used to determine the preliminary judgment; that is because the auditor decides that the preliminary judgment was too large or too small. For example, a preliminary judgment about materiality is often determined before year-end and is based on prior years' financial statements or interim financial statement information. The judgment may be reevaluated after current financial statements are available. Or, client circumstances may have changed due to qualitative events, such as the issuance of debt or increase of the company's capital that created a new class of financial statement users. Also, the auditor should consider this revision in the context of the audit procedures already performed and determine whether the nature, timing, and extent of such procedures still remain appropriate. For example, if during the audit it was discovered that the actual financial results would be different from the projected financial results used to calculate the materiality, the auditor should revise materiality and document the reasons for using such a different materiality threshold.

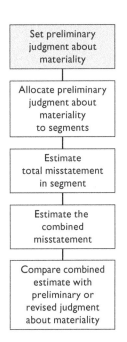

Revised judgment about materiality

A change in the auditor's preliminary judgment made when the auditor determines that the preliminary judgment was too large or too small.

Factors Affecting Preliminary Materiality Judgment

Several factors affect the auditor's preliminary judgment about materiality for a given set of financial statements. The most important of these are described in the following paragraphs.

Materiality is a Relative Rather than an Absolute Concept A misstatement of a given magnitude might be material for a small company, whereas the same dollar misstatement could be immaterial for a large one. This makes it impossible to establish dollar-value guidelines for a preliminary judgment about materiality that are applicable to all audit clients. For example, a total misstatement of US$10 million would be extremely material for Arabian Hardware Co. because, as shown in its financial statements, total assets are about US$61 million and net income before taxes is less than US$6 million. A misstatement of the same amount is almost certainly immaterial for a company such as IBM, which has total assets and net income of several billion dollars.

Bases are Needed for Evaluating Materiality Because materiality is relative, it is necessary to have bases for establishing whether misstatements are material. *Net income before taxes* is often the primary base for deciding what is material for profit-oriented businesses because it is regarded as a critical item of information for users. Some firms use a different primary base, because net income often fluctuates considerably from year to year and therefore does not provide a stable base, or when the entity is a not-for-profit organization. In such situations, total revenue or total expenses might be appropriate bases. Other primary bases include net sales, gross profit, and total or net assets. For example, net asset value or total equity are used by audit firms for asset-based entities (e.g. investment funds). After establishing a primary base, auditors should also decide whether the misstatements could materially affect the reasonableness of other bases such as current assets, total assets, current liabilities, and owners' equity. Auditing standards require the auditor to document in the audit files the basis used to determine the preliminary judgment about materiality.

Additional factors that may affect the identification of an appropriate base include:

- Whether there are items which attract the user's attention in relation to the financial statements based on auditors' experience or previous audit results.
- The nature of the entity and its life cycle; the industry and economic environment in which the entity operates.
- The entity's ownership structure and how it finances its activities. (ISA 320, Para. A3.)

Bases must relate to a percentage to calculate the preliminary judgment. A common rule of thumb is using 5 percent of profit before tax for profit-oriented entities. However, auditors are advised to apply the average of the previous years' profits or change the base of net profit before tax if the current year profit before tax is not stable or the company is close to breaking even or making losses. For example, suppose that a company made a profit before tax in 2010 of US$5 million and the auditor used 5 percent as a percentage to calculate the preliminary judgment. If in 2011, the profit before tax dropped to only US$500,000 due to loss of product markets or decrease in sales prices, the auditor should apply the 5 percent threshold not to 2011 profit before tax but to an average of the last three or five years' net profit before tax or another base such as total assets or total revenues.

Also, assume that for a given company, an auditor decided that a misstatement of income before taxes of US$100,000 or more would be material, but a misstatement would need to be US$250,000 or more to be material for current assets. It is not appropriate for the auditor to use a preliminary judgment about materiality of US$250,000 for both income before tax and current assets. Instead, the auditor must plan to find all misstatements affecting income before tax that exceed the preliminary judgment about materiality of US$100,000. Because almost all misstatements affect both the income statement and balance sheet, the auditor uses a primary preliminary materiality level of US$100,000 for most tests. The only other misstatements that will affect current assets are misclassifications within balance sheet accounts, such as misclassifying a long-term asset as a current one. So, in addition to the primary preliminary judgment of materiality of US$100,000, the auditor will also need to plan the audit with the US$250,000 preliminary judgment about materiality for misclassifications of current assets.

Qualitative Factors Also Affect Materiality Certain types of misstatements are likely to be more important to users than others, even if the dollar amounts are the same. For example:

- Amounts involving fraud are usually considered more important than unintentional errors of equal dollar amounts because fraud reflects on the honesty and reliability of the management or other personnel involved. For example, most users consider an intentional misstatement of inventory more important than clerical errors in inventory of the same dollar amount.
- Misstatements that are otherwise minor may be material if there are possible consequences arising from contractual obligations. Say that net working capital included in the financial statements is only a few hundred dollars more than the required minimum in a loan agreement. If the correct net working capital were less than the required minimum, putting the loan in default, the current and noncurrent liability classifications would be materially affected.
- Misstatements that are otherwise immaterial may be material if they affect a trend in earnings. For example, if reported income has increased by 3 percent annually for the past five years but income for the current year has declined by 1 percent, that change may be material. Similarly, a misstatement that would cause a loss to be reported as a profit may be of concern.

Illustrative Guidelines

Accounting and auditing standards do not provide specific materiality guidelines to practitioners. The concern is that such guidelines might be applied without considering all the complexities that should affect the auditor's final decision. However, in this chapter, we do provide guidelines to illustrate the application of materiality. These are intended only to help you better understand the concept of applying materiality in practice. The guidelines are stated in Figure 9-2 in the form of policy guidelines of an auditing firm. Notice that the guidelines are formulas using one or more bases and a

| FIGURE 9-2 | Illustrative Materiality Guidelines |

HABIBA AND KHALDOON, CPAs
Dubai, United Arab Emirates

POLICY STATEMENT   Habiba Khaldoon
Title: Materiality Guidelines   Samih Khaldoon
                                                                   Masbah Droub

Professional judgment is to be used at all times in setting and applying materiality guidelines. As a general guideline, the following policies are to be applied:

1. The combined total of misstatements in the financial statements exceeding 6 percent is normally considered material. A combined total of less than 3 percent is presumed to be immaterial in the absence of qualitative factors. Combined misstatements between 3 percent and 6 percent require the greatest amount of professional judgment to determine their materiality.

2. The 3 percent to 6 percent must be measured in relation to the appropriate base. Many times there is more than one base to which misstatements should be compared. The following guides are recommended in selecting the appropriate base:

   a. *Income statement.* Combined misstatements in the income statement should ordinarily be measured at 3 percent to 6 percent of operating income before taxes. A guideline of 3 percent to 6 percent may be inappropriate in a year in which income is unusually large or small. When operating income in a given year is not considered representative, it is desirable to substitute as a base a more representative income measure. For example, average operating income for a 3-year period may be used as the base.

   b. *Balance sheet.* Combined misstatements in the balance sheet should originally be evaluated for current assets, current liabilities, and total assets. For current assets and current liabilities, the guidelines should be between 3 percent and 6 percent, applied in the same way as for the income statement. For total assets, the guidelines should be between 1 percent and 3 percent, applied in the same way as for the income statement.

3. Qualitative factors should be carefully evaluated on all audits. In many instances, they are more important than the guidelines applied to the income statement and balance sheet. The intended uses of the financial statements and the nature of the information in the statements, including footnotes, must be carefully evaluated.

range of percentages. The application of guidelines, such as the ones we present here, requires considerable professional judgment.

Using the illustrative guidelines in Figure 9-2, let's examine a preliminary judgment about materiality for Arabian Hardware Co. The guidelines are as follows:

Preliminary Judgment About Materiality (Rounded, in Thousands)				
	Minimum		Maximum	
	Percentage	Dollar Amount (US$)	Percentage	Dollar Amount (US$)
Earnings from operations	3	221	6	442
Current assets	3	1,531	6	3,062
Total assets	1	614	3	1,841
Current liabilities	3	396	6	793

If the auditor for Arabian Hardware Co. decides that the general guidelines are reasonable, the first step is to evaluate whether any qualitative factors significantly affect the materiality judgment. Assuming no qualitative factors exist, if the auditor concludes at the end of the audit that combined misstatements of operating income before taxes are less than US$221,000, the statements will be considered fairly stated. If the combined misstatements exceed US$442,000, the statements will not be considered fairly stated. If the misstatements are between US$221,000 and US$442,000, a more careful consideration of all facts will be required. The auditor then applies the same process to the other three bases.

ALLOCATE PRELIMINARY JUDGMENT ABOUT MATERIALITY TO SEGMENTS (TOLERABLE MISSTATEMENT)

OBJECTIVE 9-3

Allocate preliminary materiality to segments of the audit during planning.

Allocation of the preliminary judgment about materiality

The process of assigning to each balance sheet account the misstatement amount considered to be material for that account based on the auditor's preliminary judgment.

The **allocation of the preliminary judgment about materiality** to segments (Step 2 in Figure 9-1) is necessary because auditors accumulate evidence by segments rather than for the financial statements as a whole. If auditors have a preliminary judgment about materiality for each segment, it helps them decide the appropriate audit evidence to accumulate. For an accounts receivable balance of US$1 million, for example, the auditor should accumulate more evidence if a misstatement of US$50,000 is considered material than if US$300,000 were considered material.

Most practitioners allocate materiality to balance sheet rather than income statement accounts, because most income statement misstatements have an equal effect on the balance sheet due to the nature of double-entry accounting. For example, a US$20,000 overstatement of accounts receivable is also a US$20,000 overstatement of sales. It is inappropriate to allocate the preliminary judgment to both income statement and balance sheet accounts because doing so will result in double counting, which will in turn lead to smaller tolerable misstatements than is desirable due to the allocation among a large number of accounts. This enables auditors to allocate materiality to either income statement or balance sheet accounts. Because there are fewer balance sheet than income statement accounts in most audits, and because most audit procedures focus on balance sheet accounts, materiality should be allocated only to balance sheet accounts.

Tolerable misstatement

The materiality allocated to any given account balance; used in audit planning.

When auditors allocate the preliminary judgment about materiality to account balances, the materiality allocated to any given account balance is referred to as **tolerable misstatement**. For example, if an auditor decides to allocate US$100,000 of a total preliminary judgment about materiality of US$200,000 to accounts receivable, tolerable misstatement for accounts receivable is US$100,000. This means that the auditor is willing to consider accounts receivable fairly stated if it is misstated by US$100,000 or less.

Some balance sheet accounts can have a lower materiality level. The factors leading to this conclusion are:

- Whether law, regulation, or the application of accounting standards framework affects users' expectations about specific accounts balances and disclosures such as related party transactions and the remuneration of the management, board of directors, and those charged with governance.
- Whether the results of the previous audits indicate significant misstatements related to the accounts balance and its disclosures even if such misstatements were corrected at the auditors' request.
- Whether an important event occurred such as a merger or acquisition of a company requiring detailed investigation of the effects of such a transaction on the financial statements and specific account balances.

Auditors face three major difficulties in allocating materiality to balance sheet accounts:

1. Auditors expect certain accounts to have more misstatements than others.
2. Both overstatements and understatements must be considered.
3. Relative audit costs affect the allocation.

All three of these difficulties are considered in the allocation in Figure 9-3. It is worth keeping in mind that at the end of the audit, the auditor must combine all actual and estimated misstatements and compare them to the preliminary judgment about materiality. In allocating tolerable misstatement, the auditor is attempting to do the audit as efficiently as possible.

FIGURE 9-3	Tolerable Misstatement Allocated to Arabian Hardware Co.

	Balance Dec 31, 2012 (in Thousands)	Tolerable Misstatement (in Thousands)
Cash	US$ 828	US$ 6 (a)
Trade accounts receivable (net)	18,957	265 (b)
Inventories	29,865	265 (b)
Other current assets	1,377	60 (c)
Property, plant, and equipment	10,340	48 (d)
Total assets	US$61,367	
Trade accounts payable	US$ 4,720	108 (e)
Notes payable—total	28,300	0 (a)
Accrued payroll and payroll tax	1,470	60 (c)
Accrued interest and dividends payable	2,050	0 (a)
Other liabilities	2,364	72 (c)
Capital stock and capital in excess of par	8,500	0 (a)
Retained earnings	13,963	NA (f)
Total liabilities and equity	US$61,367	US$884 (2 × US$442)

NA = Not applicable
(a) Zero or small tolerable misstatement because account can be completely audited at low cost and no misstatements are expected.
(b) Large tolerable misstatement because account is large and requires extensive sampling to audit the account.
(c) Large tolerable misstatement as a percent of account because account can be verified at extremely low cost, probably with analytical procedures, if tolerable misstatement is large.
(d) Small tolerable misstatement as a percent of account balance because most of the balance is in land and buildings, which is unchanged from the prior year and need not be audited further this year.
(e) Moderately large tolerable misstatement because a relatively large number of misstatements are expected.
(f) Not applicable—retained earnings is a residual account that is affected by the net amount of the misstatements in the other accounts.

Allocation Illustrated

Figure 9-3 illustrates the allocation approach followed by the senior, Hosni Abdel Latif, for the audit of Arabian Hardware Co. It summarizes the balance sheet, combining certain accounts, and shows the allocation of total materiality of US$442,000 (6 percent of earnings from operations). Abdel Latif's allocation approach uses judgment in the allocation, subject to the following two arbitrary requirements established by Berger and Mahmoud, CPAs:

- Tolerable misstatement for any account cannot exceed 60 percent of the preliminary judgment (60 percent of US$442,000 = US$265,000, rounded).
- The sum of all tolerable misstatements cannot exceed twice the preliminary judgment about materiality (2 × US$442,000 = US$884,000).

The first requirement keeps the auditor from allocating all of total materiality to one account. If, for example, all of the preliminary judgment of US$442,000 is allocated to trade accounts receivable, a US$442,000 misstatement in that account will be acceptable. However, it may not be acceptable to have such a large misstatement in one account, and even if it is acceptable, it does not allow for any misstatements in other accounts.

There are two reasons for the second requirement, permitting the sum of the tolerable misstatement to exceed overall materiality:

- It is unlikely that all accounts will be misstated by the full amount of tolerable misstatement. If, for example, other current assets have a tolerable misstatement

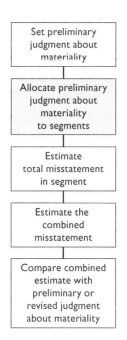

of US$100,000 but no misstatements are found in auditing those accounts, it means that the auditor, after the fact, could have allocated zero or a small tolerable misstatement to other current assets. It is common for auditors to find fewer misstatements than tolerable misstatement.

- Some accounts are likely to be overstated, whereas others are likely to be understated, resulting in a net amount that is likely to be less than the preliminary judgment.

Notice in the allocation that the auditor is concerned about the combined effect on operating income of the misstatement of each balance sheet account. An overstatement of an asset account will therefore have the same effect on the income statement as an understatement of a liability account. In contrast, a misclassification in the balance sheet, such as a classification of a note payable as an account payable, will have no effect on operating income. Therefore, the materiality of items not affecting the income statement must be considered separately.

Figure 9-3 also includes the rationale that Abdel Latif followed in deciding tolerable misstatement for each account. For example, he concluded that it was unnecessary to assign any tolerable misstatement to notes payable, even though it is as large as inventories. If he had assigned US$132,500 to each of those two accounts, more evidence would have been required in inventories, but the confirmation of the balance in notes payable would still have been necessary. It was therefore more efficient to allocate US$265,000 to inventories and none to notes payable. Similarly, he allocated US$60,000 to other current assets and accrued payroll and payroll tax, both of which are large compared with the recorded account balance. Wagdi did so because he believes that these accounts can be verified within US$60,000 by using only analytical procedures, which are low cost. If tolerable misstatement were set lower, he would have to use more costly audit procedures such as inspection and confirmation.

In practice, it is often difficult to predict in advance which accounts are most likely to be misstated and whether misstatements are likely to be overstatements or understatements. Accordingly, many accounting firms have developed rigorous guidelines and sophisticated statistical methods for doing so. These guidelines also help ensure the auditor appropriately documents the tolerable misstatement amounts and the related basis used to determine those amounts in the audit files.

To summarize, the purpose of allocating the preliminary judgment about materiality to balance sheet accounts is to help the auditor decide the appropriate evidence to accumulate for each account on both the balance sheet and income statement. An aim of the allocation is to minimize audit costs without sacrificing audit quality. Regardless of how the allocation is done, when the audit is completed, the auditor must be confident that the combined misstatements in all accounts are less than or equal to the preliminary (or revised) judgment about materiality.

ESTIMATE MISSTATEMENT AND COMPARE WITH PRELIMINARY JUDGMENT

OBJECTIVE 9-4

Use materiality to evaluate audit findings.

The first two steps in applying materiality involve planning (see Figure 9-1) and are our primary concern in this chapter. The last three steps result from performing audit tests. These steps are introduced here and discussed in more detail in subsequent chapters.

When auditors perform audit procedures for each segment of the audit, they keep a worksheet of all misstatements found. Misstatements in an account can be of two types:

known misstatements and likely misstatements. **Known misstatements** are those where the auditor can determine the amount of the misstatement in the account. For example, when auditing property, plant, and equipment, the auditor may identify capitalized leased equipment that should be expensed because it is an operating lease. There are two types of **likely misstatements**. The first are misstatements that arise from differences between management's and the auditor's judgment about estimates of account balances. Examples are differences in the estimate for the allowance for uncollectible accounts or for warranty liabilities. The second are projections of misstatements based on the auditor's tests of a sample from a population. For example, assume the auditor finds six client misstatements in a sample of 200 in testing inventory costs. The auditor uses these misstatements to estimate the *total* likely misstatements in inventory (Step 3). The total is called an estimate or a 'projection' or 'extrapolation' because only a sample, rather than the entire population, was audited. The projected misstatement amounts for each account are combined on the worksheet (Step 4), and then the combined likely misstatement is compared with materiality (Step 5).

Table 9-1 illustrates the last three steps in applying materiality. For simplicity, only three accounts are included. The misstatement in cash of US$2,000 is a known misstatement related to unrecorded bank service charges detected by the auditor. Unlike for cash, the misstatements for accounts receivable and inventory are based on samples. The auditor calculates likely misstatements for accounts receivable and inventory using known misstatements detected in those samples. To illustrate the calculation, assume that in auditing inventory the auditor found US$3,500 of net overstatement amounts in a sample of US$50,000 of the total population of US$450,000. The US$3,500 identified misstatement is a known misstatement. To calculate the estimate of the likely misstatements for the total population of US$450,000, the auditor makes a direct projection of the known misstatement from the sample to the population and adds an estimate for sampling error. The calculation of the **direct projection estimate of misstatement** is:

$$\frac{\text{Net misstatements in the sample (US\$3,500)}}{\text{Total sampled (US\$50,000)}} \times \frac{\text{Total recorded}}{\text{population value}} = \frac{\text{Direct projection estimate of}}{\text{misstatement}}$$
$$\text{(US\$450,000)} \quad \text{(US\$31,500)}$$

(Note that the direct projection of likely misstatement for accounts receivable of US$12,000 is not illustrated.)

Known misstatements

Specific misstatements in a class of transactions or account balance identified during the audit.

Likely misstatements

Misstatements that arise from either differences between management's and the auditor's judgment about estimates of account balances or from projections of misstatements based on the auditor's test of a sample from a population.

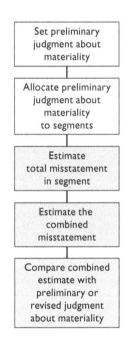

Direct projection estimate of misstatement

Estimate of likely misstatement in a population based on a sample, excluding sampling risk, and calculated as net misstatements in the sample, divided by the total sampled, multiplied by the total recorded population value.

TABLE 9-1	Illustration of Comparison of Estimated Total Misstatement to Preliminary Judgment about Materiality				
		Estimated Misstatement Amount			
Account	Tolerable Misstatement	Known Misstatement and Direct Projection	Sampling Error	Total	
Cash	US$ 4,000	US$ 2,000	US$ NA	US$ 2,000	
Accounts receivable	20,000	12,000	6,000	18,000	
Inventory	36,000	31,500	15,750	47,250	
Total estimated misstatement amount		US$45,500	US$16,800	US$62,300	
Preliminary judgment about materiality	US$50,000				
NA = Not applicable. Cash audited 100 percent					

Sampling error

Errors that result because the auditor has sampled only a portion of the population.

The estimate for **sampling error** results because the auditor has sampled only a portion of the population and there is a risk that the sample does not accurately represent the population. (We'll discuss this in more detail in Chapters 15 and 17.) In this simplified example, we'll assume the estimate for sampling error is 50 percent of the direct projection of the misstatement amounts for the accounts where sampling was used (accounts receivable and inventory). There is no sampling error for cash because the total amount of misstatement is known, not estimated.

In combining the misstatements in Table 9-1, we can observe that the known misstatements and direct projection of likely misstatements for the three accounts adds to US$45,500. However, the total sampling error is less than the sum of the individual sampling errors. This is because sampling error represents the maximum misstatement in account details not audited. It is unlikely that this maximum misstatement amount exists in all accounts subjected to sampling.

Table 9-1 shows that total estimated likely misstatement of US$62,300 exceeds the preliminary judgment about materiality of US$50,000. The major area of difficulty is inventory, where estimated misstatement of US$47,250 is significantly greater than tolerable misstatement of US$36,000. Because the estimated combined misstatement exceeds the preliminary judgment, the financial statements are not acceptable. The auditor can either determine whether the estimated likely misstatement actually exceeds US$50,000 by performing additional audit procedures or require the client to make an adjustment for estimated misstatements. If the auditor decides to perform additional audit procedures, they will be concentrated in the inventory area.

If the estimated net overstatement amount for inventory had been US$28,000 (US$18,000 plus US$10,000 sampling error), the auditor probably would not have needed to expand audit tests because it would have met both the tests of tolerable misstatement (US$36,000) and the preliminary judgment about materiality (US$2,000 + US$18,000 + US$28,000 = US$48,000 < US$50,000). In fact, the auditor would have had some leeway with that amount because the results of cash and accounts receivable procedures indicate that those accounts are within their tolerable misstatement limits. If the auditor approaches the audit of the accounts in a sequential manner, the findings of the audit of accounts audited earlier can be used to revise the tolerable misstatement established for accounts audited later. In the illustration, if the auditor had audited cash and accounts receivable before inventories, tolerable misstatement for inventories could have been increased if the auditors have confidence in the company's accounting and internal control systems and no significant misstatements were found in such accounts in the previous period.

Assume that an auditor undertakes tests on sales invoices and the value of the invoices tested was US$50,000 out of total sales of US$200,000. The auditor decides to divide his tests according to the following:

a. The auditor tests all material items amounting to US$30,000 which include an error of US$1,000. Since the auditor has tested all material items, these errors will not be reproduced in the population which has not been tested and the likely error from this source is, therefore, limited to US$1,000.

b. The auditor tests a number of other sales invoices amounting to US$25,000 and found an error of US$500.

The error in the sample could be reproduced in the population. In this case the population and sample are limited to the non-material items. The projected error by extrapolation will be:

the error discovered (US$500) × the population (US$200,000−30,000) ÷ the sample (US$25,000), i.e. US$3400.

The total projected error is, therefore: US$1,000 + US$3,400 = US$4,400.

The auditor is advised to communicate to the appropriate level of management and those charged with governance, on an interim basis, any misstatements identified during the audit. The auditor should request that management correct those misstatements so that an unmodified audit report can be issued. If management refuses to correct misstatements communicated, the auditor should study and investigate the reasons for not correcting such misstatements and form his audit opinion according to the level of materiality of such misstatements.

Table 9-2 presents examples of situations that may be assessed by auditors when considering materiality of uncorrected misstatements. The examples discussed will help auditors evaluate whether misstatements (including prior years' misstatements) are individually or in aggregate material requiring qualified or adverse opinion.

RISK

Audit risk is the risk that the auditor expresses an erroneous or incorrect audit opinion when the financial statements are materially misstated. The auditor is required to perform appropriate and sufficient audit tests to reduce audit risk to a low level to present an opinion about the financial statements of a client. There is a close relationship between materiality and risk. In Table 9-1, the auditor estimated a US$6,000 sampling error for accounts receivable, which was used to calculate the total estimated misstatement of US$18,000 for comparison to tolerable misstatement of US$20,000. The US$6,000 sampling error *includes a risk* resulting from sampling. This is only one of several kinds of risks auditors must address.

As we saw in Chapter 8, auditors accept some level of **risk** or uncertainty in performing the audit function. The auditor recognizes, for example, the inherent uncertainty about the appropriateness of evidence, uncertainty about the effectiveness of a client's internal controls, and uncertainty about whether the financial statements are fairly stated when the audit is completed. An effective auditor recognizes that risks exist and deals with those risks in an appropriate manner. Most risks auditors encounter are difficult to measure and require careful consideration before the auditor can respond appropriately. Responding to these risks properly is critical to achieving a high-quality audit.

OBJECTIVE 9-5

Define risk in auditing.

Risk

The acceptance by auditors that there is some level of uncertainty in performing the audit function.

Illustration Concerning Risks and Evidence

International Standards on Auditing require the auditor to obtain an understanding of the entity and its environment, including its internal control, to assess the risk of material misstatements in the client's financial statements. Chapter 8 described how the auditor begins by gaining an understanding of the client's business and industry and assessing client business risk. Auditors use the audit risk model to further identify the potential for misstatements in the overall financial statements and specific account balances, classes of transactions, and disclosures where misstatements are most likely to occur. The International Standards on Auditing require auditors to apply the audit risk model when they form their opinions about the company's financial statements.

In order to provide students with a comprehensive view about the application of the audit risk model we will provide illustration of the application of the audit risk model for both the financial statements and the company's internal control. In the U.S., PCAOB auditing standards note that the auditor's risk assessment procedures apply to both the audit of financial statements and the audit of internal control over financial reporting. Before we discuss the audit risk model, review the illustration for a hypothetical company in Table 9-2. Let's walk through the illustration point by point:

- The first row in the table shows the differences among cycles in the frequency and size of expected misstatements (A). Almost no misstatements are expected in payroll and personnel, but many are expected in inventory and warehousing. It is possible the payroll transactions are routine, while considerable complexities exist in recording inventory.
- Similarly, internal control is believed to differ in effectiveness among the five cycles (B). For example, internal controls in payroll and personnel are considered highly effective, whereas those in inventory and warehousing are considered ineffective.
- Finally, the auditor has decided on a low willingness that material misstatements exist after the audit is complete for all five cycles (C). It is common for auditors to want an equally low likelihood of misstatements for each cycle after the audit is finished to permit the issuance of an unmodified opinion.
- These considerations (A, B, C) affect the auditor's decision about the appropriate extent of evidence to accumulate (D). For example, because the auditor expects few misstatements in payroll and personnel (A) and internal controls are effective (B), the auditor plans for less evidence (D) than for inventory and warehousing.

OBJECTIVE 9-6

Describe the audit risk model and its components.

Audit risk model

A formal model reflecting the relationships between acceptable audit risk (AAR), inherent risk (IR), control risk (CR), and planned detection risk (PDR);

$PDR = \dfrac{AAR}{(IR \times CR)}$.

Audit Risk Model for Planning

Auditors deal with risk in planning audit evidence primarily by applying the **audit risk model**. This model comes from the professional literature on audit sampling and materiality and risk. You will need a thorough understanding of the model to conduct effective audit planning and to master the content presented in the remaining chapters of this book.

TABLE 9-2   Illustration of Differing Evidence Among Cycles

		Sales and Collection Cycle	Acquisition and Payment Cycle	Payroll and Personnel Cycle	Inventory and Warehousing Cycle	Capital Acquisition and Repayment Cycle
A	Auditor's assessment of expectation of material misstatement before considering internal control (inherent risk)	Expect some misstatements (medium)	Expect many misstatements (high)	Expect few misstatements (low)	Expect many misstatements (high)	Expect few misstatements (low)
B	Auditor's assessment of effectiveness of internal controls to prevent or detect material misstatements (control risk)	Medium effectiveness (medium)	High effectiveness (low)	High effectiveness (low)	Low effectiveness (high)	Medium effectiveness (medium)
C	Auditor's willingness to permit material misstatements to exist after completing the audit (acceptable audit risk)	Low willingness (low)	Low willingness (low)	Low willingness (low)	Low willingness (low)	Low willingness (low)
D	Extent of evidence the auditor plans to accumulate (planned detection risk)	Medium level (medium)	Medium level (medium)	Low level (high)	High level (low)	Medium level (medium)

The audit risk model helps auditors decide how much and what types of evidence to accumulate in each cycle. It is usually stated as follows:

$$PDR = \frac{AAR}{IR \times CR}$$

where:

$$PDR = planned\ detection\ risk$$
$$AAR = acceptable\ audit\ risk$$
$$IR = inherent\ risk$$
$$CR = control\ risk$$

Below, we provide a numerical example for discussion, even though it is not practical to measure as precisely as these numbers imply. The numbers used are for the inventory and warehousing cycle in Table 9-2.

$$IR = 100\%$$
$$CR = 100\%$$
$$AAR = 5\%$$
$$PDR = \frac{.05}{1.0 \times 1.0} = .05\ or\ 5\%$$

Figure 9-4 shows the relationship between the audit risk model and the understanding of the client's business and industry discussed in Chapter 8. Auditors use the audit risk model to further identify the potential for misstatements in the overall financial statements and specific account balances, classes of transactions, and disclosures where misstatements are most likely to occur.

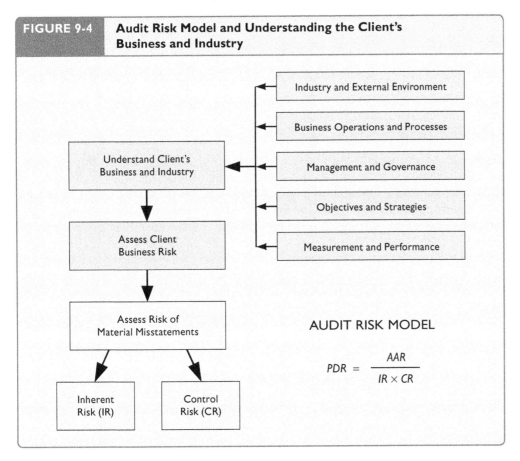

FIGURE 9-4   Audit Risk Model and Understanding the Client's Business and Industry

TYPES OF RISKS

Each of the four risks in the audit risk model is sufficiently important to merit detailed discussion. This section briefly discusses all four to provide an overview of the risks. Acceptable audit risk and inherent risk are discussed in greater detail later in this chapter. Control risk is examined in Chapter 10.

Planned Detection Risk

Planned detection risk

A measure of the risk that audit evidence for a segment will fail to detect misstatements exceeding a tolerable amount, should such misstatements exist;

$PDR = AAR / (IR \times CR)$.

Planned detection risk is the risk that audit evidence for a segment will fail to detect misstatements exceeding tolerable misstatement. Planned detection risk is determined by the effectiveness of the audit procedures and how these audit procedures are effectively performed by the auditor. Planned detection risk cannot be reduced to zero as auditors rarely test 100 percent of the segments (sampling risk). Also, the audit evidence is subject to what is called non-sampling risk, the risk that the auditor may select inadequate audit evidence, misapply an audit evidence or misinterpret the audit results. The non-sampling risk can be reduced through proper planning of the audit engagement, proper allocation of audit personnel, proper consideration of the professional skepticism concept, supervision and assessment of the audit performed, and continued application of the quality control standards for completed audit work.

Moreover, there are two key points to know about planned detection risk. Planned detection risk is dependent on the other three factors in the model. It will change only if the auditor changes one of the other risk model factors.

Planned detection risk determines the amount of substantive evidence that the auditor plans to accumulate, inversely with the size of planned detection risk. If planned detection risk is reduced, the auditor needs to accumulate more evidence to achieve the reduced planned risk. For example, in Table 9-2, planned detection risk (D) is low for inventory and warehousing, which causes planned evidence to be high. The opposite is true for payroll and personnel.

In the preceding numerical example, the planned detection risk (PDR) of .05 means the auditor plans to accumulate evidence until the risk of misstatements exceeding tolerable misstatement is reduced to 5 percent. If control risk (CR) was .50 instead of 1.0, planned detection risk (PDR) would be .10, and planned evidence could therefore be reduced.

Inherent Risk

Inherent risk measures the auditor's assessment of the likelihood that there are material misstatements (errors or fraud) in a segment before considering the effectiveness of internal control. If the auditor concludes that a high likelihood of misstatement exists, ignoring internal controls, the auditor will conclude that inherent risk is high. Internal controls are ignored in setting inherent risk because they are considered separately in the audit risk model as control risk. In Table 9-2 inherent risk (A) was assessed high for inventory and warehousing and lower for payroll and personnel and capital acquisition and repayment. Such assessments are typically based on discussions with management, knowledge of the company, and results in audits of previous years.

Inherent risk is inversely related to planned detection risk and directly related to evidence. Inherent risk for inventory and warehousing in Table 9-2 is high, which results in a lower planned detection risk and more planned evidence than if inherent risk were lower. We'll examine this in greater detail later in the chapter.

In addition to increasing audit evidence for a higher inherent risk in a given audit area, auditors commonly assign more experienced staff to that area and review the completed audit tests more thoroughly. For example, if inherent risk for inventory obsolescence is extremely high, it makes sense for the audit firm to assign an experienced staff person to perform more extensive tests for inventory obsolescence and to more carefully review the audit results.

Control Risk

Control risk measures the auditor's assessment of whether misstatements exceeding a tolerable amount in a segment will be prevented or detected on a timely basis by the client's internal controls. Control risk is a function of the effectiveness of the design and operation of the elements of internal control in meeting the entity's objectives for the preparation of a client's financial statements. There is always a risk associated with the internal control due to the inherent limitations of internal control which is the function of the entity and its environment. Assume that the auditor concludes that internal controls are completely ineffective to prevent or detect misstatements. That is the likely conclusion for inventory and warehousing (B) in Table 9-2. The auditor will therefore assign a high, perhaps 100 percent, risk factor to control risk. The more effective the internal controls, the lower the risk factor that can be assigned to control risk.

The audit risk model shows the close relationship between inherent and control risks. For example, an inherent risk of 40 percent and a control risk of 60 percent affect planned detection risk and planned evidence the same as an inherent risk of 60 percent and a control risk of 40 percent. In both cases, multiplying *IR* by *CR* results in a denominator in the audit risk model of 24 percent. The combination of inherent risk and control risk is referred to as the **risk of material misstatement**. The auditor may make a combined assessment of the risk of material misstatement or the auditor can separately assess inherent risk and control risk. (Remember, inherent risk is the expectation of misstatements *before* considering the effect of internal control.)

As with inherent risk, the relationship between control risk and planned detection risk is inverse, whereas the relationship between control risk and substantive evidence is direct. If the auditor concludes that internal controls are effective, planned detection risk can be increased and evidence therefore decreased. The auditor can increase planned detection risk when controls are effective because effective internal controls reduce the likelihood of misstatements in the financial statements.

Before auditors can set control risk less than 100 percent, they must obtain an understanding of internal control, evaluate how well it should function based on the understanding, and test the internal controls for effectiveness. Obtaining an understanding of internal control is required for all audits. The latter two are assessment of control risk steps that are required only when the auditor assesses control risk below maximum.

In most countries in the world, including those in the Arab world, auditors of publicly listed companies choose to rely extensively on controls because they must test the effectiveness of internal control over financial reporting when they form their opinions about the company's financial statements. Auditors of private companies and other entities are also likely to rely on controls that are effective, especially when day-to-day transaction processing involves highly automated procedures. When controls are likely to be ineffective and inherent risk is high, which is the situation in some Arab countries due to insufficient resources to establish such controls, the use of the audit risk model causes the auditor to decrease planned detection risk and thereby increase planned evidence. We devote the entire next chapter to understanding internal control, assessing control risk, and evaluating their impact on evidence requirements.

Acceptable Audit Risk

Acceptable audit risk is a measure of how willing the auditor is to accept that the financial statements may be materially misstated after the audit is completed and an unmodified opinion has been issued. When auditors decide on a lower acceptable audit

Control risk

A measure of the auditor's assessment of the likelihood that misstatements exceeding a tolerable amount in a segment will not be prevented or detected by the client's internal controls.

Risk of material misstatement

The combination of inherent risk and control risk (IR × CR).

risk, they want to be more certain that the financial statements are *not* materially misstated. Zero risk is certainty, and a 100 percent risk is complete uncertainty. Complete assurance (zero risk) of the accuracy of the financial statements is not economically practical. Moreover, as we discussed in Chapter 6, the auditor cannot guarantee the complete absence of material misstatements.

Audit assurance

A complement to acceptable audit risk; an acceptable audit risk of 2 percent is the same as audit assurance of 98 percent; also called overall assurance and level of assurance.

Often, auditors refer to the term **audit assurance** (also called *overall assurance* or *level of assurance*) instead of acceptable audit risk. Audit assurance or any of the equivalent terms is the complement of acceptable audit risk, that is, one minus acceptable audit risk. In other words, acceptable audit risk of 2 percent is the same as audit assurance of 98 percent.

The concept of acceptable audit risk can be more easily understood by thinking in terms of a large number of audits, say, 10,000. What portion of these audits can include material misstatements without having an adverse effect on society? Certainly, the portion is below 10 percent, the threshold of materiality. It is probably much closer to 1 percent or less. If an auditor believes that the appropriate percentage is 1 percent, then acceptable audit risk should be set at 1 percent, or perhaps lower, based on the specific circumstances.

When employing the audit risk model, there is a direct relationship between acceptable audit risk and planned detection risk, and an inverse relationship between acceptable audit risk and planned evidence. If the auditor decides to reduce acceptable audit risk, planned detection risk is thereby reduced, and planned evidence must be increased. For a client with lower acceptable audit risk, auditors also often assign more experienced staff or review the audit files more extensively.

Distinction Among Risks in the Audit Risk Model

There are important distinctions in how the auditor assesses the four risk factors in the audit risk model. For acceptable audit risk, the auditor decides the risk the audit firm is *willing to take* that the financial statements are misstated after the audit is completed, based on certain client related factors. An example of a client where the auditor will accept very little risk (low acceptable audit risk) is for an initial public offering (IPO). We will discuss factors affecting acceptable audit risk shortly. Inherent risk and control risk are based on auditor's *expectations or predictions* of clients' conditions. An example of a high inherent risk is inventory that has not been sold for two years. An example of a low control risk is adequate separation of duties between asset custody and accounting. The auditor cannot change these clients' conditions, but can only make a likelihood assessment. Inherent risk factors are discussed later in the chapter and control risk is covered in Chapter 10. Detection risk is *dependent completely on the other three risks*. It can be determined only after the auditor assesses the other three risks.

ASSESSING ACCEPTABLE AUDIT RISK

OBJECTIVE 9-7

Consider the impact of business risk on acceptable audit risk.

Business risks are risks associated with significant conditions, events, circumstances, and actions or inactions that may negatively affect management's ability to achieve its objectives or may result in determining or identifying inadequate objectives or strategies. For example, there is a risk associated with inability of the audit client to collect its receivables. Also, risks are always related with the development of a new product due to possible failure to sell it or defects in the product resulting in lawsuits or damage to the company's reputation.

It is important for the auditor to understand the entity and its environment to assess the business risks. Based on the auditor's understanding of the entity's business risks and the degree of control the entity has got over those risks, the auditor assesses the acceptable audit risk or risk of material misstatement in segments. A number of factors affect the auditor's understanding of the entity and its environment including

- *Client's industry and regulations.* Some industries are known for their unstable operating conditions, cyclical or seasonal activities, fluctuating market and competitive environment including demand and prices, and fast-changing product technology. For example, tour companies' activities in countries like Tunisia, Morocco, Jordan, and Egypt have declined significantly due to the impact of terrorism. Severe competition in the telecommunications industry resulted in a significant decrease in profitability of telecoms companies operating in Algeria, Egypt, and Saudi Arabia after several other companies entered the market providing the same services. These industries are subject to the risk of material misstatements. Financial institutions and banks need to continue to assess the adequacy of the loss reserves for their loans or their financial assets portfolios, based on historical and future cash flows, may be subject to misstatement. During 1997–2006, most of the banks operating in the Egyptian banking sector discovered defaults worth billions of Egyptian pounds in their loan portfolios. These large misstatements in the banks' financial statements necessitated government action, resulting in the sale of a significant number of Egyptian banks to international financial institutions, such as HSBC, Barclays, BNP Paribas, Citibank, and San Paolo, and Lebanese banks such as El Mashreq and Audi and others. Legislation may also significantly affect an entity's operations especially with regard to taxation, environmental requirements, and governmental policies related to acquiring or selling the company's products. All these elements, in addition to factors related to the level of economic activity within the country, including interest rates, the inflation rate, and currency revaluations, should inform the auditor's understanding of the client's business environment.
- *The nature of the client.* The auditor is required to understand the nature of the client's operations and systems. Such understanding requires the auditor's knowledge of the client's organizational structure, job descriptions and qualifications of personnel, the client's operating characteristics including its size and complexity, and key suppliers and customers. The auditor also needs to understand the process of financial reporting and the accounting framework used where the reliance is more for historical or fair values, the type of investments and sources of the client's earning process, and the key products and services. Understanding these elements will help the auditor to assess risks of material misstatements in particular segments.
- *The objectives, strategies and accounting policies.* The current and prospective strategies and objectives of the client should be understood by the auditor including new products and services, business expansion plans and current and prospective financing requirements. The auditor is required to assess whether the accounting policies used to prepare the financial statements are adequate for the business and consistent with applicable reporting framework. For example, auditors should ensure that management applies the equity method in recording investments with more than 20 percent of ownership. Auditors should also understand the methods used by management to account for unusual transactions.
- *The client's corporate governance environment.* Corporate governance represents the client's policies and procedures designed to ensure that management complies with the different regulations and requirements in achieving

the company's objectives. Examples of corporate governance factors include: an active board of directors and audit committee with independent members; an effective risk evaluation process; competent and experienced internal audit personnel; and effective control activities including proper authorizations, adequate segregation of duties, and monitoring of controls where, for example, supervisors undertake spot counts of inventory or assets.

In the Arab world, many publicly listed companies in U.A.E., Lebanon, Egypt, Saudi Arabia, Kuwait, and Jordan have established audit committees to oversee the work of the board, the external auditor(s), and the internal audit department(s). These companies are continuing to develop audit committees, and procedures to be implemented to help members of the audit committee assess the company's internal controls and their effects on proper financial reporting. Private companies in most Arab countries are still struggling to make available sufficient resources to establish such supervisory committees within their organizational structure.

The auditor should understand and assess business risk in order to evaluate the likelihood of misstatements in the financial statements affecting acceptable audit risk. There is an inverse relationship between business risk and acceptable audit risk, and a direct relationship between business risk and substantive evidence. So whenever the auditor assesses such business risk as high he needs to set acceptable audit risk at low and perform extensive substantive tests.

Impact of Business Risk on Acceptable Audit Risk

OBJECTIVE 9-8

Consider the impact of engagement risk on acceptable audit risk.

Engagement risk

The risk that the auditor or audit firm will suffer harm because of a client relationship, even though the audit report rendered for the client was correct.

Auditors must decide the appropriate acceptable audit risk for an audit, preferably during audit planning. First, auditors decide engagement risk and then use engagement risk to modify acceptable audit risk.

Engagement Risk **Engagement risk** is the risk that the auditor or audit firm will suffer harm after the audit is finished, even though the audit report was correct. Engagement risk is closely related to client business risk. For example, if a client declares bankruptcy after an audit is completed, the likelihood of a lawsuit against the audit firm is reasonably high, even if the quality of the audit was good.

It is worth noting that auditors disagree about whether engagement risk should be considered in planning the audit. Opponents of modifying evidence for engagement risk contend that auditors do not provide audit opinions for different levels of assurance and therefore should not provide more or less assurance because of engagement risk. Proponents contend that it is appropriate for auditors to accumulate additional but limited evidence, assign more experienced personnel, and review the audit more thoroughly on audits where legal exposure is high or other potential adverse actions affecting the auditor exist.

When auditors modify evidence for engagement risk, it is done by control of acceptable audit risk. We believe that a reasonably low acceptable audit risk is always desirable, but in some circumstances an even lower risk is needed because of engagement risk factors. Research points to several factors affecting engagement risk and, therefore, acceptable audit risk. Only three of those are discussed here: the degree to which external users rely on the statements, the likelihood that a client will have financial difficulties after the audit report is issued, and the integrity of management.

The Degree to Which External Users Rely on the Statements When external users place heavy reliance on the financial statements, it is appropriate to decrease acceptable audit risk. When the statements are heavily relied on, a great social harm can result if a significant misstatement remains undetected in the financial statements. Auditors can more easily justify the cost of additional evidence when the loss to users from material misstatements is substantial. Several factors are good indicators of the degree to which statements are relied on by external users:

- *Client's size.* Generally speaking, the larger a client's operations, the more widely the statements are used. The client's size, measured by total assets or total revenues, will have an effect on acceptable audit risk.
- *Distribution of ownership.* The statements of publicly held corporations are normally relied on by many more users than those of closely held corporations. For these companies, the interested parties include the financial supervisory boards, stock exchanges, financial analysts, and the general public.
- *Nature and amount of liabilities.* When statements include a large amount of liabilities, they are more likely to be used extensively by actual and potential creditors than when there are few liabilities.

The Likelihood that a Client Will Have Financial Difficulties After the Audit Report is Issued If a client is forced to file for bankruptcy or suffers a significant loss after completion of the audit, auditors face a greater chance of being required to defend the quality of the audit than if the client were under no financial strain. The natural tendency for those who lose money in a bankruptcy, or because of a stock price reversal, is to file suit against the auditor. This can result both from the honest belief that the auditor failed to conduct an adequate audit and from the users' desire to recover part of their loss regardless of the adequacy of the audit work.

In situations in which the auditor believes the chance of financial failure or loss is high and a corresponding increase in engagement risk occurs, acceptable audit risk should be reduced. If a subsequent challenge occurs, the auditor will be in a better position to defend the audit results successfully. Total audit evidence and costs will increase, but this is justifiable because of the additional risk of lawsuits that the auditor faces.

It is difficult for an auditor to predict financial failure before it occurs, but certain factors are good indicators of its increased probability:

- *Liquidity position.* If a client is constantly short of cash and working capital, it indicates a future problem in paying bills. The auditor must assess the likelihood and significance of a steadily declining liquidity position.
- *Profits (losses) in previous years.* When a company has rapidly declining profits or increasing losses for several years, the auditor should recognize the future solvency problems that the client is likely to encounter. It is also important to consider the changing profits relative to the balance remaining in retained earnings.
- *Method of financing growth.* The more a client relies on debt as a means of financing, the greater the risk of financial difficulty if the client's operating success declines. Auditors should evaluate whether fixed assets are being financed with short- or long-term loans, as large amounts of required cash outflows during a short time can force a company into bankruptcy.
- *Nature of the client's operations.* Certain types of businesses are inherently riskier than others. For example, other things being equal, a start-up technology company dependent on one product is much more likely to go bankrupt than a diversified food manufacturer.
- *Competence of management.* Competent management is constantly alert for potential financial difficulties and modifies its operating methods to minimize the effects of short-run problems. Auditors must assess the ability of management as a part of the evaluation of the likelihood of bankruptcy.

The Auditor's Evaluation of Management's Integrity As we discussed in Chapter 8 as a part of new client investigation and continuing client evaluation, if a client has questionable integrity, the auditor is likely to assess a lower acceptable audit

PROBE INTO DUBAI US$100M FRAUD ALLEGATIONS

Police are investigating fraud allegations against the chairman of one of Dubai's largest private real estate companies as dozens of aggrieved investors claim he defrauded them of more than US$100m.

The chairman of Dynasty Zarooni was arrested on allegations of fraud. At least ten members of Dynasty Zarooni's investment club, which promised vast profits from the company's preferential access to real estate deals, have lodged complaints against the chairman, an Indian national, his Emirati business partner, their joint venture Dynasty Zarooni, and two other employees.

Investors say that the chairman received subscription fees of AED 300,000 (approximately US$82,000) from 12 members. He promised them returns of AED 6m after a few months.

One British loser says he was encouraged by initial profits made by another club member, who had reinvested the proceeds into the scheme rather than taking the cash.

Lawyers say more than 100 other investors are preparing cases against Dynasty Zarooni over misrepresentation during the sale of its real estate projects.

One aggrieved investor, who placed a 20 percent deposit on an apartment in Ebony Tower 1, opposite the Dubai Marina, for AED 650,000 (approximately US$177,000), lodged a complaint with the police against Dynasty Zarooni and their development partners, Al Fajer Properties, for allegedly misleading him about the progress made on the building's

construction, thereby raising the supposed value of the property. "I have been cheated and am very distressed," he said.

Dubai's Real Estate Regulatory Agency (RERA) is cracking down on property developers without its registration. According to a RERA senior official no memorandums of understandings, sale agreements, or property contracts will be legally acceptable if they are not registered with the Dubai Land Department (DLD). Real estate developers who are not registered with RERA or any of the unregistered projects would not be permitted to sell their properties.

One wonders what type of evidence the auditors of this huge real estate company have collected to uncover such corruption. A large number of overseas property investors who purchased property in Dubai did so in stages: generally a deposit of 10 percent of the property value was put down to reserve a unit, with the remaining balance being paid in stages until the completion date. Now under the new property laws the payment schedule should be set out in an initial contract. It seems that these laws have been designed to protect investors.

Sources: Based on I. S. Kerr, 'Probe into Dubai 100m fraud allegations,' *Financial Times*, January 11, 2009, www.ft.com; and N. Shahzad, 'Onslaught On Scam To Win Confidence Of Suspicious Dubai Property Investors,' *Inman News*, October 16, 2008, www.inman.com.

risk. Companies with low integrity often conduct their business affairs in a manner that results in conflicts with their stockholders, regulators, and customers. In turn, these conflicts often reflect on the users' perceived quality of the audit and can result in lawsuits and other disagreements. A prior criminal conviction of key management personnel is an obvious example of questionable management integrity. Other examples of questionable integrity might include frequent disagreements with previous auditors, the tax authorities, and the financial supervisory boards. Frequent turnover of key financial and internal audit personnel and ongoing conflicts with labor unions and employees may also indicate integrity problems.

Making the Acceptable Audit Risk Decision

To assess acceptable audit risk, the auditor must first assess each of the factors affecting engagement risk which in turn affects acceptable audit risk. Table 9-3 illustrates the methods used by auditors to assess each of the three factors already discussed. After examining Table 9-3, it is easy to observe that the assessment of each of the factors is highly subjective, meaning overall assessment of acceptable audit risk is also highly subjective. A typical evaluation of acceptable audit risk is high, medium, or low, where a low acceptable audit risk assessment means a 'risky' client requiring more extensive evidence, assignment of more experienced personnel, and/or a more extensive review of audit documentation. As the engagement progresses, auditors obtain additional information about the client, and acceptable audit risk may be modified.

TABLE 9-3	Methods Practitioners Use to Assess Acceptable Audit Risk
Factors	**Methods Used to Assess Acceptable Audit Risk**
External users' reliance on financial statements	• Examine the financial statements, including footnotes. • Read minutes of board of directors' meetings to determine future plans. • Examine Form 10K for a publicly held company. • Discuss financing plans with management.
Likelihood of financial difficulties	• Analyze the financial statements for financial difficulties using ratios and other analytical procedures. • Examine historical and projected cash flow statements for the nature of cash inflows and outflows.
Management integrity	• Follow the procedures discussed in Chapter 8 for client acceptance and continuance.

ASSESSING INHERENT RISK

The inclusion of inherent risk in the audit risk model is one of the most important concepts in auditing. It implies that auditors should attempt to predict where misstatements are most and least likely in the financial statement segments. This information affects the amount of evidence that the auditor needs to accumulate, the assignment of staff, and the review of audit documentation.

> **OBJECTIVE 9-9**
>
> Consider the impact of several factors on the assessment of inherent risk.

Factors Affecting Inherent Risk

The auditor must assess the factors that make up the risk and modify audit evidence to take them into consideration. The auditor should consider several major factors when assessing inherent risk:

- Nature of the client's business
- Results of previous audits
- Initial versus repeat engagement
- Related parties
- Nonroutine transactions
- Judgment required to correctly record account balances and transactions
- Makeup of the population
- Factors related to fraudulent financial reporting
- Factors related to misappropriation of assets

AICPA INDUSTRY AUDIT RISK ALERTS FOR SPECIALIZED INDUSTRIES

Many companies operate in specialized industries that have unique economic, regulatory, and accounting issues. In an effort to provide auditors with current guidance on assessing inherent risks for clients in specialized industries, AICPA annually issues a series of *Industry Audit Risk Alerts*. Some of the industries covered by the publications are banks and savings institutions, construction contractors, healthcare providers, not-for-profit organizations, public utilities, and real estate. AICPA issues new or revised risk alerts whenever it concludes that auditors should be aware of recent economic, regulatory, or technical developments for companies in specific industries. Auditors in different regions of the world can use these industry risk alerts to understand the environment in which many multinationals operate and help auditors understand and assess the operating and financial risks for these specific industries. Unfortunately, the industry risk alerts have yet to be introduced and published in many Arab countries in similar forms to those AICPA guides, with guidelines provided to auditors and other interested parties to consider when providing their services to these industries.

Nature of the Client's Business Inherent risk for certain accounts is affected by the nature of the client's business. For example, an electronics manufacturer faces a greater likelihood of obsolete inventory than a steel fabricator does. Inherent risk is most likely to vary from business to business for accounts such as inventory, accounts and loans receivable, and property, plant, and equipment. The nature of the client's business should have little or no effect on inherent risk for accounts such as cash, notes, and mortgages payable. Information gained while obtaining knowledge about the client's business and industry and assessing client business risk, is useful for assessing this factor.

Results of Previous Audits Misstatements found in the previous year's audit have a high likelihood of occurring again in the current year's audit, because many types of misstatements are systemic in nature, and organizations are often slow in making changes to eliminate them. Therefore, an auditor is negligent if the results of the preceding year's audit are ignored during the development of the current year's audit program. For example, if the auditor found a significant number of misstatements in pricing inventory in last year's audit, the auditor will likely assess inherent risk as high in the current year's audit, and extensive testing will have to be done as a means of determining whether the deficiency in the client's system has been corrected. If, however, the auditor found no misstatements for the past several years in conducting tests of an audit area, the auditor is justified in reducing inherent risk, provided that changes in relevant circumstances have not occurred.

Initial Versus Repeat Engagement Auditors gain experience and knowledge about the likelihood of misstatements after auditing a client for several years. The lack of previous years' audit results causes most auditors to assess a higher inherent risk for initial audits than for repeat engagements in which no material misstatements were previously found. Most auditors set a high inherent risk in the first year of an audit and reduce it in subsequent years as they gain more knowledge about the client.

Related Parties Transactions between parent and subsidiary companies, and those between management and the corporate entity, are examples of related-party transactions. Because these transactions do not occur between two independent parties dealing at 'arm's length,' a greater likelihood exists that they might be misstated, causing an increase in inherent risk. We discussed related parties transactions in Chapter 8.

Nonroutine Transactions Transactions that are unusual for a client are more likely to be incorrectly recorded than routine transactions because the client often lacks experience recording them. Examples include fire losses, major property acquisitions, and lease agreements. By knowing the client's business and reviewing minutes of meetings, the auditor can assess the consequences of nonroutine transactions.

Judgment Required to Correctly Record Account Balances and Transactions Many account balances such as certain investments recorded at fair value, allowances for uncollectible accounts receivable, obsolete inventory, liability for warranty payments, major repairs versus partial replacement of assets, and bank loan loss reserves require estimates and a great deal of management judgment. Because they require considerable judgment, the likelihood of misstatements increases, and as a result the auditor should increase inherent risk.

Makeup of the Population Often, individual items making up the total population also affect the auditor's expectation of material misstatement. Most auditors use a higher inherent risk for accounts receivable where most accounts are significantly overdue than where most accounts are current. Examples of items requiring a higher inherent risk include transactions with affiliated companies, amounts due from officers, cash disbursements made payable to cash, and accounts receivable outstanding for several months. These situations require greater investigation because of a greater likelihood of misstatement than occurs with more typical transactions.

Factors Related to Fraudulent Financial Reporting and Misappropriation of Assets In Chapter 6, we discussed the auditor's responsibilities to assess the risk of fraudulent financial reporting and misappropriation of assets. It is difficult in concept and practice to separate fraud risk factors into acceptable audit risk, inherent risk, or control risk. For example, management that lacks integrity and is motivated to misstate financial statements is one of the factors in acceptable audit risk, but it may also affect control risk. Similarly, several of the other risk factors influencing management characteristics are a part of the control environment, as we'll discuss in Chapter 10. These include the attitude, actions, and policies that reflect the overall attitudes of top management about integrity, ethical values, and commitment to competence.

To satisfy the requirements of auditing standards, it is more important for the auditor to assess the risks and to respond to them than it is to categorize them into a risk type. For this reason, many audit firms assess fraud risk separately from the assessment of the audit risk model components.

The risk of fraud can be assessed for the entire audit or by cycle, account, and objective. For example, a strong incentive for management to meet unduly aggressive earnings expectations may affect the entire audit, while the susceptibility of inventory to theft may affect only the inventory account. For both the risk of fraudulent financial reporting and the risk of misappropriation of assets, auditors focus on specific areas of increased fraud risk and designing audit procedures or changing the overall conduct of the audit to respond to those risks. The specific response to an identified risk of fraud can include revising assessments of acceptable audit risk, inherent risk, and control risk. Assessing fraud risk will be the focus of Chapter 11.

Making the Inherent Risk Decision

The auditor must evaluate the information affecting inherent risk and decide on an appropriate inherent risk level for each cycle, account, and, many times, for each audit objective. Some factors, such as an initial versus repeat engagement, will affect many or perhaps all cycles, whereas others, such as nonroutine transactions, will affect only specific accounts or audit objectives. Although the profession has not established

---

GLOBAL ADVERTISING FIRM CHARGED IN ACCOUNTING FRAUD INVOLVING INTER-COMPANY RECEIVABLES

The Securities and Exchange Commission filed enforcement actions in 2008 against global advertising network McCann-Erickson Worldwide and two former executives for their roles in an accounting fraud involving intercompany transactions. The SEC complaint alleges that McCann, which owns hundreds of regional and local advertising agencies throughout the world (including some in Arab countries), fraudulently misstated its financial results by improperly failing to expense intercompany charges that were instead recorded as receivables. Its holding company, Interpublic Group of Companies, Inc. (IPG), negligently failed to address the accounting problems at McCann, its largest subsidiary, resulting in material misstatements in its own financial reporting.

McCann's management failed to reconcile intercompany accounts for at least six years covering the period 1997–2002. At times,

McCann's management intentionally delayed reconciling intercompany accounts because they knew it would result in write-offs that would interfere with the company's efforts to hit profit targets. In fact, every year from 1997 to 2002 the firm's auditor listed pressure to produce results in line with budgets as part of its risk assessment, and described the failure to reconcile the intercompany accounts as a fundamental breakdown in internal controls. IPG and McCann agreed to settle the SEC's charges, and McCann agreed to pay a US$12 million penalty.

Source: United States District Court Southern District of New York, *Securities and Exchange Commission v. Interpublic Group of Companies, Inc. and McCann-Erickson Worldwide, Inc.,* April 30, 2008.

standards or guidelines for setting inherent risk, we believe that auditors are generally conservative in making such assessments. Assume that in the audit of inventory the auditor notes that (1) a large number of misstatements were found in the previous year and (2) inventory turnover has slowed in the current year. Auditors will likely set inherent risk at a relatively high level (some will use 100 percent) for each audit objective for inventory in this situation.

Obtain Information to Assess Inherent Risk

Auditors begin their assessments of inherent risk during the planning phase and update the assessments throughout the audit. Chapter 8 discussed how auditors gather information relevant to inherent risk assessment during the planning phase. For example, to obtain knowledge of the client's business and industry, auditors may tour the client's plant and offices and identify related parties. This and other information about the entity and its environment discussed in Chapter 8 pertain directly to inherent risk assessment. Also, several of the items discussed earlier under factors affecting inherent risk, such as the results of previous audits and nonroutine transactions are evaluated separately to help assess inherent risk. As audit tests are performed during an audit, the auditor may obtain additional information that affects the original assessment.

RELATIONSHIP OF RISKS TO EVIDENCE AND FACTORS INFLUENCING RISKS

OBJECTIVE 9-10

Discuss the relationship of risks to audit evidence.

Figure 9-5 summarizes factors that determine each of the risks, the effect of the three component risks on the determination of planned detection risk, and the relationship of all four risks to planned audit evidence. 'D' in the figure indicates a direct relationship between a component risk and planned detection risk or planned evidence. 'I' indicates an inverse relationship. For example, an increase in acceptable audit risk results in an increase in planned detection risk (D) and a decrease in planned audit evidence (I). Compare Figure 9-3 to Table 9-2 and observe that these two illustrations include the same concepts.

Auditors respond to risk primarily by changing the extent of testing and types of audit procedures, including incorporating unpredictability from the management point of view in the audit procedures used. For example, auditors can use confirmation for specific receivable debts in addition to their review of the client's aging schedule. In addition to modifying audit evidence, there are two other ways that auditors can change the audit to respond to risks:

1. *The engagement may require more experienced staff.* Auditing firms should staff all engagements with qualified staff. For low acceptable audit risk clients, special care is appropriate in staffing, and the importance of professional skepticism should be emphasized. Similarly, if an audit area such as inventory has a high inherent risk, it is important to assign that area to someone with experience in auditing inventory.

2. *The engagement will be reviewed more carefully than usual.* Auditing firms need to ensure adequate review of the audit files that document the auditor's planning, evidence accumulation and conclusions, and other matters in the audit. When acceptable audit risk is low, more extensive review is often warranted, including a review by personnel who were not assigned to the engagement. If the risk of material misstatement (the combination of inherent risk and control risk) is high for certain accounts, the reviewer will likely spend more time making sure the evidence was appropriate and correctly evaluated.

FIGURE 9-5	Relationship of Factors Influencing Risks to Risks and Risks to Planned Evidence

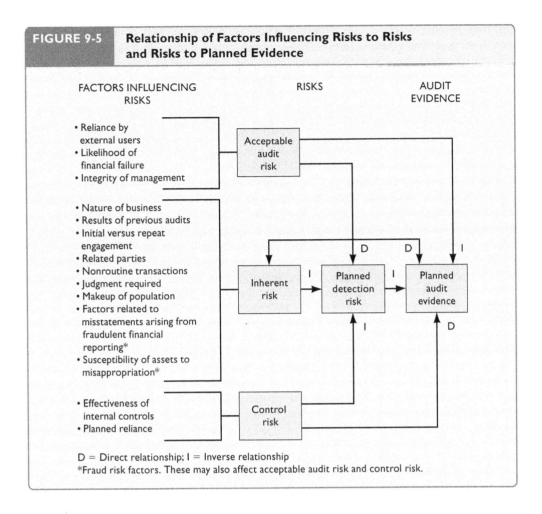

D = Direct relationship; I = Inverse relationship
*Fraud risk factors. These may also affect acceptable audit risk and control risk.

Audit Risk For Segments

Neither control risk nor inherent risk is assessed for the overall audit. Instead, both control risk and inherent risk are assessed for each cycle, each account within a cycle, and sometimes even each audit objective for the account. The assessments are likely to vary on the same audit from cycle to cycle, account to account, and objective to objective. For example, internal controls may be more effective for inventory-related accounts than for those related to fixed assets. Control risk will therefore be lower for inventory than for fixed assets. Factors affecting inherent risk, such as susceptibility to misappropriation of assets and routineness of the transactions, are also likely to differ from account to account. For that reason, it is normal to have inherent risk vary for different accounts in the same audit.

Acceptable audit risk is ordinarily assessed by the auditor during planning and held constant for each major cycle and account. Auditors normally use the same acceptable audit risk for each segment because the factors affecting acceptable audit risk are related to the entire audit, not individual accounts. For example, the extent to which external users' decisions rely upon financial statements is usually related to the overall financial statements, not just one or two accounts.

In some cases, however, a *lower* acceptable audit risk may be more appropriate for one account than for others. If an auditor decided to use a medium acceptable audit risk for the audit as a whole, the auditor might decide to reduce acceptable audit risk to low for inventory if inventory is used as collateral for a short-term loan.

Some auditors use the same acceptable audit risk for all segments based on their belief that at the end of the audit, financial statement users should have the same level of assurance for every segment of the financial statements. Other auditors use a different level of assurance for different segments based on their belief that financial statement users may be more concerned about certain account balances relative to other accounts in a given audit. For illustrations in this and subsequent chapters, we use the same acceptable audit risk for all segments in the audit. Note, however, that changing the risk for different segments is also acceptable.

Like control risk and inherent risk, planned detection risk and required audit evidence will vary from cycle to cycle, account to account, or objective to objective. This conclusion should not be surprising. As the circumstances of each engagement differ, the extent of evidence needed will depend on the unique circumstances. For example, inventory might require extensive testing on an engagement because of weak internal controls and the auditor's concerns about obsolescence resulting from technological changes in the industry. On the same engagement, accounts receivable may require little testing because of effective internal controls, fast collection of receivables, excellent relationships between the client and customers, and good audit results in previous years. Similarly, for a given audit of inventory, an auditor may assess a higher inherent risk of a realizable value misstatement because of the higher potential for obsolescence but a low inherent risk of a classification misstatement because there is only purchased inventory.

Relating Tolerable Misstatement and Risks to Balance-Related Audit Objectives

Although it is common in practice to assess inherent and control risks for each balance-related audit objective, it is not common to allocate materiality to those objectives. Auditors are able to effectively associate most risks with different objectives, and it is reasonably easy to determine the relationship between a risk and one or two objectives. For example, obsolescence in inventory is unlikely to affect any objective other than realizable value. It is more difficult to decide how much of the materiality allocated to a given account should in turn be allocated to one or two objectives. Therefore, most auditors do not attempt to do so.

Measurement Limitations

One major limitation in the application of the audit risk model is the difficulty of measuring the components of the model. Despite the auditor's best efforts in planning, the assessments of acceptable audit risk, inherent risk, and control risk, and therefore planned detection risk, are highly subjective and are only approximations of reality. Imagine, for example, attempting to precisely assess inherent risk by determining the impact of factors such as the misstatements discovered in prior years' audits and technology changes in the client's industry.

To offset this measurement problem, many auditors use broad and subjective measurement terms, such as *low*, *medium*, and *high*. As Table 9-4 shows, auditors can use this information to decide on the appropriate amount of evidence to accumulate. For example, in situation 1, the auditor has decided on a high acceptable audit risk for an account or objective. The auditor has concluded that a low risk of misstatement in the financial statements exists and that internal controls are effective. Therefore, a high planned detection risk is appropriate. As a result, a low level of evidence is needed. Situation 3 is at the opposite extreme. If both inherent and control risks are high and the auditor wants a low acceptable audit risk, considerable evidence is required. The other three situations fall between these two extremes.

It is equally difficult to measure the amount of evidence implied by a given planned detection risk. A typical audit program intended to reduce detection risk to the planned level is a combination of several audit procedures, each using a different type of evidence which is applied to different audit objectives. Auditors' measurement

TABLE 9-4	Relationships of Risk to Evidence				
Situation	Acceptable Audit Risk	Inherent Risk	Control Risk	Planned Detection Risk	Amount of Evidence Required
1	High	Low	Low	High	Low
2	Low	Low	Low	Medium	Medium
3	Low	High	High	Low	High
4	Medium	Medium	Medium	Medium	Medium
5	High	Low	Medium	Medium	Medium

methods are too imprecise to permit an accurate quantitative measure of the combined evidence. Instead, auditors subjectively evaluate whether sufficient evidence has been planned to satisfy a planned detection risk of low, medium, or high. Presumably, measurement methods are sufficient to permit an auditor to determine whether more evidence is needed to satisfy a low planned detection risk than for medium or high. Considerable professional judgment is needed to decide how much more.

In applying the audit risk model, auditors are concerned about both over-auditing and under-auditing. Most auditors are more concerned about the latter, as under-auditing exposes the audit firm to legal liability and loss of professional reputation. Because of the concern to avoid under-auditing, auditors typically assess risks conservatively. For example, an auditor might not assess either control risk or inherent risk below .5 even when the likelihood of misstatement is low. In these audits, a low risk might be .5, medium .8, and high 1.0, if the risks are quantified.

Tests of Details of Balances Evidence-Planning Worksheet

Practicing auditors develop various types of worksheets to help associate considerations affecting audit evidence with the appropriate evidence to accumulate. One such worksheet is included in Figure 9-6 for the audit of accounts receivable for Arabian Hardware Co. The eight balance-related audit objectives introduced in Chapter 6 are included in the columns at the top of the worksheet. Rows one and two are acceptable audit risk and inherent risk. Tolerable misstatement is included at the bottom of the worksheet. The engagement in-charge, Hosni Abdel Latif, made the following decisions in the audit of the company:

- *Tolerable misstatement.* The preliminary judgment about materiality was set at US$442,000 (approximately 6 percent of earnings from operations of US$7,370,000). He allocated US$265,000 to the audit of accounts receivable (see page 281).
- *Acceptable audit risk.* Hosni assessed acceptable audit risk as high because of the good financial condition of the company, high management integrity, and the relatively few users of the financial statements. Although Arabian is a publicly traded company, its stock is not widely held or extensively followed by financial analysts.
- *Inherent risk.* Hosni assessed inherent risk as medium for existence and cutoff because of concerns over revenue recognition. Hosni also assessed inherent risk as medium for realizable value. In past years, audit adjustments to the allowance for uncollectible accounts were made because it was found to be understated. Inherent risk was assessed as low for all other objectives.

Planned detection risk would be approximately the same for each balance-related audit objective in the audit of accounts receivable, if the only three factors

FIGURE 9-6	Evidence-Planning Worksheet to Decide Tests of Details of Balances for Arabian Hardware Co.—Accounts Receivable

	Detail tie-in	Existence	Completeness	Accuracy	Classification	Cutoff	Realizable value	Rights
Acceptable audit risk	High	High	High	High	High	High	High	High
Inherent risk	Low	Medium	Low	Low	Low	Medium	Medium	Low
Control risk—Sales								
Control risk—Cash receipts								
Control risk—Additional controls								
Substantive tests of transactions—Sales								
Substantive tests of transactions—Cash receipts								
Analytical procedures								
Planned detection risk for tests of details of balances								
Planned audit evidence for tests of details of balances								

Tolerable misstatement   US$265,000

the auditor needed to consider were acceptable audit risk, inherent risk, and tolerable misstatement. The evidence-planning worksheet shows that other factors must also be considered before making the final evidence decisions. (These are studied in subsequent chapters and will be integrated into the evidence-planning worksheet at that time.)

Relationship of Risk and Materiality to Audit Evidence

The concepts of materiality and risk in auditing are closely related and inseparable. Risk is a measure of uncertainty, whereas materiality is a measure of magnitude or size. Taken together, they measure the uncertainty of amounts of a given magnitude. For example, the statement that the auditor plans to accumulate evidence such that there is only a 5 percent risk (acceptable audit risk) of failing to uncover misstatements exceeding tolerable misstatements of US$265,000 (materiality) is a precise and meaningful statement. If the statement eliminates either the risk or materiality portion, it is meaningless. A 5 percent risk without a specific materiality measure could

FIGURE 9-7	Relationship of Tolerable Misstatement and Risks to Planned Evidence

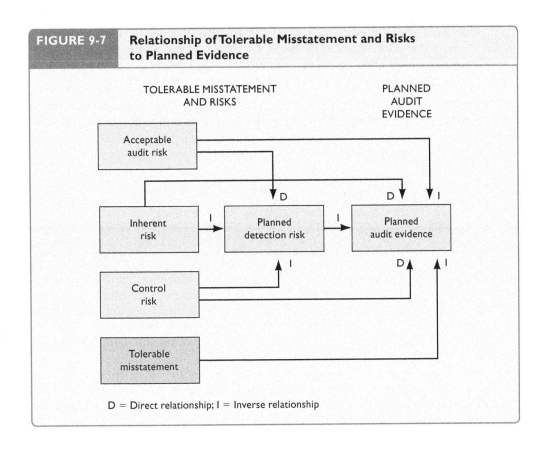

D = Direct relationship; I = Inverse relationship

imply that a US$100 or US$1 million misstatement is acceptable. A US$265,000 overstatement without a specific risk could imply that a 1 percent or 80 percent risk is acceptable.

The relationships among tolerable misstatement and the four risks to planned audit evidence are shown in Figure 9-7. This figure expands Figure 9-5 by including tolerable misstatement. Observe that tolerable misstatement does not affect any of the four risks, and the risks have no effect on tolerable misstatement, but together they determine planned evidence. Stated differently, tolerable misstatement is not a part of the audit risk model, but the combination of tolerable misstatement and the audit risk model factors determine planned audit evidence.

Revising Risks and Evidence

The audit risk model is primarily a planning model and is, therefore, of limited use in evaluating results. No difficulties occur when the auditor accumulates planned evidence and concludes that the assessment of each of the risks was reasonable or better than originally thought. The auditor will conclude that sufficient appropriate evidence has been collected for that account or cycle.

However, special care must be exercised when the auditor decides, on the basis of accumulated evidence, that the original assessment of control risk or inherent risk was understated or acceptable audit risk was overstated. In such a circumstance, the auditor should follow a two-step approach.

1. The auditor must revise the original assessment of the appropriate risk. It violates due care to leave the original assessment unchanged if the auditor knows it is inappropriate.
2. The auditor should consider the effect of the revision on evidence requirements, *without use of the audit risk model*. If a revised risk is used in the audit risk model to determine a revised planned detection risk, there is a danger of

not increasing the evidence sufficiently. Instead, the auditor should carefully evaluate the implications of the revision of the risk and modify evidence appropriately, outside of the audit risk model.

For example, assume that the auditor confirms accounts receivable and, based on the misstatements found, concludes that the original control risk assessment as low was inappropriate. The auditor should revise the estimate of control risk upward and carefully consider the effect of the revision on the additional evidence needed in the audit of receivables and the sales and collection cycle. Based on the results of the additional tests performed, the auditor should carefully evaluate whether sufficient appropriate evidence has been gathered in the circumstances to reduce audit risk to an acceptable level.

SUMMARY

Materiality and risk are fundamental concepts important to audit planning. Both concepts require significant auditor judgment and they directly impact the auditor's planned audit evidence. Materiality is important because the auditor provides assurance to financial statement users that the financial statements are free of material misstatements. Thus, the auditor must develop a preliminary judgment about materiality to be able to design an audit plan that will provide a basis for that assurance. Furthermore, because auditors accept some level of uncertainty in performing the audit function, the consideration of risk as defined by the audit risk model is necessary for the auditor to effectively address those risks in the most appropriate manner. The auditor's understanding of the entity and its environment, including its internal control, provide a basis for the auditor's assessment of the risk of material misstatement. Using the audit risk model and tolerable misstatements for each account, the auditor determines the audit evidence needed to achieve an acceptable level of audit risk for the financial statements as a whole.

ESSENTIAL TERMS

Allocation of the preliminary judgment about materiality   p. 280

Audit assurance   p. 290

Audit risk model   p. 286

Control risk   p. 289

Direct projection estimate of misstatement   p. 283

Engagement risk   p. 292

Known misstatements   p. 283

Likely misstatements   p. 283

Materiality   p. 275

Planned detection risk   p. 288

Preliminary judgment about materiality   p. 276

Revised judgment about materiality   p. 277

Risk   p. 285

Risk of material misstatement   p. 289

Sampling error   p. 284

Tolerable misstatement   p. 280

REVIEW QUESTIONS

9-1 (Objective 9-1) Chapter 8 introduced the eight parts of the planning phase of an audit. Which part is the evaluation of materiality and risk?

9-2 (Objective 9-1) Define the meaning of the term *materiality* as it is used in accounting and auditing. What is the relationship between materiality and the phrase *obtain reasonable assurance* used in the auditor's report?

9-3 (Objectives 9-1, 9-2) Explain why materiality is important but difficult to apply in practice.

9-4 (Objective 9-2) What is meant by setting a preliminary judgment about materiality? Identify the most important factors affecting the preliminary judgment.

9-5 (Objective 9-2) What is meant by using bases for setting a preliminary judgment about materiality? How will those bases differ for the audit of a manufacturing company and a government unit such as a school district?

9-6 (Objective 9-2) Assume that Karim Abdel Allem, CPA, is using 5 percent of net income before taxes, current assets, or current liabilities as his major guidelines for evaluating materiality. What qualitative factors should he also consider in deciding whether misstatements may be material?

9-7 (Objectives 9-2, 9-3) Distinguish between the terms *tolerable misstatement* and *preliminary judgment about materiality*. How are they related to each other?

9-8 (Objective 9-3) Assume a company with the following balance sheet accounts:

Account	Amount	Account	Amount
Cash	US$10,000	Long-term loans	US$30,000
Fixed assets	60,000	E. Nadim, proprietor	40,000
	US$70,000		US$70,000

You are concerned only about overstatements of owner's equity. Set tolerable misstatement for the three relevant accounts such that the preliminary judgment about materiality does not exceed US$5,000. Justify your answer.

9-9 (Objective 9-4) Explain what is meant by making an estimate of the total misstatement in a segment and in the overall financial statements. Why is it important to make these estimates? What is done with them?

9-10 (Objective 9-2) How will the conduct of an audit of a medium-sized company be affected by the company's being a small part of a large conglomerate as compared with it being a separate entity?

9-11 (Objective 9-6) Define the audit risk model and explain each term in the model. Also describe which two factors of the model when combined reflect the risk of material misstatement.

9-12 (Objective 9-6) What is meant by planned detection risk? What is the effect on the amount of evidence the auditor must accumulate when planned detection risk is increased from medium to high?

9-13 (Objective 9-6) Explain the causes of an increased or decreased planned detection risk.

9-14 (Objectives 9-6, 9-9) Define what is meant by inherent risk. Identify four factors that make for high inherent risk in audits.

9-15 (Objective 9-9) Explain why inherent risk is set for segments rather than for the overall audit. What is the effect on the amount of evidence the auditor must accumulate when inherent risk is increased from medium to high for a segment? Compare your answer with the one for question 9-12.

9-16 (Objective 9-9) Explain the effect of extensive misstatements found in the prior year's audit on inherent risk, planned detection risk, and planned audit evidence.

9-17 (Objectives 9-6, 9-8) Explain what is meant by the term *acceptable audit risk*. What is its relevance to evidence accumulation?

9-18 (Objective 9-8) Explain the relationship between acceptable audit risk and the legal liability of auditors.

9-19 (Objective 9-8) State the three categories of factors that affect acceptable audit risk and list the factors that the auditor can use to indicate the degree to which each category exists.

9-20 (Objective 9-10) Auditors have not been successful in measuring the components of the audit risk model. How is it possible to use the model in a meaningful way without a precise way of measuring the risk?

9-21 (Objective 9-11) Explain the circumstances when the auditor should revise the components of the audit risk model and the effect of the revisions on planned detection risk and planned evidence.

MULTIPLE CHOICE QUESTIONS FROM CPA EXAMINATIONS

9-22 (Objectives 9-1, 9-2) The following questions deal with materiality. Choose the best response.

a. Which one of the following statements is correct concerning the concept of materiality?
   (1) Materiality is determined by reference to guidelines established by the IFAC or AICPA.
   (2) Materiality depends only on the dollar amount of an item relative to other items in the financial statements.
   (3) Materiality depends on the nature of an item rather than the dollar amount.
   (4) Materiality is a matter of professional judgment.

b. The concept of materiality will be least important to the auditor in determining the
   (1) scope of the audit of specific accounts.
   (2) specific transactions that should be reviewed.
   (3) effects of audit exceptions upon the opinion.
   (4) effects of the CPA's direct financial interest in a client upon the CPA's independence.

c. In considering materiality for planning purposes, an auditor believes that misstatements aggregating US$10,000 will have a material effect on an entity's income statement, but that misstatements will have to aggregate US$20,000 to materially affect the balance sheet. Ordinarily, it is appropriate to design audit procedures that are expected to detect misstatements that aggregate
   (1) US$10,000
   (2) US$15,000
   (3) US$20,000
   (4) US$30,000

9-23 (Objectives 9-1, 9-6, 9-9) The following questions concern materiality and risk. Choose the best response.

a. Future Corporation has a few large accounts receivable that total US$1,400,000. Love Corporation has a great number of small accounts receivable that also total US$1,400,000. The importance of a misstatement in any one account is therefore greater for Future than for Love. This is an example of the auditor's concept of
   (1) materiality.
   (2) comparative analysis.
   (3) reasonable assurance.
   (4) relative risk.

b. Which of the following elements ultimately determines the specific auditing procedures that are necessary in the circumstances to afford a reasonable basis for an opinion?
   (1) Auditor judgment
   (2) Materiality

(3) Inherent risk

(4) Reasonable assurance

c. Which of the following *best* describes the element of inherent risk that underlies the application of auditing standards?

(1) Cash audit work may have to be carried out in a more conclusive manner than inventory audit work.

(2) Intercompany transactions are usually subject to less detailed scrutiny than arm's-length transactions with outside parties.

(3) Inventories may require more attention by the auditor on an engagement for a merchandising enterprise than on an engagement for a public utility.

(4) The scope of the audit need *not* be expanded if misstatements that arouse suspicion of fraud are of relatively insignificant amounts.

9-24 (Objectives 9-1, 9-2, 9-5, 9-6, 9-9) The following questions deal with materiality and risk. Choose the best response.

a. Which of the following statements is *not* correct about materiality?

(1) The concept of materiality recognizes that some matters are important for fair presentation of financial statements in conformity with accounting standards, whereas other matters are *not* important.

(2) An auditor considers materiality for planning purposes in terms of the largest aggregate level of misstatements that could be material to any one of the financial statements.

(3) Materiality judgments are made in light of surrounding circumstances and necessarily involve both quantitative and qualitative judgments.

(4) An auditor's consideration of materiality is influenced by the auditor's perception of the needs of a reasonable person who will rely on the financial statements.

b. Inherent risk and control risk differ from planned detection risk in that they

(1) arise from the misapplication of auditing procedures.

(2) may be assessed in either quantitative or nonquantitative terms.

(3) exist independently of the financial statement audit.

(4) can be changed at the auditor's discretion.

c. Based on evidence gathered and evaluated, an auditor decides to increase the assessed level of control risk from that originally planned. To achieve an overall audit risk level that is substantially the same as the planned audit risk level, the auditor could

(1) decrease detection risk.

(2) increase materiality levels.

(3) decrease substantive testing.

(4) increase inherent risk.

DISCUSSION QUESTIONS AND PROBLEMS

9-25 (Objectives 9-2, 9-3, 9-4) You are evaluating audit results for current assets in the audit of Sakim's Manufactured Goods. You set the preliminary judgment about materiality for current assets at US$15,000 for overstatements and at US$22,500 for understatements. The preliminary and actual estimates are shown next.

	Tolerable Misstatement		Estimate of Total Misstatement	
	Over-	Under-	Over-	Under-
Account	statements	statements	statements	statements
Cash	US$ 2,000	US$ 3,000	US$ 1,000	US$
Accounts receivable	10,000	15,000	9,000	8,000
Inventory	15,000	22,000	14,000	5,000
Prepaid expenses	3,000	5,000	2,000	1,000
Total	US$30,000	US$45,000	US$26,000	US$14,000

Required

a. How is it possible to have a lower preliminary judgment about materiality for over-statements than understatements in this situation?

b. Why do the totals of the tolerable misstatements exceed the preliminary judgments about materiality for both understatements and overstatements?

c. How is it possible that three of the estimates of total misstatement have both an over-statement and an understatement?

d. Assume that you are not concerned whether the estimate of misstatement exceeds tolerable misstatement for individual accounts if the total estimate is less than the pre-liminary judgment.
   (1) Given the audit results, should you be more concerned about the existence of material overstatements or understatements at this point in the audit of Sakim's Manufactured Goods?
   (2) Which account or accounts will you be most concerned about in question (1)? Explain.

e. Assume that the estimate of total overstatement amount for each account is less than tolerable misstatement, but that the total overstatement estimate exceeds the prelimi-nary judgment of materiality.
   (1) Explain why this would occur.
   (2) Explain what the auditor should do.

9-26 (Objectives 9-2, 9-3, 9-4) You are evaluating audit results for assets in the audit of Saber Manufacturing. You set the preliminary judgment about materiality at US$50,000. The account balances, tolerable misstatement, and estimated overstatements in the accounts are shown next.

Account	Account Balance	Tolerable Misstatement	Estimate of Total Overstatements
Cash	US$ 50,000	US$ 5,000	US$ 1,000
Accounts receivable	1,200,000	30,000	20,000
Inventory	2,500,000	50,000	?
Other assets	250,000	15,000	12,000
Total	US$4,000,000	US$100,000	?

Required

a. Assume you tested inventory amounts totaling US$1 million and found US$10,000 in overstatements. Ignoring sampling risk, what is your estimate of the total misstate-ment in inventory?

b. Based on the audit of the assets accounts and ignoring other accounts, are the overall financial statements acceptable? Explain.

c. What do you believe the auditor should do in the circumstances?

9-27 (Objectives 9-6, 9-8) Describe what is meant by acceptable audit risk. Explain why each of the following statements is true:

a. An audit firm should attempt to achieve the same audit risk for all audit clients when circumstances are similar.

b. An audit firm should decrease acceptable audit risk for audit clients when external users rely heavily on the statements.

c. An audit firm should decrease acceptable audit risk for audit clients when there is a reasonably high likelihood of a client filing bankruptcy.

d. Different audit firms should attempt to achieve reasonably similar audit risks for cli-ents with similar circumstances.

9-28 (Objectives 9-2, 9-3, 9-4, 9-6, 9-8, 9-9, 9-11) The following are concepts discussed in this chapter:

1. Preliminary judgment about materiality

2. Estimate of the combined misstatement

3. Acceptable audit risk
4. Tolerable misstatement
5. Inherent risk
6. Risk of fraud
7. Estimated total misstatement in a segment

8. Control risk
9. Planned detection risk
10. Risk of material misstatement

a. Identify which items are *audit planning decisions* requiring professional judgment.

Required

b. Identify which items are *audit conclusions* resulting from application of audit procedures and requiring professional judgment.

c. Under what circumstances is it acceptable to change those items in part (a) after the audit is started? Which items can be changed after the audit is 95% completed?

9-29 (Objectives 9-6, 9-11) Using the audit risk model, state the effect on control risk, inherent risk, acceptable audit risk, and planned evidence for each of the following independent events. In each of the events a to j, circle one letter for each of the three independent variables and planned evidence: I = increase, D = decrease, N = no effect, and C = cannot determine from the information provided.

a. The client's management materially increased long-term contractual debt:

| Control risk | I D N C | Acceptable audit risk | I D N C |
| Inherent risk | I D N C | Planned evidence | I D N C |

b. The company changed from a privately held company to a publicly held company:

| Control risk | I D N C | Acceptable audit risk | I D N C |
| Inherent risk | I D N C | Planned evidence | I D N C |

c. The auditor decided to set assessed control risk below maximum (it was previously assessed at maximum):

| Control risk | I D N C | Acceptable audit risk | I D N C |
| Inherent risk | I D N C | Planned evidence | I D N C |

d. The account balance increased materially from the preceding year without apparent reason:

| Control risk | I D N C | Acceptable audit risk | I D N C |
| Inherent risk | I D N C | Planned evidence | I D N C |

e. You determined through the planning phase that working capital, debt-to-equity ratio, and other indicators of financial condition improved during the past year:

| Control risk | I D N C | Acceptable audit risk | I D N C |
| Inherent risk | I D N C | Planned evidence | I D N C |

f. This is the second year of the engagement, and there were a few misstatements found in the previous year's audit. The auditor also decided to increase reliance on internal control:

| Control risk | I D N C | Acceptable audit risk | I D N C |
| Inherent risk | I D N C | Planned evidence | I D N C |

g. The client began selling products online to customers through its web page during the year under audit. The online customer ordering process is not integrated with the company's accounting system. Client sales staff print out customer order information and enter that data into the sales accounting system:

| Control risk | I D N C | Acceptable audit risk | I D N C |
| Inherent risk | I D N C | Planned evidence | I D N C |

h. In discussions with management, you conclude that management is planning to sell the business in the next few months. Because of the planned changes, several key accounting personnel quit several months ago for alternative employment. You also observe that the gross margin percent has significantly increased compared with that of the preceding year:

Control risk	I D N C	Acceptable audit risk	I D N C
Inherent risk	I D N C	Planned evidence	I D N C

i. There has been a change in several key management personnel. You believe that management is somewhat lacking in personal integrity compared with the previous management. You believe it is still appropriate to do the audit:

Control risk	I D N C	Acceptable audit risk	I D N C
Inherent risk	I D N C	Planned evidence	I D N C

j. In auditing inventory, you obtain an understanding of internal control and perform tests of controls. You find it significantly improved compared with that of the preceding year. You also observe that because of technology changes in the industry, the client's inventory may be somewhat obsolete:

Control risk	I D N C	Acceptable audit risk	I D N C
Inherent risk	I D N C	Planned evidence	I D N C

9-30 (Objective 9-6) Below are ten independent risk factors:

1. The client lacks sufficient working capital to continue operations.
2. The client fails to detect employee theft of inventory from the warehouse because there are no restrictions on warehouse access and the client does not reconcile inventory on hand to recorded amounts on a timely basis.
3. The company is publicly traded.
4. The auditor has identified numerous material misstatements during prior-year audit engagements.
5. The assigned staff on the audit engagement lack the necessary skills to identify actual errors in an account balance when examining audit evidence accumulated.
6. The client is one of the industry's largest based on its size and market share.
7. The client engages in several material transactions with entities owned by family members of several of the client's senior executives.
8. The allowance for doubtful accounts is based on significant assumptions made by management.
9. The audit plan omits several necessary audit procedures.
10. The client fails to reconcile bank accounts to recorded cash balances.

Required   Identify which of the following audit risk model components relates most directly to each of the ten risk factors:

- Acceptable audit risk
- Inherent risk
- Control risk
- Planned detection risk

CASE

9-31 (Objectives 9-2, 9-3, 9-4) On the following pages are statements of income and financial position for Nuqul Industries.

Required   a. Use professional judgment in deciding on the preliminary judgment about materiality for earnings, current assets, current liabilities, and total assets. Your conclusions should be stated in terms of percentages and dollars.

b. Assume that you define materiality for this audit as a combined misstatement of earnings from continuing operations before income taxes of 5 percent. Also assume that you believe there is an equal likelihood of a misstatement of every account in the financial statements, and each misstatement is likely to result in an overstatement of earnings. Allocate materiality to these financial statements as you consider appropriate.

c. As discussed in part b, net earnings from continuing operations *before* income taxes was used as a base for calculating materiality for the Nuqul Industries audit. Discuss why most auditors use *before*-tax net earnings instead of *after*-tax net earnings when calculating materiality based on the income statement.

d. Now, assume that you have decided to allocate 75 percent of your preliminary judgment to accounts receivable, inventories, and accounts payable because you believe all other accounts have a low inherent and control risk. How does this affect evidence accumulation on the audit?

e. Assume that you complete the audit and conclude that your preliminary judgment about materiality for current assets, current liabilities, and total assets has been met. The actual estimate of misstatements in earnings exceeds your preliminary judgment. What should you do?

Consolidated Statements of Income
Nuqul Industries (in thousands)

	For the 53 Weeks Ended March 30, 2012	For the 52 Weeks Ended March 31, 2011	April 1, 2010
Revenue			
Net sales	US$8,351,149	US$6,601,255	US$5,959,587
Other income	59,675	43,186	52,418
	8,410,824	6,644,441	6,012,005
Costs and expenses			
Cost of sales	5,197,375	4,005,548	3,675,369
Marketing, general, and administrative expenses	2,590,080	2,119,590	1,828,169
Provision for loss on restructured operations	64,100	—	—
Interest expense	141,662	46,737	38,546
	7,993,217	6,171,875	5,542,084
Income from continuing operations before income taxes	417,607	472,566	469,921
Income taxes	(196,700)	(217,200)	(214,100)
Income from continuing operations	220,907	255,366	255,821
Provision for loss on discontinued operations, net of income taxes	(20,700)	—	—
Net Income	US$ 200,207	US$ 255,366	US$ 255,821

(continued on next page)

Consolidated Statements of Financial Position
Nuqul Industries (in thousands)

Assets	March 30, 2012	March 31, 2011
Current assets		
Cash	US$ 39,683	US$ 37,566
Temporary investments, including time deposits of US$65,361 in 2012 and US$181,589 in 2011 (at cost, which approximates market)	123,421	271,639
Receivables, less allowances of US$16,808 in 2012 and US$17,616 in 2011	899,752	759,001
Inventories		
Finished product	680,974	550,407
Raw materials and supplies	443,175	353,795
	1,124,149	904,202
Deferred income tax benefits	9,633	10,468
Prepaid expenses	57,468	35,911
Current assets	**2,254,106**	**2,018,787**
Land, buildings, and equipment, at cost, less accumulated depreciation	1,393,902	1,004,455
Investments in affiliated companies and sundry assets	112,938	83,455
Goodwill and other intangible assets	99,791	23,145
Total	**US$3,860,737**	**US$3,129,842**

Liabilities and Stockholders' Equity	March 30, 2012	March 31, 2011
Current liabilities		
Notes payable	US$ 280,238	US$ 113,411
Current portion of long-term debt	64,594	12,336
Accounts and drafts payable	359,511	380,395
Accrued salaries, wages, and vacations	112,200	63,557
Accrued income taxes	76,479	89,151
Other accrued liabilities	321,871	269,672
Current liabilities	**1,214,893**	**928,522**
Long-term debt	**730,987**	**390,687**
Other noncurrent liabilities	**146,687**	**80,586**
Deferred income taxes	**142,344**	**119,715**
Stockholders' equity		
Common stock issued, 51,017,755 shares in 2012 and 50,992,410 in 2011	51,018	50,992
Additional paid-in capital	149,177	148,584
Cumulative foreign currency translation adjustment	(76,572)	—
Retained earnings	1,554,170	1,462,723
Common stock held in treasury, at cost, 1,566,598 shares	(51,967)	(51,967)
Stockholders' equity	**1,625,826**	**1,610,332**
Total	**US$3,860,737**	**US$3,129,842**

MYLAB ACTIVITY

Visit MyAccountingLab and complete the following activity:

→ Integrated Case Application: Pinnacle Manufacturing: Part II

INTERNAL CONTROL AND CONTROL RISK

AED 49m Mizin Corruption Case Referred to Court

An auditor discovered while checking accounts that a Lebanese businessman who bought land from property developer Mizin was allegedly given higher discounts than other customers. Tatweer auditor, Mustafa Ramadan, said he was examining the accounts of Mizin's Remraam project when he noticed that the businessman, JH, was given discounts of 3 percent while other buyers received just 2 percent. JH allegedly bought land for AED 120 (approximately US$33) per square foot for which he should have paid AED 150 (approximately US$41). Another plot of land was sold to him for AED 145 (approximately US$39) per square foot while the set price was AED 155 (approximately US$42).

Ramadan told Dubai Criminal Court that the sale contracts were allegedly approved and signed by former Mizin CEO, SH.

Dubai Public Prosecution has charged SH with accepting illegal gifts, harming the company's interests, and facilitating the transfer of company funds to an unauthorized person. Mizin is said to have lost AED 22 million (approximately US$6million) because of the alleged special arrangements made for JH.

Ramadan said the payment period for JH was extended to four years from two-and-a-half years. In violation of Mizin policy, the company allegedly split one plot of land into two parts to enable SH to sell it more quickly.

The court allowed JH to ask Ramadan why there had been no offers for 25 out of the 60 plots belonging to Mizin. Ramadan attributed the lack of offers to the absence of a clear policy on the part of the sales managers of Mizin.

Mizin is part of Tatweer, which is in turn owned by Dubai Holding. Ramadan was asked which party gave instructions to Mizin. He replied that Dubai Holding set the strategy as the owner company while Tatweer drew up policy. Mizin operated in line with the strategy and policy. Asked whether Tatweer had the right to monitor Mizin, he said it did, adding that Tatweer halted the land sales in 2007 pending the completion of the audit and a review.

Source: M. Elsidafy, 'Auditor testifies in Mizin financial fraud case,' Emirates24|7 News, August 17, 2009 (http://www.emirates247.com/eb247/news/national/auditor-testifies-in-mizin-financial-fraud-case-2009-08-17-1.30038).

LEARNING OBJECTIVES

After studying this chapter, you should be able to

10-1 Describe the three primary objectives of effective internal control.

10-2 Contrast management's responsibilities for maintaining internal control with the auditor's responsibilities for evaluating and reporting on internal control.

10-3 Explain the five components of the COSO internal control framework.

10-4 Obtain and document an understanding of internal control.

10-5 Assess control risk by linking key controls and control deficiencies to transaction-related audit objectives.

10-6 Describe the process of designing and performing tests of controls.

10-7 Understand the requirements of Section 404 of the U.S. Sarbanes–Oxley Act for auditor reporting on internal control.

10-8 Describe the differences in evaluating, reporting, and testing internal control for nonpublic companies.

The opening story involving Mizin demonstrates how deficiencies in internal control related to the sale and pricing of lands can cause significant losses resulting in material misstatements in financial statements. In the U.S., financial reporting problems at companies such as Enron and WorldCom also exposed serious deficiencies in internal control. To address these concerns auditing standards and the U.S. Sarbanes–Oxley Act (Section 404) require auditors of U.S. public companies to assess and report on the effectiveness of internal control over financial reporting, in addition to their report on the audit of the financial statements. In Arab countries, internal controls are assessed as part of the auditors forming their opinion about the company's financial statements.

This is the third chapter dealing with planning the audit. It shows how effective internal controls can reduce planned audit evidence in the audit of financial statements. To support the assessment of the control risk component of the audit risk model (i.e. risk that the internal control system may fail to present or detect material misstatements), auditors must obtain an understanding of internal control and gather evidence to support that assessment. The chart in the margin (on page 315) shows where these tasks fit into planning the audit. Most of the chapter describes how public company auditors integrate evidence to provide a basis for their report on the effectiveness of internal control over financial reporting with the assessment of control risk in the financial statement audit. The end of the chapter identifies and discusses the differences in assessing control risk and testing controls for nonpublic companies compared to public companies. By the end of the chapter, you will see that there are more similarities than differences in the two approaches.

Relevant International Standards on Auditing and other Accounting and Auditing Pronouncements	
COSO	Internal Control - Integrated Framework, 1992
COSO	Enterprise Risk Management — Integrated Framework, 2004
COSO	Guidance on Monitoring Internal Control Systems, 2009
ISA 230	Audit Documentation
ISA 250	Consideration of Laws and Regulations in an Audit of Financial Statements
ISA 265	Communicating Deficiencies in Internal Control to Those Charged with Governance and Management
ISA 315	Identifying and Assessing the Risks of Material Misstatement through Understanding the Entity and Its Environment

INTERNAL CONTROL OBJECTIVES

OBJECTIVE 10-1

Describe the three primary objectives of effective internal control.

A system of internal control consists of policies and procedures designed to provide management with reasonable assurance that the company achieves its objectives and goals in an efficient and effective way. These policies and procedures are often called controls, and collectively, they make up the entity's **internal control**. Management typically has three broad objectives in designing an effective internal control system:

1. *Reliability of financial reporting.* As we discussed in Chapter 6, management is responsible for preparing financial statements for investors, creditors, and other users. Management has both a legal and professional responsibility to be sure that the information is fairly presented in accordance with reporting requirements such as IFRS, GAAP, or other local accounting standards. The objective of effective internal control over financial reporting is to fulfill these financial reporting responsibilities.

2. *Efficiency and effectiveness of operations.* Controls within a company encourage efficient and effective use of its resources to optimize the company's goals. An important objective of these controls is accurate financial and nonfinancial information about the company's operations for decision making.

3. *Compliance with laws and regulations.* The auditing standards require auditors to ensure that management comply with laws and regulations governing the company's activities. For example, auditors need to ensure that management before distributing dividends made all necessary provisions for receivables and other debit account balances. In the U.S., Section 404 of the Sarbanes–Oxley Act includes more strict requirements for internal control reporting compared with auditing standards. Section 404 requires all public companies in the U.S. to issue a report about the operating effectiveness of internal control over financial reporting. In addition to the legal provisions of Section 404, public, non-public, and not-for-profit organizations are required to follow many laws and regulations. Some relate to accounting only indirectly, such as environmental protection and civil rights laws. Others are closely related to accounting, such as income tax regulations and anti-fraud legal provisions.

See Figure 10-1 for an example of a management report on internet control over financial reporting.

In Arab countries, there is a continued need for auditors to be fully aware of the requirements of Section 404 of the Sarbanes–Oxley Act in relation to evaluating the effectiveness of internal controls. Non-U.S. auditors are involved in assisting multinational companies with subsidiaries in many of the Arab countries to comply with the requirements of the Sarbanes–Oxley Act. A large number of non-U.S. companies are registered and required to file reports with the U.S. Securities and Exchange Commission (SEC). The current situation in most Arab countries is that auditors assess a company's

Internal control

A process designed to provide reasonable assurance regarding the achievement of management's objectives in the following categories: (1) reliability of financial reporting, (2) effectiveness and efficiency of operations, and (3) compliance with applicable laws and regulations.

| FIGURE 10-1 | **Example of Management's Report on Internal Control over Financial Reporting** |

Management is responsible for establishing and maintaining adequate internal control over financial reporting of the company. Internal control over financial reporting is a process designed to provide reasonable assurance regarding the reliability of financial reporting and the preparation of financial statements for external purposes in accordance with accounting principles generally accepted in the United States of America.

The company's internal control over financial reporting includes those policies and procedures that (i) pertain to the maintenance of records that, in reasonable detail, accurately and fairly reflect the transactions and dispositions of the assets of the company; (ii) provide reasonable assurance that transactions are recorded as necessary to permit preparation of financial statements in accordance with accounting principles generally accepted in the United States of America, and that receipts and expenditures of the company are being made only in accordance with authorizations of management and directors of the company; and (iii) provide reasonable assurance regarding prevention or timely detection of unauthorized acquisition, and use of disposition of the company's assets that could have a material effect on the financial statements.

Because of its inherent limitations, internal control over financial reporting may not prevent or detect misstatements. Also projections of any evaluation of effectiveness to future periods are subject to the risk that controls may become inadequate because of changes in conditions, or that the degree of compliance with the policies or procedures may deteriorate.

Management conducted an evaluation of the effectiveness of internal control over financial reporting based on the framework in *Internal Control - Integrated Framework* issued by the Committee of Sponsoring Organizations of the Treadway Commission (COSO). Based on this evaluation, management concluded that the company's internal control over financial reporting was effective as of December 31, 2008.

Samuel J. Palmisano
Chairman of the board.
President and Chief Executive Officer
February 24, 2009

Mark Loughridge
Senior Vice President.
Chief Financial President
February 24, 2009

internal controls as part of their responsibility to form an opinion about the company's financial statements. No separate report is prepared for the results of assessing internal controls over financial reporting like in the U.S.

It is important that students understand the requirements of Section 404 as it is expected that ISAs will include similar requirements as Section 404 in the near future.

MANAGEMENT AND AUDITOR RESPONSIBILITIES FOR INTERNAL CONTROL

OBJECTIVE 10-2

Contrast management's responsibilities for maintaining internal control with the auditor's responsibilities for evaluating and reporting on internal control.

Responsibilities for internal controls differ between management and the auditor. Management is responsible for establishing and maintaining the entity's internal controls. The reporting of management on the design and effectiveness of the internal control depends on the regulations and accounting standards governing the preparation of the public versus nonpublic companies' financial statements. In the U.S., management of public companies is required by Section 404 to publicly report on the operating effectiveness of the internal controls. In contrast, the auditor's responsibilities include understanding and testing internal control over financial reporting. The auditor is also required by Section 404 to issue an audit report on the operating effectiveness of those controls for public companies. The independent reporting responsibility of the auditor over internal control does not exist in many Arab countries. Even though ISAs have expanded the auditor's responsibility to examine internal control and communicate deficiencies in the internal control system during the financial statement audit, auditors are not required to independently express an opinion on the effectiveness of Internal Control over Financial Reporting (ICFR). In case auditors are required to report on ICFR, they should perform their examination in accordance with the International Standards on assurance engagements.

Management's Responsibilities for Establishing Internal Control

Management, not the auditor, must establish and maintain the entity's internal controls. This concept is consistent with the requirement that management, not the auditor, is responsible for the preparation of financial statements in accordance with IFRS, GAAP, or local accounting standards. Two key concepts underlie management's design and implementation of internal control—reasonable assurance and inherent limitations.

Reasonable Assurance A company should develop internal controls that provide reasonable, but not absolute, assurance that the financial statements are fairly stated. Internal controls are developed by management after considering both the costs and benefits of the controls. The concept of reasonable assurance allows for only a remote likelihood that material misstatements will not be prevented or detected on a timely basis by internal control. For example, if the auditor properly assesses the risk associated with internal control and performs tests of such control in accordance with the requirements of ISAs 315 and 265, the auditor is not responsible for the complete assurance that such controls will prevent and detect errors and fraud in the company's accounts and transactions.

Inherent Limitations Internal controls can never be completely effective, regardless of the care followed in their design and implementation. Even if systems personnel can design an ideal system, its effectiveness depends on the competency and dependability of the people using it. Assume, for example, that a carefully developed procedure for counting inventory requires two employees to count independently. If neither of the employees understands the instructions or if both are careless in doing the counts, the inventory count is likely to be wrong. Even if the count is correct, management might override the procedure and instruct an employee to increase the count to improve reported earnings. Similarly, the employees might decide to overstate the counts to intentionally cover up a theft of inventory by one or both of them. An act of two or more employees who conspire to steal assets or misstate records is called **collusion**.

Management's Section 404 Reporting Responsibilities

In the U.S., Section 404 of the Sarbanes–Oxley Act requires management of all public companies to issue an internal control report that includes the following:

- A statement that management is responsible for establishing and maintaining an adequate internal control structure and procedures for financial reporting
- An assessment of the effectiveness of the internal control structure and procedures for financial reporting as of the end of the company's fiscal year

Management must also identify the framework used to evaluate the effectiveness of internal control. The internal control framework used by most U.S. companies is the Committee of Sponsoring Organizations of the Treadway Commission (COSO) *Internal Control - Integrated Framework*. Other internal control frameworks exist around the world, such as the United Kingdom's *Internal Control: Guidance for Directors on the Combined Code* (known as the Turnbull Report) and Canada's *Guidance on Assessing Control* (known as 'CoCo'). In the Arab countries, COSO is the framework applied by the manager of the business to design and evaluate internal controls.

Management's assessment of internal control over financial reporting consists of two key components. First, management must evaluate the *design* of internal control over financial reporting. Second, management must test the *operating effectiveness* of those controls.

Design of Internal Control Management must evaluate whether the controls are designed and put in place to prevent or detect material misstatements in the financial statements. Management's focus is on controls that address risks related to all relevant assertions for all significant accounts and disclosures in the financial statements. This includes evaluating how significant transactions are initiated, authorized, recorded, processed, and reported to identify points in the flow of transactions where material misstatements due to error or fraud could occur.

Operating Effectiveness of Controls In addition, management must test the operating effectiveness of controls. The testing objective is to determine whether the controls are operating as designed and whether the person performing the control possesses the necessary authority and qualifications to perform the control effectively. Management must disclose any material weakness in internal control. Even if only one material weakness is present, management must conclude that the company's internal control over financial reporting is not effective.

In the U.S., the SEC requires management to include its report on internal control in its annual set of SEC filings (i.e. Form 10-K report) with the SEC. Figure 10-2 includes an example of a management's report on internal control that complies with Section 404 requirements and related SEC rules.

Auditor Responsibilities for Understanding Internal Control

Auditing standards require that the auditor must obtain a sufficient understanding of the entity and its environment, *including its internal control*, to assess the risk of material misstatement of the financial statements whether due to error or fraud and to determine the nature, timing, and extent of substantive audit procedures (ISA 315).

FIGURE 10-2   **Example Section 404 Management Report on Internal Control Over Financial Reporting**

The management of Marble Corporation is responsible for establishing and maintaining adequate internal control over financial reporting. Marble's internal control system was designed to provide reasonable assurance to the company's management and board of directors regarding the preparation and fair presentation of published financial statements.

Marble management assessed the effectiveness of the company's internal control over financial reporting as of December 31, 2009. In making this assessment, it used the criteria set forth by the Committee of Sponsoring Organizations of the Treadway Commission (COSO) in *Internal Control - Integrated Framework*. Based on our assessment, we believe that, as of December 31, 2009, the company's internal control over financial reporting is effective based on those criteria.

Marble's independent auditors have issued an audit report on our assessment of the company's internal control over financial reporting. This report appears on the following page.

February 15, 2010

Fred Narsky, President   Karen Wilson, Chief Financial Officer

---

The auditor obtains the understanding of internal control to assess control risk in every audit. Auditors are primarily concerned about controls over the reliability of financial reporting and controls over classes of transactions.

Controls Over the Reliability of Financial Reporting Financial statements are not likely to correctly reflect the accounting standard framework if internal controls over financial reporting are inadequate. Unlike the client, the auditor is less concerned with controls that affect the efficiency and effectiveness of company operations, because such controls may not influence the fair presentation of financial statements. Auditors should not, however, ignore controls affecting internal management information, such as budgets and internal performance reports. These types of information are often important sources used by management to run the business and can be important sources of evidence that help the auditor decide whether the financial statements are fairly presented. If the controls over these internal reports are inadequate, the value of the reports as evidence diminishes.

Controls over Classes of Transactions Auditors emphasize internal control over classes of transactions rather than account balances because the accuracy of accounting system outputs (account balances) depends heavily on the accuracy of inputs and processing (transactions). For example, if products sold, units shipped, or unit selling prices are wrong in billing customers for sales, both sales and accounts receivable will be misstated. On the other hand, if controls are adequate to ensure correct billings, cash receipts, sales returns and allowances, and write-offs, the ending balance in accounts receivable is likely to be correct. Because of the emphasis on classes of transactions, auditors are primarily concerned with the transaction-related audit objectives discussed in Chapter 6 when assessing internal controls over financial reporting. Table 10-1 illustrates the development of transaction-related audit objectives for sales transactions.

Even though auditors emphasize transaction-related controls, the auditor must also gain an understanding of controls over ending account balance and presentation and disclosure objectives.

Auditor Responsibilities for Testing Internal Control

Auditing standards require the auditor to assess the effectiveness of internal control over financial reporting when reporting on the company's financial statements. To assess the effectiveness of these controls, the auditor obtains an understanding of and performs

TABLE 10-1	Sales Transaction-Related Audit Objectives
Transaction-Related Audit Objective—General Form	**Sales Transaction-Related Audit Objectives**
Recorded transactions exist (occurrence).	Recorded sales are for shipments made to existing customers.
Existing transactions are recorded (completeness).	Existing sales transactions are recorded.
Recorded transactions are stated at the correct amounts (accuracy).	Recorded sales are for the amount of goods shipped and are correctly billed and recorded.
Recorded transactions are correctly included in the master files and are correctly summarized (posting and summarization).	Sales transactions are correctly included in the master files and are correctly summarized.
Transactions are correctly classified (classification).	Sales transactions are correctly classified.
Transactions are recorded on the correct dates (timing).	Sales are recorded on the correct dates.
Transactions are the rights of the company (rights and obligations).	The company has rights for the amounts of sales made.

tests of controls for all significant account balances, classes of transactions, and disclosures and related assertions in the financial statements. We will discuss tests of controls later in the chapter and in considerable detail in several other chapters throughout the text. Auditor reporting on internal control is also discussed later in the chapter.

COSO COMPONENTS OF INTERNAL CONTROL

COSO's *Internal Control - Integrated Framework* is the most widely accepted internal control framework in the United States, and in many other countries including Arab countries such as Lebanon, Jordan, Bahrain, Kuwait, United Arab Emirates, and Egypt. It describes five components of internal control that management designs and implements to provide reasonable assurance that its control objectives will be met. Each component contains many controls, but auditors concentrate on those designed to prevent or detect material misstatements in the financial statements. The COSO internal control components include the following:

1. Control environment
2. Risk assessment
3. Control activities
4. Information and communication
5. Monitoring

As illustrated in Figure 10-3, the control environment serves as the umbrella for the other four components. Without an effective control environment, the other four are unlikely to result in effective internal control, regardless of their quality.

FIGURE 10-3	Five Components of Internal Control

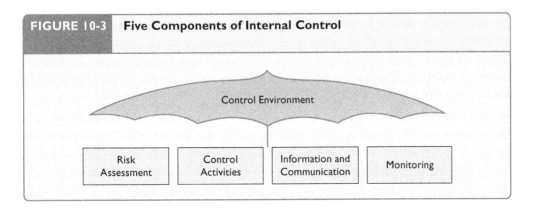

The Control Environment

The essence of an effectively controlled organization lies in the attitude of its management. If top management believes that control is important, others in the organization will sense this commitment and respond by conscientiously observing the controls established. If members of the organization believe that control is not an important concern to top management, it is almost certain that management's control objectives will not be effectively achieved.

Control environment

The actions, policies, and procedures that reflect the overall attitudes of top management, directors, and owners of an entity about internal control and its importance to the entity.

The **control environment** consists of the actions, policies, and procedures that reflect the overall attitudes of top management, directors, and owners of an entity about internal control and its importance to the entity. To understand and assess the control environment, auditors should consider the most important control subcomponents.

Integrity and Ethical Values Integrity and ethical values are the product of the entity's ethical and behavioral standards, as well as how they are communicated and reinforced in practice. They include management's actions to remove or reduce incentives and temptations that might prompt personnel to engage in dishonest, illegal, or unethical acts. They also include the communication of entity values and behavioral standards to personnel through policy statements, codes of conduct, and by example.

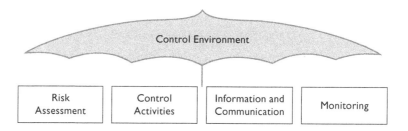

Commitment to Competence Competence is the knowledge and skills necessary to accomplish tasks that define an individual's job. Commitment to competence includes management's consideration of the competence levels for specific jobs and how those levels translate into requisite skills and knowledge.

Board of Directors or Audit Committee Participation The board of directors is essential for effective corporate governance because it has ultimate responsibility to make sure management implements proper internal control and financial reporting processes. An effective board of directors is independent of management, and its members stay involved in and scrutinize management's activities. Although the board delegates responsibility for internal control to management, it must regularly assess these controls. In addition, an active and objective board can reduce the likelihood that management overrides existing controls.

NEED TO ENSURE EFFECTIVENESS OF AUDIT COMMITTEES IN THE ARAB WORLD

A member of the audit committee in a top mortgage company said in a private interview that the committee failed to replace the company's auditors for a period exceeding five years. During that period, the auditor did not submit any management letter showing the results of his audit of both the company's internal control and the financial statements. Even though several members of the audit committee were convinced that there was a need to replace the external auditor due to his inability to provide a high quality audit in accordance with acceptable auditing standards, the decision was not made because the principal partner in the audit firm was a member of both the Central Bank as well as the governing body organizing the mortgage sector in the Arab country. This example of inefficient functioning of an audit committee confirms the need for more development in the control and supervision over the operations and roles of the audit committee in many Arab countries.

To assist the board in its oversight, the board creates an audit committee that is charged with oversight responsibility for financial reporting. The audit committee is also responsible for maintaining ongoing communication with both external and internal auditors, including the approval of audit and nonaudit services done by auditors for public companies. This allows the auditors and directors to discuss matters that might relate to such things as management integrity or the appropriateness of actions taken by management.

The audit committee's independence from management and knowledge of financial reporting issues are important determinants of its ability to effectively evaluate internal controls and financial statements prepared by management. All major stock exchanges require that listed companies have an audit committee composed entirely of independent directors who are financially literate. In the U.S., PCAOB Standard 5 requires explicitly that the auditor evaluate the effectiveness of the audit committee's oversight of the company's external financial reporting and internal control over financial reporting. No similar requirements for the assessment of the audit committee oversight responsibilities exist in Arab countries yet.

Many privately held companies also create an effective audit committee. For other privately held companies, governance may be provided by owners, partners, trustees, or a committee of management, such as finance or budget committee. Figure 10-4 shows the elements as set out by Hawkamah (the Institute for Corporate Governance in the United Arab Emirates). Individuals responsible for overseeing the strategic direction of the entity and the accountability of the entity, including financial reporting and disclosure, are called **those charged with governance** by auditing standards.

Those charged with governance

The person(s) with responsibility for overseeing the strategic direction of the entity and its obligations related to the accountability of the entity, including overseeing the financial reporting and disclosure process.

Management's Philosophy and Operating Style   Management, through its activities, provides clear signals to employees about the importance of internal control. For example, does management take significant risks, or is it risk averse? Are sales and earnings targets unrealistic, and are employees encouraged to take aggressive actions to meet those targets? Can management be described as 'fat and bureaucratic,' 'lean and mean,' dominated by one or a few individuals, or is it 'just right'? Understanding these and similar aspects of management's philosophy and operating style gives the auditor a sense of management's attitude about internal control.

Organizational Structure   The entity's organizational structure defines the existing lines of responsibility and authority. By understanding the client's organizational structure, the auditor can learn the management and functional elements of the business and

FIGURE 10-4   Corporate Governance in U.A.E.

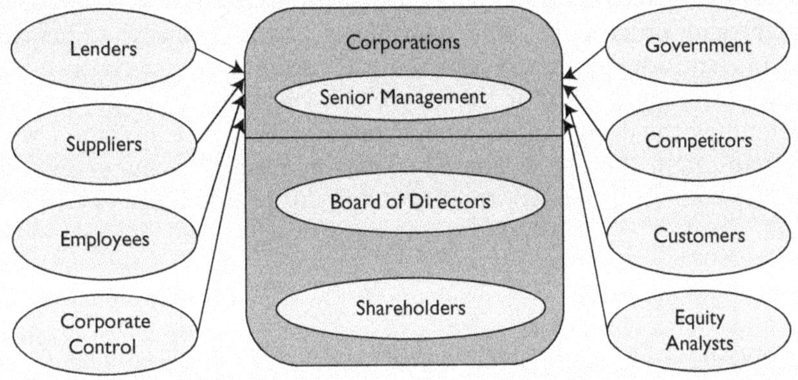

Hawkamah, U.A.E. Regulatory Requirements

CORPORATE GOVERNANCE IN MIDDLE EAST AND NORTH AFRICA

Hawkamah (the Institute for Corporate Governance) and the International Finance Corporation (the private-sector arm of the World Bank Group) have published a comprehensive study of corporate governance in the MENA region. The study reveals that a majority of participating banks and listed companies are unable to properly define corporate governance. What's more, only 3 percent follow good practice and none follows best practice, while 56 percent of boards have no more than one independent director, a situation that makes proper oversight difficult, according to the study.

The report outlines several ways that good corporate governance can benefit companies, including achieving a higher long-term return on investment, better protection of shareholder rights and greater access to capital at a lower cost.

Among the most significant findings and recommendations:

- The 42.3 percent of companies that still combine the function of chairman and CEO should separate these roles to comply with best practice.

- According to the study, only 25 percent of banks and listed firms provide information on their dividend policies online and just 12 percent have online information on key executives' remuneration.
- Most respondents view disclosure from a compliance point of view, rather than see it as an effective tool for managing stakeholder relations and adding value to their business.
- Only 50 percent of listed family-owned enterprises (FOEs) had adopted a family constitution, while only 25 percent had family councils in place. Three-quarters of FOEs said their boards are composed of a majority of family members.

Source: Adapted from 'Report from Hawkamah and IFC Outlines Scope for Improvement in MENA Corporate Governance,' Hawkamah website, accessed at http://www.hawkamah.org/publications/IFC/.

---

perceive how controls are implemented. An example of poor organizational structure would be if the managing director supervises more than five to seven divisions headed by a similar number of managers; it is expected that his ability to observe malpractices would be affected significantly, allowing for such malpractices to occur without being detected.

Human Resource Policies and Practices The most important aspect of internal control is personnel. If employees are competent and trustworthy, other controls can be absent, and reliable financial statements will still result. Incompetent or dishonest people can ruin the whole system—even if there are numerous controls in place. Honest, efficient people are able to perform at a high level even when there are few other controls to support them. However, even competent and trustworthy people can have shortcomings. For example, they can become bored or dissatisfied, personal problems can disrupt their performance, or their goals may change.

Because of the importance of competent, trustworthy personnel in providing effective control, the methods by which persons are hired, evaluated, trained, promoted, and compensated are an important part of internal control.

After obtaining information about each of the subcomponents of the control environment, the auditor uses this understanding as a basis for assessing management's and directors' attitudes and awareness about the importance of control. For example, the auditor might determine the nature of a client's budgeting system as a part of understanding the design of the control environment. The operation of the budgeting system might then be evaluated in part by inquiry of budgeting personnel to determine budgeting procedures and follow-up of differences between budget and actual.

Risk assessment

Management's identification and analysis of risks relevant to the preparation of financial statements in accordance with generally accepted accounting principles.

Risk Assessment

Risk assessment for financial reporting is management's identification and analysis of risks relevant to the preparation of financial statements in conformity with IFRS, GAAP, or other local accounting standards. For example, if a company frequently sells products at a price below inventory cost because of rapid technology changes, it is essential for the company to incorporate adequate controls to address the risk of overstating inventory. Similarly, failure to meet prior objectives, quality of personnel, geographic dispersion of company operations, significance and complexity of core business processes, introduction of new information technologies, and entrance of new competitors are examples of factors that may lead to increased risk. Also, once management identifies a risk, it estimates the significance of that risk, assesses the likelihood of the risk occurring, and develops specific actions that need to be taken to reduce the risk to an acceptable level. Of course, there is no cost-beneficial way to eliminate risk entirely.

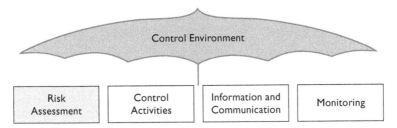

For example, in case of financial crises affecting the world economy or a country economic system, management must assess the impact of such crises on the company's sales, supply of raw materials and their prices, profitability, leverage and the ability of the company to maintain its stream of current cash flows. Management must respond to the effect of the above risk factors on the company ability to continue in existence and the need to show a fair presentation of the company's financial results and financial position.

Management's risk assessment differs from but is closely related to the auditor's risk assessment discussed in Chapter 9. While management assesses risks as a part of designing and operating internal controls to minimize errors and fraud, auditors assess risks to decide the evidence needed in the audit. If management effectively assesses and responds to risks, the auditor will typically accumulate less evidence than when management fails to identify or respond to significant risks.

Auditors obtain knowledge about management's risk assessment process using questionnaires and discussions with management to determine how management identifies risks relevant to financial reporting, evaluates the significance and likelihood of the risks occurring, and decides the actions needed to address the risks.

Control Activities

Control activities are the policies and procedures, in addition to those included in the other four control components, that help ensure that necessary actions are taken to address risks to the achievement of the entity's objectives. There are potentially many such control activities in any entity, including both manual and automated controls. The control activities generally fall into the following five types, which are discussed next:

1. Adequate separation of duties
2. Proper authorization of transactions and activities
3. Adequate documents and records
4. Physical control over assets and records
5. Independent checks on performance

Control activities

Policies and procedures, in addition to those included in the other four components of internal control, that help ensure that necessary actions are taken to address risks in the achievement of the entity's objectives; they typically include the following five specific control activities: (1) adequate separation of duties, (2) proper authorization of transactions and activities, (3) adequate documents and records, (4) physical control over assets and records, and (5) independent checks on performance.

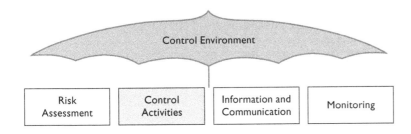

Separation of duties

Separation of the following activities in an organization: (1) custody of assets from accounting, (2) authorization from custody of assets, (3) operational responsibility from record keeping, and (4) IT duties from outside users of IT.

Adequate Separation of Duties Four general guidelines for adequate **separation of duties** to prevent both fraud and errors are especially significant for auditors.

Separation of the Custody of Assets from Accounting To protect a company from embezzlement, a person who has temporary or permanent custody of an asset should not account for that asset. Allowing one person to perform both functions increases the risk of that person disposing of the asset for personal gain and adjusting the records to cover up the theft. If the cashier, for example, receives cash and is responsible for data entry for cash receipts and sales, that person could pocket the cash received and adjust the customer's account by failing to record a sale or by recording a fictitious credit to the account.

Separation of the Authorization of Transactions from the Custody of Related Assets To reduce the likelihood of embezzlement, members of staff who authorize transactions should not also have control over the related asset. For example, the same person should not authorize the payment of a vendor's invoice and then sign the check in settlement of the invoice. A sales manager who authorizes the sale of merchandise to a customer should not be allowed to accept the customer's check in payment.

Separation of Operational Responsibility from Record-Keeping Responsibility To ensure unbiased information, record keeping is typically included in a separate department under the controller. For example, if a department or division prepares its own records and reports, it might change the results to improve its reported performance.

Separation of IT Duties from User Departments As the level of complexity of IT systems increases, the separation of authorization, record keeping, and custody often becomes blurred. For example, sales agents may enter customer orders online. The computer authorizes those sales based on its comparison of customer credit limits to the master file and posts all approved sales in the sales cycle journals. Therefore, the computer plays a significant role in the authorization and record keeping of sales transactions. To compensate for these potential overlaps of duties, it is important for companies to separate major IT-related functions from key user department functions. In this example, responsibility for designing and controlling accounting software programs that contain the sales authorization and posting controls should be under the authority of IT, whereas the ability to update information in the master file of customer credit limits should reside in the company's credit department outside the IT function.

COSO ENTERPRISE RISK MANAGEMENT— INTEGRATED FRAMEWORK

An increased concern and focus on risk management illustrated the need for a framework to identify, assess, and manage risk. As a result, COSO issued *Enterprise Risk Management – Integrated Framework* to expand on internal control to provide key risk management principles and concepts, as well as direction and guidance for management.

Companies exist to provide value for stakeholders, and also face uncertainty in their attempts to grow stakeholder value. A challenge for management is to determine how much uncertainty to accept, and how to effectively deal with uncertainty and associated risks. Enterprise risk management encompasses:

- Aligning risk appetite and strategy
- Enhancing risk response decisions

- Reducing operational surprises and losses
- Identifying and managing multiple and cross enterprise risks
- Seizing opportunities
- Improving deployment of capital

Risk management is an ongoing process applied across all levels of the enterprise. Effective risk management can help management achieve its strategic objectives, while avoiding pitfalls and surprises.

Source: *Enterprise Risk Management – Integrated Framework*, Executive Summary, Committee of Sponsoring Organizations of the Treadway Commission, 2004 & 2007.

Proper Authorization of Transactions and Activities Every transaction must be properly authorized if controls are to be satisfactory. If any person in an organization could acquire or dispose of assets at will, complete chaos would result. Authorization can be either general or specific. Under **general authorization**, management establishes policies and subordinates are instructed to implement these general authorizations by approving all transactions within the limits set by the policy. General authorization decisions include the issuance of fixed price lists for the sale of products, credit limits for customers, and fixed reorder points for making acquisitions. General authorizations are found in the company's various operating manuals such as financial, sales and acquisition, and warehousing manuals. These operating manuals are prepared and implemented at the establishment of the company's activities and are updated with any change in the company's policies and operating instructions. Management is required to adhere to requirements of those manuals especially in relation to various authorizations of the company's transactions.

General authorization

Companywide policies for the approval of all transactions within stated limits.

Specific authorization applies to individual transactions. For certain transactions, management prefers to authorize each transaction. An example is the authorization of the board of directors for the chairman to sign a loan contract needed for the company's operations. Another example is the authorization of a sales transaction by the sales manager for a used-car company (i.e. specific authorization for the sale of a specific asset of the company).

Specific authorization

Case-by-case approval of transactions not covered by companywide policies.

The distinction between authorization and approval is also important. Authorization is a policy decision for either a general class of transactions (i.e. the credit manager authorizes the sale to a client after checking his credit limit) or specific transactions (i.e. the board of directors authorizes the sale of one of the company's assets). Approval is the implementation of management's general authorization decisions. An example of a general authorization is management setting a policy authorizing the ordering of inventory when less than a three-week supply is on hand. When a department orders inventory, the clerk responsible for maintaining the perpetual record approves the order to indicate that the authorization policy has been met. In other cases, the computer approves the transactions by comparing quantities of inventory on hand to a master file of reorder points and automatically submits purchase orders to authorized suppliers in the vendor master file. In this case, the computer is performing the approval function using preauthorized information contained in the master files.

NOT SURPRISING... THE PRIME MINISTER OVERRIDES TENDER PROCEDURES

Even though the Egyptian tender law requires that all purchases using public funds must be made after such purchases have been put out to tender and bids for the tender have been received, the Prime Minister overrode such procedures when putchasing registered vehicles plates during the period 2006–2010. The direct purchase order made with a German company cost €92 million (each plastic plate cost EGP 40). The Egyptian prosecutor found that a bid had been made by a local Egyptian company at 50 percent of the price agreed with the German company (i.e. EGP 20). Another company had offered to build a factory to produce the plates without any capital expenditure by the Government except for the purchase price of the plates. This situation resulted in a total loss to Egyptian public funds of EGP 100 million or €46 million.

The Prime Minister approved the purchase of the plates using the authority allowing him to make such a decision in cases of urgency. To the prosecutor's surprise, the matter appeared not to be that urgent as the procedures for contracting with the German company were delayed for more than a year after the Prime Minister approved the purchase. The prosecutor claimed that the Minister of Finance, Dr Youssef Ghali, owned shares in the German company and the plates were sold to Egyptian drivers at EGP 135 per plate. The above misappropriation of government public funds confirms that the overriding of internal control procedures can be found in all sectors and industries as well as all levels of management as long as there are some financial benefits to the parties involved in the fraud.

Source: Translated and adapted from *Al Masry Al Youm*, No 2493 & 2494, Monday April 11, 2011 and Tuesday April 12, 2011, page 5, and *El-Shorouk Newspaper*, Tuesday April 12, 2011, page 6.

Adequate Documents and Records Documents and records are the records upon which transactions are entered and summarized. They include such diverse items as sales invoices, purchase orders, subsidiary records, sales journals, and employee time cards. Many of these documents and records are maintained in electronic rather than paper formats. Adequate documents are essential for correct recording of transactions and control of assets. For example, if the receiving department completes an electronic receiving report when material is received, the accounts payable computer application can verify the quantity and description on the vendor's invoice by comparing it with the information on the receiving report, with exceptions resolved by the accounts payable department.

Certain principles dictate the proper design and use of documents and records. Documents and records should be:

- Prenumbered consecutively to facilitate control over missing documents and as an aid in locating documents when they are needed at a later date. Prenumbered documents are important for the completeness transaction-related audit objective.
- Prepared at the time a transaction takes place, or as soon as possible thereafter, to minimize timing errors.
- Designed for multiple use, when possible, to minimize the number of different forms. For example, a properly designed and used shipping document can be the basis for releasing goods from storage to the shipping department, informing billing of the quantity of goods to bill to the customer and the appropriate billing date, and updating the perpetual inventory records.
- Constructed in a manner that encourages correct preparation. This can be done by providing internal checks within the form or record. For example, a document might include instructions for proper routing, blank spaces for authorizations and approvals, and designated column spaces for numerical data.

When transaction data are entered online into the computer, the design of the input screen is important to minimize errors and to improve efficiencies in the input process. For example, automatic prompts that provide instructional messages assist input personnel in identifying information needed for input. Similarly, screen controls can validate the information entered, such as when an invalid general ledger account number is automatically rejected when the account number does not match the chart of accounts master file.

A control closely related to documents and records is the **chart of accounts**, which classifies transactions into individual balance sheet and income statement accounts.

Chart of accounts

A listing of all the entity's accounts, which classifies transactions into individual balance sheet and income statement accounts.

PHANTOM BOOKS

Senior executives at Livent Inc., the Toronto, Canada theater owner and producer of Broadway-style shows including *Show Boat, Ragtime,* and *Phantom of the Opera,* took their theatrics to a new level when they allegedly engaged in a pervasive fraud to materially distort their financial statements over an eight-year period. According to charges filed by the Securities and Exchange Commission, the former chairman and CEO and former president together coaxed several of their longtime company associates, including the CFO and IT manager, to participate in a multifaceted scheme to manipulate profits.

In addition to orchestrating vendor kickback schemes to siphon off millions of dollars and numerous customer side-agreements to falsify revenues, senior management manipulated the accounting records to shift costs of shows to fixed assets from expenses. Their techniques included alteration of computer programs to lower expenses without a trace in order to hide the fraud from Livent auditors. In addition, they created 'phantom' accounting records showing the adjustments so senior management could track the fraudulent entries and know the company's true financial condition. Ultimately, their distortions were revealed, and the executives faced charges both in the United States and Canada. Livent filed for bankruptcy and was subsequently sold to a team headed by a former Walt Disney Company executive.

Sources: 1. Securities and Exchange Commission, Litigation Release No. 16022, Washington, DC, U.S., January 1999. 2. Canadian Broadcasting Company, 'Livent Founders Charged with Fraud,' *Arts Now,* Toronto, Canada, October 10, 2002.

The chart of accounts is helpful in preventing classification errors if it accurately describes which type of transactions should be in each account.

Physical Control Over Assets and Records To maintain adequate internal control, assets and records must be protected. If assets are left unprotected, they can be stolen. If records are not adequately protected, they can be stolen, damaged, or lost, which can seriously disrupt the accounting process and business operations. When a company is highly computerized, its computer equipment, programs, and data files must be protected. The data files are the records of the company and, if damaged, could be costly or even impossible to reconstruct.

The most important type of protective measure for safeguarding assets and records is the use of physical precautions. An example is the use of storerooms for inventory to guard against theft. When the storeroom is under the control of a competent employee, there is further assurance that theft is minimized. Fireproof safes and safety deposit vaults for the protection of assets such as currency and securities are other important physical safeguards in addition to off-site backup of computer software and data files.

Independent Checks on Performance The last category of control activities is the careful and continuous review of the other four, often called **independent checks** or internal verification. The need for independent checks arises because internal controls tend to change over time, unless there is frequent review. Personnel are likely to forget or intentionally fail to follow procedures, or they may become careless unless someone observes and evaluates their performance. Regardless of the quality of the controls, personnel can make errors or commit fraud.

Independent checks
Internal control activities designed for the continuous internal verification of other controls.

Personnel responsible for performing internal verification procedures must be independent of those originally responsible for preparing the data. The least expensive means of internal verification is the separation of duties in the manner previously discussed. For example, when the bank reconciliation is done by a person independent of the accounting records and handling of cash, there is an opportunity for verification without incurring significant additional costs.

Computerized accounting systems can be designed so that many internal verification procedures can be automated as part of the system. For example, the computer can prevent processing payment on a vendor invoice if there is no matching purchase order number or receiving report number for that invoice included in the system.

Auditing standards require the auditor to obtain an understanding of the process company employees follow to reconcile detail records supporting a significant account balance to the general ledger for those accounts to help the auditor more effectively design and perform audit procedures. For example, an auditor is likely to send confirmations of customer accounts receivable selected from accounts receivable master files. Before planning the confirmation procedures the auditor needs to understand the design and implementation of controls that company personnel use to reconcile the accounts receivable master file to the related general ledger account balance.

SERIOUS CORRUPTION IN THE EXPORT SUPPORT FUND BY A GROUP OF OFFICIALS

The Egyptian Attorney General is investigating corruption at the Export Support Fund amounting to EGP 12,730 million (approximately US$2 million). The investigation showed that the former Minister of Industry and Trade, in cooperation with the Executive Director of the fund and a prominent businessman, made funds available in the form of support for exports to a number of companies in which they have a percentage of ownership. The Executive Director of the Export Support Fund approved the payment of EGP 2,206 million (approximately US$370,000) from the fund to a not-for-profit organization of which he is the Treasurer. The former Minister of Industry and Trade also ordered the payment of EGP 2,514 million (approximately US$412,000) from the Fund to a number of companies in which he is heavily involved.

Source: Translated and adapted from *El Masry El Youm*, 4/6/2011, issue no 2547, p. 7.

Information and Communication

The purpose of an entity's accounting **information and communication** system is to initiate, record, process, and report the entity's transactions and to maintain accountability for the related assets. An accounting information and communication system has several subcomponents, typically made up of classes of transactions such as sales, sales returns, cash receipts, acquisitions, and so on. For each class of transactions, the accounting system must satisfy all of the six transaction-related audit objectives identified earlier in Table 10-1. For example, the sales accounting system should be designed to ensure that all shipments of goods are correctly recorded as sales (completeness and accuracy objectives) and are reflected in the financial statements in the proper period (timing objective). The system must also avoid duplicate recording of sales and recording a sale if a shipment did not occur (occurrence objective).

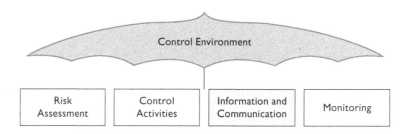

To understand the design of the accounting information system, the auditor determines (1) the major classes of transactions of the entity; (2) how those transactions are initiated and recorded; (3) what accounting records exist and their nature; (4) how the system captures other events that are significant to the financial statements, such as declines in asset values; and (5) the nature and details of the financial reporting process followed, including procedures to enter transactions and adjustments in the general ledger.

Monitoring

Monitoring activities deal with ongoing or periodic assessment of the quality of internal control by management to determine that controls are operating as intended and that they are modified as appropriate for changes in conditions. The information being assessed comes from a variety of sources, including studies of existing internal controls, internal auditor reports, exception reporting on control activities, reports by regulators such as bank regulatory agencies, feedback from operating personnel, and complaints from customers about billing charges.

For many companies, especially larger ones, an internal audit department is essential for effective monitoring of the operating performance of internal controls. To be effective, the internal audit function must be performed by staff independent of both the operating and accounting departments and report directly to a high level of authority within the organization, either top management or the audit committee of the board of directors.

In addition to its role in monitoring an entity's internal control, an adequate internal audit staff can reduce external audit costs by providing direct assistance to the external auditor. In general, if the external auditor obtains evidence that supports the competence, integrity, and objectivity of internal auditors, the external auditor can rely on the internal auditor's work in a number of ways. The external auditor can take the results of examination made by internal auditors for specific transactions and procedures and direct his attention to more riskier accounts' balances.

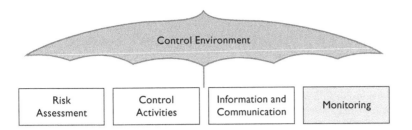

COSO's five components of internal control discussed in the preceding sections are summarized in Table 10-2. Certain control elements within the five COSO control components have a pervasive effect on the entity's system of internal control, and are referred to as **entity-level controls**. Examples include the board and audit committee element of the control environment, the entity's risk assessment process, and internal audit's role in monitoring controls.

Entity-level controls

Controls that have a pervasive effect on the entity's system of internal control; also referred to as 'company-level controls.'

TABLE 10-2	COSO Components of Internal Control

	INTERNAL CONTROL	
Component	**Description of Component**	**Further Subdivision (if applicable)**
Control environment	Actions, policies, and procedures that reflect the overall attitude of top management, directors, and owners of an entity about internal control and its importance	Subcomponents of the control environment: • Integrity and ethical values • Commitment to competence • Board of directors and audit committee participation • Management's philosophy and operating style • Organizational structure • Human resource policies and practices
Risk assessment	Management's identification and analysis of risks relevant to the preparation of financial statements in accordance with IFRS, GAAP or other local accounting standards	Risk assessment processes: • Identify factors affecting risks • Assess significance of risks and likelihood of occurrence • Determine actions necessary to manage risks Categories of management assertions that must be satisfied: • Assertions about classes of transactions and other events • Assertions about account balances • Assertions about presentation and disclosure
Control activities	Policies and procedures that management has established to meet its objectives for financial reporting	Types of specific control activities: • Adequate separation of duties • Proper authorization of transactions and activities • Adequate documents and records • Physical control over assets and records • Independent checks on performance
Information and communication	Methods used to initiate, record, process, and report an entity's transactions and to maintain accountability for related assets	Transaction-related audit objectives that must be satisfied: • Occurrence • Completeness • Accuracy • Posting and summarization • Classification • Timing • Rights and obligations
Monitoring	Management's ongoing and periodic assessment of the quality of internal control performance to determine whether controls are operating as intended and are modified when needed	Not applicable

COSO MONITORING GUIDANCE

The Committee of Sponsoring Organizations of the Treadway Commission (COSO) has developed guidance that provides more extensive understanding of the monitoring component of the COSO *Internal Control–Integrated Framework*. This guidance is in response to observations that organizations are often not fully utilizing the monitoring component of internal control. For example, some public companies perform separate procedures to evaluate the operating effectiveness of internal control over financial reporting to comply with Section 404 responsibilities, even though the entity's existing monitoring activities generate sufficient evidence for management's Section 404 reporting.

COSO's *Guidance on Monitoring Internal Control Systems* is intended to help organizations improve the effectiveness and efficiency of their internal control systems, through more efficient and effective monitoring procedures. The guidance should help management, boards of directors, and internal and external auditors recognize effective monitoring where it exists and identify and correct weaknesses in the monitoring component of internal control.

Source: *Exposure Draft of Guidance on Monitoring Internal Control Systems*, Committee of Sponsoring Organizations of the Treadway Commission (COSO), 2008, www.coso.org.

OBTAIN AND DOCUMENT UNDERSTANDING OF INTERNAL CONTROL

OBJECTIVE 10-4

Obtain and document an understanding of internal control.

Figure 10-5 provides an overview of the process of understanding internal control and assessing control risk for an integrated audit of the financial statements and the effectiveness of internal control over financial reporting. The figure shows that there are four phases in the process. Each of these four phases is discussed in this section.

The level of understanding internal control and extent of testing required for the audit of internal control exceeds what is required for an audit of only the financial statements. Therefore, when auditors first focus on the understanding and testing of internal control for the audit of internal controls, they will have met the requirements for assessing internal control for the financial statement audit.

| FIGURE 10-5 | Process for Understanding Internal Control and Assessing Control Risk |

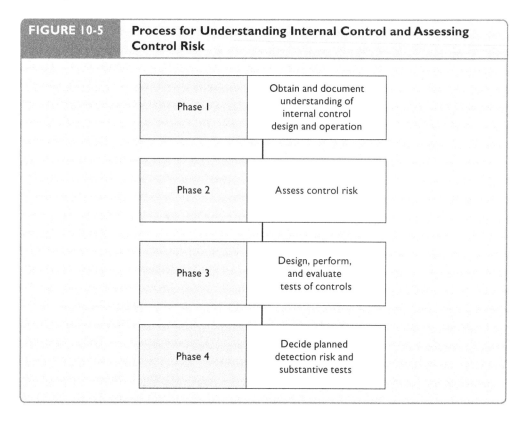

Phase 1 — Obtain and document understanding of internal control design and operation

Phase 2 — Assess control risk

Phase 3 — Design, perform, and evaluate tests of controls

Phase 4 — Decide planned detection risk and substantive tests

As discussed earlier, using the model of the U.S. for understanding internal control, Section 404 requires management to document its processes for assessing the effectiveness of the company's internal control over financial reporting. Management must document the design of controls, including all five control components, and also the results of its testing and evaluation. The types of information gathered by management to assess and document internal control effectiveness can take many forms, including policy manuals, flowcharts, narratives, documents, questionnaires, and other paper and electronic forms.

Obtain and Document Understanding of Internal Control

Auditing standards require auditors to obtain and document their understanding of internal control for every audit. This understanding is necessary for both the audit of internal controls over financial reporting and the audit of financial statements. Management's documentation is a major source of information in gaining the understanding.

As part of the auditor's risk assessment procedures, the auditor uses **procedures to obtain an understanding**, which involve gathering evidence about the design of internal controls and whether they have been implemented, and then uses that information as a basis for the integrated audit. The auditor generally uses four of the eight types of evidence described in Chapter 7 to obtain an understanding of the design and implementation of controls: inspection, inquiry of entity personnel, observation of employees performing control processes, and reperformance by tracing one or a few transactions through the accounting system from start to finish.

Auditors commonly use three types of documents to obtain and document their understanding of the design of internal control: narratives, flowcharts, and internal control questionnaires. In the U.S., because Section 404 requires management to assess and document the design effectiveness of internal control over financial reporting, they have usually already prepared this documentation. In the Arab countries, it is up to the auditor in those countries to determine which of those methods will be used to understand, document, and assess internal control. Factors influencing the auditor's decision to select one or more of the above methods include: size of the client, competency and experience of the audit team, level of documentation of the internal control by management, and deficiencies in internal control from previous periods assessment.

Narrative A **narrative** is a written description of a client's internal controls. A proper narrative of an accounting system and related controls describes four things:

1. *The origin of every document and record in the system.* For example, the description should state where customer orders come from and how sales invoices are generated.
2. *All processing that takes place.* For example, if sales amounts are determined by a computer program that multiplies quantities shipped by standard prices contained in price master files, that process should be described.
3. *The disposition of every document and record in the system.* The filing of documents, sending them to customers, or destroying them should be described.
4. *An indication of the controls relevant to the assessment of control risk.* These typically include separation of duties (such as separating recording cash from handling cash), authorizations and approvals (such as credit approvals), and internal verification (such as comparison of unit selling price to sales contracts).

Flowchart An internal control **flowchart** is a diagram of the client's documents and their sequential flow in the organization. An adequate flowchart includes the same four characteristics identified for narratives.

Well prepared flowcharts are advantageous primarily because they provide a concise overview of the client's system, which helps auditors identify controls and deficiencies in the client's system. Flowcharts have two advantages over narratives: typically

Procedures to obtain an understanding

Procedures used by the auditor to gather evidence about the design and implementation of specific controls.

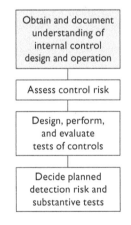

Narrative

A written description of a client's internal controls, including the origin, processing, and disposition of documents and records, and the relevant control procedures.

Flowchart

A diagrammatic representation of the client's documents and records and the sequence in which they are processed.

they are easier to read and easier to update. It is unusual to use both a narrative and a flowchart to describe the same system because both present the same information.

Internal control questionnaire

A series of questions about the controls in each audit area used as a means of indicating to the auditor aspects of internal control that may be inadequate.

Internal Control Questionnaire An **internal control questionnaire** asks a series of questions about the controls in each audit area as a means of identifying internal control deficiencies. Most questionnaires require a 'yes' or a 'no' response, with 'no' responses indicating potential internal control deficiencies. By using a questionnaire, auditors cover each audit area reasonably quickly. The two main disadvantages of questionnaires are their inability to provide an overview of the system and their inapplicability for some audits, especially smaller ones.

Figure 10-6 illustrates part of an internal control questionnaire for the sales and collection cycle of Arabian Hardware Co. Notice how the questionnaire incorporates the six transaction-related audit objectives A through F as each applies to sales transactions (see shaded portions). The same is true for all other audit areas.

The use of questionnaires and flowcharts together is useful for understanding the client's internal control design and identifying internal controls and deficiencies. Flowcharts provide an overview of the system, while questionnaires offer useful checklists to remind the auditor of the many different types of internal controls that should exist.

Evaluating Internal Control Implementation

In addition to understanding the design of the internal controls, the auditor must also evaluate whether the designed controls are implemented. In practice, the understanding of the design and implementation are often done simultaneously. Following are common methods.

Update and Evaluate Auditor's Previous Experience with the Entity Most audits of a company are done annually by the same audit firm. After the first year's audit, the auditor begins with a great deal of information from prior years about the client's internal control. It is especially useful to determine whether controls that were not previously operating effectively have been improved.

Identify Financial Reporting Risks and Related Controls Auditors must identify and assess the risk that a misstatement could result in a material misstatement of the financial statements. Auditors should consider the company's characteristics such as the size, complexity, and organizational structure, and its processes and financial reporting environment. Then, the auditor should identify controls that are in place to address financial reporting risks including entity level and transactions/processes controls. Table 10-3 gives some examples of financial statements or entity level control risks.

Make Inquiries of Client Personnel Auditors should ask management, supervisors, and staff to explain their duties. Careful questioning of appropriate personnel helps auditors evaluate whether employees understand their duties and do what is described in the client's control documentation.

Examine Documents and Records The five components of internal control all involve the creation of many documents and records. By examining completed documents, records, and computer files, the auditor can evaluate whether information described in flowcharts and narratives has been implemented.

Observe Entity Activities and Operations When auditors observe client personnel carrying out their normal accounting and control activities, including their preparation of documents and records, it further improves their understanding and knowledge that controls have been implemented. Auditors should consider whether the control is operating as designed, and whether the person performing the control possesses the appropriate authority and competence to implement such controls

FIGURE 10-6   Partial Internal Control Questionnaire for Sales

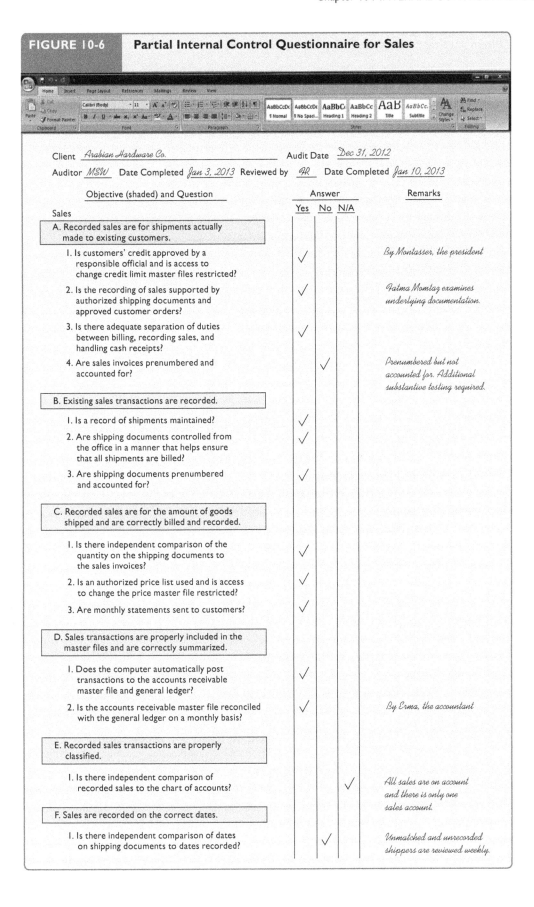

Client _Arabian Hardware Co._ _____ Audit Date _Dec 31, 2012_

Auditor _MSW_   Date Completed _Jan 3, 2013_ Reviewed by _4R_ Date Completed _Jan 10, 2013_

Objective (shaded) and Question	Answer			Remarks
	Yes	No	N/A	
Sales				
A. Recorded sales are for shipments actually made to existing customers.				
1. Is customers' credit approved by a responsible official and is access to change credit limit master files restricted?	✓			_By Montasser, the president_
2. Is the recording of sales supported by authorized shipping documents and approved customer orders?	✓			_Fatma Momtaz examines underlying documentation._
3. Is there adequate separation of duties between billing, recording sales, and handling cash receipts?	✓			
4. Are sales invoices prenumbered and accounted for?		✓		_Prenumbered but not accounted for. Additional substantive testing required._
B. Existing sales transactions are recorded.				
1. Is a record of shipments maintained?	✓			
2. Are shipping documents controlled from the office in a manner that helps ensure that all shipments are billed?	✓			
3. Are shipping documents prenumbered and accounted for?	✓			
C. Recorded sales are for the amount of goods shipped and are correctly billed and recorded.				
1. Is there independent comparison of the quantity on the shipping documents to the sales invoices?	✓			
2. Is an authorized price list used and is access to change the price master file restricted?	✓			
3. Are monthly statements sent to customers?	✓			
D. Sales transactions are properly included in the master files and are correctly summarized.				
1. Does the computer automatically post transactions to the accounts receivable master file and general ledger?	✓			
2. Is the accounts receivable master file reconciled with the general ledger on a monthly basis?	✓			_By Erma, the accountant_
E. Recorded sales transactions are properly classified.				
1. Is there independent comparison of recorded sales to the chart of accounts?			✓	_All sales are on account and there is only one sales account._
F. Sales are recorded on the correct dates.				
1. Is there independent comparison of dates on shipping documents to dates recorded?		✓		_Unmatched and unrecorded shippers are reviewed weekly._

TABLE 10-3	Examples of Financial Statements or Entity Level Control Risks

- The company's risk assessment process and control deficiencies identified in previous period and communicated to management and the audit committee.
- The volume of activity, and relative complexity of the company's operations.
- Elements of control environment including tone at the top, assignment of authority and responsibility, management's philosophy and operating style, consistent policies and procedures, codes of conduct and ethical values, and fraud prevention and detection procedures.
- Matters affecting the industry at which the company operates.
- Issues relating to the entity's business, including its organization, operating characteristics, and capital structure.
- Centralized processing of information, transactions, and controls to monitor the results of the company's procedures.
- Independent controls over transactions such as internal audit function, the audit committee, and other self-assessment activities and initiatives such as considering key performance indicators.
- Controls over the preparation of the company's interim and end of the year financial statements.
- Company's strategies and policies to address business and management practice risks.
- Susceptibility of accounts to misstatement due to errors and fraud.
- Possibility of significant contingent liabilities arising from the activities reflected in the account or disclosure.

Source: Based on PCAOB, AS 5, para. 29 & 40.

effectively. Auditors should devote more attention to areas, transactions, and processes that have a high risk of material weakness. The following is a list of controls that should be considered:

- Controls over initiating, authorizing, recording, processing, and reporting significant accounts and disclosures and related objectives included in the financial statements.
- Controls over significant, unusual transactions, particularly those that result in late or unusual journal entries.
- Controls over journal entries and adjustments made in the period-end financial reporting process.
- Controls over related-party transactions.
- Controls over the proper application of accounting standards in recording the company's transactions and preparing the financial statements.
- Management anti-fraud programs and procedures.
- Information technology general and specific controls.
- Controls over routine versus nonroutine transactions, management estimates, and judgments.

Walkthrough

The tracing of selected transactions through the accounting system to determine that controls are in place.

Perform Walkthroughs of the Accounting System In a **walkthrough**, the auditor selects one or a few documents of a transaction type and traces them from initiation through the entire accounting process. At each stage of processing, the auditor makes inquiries, observes activities, and examines completed documents and records. Walkthroughs conveniently combine observation, inspection, and inquiry to assure that the controls designed by management have been implemented.

Auditors should assess all types of controls. They should understand and test controls that operate continuously (e.g. controls over the processing of routine purchase transactions) and those that operate only occasionally (e.g. monthly bank reconciliations and end-of-the-month adjusting entries). For routine transactions, auditors should examine routine processing controls, such as verification of data entry, edit checks and validation controls, completeness controls, and so forth. As for nonroutine transactions, auditors should pay attention to those involving estimation, review, and approval controls.

Auditors should consider which locations within the company operations to include in testing and assessment. When controls addressing transactions and financial reporting risks are implemented at more than one location or business unit, auditors need to assess evidence of the operations of controls at the individual locations or business units.

ASSESS CONTROL RISK

The auditor obtains an understanding of the design and implementation of internal control to make a preliminary assessment of control risk as part of the auditor's overall assessment of the risk of material misstatements. As described in Chapter 9, the auditor uses this preliminary assessment of control risk to plan the audit for each material class of transactions. However, in some instances the auditor may learn that the control deficiencies are significant such that the client's financial statements may not be auditable. So, before making a preliminary assessment of control risk for each material class of transactions, the auditor must first decide whether the entity is auditable.

> **OBJECTIVE 10-5**
>
> Assess control risk by linking key controls and control deficiencies to transaction-related audit objectives.

Assess Whether the Financial Statements are Auditable

Two primary factors determine auditability: the integrity of management and the adequacy of accounting records. The importance of management integrity was discussed in Chapter 8 under client acceptance and continuance. If management lacks integrity, most auditors will not accept the engagement.

The accounting records are an important source of audit evidence for most audit objectives. If the accounting records are deficient, necessary audit evidence may not be available. For example, if the client has not kept duplicate sales invoices and vendors' invoices, it is usually impractical to do an audit.

In complex IT environments, much of the transaction information is available only in electronic form without generating a visible audit trail of documents and records. Auditors must assess whether they have the necessary skills to gather evidence that is in electronic form.

Determine Assessed Control Risk Supported by the Understanding Obtained, Assuming the Controls are Being Followed

After obtaining an understanding of internal control, the auditor makes a preliminary **assessment of control risk** as part of the auditor's overall assessment of the risk of material misstatement. This assessment is a measure of the auditor's expectation that internal controls will prevent material misstatements from occurring or detect and correct them if they have occurred.

The auditor makes the preliminary assessment for each transaction-related audit objective for each major type of transaction in each transaction cycle. For example, in the sales and collection cycle, the types of transactions usually involve sales, sales returns and allowances, cash receipts, and the provision for and write-off of uncollectible accounts. The auditor also makes the preliminary assessment for controls affecting audit objectives for balance sheet accounts and presentations and disclosures in each cycle.

> **Assessment of control risk**
>
> A measure of the auditor's expectation that internal controls will neither prevent material misstatements from occurring nor detect and correct them if they have occurred; control risk is assessed for each transaction-related audit objective in a cycle or class of transactions.

Use of a Control Risk Matrix to Assess Control Risk

Many auditors use a **control risk matrix** to assist in the control risk assessment process. The purpose is to provide a convenient way to organize assessing control risk for each audit objective. Figure 10-7 illustrates the use of a control risk matrix for sales transaction audit objectives of Arabian Hardware Co. While Figure 10-7 only illustrates the control risk matrix for transaction-related audit objectives, auditors use a similar control risk matrix format to assess control risk for balance-related and presentation and disclosure-related audit objectives. We now discuss the preparation of the matrix.

> **Control risk matrix**
>
> A methodology used to help the auditor assess control risk by matching key internal controls and internal control deficiencies with transaction-related audit objectives.

FIGURE 10-7   Control Risk Matrix for Sales

INTERNAL CONTROL	Recorded sales are for shipments actually made to nonfictitious customers (occurrence).	Existing sales transactions are recorded (completeness).	Recorded sales are for the amount of goods shipped and are correctly billed and recorded (accuracy).	Sales transactions are correctly included in the accounts receivable master file and are correctly summarized (posting and summarization).	Sales transactions are correctly classified (classification).	Sales are recorded on the correct dates (timing).	Sales pertain to the company (rights).
SALES TRANSACTION-RELATED AUDIT OBJECTIVES							
Credit is approved automatically by computer by comparison to authorized credit limits (C1).	C						
Recorded sales are supported by invoices, authorized shipping documents and approved customer orders (C2).	C		C				C
Separation of duties exists among billing, recording of sales, and handling of cash receipts (C3).	C	C		C			
Shipping documents are forwarded to billing daily and are billed the subsequent day (C4).	C					C	
Shipping documents are prenumbered and accounted for weekly (C5).		C				C	
Batch totals of quantities shipped are compared with quantities billed (C6).	C	C	C				
Unit selling prices are obtained from the price list master file of approved prices (C7).			C				
Sales transactions are internally verified (C8).					C		
Statements are mailed to customers each month (C9).	C		C	C			
Computer automatically posts transactions to the accounts receivable subsidiary records and to the general ledger (C10).				C			
Accounts receivable master file is reconciled to the general ledger on a monthly basis (C11).				C			
There is a lack of internal verification for the possibility of sales invoices being recorded more than once (D1).	D						
There is a lack of control to test for timely recording (D2).						D	
Assessed control risk	Med.	Low	Low	Low	Low*	Med.	

*Because there are no cash sales, classification is not a problem.

C = Control; D = Significant Deficiency or Material Weakness.

Note: This matrix was developed using an internal control questionnaire, part of which is included in Figure 10-6 (p. 333), as well as flowcharts and other documentation of the auditor's understanding of internal control.

Identify Audit Objectives The first step in the assessment is to identify the audit objectives for classes of transactions, account balances, and presentation and disclosure to which the assessment applies. For example, this is done for classes of transactions by applying the specific transaction-related audit objectives introduced earlier, which were stated in general form, to each major type of transaction for the entity. Transaction-related audit objectives are shown for sales transactions for Arabian Hardware at the top of Figure 10-7.

Identify Existing Controls Next, the auditor uses the information discussed in the previous section on obtaining and documenting an understanding of internal control to identify the controls that contribute to accomplishing transaction-related audit objectives. One way for the auditor to do this is to identify controls to satisfy each objective. For example, the auditor can use knowledge of the client's system to identify controls that are likely to prevent errors or fraud in the occurrence transaction-related audit objective. The same thing can be done for all other objectives. It is also helpful for the auditor to use the five control activities as reminders of controls. For example: Is there adequate separation of duties and how is it achieved? Are transactions properly authorized? Are prenumbered documents properly accounted for? Are key master files properly restricted from unauthorized access?

The auditor should identify and include only those controls that are expected to have the greatest effect on meeting the transaction-related audit objectives. These are often called **key controls**. The reason for including only key controls is that they will be sufficient to achieve the transaction-related audit objectives and also provide audit efficiency. Examples of key controls for Arabian Hardware Co. are shown in Figure 10-6.

> **Key controls**
>
> Controls that are expected to have the greatest effect on meeting the audit objectives.

Associate Controls with Related Audit Objectives Each control satisfies one or more related audit objectives. This can be seen in Figure 10-7 for transaction-related audit objectives. The body of the matrix is used to show how each control contributes to the accomplishment of one or more transaction-related audit objectives. In this illustration, a C was entered in each cell where a control partially or fully satisfied an objective. A similar control risk matrix would be completed for balance-related and presentation and disclosure-related audit objectives. For example, the mailing of statements to customers satisfies three objectives in the audit of Arabian Hardware, which is indicated by the placement of each C on the row in Figure 10-7 describing that control.

Identify and Evaluate Control Deficiencies, Significant Deficiencies, and Material Weaknesses Auditors must evaluate whether key controls are absent in the design of internal control over financial reporting as a part of evaluating control risk and the likelihood of financial statement misstatements. Auditing standards define three levels of the absence of internal controls:

1. *Control deficiency*. A **control deficiency** exists if the design or operation of controls does not permit company personnel to prevent or detect misstatements on a timely basis. A *design deficiency* exists if a necessary control is missing or not properly designed. An *operation deficiency* exists if a well-designed control does not operate as designed or if the person performing the control is insufficiently qualified or authorized.
2. *Significant deficiency*. A **significant deficiency** exists if one or more control deficiencies exist that is less severe than a material weakness (defined below), but important enough to merit attention by those responsible for oversight of the company's financial reporting.
3. *Material weakness*. A **material weakness** exists if a significant deficiency, by itself, or in combination with other significant deficiencies, results in a reasonable possibility that internal control will not prevent or detect material financial statement misstatements on a timely basis.

> **Control deficiency**
>
> A deficiency in the design or operation of controls that does not permit company personnel to prevent or detect misstatements on a timely basis.
>
> **Significant deficiency**
>
> One or more control deficiencies exist that is less severe than a material weakness, but important enough to merit attention by those responsible for oversight of the company's financial reporting.
>
> **Material weakness**
>
> A significant deficiency in internal control that, by itself, or in combination with other significant deficiencies, results in a reasonable possibility that a material misstatement of the financial statements will not be prevented or detected.

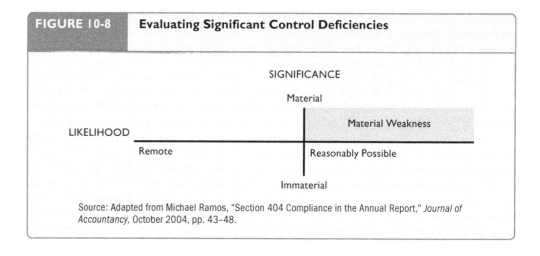

FIGURE 10-8   **Evaluating Significant Control Deficiencies**

Source: Adapted from Michael Ramos, "Section 404 Compliance in the Annual Report," *Journal of Accountancy,* October 2004, pp. 43–48.

To determine if a significant internal control deficiency or deficiencies are a material weakness, they must be evaluated along two dimensions: likelihood and significance. The horizontal line in Figure 10-8 depicts the likelihood of a misstatement resulting from the significant deficiency, while the vertical line depicts its significance. If there is more than a reasonable possibility (likelihood) that a material misstatement (significance) could result from the significant deficiency or deficiencies, then it is considered a material weakness.

Identify Deficiencies, Significant Deficiencies, and Material Weaknesses

A five-step approach can be used to identify deficiencies, significant deficiencies, and material weaknesses:

1. *Identify existing controls.* Because deficiencies and material weaknesses are the absence of adequate controls, the auditor must first know which controls exist. The methods for identifying controls have already been discussed.
2. *Identify the absence of key controls.* Internal control questionnaires, flowcharts, and walkthroughs are useful tools to identify where controls are lacking and the likelihood of misstatement is therefore increased. It is also useful to examine the control risk matrix, such as the one in Figure 10-7, to look for objectives where there are no or only a few controls to prevent or detect misstatements.
3. *Consider the possibility of compensating controls.* A **compensating control** is one elsewhere in the system that offsets the absence of a key control. A common example in a small business is the active involvement of the owner.
4. *Decide whether there is a significant deficiency or material weakness.* The likelihood of misstatements and their materiality are used to evaluate if there are significant deficiencies or material weaknesses.
5. *Determine potential misstatements that could result.* This step is intended to identify specific misstatements that are likely to result because of the significant deficiency or material weakness. The importance of a significant deficiency or material weakness is directly related to the likelihood and materiality of potential misstatements.

Compensating control

A control elsewhere in the system that offsets the absence of a key control.

Risk factors that affect whether control deficiency, or a combination of control deficiencies, will result in a misstatement of an account balance or disclosure, include:[10]

- The nature of the financial statement accounts, disclosures, and assertions involved.
- The susceptibility of the related asset or liability to loss or fraud.

- The subjectivity, complexity, or extent of judgment required to determine the amount involved.
- The interaction or relationship of the control with other controls, including whether they are interdependent or redundant.
- The interaction and effect of the deficiencies on the company's transactions and financial statements.

Figure 10-9 for Arabian Hardware includes two significant deficiencies but no material weaknesses.

Associate Significant Deficiencies and Material Weaknesses with Related Audit Objectives The same as for controls, each significant deficiency or material weakness can apply to one or more related audit objectives. In the case of Arabian Hardware in Figure 10-7, there are two significant deficiencies, and each applies to only one transaction-related objective. The significant deficiencies are shown in the body of the figure by a D in the appropriate objective column.

Assess Control Risk for Each Related Audit Objective After controls, significant deficiencies and material weaknesses are identified and associated with transaction-related audit objectives, the auditor can assess control risk for transaction-related audit objectives. This is the critical decision in the evaluation of internal control.

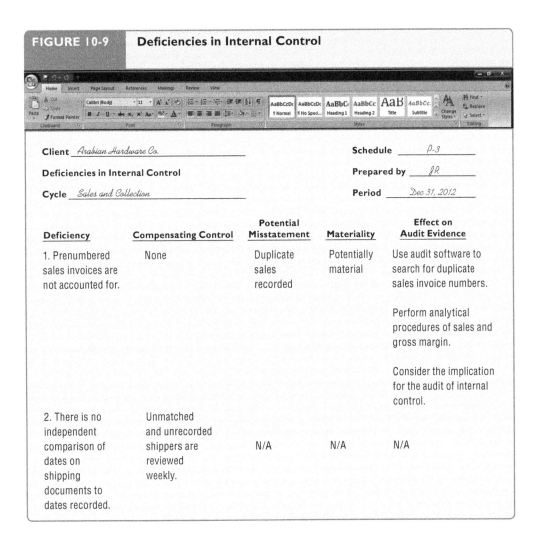

FIGURE 10-9   Deficiencies in Internal Control

Client _Arabian Hardware Co._   Schedule _P-3_

Deficiencies in Internal Control   Prepared by _JR_

Cycle _Sales and Collection_   Period _Dec 31, 2012_

Deficiency	Compensating Control	Potential Misstatement	Materiality	Effect on Audit Evidence
1. Prenumbered sales invoices are not accounted for.	None	Duplicate sales recorded	Potentially material	Use audit software to search for duplicate sales invoice numbers. Perform analytical procedures of sales and gross margin. Consider the implication for the audit of internal control.
2. There is no independent comparison of dates on shipping documents to dates recorded.	Unmatched and unrecorded shippers are reviewed weekly.	N/A	N/A	N/A

The auditor uses all of the information discussed previously to make a subjective control risk assessment for each objective. There are different ways to express this assessment. Some auditors use a subjective expression such as high, moderate, or low. Others use numerical probabilities such as 1.0, 0.6, or 0.2.

Again, the control risk matrix is a useful tool for making the assessment. Referring to Figure 10-7, the auditor assessed control risk for each objective for Arabian's sales by reviewing each column for pertinent controls and significant deficiencies and asking, what is the likelihood that a material misstatement would not be prevented or detected, or corrected if it occurred, by these controls, and what is the effect of the deficiencies or weaknesses? If the likelihood is low, then control risk is low, and so forth. Figure 10-7 for Arabian Hardware shows that all objectives are assessed as low except occurrence and timing, which are medium.

This assessment is not the final one. Before making the final assessment at the end of the integrated audit, the auditor will test controls and perform substantive tests. These procedures can either support the preliminary assessment or cause the auditor to make changes. In some cases, management can correct deficiencies and material weaknesses before the auditor does significant testing, which may permit a reduction in control risk.

After a preliminary assessment of control risk is made for sales and cash receipts, the auditor can complete the three control risk rows of the evidence-planning worksheet that was introduced in Chapter 9. If tests of controls results do not support the preliminary assessment of control risk, the auditor must modify the worksheet later. Alternatively, the auditor can wait until tests of controls are done to complete the three control risk rows of the worksheet. An evidence-planning worksheet for Arabian Hardware with the three rows for control risk completed is illustrated in Figure 15-6 on page 520.

Communications to Those Charged with Governance and Management Letters

As part of understanding internal control and assessing control risk, the auditor is required to communicate certain matters to those charged with governance. This information and other recommendations about controls are also often communicated to management.

Communications to Those Charged with Governance The auditor must communicate significant deficiencies and material weaknesses in writing to those charged with governance as soon as the auditor becomes aware of their existence (ISA 265). The communication is usually addressed to the audit committee and to management. Timely communications may provide management with an opportunity to address control deficiencies before management's report on internal control must be issued. In some instances, deficiencies can be corrected sufficiently early such that both management and the auditor can conclude that controls are operating effectively as of the balance sheet date. In the U.S., the Sarbanes–Oxley Act and SEC regulations require that such communications must be made no later than 60 days following the audit report release. No similar requirements exist in ISAs. Thus, no formal requirements exist in Arab countries for the preparation of a separate report for the assessment of internal control over financial reporting but it is just a part of auditor's reporting about the company's financial statements.

Management Letters In addition to these matters, auditors often identify less significant internal control-related issues, as well as opportunities for the client to make operational improvements. These should also be communicated to the client. The form of communication is often a separate letter for that purpose, called a **management letter**. Although management letters are not required by auditing standards, auditors generally prepare them as a value-added service of the audit.

Management letter

An optional letter written by the auditor to a client's management containing the auditor's recommendations for improving any aspect of the client's business.

TESTS OF CONTROLS

We've examined how auditors link controls, significant deficiencies, and material weaknesses in internal control to related audit objectives to assess control risk for each objective. Now we'll address how auditors test those controls that are used to support a control risk assessment. For example, each key control in Figure 10-7 that the auditor intends to rely on to support a control risk of medium or low must be supported by sufficient tests of controls. We will deal with tests of controls for both audits of internal control for financial reporting and audits of financial statements.

OBJECTIVE 10-6

Describe the process of designing and performing tests of controls.

Purpose of Tests of Controls

Assessing control risk requires the auditor to consider both the design and operation of controls to evaluate whether they will likely be effective in meeting related audit objectives. During the understanding phase, the auditor will have already gathered some evidence in support of both the design of the controls and their implementation by using procedures to obtain an understanding of such a control system. In most cases, the auditor *will not* have gathered enough evidence to reduce assessed control risk to a sufficiently low level. The auditor must therefore obtain additional evidence about the operating effectiveness of controls throughout all, or at least most, of the period under audit. The procedures to test effectiveness of controls in support of a reduced assessed control risk are called tests of controls.

If the results of tests of controls support the design and operation of controls as expected, the auditor uses the same assessed control risk as the preliminary assessment. If, however, the tests of controls indicate that the controls did not operate effectively, the assessed control risk must be reconsidered. For example, the tests may indicate that the application of a control was curtailed midway through the year or that the person applying it made frequent misstatements. In such situations, the auditor uses a higher assessed control risk, unless compensating controls for the same related audit objectives are identified and found to be effective. Of course, the auditor must also consider the impact of those controls that are not operating effectively on the auditor's report on internal control.

Procedures for Tests of Controls

The auditor is likely to use four types of procedures to support the operating effectiveness of internal controls. Management's testing of internal control will likely include the same types of procedures. The four types of procedures are as follows:

1. *Make inquiries of appropriate client personnel.* Although inquiry is not a highly reliable source of evidence about the effective operation of controls, it is still appropriate. For example, to determine that unauthorized personnel are denied access to computer files, the auditor may make inquiries of the person who controls the computer library and of the person who controls online access security password assignments.
2. *Examine documents, records, and reports.* Many controls leave a clear trail of documentary evidence that can be used to test controls. Suppose, for example,

Obtain and document
understanding of
internal control
design and operation

Assess control risk

Design, perform,
and evaluate
tests of controls

Decide planned
detection risk and
substantive tests

that when a customer order is received, it is used to create a customer sales order, which is approved for credit. (See the first and second key controls in Figure 10-7.) Then the customer order is attached to the sales order as authorization for further processing. The auditor can test the control by examining the documents to make sure that they are complete and properly matched and that required signatures or initials are present.

3. *Observe control-related activities.* Some controls do not leave an evidence trail, which means that it is not possible to examine evidence that the control was executed at a later date. For example, separation of duties relies on specific persons performing specific tasks, and there is typically no documentation of the separate performance. (See the third key control in Figure 10-7.) For controls that leave no documentary evidence, the auditor generally observes them being applied at various points during the year.

4. *Reperform client procedures.* There are also control-related activities for which there are related documents and records, but their content is insufficient for the auditor's purpose of assessing whether controls are operating effectively. For example, assume that prices on sales invoices are obtained from the master price list, but no indication of the control is documented on the sales invoices. (See the seventh key control in Figure 10-7.) In these cases, it is common for the auditor to reperform the control activity to see whether the proper results were obtained. For this example, the auditor can reperform the procedure by tracing the sales prices to the authorized price list in effect at the date of the transaction. If no misstatements are found, the auditor can conclude that the procedure is operating as intended.

Extent of Procedures

The extent to which tests of controls are applied depends on the preliminary assessed control risk. If the auditor wants a lower assessed control risk, more extensive tests of controls are applied, both in terms of the number of controls tested and the extent of the tests for each control. For example, if the auditor wants to use a low assessed control risk, a larger sample size for inspection, observation, and reperformance procedures should be applied. The extent of testing also depends on the frequency of the operation of the controls, and whether it is manual or automated.

Reliance on Evidence from the Prior Year's Audit If auditors determine that a key control has been changed since it was last tested, they should test it in the current year. When there are a number of controls tested in prior audits that have not been changed, auditing standards require auditors to test some of those controls each year to ensure there is a rotation of controls testing throughout a three-year period. In the U.S., when auditors plan to use evidence about the operating effectiveness of internal control obtained in prior audits, auditing standards (AU 318) require tests of the controls' effectiveness at least once every third year. There are no similar requirements in Arab countries. Auditors are required under ISA to assess internal control as part of forming their independent opinion about the client's financial statements.

Significant risks

Risks the auditor believes require special audit consideration; the auditor is required to test the operating effectiveness of controls that mitigate these risks in the current year audit, if control risk is to be assessed below the maximum.

Testing of Controls Related to Significant Risks **Significant risks** are those risks that the auditor believes require special audit consideration. When the auditor's risk assessment procedures identify significant risks, the auditor is required to test the operating effectiveness of controls that mitigate these risks in the current year audit, if the auditor plans to rely on those controls to support a control risk assessment below 100 percent. The greater the risk, the more audit evidence the auditor should obtain that controls are operating effectively.

Testing Less Than the Entire Audit Period The timing of the auditor's tests of controls depends on the nature of the controls and when the company uses them. For controls that are applied throughout the accounting period, it is usually practical to test them at an interim date. The auditor will then determine later if changes in controls occurred in the period not tested and decide the implication of any change. Controls dealing with financial statement preparation occur only quarterly or at year-end and must therefore also be tested at quarter and year-end. PCAOB Standard 5 requires the auditor to perform tests of controls that are adequate to determine whether controls are operating effectively at year-end.

Relationship between Tests of Controls and Procedures to Obtain an Understanding

There is a significant overlap between tests of controls and procedures to obtain an understanding. Both include inquiry, inspection, and observation. There are two primary differences in the application of these common procedures.

1. In obtaining an understanding of internal control, the procedures to obtain an understanding are applied to all controls identified during that phase. Tests of controls, on the other hand, are applied only when the assessed control risk has not been satisfied by the procedures to obtain an understanding.
2. Procedures to obtain an understanding are performed only on one or a few transactions or, in the case of observations, at a single point in time. Tests of controls are performed on larger samples of transactions (perhaps 20 to 100 percent), and often, observations are made at more than one point in time.

For key controls, tests of controls other than reperformance are essentially an extension of procedures to obtain an understanding. Therefore, assuming the auditors plan to obtain a low assessed control risk from the beginning of the integrated audit, they will likely combine both types of procedures and perform them simultaneously. Table 10-4 illustrates this concept in more detail. One option is to perform the audit procedures separately, as shown in Table 10-4, where minimum procedures to obtain an understanding of design and operation are performed, followed by additional tests of controls. An alternative is to combine both columns and do them simultaneously. The same amount of evidence is accumulated in the second approach, but more efficiently.

The determination of the appropriate sample size for tests of controls is an important audit decision. That topic is covered in Chapter 15.

TABLE 10-4	**Relationship of Assessed Control Risk and Extent of Procedures**	
	Assessed Control Risk	
Type of Procedure	**High Level: Procedures to Obtain an Understanding**	**Low Level: Tests of Controls***
Inquiry	Yes—extensive	Yes—some
Inspection	Yes—with transaction walkthrough	Yes—using sampling
Observation	Yes—with transaction walkthrough	Yes—at multiple times
Reperformance	No	Yes—using sampling

Note: In an integrated audit for a public company, the auditor will likely combine procedures to obtain an understanding with tests of controls and perform them simultaneously.

DECIDE PLANNED DETECTION RISK AND DESIGN SUBSTANTIVE TESTS

Obtain and document
understanding of
internal control
design and operation

Assess control risk

Design, perform,
and evaluate
tests of controls

Decide planned
detection risk and
substantive tests

We've focused on how auditors assess control risk for each related audit objective and support control risk assessments with tests of controls. The completion of these activities is sufficient for the audit of internal control over financial reporting, even though the report will not be finalized until the auditor completes the audit of financial statements.

The auditor uses the control risk assessment and results of tests of controls to determine planned detection risk and related substantive tests for the audit of financial statements. The auditor does this by linking the control risk assessments to the balance-related audit objectives for the accounts affected by the major transaction types and to the four presentations and disclosure audit objectives. The appropriate level of detection risk for each balance-related audit objective is then decided using the audit risk model. The relationship of transaction-related audit objectives to balance-related audit objectives and the selection and design of audit procedures for substantive tests of financial statement balances are discussed and illustrated in Chapter 13.

SECTION 404 REPORTING ON INTERNAL CONTROL

OBJECTIVE 10-7

Understand requirements of Section 404 of the U.S. Sarbanes–Oxley Act for auditor reporting on internal control.

It is important to understand the requirements of Section 404 since it is expected that the ISA (applied in many Arab countries) will include similar requirements in the near future.

The scope of the auditor's report on internal control is limited to obtaining reasonable assurance that material weaknesses in internal control are identified. Thus, the audit is not designed to detect deficiencies in internal control that individually, or in the aggregate, are less severe than a material weakness. The distinction between deficiencies, significant deficiencies, and material weaknesses was discussed earlier.

In Auditing Standard 5, para. A5, the PCAOB defines *Internal Control over Financial Reporting* as:

> "...a process designed by, or under the supervision of, the company's principal executive and principal financial officers, or persons performing similar functions, and effected by the company's board of directors, management, and other personnel, to provide reasonable assurance regarding the reliability of financial reporting and the preparation of financial statements for external purposes in accordance with GAAP, and includes those policies and procedures that:
>
> 1. Pertain to the maintenance of records that, in reasonable detail, accurately and fairly reflect the transactions and dispositions of the assets of the company;
> 2. Provide reasonable assurance that transactions are recorded as necessary to permit preparation of financial statements in accordance with GAAP, and that receipts and expenditures of the company are being made only in accordance with authorizations of management and directors of the company; and
> 3. Provide reasonable assurance regarding prevention or timely detection of unauthorized acquisition, use or disposition of the company's assets that could have a material effect on the financial statements.

It is worth noting that the objectives of internal control in the PCAOB definition above are much more specific than the objectives listed in the COSO requirements.

It is agreed that management must fulfill the following responsibilities and tasks for the auditor to complete an audit of ICFR under Section 404:

- Accept responsibility for the effectiveness of the company's ICFR.
- Assess the effectiveness of the company's ICFR using suitable control criteria— usually COSO.
- Properly document the results of the assessment of internal control giving required evidence.
- Report on the assessment of the effectiveness of the company's internal control as at the end of the accounting period.

The auditor's objective in an audit of ICFR is to express an opinion on the effectiveness of the company's internal control over financial reporting. This is in addition to the auditor's responsibility to express an opinion on the fair presentation of the company's financial statements.

Types of Opinions

Unmodified Opinion
The auditor will issue an unmodified opinion on internal control over financial reporting when two conditions exist:

- There are no identified material weaknesses in the design or operations of the internal control.
- There have been no restrictions on the scope of the auditor's work.

A control deficiency exists when the design or operation of a control will not help management in performing the normal activities of the company, or prevent or detect misstatements on a timely basis. The determination of the significance of control deficiency requires a great deal of professional judgment on the part of both management and the auditor. Management as well as auditors must also consider the existence and effectiveness of compensating controls that would prevent or detect a misstatement that could be material.

Adverse Opinion
When material weaknesses exist, the auditor must express an adverse opinion on the effectiveness of internal control. The most common cause of an adverse opinion in the auditor's report on internal control is when management identified a material weakness in its report.

Qualified or Disclaimer of Opinion
A scope limitation requires the auditor to express a qualified opinion or a disclaimer of opinion on internal control over financial reporting. This type of opinion is issued when the auditor is unable to determine if there are material weaknesses, due to a restriction on the scope of the audit of internal control over financial reporting or other circumstances where the auditor is unable to obtain sufficient evidence.

Because the audit of the financial statements and the audit of internal control over financial reporting are integrated, the auditor must consider the results of audit procedures performed to issue the audit report on the financial statements when issuing the audit report on internal control. For example, assume the auditor identifies a material misstatement in the financial statements that was not initially identified by the company's internal controls. The following four responses to this finding are likely:

1. Because there is a material error in the financial statements, the auditor should consider whether the misstatement indicates the existence of a material weakness. Determining if the misstatement is in fact a material weakness or a significant deficiency involves judgment and depends on the nature and size of the misstatement.
2. The auditor can issue an unqualified opinion on the financial statements if the client adjusts the statements to correct the misstatement prior to issuance.

Report of Independent Registered Public Accounting Firm

[Definition of material weakness paragraph]

A **material weakness** is a deficiency, or combination of deficiencies, in internal control over financial reporting, such that there is a **reasonable possibility** that a material misstatement of the company's interim or annual financial statements will not be prevented or detected on a timely basis.

[Opinion paragraph]

In our opinion, because of the effect of the material weakness described above on the achievement of the objectives of the control criteria, Kincannon Company has not maintained effective internal control over financial reporting as of December 31, 2009, based on criteria established in *Internal Control - Integrated Framework* issued by the Committee of Sponsoring Organizations of the Treadway Commission (COSO).

Kellum & Kellum, LLP
Brentwood, Tennessee, U.S.

February 2, 2010

*The introductory scope, definition of internal control, inherent limitations of internal control, and reference to the opinion on the financial statements paragraphs use standard wording and are not included. The explanatory paragraph describing the nature of the weakness is also not included.

3. Management is likely to change its report on internal control to assert that the controls are not operating effectively.
4. The auditor must issue an adverse opinion on internal control over financial reporting if the deficiency is considered a material weakness.

Figure 10-10 illustrates the definition of material weakness and opinion paragraphs from an auditor's separate report on internal control when the auditor expresses an adverse opinion on the effectiveness of internal control over financial reporting because of the existence of a material weakness. If the material weakness has not been included in management's assessment, the report should note that a material weakness has been identified but not included in management's assessment.

EVALUATING, REPORTING, AND TESTING INTERNAL CONTROL FOR NONPUBLIC COMPANIES

OBJECTIVE 10-8

Describe the differences in evaluating, reporting, and testing internal control for nonpublic companies.

This section deals with the differences in evaluating, reporting, and testing internal control for nonpublic companies.

A common misconception of nonpublic companies is that they are automatically small and less sophisticated than public companies. While it is true that many nonpublic companies are small, others are large and have sophisticated internal controls.

The following identifies and discusses the most important differences in evaluating, reporting, and testing internal control for nonpublic companies in many countries all over the world including the Arab world.

1. *Reporting requirements.* In audits of nonpublic companies, there is no requirement for an audit of internal control over financial reporting. The auditor, therefore, focuses on internal control only to the extent needed to do a quality audit of financial statements.

2. *Extent of required internal controls.* Management, not the auditor, is responsible for establishing adequate internal controls in nonpublic companies, just like management for public companies. If the control environment or documentation is inadequate, the auditor may decide to withdraw from the engagement or issue a disclaimer of opinion on the financial statements. Also, well-run nonpublic companies understand the importance of effective controls to reduce the likelihood of errors and fraud, and to improve effectiveness and efficiency.

   A company's size has a significant effect on the nature of internal control and the specific controls that are implemented. Obviously, it is more difficult to establish adequate separation of duties in a small company. It is also unreasonable to expect a small firm to have internal auditors. However, if the various components of internal control are examined, it becomes apparent that most are applicable to both large and small companies. It is certainly possible for a small company to have (1) competent, trustworthy personnel with clear lines of authority; (2) proper procedures for authorization, execution, and recording of transactions; (3) adequate documents, records, and reports; (4) physical controls over assets and records; and, to a limited degree, (5) independent checks on performance.

   A major control available in a small company is the knowledge and concern of the top operating person, who is often an owner–manager. A personal interest in the organization and a close relationship with personnel make careful evaluation of the competence of the employees and the effectiveness of the overall system possible. For example, internal control can be significantly strengthened if the owner conscientiously performs such duties as signing all checks after carefully reviewing supporting documents, reviewing bank reconciliations, examining accounts receivable statements sent to customers, approving credit, examining all correspondence from customers and vendors, and approving bad debts.

   Some nonpublic companies are unwilling to implement ideal internal control systems because of costs. For a small nonpublic company, hiring additional personnel might achieve only small improvements in the reliability of accounting data. Instead, it is often less expensive for nonpublic companies to have auditors do more extensive auditing than to incur higher internal control costs.

3. *Extent of understanding needed.* Auditing standards require that the auditor obtain a sufficient understanding of internal control to assess control risk. In practice, the procedures to gain an understanding of internal control vary considerably from client to client. For smaller nonpublic clients, many auditors obtain a level of understanding sufficient only to assess whether the statements are auditable and to evaluate the control environment for management's attitude toward internal control. If the auditor determines that the overall attitude of management about the importance of internal control is inadequate to support the other four components of internal control, the auditor assesses control risk at maximum and designs and performs detailed substantive procedures. For larger clients, the understanding can be the same as that described for public companies.

4. *Assessing control risk.* The most important difference in a nonpublic company in assessing control risk is the assessment of control risk at maximum for any or all control-related objectives when internal controls for the objective or objectives are nonexistent or ineffective. Because of the expectation that public companies should have effective internal controls for all significant transactions and accounts, there is an initial presumption that control risk is low in the audit of public company financial statements. Thus, it is unlikely that a public company auditor will make a preliminary assessment of control risk at maximum. This is due to the unique characteristics of large public companies represented in their size, complexity, and organizational structure, and their processes and financial reporting environment. Auditors are advised to follow a top-down risk-based approach for evaluating and assessing the internal control. This approach begins with the auditor's understanding of the risks at the financial statements levels

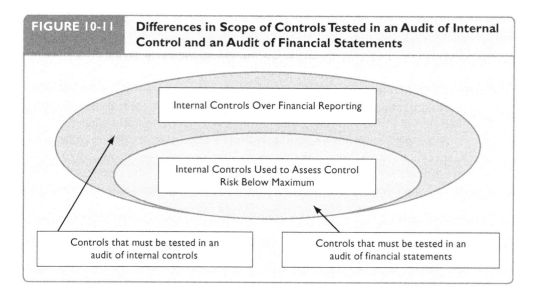

FIGURE 10-11   **Differences in Scope of Controls Tested in an Audit of Internal Control and an Audit of Financial Statements**

Internal Controls Over Financial Reporting

Internal Controls Used to Assess Control Risk Below Maximum

Controls that must be tested in an audit of internal controls

Controls that must be tested in an audit of financial statements

and entity level controls and works down to significant accounts and disclosures and their relevant assertions. This approach should include: (1) identify financial reporting risks and related controls, (2) evaluate evidence about the operating effectiveness of internal control including considering which locations, processes, accounts, and transactions to include in the evaluation, and (3) report the findings of the evaluation of the internal control.

As with public company audits, it is useful for auditors to use a control risk matrix for nonpublic company audits. The same format suggested in Figure 10-7 is appropriate.

5. *Extent of tests of controls needed.* The auditor will not perform tests of controls when the auditor assesses control risk at maximum because of inadequate controls. When control risk is assessed below the maximum for a nonpublic company, the auditor designs and performs a combination of tests of controls and substantive procedures to obtain reasonable assurance that the financial statements are fairly stated.

In contrast, the number of controls tested by auditors to express an opinion on internal controls for a public company is significantly greater than that tested solely to express an opinion on the financial statements. This is illustrated in Figure 10-11. To express an opinion on internal controls for a public company, the auditor obtains an understanding of and performs tests of controls for all significant account balances, classes of transactions, and disclosures and related assertions in the financial statements. Those controls might or might not be tested in a financial statement audit of a nonpublic company.

SUMMARY

This chapter focused on management's and the auditor's responsibility for understanding, evaluating, and testing internal control for an integrated audit of financial statements and internal control over financial reporting. The chapter also discussed the auditor's responsibility in relation to reports on Internal Control over Financial Reporting (ICFR) as required under Sarbanes–Oxley Act in the U.S. The chapter discussed the requirements of Section 404 of the Sarbanes–Oxley Act and PCAOB requirements as these include specific regulations aimed at protecting investors' funds. In the Arab countries, auditors understand and test internal controls as part of their audit of the clients' financial statements as stated in the International Standards on Auditing. To rely on a client's internal controls and to reduce planned audit evidence for audits of financial statements, the auditor must first obtain an understanding of each of the five components of internal control. Knowledge about the design of the client's control environment, risk assessment, control activities, information and communication, and monitoring activities and information about whether internal control components have been implemented assist the auditor in assessing control risk for each transaction-related audit objective.

The chapter showed that the assessment of these five components of the internal controls exist in Arab countries but the tools used by auditors to achieve the objective of assessing these components are still being developed. Auditors in the Arab world are developing their IT capabilities, improving the risk assessment process by developing published industry alerts, and looking for more practical means by which control activities are effectively implemented by management.

The chapter ended with a discussion of the differences in the audit of nonpublic companies compared to public companies in relation to reporting on internal control over financial reporting. For nonpublic companies, auditors have the option of assessing a higher level of control risk, depending on the quality of the client's internal controls and cost–benefit considerations.

The process followed by auditors in assessing control risk for public and nonpublic companies is summarized in Figure 10-12.

FIGURE 10-12	Summary of Understanding Internal Control and Assessing Control Risk

Nonpublic Company		Public Company	
Sufficient to audit financial statements	Obtain an understanding of internal control design and operation	Sufficient to audit internal control over financial reporting	PHASE 1
Varies depending on extent and effectiveness of controls and the auditor's planned reliance on controls	Decide control risk at the objective level for each transaction type	Decide low for all objectives unless there are significant deficiencies or material weaknesses	PHASE 2
	Three alternatives		
	Maximum Intermediate Low		
Varies depending on assessed level of control risk	Plan and perform tests of controls and evaluate results	Extensive tests for all objectives	PHASE 3
Revise for tests of controls results	Revise assessed control risk if appropriate	Revise for tests of controls results	
Likely to be more reliance on substantive tests, depending on assessed control risk option selected	Plan detection risk and perform substantive tests considering control risk and other audit risk model factors	Likely to be less reliance on substantive tests due to extensive tests of controls	PHASE 4
Must communicate in writing to those charged with governance describing significant deficiencies or material weaknesses	Issue internal control report or letter	Must issue report on internal control over financial reporting and issue a written communication to audit committee describing significant deficiencies or material weaknesses	

ESSENTIAL TERMS

Assessment of control risk   p. 335

Chart of accounts   p. 326

Collusion   p. 317

Compensating control   p. 338

Control activities   p. 323

Control deficiency   p. 337

Control environment   p. 320

Control risk matrix   p. 335

Entity-level controls   p. 329

Flowchart   p. 331

General authorization   p. 325

Independent checks   p. 327

Information and communication   p. 328

Internal control   p. 314

Internal control questionnaire   p. 332

Key controls   p. 337

Management letter   p. 341

Material weakness   p. 337

Monitoring   p. 328

Narrative   p. 331

Procedures to obtain an
understanding   p. 331

Risk assessment   p. 322

Separation of duties   p. 324

Significant deficiency   p. 337

Significant risks   p. 342

Specific authorization   p. 325

Those charged with
governance   p. 321

Walkthrough   p. 334

REVIEW QUESTIONS

10-1 (Objective 10-1) Describe the three broad objectives management has when design-ing effective internal control.

10-2 (Objective 10-1) Describe which of the three categories of broad objectives for inter-nal controls are considered by the auditor in an audit of both the financial statements and internal control over financial reporting.

10-3 (Objective 10-2) Section 404 of the U.S. Sarbanes–Oxley Act requires management to issue a report on internal control over financial reporting. Identify the specific Section 404 reporting requirements for management. Are there similar requirements for reporting on internal control in the Arab countries? Why have such measures not yet been introduced in your country?

10-4 (Objectives 10-2, 10-7) What two components of internal control must management assess when reporting on internal control to comply with Section 404 of the Sarbanes–Oxley Act? Are similar components required under laws in your country?

10-5 (Objective 10-2) Chapter 8 introduced the eight parts of the planning phase of audits. Which part is understanding internal control and assessing control risk? What parts pre-cede and follow that understanding and assessing?

10-6 (Objectives 10-2, 10-4, 10-7, 10-8) What is the auditor's responsibility for obtaining an understanding of internal control? How does that responsibility differ for audits of pub-lic and nonpublic companies?

10-7 (Objectives 10-2, 10-7) When auditing a public company, how do the auditor's responsibilities related to internal control as required by the U.S. PCAOB standards com-pare with requirements in the Arab world?

10-8 (Objectives 10-2, 10-3, 10-7) Management must identify the framework used to eval-uate the effectiveness of internal control over financial reporting. What framework is used widely under IFAC and in most U.S. public companies?

10-9 (Objective 10-3) What are the five components of internal control in the COSO internal control framework?

10-10 (Objective 10-3) What is meant by the control environment? What are the factors the auditor must evaluate to understand it?

10-11 (Objective 10-3) What is the relationship among the five components of internal control?

10-12 (Objective 10-3) List the types of specific control activities and provide one specific illustration of a control in the sales area for each control activity.

10-13 (Objective 10-3) The separation of operational responsibility from record keeping is meant to prevent different types of misstatements than the separation of the custody of assets from accounting. Explain the difference in the purposes of these two types of separation of duties.

10-14 (Objective 10-3) For each of the following, give an example of a physical control the client can use to protect the asset or record:

1. Petty cash
2. Cash received by retail clerks
3. Accounts receivable records
4. Raw material inventory
5. Machinery and other miscellaneous tools
6. Manufacturing equipment
7. Marketable securities

10-15 (Objective 10-3) Explain what is meant by independent checks on performance and give three specific examples.

10-16 (Objective 10-4) Describe the four phases performed by the auditor when obtaining an understanding of internal control and assessing control risk.

10-17 (Objective 10-4) What two aspects of internal control must the auditor assess when performing procedures to obtain an understanding of internal control?

10-18 (Objective 10-4) What is a walkthrough of internal control? What is its purpose?

10-19 (Objective 10-5) Describe what is meant by a key control and a control deficiency.

10-20 (Objectives 10-5, 10-7) Distinguish a significant deficiency in internal control from a material weakness in internal control. How will the presence of one significant deficiency affect an auditor's report on internal control under PCAOB and IFAC standards? How will the presence of one material weakness affect an auditor's report on internal control under PCAOB and IFAC standards?

10-21 (Objectives 10-3, 10-5) Heidi Helmy, a highly competent employee of Vidi-Ad Sales Corporation, had been responsible for accounting-related matters for two decades. Her devotion to the firm and her duties had always been exceptional, and over the years, she had been given increased responsibility. Both the president of Vidi-Ad and the partner of an independent audit firm in charge of the audit were shocked and dismayed to discover that Heidi had embezzled more than US$500,000 over a ten-year period by not recording billings in the sales journal and subsequently diverting the cash receipts. What major factors permitted the embezzlement to take place?

10-22 (Objective 10-5) Aisha Mubarak, CPA, believes that it is appropriate to obtain an understanding of internal control about halfway through the audit, after she is familiar with the client's operations and the way the system actually works. She has found through experience that filling out internal control questionnaires and flowcharts early in the engagement is not beneficial because the system rarely functions the way it is supposed to. Later in the engagement, the auditor can prepare flowcharts and questionnaires with relative ease because of the knowledge already obtained on the audit. Evaluate her approach.

10-23 (Objectives 10-6, 10-8) Distinguish the auditor's responsibility for testing controls in an audit of a public company from the responsibility to test controls in an audit of a nonpublic company.

10-24 (Objective 10-6) How does the sufficiency of evidence differ between procedures to obtain an understanding of internal control and tests of controls?

10-25 (Objective 10-6) During the prior year audits of Kuwait Trading Co., a private company, the auditor did tests of controls for all relevant financial statement assertions. Some of the related controls are manual while others are automated. Describe the extent the auditor can rely on tests of controls performed in prior years.

MULTIPLE CHOICE QUESTIONS FROM CPA EXAMINATIONS

10-26 (Objectives 10-1, 10-2, 10-7) The following are general questions about internal control. Choose the best response.

a. When considering internal control, an auditor must be aware of the concept of reasonable assurance, which recognizes that the
   (1) employment of competent personnel provides assurance that management's control objectives will be achieved.
   (2) establishment and maintenance of internal control is an important responsibility of management and not of the auditor.
   (3) cost of internal control should not exceed the benefits expected to be derived therefrom.
   (4) separation of incompatible functions is necessary to ascertain that the internal control is effective.

b. When an auditor issues an unqualified opinion about internal control over financial reporting for a public company in the U.S., the auditor has obtained reasonable assurance that
   (1) the likelihood of fraud is minimal.
   (2) there are no control deficiencies.
   (3) internal control over financial reporting is operating effectively.
   (4) the financial statements are fairly presented in all material respects.

c. Which of the following most accurately describe the auditor's responsibilities for reporting on internal control required by PCAOB standards? The auditor tested
   (1) all controls related to the objectives of reliable financial reporting, efficiency and effectiveness of operations, and compliance with laws and regulations.
   (2) controls solely related to the reliability of financial reporting objective.
   (3) controls related to the compliance with laws and regulations objective.
   (4) controls related to the reliability of financial reporting objective in addition to those controls related to operations and compliance with laws and regulations objectives that could materially affect financial reporting.

d. What is the independent auditor's principal purpose for obtaining an understanding of internal control and assessing control risk in a financial statement audit under ISA?
   (1) To comply with International Financial Reporting Standards.
   (2) To obtain a measure of assurance of management's efficiency.
   (3) To maintain a state of independence in mental attitude during the audit.
   (4) To determine the nature, timing, and extent of subsequent audit work.

10-27 (Objectives 10-5, 10-7) The following questions deal with deficiencies in internal control. Choose the best response.

a. In general, an internal control deficiency may be defined as a condition under which misstatements would ordinarily not be detected within a timely period by
   (1) an auditor during the typical obtaining of an understanding of internal control and assessment of control risk.

    (2) a controller when reconciling accounts in the general ledger.

    (3) employees in the normal course of performing their assigned functions.

    (4) the chief financial officer when reviewing interim financial statements.

b. A material weakness in internal control represents a control deficiency that

    (1) more than remotely adversely affects a company's ability to initiate, authorize, record, process, or report external financial statements reliably.

    (2) results in a reasonable possibility that internal control will not prevent or detect material financial statement misstatements.

    (3) exists because a necessary control is missing or not properly designed.

    (4) reduces the efficiency and effectiveness of the entity's operations.

c. When a nonpublic company auditor's tests of controls identify deficiencies in internal control over financial reporting, the auditor

    (1) must communicate to management all deficiencies identified.

    (2) must communicate both significant deficiencies and material weaknesses to those charged with governance.

    (3) may communicate orally or in writing to the board all significant deficiencies and material weaknesses identified.

    (4) must issue an adverse opinion on the financial statements.

10-28 (Objectives 10-5, 10-6, 10-8) The following questions deal with assessing control risk in a financial statement audit. Choose the best response.

a. The ultimate purpose of assessing control risk is to contribute to the auditor's evaluation of the

    (1) factors that raise doubts about the auditability of the financial statements.

    (2) operating effectiveness of internal controls.

    (3) risk that material misstatements exist in the financial statements.

    (4) possibility that the nature and extent of substantive tests may be reduced.

b. An auditor uses assessed control risk to

    (1) evaluate the effectiveness of the entity's internal controls.

    (2) identify transactions and account balances where inherent risk is at the maximum.

    (3) indicate whether materiality thresholds for planning and evaluation purposes are sufficiently high.

    (4) determine the acceptable level of detection risk for financial statement assertions.

c. On the basis of audit evidence gathered and evaluated, an auditor decides to increase assessed control risk from that originally planned. To achieve an audit risk level (AcAR) that is substantially the same as the planned audit risk level (AAR), the auditor will

    (1) increase inherent risk.

    (2) increase materiality levels.

    (3) decrease substantive testing.

    (4) decrease planned detection risk.

d. Which of the following statements about tests of controls is incorrect? Tests of controls

    (1) must be done in every audit of a public company's financial statements.

    (2) provide persuasive evidence that a material misstatement exists when the auditor determines that the control is not being consistently applied.

    (3) are often based on the same types of audit techniques used to gain an understanding of internal controls, except the extent of testing is generally greater when testing controls.

    (4) allow a reduction in the extent of substantive testing, as long as the results of the tests of controls are equal to or better than what the auditor expects.

DISCUSSION QUESTIONS AND PROBLEMS

10-29 (Objectives 10-3, 10-4, 10-5, 10-6) Each of the following internal controls has been taken from a standard internal control questionnaire used by an auditing firm for assessing control risk in the payroll and personnel cycle.

1. Approval of department head or foreman on time cards is required before preparing payroll.
2. All prenumbered time cards are accounted for before beginning data entry for preparation of checks.
3. The payroll accounting software application will not accept data input for an employee number not contained in the employee master file.
4. Persons preparing the payroll do not perform other payroll duties (timekeeping, distribution of checks) or have access to payroll data master files or cash.
5. The computer calculates gross and net pay based on hours inputted and information in employee master files, and payroll accounting personnel double-check the mathematical accuracy on a test basis.
6. All voided and spoiled payroll checks are properly mutilated and retained.
7. Human resources policies require an investigation of an employment application from new employees. Investigation includes checking the employee's background, former employers, and references.
8. Written termination notices, with properly documented reasons for termination, and approval of an appropriate official are required.
9. All checks not distributed to employees are returned to the treasurer for safekeeping.
10. Online ability to add employees or change pay rates to the payroll master file is restricted via passwords to authorized human resource personnel.

Required

a. For each internal control, identify the type(s) of specific control activity (activities) to which it applies (such as adequate documents and records or physical control over assets and records).

b. For each internal control, identify the transaction-related audit objective(s) to which it applies.

c. For each internal control, identify a specific misstatement that is likely to be prevented if the control exists and is effective.

d. For each control, list a specific misstatement that could result from the absence of the control.

e. For each control, identify one audit test that the auditor could use to uncover misstatements resulting from the absence of the control.

10-30 (Objectives 10-3, 10-4, 10-5, 10-8) The following are misstatements that have occurred in Fresh Foods Grocery Store, a retail and wholesale grocery company:

1. The incorrect price was used on sales invoices for billing shipments to customers because the wrong price was entered into the computer master file of prices.
2. A vendor's invoice was paid twice for the same shipment. The second payment arose because the vendor sent a duplicate copy of the original two weeks after the payment was due.
3. On the last day of the year, a truckload of beef was set aside for shipment but was not shipped. Because it was still on hand the inventory was counted. The shipping document was dated the last day of the year, so it was also included as a current-year sale.
4. A vendor invoice was paid even though no merchandise was ever received. The accounts payable software application does not require the input of a valid receiving report number before payment can be made.
5. Employees in the receiving department took sides of beef for their personal use. When a shipment of meat was received, the receiving department filled out a receiving report and forwarded it to the accounting department for the amount of goods

actually received. At that time, two sides of beef were put in an employee's pickup truck rather than in the storage freezer.

6. During the physical count of inventory of the retail grocery, one counter wrote down the wrong description of several products and miscounted the quantity.

7. A salesperson sold an entire carload of lamb at a price below cost because she did not know the cost of lamb had increased in the past week.

8. An accounts payable clerk processed payments to himself by adding a fictitious vendor address to the approved vendor master file.

a. For each misstatement, identify one or more types of controls that were absent.   **Required**

b. For each misstatement, identify the transaction-related audit objectives that have not been met.

c. For each misstatement, suggest a control to correct the deficiency.

10-31 (Objective 10-3) The division of the following duties is meant to provide the best possible controls for the Sultan Paint Company, a small wholesale store:

1. Assemble supporting documents for general and payroll cash disbursements.
2. Sign general cash disbursement checks.
3. Input information to prepare checks for signature, record checks in the cash disbursements journal, and update the appropriate master files.
4. Mail checks to suppliers and deliver checks to employees.
5. Cancel supporting documents to prevent their reuse.
6. Approve credit for customers included in the customer credit master file.
7. Input shipping and billing information to bill customers, record invoices in the sales journal, and update the accounts receivable master file.
8. Open the mail and prepare a prelisting of cash receipts.
9. Enter cash receipts data to prepare the cash receipts journal and update the accounts receivable master file.
10. Prepare daily cash deposits.
11. Deliver daily cash deposits to the bank.
12. Assemble the payroll time cards and input the data to prepare payroll checks and update the payroll journal and payroll master files.
13. Sign payroll checks.
14. Update the general ledger at the end of each month and review all accounts for unexpected balances.
15. Reconcile the accounts receivable master file with the control account and review accounts outstanding more than 90 days.
16. Prepare monthly statements for customers by printing the accounts receivable master file; then mail the statements to customers.
17. Reconcile the monthly statements from vendors with the accounts payable master file.
18. Reconcile the bank account.

You are to divide the accounting-related duties 1 through 18 among Ahmed Ismail,   **Required** Ibrahim Moftah, and Jasmine Fouad. All of the responsibilities are assumed to take about the same amount of time and must be divided equally between Ismail and Ibrahim. Both employees are equally competent. Jasmine Fouad, who is president of the company, is willing to perform functions related to her role as the president of the company.

10-32 (Objectives 10-3, 10-5) The following are partial descriptions of internal controls for companies engaged in the manufacturing business:

1. When Mr. Hassan orders materials for his machine-rebuilding plant, he sends a duplicate purchase order to the receiving department. During the delivery of materials, Mr. Fayez, the receiving clerk, records the receipt of shipment on this purchase order. After recording, Mr. Fayez sends the purchase order to the accounting department, where it is used to record materials purchased and accounts payable. The materials are transported to the storage area by forklifts. The additional purchased quantities are recorded on storage records.

2. Every day, hundreds of employees clock in using time cards at Saudi Arabia Jamil Motors Corporation. The timekeepers collect these cards once a week and deliver them to the computer department. There, the data on these time cards are entered into the computer. The information entered into the computer is used in the preparation of the labor cost distribution records, the payroll journal, and the payroll checks. The treasurer, Mr. Suleiman, compares the payroll journal with the payroll checks, signs the checks, and returns them to Mr. Hamza, the supervisor of the computer department. The payroll checks are distributed to the employees by Mr. Hayek.

3. The smallest branch of Dead Sea Cosmetics in Amman employs Fatma Abdel Aziz, the branch manager, and her sales assistant, Samar Youssef. The branch uses a bank account in Amman to pay expenses. The account is kept in the name of Dead Sea Cosmetics—Special Account. To pay expenses, checks must be signed by Fatma Abdel Aziz or by the treasurer of Dead Sea Cosmetics, Mohamed Salah. Abdel Aziz receives the cancelled checks and bank statements. She reconciles the branch account herself and files cancelled checks and bank statements in her records. She also periodically prepares reports of cash disbursements and sends them to the home office.

Required

a. List the deficiencies in internal control for each of these situations. To identify the deficiencies, use the methodology that was discussed in this chapter.

b. For each deficiency, state the type(s) of misstatement(s) that is (are) likely to result. Be as specific as possible.

c. How would you improve internal controls for each of the three companies?

CASE

10-33 (Objective 10-5) The Cotton Company, a retail store dealing in expensive linens and clothing, has a staff of about 20 salesclerks. The sales are done in cash or credit, using the store's own billing rather than credit cards. Most of the larger sales are on credit.

Each salesclerk has his own sales book with prenumbered, three-copy, multicolored sales slips attached, but perforated. Only a central cash register is used, run by the store manager. He's been working for Zafir Diab, the store owner, for over 15 years. The cash register is physically positioned to monitor the entire store and the front door.

All transactions are recorded in the salesclerks' sales books. The original and second copies for each sale are given to the cashier. The third copy is retained by the salesclerk in the sales book. When the sale is for cash, the customer pays the salesclerk, who marks all three copies 'paid' and takes the money to the supervisor.

The supervisor compares the clothing to the description on the invoice and the price on the sales tag. He also rechecks the clerk's calculations. Any corrections are approved by the salesclerk. The clerk changes his sales book at that time, and the items are packaged and given to the customer.

A credit sale must be approved by the supervisor from an approved credit list after the salesclerk prepares the three-part invoice. Next, the supervisor enters the sale in his cash register as a credit or cash sale. The second copy of the invoice, which has been validated by the cash register, is given to the customer. Diab must approve of any credit sales that exceed US$500.

At the end of the day, the sales clerks give their books to the supervisor, and the supervisor compares the totals to the cash register tape. He then creates a summary of the day's transactions. The cash is deposited in the bank the next morning by Diab, and he receives a deposit slip, which he gives to the accounts receivable clerk. If Diab is unable to deposit the money, the supervisor goes instead. The cashier's copies of the invoices are also given to the accounts receivable clerk along with a summary of the day's receipts.

Khalid, the accounts receivable clerk, reviews the sales books and the register tape. He inputs all sales invoice information into the firm's computer, which provides a complete printout of all input and summaries. The accounting summary includes sales by the salesclerks, cash sales, credit sales, and total sales. Khalid compares this output with the summary and reconciles all differences.

The computer updates accounts receivable, inventory, and general ledger master files. After the update procedure has been run on the computer, Khalid's assistant files all sales included in the sales printout. Khalid uses these files to create bills that are mailed to the customers. The mail is opened each morning by Diab's secretary. She gives all correspondence to Diab and all payments to the supervisor. The supervisor totals the amounts and adds this cash to the register for later deposit. He gives the total to Khalid to update customer accounts on the computer. Khalid uses this list and all the remittances to record cash receipts and update accounts receivable, again by computer. He reconciles the total receipts on the prelist to the deposit slip and to her printout. At the same time, he compares the deposit slip received from the bank for cash sales to the cash receipts journal. He has online access to the store's bank account, which he accesses monthly to pay the store's bills online.

The computer generates a weekly aged trial balance of accounts receivable. A separate listing of all unpaid bills is also automatically prepared, and both are given to Diab. He approves all write-offs of uncollectible items and forwards the list to Khalid, who writes them off.

Each month Khalid mails computer-generated statements to customers. Complaints and disagreements are resolved by Diab, who then informs Khalid in writing of any write-downs or misstatements that require correction.

The computer system also automatically totals the journals and posts the totals to the general ledger. A general ledger trial balance is printed out, from which Khalid prepares financial statements. Khalid also prepares monthly bank reconciliations and reconciles the general ledger to the aged accounts receivable trial balance.

Because of the importance of inventory control, Khalid prints out the inventory perpetual totals monthly, on the last day of each month. Salesclerks count all inventory after store hours on the last day of each month for comparison with the perpetuals. An inventory shortage report is provided to Diab. The perpetuals are adjusted by Khalid after Diab has approved the adjustments.

a. For each sales transaction-related audit objective, identify one or more existing controls.
b. For each cash receipts transaction-related audit objective, identify one or more existing controls.
c. What are some possible deficiencies in the store's system? How would you, as the auditor, suggest ways to improve their system?

Required

MYLAB ACTIVITY

Visit MyAccountingLab and complete the following activity:
→ Integrated Case Application: Pinnacle Manufacturing: Part III

CHAPTER 11

FRAUD AUDITING

Longest Jail Term Yet in Dubai in Corruption Inquiry

CT, a British senior manager at Istithmar World, the overseas investment arm of Dubai World, was sentenced to five years in jail and ordered
to pay almost AED 10 million (US$2.7 million) in fines and restitution after
being found guilty of embezzling AED 4.9 million (US$1.34 million). CT was
accused of purchasing stocks for Istithmar from a British brokerage company
that he owned, then pocketing a portion of the funds. Abdel Wahid Abdel
Rahman, 31, a board member of Dubai World, told prosecutors CT had
been hired to head Istithmar's risk assessment department. He was asked to
establish procedures to combat and prevent fraud within the company. "In
2008 God sent us an angel to alert us of the fraud taking place by the person
entrusted to prevent it," Mr. Abdel Rahman said in Dubai Criminal Court. He
testified that company investigators discovered CT had signed agreements
to purchase stocks worth GBP 2 million (AED 12.11 million) from Newland
Brokerage, a British company. "The defendant purchased stocks in the name
of Istithmar, which he is not entitled to do," Mr. Abdel Rahman said. "Our
investigations revealed that CT transferred US$1.3 million to his account
after the agreements were done. Furthermore, we found out that the company in the U.K. belonged to him and he was its managing director." The court
ordered CT to repay the US$1.3 million and fined him the same amount. He
was further ordered to be dismissed from his position. Thousands of investors and employees were amazed at the way the fraud was committed and
everyone asked "Where were the auditors?" The accounting profession in
this Gulf state was under immense political pressure from reform-minded
lawmakers, and the negative publicity surrounding the perceived audit failure
cast all CPAs in the most unfavourable light.

Source: Adapted from 'Longest Jail Term in Corruption Inquiry,' *The National News*,
November 4, 2009.

The classic fraud at Istithmar World illustrates that fraud is nothing new. In the wake of that scandal, the auditing profession in U.A.E. and other Arab countries responded by confirming the need of audit firms to comply with standards for auditing procedures. Those standards required confirmation of investments, plus more guidance on the auditor's responsibilities for detecting fraud.

In the U.S., in response to recent frauds, the Sarbanes–Oxley Act was passed in 2002 and AICPA developed specific auditing standards to deal with fraud risk assessment and detection. Internationally, the IFAC redrafted a number of its International Standards on Auditing to include more guidelines and measures to help auditors uncover fraud instances. In this chapter we will discuss the auditor's responsibility to assess the risk of fraud and detect material misstatements due to fraud, and describe major areas of fraud risk, as well as controls to prevent fraud and audit procedures to detect fraud.

Relevant International Standards on Auditing	
IESBA	The Code of Ethics for Professional Accountants
ISA 220	Quality Control for an Audit of Financial Statements
ISA 230	Audit Documentation
ISA 240	The Auditor's Responsibilities Relating to Fraud in an Audit of Financial Statements
ISA 260	Communication with Those Charged with Governance
ISA 315	Identifying and Assessing the Risks of Material Misstatement through Understanding the Entity and Its Environment
ISA 450	Evaluation of Misstatements Identified during the Audit
ISA 700	Forming an Opinion and Reporting on Financial Statements

TYPES OF FRAUD

OBJECTIVE 11-1

Define fraud and distinguish between fraudulent financial reporting and misappropriation of assets.

Generally speaking, misstatements can result from error or fraud. A misstatement due to error or fraud can be defined as:

a difference between the amount, classification, or presentation of a reported financial statement element, account or item and the amount, classification or presentation that would have been reported under the applicable financial reporting framework.

Source: Eiligsen, A, Messier, W, Glover, S, and Prawitt, D. (2010), *Auditing & Assurance Services*, McGraw-Hill, p. 87

Practitioners in the auditing profession have identified a number of situations where misstatements from error and fraud may result from:

- An inaccuracy in gathering or processing transactions' data from which the financial statements are prepared.
- An omission of a transaction, an amount, or disclosure related to a company's activities.
- An incorrect accounting estimate due to overlooking or improper misinterpretation of facts.
- Management's inappropriate selection and application of accounting policies or judgments concerning accounting estimates that the auditor considers unreasonable, including related disclosures.

Fraud describes any intentional deceit meant to deprive another person or party of their property or rights. In the context of auditing financial statements, fraud is defined as an intentional misstatement of financial statements. The two main categories are fraudulent financial reporting and misappropriation of assets, which we introduced when defining the auditor's responsibilities for detecting material misstatements in Chapter 6.

Fraudulent Financial Reporting

Fraudulent financial reporting is an intentional misstatement or omission of amounts or disclosures with the intent to deceive users. Most cases involve the intentional misstatement of amounts, rather than disclosures. For example, in the Istithmar World case, the investment manager defrauded the company US$1.34 million through illegal transactions with his own company in London. Also, WorldCom, the U.S. company hit by a major fraud scandal in 2002, is reported to have capitalized as fixed assets billions of dollars that should have been expensed. Omissions of amounts are less common, but a company can overstate income by omitting accounts payable and other liabilities. Some of the most famous fraudulent financial reporting acts include:

- Manipulation, falsification, or alteration of accounting records or supporting documents used to prepare financial statements.
- Misrepresentation in, or intentional omission from, the financial statements of events, transactions, or other significant information.
- Intentional misapplication of accounting policies related to amounts, classification, presentation, or disclosure of accounting information.

While most cases of fraudulent financial reporting involve an attempt to overstate income—either by overstatement of assets and income or by omission of liabilities and expenses—companies also deliberately understate income. At privately held companies, this may be done in an attempt to reduce income taxes. Companies may also intentionally understate income when earnings are high to create a reserve of earnings or 'cookie jar reserves' that may be used to increase earnings in future periods. Such practices are called income smoothing and earnings management. **Earnings management** involves deliberate actions taken by management to meet earnings objectives. **Income smoothing** is a form of earnings management in which revenues and expenses are shifted between periods to reduce fluctuations in earnings. One technique to smooth income is to reduce the value of inventory and other assets of an acquired company at the time of acquisition, resulting in higher earnings when the assets are later sold. Companies may also deliberately overstate inventory obsolescence reserves and allowances for doubtful accounts to counter higher earnings.

Although less frequent, several notable cases of fraudulent financial reporting involve inadequate disclosure. For example, the investment manager of Istithmar did not disclose his ownership of the British brokerage firm he owned in London and used it to transfer million of dollars illegally. A central issue in the Enron case in the U.S. was whether the company adequately disclosed obligations to affiliates known as special purpose entities.

Earnings management

Deliberate actions taken by management to meet earnings objectives.

Income smoothing

Form of earnings management in which revenues and expenses are shifted between periods to reduce fluctuations in earnings.

Misappropriation of Assets

Misappropriation of assets is fraud that involves theft of an entity's assets. This is sometimes referred to as defalcations. Examples of misappropriation of assets include:

- Embezzling cash received.
- Stealing assets or the company's funds.
- Collusion among employees/outside parties to make the entity pay for goods or services not received.

FRAUDULENT FINANCIAL REPORTING STATISTICS

In the U.S., the two most common techniques used by management to misstate financial statement information involve improper revenue recognition and overstatements of assets. According to a study commissioned by COSO, 50 percent of U.S. companies committing financial statement fraud between 1987 and 1997 recorded revenues prematurely or created fictitious revenue transactions.

In addition to these revenue and receivable overstatements, half of the identified fraudulent companies also overstated assets by either overvaluing existing assets, recording fictitious assets or assets not owned, or capitalizing items that should have been expensed. The companies typically overstated assets such as inventory, net accounts receivable due to understated allowances for doubtful accounts, and property, plant, and equipment. Only 18 percent of the fraud companies understated expenses or liabilities. Most of the financial statement fraud instances involved intentionally misstating financial information; only 12 percent of the fraud cases involved misappropriation of company assets.

Eighty-three percent of the fraud cases were perpetrated by the chief executive officer (CEO) and/or the chief financial officer (CFO). These individuals allegedly engaged in the fraud to avoid reporting a pretax loss, to maintain requirements to continue trading company stock on one of the national stock exchanges, or to increase stock prices. The motivation to commit the fraud was high because, on average, company officers and members of the board of directors owned 32 percent of the company stock.

Consequences of these frauds were significant. More than half of the companies where fraudulent activity was identified filed for bankruptcy or changed form of ownership following the fraud period. Many of the individuals involved were forced to resign, were terminated as a result of the fraud, and, in some cases, were jailed. Additionally, both companies and individuals faced lawsuits filed by shareholders and the SEC.

Source: Adapted from *Fraudulent Financial Reporting: 1987–1997, An Analysis of U.S. Public Companies*, Committee of Sponsoring Organizations of the Treadway Commission, New York, U. S., 1999 (www.coso.org).

Misappropriation of assets is usually accompanied by false or misleading records or documents, possibly created by circumventing controls. Misappropriation of assets may involve one or more individuals among management, employees, or third parties.

In many cases, but not all, the amounts involved are not material to the financial statements. However, the theft of company assets is often a management concern, regardless of the materiality of the amounts involved, because small thefts can easily increase in size over time.

The term misappropriation of assets is normally used to refer to theft involving employees and others internal to the organization. According to estimates of the Association of Certified Fraud Examiners, the average company loses 7 percent of its revenues to fraud, although much of this fraud involves external parties, such as shoplifting by customers and cheating by suppliers.

Misappropriation of assets is normally perpetrated at lower levels of the organization hierarchy. In some notable cases, however, top management is involved in the theft of company assets. Because of management's greater authority and control over organization assets, embezzlements involving top management can involve significant amounts. As we have seen in the introductory case of the chapter, Istithmar World hired a senior manager to establish procedures to combat and prevent fraud within the company and he himself overrode the company system and stole US$1.34 million (AED 4.9 million). In another extreme example, in the U.S., the former CEO of Tyco International was charged by the SEC with stealing over US$100 million in assets. A fraud survey conducted by the Association of Certified Fraud Examiners found that asset misappropriations are the most common fraud scheme, although the size of the fraud is much greater for fraudulent financial reporting.

Table 11-1 highlights major types of fraud in various industry sectors showing the most affected industries are financial services and construction. Also, the types of fraud which have the highest percentages are theft of physical assets or stocks, corruption and bribery, management conflict of interest, and fraudulent financial reporting.

TABLE 11-1	Examples and Statistics Concerning Global Fraud and Affected Sectors									
	Financial services	Professional services	Manufacturing	Healthcare, pharmaceuticals, & biotechnology	Technology, media & telecoms	Natural resources	Travel, leisure, & transportation	Retail, wholesale, & distribution	Consumer goods	Construction
Corruption and bribery	16%	14%	24%	13%	16%	24%	20%	22%	19%	33%
Theft of physical assets or stock	28%	23%	46%	35%	30%	43%	43%	51%	44%	37%
Money laundering	11%	4%	4%	4%	3%	4%	6%	2%	1%	5%
Financial mismanagement	25%	17%	24%	24%	17%	17%	22%	21%	15%	30%
Regulatory or compliance breach	28%	17%	21%	30%	17%	21%	21%	14%	21%	25%
Internal financial fraud or theft	27%	10%	19%	18%	9%	20%	28%	22%	18%	17%
Information theft, loss, or attack	25%	28%	23%	22%	29%	24%	23%	25%	22%	19%
Vendor, supplier, or procurement fraud	12%	16%	21%	18%	17%	21%	19%	25%	28%	23%
IP theft, piracy, or counterfeiting	7%	15%	21%	20%	19%	11%	9%	14%	21%	9%
Management conflict of interest	23%	23%	18%	24%	15%	33%	30%	18%	18%	24%

Source: Kroll Global Fraud Report, 2009/10.

CONDITIONS FOR FRAUD

Three conditions for fraud arising from fraudulent financial reporting and misappropriations of assets are described in ISAs 240, 315, and 450. As shown in Figure 11-1, these three conditions are referred to as the **fraud triangle**.

OBJECTIVE 11-2

Describe the fraud triangle and identify conditions for fraud.

Fraud triangle

The three conditions of fraud: incentives/pressures, opportunities, and attitudes/rationalization.

FIGURE 11-1	The Fraud Triangle

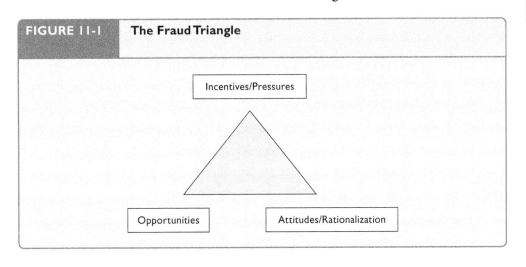

Incentives/Pressures

Opportunities   Attitudes/Rationalization

1. *Incentives/Pressures.* Management or other employees have incentives or pressures to commit fraud.
2. *Opportunities.* Circumstances provide opportunities for management or employees to commit fraud.
3. *Attitudes/Rationalization.* An attitude, character, or set of ethical values exists that allows management or employees to commit a dishonest act, or they are in an environment that imposes sufficient pressure that causes them to rationalize committing a dishonest act.

Risk Factors for Fraudulent Financial Reporting

Fraud risk factors

Entity factors that increase the risk of fraud.

An essential consideration by the auditor in uncovering fraud is identifying factors that increase the risk of fraud. Table 11-2 provides examples of these **fraud risk factors** for each of the three conditions of fraud for fraudulent financial reporting. In the fraud triangle, fraudulent financial reporting and misappropriation of assets share the same three conditions, but the risk factors differ. We'll first address the risk factors for fraudulent financial reporting, and then discuss those for misappropriation of assets. Later in the chapter, the auditor's use of the risk factors in uncovering fraud is discussed.

Incentives/Pressures A common incentive for companies to manipulate financial statements is a decline in the company's financial prospects. For example, a decline in earnings may threaten the company's ability to obtain financing. Companies may

TABLE 11-2	Examples of Risk Factors for Fraudulent Financial Reporting	
THREE CONDITIONS OF FRAUD		
Incentives/Pressures	**Opportunities**	**Attitudes/Rationalization**
Management or other employees have incentives or pressures to materially misstate financial statements.	Circumstances provide an opportunity for management or employees to misstate financial statements.	An attitude, character, or set of ethical values exists that allows management or employees to intentionally commit a dishonest act, or they are in an environment that imposes sufficient pressure that causes them to rationalize committing a dishonest act.
Examples of Risk Factors	**Examples of Risk Factors**	**Examples of Risk Factors**
Financial stability or profitability is threatened by economy, industry, severe competition with declining profit margin or entity operating conditions. Examples include significant declines in customer demand, recurring losses, high vulnerability to rapid changes in technology, and increasing business failures in either the industry or overall economy.	Significant accounting estimates involve subjective judgments, unusual or significant transactions or uncertainties that are difficult to verify (related parties transactions).	Inappropriate or ineffective communication and support of the entity's values.
Excessive pressure for management to meet debt repayment or other debt covenant requirements due to investment analysts' expectations related to profit. Also, financial loss of management due to entity's bad performance.	Ineffective board of directors, deficient internal control, complex organizational structure, ineffective monitoring of management or audit committee oversight over financial reporting.	Known history of violations of securities laws or other laws and regulations.
Management or the board of directors' personal net worth is materially threatened by the entity's financial performance.	High turnover or ineffective accounting, internal audit, or information technology staff.	Management's practice of making overly aggressive or unrealistic forecasts to analysts, creditors, and other third parties.

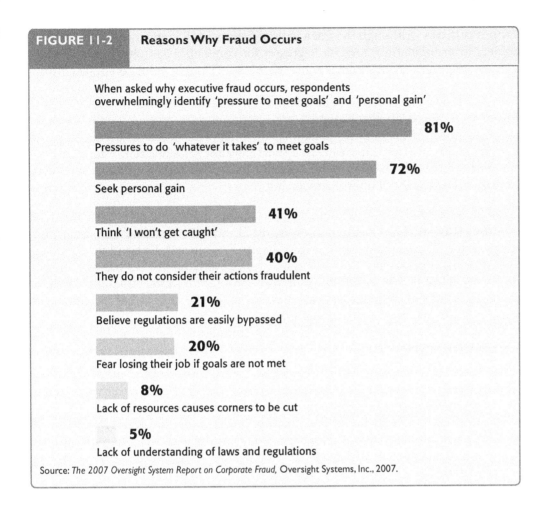

FIGURE 11-2 **Reasons Why Fraud Occurs**

When asked why executive fraud occurs, respondents overwhelmingly identify 'pressure to meet goals' and 'personal gain'

81%
Pressures to do 'whatever it takes' to meet goals

72%
Seek personal gain

41%
Think 'I won't get caught'

40%
They do not consider their actions fraudulent

21%
Believe regulations are easily bypassed

20%
Fear losing their job if goals are not met

8%
Lack of resources causes corners to be cut

5%
Lack of understanding of laws and regulations

Source: *The 2007 Oversight System Report on Corporate Fraud,* Oversight Systems, Inc., 2007.

also manipulate earnings to meet analysts' forecasts or benchmarks such as prior year earnings, to meet debt covenant restrictions, or to artificially inflate stock prices. In some cases, management may manipulate earnings just to preserve their reputation. Figure 11-2 highlights a recent Oversight Systems Inc. survey finding that the pressure to do 'whatever it takes' to meet goals and the desire for personal gain are often cited as primary incentives to engage in fraudulent actions.

LAST DEAL FOR TURNAROUND ARTIST

Albert J. 'Chainsaw Al' Dunlap was a legendary turn-around artist known for his reputation of slashing jobs and other costs. In July 1996, news that he was joining Sunbeam caused its stock to rise by nearly 60 percent, at that time, the largest one-day jump in the history of the New York Stock Exchange in the U.S. Two years later, however, he was ousted from the company by the board of directors amid charges that he had cooked the books to hide Sunbeam's true financial condition from investors.

To increase income and create the impression of revenue growth, the company borrowed revenues from future periods through a procedure known as 'channel stuffing.' Sunbeam offered discounts and inducements to customers to buy merchandise immediately that was normally sold in later periods. For example, customers were encouraged to take delivery of outdoor grills during the winter, even though there was little demand for these items at that time.

Sunbeam ultimately entered bankruptcy in 2001. Al Dunlap was fined US$500,000 by the SEC, a proverbial slap on the wrist compared to his compensation from Sunbeam and his accumulated wealth. He also agreed to a lifetime ban from serving as an officer or director of a public company.

Sources: Adapted from 1. John Byrne, 'Chainsaw Al Dunlap Cuts His Last Deal,' *BusinessWeek* (September 5, 2002). 2. Securities and Exchange Commission Accounting and Auditing Enforcement Release 1623, September 4, 2002 (www.sec.gov/litigation/litreleases/lr17710.htm)

Opportunities Although the financial statements of all companies are potentially subject to manipulation, the risk is greater for companies in industries where significant judgments and estimates are involved. For example, valuation of inventories is subject to greater risk of misstatement for companies with diverse inventories in many locations. The risk of misstatement of inventories is further increased if those inventories are potentially obsolete.

A turnover in accounting personnel or other weaknesses in accounting and information processes can create an opportunity for misstatement. Many cases of fraudulent financial reporting were caused by ineffective audit committee and board of directors' oversight of financial reporting.

Attitudes/Rationalization The attitude of top management toward financial reporting is a critical risk factor in assessing the likelihood of fraudulent financial statements. If the CEO or other top managers display a significant disregard for the financial reporting process, such as consistently issuing overly optimistic forecasts, or they are overly concerned about meeting analysts' earnings forecasts, fraudulent financial reporting is more likely. Management's character or set of ethical values also may make it easier for them to rationalize a fraudulent act.

Risk factors associated with management attitude/rationalization for fraudulent financial reporting include:

- Ineffective communication, support, and enforcement of the entity's values or ethical standards by management, or those charged with governance or the communication of inappropriate values or ethical standards.
- Improper selection of accounting policies or the determination of significant estimates affecting company results and recurring attempts by management to justify marginal or inappropriate accounting on the basis or materiality.
- History of violations of companies acts, securities laws, or other laws and regulations, or claims against the entity, its senior management, or those charged with governance alleging fraud or violations of laws and regulations.
- Intentional motivation by management to increase the entity's stock price or earnings trend.
- Management commitment to meet analysts, creditors, and other third parties to achieve aggressive or unrealistic forecasts.

Auditors should carefully study these risk factors and make necessary inquiries to ensure that no incident of fraudulent financial reporting occurred.

Risk Factors for Misappropriation of Assets

The same three conditions apply to misappropriation of assets. However, in assessing risk factors, greater emphasis is placed on individual incentives and opportunities for theft. Table 11-3 provides examples of fraud risk factors for each of the three conditions of fraud for misappropriation of assets.

Incentives/Pressures Financial pressures are a common incentive for employees who misappropriate assets. Employees with excessive financial obligations, or other problems, may steal to meet their personal needs. In other cases, dissatisfied employees may steal from a sense of entitlement or as a form of attack against their employers.

TABLE 11-3	Examples of Risk Factors for Misappropriation of Assets	
THREE CONDITIONS OF FRAUD		
Incentives/Pressures	Opportunities	Attitudes/Rationalization
Management or other employees have incentives or pressures to misappropriate material assets.	*Circumstances provide an opportunity for management or employees to misappropriate assets.*	*An attitude, character, or set of ethical values exists that allows management or employees to intentionally commit a dishonest act, or they are in an environment that imposes sufficient pressure that causes them to rationalize committing a dishonest act.*
Examples of Risk Factors	**Examples of Risk Factors**	**Examples of Risk Factors**
Personal financial obligations create pressure for those with access to cash or other assets susceptible to theft to misappropriate those assets.	Presence of large amounts of cash on hand or inventory items that are small, of high value, or are in high demand.	Disregard for the need to monitor or reduce risk of misappropriating assets.
Adverse relationships between management and employees with access to assets susceptible to theft motivate employees to misappropriate those assets. Examples include the following: • Known or expected employee layoffs. • Promotions, compensation, or other rewards inconsistent with expectations.	Inadequate internal control over assets due to lack of the following: • Appropriate segregation of duties or independent checks. • Job applicant screening for employees with access to assets. • Mandatory vacations for employees with access to assets. • Adequate management oversight of employees handling cash.	Disregard for internal controls by overriding existing controls or failing to correct known internal control deficiencies.

Opportunities Opportunities for theft exist in all companies. However, opportunities are greater in companies with accessible cash or with inventory or other valuable assets, especially if they are small or easily removed. For example, thefts of laptop computers are much more frequent than thefts of desktop systems.

Weak internal controls create opportunities for theft. Inadequate separation of duties is practically a license for employees to steal. Whenever employees have custody or even temporary access to assets and maintain the accounting records for those assets, the potential for theft exists. If inventory storeroom employees also maintain inventory records, they can easily take inventory items and cover the theft by adjusting the accounting records.

Fraud is more prevalent in smaller businesses and not-for-profit organizations because it is more difficult for these entities to maintain adequate separation of duties. However, even large organizations may fail to maintain adequate separation in critical areas. Barings Bank was the oldest merchant bank in London until it collapsed in 1995 after incurring losses in excess of US$1 billion from the activities of one trader because of inadequate separation of duties.

Attitudes/Rationalization Management's attitude toward controls and ethical conduct may allow employees and managers to rationalize the theft of assets. If management cheats customers through overcharging for goods or engaging in high-pressure sales tactics, employees may feel that it is acceptable for them to behave in the same fashion by cheating on expense or time reports.

| DUBAI ISLAMIC BANK AED 1.8 BILLION FRAUD CASE REFERRED TO COURT | The authorities' campaign against corruption continues with the case of seven suspects who reportedly swindled AED 1.8 billion from Dubai Islamic Bank (DIB) being referred to court. The public prosecution referred five businessmen and two former senior executives of DIB to court where they will be prosecuted on charges of swindling, forgery and bribery. The public prosecution charged three businessmen with defrauding DIB of AED 1.8 billion the equivalent to US$501 million. AI and CM, who worked for one of DIB's business partners, reportedly collaborated with RL (who established a number of companies) and fabricated documents of bogus transactions (with the intention to con the bank), then submitted those documents to DIB to finance their projects. The ex-DIB Pakistani executives assisted the businessmen by accepting their transactions and granting them more credit facilities to finance their projects. The employees | of the bank abused their duties in the bank and allegedly accepted US$950,000 (AED 3.48 million) and US$750,000 (AED 2.75 million) in bribes, respectively. A sixth American businessman ZU (who is at large) has been arraigned for reportedly defrauding DIB of US$2 million (AED 7.34 million). He did it by means of establishing a company and fabricating documents and bills related to bogus transactions. He then submitted them to the bank's business partner as real deals, which deceived the bank and caused it to hand in the swindled amount, according to the arraignment sheet. ZU has been additionally charged with forging documents and using them. Finally, a 58-year-old British businessman, AF, has been charged with aiding and abetting AI, CM, and RL.

Source: Extracts from B. Za'za, 'Dubai Islamic Bank AED 1.8 billion fraud case referred to court,' *Gulf News*, March 9, 2009. |

ASSESSING THE RISK OF FRAUD

OBJECTIVE 11-3

Understand the auditor's responsibility for assessing the risk of fraud and detecting material misstatements due to fraud.

Auditing standards (ISA 240) provide guidance to auditors in assessing the risk of fraud. Auditors must maintain a level of professional skepticism as they consider a broad set of information, including fraud risk factors, to identify and respond to fraud risk. As we discussed in Chapter 6, the auditor has a responsibility to respond to fraud risk by planning and performing the audit to obtain reasonable assurance that material misstatements, whether due to errors or fraud, are detected. Kroll's *Global Fraud Report* 2009/10 highlights some of the measures used by companies to prevent, detect, or mitigate fraud:

- Financial: financial controls, fraud detection, internal audit, external audit, anti-money laundering policies
- Staff: background screening
- Staff: training, whistleblower hotline
- Partners, clients, and vendors: due diligence
- Reputation: media monitoring, compliance controls and training, legal review
- Risk: risk officer and risk management system
- IP: intellectual property and trademarks monitoring program
- Assets: physical security systems, stock inventories, tagging, asset register
- Information: IT security, technical countermeasures
- Management: management controls, incentives, external supervising e.g. audit committee

Professional Skepticism

Professional skepticism

An attitude of the auditor that neither assumes management is dishonest nor assumes unquestioned honesty.

Auditing standards state that, in exercising **professional skepticism**, an auditor *neither assumes that management is dishonest nor assumes unquestioned honesty*. In practice, maintaining this attitude of professional skepticism can be difficult because, despite some recent high-profile examples of fraudulent financial statements, material frauds are infrequent compared to the number of audits of financial statements conducted annually. The auditor should conduct the engagement assuming there is a possibility that a material

PCAOB CONSIDERATION OF AUDITOR RESPONSIBILITY FOR FRAUD DETECTION

As part of their inspections of audits performed by audit firms, PCAOB staff often observes common deficiencies in the audit process. Periodically, the PCAOB releases a report, often described as a "4010 Report," that highlights these observations. The staff noted the following:

- Auditors often documented their consideration of fraud merely by checking off items on standard audit programs and checklists, without any documentation of the performance of certain procedures outlined in the programs and checklists.
- Auditors failed to expand audit procedures when addressing identified fraud risk factors.
- Audit teams were unable to demonstrate that brainstorming sessions were held or audit teams were found to conduct the brainstorming session after planning and substantive fieldwork had begun.
- There was no documentation that the auditor made the required inquiries of the audit committee, management, or others about their knowledge of fraud and fraud risks.
- Auditors failed to perform adequate procedures to address the risk of management override of controls, particularly with respect to the examination of journal entries and accounting estimates.

Source: *Observations on Auditor's Implementation of PCAOB Standards Relating to Auditors' Responsibilities with Respect to Fraud*, PCAOB Release No. 2007-001, January 22, 2007.

misstatement due to fraud could be present, regardless of any prior beliefs or past experience with the entity and regardless of the auditor's belief about management's honesty and integrity.

Questioning Mind Auditing standards emphasize consideration of a client's susceptibility to fraud, regardless of the auditor's beliefs about the likelihood of fraud and management's honesty and integrity. During audit planning for every audit, the engagement team must discuss the need to maintain a questioning mind throughout the audit to identify fraud risks and critically evaluate audit evidence.

Critical Evaluation of Audit Evidence Upon discovering information or other conditions that indicate a material misstatement due to fraud may have occurred, auditors should thoroughly probe the issues, acquire additional evidence as needed, and consult with other team members. For example, the auditor should be alert to audit evidence that contradict other audit evidence obtained and information that brings into question the reliability of documents and responses to inquiries to be used as audit evidence. Auditors must be careful not to rationalize or assume a misstatement is an isolated incident. For example, say an auditor uncovers a current-year sale that should properly be reflected as a sale in the following year. The auditor should evaluate the reasons for the misstatement, determine whether it was unintentional or a fraud, and consider whether other such misstatements are likely to have occurred.

Sources of Information to Assess Fraud Risks

Figure 11-3 summarizes the information used to assess fraud risk. The six sources of information to assess these fraud risks on the top of the figure are discussed further in this section.

Communications Among Audit Team Auditing standards (ISA 240 and ISA 315) require that the engagement team have discussions to share insights from more experienced audit team members and to 'brainstorm' ideas that address the following:

1. How and where they believe the entity's financial statements might be susceptible to material misstatement due to fraud. This should include consideration of known external and internal factors affecting the entity that might:
   - create an incentive or pressure for management to commit fraud.

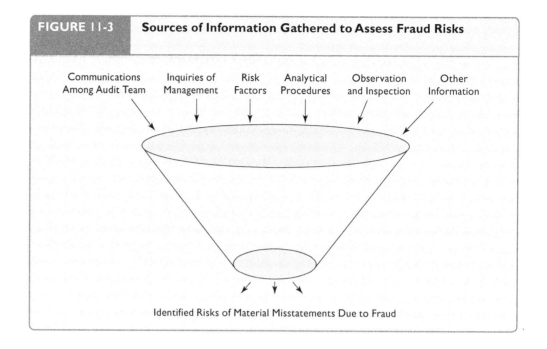

FIGURE 11-3   Sources of Information Gathered to Assess Fraud Risks

Communications Among Audit Team · Inquiries of Management · Risk Factors · Analytical Procedures · Observation and Inspection · Other Information

Identified Risks of Material Misstatements Due to Fraud

- provide the opportunity for fraud to be perpetrated.
- indicate a culture or environment that enables management to rationalize fraudulent acts.

2. How management could perpetrate and conceal fraudulent financial reporting.
3. How anyone might misappropriate assets of the entity.
4. How the auditor might respond to the susceptibility of material misstatements due to fraud.

These discussions about fraud risks will likely take place at the same time as discussions about the susceptibility of the entity's financial statements to other types of material misstatement, which was addressed in Chapter 8.

Inquiries of Management Auditing standards (ISA 260) require the auditor to make specific inquiries about fraud in every audit. Inquiries of management, those charged with governance and others within the company, provide employees with an opportunity to tell the auditor information that otherwise might not be communicated. The inquiry of management includes employees involved in initiating, processing, or recording complex or unusual transactions, in-house legal consultant and production, marketing, sales, and other personnel. Moreover, their responses to the auditor's questions often reveal information on the likelihood of fraud.

The auditor's inquiries of management should ask whether management has knowledge of any fraud or suspected fraud within the company. Auditors should also inquire about management's process of assessing fraud risks, the nature of fraud risks identified by management, any internal controls implemented to address those risks, related parties transactions, accounting estimates and their revisions and any information about fraud risks and related controls that management has reported to those charged with governance, such as the audit committee.

The audit committee and the internal audit department often assume an active role in overseeing management's fraud risk assessment and response processes. The auditor must inquire of the audit committee, the internal auditor or others charged with governance about their views of the risks of fraud and whether they have knowledge of any fraud or suspected fraud.

Auditing standards (ISAs 240 and 315) also require the auditor to make inquiries of others within the entity whose duties lie outside the normal financial reporting lines of responsibility. When coming into contact with company personnel, such as the inventory warehouse manager or purchasing agents, the auditor may inquire about the existence or suspicion of fraud. Throughout the audit, inquiries of executives and a wide variety of other employees provide opportunities for the auditor to learn about risks of fraud. When responses are inconsistent, the auditor should obtain additional audit evidence to resolve the inconsistency and to support or refute the original risk assessment.

Risk Factors Auditing standards require the auditor to evaluate whether fraud risk factors indicate incentives or pressures to perpetrate fraud, opportunities to carry out fraud, or attitudes or rationalizations used to justify a fraudulent action. Tables 11-2 and 11-3 outline examples of the fraud risk factors auditors should consider. The existence of fraud risk factors does not mean fraud exists, only that the likelihood of fraud is higher. Auditors should consider these factors along with any other information used to assess the risks of fraud. Auditors should understand these elements when they study the entity control environment. Auditors should ensure management compliance with the entity risk assessment process and check whether it is operating effectively or not. In the case where management does not respond to identified fraud risks, auditors should develop independent tests to determine whether any fraud exists in the entity's transactions and/or account balances.

Analytical Procedures As we discussed in Chapter 8, auditors must perform analytical procedures during the planning and completion phases of the audit to help identify unusual transactions or events that might indicate the presence of material misstatements in the financial statements. When results from analytical procedures differ from the auditor's expectations, the auditor evaluates those results in light of other information obtained about the likelihood of fraud to determine if fraud risk is heightened.

Because occurrences of fraudulent financial reporting often involve manipulation of revenue, auditing standards require the auditor to perform analytical procedures on revenue accounts. The objective is to identify unusual or unexpected relationships involving revenue accounts that may indicate fraudulent financial reporting. By comparing the sales volume based on recorded revenue with actual production capacity, for example, the auditor can reveal revenues beyond the entity's production capabilities.

Observation and Inspection Observation and inspection may include the auditor observing the actual implementation of the entity's operations, reading reports prepared by management, those charged with governance and internal audit, visits and observing operations within the entity's premises and plant facilities, and applying walkthrough tests from the initiation of a transaction until it is completed. Auditors also must inspect documents supporting the entity's transactions and account balances including business plans, records, and internal control manuals. Auditors should be alert for risks of fraud while observing and inspecting the entity's operations and documents. The auditor should also read and study carefully industry developments and trends, and interim financial statements, and assess regulatory and financial publications.

Other Information Auditors should consider all information they have obtained in any phase or part of the audit as they assess the risk of fraud. Many of the risk assessment procedures that the auditor performs during planning to assess the risk of material misstatement may indicate a heightened risk of fraud. For example, information about management's integrity and honesty obtained during client acceptance procedures, inquiries and analytical procedures done in connection with the auditor's review of the client's quarterly financial statements, and information considered in assessing inherent and control risks may lead to auditor concerns about the likelihood of misstatements due to fraud.

Documenting Fraud Assessment

Auditing standards (ISA 230) require that auditors document the following matters related to the auditor's consideration of material misstatements due to fraud:

- The discussion among engagement team personnel in planning the audit about the susceptibility of the entity's financial statements to material fraud.
- Procedures performed to obtain information necessary to identify and assess the risks of material fraud.
- Specific risks of material fraud that were identified, and a description of the auditor's response to those risks.
- Reasons supporting a conclusion that there is not a significant risk of material improper revenue recognition.
- Results of the procedures performed to address the risk of management override of controls.
- Other conditions and analytical relationships indicating that additional auditing procedures or other responses were required, and the actions taken by the auditor.
- The nature of communications about fraud made to management, the audit committee, or others.

After fraud risks are identified and documented, the auditor should evaluate factors that reduce fraud risk before developing an appropriate response to the risk of fraud. Corporate governance and other control factors that reduce fraud risks are discussed in the next section.

CORPORATE GOVERNANCE OVERSIGHT TO REDUCE FRAUD RISKS

OBJECTIVE 11-4

Identify corporate governance and other control environment factors that reduce fraud risks.

Management is responsible for implementing corporate governance and control procedures to minimize the risk of fraud, which can be reduced through a combination of prevention, deterrence, and detection measures. Because collusion and false documentation make detection of fraud a challenge, it is often more effective and economical for companies to focus on fraud prevention and deterrence. By implementing antifraud programs and controls, management can prevent fraud by reducing opportunity. By communicating fraud detection and punishment policies, management can deter employees from committing fraud.

Guidance developed by the AICPA identifies three elements to prevent, deter, and detect fraud:

1. Culture of honesty and high ethics
2. Management's responsibility to evaluate risks of fraud
3. Audit committee oversight

Let's examine these elements closely, as auditors should have a thorough understanding of each to assess the extent to which clients have implemented fraud-reducing activities.

Culture of Honesty and High Ethics

Research indicates that the most effective way to prevent and deter fraud is to implement antifraud programs and controls that are based on core values embraced by the company. Such values create an environment that reinforces acceptable behavior and expectations that employees can use to guide their actions. These

GUIDANCE FOR MANAGING FRAUD RISK	All organizations are subject to fraud risks, and regulations around the world have increased management's responsibility for managing fraud risk. Governance principles place high expectations on boards of directors to ensure overall high ethical behavior in the organization, with a particular emphasis on senior management's ethical attitude and leadership within the organization. In addition to the board, personnel at all levels of an organization have responsibility for dealing with fraud risk.

All organizations are subject to fraud risks, and regulations around the world have increased management's responsibility for managing fraud risk. Governance principles place high expectations on boards of directors to ensure overall high ethical behavior in the organization, with a particular emphasis on senior management's ethical attitude and leadership within the organization. In addition to the board, personnel at all levels of an organization have responsibility for dealing with fraud risk.

The American Institute of CPAs, The Institute of Internal Auditors, and the Association of Certified Fraud Examiners jointly created *Managing the Business Risk of Fraud: A Practical Guide*, to assist boards, senior management, and internal auditors in their management of fraud risk within organizations. This guide can certainly be used by any organization in the Arab countries to manage risk of fraud. The guide defines the following five principles for fraud risk management:

Principle 1: As part of an organization's governance structure, a fraud risk management program should be in place, including a written policy (or policies) to convey the expectations of the board of directors and senior management regarding managing fraud risk.

Principle 2: Fraud risk exposure should be assessed periodically by the organization to identify specific potential schemes and events that the organization needs to mitigate.

Principle 3: Prevention techniques to avoid potential key fraud risk events should be established, where feasible, to mitigate possible impacts on the organization.

Principle 4: Detection techniques should be established to uncover fraud events when preventive measures fail or unmitigated risks are realized.

Principle 5: A reporting process should be in place to solicit input on potential fraud, and a coordinated approach to investigation and corrective action should be used to help ensure potential fraud is addressed appropriately and timely.

Source: *Managing the Business Risk of Fraud: A Practical Guide*, The Institute of Internal Auditors, The American Institute of Certified Public Accountants, and the Association of Certified Fraud Examiners, 2008.

values help create a culture of honesty and ethics that provides the foundation for employees' job responsibilities. Creating a culture of honesty and high ethics includes six elements.

Setting the Tone at the Top Management and the board of directors are responsible for setting the 'tone at the top' for ethical behavior in the company. Honesty and integrity by management reinforces honesty and integrity to employees throughout the organization. Management cannot act one way and expect others in the company to behave differently. Through its actions and communications, management can show that dishonest and unethical behaviors are not tolerated, even if the results benefit the company.

A tone at the top based on honesty and integrity provides the foundation upon which a more detailed code of conduct can be developed to provide more specific guidance about permitted and prohibited behavior. Table 11-4 provides an example of the key contents of an effective code of conduct.

Creating a Positive Workplace Environment Research shows that wrongdoing occurs less frequently when employees have positive feelings about their employer than when they feel abused, threatened, or ignored. A positive workplace can generate improved employee morale, which may reduce employees' likelihood of committing fraud against the company.

Employees should also have the ability to obtain advice internally before making decisions that appear to have legal or ethical implications. Many organizations have a whistle-blowing process for employees to report actual or suspected wrongdoing or potential violations of the code of conduct or ethics policy—for an example see Figure 11-4.

Hiring and Promoting Appropriate Employees There can be risks when an employee turns out to be dishonest. To be successful in preventing fraud, well-run companies implement effective screening policies to reduce the likelihood of hiring and

TABLE 11-4	Example Elements for a Code of Ethics or Conduct
Code of Conduct Element	**Description**
Organizational Code of Conduct	The organization and its employees must at all times comply with all applicable laws and regulations, with all business conduct well above the minimum standards required by law.
General Employee Conduct	The organization expects its employees to conduct themselves in a businesslike manner and prohibits unprofessional activities, such as drinking, gambling, fighting, and swearing, while on the job.
Conflicts of Interest	The organization expects that employees will perform their duties conscientiously, honestly, and in accordance with the best interests of the organization and will not use their positions or knowledge gained for private or personal advantage.
Outside Activities, Employment, and Directorships	All employees share a responsibility for the organization's good public relations. Employees should avoid activities outside the organization that create an excessive demand on their time or create a conflict of interest.
Relationships with Clients and Suppliers	Employees should avoid investing in or acquiring a financial interest in any business organization that has a contractual relationship with the organization.
Gifts, Entertainment, and Favors	Employees must not accept entertainment, gifts, or personal favors that could influence or appear to influence business decisions in favor of any person with whom the organization has business dealings.
Kickbacks and Secret Commissions	Employees may not receive payment or compensation of any kind, except as authorized under organizational remuneration policies.
Organization Funds and Other Assets	Employees who have access to organization funds must follow prescribed procedures for recording, handling, and protecting money.
Organization Records and Communications	Employees responsible for accounting and record keeping must not make or engage in any false record or communication of any kind, whether external or internal.
Dealing with Outside People and Organizations	Employees must take care to separate their personal roles from their organizational positions when communicating on matters not involving the organization's business.
Prompt Communications	All employees must make every effort to achieve complete, accurate, and timely communications in all matters relevant to customers, suppliers, government authorities, the public, and others within the organization.
Privacy and Confidentiality	When handling financial and personal information about customers and others with whom the organization has dealings, employees should collect, use, and retain only the information necessary for the organization's business; internal access to information should be limited to those with a legitimate business reason for seeking that information.

Source: Adapted from *CPA's Handbook of Fraud and Commercial Crime Prevention*, AICPA.

promoting individuals with low levels of honesty, especially those who hold positions of trust. Such policies may include background checks on individuals being considered for employment or for promotion to positions of trust. Background checks verify a candidate's education, employment history, and personal references, including references about character and integrity. After an employee is hired, continuous evaluation of employee compliance with the company's values and code of conduct also reduces the likelihood of fraud.

Training All new employees should be trained about the company's expectations of employees' ethical conduct. Employees should be told of their duty to communicate actual or suspected fraud and the appropriate way to do so. In addition, fraud awareness training should be tailored to employees' specific job responsibilities with, for example, different training for purchasing agents and sales agents.

Confirmation Most companies require employees to periodically confirm their responsibilities for complying with the code of conduct. Employees are asked to state

FIGURE 11-4	Nuqul Group Corporate Integrity Hotline

What is NUQUL Group Corporate Integrity Hotline?

It is an independent and anonymous system whereby employees can report misconduct which does not comply with Nuqul Group values and ethics directly to the Board of Directors. While you are encouraged to report compliance issues directly to your immediate supervisor, Nuqul Group recognizes that this may not always be an option and has made available the Hotline for this reason.

The Hotline is available to all Nuqul Group employees working at facilities inside Jordan or in any country where the Group has operations. Methods of reporting employees concerns will be available at all locations.

What if I only suspect that something is wrong?

In general, you should have reasonable grounds for suspecting a violation and must do so in good faith. Most instances of fraud and abuse are discovered through tips and complaints from honest people who are not sure of all the facts. This type of calls is encouraged as well as acceptable.

Those are the company's problems. Why should I care?

Losses due to illegal, unethical and irresponsible activities can affect all of us. We pay in many ways:

- Employee morale may be harmed.
- The financial losses may mean fewer growth opportunities.
- Our personal safety and security may be at risk.

What should be reported?

The Hotline is not for general complaints or suggestions. Other means are available for resolving personnel problems or recommending cost-saving measures. This Hotline is reserved for reporting violations such as—but not restricted to—the following:

- Theft
- Bribery
- Fraud
- Abuse
- Gross negligence
- Violation of local laws
- Collusion with customers
- Accounting irregularities
- Harassment/Discrimination
- Violation of the Group Code of Conduct
- Falsifying company records
- Waste of company funds resources

Will anyone know about my call?

Communications via the Hotline are not traced and the information is treated in strict confidentiality. You do not have to reveal your identity to call the Hotline. No one will know you called unless you tell. Nuqul Group strictly prohibits retaliation against employees who raise concerns regarding unethical business behaviors or any violations to the company's policies and procedures.

Unethical behavior is against our core values.

Remember......
Hotline is confidential
Prompt feedback
Better workplace
Call now

Source: Nuqul Group Corporate Integrity Hotline Brochure, accessed at http://www.nuqulgroup.com/LinkClick.aspx?fileticket=Geg1Fyems74%3d&tabid=106

EVERYDAY VALUES: THE HARLEY-DAVIDSON CODE OF BUSINESS CONDUCT

The Harley-Davidson Motor Company, founded over 100 years ago, has grown to be recognized as one of the leading U.S. companies. Both *Fortune* and *Forbes* magazines have named Harley-Davidson several times as one of their most admired companies. The company has an incredible following of avid motorcycle enthusiasts, often referred to as 'H.O.G.s'

The company places tremendous emphasis on preserving the Harley-Davidson legacy. To help its employees make the right decisions on the job, management developed a detailed guide, *Everyday Values: Code of Business Conduct*, which applies to the board of directors and all employees of the company. The guide is built around these five basic Arab and Islamic traditions values:

- Tell the truth
- Be fair
- Keep your promises
- Respect the individual
- Encourage intellectual curiosity

The guide is intended to promote honest and ethical conduct, and it addresses a wide range of activities and situations in which employees may need to make decisions.

that they understand the company's expectations and have complied with the code, and that they are unaware of any violations. These confirmations help reinforce the code of conduct policies and also help deter employees from committing fraud or other ethics violations. By following-up on disclosures and non-replies, internal auditors or others may uncover significant issues.

Discipline Employees must know that they will be held accountable for failing to follow the company's code of conduct. Enforcement of violations of the code, regardless of the level of the employee committing the act, sends clear messages to all employees that compliance with the code of conduct and other ethical standards is important and expected. Thorough investigation of all violations and appropriate and consistent responses can be effective deterrents to fraud.

Management's Responsibility to Evaluate Risks of Fraud

Fraud cannot occur without a perceived opportunity to commit and conceal the act. Management is responsible for identifying and measuring fraud risks, taking steps to mitigate identified risks, and monitoring internal controls that prevent and detect fraud.

Identifying and Measuring Fraud Risks Effective fraud oversight begins with management's recognition that fraud is possible and that almost any employee is capable of committing a dishonest act under the right circumstances. This recognition increases the likelihood that effective fraud prevention, deterrence, and detection programs and controls are implemented. Figure 11-5 summarizes factors that management should consider that may contribute to fraud in an organization.

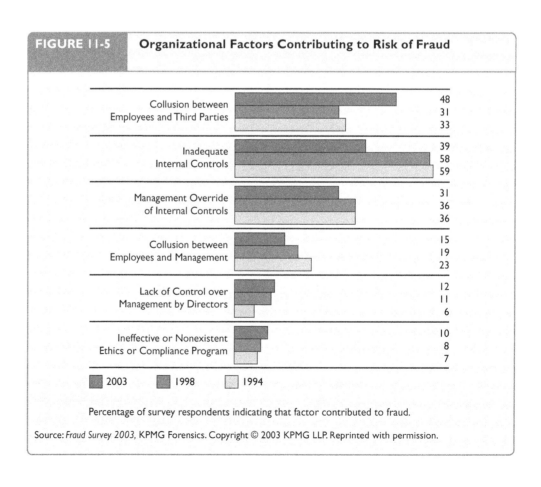

FIGURE 11-5   Organizational Factors Contributing to Risk of Fraud

	2003	1998	1994
Collusion between Employees and Third Parties	48	31	33
Inadequate Internal Controls	39	58	59
Management Override of Internal Controls	31	36	36
Collusion between Employees and Management	15	19	23
Lack of Control over Management by Directors	12	11	6
Ineffective or Nonexistent Ethics or Compliance Program	10	8	7

Percentage of survey respondents indicating that factor contributed to fraud.

Source: *Fraud Survey 2003*, KPMG Forensics. Copyright © 2003 KPMG LLP. Reprinted with permission.

Mitigating Fraud Risks Management is responsible for designing and implementing programs and controls to mitigate fraud risks, and it can change business activities and processes prone to fraud to reduce incentives and opportunities for fraud. For example, management can outsource certain operations, such as transferring cash collections from company personnel to a bank lockbox system. Other programs and controls may be implemented at a company-wide level, such as the training of all employees about fraud risks, and strengthening employment and promotion policies.

Monitoring Fraud Prevention Programs and Controls For high fraud risk areas, management should periodically evaluate whether appropriate antifraud programs and controls have been implemented and are operating effectively. For example, management's review and evaluation of operating units' or subsidiaries' financial results increase the likelihood that manipulated results will be detected.

Internal audit plays a key role in monitoring activities to ensure that antifraud programs and controls are operating effectively. Internal audit activities can both deter and detect fraud. Internal auditors assist in deterring fraud by examining and evaluating internal controls that reduce fraud risk. They assist in fraud detection by performing audit procedures that may uncover fraudulent financial reporting and misappropriation of assets.

Audit Committee Oversight

The audit committee has primary responsibility to oversee the organization's financial reporting and internal control processes. In fulfilling this responsibility, the audit committee considers the potential for management override of internal controls and oversees management's fraud risk assessment process, as well as antifraud programs and controls. The audit committee also assists in creating an effective 'tone at the top' about the importance of honesty and ethical behavior by reinforcing management's zero tolerance for fraud.

Audit committee oversight also serves as a deterrent to fraud by senior management. Oversight may include:

- Direct reporting of key findings by internal audit to the audit committee
- Periodic reports by ethics officers about whistle-blowing
- Other reports about lack of ethical behavior or suspected fraud

Because the audit committee plays an important role in establishing a proper tone at the top and in overseeing the actions of management, auditing standards require the

---

ANHEUSER-BUSCH'S AUDIT COMMITTEE CHARTER

The audit committee charter for Anheuser-Busch, Inc. assigns the audit committee of the board of directors primary responsibility for financial reporting and internal control oversight. While management is responsible for ensuring that overall controls are adequate to meet operating, financial, and compliance objectives, the audit committee is responsible for monitoring, reviewing, and challenging management and the independent auditors to ensure that the company's financial statements are materially complete and accurate. The charter explicitly notes that the audit committee is responsible for reviewing with management the company's major financial risk exposures and the steps management has taken to monitor, mitigate, and control those exposures.

In addition, the audit committee is responsible for receiving and reviewing reports about fraud involving senior management and any fraud that causes a material misstatement of the financial statements. The audit committee is also charged with establishing procedures for the receipt, retention, and treatment of complaints received by the company regarding accounting, internal control, or auditing matters, and the confidential anonymous submission by employees of concerns regarding questionable accounting or auditing matters.

Source: Anheuser-Busch Inc., Audit Committee Charter, as amended February 28, 2007 (www.anheuser-busch.com)

auditor to give particular attention when auditing a public company to evaluate the effectiveness of the board and audit committee as part of the auditor's evaluation of the financial statements. This is also emphasized by PCAOB Standard 5 which requires the auditor to undertake similar evaluation tests as part of forming his opinion about operating effectiveness of internal control over financial reporting. As part of the evaluation, the auditor might consider the audit committee's independence from management and the level of understanding between management and the audit committee regarding the latter's responsibilities. An external auditor may gather insights by observing interactions between the audit team, the audit committee, and internal audit regarding the level of audit committee commitment to overseeing the financial reporting process. The above process may be applied by external auditors when auditing the financial statements of organizations operating in many of the Arab countries. In the U.S., PCAOB Standard 5 notes that ineffective oversight by the audit committee may be a strong indicator of a material weakness in internal control over financial reporting.

RESPONDING TO THE RISK OF FRAUD

OBJECTIVE 11-5

Develop responses to identified fraud risks.

When risks of material misstatements due to fraud are identified, the auditor should first discuss these findings with management and obtain management's views of the potential for fraud and existing controls designed to prevent or detect misstatements. Auditors should then consider whether management's internal antifraud programs and controls mitigate the identified risks of material misstatements due to fraud or whether control deficiencies increase the risk of fraud. Auditor responses to fraud risk include the following:

1. Change the overall conduct of the audit
2. Design and perform audit procedures to address fraud risks
3. Design and perform procedures to address management override of controls

Change the Overall Conduct of the Audit

Auditors can choose among several overall responses to an increased fraud risk. If the risk of misstatement due to fraud is increased, more experienced personnel may be assigned to the audit. In some cases, a fraud specialist may be assigned to the audit team.

Fraud perpetrators are often knowledgeable about audit procedures. For this reason, auditing standards require auditors to incorporate unpredictability in the audit plan. For example, auditors may visit inventory locations or test accounts that were not tested in prior periods. Auditors should also consider tests that address misappropriation of assets, even when the amounts are not typically material.

Design and Perform Audit Procedures to Address Fraud Risks

The appropriate audit procedures used to address specific fraud risks depend on the account being audited and type of fraud risk identified. For example, if concerns are raised about revenue recognition because of cutoff or channel stuffing (i.e. transferring revenues to be recorded from one department's unit to another or from one branch to another one), the auditor may review the sales journal for unusual activity near the end of the period and review the terms of sales. Later in this chapter, procedures for specific fraud risk areas are discussed.

Auditors should also consider management's choice of accounting principles. Careful attention should be placed on accounting principles that involve subjective measurements or complex transactions. Because auditors presume fraud risk in revenue recognition, they should also evaluate the company's revenue recognition policies.

Design and Perform Procedures to Address Management Override of Controls

The risk of management override of controls exists in almost all audits. Because management is in a unique position to perpetrate fraud by overriding controls that are otherwise operating effectively, auditors must perform procedures in every audit to address the risk of management override. Three procedures must be performed in every audit.

Examine Journal Entries and Other Adjustments for Evidence of Possible Misstatements Due to Fraud Fraud often results from adjustments to amounts reported in the financial statements, even when effective internal controls exist over the rest of the recording processes. The auditor should first obtain an understanding of the entity's financial reporting process, as well as controls over journal entries and other adjustments, and inquire of employees involved in the financial reporting process about inappropriate or unusual activity in processing journal entries and other adjustments. Auditing standards require testing of journal entries and other financial statement adjustments. The extent of testing is affected by the effectiveness of controls and results of the inquiries.

Review Accounting Estimates for Biases Fraudulent financial reporting is often accomplished through intentional misstatement of accounting estimates. Auditing standards require the auditor to consider the potential for management bias when reviewing current-year estimates. The auditor is required to 'look back' at significant prior year estimates to identify any changes in the company's processes or management's judgments and assumptions that might indicate a potential bias. For example, management's estimates may have been clustered at the high end of the range of acceptable amounts in the prior year and at the low end in the current year.

Evaluate the Business Rationale for Significant Unusual Transactions Auditing standards place greater focus than was previously required on understanding the underlying business rationale for significant unusual transactions that might be outside the normal course of business for the company. The auditor should gain an understanding of the purposes of significant transactions to assess whether transactions have been entered into to engage in fraudulent financial reporting. For example, the company may engage in financing transactions to avoid reporting liabilities on the balance sheet. The auditor should determine whether the accounting treatment for any unusual transaction is appropriate in the circumstances, and whether information about the transaction is adequately disclosed in the financial statements.

Update Risk Assessment Process

The auditor's assessment of the risks of material misstatement due to fraud should be ongoing throughout the audit and coordinated with the auditor's other risk assessment procedures. Auditors should be alert for the following conditions when doing the audit:

- Discrepancies in the accounting records
- Conflicting or missing audit evidence
- Problematic or unusual relationships between the auditor and management
- Results from substantive or final review stage analytical procedures that indicate a previously unrecognized fraud risk
- Responses to inquiries made throughout the audit that have been vague or implausible or that have produced evidence that is inconsistent with other evidence

Figure 11-6 outlines the process to be used by the auditor when assessing risk of material misstatements.

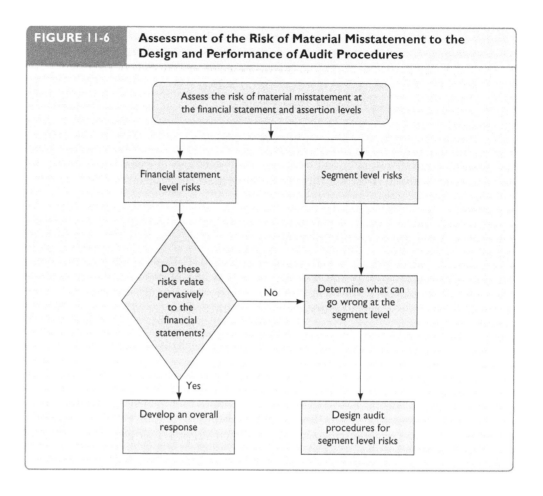

FIGURE 11-6   **Assessment of the Risk of Material Misstatement to the Design and Performance of Audit Procedures**

The auditor starts by assessing the risk of fraud on the financial statements level and determine the effect—if any—on the segment level. Whenever the auditor assessment indicates potential risk for fraud, the auditor is expected to apply all or some of the sources of information including detailed substantive tests.

When the risks relate to a segment or set of segments for the same business process or account, the auditor should consider the entity's internal controls. The auditor needs to consider the design and operation of controls within a business process to determine if they prevent, or detect and correct misstatements. If the controls are properly designed, and the auditor intends to rely on those controls, the auditor will test the operating effectiveness of the controls. Depending on the operating effectiveness of the entity's controls, the auditor will design and perform substantive tests directed at the potential misstatements that may result from the identified risks.

ISA 315 (para. 27–29) requires the auditors to consider with great attention and professional judgment what is called significant risks. Examples of the types of items that may result in significant risks include:

- Nonroutine or unsystematically processed transactions
- Significant accounting estimates and judgments
- Highly complex transactions
- Significant transactions with related parties
- Significant transactions outside the normal course of business of the entity, or considered unusual considering the nature of the company's activities and its environment
- Application of new accounting standards
- Revenue recognition in certain industries or for certain types of transactions
- Industry-specific issues

The auditor always treats assessed risks of material misstatement due to fraud as significant risks (ISA 240 para. 27). Accounting estimates having high estimation uncertainty such as estimates highly dependent upon judgment give rise to significant risks.

When the auditor has determined that a significant risk exists, the auditor should, to the extent not already done, obtain an understanding of the entity's controls, including control activities, relevant to that risk (ISA 315 para. 29). The auditor should always perform substantive procedures that directly respond to the significant risk at the assertion level (ISA 330 para. 21). For example, for accounting estimates that give rise to significant risks, the auditor should test the reasonableness of management's assumptions and how estimation uncertainty has been addressed. When the auditor plans to rely on controls over a significant risk, the auditor tests those controls in the current period (ISA 330 para. 15).

SPECIFIC FRAUD RISK AREAS

Depending on the client's industry, certain accounts are especially susceptible to manipulation or theft. Specific high-risk accounts are discussed next, including warning signs of fraud (i.e. red flags). But even when auditors are armed with knowledge of these warning signs, fraud remains extremely difficult to detect. However, an awareness of warning signs and other fraud detection techniques increases an auditor's likelihood of identifying misstatements due to fraud.

> **OBJECTIVE 11-6**
>
> Recognize specific fraud risk areas and develop procedures to detect fraud.

Revenue and Accounts Receivable Fraud Risks

Revenue and related accounts receivable and cash accounts are especially susceptible to manipulation and theft. A COSO study in the U.S. found that more than half of financial statement frauds involve revenues and accounts receivable. Similarly, because sales are often made for cash or are quickly converted to cash, cash is also highly susceptible to theft.

Fraudulent Financial Reporting Risk for Revenue As a result of the frequency of financial reporting frauds involving revenue recognition, the auditing standards issued guidelines for dealing with revenue recognition. Auditing standards specifically require auditors to identify revenue recognition as a fraud risk in most audits.

Several reasons make revenue susceptible to manipulation. Most important, revenue is almost always the largest account on the income statement, therefore a misstatement only representing a small percentage of revenues can still have a large effect on income. An overstatement of revenues often increases net income by an equal amount, because related costs of sales are usually not recognized on fictitious or prematurely recognized revenues. Another reason revenue is susceptible to manipulation is the difficulty of determining the appropriate timing of revenue recognition in many situations.

Three main types of revenue manipulations are:

1. Fictitious revenues
2. Premature revenue recognition
3. Manipulation of adjustments to revenues

Fictitious Revenues The most egregious forms of revenue fraud involve creating fictitious revenues. You may be aware of several recent cases involving fictitious revenues, but this type of fraud is not new. The 1931 *Ultramares* case described in Chapter 4 involved fictitious revenue entries in the general ledger.

Fraud perpetrators often go to great lengths to support fictitious revenue. For example, in Kuwait an investment holding company specializing in investing in a variety of listed and unlisted companies in the Kuwait Stock Market and markets in other Arab countries recognized a fictitious capital gain on the revaluation of shares of a subsidiary due to the overstated valuation of land owned by the subsidiary. The auditors of the holding company discovered that the land owned by the subsidiary is under dispute with the government due to noncompliance with the conditions of the agreements regarding the acquisition of the land.

Premature revenue recognition

Recognition of revenue before IFRS or local accounting standards' requirements for recording revenue have been met.

Premature Revenue Recognition Companies often accelerate the timing of revenue recognition to meet earnings or sales forecasts. **Premature revenue recognition**, the recognition of revenue before IFRS or local accounting standards' requirements for recording revenue have been met, should be distinguished from cutoff errors, in which transactions are inadvertently recorded in the incorrect period. In the simplest form of accelerated revenue recognition, sales that should have been recorded in the subsequent period are recorded as current period sales.

One method of fraudulently accelerating revenue is a 'bill-and-hold' sale. Sales are normally recognized at the time goods are shipped, but in a bill-and-hold sale, the goods are invoiced before they are shipped. Another method involves issuing side agreements that modify the terms of the sales transaction. For example, revenue recognition is likely to be inappropriate if a major customer agrees to 'buy' a significant amount of inventory at year-end, but a side agreement provides for more favorable pricing and unrestricted return of the goods if not sold by the customer. In some cases, as a result of the terms of the side agreement, the transaction does not qualify as a sale under IFRS or local accounting standards.

One notable example of premature revenue recognition in the U.S. used to clarify the nature of such fraud involves Bausch and Lomb. Items were shipped that were not ordered by customers, with unrestricted right of return and promises that the goods did not have to be paid for until sold.

Manipulation of Adjustments to Revenues The most common adjustment to revenue involves sales returns and allowances. A company may hide sales returns from the auditor to overstate net sales and income. If the returned goods are counted as part of physical inventory, the return may increase reported income. In this case, an asset increase is recognized through the counting of physical inventory, but the reduction in the related accounts receivable balance is not made.

Companies may also understate bad debt expense, in part because significant judgment is required to determine the correct amount. Companies may attempt to reduce bad debt expense by understating the allowance for doubtful accounts. Because the required allowance depends on the age and quality of accounts receivable, some companies have altered the aging of accounts receivable to make them appear more current.

Warning Signs of Revenue Fraud Many potential warning signals or symptoms indicate revenue fraud. Two of the most useful are analytical procedures and documentary discrepancies.

Analytical Procedures Analytical procedures often signal revenue frauds, especially gross margin percentage and accounts receivable turnover. Fictitious revenue overstates the gross margin percentage, and premature revenue recognition also overstates gross margin if the related cost of sales is not recognized. Fictitious revenues also lower accounts receivable turnover, because the fictitious revenues are also included in uncollected receivables. Table 11-5 includes comparative sales, cost of sales, and accounts receivable data for Jabal Ali Vacuum Company, including the year before the fraud and the two fraud years. Notice how both a higher gross profit percentage and lower accounts receivable turnover ratio in the most recent two years that include the fraud helped signal fictitious accounts receivable.

TABLE 11-5	Example of the Effect of Fictitious Receivables on Accounting Ratios Based on Jabal Ali Vacuum Company		
	Year Ended June 30		
	2011	**2010**	**2009**
Sales	US$181,123	US$126,234	US$76,144
Cost of sales	(94,934)	(70,756)	(46,213)
Gross profit	86,189	55,478	29,931
Gross profit percentage	47.6%	43.9%	39.3%
Year-end accounts receivable	51,076	27,801	14,402
Accounts receivable turnover[a]	3.55	4.54	5.29

[a]Accounts receivable turnover calculated as Sales/Ending accounts receivable

In some frauds, management generated fictitious revenues to make analytical procedures results, such as gross margin, similar to the prior year. In frauds like this, analytical procedures are typically not useful to signal the fraud.

Documentary Discrepancies Despite the best efforts of fraud perpetrators, fictitious transactions rarely have the same level of documentary evidence as legitimate transactions. For example, in the well-known fraud at ZZZZ Best, insurance restoration contracts worth millions of dollars were supported by one or two page agreements and lacked many of the supporting details and evidence, such as permits, that are normally associated with these types of contracts.

Auditors should be aware of unusual markings and alterations on documents, and they should rely on original rather than duplicate copies of documents. Because fraud perpetrators attempt to conceal fraud, even one unusual transaction in a sample should be considered to be a potential indicator of fraud that should be investigated.

Misappropriation of Receipts Involving Revenue

Although misappropriation of cash receipts is rarely as material as fraudulent reporting of revenues, such frauds can be costly to the organization because of the direct loss of assets. A typical misappropriation of cash involves failure to record a sale or an adjustment to customer accounts receivable to hide the theft.

Failure to Record a Sale One of the most difficult frauds to detect is when a sale is not recorded and the cash from the sale is stolen. Such frauds are easier to detect when goods are shipped on credit to customers. Tracing shipping documents to sales entries in the sales journal and accounting for all shipping documents can be used to verify that all sales have been recorded.

POCKETING PARKING CASH

Zeid Nasser was in charge of a university parking lot. He was supposed to place a parking receipt on the dashboard of the car when he received cash from the driver, but he would often collect the cash and wave the driver in without a receipt, particularly for sporting events. The university considered it too expensive to have two employees handle parking, and it was difficult to count the paid vehicles in a lot because some cars were parked by university employees with passes.

After several years, the university rotated Zeid to another lot. An employee in the accounting office noticed that revenues collected from the lot seemed to increase after Zeid's departure. Further investigation revealed that average revenues declined at the new lot to which Zeid had been assigned. Confronted with the evidence, Zeid confessed that he stole cash from revenues collected and was terminated from employment.

It is much more difficult to verify that all cash sales have been recorded, especially if no shipping documents exist to verify the completeness of sales, and no customer accounts receivable records support the sale. In such cases, other documentary evidence is necessary to verify that all sales are recorded. For example, a retail establishment may require that all sales be recorded on a cash register. Recorded sales can then be compared to the total amount of sales on the cash register tape. If the sale is not included in the cash register it is almost impossible to detect the fraud.

Theft of Cash Receipts After a Sale is Recorded It is much more difficult to hide the theft of cash receipts after a sale is recorded. If a customer's payment is stolen, regular billing of unpaid accounts will quickly uncover the fraud. As a result, to hide the theft, the fraud perpetrator must reduce the customer's account in one of three ways:

1. Record a sales return or allowance
2. Write off the customer's account
3. Apply the payment from another customer to the customer's account, which is also known as lapping

Warning Signs of Misappropriation of Revenues and Cash Receipts
Relatively small thefts of sales and related cash receipts are best prevented and detected by internal controls designed to minimize the opportunity for fraud. For detecting larger frauds, analytical procedures and other comparisons may be useful.

Inventory Fraud Risks

Inventory is often the largest account on many companies' balance sheets, and auditors often find it difficult to verify the existence and valuation of inventories. As a result, inventory is susceptible to manipulation by managers who want to achieve certain financial reporting objectives. Because it is also usually readily saleable, inventory is also susceptible to misappropriation.

Fraudulent Financial Reporting Risk for Inventory Fictitious inventory has been at the center of several major cases of fraudulent financial reporting. Many large companies have varied and extensive inventory in multiple locations, making it relatively easy for the company to add fictitious inventory to accounting records.

While auditors are required to verify the existence of physical inventories, audit testing is done on a sample basis, and not all locations with inventory are typically tested. In some cases involving fictitious inventories, auditors informed the client in advance which inventory locations were to be tested. As a result, it was relatively easy for the client to transfer inventories to the locations being tested.

Warning Signs of Inventory Fraud Similar to deceptions involving accounts receivable, many potential warning signals or symptoms point to inventory fraud. Analytical procedures are useful for detecting inventory fraud.

Analytical Procedures Analytical procedures, especially gross margin percentage and inventory turnover, often help uncover inventory fraud. Fictitious inventory understates cost of goods sold and overstates the gross margin percentage. Fictitious inventory also lowers inventory turnover. Table 11-6 is an example of the effects of fictitious inventory on inventory turnover, based on the Crazy Eddie fraud. Note that the gross profit percentage did not signal the existence of fictitious inventories, but the significant decrease in inventory turnover was a sign of fictitious inventories.

Purchases and Accounts Payable Fraud Risks

Cases of fraudulent financial reporting involving accounts payable are relatively common although less frequent than frauds involving inventory or accounts receivable. The deliberate understatement of accounts payable generally results in an under-

TABLE 11-6	Example of the Effect of Fictitious Inventory on Inventory Turnover, Based on Crazy Eddie, Inc.		
	Year Ended March 1, 2007	Year Ended March 2, 2006	9 Months Ended March 3, 2005
Sales	US$352,523	US$262,268	US$136,319
Cost of sales	(272,255)	(194,371)	(103,421)
Gross profit	80,268	67,897	32,898
Gross profit percentage	22.8%	25.9%	24.1%
Year-end inventories	109,072	59,864	26,543
Inventory turnover[a]	2.50	3.20	5.20[b]

[a]Inventory turnover calculated as Cost of sales/Ending inventory.
[b]Inventory turnover calculated based on annualized Cost of sales.

statement of purchases and cost of goods sold and an overstatement of net income. Significant misappropriations involving purchases can also occur in the form of payments to fictitious vendors, as well as kickbacks and other illegal arrangements with suppliers.

Fraudulent Financial Reporting Risk for Accounts Payable Companies may engage in deliberate attempts to understate accounts payable and overstate income. This can be accomplished by not recording accounts payable until the subsequent period or by recording fictitious reductions to accounts payable.

All purchases received before the end of the year should be recorded as liabilities. This is relatively easy to verify if the company accounts for prenumbered receiving reports. However, if the receiving reports are not prenumbered or the company deliberately omits receiving reports from the accounting records, it may be difficult for the auditor to verify whether all liabilities have been recorded. In such cases, analytical evidence, such as unusual changes in ratios, may signal that accounts payable are understated.

Companies often have complex arrangements with suppliers that result in reductions to accounts payable for advertising credits and other allowances. These arrangements are often not as well documented as acquisition transactions. Some companies have used fictitious reductions to accounts payable to overstate net income. Therefore, auditors should read agreements with suppliers when amounts are material and make sure the financial statements reflect the substance of the agreements.

Misappropriations in the Acquisition and Payment Cycle The most common fraud in the acquisitions area is for the perpetrator to issue payments to fictitious vendors and deposit the cash in a fictitious account. These frauds can be prevented by allowing payments to be made only to approved vendors and by carefully scrutinizing documentation supporting the acquisitions by authorized personnel before payments are made. In other misappropriation cases, the accounts payable clerk or other employee steals a check to a legitimate vendor. Documentation related to the purchase is then resubmitted for payment to the vendor. Such fraud can be prevented by canceling supporting documents to prevent their use as support for multiple payments.

Other Areas of Fraud Risk

Although some accounts are more susceptible than others, almost every account is subject to manipulation. Let's examine some other accounts with specific risks of fraudulent financial reporting or misappropriation.

Fixed Assets   Fixed assets, a large balance sheet account for many companies, are often based on subjectively determined valuations. As a result, fixed assets may be a target for manipulation, especially for companies without material receivables or inventories. For example, companies may capitalize repairs or other operating expenses as fixed assets. Such frauds are relatively easy to detect if the auditor examines evidence supporting fixed asset additions. Nevertheless, prior cases of fraudulent financial reporting, such as Enron and WorldCom, have involved improper capitalization of assets.

Because of their value and salability, fixed assets are also targets for theft. This is especially true for fixed assets that are readily portable, such as laptop computers. To reduce the potential for theft, fixed assets should be physically protected whenever possible, engraved, or otherwise permanently labeled, and should be periodically inventoried.

Payroll Expenses   Payroll is rarely a significant risk area for fraudulent financial reporting. However, companies may overstate inventories and net income by recording excess labor costs in inventory. Company employees are sometimes used to construct fixed assets. Excess labor cost may also be capitalized as fixed assets in these circumstances. Material fringe benefits, such as retirement benefits, are also subject to manipulation.

Payroll fraud involving misappropriation of assets is fairly common, but the amounts involved are often immaterial. The two most common areas of fraud are the creation of fictitious employees and overstatement of individual payroll hours. The existence of fictitious employees can usually be prevented by separation of the human resource and payroll functions. Overstatement of hours is typically prevented by use of time clocks or approval of payroll hours.

CORPORATE FRAUD IN THE ARAB COUNTRIES

OBJECTIVE 11-7

Analyze corporate fraud and risk mitigation in the Arab countries.

The culture of the Arab world makes it a crime of dignity and reputation if a member of the public commits fraud or any sort of corrupt act. People look at that person as an outsider who will not receive the respect of his family and people at large. Islamic rules contain strict penalties for those who commit fraud acts, especially crimes related to the theft of assets and public funds. However, in recent times due to the poverty affecting many of the largely populated Arab countries, many corporations and business groups in the Arab countries have been exposed to corporate frauds.

The perception of fraud coupled with heavy corruptions remains a serious problem in the Arab countries. The United Arab Emirates launched a major crackdown on corruption resulting in an improvement of the country from 35th in the corruption perception index in 2008 to 30th in the 2009 index. Elsewhere in the Arab world, Oman was ranked 39th, Bahrain 46th, Saudi Arabia 63rd—a leap of 17 places on its 2008 ranking—and Kuwait came in at number 66. Table 11-7 describes the type of fraud usually committed in Arab countries.

A prominent consulting company in the areas of governance, risk, and compliance[11] recently made a presentation showing the importance of mitigating the risks of fraud in the Middle East. Among the cases cited in the presentation were:

- A smelting firm in Bahrain seeking more than US$1 billion in a lawsuit against a leading aluminum manufacturer, accusing it of a 15-year conspiracy involving overcharging, fraud, and bribery.
- A lawsuit filed by a customer in Qatar against a leading European bank because in one single day more than US$45 million was withdrawn from the customer's account without his knowledge. This incident emphasized the

TABLE 11-7	Types of Fraud Committed in Arab Countries		
Countries	Management	Non-Management	External Parties
Bahrain	Funds obtained through misrepresentation	Credit card, petty cash fraud	Accounts receivable fraud
Saudi Arabia	False invoicing	Manipulation of financial statements, theft of cash receipts	Electronic fund transfer kickbacks, bribery, and procurement fraud
Kuwait	Fraudulent expense claims	Accounts receivable fraud	Check forgery
Qatar	Kickbacks, bribery, and procurement fraud	Petty cash fraud	Credit card and petty cash fraud
Oman	Theft of cash receipts	Theft of inventory and plant, purchase for personal use	Theft of inventory and plant, purchase for personal use
U.A.E.	Payroll fraud	False invoicing, theft of inventory and plant, manipulation of financial statements	Credit card fraud and check forgery

Source: Based on *2008 GCC Fraud Survey*, KPMG, p. 12, http://www.metransparent.net/IMG/pdf/2008_GCC_Fraud_Survey_English_1_.pdf

need to find ways of combating fraud and corruption especially with regard to money laundering.

- In Saudi Arabia, authorities took severe action against an entrepreneur involved in the biggest corporate scandal to hit the Gulf area when US$151 million of loans were taken out by this entrepreneur in financing facilities and credit lines and he defaulted on the repayment of these loans.
- A Kuwaiti logistics company was served a civil suit and criminal charges by the U.S. government accusing the company of deliberately overcharging the U.S. military by more than US$62 million (AED 227.7 million) to supply food to troops across the Middle East.

Table 11-8 presents an overview of the types of fraud in the Middle East with related percentage of occurrence. The table shows that the high vulnerability areas are corruption and bribery, and management conflict of interest.

The known incidents of corporate fraud place more responsibilities on Arab professional societies and governments to take measures to mitigate the risk of fraud. These measures may include:

- More management commitment and motivation in corporate businesses to adopt best practices of corporate governance and business excellence awards to control fraud. This should be a continuous process followed by the management who should periodically assess fraud risk exposure to identify specific potential schemes and events that the organization needs to mitigate.
- Development of complete and integrated business process manuals prepared in accordance with international compliance standards as laid down in the International Organization for Standardization (ISO) quality standards, the Basel declaration, and local corporate laws. This may include modifying an organization's governance structure to consider a fraud risk management program to convey the strategies, policies, and techniques of the board of directors, senior management, and the audit committee to prevent, detect, and mitigate risks of fraud.
- More initiatives in mapping of corporate fraud and forensic accounting to better understand and reduce the risks of fraud and corruption.
- Development of reporting systems to update those charged with governance as well as top management about the existence of fraud risks, with a coordinated approach for investigation and corrective action, to help ensure potential fraud is addressed appropriately and on a timely basis.

TABLE 11-8	Fraud Overview in Middle East	
	2009	2008
Financial Loss: Average loss per company over last three years	US$11.5 million (147% of average)	US$5.6 million (68% of average)
Prevalence: Companies suffering fraud loss over last three years	88%	91%
High Vulnerability Areas: Percentage of firms calling themselves highly vulnerable	Corruption and bribery (27%) Vendor, supplier, or procurement fraud (22%)	IP theft, piracy, or counterfeiting (24%) Information theft, loss, or attack (23%) Management conflict of interest (22%) Corruption and bribery (21%)
Areas of Frequent Loss: Percentage of firms reporting loss to this type of fraud in last three years	Theft of physical assets or stock (38%) Corruption and bribery (34%) Vendor, supplier, or procurement fraud (33%) Management conflict of interest (31%) Financial mismanagement (31%) Internal financial fraud or theft (27%) Information theft, loss, or attack (26%) Regulatory or compliance breach (23%) IP theft, piracy, or counterfeiting (22%)	Theft of physical assets or stock (46%) Management conflict of interest (43%) Financial mismanagement (38%) Corruption and bribery (34%) Information theft, loss, or attack (29%) Internal financial fraud or theft (27%) Vendor, supplier, or procurement fraud (24%) Regulatory or compliance breach (23%)

Source: *Kroll Global Fraud Report, 2009/2010,* http://www.acl.com/pdfs/200910_Kroll_Fraud_Report.pdf p.29

In order to combat all these fraud and corruption situations, many Arab countries attempt to apply effective corporate governance elements and impose severe penalties for fraud. In most Arab countries, a private employee convicted of fraud or corruption would face between six months and three years in jail and a public official would face 3 to 15 years in prison. All sentences would be in addition to the court assessment of the losses realized from the fraud and the court's decision to compensate investors or the government for the funds or misappropriation of assets.

The U.A.E. is making significant efforts and establishing strict regulations to reduce corporate fraud in the region. The government of Dubai established the Real Estate Regulatory Agency (RERA) for monitoring real estate transactions and implementation of the escrow system to protect investors. It also established Hawkamah, the Institute of Corporate Governance, with the objective to promote corporate sector reform and good governance in the region.

RESPONSIBILITIES WHEN FRAUD IS SUSPECTED

OBJECTIVE 11-8

Understand interview techniques and other activities after fraud is suspected.

Fraud is often detected through the receipt of an anonymous tip or by accident, internal controls, or the internal audit function. Figure 11-7 highlights that external auditors detect a higher percentage of the largest frauds relative to the detection of all cases, likely attributable to their focus on material misstatements.

Responding to Misstatements That May Be the Result of Fraud

Throughout an audit, the auditor continually evaluates whether evidence gathered and other observations made indicate material misstatement due to fraud. All misstatements the auditor finds during the audit should be evaluated for any indication of fraud. When fraud is suspected, the auditor gathers additional information to

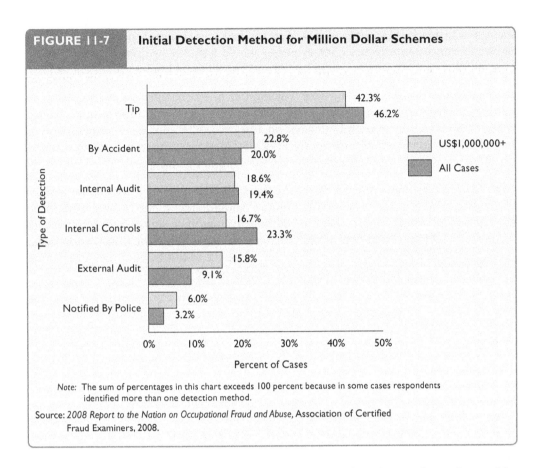

FIGURE 11-7 **Initial Detection Method for Million Dollar Schemes**

Note: The sum of percentages in this chart exceeds 100 percent because in some cases respondents identified more than one detection method.

Source: *2008 Report to the Nation on Occupational Fraud and Abuse,* Association of Certified Fraud Examiners, 2008.

determine whether fraud actually exists. Often, the auditor begins by making additional inquiries of management and others.

Use of Inquiry Inquiry can be an effective audit evidence gathering technique, as we discussed in Chapter 7. Interviewing allows the auditor to clarify unobservable issues and observe the respondent's verbal and nonverbal responses. Interviewing can also help identify issues omitted from inspection or confirmations. The auditor can also modify questions during the interview based on the interviewee's responses.

Inquiry as an audit evidence technique should be tailored to the purpose for which it is being used. Depending on the purpose, the auditor may ask different types of questions and change the tone of the interview. One or more of three categories of inquiry can be used, depending on the auditor's objectives.

Categories of Inquiry An auditor uses **informational inquiry** to obtain information about facts and details that the auditor does not have, usually about past or current events or processes. Auditors often use informational inquiry when gathering follow-up evidence about programs and controls or other evidence involving a misstatement or suspected fraud uncovered during the audit. Auditors can most effectively use informational inquiry by posing open-ended questions about details of events, processes, or circumstances.

An auditor uses **assessment inquiry** to corroborate or contradict prior information. The auditor often starts assessment inquiry with broad, open-ended questions that allow the interviewee to provide detailed responses that can later be followed up with more specific questions. One common use of assessment inquiry is to corroborate management responses to earlier inquiries by asking questions of other employees.

Interrogative inquiry is often used to determine if the individual is being deceptive or purposefully omitting disclosure of key knowledge of facts, events, or circumstances. Often, interrogative inquiry (seeking a 'yes' or 'no' response) is confrontational, given

Informational inquiry

Inquiry to obtain information about facts and details the auditor does not have.

Assessment inquiry

Inquiry to corroborate or contradict prior information obtained.

Interrogative inquiry

Inquiry used to determine if the interviewee is being deceptive or purposefully omitting disclosure of key knowledge of facts, events, or circumstances.

that subjects may be defensive, as they cover up their knowledge of specific facts, events, or circumstances. Interrogative interviewing should typically be done by senior members of the audit team who are experienced and knowledgeable about the client's affairs.

Evaluating Responses to Inquiry For inquiry to be effective, an auditor needs to be skilled at listening and evaluating responses to questions. Typically, the interviewee's initial response will omit useful information. Effective follow-up questions often lead to better information to assess whether fraud exists. Good listening techniques and observation of behavioral cues strengthen the auditor's inquiry techniques.

Listening Techniques It is critical for the auditor to use effective listening skills throughout the inquiry process. The auditor should stay attentive by maintaining eye contact, nodding in agreement, or demonstrating other signs of comprehension. Auditors should also attempt to avoid preconceived ideas about the information being provided. Good listeners also take advantage of silence to think about the information provided and to prioritize and review information heard.

Observing Behavioral Cues An auditor who is skilled in using inquiry evaluates verbal and nonverbal cues when listening to the interviewee. Verbal cues, such as those outlined in Table 11-9, may indicate the responder's nervousness, lack of knowledge, or even deceit. In addition to observing verbal cues, the use of inquiry allows the auditor to observe nonverbal behaviors. Expert investigators note that subjects who are uncomfortable providing a response to an inquiry often exhibit many of the nonverbal behaviors shown in Table 11-10. Students in the Arab countries should study the cues listed in Table 11-10 and think about the Arabic terms which might be verbal cues for auditors to look out for while undertaking their usual inquiries.

The key is to identify when the individual's behavior begins to change from his or her normal behavior.

Other Responsibilities When Fraud is Suspected When the auditor suspects that fraud may be present, auditing standards require the auditor to obtain additional evidence to determine whether material fraud has occurred. Auditors often use inquiry, as previously discussed, as part of that information-gathering process.

Audit Software Analysis Auditors often use audit software such as ACL or IDEA to determine whether fraud may exist. For example, software tools can be used to search for fictitious revenue transactions by searching for duplicate sales invoice numbers or by reconciling databases of sales invoices to databases of shipping records, to ensure that all sales are supported by evidence of shipping. Similarly, these tools provide efficient searches for breaks in document sequences, which may indicate misstatements related to the completeness objective for liabilities and expense accounts. Auditors use audit software, including basic spreadsheet tools such as Excel, to sort transactions or account balances into subcategories for further audit testing. For example, an auditor may use spreadsheet options to sort transactions exceeding a certain size or consisting of other unusual characteristics such as non-standard account numbers or unusual dollar balances (for example, transactions with rounded dollar amounts may be unusual for certain industries).

Auditors also use basic spreadsheet tools, such as Excel, to perform analytical procedures at disaggregated levels. For example, sales can be sorted to disaggregate the data by location, by product type, and across time (monthly) for further analytical procedure analysis. Unusual trends not observable at the aggregate level may be detected when the data is analyzed in greater detail.

Expanded Substantive Testing Auditors may also expand other substantive procedures to address heightened risks of fraud. For example, when there is a risk that sales terms may have been altered to prematurely record revenues, the auditor may modify

TABLE 11-9	Observing Verbal Cues During Inquiry
Verbal Cue Examples	**Implications**
Extensive use of modifiers, such as "generally," "usually," "often," "normally," etc.	Auditors should probe further to determine whether the use of the modifier indicates that there are exceptions to the processes or circumstances being examined.
Frequent rephrasing by the interviewee of the auditor's question.	Skilled auditors recognize that rephrasing often indicates that the interviewee is uncertain about his or her response or is attempting to stall for time.
Filler terms, such as "um," "well," "to tell you the truth," etc.	Auditors should be alert for filler terms, given that they often suggest that the interviewee is hesitant or unable to respond to the inquiry.
Forgetfulness and acknowledgments of nervousness, such as "I'm a bit nervous," or "I just can't remember."	When this continues to occur, auditors should be concerned about the possibility of deception.
Tolerant attitudes, such as "it depends on the circumstances," and overqualified responses, such as "to the best of my memory."	Dishonest people are often tolerant toward someone who may have committed fraud.
Reluctance to end an interview.	Someone who has been honest generally is ready to terminate an interview. Those trying to deceive may try to continue the inquiry process to convince the auditor that they are telling the truth.

Source: Reprinted by permission of The Association of Fraud Examiners.

TABLE 11-10	Observing Nonverbal Cues During Inquiry
Nonverbal Cue Examples	**Implications**
Physical Barriers—Interviewees may • Block their mouth with their hands, pens, pencils, papers, etc. • Cross their arms or legs. • Use distracting noises, such as finger tapping or drumming. • Lean away from the auditor, usually toward the door or window, in an effort to create spatial distance.	When the interviewee feels uncomfortable with a specific inquiry, he or she may put up nonverbal barriers to try to keep the auditor at a comfortable distance.
Signs of Stress—Interviewees under stress may • Show signs of having a dry mouth. • Lick lips, swallow, or clear their throats frequently. • Fidget, tap their foot, or shake a leg. • Sweat or become flushed in the face. • Avoid eye contact.	In most people, lying will produce stress, which can manifest itself physically.

Source: Copyright © 2004, Conducting Internal Auditing Interviews by the Institute of Internal Auditing Research Foundation, 247 Maitland Avenue, Altamonte Springs, FL 32701-4201. USA. Reprinted with permission.

the accounts receivable confirmation requests to obtain more detailed responses from customers about specific terms of the transactions, such as payment, transfer of custody, and return policy terms. In some instances, the auditor may confirm individual transactions rather than entire account balances, particularly for large transactions recorded close to year-end.

Often the risk of fraud is high for accounts that are based on management's subjective estimation. To respond to heightened risks that management used inappropriate assumptions to estimate account balances, such as the allowance for inventory obsolescence, the auditor may use specialists to assist in evaluating the accuracy and reasonableness of key assumptions. For example, auditors may rely on inventory specialists to assess the obsolescence of electronic parts inventories and business valuation experts to assess the reasonableness of market value assumptions made for certain investments.

Other Audit Implications Auditing standards require the auditor to consider the implications for other aspects of the audit. For example, fraud involving the misappropriation of cash from a small petty cash fund normally is of little significance to the auditor, unless the matter involves higher-level management, which may indicate a more pervasive problem involving management's integrity. This may indicate to the auditor a need to reevaluate the fraud risk assessment and the impact on the nature, timing, and extent of audit evidence.

When the auditor determines that fraud may be present, auditing standards require the auditor to discuss the matter and audit approach for further investigation with an appropriate level of management, even if the matter might be considered inconsequential. The appropriate level of management should be at least one level above those involved, as well as senior management and the audit committee. If the auditor believes that senior management may be involved in the fraud, the auditor should discuss the matter directly with the audit committee.

Sometimes, auditors identify risks of material misstatements due to fraud that have internal control implications. In some cases, the auditor's consideration of management's antifraud programs and controls identifies deficiencies that fail to mitigate these risks of fraud. The auditor must communicate those items to management and those charged with governance, such as the audit committee, if they are considered significant deficiencies or material weaknesses. When auditing the financial statements of a public company, the auditor should consider those deficiencies when auditing internal controls over financial reporting, as we described in Chapter 10.

The disclosure of possible fraud to parties other than the client's senior management and its audit committee ordinarily is not part of the auditor's responsibility. As described in Chapter 5, such disclosure is prevented by the auditor's code of ethics for professional accountants and may violate legal obligations of confidentiality.

The results of the auditor's procedures may indicate such a significant risk of material misstatement due to fraud that the auditor should consider withdrawing from the audit. Withdrawal may depend on management's integrity and the diligence and cooperation of management and the board of directors in investigating the potential fraud and taking appropriate action.

SUMMARY

This chapter examined the two types of fraud considered by auditors when auditing financial statements: fraudulent financial reporting and misappropriations of assets. Auditors are responsible for obtaining reasonable assurance that material misstatements are detected, whether due to errors or fraud. The chapter described the way auditors gather information to assess fraud risk in every audit and develop appropriate responses to identified fraud risks, after considering the effectiveness of management's antifraud programs and controls. Several illustrations of typical fraud techniques highlighted areas subject to greater fraud risk and provided examples of effective audit procedures to address those risk areas. Once auditors suspect fraud, they gather additional evidence, often through inquiry, and are responsible for making certain communications about suspected or detected fraud to senior management and the audit committee. Auditors of public companies must consider the implications of their fraud risk assessments, including any suspected fraud, when arriving at their opinion on the companies' financial statements. The chapter also showed that the major types of fraud in the Arab countries are corruption and bribery, management conflict of interest, financial mismanagement, and regulatory and compliance breach.

ESSENTIAL TERMS

Assessment inquiry   p. 389

Earnings management   p. 361

Fraud risk factors   p. 364

Fraud triangle   p. 363

Income smoothing   p. 361

Informational inquiry   p. 389

Interrogative inquiry   p. 389

Premature revenue
recognition   p. 382

Professional skepticism   p. 368

REVIEW QUESTIONS

11-1 (Objective 11-1) Define fraudulent financial reporting and give two examples that illustrate fraudulent financial reporting. Explain how fraud cases may differ in Arab countries compared with developed countries.

11-2 (Objective 11-1) Define misappropriation of assets and give two examples of misappropriation of assets.

11-3 (Objective 11-1) Distinguish fraudulent financial reporting from misappropriation of assets.

11-4 (Objective 11-2) What are the three conditions of fraud often referred to as 'the fraud triangle?'

11-5 (Objective 11-2) Give examples of risk factors for fraudulent financial reporting for each of the three fraud conditions: incentives/pressures, opportunities, and attitudes/rationalization.

11-6 (Objective 11-2) Give examples of risk factors for misappropriation of assets for each of the three fraud conditions: incentives/pressures, opportunities, and attitudes/rationalization.

11-7 (Objective 11-3) What sources are used by the auditor to gather information to assess fraud risks?

11-8 (Objective 11-3) What should the audit team consider in its planning discussion about fraud risks?

11-9 (Objective 11-3) Auditors are required to make inquiries of individuals in the company when gathering information to assess fraud risk. Identify those with whom the auditor must make inquiries.

11-10 (Objective 11-4) Describe the purpose of corporate codes of ethics or conducts and identify three examples of items addressed in a typical code of ethics/conduct.

11-11 (Objective 11-4) Discuss the importance of the control environment, or 'setting the tone at the top,' in establishing a culture of honesty and integrity in a company.

11-12 (Objective 11-4) Distinguish management's responsibility from the audit committee's responsibility for designing and implementing antifraud programs and controls within a company.

11-13 (Objective 11-5) What are the three categories of auditor responses to fraud risks?

11-14 (Objective 11-5) What three auditor actions are required to address the potential for management override of controls?

11-15 (Objective 11-6) Describe the three main techniques used to manipulate revenue.

11-16 (Objective 11-6) You go through the drive-through window of a fast food restaurant and notice a sign that reads "Your meal is free if we fail to give you a receipt." Why would the restaurant post this sign?

11-17 (Objective 11-7) Discuss some of the statistics associated with the type of fraud in Arab countries. Compare the above statistics with those found in developed countries.

11-18 (Objective 11-8) Name the three categories of inquiry and describe the purpose of each when used by an auditor to obtain additional information about a suspected fraud.

11-19 (Objective 11-8) Identify three verbal and three nonverbal cues that may be observed when making inquiries of an individual who is being deceitful. Identify main differences between those cues and the ones to be applied in your country. Justify your answer.

11-20 (Objective 11-8) You have identified a suspected fraud involving the company's controller. What must you do in response to this discovery? How might this discovery affect your report on internal control when auditing a public company in the U.S. compared with a similar company in Arab countries?

MULTIPLE CHOICE QUESTIONS FROM CPA EXAMINATIONS

11-21 (Objectives 11-2, 11-3) The following questions address fraud risk factors and the assessment of fraud risk.

a. Because of the risk of material misstatements due to fraud (fraud risk), an audit of financial statements in accordance with international standards on auditing should be performed with an attitude of
   (1) objective judgment.
   (2) independent integrity.
   (3) professional skepticism.
   (4) impartial conservatism.

b. Which of the following circumstances is most likely to cause an auditor to consider whether material misstatements due to fraud exist in an entity's financial statements?
   (1) Management places little emphasis on meeting earnings projections of external parties.
   (2) The board of directors oversees the financial reporting process and internal control.
   (3) Significant deficiencies in internal control previously communicated to management have been corrected.
   (4) Transactions selected for testing are not supported by proper documentation.

c. Which of the following characteristics is most likely to heighten an auditor's concern about the risk of material misstatements due to fraud in an entity's financial statements?
   (1) The entity's industry is experiencing declining customer demand.
   (2) Employees who handle cash receipts are not bonded.
   (3) Internal auditors have direct access to the board of directors and the entity's management.
   (4) The board of directors is active in overseeing the entity's financial reporting policies.

d. Which of the following circumstances is most likely to cause an auditor to increase the assessment of the risk of material misstatement of the financial statements due to fraud?
   (1) Property and equipment are usually sold at a loss before being fully depreciated.
   (2) Unusual discrepancies exist between the entity's records and confirmation replies.
   (3) Monthly bank reconciliations usually include several in-transit items.
   (4) Clerical errors are listed on a computer-generated exception report.

11-22 (Objective 11-5) The following questions concern the auditor's responses to the possibility of fraud.

a. If an independent audit leading to an opinion on financial statements causes the auditor to believe that a material misstatement due to fraud exists, the auditor should first
(1) consider the implications for other aspects of the audit and discuss the matter with the appropriate levels of management.
(2) make the investigation necessary to determine whether fraud has actually occurred.
(3) request that management investigate to determine whether fraud has actually occurred.
(4) consider whether fraud was the result of a failure by employees to comply with existing controls.

b. As a result of analytical procedures, the auditor determines that the gross profit percentage has increased from 30 percent in the preceding year to 40 percent in the current year. The auditor should
(1) document management's plans for maintaining this trend.
(2) evaluate management's performance in causing the improvement in gross profit.
(3) require footnote disclosure.
(4) increase the auditor's assessment of the risk of revenue misstatements, including fraud.

11-23 (Objective 11-6) The following questions address fraud risks in specific audit areas and accounts.

a. Cash receipts from sales on account have been misappropriated. Which of the following acts will conceal this embezzlement and be least likely to be detected by the auditor?
(1) Understating the sales journal.
(2) Overstating the accounts receivable control account.
(3) Overstating the accounts receivable subsidiary records.
(4) Understating the cash receipts journal.

b. An auditor discovers that a client's accounts receivable turnover is substantially lower for the current year than for the prior year. This trend may indicate that
(1) fictitious credit sales have been recorded during the year.
(2) employees have stolen inventory just before year-end.
(3) the client recently tightened its credit-granting policies.
(4) an employee has been lapping receivables in both years.

c. Which of the following internal controls will best detect the theft of valuable items from an inventory that consists of hundreds of different items selling for US$1 to US$10 and a few items selling for hundreds of dollars?
(1) Maintain a perpetual inventory of only the more valuable items, with frequent periodic verification of the validity of the perpetual inventory records.
(2) Have an independent auditing firm examine and report on management's assertion about the design and operating effectiveness of the control activities relevant to inventory.
(3) Have separate warehouse space for the more valuable items, with sequentially numbered tags.
(4) Require an authorized officer's signature on all requisitions for the more valuable items.

DISCUSSION QUESTIONS AND PROBLEMS

11-24 (Objective 11-2) During audit planning, an auditor obtained the following information:

1. Management has a strong interest in employing inappropriate means to minimize reported earnings for tax-motivated reasons.

2. Assets and revenues are based on significant estimates that involve subjective judgments and uncertainties that are hard to corroborate.
3. The company is marginally able to meet exchange listing and debt covenant requirements.
4. Significant operations are located and conducted across international borders in jurisdictions where differing business environments and cultures exist.
5. There are recurring attempts by management to justify marginal or inappropriate accounting on the basis of materiality.
6. The company's financial performance is threatened by a high degree of competition and market saturation.

Required

Classify each of the six factors into one of these fraud conditions: incentives/pressures, opportunities, or attitudes/rationalization.

11-25 (Objectives 11-1, 11-4, 11-6) The following misstatements are included in the accounting records of the Jasmine Manufacturing Company:

1. Several key-entry mistakes resulted in the exclusion of three invoices.
2. A customer complained when he received a bill, saying he has already paid. He produced a receipt, but there was no record of the payment in the books.
3. A shipment to a customer was not billed because of the loss of the bill of lading.
4. Merchandise was shipped to a customer, but no bill of lading was prepared. Because billings are prepared from bills of lading, the customer was not billed.
5. Commercial and residential customers are not differentiated on bills of lading.
6. Sales generated through the company's website are recorded at the point the customers submit the orders online.
7. A shipment of goods was recorded as being paid at the end of the year, but was recorded as unpaid at the beginning of the next year.
8. Several invoices were lost when the office moved to a new location.

Required

a. Identify whether each misstatement is an error or fraud.

b. For each misstatement, list one or more controls that should have prevented it from occurring on a continuing basis.

c. For each misstatement, identify evidence the auditor can use to uncover it.

11-26 (Objectives 11-2, 11-3, 11-4, 11-6) Fateen Shakran, store supervisor, is responsible for creating a summary of the store's transactions at the end of each day. He is also responsible for checking the register tape against the credit slips and cash in the register, and then depositing the money in the morning. Fateen recently took on a new role as head bookkeeper, when the former one retired. Fateen would occasionally change a transaction on the register and pocket the extra money. Now, he waits until the end of the year for the store manager to go on holiday break. He writes a check for himself in the amount of an invoice, then cancels the check originally written to pay for the invoice. He cashes the check for himself, and waits a few weeks before resubmitting the invoice. When the owner writes the second check, Fateen records this in the cash disbursements journal, and then deposits the check. He then files it with all other paid invoices. Fateen has been following this practice successfully for several years and feels confident that he has developed a foolproof method to earn some extra income.

Required

a. What is the auditor's responsibility for discovering this type of embezzlement?

b. What deficiencies exist in the client's internal control?

c. What evidence can the auditor use to uncover the fraud?

11-27 (Objectives 11-2, 11-4, 11-6) Appliances Repair and Service Company bills all customers rather than collecting in cash when services are provided. All mail is opened by Esam Galal, treasurer. Galal, a CPA, is the most qualified person in the company who is in the office daily. Therefore, he can solve problems and respond to customers' needs quickly. Upon receipt of cash, he immediately prepares a listing of the cash and a duplicate deposit slip. Cash is deposited daily. Galal uses the listing to enter the financial transactions in the computerized accounting records. He also contacts customers about uncollected accounts receivable. Because he is so knowledgeable about the business and each customer, he grants credit, authorizes all sales allowances, and charges off uncollectible accounts. The owner is extremely pleased with the efficiency of the company. He can run the business without spending much time there because of Galal's effectiveness.

Imagine the owner's surprise when he discovers that Galal has committed a major theft of the company's cash receipts. He did so by not recording sales, recording improper credits to recorded accounts receivable, and overstating receivables.

a. Given that cash was prelisted, went only to the treasurer, and was deposited daily, what internal control deficiency permitted the fraud?   **Required**

b. What are the benefits of a prelisting of cash? Who should prepare the prelisting and what duties should that person not perform?

c. Assume that an appropriate person, as discussed in part b, prepares a prelisting of cash. What is to prevent that person from taking the cash after it is prelisted but before it is deposited?

d. Who should deposit the cash, given your answer to part b?

11-28 (Objectives 11-2, 11-4, 11-6) The First Manufacturing Company employs about 50 production workers and has the following payroll procedures.

The factory foreman interviews applicants and on the basis of the interview either hires or rejects them. When applicants are hired, they complete an information form and give it to the foreman. The foreman fills in the hourly rate of pay for the new employee and then gives the form to a payroll clerk as notice that the worker has been employed. The foreman verbally advises the payroll department of rate adjustments.

A supply of blank time cards is kept in a box near the entrance to the factory. Each worker takes a time card on Sunday morning, fills in his or her name, and notes in pencil their daily arrival and departure times. At the end of the week, the workers drop the time cards in a box near the door to the factory.

On Sunday morning, the completed time cards are taken from the box by a payroll clerk. One of the payroll clerks then records the payroll transactions using a computer system, which records all information for the payroll journal that was calculated by the clerk and automatically updates the employees' earnings records and general ledger. Employees are automatically removed from the payroll when they fail to turn in a time card.

The payroll checks are manually signed by the chief accountant and given to the foreman. The foreman distributes the checks to the workers in the factory and arranges for the delivery of the checks to the workers who are absent. The payroll bank account is reconciled by the chief accountant, who also prepares the various quarterly and annual payroll tax reports.

a. List the most important deficiencies in internal control and state the misstatements that are likely to result from each deficiency.   **Required**

b. For each deficiency that increases the likelihood of fraud, identify whether the likely fraud is misappropriation of assets or fraudulent financial reporting.[12]

ACL PROBLEM

11-29 (Objective 11-6) This problem requires the use of ACL software, which is included in the MyAccountingLab. Information about installing and using ACL and solving this problem can be found in the Appendix, pages 855–859. You should read all of the reference material preceding the instructions about 'Quick Sort' before locating the appropriate command to answer questions a–f. For this problem use the Metaphor_APTrans_2002 file in ACL_Demo. The suggested command or other source of information needed to solve the problem requirement is included at the end of each question.

a. Total the Invoice Amount column for comparison to the general ledger. (Total Field)

b. Recalculate unit cost times quantity and identify any extension misstatements. (Filter)

c. Products that Metaphor purchases should not exceed US$100 per unit. Print any purchases for subsequent follow-up where unit cost exceeded that amount. (Filter)

d. Identify the three vendors from which the largest total dollar accounts payable transactions occurred in 2002. (Summarize and Quick Sort)

e. For each of the three vendors in question d, list any transactions that exceeded US$15,000 for subsequent follow-up. Include the vendor number, invoice number, and invoice amount. (Filter)

f. Vendor numbers 10134 and 13440 are related parties to Metaphor. Print any accounts payable transactions with those two vendors. (Filter) Also, determine the total amount of transactions with vendor 10134. (Total Field)

CHAPTER 12

THE IMPACT OF INFORMATION TECHNOLOGY ON THE AUDIT PROCESS

Just Because The Computer Did The Work Doesn't Mean It's Right

Mohy Gamal's audit client, Magnum Department Stores Inc., installed a software program (Infinity) that processed and aged customer accounts receivable. The aging, which indicated how long the customers' accounts were outstanding, was useful to Mohy when evaluating the collectibility of those accounts.

Because Mohy didn't know whether the aging totals were computed correctly, he decided to test Magnum's aging by using his own firm's ACL audit software to recalculate the aging, using an electronic copy of Magnum's accounts receivable data file. He reasoned that if the aging produced by his audit software was in reasonable agreement with Magnum's aging, he would have evidence that Magnum's aging was correct.

Mohy was shocked when he found a material difference between his and Magnum's calculated aging. Ihab Ismail, the manager of Magnum's information technology (IT) function, investigated the discrepancy and discovered that programmer errors had resulted in design flaws in Magnum's software used to calculate the aging. This outcome caused Mohy to substantially increase the amount of his testing of the year-end balance of the allowance for uncollectible accounts.

LEARNING OBJECTIVES

After studying this chapter, you should be able to

12-1 Describe how IT improves internal control.

12-2 Identify risks that arise from using an IT-based accounting system.

12-3 Explain how general controls and application controls reduce IT risks.

12-4 Describe how general controls affect the auditor's testing of application controls.

12-5 Use test data, parallel simulation, and embedded audit module approaches when auditing through the computer.

12-6 Identify issues for e-commerce systems and other specialized IT systems.

Auditors cannot rely on information just because it is generated by a computer, as illustrated in the opening story about Magnum's overreliance on the accuracy of the computer-produced accounts receivable aging. People often assume "the information is correct because the computer produced it." Unfortunately, auditors sometimes depend on the untested accuracy of computer-generated output because they forget that computers perform only as well as they are programmed. Before concluding that computer-generated information is reliable, auditors must understand and test computer-based controls.

This chapter builds on Chapter 10's coverage of internal control and how the auditor obtains an understanding of internal control, assesses control risk, and does tests of controls. We will examine how the client's integration of information technology (IT) into the accounting system affects risks and internal control.

The use of IT can improve internal control by adding new control procedures done by the computer and by replacing manual controls subject to human error. At the same time, IT can introduce new risks, which the client can manage by using controls specific to IT systems. In this chapter, we highlight risks specific to IT systems, identify controls that can be implemented to address those risks, and explain how IT-related controls affect the audit. However, it should be noted that in the Arab world, IT has seen great development in the areas of communication and software development, where a number of accounting software packages such as Alfa, El Motamem, Infinity, El Motakamel, and other newly developed software are distributed in many Arab countries. Auditors still rely on ACL and IDEA as effective audit tools but as yet Arab software has not been developed to help auditors achieve the objectives of continuous audit.

Relevant International Standards on Auditing

IAPS 1013	Electronic Commerce—Effect on the Audit of Financial Statements
ISA 315	Identifying and Assessing the Risks of Material Misstatement through Understanding the Entity and Its Environment
ISA 330	The Auditor's Responses to Assessed Risks
ISA 500	Audit Evidence
ISA 620	Using the Work of an Auditor's Expert

HOW INFORMATION TECHNOLOGIES IMPROVE INTERNAL CONTROL

OBJECTIVE 12-1

Describe how IT improves internal control.

Most entities, including small, family-owned businesses, rely on IT to record and process business transactions. As a result of explosive advancements in IT, even relatively small businesses use personal computers with commercial accounting software for their accounting. As businesses grow and have increased information needs, they typically upgrade their IT systems. The accounting function's use of complex IT networks, the internet, and centralized IT functions is now commonplace.

Let's examine several changes in internal control resulting from the integration of IT into accounting systems:

- *Computer controls replace manual controls.* The obvious benefit of IT is the ability to handle large amounts of complex business transactions cost-effectively. Because computers process information consistently, IT systems can potentially reduce misstatements by replacing manual procedures with automated controls that apply checks and balances to each processed transaction. This reduces the human errors that often occur in manually processed transactions.

    Computers now do many internal control activities that once were done by employees, including comparing customer and product numbers with master files and comparing sales transaction amounts with preprogrammed credit limits. Online security controls in applications, databases, and operating systems can improve separation of duties, which reduces opportunities for fraud.

- *Higher-quality information is available.* Complex IT activities are usually administered effectively because the complexity requires effective organization, procedures, and documentation. This typically results in providing management with more and higher-quality information, faster than most manual systems. Once management is confident that information produced by IT is reliable, management is likely to use the information for better management decisions.

ASSESSING RISKS OF INFORMATION TECHNOLOGY

Although IT can improve a company's internal control, it can also affect the company's overall control risk. Many risks in manual systems are reduced and in some cases eliminated. However, new risks specific to IT systems are created and can lead to substantial losses if ignored. If IT systems fail, organizations can be paralyzed by the inability to retrieve information or by the use of unreliable information caused by processing errors. These risks increase the likelihood of material misstatements in financial statements. Specific risks to IT systems include:

> **OBJECTIVE 12-2**
>
> Identify risks that arise from using an IT-based accounting system.

1. Risks to hardware and data
2. Reduced audit trail
3. Need for IT experience and separation of IT duties

Risks to Hardware and Data

Although IT provides significant processing benefits, it also creates unique risks in protecting hardware and data, as well as introducing potential for new types of errors. Specific risks include the following:

- *Reliance on the functioning capabilities of hardware and software.* Without proper physical protection, hardware or software may not function or may function improperly. Therefore, it is critical to physically protect hardware, software, and related data from physical damage that might result from inappropriate use, sabotage, or environmental damage (such as fire, heat, humidity, or water).
- *Systematic versus random errors.* When organizations replace manual procedures with technology-based procedures, the risk of random error from human involvement decreases. However, the risk of systematic error increases because once procedures are programmed into computer software, the computer processes information consistently for all transactions until the programmed procedures are changed. Unfortunately, flaws in software programming and changes to that software affect the reliability of computer processing, often resulting in many significant misstatements. This risk is increased if the system is not programmed to recognize and flag unusual transactions or when transaction audit trails are inadequate.
- *Unauthorized access.* IT-based accounting systems often allow online access to electronic data in master files, software, and other records. Because online access can occur from remote access points, including by external parties with remote access through the internet, there is potential for illegitimate access. Without proper online restrictions such as passwords and user IDs, unauthorized activity may be initiated through the computer, resulting in improper changes in software programs and master files.
- *Loss of data.* Much of the data in an IT system are stored in centralized electronic files. This increases the risk of loss or destruction of entire data files. This has severe ramifications, with the potential for misstated financial statements and, in certain cases, serious interruptions of the entity's operations.

Reduced Audit Trail

Misstatements may not be detected with the increased use of IT due to the loss of a visible audit trail, as well as reduced human involvement. In addition, the computer replaces traditional types of authorizations in many IT systems.

- *Visibility of audit trail.* Because much of the information is entered directly into the computer, the use of IT often reduces or even eliminates source documents and records that allow the organization to trace accounting information. These documents and records are called the audit trail. Because of the loss of the audit trail, other controls must be put into place to replace the traditional ability to compare output information with hard-copy data.
- *Reduced human involvement.* In many IT systems, employees who deal with the initial processing of transactions never see the final results. Therefore, they are less able to identify processing misstatements. Even if they see the final output, it is often difficult to recognize misstatements because underlying calculations are not visible and the results are often highly summarized. Also, employees tend to regard output generated through the use of technology as 'correct' because a computer produced it.
- *Lack of traditional authorization.* Advanced IT systems can often initiate transactions automatically, such as calculating interest on savings accounts and ordering inventory when prespecified order levels are reached. Therefore, proper authorization depends on software procedures and accurate master files used to make the authorization decision.

Need for IT Experience and Reduced Separation of Duties

IT systems reduce the traditional separation of duties (authorization, record keeping, and custody) and create a need for additional IT experience.

- *Reduced separation of duties.* As organizations convert from manual to computer processes, computers do many duties that were traditionally segregated, such as authorization and record keeping. Combining activities from different parts of the organization into one IT function centralizes responsibilities that were traditionally divided. IT personnel with access to software and master files may be able to steal assets unless key duties are segregated within the IT function.
- *Need for IT experience.* Even when companies purchase simple off-the-shelf accounting software packages, it is important to have personnel with knowledge and experience to install, maintain, and use the system. As the use of IT systems increases, the need for qualified IT specialists increases. Many companies create an entire function of IT personnel, while other companies outsource the management of IT operations.

INTERNAL CONTROLS SPECIFIC TO INFORMATION TECHNOLOGY

OBJECTIVE 12-3

Explain how general controls and application controls reduce IT risks.

To address many of the risks associated with reliance on IT, organizations often implement specific IT controls. Auditing standards describe two categories of controls for IT systems: general controls and application controls.

General controls apply to all aspects of the IT function, including IT administration; separation of IT duties; systems development; physical and online security over access to hardware, software, and related data; backup and contingency planning in the

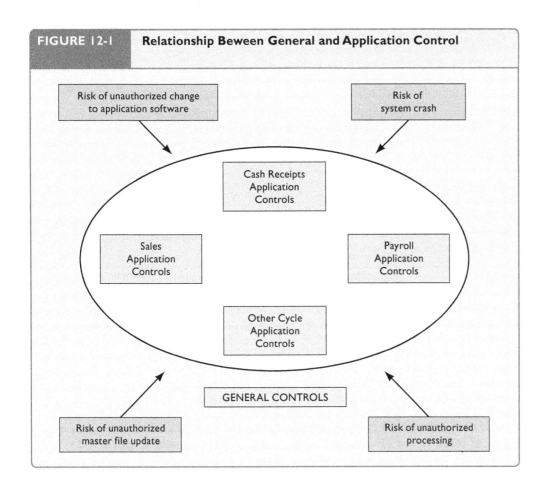

FIGURE 12-1   Relationship Beween General and Application Control

event of unexpected emergencies; and **hardware controls**. Because general controls often apply on an entity-wide basis, auditors evaluate general controls for the company as a whole.

Application controls apply to processing transactions, such as controls over the processing of sales or cash receipts. Auditors must evaluate application controls for every class of transactions or account in which the auditor plans to reduce assessed control risk because IT controls will be different across classes of transactions and accounts. Application controls are likely to be effective only when general controls are effective.

Figure 12-1 illustrates the relationship between general controls and application controls. General controls provide assurance that all application controls are effective. Strong general controls reduce the types of risks identified in the boxes outside the general controls oval in Figure 12-1.

Table 12-1 describes six categories of general controls and three categories of application controls, with specific examples for each category. Let's examine these categories of general and application controls in more detail.

General Controls

Similar to the effect that the control environment has on other components of internal control discussed in Chapter 10, the six categories of general controls have an entity-wide effect on all IT functions. Auditors typically evaluate general controls early in the audit because of their impact on application controls.

Administration of the IT Function The board of directors' and senior management's attitude about IT affect the perceived importance of IT within an organization.

General controls

Controls that relate to all parts of the IT function.

Hardware controls

Controls built into the computer equipment by the manufacturer to detect and report equipment failure.

Application controls

Controls related to a specific use of IT, such as the inputting, processing, and outputting of sales or cash receipts.

TABLE 12-1	Categories of General and Application Controls	
Control Type	**Category of Control**	**Example of Control**
General controls	Administration of the IT function	Chief information officer or IT manager reports to senior management and board.
	Separation of IT duties	Responsibilities for programming, operations, and data control are separated.
	Systems development	Teams of users, systems analysts, and programmers develop and thoroughly test software.
	Physical and online security	Access to hardware is restricted, passwords and user IDs limit access to software and data files, and encryption and firewalls protect data and programs from external parties.
	Backup and contingency planning	Written backup plans are prepared and tested regularly throughout the year.
	Hardware controls	Memory failure or hard drive failure causes error messages on the monitor.
Application controls	Input controls	Preformatted screens prompt data input personnel for information to be entered.
	Processing controls	Reasonableness tests review unit-selling prices used to process a sale.
	Output controls	The sales department does post-processing review of sales transactions.

Their oversight, resource allocation, and involvement in key IT decisions each signal the importance of IT. In complex environments, management may establish IT steering committees to help monitor the organization's technology needs. In less complex organizations, the board may rely on regular reporting by a chief information officer (CIO) or other senior IT manager to keep management informed. In contrast, when management assigns technology issues exclusively to lower-level employees or outside consultants, an implied message is sent that IT is not a high priority. The result is often an understaffed, underfunded, and poorly controlled IT function.

Separation of IT Duties To respond to the risk of combining traditional custody, authorization, and record-keeping responsibilities by having the computer perform those tasks, well-controlled organizations respond by separating key duties within IT. For example there should be separation of IT duties to prevent IT personnel from authorizing and recording transactions to cover the theft of assets. Figure 12-2 shows

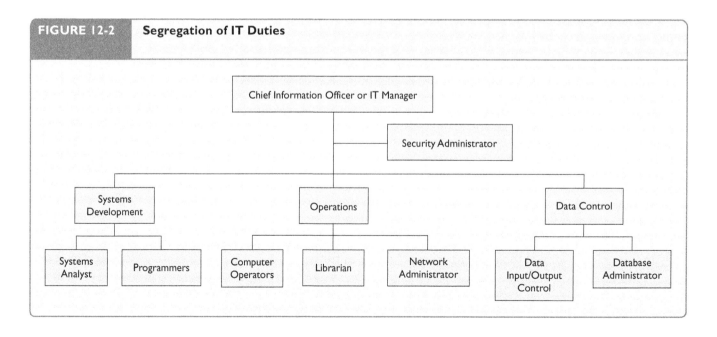

FIGURE 12-2   Segregation of IT Duties

an ideal separation of duties. Ideally, responsibilities for IT management, systems development, operations, and data control should be separated as follows:

- *IT management.* The CIO or IT manager should be responsible for oversight of the IT function to ensure that activities are carried out consistent with the IT strategic plan. A security administrator should monitor both physical and online access to hardware, software, and data files and investigate all security breaches.
- *Systems development.* Systems analysts, who are responsible for the overall design of each application system, coordinate the development and changes to IT systems by IT personnel responsible for programming the application and personnel outside IT who will be the primary system users (such as accounts receivable personnel). Programmers develop flowcharts for each new application, prepare computer instructions, test the programs, and document the results.

   Programmers should not have access to input data or computer operations to avoid using their knowledge of the system for personal benefit. They should be allowed to work only with test copies of programs and data so they can only make software changes after proper authorization.
- *Operations.* Computer operators are responsible for the day-to-day operations of the computer following the schedule established by the CIO. They also monitor computer consoles for messages about computer efficiency and malfunctions.

   A librarian is responsible for controlling the use of computer programs, transaction files, and other computer records and documentation. The librarian releases them to operators only when authorized. For example, programs and transaction files are released to operators only when a job is scheduled to be processed. Similarly, the librarian releases a test copy to programmers only on approval by senior management. Network administrators also affect IT operations as they are responsible for planning, implementing, and maintaining operation of the network of servers that link users to various applications and data files.
- *Data control.* Data input/output control personnel independently verify the quality of input and the reasonableness of output. For organizations that use databases to store information shared by accounting and other functions, database administrators are responsible for the operation and access security of shared databases.

Naturally, the extent of separation of duties depends on the organization's size and complexity. In many small companies, it is not practical to segregate the duties to the extent illustrated in Figure 12-2.

Systems Development Systems development includes:

- Purchasing software or developing in-house software that meets the organization's needs. A key to implementing the right software is to involve a team of both IT and non-IT personnel, including key users of the software and internal auditors. This combination increases the likelihood that information needs as well as software design and implementation concerns are properly addressed. Involving users also results in better acceptance by key users.
- Testing all software to ensure that the new software is compatible with existing hardware and software and determining whether the hardware and software can handle the needed volume of transactions. Whether software is purchased or developed internally, extensive testing of all software with realistic data is critical. Companies typically use one or a combination of the following two test approaches:

   1. **Pilot testing**: A new system is implemented in one part of the organization while other locations continue to rely on the old system.
   2. **Parallel testing**: The old and new systems operate simultaneously in all locations.

Pilot testing

A company's computer testing approach that involves implementing a new system in just one part of the organization, while maintaining the old system at other locations.

Parallel testing

A company's computer testing approach that involves operating the old and new systems simultaneously.

Proper documentation of the system is required for all new and modified software. After the software has been successfully tested and documented, it is transferred to the librarian in a controlled manner to ensure only authorized software is ultimately accepted as the authorized version.

Physical and Online Security   Physical controls over computers and restrictions to online software and related data files decrease the risk of unauthorized changes to programs and improper use of programs and data files. Security plans should be in writing and monitored. Security controls include both physical controls and online access controls.

- *Physical controls.* Proper physical controls over computer equipment restrict access to hardware, software, and backup data files on magnetic tapes or disks, hard drives, CDs, and external disks. Common examples to physically restrict unauthorized use include keypad entrances, badge-entry systems, security cameras, and security personnel. More sophisticated controls only allow physical and online access after employee fingerprints are read or employee retinas are scanned and matched with an approved database. Other physical controls include monitoring of cooling and humidity to ensure that the equipment functions properly and installing fire-extinguishing equipment to reduce fire damage.
- *Online access controls.* Proper user IDs and passwords control access to software and related data files, reducing the likelihood that unauthorized changes are made to software applications and data files. Separate add-on security software packages, such as firewall and encryption programs, can be installed to improve a system's security. (See page 416 for a description of firewall and encryption programs.)

Backup and Contingency Planning   Power failures, fire, excessive heat or humidity, water damage, or even sabotage can have serious consequences to businesses using IT. To prevent data loss during power outages, many companies rely on battery backups or on-site generators. For more serious disasters, organizations need detailed backup and contingency plans such as off-site storage of critical software and data files or outsourcing to firms that specialize in secure data storage.

Backup and contingency plans should also identify alternative hardware that can be used to process company data. Companies with small IT systems can purchase replacement computers in an emergency and reprocess their accounting records by using backup copies of software and data files. Larger companies often contract with IT data centers that specialize in providing access to off-site computers and other IT services for use in the event of an IT disaster.

Hardware Controls   Hardware controls are built into computer equipment by manufacturers to detect and report equipment failures. Auditors are more concerned with how the client handles errors identified by the hardware controls than with their adequacy. Regardless of the quality of hardware controls, output will be corrected only if the client has provided for handling machine errors.

Application Controls

Application controls are designed for each software application and are intended to help a company satisfy the transaction-related audit objectives discussed in previous chapters. Although some application controls affect one or only a few transaction-related audit objectives, most controls prevent or detect several types of misstatements. Other application controls concern account balance and presentation and disclosure objectives.

Application controls may be done by computers or client personnel. When they are done by client personnel, they are called **manual controls**. The effectiveness of manual controls depends on both the competence of the people performing the controls and

Manual controls

Application controls done by people.

the care they exercise when doing them. For example, when credit department personnel review exception reports that identify credit sales exceeding a customer's authorized credit limit, the auditor may need to evaluate both the person's ability to make the assessment and test the accuracy of the exception report. When controls are done by computers, they are called **automated controls**. Because of the nature of computer processing, automated controls, if properly designed, lead to consistent operation of the controls.

Application controls fall into three categories: input, processing, and output. Although the objectives for each category are the same, the procedures for meeting the objectives vary considerably. Let's examine each more closely.

Input Controls **Input controls** are designed to ensure that the information entered into the computer is authorized, accurate, and complete. They are critical because a large portion of errors in IT systems result from data entry errors and, of course, regardless of the quality of information processing, input errors result in output errors. Typical controls developed for manual systems are still important in IT systems, such as:

- Management's authorization of transactions
- Adequate preparation of input source documents
- Competent personnel

Controls specific to IT include:

- Adequately designed input screens with preformatted prompts for transaction information
- Pull-down menu lists of available software options
- Computer-performed validation tests of input accuracy, such as the validation of customer numbers against customer master files
- Online based input controls for e-commerce applications where external parties, such as customers and suppliers, perform the initial part of the transaction inputting
- Immediate error correction procedures, to provide for early detection and correction of input errors
- Accumulation of errors in an error file for subsequent follow-up by data input personnel

For IT systems that group similar transactions together into batches, the use of financial batch totals, hash totals, and record count totals helps increase the accuracy and completeness of input. Batch input controls are described in Table 12-2.

Processing Controls **Processing controls** prevent and detect errors while transaction data are processed. General controls, especially controls related to systems development and security, provide essential control for minimizing errors. Specific application processing controls are often programmed into software to prevent, detect, and correct processing errors. Examples of processing controls are illustrated in Table 12-3.

Automated controls

Application controls done by the computer.

Input controls

Controls designed by an organization to ensure that the information to be processed by the computer is authorized, accurate, and complete.

Processing controls

Controls designed to ensure that data input into the system are accurately and completely processed.

TABLE 12-2	Batch Input Controls	
Control	**Definition**	**Examples**
Financial total	Summary total of field amounts for all records in a batch that represent a meaningful total such as dollars or amounts	The total of dollars of all vendor invoices to be paid
Hash total	Summary total of codes from all records in a batch that do not represent a meaningful total	The total of all vendor account numbers for vendor invoices to be paid
Record count	Summary total of physical records in a batch	The total number of vendor invoices to be processed

TABLE 12-3	**Processing Controls**	
Type of Processing Control	**Description**	**Example**
Validation test	Ensures the use of the correct master file, database, and programs in processing	Does the internal label on the payroll master file tape match the file label indicated in the application software?
Sequence test	Determines that data submitted for processing are in the correct order	Has the file of payroll input transactions been sorted in departmental order before processing?
Arithmetic accuracy test	Checks the accuracy of processed data	Does the sum of net pay plus withholdings equal gross pay for the entire payroll?
Data reasonableness test	Determines whether data exceed prespecified amounts	Does employee's gross pay exceed 60 hours or US$1,999 for the week?
Completeness test	Determines that every field in a record has been completed	Are employee number, name, number of regular hours, number of overtime hours, department number, etc., included for each employee?

Output controls

Controls designed to ensure that computer-generated data are valid, accurate, complete, and distributed only to authorized people.

Output Controls   **Output controls** focus on detecting errors after processing is completed, rather than on preventing errors. The most important output control is review of the data for reasonableness by someone knowledgeable about the output. Users can often identify errors because they know the approximate correct amounts. Several common controls for detecting errors in outputs include:

- Reconcile computer-produced output to manual control totals
- Compare the number of units processed to the number of units submitted for processing
- Compare a sample of transaction output to input source documents
- Verify dates and times of processing to identify any out-of-sequence processing

For sensitive computer output, such as payroll checks, control can be improved by requiring employees to present employee identification before they receive their checks or by requiring the use of direct deposit into the employees' pre-approved bank accounts. Also, access to sensitive output stored in electronic files or transmitted across networks, including the internet, are often restricted by requiring passwords, user IDs, and encryption techniques.

IMPACT OF INFORMATION TECHNOLOGY ON THE AUDIT PROCESS

OBJECTIVE 12-4

Describe how general controls affect the auditor's testing of application controls.

Because auditors are responsible for obtaining an understanding of internal control, they must be knowledgeable about general and application controls, whether the client's use of IT is simple or complex. Knowledge of general controls increases the auditor's ability to assess and rely on effective application controls to reduce control risk for related audit objectives. In the U.S., public company auditors must issue an opinion on internal control over financial reporting and therefore knowledge of both general and application IT controls is essential. In the Arab world, there is no formal requirement for auditors to issue a specific report on internal control or to be knowledgeable about general and application IT controls. However, in most multinational companies, banks, and financial institutions, auditors either use their own IT departments or get the assistance of an IT expert to evaluate the IT system of those businesses, and report deficiencies and recommendations for improvement to those charged with governance and management.

Effect of General Controls on Control Risk

Auditors should evaluate the effectiveness of general controls before evaluating application controls. As illustrated in Figure 12-1, general controls have a pervasive effect on the effectiveness of application controls, so auditors should first evaluate those controls before concluding whether application controls are effective.

Effects of General Controls on System-Wide Applications

Ineffective general controls create the potential for material misstatements across all system applications, regardless of the quality of individual application controls. For example, if IT duties are inadequately separated such that computer operators also work as programmers and have access to computer programs and files, the auditor should be concerned about the potential for unauthorized software program or data file changes that might lead to fictitious transactions or unauthorized data and omissions in accounts such as sales, purchases, and salaries. Similarly, if the auditor observes that data files are inadequately safeguarded, the auditor may conclude that there is a significant risk of loss of data for every class of transaction that relies on that data to conduct application controls. In this situation, the auditor may need to expand audit testing in several areas such as cash receipts, cash disbursements, and sales to satisfy the completeness objective.

On the other hand, if general controls are effective, the auditor may be able to place greater reliance on application controls whose functionality is dependent on IT. Auditors can then test those application controls for operating effectiveness and rely on the results to reduce substantive testing.

Effect of General Controls on Software Changes

Client changes to application software affect the auditor's reliance on automated controls. When the client changes the software, the auditor must evaluate whether additional testing is needed. If general controls are effective, the auditor can easily identify when software changes are made. But in companies where general controls are weak, it may be difficult to identify software changes. As a result, when general controls are weak, auditors must then consider doing tests of application controls that depend on IT throughout the current year audit.

Obtaining an Understanding of Client General Controls

Auditors typically obtain information about general and application controls through the following ways:

- Interviews with IT personnel and key users
- Examination of system documentation such as flowcharts, user manuals, program change requests, and system testing results
- Reviews of detailed questionnaires completed by IT staff

In most cases, auditors should use several of these approaches because each offers different information. For example, interviews with the CIO and systems analysts provide useful information about the operation of the entire IT function, the extent of software development and hardware changes made to accounting application software, and an overview of any planned changes. Reviews of program change requests and system test results are useful to identify program changes in application software. Questionnaires help auditors identify specific internal controls.

Effect of IT Controls on Control Risk and Substantive Tests

The following discussion of control risk may seem familiar because auditors link IT controls to audit objectives following the same principles and approaches which were covered in Chapter 10. You may recall that auditors relate controls and deficiencies in internal control to specific audit objectives. Based on those controls and deficiencies, the auditor assesses control risk for each related audit objective. The same approach is used when controls are done by IT.

Relating IT Controls to Transaction-Related Audit Objectives Auditors do not normally link controls and deficiencies in general controls to specific transaction-related audit objectives. Because general controls affect audit objectives in several cycles, if the general controls are ineffective, the auditor's ability to rely on IT-related application controls to reduce control risk in all cycles is reduced. Conversely, if general controls are effective, it increases the auditor's ability to rely on IT-based application controls for all cycles.

Auditors can use a control risk matrix, much like the one we discussed in Chapter 10, to help them identify both manual and automated application controls and control deficiencies for each related audit objective. For example, to prevent payments to fictitious employees, a computer comparison of inputted employee identification numbers with the employee master file might reduce control risk for the occurrence objective for payroll transactions. Auditors can identify manual and automated controls at the same time or separately, but they should not identify deficiencies or assess control risk until both types of controls have been identified.

Effect of IT Controls on Substantive Testing After identifying specific IT-based application controls that can be used to reduce control risk, auditors can reduce substantive testing. The systematic nature of automated application controls may allow auditors to reduce sample sizes used to test those controls in both an audit of financial statements and an audit of internal control over financial reporting. Auditors may also be able to rely on prior year testing of automated controls as described in Chapter 10 when general controls are effective and the automated control has not been changed since testing by the auditor. Auditors often use their own software to test the controls. These factors, when combined, often lead to extremely effective and efficient audits.

The impact of general controls and application controls on audits is likely to vary depending on the level of complexity in the IT environment. We discuss that next.

Auditing in Less Complex IT Environments

Many organizations design and use accounting software to process business transactions so that source documents are retrievable in a readable form and can be traced easily through the accounting system to output. Such systems retain many of the traditional source documents such as customer purchase orders, shipping and receiving records, and sales and vendor invoices. The software also produces printed journals and ledgers that allow the auditor to trace transactions through the accounting records. Internal controls in these systems often include client personnel comparing computer-produced records with source documents.

In these situations, the use of IT does not significantly impact the audit trail. Typically, auditors obtain an understanding of internal control and do tests of controls, substantive tests of transactions, and account balance verification procedures in the same way they do when testing manual accounting systems. The auditor is still responsible for obtaining an understanding of general and application computer controls because such knowledge is useful in identifying risks that may affect the financial statements. But, the auditor typically does not test automated controls. This approach to auditing is often called **auditing around the computer** because the auditor is not using automated controls to reduce assessed control risk. Instead, the auditor uses manual controls to support a reduced control risk assessment.

Auditors in smaller companies often audit around the computer when general controls are less effective than in more complex IT environments. Often, smaller companies lack dedicated IT personnel, or they rely on periodic involvement of IT consultants to assist in installing and maintaining hardware and software. The responsibility of the IT function is often assigned to user departments, such as the accounting department, where the hardware physically resides. Auditing around the computer is effective because these systems often produce sufficient audit trails to permit auditors to compare source documents such as vendors' and sales invoices to output, and there may be manual

Auditing around the computer

Auditing without relying on and testing automated controls embedded in computer application programs, which is acceptable when the auditor has access to readable source documents that can be reconciled to detailed listings of output or when sufficient nonautomated controls exist.

controls over the input and output processes that operate effectively to prevent and detect material financial statement misstatements.

Many organizations with non-complex IT environments often heavily rely on microcomputers to do accounting system functions. The use of microcomputers creates the following unique audit considerations:

- *Limited reliance on automated controls.* Even in less sophisticated IT environments, automated controls can often be relied on. For example, software programs in microcomputers can be loaded on the computer's hard drive in a format that does not permit changes by client personnel, making the risk of unauthorized changes in the software low. Before relying on controls built into that software, auditors must be confident that the software vendor has a reputation for quality.
- *Access to master files.* When clients use microcomputers, auditors should be concerned about access to master files by unauthorized people. Appropriate separation of duties between personnel with access to master files and responsibilities for processing is critical. Regular owner–manager review of transaction output improves internal control.
- *Risk of computer viruses.* Computer viruses can lead to the loss of data and programs. Certain viruses can damage electronic files or shut down an entire network of computers. Regularly updated virus protection software that screens for virus infections improves controls.

A public company's use of microcomputers in the financial reporting process may affect the audit of internal control over financial reporting. If the auditor concludes that general controls are ineffective, the auditor's tests of automated application controls may need to be increased. The auditor must also consider the implications of the lack of effective general controls on the opinion about the operating effectiveness of internal control over financial reporting.

AUDITING IN MORE COMPLEX IT ENVIRONMENTS

OBJECTIVE 12-5

Use test data, parallel simulation, and embedded audit module approaches when auditing through the computer.

As organizations expand their use of IT, internal controls are often embedded in applications that are available only electronically. When traditional source documents such as invoices, purchase orders, billing records, and accounting records such as sales journals, inventory listings, and accounts receivable subsidiary records exist only electronically, auditors must change their approach to auditing. This approach is often called **auditing through the computer**. Table 12-4 illustrates some differences between auditing around the computer and auditing through the computer.

Auditors use three categories of testing approaches when auditing through the computer: test data approach, parallel simulation, and embedded audit module approach.

Test Data Approach In the **test data approach**, auditors process their own test data using the client's computer system and application programs to determine whether the automated controls correctly process the test data. Auditors design the test data to include transactions that the client's system should either accept or reject. After the test data are processed on the client's system, auditors compare the actual output to the expected output to assess the effectiveness of the application program's automated controls. Figure 12-3 illustrates the use of the test data approach.

When using the test data approach, auditors have three main considerations:

1. *Test data should include all relevant conditions that the auditor wants tested.* Auditors should design test data to test all key computer-based controls and include realistic data that are likely to be a part of the client's normal processing, including both valid and invalid transactions.

Auditing through the computer

Auditing by testing automated internal controls and account balances electronically, generally because strong general controls exist.

Test data approach

A method of auditing an IT system that uses the auditor's test data to determine whether the client's computer program correctly processes valid and invalid transactions.

TABLE 12-4	Examples of Auditing Around and Through the Computer		
Auditing Around the Computer Approach	**Internal Control**	**Auditing Through the Computer Approach**	
Select a sample of sales transactions from the sales journal and obtain the related customer sales order to determine that the credit manager's initials are present, indicating approval of sales on account.	Credit is approved for sales on account.	Obtain a copy of the client's sales application program and related credit limit master file and process a test data sample of sales transactions to determine whether the application software properly rejects those test sales transactions that exceed the customer's credit limit amount and accepts all other transactions.	
Select a sample of payroll disbursements from the payroll journal and verify by reviewing human resource department files that the payee is currently employed.	Payroll is processed only for individuals currently employed.	Create a test data file of valid and invalid employee ID numbers and process that file using a controlled copy of the client's payroll application program to determine that all invalid employee ID numbers are rejected and that all valid employee ID numbers are accepted.	
Obtain a printout of the cash disbursements journal and manually foot each column to verify the accuracy of the printed column totals.	Column totals for the cash disbursements journal are subtotaled automatically by the computer.	Obtain an electronic copy of the cash disbursements journal transactions and use generalized audit software to verify the accuracy of the column totals.	

For example, assume the client's payroll application contains a limit check that disallows a payroll transaction that exceeds 80 hours per week. To test this control, the auditor can prepare payroll transactions with 79, 80, and 81 hours for each sampled week and process them through the client's system in a manner shown in Figure 12-3. If the limit check control is operating effectively, the

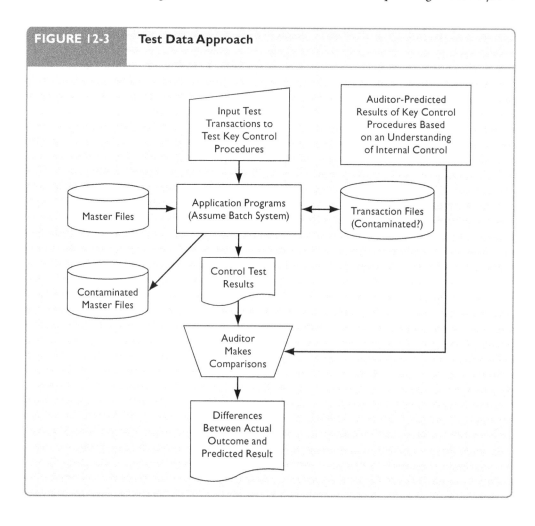

FIGURE 12-3   Test Data Approach

client's system should reject the transaction for 81 hours, and the client's error listing should report the 81-hour transaction error.

2. *Application programs tested by auditors' test data must be the same as those the client used throughout the year.* One approach is to run the test data on a surprise basis, possibly at random times throughout the year, even though doing so is costly and time-consuming. Another method is to rely on the client's general controls in the librarian and systems development functions to ensure that the program tested is the one used in normal processing.

3. *Test data must be eliminated from the client's records.* If auditors process test data while the client is processing its own transactions, auditors must eliminate the test data in the client's master files after the tests are completed. Auditors can do this by developing and processing data that reverses the effect of the test data.

Because of the complexities of many clients' application software programs, auditors who use the test data approach often obtain assistance from a computer audit specialist. Many larger CPA firms have staff dedicated to assisting in testing client application controls.

Parallel Simulation Auditors often use auditor-controlled software to do the same operations that the client's software does, using the same data files. The purpose is to determine the effectiveness of automated controls and to obtain evidence about electronic account balances. This testing approach is called **parallel simulation testing**. Figure 12-4 shows a typical parallel simulation. Whether testing controls or ending balances, the auditor compares the output from the auditor's software to output from the client's system to test the effectiveness of the client's software and to determine if the client's balance is correct. A variety of software is available to assist auditors.

Parallel simulation testing

An audit testing approach that involves the auditor's use of audit software, either purchased or programmed by the auditor, to replicate some part of a client's application system.

FIGURE 12-4   Parallel Simulation

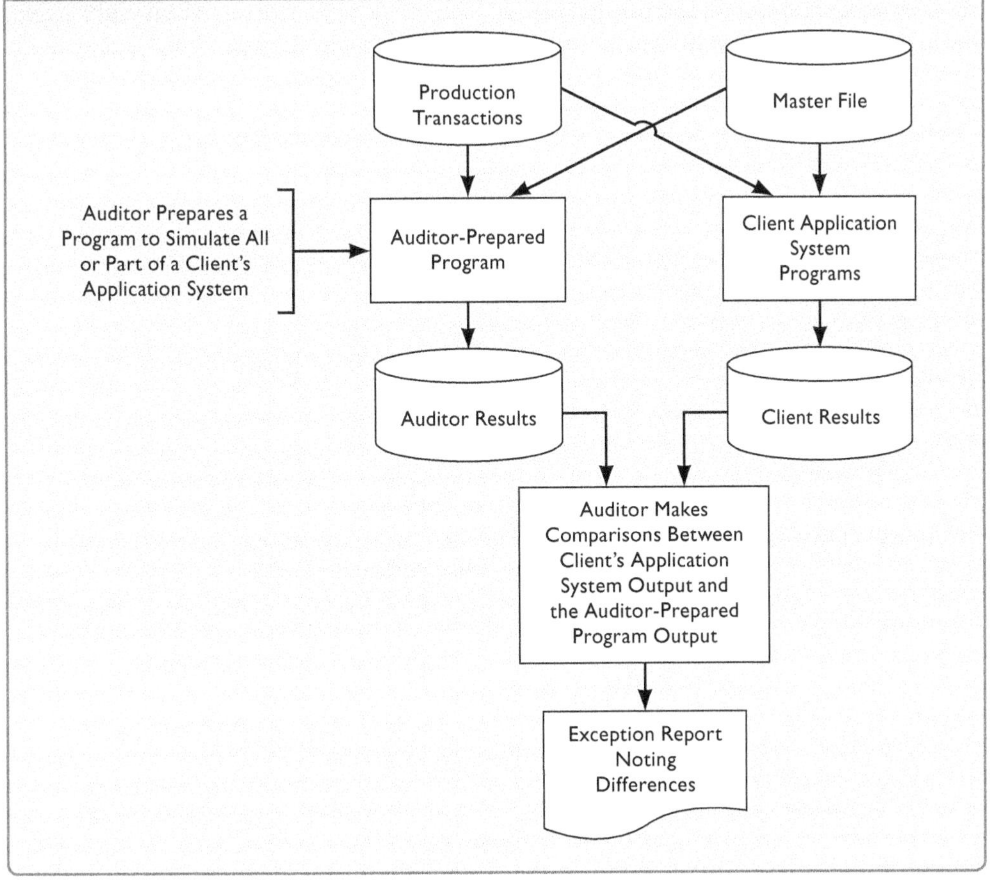

Generalized audit software (GAS)

Computer programs used by auditors that provide data retrieval, data manipulation, and reporting capabilities specifically oriented to the needs of auditors.

Auditors commonly do parallel simulation testing using **generalized audit software (GAS)**, which are programs designed specifically for auditing purposes. Commercially available audit software, such as ACL or IDEA, can be easily operated on auditors' desktops or laptop computers. Auditors obtain copies of machine-readable client databases or master files and use the generalized audit software to do a variety of tests of the client's electronic data. Instead of GAS, some auditors use spreadsheet software to do simple parallel simulation tests. Others develop their own customized audit software.

Generalized audit software provides three advantages: it is relatively easy to train audit staff in its use, even if they have had little audit-related IT training, the software can be applied to a wide variety of clients with minimal customization, and it has the ability to do audit tests much faster and in more detail than using traditional manual procedures. Table 12-5 includes some of the common uses of GAS. Two are examined in detail:

1. *Generalized audit software is used to test automated controls.* An auditor obtains copies of a client's customer credit limit master file and a customer order file, and then instructs the auditor's computer to list transactions that exceed the customer's authorized credit limit. The auditor then compares the audit output to the client's list of customer orders that were rejected for exceeding authorized credit limits.

2. *Generalized audit software is used to verify the client's account balances.* An auditor can use the software to sum the master file of customer accounts receivable to determine whether the total agrees with the general ledger balance.

Embedded audit module approach

A method of auditing transactions processed by IT whereby the auditor embeds a module in the client's application software to identify transactions with characteristics that are of interest to the auditor; the auditor is then able to analyze these transactions on a real-time, continuous basis as client transactions are processed.

Embedded Audit Module Approach When using the **embedded audit module approach**, auditors insert an audit module in the client's application system to identify specific types of transactions. For example, auditors might want to use an embedded module to identify all purchases exceeding US$25,000 for follow-up with more detailed examination for the occurrence and accuracy transaction-related audit objectives. In some cases, auditors later copy the identified transactions to a separate data file

TABLE 12-5	Common Uses of Generalized Audit Software	
Uses	**Description**	**Examples**
Verify extensions and footings.	Verify the accuracy of the client's computations by calculating information independently.	Foot accounts receivable trial balance.
Examine records for quality, completeness, consistency, and correctness.	Scan all records using specified criteria.	Review payroll files for terminated employees.
Compare data on separate files.	Determine that information in two or more data files agrees.	Compare changes in accounts receivable balances between two dates using sales and cash receipts in transaction files.
Summarize or resequence data and do analyses.	Change or aggregate data.	Resequence inventory items by location to facilitate physical observation.
Select audit samples.	Select samples from machine-readable data.	Randomly select accounts receivable for confirmation.
Print confirmation requests.	Print data for sample items selected for confirmation testing.	Print customer name, address, and account balance information from master files.
Compare data obtained through other audit procedures with company records.	Compare machine-readable data with audit evidence gathered manually, which is converted to machine-readable form.	Compare confirmation responses with accounts receivable master files.

and then process those transactions using parallel simulation to duplicate the function done by the client's system. The auditor then compares the client's output with the auditor's output. Discrepancies are printed on an exception report for auditor follow-up.

The embedded audit module approach allows auditors to continuously audit transactions by identifying actual transactions processed by the client as compared to test data and parallel simulation approaches, which only allow intermittent testing. Internal audit may also find this technique useful.

Although auditors may use one or any combination of testing approaches, they typically use:

- Test data to do tests of controls and substantive tests of transactions
- Parallel simulation for substantive testing, such as recalculating transaction amounts and footing master file subsidiary records of account balances
- Embedded audit modules to identify unusual transactions for substantive testing

ISSUES FOR DIFFERENT IT ENVIRONMENTS

So far, we have addressed the effect of IT on the audit process for organizations that centralize the IT function. Although all organizations need good general controls regardless of the structure of their IT function, some general control issues vary depending on the IT environment. Next, we'll examine IT issues for clients who use networks, database management systems, e-commerce systems, and outsourced computer service centers.

OBJECTIVE 12-6

Identify issues for e-commerce systems and other specialized IT systems.

Issues for Network Environments

The use of networks that link equipment such as microcomputers, midrange computers, mainframes, workstations, servers, and printers is common for most businesses. **Local area networks (LANs)** link equipment within a single or small cluster of buildings, and are used only within a company. LANs are often used to transfer data and programs from one computer or workstation using network system software that allow all of the devices to function together. **Wide area networks (WANs)** link equipment in larger geographic regions, including global operations.

In networks, application software and data files used to process transactions are included on several computers that are linked together. Access to the application from microcomputers or workstations is managed by network server software. Even small companies can have several computer servers linked together on a network, while larger companies may have hundreds of servers in dozens of locations networked together.

Most of the general controls discussed in this chapter apply to large client networks, because IT support and user involvement is centralized. For other companies, networks present control issues that the auditor must consider in planning the audit. For example, auditors often increase control risk when companies have networks consisting of servers located throughout various parts of the organization because decentralized network operations often lack security and management supervision over the various connected servers.

When clients have accounting applications processed in a network, the auditor should learn about the network configuration, including the location of computer servers and workstations linked to one another, network software used to manage the system, and controls over access and changes to application programs and data files located on servers. This knowledge may have implications for the auditor's control risk assessment when planning the audit of the financial statements and when testing controls in an audit of internal control over financial reporting.

Local area networks (LANs)

Networks that connect computer equipment, data files, software, and peripheral equipment within a local area, such as a single building or a small cluster of buildings, for intracompany use.

Wide area networks (WANs)

Networks that connect computer equipment, databases, software, and peripheral equipment that reside in many geographic locations, such as client offices located around the world.

Issues for Database Management Systems

Database management systems

Hardware and software systems that allow clients to establish and maintain databases shared by multiple applications.

Database management systems allow clients to create databases that include information that can be shared across multiple applications. In nondatabase systems, each application has its own data file, whereas in database management systems, many applications share files. Clients implement database management systems to reduce data redundancy, improve control over data, and provide better information for decision making by integrating information throughout functions and departments. For example, customer data, such as the customer's name and address, can be shared in the sales, credit, accounting, marketing, and shipping functions, resulting in consistent information for all users and significant cost reductions. Companies often integrate database management systems within the entire organization using enterprise software programs.

Controls often improve when data are centralized in a database management system by eliminating duplicate data files. However, database management systems also can create internal control risks. Risks increase when multiple users, including individuals outside of accounting, can access and update data files. To counter the risks of unauthorized, inaccurate, and incomplete data files, companies must implement proper database administration and access controls. With the centralization of data in a single system, they must also ensure proper backup of data on a regular basis.

Auditors of clients using database management systems should understand the clients' planning, organization, and policies and procedures to determine how well the systems are managed. This understanding may affect the auditor's assessment of control risk and the auditor's opinion about the operating effectiveness of internal control over financial reporting.

Issues for E-Commerce Systems

Companies using e-commerce systems to transact business electronically link their internal accounting systems to external parties' systems, such as customers and suppliers. As a result, a company's risks depend in part on how well its e-commerce partners identify and manage risks in their own IT systems. To manage these interdependency risks, companies must ensure that their business partners manage IT system risks before conducting business with them electronically. Some of the assurance services discussed in Chapter 1, such as *SysTrust*, provide objective information about the reliability of a business partner's IT system.

The use of e-commerce systems also exposes sensitive company data, programs, and hardware to potential interception or sabotage by external parties. To limit these exposures, companies use firewalls, encryption techniques, and digital signatures.

Firewall

A system of hardware and software that monitors and controls the flow of e-commerce communications by channeling all network connections through a control gateway.

A **firewall** protects data, programs, and other IT resources from unauthorized external users accessing the system through networks, such as the internet. A firewall is a system of hardware and software that monitors and controls the flow of e-commerce communications by channeling all network connections through controls that verify external users, grant accesses to authorized users, deny access to unauthorized users, and direct authorized users to requested programs or data.

Encryption techniques

Computer programs that change a standard message into one that is coded, then decoded by the recipient using a decryption program.

Encryption techniques protect the security of electronic communication when information is transmitted and when it is stored. Computerized encryption changes a standard message or data file into one that is coded (encrypted), requiring the receiver of the electronic message or user of the encrypted data file to use a decryption program to decode the message or data. A public key encryption technique is often used, where one key (the public key) is used for encoding the message and another key (the private key) is used to decode the message. The public key is distributed to all approved users of the e-commerce system. The private key is distributed only to internal users with the authority to decode the message.

To authenticate the validity of a trading partner conducting business electronically, companies may rely on external certification authorities who verify the source of the public key by using **digital signatures**. A trusted certification authority issues a digital certificate to individuals and companies engaging in e-commerce. The digital signature contains the holder's name and its public key. It also contains the name of the certification authority and the certificate's expiration date and other specified information. To guarantee integrity and authenticity, each signature is digitally signed by the private key maintained by the certification authority.

Auditors should understand the nature of firewall and encryption controls to ensure that they are properly implemented and monitored. An inadequate firewall may increase the likelihood of unauthorized changes to software and data. Thus, the auditor may need to test controls surrounding the use of the firewall to ensure that automated application controls used to support assessed control risk below the maximum have not been changed without the auditor's knowledge. Similarly, auditors may need to understand and test encryption controls to satisfy transaction and account balance objectives. Failure to adequately encrypt transaction or account data may result in changes in amounts supporting transactions or account balances.

Digital signatures

Electronic certificates that are used to authenticate the validity of individuals and companies conducting business electronically.

Issues When Clients Outsource IT

Many clients outsource some or all of their IT needs to an independent computer **service center**, including **application service providers (ASPs)**, rather than maintain an internal IT center. Smaller companies often outsource their payroll function because payroll is reasonably standard from company to company, and many reliable providers of payroll services are available. Companies also outsource their e-commerce systems to external website service providers. Like all outsourcing decisions, companies decide whether to outsource IT on a cost–benefit basis.

When outsourcing to a computer service center, the client submits input data, which the service center processes for a fee, and returns the agreed-upon output and the original input. For payroll, the company submits data from time cards, and pay rates to the service center. The service center returns payroll checks, journals, and input data each week. The service center is responsible for designing the computer system and providing adequate controls to ensure that the processing is reliable.

Service center

An organization that provides IT services for companies on an outsourcing basis.

Application service providers (ASPs)

A third-party entity that manages and supplies software applications or software-related services to customers through the internet.

CLOUD COMPUTING

An increasingly popular software model is emerging that is widely known as 'cloud computing.' Cloud computing is a service where users save money by paying a monthly fee to access software applications that run on someone else's hardware and rely on others' application designs. Cloud computing helps users spare the expense of acquiring their own servers, storage and backup systems, hiring and retaining IT professionals to keep the systems running, and other high-cost IT support activities. Instead of running their own systems, users pay vendors to host the application and store related data. Systems are accessed through the internet, which means they can be used on any computer with an internet connection. Cloud computing solutions are appearing in a number of business process areas, including customer relationship management, human resources, payroll, billing, and help desk management.

Relying on cloud computing solutions does come with risks that need to be managed. Data is transmitted and then stored in environments not directly controlled by users and another entity hosts the software. As a result, the underlying code for the software is basically the same for all users, which restricts user customization. And, when systems are down, user access depends on restoration by the vendor. Backup options may also not be available for users since their decision to contract with a cloud computing vendor is often driven by a desire to avoid costs of buying servers and hardware to host the software.

Not only are individual cloud computing solutions becoming available, but massive scale cloud computing environments are emerging as well. IBM unveiled plans in late 2007 for Blue Cloud, a series of cloud computing offerings that will allow corporate data centers to operate more like the internet by enabling computing across a widely distributed, global super powerful computer.

Sources: Adapted from Alan Cohen, 'Cloud Computing: Is it Safe?,' *Law.com*, October 31, 2008 (www.law.com); IBM, Inc., 'IBM Introduces Ready-to-Use Cloud Computing,' www.ibm.com, November 15, 2007.

Understanding Internal Controls in Outsourced Systems The auditor faces a difficulty when obtaining an understanding of the client's internal controls in these situations because many of the controls reside at the service center, and the auditor cannot assume that the controls are adequate simply because it is an independent enterprise. Auditing standards require the auditor to consider the need to obtain an understanding and test the service center's controls if the service center application involves processing significant financial data. For example, many of the controls for payroll transaction-related audit objectives reside within the software program maintained and supported by the payroll services company, not the audit client.

When obtaining an understanding and testing the service center's controls, the auditor should use the same criteria that was used in evaluating a client's internal controls. If the auditor concludes that active involvement at the service center is the only way to conduct the audit, it may be necessary to obtain an understanding of internal controls at the service center and test controls using test data and other tests of controls.

Reliance on Service Center Auditors In recent years, it has become increasingly common for the service center to engage a CPA firm to obtain an understanding and test internal controls of the service center and issue a report for use by all customers and their independent auditors. The purpose of this independent assessment is to provide service center customers reasonable assurance about the adequacy of the service center's general and application controls and to eliminate the need for redundant audits by customers' auditors.

For service center organizations, auditors may issue two types of reports:

- Report on controls that have been implemented
- Report on controls that have been implemented and tested for operating effectiveness

A report on controls that have been implemented helps auditors obtain an understanding of internal control to plan the audit. However, auditors also require evidence about the operating effectiveness of controls to assess control risk, especially when auditing internal control over financial reporting for public companies. This evidence can:

- Be based on the service auditor's report on controls that have been implemented and tests of operating effectiveness
- Come from tests of the user organization's controls over the activities of the service organization
- Be created when the user auditor does appropriate tests at the service organization

If the user auditor decides to rely on the service auditor's report, appropriate inquiries should be made about the service auditor's reputation. Auditing standards state that the user auditor should not make reference to the report of the service auditor in the opinion on the user organization's financial statements.

SUMMARY

This chapter studied how IT influences the audit process. Even when a client's use of IT leads to improved internal control, the use of IT-based accounting systems introduces new risks typically not associated with traditional manual systems. Well-managed companies recognize these new risks and respond by implementing effective general and application controls in the IT system to reduce the impact of these risks on financial reporting. The auditor must be knowledgeable about these risks and obtain an understanding of the client's general and application controls to effectively plan an audit. Knowledge about general controls provides a basis for the auditor to rely on automated application controls and may reduce the extent of tests of key automated controls in audits of financial statements and internal controls. Some of the auditor's tests of controls can be done by the computer, often as a way to achieve more effective and efficient audits. Reliance on general and application controls to reduce control risk is likely to change when clients use microcomputers, networks, database management systems, e-commerce systems, and outsourced computer service centers instead of centralized IT systems.

ESSENTIAL TERMS

Application controls   p. 403

Application service providers (ASPs)   p. 417

Auditing around the computer   p. 410

Auditing through the computer   p. 411

Automated controls   p. 407

Database management systems   p. 416

Digital signatures   p. 417

Embedded audit module approach   p. 414

Encryption techniques   p. 416

Firewall   p. 416

General controls   p. 403

Generalized audit software (GAS)   p. 414

Hardware controls   p. 403

Input controls   p. 407

Local area networks (LANs)   p. 415

Manual controls   p. 406

Output controls   p. 408

Parallel simulation testing   p. 413

Parallel testing   p. 405

Pilot testing   p. 405

Processing controls   p. 407

Service center   p. 417

Test data approach   p. 411

Wide area networks (WANs)   p. 415

REVIEW QUESTIONS

12-1 (Objective 12-1) Explain how client internal controls can be improved through the proper installation of IT.

12-2 (Objective 12-2) Identify risks for accounting systems that rely heavily on IT functions.

12-3 (Objective 12-2) Define what is meant by an audit trail and explain how it can be affected by the client's integration of IT.

12-4 (Objective 12-2) Distinguish between random error resulting from manual processing and systematic error resulting from IT processing and give an example of each category of error.

12-5 (Objective 12-2) Identify the traditionally segregated duties in noncomplex IT systems and explain how increases in the complexity of the IT function affect that separation.

12-6 (Objective 12-3) Distinguish between general controls and application controls and give two examples of each.

12-7 (Objective 12-3) Identify the typical duties within an IT function and describe how those duties should be segregated among IT personnel.

12-8 (Objective 12-4) Explain how the effectiveness of general controls affects the auditor's tests of automated application controls, including the auditor's ability to rely on tests done in prior audits.

12-9 (Objective 12-4) Explain the relationship between application controls and transaction-related audit objectives.

12-10 (Objective 12-4) Explain what is meant by auditing around the computer and describe what must be present for this approach to be effective when auditing clients who use IT to process accounting information.

12-11 (Objective 12-5) Explain what is meant by the test data approach. What are the major difficulties with using this approach? Define parallel simulation with audit software and provide an example of how it can be used to test a client's payroll system.

12-12 (Objective 12-6) Describe risks that are associated with purchasing software to be installed on microcomputer hard drives. What precautions can clients take to reduce those risks?

12-13 (Objective 12-6) Compare the risks associated with network systems to those associated with centralized IT functions.

12-14 (Objective 12-6) How does the use of a database management system affect risks?

12-15 (Objective 12-6) An audit client is in the process of creating an online web-based sales ordering system for customers to purchase products using personal credit cards for payment. Identify three risks related to an online sales system that management should consider. For each risk, identify an internal control that could be implemented to reduce that risk.

12-16 (Objective 12-6) Explain why it is unacceptable for an auditor to assume that an independent computer service center is providing reliable accounting information to an audit client. What can the auditor do to test the service center's internal controls?

MULTIPLE CHOICE QUESTIONS FROM CPA EXAMINATIONS

12-17 (Objectives 12-1, 12-4) The following questions concern the characteristics of IT systems. Choose the best response.

a. An IT system is designed to ensure that management possesses the information it needs to carry out its functions through the integrated actions of
   (1) data-gathering, analysis, and reporting functions.
   (2) a computer-based information retrieval and decision-making system.
   (3) statistical and analytical procedures functions.
   (4) production budgeting and sales forecasting activities.

b. Which of the following conditions will not normally cause the auditor to question whether material misstatements exist?
   (1) Bookkeeping errors are listed on an IT-generated error listing.
   (2) Differences exist between control accounts and supporting master files.
   (3) Transactions are not supported by proper documentation.
   (4) Differences are disclosed by confirmations.

c. As general IT controls weaken, the auditor is most likely to
   (1) reduce testing of automated application controls done by the computer.
   (2) increase testing of general IT controls to conclude whether they are operating effectively.
   (3) expand testing of automated application controls used to reduce control risk to cover greater portions of the fiscal year under audit.
   (4) ignore obtaining knowledge about the design of general IT controls and whether they have been implemented.

d. Which of the following is an example of an application control?
   (1) The client uses access security software to limit access to each of the accounting applications.
   (2) Employees are assigned a user ID and password that must be changed every quarter.
   (3) The sales system automatically computes the total sale amount and posts the total to the sales journal master file.
   (4) Systems programmers are restricted from doing applications programming functions.

12-18 (Objectives 12-2, 12-4) The following questions concern auditing complex IT systems. Choose the best response.

a. Which of the following client IT systems generally can be audited without examining or directly testing the computer programs of the system?
   (1) A system that performs relatively uncomplicated processes and produces detailed output.
   (2) A system that affects a number of essential master files and produces limited output.
   (3) A system that updates a few essential master files and produces no printed output other than final balances.
   (4) A system that does relatively complicated processing and produces little detailed output.

b. Which of the following is true of generalized audit software programs?
   (1) They can be used only in auditing online computer systems.
   (2) They can be used on any computer without modification.
   (3) They each have their own characteristics that the auditor must carefully consider before using in a given audit situation.
   (4) They enable the auditor to do all manual tests of control procedures less expensively.

c. Assume that an auditor estimates that 10,000 checks were issued during the accounting period. If an automated application control that does a limit check for each check request is to be subjected to the auditor's test data approach, the sample should include
   (1) approximately 1,000 test items.
   (2) a number of test items determined by the auditor to be sufficient under the circumstances.
   (3) a number of test items determined by the auditor's reference to the appropriate sampling tables.
   (4) one transaction.

d. An auditor will use the test data approach to obtain certain assurances with respect to the
   (1) input data.
   (2) machine capacity.
   (3) procedures contained within the program.
   (4) degree of data entry accuracy.

DISCUSSION QUESTIONS AND PROBLEMS

12-19 (Objectives 12-2, 12-3) The following are misstatements that can occur in the sales and collection cycle:

1. A data entry operator accidentally transposed a P.O. Box number in a customer's address. As a result, the bills sent to the customer are returned to the company.
2. A new online ordering service was created to increase sales and customer base. However, a glitch in the software allows only existing customers to make purchases.
3. During the night, a company lost power, which inadvertently wiped all of the previous day's entries and sales from its records. The company does not regularly backup its data.
4. A computer virus scrambled some of the contact information for several customers, which resulted in packages being sent to incorrect addresses.
5. A former employee created a fictitious account for a supplier and deposited the money paid for invoices into this account.
6. A data entry operator accidentally re-entered the sales data from a previous week's sale.
7. A data entry operator attempted to change customer information; however, a glitch in the computer program deleted the customer's profile.
8. A shipment of goods was supposed to arrive pre-priced. Upon opening the shipment, the manager found that the items were not the same items listed on the invoice that came with the shipment.

Required
  a. Identify the transaction-related audit objective(s) to which each misstatement pertains.
  b. Identify one automated control that would have likely prevented each misstatement.

12-20 (Objectives 12-2, 12-3, 12-4, 12-5) The Meyers Pharmaceutical Company has the following system for billing and recording accounts receivable:

  1. An incoming customer's purchase order is received in the order department by a clerk who prepares a prenumbered company sales order on which the pertinent information, such as the customer's name and address, customer's account number, and items and quantities ordered, is inserted. After the sales order has been prepared, the customer's purchase order is stapled to it.
  2. The sales order is then passed to the credit department for credit approval. Rough approximations of the billing values of the orders are made in the credit department for those accounts on which credit limitations are imposed. After investigation, approval of credit is noted on the sales order.
  3. Next the sales order is passed to the billing department, where a clerk key-enters the sales order information onto a data file, including unit sales prices obtained from an approved price list. The data file is used to prepare sales invoices.
     The billing application automatically accumulates daily totals of customer account numbers and invoice amounts to provide 'hash' totals and control amounts. These totals, which are inserted in a daily record book, serve as predetermined batch totals for verification of computer inputs. The billing is done on prenumbered, continuous, multi-copy forms that have the following designations:
     (a) Customer copy
     (b) Sales department copy, for information purposes
     (c) File copy
     (d) Shipping department copy, which serves as a shipping order
     Bills of lading are also prepared as carbon copy by-products of the invoicing procedure.
  4. The shipping department copy of the invoice and the bills of lading are then sent to the shipping department. After the order has been shipped, copies of the bill of lading are returned to the billing department. The shipping department copy of the invoice is filed in the shipping department.
  5. In the billing department, one copy of the bill of lading is attached to the customer's copy of the invoice and both are mailed to the customer. The other copy of the bill of lading, together with the sales order, is then stapled to the invoice file copy and filed in invoice numerical order.
  6. The data file is updated for shipments that are different from those billed earlier. After these changes are made, the file is used to prepare a sales journal in sales invoice order and to update the accounts receivable master file. Daily totals are printed to match the control totals prepared earlier. These totals are compared with the 'hash' and control totals by an independent person.

Required
  a. Identify the important controls and related sales transaction-related audit objectives.
  b. List the procedures that a CPA will use in an audit of sales transactions to test the identified controls and the substantive aspects of the sales transactions.

12-21 (Objective 12-5) The following are audit procedures taken from a CPA firm's audit program for acquisitions and cash disbursements:

  1. Foot the list of accounts payable and trace the balance to the general ledger.
  2. Select a sample of accounts payable for confirmation, emphasizing vendors with a large balance and those that the client transacts with frequently, but include several with small and zero balances.
  3. Compare the total of each account payable outstanding, including zero balances, with those in the preceding year, and examine vendors' statements for any total with a difference in excess of US$500.
  4. Compare the unit cost on a random sample of 100 vendors' invoices with catalogs or other price lists and investigate any with a difference of more than 3%.

5. Compare all transactions recorded for four days before and after the balance sheet date with related receiving reports and vendors' invoices to determine the appropriate recording period.

6. Examine a random sample of 100 acquisition transactions to determine whether each was authorized by an appropriate official and paid within the discount period to obtain the maximum cash discount.

a. For each audit procedure, identify whether it is a test of control, a substantive test of transactions, or a test of details of balances.   **Required**

b. Explain how generalized audit software can be used, at least in part, to do some or all of each audit procedure. Assume all information is both machine- and non-machine-readable. Also, identify audit procedures or parts of procedures to which the general audit software is not likely to be applicable. Use the following format:

Procedure	Data File or Files Needed	Kind of Test or Tests the Auditor Can Do Using GAS	Procedure for Which GAS is Likely to Be Inappropriate

12-22 (Objective 12-4) Following are ten key internal controls in the payroll cycle for Gilman Stores, Inc.

Key Controls

1. To input hours worked, payroll accounting personnel input the employee's Social Security number. The system does not allow input of hours worked for invalid employee numbers.

2. The system automatically computes pay at time and a half once hours worked exceed 80 in a two-week pay period.

3. The system accumulates totals each pay period of employee checks processed and debits the payroll expense general ledger account for the total amount.

4. Each pay period, payroll accounting clerks count the number of time cards submitted by department heads for processing and compare that total with the number of checks printed by the system to ensure that each time card has a check.

5. For factory personnel, the payroll system matches employee ID numbers with ID numbers listed on job costing tickets as direct labor per the cost accounting system. The purpose of the reconciliation is to verify that the amount paid to each employee matches the amount charged to production during the time period.

6. The system generates a listing by employee name of checks processed. Department heads review these listings to ensure that each employee actually worked during the pay period.

7. The payroll application is programmed so that only human resource personnel are able to add employee names to the employee master files.

8. On a test basis, payroll accounting personnel obtain a listing of pay rates and withholding information for a sample of employees from human resources to recalculate gross and net pay.

9. Input menus distinguish executive payroll, administrative payroll, and factory payroll.

10. The system automatically rejects processing an employee's pay if inputted hours exceed 160 hours for a two-week pay period.

For each control: **Required**

a. Identify whether the control is an automated application control (AC) or a manual control done by Gilman employees (MC).

b. Identify the transaction-related audit objective that is affected by the control.

c. Identify which controls, if tested within the last two prior year audits, would not have to be retested in the current year, assuming there are effective IT general controls and no changes to the noted control have been made since auditor testing was completed.

12-23 (Objectives 12-1, 12-2, 12-3, 12-4, 12-5) You are conducting an audit of sales for the Metro Department Store, a retail chain store with a computer-based sales system in which computer-based cash registers are integrated directly with accounts receivable, sales, perpetual inventory records, and sales commission expense. At the time of sale, the sales clerks key-enter the following information directly into the cash register:

- Product number
- Quantity sold
- Unit selling price
- Store code number
- Salesclerk number
- Date of sale
- Cash sale or credit sale
- Customer account number for all credit sales

The total amount of the sale, including sales tax, is automatically computed by the system and indicated on the cash register's visual display. The only printed information for cash sales is the cash register receipt, which is given to the customer. For credit sales, a credit slip is prepared and one copy is retained by the clerk and submitted daily to the accounting department.

A summary of sales is printed out daily in the accounting department. The summary includes daily and monthly totals by salesclerks for each store as well as totals for each of 93 categories of merchandise by store. Perpetual inventory and accounts receivable records are updated daily on magnetic tape, but supporting records are limited primarily to machine-readable records.

Required

a. What major problems does the auditor face in verifying sales and accounts receivable?

b. How can the concept of test data be used in the audit? Explain the difficulties the auditor will have to overcome in using test data.

c. How can generalized audit software be used in this audit? List several tests that can be conducted by using this approach.

d. The client would also like to reduce the time it takes to key-enter the information into the cash register. Suggest several ways in which this can be accomplished, considering the information now being key-entered manually.

12-24 (Objectives 12-2, 12-3) One of the firm's audit partners, Gamal Sabah, just had lunch with a good friend, Sara Siag, who is president of Fast Container Corporation. Fast Container Corp. is a growing company that has been in business for only a few years. During lunch, Sara asked Gamal for some advice and direction on how Fast Container should structure its systems development process within the Information Systems Department. Sara noted that because Fast Container has experienced such tremendous growth, the systems development process has evolved into its current state without much direction. Given Fast Container's current size, Sara questions whether its current processes are reasonable. Sara's concern is magnified by the fact that she has little understanding of information systems processes. Gamal told Sara about your information systems evaluation experience and agreed to have you look at Fast Container's current systems development procedures. Sara gave Gamal the following summary of the current processes:

Ashraf Gamry is the information systems manager at Fast Container and has been at the company for three years. Before becoming an employee, Ashraf provided software consulting services for Fast Container. Fast Container purchased a basic software package from Ashraf's former employer. Fast Container has the capability to make extensive modifications to the purchased software to adapt the software to Fast Container's specific business needs.

Program change requests are initiated by either the operations staff (two employees) or the programming staff (two employees), depending on the nature of the change. All change requests are discussed in Ashraf's office with the initiating staff. Based on that discussion, Ashraf provides a verbal approval or denial of the requested change. For approved projects, he encourages the programmers to visit with him from time to time to discuss progress on the projects. Ashraf's long and varied experience with this particular software is helpful in the evaluation of work done, and he is able to make substantive suggestions for improvement. Ashraf has complete faith in his programmers. He believes that if he controlled their activities too carefully, he would stifle their creativity.

Upon completion of the technical programming, Ashraf reviews the programs and related systems flowcharts. Ashraf only rarely identifies last-minute changes before granting his final approval for implementation. One evening a week is set aside in the computer room for program debugging and testing.

The programmers stay late on those evenings so that they can load the programs themselves. To speed up the coding, debugging, and testing process, the programmers work with the actual production program. As a safeguard, however, testing is done on copies of the data files. The original data files are locked carefully in the file storage room. Ashraf is the only person who has access to the room.

When program changes are tested to the satisfaction of the programmers, Ashraf reviews the test results. If he approves the test results, he personally takes care of all the necessary communications and documentation. This involves preparing a short narrative description of the change, usually no longer than a paragraph. A copy of the narrative is sent to the user. Another copy is filed with the systems documentation. When the narrative is complete, Ashraf instructs operations to resume normal production with the new program.

a. Describe controls in Fast Container's systems development and program change processes.

Required

b. Describe deficiencies in Fast Container's systems development and program change processes.

c. Provide recommendations for how Fast Container could improve its processes.

ACL PROBLEM

12-25 (Objective 12-5) This problem requires the use of ACL software, which is included in MyAccountingLab. Information about installing and using ACL and solving this problem can be found in the Appendix, pages 855–859. You should read all of the reference material preceding the instructions about 'Quick Sort' before locating the appropriate command to answer questions a–f. For this problem use the Metaphor_Trans_2002 file in ACL_Demo, which is a file of purchase transactions. The suggested command or other source of information needed to solve the problem requirement is included at the end of each question.

a. Use Quick Sort for each column in the table and identify any concerns you have about the data. (Quick Sort)

Required

b. Determine the total cost of all purchases, ignoring any concerns in part a. (Total)

c. Determine if there are any duplicates or missing numbers in the voucher file. (Invoice column) State your audit concerns with any gaps or duplicates. Provide a possible explanation for any gaps or duplicates that you find. (Gaps and Duplicates)

d. Determine and print the total purchases for the period by product. (Summarize) Determine if the total cost is the same as in part b. (Total) What product number has the greatest amount of purchases? (Quick Sort)

e. Determine and print the percent of total purchases by product. Save the classified file for use in requirement f. (Classify) Based on that output, what percentage is product number 024133112 of the total amount?

f. Using the classified file from requirement e, stratify and print the purchases by product. Exclude all items smaller than US$1,000. Sort the items to determine the smallest and largest amounts. Use the smallest amount as the minimum in the Stratify window. Because the largest amount is significantly larger than all other items, use the second highest amount as the maximum in the Stratify window. (Filter, Quick Sort, and Stratify)

THE OVERALL AUDIT PLAN AND AUDIT PROGRAM

How Much And What Kind Of Testing Will Get The Job Done?

Mahmoud Gazaly and Samar Soliman have known each other for years. Mahmoud is an audit partner and Samar is a professor of auditing. They get together once a month and talk about auditing theory versus practice. Following is their most recent conversation:

SAMAR: Now that PCAOB standards in the U.S. require the audit of a public company's financial statements and internal control over financial reporting to be integrated, I'm afraid that auditors are expected in the near future to over-rely on tests of controls and perform virtually no testing of details of balances. Given significant time pressures required to complete the testing of controls to comply with such requirements, firms may take the above low-cost approach compared to the current approach applied in most Arab CPA firms and reduce substantive testing instead of being concerned enough about audit quality, especially in the audit of the financial statements.

MAHMOUD: Auditors must understand internal control in every audit, regardless if the client is publicly traded or not. For all public companies and for nonpublic companies where control risk is assessed below maximum, the auditor will be performing tests of controls. But, don't forget that International Standards on Auditing also require that substantive tests be performed in *all* audits. We might concentrate on larger items in tests of details of balances. Where risks are high, we pull out all the stops and do a lot of detailed testing.

SAMAR: That sounds fine, but there are certain things that only detailed testing will find. I'm thinking specifically about misappropriation of assets. I'm sure your clients expect you to find those, but analytical procedures and tests of large items at year-end won't get that job done. What about that?

MAHMOUD: Well, our clients also tell us they want our opinion on their financial statements at as low a cost as possible. If we went looking for misappropriation of assets in every audit, our costs would go through the roof. And I'll tell you, the best way for the client to deal with fraud is to have good controls.

SAMAR: I'm not convinced. I'm concerned about the reduction in testing to search for errors as well as fraud. It seems to me you guys are taking the auditing standards' requirements and figuring out how to audit so efficiently that you're not allowing any slack in the process. I think you're creeping more and more toward being an insurer rather than an assurer of the financial statements.

MAHMOUD: What do you mean? I don't understand your theory at all.

SAMAR: Well, you guys are counting on most of your clients not having misstated financial statements, doing minimal audit work at relatively high fees, and then banking on the fact that you'll be able to absorb the cost of any damages you suffer from bad audit opinions through insurance contacts made with international insurance companies. The costs incurred by CPA firms are not that high for Big Four firms or their representatives in Arab countries.

MAHMOUD: Oh come on, Samar, sitting in this ivory tower of yours has turned you into a cynic. I hope you don't talk to your students this way. Auditors do a terrific job, and there is tremendous focus on the auditing profession right now. We want people to come into the profession with a positive attitude. Let's talk about something else. Say, I believe it's your turn to pay.

This chapter deals with the eighth and last step in the planning phase of an audit. This critical step establishes the entire audit program the auditor plans to follow, including all audit procedures, sample sizes, items to select, and timing. The chapter-opening example deals with the importance of making correct decisions in forming the overall audit plan and developing a detailed audit program, considering both the effectiveness of evidence and audit efficiency.

First, the overall audit plan is discussed, which means selecting a mix of five types of tests that will result in an effective and efficient audit. This topic includes discussion of the trade-offs among the types of tests, including consideration of the cost of each type. After deciding on the most cost-effective mix of the types of tests, the auditor designs a detailed audit program. Later in the chapter, we'll address how phase I, which includes all of the audit planning steps, relates to the other three phases of the audit.

Relevant International Standards on Auditing	
ISA 200	Overall Objectives of the Independent Auditor and the Conduct of an Audit in Accordance with International Standards on Auditing
ISA 230	Audit Documentation
ISA 300	Planning an Audit of Financial Statements
ISA 315	Identifying and Assessing the Risks of Material Misstatement through Understanding the Entity and Its Environment
ISA 320	Materiality in Planning and Performing an Audit
ISA 500	Audit Evidence
ISA 510	Initial Audit Engagements—Opening Balances
ISA 610	Using the Work of Internal Auditors
ISA 620	Using the Work of an Auditor's Expert

Types of tests

The five categories of audit tests auditors use to determine whether financial statements are fairly stated: risk assessment procedures, tests of controls, substantive tests of transactions, analytical procedures, and tests of details of balances.

TYPES OF TESTS

OBJECTIVE 13-1

Use the five types of audit tests to determine whether financial statements are fairly stated.

Further audit procedures

Combination of tests of controls, substantive tests of transactions, analytical procedures, and tests of details of balances performed in response to risks of material misstatement identified by the auditor's risk assessment procedures.

In developing an overall audit plan, auditors use five **types of tests** to determine whether financial statements are fairly stated. Auditors use risk assessment procedures to assess the risk of material misstatement, represented by the combination of inherent risk and control risk as described in Chapters 8 and 9. The other four types of tests represent **further audit procedures** performed in response to the risks identified. Each audit procedure falls into one, and sometimes more than one, of these five categories.

Figure 13-1 shows the relationship of the four types of further audit procedures to the audit risk model. As Figure 13-1 illustrates, tests of controls are performed to support a reduced assessment of control risk, while auditors use analytical procedures and tests of details of balances to satisfy planned detection risk. Substantive tests of transactions affect both control risk and planned detection risk, because they test the effectiveness of internal controls and the dollar amounts of transactions.

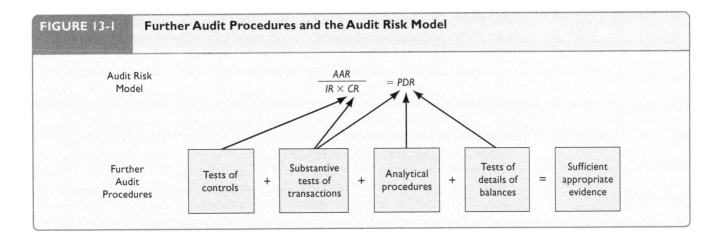

FIGURE 13-1   **Further Audit Procedures and the Audit Risk Model**

Risk Assessment Procedures

Auditing standards (ISA 300 and ISA 315) require the auditor to obtain an understanding of the entity and its environment, including its internal control, to assess the risk of material misstatement in the client's financial statements. Chapter 8 described how the auditor performs procedures to understand the client's business and industry to assess the risk of material misstatement. Chapter 9 further described how auditors perform procedures to assess inherent risk and control risk, while Chapter 10 illustrated how auditors perform procedures to obtain an understanding of internal control to assess control risk. Collectively, procedures performed to obtain an understanding of the entity and its environment, including internal controls, represent the auditor's risk assessment procedures.

Risk assessment procedures are performed to assess the risk of material misstatement in the financial statements as illustrated by Figure 13-1. The auditor performs tests of controls, substantive tests of transactions, analytical procedures, and tests of details of balances in response to the auditor's assessment of the risk of material misstatements. The combination of these four types of further audit procedures provides the basis for the auditor's opinion, as illustrated by Figure 13-1.

Tests of Controls

The auditor's understanding of internal control is used to assess control risk for each transaction-related audit objective. Examples are assessing the accuracy objective for sales transactions represented in proper recording of the values of such transactions as low and the occurrence objective (the transaction did actually occur) as moderate. When control policies and procedures are believed to be effectively designed, the auditor assesses control risk at a level that reflects the relative effectiveness of those controls. To obtain sufficient appropriate evidence to support that assessment, the auditor performs tests of controls.

Tests of controls, either manual or automated, may include the following types of evidence. (Note that the first three procedures are the same as those used to obtain an understanding of internal control.)

- Make inquiries of appropriate client personnel
- Examine documents, records, and reports
- Observe control-related activities
- Reperform client procedures

Auditors perform a system walkthrough as part of procedures to obtain an understanding to help them determine whether controls are in place. The walkthrough is normally applied to one or a few transactions and follows that transaction through the entire process. For example, the auditor may select one sales transaction for a system walkthrough of the credit approval process, then follow the credit approval process from initiation of the sales transaction through to the granting of credit.

Tests of controls are also used to determine whether these controls are effective and usually involve testing a sample of transactions. As a test of the operating effectiveness of the credit approval process, for example, the auditor might examine a sample of 50 sales transactions from throughout the year to determine whether credit was granted before the shipment of goods. Procedures to obtain an understanding of internal control generally do not provide sufficient appropriate evidence that a control is operating effectively. An exception may apply for automated controls because of their consistent performance. The auditor's procedures to determine whether the automated control has been implemented may also serve as the test of that control. If the auditor determines there is minimal risk that the automated control has been changed since the understanding was obtained, then no additional tests of controls would be required. The amount of additional evidence required for tests of controls depends on two things:

1. The extent of evidence obtained in gaining the understanding of internal control
2. The planned reduction in control risk after its assessment at the planning phase

Figure 13-2 shows the role of tests of controls in the audit of the sales and collection cycle relative to other tests performed to provide sufficient appropriate evidence for the auditor's opinion. Note the unshaded circles with the words 'Audited by TOC.' For simplicity, we make two assumptions: Only sales and cash receipts transactions and three general ledger balances make up the sales and collection cycle, and the beginning balances in cash and accounts receivable were audited in the previous year and are considered correct.

If auditors verify that sales and cash receipts transactions are correctly recorded in the accounting records and posted to the general ledger, they can conclude that

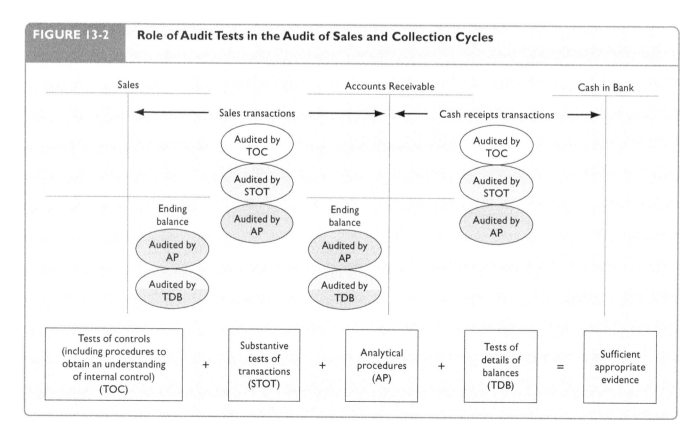

FIGURE 13-2   Role of Audit Tests in the Audit of Sales and Collection Cycles

the ending balances in accounts receivable and sales are correct. (Cash disbursements transactions will have to be audited before the auditor can reach a conclusion about the ending balance in the cash account.) One way the auditor can verify recording of transactions is to perform tests of controls. If controls are in place over sales and cash receipts transactions, the auditor can perform tests of controls to determine whether the seven transaction-related audit objectives are being met for that cycle. Substantive tests of transactions, which we will examine in the next section, also affect audit assurance for sales and cash receipts transactions.

Table 13-1 identifies tests of controls that might be performed to test effectiveness.

Substantive Tests of Transactions

Substantive tests are procedures designed to test for dollar misstatements (often called *monetary misstatements*) that directly affect the correctness of financial statement balances. Auditors rely on three types of substantive tests: substantive tests of transactions, substantive analytical procedures, and tests of details of balances.

Substantive tests of transactions are used to determine whether all seven transaction-related audit objectives studied in Chapter 6 have been satisfied for each class of transactions. Two of those objectives for sales transactions are recorded sales transactions exist (occurrence objective) and existing sales transactions are recorded (completeness objective).

When auditors are confident that all transactions were correctly recorded in the journals and correctly posted, considering all seven transaction-related audit objectives, they can be confident that general ledger totals are correct.

Substantive tests

Audit procedures designed to test for dollar (monetary) misstatements of financial statement balances.

TABLE 13-1	Illustration of Tests of Controls
Illustrative Key Controls	**Typical Tests of Controls**
Credit is approved automatically by the computer by comparison to authorized credit limits (C1).	Examine a sample of sales invoices and compare customer order to authorized credit limit (reperformance).
Recorded sales are supported by authorized shipping documents and approved customer orders (C2).	Examine a sample of duplicate sales invoices to determine that each one is supported by an attached authorized shipping document and approved customer order (Inspection).
Separation of duties exists among billing, recording of sales, and handling of cash receipts (C3).	Observe whether personnel responsible for handling cash have no accounting responsibilities and inquire as to their duties (observation and inquiry).
Shipping documents are forwarded to billing daily and are billed the subsequent day (C4).	Observe whether shipping documents are forwarded daily to billing and observe when they are billed (observation).
Shipping documents are prenumbered and accounted for weekly (C5).	Account for a sequence of shipping documents and trace each to the sales journal (inspection and reperformance).
Batch totals of quantities shipped are compared with quantities billed (C6).	Examine a sample of daily batches, recalculate the shipping quantities, and trace totals to reconciliation with input reports (reperformance).
Unit selling prices are obtained from the price list master file of approved prices (C7).	Examine a sample of sales invoices and agree prices to authorized computer price list. Review changes to price file throughout the year for proper approval (reperformance and inspection).
Sales transactions are internally verified (C8).	Examine document package for internal verification (inspection).
Statements are mailed to customers each month (C9).	Observe whether statements are mailed for one month and inquire about who is responsible for mailing the statements (observation and inquiry).
Computer automatically posts transactions to the accounts receivable subsidiary records and to the general ledger (C10).	Use audit software to trace postings from the batch of sales transactions to the subsidiary records and general ledger (reperformance).
Accounts receivable master file is reconciled to the general ledger on a monthly basis (C11).	Examine evidence of reconciliation for test month, and test accuracy of reconciliation (inspection and reperformance).

Figure 13-2 illustrates the role of substantive tests of transactions in the audit of the sales and collection cycle by lightly shaded circles with the words 'Audited by STOT.' Observe that both tests of controls and substantive tests of transactions are performed for transactions in the cycle, not on the ending account balances. The auditor verifies the recording and summarizing of sales and cash receipts transactions by performing substantive tests of transactions. Figure 13-2 shows one set of tests for sales and another for cash receipts.

Auditors can perform tests of controls separately from all other tests, but it's often more efficient to do them at the same time as substantive tests of transactions. For example, auditors can usually apply tests of controls involving inspection and reperformance to the same transactions tested for monetary misstatements. (Reperformance simultaneously provides evidence about both controls and monetary correctness.) In the rest of this book, we will assume that tests of controls and substantive tests of transactions are done at the same time.

Analytical Procedures

As we first discussed in Chapter 7, analytical procedures involve comparisons of recorded amounts to expectations developed by the auditor. Auditing standards require that they be done during planning and completing the audit. Although not required, analytical procedures may also be performed to audit an account balance. The two most important purposes of analytical procedures in the audit of account balances are to:

1. Indicate possible misstatements in the financial statements
2. Provide substantive evidence

Analytical procedures done during planning typically differ from those done in the testing phase. Even if, for example, auditors calculate the gross margin during planning, they probably do it using interim data. Later, during the tests of the ending balances, they will recalculate the ratio using full-year data. If auditors believe that analytical procedures indicate a reasonable possibility of misstatement, they may perform additional analytical procedures or decide to modify tests of details of balances.

When the auditor develops expectations using analytical procedures and concludes that the client's ending balances in certain accounts appear reasonable, certain tests of details of balances may be eliminated or sample sizes reduced. Auditing standards state that analytical procedures are a type of substantive test (referred to as substantive analytical procedures), when they are performed to provide evidence about an account balance. The extent to which auditors may be willing to rely on substantive analytical procedures in support of an account balance depends on several factors, including the precision of the expectation developed by the auditor, materiality, and the risk of material misstatement.

Figure 13-2 illustrates the role of substantive analytical procedures in the audit of the sales and collection cycle by the dark shaded circles with the words 'Audited by AP.' Observe that the auditor performs substantive analytical procedures on sales and cash receipts transactions, as well as on the ending balances of the accounts in the cycle.

Tests of Details of Balances

Tests of details of balances focus on the ending general ledger balances for both balance sheet and income statement accounts. The primary emphasis in most tests of details of balances is on the balance sheet. Examples include confirmation of customer balances for accounts receivable, physical examination of inventory, and examination of vendors' statements for accounts payable. Tests of ending balances are essential because the evidence is usually obtained from a source independent of the client, which is considered highly reliable. Much like for transactions, the auditor's tests of details of balances must satisfy all balance-related audit objectives for each significant balance sheet account. These objectives were introduced in Chapter 6.

Figure 13-2 illustrates the role of tests of details of balances by the circles with half dark and half light shading and the words 'Audited by TDB.' Auditors perform detailed tests of the ending balances for sales and accounts receivable, including procedures such as confirmation of account receivable balances and sales cutoff tests. The extent of these tests depends on the results of tests of controls, substantive tests of transactions, and substantive analytical procedures for these accounts.

Tests of details of balances help establish the monetary correctness of the accounts they relate to and therefore are substantive tests. For example, confirmations test for monetary misstatements in accounts receivable and are therefore substantive tests. Similarly, counts of inventory and cash on hand are also substantive tests.

SELECTING WHICH TYPES OF TESTS TO PERFORM

Several factors influence the auditor's choice of the types of tests to select, including the availability of the eight types of evidence, the relative costs of each type of test, the effectiveness of internal controls, and inherent risks. The last two of these were discussed in earlier chapters.

OBJECTIVE 13-2

Select the appropriate types of audit tests.

Availability of Types of Evidence for Further Audit Procedures

Each of the four types of further audit procedures involves only certain types of evidence (confirmation, inspection, and so forth). Table 13-2 summarizes the relationship between further audit procedures and types of evidence. Note that:

- More types of evidence, six in total, are used for tests of details of balances than for any other type of test.
- Only tests of details of balances involve physical examination and confirmation.
- Inquiries of the client are made for every type of test.
- Inspection is used in every type of test except analytical procedures.
- Reperformance is used in every type of test except analytical procedures. Auditors may reperform a control as part of a transaction walkthrough or to test a control that is not supported by sufficient documentary evidence.

| TABLE 13-2 | Relationship Between Further Audit Procedures and Evidence |

| | Type of Evidence | | | | | | | |
Further Audit Procedures	Physical Examination	Confirmation	Inspection	Observation	Inquiries of the Client	Reperformance	Analytical Procedures	Recalculation
Tests of controls (including procedures to obtain an understanding of internal control)			√	√	√	√		
Substantive tests of transactions			√		√	√		√
Analytical procedures					√		√	
Tests of details of balances	√	√	√		√	√		√

- Recalculation is used to verify the mathematical accuracy of transactions when performing substantive test of transactions and account balances when performing tests of details of balances.

Relative Costs

When auditors must decide which type of test to select for obtaining sufficient appropriate evidence, the cost is an important consideration. The types of tests are listed below in order of increasing cost:

- Analytical procedures
- Risk assessment procedures, including procedures to obtain an understanding of internal control
- Tests of controls
- Substantive tests of transactions
- Tests of details of balances

Analytical procedures are the least costly because of the relative ease of making calculations and comparisons. Often, considerable information about potential misstatements can be obtained by simply comparing two or three numbers.

Risk assessment procedures, including procedures to obtain an understanding of internal control, are not as costly as other audit tests because auditors can easily make inquiries and observations and perform planning analytical procedures.

Because tests of controls also involve inquiry, observation, and inspection, their relative costs are also low compared to substantive tests. However, tests of controls are more costly relative to the auditor's risk assessment procedures due to a greater extent of testing required to obtain evidence that a control is operating effectively, especially when those tests of controls involve reperformance. Often, auditors can perform a large number of tests of controls quickly using audit software. Such software can test controls in clients' computerized accounting systems, such as in computerized accounts receivable systems that automatically authorize sales to existing customers by comparing the proposed sales amount and existing accounts receivable balance with the customer's credit limit.

Substantive tests of transactions cost more than tests of controls that do not include reperformance because the former often require recalculations and tracings. In a computerized environment, however, the auditor can often perform substantive tests of transactions quickly for a large sample of transactions.

Tests of details of balances almost always cost considerably more than any of the other types of procedures because of the cost of procedures such as sending confirmations and counting inventories. Because of the high cost of tests of details of balances, auditors usually try to plan the audit to minimize their use.

Naturally, the cost of each type of evidence varies in different situations. For example, the cost of an auditor's test-counting inventory (a substantive test of the details of the inventory balance) often depends on the type and dollar value of the inventory, its location, and the number of different items.

Relationship Between Tests of Controls and Substantive Tests

To better understand tests of controls and substantive tests, let's examine how they differ. An exception in a test of control only *indicates* the likelihood of misstatements affecting the dollar value of the financial statements, whereas an exception in a substantive test of transactions or a test of details of balances is a financial statement misstatement. Exceptions in tests of controls are called *control test deviations*.

From Chapter 10, you may recall the three levels of control deficiencies: deficiencies, significant deficiencies, and material weaknesses. Auditors are most likely to believe material dollar misstatements exist in the financial statements when control test deviations are considered to be significant deficiencies or material weaknesses. Auditors should then perform substantive tests of transactions or tests of details of balances to determine whether material dollar misstatements have actually occurred.

Assume that the client's controls require an independent clerk to verify the quantity, price, and extension of each sales invoice, after which the clerk must initial the duplicate invoice to indicate performance. A test of control audit procedure is to inspect a sample of duplicate sales invoices for the initials of the person who verified the information. If a significant number of documents lack initials, the auditor should consider implications for the audit of internal control and follow up with substantive tests for the financial statement audit. This can be done by extending tests of duplicate sales invoices to include verifying prices, extensions, and footings (substantive tests of transactions) or by increasing the sample size for the confirmation of accounts receivable (substantive test of details of balances). Even though the control is not operating effectively, the invoices may still be correct, especially if the person originally preparing the sales invoices did a conscientious and competent job.

On the other hand, if no documents or only a few of them are missing initials, the control will be considered effective and the auditor can therefore reduce substantive tests of transactions and tests of details of balances. However, some reperformance and recalculation substantive tests are still necessary to provide the auditor assurance that the clerk did not initial documents without actually performing the control procedure or performed it carelessly. Because of the need to complete some reperformance and recalculation tests, many auditors perform them as a part of the original tests of controls. Others wait until they know the results of the tests of controls and then determine the total sample size needed.

Relationship Between Analytical Procedures and Substantive Tests

Like tests of controls, analytical procedures only *indicate* the likelihood of misstatements affecting the dollar value of the financial statements. Unusual fluctuations in the relationships of an account to other accounts, or to nonfinancial information, may indicate an increased likelihood that material misstatements exist without necessarily providing direct evidence of a material misstatement. When analytical procedures identify unusual fluctuations, auditors should perform substantive tests of transactions or tests of details of balances to determine whether dollar misstatements have actually occurred. If the auditor performs substantive analytical procedures and believes that the likelihood of material misstatement is small, other substantive tests can be reduced. For accounts with small balances and only minimal potential for material misstatements, such as many supplies and prepaid expense accounts, auditors often limit their tests to substantive analytical procedures if they conclude the accounts are reasonably stated.

Trade-off Between Tests of Controls and Substantive Tests

There is a trade-off between tests of controls and substantive tests. During planning, auditors decide whether to assess control risk below the maximum. When they do, they must then perform tests of controls to determine whether the assessed level of control risk is supported. If tests of controls support the control risk assessment, planned detection risk in the audit risk model is increased, and planned substantive tests can therefore be reduced. In the Arab world, auditors assess control risk below maximum for a publicly listed company whenever the company has strong and effective internal controls. However, if the company is a new audit client or does not maintain strong internal controls then the auditor estimates control risk as high and performs extensive

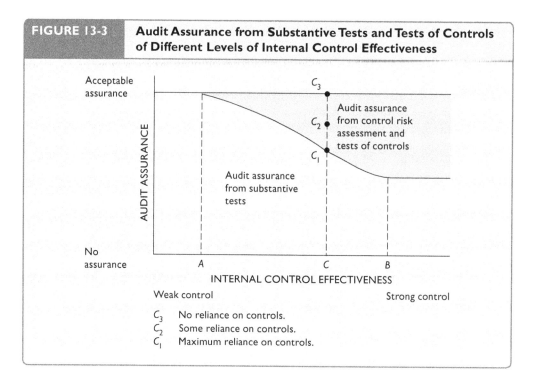

FIGURE 13-3 | **Audit Assurance from Substantive Tests and Tests of Controls of Different Levels of Internal Control Effectiveness**

C_3 No reliance on controls.
C_2 Some reliance on controls.
C_1 Maximum reliance on controls.

substantive tests including tests of details of transactions and balances. Figure 13-3 shows the relationship between substantive tests and control risk assessment (including tests of controls) at differing levels of internal control effectiveness.

The shaded area in Figure 13-3 is the maximum assurance obtainable from control risk assessment and tests of controls. At any point to the left of point A, assessed control risk is 1.0 because the auditor initially evaluated internal controls as ineffective based on the performance of risk assessment procedures. Any point to the right of point B results in no further reduction of control risk because the auditing firm has established a minimum assessed control risk. Notice in Figure 13-3 that an audit of financial statements always requires some substantive procedures.

The auditor's understanding of internal control performed as part of risk assessment procedures provides the basis for the auditor's initial assessment of control risk. Assuming that the auditor determines that the design of internal control is effective and the controls are implemented, the auditor selects a point within the shaded area of Figure 13-3 that is consistent with the assessed control risk the auditor decides to support with tests of controls. Assume the auditor contends that internal control effectiveness is at point C. Tests of controls at the C_1 level will be extensive to support the low

INTERNAL CONTROL PROCEDURES STILL NOT FOLLOWED— A SHOCKING CASE

The managing director of a public sector sporting club in a North African Arab country overrode internal control procedures and government regulations, as he approved the sale of land owned by the club to the owner of an hotel managed by Sonesta International Management Company. The managing director of the club and the former governor of the city approved the sale of the land, which contained an Olympic swimming pool facing the famous river in this beautiful Mediterranean city and was used by the people of the governorate, to the owner of Sonesta Hotel, a well-known businessman. He purchased the land for the price of US$21 million based on price per square meter of US$3,200, while the market price of the land was equal to US$48 million representing US$15,000 per square meter. Both the managing director and the former governor of the city violated the internal control procedures related to the sale of the land at its fair value. To ensure the sale of the land, the former governor of the city colluded with the managing director and ordered the closure of the Olympic swimming pool, which meant that no benefits would accrue from maintaining the land in the assets of the sporting club.

assessment of control risk. The auditor may then determine through the performance of tests of controls that the initial low assessment of control risk at point C is not supported and that internal control is not operating effectively. Then, the auditor's revised control risk assessment would be at the maximum (point C_3) and audit assurance will be obtained from substantive tests. Any point between the two, such as C_2, represents situations where the audit assurance obtained from tests of controls is less than the maximum level of assurance represented by point C_1. If C_2 is selected, the audit assurance from tests of controls is $C_3 - C_2$ and from substantive tests is $C - C_2$. The auditor will likely select C_1, C_2, or C_3 based on the relative cost of tests of controls and substantive tests.

IMPACT OF INFORMATION TECHNOLOGY ON AUDIT TESTING

> **OBJECTIVE 13-3**
>
> Understand how information technology affects audit testing.

Auditing standards and auditing textbooks provide guidance for auditors of entities that transmit, process, maintain, or access significant information electronically. Examples of electronic evidence include records of electronic fund transfers and purchase orders transmitted through electronic data interchange (EDI). Evidence of the performance of automated controls, such as the computer's comparison of proposed sales orders to customer credit limits, may also only be in electronic form.

The standards recognize that when a significant amount of audit evidence exists in electronic form, it may not be practical or possible to reduce detection risk to an acceptable level by performing only substantive tests. For example, the potential for improper initiation or alteration of information may be greater if information is maintained only in electronic form. In these circumstances, the auditor should perform tests of controls to gather evidence in support of an assessed level of control risk below maximum for the affected financial statement assertions. Although some substantive tests are still required, the auditor can significantly reduce substantive tests if the results of tests of controls support the effectiveness of controls.

Because of the inherent consistency of IT processing, however, the auditor may be able to reduce the extent of testing of an automated control. For example, a software-based control is almost certain to function consistently unless the program is changed. Once auditors determine an automated control is functioning properly, they can focus subsequent tests on assessing whether any changes have occurred that will limit the effectiveness of the control. Such tests might include determining whether any changes have occurred to the program and whether these changes were properly authorized and tested prior to implementation.

> **Evidence mix**
>
> The combination of the types of tests to obtain sufficient appropriate evidence for a cycle; there are likely to be variations in the mix from cycle to cycle depending on the circumstances of the audit.

EVIDENCE MIX

> **OBJECTIVE 13-4**
>
> Understand the concept of evidence mix and how it should be varied in different circumstances.

The choice of which types of tests to use and how extensively they need to be performed can vary widely among audits for differing levels of internal control effectiveness and inherent risks. Even within a given audit, variations may occur from cycle to cycle. To obtain sufficient appropriate evidence in response to risks identified through risk assessment procedures, auditors employ a combination of the four remaining types of tests. This combination is often called the **evidence mix**, which is illustrated in Table 13-3 for four different audits. In each case, assume that sufficient appropriate evidence was accumulated. In each audit, you should be able to determine the description of the client from the evidence mix in Table 13-3.

Analysis of Audit 1 This client is a large company with sophisticated internal controls and low inherent risk. Therefore, the auditor performs extensive tests of controls and relies heavily on the client's internal controls to reduce substantive tests. Extensive

TABLE 13-3	Variations in Evidence Mix			
	Tests of Controls	Substantive Tests of Transactions	Analytical Procedures	Tests of Details of Balances
Audit 1	E	S	E	S
Audit 2	M	M	E	M
Audit 3	N	E	M	E
Audit 4	M	E	E	E

E = Extensive amount of testing; M = Medium amount of testing; S = Small amount of testing; N = No testing.

substantive analytical procedures are also performed to reduce other substantive tests. Substantive tests of transactions and tests of details of balances are therefore minimized saving the cost of an audit.

Analysis of Audit 2 This company is medium sized, with some controls and a few inherent risks. The auditor has decided to do a medium amount of testing for all types of tests except substantive analytical procedures, which will be done extensively. More extensive testing will be required if specific inherent risks are discovered.

Analysis of Audit 3 This company is medium sized but has few effective controls and significant inherent risks. Perhaps management has decided that better internal controls are not cost-effective. Because of the lack of effective internal control, we can assume this company is probably a nonpublic company. No tests of controls are done because reliance on internal controls is inappropriate when controls are insufficient for a nonpublic company. The auditor emphasizes tests of details of balances and substantive tests of transactions, but some substantive analytical procedures are also done. Because of the reliance on substantive tests and the costs associated with them, substantive analytical procedures are usually performed to reduce the substantive tests of transactions and balances because they provide evidence about the likelihood of material misstatements. Based on the results of the analytical procedures, auditors may concentrate their tests on specific accounts balances minimizing the costs of performing extensive tests for all account balances. If the auditor already expects to find material misstatements in the account balances, additional analytical procedures are not cost-effective. The cost of the audit is likely to be relatively high because of the amount of detailed substantive testing.

Analysis of Audit 4 The original plan on this audit was to follow the approach used in Audit 2. However, the auditor likely found extensive control test deviations and significant misstatements while performing substantive tests of transactions and substantive analytical procedures. Therefore, the auditor concluded that the internal controls were not effective. Extensive tests of details of balances are performed to offset the unacceptable results of the other tests. The cost of this audit is higher because tests of controls and substantive tests of transactions were performed but can not be used to reduce tests of details of balances.

DESIGN OF THE AUDIT PROGRAM

OBJECTIVE 13-5

Design an audit program.

After the auditor uses risk assessment procedures to determine the appropriate emphasis on each of the other four types of tests, the specific audit procedures for each type must be designed. These audit procedures are then combined to form the audit program. In most audits, the engagement in-charge auditor recommends the evidence mix to the engagement manager. After the evidence mix is approved, the in-charge prepares the audit program or modifies an existing program to satisfy all audit objectives, considering such things as materiality, evidence mix, inherent risk, control risk, and any identified fraud risks, as well as the need for an integrated audit for a public company. The in-charge is also likely to get approval from the manager before performing the audit procedures or delegating their performance to an assistant.

Let's focus on designing audit programs to satisfy transaction-related and balance-related audit objectives. In addition to the section of the audit program that contains the risk assessment procedures performed in planning, the audit program for most audits is designed in three additional parts: tests of controls and substantive tests of transactions, substantive analytical procedures, and tests of details of balances.

Each transaction cycle will likely be evaluated using a separate set of sub-audit programs. In the sales and collection cycle, for example, the auditor might use:

- A test of controls and substantive tests of transactions audit program for sales and cash receipts
- A substantive analytical procedures audit program for the entire cycle
- Tests of details of balances audit programs for cash, accounts receivable, bad debt expense, allowance for uncollectible accounts, and miscellaneous accounts receivable

Tests of Controls and Substantive Tests of Transactions

The tests of controls and substantive tests of transactions audit program normally includes a descriptive section documenting the understanding of internal control obtained during the performance of risk assessment procedures. The program is also likely to include a description of the procedures performed to obtain an understanding of internal control and a description of the assessed level of control risk. The auditor uses this information to develop the tests of controls and substantive tests of transactions audit program. Figure 13-4 illustrates the methodology used to design these tests.

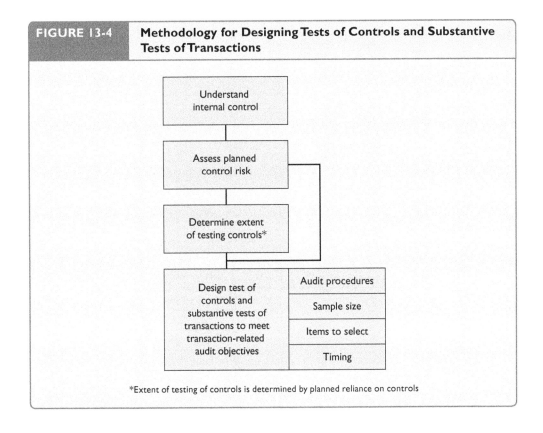

FIGURE 13-4   Methodology for Designing Tests of Controls and Substantive Tests of Transactions

Understand internal control

Assess planned control risk

Determine extent of testing controls*

Design test of controls and substantive tests of transactions to meet transaction-related audit objectives

Audit procedures

Sample size

Items to select

Timing

*Extent of testing of controls is determined by planned reliance on controls

(We previously discussed these steps in Chapter 10.) The audit procedures include both tests of controls and substantive tests of transactions, which vary depending on assessed control risk. When controls are effective and control risk is assessed as low, auditors put heavy emphasis on tests of controls. Some substantive tests of transactions will also be included. If control risk is assessed at maximum, only substantive tests of transactions will be used, assuming the audit is of a nonpublic company.

Audit Procedures When designing tests of controls and substantive tests of transactions, auditors emphasize satisfying the transaction-related audit objectives developed in Chapter 6. Auditors follow a four-step approach to reduce assessed control risk.

1. Apply the transaction-related audit objectives to the class of transactions being tested, such as sales.
2. Identify key controls that should reduce control risk for each transaction-related audit objective.
3. Develop appropriate tests of controls for all internal controls that are used to reduce the preliminary assessment of control risk below maximum (key controls).
4. For potential types of misstatements related to each transaction-related audit objective, design appropriate substantive tests of transactions, considering deficiencies in internal control and expected results of the tests of controls in Step 3.

Figure 13-5 summarizes this four-step approach to designing tests of controls and substantive tests of transactions.

Analytical Procedures

Because analytical procedures are relatively inexpensive, many auditors perform them on all audits. Analytical procedures performed during substantive testing, such as

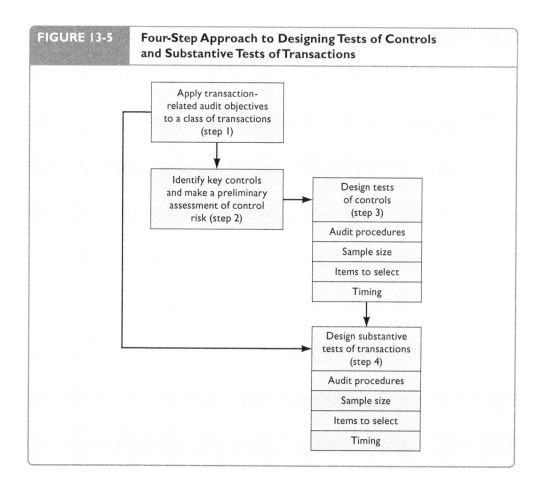

FIGURE 13-5   Four-Step Approach to Designing Tests of Controls and Substantive Tests of Transactions

for the audit of accounts receivable, are typically more focused and more extensive than those done as part of planning. The auditor is likely to use disaggregated data to increase the precision of the auditor's expectations. During planning, the auditor might calculate the gross margin percentage for total sales, while during substantive testing of accounts receivable, the auditor might calculate gross margin percentage by month or by line of business, or possibly both. Analytical procedures calculated using monthly amounts will typically be more effective in detecting misstatements than those calculated using annual amounts, and comparisons by line of business will usually be more effective than company-wide comparisons.

If sales and accounts receivable are based on predictable relationships with non-financial data, the auditor often uses that information for analytical procedures. For example, if revenue billings are based on the number of hours professionals charge to clients, such as in law firms and other organizations that provide services, the auditor can estimate total revenue by multiplying hours billed by the average billing rate.

When the auditor plans to use analytical procedures to provide substantive assurance about an account balance, the data used in the calculations must be considered sufficiently reliable. This is true for all data, especially nonfinancial data. For example, if auditors estimate total revenue using hours billed and the average billing rate, they must be confident that both numbers are reasonably reliable.

Tests of Details of Balances

To design tests of details of balances audit procedures, auditors use a methodology oriented to the balance-related audit objectives we covered in Chapter 6. If the auditor is verifying accounts receivable, for example, the planned audit procedures must be sufficient to satisfy each of the balance-related audit objectives. In planning tests of details of balances audit procedures to satisfy these objectives, many auditors follow a methodology such as the one shown in Figure 13-6 for accounts receivable. The design of these procedures is normally the most difficult part of the entire planning process because it is subjective and requires considerable professional judgment.

Let's discuss the key decisions in designing tests of details of balances audit procedures as shown in Figure 13-6.

Identify Client Business Risks Affecting Accounts Receivable As part of gaining an understanding of the client's business and industry, the auditor identifies and evaluates significant client business risks to determine whether they result in increased risk of material misstatements in the financial statements. If any of the identified client business risks affect accounts receivable, they should be incorporated in the auditor's evaluation of inherent risk or control risk. These risks will then affect the appropriate extent of evidence.

SEC SANCTIONS AUDITOR FOR LACK OF AUDIT PROGRAM

Norman Stumacher was the auditor from April 2001 to February 2005 for Video Without Boundaries, Inc. (Video), a consumer electronics company based in Fort Lauderdale, Florida U.S. Video recorded fictitious revenues and assets through improper revenue recognition and other accounting schemes. These methods included recognizing revenue for services that were never provided in return for shares of stock in a company that went bankrupt. Video also recorded revenue for shipments to a distributor's warehouse, although the distributor was not obligated to pay for the products until they were sold to third-party customers.

Stumacher did not create any audit programs or other documentation to support his unmodified opinions on Video's financial statements. As a result of his improper professional conduct and violations of Rule 10b-5, Stumacher was prohibited from acting as an accountant before the SEC.

Source: Securities and Exchange Commission Accounting and Auditing Enforcement Release No. 2883, September 23, 2008 (http://www.sec.gov/litigation/admin/2008/34-58624.pdf).

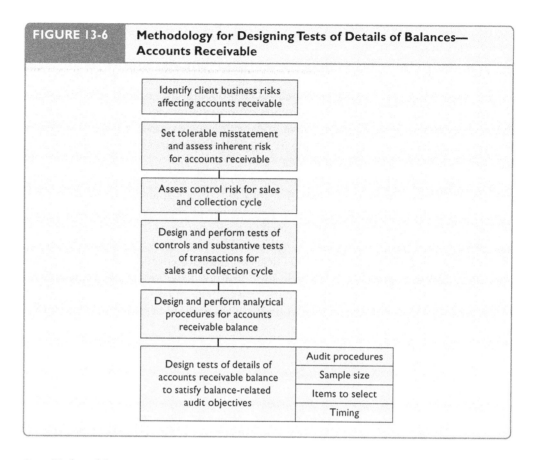

FIGURE 13-6 | **Methodology for Designing Tests of Details of Balances—Accounts Receivable**

Set Tolerable Misstatement and Assess Inherent Risk for Accounts Receivable Auditors must decide the preliminary judgment about materiality for the audit as a whole and then allocate the total to account balances, to establish tolerable misstatement for each significant balance. For a lower tolerable misstatement, more testing of details is required, and vice versa. Some auditors allocate tolerable misstatement to individual balance-related audit objectives, but most do not.

Inherent risk is assessed by identifying any aspect of the client's history, environment, or operations that indicates a high likelihood of misstatement in the current year's financial statements. Considerations affecting inherent risk that may apply to accounts receivable include makeup of accounts receivable, nature of the client's business, initial engagement, and other inherent risk factors discussed in Chapter 9. An account balance for which inherent risk has been assessed as high will result in more evidence accumulation than for an account with low inherent risk.

Inherent risk also can be extended to individual balance-related audit objectives. For example, adverse economic conditions in the client's industry may make the auditor conclude that a high risk of uncollectible accounts receivable (realizable value objective) exists. Inherent risk can still be low for all other objectives.

Assess Control Risk for the Sales and Collection Cycle The methodology for evaluating control risk will be applied to both sales and cash receipts in the audit of accounts receivable. Effective controls will reduce control risk and, along with it, the amount of evidence required for substantive tests of transactions and tests of details of balances. Inadequate controls will increase the substantive evidence needed.

Design and Perform Tests of Controls and Substantive Tests of Transactions for the Sales and Collection Cycle Tests of controls and substantive tests of transactions are designed with the expectation that certain results will be obtained. These predicted results affect the design of tests of details of balances.

For example, typically, the auditor plans to do extensive tests of controls when control risk is assessed as low. This will permit less extensive substantive testing of accounts receivable balances.

Design and Perform Analytical Procedures for Accounts Receivable Balance Auditors perform substantive analytical procedures for an account such as accounts receivable for two purposes: to identify possible misstatements in the account balance and to reduce detailed audit tests. The results of substantive analytical procedures directly affect the extent of tests of details of balances.

Design Tests of Details of Accounts Receivable Balance to Satisfy Balance-Related Audit Objectives The planned tests of details of balances include audit procedures, sample size, items to select, and timing. Procedures must be selected and designed for each account and each balance-related audit objective within each account.

A difficulty auditors face in designing tests of details of balances is the need to predict the outcome of the tests of controls, substantive tests of transactions, and substantive analytical procedures before they are performed. This is necessary because the auditor should design tests of details of balances during the planning phase, but the appropriate design depends on the outcome of the other tests. In planning tests of details of balances, the auditor usually predicts few or no exceptions will occur in tests of controls, substantive tests of transactions, and substantive analytical procedures. If the results of the tests of controls, substantive tests of transactions, and substantive analytical procedures are *not* consistent with the predictions, auditors will need to change the tests of details of balances as the audit progresses including the type of audit evidence, sample size, and items to be tested.

Figure 13-7 summarizes the discussion about the approach to designing tests of details of balances applied to accounts receivable. The light shaded boxes on the left side of the figure correspond to the design of tests of controls and substantive tests of transactions, as presented in Figure 13-5. Figure 13-7 builds on Figure 13-5 by also showing how tests of controls and substantive tests of transactions affect the design of the tests of details of balances. Other factors affecting that decision are shown in the darker shaded boxes on the right side of the figure.

One of the most challenging parts of auditing is properly applying the factors that affect tests of details of balances. Each of the factors is subjective. Moreover, the impact of each factor on tests of details of balances is equally subjective. For example, if inherent risk is reduced from medium to low, there is agreement that tests of details of balances can be reduced. Auditors need to use considerable professional judgment to decide the specific effects of such a change on audit procedures, sample size, items to select, and timing.

Level of Disaggregation of Planning Activities

The various planning activities we discussed in Chapters 6 through 13 are applied at different levels of disaggregation, depending on the nature of the activity. Figure 13-8 shows the primary planning activities and the levels of disaggregation normally applied. These levels of disaggregation range from the overall audit to the balance-related audit objective for each account. For example, risk assessment procedures related to obtaining background information about the client's business and industry pertain to the overall audit. Auditors will first use that information in assessing acceptable audit risk for the engagement as whole. They will then use information about the client and industry obtained through risk assessment procedures to assess inherent risk for specific audit objectives. As the audit progresses, they will likely use that information when making decisions about tests of details of balances. Similarly, the auditor will first assess the risk

FIGURE 13-7   **Approach to Designing Tests of Details of Balances**

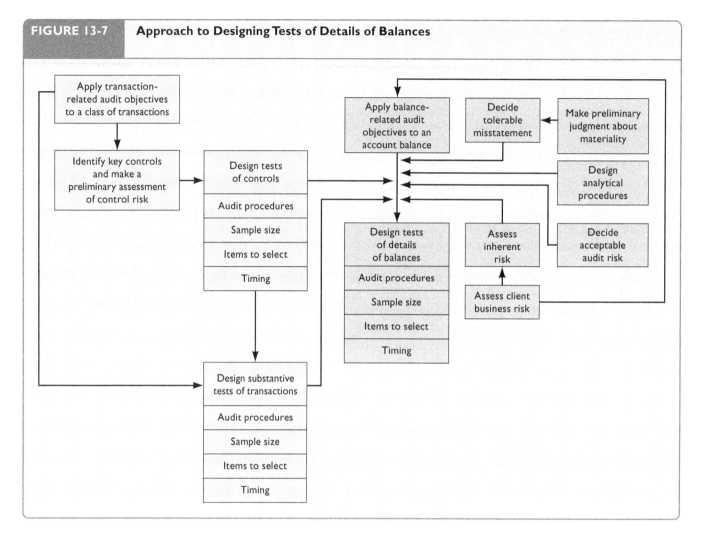

of fraud for the overall audit, and later consider whether any fraud risks exist that may affect fraud risk assessments for specific accounts and the audit procedures and sample sizes for tests of details of balances for accounts that are affected.

Illustrative Audit Program

Auditing standards require the auditor to use a written audit program. Table 13-4 shows the tests of details of balances segment of an audit program for accounts receivable. The format used relates the audit procedures to the balance-related audit objectives. Notice that most procedures satisfy more than one objective, and that more than one audit procedure is used for each objective. Audit procedures can be added or deleted as the auditor deems necessary. For most audit procedures, sample size, items to select, and timing can also be changed.

The audit program in Table 13-4 was developed after consideration of all factors affecting tests of details of balances and is based on several assumptions about inherent risk, control risk, and the results of tests of controls, substantive tests of transactions, and substantive analytical procedures. As indicated, if those assumptions are materially incorrect, the planned audit program will likely need revision. For example, analytical procedures performed near the end of the audit can indicate potential misstatements for several balance-related audit objectives, requiring a revision of the audit plan to gather additional evidence.

Audit programs are often computerized. The simplest approach is to save the audit program file from one year to the next to facilitate changes and updating.

FIGURE 13-8	Disaggregation Level to Which Planning Activities are Applied

PLANNING ACTIVITY	Overall Audit	Cycle	Account	Transaction-Related Audit Objective	Balance-Related Audit Objective
			LEVEL OF DISAGGREGATION		
Accept client and perform initial planning	P				
Understand client's business and industry	P				
Assess client business risk	P				
Gather information to assess fraud risks	P				

Understand internal control:
  Control environment
  Risk assessment
  Control activities
  Information and communication
  Monitoring
	P	P
		P
		P
		P			

Identify key internal controls				P	
Identify internal control deficiencies				P	
Design tests of controls				P	
Design substantive tests of transactions				P	
Assess control risk				P	
Assess inherent risk			P		P
Assess acceptable audit risk	P				
Set preliminary judgment about materiality	P				
Set tolerable misstatement			P		
Design substantive analytical procedures			P		P
Design tests of details of balances					P

P = Primary level to which planning activity is applied

Relationship of Transaction-Related Audit Objectives to Balance-Related and Presentation and Disclosure-Related Audit Objectives

Table 13-5 gives a general presentation of the relationship between balance-related audit objectives for each account and how the extent of these tests can be reduced when transaction-related audit objectives have been satisfied by tests of controls or substantive tests of transactions. The table also helps auditors understand how each transaction-audit objective relates to each balance-related audit objective.

This chapter emphasizes the relationship between audit procedures performed to satisfy transaction-related audit objectives and balance-related audit objectives. The chapter also helps auditors understand how each transaction-related audit objective relates to each balance-related audit objective. The auditor also performs audit procedures to obtain assurance about the three presentation and disclosure-related

> **OBJECTIVE 13-6**
>
> Compare and contrast transaction-related audit objectives with balance-related and presentation and disclosure-related audit objectives.

TABLE 13-4	Tests of Details of Balances Audit Program for Accounts Receivable

				Accounts Receivable Balance-Related Audit Objectives							
Tests of Details of Balances Audit Procedures	Sample Size for Each Audit Procedure	Items to Select from the Population	Timing of the Test	Detail tie-in	Existence	Completeness	Accuracy	Classification	Cutoff	Realizable value	Rights
1. Obtain an aged list of receivables: trace accounts to the master file, foot schedule, and trace to general ledger.	Trace 20 items; foot 2 pages and all subtotals	Random	I	X							
2. Obtain an analysis of the allowance for doubtful accounts and bad debt expense: test accuracy, examine authorization for write-offs, and trace to general ledger.	All	All	Y	X	X	X	X			X	
3. Obtain direct confirmation of accounts receivable and perform alternative procedures for nonresponses.	50	10 largest 40 random	I		X		X	X	X		X
4. Review accounts receivable control account for the period. Investigate the nature of and review support for any large or unusual entries or any entries not arising from normal journal sources. Also investigate any significant increases or decreases in sales toward year-end.	NA	NA	Y		X		X	X	X		X
5. Review receivables for any that have been assigned or discounted.	All	All	Y								X
6. Investigate collectibility of account balances.	NA	NA	Y							X	
7. Review lists of balances for amounts due from related parties or employees, credit balances, and unusual items, as well as notes receivable due after one year.	All	All	Y		X			X			
8. Determine that proper cutoff procedures were applied at the balance sheet date to ensure that sales, cash receipts, and credit memos have been recorded in the correct period.	20 transactions for sales and cash receipts; 10 for credit memos	50% before and 50% after year-end	Y						X		

I = Interim; Y = Year-end; NA = Not applicable.

<table>
<tr><td>REVISING AUDIT PROGRAMS FOR GREATER EFFICIENCY</td><td>The audit program should be carefully reviewed during audit planning to determine whether any audit procedures should be increased or eliminated. Generally, some CPAs advise that risk assessments should affect audit procedures. Risk assessments should result in a reduction of testing in low-risk areas and greater focus on trouble spots.

Other CPAs find that firms often overaudit and don't know why. One CPA frequently asks the purpose of an audit schedule. Responses include: "I don't know why we audited these accounts balances.</td><td>We've always done it that way in the previous audits." "We need to ensure that proper justification is provided for every type of audit test." Auditors should carefully plan and review the audit program to ensure that significant time savings are achieved.

Source: Partly adapted from an article by Anita Dennis, 'Best Practices for Audit Efficiency,' *Journal of Accountancy* (September 2000) pp. 65–68; also based on author's interview with a leading CPA in one of the Big Four firms in Bahrain.</td></tr>
</table>

TABLE 13-5 **Relationship of Transaction-Related Audit Objectives to Balance-Related Audit Objectives**

Transaction-Related Audit Objective	Balance-Related Audit Objective	Nature of Relationship	Explanation
Occurrence	Existence or completeness	Direct	There is a direct relationship of the occurrence transaction-related audit objective to the existence balance-related audit objective if a class of transactions increases the related account balance (e.g. sales transactions increase accounts receivable). There is a direct relationship of the occurrence transaction-related audit objective to the completeness balance-related audit objective if a class of transactions decreases the related account balance (e.g. cash receipts transactions decrease accounts receivable).
Completeness	Completeness or existence	Direct	See comments above for existence objective.
Accuracy	Accuracy	Direct	—
Posting and summarization	Detail tie-in	Direct	—
Classification	Classification	Direct	—
Timing	Cutoff	Direct	—
	Realizable value	None	Few internal controls over realizable value are related to classes of transactions, but the credit approval process affects the extent of tests.
Rights and obligations	Rights and obligations	None	Few internal controls over rights and obligations are related to classes of transactions.

audit objectives described in Chapter 6. The auditor's approach to obtaining evidence related to presentation and disclosure-related audit objectives is consistent with the approach described in this chapter. The auditor performs tests of controls and substantive procedures to obtain assurance that all audit objectives are achieved for information and amounts included in those disclosures.

SUMMARY OF KEY EVIDENCE-RELATED TERMS

Several evidence-related terms have been used in the past few chapters. To help you distinguish and understand each of these terms, we summarize them in Table 13-6.

Phases of the Audit Process The four phases of the audit process in the first column are the primary way that audits are organized, as described in Chapter 6. Figure 13-9 shows the key components of these four phases of the audit process.

TABLE 13-6	Relationship Among Five Key Evidence-Related Terms			
Phases of the Audit Process	**Audit Objectives**	**Types of Tests**	**Evidence Decisions**	**Types of Evidence**
Plan and Design an Audit Approach (Phase I)		Risk assessment procedures • Procedures to understand client business and industry • Procedures to understand internal control • Planning analytical procedures	• Audit procedures • Timing	Inspection Inquiries of client Analytical procedures
Perform Tests of Controls and Substantive Tests of Transactions (Phase II)	Transaction-related audit objectives • Occurrence • Completeness • Accuracy • Posting and Summarization • Classification • Timing • Rights and Obligations	Procedures to obtain an understanding and tests of controls Substantive tests of transactions	• Audit procedures • Sample size • Items to select • Timing • Audit procedures • Sample size • Items to select • Timing	Inspection Observation Inquiries of client Reperformance Recalculation
Perform Analytical Procedures and Tests of Details of Balances (Phase III)	Balance-related audit objectives • Existence • Completeness • Accuracy • Classification • Cutoff • Detail tie-in • Realizable value • Rights and Obligations	Analytical procedures Tests of details of balances	• Audit procedures • Timing • Audit procedures • Sample size • Items to select • Timing	Physical examination Confirmation Inspection Inquiries of client Reperformance Analytical procedures Recalculation
Complete the Audit and Issue an Audit Report (Phase IV)	Presentation and disclosure-related audit objectives • Completeness • Valuation and Accuracy • Classification and Understandability	Analytical procedures Tests of details of balances	• Audit procedures • Timing • Audit procedures • Sample size • Items to select • Timing	Analytical procedures Inspection Inquiries of client

Audit Objectives These are the objectives on an audit that must be met before the auditor can conclude that any given class of transactions or account balance is fairly stated. There are seven transaction-related, eight balance-related, and three presentation and disclosure-related audit objectives, all of which are listed in Table 13-6. Observe that all transaction-related audit objectives are primarily addressed in phase II, balance-related audit objectives in phase III, and presentation and disclosure-related audit objectives in phase IV.

Types of Tests The five types of audit tests discussed earlier in the chapter that auditors use to determine whether financial statements are fairly stated are included in the third column in Table 13-6. Observe that analytical procedures are used in Phase III and Phase IV. Keep in mind that planning analytical procedures are also performed as part of the risk assessment procedures in Phase I. Recall that analytical procedures are also required at the completion of the audit, which is why they

FIGURE 13-9   **Summary of the Audit Process**

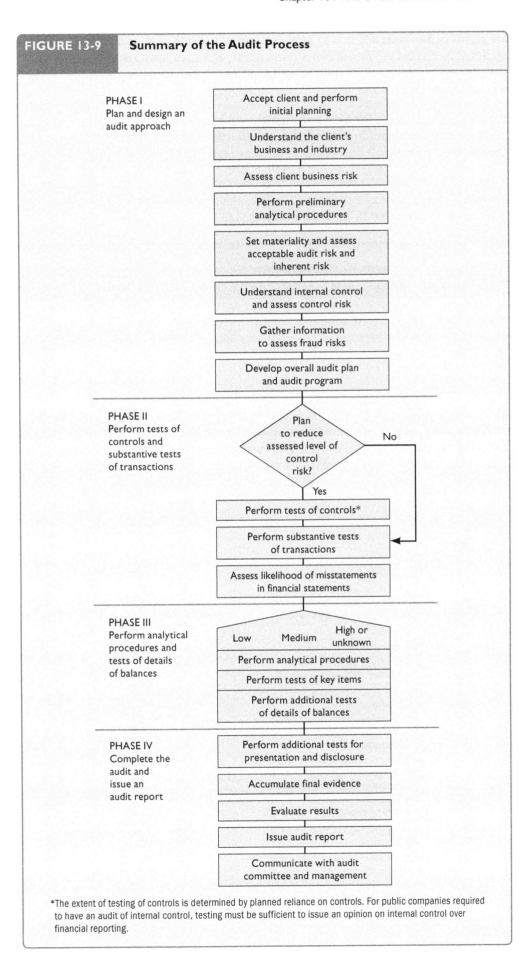

PHASE I
Plan and design an
audit approach

Accept client and perform
initial planning

Understand the client's
business and industry

Assess client business risk

Perform preliminary
analytical procedures

Set materiality and assess
acceptable audit risk and
inherent risk

Understand internal control
and assess control risk

Gather information
to assess fraud risks

Develop overall audit plan
and audit program

PHASE II
Perform tests of
controls and
substantive tests
of transactions

Plan
to reduce
assessed level of
control
risk?

No

Yes

Perform tests of controls*

Perform substantive tests
of transactions

Assess likelihood of misstatements
in financial statements

PHASE III
Perform analytical
procedures and
tests of details
of balances

Low   Medium   High or
unknown

Perform analytical procedures

Perform tests of key items

Perform additional tests
of details of balances

PHASE IV
Complete the
audit and
issue an
audit report

Perform additional tests for
presentation and disclosure

Accumulate final evidence

Evaluate results

Issue audit report

Communicate with audit
committee and management

*The extent of testing of controls is determined by planned reliance on controls. For public companies required
to have an audit of internal control, testing must be sufficient to issue an opinion on internal control over
financial reporting.

are included in Phase IV. It may appear unusual to have tests of details of balances included in Phase IV. We will explain the nature of the procedures auditors use during completing the audit, including meeting the presentation and disclosure-related objectives, in Chapter 24.

Evidence Decisions The four subcategories of decisions the auditor makes in accumulating audit evidence are included in the fourth column in Table 13-6. Except for analytical procedures, all four evidence decisions apply to each type of test.

Types of Evidence The eight broad categories of evidence auditors accumulate are included in the last column of Table 13-6. The relationship of types of evidence to types of tests was summarized in Table 13-2 on page 433.

SUMMARY OF THE AUDIT PROCESS

OBJECTIVE 13-7

Integrate the four phases of the audit process.

Figure 13-9 shows the four phases for the entire audit process, and Table 13-7 shows the timing of the tests in each phase for an audit with a December 31 balance sheet date.

Phase I: Plan and Design an Audit Approach

Auditors use information obtained from risk assessment procedures related to client acceptance and initial planning, understanding the client's business and industry, assessing the client's business risks, and performing preliminary analytical procedures (first four boxes in Figure 13-9) primarily to assess inherent risk and acceptable audit risk. Auditors use assessments of materiality, acceptable audit risk, inherent

TABLE 13-7	Timing of Tests		
Phase I	Plan and design audit approach. Update understanding of internal control. Update audit program. Perform preliminary analytical procedures.	Aug 31, 2011	
Phase II	Perform tests of controls and substantive tests of transactions for first 9 months of the year.	Sept 30, 2011	
Phase III	Confirm accounts receivable. Observe inventory.	Oct 31, 2011	
	Count cash. Perform cutoff tests. Request various other confirmations.	Dec 31, 2011	Balance sheet date
	Perform analytical procedures, complete tests of controls and substantive tests of transactions, and complete most tests of details of balances.	Jan 7, 2012	Books closed
Phase IV	Perform procedures to support presentation and disclosure-related audit objectives, summarize results, accumulate final evidence (including analytical procedures), and finalize audit.	Feb 15, 2012	Last date of field work
	Issue audit report.	Feb 25, 2012	

risk, control risk, and any identified fraud risks to develop an overall audit plan and audit program.

At the end of phase I, the auditor should have a well-defined audit plan and a specific audit program for the entire audit.

Phase II: Perform Tests of Controls and Substantive Tests of Transactions

Auditors perform tests of controls and substantive tests of transactions during this phase. The objectives of phase II are to:

1. Obtain evidence in support of the specific controls that contribute to the auditor's assessed control risk (that is, where it is reduced below the maximum) for audits of financial statements.
2. Obtain evidence in support of the monetary correctness of transactions.

The first objective is met by performing tests of controls, and the second by performing substantive tests of transactions. Frequently both types of tests are done simultaneously on the same transactions. When controls are not considered effective or when the auditor finds deviations, substantive tests can be expanded in this phase or in phase III.

Because the results of tests of controls and substantive tests of transactions are a major determinant of the extent of tests of details of balances, they are often done two or three months before the balance sheet date. This helps the auditor revise the tests of details of balance audit program for unexpected results in the earlier tests and to complete the audit as soon as possible after the balance sheet date. This approach is also used in the audit of public companies to allow management an opportunity to correct control deficiencies in time to allow auditor testing of the newly implemented controls before year-end. Auditors update their testing of internal controls near year-end to verify that the controls continue to operate effectively.

Phase III: Perform Analytical Procedures and Tests of Details of Balances

The objective of phase III is to obtain sufficient additional evidence to determine whether the ending balances and footnotes in financial statements are fairly stated. The nature and extent of the work will depend heavily on the findings of the two previous phases.

The two general categories of phase III procedures are:

1. Substantive analytical procedures that assess the overall reasonableness of transactions and balances.
2. Tests of details of balances, which are audit procedures to test for monetary misstatements in the balances in the financial statements.

Table 13-7 shows analytical procedures are performed before and after the balance sheet date. Because of their low cost, analytical procedures are commonly used whenever they are relevant. They are often performed early, using preliminary data before year-end, as a means of planning and directing other audit tests to specific areas. But the greatest benefit from calculating ratios and making comparisons occurs after the client has finished preparing its financial statements. Ideally, these analytical procedures are done before tests of details of balances so they can then be used to determine how extensively to test balances. They are also used as a part of performing tests of balances and during the completion phase of the audit.

Table 13-7 also shows that tests of details of balances are normally done last. On some audits, all are done after the balance sheet date. When clients want to issue statements soon after the balance sheet date, the more time-consuming tests of details of balances are done at interim dates before year-end with additional work being done to roll-forward the audited interim-date balances to year-end. Substantive tests of balances performed before year-end provide less assurance and are normally only done when internal controls are effective.

Phase IV: Complete the Audit and Issue an Audit Report

After the first three phases are completed, auditors must accumulate additional evidence related to presentation and disclosure-related objectives, summarize the results, issue the audit report, and perform other forms of communication. As shown in Figure 13-9, this phase has several parts.

Perform Additional Tests for Presentation and Disclosure The procedures auditors perform to support the three presentation and disclosure-related objectives are similar to audit procedures performed to support both transaction- and balance-related audit objectives. For example, management implements internal controls to ensure that all required footnote disclosures are included and that amounts and other information disclosed are accurate. Auditor tests of those controls provide evidence supporting the *completeness* and *accuracy* presentation and disclosure-related audit objectives. Auditors also perform substantive tests to obtain sufficient appropriate evidence that information disclosed in the financial statements are presented under the correct headings to support the *classification* objective.

During this last phase of the audit, auditors perform audit procedures related to contingent liabilities and subsequent events. Contingent liabilities are potential liabilities that must be disclosed in the client's footnotes. Auditors must make sure that the disclosure is complete and accurate. Subsequent events represent events that occasionally occur after the balance sheet date, but before the issuance of the financial statements and auditor's report, that have an effect on the financial statements. Specific review procedures are designed to bring to the auditor's attention any subsequent events that affect the financial statements. Both contingent liabilities and subsequent events are studied in Chapter 24.

Accumulate Final Evidence In addition to the evidence obtained for each cycle during phases I and II, and for each account during phase III, auditors must gather the following evidence for the financial statements as a whole during the completion phase:

- Perform final analytical procedures
- Evaluate the going-concern assumption
- Obtain a client representation letter
- Read information in the annual report to make sure that it is consistent with the financial statements

Issue Audit Report The type of audit report issued depends on the evidence accumulated and the audit findings. The appropriate reports for differing circumstances were studied in Chapter 3.

Communicate with Audit Committee, Management, and Those Charged with Governance The auditor is required to communicate significant deficiencies in internal control to the audit committee or senior management. Auditing standards also require the auditor to communicate certain other matters to those charged with governance, such as the audit committee or a similarly designated body upon completion of the audit, if not sooner. Although not required, auditors often also make suggestions to management to improve business performance.

SUMMARY

This chapter summarized important issues discussed in previous chapters, mainly Chapters 6, 7, 8, 9 and 10, emphasizing the steps that must be followed by the auditor from planning the audit engagement until the auditor issues the audit report. The chapter showed the interrelationships between the various types of audit tests, including tests of internal control, tests of details of transactions, analytical procedures, and tests of details of balances. The timing and costs related to these types of tests were provided given various audit situations for clarification purposes. Also, an overview of the relationship between transaction- and balance-related audit objectives was presented with emphasis on presentation and disclosure-related audit objectives.

ESSENTIAL TERMS

Evidence mix   p. 437

Further audit procedures   p. 428

Substantive tests   p. 431

Types of tests   p. 428

REVIEW QUESTIONS

13-1 (Objective 13-1) What are the five types of tests auditors use to determine whether financial statements are fairly stated? Identify which tests are performed to reduce control risk and which tests are performed to reduce planned detection risk.

13-2 (Objective 13-1) What is the purpose of risk assessment procedures and how do they differ from the four other types of audit tests?

13-3 (Objective 13-1) What is the purpose of tests of controls? Identify specific accounts on the financial statements that are affected by performing tests of controls for the acquisition and payment cycle.

13-4 (Objective 13-1) Distinguish between a test of control and a substantive test of transactions. Give two examples of each.

13-5 (Objectives 13-1, 13-4) State a test of control audit procedure to test the effectiveness of the following control: Approved wage rates are used in calculating employees' earnings. State a substantive test of transactions audit procedure to determine whether approved wage rates are actually used in calculating employees' earnings.

13-6 (Objective 13-1) A considerable portion of the tests of controls and substantive tests of transactions are performed simultaneously as a matter of audit convenience. But the substantive tests of transactions' procedures and sample size, in part, depend on the results of the tests of controls. How can the auditor resolve this apparent inconsistency?

13-7 (Objectives 13-2, 13-4) Evaluate the following statement: "Tests of sales and cash receipts transactions are such an essential part of every audit that I like to perform them as near the end of the audit as possible. By that time I have a fairly good understanding of the client's business and its internal controls because confirmations, cutoff tests, and other procedures have already been completed."

13-8 (Objectives 13-1, 13-2) Explain how the calculation and comparison to previous years of the gross margin percentage and the ratio of accounts receivable to sales are related to the confirmation of accounts receivable and other tests of the accuracy of accounts receivable.

13-9 (Objective 13-1) Distinguish between substantive tests of transactions and tests of details of balances. Give one example of each for the acquisition and payment cycle.

13-10 (Objective 13-3) The auditor of Hamas Textile, Inc., identified two internal controls in the sales and collection receipts cycle for testing. In the first control, the computer verifies that a planned sale on account will not exceed the customer's credit limit entered in the accounts receivable master file. In the second control, the accounts receivable clerk matches bills of lading, sales invoices, and customer orders before recording in the sales journal. Describe how the presence of general controls over software programs and master file changes affects the extent of audit testing of each of these two internal controls.

13-11 (Objective 13-4) Assume that the client's internal controls over the recording and classifying of fixed asset additions are considered deficient because the individual responsible for recording new acquisitions has inadequate technical training and limited experience in accounting. How will this situation affect the evidence you should accumulate in auditing fixed assets as compared with another audit in which the controls are excellent? Be as specific as possible.

13-12 (Objective 13-2) For each of the eight types of evidence discussed in Chapter 7, identify whether it is applicable for risk assessment procedures, tests of controls, substantive tests of transactions, analytical procedures, and tests of details of balances.

13-13 (Objective 13-2) Rank the following types of tests from most costly to least costly: analytical procedures, tests of details of balances, risk assessment procedures, tests of controls, and substantive tests of transactions.

13-14 (Objective 13-2) In Figure 13-3, explain the difference among C_3, C_2, and C_1. Explain the circumstances under which it will be a good decision to obtain audit assurance from substantive tests at point C_1. Do the same for points C_2 and C_3.

13-15 (Objective 13-4) Table 13-3 illustrates variations in the emphasis on different types of audit tests. What are the benefits to the auditor of identifying the best mix of tests?

13-16 (Objective 13-5) State the four-step approach to designing tests of controls and substantive tests of transactions.

13-17 (Objective 13-5) Explain the relationship between the methodology for designing tests of controls and substantive tests of transactions in Figure 13-5 to the methodology for designing tests of details of balances in Figure 13-7.

13-18 (Objective 13-5) Why is it desirable to design tests of details of balances before performing tests of controls and substantive tests of transactions? State the assumptions that the auditor must make in doing that. What does the auditor do if the assumptions are wrong?

13-19 (Objective 13-5) Explain the relationship of tolerable misstatement, inherent risk, and control risk to planned tests of details of balances.

13-20 (Objective 13-5) List the eight balance-related audit objectives in the verification of the ending balance in inventory and provide one useful audit procedure for each of the objectives.

13-21 (Objective 13-7) Why do auditors often consider it desirable to perform audit tests throughout the year rather than wait until year-end? List several examples of evidence that can be accumulated before year-end.

MULTIPLE CHOICE QUESTIONS FROM CPA EXAMINATIONS

13-22 (Objectives 13-1, 13-5, 13-7) The following questions concern types of audit tests. Choose the best response.

a. The auditor looks for an indication on duplicate sales invoices to see whether the invoices have been verified. This is an example of
   (1) a test of details of balances.
   (2) a test of control.
   (3) a substantive test of transactions.
   (4) both a test of control and a substantive test of transactions.

b. Analytical procedures may be classified as being primarily
   (1) tests of controls.   (3) tests of ratios.
   (2) substantive tests.   (4) tests of details of balances.

c. The auditor faces a risk that the audit will not detect material misstatements that occur in the accounting process. To minimize this risk, the auditor relies primarily on
   (1) substantive tests.   (3) internal control.
   (2) tests of controls.   (4) statistical analysis.

d. A conceptually logical approach to the auditor's evaluation of internal control consists of the following four steps:
   I. Determining the internal controls that should prevent or detect errors and fraud.
   II. Identifying control deficiencies to determine their effect on the nature, timing, or extent of auditing procedures to be applied and suggestions to be made to the client.
   III. Determining whether the necessary internal control procedures are prescribed and are being followed satisfactorily.
   IV. Considering the types of errors and fraud that can occur.

   What should be the order in which these four steps are performed?
   (1) i, ii, iii, and iv   (3) iii, iv, i, and ii
   (2) i, iii, iv, and ii   (4) iv, i, iii, and ii

13-23 (Objective 13-1) The following questions deal with tests of controls. Choose the best response.

a. Which of the following statements about tests of controls is most accurate?
   (1) Auditing procedures cannot concurrently provide both evidence of the effectiveness of internal control procedures and evidence required for substantive tests.
   (2) Tests of controls include observations of the proper segregation of duties.
   (3) Tests of controls provide direct evidence about monetary misstatements in transactions.
   (4) Tests of controls ordinarily should be performed as of the balance sheet date or during the period subsequent to that date.

b. To support the auditor's initial assessment of control risk below maximum, the auditor performs procedures to determine that internal controls are operating effectively. Which of the following audit procedures is the auditor performing?
   (1) Tests of details of balances   (3) Tests of controls
   (2) Substantive tests of transactions   (4) Tests of trends and ratios

c. The primary objective of performing tests of controls is to obtain
   (1) a reasonable degree of assurance that the client's internal controls are operating effectively on a consistent basis throughout the year.
   (2) sufficient, appropriate audit evidence to afford a reasonable basis for the auditor's opinion, without the need for additional evidence.
   (3) assurances that informative disclosures in the financial statements are reasonably adequate.
   (4) knowledge and understanding of the client's prescribed procedures and methods.

d. Which of the following is ordinarily considered a test of control audit procedure?
   (1) Sending confirmation letters to banks.
   (2) Counting and listing cash on hand.
   (3) Examining signatures on checks.
   (4) Preparing reconciliations of bank accounts as of the balance sheet date.

DISCUSSION QUESTIONS AND PROBLEMS

13-24 (Objectives 13-1, 13-2) The following are 11 audit procedures taken from an audit program:

1. Foot the accounts payable trial balance and compare the total with the general ledger.
2. Examine vendors' invoices to verify the ending balance in accounts payable.
3. Compare the balance in payroll tax expense with previous years. The comparison takes the increase in payroll tax rates into account.
4. Examine the internal auditor's initials on monthly bank reconciliations as an indication of whether they have been reviewed.
5. Examine vendors' invoices and other documentation in support of recorded transactions in the acquisitions journal.
6. Multiply the commission rate by total sales and compare the result with commission expense.
7. Examine vendors' invoices and other supporting documents to determine whether large amounts in the repair and maintenance account should be capitalized.
8. Discuss the duties of the cash disbursements clerk with him and observe whether he has responsibility for handling cash or preparing the bank reconciliation.
9. Confirm accounts payable balances directly with vendors.
10. Account for a sequence of checks in the cash disbursements journal to determine whether any have been omitted.
11. Inquire about the accounts payable supervisor's monthly review of a computer-generated exception report of receiving reports and purchase orders that have not been matched with a vendor invoice.

Required
a. Indicate whether each procedure is a test of control, substantive test of transactions, analytical procedure, or a test of details of balances.
b. Identify the type of evidence for each procedure.

13-25 (Objectives 13-1, 13-2, 13-3, 13-6) The following are audit procedures from different transaction cycles:

1. Use audit software to foot and cross-foot the cash disbursements journal and trace the balance to the general ledger.
2. Select a sample of entries in the acquisitions journal and trace each one to a related vendor's invoice to determine whether one exists.
3. Examine documentation for acquisition transactions before and after the balance sheet date to determine whether they are recorded in the proper period.
4. Inquire of the credit manager whether each account receivable on the aged trial balance is collectible.
5. Compute inventory turnover for each major product and compare with previous years.

6. Confirm a sample of notes payable balances, interest rates, and collateral with lenders.
7. Use audit software to foot the accounts payable trial balance and compare the balance with the general ledger.

Required

a. For each audit procedure, identify the transaction cycle being audited.
b. For each audit procedure, identify the type of evidence.
c. For each audit procedure, identify whether it is a test of control or a substantive test.
d. For each substantive audit procedure, identify whether it is a substantive test of transactions, a test of details of balances, or an analytical procedure.
e. For each test of control or substantive test of transactions procedure, identify the transaction-related audit objective or objectives being satisfied.
f. For each analytical procedure or test of details of balances procedure, identify the balance-related audit objective or objectives being satisfied.

13-26 (Objectives 13-1, 13-5, 13-6) The following are independent internal controls commonly found in the acquisition and payment cycle. Each control is to be considered independently.

1. At the end of each month, an accounting clerk accounts for all prenumbered receiving reports (documents evidencing the receipt of goods) issued during the month, and traces each one to the related vendor's invoice and acquisitions journal entry. The clerk's tests do not include testing the quantity or description of the merchandise received.
2. The cash disbursements clerk is prohibited from handling cash. The bank account is reconciled by another person even though the clerk has sufficient expertise and time to do it.
3. Before a check is prepared to pay for acquisitions by the accounts payable department, the related purchase order and receiving report are attached to the vendor's invoice being paid. A clerk compares the quantity on the invoice with the receiving report and purchase order, compares the price with the purchase order, recomputes the extensions, re-adds the total, and examines the account number indicated on the invoice to determine whether it is correctly classified. He indicates his performance of these procedures by initialing the invoice.
4. Before a check is signed by the controller, she examines the supporting documentation accompanying the check. At that time, she initials each vendor's invoice to indicate her approval.
5. After the controller signs the checks, her secretary writes the check number and the date the check was issued on each of the supporting documents to prevent their reuse.

Required

a. For each of the internal controls, state the transaction-related audit objective(s) the control is meant to fulfill.
b. For each control, list one test of control the auditor could perform to test the effectiveness of the control.
c. For each control, list one substantive test the auditor could perform to determine whether financial misstatements are actually taking place.

13-27 (Objectives 13-1, 13-5, 13-6) The following internal controls for the acquisition and payment cycle were selected from a standard internal control questionnaire.

1. Vendors' invoices are recalculated before payment.
2. Approved price lists are used for acquisitions.
3. Prenumbered receiving reports are prepared as support for acquisitions and numerically accounted for.
4. Dates on receiving reports are compared with vendors' invoices before entry into the acquisitions journal.
5. The accounts payable master file is updated, balanced, and reconciled to the general ledger monthly.

6. Account classifications are reviewed by someone other than the preparer.
7. All checks are signed by the owner or manager.
8. The check signer compares data on supporting documents with checks.
9. All supporting documents are cancelled after the checks are signed.
10. Checks are mailed by the owner or manager or a person under her supervision after signing.

Required

a. For each control, identify which element of the five categories of control activities is applicable (separation of duties, proper authorization, adequate documents or records, physical control over assets and records, or independent checks on performance).
b. For each control, state which transaction-related audit objective(s) is (are) applicable.
c. For each control, write an audit procedure that could be used to test the control for effectiveness.
d. For each control, identify a likely misstatement, assuming that the control does not exist or is not functioning.
e. For each likely misstatement, identify a substantive audit procedure to determine whether the misstatement exists.

13-28 (Objectives 13-4, 13-5) Following are several decisions that the auditor must make in an audit of a nonpublic company. Letters indicate alternative conclusions that could be made.

Decisions	Alternative Conclusions
1. Determine whether it is cost-effective to perform tests of controls.	A It is cost-effective B It is not cost-effective
2. Perform substantive tests of details of balances.	C Perform reduced tests D Perform expanded tests
3. Complete initial assessment of control risk.	E Controls are effective F Controls are ineffective
4. Perform tests of controls.	G Controls are effective H Controls are ineffective

Required

a. Identify the sequence in which the auditor should make decisions 1 to 4.
b. For the audit of the sales and collection cycle and accounts receivable, an auditor reached the following conclusions: A, D, E, H. Put the letters in the appropriate sequence and evaluate whether the auditor's logic was reasonable. Explain your answer.
c. For the audit of inventory and related inventory cost records, an auditor reached the following conclusions: B, C, E, G. Put the letters in the appropriate sequence and evaluate whether the auditor used good professional judgment. Explain your answer.
d. For the audit of property, plant, and equipment and related acquisition records, an auditor reached the following conclusions: A, C, F, G. Put the letters in the appropriate sequence and evaluate whether the auditor used good professional judgment. Explain your answer.
e. For the audit of payroll expenses and related liabilities, an auditor recorded the following conclusions: D, F. Put the letters in the appropriate sequence and evaluate whether the auditor used good professional judgment. Explain your answer.

13-29 (Objective 13-3) Omar Afindi, Inc. specializes in bed and bath furnishings. Its inventory system is linked through the internet to key suppliers. The auditor identified the following internal controls in the inventory cycle:

1. The computer initiates an order only when perpetual inventory levels fall below pre-specified inventory levels in the inventory master file.
2. The sales and purchasing department managers review inventory reorder points on a monthly basis for reasonableness. Approved changes to reorder points are entered into the master file by the purchasing department manager and an updated printout is generated for final review. Both managers verify that all changes were entered

correctly and initial the final printout indicating final approval. These printouts are maintained in the purchasing department.

3. The computer will initiate a purchase order only for inventory product numbers maintained in the inventory master file.

4. The purchasing department manager reviews a computer-generated exception report that highlights weekly purchases that exceed US$20,000 per vendor.

5. Sales clerks send damaged merchandise on the store shelves to the back storage room. The sales department manager examines the damaged merchandise each month and prepares a listing showing the estimated salvage value by product number. The accounting department uses the listing to prepare a monthly adjustment to recorded inventory values.

a. Consider each of the preceding controls separately. Identify whether the control **Required** is a(n)
   (1) automated control embedded in computer software.
   (2) manual control with effectiveness based significantly on IT-generated information.
   (3) manual control with effectiveness not significantly reliant on IT-generated information.

b. Describe how the extent of testing of each control will be affected in subsequent years if general controls are effective, particularly controls over program and master file changes.

13-30 (Objectives 13-5, 13-7) Following are evidence decisions for the three audits described in Figure 13-3 on page 436:

Audit A	Ineffective client internal controls
Audit B	Very effective client internal controls
Audit C	Somewhat effective client internal controls

Evidence Decisions

1. The auditor performed extensive positive confirmations at the balance sheet date.
2. The auditor performed extensive tests of controls and minimal substantive tests.
3. The auditor decided it was possible to assess control risk below the maximum.
4. The auditor performed substantive tests.
5. This audit was likely the least expensive to conduct.
6. The auditor confirmed receivables at an interim date.
7. The auditor identified effective controls and also identified some deficiencies in controls.
8. The auditor performed tests of controls.

a. Explain why Audit B represents the maximum amount of reliance that can be placed **Required** on internal control. Why can't all the audit assurance be obtained by tests of controls?

b. Explain why the auditor may not place the maximum extent of reliance on controls in Audit B and Audit C.

c. For each of the eight evidence decisions, indicate whether the evidence decision relates to each of the audits described above. Every evidence decision relates to at least one of the audits, and some may relate to two or all three audits.

13-31 (Objectives 13-5, 13-7) The following are parts of a typical audit for a company with a fiscal year-end of July 31.

1. Confirm accounts payable.
2. Do tests of controls and substantive tests of transactions for the acquisition and payment and payroll and personnel cycles.
3. Do other tests of details of balances for accounts payable.
4. Do tests for review of subsequent events.

5. Accept the client.
6. Issue the audit report.
7. Understand internal control and assess control risk.
8. Do analytical procedures for accounts payable.
9. Set acceptable audit risk and decide preliminary judgment about materiality and tolerable misstatement.

Required

a. Put parts 1 through 9 of the audit in the sequential order in which you will expect them to be performed in a typical audit.
b. Identify those parts that will frequently be done before July 31.

13-32 (Objective 13-4) The following are three situations, all involving nonpublic companies, in which the auditor is required to develop an audit strategy:

1. The client has inventory at approximately 50 locations in a three-governorates region. The inventory is difficult to count and can be observed only by traveling by automobile. The internal controls over acquisitions, cash disbursements, and perpetual records are considered effective. This is the fifth year that you have done the audit, and audit results in past years have always been excellent. The client is in excellent financial condition and is privately held.

2. This is the first year of an audit of a medium-sized company that is considering selling its business because of severe under-financing. A review of the acquisition and payment cycle indicates that controls over cash disbursements are excellent but controls over acquisitions cannot be considered effective. The client lacks receiving reports and a policy as to the proper timing to record acquisitions. When you review the general ledger, you observe that there are many large adjusting entries to correct accounts payable.

3. You are doing the audit of a small loan company with extensive receivables from customers. Controls over granting loans, collections, and loans outstanding are considered effective, and there is extensive follow-up of all outstanding loans weekly. You have recommended a new computer system for the past two years, but management believes the cost is too great, given their low profitability. Collections are an ongoing problem because many of the customers have severe financial problems. Because of adverse economic conditions, loans receivable have significantly increased and collections are less than normal. In previous years, you have had relatively few adjusting entries.

Required

a. For audit 1, recommend an evidence mix for the five types of tests for the audit of inventory and cost of goods sold. Justify your answer. Include in your recommendations both tests of controls and substantive tests.
b. For audit 2, recommend an evidence mix for the audit of the acquisition and payment cycle, including accounts payable. Justify your answer.
c. For audit 3, recommend an evidence mix for the audit of outstanding loans. Justify your answer.

CASE

13-33 (Objectives 13-4, 13-5) El Sherif Plastics has been an audit client of Samaha, Sameh & Co., CPAs, for several years. El Sherif Plastics was started by Abdel Latif Sherif, who owns 51 percent of the company's stock. The balance is owned by about 20 stockholders who are investors with no operational responsibilities. El Sherif Plastics makes products that have plastic as their primary material. Some are made to order, but most products are made for inventory. An example of an El Sherif-manufactured product is a plastic chair pad that is used in a carpeted office. Another is a plastic bushing that is used with certain fastener systems.

El Sherif has grown from a small, two-product company, when they first engaged Samaha, Sameh & Co., to a successful diverse company. At the time Ibrahim Ouf of Samaha & Sameh became manager of the audit, annual sales had grown to US$200 million and profits to US$10.9 million. Historically, the company presented no unusual audit problems, and Samaha & Sameh had issued an unmodified opinion every year.

The audit approach Samaha & Sameh always used on the audit of El Sherif Plastics was a 'substantive' audit approach. Under this approach, the in-charge auditor obtained an understanding of internal control as part of the risk assessment procedures, but control risk was assessed at the maximum (100 percent). Extensive analytical procedures were done on the income statement, and unusual fluctuations were investigated. Detailed audit procedures emphasized balance sheet accounts. The theory was that if the balance sheet accounts were correct at year-end and had been audited as of the beginning of the year, then retained earnings and the income statement must be correct.

Part I

In evaluating the audit approach for El Sherif for the current year's audit, Ibrahim believed that a substantive approach was really only appropriate for the audits of small nonpublic companies. In his judgment, El Sherif Plastics, with sales of US$200 million and 146 employees, had reached the size where it was not economical, and probably not wise, to concentrate all the tests on the balance sheet. Furthermore, although El Sherif is not a public company, Ibrahim recognized that similar public companies are required to have an integrated audit of the financial statements including testing internal control. Therefore, he designed an audit program that emphasized identifying internal controls in all major transaction cycles and included tests of controls. The intended economic benefit of this 'reducing control risk' approach was that the time spent testing controls will be more than offset by reduced tests of details of the balance sheet accounts.

In planning tests of inventories, Ibrahim used the audit risk model included in auditing standards to determine the number of inventory items Samaha & Sameh will test at year-end. Because of the number of different products, features, sizes, and colors, El Sherif's inventory consisted of 2,450 different items. These were maintained on a perpetual inventory management system that used a relational database.

In using the audit risk model for inventories, Ibrahim believed that an audit risk of 5 percent was acceptable. He assessed inherent risk as high (100 percent) because inventory, by its nature, is subject to many types of misstatements. Based on his understanding of the relevant transaction cycles, Ibrahim believed that internal controls were good. He therefore assessed control risk as low (50 percent) before performing tests of controls. Ibrahim also planned to use analytical procedures for tests of inventory. These planned tests included comparing gross profit margins by month and reviewing for slow-moving items. Ibrahim believed that these tests will provide assurance of 40 percent. Substantive tests of details will include tests of inventory quantities, costs, and net realizable values at an interim date two months before year-end. Cutoff tests will be done at year-end. Inquiries and analytical procedures will be relied on for assurance about events between the interim audit date and fiscal year-end.

a. Decide which of the following will likely be done under both a reducing control risk approach and a substantive approach: **Required**
   (1) Assess acceptable audit risk.
   (2) Assess inherent risk.
   (3) Obtain an understanding of internal control.
   (4) Assess control risk at less than 100%.
   (5) Perform analytical procedures.
   (6) Assess planned detection risk.

b. What advantages does the reducing control risk approach Ibrahim plans to use have over the substantive approach previously used in the audit of El Sherif Plastics?

c. What advantages did the substantive approach have over the reducing control risk approach?

Part II

The engagement partner agreed with Ibrahim's recommended approach. In planning the audit evidence for detailed inventory tests, the audit risk model was applied with the following results:

$$TDR = \frac{AAR}{IR \times CR \times APR}$$

where:

$$
\begin{aligned}
TDR &= \text{test of details risk} \\
AAR &= \text{acceptable audit risk} \\
IR &= \text{inherent risk} \\
CR &= \text{control risk} \\
APR &= \text{analytical procedues risk}
\end{aligned}
$$

Therefore, using Ibrahim's assessments and judgments as described previously,

$$TDR = \frac{.05}{1.0 \times .5 \times .6}$$

$$TDR = .17$$

Required

a. Explain what .17 means in this audit.

b. Calculate *TDR* assuming that Ibrahim had assessed control risk at 100% and all other risks as they are stated.

c. Explain the effect of your answer in requirement b on the planned audit procedures and sample size in the audit of inventory compared with the .17 calculated by Ibrahim.

Part III

Although the planning went well, the actual testing yielded some surprises. When conducting tests of controls over acquisitions and additions to the perpetual inventory, the staff person performing the tests found that the exception rates for several key controls were significantly higher than expected. As a result, the staff person considered internal control to not be operating effectively, supporting an 80 percent control risk rather than the 50 percent level used. Accordingly, the staff person 'reworked' the audit risk model as follows:

$$TDR = \frac{.05}{1.0 \times .8 \times .6}$$

$$TDR = .10$$

A 10 percent test of details risk still seemed to the staff person to be in the 'moderate' range, so he recommended no increase in planned sample size for substantive tests.

Do you agree with the staff person's revised judgments about the effect of tests of controls   **Required**
on planned substantive tests? Explain the nature and basis of any disagreement.

MYLAB ACTIVITY

Visit MyAccountingLab and complete the following activity:
→ Internet Problem 13-1: Assessing Effects Of Evidence Mix.

PART 3

APPLICATION OF THE AUDIT PROCESS TO THE SALES AND COLLECTION CYCLE

For you to appreciate how auditing is done in practice, you need to understand how auditing concepts are applied to specific auditing areas. We'll first look at one important part of every audit, the sales and collection cycle, to examine the practical application of auditing concepts.

The four chapters of **Part 3** apply the concepts you learned in Part 2 to the audit of sales, cash receipts, and the related income statement and balance sheet accounts in the cycle.

- **Chapter 14** will help you learn the methodology for designing tests of controls and substantive tests of transactions audit procedures for sales, cash receipts, and the other classes of transactions in the sales and collection cycle.
- **Chapter 15** deals with nonstatistical and statistical sampling methods for tests of controls and substantive tests of transactions.
- **Chapter 16** presents the methodology for designing audit procedures for the audit of accounts receivable and other account balances in the sales and collection cycle.
- **Chapter 17** covers audit sampling for tests of details of balances.

CHAPTER 14

AUDIT OF THE SALES AND COLLECTION CYCLE: TESTS OF CONTROLS AND SUBSTANTIVE TESTS OF TRANSACTIONS

The Choice Is Simple—Rely On Internal Control Or Resign From The Audit

Silver Stone Company is the largest client managed by a major accountancy firm. It is a financial services conglomerate with almost 200 offices in the region, and corresponding offices in a number of African countries. The company's records contain more than 100,000 accounts receivable and it processes millions of revenues and other transactions annually.

The company's computer data center is in a large, environmentally controlled room that contains several large computer servers and a great deal of ancillary equipment. There are two complete online systems, one serving as a backup for the other, as systems failure would preclude operations in all of the company's branches.

The company has an unusual system of checks and balances in which branch office transaction records are reconciled to data processing controls daily, which, in turn, are reconciled to outside bank account records monthly. Whenever this reconciliation process indicates a significant out-of-balance condition, procedures are initiated to resolve the problem as quickly as possible. A large internal audit staff oversees any special investigative efforts.

Because Silver Stone is a public company, it must file its annual financial report with appropriate financial supervisory authority within 90 days after its fiscal year-end. In addition, the company likes to announce annual earnings and issue its annual report as soon after year-end as reasonably feasible. Under these circumstances, there is always a great deal of pressure on the auditing firm to complete the audit quickly.

A standard audit planning question is: 'How much shall we rely on internal control?' In the case of the Silver Stone audit, the only possible answer is: 'As much as we can.'

Auditing standards require the auditor to test controls as part of the audit of the company's financial statements. Furthermore, it would be difficult to complete the audit within the reporting deadlines without extensively testing key controls. Accordingly, the audit firm conducts the audit with significant reliance on IT controls, reconciliation processes, and internal audit procedures. In all honesty, if Silver Stone did not have excellent internal controls, the auditing firm admits that an audit of the company just could not be done.

The circumstances of Silver Stone in the opening story illustrate an audit in which extensive reliance on internal controls in the sales and collection cycle will likely require the auditor to do extensive tests of controls and substantive tests of transactions. In other situations not involving the audit of a public company, the auditor may rely far less on internal controls but, as was shown in Chapter 10, will still need to understand the internal controls over sales and cash receipts. Auditors need to know when they should rely extensively on internal controls and when they shouldn't. This chapter studies assessing control risk and designing tests of controls and substantive tests of transactions for each of the classes of transactions in the sales and collection cycle.

Before we study assessing control risk and designing tests of controls and substantive tests of transactions for each class of transactions in detail, we will cover two related topics.

1. You need to know the sales and collection cycle classes of transactions and account balances in a typical company. We discussed these earlier, but we review them again here.
2. Because a considerable portion of the audit of transactions in the sales and collection cycle involves documents and records, it is essential to understand the typical documents and records used in the cycle.

Relevant International Standards on Auditing	
ISA 200	Overall Objectives of the Independent Auditor and the Conduct of an Audit in Accordance with International Standards on Auditing
ISA 230	Audit Documentation
ISA 265	Communicating Deficiencies in Internal Control to Those Charged with Governance and Management
ISA 300	Planning an Audit of Financial Statements
ISA 315	Identifying and Assessing the Risks of Material Misstatement through Understanding the Entity and Its Environment
ISA 450	Evaluation of Misstatements Identified during the Audit
ISA 500	Audit Evidence
ISA 520	Analytical Procedures
ISA 610	Using the Work of Internal Auditors

ACCOUNTS AND CLASSES OF TRANSACTIONS IN THE SALES AND COLLECTION CYCLE

OBJECTIVE 14-1

Identify the accounts and the classes of transactions in the sales and collection cycle.

Sales and collection cycle

Involves the decisions and processes necessary for the transfer of the ownership of goods and services to customers after they are made available for sale; it begins with a request by a customer and ends with the conversion of material or service into an account receivable, and ultimately into cash.

The overall objective in the audit of the **sales and collection cycle** is to evaluate whether the account balances affected by the cycle are fairly presented in accordance with IFRS or local accounting standards. Figure 14-1 shows typical accounts included in the sales and collection cycle using T accounts. The nature of the accounts may vary, of course, depending on the industry and client involved. Let's assume we're dealing with a wholesale merchandising company.

Figure 14-1 shows the way accounting information flows through the various accounts in the sales and collection cycle. This figure shows that there are five **classes of transactions in the sales and collection cycle**:

1. Sales (cash and sales on account)
2. Cash receipts
3. Sales returns and allowances
4. Write-off of uncollectible accounts
5. Estimate of bad debt expense

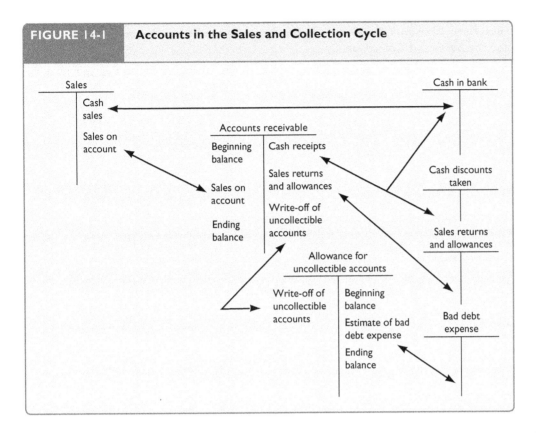

FIGURE 14-1   Accounts in the Sales and Collection Cycle

Classes of transactions in the sales and collection cycle

The categories of transactions for the sales and collection cycle in a typical company: sales, cash receipts, sales returns and allowances, write-off of uncollectible accounts, and bad debt expense.

Figure 14-1 also shows that, with the exception of cash sales, every transaction and amount is ultimately included in one of two balance sheet accounts, accounts receivable or allowance for uncollectible accounts. For simplicity, we assume that the same internal controls exist for both cash and credit sales.

BUSINESS FUNCTIONS IN THE CYCLE AND RELATED DOCUMENTS AND RECORDS

The sales and collection cycle involves the decisions and processes necessary for the transfer of the ownership of goods and services to customers after they are made available for sale. It begins with a request by a customer and ends with the conversion of material or service into an account receivable, and ultimately into cash.

The eight **business functions for the sales and collection cycle** are shown in the third column of Table 14-1. They occur in every business in the recording of the five classes of transactions in the sales and collection cycle. Under 'Business Functions,' observe that the first four processes are for recording sales, while every other class of transactions includes only one business function. In this section, we'll explain each of the eight business functions and describe typical documents and records for each function, which appear in the fourth column of Table 14-1. Before auditors can assess control risk and design tests of controls and substantive tests of transactions, they need to understand the business functions and documents and records in a business.

OBJECTIVE 14-2

Describe the business functions and the related documents and records in the sales and collection cycle.

Business functions for the sales and collection cycle

The key activities that an organization must complete to execute and record business transactions for sales, cash receipts, sales returns and allowances, write-off of uncollectible accounts, and bad debt expense.

Processing Customer Orders

A customer's request for goods initiates the entire cycle. Legally, it is an offer to buy goods under specified terms. The receipt of a customer order often results in the immediate creation of a sales order.

TABLE 14-1	Classes of Transactions, Accounts, Business Functions, and Related Documents and Records for the Sales and Collection Cycle		
Classes of Transactions	Accounts	Business Functions	Documents and Records
Sales	Sales Accounts receivable	Processing customer orders Granting credit Shipping goods Billing customers and recording sales	Customer order Sales order Customer order or sales order Shipping document Sales invoice Sales transaction file Sales journal or listing Accounts receivable master file Accounts receivable trial balance Monthly statement

Cash receipts	Cash in bank (debits from
	    cash receipts)
	Accounts receivable
		Processing and recording
		    cash receipts
			Remittance advice
			Prelisting of cash receipts
			Cash receipts transaction file
			Cash receipts journal or listing

Sales returns and
    allowances
	Sales returns and allowances
	Accounts receivable
		Processing and recording sales
		    returns and allowances
			Credit memo
			Sales returns and allowances journal

Write-off of uncollectible
    accounts
	Accounts receivable
	Allowance for uncollectible
	    accounts
		Writing off uncollectible accounts
		    receivable
			Uncollectible account authorization
			    form
			General journal

Bad debt expense	Bad debt expense Allowance for uncollectible accounts	Providing for bad debts	General journal

Customer Order A customer order is a request for merchandise by a customer. It may be received by telephone, letter, a printed form that has been sent to prospective and existing customers, through salespeople, electronic submission of the customer order through the internet, or other network linkage between the supplier and the customer.

Sales Order A sales order is a document for communicating the description, quantity, and related information for goods ordered by a customer. This is often used to indicate credit approval and authorization for shipment. Figure 14-2 shows an example of a sales order form.

Granting Credit

Before goods are shipped, a properly authorized person must approve credit to the customer for sales on account. Weak practices in credit approval often result in excessive bad debts and accounts receivable that may be uncollectible. An indication of credit approval on the sales order often serves as the approval to ship the goods. In some companies, the computer automatically approves a credit sale based on preapproved credit limits maintained in a customer master file. The computer allows the sale to proceed only when the proposed sales order total plus the existing customer balance is less than the credit limit in the master file.

Shipping Goods

This critical function is the first point in the cycle at which the company gives up assets. Most companies recognize sales when goods are shipped. A shipping document is prepared at the time of shipment, which can be done automatically by a computer, based on sales order information. The shipping document, which is often a multicopy bill of lading, is essential to the proper billing of shipments to customers. Companies that maintain perpetual inventory records also update them based on shipping records.

FIGURE 14-2	Example of Sales Order Form

Sales Order form

Number
Date
Salesperson

Address

Sold to	Ship to
Phone	Ship by

Quantity	Item/Description	Price/Item	Subtotal

		Sales Tax	
		Total	
		Shipping Charge	
		Amount Due	

Shipping Document A shipping document is prepared to initiate shipment of the goods, indicating the description of the merchandise, the quantity shipped, and other relevant data. The company sends the original to the customer and retains one or more copies. The shipping document serves as a signal to bill the customer and may be in electronic or paper form.

One type of shipping document is a bill of lading, which is a written contract between the carrier and the seller of the receipt and shipment of goods. Often, bills of lading include only the number of boxes or pounds shipped, rather than complete details of quantity and description. (For the purpose of this textbook, however, we will assume that complete details are included on bills of lading.)

The bill of lading is often transmitted electronically, once goods have been shipped, and automatically generates the related sales invoice as well as the entry in the sales journal. Many companies use bar codes and handheld computers to record removal of inventory from the warehouse. This information is used to update the perpetual inventory records.

STEALING COMPANY FUNDS AND USING SICK LEAVE AS A COVER	It is difficult for an external auditor to uncover cases of employee corruption and intent to steal, and procedures and policies should be established to ensure that all cash collected during one day should be deposited on the same day. The management of one of the industrial companies in the Kingdom of Saudi Arabia discovered that one of its collection representatives reported to the management of the company that he had been taken ill and requested sick leave for a few days, although he was due to collect amounts due from a number of the company's customers, and	to give the customers receipts for the amounts collected. When the company tried to contact the representative after some days to inquire after his health and to ask him to deliver the cash collected before his sick leave, he informed the human resource manager that he was so ill that he couldn't get out of bed. After more than 15 days he closed down his cell phone account. To its surprise the company's management discovered that the representative had stolen all the money he had collected and had left the country without even collecting his passport from the company's head office.

Billing Customers and Recording Sales

Because billing customers is the means by which the customer is informed of the amount due for the goods, it must be done correctly and on a timely basis. The most important aspects of billing are:

- All shipments made have been billed (completeness)
- No shipment has been billed more than once (occurrence)
- Each one is billed for the proper amount (accuracy)

Billing the proper amount is dependent on charging the customer for the quantity shipped at the authorized price, which includes consideration for freight charges, insurance, and terms of payments.

In most systems, billing of the customer includes preparation of a multicopy sales invoice and simultaneous updating of the sales transactions file, accounts receivable master file, and general ledger master file for sales and accounts receivable. This information is used to generate the sales journal and, along with cash receipts and miscellaneous credits, allows preparation of the accounts receivable trial balance.

Sales Invoice A sales invoice is a document or electronic record indicating the description and quantity of goods sold, the price, freight charges, insurance terms, and other relevant data. The sales invoice is the method of indicating to the customer the amount of a sale and the payment due date. Companies send the original to the customer, and retain one or more copies. Typically, the computer automatically prepares the sales invoice after the customer number, quantity, destination of goods shipped, and sales terms are entered. The computer calculates the invoice extensions and total sales amount using the information entered, along with prices in the inventory master file.

Sales Transaction File This is a computer-generated file that includes all sales transactions processed by the accounting system for a period, which could be a day, week, or month. It includes all information entered into the system and information for each transaction, such as customer name, date, amount, account classification or classifications, salesperson, and commission rate. The file can also include returns and allowances or there can be a separate file for those transactions.

The information in the sales transaction file is used for a variety of records, listings, or reports, depending on the company's needs. These may include a sales journal, accounts receivable master file, and transactions for a certain account balance or division.

Sales Journal or Listing This is a listing or report generated from the sales transaction file that typically includes the customer name, date, amount, and account classification or classifications for each transaction, such as division or product line. It also identifies whether the sale was for cash or accounts receivable. The journal or listing is usually for a month but can cover any period of time. Typically, the journal or listing includes totals of every account number for the time period. The same transactions included in the journal or listing are also posted simultaneously to the general ledger and, if they are on account, to the accounts receivable master file. The journal or listing can also include returns and allowances or there can be a separate journal or listing of those transactions.

Accounts Receivable Master File This is a computer file used to record individual sales, cash receipts, and sales returns and allowances for each customer and to maintain customer account balances. The master file is updated from the sales, sales returns and allowances, and cash receipts computer transaction files. The total of the individual account balances in the master file equals the total balance of accounts receivable in the general ledger. A printout of the accounts receivable master file shows, by customer, the beginning balance in accounts receivable, each sales transaction, sales returns and allowances, cash receipts, and the ending balance.

In this book, we use the term *master file* to refer to either the computer file or a printout of that file, but it is sometimes called the accounts receivable subsidiary ledger or subledger.

Accounts Receivable Trial Balance This list or report shows the amount receivable from each customer at a point in time. It is prepared directly from the accounts receivable master file, and is usually an *aged* trial balance that includes the total balance outstanding and the number of days the receivable has been outstanding, by category of days (such as less than 30 days, 31 to 60 days and so on).

Monthly Statement This is a document sent by mail or electronically to each customer indicating the beginning balance of their accounts receivable, the amount and date of each sale, cash payments received, credit memos issued, and the ending balance due. It is, in essence, a copy of the customer's portion of the accounts receivable master file.

Processing and Recording Cash Receipts

The four sales transaction functions are necessary for getting the goods into the hands of customers, correctly billing them, and reflecting the information in the accounting records. The remaining four functions involve the collection and recording of cash, sales returns and allowances, write-off of uncollectible accounts, and providing for bad debt expense.

Processing and recording cash receipts includes receiving, depositing, and recording cash. Cash includes currency, checks, and electronic funds transfers. The most important concern is the possibility of theft. Theft can occur before receipts are entered in the records or later. It is important that all cash receipts are deposited in the bank at the proper amount on a timely basis and recorded in the cash receipts transaction file. This file is used to prepare the cash receipts journal and update the accounts receivable and general ledger master files.

Remittance Advice A remittance advice is a document mailed to the customer and typically returned to the seller with the cash payment. It indicates the customer name, the sales invoice number, and the amount of the invoice. A remittance advice is used as a record of the cash received to permit the immediate deposit of cash and to improve control over the custody of assets. If the customer fails to include the remittance advice with the payment, it is common for the person opening the mail to prepare one at that time.

Prelisting of Cash Receipts This is a list prepared when cash is received by someone who has no responsibility for recording sales, accounts receivable, or cash, and who has no access to accounting records. It is used to verify whether cash received was recorded and deposited at the correct amounts and on a timely basis.

Many companies use a bank to process cash receipts from customers. Some companies use a lockbox system in which customers mail payments directly to an address maintained by the bank. The bank is responsible for opening all receipts, maintaining records of all customer payments received at the lockbox address, and depositing receipts into the company's bank account on a timely basis. In other cases, receipts are submitted electronically from a customer's bank account to a company bank account through the use of electronic funds transfer (EFT). When customers purchase goods by credit card, the issuer of the credit card uses EFT to transfer funds into the company's bank account. For both lockbox systems and EFT transactions, the bank provides information to the company to prepare the cash receipt entries in the accounting records.

Cash Receipts Transaction File This is a computer-generated file that includes all cash receipts transactions processed by the accounting system for a period, such as a day, week, or month. It includes the same type of information as the sales transaction file.

Cash Receipts Journal or Listing This listing or report is generated from the cash receipts transaction file and includes all transactions for a time period. The same transactions, including all relevant information, are included in the accounts receivable master file and general ledger.

Processing and Recording Sales Returns and Allowances

When a customer is dissatisfied with the goods, the seller often accepts the return of the goods or grants a reduction in the charges. The company prepares a receiving report for returned goods and returns them to storage. Returns and allowances are recorded in the sales returns and allowances transaction file, as well as the accounts receivable master file. Credit memos are issued for returns and allowances to aid in maintaining control and to facilitate record keeping.

Credit Memo A credit memo indicates a reduction in the amount due from a customer because of returned goods or an allowance. It often takes the same general form as a sales invoice, but it supports reductions in accounts receivable rather than increases.

Sales Returns and Allowances Journal This is the journal used to record sales returns and allowances. It performs the same function as the sales journal. Many companies record these transactions in the sales journal rather than in a separate journal.

Writing Off Uncollectible Accounts Receivable

Regardless of the diligence of credit departments, some customers do not pay their bills. After concluding that an amount cannot be collected, the company must write it off. Typically, this occurs after a customer files for bankruptcy or the account is turned over to a collection agency. Proper accounting requires an adjustment for these uncollectible accounts.

Uncollectible Account Authorization Form This is a document used internally to indicate authority to write an account receivable off as uncollectible.

Providing for Bad Debts

Because companies cannot expect to collect on 100 percent of their sales, accounting standards require them to record bad debt expense for the amount they do not expect to collect. Most companies record this transaction at the end of each month or quarter.

METHODOLOGY FOR DESIGNING TESTS OF CONTROLS AND SUBSTANTIVE TESTS OF TRANSACTIONS FOR SALES

OBJECTIVE 14-3

Understand internal control, and design and perform tests of controls and substantive tests of transactions for sales.

In this chapter, we've discussed account balances, classes of transactions, business functions, and related documents and records for the sales and collection cycle. Now, we will study the design of tests of controls and substantive tests of transactions for each of the five classes of transactions in the cycle.

Figure 14-3 illustrates the methodology for obtaining an understanding of internal control and designing tests of controls and substantive tests of transactions for sales. The content of the figure was introduced and explained in Chapter 13. We will organize the following discussion around this illustration and apply it to sales (revenues) and cash receipts for Arabian Hardware Co.

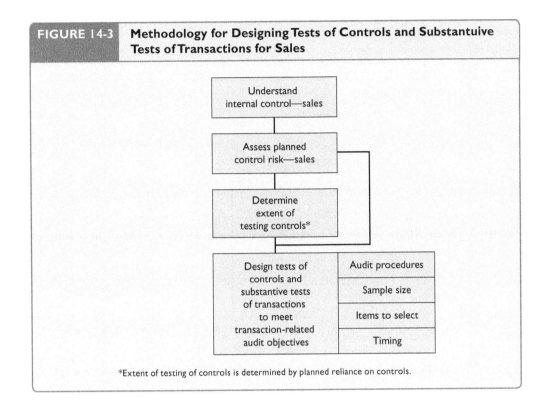

FIGURE 14-3   Methodology for Designing Tests of Controls and Substantuive Tests of Transactions for Sales

*Extent of testing of controls is determined by planned reliance on controls.

Understand Internal Control—Sales

How do auditors obtain an understanding of internal control? Using one typical approach for sales, auditors study the client's flowcharts, make inquiries of the client using an internal control questionnaire, and perform walkthrough tests of sales. We will examine the flowchart of the sales (revenues) and cash receipts function for Arabian Hardware Co. in Figure 14-4 to demonstrate the design of tests of controls and substantive tests of transactions audit procedures.

Assess Planned Control Risk—Sales

The auditor uses the information obtained in understanding internal control to assess control risk. Four steps are essential steps to this assessment.

1. The auditor needs a framework for assessing control risk. The seven transaction-related audit objectives provide this framework. These are shown for sales for Arabian Hardware in Figure 10-7 (page 336). These seven objectives are the same for every audit of sales.
2. The auditor must identify the key internal controls and deficiencies for sales, also shown in Figure 10-7. These will differ for every audit because every client has different internal controls. The controls and deficiencies for Arabian Hardware were identified from the flowchart in Figure 14-3 and the internal control checklist in Figure 10-6 in Chapter 10.
3. After identifying the controls and deficiencies, the auditor associates them with the objectives, as shown with C's and D's in appropriate columns in Figure 10-7.
4. The auditor assesses control risk for each objective by evaluating the controls and deficiencies for each objective. This step is critical because it affects the auditor's decisions about both tests of controls and substantive tests. It is a highly subjective decision. The bottom row of Figure 10-7 labeled 'Assessed control risk' shows the auditor's conclusions about assessed control risk for Arabian Hardware.

FIGURE 14-4   Arabian Hardware—Flowchart of Sales and Cash Receipts

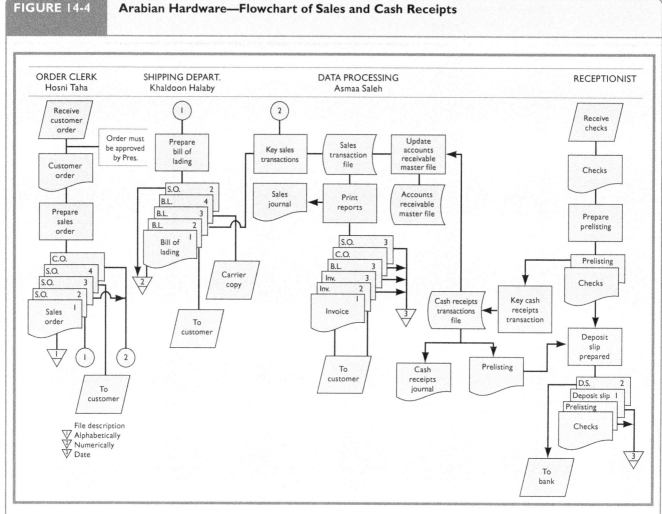

NOTES

1. All correspondence is sent to the president.
2. All sales order numbers are accounted for weekly by the controller.
3. All bills of lading numbers are accounted for weekly by the controller.
4. Sales amount recorded on sales invoice is based on standard price list. The price list is stored in the inventory master file and can be changed only with authorization of the vice president of sales.
5. Duplicate sales invoice is compared with bill of lading daily by the Order Clerk for descriptions and quantities and the sales invoice is reviewed for reasonableness of the extensions and footing. She initials a copy of the invoice before the original is mailed to the customer.
6. Sales are batched daily by the Order Clerk. The batch totals are compared with the sales journal weekly.
7. Statements are sent to customers monthly.
8. Accounts receivable master file total is compared with general ledger by the controller on a monthly basis.

9. Unpaid invoices are filed separately from paid invoices.
10. The receptionist stamps incoming checks with a restrictive endorsement immediately upon receipt.
11. There are no cash sales.
12. Deposits are made daily.
13. Cash receipts are batched daily by the receptionist. The batch totals are compared with the cash receipts journal weekly.
14. The bank account is reconciled by the controller on a monthly basis.
15. All bad debt expense and write-off of bad debts are approved by the president after being initiated by the controller.
16. Financial statements are printed monthly by the controller and reviewed by the president.
17. All errors are reviewed daily by the controller immediately after the updating run. Corrections are made the same day.

We next examine key control activities for sales. Knowledge of these control activities assists in identifying the key controls and deficiencies for sales.

Adequate Separation of Duties   Proper separation of duties helps prevent various types of misstatements due to both errors and fraud. To prevent fraud, management should deny cash access to anyone responsible for entering sales and cash receipts transaction information into the computer. The credit-granting function should be separated from the sales function, because credit checks are intended to offset the natural tendency of sales personnel to optimize volume even at the expense of high bad debt write-offs. Personnel responsible for doing internal comparisons should be independent of

| FORGERY BY SALES REPRESENTATIVE | A salesperson at a large company stole payments received from clients in respect of company products which they had purchased. The company's sales procedures include issuing sales invoices and a receipt showing the amount of products sold. The sales representative telephoned the distribution department and changed the location for delivery of the products. This was in breach of the company's procedures which stated that goods should be delivered either to the client's head office or to a previously designated branch.

The sales representative arranged for some of his friends to collect the client's goods and to sign for the goods while pretending to be the client. The representative then added the value of the sold goods to the real client's account.

Although company procedures were that confirmations should be sent to various clients on an | interim basis to check the accuracy of the receivables balances, the sales representative forged the client's documents to ensure the accuracy of the receivables.

The client is a charity organization and because the fraud was related to the client's activity and the unexpectedly large amount of the receivable balances, and the fact that goods that were being sold to the client were different from the goods which they usually ordered, the company's external auditor uncovered the fraud after doubting the accuracy of this client's balance.

The causes of this fraud were noncompliance with the company's procedures for the delivery of goods to the client's premises and the inappropriate application of the confirmations without the existence of appropriate segregation of duties. |
|---|---|---|

those entering the original data. For example, comparison of batch control totals with summary reports and comparison of the accounts receivable master file totals with the general ledger balance should be done by someone independent of those who input sales and cash receipt transactions.

Proper Authorization The auditor is concerned about authorization at *three key points:*

1. Credit must be properly authorized before a sale takes place.
2. Goods should be shipped only after proper authorization.
3. Prices, including basic terms, freight, and discounts, must be authorized.

The first two controls are meant to prevent the loss of company assets by shipping to fictitious customers or those who will fail to pay for the goods. Price authorization is meant to ensure that the sale is billed at the price set by company policy. Authorization may be done for each individual transaction or general authorization may be given for specific classes of transactions. General authorizations are often done automatically by computer.

Adequate Documents and Records Because each company has a unique system of originating, processing, and recording transactions, auditors may find it difficult to evaluate whether each client's procedures are designed for maximum control. Nevertheless, adequate record-keeping procedures must exist before most of the transaction-related audit objectives can be met. Some companies, for example, automatically prepare a multicopy prenumbered sales invoice at the time a customer order is received. Copies of this document are used to approve credit, authorize shipment, record the number of units shipped, and bill customers. This system greatly reduces the chance of the failure to bill a customer if all invoices are accounted for periodically, but controls have to exist to ensure the sale isn't recorded until shipment occurs.

Prenumbered Documents Prenumbering is meant to prevent both the *failure* to bill or record sales and the occurrence of *duplicate* billings and recordings. Of course, it does not do much good to have prenumbered documents unless they are properly accounted for. To use this control effectively, a billing clerk will file a copy of all shipping documents in sequential order after each shipment is billed, while someone else will periodically account for all numbers and investigate the reason for any missing documents.

Monthly Statements Sending monthly statements is a useful control because it encourages customers to respond if the balance is incorrectly stated. These statements should be controlled by persons who have no responsibility for handling cash or recording sales or accounts receivable to avoid the intentional failure to send the statements. For maximum effectiveness, all disagreements about the account balance should be directed to a designated person who has no responsibility for handling cash or recording sales or accounts receivable.

Internal Verification Procedures Computer programs or independent personnel should check that the processing and recording of sales transactions fulfill each of the seven transaction-related audit objectives. Examples include accounting for the numerical sequence of prenumbered documents, checking the accuracy of document preparation, and reviewing reports for unusual or incorrect items.

Determine Extent of Testing Controls

After auditors identify the key internal controls and control deficiencies, they assess control risk, often using a matrix format similar to Figure 10-7 in Chapter 10. The auditors must perform tests of key controls and evaluate the impact of the deficiencies on the auditor's report on financial statements. The extent of testing of controls depends on the effectiveness of the controls and the extent to which the auditor believes they can be relied on to reduce control risk within an acceptable audit cost. A lower assessed level of control risk will result in increased testing of controls to support the lower control risk, with a corresponding increase in detection risk and decrease in the amount of substantive tests.

Design Tests of Controls For Sales

For each key control, one or more tests of controls must be designed to verify its effectiveness. In most audits, it is relatively easy to determine the nature of the test of the control from the nature of the control. For example, if the internal control is to initial customer orders after they have been approved for credit, the test of control is to examine the customer order for proper initials.

The first three columns of Table 14-2 illustrate the design of tests of controls for sales for Arabian Hardware. Column three shows one test of control for each key internal control in column two. Observe that this table is organized by transaction-related audit objective. For example, the second key internal control for the occurrence objective is 'sales are supported by authorized shipping documents and approved customer orders.' The test of control is to 'examine sales invoice for supporting bill of lading and customer order.' For this test, the auditor should start with sales invoices and examine documents in support of the sales invoices rather than going in the opposite direction. If the auditor traced from shipping documents to sales invoices, it is a test of completeness. (Direction of tests is discussed further later in the chapter.)

As shown in the third column of Table 14-2 for the completeness objective, a common test of control for sales is to account for a sequence of various types of documents. For example, accounting for a sequence of shipping documents and tracing each one to the duplicate sales invoice and recording in the sales journal provides evidence of completeness.

To simultaneously provide evidence of both the occurrence and completeness objectives, an auditor can check the sequence of sales invoices selected from the sales journal and watch for duplicate and omitted numbers or invoices outside the normal sequence. Assume the auditor selects sales invoices #18100 to #18199. The completeness objective for this procedure will be satisfied if all 100 sales invoices are recorded. The occurrence objective will be satisfied if there is no duplicate recording of any of the invoice numbers. As indicated in Table 14-2, the lack of verification to prevent the possibility of duplicate recording of sales invoices is a deficiency at Arabian Hardware.

TABLE 14-2 Transaction-Related Audit Objectives, Key Existing Controls, Tests of Controls, Deficiencies, and Substantive Tests of Transactions for Sales—Arabian Hardware Co.

Transaction-Related Audit Objectives	Key Existing Controls*	Test of Controls†	Deficiencies*	Substantive Tests of Transactions†
Recorded sales are for shipments actually made to nonfictitious customers (occurrence).	Credit is approved automatically by computer by comparison to authorized credit limits (C1). Sales are supported by invoices, authorized shipping documents and approved customer orders (C2). Batch totals of quantities shipped are compared with quantities billed (C6). Statements are sent to customers each month (C9).	Examine customer order for evidence of credit approval (13e). Examine sales invoice for supporting bill of lading and customer order (13b). Examine file of batch totals for initials of data control clerk (8). Observe whether monthly statements are sent (6).	There is a lack of internal verification for the possibility of sales invoices being recorded more than once (D1).	Account for a sequence of sales invoices (12). Review sales journal and master file for unusual transactions and amounts (1). Trace sales journal entries to supporting documents, including duplicate sales invoice, bill of lading, sales order, and customer order (14).
Existing sales transactions are recorded (completeness).	Shipping documents are prenumbered and accounted for weekly (C5). Batch totals of quantities shipped are compared with quantities billed (C6).	Account for a sequence of shipping documents (10). Examine file of batch totals for initials of data control clerk (8).		Trace selected shipping documents to the sales journal to be sure that each one is included (11).
Recorded sales are for the amount of goods shipped and are correctly billed and recorded (accuracy).	Sales are supported by invoices, authorized shipping documents and approved customer orders (C2). Batch totals of quantities shipped are compared with quantities billed (C6). Unit selling prices are obtained from the price list master file of approved prices (C7). Statements are sent to customers each month (C9).	Examine sales invoice for supporting documents (13b). Examine file of batch totals for initials of data control clerk (8). Examine the approved price list for accuracy and proper authorization (9). Observe whether monthly statements are sent (6).		Trace entries in sales journal to sales invoices (13b). Recompute prices and extensions on sales invoices (13b). Trace details on sales invoices to: shipping documents (13c) sales order (13d) customer order (13e).
Sales transactions are correctly included in the accounts receivable master file and are correctly summarized (posting and summarization).	Computer automatically posts transactions to the accounts receivable master file and general ledger (C10). Accounts receivable master file is reconciled to the general ledger on a monthly basis (C11). Statements are sent to customers each month (C9).	Examine evidence that accounts receivable master file is reconciled to the general ledger (7). Examine evidence that accounts receivable master file is reconciled to the general ledger (7). Observe whether monthly statements are sent (6).		Trace selected sales invoices from the sales journal to the accounts receivable master file and test for amount, date, and invoice number (13a). Use audit software to foot and cross-foot the sales journal and trace totals to the general ledger (2).

(Table 14-2 continued on next page)

TABLE 14-2	Transaction-Related Audit Objectives, Key Existing Controls, Tests of Controls, Deficiencies, and Substantive Tests of Transactions for Sales—Arabian Hardware Co. *(Cont.)*			
Transaction-Related Audit Objectives	**Key Existing Controls***	**Test of Controls†**	**Deficiencies***	**Substantive Tests of Transactions†**
Sales transactions are correctly classified (classification).	Account classifications are internally verified (C8).	Examine document package for internal verification (13b).		Examine duplicate sales invoice for proper account classification (13b).
Sales are recorded on the correct dates (timing).	Shipping documents are prenumbered and accounted for weekly by the accountant (C5).	Account for a sequence of shipping documents (10).	There is a lack of control to test for timely recording (D2).	Compare date of recording of sale in sales journal with duplicate sales invoice and bill of lading (13b and 13c).
Sales pertain to the company (rights).	Sales are supported by invoices, authorized shipping documents and approved customers orders (C2).	Examine sales invoices for internal verification of company's name (13b).		Account for a sequence of sales invoices to ensure all are in company's name (12).

*Controls (C) and Deficiencies (D) are from the control matrix for sales in Figure 10-7 in Chapter 10. Controls C3 and C4 from the control matrix are not included here.

†The number in parentheses after each test of control and substantive test of transaction refers to an audit procedure in the audit program in Figure 14-8.

The appropriate tests of controls for separation of duties are ordinarily restricted to the auditor's observations of activities and discussions with personnel. For example, it is possible to observe whether the billing clerk has access to cash when incoming mail is opened or cash is deposited. It is usually also necessary to ask personnel what their responsibilities are and if there are any circumstances where their responsibilities are different from the normal policy. For example, the employee responsible for billing customers may state that he or she does not have access to cash. Further discussion may reveal that he or she actually takes over the cashier's duties when the cashier is on vacation.

Several of the tests of controls in Table 14-2 can be performed using the computer. For example, the auditor can test whether credit is properly authorized by the computer by attempting to initiate transactions that exceed a customer's credit limit. If the control is working effectively, the proposed sales order should be rejected. The occurrence of sales can be similarly tested by attempting to input nonexistent customer numbers, which should be rejected by the computer. This key control will reduce the likelihood of fictitious sales.

Design Substantive Tests of Transactions for Sales

In deciding substantive tests of transactions, auditors commonly use some procedures on every audit regardless of the circumstances, whereas others are dependent on the adequacy of the controls and the results of the tests of controls. In the fifth column of Table 14-2, the substantive tests of transactions are related to the transaction-related audit objectives in the first column and are designed to determine whether any monetary misstatements for that objective exist in the transaction. The audit procedures used are affected by the internal controls and tests of controls for that objective. Materiality, results of the prior year, and the other factors discussed in Chapter 9 also influence the procedures used.

Determining the proper substantive tests of transactions procedures for sales is relatively difficult because they vary considerably depending on the circumstances. Table 14-2 addresses the substantive tests of transactions procedures in the order of the sales transaction-related audit objectives. Note that some audit procedures fulfill more than one transaction-related audit objective (For example, audit procedure (13b) is included for three objectives.)

The following paragraphs discuss substantive tests of transaction audit procedures that are done only when there are specific circumstances that require special audit attention, such as when there is a deficiency in internal control.

Recorded Sales Occurred For this objective, the auditor is concerned with the possibility of *three types of misstatements:*

1. Sales included in the journals for which no shipment was made.
2. Sales recorded more than once.
3. Shipments made to nonexistent customers and recorded as sales.

The first two types of misstatements can be due to an error or fraud. The last type is always a fraud. The potential consequences of all three are significant because they lead to an overstatement of assets and income.

Unintentional overstatements of sales are typically more easily discovered than fraudulent overstatements. An unintentional overstatement normally also results in an overstatement of accounts receivable, which the client can detect by sending monthly statements to customers. Unintentional misstatements at year-end can often be easily found by the auditor through confirmation procedures. With fraudulent overstatements, the perpetrator will attempt to conceal the overstatement, making it more difficult for auditors to find. Substantive tests of transactions may be necessary to discover overstated sales in these circumstances.

The appropriate substantive tests of transactions for testing the occurrence objective depend on where the auditor believes misstatements are likely. Many auditors do substantive tests of transactions for the occurrence objective only if they believe that a control deficiency exists. Therefore, the nature of the tests depends on the nature of the potential misstatement as follows:

Recorded Sale for Which There Was No Shipment The auditor can vouch selected entries in the sales journal to related copies of shipping and other supporting documents to make sure they occurred. If the auditor is concerned about the possibility of a fictitious duplicate copy of a shipping document, it may be necessary to trace the amounts to the perpetual inventory records as a test of whether inventory was reduced.

Sale Recorded More Than Once Duplicate sales can be determined by reviewing a numerically sorted list of recorded sales transactions for duplicate numbers. The auditor can also test for the proper cancellation of shipping documents. Proper cancellation decreases the likelihood that a shipping document will be used to record another sale.

Shipment Made to Nonexistent Customers This type of fraud normally occurs only when the person recording sales is also in a position to authorize shipments. Weak internal controls make it difficult to detect fictitious shipments, such as shipments to other locations of the company. To test for nonexistent customers, the auditor can trace customer information on the sales invoice to the customer master file. These revenue frauds are often referred to as 'sham sales.'

Another effective approach to detecting the three types of misstatements of sales transactions just discussed is to trace the *credit* in the accounts receivable master file to its source. If the receivable was actually collected in cash or the goods were returned, a sale must have originally occurred. If the credit was for a bad debt write-off or a credit memo, or if the account was still unpaid at the time of the audit, this could indicate an inappropriately recorded sales transaction. The auditor must examine shipping and customer order documents to determine if there is adequate support that a sales transaction actually occurred.

Auditing standards indicate that the auditor should normally identify improper revenue recognition as a fraud risk. However, substantive tests of transactions should be necessary for improper revenue recognition only if the auditor is concerned about fraud due to inadequate controls. However, if controls are adequate their substantive tests of transactions are necessary to double check the nonexistence of fraud.

Existing Sales Transactions are Recorded In many audits, no substantive tests of transactions are done for the completeness objective. This is because overstatements of assets and income from sales transactions are more likely than understatements, and overstatements also represent a greater source of audit risk. If controls are inadequate, which is likely if the client does no independent internal tracing from shipping documents to the sales journal, substantive tests are necessary.

To test for unbilled shipments, auditors can trace selected shipping documents from a file in the shipping department to related duplicate sales invoices and the sales journal. To conduct a meaningful test using this procedure, the auditor must be confident that all shipping documents are included in the file. This can be done by accounting for a numerical sequence of the documents.

Direction of Tests Auditors need to understand the difference between tracing from source documents to the journals and vouching from the journals back to source documents. The former tests for *omitted transactions* (completeness objective); the latter tests for *nonexistent transactions* (occurrence objective).

To test for the occurrence objective, the auditor starts by selecting a sample of invoice numbers *from* the journal and vouches them *to* duplicate sales invoices, shipping documents, and customer orders. In testing for the completeness objective, the auditor typically starts by selecting a sample of shipping documents and traces them *to* duplicate sales invoices and the sales journal as a test of omissions.

When designing audit procedures for the occurrence and completeness objectives, the starting point for the test is essential. This is called the direction of tests and is illustrated in Figure 14-5. For example, if the auditor is concerned about the occurrence objective but tests in the wrong direction (from shipping documents to the journals), a serious audit deficiency exists. In testing for the other five transaction-related audit objectives, the direction of tests is usually not relevant. For example, the accuracy of sales transactions can be tested by testing from a duplicate sales invoice to a shipping document or vice versa.

Sales Are Accurately Recorded The accurate recording of sales transactions concerns:

- Shipping the amount of goods ordered
- Accurately billing for the amount of goods shipped
- Accurately recording the amount billed in the accounting records

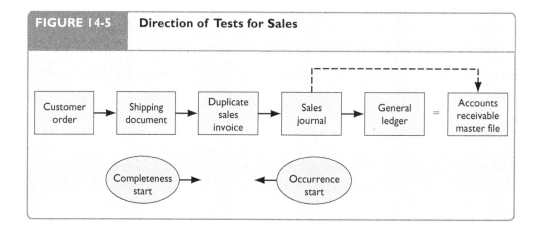

FIGURE 14-5   Direction of Tests for Sales

Auditors typically do substantive tests of transactions in every audit to ensure that each of these three aspects of accuracy are done correctly by recalculating information in the accounting records and comparing information on different documents. Auditors commonly compare prices on duplicate sales invoices with an approved price list, recalculate extensions and footings, and compare the details on the invoices with shipping records for description, quantity, and customer identification. Often, auditors also examine customer orders and sales orders for the same information.

The comparison of tests of controls and substantive tests of transactions for the accuracy objective is a good example of how audit time can be saved when effective internal controls exist. Obviously, the test of control for this objective takes almost no time because it involves examining only initial or other evidence of internal verification. If this control is effective, the sample size for substantive tests of transactions can be reduced, yielding significant savings.

When sales invoices are automatically calculated and posted by a computer, the auditor may be able to reduce substantive tests of transactions for the accuracy objective. If the auditor determines that the computer is programmed accurately and the price list master file is authorized and correct, detailed invoice computations can be reduced or eliminated. In this case, the auditor focuses on determining that effective computer controls exist to ensure that the computer is properly programmed and has not been altered since it was last tested by the auditor. Tests of controls would focus on the authorization and accuracy of changes to the price list master file.

Sales Transactions are Correctly Included in the Master File and Correctly Summarized The proper inclusion of all sales transactions in the accounts receivable master file is essential because the accuracy of these records affects the client's ability to collect outstanding receivables. Similarly, the sales journal must be correctly totaled

---

FIGURE 14-6   Extracts from an Audit Management Letter

A management letter includes the auditor's remarks, whether material or not, concerning his examination and assessment of the client's internal controls, transactions, and accounts balances:

a) We discovered when reviewing the aging report as of December 31 2011, and the aging report as of December 31 2012 that some clients did not pay invoices in 2011, although they paid invoices during the current year of 2012. Examples are: Coral Travel paid invoices raised in December 2011, and other invoices raised in January 2012 although there were invoices outstanding since October and November 2011. Also, Tooty Travco paid invoices raised in January and February 2012, although there are still amounts outstanding since August, October, November, and December 2011.

  • We recommend taking the necessary steps for collection of outstanding balances on those clients.

b) We discovered upon reviewing the statement of Marhaba Tours that it included collecting an amount of US$109,198 relating to invoices raised in 2012. The invoices paid had not been adjusted with that amount, which affected the accuracy of the aging report prepared at 31 December 2012 for that client.

  • We recommend adjusting the client's account at that date to facilitate obtaining the real account balance of such client.

c) We discovered upon reviewing the statement of Tooty Travco that it included US$72,143 added as an adjustment to the client's account, without any supporting documents.

  • We recommend studying the amounts added to the client's account and presenting supporting documents.

d) We discovered that the computer accounting program relating to clients cannot display the balance of each client in different currencies. It can only display the ending balance in local currency, which makes the process of checking balances with customers difficult. It is also difficult to evaluate the balances in the local currency according to the exchange rates prevailing at the date of preparing the annual financial statements of the resort.

  • We recommend adjusting the computer program so that it can display the balance of each client in different currencies at all times to facilitate checking balances with suppliers, as well as evaluating balances when preparing the final financial statements.

and posted to the general ledger if the financial statements are to be correct. In most engagements, auditors perform some clerical accuracy tests, such as footing the journals and tracing the totals and details to the general ledger and the master file, to check whether there are errors or fraud in the processing of sales transactions. The extent to which such tests are needed is determined by the quality of internal controls.

Tracing from the sales journal to the master file is typically done as a part of fulfilling other transaction-related audit objectives, but footing the sales journal and tracing the totals to the general ledger are done as separate procedures.

Posting and summarization tests differ from those for other transaction-related audit objectives because they include footing journals, master file records, and ledgers, and tracing from one to the other among these three.

When footing and comparisons are restricted to these three records, the transaction-related audit objective is posting and summarization. When the journals, master files, or ledgers are traced to or from a document, the objective is one of the other five objectives, depending on what is being verified. To illustrate, when an auditor compares an amount on a duplicate sales invoice with either the sales journal or master file entry, it is an accuracy audit objective procedure. When an auditor traces an entry from the sales journal to the master file, it is a posting and summarization procedure.

Recorded Sales are Correctly Classified Although it is less of a problem in sales than in some transaction cycles, auditors must still be concerned that transactions are charged to the correct general ledger account. With cash and credit sales, company personnel should not debit accounts receivable for a cash sale or credit sales for collection of a receivable. They should also not classify sales of operating assets, such as buildings, as sales. For those companies using more than one sales classification, such as companies issuing segmented earnings statements, proper classification is essential.

Sales are Recorded on the Correct Dates Sales should be billed and recorded as soon after shipment takes place as possible to prevent the unintentional omission of transactions from the records and to make sure that sales are recorded in the proper period. Timely recorded transactions are also less likely to contain misstatements. When auditors do substantive tests of transactions procedures for accuracy they commonly compare the date on selected bills of lading or other shipping documents with the date on related duplicate sales invoices, the sales journal, and the accounts receivable master file. Significant differences indicate potential cutoff problems in the test of year-end balances.

Sales Pertain to the Company Auditors should examine a sample of sales invoices and related documents such as shipping documents, credit memos, and customer orders to ensure that sales transactions pertain to the company. This will require the auditor checking the nature of the transactions, and making sure that they relate to the company's activities and operations.

Design of Audit Programs

The information presented in Table 14-2 is intended to help auditors design audit programs that satisfy the transaction-related audit objectives in a given set of circumstances. This methodology helps the auditor design an effective and efficient audit program that responds to the unique risks of material misstatements at each client.

After the appropriate audit procedures for a given set of circumstances have been designed, they must, of course, be performed.

Figure 14-7 illustrates an audit program for sales and cash receipts for Arabian Hardware. It is a summary of the audit procedures in Tables 14-2 and 14-3. The numbers for the audit procedures in Figure 14-7 correspond to the numbers at the end of the tests of control and substantive audit procedures in Tables 14-2 and 14-3. These numbers are included to help you see the relationship between the two tables and Figure 14-7.

FIGURE 14-7	Control Risk for Arabian Hardware Co.—Cash Receipts

CASH RECEIPTS TRANSACTION-RELATED AUDIT OBJECTIVES

INTERNAL CONTROL	Recorded cash receipts are for funds actually received by the company (occurrence).	Cash received is recorded in the cash receipts journal (completeness).	Cash receipts are deposited and recorded at the amounts received (accuracy).	Cash receipts are correctly included in the accounts receivable master file and are correctly summarized (posting and summarization).	Cash receipts transactions are correctly classified (classification).	Cash receipts are recorded on the correct dates (timing).	Cash receipts pertain to the company (rights).
Accountant independently reconciles bank account (C1).	C		C				
Prelisting of cash receipts is prepared (C2).		C					
Checks are restrictively endorsed (C3).		C					
Batch totals of cash receipts are compared with computer summary reports (C4).	C	C	C				
Statements are sent to customers each month (C5).		C	C	C			
Cash receipts transactions are internally verified (C6).					C		
Procedures require recording of cash on a daily basis (C7).						C	
Computer automatically posts transactions to the accounts receivable master file and to the general ledger (C8).				C			
Accounts receivable master file is reconciled to the general ledger on a monthly basis (C9).				C			
Procedures require that cash relates to sales invoices (C10).							C
DEFICIENCY Prelisting of cash is not used to verify recorded cash receipts (D1).		D					
Assessed control risk	Low	Medium	Low	Low	Low	Low	Low

C = Control; D = Significant deficiency or material weakness

SALES RETURNS AND ALLOWANCES

The transaction-related audit objectives and the client's methods of controlling misstatements are essentially the same for processing credit memos as those described for sales, with two differences. The first is *materiality*. In many instances, sales returns and allowances are so immaterial the auditor can ignore them.

The second difference is *emphasis on the occurrence objective*. For sales returns and allowances, auditors usually emphasize testing recorded transactions to uncover any

OBJECTIVE 14-4

Apply the methodology for controls over sales transactions to controls over sales returns and allowances.

theft of cash from the collection of accounts receivable that was covered up by a fictitious sales return or allowance. (Although auditors usually emphasize the occurrence objective for sales returns and allowances transactions, the *completeness* objective is especially important in tests of account balances to determine if sales and returns are understated at year-end.)

Naturally, other objectives should not be ignored. But because the objectives and methodology for auditing sales returns and allowances are essentially the same as for sales, we do not include a detailed study of them. If you need to audit sales returns and allowances, you should be able to apply the same logic to arrive at suitable controls, tests of controls, and substantive tests of transactions to verify the amounts.

METHODOLOGY FOR DESIGNING TESTS OF CONTROLS AND SUBSTANTIVE TESTS OF TRANSACTIONS FOR CASH RECEIPTS

OBJECTIVE 14-5

Understand internal control, and design and perform tests of controls and substantive tests of transactions for cash receipts.

Cash receipts tests of controls and substantive tests of transactions audit procedures are developed around the same framework used for sales, but of course the specific objectives are applied to cash receipts. Given the transaction-related audit objectives, the auditor follows this process:

- Determine key internal controls for each audit objective
- Design tests of control for each control used to support a reduced control risk
- Design substantive tests of transactions to test for monetary misstatements for each objective

As in all other audit areas, the tests of controls depend on the controls the auditor identifies, and the extent they will be relied on to reduce assessed control risk.

Figure 14-7 presents the control risk matrix for cash receipts for Arabian Hardware. It is based on the information in the sales and cash receipts flowchart in Figure 14-4.

Table 14-3 lists key internal controls, common tests of controls, and common substantive tests of transactions to satisfy each of the transaction-related audit objectives for cash receipts for Arabian Hardware Co. Table 14-3 follows the same format used for sales as shown in Table 14-2. The tests of controls and substantive tests of transactions

TABLE 14-3	Transaction-Related Audit Objectives, Key Existing Controls, Tests of Controls, Deficiencies, and Substantive Tests of Transactions for Cash Receipts—Arabian Hardware Co.			
Transaction-Related Audit Objectives	Key Existing Controls*	Tests of Controls†	Deficiencies*	Substantive Tests of Transactions†
Recorded cash receipts are for funds actually received by the company (occurrence).	Accountant independently reconciles bank account (C1). Batch totals of cash receipts are compared with computer summary reports (C4).	Observe whether accountant reconciles bank account (3). Examine file of batch totals for initials of data control clerk (8).		Review cash receipts journal and master file for unusual transactions and amounts (1). Trace cash receipts entries from the cash receipts journal entries to the bank statement (19). Prepare a proof of cash receipts (18).
Cash received is recorded in the cash receipts journal (completeness).	Prelisting of cash receipts is prepared (C2). Checks are restrictively endorsed (C3). Batch totals of cash receipts are compared with computer summary reports (C4). Statements are sent to customers each month (C5).	Observe prelisting of cash receipts (4). Observe endorsement of incoming checks (5). Examine file of batch totals for initials of data control clerk (8). Observe whether monthly statements are sent (6).	Prelisting of cash is not used to verify recorded cash receipts (D1).	Obtain prelisting of cash receipts and trace amounts to the cash receipts journal, testing for names, amounts, and dates (15). Compare the prelisting with the duplicate deposit slip (16).
Cash receipts are deposited and recorded at the amounts received (accuracy).	Accountant independently reconciles bank account (C1). Batch totals of cash receipts are compared with computer summary reports (C4). Statements are sent to customers each month (C5).	Observe whether accountant reconciles bank account (3). Examine file of batch totals for initials of data control clerk (8). Observe whether monthly statements are sent (6).		Obtain prelisting of cash receipts and trace amounts to the cash receipts journal, testing for names, amounts, and dates (15). Prepare proof of cash receipts (18).
Cash receipts are correctly included in the accounts receivable master file and are correctly summarized (posting and summarization).	Statements are sent to customers each month (C5). Computer automatically posts transactions to the accounts receivable master file and general ledger (C8). Accounts receivable master file is reconciled to the general ledger on a monthly basis (C9).	Observe whether monthly statements are sent (6). Examine evidence that accounts receivable master file is reconciled to general ledger (7).		Trace selected entries from the cash receipts journal to the accounts receivable master file and test for dates and amounts (20). Trace selected credits from the accounts receivable master file to the cash receipts journal and test for dates and amounts (21). Use audit software to foot and cross-foot the sales journal and trace totals to the general ledger (2).
Cash receipts transactions are correctly classified (classification).	Cash receipts transactions are internally verified (C6).	Examine evidence of internal verification (15).		Examine prelisting for proper account classification (17).
Cash receipts are recorded on the correct dates (timing).	Procedures require recording of cash on a daily basis (C7).	Observe unrecorded cash at a point in time (4).		Compare date of deposit per bank statement to the dates in the cash receipts journal and prelisting of cash receipts (16).
Cash receipts pertain to the company (rights).	Procedures require that cash relates to sales invoices (C10).	Examine evidence of internal verification that cash receipts pertain to the company (15).		Trace selected entries from the cash receipts journal to sales invoices recorded in sales journals (20).

*Controls (C) and Deficiencies (D) are from control matrix for cash receipts in Figure 14-7 (p. 483).

†The number in parentheses after each test of control and substantive test of transaction refers to an audit procedure in the performance format audit program in Figure 14-8 (p. 486).

for cash receipts are combined with those for sales in the performance format audit program in Figure 14-8.

Because the methodology for cash receipts is similar to that for sales, our discussion is not as detailed as our discussion of the internal controls, tests of controls, and substantive tests of transactions for the audit of sales. Instead, we focus on the substantive audit procedures that are most likely to be misunderstood.

FIGURE 14-8	Audit Program for Tests of Controls and Substantive Tests of Transactions for Sales and Cash Receipts for Arabian Hardware

ARABIAN HARDWARE CO.
Tests of Controls and Substantive Tests of Transactions Audit Procedures
for Sales and Cash Receipts
(Sample size and the items in the sample are not included.)
General
1. Review journals and master file for unusual transactions and amounts.
2. Use audit software to foot and cross-foot the sales and cash receipts journals and trace the totals to the general ledger.
3. Observe whether accountant reconciles the bank account.
4. Observe whether cash is prelisted and the existence of any unrecorded cash.
5. Observe whether restrictive endorsement is used on cash receipts.
6. Observe whether monthly statements are sent.
7. Observe whether accountant compares master file total with general ledger account.
8. Examine file of batch totals for initials of data control clerk.
9. Examine the approved price list in the inventory master file for accuracy and proper authorization.

Shipment of Goods
10. Account for a sequence of shipping documents.
11. Trace selected shipping documents to the sales journal to be sure that each one has been included.

Billing of Customers and Recording the Sales in the Records
12. Account for a sequence of sales invoices in the sales journal.
13. Trace selected sales invoice numbers from the sales journal to
   a. accounts receivable master file and test for amount, date, and invoice number.
   b. duplicate sales invoice and check for the total amount recorded in the journal, date, customer name, and account classification. Check the pricing, extensions, and footings. Examine underlying documents for indication of internal verification.
   c. bill of lading and test for customer name, product description, quantity, and date.
   d. duplicate sales order and test for customer name, product description, quantity, date, and indication of internal verification.
   e. customer order and test for customer name, product description, quantity, date, and credit approval.
14. Trace recorded sales from the sales journal to the file of supporting documents, which includes a duplicate sales invoice, bill of lading, sales order, and customer order.

Processing Cash Receipts and Recording the Amounts in the Records
15. Obtain the prelisting of cash receipts and trace amounts to the cash receipts journal, testing for names, amounts, dates, and internal verification.
16. Compare the prelisting of cash receipts with the duplicate deposit slip, testing for names, amounts, and dates. Trace the total from the cash receipts journal to the bank statement, testing for a delay in deposit.
17. Examine prelisting for proper account classification.
18. Prepare a proof of cash receipts.
19. Trace cash receipt entries from the cash receipts journal to the bank statement, testing for dates and amounts of deposits.
20. Trace selected entries from the cash receipts journal to sales invoices recorded in the sales journal and to entries in the accounts receivable master file and test for dates and amounts.
21. Trace selected credits from the accounts receivable master file to the cash receipts journal and test for dates and amounts.

An essential part of the auditor's responsibility in auditing cash receipts is to identify deficiencies in internal control that increase the likelihood of fraud. To expand on Table 14-3, we emphasize those audit procedures that are designed primarily for the discovery of fraud. We omit discussion of some procedures only because their purpose and the methodology for applying them should be apparent from the description provided in Table 14-3.

Determine Whether Cash Received Was Recorded

The most difficult type of cash embezzlement for auditors to detect is when it occurs *before the cash is recorded* in the cash receipts journal or other cash listing, especially if the sale and cash receipt are recorded simultaneously. For example, if a grocery store clerk takes cash and intentionally fails to record the sale and receipt of cash on the cash register, it is extremely difficult to discover the theft. To prevent this type of fraud, internal controls such as those included in the second objective in Table 14-3 are implemented by many companies. The type of control will, of course, depend on the type of business. For example, the controls for a retail store in which the cash is received by the same person who sells the merchandise and enters cash receipts in a cash register should be different from the controls for a company in which all receipts are received through the mail several weeks after the sales have taken place.

It is normal practice to trace from prenumbered remittance advices or prelists of cash receipts to the cash receipts journal and subsidiary accounts receivable records as a substantive test of the recording of actual cash received. This test will be effective only if a cash register tape or some other prelisting was prepared at the time cash was received.

Prepare Proof of Cash Receipts

A useful audit procedure to test whether all recorded cash receipts have been deposited in the bank account is a **proof of cash receipts**. In this test, the total cash receipts recorded in the cash receipts journal for a given period, such as a month, are reconciled with the actual deposits made to the bank during the same period. A difference in the two may be the result of deposits in transit and other items, but the amounts can be reconciled and compared. This procedure is not useful in discovering cash receipts that have not been recorded in the journals or time lags in making deposits, but it can help uncover recorded cash receipts that have not been deposited, unrecorded deposits, unrecorded loans, bank loans deposited directly into the bank account, and similar misstatements. Ordinarily, this somewhat time-consuming procedure is used only when the controls are deficient.

Proof of cash receipts

An audit procedure to test whether all recorded cash receipts have been deposited in the bank account by reconciling the total cash receipts recorded in the cash receipts journal for a given period with the actual deposits made to the bank.

Test to Discover Lapping of Accounts Receivable

Lapping of accounts receivable is the postponement of entries for the collection of receivables to *conceal an existing cash shortage*. The embezzlement is perpetrated by a person who handles cash receipts and then enters them into the computer system. He or she defers recording the cash receipts from one customer and covers the shortages with receipts of another. These in turn are covered from the receipts of a third customer a few days later. The employee must continue to cover the shortage through repeated lapping, replace the stolen money, or find another way to conceal the shortage.

This embezzlement can be easily prevented by separation of duties and a mandatory vacation policy for employees who both handle cash and enter cash receipts into the system. It can be detected by comparing the name, amount, and dates shown on remittance advices with cash receipts journal entries and related duplicate deposit slips. Because this procedure is relatively time-consuming, it is ordinarily performed only when specific concerns with embezzlement exist because of a deficiency in internal control.

Lapping of accounts receivable

The postponement of entries for the collection of receivables to conceal an existing cash shortage.

AUDIT TESTS FOR THE WRITE-OFF OF UNCOLLECTIBLE ACCOUNTS

OBJECTIVE 14-6

Apply the methodology for controls over the sales and collection cycle to write-offs of uncollectible accounts receivable.

The same as for sales returns and allowances, the auditor's primary concern in the audit of the write-off of uncollectible accounts receivable is the possibility of client personnel covering up an embezzlement by writing off accounts receivable that have already been collected (the occurrence transaction-related audit objective). The major control for preventing this fraud is proper authorization of the write-off of uncollectible accounts by a designated level of management only after a thorough investigation of the reason the customer has not paid.

Normally, verification of the accounts written off takes relatively little time. Typically, the auditor examines approvals by the appropriate persons. For a sample of accounts written off, it is also usually necessary for the auditor to examine correspondence in the client's files establishing their uncollectibility. After the auditor has concluded that the accounts written off by general journal entries are proper, selected items should be traced to the accounts receivable master file to test whether the write-off was properly recorded.

The estimation of bad debt expense, which is the fifth class of transactions in the sales and collection cycle, obviously relates to the write-off of uncollectible accounts. However, because the estimation of bad debts is based on the year-end accounts receivable balances, the auditor evaluates the estimate for uncollectible accounts as part of the tests of details of ending accounts receivable balances.

EFFECT OF RESULTS OF TESTS OF CONTROLS AND SUBSTANTIVE TESTS OF TRANSACTIONS

The results of the tests of controls and substantive tests of transactions have a significant effect on the remainder of the audit, especially on substantive tests of details of balances. The parts of the audit most affected by the tests of controls and substantive tests of transactions for the sales and collection cycle are the balances in accounts receivable, cash, bad debt expense, and allowance for doubtful accounts.

Furthermore, if the test results are unsatisfactory, it is necessary to do additional substantive testing of sales, sales returns and allowances, write-off of uncollectible accounts, and processing cash receipts. Auditors of companies must also consider the impact of the unsatisfactory test results on the audit of internal control over financial reporting.

At the completion of the tests of controls and substantive tests of transactions, auditors must analyze each exception, for both public and nonpublic audits, to determine its cause and the implication of the exception on assessed control risk, which may affect the supported detection risk and related remaining substantive tests. The methodology and implications of exceptions analysis are explained more fully in the next chapter.

The most significant effect of the results of the tests of controls and substantive tests of transactions in the sales and collection cycle is on the confirmation of accounts receivable. The type of confirmation, the size of the sample, and the timing of the test are all affected. The effect of the tests on accounts receivable, bad debt expense, and allowance for uncollectible accounts is considered in Chapter 16.

Figure 14-9 illustrates the major accounts in the sales and collection cycle and the types of audit tests used to audit these accounts. This figure was introduced in the preceding chapter (page 430) and is presented here for further review.

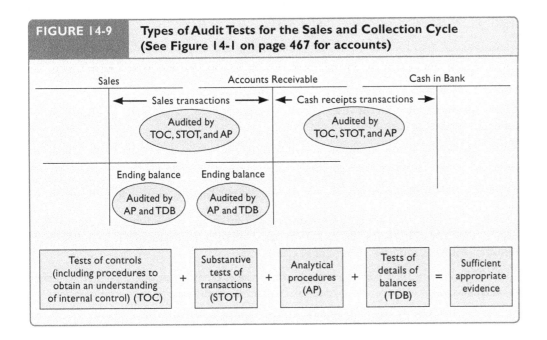

FIGURE 14-9 Types of Audit Tests for the Sales and Collection Cycle (See Figure 14-1 on page 467 for accounts)

SUMMARY

This chapter deals with designing tests of controls and substantive tests of transactions for each of the five classes of transactions in the sales and collection cycle, including sales, cash receipts, sales returns and allowances, write-off of uncollectible accounts receivable, and bad debt expense.

The methodology for designing tests of controls and substantive tests of transactions is, in concept, the same for each of the five classes of transactions and includes the following steps:

- Understand internal control
- Assess planned control risk
- Determine the extent of testing controls
- Design tests of controls and substantive tests of transactions to meet transaction-related audit objectives

In designing tests of controls for each class of transactions, auditors focus on testing internal controls that they intend to rely upon to reduce control risk. First, the auditor identifies internal controls, if any exist, for each transaction-related audit objective. After assessing control risk for each objective, the auditor then determines the extent of tests of controls that must be performed. The more the controls are applied and effective, the fewer substantive tests of transactions are undertaken.

For audits of public companies, extensive tests of controls must be performed to ensure the accuracy of the accounts balance as a large number of shareholders rely on the audited financial statement for their investment decisions. This is the basis for the auditor's report on internal control over financial reporting. For audits of nonpublic companies, the decision to perform tests of controls is based on the effectiveness of controls and the extent to which the auditor intends to rely on them to reduce control risk.

The auditor also designs substantive tests of transactions for each class of transactions to determine whether the monetary amounts of transactions are correctly recorded. Like tests of controls, substantive tests of transactions are designed for each transaction-related audit objective.

After the design of tests of controls and substantive tests of transactions for each audit objective and each class of transactions is completed, the auditor organizes the audit procedures into an audit program. The purpose of this audit program is to help the auditor complete the audit tests efficiently.

ESSENTIAL TERMS

Business functions for the sales
and collection cycle   p. 467

Classes of transactions in the sales
and collection cycle   p. 466

Lapping of accounts receivable   p. 487

Proof of cash receipts   p. 487

Sales and collection cycle   p. 466

REVIEW QUESTIONS

14-1 (Objective 14-2) Describe the nature of the following documents and records and explain their use in the sales and collection cycle: bill of lading, sales invoice, credit memo, remittance advice, monthly statement to customers.

14-2 (Objective 14-2) Explain the importance of proper credit approval for sales. What effect do adequate controls in the credit function have on the auditor's evidence accumulation?

14-3 (Objective 14-2) Distinguish between the sales journal and the accounts receivable master file. What type of information is recorded in each and how do these accounting records relate?

14-4 (Objective 14-2) BestSellers.com sells fiction and nonfiction books to customers through the company's website. Customers place orders for books via the website by providing their name, address, credit card number, and expiration date. What internal controls could BestSellers.com implement to ensure that shipments of books occur only for customers who have the ability to pay for those books? At what point will BestSellers.com be able to record the sale as revenue?

14-5 (Objective 14-3) List the transaction-related audit objectives for the audit of sales transactions. For each objective, state one internal control that the client can use to reduce the likelihood of misstatements.

14-6 (Objective 14-3) State one test of control and one substantive test of transactions that the auditor can use to verify the following sales transaction-related audit objective: Recorded sales are stated at the proper amounts.

14-7 (Objective 14-3) List the most important duties that should be segregated in the sales and collection cycle. Explain why it is desirable that each duty be segregated.

14-8 (Objective 14-3) Explain how prenumbered shipping documents and sales invoices can be useful controls for preventing misstatements in sales.

14-9 (Objective 14-3) What three types of authorizations are commonly used as internal controls for sales? For each authorization, state a substantive test that the auditor could use to verify whether the control was effective in preventing misstatements.

14-10 (Objective 14-3) Explain the purpose of footing and cross-footing the sales journal and tracing the totals to the general ledger.

14-11 (Objective 14-4) What is the difference between the auditor's approach in verifying sales returns and allowances and that for sales? Explain the reasons for the difference.

14-12 (Objective 14-5) Explain why auditors usually emphasize the detection of fraud in the audit of cash receipts. Is this consistent or inconsistent with the auditor's responsibility in the audit? Explain.

14-13 (Objective 14-5) List the transaction-related audit objectives for the verification of cash receipts. For each objective, state one internal control that the client can use to reduce the likelihood of misstatements.

14-14 (Objective 14-5) List several audit procedures that the auditor can use to determine whether all cash received was recorded.

14-15 (Objective 14-5) Explain what is meant by a proof of cash receipts and state its purpose.

14-16 (Objective 14-5) Explain what is meant by lapping and discuss how the auditor can uncover it. Under what circumstances should the auditor make a special effort to uncover lapping?

14-17 (Objective 14-6) What audit procedures are most likely to be used to verify accounts receivable written off as uncollectible? State the purpose of each of these procedures.

14-18 (Objectives 14-3, 14-5) State the relationship between the confirmation of accounts receivable and the results of the tests of controls and substantive tests of transactions.

14-19 (Objectives 14-3, 14-5) Under what circumstances is it acceptable to perform tests of controls and substantive tests of transactions for sales and cash receipts at an interim date?

14-20 (Objective 14-3) Elie Khoury, CPA, performed tests of controls and substantive tests of transactions for sales for the month of March in an audit of the financial statements for the year ended December 31, 2011. Based on the excellent results of both the tests of controls and the substantive tests of transactions, he decided to significantly reduce his substantive tests of details of balances at year-end. Evaluate this decision.

MULTIPLE CHOICE QUESTIONS FROM CPA EXAMINATIONS

14-21 (Objectives 14-3, 14-4, 14-5, 14-6) The following questions deal with internal controls in the sales and collection cycle. Choose the best response.

a. When a customer fails to include a remittance advice with a payment, it is common for the person opening the mail to prepare one. Consequently, mail should be opened by which of the following four company employees?
   (1) Credit manager   (3) Accounts receivable clerk
   (2) Sales manager   (4) Receptionist

b. A key internal control in the sales and collection cycle is the separation of duties between cash handling and record keeping. The objective most directly associated with this control is to verify that
   (1) cash receipts recorded in the cash receipts journal are reasonable.
   (2) cash receipts are correctly classified.
   (3) recorded cash receipts result from legitimate transactions.
   (4) existing cash receipts are recorded.

c. Company personnel account for the sequence of shipping documents and verify that an entry for each shipment is included in the sales journal. This control relates most directly to the sales transaction-related audit objective of
   (1) occurrence.   (3) completeness.
   (2) accuracy.   (4) timing.

14-22 (Objectives 14-3, 14-4) For each of the following types of misstatements (parts a through d), select the control that should have prevented the misstatement:

a. A manufacturing company received a substantial sales return in the last month of the year, but the credit memorandum for the return was not prepared until after the auditors had completed their testing. The returned merchandise was included in the physical inventory.

    (1) Aged trial balance of accounts receivable is prepared.

    (2) Credit memoranda are prenumbered and all numbers are accounted for.

    (3) A reconciliation of the trial balance of customers' accounts with the general ledger control is prepared periodically.

    (4) Receiving reports are prepared for all materials received and such reports are accounted for on a regular basis.

b. Which of the following controls most likely will be effective in offsetting the tendency of sales personnel to maximize sales volume at the expense of high bad debt write-offs?

    (1) Employees responsible for authorizing sales and bad debt write-offs are denied access to cash.

    (2) Shipping documents and sales invoices are matched by an employee who does not have the authority to write off bad debts.

    (3) Employees involved in the credit-granting function are separated from the sales function.

    (4) Subsidiary accounts receivable records are reconciled to the control account by an employee independent of the authorization of credit.

c. A sales invoice for US\$5,200 was computed correctly but, by mistake, was key-entered as US\$2,500 to the sales journal and to the accounts receivable master file. The customer remitted only US\$2,500, the amount on his monthly statement.

    (1) Prelistings and predetermined totals are used to control postings.

    (2) Sales invoice numbers, prices, discounts, extensions, and footings are independently checked.

    (3) The customers' monthly statements are verified and mailed by a responsible person other than the bookkeeper who prepared them.

    (4) Unauthorized remittance deductions made by customers or other matters in dispute are investigated promptly by a person independent of the accounts receivable function.

d. Copies of sales invoices show different unit prices for apparently identical items.

    (1) All sales invoices are checked as to all details after their preparation.

    (2) Differences reported by customers are satisfactorily investigated.

    (3) Statistical sales data are compiled and reconciled with recorded sales.

    (4) All sales invoices are compared with the customers' purchase orders.

14-23 (Objectives 14-1, 14-3) The following questions deal with audit evidence for the sales and collection cycle. Choose the best response.

a. An auditor is performing substantive tests of transactions for sales. One step is to trace a sample of debit entries from the accounts receivable master file back to the supporting duplicate sales invoices. What will the auditor intend to establish by this step?

    (1) Sales invoices represent existing sales.

    (2) All sales have been recorded.

    (3) All sales invoices have been correctly posted to customer accounts.

    (4) Debit entries in the accounts receivable master file are correctly supported by sales invoices.

b. To verify that all sales transactions have been recorded, a substantive test of transactions should be completed on a representative sample drawn from

    (1) entries in the sales journal.

    (2) the billing clerk's file of sales orders.

    (3) a file of duplicate copies of sales invoices for which all prenumbered forms in the series have been accounted.

    (4) the shipping clerk's file of duplicate copies of bills of lading.

c. Which audit procedure is most effective in testing credit sales for overstatement?

    (1) Trace a sample of postings from the sales journal to the sales account in the general ledger.

    (2) Vouch a sample of recorded sales from the sales journal to shipping documents.

    (3) Prepare an aging of accounts receivable.

    (4) Trace a sample of initial sales orders to sales recorded in the sales journal.

DISCUSSION QUESTIONS AND PROBLEMS

14-24 (Objectives 14-2, 14-3, 14-4, 14-5) Items 1 through 9 are selected questions of the type generally found in internal control questionnaires used by auditors to obtain an understanding of internal control in the sales and collection cycle. In using the questionnaire for a client, a "yes" response to a question indicates a possible internal control, whereas a "no" indicates a potential deficiency.

1. Are sales invoices independently compared with customers' orders for prices, quantities, extensions, and footings?
2. Are sales orders, invoices, and credit memoranda issued and filed in numerical sequence and are the sequences accounted for periodically?
3. Are the selling and cash register functions independent of the cash receipts, shipping, delivery, and billing functions?
4. Are sales generated through the company's website automatically recorded in the sales system?
5. Are all Certificates of Deposits (COD), scrap, equipment, and cash sales accounted for in the same manner as charge sales and is the record keeping independent of the collection procedure?
6. Is the collection function independent of and does it constitute a check on billing and recording sales?
7. Are accounts receivable master files balanced regularly to control accounts by an employee independent of billing functions?
8. Are cash receipts recorded by persons independent of the mail-opening and receipts-listing functions?
9. Are receipts deposited intact daily on a timely basis?

a. For each of the preceding questions, state the transaction-related audit objectives being fulfilled if the control is in effect.   **Required**
b. For each control, list a test of control to test its effectiveness.
c. For each of the preceding questions, identify the nature of the potential financial misstatements.
d. For each of the potential misstatements in part c, list the type of audit evidence required to determine whether a material misstatement exists.

14-25 (Objectives 14-3, 14-4, 14-5) The following are commonly performed tests of controls and substantive tests of transactions audit procedures in the sales and collection cycle:

1. Account for a sequence of shipping documents and examine each one to make sure that a duplicate sales invoice is attached.
2. Account for a sequence of sales invoices and examine each one to make sure that a duplicate copy of the shipping document is attached.
3. Compare the quantity and description of items on shipping documents with the related duplicate sales invoices.
4. Trace recorded sales in the sales journal to the related accounts receivable master file and compare the customer name, date, and amount for each one.
5. Examine sales returns for approval by an authorized official.
6. Review the prelisting of cash receipts to determine whether cash is prelisted daily.
7. Reconcile the recorded cash receipts on the prelisting with the cash receipts journal and the bank statement for a one-month period.

a. Identify whether each audit procedure is a test of control or a substantive test of transactions.   **Required**
b. State which of the seven transaction-related audit objectives each of the audit procedures fulfills.
c. Identify the type of evidence used for each audit procedure, such as confirmation and observation.

14-26 (Objective 14-3) The following are possible errors and fraud involving sales (1 through 8) and controls (a through k) that may prevent or detect the errors and fraud:

Possible Errors or Fraud

1. Invoices for goods sold are posted to incorrect customer accounts.
2. Goods ordered by customers are shipped, but are not billed to anyone.
3. Invoices are sent for shipped goods, but are not recorded in the sales journal.
4. Invoices are sent for shipped goods and are recorded in the sales journal, but are not posted to any customer account.
5. Credit sales are made to individuals with unsatisfactory credit ratings.
6. Goods are removed from inventory for unauthorized orders.
7. Goods shipped to customers do not agree with goods ordered by customers.
8. Invoices are sent to colluding parties in a fraudulent scheme and sales are recorded for fictitious transactions.

Controls

a. Shipping clerks compare goods received from the warehouse with the details on the shipping documents.
b. Approved sales orders are required for goods to be removed from the warehouse.
c. Monthly statements are mailed to all customers with outstanding balances.
d. Shipping clerks compare goods received from the warehouse with approved sales orders.
e. Customer orders are compared with the inventory master file to determine whether items ordered are in stock.
f. Daily sales summaries are compared with control totals of invoices.
g. Shipping documents are compared with sales invoices when goods are shipped.
h. Sales invoices are compared with shipping documents and approved customer orders before invoices are mailed.
i. Customer orders are compared to an approved customer list.
j. Sales orders are prepared for each customer order.
k. Control amounts posted to the accounts receivable ledger are compared with control totals of invoices.

Required   For each error or fraud, select one internal control that, if properly designed and implemented, most likely would be effective in preventing or detecting the errors and fraud. Each response in the list of controls may be used once, more than once, or not at all.[13]

14-27 (Objectives 14-3, 14-5) The following are common audit procedures for tests of sales and cash receipts:

1. Compare the quantity and description of items on duplicate sales invoices with related shipping documents.
2. Trace recorded cash receipts in the accounts receivable master file to the cash receipts journal and compare the customer name, date, and amount of each one.
3. Examine duplicate sales invoices for an indication that unit selling prices were compared to the approved price list.
4. Examine duplicate sales invoices to determine whether the account classification for sales has been included on the document.
5. Examine the sales journal for related-party transactions, notes receivable, and other unusual items.
6. Select a sample of customer orders and trace the document to related shipping documents, sales invoices, and the accounts receivable master file for comparison of name, date, and amount.

7. Perform a proof of cash receipts.
8. Examine a sample of remittance advices for approval of cash discounts.
9. Account for a numerical sequence of remittance advices and determine whether there is a cross-reference mark for each one, indicating that it has been recorded in the cash receipts journal.

a. Identify whether each audit procedure is a test of control or substantive test of trans-   **Required**
actions.

b. State which transaction-related audit objective(s) each of the audit procedures fulfills.

c. For each test of control in part a, state a substantive test that could be used to determine whether there was a monetary misstatement.

14-28 (Objectives 14-2, 14-3) The following sales procedures were encountered during the annual audit of Metro Distribution Company. Customer orders are received by the sales order department. A clerk computes the approximate dollar amount of the order and sends it to the credit department for approval. Credit approval is stamped on the order and sent to the accounting department. A computer is then used to generate two copies of a sales invoice. The order is filed in the customer order file.

The customer copy of the sales invoice is held in a pending file awaiting notification that the order was shipped. The shipping copy of the sales invoice is routed through the warehouse, and the shipping department has authority for the respective departments to release and ship the merchandise. Shipping department personnel pack the order and manually prepare a three-copy bill of lading: The original copy is mailed to the customer, the second copy is sent with the shipment, and the other is filed in sequence in the bill of lading file. The sales invoice shipping copy is sent to the accounting department with any changes resulting from lack of available merchandise.

A clerk in accounting matches the received sales invoice shipping copy with the sales invoice customer copy from the pending file. Quantities on the two invoices are compared and prices are compared to an approved price list. The customer copy is then mailed to the customer, and the shipping copy is sent to the data processing department.

The data processing clerk in accounting enters the sales invoice data into the computer, which is used to prepare the sales journal and update the accounts receivable master file. She files the shipping copy in the sales invoice file in numerical sequence.

a. To determine whether the internal controls operated effectively to minimize instances   **Required**
of failure to post invoices to customers' accounts receivable master file, the auditor would select a sample of transactions from the population represented by the
(1) customer order file.   (3) customers' accounts receivable master file.
(2) bill of lading file.   (4) sales invoice file.

b. To determine whether the internal controls operated effectively to minimize instances of failure to invoice a shipment, the auditor would select a sample of transactions from the population represented by the
(1) customer order file.   (3) customers' accounts receivable master file.
(2) bill of lading file.   (4) sales invoice file.

c. To gather audit evidence that uncollected items in customers' accounts represented existing trade receivables, the auditor would select a sample of items from the population represented by the
(1) customer order file.   (3) customers' accounts receivable master file.
(2) bill of lading file.   (4) sales invoice file.[14]

14-29 (Objectives 14-3, 14-5) Items 1 through 10 present various internal control strengths or internal control deficiencies.

1. Credit is granted by a credit department.
2. Sales returns are presented to a sales department clerk who prepares a written, prenumbered receiving report.

3. Statements are sent monthly to customers.
4. Write-offs of accounts receivable are approved by the controller.
5. Cash receipts received in the mail are received by a secretary with no record-keeping responsibility.
6. Cash receipts received in the mail are forwarded unopened with remittance advices to accounting.
7. The cash receipts journal is prepared by the treasurer's department.
8. Cash is deposited weekly.
9. Once shipment occurs and is recorded in the sales journal, all shipping documents are marked 'recorded' by the accounting staff.
10. The bank reconciliation is prepared by individuals independent of cash receipts record-keeping.

Required

a. For each of the preceding 1–10 items, indicate whether the item represents an:
  (1) internal control strength for the sales and collection cycle.
  (2) internal control deficiency for the sales and collection cycle.

b. For each item that you answered (1), indicate the transaction-related audit objective(s) to which the control relates.

c. For each item that you answered (2), indicate the nature of the deficiency.[15]

ACL PROBLEM

14-30 (Objectives 14-4, 14-5) This problem requires the use of ACL software, which is included in the MyAccountingLab. Information about installing and using ACL and solving this problem can be found in the Appendix, pages 855–859. You should read all of the reference material preceding the instructions for 'Quick Sort' before locating the appropriate command to answer questions a–e. For this problem use the Metaphor_AR_2002 file in ACL_Demo. The suggested command or other source of information needed to solve the problem requirement is included at the end of each question.

Required

a. Determine the total number and amount of September 2002 transactions in the file. (Filter, Count, and Total Field)

b. Determine and print the total amount for each of the five types of 2002 transactions for comparison to the general ledger. (Summarize) Which transaction type has the highest count?

c. For sales invoices (IN), determine the number of transactions, total amount, largest amount, and average size. (Filter and Statistics)

d. Determine the number of days difference between the invoice date (DATE1) and the due date (DUE) for sales invoices (IN) and evaluate the internal controls over these two dates. (Computed Field)

e. To better decide the sales invoices to select for testing, you decide to stratify 2002 sales invoices (IN) after excluding all invoices less than US$300. Print the output. (Filter and Stratify)

MYLAB ACTIVITIES

Visit the MyAccountingLab and complete the following activities:
→ Integrated Case Application: Pinnacle Manufacturing: Part IV
→ Internet Problem 14-1: Point of Sales Systems Controls

AUDIT SAMPLING FOR TESTS OF CONTROLS AND SUBSTANTIVE TESTS OF TRANSACTIONS

LEARNING OBJECTIVES

After studying this chapter,
you should be able to

15-1 Explain the concept of representative sampling.

15-2 Distinguish between statistical and nonstatistical sampling and between probabilistic and non-probabilistic sample selection.

15-3 Select representative samples.

15-4 Define and describe audit sampling for exception rates.

15-5 Use nonstatistical sampling in tests of controls and substantive tests of transactions.

15-6 Define and describe attributes sampling and a sampling distribution.

15-7 Use attributes sampling in tests of controls and substantive tests of transactions.

If You Are Not Going To Believe It, Don't Use It

El Gabry & Co., CPAs, uses random samples when performing audit tests whenever possible. They believe that this gives them the best chance of getting representative samples of their clients' accounting information. In the audit of Halab Manufacturing Products, a random sample of 30 inventory items was taken from a population of 1,800 items for testing unit and total costs. Only 1 of the 30 items was in error, but it was large. In investigating the error, Nabil Ghanam, the audit staff person doing the test, was told by Halab Manufacturing Products' controller that the error occurred while the regular inventory clerk was on vacation and was really only an isolated error.

Nabil knew auditing standards require errors in random samples to be projected to the entire population. In this case, such a projection involved multiplying the error found by a factor of 60 (1,800 divided by 30). This would result in an audit adjustment or additional audit work. Nabil knew that the client would not be happy about this because the adjustment would reduce an already 'strained' net income figure and additional auditing would increase the audit fee. If the error was, in fact, an isolated one, it would not be significant enough to require an audit adjustment.

Nabil decided to look at the situation in terms of the probability of the error being an isolated occurrence. He calculated the odds to be about 1 in 60 for a sample of 30 from a population of 1,800 to include an isolated error. He then looked at accepting the client's representation about the uniqueness of the error as a bet. If he accepted the representation and didn't do the projection and act on it, he was in effect betting his career on a situation where the odds were 60 to 1 against him. It didn't take Nabil long to recognize the wisdom of the professional standards and conclude that the projection should be done.

Audit sampling

Testing less than 100 percent of a population for the purpose of making inferences about that population.

Chapter 14 dealt with designing tests of controls and substantive tests of transactions for tests of the sales and collection cycle. Before these tests can be performed, the auditor needs to decide for each audit procedure the sample size and sample items to select from the population. When the auditor decides to select less than 100 percent of the population for testing to make inferences about the population, it is called **audit sampling**. As demonstrated by the story about El Gabry & Co., CPAs, evaluating audit samples is an essential and often challenging part of auditing. When is a sample size sufficiently large to evaluate a population? Does a given sample accurately represent the accounting information? This chapter discusses sampling issues such as these for tests of controls and substantive tests of transactions. The discussion is limited to the sales and collection cycle, but the sampling concepts apply equally to all other cycles.

Relevant International Standards on Auditing	
ISA 200	Overall Objectives of the Independent Auditor and the Conduct of an Audit in Accordance with International Standards on Auditing
ISA 230	Audit Documentation
ISA 300	Planning an Audit of Financial Statements
ISA 320	Materiality in Planning and Performing an Audit
ISA 450	Evaluation of Misstatements Identified during the Audit
ISA 500	Audit Evidence
ISA 530	Audit Sampling

REPRESENTATIVE SAMPLES

OBJECTIVE 15-1

Explain the concept of representative sampling.

Representative sample

A sample with characteristics the same as those of the population.

When selecting a sample from a population, the auditor strives to obtain a representative sample. A **representative sample** is one in which the characteristics in the sample are approximately the same as those of the population. This means that the sampled items are similar to the items not sampled. Assume a client's internal controls require a clerk to attach a shipping document to every duplicate sales invoice, but the clerk fails to follow the procedure exactly 3 percent of the time. If the auditor selects a sample of 100 duplicate sales invoices and finds three are missing attached shipping documents, the sample is highly representative. If two or four such items are found in the sample, the sample is reasonably representative. If no or many missing items are found, the sample is nonrepresentative.

In practice, auditors never know whether a sample is representative, even after all testing is complete. (The only way to know if a sample is representative is to subsequently audit the entire population.) However, auditors can increase the likelihood of a sample being representative by using care in designing the sampling process, sample selection, and evaluation of sample results. A sample result can be nonrepresentative due to nonsampling error or sampling error. The risk of these two types of errors occurring is called nonsampling risk and sampling risk. Both of these can be controlled.

Nonsampling risk

The risk that the auditor fails to identify existing exceptions in the sample; nonsampling risk (nonsampling error) is caused by failure to recognize exceptions and by inappropriate or ineffective audit procedures.

Nonsampling risk is the risk that audit tests do not uncover existing exceptions in the sample. The two causes of nonsampling risk are the auditor's failure to recognize exceptions and inappropriate or ineffective audit procedures.

An auditor might fail to recognize an exception because of exhaustion, boredom, or lack of understanding of what to look for. In the preceding example, assume three shipping documents were not attached to duplicate sales invoices in a sample of 100. If the auditor concluded that no exceptions existed, that is a nonsampling error.

An ineffective audit procedure for detecting the exceptions in question would be to examine a sample of shipping documents and determine whether each is attached to a duplicate sales invoice, rather than to examine a sample of duplicate sales invoices to determine if shipping documents are attached. In this case, the auditor has done the test in the wrong direction by starting with the shipping document instead of the duplicate sales invoice. Careful design of audit procedures, proper instruction, supervision, and review are ways to control nonsampling risk.

Sampling risk is the risk that an auditor reaches an incorrect conclusion because the sample is not representative of the population. Sampling risk is an inherent part of sampling that results from testing less than the entire population. For example, assume the auditor decided that a control is not effective if there is a population exception rate of 6 percent. Assume the auditor accepts the control as effective based on tests of the control with a sample of 100 items that had two exceptions. If the population actually has an 8 percent exception rate, the auditor incorrectly accepted the population because the sample was not sufficiently representative of the population.

Auditors have two ways to control sampling risk:

1. Adjust sample size
2. Use an appropriate method of selecting sample items from the population

Increasing sample size reduces sampling risk, and vice versa. At one extreme, a sample of all the items of a population has a zero sampling risk. At the other extreme, a sample of one or two items has an extremely high sampling risk.

Using an appropriate sample selection method increases the likelihood of representativeness. This does not eliminate or even reduce sampling risk, but it does allow the auditor to measure the risk associated with a given sample size if statistical methods of sample selection and evaluation are used.

Sampling risk

Risk of reaching an incorrect conclusion inherent in tests of less than the entire population because the sample is not representative of the population; sampling risk may be reduced by using an increased sample size and an appropriate method of selecting sample items from the population.

STATISTICAL VERSUS NONSTATISTICAL SAMPLING AND PROBABILISTIC VERSUS NONPROBABILISTIC SAMPLE SELECTION

Before discussing the methods of sample selection to obtain representative samples, it is useful to make distinctions between statistical versus nonstatistical sampling, and probabilistic versus nonprobabilistic sample selection.

OBJECTIVE 15-2

Distinguish between statistical and nonstatistical sampling and between probabilistic and nonprobabilistic sample selection.

Statistical Versus Nonstatistical Sampling

Audit sampling methods can be divided into two broad categories: statistical sampling and nonstatistical sampling. These categories are similar in that they both involve three phases:

1. Plan the sample
2. Select the sample and perform the tests
3. Evaluate the results

The purpose of planning the sample is to make sure that the audit tests are performed in a manner that provides the desired sampling risk and minimizes the likelihood of nonsampling error. Selecting the sample involves deciding how a sample is selected from the population. The auditor can perform the audit tests only after the sample items are selected. Evaluating the results is the drawing of conclusions based on the audit tests.

Assume that an auditor selects a sample of 100 duplicate sales invoices from a population, tests each to determine whether a shipping document is attached, and determines that there are three exceptions. Let's look at those actions step-by-step:

Action	Step
• Decide that a sample size of 100 is needed.	1. Plan the sample
• Decide which 100 items to select from the population. • Perform the audit procedure for each of the 100 items and determine that three exceptions exist.	2. Select the sample Perform the tests
• Reach conclusions about the likely exception rate in the total population when the sample exception rate equals 3 percent.	3. Evaluate the results

Statistical sampling

The use of mathematical measurement techniques to calculate formal statistical results and quantify sampling risk.

Nonstatistical sampling

The auditor's use of professional judgment to select sample items, estimate the population values, and estimate sampling risk.

Statistical sampling differs from nonstatistical sampling in that, by applying mathematical rules, auditors can quantify (measure) sampling risk in planning the sample (step 1) and in evaluating the results (step 3). (You may remember calculating a statistical result at a 95 percent confidence level in a statistics course. A 95 percent confidence level provides a 5 percent sampling risk.)

In **nonstatistical sampling**, auditors do not quantify sampling risk. Instead, auditors select sample items they believe will provide the most useful information, given the circumstances, and reach conclusions about populations on a judgmental basis. For that reason, the use of nonstatistical sampling is often termed judgmental sampling.

Probabilistic Versus Nonprobabilistic Sample Selection

Probabilistic sample selection

A method of selecting a sample such that each population item has a known probability of being included in the sample and the sample is selected by a random process.

Nonprobabilistic sample selection

A method of sample selection in which the auditor uses professional judgment to select items from the population.

Both probabilistic and nonprobabilistic sample selection fall under step 2. When using **probabilistic sample selection** the auditor randomly selects items such that each population item has a known probability of being included in the sample. This process requires great care and uses one of several methods discussed shortly. In **nonprobabilistic sample selection**, the auditor selects sample items using professional judgment rather than probabilistic methods. Auditors can use one of several nonprobabilistic sample selection methods.

Applying Statistical and Nonstatistical Sampling in Practice and Sample Selection Methods

Auditing standards permit auditors to use either statistical or nonstatistical sampling methods. However, it is essential that either method be applied with due care. All steps of the process must be followed carefully. When statistical sampling is used, the sample *must be a probabilistic one* and appropriate statistical evaluation methods must be used with the sample results to make the sampling risk computations. Auditors may make nonstatistical evaluations when using probabilistic selection, but it is never acceptable to evaluate a nonprobabilistic sample using statistical methods.

Three types of sample selection methods are commonly associated with nonstatistical audit sampling. All three methods are nonprobabilistic. Four types of sample selection methods are commonly associated with statistical audit sampling. All four methods are probabilistic.

Nonprobabilistic (judgmental) sample selection methods include the following:

1. Directed sample selection
2. Block sample selection
3. Haphazard sample selection

Probabilistic sample selection methods include the following:

1. Simple random sample selection
2. Systematic sample selection
3. Probability proportional to size sample selection
4. Stratified sample selection

We will now discuss each of these seven sample selection methods, starting with nonprobabilistic methods.

NONPROBABILISTIC SAMPLE SELECTION METHODS

Nonprobabilistic sample selection methods are those that do not meet the technical requirements for probabilistic sample selection. Because these methods are not based on mathematical probabilities, the representativeness of the sample may be difficult to determine.

Directed Sample Selection

In **directed sample selection** auditors deliberately select each item in the sample based on their own judgmental criteria instead of using random selection. Commonly used approaches include:

Items Most Likely to Contain Misstatements Auditors are often able to identify which population items are most likely to be misstated. Examples are accounts receivable outstanding for a long time, purchases from and sales to officers and affiliated companies, obsolete inventory items, allowance for legal claims, outstanding tax payable, and unusually large or complex transactions. The auditor can efficiently investigate these types of items and the results can be applied to the population judgmentally. In evaluating such samples, auditors typically reason that if none of the items selected is misstated, it is unlikely that the population is materially misstated.

Items Containing Selected Population Characteristics By selecting one or more items with different population characteristics, the auditor may be able to design the sample to be representative. For example, the auditor might select a sample of cash disbursements that includes some from each month, each bank account or location, and each major type of acquisition.

Large Currency (Dollar, Dinar, Pounds, Riyal) Coverage Auditors can sometimes select a sample that includes a large portion of total population currency and thereby reduce the risk of drawing an improper conclusion by not examining small items. This is a practical approach on many audits, especially smaller ones, where a few population items make up a large portion of the total population value. Some statistical sampling methods are also designed to accomplish the same effect.

Block Sample Selection

In **block sample selection** auditors select the first item in a block, and the remainder of the block is chosen in sequence. For example, assume the block sample will be a sequence of 100 sales transactions from the sales journal for the third week of March. Auditors can select the total sample of 100 by taking 5 blocks of 20 items, 10 blocks of 10, 50 blocks of 2 or one block of 100.

It is ordinarily acceptable to use block samples only if a reasonable number of blocks is used. If few blocks are used, the probability of obtaining a nonrepresentative

Directed sample selection

A nonprobabilistic method of sample selection in which each item in the sample is selected based on some judgmental criteria established by the auditor.

Block sample selection

A nonprobabilistic method of sample selection in which items are selected in measured sequences.

sample is too great, considering the possibility of employee turnover, changes in the accounting system, and the seasonal nature of many businesses. For example, in the previous example, sampling 10 blocks of 10 from the third week of March is far less appropriate than selecting 10 blocks of 10 from 10 different months.

Block sampling can also be used to supplement other samples when there is a high likelihood of misstatement for a known period. For example, the auditor might select all 100 cash receipts from the third week of March if that is when the accounting clerk was on vacation and an inexperienced temporary employee processed the cash receipt transactions.

Haphazard Sample Selection

Haphazard sample selection

A nonprobabilistic method of sample selection in which items are chosen without regard to their size, source, or other distinguishing characteristics.

Haphazard sample selection is the selection of items without any conscious bias by the auditor. In such cases, the auditor selects population items without regard to their size, source, or other distinguishing characteristics.

The most serious shortcoming of haphazard sample selection is the difficulty of remaining completely unbiased in the selection. Because of the auditor's training and unintentional bias, certain population items are more likely than others to be included in the sample.

Although haphazard and block sample selection appear to be less logical than directed sample selection, they are often useful in situations where the cost of more complex sample selection methods outweighs the benefits obtained from using these approaches. For example, assume that the auditor wants to trace credits from the accounts receivable master files to the cash receipts journal and other authorized sources as a test for fictitious credits in the master files. In this situation, many auditors use a haphazard or block approach, because it is simpler and much less costly than other selection methods.

PROBABILISTIC SAMPLE SELECTION METHODS

OBJECTIVE 15-3

Select representative samples.

Statistical sampling requires a probabilistic sample to measure sampling risk. For probabilistic samples, the auditor uses no judgment about which sample items are selected, except in choosing which of the four selection methods to use.

Simple Random Sample Selection

Random sample

A sample in which every possible combination of elements in the population has an equal chance of constituting the sample.

In a simple **random sample** selection, every possible combination of population items has an equal chance of being included in the sample. Auditors use simple random sampling to sample populations when there is no need to emphasize one or more types of population items. Say, for example, auditors want to sample a client's cash disbursements for the year. They might select a simple random sample of 60 items from the cash disbursements journal, apply appropriate auditing procedures to the 60 items selected, and draw conclusions about all recorded cash disbursement transactions.

Random number table

A listing of independent random digits conveniently arranged in tabular form to facilitate the selection of random numbers with multiple digits.

Random Number Tables   When auditors obtain a simple random sample, they must use a method that ensures all items in the population have an equal chance of selection. Suppose an auditor decides to select a sample from a total of 12,000 cash disbursement transactions for the year. A simple random sample of one transaction will be such that each of the 12,000 transactions has an equal chance of being selected. The auditor will select one random number between 1 and 12,000. Assume that number is 3,895. The auditor will select and test only the 3,895th cash disbursement transaction. For a random sample of 100, each population item also has an equal chance of being selected.

Random numbers are a series of digits that have equal probabilities of occurring over long runs and which have no identifiable pattern. A **random number table** has random digits in table form with numbered rows and columns. The auditor chooses a random sample by first establishing a correspondence between the client's document numbers to be selected and the digits in the random number table. After selecting a random starting point, the auditor reads down the table and finds the first random number that falls within the sequence of the document numbers being tested. The process continues until the final sample item is selected.

Computer Generation of Random Numbers Auditors most often generate random samples by using one of three computer selection techniques: electronic spreadsheets, random number generators, and generalized audit software.

Computer programs offer several advantages: time savings, reduced likelihood of auditor error in selecting the numbers, and automatic documentation.

Figure 15-1 shows the random selection of sales invoices for the audit of Arabian Hardware Co. using an electronic spreadsheet program. In the example, the auditor wants 50 sample items from a population of sales invoices numbered from 3689 to 9452. The program requires only input parameters to create a sample for the auditor to select. Programs possess great flexibility, and are able to generate random dates or ranges of sets of numbers (such as page and line numbers or check numbers for multiple bank accounts), and provide output in either sorted or selection order.

Random numbers may be obtained with or without replacement. With replacement means an element in the population can be included in the sample more than once. In selection without replacement, an item can be included only once. Although both selection approaches are consistent with sound statistical theory, auditors rarely use replacement sampling.

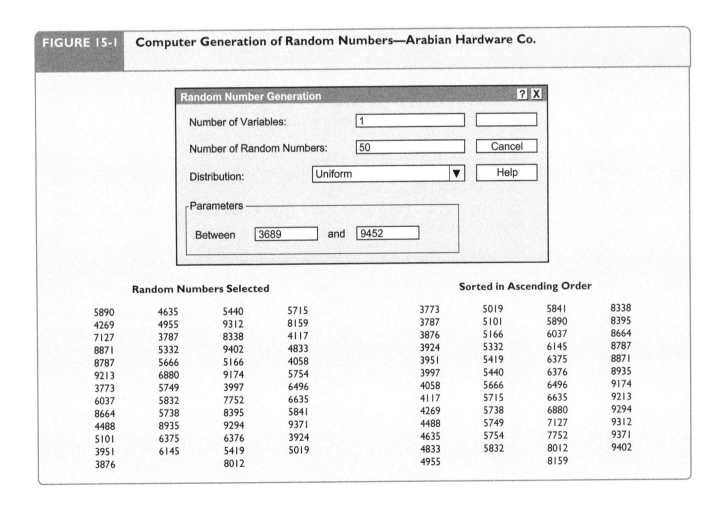

FIGURE 15-1   Computer Generation of Random Numbers—Arabian Hardware Co.

Random Number Generation

Number of Variables: 1

Number of Random Numbers: 50   Cancel

Distribution: Uniform   Help

Parameters

Between 3689 and 9452

Random Numbers Selected

5890	4635	5440	5715
4269	4955	9312	8159
7127	3787	8338	4117
8871	5332	9402	4833
8787	5666	5166	4058
9213	6880	9174	5754
3773	5749	3997	6496
6037	5832	7752	6635
8664	5738	8395	5841
4488	8935	9294	9371
5101	6375	6376	3924
3951	6145	5419	5019
3876		8012	

Sorted in Ascending Order

3773	5019	5841	8338
3787	5101	5890	8395
3876	5166	6037	8664
3924	5332	6145	8787
3951	5419	6375	8871
3997	5440	6376	8935
4058	5666	6496	9174
4117	5715	6635	9213
4269	5738	6880	9294
4488	5749	7127	9312
4635	5754	7752	9371
4833	5832	8012	9402
4955		8159	

Systematic Sample Selection

In **systematic sample selection** (also called systematic sampling), the auditor calculates an interval and then selects the items for the sample based on the size of the interval. The interval is determined by dividing the population size by the desired sample size. In a population of sales invoices ranging from 652 to 3151, with a desired sample size of 125, the interval is 20 [(3,151 − 651)/125]. The auditor first selects a random number between 0 and 19 (the interval size) to determine the starting point for the sample. If the randomly selected number is 9, the first item in the sample will be invoice number 661 (652 + 9). The remaining 124 items will be 681 (661 + 20), 701 (681 + 20), and so on through to item 3141.

The advantage of systematic selection is its ease of use. In most populations, a systematic sample can be drawn quickly and the approach automatically puts the numbers in sequence, making it easy to develop the appropriate documentation.

A concern with systematic selection is the possibility of bias. Because of the way systematic selection is done, once the first item in the sample is selected, all other items are chosen automatically. This causes no problem if the characteristic of interest, such as a possible control deviation, is distributed randomly throughout the population, which may not always be the case. For example, if a control deviation occurred at a certain time of the month or only with certain types of documents, a systematic sample can have a higher likelihood of failing to be representative than a simple random sample. Therefore, when auditors use systematic selection, they must consider possible patterns in the population data that can cause sample bias.

Probability Proportional to Size and Stratified Sample Selection

In many auditing situations, it is advantageous to select samples that emphasize population items with larger recorded amounts. There are two ways to obtain such samples:

1. Take a sample in which the probability of selecting any individual population item is proportional to its recorded amount. This method is called sampling with probability proportional to size (PPS), and it is evaluated using nonstatistical sampling or monetary unit statistical sampling.
2. Divide the population into subpopulations, usually by dollar size, and take larger samples from the subpopulations with larger sizes. This is called stratified sampling, and it is evaluated using nonstatistical sampling or variables statistical sampling.

These selection methods and their related evaluation methods are discussed in more detail in Chapter 17.

SAMPLING FOR EXCEPTION RATES

Auditors use sampling for tests of controls and substantive tests of transactions to estimate the percent of items in a population containing a characteristic or **attribute** of interest. This percent is called the **occurrence rate** or **exception rate**. For example, if an auditor determines that the exception rate for the internal verification of sales invoices is approximately 3 percent, then on average 3 of every 100 invoices are not properly verified.

Auditors are interested in the following types of exceptions in populations of accounting data:

1. Deviations from client's established controls
2. Monetary misstatements in populations of transaction data
3. Monetary misstatements in populations of account balance details

Knowing the exception rate is particularly helpful for the first two types of exceptions, which involve transactions. Therefore, auditors make extensive use of audit sampling that measures the exception rate in doing tests of controls and substantive tests of transactions. With the third type of exception, auditors usually need to estimate the total dollar amount of the exceptions because they must decide whether the misstatements are material. When auditors want to know the total amount of a misstatement, they use methods that measure dollars, not the exception rate.

The exception rate in a sample is used to estimate the exception rate in the entire population, meaning it is the auditor's 'best estimate' of the population exception rate. The term *exception* should be understood to refer to both deviations from the client's control procedures and amounts that are not monetarily correct, whether because of an unintentional accounting error or any other cause. The term *deviation* refers specifically to a departure from prescribed controls.

Assume, for example, that the auditor wants to determine the percentage of duplicate sales invoices that do not have shipping documents attached. Because the auditor cannot check every invoice, the actual percentage of missing shipping documents remains unknown. The auditor obtains a sample of duplicate sales invoices and determines the percentage of the invoices that do not have shipping documents attached. The auditor then concludes that the sample exception rate is the best estimate of the population exception rate.

Because the exception rate is based on a sample, there is a significant likelihood that the sample exception rate differs from the actual population exception rate. This difference is called the *sampling error*. The auditor is concerned with both the estimate of the sampling error and the reliability of that estimate, called *sampling risk*. Assume the auditor determines a 3 percent sample exception rate, and a sampling error of 1 percent, with a sampling risk of 10 percent. The auditor can state that the interval estimate of the population exception rate is between 2 percent and 4 percent (3 percent $\pm$ 1) with a 10 percent risk of being wrong (and a 90 percent chance of being right).

In using audit sampling for exception rates, the auditor wants to know the *most* the exception rate is likely to be, rather than the width of the confidence interval. So, the auditor focuses on the upper limit of the interval estimate, which is called the estimated or **computed upper exception rate (CUER)** in tests of controls and substantive tests of transactions. Using figures from the preceding example, an auditor might conclude that the CUER for missing shipping documents is 4 percent at a 5 percent sampling risk, meaning the auditor concludes that the exception rate in the population is no greater than 4 percent with a 5 percent risk of the exception rate exceeding 4 percent. Once it is calculated, the auditor can consider CUER in the context of specific audit objectives. If testing for missing shipping documents, for example, the auditor must determine whether a 4 percent exception rate indicates an acceptable control risk for the occurrence objective.

In many Arab countries, tax authorities are in the process of applying systems for selecting tax returns for testing according to a system where only a sample of transactions is being examined by the tax inspectors.

Exception rate

The percent of items in a population that include exceptions in prescribed controls or monetary correctness.

Computed upper exception rate (CUER)

The upper limit of the probable population exception rate; the highest exception rate in the population at a given ARACR.

APPLICATION OF NONSTATISTICAL AUDIT SAMPLING

We will now examine the application of nonstatistical audit sampling in testing transactions for control deviations and monetary misstatements. Statistical sampling is examined later in this chapter. Before doing so, key terminology are defined and summarized in Table 15-1. The same terminology is used for statistical sampling.

Auditors use 14 well-defined steps to apply audit sampling to tests of controls and substantive tests of transactions. These steps are divided into the three phases described earlier. Auditors should follow these steps carefully to ensure proper application of

OBJECTIVE 15-5

Use nonstatistical sampling in tests of controls and substantive tests of transactions.

TABLE 15-1	Terms Used in Audit Sampling

Term	Definition
Terms Related to Planning	
Characteristics or attribute	The characteristic being tested in the application
Acceptable risk of assessing control risk too low (ARACR)	The risk that the auditor is willing to take of accepting a control as effective or a rate of monetary misstatements as tolerable, when the true population exception rate is greater than the tolerable exception rate
Tolerable exception rate (TER)	Exception rate that the auditor will permit in the population and still be willing to conclude the control is operating effectively and/or the amount of monetary misstatements in the transactions established during planning is acceptable
Estimated population exception rate (EPER)	Exception rate that the auditor expects to find in the population before testing begins
Initial sample size	Sample size decided after considering the above factors in planning
Terms Related to Evaluating Results	
Exception	Exception from the attribute in a sample item
Sample exception rate (SER)	Number of exceptions in the sample divided by the sample size
Computed upper exception rate (CUER)	The highest estimated exception rate in the population at a given ARACR

both the auditing and sampling requirements. We use the example audit of Arabian Hardware Co. to illustrate the steps in the following discussion.

Plan the Sample

1. State the objectives of the audit test.
2. Decide whether audit sampling applies.
3. Define attributes and exception conditions.
4. Define the population.
5. Define the sampling unit.
6. Specify the tolerable exception rate.
7. Specify acceptable risk of assessing control risk too low.
8. Estimate the population exception rate.
9. Determine the initial sample size.

Select the Sample and Perform the Audit Procedures

10. Select the sample.
11. Perform the audit procedures.

Evaluate the Results

12. Generalize from the sample to the population.
13. Analyze exceptions.
14. Decide the acceptability of the population.

State the Objectives of the Audit Test

The objectives of the test must be stated in terms of the transaction cycle being tested. Typically, auditors define the objectives of tests of controls and substantive tests of transactions:

- Test the operating effectiveness of controls
- Determine whether the transactions contain monetary misstatements

The objectives of these tests in the sales and collection cycle are usually to test the effectiveness of internal controls over sales and cash receipts and to determine whether sales and cash receipts transactions contain monetary misstatements. Auditors normally define these objectives as a part of designing the audit program, which was discussed for the sales and collection cycle in Chapter 14. You can find the audit program for the sales and collection cycle for Arabian Hardware Co. in Figure 14-8.

Decide Whether Audit Sampling Applies

Audit sampling applies whenever the auditor plans to reach conclusions about a population based on a sample. The auditor should examine the audit program and select those audit procedures where audit sampling applies. To illustrate, assume the following partial audit program:

1. Review sales transactions for large and unusual amounts (analytical procedure).
2. Observe whether the duties of the accounts receivable clerk are separate from handling cash (test of control).
3. Examine a sample of duplicate sales invoices for
   a. credit approval by the credit manager (test of control).
   b. existence of an attached shipping document (test of control).
   c. inclusion of a chart of accounts number (test of control).
4. Select a sample of shipping documents and trace each to related duplicate sales invoices (test of control).
5. Compare the quantity on each duplicate sales invoice with the quantity on related shipping documents (substantive test of transactions).

Audit sampling does not apply for the first two procedures in this audit program. The first is an analytical procedure for which sampling is inappropriate. The second is an observation procedure for which no documentation exists to perform audit sampling. Audit sampling can be used for the remaining three procedures. Table 15-2 indicates the audit procedures for the sales cycle for Arabian Hardware Co. where audit sampling is appropriate.

Define Attributes and Exception Conditions

When audit sampling is used, auditors must carefully define the characteristics (attributes) being tested and the exception conditions. Unless they carefully define each attribute in advance, the staff person who performs the audit procedures will have no guidelines to identify exceptions.

Attributes of interest and exception conditions for audit sampling are taken directly from the auditor's audit procedures. Table 15-3 shows nine attributes of interest and exception conditions taken from audit procedures 12 through 14 in the audit of Arabian Hardware's billing function. Samples of sales invoices will be used to verify these attributes. The absence of the attribute for any sample item will be an exception for that attribute. Both missing documents and immaterial misstatements result in exceptions unless the auditor specifically states otherwise in the exception conditions.

Define the Population

The population is those items about which the auditor wishes to generalize. Auditors can define the population to include any items they want, but when they select the sample, it must be selected from the entire population as it has been defined. The auditor should test the population for completeness and detail tie-in before a sample is selected to ensure that all population items are subjected to sample selection.

The auditor may generalize *only* about that population that has been sampled. For example, when performing tests of controls and substantive tests of sales transactions, the auditor generally defines the population as all recorded sales invoices for the year. If the auditor samples from only one month's transactions, it is invalid to draw conclusions about the invoices for the entire year.

The auditor must carefully define the population in advance, consistent with the objectives of the audit tests. In some cases, it may be necessary to define separate populations for different audit procedures. For example, in the audit of the sales and collection cycle for Arabian Hardware Co., the direction of testing in audit procedures 12 through 14 (in Table 15-2) proceeds from sales invoices in the sales journal to source documentation.

TABLE 15-2	Audit Procedures—Arabian Hardware Co.
Procedure	**Comment**
Shipment of Goods	
10. Account for a sequence of shipping documents.	It is possible to do this by selecting a random sample and accounting for all shipping documents selected. This requires a separate set of random numbers because the sampling unit is different from that used for the other tests.
11. Trace selected shipping documents to the sales journal to be sure that each one has been included.	No exceptions are expected, and a 6 percent TER is considered acceptable at an ARACR of 10 percent. A sample size of 40 is selected. The shipping documents are traced to the sales journal. This is done for all 40 items. There are no exceptions for either test. The results are considered acceptable. There is no further information about this portion of the tests in this illustration.
Billing of Customers and Recording the Sales in the Records	
12. Account for a sequence of sales invoices in the sales journal.	The audit procedures for billing and recording sales (procedures 12 to 14) are the only ones included for illustration throughout this chapter.
13. Trace selected sales invoice numbers from the sales journal to a. accounts receivable master file and test for amount, date, and invoice number. b. duplicate sales invoice and check for the total amount recorded in the journal, date, customer name, and account classification. Check the pricing, extensions, and footings. Examine underlying documents for indication of internal verification. c. bill of lading and test for customer name, product description, quantity, and date. d. duplicate sales order and test for customer name, product description, quantity, date, and indication of internal verification. e. customer order and test for customer name, product description, quantity, date, and credit approval.	
14. Trace recorded sales from the sales journal to the file of supporting documents, which includes a duplicate sales invoice, bill of lading, sales order, and customer order.	

Note: Random selection and statistical sampling are not applicable for the nine general audit procedures in Figure 14-8 (p. 486). Advanced statistical techniques, such as regression analysis, can be applicable for analysis of the results of analytical procedures. Random selection can be used for procedure 2.

In contrast, the direction of testing for audit procedures 10 and 11 proceeds from the shipping documents to the sales journal. Thus, the auditor defines two populations—a population of sales invoices in the sales journal and a population of shipping documents.

Define the Sampling Unit

The sampling unit is defined by the auditor based on the definition of the population and objective of the audit test. The sampling unit is the physical unit that corresponds to the random numbers the auditor generates. It is often helpful to think of the sampling unit as the starting point for doing the audit tests. For the sales and collection cycle, the sampling unit is typically a sales invoice or shipping document number. For example, if the auditor wants to test the occurrence of sales, the appropriate sampling unit is sales invoices recorded in the sales journal. If the objective is to determine whether the quantity of the goods described on the customer's order is accurately shipped and billed, the auditor can define the sampling unit as the customer's order, the shipping document, or the duplicate sales invoice, because the direction of the audit test doesn't matter for this audit procedure.

TABLE 15-3	Attributes Defined—Tests of Arabian Hardware Co.'s Billing Function
Attribute	**Exception Condition**
1. Existence of the sales invoice number in the sales journal (procedure 12).	No record of sales invoice number in the sales journal.
2. Amount and other data in the master file agree with sales journal entry (procedure 13a).	The amount recorded in the master file differs from the amount recorded in the sales journal.
3. Amount and other data on the duplicate sales invoice agree with the sales journal entry (procedure 13b).	Customer name and account number on the invoice differ from the information recorded in the sales journal.
4. Evidence that pricing, extensions, and footings are checked (initials and correct amounts) (procedure 13b).	Lack of initials indicating verification of pricing, extensions, and footings.
5. Quantity and other data on the bill of lading agree with the duplicate sales invoice and sales journal (procedure 13c).	Quantity of goods shipped differs from quantity on the duplicate sales invoice.
6. Quantity and other data on the sales order agree with the duplicate sales invoice (procedure 13d).	Quantity on the sales order differs from the quantity on the duplicate sales invoice.
7. Quantity and other data on the customer order agree with the duplicate sales invoice (procedure 13e).	Product number and description on the customer order differ from information on the duplicate sales invoice.
8. Credit is approved (procedure 13e).	Lack of initials indicating credit approval.
9. For recorded sales in the sales journal, the file of supporting documents includes a duplicate sales invoice, bill of lading, sales order, and customer order (procedure 14).	Bill of lading is not attached to the duplicate sales invoice and the customer order.

Audit procedure 14 in Table 15-2 is a test for the occurrence of recorded sales. What is the appropriate sampling unit? It is the duplicate sales invoice. Is the appropriate sampling unit for audit procedure 11 the shipping document? Yes, because this tests that existing sales are recorded (completeness). Either the duplicate sales invoice or the shipping document is appropriate for audit procedures 13a through 13e because these are all nondirectional tests.

To perform audit procedures 12 through 14, the auditor will define the sampling unit as the duplicate sales invoice. Audit procedures 10 and 11 will have to be tested separately using a sample of shipping documents.

Specify the Tolerable Exception Rate

Establishing the **tolerable exception rate** for each attribute requires an auditor's professional judgment. TER represents the highest exception rate the auditor will permit in the control being tested and still be willing to conclude the control is operating effectively (and/or the rate of monetary misstatements in the transactions is acceptable). For example, assume that the auditor decides that TER for attribute 8 in Table 15-3 is 9 percent. That means that the auditor has decided that even if 9 percent of the duplicate sales invoices are not approved for credit, the credit approval control is still effective in terms of the assessed control risk included in the audit plan.

The suitable TER is a question of materiality and is therefore affected by both the definition and the importance of the attribute in the audit plan. If only one internal control is used to support a low control risk assessment for an objective, TER will be lower for the attribute than if multiple controls are used to support a low control risk assessment for the same objective.

Tolerable exception rate (TER)

The exception rate that the auditor will permit in the population and still be willing to conclude the control is operating effectively and/or the amount of monetary misstatements in the transactions established during planning is acceptable.

TER can have a significant impact on sample size. A larger sample size is needed for a low TER than for a high TER. For example, a larger sample size is needed for the test of credit approval (attribute 8) if the TER is decreased from 9 percent to 6 percent. Since a lower TER is used for significant account balances, the auditor requires a larger sample size to gather sufficient evidence about the effectiveness of the control or absence of monetary misstatements.

Most auditors use some type of preprinted form to document each sampling application. Figure 15-2 shows one example of a commonly used form. Notice that the top part of the form includes a definition of the objective, the population, and the sampling unit.

| **FIGURE 15-2** | **Sampling Data Sheet: Tests of Arabian Hardware Co.'s Billing Function** |

Client: Arabian Hardware   **Year-end:** 12/31/12
Audit Area: Tests of Controls and Substantive Tests of Transactions—   **Pop. size:** 5,764
Billing Function

Define the objective(s): Examine duplicate sales invoices and related documents to determine whether the system has functioned as intended and as described in the audit program.

Define the population precisely (including stratification, if any): Sales invoices for the period 1/1/12 to 10/31/12. First invoice number = 3689. Last invoice number = 9452.

Define the sampling unit, organization of population items, and random selection procedures: Sales invoice number, recorded in the sales journal sequentially; computer generation of random numbers.

Description of Attributes	Planned Audit				Actual Results			
	EPER	TER	ARACR	Initial sample size	Sample size	Number of exceptions	Sample exception rate	Calculated sampling error (TER − SER)
1. Existence of the sales invoice number in the sales journal (procedure 12).	0	4	Low	75				
2. Amount and other data in the master file agree with sales journal entry (procedure 13a).	1	5	Low	100				
3. Amount and other data on the duplicate sales invoice agree with the sales journal entry (procedure 13b).	1	5	Low	100				
4. Evidence that pricing, extensions, and footings are checked (initials and correct amounts) (procedure 13b).	1	5	Low	100				
5. Quantity and other data on the bill of lading agree with the duplicate sales invoice and sales journal (procedure 13c).	1	5	Low	100				
6. Quantity and other data on the sales order agree with the duplicate sales invoice (procedure 13d).	1	7	Low	65				
7. Quantity and other data on the customer order agree with the duplicate sales invoice (procedure 13e).	1.5	9	Low	50				
8. Credit is approved (procedure 13e).	1.5	9	Low	50				
9. For recorded sales in the sales journal, the file of supporting documents includes a duplicate sales invoice, bill of lading, sales order, and customer order (procedure 14).	1	7	Low	65				

Intended use of sampling results:

1. Effect on Audit Plan:

2. Recommendations to Management:

Auditors determine the TER for each attribute being tested in audit procedures 12 through 14 in Table 15-3 by deciding what exception rate is material. As Figure 15-2, indicates:

- For attribute 1, the failure to record a sales invoice would be highly significant, so the lowest TER (4 percent) is chosen.
- For attributes 2–5, the incorrect billing to a customer and recording the transaction is potentially significant, but no misstatement is likely to be for the full amount of the invoice. As a result, the auditor chose a 5 percent TER for each of these attributes.
- Attributes 6–9 have higher TERs because they are of less importance in the audit.

Specify Acceptable Risk of Assessing Control Risk Too Low

Whenever auditors take a sample, they risk making incorrect conclusions about the population. Unless 100 percent of the population is tested, this is true for both nonstatistical and statistical sampling.

For audit sampling in tests of controls and substantive tests of transactions, that risk is called the **acceptable risk of assessing control risk too low (ARACR)**. ARACR measures the risk the auditor is willing to take of accepting a control as effective (or a rate of misstatements as tolerable) when the true population exception rate is greater than TER. ARACR represents the auditor's measure of sampling risk. Assume that TER is 6 percent, ARACR is high, and the true population exception rate is 8 percent. The control in this case is not acceptable because the true exception rate of 8 percent exceeds TER. The auditor, of course, does not know the true population exception rate. The ARACR of high means that the auditor is willing to take a fairly substantial risk of concluding that the control is effective after all testing is completed, even when it is ineffective. If the control were found to be effective in this illustration, the auditor would have overrelied on the system of internal control (used a lower assessed control risk than was justified).

In choosing the appropriate ARACR for each attribute, auditors must use their best judgment. Their main consideration is the extent to which they plan to reduce assessed control risk as a basis for the extent of tests of details of balances. Auditors normally assess ARACR at a lower level when auditing a new company because the auditor needs to be confident that the internal controls are effective to support the opinion on financial statements. In audits of private companies, the appropriate ARACR and extent of tests of controls depend on assessed control risk. For audits where there is extensive reliance on internal control, control risk will be assessed at low and therefore ARACR will also be low.

For nonstatistical sampling, it is common for auditors to use ARACR of high, medium, or low instead of a percentage. For statistical sampling it is common for auditors to use a percent, such as 5 percent or 10 percent. A low ARACR implies that the tests of controls are important and will correspond to a low assessed control risk and reduced substantive tests of details of balances. As summarized in Figure 15-2, ARACR for the audit of the billing function at Arabian Hardware Co. is assessed as low for all attributes, because it is a listed company and the auditor's tests of controls must provide a basis for the opinion on financial statements.

Like for TER, there is an inverse relationship between ARACR and planned sample size. If the auditor reduces ARACR from high to low, planned sample size must be increased. ARACR represents the auditor's risk of incorrectly accepting the control as effective, and a larger sample size is required to lower this risk.

The auditor can establish different TER and ARACR levels for different attributes of an audit test, depending on the importance of the attribute and related control. For example, auditors commonly use higher TER and ARACR levels for tests of credit approval than for tests of the occurrence of duplicate sales invoices and bills of lading.

Acceptable risk of assessing control risk too low (ARACR)

The risk that the auditor is willing to take of accepting a control as effective or a rate of monetary misstatements as tolerable when the true population exception rate is greater than the tolerable exception rate.

TABLE 15-4	Guidelines for ARACR and TER for Nonstatistical Sampling: Tests of Controls	
Factor	**Judgment**	**Guideline**
Assessed control risk. Consider:	• Lowest assessed control risk	• ARACR of low
Need to issue a separate report on internal control over financial reporting for public companies	• Moderate assessed control risk	• ARACR of medium
Nature, extent, and timing of substantive tests (extensive planned substantive tests relate to higher assessed control risk and vice versa)	• Higher assessed control risk	• ARACR of high
Quality of evidence available for tests of controls (a lower quality of evidence available results in a higher assessed control risk and vice versa)	• 100% assessed control risk	• ARACR is not applicable
Significance of the transactions and related account balances that the internal controls are intended to affect	• Highly significant balances	• TER of 4%
	• Significant balances	• TER of 5%
	• Less significant balances	• TER of 6%

Note: The guidelines should recognize that there may be variations in ARACRs based on audit considerations. The guidelines above are the most conservative that should be followed.

This makes sense because the exceptions for the latter are likely to have a more direct impact on the correctness of the financial statements than the former.

Tables 15-4 and 15-5 present illustrative guidelines for establishing TER and ARACR. The guidelines should not be interpreted as representing broad professional standards. However, they are typical of the types of guidelines CPA firms issue to their staff.

Estimate the Population Exception Rate

Estimated population exception rate (EPER)

Exception rate the auditor expects to find in the population before testing begins.

Auditors should make an advance estimate of the population exception rate to plan the appropriate sample size. If the **estimated population exception rate** is low, a relatively small sample size will satisfy the auditor's tolerable exception rate, because a less precise estimate is required.

Auditors often use the preceding year's audit results to estimate EPER. If prior-year results are not available, or if they are considered unreliable, the auditor can take a small preliminary sample of the current year's population for this purpose. It is not critical that the estimate be precise because the current year's sample exception rate is ultimately used to estimate the population characteristics. If a preliminary sample is used, it can be included in the total sample, as long as appropriate sample selection

TABLE 15-5	Guidelines for ARACR and TER for Nonstatistical Sampling: Substantive Tests of Transactions			
Planned Reduction in Substantive Tests of Details of Balances	**Results of Understanding Internal Control and Tests of Controls**	**ARACR for Substantive Tests of Transactions**	**TER for Substantive Tests of Transactions**	
Large	Excellent[1]	High	Percent or amount based on materiality considerations for related accounts	
	Good	Medium		
	Not good	Low		
Moderate	Excellent[1]	High	Percent or amount based on materiality considerations for related accounts	
	Good	Medium		
	Not good	Medium-low		
Small[2]	Excellent[1]	High	Percent or amount based on materiality considerations for related accounts	
	Good	Medium-high		
	Not good	Medium		

Note: The guidelines should also recognize that there may be variations in ARACRs based on audit considerations. The guidelines above are the most conservative that should be followed.

[1] In this situation, both internal control and evidence about it are good. Substantive tests of transactions are least likely to be performed in this situation.

[2] In this situation, little emphasis is being placed on internal controls. Neither tests of controls nor substantive tests of transactions are likely in this situation.

procedures are followed. In the Arabian Hardware Co. audit, the estimated population exception rates for the attributes in Figure 15-2 are based on the previous year's results, modified slightly to account for the change in personnel.

Determine the Initial Sample Size

Four factors determine the **initial sample size** for audit sampling: population size, TER, ARACR, and EPER. Population size is not a significant factor and typically can be ignored, especially for large populations. Auditors using nonstatistical sampling decide the sample size using professional judgment rather than using a statistical formula. Once the three major factors affecting sample size have been determined, the auditor can decide an initial sample size. It is called an initial sample size because the exceptions in the actual sample must be evaluated before auditors can decide whether the sample is sufficiently large to achieve the objectives of the tests.

Initial sample size

Sample size determined by professional judgment (nonstatistical sampling) or by statistical tables (attributes sampling).

Sensitivity of Sample Size to a Change in the Factors To understand the concepts underlying sampling in auditing, you need to understand the effect of increasing or decreasing any of the four factors that determine sample size, while the other factors are held constant. Table 15-6 shows the effect on sample size of independently increasing each factor. The opposite effect will occur for decreasing each factor.

A combination of two factors has the greatest effect on sample size: TER minus EPER. The difference between the two factors is the *precision* of the initial sample estimate. A smaller precision, which is called a more precise estimate, requires a larger sample. At one extreme, assume TER is 4 percent and EPER is 3 percent. In this case, precision is 1 percent, which will result in a large sample size. Now assume TER is 8 percent and EPER is zero for an 8 percent precision. In this case the sample size can be small and still give the auditor confidence that the actual exception rate is less than 8 percent, assuming no exceptions are found when auditing the sample.

Figure 15-2 summarizes the different sample sizes selected for testing attributes 1 through 9 for the Arabian audit. The largest sample (a size of 100) is selected for tests of attributes 2 through 5, because of the degree of precision required. For those attributes, the difference between TER and EPER is smallest, thus requiring a larger sample size than attributes 6 through 9. Although the difference between TER and EPER for attribute 1 is the same as that between attributes 2 through 5, the EPER of zero justifies a smaller sample of 75 items. Because a less precise estimate is needed (TER minus EPER is larger) for attributes 7 and 8, a sample size of only 50 items is needed.

Select the Sample

After auditors determine the initial sample size for the audit sampling application, they must choose the items in the population to include in the sample. Auditors can choose the sample using any of the probabilistic or nonprobabilistic methods we discussed earlier in this chapter. To minimize the possibility of the client altering the sample items, the auditor should not inform the client too far in advance of the sample items selected. The auditor should also control the sample after the client provides the documents.

TABLE 15-6	Effect on Sample Size of Changing Factors
Type of Change	**Effect on Initial Sample Size**
Increase acceptable risk of assessing control risk too low	Decrease
Increase tolerable exception rate	Decrease
Increase estimated population exception rate	Increase
Increase population size	Increase (minor effect)

Several additional sample items may be selected as extras to replace any voided items in the original sample.

The random selection for the Arabian audit procedures is straightforward except for the different sample sizes needed for different attributes. To overcome this problem, auditors can select a random sample of 50 for use on all nine attributes, followed by another sample of 15 for all attributes except attributes 7 and 8, an additional 10 for attributes 1 through 5, and 25 more for attributes 2 through 5.

Figure 15-1 illustrates the selection of the first 50 sample items for the company's audit using computer generation of random numbers.

Perform the Audit Procedures

The auditor performs the audit procedures by examining each item in the sample to determine whether it is consistent with the definition of the attribute and by maintaining a record of all the exceptions found. When audit procedures have been completed for a sampling application, the auditor will have a sample size and number of exceptions for each attribute.

To document the tests and provide information for review, auditors commonly include a schedule of the results. Some auditors prefer to include a schedule listing all items in the sample; others prefer to limit the documentation to identifying the exceptions. This latter approach is followed in Figure 15-3.

Generalize from the Sample to the Population

Sample exception rate (SER)

Number of exceptions in the sample divided by the sample size.

The **sample exception rate** can be easily calculated from the actual sample results. SER equals the actual number of exceptions divided by the actual sample size. Figure 15-3 summarizes the exceptions found for tests of attributes 1 through 9. In this example, the auditor found zero exceptions for attribute 1 and two exceptions for attribute 2, making the SER 0 percent ($0 \div 75$) for attribute 1, and 2 percent for attribute 2 ($2 \div 100$).

It is improper for the auditor to conclude that the population exception rate is exactly the same as the SER, as there is only a slight chance they are identical. For nonstatistical methods, auditors use two ways to generalize from the sample to the population.

1. Add an estimate of sampling error to SER to arrive at a CUER for a given ARACR. It is extremely difficult for auditors to make sampling error estimates using nonstatistical sampling because of the judgment required to do so; therefore, they usually do not use this approach.
2. Subtract the SER from the tolerable exception rate to find the calculated sampling error (TER – SER), and evaluate whether it is sufficiently large to conclude that the true population exception rate is acceptable. Under this approach, the auditor does not make an estimate of the CUER. Most auditors using nonstatistical sampling follow this approach. For example, if an auditor takes a sample of 100 items for an attribute and finds no exceptions (SER = 0) and TER is 5 percent, calculated sampling error is 5 percent (TER of 5 percent – SER of 0 = 5 percent). If the auditors had found four exceptions, calculated sampling error would have been 1 percent (TER of 5 percent – SER of 4 percent). It is much more likely that the true population exception rate is less than or equal to the TER in the first case than in the second one. Therefore, most auditors would probably find the population acceptable based on the first sample result and not acceptable based on the second.

When SER exceeds the EPER used in designing the sample, auditors usually conclude that the sample results do not support the preliminary assessed control risk.

FIGURE 15-3	Inspection of Sample Items for Attributes

CLIENT: Arabian Hardware
INSPECTION OF SAMPLE ITEMS FOR ATTRIBUTES
YEAR-END: DECEMBER 31, 2012

Prepared by MSW
Date Nov 15, 2012

Identity of Item Selected	Attributes											X = Exception
Invoice no.	1	2	3	4	5	6	7	8	9	10	11	
3787					X							
3924				X				X				
3990				X								
4058		X		X								
4117								X				
4222					X							
4488								X				
4635				X	X							
4955						X		X				
4969				X								
5101								X				
5166								X				
5419								X				
5832								X				
5890								X				
6157		X		X								
6229				X								
6376								X				
6635					X							
7127				X								
8338								X				
8871				X								
9174								X				
9371				X								
No. Exceptions	0	2	0	10	4	1	0	12	0			
Sample Size	75	100	100	100	100	65	50	50	65			

In that case, auditors are likely to conclude that there is an unacceptably high risk that the true deviation rate in the population exceeds TER.

The auditor's consideration of whether sampling error is sufficiently large also depends on the sample size used. If the sample size in the previous example had been only 20 items, the auditor would have been much less confident that finding no exceptions was an indication that the true population exception rate does not exceed TER.

The SER and the calculated sampling error (TER − SER) for Arabian Hardware are summarized in Figure 15-4.

FIGURE 15-4   **Sampling Data Sheet: Tests of Arabian Hardware Co.'s Billing Function**

Client: Arabian Hardware   **Year-end:** 12/31/12
Audit Area: Tests of Controls and Substantive Tests of Transactions—   **Pop. size:** 5,764
Billing Function

Define the objective(s): Examine duplicate sales invoices and related documents to determine whether the system has functioned as intended and as described in the audit program.

Define the population precisely (including stratification, if any): Sales invoices for the period 1/1/12 to 10/31/12. First invoice number = 3689. Last invoice number = 9452.

Define the sampling unit, organization of population items, and random selection procedures: Sales invoice number, recorded in the sales journal sequentially; computer generation of random numbers.

Description of Attributes	Planned Audit				Actual Results			
	EPER	TER	ARACR	Initial sample size	Sample size	Number of exceptions	Sample exception rate	Calculated sampling error (TER − SER)
1. Existence of the sales invoice number in the sales journal (procedure 12).	0	4	Low	75	75	0	0	4.0
2. Amount and other data in the master file agree with sales journal entry (procedure 13a).	1	5	Low	100	100	2	2	3.0
3. Amount and other data on the duplicate sales invoice agree with the sales journal entry (procedure 13b).	1	5	Low	100	100	0	0	5.0
4. Evidence that pricing, extensions, and footings are checked (initials and correct amounts) (procedure 13b).	1	5	Low	100	100	10	10	SER exceeds TER
5. Quantity and other data on the bill of lading agree with the duplicate sales invoice and sales journal (procedure 13c).	1	5	Low	100	100	4	4	1.0
6. Quantity and other data on the sales order agree with the duplicate sales invoice (procedure 13d).	1	7	Low	65	65	1	1.5	5.5
7. Quantity and other data on the customer order agree with the duplicate sales invoice (procedure 13e).	1.5	9	Low	50	50	0	0	9.0
8. Credit is approved (procedure 13e).	1.5	9	Low	50	50	12	24	SER exceeds TER
9. For recorded sales in the sales journal, the file of supporting documents includes a duplicate sales invoice, bill of lading, sales order, and customer order (procedure 14).	1	7	Low	65	65	0	0	7.0

Intended use of sampling results:

1. Effect on Audit Plan: Controls tested through attributes 1, 3, 6, 7, and 9 can be viewed as operating effectively given the size of the allowance for sampling error (e.g. TER − SER). Additional emphasis is needed in confirmation, allowance for uncollectible accounts, cutoff tests, and price tests for the financial statement audit due to results of tests for attributes 2, 4, 5, and 8.

2. Effect on Report on Internal Control: The allowance for sampling error is too small or SER exceeds TER for attributes 2, 4, 5, and 8. These findings have been communicated to management to allow an opportunity for correction of the control deficiency to be made before year-end. If timely correction is made by management, the corrected controls will be tested before year-end for purposes of reporting on internal control over financial reporting.

3. Recommendations to Management: Each of the exceptions should be discussed with management. Specific recommendations are needed to correct the internal verification of sales invoices and to improve the approach to credit approvals.

Analyze Exceptions

In addition to determining SER for each attribute and evaluating whether the true (but unknown) exception rate is likely to exceed the TER, auditors must analyze individual exceptions to determine the breakdown in the internal controls that allowed them to happen. Exceptions can be caused by many factors, such as carelessness of employees, misunderstood instructions, or intentional failure to perform procedures. The nature of an exception and its causes have a significant effect on the qualitative evaluation of the system. For example, if all the exceptions in the tests of internal verification of sales invoices occurred while the person normally responsible for performing the tests was on vacation, this will affect the auditor's evaluation of the internal controls and the subsequent investigation differently than if the exceptions arose from the incompetence of the regular employee.

The exception analysis is illustrated for Arabian Hardware in Figure 15-5.

Decide the Acceptability of the Population

When generalizing from the sample to the population, most auditors using nonstatistical sampling subtract SER from TER and evaluate whether the difference (calculated sampling error) is sufficiently large. If the auditor concludes the difference is sufficiently large, the control being tested can be used to reduce assessed control risk as planned, assuming a careful analysis of the exceptions does not indicate the possibility of other significant problems with internal controls.

As Figure 15-4 illustrates, SER exceeds TER for attributes 4 and 8. Although SER is less than TER for attributes 2 and 5, the auditor concluded that the calculated allowance for sampling error is too small and the results of these tests are therefore also unacceptable.

When the auditor concludes that TER − SER is too small to conclude that the population is acceptable, or when SER exceeds TER, the auditor must follow one of four following courses of action.

Revise TER or ARACR This alternative should be followed only when the auditor has concluded that the original specifications were too conservative. Relaxing either TER or ARACR may be difficult to defend if the auditor is ever subject to review by a court or a commission.

Expand the Sample Size An increase in the sample size has the effect of decreasing the sampling error if the actual SER does not increase. Of course, SER may also increase or decrease if additional items are selected. Increasing the sample size is appropriate if the auditor believes the initial sample was not representative, or if it is important to obtain evidence that the control is operating effectively. This is likely if the control relates to highly significant account balances such as receivables or inventory.

Revise Assessed Control Risk If the results of the tests of controls and substantive tests of transactions do not support the preliminary assessed control risk, the auditor should revise assessed control risk upward. This will likely result in the auditor increasing substantive tests of transactions and tests of details of balances. For example, if tests of controls of internal verification procedures for verifying prices, extensions, and quantities on sales invoices indicate that those procedures are not being followed, the auditor should increase substantive tests of transactions for the accuracy of sales.

FIGURE 15-5	Analysis of Exceptions

CLIENT: Arabian Hardware
ANALYSIS OF EXCEPTIONS   **Prepared by:** MSW
YEAR-END: December 31, 2012   **Date:** Nov 15, 2012

Attribute	Number of exceptions	Nature of exceptions	Effect on the financial statement audit and other comments*
2	2	Both errors were posted to the wrong account and were still outstanding after several months. The amounts were for US$2,500 and US$7,900.	Because the allowance for sampling error is small (e.g. TER – SER), additional substantive work is needed. Perform expanded confirmation procedures and review older uncollected balances thoroughly.
4	10	—In six cases there were no initials for internal verification. —In two cases the wrong price was used but the errors were under US$200 in each case. —In one case there was a pricing error of US$5,000. —In one case freight was not charged. (Three of the last four exceptions had initials for internal verification.)	As a result, have independent client personnel recheck a random sample of 500 duplicate sales invoices under our control. Also, expand the confirmation of accounts receivable.
5	4	In each case the date on the duplicate sales invoice was several days later than the shipping date.	Do extensive tests of the sales cutoff by comparing recorded sales with the shipping documents.
6	1	Just 106 items were shipped and billed though the sales order was for 112 items. The reason for the difference was an error in the perpetual inventory master file. The perpetuals indicated that 112 items were on hand, when there were actually 106. The system does not backorder for undershipments smaller than 25%.	No expansion of tests of controls or substantive tests. The system appears to be working effectively.
8	12	Credit was not approved. Four of these were for new customers. Discussed with Chulick, who stated his busy schedule did not permit approving all sales.	Expand the year-end procedures extensively in evaluating allowance for uncollectible accounts. This includes scheduling of cash receipts subsequent to year-end for all outstanding accounts receivable to determine collectibility at year-end.

*This column documents conclusions about implications for the financial statement audit. The control deficiencies have been communicated to management to allow an opportunity for correction of the deficiency before year-end. If timely correction is made by management, the corrected controls will be tested before year-end for purposes of reporting on internal control over financial reporting.

The auditor should decide whether to increase sample size or to revise assessed control risk on the basis of cost versus benefit. If the sample is not expanded, the auditor must revise assessed control risk upward and therefore perform additional substantive tests. The cost of additional tests of controls must be compared with that of additional substantive tests. If an expanded sample continues to produce unacceptable results, additional substantive tests will still be necessary.

Communicate with the Audit Committee or Management Communication is desirable, in combination with one of the other three actions just described, regardless of the nature of the exceptions. When the auditor determines that the internal controls are not operating effectively, management should be informed in a timely manner. If the tests were performed prior to year-end, this may allow management to correct the deficiency before year-end. The auditor is required to communicate *in writing* to those charged with governance, such as the audit committee, regarding significant deficiencies and material weaknesses in internal control.

In some instances, it may be acceptable to limit the action to writing a letter to management when TER − SER is too small. This occurs if the auditor has no intention of reducing the assessed control risk or has already carried out sufficient procedures to his or her own satisfaction as a part of substantive tests of transactions.

As Figure 15-4 illustrates, in the Arabian Hardware audit, SER exceed TER for two attributes (4 and 8). Because the sales transactions tested at the company represented transactions recorded only through to October 31, 2011, timely communication of these deficiencies may allow the company management to correct the noted deficiencies in time for the auditor to test the corrected controls before year-end for purposes of auditing the internal control system.

In Figure 15-5, the last column summarizes the follow-up actions the auditor plans to do regardless of whether the control deficiencies were corrected. Because the difference between SER and TER was small for attributes 2 and 5, Figure 15-5 includes follow-up actions in the financial statement audit for those attributes. No follow-up actions are required to address the exception noted for attribute 6, given the large difference between SER and TER. The conclusions reached about each attribute are also documented at the bottom of Figure 15-4.

Adequate Documentation

The auditor needs to retain adequate records of the procedures performed, the methods used to select the sample and perform the tests, the results found in the tests, and the conclusions reached. Documentation is needed for both statistical and nonstatistical sampling to evaluate the combined results of all tests and to defend the audit if the need arises. Figures 15-2 through 15-6 illustrate the type of documentation commonly found in practice.

Figure 15-6 illustrates the evidence-planning worksheet used in the audit of Arabian Hardware to decide the tests of balances for accounts receivable. After completing tests of controls and substantive tests of transactions, the auditor should complete rows 3 through 7 of the worksheet. (You may recall that rows 1 and 2 were completed in Chapter 9.) Rows 3 through 5 document control risk for sales, cash receipts, and additional controls. The control risk assessments in Figure 15-6 are the same as the preliminary assessments in the control risk matrices for Arabian Hardware with the following modifications:

- Control risk is high for the accuracy objective for sales because of the unsatisfactory results for attribute 4 (procedure 13b).
- Control risk is high for the realizable value objective for sales based on the results for attribute 8 (procedure 13e).
- The occurrence (completeness) objective for cash receipts relates to the completeness (existence) objective for accounts receivable.

Finally, note in Figure 15-6 that all substantive tests of transactions results were satisfactory except for the accuracy and cutoff objectives for sales. Refer back to Figure 15-5 and you can see that:

- Substantive tests of transactions results for the accuracy objective were only fair because of exceptions found for attribute 2 (procedure 13a).
- Results were unacceptable for the cutoff objective because of unsatisfactory results for attribute 5 (procedure 13c).

All of the steps involved in nonstatistical sampling are summarized in Figure 15-7. Although this figure deals with nonstatistical sampling, the 14 steps in the figure also apply to statistical sampling, which is covered next.

FIGURE 15-6	Evidence-Planning Worksheet to Decide Tests of Details of Balances for Arabian Hardware Co.—Accounts Receivable

	Detail tie-in	Existence	Completeness	Accuracy	Classification	Cutoff	Realizable value	Rights
Acceptable audit risk	Medium	Medium	Medium	Medium	Medium	Medium	Medium	Medium
Inherent risk	Low	Medium	Low	Low	Low	Medium	Medium	Low
Control risk— Sales	Low	Medium	Low	High	Low	Medium	High	Not applicable
Control risk— Cash receipts	Low	Medium	Low	Low	Low	Low	Not applicable	Not applicable
Control risk— Additional controls	None	None	None	None	None	None	None	Low
Substantive tests of transactions— Sales	Good results	Good results	Good results	Fair results	Good results	Unacceptable results	Not applicable	Not applicable
Substantive tests of transactions— Cash receipts	Good results	Good results	Good results	Good results	Good results	Good results	Not applicable	Not applicable
Analytical procedures								
Planned detection risk for tests of details of balances								
Planned audit evidence for tests of details of balances								

Tolerable misstatement <u>US$265,000</u>

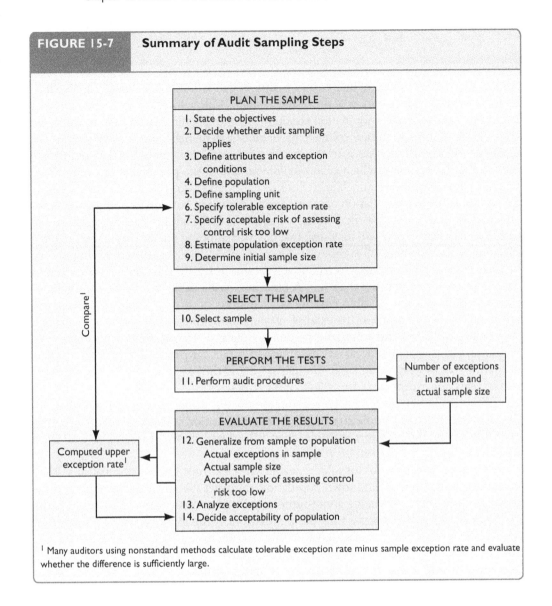

FIGURE 15-7 | **Summary of Audit Sampling Steps**

PLAN THE SAMPLE
1. State the objectives
2. Decide whether audit sampling applies
3. Define attributes and exception conditions
4. Define population
5. Define sampling unit
6. Specify tolerable exception rate
7. Specify acceptable risk of assessing control risk too low
8. Estimate population exception rate
9. Determine initial sample size

SELECT THE SAMPLE
10. Select sample

PERFORM THE TESTS
11. Perform audit procedures

Number of exceptions in sample and actual sample size

EVALUATE THE RESULTS
12. Generalize from sample to population
   Actual exceptions in sample
   Actual sample size
   Acceptable risk of assessing control risk too low
13. Analyze exceptions
14. Decide acceptability of population

Computed upper exception rate[1]

Compare[1]

[1] Many auditors using nonstandard methods calculate tolerable exception rate minus sample exception rate and evaluate whether the difference is sufficiently large.

STATISTICAL AUDIT SAMPLING

The statistical sampling method most commonly used for tests of controls and substantive tests of transactions is **attributes sampling.** (When the term *attributes sampling* is used in this text, it refers to attributes statistical sampling. Nonstatistical sampling also has attributes, which are the characteristics being tested for in the population, but attributes sampling is a statistical method.)

The application of attributes sampling for tests of controls and substantive tests of transactions has far more similarities to nonstatistical sampling than differences. The same 14 steps are used for both approaches, and the terminology is essentially the same. The main differences are the calculation of initial sample sizes using tables developed from statistical probability distributions and the calculation of estimated upper exception rates using tables similar to those for calculating sample sizes.

OBJECTIVE 15-6

Define and describe attributes sampling and a sampling distribution.

Attributes sampling

A statistical, probabilistic method of sample evaluation that results in an estimate of the proportion of items in a population containing a characteristic or attribute of interest.

SAMPLING DISTRIBUTION

Sampling distribution

A frequency distribution of the results of all possible samples of a specified size that could be obtained from a population containing some specific parameters.

Auditors base their statistical inferences on sampling distributions. A **sampling distribution** is a frequency distribution of the results of all possible samples of a specified size that could be obtained from a population containing some specific characteristics. Sampling distributions allow the auditor to make probability statements about the likely representativeness of any sample that is in the distribution. Attributes sampling is based on the binomial distribution, in which each possible sample in the population has one of two possible values, such as yes/no, black/white, or control deviation/no control deviation.

Assume that in a population of sales invoices, 5 percent have no shipping documents attached as required by the client's internal controls. If the auditor takes a sample of 50 sales invoices, how many will be found that have no shipping documents? Simple multiplication would estimate 2.5 exceptions (5 percent of 50), but that number is impossible because there is no such thing as half an exception. In reality, the sample could contain no exceptions or even more than ten. A binomial-based sampling distribution tells us the probability of each possible number of exceptions occurring. Table 15-7 illustrates the sampling distribution for the example population with a sample of 50 items from a very large population and an exception rate of 5 percent. To calculate the probability of obtaining a sample with at least one exception, subtract the probability of no exceptions occurring from 1 (100 percent). By doing so, we find the likelihood of finding a sample with at least one exception is 1 − .0769, or 92.31 percent.

Each population exception rate and sample size has a unique sampling distribution. The distribution for a sample size of 100 from a population with a 5 percent exception rate differs from the previous example, as will the distribution for a sample of 50 from a population with a 3 percent exception rate.

Of course, auditors do not take repeated samples from known populations. They take one sample from an unknown population and get a specific number of exceptions in that sample. But knowledge about sampling distributions enables auditors to make statistically valid statements about the population. If the auditor selects a sample of 50 sales invoices to test for attached shipping documents and finds one exception, the auditor could examine the probability table in Table 15-7 and know there is a 20.25 percent probability that the sample came from a population with a 5 percent exception rate, and a 79.75 percent (1 − .2025) probability that the sample was taken from a population having some other exception rate. Based on the cumulative probabilities column in Table 15-7, an auditor could estimate a 27.94 percent probability that the sample came from a population with more than a 5 percent exception rate and a 72.06 percent (1 − .2794) probability that the sample was taken from a population having an

TABLE 15-7	Probability of Each Exception Rate—5 Percent Population Exception Rate and Sample Size of 50		
Number of Exceptions	Percentage of Exception	Probability	Cumulative Probability
0	0	.0769	.0769
1	2	.2025	.2794
2	4	.2611	.5405
3	6	.2199	.7604
4	8	.1360	.8964
5	10	.0656	.9620
6	12	.0260	.9880
7	14	.0120	1.0000

exception rate of 5 percent or less. Because it is also possible to calculate the probability distributions for other population exception rates, auditors use these to draw statistical conclusions about the unknown population being sampled. These sampling distributions are the basis for the tables used by auditors for attributes sampling.

APPLICATION OF ATTRIBUTES SAMPLING

While the 14 steps discussed for nonstatistical sampling are equally applicable to attributes sampling, in this section, we'll focus on the differences between the two.

OBJECTIVE 15-7

Use attributes sampling in tests of controls and substantive tests of transactions.

Plan the Sample

1. *State the objectives of the audit test.* Same for attributes and nonstatistical sampling.
2. *Decide whether audit sampling applies.* Same for attributes and nonstatistical sampling.
3. *Define attributes and exception conditions.* Same for attributes and nonstatistical sampling.
4. *Define the population.* Same for attributes and nonstatistical sampling.
5. *Define the sampling unit.* Same for attributes and nonstatistical sampling.
6. *Specify the tolerable exception rate.* Same for attributes and nonstatistical sampling.
7. *Specify acceptable risk of assessing control risk too low.* The concepts of specifying this risk are the same for both statistical and nonstatistical sampling, but the method of quantification is usually different. For nonstatistical sampling, most auditors use low, medium, or high acceptable risk, whereas auditors using attributes sampling assign a specific amount, such as 10 percent or 5 percent risk. The methods differ because auditors need to evaluate results statistically.
8. *Estimate the population exception rate.* Same for attributes and nonstatistical sampling.
9. *Determine the initial sample size.* Four factors determine the initial sample size for both statistical and nonstatistical sampling: population size, TER, ARACR, and EPER. In attributes sampling, auditors determine sample size by using computer programs or tables developed from statistical formulas.

The two tables in Table 15-8 come from the AICPA *Audit Sampling Guide*. The top one shows sample sizes for a 5 percent ARACR, while the bottom one is for a 10 percent ARACR.

Use of the Tables   When auditors use the tables to determine initial sample size, they follow these four steps:

  i.   Select the table corresponding to the ARACR.
 ii.   Locate the TER at the top of the table.
iii.   Locate the EPER in the far left column.
 iv.   Read down the appropriate TER column until it intersects with the appropriate EPER row. The number at the intersection is the initial sample size.

Using our Arabian Hardware Co. example, assume that an auditor is willing to reduce assessed control risk for the agreement between sales orders and invoices if the number of exceptions in the population (attribute 6 in Table 15-3) does not exceed 7 percent (TER), at a 5 percent ARACR. On the basis of past experience, the auditor sets EPER at 1 percent. On the 5 percent ARACR table, locate the 7 percent TER column, and read down the column until it intersects with the 1 percent EPER row. The initial sample size is 66.

Is 66 a large enough sample size for this audit? It is not possible to decide until after the tests have been performed. If the actual exception rate in the sample turns out to be

TABLE 15-8	Determining Sample Size for Attributes Sampling

5 PERCENT ARACR

Estimated Population Exception Rate (in Percent)	Tolerable Exception Rate (in Percent)										
	2	3	4	5	6	7	8	9	10	15	20
0.00	149	99	74	59	49	42	36	32	29	19	14
0.25	236	157	117	93	78	66	58	51	46	30	22
0.50	*	157	117	93	78	66	58	51	46	30	22
0.75	*	208	117	93	78	66	58	51	46	30	22
1.00	*	*	156	93	78	66	58	51	46	30	22
1.25	*	*	156	124	78	66	58	51	46	30	22
1.50	*	*	192	124	103	66	58	51	46	30	22
1.75	*	*	227	153	103	88	77	51	46	30	22
2.00	*	*	*	181	127	88	77	68	46	30	22
2.25	*	*	*	208	127	88	77	68	61	30	22
2.50	*	*	*	*	150	109	77	68	61	30	22
2.75	*	*	*	*	173	109	95	68	61	30	22
3.00	*	*	*	*	195	129	95	84	61	30	22
3.25	*	*	*	*	*	148	112	84	61	30	22
3.50	*	*	*	*	*	167	112	84	76	40	22
3.75	*	*	*	*	*	185	129	100	76	40	22
4.00	*	*	*	*	*	*	146	100	89	40	22
5.00	*	*	*	*	*	*	*	158	116	40	30
6.00	*	*	*	*	*	*	*	*	179	50	30
7.00	*	*	*	*	*	*	*	*	*	68	37

10 PERCENT ARACR

Estimated Population Exception Rate (in Percent)	Tolerable Exception Rate (in Percent)										
	2	3	4	5	6	7	8	9	10	15	20
0.00	114	76	57	45	38	32	28	25	22	15	11
0.25	194	129	96	77	64	55	48	42	38	25	18
0.50	194	129	96	77	64	55	48	42	38	25	18
0.75	265	129	96	77	64	55	48	42	38	25	18
1.00	*	176	96	77	64	55	48	42	38	25	18
1.25	*	221	132	77	64	55	48	42	38	25	18
1.50	*	*	132	105	64	55	48	42	38	25	18
1.75	*	*	166	105	88	55	48	42	38	25	18
2.00	*	*	198	132	88	75	48	42	38	25	18
2.25	*	*	*	132	88	75	65	42	38	25	18
2.50	*	*	*	158	110	75	65	58	38	25	18
2.75	*	*	*	209	132	94	65	58	52	25	18
3.00	*	*	*	*	132	94	65	58	52	25	18
3.25	*	*	*	*	153	113	82	58	52	25	18
3.50	*	*	*	*	194	113	82	73	52	25	18
3.75	*	*	*	*	*	131	98	73	52	25	18
4.00	*	*	*	*	*	149	98	73	65	25	18
4.50	*	*	*	*	*	218	130	87	65	34	18
5.00	*	*	*	*	*	*	160	115	78	34	18
5.50	*	*	*	*	*	*	*	142	103	34	18
6.00	*	*	*	*	*	*	*	182	116	45	25
7.00	*	*	*	*	*	*	*	*	199	52	25
7.50	*	*	*	*	*	*	*	*	*	52	25
8.00	*	*	*	*	*	*	*	*	*	60	25
8.50	*	*	*	*	*	*	*	*	*	68	32

*Sample is too large to be cost-effective for most audit applications.

Notes: 1. This table assumes a large population. 2. Sample sizes are the same in certain columns even when estimated population exception rates differ because of the method of constructing the tables. Sample sizes are calculated for attributes sampling by using the expected number of exceptions in the population, but auditors can deal more conveniently with estimated population exception rates. For example, in the 15 percent column for tolerable exception rate, at an ARACR of 5 percent, the initial sample size for most EPERs is 30. One exception, divided by a sample size of 30, is 3.3 percent. Therefore, for all EPERs greater than zero but less than 3.3 percent, the initial sample size is the same.

greater than 1 percent, the auditor will be unsure of the effectiveness of the control. The reasons will become apparent in the following sections.

Effect of Population Size In the preceding discussion, auditors ignored the size of the population in determining the initial sample size. Statistical theory shows that in populations where attributes sampling applies, population size is a minor consideration in determining sample size. Because most auditors use attributes sampling for reasonably large populations, the reduction of sample size for smaller populations is ignored here.

Select the Sample and Perform the Audit Procedures

10. *Select the sample.* The only difference in sample selection for statistical and non-statistical sampling is the requirement that probabilistic methods must be used for statistical sampling. Either simple random or systematic sampling is used for attributes sampling.
11. *Perform the audit procedures.* Same for attributes and nonstatistical sampling.

Evaluate the Results

12. *Generalize from the sample to the population.* For attributes sampling, the auditor calculates an upper precision limit (CUER) at a specified ARACR, again using special computer programs or tables developed from statistical formulas. The calculations are illustrated in tables like Table 15-9. These are 'one-sided tables,' meaning they represent the upper exception rate for a given ARACR.

Use of the Tables Use of tables to compute CUER involves four steps:

i. Select the table corresponding to the auditor's ARACR. This ARACR should be the same as the ARACR used for determining the initial sample size.
ii. Locate the actual number of exceptions found in the audit tests at the top of the table.
iii. Locate the actual sample size in the far left column.
iv. Read down the appropriate actual number of exceptions column until it intersects with the appropriate sample size row. The number at the intersection is the CUER.

To use the evaluation table for our Arabian Hardware, assume an actual sample size of 70 and one exception in attribute 6. Using an ARACR of 5 percent, CUER equals 6.6 percent. In other words, the CUER for attribute 6 is 6.6 percent at a 5 percent ARACR. Does this mean that if 100 percent of the population were tested, the true exception rate will be 6.6 percent? No, the true exception rate remains unknown. What this result means is this: if the auditor concludes that the true exception rate does not exceed 6.6 percent, there is a 95 percent probability that the conclusion is right and a 5 percent chance that it is wrong.

It is possible to have a sample size that is not equal to those provided for in the attributes sampling evaluation tables. When this occurs, it is common for auditors to interpolate to estimate the data points that fall between those listed in the table.

These tables assume a very large (infinite) population size, which results in a more conservative CUER than for smaller populations. As with sample size, the effect of population size on CUER is typically very small, so it is ignored.

13. *Analyze exceptions.* Same for attributes and nonstatistical sampling.
14. *Decide the acceptability of the population.* The methodology for deciding the acceptability of the population is essentially the same for attributes and non-statistical sampling. For attributes sampling, the auditor compares CUER with TER for each attribute. Before the population can be considered acceptable, the CUER determined on the basis of the actual sample results must be *less than or equal to* TER when both are based on the same ARACR. In our example, when the auditor specified a TER of 7 percent at a 5 percent ARACR and the CUER was 6.6 percent, the requirements of the sample have been met.

TABLE 15-9	Evaluating Sample Results Using Attributes Sampling

5 PERCENT ARACR

Actual Number of Exceptions Found

Sample Size	0	1	2	3	4	5	6	7	8	9	10
25	11.3	17.6	*	*	*	*	*	*	*	*	*
30	9.5	14.9	19.6	*	*	*	*	*	*	*	*
35	8.3	12.9	17.0	*	*	*	*	*	*	*	*
40	7.3	11.4	15.0	18.3	*	*	*	*	*	*	*
45	6.5	10.2	13.4	16.4	19.2	*	*	*	*	*	*
50	5.9	9.2	12.1	14.8	17.4	19.9	*	*	*	*	*
55	5.4	8.4	11.1	13.5	15.9	18.2	*	*	*	*	*
60	4.9	7.7	10.2	12.5	14.7	16.8	18.8	*	*	*	*
65	4.6	7.1	9.4	11.5	13.6	15.5	17.4	19.3	*	*	*
70	4.2	6.6	8.8	10.8	12.6	14.5	16.3	18.0	19.7	*	*
75	4.0	6.2	8.2	10.1	11.8	13.6	15.2	16.9	18.5	20.0	*
80	3.7	5.8	7.7	9.5	11.1	12.7	14.3	15.9	17.4	18.9	*
90	3.3	5.2	6.9	8.4	9.9	11.4	12.8	14.2	15.5	16.8	18.2
100	3.0	4.7	6.2	7.6	9.0	10.3	11.5	12.8	14.0	15.2	16.4
125	2.4	3.8	5.0	6.1	7.2	8.3	9.3	10.3	11.3	12.3	13.2
150	2.0	3.2	4.2	5.1	6.0	6.9	7.8	8.6	9.5	10.3	11.1
200	1.5	2.4	3.2	3.9	4.6	5.2	5.9	6.5	7.2	7.8	8.4

10 PERCENT ARACR

Actual Number of Exceptions Found

Sample Size	0	1	2	3	4	5	6	7	8	9	10
20	10.9	18.1	*	*	*	*	*	*	*	*	*
25	8.8	14.7	19.9	*	*	*	*	*	*	*	*
30	7.4	12.4	16.8	*	*	*	*	*	*	*	*
35	6.4	10.7	14.5	18.1	*	*	*	*	*	*	*
40	5.6	9.4	12.8	16.0	19.0	*	*	*	*	*	*
45	5.0	8.4	11.4	14.3	17.0	19.7	*	*	*	*	*
50	4.6	7.6	10.3	12.9	15.4	17.8	*	*	*	*	*
55	4.1	6.9	9.4	11.8	14.1	16.3	18.4	*	*	*	*
60	3.8	6.4	8.7	10.8	12.9	15.0	16.9	18.9	*	*	*
70	3.3	5.5	7.5	9.3	11.1	12.9	14.6	16.3	17.9	19.6	*
80	2.9	4.8	6.6	8.2	9.8	11.3	12.8	14.3	15.8	17.2	18.6
90	2.6	4.3	5.9	7.3	8.7	10.1	11.5	12.8	14.1	15.4	16.6
100	2.3	3.9	5.3	6.6	7.9	9.1	10.3	11.5	12.7	13.9	15.0
120	2.0	3.3	4.4	5.5	6.6	7.6	8.7	9.7	10.7	11.6	12.6
160	1.5	2.5	3.3	4.2	5.0	5.8	6.5	7.3	8.0	8.8	9.5
200	1.2	2.0	2.7	3.4	4.0	4.6	5.3	5.9	6.5	7.1	7.6

*More than 20 percent.

Note: This table presents computed upper exception rates as percentages. Table assumes a large population.

In this case, the control being tested can be used to reduce assessed control risk as planned, provided a careful analysis of the cause of exceptions does not indicate the possibility of a significant problem in an aspect of the control not previously considered.

When the CUER is greater than the TER, it is necessary to take specific action. The four courses of action discussed for nonstatistical sampling are equally applicable to attributes sampling.

Figure 15-8 illustrates the sampling documentation completed for the tests of attributes 1 through 9 in Table 15-3 for the Arabian Hardware Co. using attributes sampling. Notice that much of the information in Figure 15-8 is consistent with information presented in the nonstatistical sampling example illustrated in Figure 15-4. The key differences between Figures 15-4 and 15-8 are the auditor's judgment about

FIGURE 15-8   Attributes Sampling Data Sheet: Tests for Arabian Hardware Co.'s Billing Function

Client: Arabian Hardware   **Year-end:** 12/31/12
Audit Area: Tests of Controls and Substantive Tests of Transactions—   **Pop. size:** 5,764
Billing Function

Define the objective(s): Examine duplicate sales invoices and related documents to determine whether the system has functioned as intended and as described in the audit program.

Define the population precisely (including stratification, if any): Sales invoices for the period 1/1/12 to 10/31/12. First invoice number = 3689. Last invoice number = 9452.

Define the sampling unit, organization of population items, and random selection procedures: Sales invoice number, recorded in the sales journal sequentially; computer generation of random numbers.

Description of Attributes	Planned Audit				Actual Results			
	EPER	TER	ARACR	Initial sample size	Sample size	Number of exceptions	Sample exception rate	CUER
1. Existence of the sales invoice number in the sales journal (procedure 12).	0	4	5	74	75	0	0	4.0
2. Amount and other data in the master file agree with sales journal entry (procedure 13a).	1	5	5	93	100	2	2	6.2
3. Amount and other data on the duplicate sales invoice agree with the sales journal entry (procedure 13b).	1	5	5	93	100	0	0	3.0
4. Evidence that pricing, extensions, and footings are checked (initials and correct amounts) (procedure 13b).	1	5	5	93	100	10	10	16.4
5. Quantity and other data on the bill of lading agree with the duplicate sales invoice and sales journal (procedure 13c).	1	5	5	93	100	4	4	9.0
6. Quantity and other data on the sales order agree with the duplicate sales invoice (procedure 13d).	1	7	5	66	70	1	1.5	6.6
7. Quantity and other data on the customer order agree with the duplicate sales invoice (procedure 13e).	1.5	9	5	51	50	0	0	5.9
8. Credit is approved (procedure 13e).	1.5	9	5	51	50	12	24	>20
9. For recorded sales in the sales journal, the file of supporting documents includes a duplicate sales invoice, bill of lading, sales order, and customer order (procedure 14).	1	7	5	66	65	0	0	4.6

Intended use of sampling results:

1. Effect on Audit Plan: Controls tested through attributes 1, 3, 6, 7, and 9 can be viewed as operating effectively given that TER equals or exceeds CUER. Additional emphasis is needed in confirmation, allowance for uncollectible accounts, cutoff tests, and price tests for the financial statement audit due to results of tests for attributes 2, 4, 5, and 8.

2. Effect on Report on Internal Control: CUER exceeds TER for attributes 2, 4, 5, and 8. These findings have been communicated to management to allow an opportunity for correction of the control deficiency to be made before year-end. If timely correction is made by management, the corrected controls will be tested before year-end for purposes of reporting on internal control over financial reporting.

3. Recommendations to Management: Each of the exceptions should be discussed with management. Specific recommendations are needed to correct the internal verification of sales invoices and to improve the approach to credit approvals.

ARACR and the initial sample size determined when planning the audit, and the calculation of CUER using the actual test results. Notice that the ARACR judgment is numerical (5 percent) in the attributes sampling application (Figure 15-8). The numerical judgment about ARACR is considered along with the assessments of EPER and TER to determine the initial sample sizes for each attribute using Table 15-8. The CUER in Figure 15-8 is determined using Table 15-9 based on the sample exceptions identified and the actual sample size tested.

Need for Professional Judgment

A criticism occasionally leveled against statistical sampling is that it reduces the auditor's use of professional judgment. A comparison of the 14 steps discussed in this chapter for nonstatistical and attributes sampling shows that this criticism is unwarranted. For proper application, attributes sampling requires auditors to use professional judgment in most of the steps. To select the initial sample size, auditors depend primarily on TER and ARACR, which require a high level of professional judgment, as well as EPER, which requires a careful estimate. Similarly, the final evaluation of the adequacy of the entire application of attributes sampling, including the adequacy of the sample size, must also be based on high-level professional judgment.

SUMMARY

In this chapter we described representative samples and discussed the differences between statistical and nonstatistical sampling and probabilistic and nonprobabilistic sample selection. We also described the 14 steps in sampling for exception rates used in tests of controls and substantive tests of transactions. Nonstatistical and statistical attributes sampling for exception rates were illustrated for the Arabian Hardware Co.

ESSENTIAL TERMS

Acceptable risk of assessing control risk too low (ARACR)   p. 511

Attribute   p. 504

Attributes sampling   p. 521

Audit sampling   p. 498

Block sample selection   p. 501

Computed upper exception rate (CUER)   p. 505

Directed sample selection   p. 501

Estimated population exception rate (EPER)   p. 512

Exception rate   p. 504

Haphazard sample selection   p. 502

Initial sample size   p. 513

Nonprobabilistic sample selection   p. 500

Nonsampling risk   p. 498

Nonstatistical sampling   p. 500

Occurrence Rate   p. 504

Probabilistic sample selection   p. 500

Random number table   p. 502

Random sample   p. 502

Representative sample   p. 498

Sample exception rate (SER)   p. 514

Sampling distribution   p. 522

Sampling risk   p. 499

Statistical sampling   p. 500

Systematic sample selection   p. 504

Tolerable exception rate (TER)   p. 509

15-1 (Objective 15-1) State what is meant by a representative sample and explain its importance in sampling audit populations.

15-2 (Objective 15-2) Explain the major difference between statistical and nonstatistical sampling. What are the three main parts of statistical and nonstatistical methods?

15-3 (Objective 15-3) Explain the difference between replacement sampling and nonreplacement sampling. Which method do auditors usually follow? Why?

15-4 (Objective 15-3) What are the two types of simple random sample selection methods? Which of the two methods is used most often by auditors and why?

15-5 (Objective 15-3) Describe systematic sample selection and explain how an auditor will select 35 numbers from a population of 1,750 items using this approach. What are the advantages and disadvantages of systematic sample selection?

15-6 (Objective 15-4) What is the purpose of using nonstatistical sampling for tests of controls and substantive tests of transactions?

15-7 (Objective 15-2) Explain what is meant by block sample selection and describe how an auditor can obtain five blocks of 20 sales invoices from a sales journal.

15-8 (Objective 15-5) Define each of the following terms:
   a. Acceptable risk of assessing control risk too low (ARACR)
   b. Computed upper exception rate (CUER)
   c. Estimated population exception rate (EPER)
   d. Sample exception rate (SER)
   e. Tolerable exception rate (TER)

15-9 (Objective 15-5) Describe what is meant by a sampling unit. Explain why the sampling unit for verifying the occurrence of recorded sales differs from the sampling unit for testing for the possibility of omitted sales.

15-10 (Objective 15-5) Distinguish between the TER and the CUER. How is each determined?

15-11 (Objective 15-1) Distinguish between a sampling error and a nonsampling error. How can each be reduced?

15-12 (Objective 15-4) What is meant by an attribute in sampling for tests of controls and substantive tests of transactions? What is the source of the attributes that the auditor selects?

15-13 (Objective 15-4) Explain the difference between an attribute and an exception condition. State the exception condition for the audit procedure: The duplicate sales invoice has been initialed indicating the performance of internal verification.

15-14 (Objective 15-5) Identify the factors an auditor uses to decide the appropriate TER. Compare the sample size for a TER of 6% with that of 3%, all other factors being equal.

15-15 (Objective 15-5) Identify the factors an auditor uses to decide the appropriate ARACR. Compare the sample size for an ARACR of 10% with that of 5%, all other factors being equal.

15-16 (Objective 15-5) State the relationship between the following:
   a. ARACR and sample size
   b. Population size and sample size
   c. TER and sample size
   d. EPER and sample size

15-17 (Objective 15-7) Assume that the auditor has selected 100 sales invoices from a population of 100,000 to test for an indication of internal verification of pricing and extensions. Determine the CUER at a 5% ARACR if three exceptions are found in the sample using attributes sampling. Explain the meaning of the statistical results in auditing terms.

15-18 (Objective 15-5) Explain what is meant by analysis of exceptions and discuss its importance.

15-19 (Objective 15-5) When the CUER exceeds the TER, what courses of action are available to the auditor? Under what circumstances should each of these be followed?

15-20 (Objective 15-3) Distinguish between probabilistic selection and statistical measurement. State the circumstances under which one can be used without the other.

15-21 (Objective 15-7) List the major decisions that the auditor must make in using attributes sampling. State the most important considerations involved in making each decision.

MULTIPLE CHOICE QUESTIONS FROM CPA EXAMINATIONS

15-22 (Objectives 15-5, 15-7) The following items apply to determining sample sizes using random sampling from large populations for attributes sampling. Select the most appropriate response for each question.

a. If all other factors specified in a sampling plan remain constant, changing the ARACR from 10% to 5% will cause the required sample size to
  (1) increase.
  (2) remain the same.
  (3) decrease.
  (4) become indeterminate.

b. If all other factors specified in a sampling plan remain constant, changing the TER from 8% to 12% will cause the required sample size to
  (1) increase.
  (2) remain the same.
  (3) decrease.
  (4) become indeterminate.

c. If an auditor wishes to select a random sample that must have a 10% ARACR and a TER of 10%, the size of the sample selected will decrease as the estimate of the
  (1) population exception rate increases.
  (2) population exception rate decreases.
  (3) population size increases.
  (4) ARACR increases.

d. In planning a statistical sample for tests of controls, an auditor increases the expected population exception rate from the prior year's rate because of the results of the prior year's tests of controls. As a result, the auditor will most likely increase the planned
  (1) tolerable exception rate.
  (2) allowance for sampling risk.
  (3) acceptable risk of assessing control risk too low.
  (4) sample size.

15-23 (Objectives 15-5, 15-7) The following items concern determining exception rates using random sampling from large populations using attributes sampling. Select the best response.

a. From a random sample of items listed from a client's inventory count, an auditor estimates with a 90% confidence level that the CUER is between 4% and 6%. The auditor's major concern is that there is 1 chance in 20 that the true exception rate in the population is
  (1) more than 6%.
  (2) less than 6%.

    (3) more than 4%.

    (4) less than 4%.

b. If, from a random sample, an auditor can state with a 5% ARACR that the exception rate in the population does not exceed 20%, the auditor can state that the exception rate does not exceed 25% with

    (1) 5% risk.

    (2) risk greater than 5%.

    (3) risk less than 5%.

    (4) This cannot be determined from the information provided.

c. As a result of tests of controls, an auditor assessed control risk too low and decreased substantive testing. This assessment occurred because the true deviation rate in the population was

    (1) less than the risk of assessing control risk too low, based on the auditor's sample.

    (2) less than the deviation rate in the auditor's sample.

    (3) more than the risk of assessing control risk too low, based on the auditor's sample.

    (4) more than the deviation rate in the auditor's sample.

d. An auditor who uses statistical sampling for attributes in testing internal controls should reduce the planned reliance on a prescribed control when the

    (1) sample exception rate plus the allowance for sampling risk equals the tolerable rate.

    (2) sample exception rate is less than the expected rate of exception used in planning the sample.

    (3) tolerable rate less the allowance for sampling risk exceeds the sample exception rate.

    (4) sample exception rate plus the allowance for sampling risk exceeds the tolerable rate.

15-24 (Objectives 15-1, 15-2) The following questions concern sampling for attributes. Choose the best response.

a. An advantage of statistical sampling over nonstatistical sampling is that statistical sampling helps an auditor

    (1) minimize the failure to detect errors and fraud.

    (2) eliminate the risk of nonsampling errors.

    (3) design more effective audit procedures.

    (4) measure the sufficiency of the audit evidence by quantifying sampling risk.

b. Which of the following best illustrates the concept of sampling risk?

    (1) The documents related to the chosen sample may not be available to the auditor for inspection.

    (2) An auditor may fail to recognize errors in the documents from the sample.

    (3) A randomly chosen sample may not be representative of the population as a whole for the characteristic of interest.

    (4) An auditor may select audit procedures that are not appropriate to achieve the specific objective.

c. For which of the following tests would an auditor most likely use attribute sampling?

    (1) Selecting accounts receivable for confirmation of account balances.

    (2) Inspecting employee time cards for proper approval by supervisors.

    (3) Making an independent estimate of the amount of a LIFO inventory.

    (4) Examining invoices in support of the valuation of fixed asset additions.

DISCUSSION QUESTIONS AND PROBLEMS

15-25 (Objective 15-3)

a. In each of the following independent problems, design an unbiased random sampling plan, using an electronic spreadsheet or a random number generator program. The plan should include defining the sampling unit and establishing a numbering system for the population. After the plan has been designed, select the sample using the computer. Assume that the sample size is 50 for each of (1) through (4).

    (1) Prenumbered sales invoices in a sales journal where the lowest invoice number is 1 and the highest is 6211.

    (2) Prenumbered bills of lading where the lowest document number is 21926 and the highest is 28511.

    (3) Accounts receivable on ten pages with 60 lines per page except the last page, which has only 36 full lines. Each line has a customer name and an amount receivable.

    (4) Prenumbered invoices in a sales journal where each month starts over with number 1. (Invoices for each month are designated by the month and document number.) There is a maximum of 20 pages per month with a total of 185 pages for the year. All pages have 75 invoices except for the last page for each month.

b. Using systematic sampling, select the first five sample items for populations (1) through (3) from part a, using the random starting points shown. Recall that the sample size is 50 in each case.

    (1) Invoice #67

    (2) Bill of lading #22011

    (3) Page 1, line #8

15-26 (Objectives 15-3, 15-5, 15-7) One of your clients, National Supply Company, is a medium-sized company that sells wholesale hardware supplies in Bahrain. As a result of your recommendations, it has instituted a set of exemplary internal controls for sales.

To control outgoing shipments of its products, the client uses prenumbered warehouse removal slips for every sale. Nothing should be removed from the warehouse without an authorized slip, and inventories are periodically taken to ensure that no products are unaccounted for. Once an order has been shipped, two copies of the removal slip are sent to the accounting department so that a sales invoice can be prepared. One copy is stapled to a duplicate copy of a prenumbered sales invoice, and the other is filed numerically. In certain cases, more than one warehouse removal slip may be used for billing a single sales invoice. This past year, the smallest warehouse removal slip number was 11741 and the largest was 34687. The smallest sales invoice number was 45302 and the largest was 65747.

In the yearly audit of sales, one of the company's major concerns is the effectiveness of the controls designed to ensure that all shipments are billed. To test these internal controls, you have decided to use audit sampling.

Required

a. State an effective audit procedure for testing whether shipments have been billed. What is the sampling unit for the audit procedure?

b. Assume that you expect no exceptions in the sample but are willing to accept a TER of 4%. At a 5% ARACR, what is the appropriate sample size for the audit test? You may complete this requirement using attributes sampling.

c. Design a random selection plan for selecting the sample from the population, using either systematic sampling or the computer generation of random numbers. Use the sample size determined in part b. If you use systematic sampling, use a random starting point of 11878.

d. Your supervisor suggests the possibility of performing other sales tests with the same sample as a means of efficiently using your audit time. List two other audit procedures that could conveniently be performed using the same sample and state the purpose of each procedure.

e. Is it desirable to test the occurrence of sales with the random sample you have designed in part c? Why?

15-27 (Objective 15-7) The following is a partial audit program for the audit of cash receipts.

1. Review the cash receipts journal for large and unusual transactions.

2. Trace entries from the prelisting of cash receipts to the cash receipts journal to determine whether each is recorded.

3. Compare customer name, date, and amount on the prelisting with the cash receipts journal.

4. Examine the related remittance advice for entries selected from the prelisting to determine whether cash discounts were approved.

5. Trace entries from the prelisting to the deposit slip to determine whether each has been deposited.

a. Identify which audit procedures can be tested by using attributes sampling.   **Required**

b. What is the appropriate sampling unit for the tests in part a?

c. List the attributes for testing in part a.

d. Assume an ARACR of 5% and a TER of 8% for tests of controls and 6% for substantive tests of transactions. The EPER for tests of controls is 2%, and for substantive tests of transactions it is 1%. What is the initial sample size for each attribute?

15-28 (Objective 15-7) The following are auditor judgments and attributes sampling results for six populations. Assume large population sizes.

	1	2	3	4	5	6
EPER (in percent)	2	1	1	0	3	8
TER (in percent)	6	5	20	3	8	15
ARACR (in percent)	5	5	10	5	10	10
Actual sample size	100	100	20	100	60	60
Actual number of exceptions in the sample	2	4	1	0	1	8

a. For each population, did the auditor select a smaller sample size than is indicated by   **Required**
using the attributes sampling tables in Table 15-8 (p. 524) for determining sample size? Evaluate selecting either a larger or smaller size than those determined in the tables.

b. Calculate the SER and CUER for each population.

c. For which of the six populations should the sample results be considered unacceptable? What options are available to the auditor?

d. Why is analysis of the exceptions necessary even when the populations are considered acceptable?

e. For the following terms, identify which is an audit decision, a nonstatistical estimate made by the auditor, a sample result, and a statistical conclusion about the population:

(1) EPER   (5) Actual number of exceptions in the sample
(2) TER   (6) SER
(3) ARACR   (7) CUER
(4) Actual sample size

15-29 (Objectives 15-5, 15-7) The questions below relate to determining the CUER in audit sampling for tests of controls, using the following table:

	1	2	3	4
ARACR (in percent)	10	10	5	5
Population size	5,000	50,000	5,000	50,000
Sample size	50	100	50	100
Number of exceptions	2	4	2	3
CUER	10.3	7.9	12.1	7.6

a. Calculate SER for each of columns 1 through 4 and use this to calculate the actual   **Required**
allowance for sampling risk.

b. Explain why the CUER is higher for the attribute in column 1 than the attribute in column 2.

c. Explain why the CUER is higher for the attribute in column 3 than the attribute in column 1.

d. Assume that the TER for attribute 4 is 6 percent. Your audit senior indicates that he would like to be able to rely on this control and has asked you to increase the sample by an additional 50 items. Use the appropriate statistical sampling table to evaluate whether the increase in the sample is likely to result in favorable results for the entire sample of 150 items.

15-30 (Objectives 15-5, 15-7) The following questions concern the determination of the proper sample size in audit sampling using the following table:

	1	2	3	4	5	6	7
ARACR (in percent)	10	5	5	5	10	10	5
TER	6	6	5	6	20	20	2
EPER (in percent)	2	2	2	2	8	2	0
Population size	1,000	100,000	6,000	1,000	500	500	1,000,000

Required

a. Assume that the initial sample size for column 1 using nonstatistical sampling is 90 items. For each of columns 2 through 7, use your judgment to decide the appropriate nonstatistical sample size. In deciding each sample size, consider the effects of changes in each of the four factors (ARACR, TER, EPER, and population size) compared with column 1.

b. For each of the columns numbered 1 through 7, determine the initial sample size needed to satisfy the auditor's requirements using attributes sampling from the appropriate part of Table 15-8 (p. 524).

c. Using your understanding of the relationship between the following factors and sample size, state the effect on the initial sample size (increase or decrease) of changing each of the following factors while the other three are held constant:
   (1) An increase in ARACR
   (2) An increase in the TER
   (3) An increase in the EPER
   (4) An increase in the population size

d. Explain why there is such a large difference in the sample sizes for columns 3 and 6.

e. Compare your answers in part c with the results you determined in part a (nonstatistical sampling) or part b (attributes sampling). Which of the four factors appears to have the greatest effect on the initial sample size? Which one appears to have the least effect?

f. Why is the sample size called the initial sample size?

15-31 (Objectives 15-5, 15-7) The questions below relate to determining the CUER in audit sampling for tests of controls, using the following table:

	1	2	3	4	5	6	7	8
ARACR (in percent)	10	5	5	5	5	5	5	5
Population size	5,000	5,000	5,000	50,000	500	900	5,000	500
Sample size	200	200	50	200	100	100	100	25
Number of exceptions	4	4	1	4	2	10	0	0

Required

a. Using nonstatistical sampling, calculate TER − SER for each of columns 1 through 8 and evaluate whether or not sampling error is large enough to accept the population. Assume that TER is 5% for each column.

b. For each of the columns 1 through 8, determine CUER using attributes sampling from the appropriate table.

c. Using your understanding of the relationship between the four preceding factors and the CUER, state the effect on the CUER (increase or decrease) of changing each of the following factors while the other three are held constant:
   (1) A decrease in the ARACR
   (2) A decrease in the population size
   (3) A decrease in the sample size
   (4) A decrease in the number of exceptions in the sample

d. Compare your answers in part c with the results you determined in part a (nonstatistical sampling) or part b (attributes sampling). Which of the factors appears to have the greatest effect on the CUER? Which one appears to have the least effect?

e. Why is it necessary to compare the CUER with the TER?

CASE

15-32 (Objectives 15-4, 15-5, 15-7) Sabah Ibrahim, CPA, is conducting a test of sales for 9 months of the year ended December 31, 2011, for the audit of Oman Mineral Enterprises. Included among her audit procedures are the following:

1. Foot and cross-foot the sales journal and trace the balance to the general ledger.
2. Review all sales transactions for reasonableness.
3. Select a sample of recorded sales from the sales journal and trace the customer name and amounts to duplicate sales invoices and the related shipping document.
4. Select a sample of shipping document numbers and perform the following tests:
   a. Trace the shipping document to the related duplicate sales invoice.
   b. Examine the duplicate sales invoice to determine whether copies of the shipping document, shipping order, and customer order are attached.
   c. Examine the shipping order for an authorized credit approval.
   d. Examine the duplicate sales invoice for an indication of internal verification of quantity, price, extensions, and footings, and trace the balance to the accounts receivable master file.
   e. Compare the price on the duplicate sales invoice with the approved price list and the quantity with the shipping document.
   f. Trace the total on the duplicate sales invoice to the sales journal and accounts receivable master file for customer name, amount, and date.

Required

a. Which of these procedures is/are best suited to audit sampling for exceptions?

b. Considering the audit procedures Sabah developed, what is the most appropriate sampling unit for conducting most of the audit sampling tests?

c. Set up a sampling data sheet using attributes or nonstatistical sampling. For all tests of controls, assume a TER rate of 9% and an EPER of 2.25%. For all substantive tests of transactions, use a 4% TER and a 0% EPER. Use a 5% ARACR for all tests.

MYLAB ACTIVITY

Visit the MyAccountingLab and complete the following activity:

→ Integrated Case Application: Pinnacle Manufacturing: Part V

CHAPTER 16

COMPLETING THE TESTS IN THE SALES AND COLLECTION CYCLE: ACCOUNTS RECEIVABLE

Things Aren't Always As They Appear

The Rafedeen Trading Company has been in operation for five years and has always presented strong financial positions and good results of performance. The same auditing firm has performed the audit since the inception of the company and has become very familiar with the company, its operations, and its management.

In 2011, the auditing firm decided, based on the risk assessment, to send a total of 100 positive confirmations to selected companies listed as accounts receivable on the statement of financial position. The senior auditor was put in charge of mailing and following up on the confirmations. After three weeks, busy season was now in full swing and only 30 of the confirmations had been received. The senior was very busy with other work and grumbled to herself, "What a pain, no one ever returns these things… and if they do, they are filled out incorrectly! I don't have time for all of this follow up."

The senior enlisted the help of the staff auditor on the engagement, who assisted with the follow-up of confirmations. The staff auditor didn't really have a good understanding of the process and did not have much supervision because the senior was so busy. As the weeks rolled on, the staff auditor realized that there were a few confirmations that were just never going to come back and—figuring they were immaterial amounts—she made a note about the 40 missing confirmations and marked the workpaper as complete. The other testing areas proceeded normally, and none of the reviewers noticed the note about the missing A/R confirmations on the workpaper. Rafedeen Trading Company showed positive results as usual and the auditing firm issued an unmodified opinion.

Three months later, Rafedeen Trading Company found itself facing liquidity problems and began looking frantically for outside financing. Owners of the company wondered how they had ended up in this situation, considering the results they had showed at year-end. The CEO personally looked into the financial results and through intense questioning found that the Controller and the CFO had conspired to artificially inflate the results of the company by creating fictitious accounts receivable from fictitious companies which were written off after year-end by credit memos. Both the Controller and CFO were fired immediately and the CEO went after the auditing firm next.

Was there something else the auditing firm could have done to detect this fraud during the audit? Granted, fraud committed with collusion between management can be hard to detect, but surely there must have been something else the auditing firm could have done, right?

In the preceding two chapters, we examined tests of controls and substantive tests of transactions for the sales and collection cycle. Both types of tests are part of phase II of the audit process. We now move to phase III and turn our attention to substantive analytical procedures and tests of details of balances for the sales and collection cycle.

This chapter shows that it is essential for auditors to select the appropriate evidence to verify the account balances in the sales and collection cycle, after considering tolerable misstatement, performing risk assessment procedures to assess inherent and control risks, and performing tests of controls and substantive tests of transactions. This chapter examines designing substantive analytical procedures and tests of details of balances for the two key balance sheet accounts in the cycle: accounts receivable and the allowance for uncollectible accounts.

Relevant International Standards on Auditing	
ISA 200	Overall Objectives of the Independent Auditor and the Conduct of an Audit in Accordance with International Standards on Auditing
ISA 220	Quality Control for an Audit of Financial Statements
ISA 230	Audit Documentation
ISA 240	The Auditor's Responsibilities Relating to Fraud in an Audit of Financial Statements
ISA 300	Planning an Audit of Financial Statements
ISA 315	Identifying and Assessing the Risks of Material Misstatement through Understanding the Entity and its Environment
ISA 320	Materiality in Planning and Performing an Audit
ISA 450	Evaluation of Misstatements Identified during the Audit
ISA 500	Audit Evidence
ISA 505	External Confirmations
ISA 520	Analytical Procedures
ISA 530	Audit Sampling
ISA 540	Auditing Accounting Estimates, Including Fair Value Accounting Estimates, and Related Disclosures

METHODOLOGY FOR DESIGNING TESTS OF DETAILS OF BALANCES

OBJECTIVE 16-1

Describe the methodology for designing tests of details of balances using the audit risk model.

Figure 16-1 shows the methodology auditors follow in designing the appropriate tests of details of balances for accounts receivable.

The methodology shown in Figure 16-1 relates directly to the evidence-planning worksheet first introduced in Chapter 9. The worksheet was partially completed for materiality and risk considerations (part of phase I) and for tests of controls and substantive tests of transactions in Chapter 15 (phase II). We will continue to complete the worksheet as we proceed through phase III in this chapter. For now, you might want to look at the example of a completed worksheet in Figure 16-7 to see what the completed worksheet looks like, to provide you an overview of the focus of this chapter.

The appropriate evidence to be obtained from tests of details of balances must be decided on an objective-by-objective basis. Because several interactions affect the need for evidence from tests of details of balances, this audit decision can be complex. For

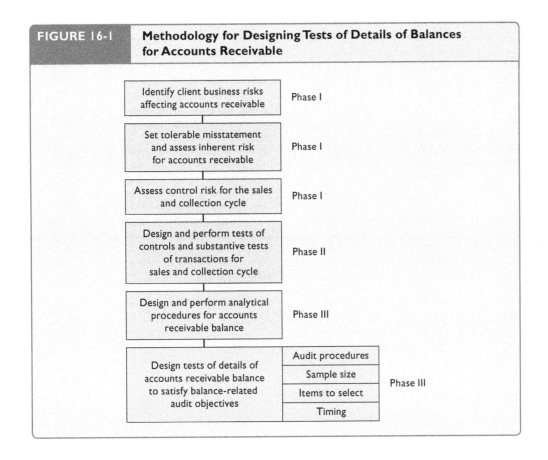

FIGURE 16-1   Methodology for Designing Tests of Details of Balances for Accounts Receivable

example, the auditor must evaluate the potential for fraud and also consider inherent risk, which may vary by objective, as well as the results of tests of controls and the related control risk assessment, which also may vary by objective. The auditor must also consider the results of substantive tests of sales and cash receipts.

In designing tests of details of balances for accounts receivable, auditors must satisfy each of the eight balance-related audit objectives discussed in Chapter 6. These eight general objectives are the same for all accounts. Specifically applied to accounts receivable, they are called **accounts receivable balance-related audit objectives** and are as follows:[16]

1. Accounts receivable in the aged trial balance agree with related master file amounts, and the total is correctly added and agrees with the general ledger. (Detail tie-in)
2. Recorded accounts receivable exist. (Existence)
3. Existing accounts receivable are included. (Completeness)
4. Accounts receivable are accurate. (Accuracy)
5. Accounts receivable are correctly classified. (Classification)
6. Cutoff for accounts receivable is correct. (Cutoff)
7. Accounts receivable is stated at realizable value. (Realizable value)
8. The client has rights to accounts receivable. (Rights)

The columns in the evidence-planning worksheet in Figure 16-7 include the balance-related audit objectives. The auditor uses the factors in the rows to aid in assessing planned detection risk for accounts receivable, by objective.

The following overview explains the methodology for designing tests of details of balances for accounts receivable.

Accounts receivable balance-related audit objectives

The eight specific audit objectives used by the auditor to decide the appropriate audit evidence for accounts receivable.

<table>
<tr><td>

RECEIVABLES AND BAD DEBTS

</td><td>

The Central Audit Organization in Egypt in its report on the financial statements of the Egyptian Etisalat Company, for the year ending December 31, 2009 included a qualification for the unsuccessful collection of more than EGP 1.3 billion (US$220 million) from clients of the company. The report discussed the management decision to reduce the debt for Minatel by EGP 20 million (US$3.3 million) from the original amount of EGP 65 million (US$10.8 million) for the acquisition of telephone boxes by Minatel, taking into consideration that management did not use the boxes until the date of the auditor's report. The Minatel debts to the company had been unpaid since 2004 due to the close relationship between the chairman of the company and the former President of Egypt. The report also included the delay in collecting the debts associated with prepaid telephone cards from a number of client companies

</td><td>

amounting to EGP 128 million (US$21.3 million) as at June 30, 2010 as well as the debts owed by the Nile University amounting to EGP 3.3 million (US$0.5 million).

Moreover, the management of the Egyptian Etisalat Company did not prepare a business contract with Etisalat Egypt (the mobile phone company) to preserve the company's rights for debts owed to the company which amounted to EGP 122 million (US$20.3 million) at June 30, 2010. There was also excess spending in remuneration and other expenses (i.e. hotel accommodation, travelling expenses and meal allowances, bonuses, recruitment costs) for the activities of a large number of committees established to solve many of the company operational problems. The remuneration of these committees amounted to EGP 1.8 million (US$0.3 million).

Source: *Al-Ahram Newspaper*, July 10, 2011.

</td></tr>
</table>

Identify Client Business Risks Affecting Accounts Receivable (Phase I)

Tests of accounts receivable are based on the auditor's risk assessment procedures that provide an understanding of the client's business and industry, discussed in Chapter 8. As part of this understanding, the auditor studies the client's industry and external environment and evaluates management objectives and business processes to identify significant client business risks that could affect the financial statements, including accounts receivable. As part of gaining this understanding, the auditor also performs preliminary analytical procedures that may indicate increased risk of misstatements in accounts receivable.

Client business risks affecting accounts receivable are considered in the auditor's evaluation of inherent risk and planned evidence for accounts receivable. For example, as a result of adverse changes in the industry's economic environment, the auditor may increase inherent risk for net realizable value of accounts receivable.

Set Tolerable Misstatement and Assess Inherent Risk (Phase I)

As studied in Chapter 9, the auditor first decides the preliminary judgment about materiality for the entire financial statements, and then allocates the preliminary judgment amount to each significant balance sheet account, including accounts receivable. This allocation is called *setting tolerable misstatement*. Accounts receivable is typically one of the most material accounts in the financial statements for companies that sell on credit. For even small accounts receivable balances, the transactions in the sales and collection cycle that affect the balance in accounts receivable are almost certain to be highly significant.

Auditors assess inherent risk for each objective for an account such as accounts receivable, considering client business risk and the nature of the client and industry. Auditing standards indicate that auditors should normally identify the likelihood of fraud risk for revenue recognition. This likely affects the auditor's assessment of inherent risk for the following objectives: existence, sales cutoff, and sales returns and

WILL AUDITORS SUCCEED IN CONVINCING MANAGEMENT TO ENHANCE INTERNAL CONTROL?

Nour Bin Arabia, the audit partner in a top auditing firm in Tunisia, had the following discussion with the credit manager of a manufacturing company concerning deficiencies in their internal control for sales and collection cycle.

NOUR: We found excesses over authorized limits for some customers. This is noncompliance with the company credit policy especially in relation to approving any renewal or increase in the authorized limits which should be subject to a full credit check.

CREDIT MANAGER: Please note that outstanding exposure is subject to rescheduling according to the rescheduling agreement signed by the customers taking into consideration that the rescheduling covers the balance at the date of agreement and no limits were increased to cover the excess.

NOUR: But this was not applied for the client, Crystal Glass.

CREDIT MANAGER: For Crystal Glass, limits increases were approved by the authorized committees based on an integrated presentation of the investment cost and cash flow of the company. The presentation also included the audited financial statements taking into consideration that the company credit facilities renewal is presented to the board of directors for approval.

NOUR: There is no valuation for some of the collateral provided by customers. The need to obtain a recent valuation for the real estate owned by customers is considered important.

CREDIT MANAGER: As per the company credit manual according to the standard the fair value of the collateral was considered before the formation of the appropriate provision. Also, the legal department opinion was obtained hence the debt can be assessed in light of the incoming cash flow.

NOUR: Finally, the authorized limits of some of the clients are not updated in accordance with the latest credit approval. The system should be updated by the credit portfolio latest data. There should be coordination between the concerned departments in respect of the available documents.

CREDIT MANAGER: A new unit was established in the risk control department for that purpose taking into consideration that there is no difference in company approved credit limit and actual debts.

allowances cutoff. It is common for clients to misstate cutoff either by error or through fraud. It is also common for clients to unintentionally or fraudulently misstate the allowance for uncollectible accounts (realizable value) because of the difficulty of the judgments to determine the correct balance.

Assess Control Risk for the Sales and Collection Cycle (Phase I)

Internal controls over sales and cash receipts and the related accounts receivable are at least reasonably effective for most companies because management is concerned with keeping accurate records to maintain good relations with customers. Auditors are especially concerned with three aspects of internal controls:

1. Controls that prevent or detect embezzlements
2. Controls over cutoff
3. Controls related to the allowance for uncollectible accounts

The auditor must relate control risk for transaction-related audit objectives to balance-related audit objectives in deciding planned detection risk and planned evidence for tests of details of balances. For the most part, this relationship is straightforward. Figure 16-2 shows the relationship for the two primary classes of transactions in the sales and collection cycle. For example, assume the auditor concluded that control risk for both sales and cash receipts transactions is low for the accuracy transaction-related audit objective. The auditor can therefore conclude that controls for the accuracy balance-related audit objective for accounts receivable are effective because the only transactions that affect accounts receivable are sales and cash receipts. Of course, if sales returns and allowances and write-off of uncollectible accounts receivable are significant, assessed control risk must also be considered for these two classes of transactions.

| FIGURE 16-2 | Relationships between Transaction-Related Audit Objectives for the Sales and Collection Cycle and Balance-Related Audit Objectives for Accounts Receivable |

CLASS OF TRANSACTIONS	TRANSACTION-RELATED AUDIT OBJECTIVES	ACCOUNTS RECEIVABLE BALANCE-RELATED AUDIT OBJECTIVES							
		Detail tie-in	Existence	Completeness	Accuracy	Classification	Cutoff	Realizable value	Rights
Sales	Occurrence		X						
	Completeness			X					
	Accuracy				X				
	Posting and summarization	X							
	Classification					X			
	Timing						X		
Cash receipts	Occurrence			X					
	Completeness		X						
	Accuracy				X				
	Posting and summarization	X							
	Classification					X			
	Timing						X		

Two aspects of the relationships in Figure 16-2 deserve special mention:

1. For sales, the occurrence transaction-related audit objective affects the existence balance-related audit objective. For cash receipts, however, the occurrence transaction-related audit objective affects the completeness balance-related audit objective. A similar relationship exists for the completeness transaction-related audit objective. The reason for this somewhat surprising conclusion is that an increase in sales increases accounts receivable, but an increase in cash receipts decreases accounts receivable. For example, recording a sale that did not occur violates the occurrence transaction-related audit objective and existence balance-related audit objective (both overstatements). Recording a cash receipt that did not occur violates the occurrence transaction-related audit objective, but it also violates the completeness balance-related audit objective for accounts receivable because a receivable that is still outstanding is no longer included in the records.

2. The realizable value and rights for accounts receivable balance-related audit objectives, as well as the presentation and disclosure-related objectives, are not affected by assessed control risk for classes of transactions. To assess control risk below the maximum for these objectives, the auditor must identify and test separate controls that support those objectives.

Figure 16-7 includes three rows for assessed control risk: one for sales, one for cash receipts, and one for additional controls related to the accounts receivable balance. The source of each control risk for sales and cash receipts is the control risk matrix assuming that the tests of controls results supported the original assessment. The auditor makes a separate assessment of control risk for objectives that are related only to the accounts receivable balance or to presentation and disclosure audit objectives.

Design and Perform Tests of Controls and Substantive Tests of Transactions (Phase II)

The results of the tests of controls determine whether assessed control risk for sales and cash receipts needs to be revised. Auditors use the results of the substantive tests of transactions to determine the extent to which planned detection risk is satisfied for each accounts receivable balance-related audit objective. The evidence-planning worksheet in Figure 16-7 shows three rows for control risk and two for substantive tests of transactions, one for sales, and the other for cash receipts.

Design and Perform Analytical Procedures (Phase III)

As discussed in Chapter 8, analytical procedures are often done during three phases of the audit: during planning, when performing detailed tests, and as a part of completing the audit. This chapter covers planning analytical procedures and substantive analytical procedures done when performing detailed tests for accounts in the sales and collection cycle.

OBJECTIVE 16-2

Design and perform analytical procedures for accounts in the sales and collection cycle.

Most analytical procedures performed during the detailed testing phase are done after the balance sheet date but before tests of details of balances. It makes little sense to perform extensive analytical procedures before the client has recorded all transactions for the year and finalized the financial statements.

Auditors perform analytical procedures for the entire sales and collection cycle, not just accounts receivable. This is necessary because of the close relationship between income statement and balance sheet accounts. If the auditor identifies a possible misstatement in sales or sales returns and allowances using analytical procedures, accounts receivable will likely be the offsetting misstatement.

Table 16-1 presents examples of ratios and comparisons for the sales and collection cycle and potential misstatements that analytical procedures may uncover. Although Table 16-1 focuses on the comparison of current year results with previous years, auditors also consider current year results compared to budgets and industry trends. Observe in the 'possible misstatement' column how both balance sheet and income statement accounts are affected. For example, when the auditor performs analytical procedures for sales, evidence is being obtained about both sales and accounts receivable.

In addition to the analytical procedures in Table 16-1, auditors should also review accounts receivable for large and unusual amounts, such as large balances, accounts that have been outstanding for a long time, receivables from affiliated companies, officers, directors, and other related parties, and credit balances. To identify these amounts the auditor should review the listing of accounts (aged trial balance) at the balance sheet date to determine which accounts should be investigated further.

To illustrate the use of analytical procedures during the detailed testing phase, Table 16-2 presents comparative trial balance information for the sales and collection cycle information for Arabian Hardware Co. Building on that information, Table 16-3 demonstrates several substantive analytical procedures. The only potential misstatement indicated in these two tables is in the allowance for uncollectible accounts. This is indicated by the ratio of the allowance to accounts receivable, as explained at the bottom of Table 16-3.

TABLE 16-1	Analytical Procedures for the Sales and Collection Cycle
Analytical Procedure	**Possible Misstatement**
Compare gross margin percentage with previous years (by product line).	Overstatement or understatement of sales and accounts receivable.
Compare sales by month (by product line) over time.	Overstatement or understatement of sales and accounts receivable.
Compare sales returns and allowances as a percentage of gross sales with previous years (by product line).	Overstatement or understatement of sales returns and allowances and accounts receivable.
Compare individual customer balances over a stated amount with previous years.	Misstatements in accounts receivable and related income statement accounts.
Compare bad debt expense as a percentage of gross sales with previous years.	Uncollectible accounts receivable that have not been provided for.
Compare number of days that accounts receivable are outstanding with previous years and related turnover of accounts receivable.	Overstatement or understatement of allowance for uncollectible accounts and bad debt expense; also may indicate fictitious accounts receivable.
Compare aging categories as a percentage of accounts receivable with previous years.	Overstatement or understatement of allowance for uncollectible accounts and bad debt expense.
Compare allowance for uncollectible accounts as a percentage of accounts receivable with previous years.	Overstatement or understatement of allowance for uncollectible accounts and bad debt expense.
Compare write-off of uncollectible accounts as a percentage of total accounts receivable with previous years.	Overstatement or understatement of allowance for uncollectible accounts and bad debt expense.

TABLE 16-2	Comparative Information for Arabian Hardware Co.—Sales and Collection Cycle

	Amount				
	Dec 31, 2012 (in Thousands)	Percent Change 2011	Dec 31, 2011 (in Thousands)	Percent Change 2010	Dec 31, 2010 (in Thousands)
Sales	US$144,328	9.0%	US$132,421	7.0%	US$123,737
Sales returns and allowances	1,242	3.9	1,195	13.6	1,052
Gross margin	39,845	9.6	36,350	7.0	33,961
Accounts receivable	20,197	15.3	17,521	3.3	16,961
Allowance for uncollectible accounts	1,240	(5.4)	1,311	21.5	1,079
Bad debt expense	3,323	(2.1)	3,394	7.3	3,162
Total current assets	51,027	2.3	49,895	1.5	49,157
Total assets	61,367	0.9	60,791	1.8	59,696
Net earnings before taxes	5,681	21.9	4,659	39.0	3,351
Number of accounts receivable	258	16.7	221	5.7	209
Number of accounts receivable with balance over US$10,000	37	15.6	32	6.7	30

The auditor's conclusions about substantive analytical procedures for the sales and collection cycle are incorporated in the evidence-planning worksheet in Figure 16-7 (p. 559) in the third row from the bottom. Because analytical procedures are substantive tests, they reduce the extent to which the auditor needs to perform detailed tests of balances, if the analytical procedure results are favorable.

TABLE 16-3	Analytical Procedures for Arabian Hardware Co.—Sales and Collection Cycle		
	Dec 31, 2012	Dec 31, 2011	Dec 31, 2010
Gross margin/net sales	27.85%	27.70%	27.68%
Sales returns and allowances/gross sales	0.9%	0.9%	0.9%
Bad debt expense/net sales	2.3%	2.6%	2.6%
Allowance for uncollectible accounts/ accounts receivable	6.1%	7.5%	6.4%
Number of days receivables outstanding*	48.09	47.96	49.32
Net accounts receivable/total current assets	37.2%	32.5%	32.3%

*Based on year-end accounts receivable only.

Comment: Allowance as a percentage of accounts receivable has declined from 6.4% to 6.1%. Number of days receivables outstanding and economic conditions do not justify this change. Potential misstatement is approximately US$60,000 (US$20,197,000 × [.064–.061]).

When analytical procedures in the sales and collection cycle uncover unusual fluctuations, the auditor should make additional inquiries of management. Management's responses should be critically evaluated to determine whether they adequately explain the unusual fluctuations and whether they are supported by corroborating evidence.

Design and Perform Tests of Details of Accounts Receivable Balance (Phase III)

The appropriate tests of details of balances depend on the factors listed in the evidence-planning worksheet in Figure 16-7. Planned detection risk for each accounts receivable balance-related audit objective is shown in the second row from the bottom in Figure 16-7. It is a subjective decision made by auditors after they have combined the conclusions reached about each of the factors listed above that row.

The task of combining the factors that determine planned detection risk is complex because the measurement for each factor is imprecise and the appropriate weight given to each factor is highly subjective. Conversely, the relationship between each factor and planned detection risk is well established. For example, auditors know that a high inherent risk or control risk decreases planned detection risk and increases planned substantive tests, whereas good results of substantive tests of transactions increase planned detection risk and decrease other planned substantive tests.

The bottom row in Figure 16-7 shows the planned audit evidence for tests of details of balances for accounts receivable, by objective. As we've discussed, planned audit evidence is the inverse of planned detection risk. After deciding whether planned audit evidence for a given objective is high, medium, or low, the auditor must then decide on the appropriate audit procedures, sample size, items to select, and timing.

For the remainder of this chapter, we will discuss how auditors decide on the specific audit procedures and their timing for auditing accounts receivable. In Chapter 17, we'll address sample size and selecting items from the population for testing.

DESIGNING TESTS OF DETAILS OF BALANCES

Even though auditors emphasize balance sheet accounts in tests of details of balances, they are not ignoring income statement accounts because the income statement accounts are tested as a by-product of the balance sheet tests. For example, if the auditor confirms accounts receivable balances and finds overstatements caused by mistakes in billing customers, then both accounts receivable and sales are overstated.

> **OBJECTIVE 16-3**
>
> Design and perform tests of details of balances for accounts receivable.

Confirmation of accounts receivable is the most important test of details of accounts receivable. We will discuss confirmation briefly as we study the appropriate tests for each of the balance-related audit objectives. We'll examine it in more detail later in this chapter.

For our discussion of tests of details of balances for accounts receivable, we will focus on balance-related audit objectives. We will also assume two things:

1. Auditors have completed an evidence-planning worksheet similar to the one in Figure 16-7.
2. They have decided planned detection risk for tests of details for each balance-related audit objective.

The audit procedures selected and their sample size will depend heavily on whether planned evidence for a given objective is low, medium, or high.

Accounts Receivable are Correctly Added and Agree with the Master File and the General Ledger

Aged trial balance

A listing of the balances in the accounts receivable master file at the balance sheet date broken down according to the amount of time passed between the date of sale and the balance sheet date.

Most tests of accounts receivable and the allowance for uncollectible accounts are based on the aged trial balance. An **aged trial balance** lists the balances in the accounts receivable master file at the balance sheet date, including individual customer balances outstanding and a breakdown of each balance by the time passed between the date of sale and the balance sheet date. Figure 16-3 illustrates a typical aged trial balance, based on the Arabian Hardware example.

Ordinarily, auditors test the information on the aged trial balance for detail tie-in before any other tests to verify that the population being tested agrees with the general ledger and accounts receivable master file. The total column and the columns depicting the aging must be test footed and the total on the trial balance compared with the general ledger. In addition, auditors should trace a sample of individual balances to supporting documents such as duplicate sales invoices to verify the customer's name, balance, and proper aging. The extent of the testing for detail tie-in depends on the

FIGURE 16-3	Aged Trial Balance for Arabian Hardware Co.

PBC

Arabian Hardware Co.
Accounts Receivable
Aged Trial Balance
Dec 31, 2012

Schedule Prepared by Client
Approved by

Date Jan 1, 2013

			Aging, Based on Invoice Date				
Account Number	Customer	Balance 31/12/12	0–30 days	31–60 days	61–90 days	91–120 days	over 120 days
01011	Adams Supply	146,589	90,220	56,369			
01044	Argonaut, Inc.	30,842	30,842				
01100	Atwater Brothers	210,389	210,389				
01191	Beekman Bearings	83,526	73,526		10,000		
01270	Brown and Phillips	60,000				60,000	
01301	Christopher Plumbing	15,789					15,789
09733	Travelers Equipment	59,576	59,576				
09742	Underhill Parts and Maintenance	179,263	179,263				
09810	UJW Co.	102,211	34,911	34,700	32,600		
09907	Zephyr Plastics	286,300	186,000	100,300			
		US$20,196,800	US$14,217,156	US$2,869,366	US$1,408,642	US$1,038,926	US$662,710

number of accounts involved, the degree to which the master file has been tested as a part of tests of controls and substantive tests of transactions, and the extent to which the schedule has been verified by an internal auditor or other independent person before it is given to the auditor. Auditors often use audit software to foot and cross-foot the aged trial balance and to recalculate the aging.

Recorded Accounts Receivable Exist

Confirmation of customers' balances is the most important test of details of balances for determining the existence of recorded accounts receivable. When customers do not respond to confirmations, auditors also examine supporting documents to verify the shipment of goods and evidence of subsequent cash receipts to determine whether the accounts were collected. Normally, auditors do not examine shipping documents or evidence of subsequent cash receipts for any account in the sample that is confirmed, but they may use these documents extensively as alternative evidence for nonresponses.

Existing Accounts Receivable are Included

It is difficult for auditors to test for account balances omitted from the aged trial balance except by relying on the self-balancing nature of the accounts receivable master file. For example, if the client accidentally excluded an account receivable from the trial balance, the only likely way it will be discovered is for the auditor to foot the accounts receivable trial balance and reconcile the balance with the control account in the general ledger.

If all sales to a customer are omitted from the sales journal, the understatement of accounts receivable is almost impossible to uncover by tests of details of balances. For example, auditors rarely send accounts receivable confirmations to customers with zero balances, in part because research shows that customers are unlikely to respond to requests that indicate their balances are understated. In addition, unrecorded sales to a new customer are difficult to identify for confirmation because that customer is not included in the accounts receivable master file. The understatement of sales and accounts receivable is best uncovered by substantive tests of transactions for shipments made but not recorded (completeness objective for tests of sales transactions) and by analytical procedures.

Accounts Receivable are Accurate

Confirmation of accounts selected from the trial balance is the most common test of details of balances for the accuracy of accounts receivable. When customers do not respond to confirmation requests, auditors examine supporting documents in the same way as described for the existence objective. Auditors perform tests of the debits and credits to individual customers' balances by examining supporting documentation for shipments and cash receipts.

Accounts Receivable are Properly Classified

Normally, auditors can evaluate the classification of accounts receivable relatively easily, by reviewing the aged trial balance for material receivables from affiliates, officers, directors, or other related parties. Auditors should verify that notes receivable or accounts that should be classified as noncurrent assets are separated from regular accounts, and significant credit balances in accounts receivable are reclassified as accounts payable.

There is a close relationship between the classification balance-related objective and the related classification and understandability presentation and disclosure objective. To satisfy the classification balance-related audit objective, the auditor must determine whether the client has correctly separated different classifications of accounts receivable. For example, the auditor will determine whether receivables from related parties have been separated on the aged trial balance. To satisfy the objective for presentation and disclosure, the auditor must make sure that the classifications are properly presented by determining whether related party transactions are correctly shown in the financial statements during the completion phase of the audit.

Cutoff for Accounts Receivable Is Correct

Cutoff misstatements

Misstatements that take place as a result of current period transactions being recorded in a subsequent period, or subsequent period transactions being recorded in the current period.

Cutoff misstatements exist when current period transactions are recorded in the subsequent period or vice versa. The objective of cutoff tests, regardless of the type of transaction, is to verify whether transactions near the end of the accounting period are recorded in the proper period. The cutoff objective is one of the most important in the cycle because misstatements in cutoff can significantly affect current period income. For example, the intentional or unintentional inclusion of several large, subsequent period sales in the current period—or the exclusion of several current period sales returns and allowances—can materially overstate net earnings.

Cutoff misstatements can occur for *sales, sales returns and allowances*, and *cash receipts*. For each one, auditors require a threefold approach to determine the reasonableness of cutoff:

1. Decide on the appropriate *criteria for cutoff*.
2. Evaluate whether the client has established *adequate procedures* to ensure a reasonable cutoff.
3. *Test* whether the cutoff was correct.

Sales Cutoff Most merchandising and manufacturing clients record a sale based on *shipment of goods* criterion. However, some companies record invoices at the time title passes, which can occur before shipment (as in the case of custom-manufactured goods), at the time of shipment, or subsequent to shipment. For the correct measurement of current period income, the method must be in accordance with International Financial Reporting Standards (IFRS) or local accounting standards and consistently applied.

EARLY REVENUE RECOGNITION BOOSTS PROFITS

Faced with declining sales for its traditional product lines, Xerox, a transnational printing equipment and documents manufacturer with offices all over the world including all Arab countries, prematurely recognized revenues to meet market expectations, according to charges filed by the SEC. The SEC stated that Xerox accelerated the recognition of equipment revenue to increase revenues by over US$3 billion and pre-tax earnings by approximately US$1.5 billion over the period 1997 through 2000. The early revenue recognition and other actions to increase earnings were significant, representing 37 percent of reported pre-tax earnings for the fourth quarters of 1997 and 1998. Without these actions to increase earnings, the SEC charged that Xerox would have fallen short of market earnings expectations for almost every reporting period from 1997 through 1999.

A primary issue was how Xerox accounted for lease revenue. The revenue in Xerox's leasing arrangements represented three components: the value of the equipment, servicing over the life of the lease, and financing. The revenue from the equipment was recorded at the beginning of the lease, but revenues from servicing and financing were recognized over the life of the lease contract. According to the SEC complaint, Xerox took a number of actions to shift servicing and financing revenue to the value of the equipment, so that more of the revenue could be recognized immediately.

The SEC alleged that these actions were set by the 'tone at the top' and ordered six senior executives to pay over US$22 million in penalties and disgorgement of profits from their actions. Without admitting or denying the allegations made in the SEC complaint, Xerox agreed to pay a US$10 million fine, at that time the largest ever for a public company.

Sources: Securities and Exchange Commission Accounting and Auditing Enforcement Release No. 1542 (April 11, 2002); and Securities and Exchange Commission Press Release 2003-70 (June 5, 2003) (www.sec.gov).

The most important part of evaluating the client's method of obtaining a reliable cutoff is to determine the procedures in use. When a client issues prenumbered shipping documents sequentially, it is usually a simple matter to evaluate and test cutoff. Moreover, the segregation of duties between the shipping and the billing function also enhances the likelihood of recording transactions in the proper period. However, if shipments are made by company truck, if the shipping records are unnumbered, and if shipping and billing department personnel are not independent of each other, it may be difficult, if not impossible, to be assured of an accurate cutoff.

When the client's internal controls are adequate, auditors can usually verify the cutoff by obtaining the shipping document number for the last shipment made at the end of the period and comparing this number with current and subsequent period recorded sales. As an illustration, assume the shipping document number for the last shipment in the current period is 1489. All recorded sales before the end of the period should bear a shipping document number preceding number 1490, and no sales recorded and shipped in the subsequent period should have a bill of lading numbered 1489 or lower. An auditor can easily test this by comparing recorded sales with the related shipping documents for the last few days of the current period and the first few days of the subsequent period.

Sales Returns and Allowances Cutoff Accounting standards require that sales returns and allowances be *matched with related sales* if the amounts are material. For example, if current period shipments are returned in the subsequent period, the sales return should appear in the current period. (The returned goods should be treated as current period inventory.) For most companies, however, sales returns and allowances are recorded in the *accounting period in which they occur*, under the assumption of approximately equal, offsetting amounts at the beginning and end of each accounting period. This approach is acceptable as long as the amounts are not material. Some companies establish a reserve, similar to the allowance for uncollectible accounts, for the expected amount of returns in the subsequent period.

When the auditor is confident that the client records all sales returns and allowances promptly, the cutoff tests are simple and straightforward. The auditor can examine supporting documentation for a sample of sales returns and allowances recorded during several weeks subsequent to the closing date to determine the date of the original sale. If auditors discover that the amounts recorded in the subsequent period are significantly different from unrecorded returns and allowances at the beginning of the period under audit, they must consider an adjustment. For example, a company may experience an increase in sales returns when it expands internet sales because customers are unable to examine the product before purchase. In addition, if the internal controls for recording sales returns and allowances are evaluated as ineffective, a larger sample is needed to verify cutoff.

Cash Receipts Cutoff For most audits, a proper cash receipts cutoff is *less important* than either the sales or the sales returns and allowances cutoff because the improper cutoff of cash affects only the cash and the accounts receivable balances, not earnings. Nevertheless, if the misstatement is material, it can affect the fair presentation of these accounts, especially when cash is a small or negative balance.

It is easy to test for a cash receipts cutoff misstatement (often called *holding the cash receipts book open*) by tracing recorded cash receipts to subsequent period bank deposits on the bank statement. If a delay of several days exists, that could indicate a cutoff misstatement.

To some degree, auditors may also rely on the confirmation of accounts receivable to uncover cutoff misstatements for sales, sales returns and allowances, and cash receipts. However, it is often difficult to distinguish a cutoff misstatement from a normal **timing difference** due to shipments and payments in transit at year end.

Timing difference

A reported difference in a confirmation from a debtor that is determined to be a timing difference between the client's and debtor's records and therefore not a misstatement.

For example, if a customer mails and records a check to a client for payment of an unpaid account on December 30 and the client receives and records the amount on January 2, the records of the two organizations will be different on December 31. This is not a cutoff misstatement, but a timing difference due to the delivery time. It may be difficult for the auditor to evaluate whether a cutoff misstatement or a timing difference occurred when a confirmation reply is the source of information. This type of situation requires additional investigation, such as inspection of supporting documents.

Accounts Receivable is Stated at Realizable Value

Realizable value of accounts receivable

The amount of the outstanding balances in accounts receivable that will ultimately be collected.

Accounting standards require that companies state accounts receivable at the amount that will ultimately be collected. The **realizable value of accounts receivable** equals gross accounts receivable less the *allowance for uncollectible accounts*. To calculate the allowance, the client estimates the total amount of accounts receivable that it expects to be uncollectible. Obviously, clients cannot predict the future precisely, but it is necessary for the auditor to evaluate whether the client's allowance is reasonable, considering all available facts. To assist with this evaluation, the auditor often prepares an audit schedule that analyzes the allowance for uncollectible accounts, as illustrated in Figure 16-4. In this example, the analysis indicates that the allowance is understated. This can be the result of the client failing to adjust the allowance or economic factors. Note that the potential understatement of the reserve was signaled by the analytical procedures in Table 16-3 for Arabian Hardware.

To begin the evaluation of the allowance for uncollectible accounts, the auditor reviews the results of the tests of controls that are concerned with the client's credit policy. If the client's credit policy has remained unchanged and the results of the tests of credit policy and credit approval are consistent with those of the preceding year, the

FIGURE 16-4	Analysis of Allowance for Uncollectible Accounts—Arabian Hardware Co.

Arabian Hardware Co.
Analysis of Allowance for Uncollectible Accounts
Dec 31, 2012

		Schedule	B-4	Date
		Prepared by	TW	Jan 8, 2013
		Approved by	SB	Jan 10, 2013

A/R Category	A/R Balance 31/12/12		Estimated Allowance Percentage		Estimated Required Allowance
0–30 days	US$14,217,156	✓	3%	×	US$ 426,515
31–60 days	2,869,366	✓	6%	×	172,162
61–90 days	1,408,642	✓	15%	×	211,296
91–120 days	1,038,926	✓	25%	×	259,732
Over 120	662,710	✓	40%	×	265,084
Total	US$20,196,800				US$1,334,789
Recorded Allowance					US$1,240,000 TB
Difference					US$ 94,789

✓ – Traced to aged accounts receivable trial balance.
× – Allowance percentages are consistent with prior year, and appear reasonable
    based on historical loss percentages documented in permanent file.
TB – Agreed to trial balance.

Conclusion: Recorded allowance appears understated based on aging analysis. Approximate amount of US$95,000 not considered material. Include on Summary of Possible Misstatements schedule on A-3. (See Figure 24-6 on page 789.)

MEDIA PRODUCTION CITY COMPANY MISSTATEMENTS

The annual general meeting of Media Production City Company (in an Arab country) was attended by the shareholders' representatives, company employees, and the external auditors. The external auditors indicated a number of important misstatements in the company's financial statements as at December 31, 2011.

1. The external auditor indicated a deficit in provisions for doubtful debts of US$26 million (the balance of the current provision being US$15 million) in addition to a deficit in provision for legal claims of US$24.3 million. A provision for a tax case amounting to US$13 million is also required. Management calculated an impairment of 25 percent of the total investment in Media Soft even though it had continued to make losses for a number of years. In addition, an impairment for a similar investment in El Hoda had not been calculated even though its accumulated losses represented 42 percent of the company's capital according to the company's financial statements at 2010.

2. The management of the company sold some land by tender. The external auditor claimed that the sale of this land is in violation of the acquisition contract of the land, which gave this asset to the company free based on a presidential decree and approval of the country's prime minister, and so therefore management is not allowed to sell the land.

3. The external auditor also indicated that one of the buyers of the land did not pay the installments due on January 11, and April 11, 2011 amounting to US$6.88 million. The total value of the land purchased was US$31.96 million. Instead of taking legal action against the buyer, management rescheduled the debts giving the buyer a grace period and adding 10.5 percent interest on the amounts outstanding. The auditor also objected to the recognition of capital gains made from the sale of the land showing the difference between the book value of the land and the market value, and asked for the recognition of the capital gain to be limited to the installments received.

4. The external auditor indicated that management did not send confirmations for clients and credit balances amounting to US$155 million in addition to non-payment of stamp tax on advertisements made by the company amounting to US$13.57 million. The external auditor also indicated non-payment of balances by clients amounting to US$21 million, which should be considered bad debts resulting in overstatement of assets by such an amount.

change in the balance in the allowance for uncollectible accounts should reflect only changes in economic conditions and sales volume. However, if the client's credit policy or the degree to which it correctly functions has significantly changed, auditors must take great care to consider the effects of these changes as well.

Auditors often evaluate the adequacy of the allowance by carefully examining the noncurrent accounts on the aged trial balance to determine which ones have not been paid subsequent to the balance sheet date. The size and age of unpaid balances can then be compared with similar information from previous years to evaluate whether the amount of noncurrent receivables is increasing or decreasing over time. Auditors also gain insights into the collectibility of the accounts by examining credit files, discussions with the credit manager, and review of the client's correspondence file. These procedures are especially important if a few large balances are noncurrent and are not being paid on a regular basis.

Bad Debt Expense After the auditor is satisfied with the allowance for uncollectible accounts, it is easy to verify bad debt expense. Assume that:

- The beginning balance in the allowance account was verified as a part of the previous audit.
- The uncollectible accounts written off were verified as a part of the substantive tests of transactions.
- The ending balance in the allowance account has been verified by various means.

Bad debt expense is then simply a residual balance that can be verified by recalculation.

PUT IT ON THE CARD

Sears, Roebuck & Co., the American retailer, was enjoying a remarkable turnaround in earnings in 1996. However, most of the increase in profits was attributable to interest on Sears credit card balances. In the early 1990s, Sears added more than 17 million new credit card customers. However, many of these new customers were not good credit risks, and they tended to carry high balances. As a result, in 1997, Sears had to increase its allowance for credit card delinquencies to US$393 million, a 44 percent increase.

Unfortunately, the delinquencies were only part of the problem. Many of these delinquent customers also filed for bankruptcy. In fact, by 1997 Sears was a creditor in more than one-third of all bankruptcies filed in the United States. Sears aggressively sought reaffirmation agreements with these customers, in which they pledged to continue making payments on their accounts. However, many of these agreements were not filed in the bankruptcy cases, which meant the company was collecting on unenforceable agreements for debt that no longer legally existed. As a result of a federal investigation, Sears was forced to pay a US$60 million fine and set aside US$475 million in reserves to cover complaints over its debt collection practices. After continuing struggles with write-offs, Sears sold its credit card business to Citigroup in 2003.

Sources: Adapted from De'Ann Weimer, 'Put the Comeback on My Card,' *BusinessWeek* (November 10, 1997), pp. 118–119; John McCormick, 'The Sorry Side of Sears,' *Newsweek* (February 22, 1999), pp. 36–39; and Robert Berner, 'The Struggle in Store for Sears,' *BusinessWeek* (July 24, 2003).

The Client Has Rights to Accounts Receivable

The client's rights to accounts receivable ordinarily cause no audit problems because the receivables usually belong to the client. In some cases, however, a portion of the receivables may have been pledged as collateral, assigned to someone else, factored, or sold at discount. Normally, the client's customers are not aware of the existence of such matters, so the confirmation of receivables will not bring them to light. To uncover instances in which the client has limited rights to receivables, the auditor may review the minutes, discuss with the client, confirm with banks, examine debt contracts for evidence of accounts receivable pledged as collateral, and examine correspondence files.

Accounts Receivable Presentation and Disclosure

Tests of the three presentation and disclosure-related audit objectives are generally done as part of the completion phase of the audit. However, some tests of presentation and disclosure are often done with tests to meet the balance-related audit objectives. For example, when testing sales and accounts receivable, the auditor must understand and evaluate the appropriateness of the client's revenue recognition policy to determine whether it is properly disclosed in the financial statements. The auditor must also decide whether the client has properly combined amounts and disclosed related party information in the statements. To evaluate the adequacy of the presentation and disclosure, the auditor must have a thorough understanding of accounting standards and presentation and disclosure requirements.

An important part of the evaluation involves deciding whether the client has separated material amounts requiring separate disclosure in the statements. For example, receivables from officers and affiliated companies must be segregated from accounts receivable from customers if the amounts are material. Similarly, companies may disclose sales and assets for different business segments separately. The proper aggregation of general ledger balances in the financial statements also requires combining account balances that are not relevant for external users of the statements. If all accounts included in the general ledger were disclosed separately on the statements, most statement users would be more confused than enlightened.

CONFIRMATION OF ACCOUNTS RECEIVABLE

The primary purpose of accounts receivable confirmation, which is considered to be highly reliable audit evidence, is to satisfy the *existence, accuracy,* and *cutoff* objectives.

Types of Confirmation

In performing confirmation procedures, the auditor must first decide the type of confirmation to use.

Positive Confirmation A **positive confirmation** is a communication addressed to the debtor requesting the recipient to confirm directly whether the balance as stated on the confirmation request is correct or incorrect. Figure 16-5 illustrates a positive confirmation in the audit of Arabian Hardware Co.

A **blank (or blind) confirmation form** is a type of positive confirmation that does not state the amount on the confirmation but requests the recipient to fill in the balance or furnish other information. Because blank forms require the recipient to determine the information requested, they are considered more reliable than confirmations that include balance information. Blank forms are rarely used in practice because they often result in lower response rates.

An **invoice confirmation** is another type of positive confirmation in which an individual invoice is confirmed, rather than the customer's entire accounts receivable balance. Many customers use voucher systems that allow them to confirm individual invoices but not balance information. As a result, the use of invoice confirmations may improve confirmation response rates. Invoice confirmations also result in fewer timing differences and other reconciling items than balance confirmations. However, invoice confirmations have the disadvantage of not directly confirming ending balances.

Sales to major customers often involve special terms or side-agreements for the return of goods that may affect the amount and timing of revenue to be recognized from the sale. To address these concerns, positive confirmations often request the customer to confirm the existence of any special terms or side-agreements between the client and customer.

OBJECTIVE 16-4

Obtain and evaluate accounts receivable confirmations.

Positive confirmation

A letter, addressed to the debtor, requesting that the recipient indicate directly on the letter whether the stated account balance is correct or incorrect and, if incorrect, by what amount.

Blank or blind confirmation form

A letter, addressed to the debtor, requesting the recipient to fill in the amount of the accounts receivable balance; it is considered a positive confirmation.

Invoice confirmation

A type of positive confirmation in which an individual invoice is confirmed, rather than the customer's entire accounts receivable balance.

FIGURE 16-5	An Example of a Positive Confirmation

Arabian Hardware Co.

Alex. February 13, 2013

MESSERS/Arabian Hardware Co.

In connection with the examination of our accounts by our auditors, please confirm the correctness of the following balance(s) being indicated by our records as of December 31, 2011.

Balance   **Currency**
4,629,396.36   Debit/~~Credit~~   US $

If there are any discrepancies, please furnish details in your reply.

Thanks for your assistance,

**Deputy Executive President
& Financial Manager**

The above statement is correct/incorrect
Name   :   _____
Title   :   _____
Discrepancies: _____

Negative confirmation

A letter, addressed to the debtor, requesting a response only if the recipient disagrees with the amount of the stated account balance.

Negative Confirmation A **negative confirmation** is also addressed to the debtor but requests a response only when the debtor disagrees with the stated amount. Figure 16-6 illustrates a negative confirmation in the audit of Arabian Hardware Co. that has been attached to a customer's monthly statement.

A positive confirmation is *more reliable* evidence because the auditor can perform follow-up procedures if a response is not received from the debtor. With a negative confirmation, failure to reply must be regarded as a correct response, even though the debtor may have ignored the confirmation request.

Offsetting the reliability disadvantage, negative confirmations are less expensive to send than positive confirmations, and thus more can be distributed for the same total cost. Negative confirmations cost less because there are no second requests and no follow-up of nonresponses.

The determination of which type of confirmation to use is an auditor's decision, and it should be based on the facts in the audit. Auditing standards state that it is acceptable to use negative confirmations only when *all* three of the following circumstances are present:

1. Accounts receivable is made up of a large number of small accounts.
2. Combined assessed control risk and inherent risk is low. The combined risk is unlikely to be low if either internal controls are ineffective or there is a high expectation of misstatements. For example, if prior years' audits indicate that accounts receivable are often disputed or inaccurate, negative confirmations are inappropriate.
3. There is no reason to believe that the recipients of the confirmations are unlikely to give them consideration. For example, if the response rate to positive confirmations in prior years was extremely high or if there are high response rates on audits of similar clients, it is likely that recipients will give negative confirmations reasonable consideration as well.

Typically, when negative confirmations are used, the auditor puts considerable emphasis on the effectiveness of internal controls, substantive tests of transactions, and analytical procedures as evidence of the fairness of accounts receivable, and assumes

---

FIGURE 16-6	An Example of a Negative Bank Confirmation

Commercial Bank CB

Beirut January 21, 2013

To Messrs/

Re: Lebanon Oil Company as of December 31, 2012

Dear Sir,
Upon our customer request, we confirm the following information as of **December 31, 2012**

1. Account No.	Balance:
03 95315948	USD 327727.57 CR
03 07310599	USD 6800.91 DR
03 95016389	EGP 2309294.36 CR
03 95317019	USD ZERO
03 07011452	EGP ZERO
2. Time Deposit	N/L
3. Loans	N/L

This certificate is issued upon our customer's request and without any responsibility on the bank or its officers.

Account Service Unit

that the large majority of the recipients will provide a conscientious reading and response to the confirmation request.

Negative confirmations are often used for audits of hospitals, retail stores, banks, and other industries in which the receivables are due from the general public. It is also common to use a combination of negative and positive confirmations by sending the latter to accounts with large balances and the former to those with small balances.

The auditor's choice of confirmation falls along a continuum, starting with the use of no confirmations in some circumstances, to using only negatives, to using both negatives and positives, to using only positives. The primary factors affecting the auditor's decision are the materiality of total accounts receivable, the number and size of individual accounts, control risk, inherent risk, the effectiveness of confirmations as audit evidence, and the availability of other audit evidence.

Timing

The most reliable evidence from confirmations is obtained when they are sent as close to the balance sheet date as possible. This permits the auditor to directly test the accounts receivable balance on the financial statements without making any inferences about the transactions taking place between the confirmation date and the balance sheet date. However, as a means of completing the audit on a timely basis, it is often necessary to confirm the accounts at an interim date. This is permissible if internal controls are adequate and can provide reasonable assurance that sales, cash receipts, and other credits are properly recorded between the date of the confirmation and the end of the accounting period. The auditor is likely to consider other factors in making the decision, including the materiality of accounts receivable and the auditor's exposure to lawsuits because of the possibility of client bankruptcy and similar risks.

If the decision is made to confirm accounts receivable before year-end, the auditor typically prepares a roll-forward schedule that reconciles the accounts receivable balance at the confirmation date to accounts receivable at the balance sheet date. In addition to performing analytical procedures on the activity during the intervening period, it may be necessary to test the transactions occurring between the confirmation date and the balance sheet date. The auditor can accomplish this by examining internal documents such as duplicate sales invoices, shipping documents, and evidence of cash receipts.

Sampling Decisions

Sample Size The major factors affecting sample size for confirming accounts receivable fall into several categories and include the following:

- Tolerable misstatement
- Inherent risk (relative size of total accounts receivable, number of accounts, prior year results, and expected misstatements)
- Control risk
- Achieved detection risk from other substantive tests (extent and results of substantive tests of transactions, analytical procedures, and other tests of details)
- Type of confirmation (negatives normally require a larger sample size)

Selection of the Items for Testing Some type of *stratification* is desirable with most confirmations. In a typical approach to stratification for selecting the balances for confirmation, an auditor considers both the dollar size of individual accounts and the length of time an account has been outstanding. In most audits, the emphasis should be on confirming larger and older balances because these are most likely to include a significant misstatement. But it is also important to sample some items from every material segment of the population. In many cases, the auditor selects all accounts above a certain dollar amount and selects a random sample from the remainder.

FALSE AUDIT CONFIRMATIONS HIDE FRAUD AT U.S. SUBSIDIARY

Confirmations are normally considered highly reliable evidence because they come from independent third parties. However, in some cases customers have colluded with audit clients and returned false audit confirmations. Such was the case at U.S. Foodservice, Inc., a U.S. subsidiary of Royal Ahold, a company headquartered in The Netherlands. The SEC complaints charged that U.S. Foodservice inflated promotional allowances from vendors by at least US$700 million for fiscal years 2001 and 2002 in order to meet earnings targets. U.S. Foodservice personnel contacted vendors and pressured them to return false confirmation

letters to the auditors. In two separate complaints, the SEC charged 16 individuals who were employees of or agents for vendors that supplied U.S. Foodservice.

Sources: Securities and Exchange Commission Accounting and Auditing Enforcement Release No. 2341, November 2, 2005 (http://www.sec .gov/litigation/litreleases/lr19454.htm); Securities and Exchange Commission Accounting and Auditing Enforcement Release No. 2167, January 13, 2005 (http://www.sec.gov/litigation/ litreleases/lr19034.htm).

When selecting a sample of accounts receivable for confirmation, the auditor should be careful to avoid being influenced by the client. If a client tries to discourage the auditor from sending confirmations to certain customers, the auditor should consider the possibility that the client is attempting to conceal fictitious or known misstatements of accounts receivable.

Maintaining Control

After the items for confirmation have been selected, the auditor must maintain control of the confirmations until they are returned from the customer. When the client assists by preparing the confirmations, enclosing them in envelopes, or putting stamps on the envelopes, close supervision by the auditor is required. A return address must be included on all envelopes to make sure that undelivered mail is received by the CPA firm. Similarly, self-addressed return envelopes accompanying the confirmations must be addressed for delivery to the CPA firm's office. It is even important to mail the confirmations *outside* the client's office. All of these steps are necessary to ensure independent communication between the auditor and the customer.

Follow-Up on Nonresponses

It is inappropriate to regard confirmations mailed but not returned by customers as significant audit evidence. For example, nonresponses to positive confirmations do not provide audit evidence. Similarly, for negative confirmations, the auditor should not conclude that the recipient received the confirmation request and verified the information requested. Negative confirmations do, however, provide some evidence of the existence assertion.

When positive confirmations are used, auditing standards require follow-up procedures for confirmations not returned by the customer. It is common to send second and sometimes even third requests for confirmations. Even with these efforts, some customers do not return the confirmation, so it is necessary to follow up with **alternative audit procedures.** The objective of alternative procedures is to determine by a means other than confirmation whether the nonconfirmed account existed and was properly stated at the confirmation date. For any positive confirmation not returned, auditors can examine the following documentation to verify the existence and accuracy of individual sales transactions making up the ending balance in accounts receivable:

Alternative audit procedures

The follow-up of a positive confirmation not returned by the debtor with the use of documentation evidence to determine whether the recorded receivable exists.

Subsequent Cash Receipts Evidence of the receipt of cash subsequent to the confirmation date includes examining remittance advices, entries in the cash receipts records, or perhaps even subsequent credits in the accounts receivable master file. On the one hand, the examination of evidence of subsequent cash receipts is a highly useful alternative procedure because it is reasonable to assume that a customer would not have made a payment unless it was an existing receivable. On the other hand, payment does not establish whether an obligation existed on the date of the confirmation. In addition, auditors should take care to match each unpaid sales transaction with evidence of its subsequent payment as a test for disputes or disagreements over individual outstanding invoices.

Duplicate Sales Invoices These are useful in verifying the actual issuance of a sales invoice and the actual date of the billing.

Shipping Documents These are important in establishing whether the shipment was actually made and as a test of cutoff.

Correspondence with the Client Usually, the auditor does not need to review correspondence as a part of alternative procedures, but correspondence can be used to disclose disputed and questionable receivables not uncovered by other means.

The extent and nature of the alternative procedures depend primarily on the materiality of the nonresponses, the types of misstatements discovered in the confirmed responses, the subsequent cash receipts from the nonresponses, and the auditor's conclusions about internal control.

It is normally desirable to account for all unconfirmed balances with alternative procedures even if the amounts are small, as a means of properly generalizing from the sample to the population. Another acceptable approach is to assume that nonresponses are 100 percent overstatement amounts.

Analysis of Differences

When the confirmation requests are returned by the customer, the auditor must determine the reason for any reported differences. In many cases, they are caused by timing differences between the client's and the customer's records. It is important to distinguish between timing differences and *exceptions*, which represent misstatements of the accounts receivable balance.

The most commonly reported types of differences in confirmations include:

Payment Has Already Been Made Reported differences typically arise when the customer has made a payment before the confirmation date, but the client has not received the payment in time for recording before the confirmation date. Such instances should be carefully investigated to determine the possibility of a cash receipts cutoff misstatement, lapping, or a theft of cash.

Goods Have Not Been Received These differences typically result because the client records the sale at the date of shipment and the customer records the acquisition when the goods are received. The time that the goods are in transit is often the cause of differences reported on confirmations. These should be investigated to determine the possibility of the customer not receiving the goods at all or the existence of a cutoff misstatement on the client's records.

The Goods Have Been Returned The client's failure to record a credit memo could have resulted from timing differences or the improper recording of sales returns and allowances. Like other differences, these must be investigated.

Clerical Errors and Disputed Amounts The most likely types of reported differences in a client's records are when the customer states that there is an error in the price charged for the goods, the goods are damaged, the proper quantity of goods was not received, and so forth. These differences must be investigated to determine whether the client is in error and the amount of the error.

In most instances, the auditor will ask the client to reconcile the difference and, if necessary, will communicate with the customer to resolve any disagreements. Naturally, the auditor must carefully verify the client's conclusions on each significant difference.

Drawing Conclusions

When all differences have been resolved, including those discovered in performing alternative procedures, the auditor must *reevaluate internal control*. Each client misstatement must be analyzed to determine whether it was consistent or inconsistent with the original assessed level of control risk. If a significant number of misstatements occurred that are inconsistent with the assessment of control risk, it is necessary to revise the assessment and consider the effect of the revision on the audit.

It is also necessary to generalize from the sample to the entire population of accounts receivable. Even though the sum of the misstatements in the sample may not significantly affect the financial statements, the auditor must consider whether the population is likely to be materially misstated. Generalizing from the sample to the population can be done using nonstatistical or statistical sampling techniques and is discussed in Chapter 17.

The auditor should always evaluate the qualitative nature of the misstatements found in the sample, regardless of the dollar amount of the estimated population misstatement. Even if the estimated misstatement is less than the tolerable misstatement for accounts receivable, the misstatements found in a sample can be symptomatic of a more serious problem.

The final decision about accounts receivable and sales is whether sufficient evidence has been obtained through tests of controls and substantive tests of transactions, analytical procedures, cutoff procedures, confirmation, and other substantive tests to justify drawing conclusions about the correctness of the stated balance.

DEVELOPING TESTS OF DETAILS AUDIT PROGRAM

OBJECTIVE 16-5

Design audit procedures for the audit of accounts receivable, using an evidence-planning worksheet as a guide.

We use Arabian Hardware Co. to illustrate the development of audit program procedures for tests of details in the sales and collection cycle, which serves as the summary of this chapter. The determination of these procedures is based on the tests of controls and substantive tests of transactions, as illustrated in Chapters 14 and 15, and the analytical procedures described earlier in this chapter.

Hosni Abdel Latif, the audit senior, prepared the evidence-planning worksheet in Figure 16-7 as an aid to help him decide the extent of planned tests of details of balances. The source of each of the rows is as follows:

- *Tolerable misstatement.* The preliminary judgment of materiality was set at US$442,000 (approximately 6 percent of earnings from operations of US$7,370,000). He allocated US$265,000 to the audit of accounts receivable (see page 559).
- *Acceptable audit risk.* Hosni assessed acceptable audit risk as high because of the good financial condition of the company, its financial stability, and the relatively small number of users of the financial statements.
- *Inherent risk.* Hosni assessed inherent risk as medium for existence and cutoff because of concerns over revenue recognition identified in SAS 99. Hosni also assessed inherent risk as medium for realizable value. In past years, the client made audit adjustments to the allowance for uncollectible accounts because it was found to be understated. Inherent risk was assessed as low for all other objectives.

FIGURE 16-7	Evidence-Planning Worksheet to Decide Tests of Details of Balances for Arabian Hardware Co.— Accounts Receivable

	Detail tie-in	Existence	Completeness	Accuracy	Classification	Cutoff	Realizable value	Rights
Acceptable audit risk	High	High	High	High	High	High	High	High
Inherent risk	Low	Medium	Low	Low	Low	Medium	Medium	Low
Control risk— Sales	Low	Medium	Low	High	Low	Medium	High	Not applicable
Control risk— Cash receipts	Low	Medium	Low	Low	Low	Low	Not applicable	Not applicable
Control risk— Additional controls	None	None	None	None	None	None	None	Low
Substantive tests of transactions— Sales	Good results	Good results	Good results	Fair results	Good results	Unacceptable results	Not applicable	Not applicable
Substantive tests of transactions— Cash receipts	Good results	Good results	Good results	Good results	Good results	Good results	Not applicable	Not applicable
Analytical procedures	Good results	Good results	Good results	Good results	Good results	Good results	Unacceptable results	Not applicable
Planned detection risk for tests of details of balances	High	Medium	High	Medium	High	Low	Low	High
Planned audit evidence for tests of details of balances	Low	Medium	Low	Medium	Low	High	High	Low

Tolerable misstatement US$265,000

- *Control risk.* Control risk assessments for each audit objective are the same as those in Figure 15-6 in Chapter 15. (Recall that results of tests of controls and substantive tests of transactions in Chapter 15 were consistent with the auditor's initial control risk assessments, except for the accuracy and realizable value objectives for sales.)
- *Substantive tests of transactions results.* These results were also taken from Figure 15-6. (Recall from Chapter 15 that all results were acceptable except for the accuracy and cutoff objectives for sales.)
- *Analytical procedures.* See Tables 16-2 and 16-3.
- *Planned detection risk* and *planned audit evidence.* These two rows are decided for each objective based on the conclusions in the other rows.

TABLE 16-4	Balance-Related Audit Objectives and Audit Program for Arabian Hardware Co.—Sales and Collection Cycle (Design Format)

Balance-Related Audit Objective	Audit Procedure
Accounts receivable in the aged trial balance agree with related master file amounts, and the total is correctly added and agrees with the general ledger (detail tie-in).	Trace ten accounts from the trial balance to accounts on master file (6). Foot two pages of the trial balance, and total all pages (7). Trace the balance to the general ledger (8).
The accounts receivable on the aged trial balance exist (existence).	Confirm accounts receivable, using positive confirmations. Confirm all amounts over US$100,000 and a nonstatistical sample of the remainder (10). Perform alternative procedures for all confirmations not returned on the first or second request (11). Review accounts receivable trial balance for large and unusual receivables (1).
Existing accounts receivable are included in the aged trial balance (completeness).	Trace five accounts from the accounts receivable master file to the aged trial balance (9).
Accounts receivable in the trial balance are accurate (accuracy).	Confirm accounts receivable, using positive confirmations. Confirm all amounts over US$100,000 and a nonstatistical sample of the remainder (10). Perform alternative procedures for all confirmations not returned on the first or second request (11). Review accounts receivable trial balance for large and unusual receivables (1).
Accounts receivable on the aged trial balance are correctly classified (classification).	Review the receivables listed on the aged trial balance for notes and related party receivables (3). Inquire of management whether there are any related party, notes, or long-term receivables included in the trial balance (4).
Transactions in the sales and collection cycle are recorded in the proper period (cutoff).	Select the last 20 sales transactions from the current year's sales journal and the first 20 from the subsequent year's and trace each to the related shipping documents, checking for the date of actual shipment and the correct recording (14). Review large sales returns and allowances before and after the balance sheet date to determine whether they are recorded in the correct period (15).
Accounts receivable is stated at realizable value (realizable value).	Trace ten accounts from the aging schedule to the accounts receivable master file to test for the correct aging on the trial balance (6). Foot the aging columns on the trial balance and total the pages (7). Cross-foot the aging columns (7). Discuss with the credit manager the likelihood of collecting older accounts. Examine subsequent cash receipts and the credit file on all accounts over 90 days and evaluate whether the receivables are collectible (12). Evaluate whether the allowance is adequate after performing other audit procedures for collectibility of receivables (13).
The client has rights to accounts receivable on the trial balance (rights).	Review the minutes of the board of directors' meetings for any indication of pledged or factored accounts receivable (5). Inquire of management whether any receivables are pledged or factored (5).

Table 16-4 shows the tests of details audit program for accounts receivable, by objective, and for the allowance for uncollectible accounts. The audit program reflects the conclusions for planned audit evidence on the evidence-planning worksheet in Figure 16-7.

A summary of the audit procedures contained in Table 16-5 shows audit program for receivables. The audit procedures are identical to those in Table 16-4 except for procedure 2, which is an analytical procedure. The numbers in parentheses are a cross reference between the two tables.

TABLE 16-5	Test of Details of Balances Audit Program for Arabian Hardware Company—Sales and Collection Cycle (Performance Format)

1. Review accounts receivable trial balance for large and unusual receivables.

2. Calculate analytical procedures indicated in carry-forward audit schedules (not included) and follow up on any significant changes from prior years.

3. Review the receivables listed on the aged trial balance for notes and related party receivables.

4. Inquire of management whether there are any related party, notes, or long-term receivables included in the trial balance.

5. Review the minutes of the board of directors' meetings and inquire of management to determine whether any receivables are pledged or factored.

6. Trace ten accounts from the trial balance to the accounts receivable master file for aging and the balance.

7. Foot two pages of the trial balance for aging columns and balance, total all pages and cross-foot the aging.

8. Trace the balance to the general ledger.

9. Trace five accounts from the accounts receivable master file to the aged trial balance.

10. Confirm accounts receivable, using positive confirmations. Confirm all amounts over US$100,000 and a nonstatistical sample of the remainder.

11. Perform alternative procedures for all confirmations not returned on the first or second request.

12. Discuss with the credit manager the likelihood of collecting older accounts. Examine subsequent cash receipts and the credit file on all larger accounts over 90 days and evaluate whether the receivables are collectible.

13. Evaluate whether the allowance is adequate after performing other audit procedures for collectibility of receivables.

14. Select the last 20 sales transactions from the current year's sales journal and the first 20 from the subsequent year's and trace each to the related shipping documents, checking for the date of actual shipment and the correct recording.

15. Review large sales returns and allowances before and after the balance sheet date to determine whether they are recorded in the correct period.

SUMMARY

This chapter introduced the procedures related to the test of balances of the sales and collection cycle. This cycle is considered an important process in the audit of business enterprises mainly for manufacturing companies. Documents and procedures related to the test of details of balances and the application of analytical procedures for the sales and collection cycle were presented showing the role of the external auditor in checking the reliability of accounts associated with the cycle. Various audit objectives were analyzed showing how auditors can use various audit evidence to achieve these objectives taking into consideration the effects of the auditor's assessment of the internal control on financial reporting.

ESSENTIAL TERMS

Accounts receivable balance-related audit objectives   p. 539

Aged trial balance   p. 546

Alternative audit procedures   p. 556

Blank or blind confirmation form   p. 553

Cutoff misstatements   p. 548

Invoice confirmation   p. 553

Negative confirmation   p. 554

Positive confirmation   p. 553

Realizable value of accounts receivable   p. 550

Timing difference   p. 549

REVIEW QUESTIONS

16-1 (Objective 16-1) Distinguish among tests of details of balances, tests of controls, and substantive tests of transactions for the sales and collection cycle. Explain how the tests of controls and substantive tests of transactions affect the tests of details of balances.

16-2 (Objective 16-1) Mohamed El Batran, an auditor, expresses the following viewpoint: "I do not believe in performing tests of controls and substantive tests of transactions for the sales and collection cycle. As an alternative, I send a lot of negative confirmations on every audit at an interim date. If I find a lot of misstatements, I analyze them to determine their cause. If internal controls are inadequate, I send positive confirmations at year-end to evaluate the amount of misstatements. If the negative confirmations result in minimal misstatements, which is often the case, I have found that the internal controls are effective without bothering to perform tests of controls and substantive tests of transactions, and the confirmation requirement has been satisfied at the same time. In my opinion, the best test of internal controls is to go directly to third parties." Evaluate his point of view.

16-3 (Objective 16-2) List five analytical procedures for the sales and collection cycle. For each test, describe a misstatement that could be identified.

16-4 (Objective 16-3) Identify the eight accounts receivable balance-related audit objectives. For each objective, list one audit procedure.

16-5 (Objective 16-3) Which of the eight accounts receivable balance-related audit objectives can be partially satisfied by confirmations with customers?

16-6 (Objective 16-3) State the purpose of footing the total column in the client's accounts receivable trial balance, tracing individual customer names and amounts to the accounts receivable master file, and tracing the total to the general ledger. Is it necessary to trace each amount to the master file? Why?

16-7 (Objective 16-3) Distinguish between accuracy tests of gross accounts receivable and tests of the realizable value of receivables.

16-8 (Objective 16-3) Explain why you agree or disagree with the following statement: "In most audits, it is more important to test carefully the cutoff for sales than for cash receipts." Describe how you perform each type of test, assuming documents are prenumbered.

16-9 (Objective 16-4) Evaluate the following statement: "In many audits in which accounts receivable is material, the requirement of confirming customer balances is a waste of time and would not be performed by competent auditors if it were not required by auditing standards. When internal controls are excellent and there are a large number of small receivables from customers who do not recognize the function of confirmation, it is a meaningless procedure. Examples include well-run utilities and retail stores. In these situations, tests of controls and substantive tests of transactions are far more effective than confirmations."

16-10 (Objective 16-4) Distinguish between a positive and a negative confirmation and state the circumstances in which each should be used. Why do auditing firms sometimes use a combination of positive and negative confirmations on the same audit?

16-11 (Objective 16-4) Under what circumstances is it acceptable to confirm accounts receivable before the balance sheet date?

16-12 (Objective 16-4) State the most important factors affecting the sample size in confirmations of accounts receivable.

16-13 (Objective 16-4) In Chapter 15, one of the points brought out was the need to obtain a representative sample of the population. How can this concept be reconciled with the statement in this chapter that the emphasis should be on confirming larger and older balances because these are most likely to contain misstatements?

16-14 (Objective 16-4) Define what is meant by alternative procedures in the confirmation of accounts receivable and explain their purpose. Which alternative procedures are the most reliable? Why?

16-15 (Objective 16-4) Explain why the analysis of differences is important in the confirmation of accounts receivable, even if the misstatements in the sample are not material.

16-16 (Objective 16-4) State three types of differences that might be observed in the confirmation of accounts receivable that do not constitute misstatements. For each, state an audit procedure that will verify the difference.

16-17 (Objective 16-1) What is the relationship of each of the following to the sales and collection cycle: flowcharts, assessing control risk, tests of controls, and tests of details of balances?

16-18 (Objective 16-3) Customers purchasing products through a company's internet website generally pay for those goods by providing their personal credit card information. Describe how a company's sale of products through its website affects the auditor's tests of accounts receivable in the financial statement audit.

MULTIPLE CHOICE QUESTIONS FROM CPA EXAMINATIONS

16-19 (Objective 16-2) The following questions concern analytical procedures in the sales and collection cycle. Choose the best response.

a. As a result of analytical procedures, the auditor determines that the gross profit percentage has declined from 30% in the preceding year to 20% in the current year. The auditor should
   (1) express a qualified opinion due to inability of the client company to continue as a going concern.
   (2) evaluate management's performance in causing this decline.
   (3) require footnote disclosure.
   (4) consider the possibility of a misstatement in the financial statements.

b. After an auditor has determined that accounts receivable have increased as a result of slow collections in a 'tight money' environment, the auditor will be likely to
   (1) increase the balance in the allowance for bad debt account.
   (2) review the going concern ramifications.
   (3) review the credit and collection policy.
   (4) expand tests of collectibility.

c. In connection with his review of key ratios, the auditor notes that Hassan Kamal had accounts receivable equal to 30 days' sales at December 31, 2010, and to 45 days' sales at December 31, 2011. Assuming that there have been no changes in economic conditions, clientele, or sales mix, this change most likely will indicate
   (1) a steady increase in sales in 2011.
   (2) an easing of credit policies in 2011.
   (3) a decrease in accounts receivable relative to sales in 2011.
   (4) a steady decrease in sales in 2011.

16-20 (Objective 16-4) The following questions deal with confirmation of accounts receivable. Choose the best response.

a. The negative form of accounts receivable confirmation request is useful *except* when
   (1) internal control surrounding accounts receivable is considered to be effective.
   (2) a large number of small balances are involved.
   (3) the auditor has reason to believe the persons receiving the requests are likely to give them consideration.
   (4) individual account balances are relatively large.

b. The return of a positive confirmation of accounts receivable without an exception attests to the
   (1) collectibility of the receivable balance.
   (2) accuracy of the receivable balance.
   (3) accuracy of the aging of accounts receivable.
   (4) accuracy of the allowance for uncollectible accounts.

c. In confirming a client's accounts receivable in prior years, an auditor found that there were many differences between the recorded account balances and the confirmation responses. These differences, which were not misstatements, required substantial time to resolve. In defining the sampling unit for the current year's audit, the auditor will most likely choose
   (1) individual overdue balances.   (2) individual invoices.
   (3) small account balances.   (4) large account balances.

16-21 (Objective 16-3) The following questions concern audit objectives and management assertions for accounts receivable. Choose the best response.

a. When evaluating the adequacy of the allowance for uncollectible accounts, an auditor reviews the entity's aging of receivables to support management's balance-related assertion of
   (1) existence.
   (2) completeness.
   (3) valuation and allocation.
   (4) rights and obligations.

b. Which of the following audit procedures will best uncover an understatement of sales and accounts receivable?
   (1) Test a sample of sales transactions, selecting the sample from prenumbered shipping documents.
   (2) Test a sample of sales transactions, selecting the sample from sales invoices recorded in the sales journal.
   (3) Confirm accounts receivable.
   (4) Review the aged accounts receivable trial balance.

DISCUSSION QUESTIONS AND PROBLEMS

16-22 (Objective 16-3) The following are the eight balance-related audit objectives, six tests of details of balances for accounts receivable, and seven tests of controls or substantive tests of transactions for the sales and collection cycle:

Balance-Related Audit Objectives

Detail tie-in	Classification
Existence	Cutoff
Completeness	Realizable value
Accuracy	Rights

Test of Details of Balances, Test of Control, or Substantive Test of Transactions Audit Procedure

1. Confirm accounts receivable.
2. Review sales returns after the balance sheet date to determine whether any are applicable to the current year.
3. Compare dates on shipping documents and the sales journal throughout the year.
4. Perform alternative procedures for nonresponses to confirmation.

5. Examine sales transactions for related party or employee sales recorded as regular sales.
6. Examine duplicate sales invoices for consignment sales and other shipments for which title has not passed.
7. Trace a sample of accounts from the accounts receivable master file to the aged trial balance.
8. Trace recorded sales transactions to shipping documents to determine whether a document exists.
9. Examine duplicate sales invoices for initials that indicate internal verification of extensions and footings.
10. Trace a sample of shipping documents to related sales invoice entries in the sales journal.
11. Compare amounts and dates on the aged trial balance and accounts receivable master file.
12. Trace from the sales journal to the accounts receivable master file to make sure the information is the same.
13. Inquire of management whether there are notes from related parties included with trade receivables.

a. Identify which procedures are tests of details of balances, which are tests of controls, and which are substantive tests of transactions.

b. Identify one test of details and one test of control or substantive test of transactions that will partially satisfy each balance-related audit objective. Each procedure must be used at least once.

16-23 (Objective 16-3) The following are common tests of details of balances for the audit of accounts receivable:

1. Obtain a list of aged accounts receivable, foot the list, and trace the total to the general ledger.
2. Trace 35 accounts to the accounts receivable master file for name, amount, and age categories.
3. Examine and document cash receipts on accounts receivable for 20 days after the engagement date.
4. Request 25 positive and 65 negative confirmations of accounts receivable.
5. Perform alternative procedures on accounts not responding to second requests by examining subsequent cash receipts documentation and shipping reports or sales invoices.
6. Test the sales cutoff by tracing entries in the sales journal for 15 days before and after the balance sheet date to shipping documents, if available, and/or sales invoices.
7. Determine whether any accounts receivable have been pledged, discounted, sold, assigned, or guaranteed by others.
8. Evaluate the materiality of credit balances in the aged trial balance.

For each audit procedure, identify the balance-related audit objective or objectives it   **Required**
partially or fully satisfies.

16-24 (Objective 16-3) The following misstatements are sometimes found in the sales and collection cycle's account balances:

1. Several accounts receivable in the accounts receivable master file are not included in the aged trial balance.
2. One account receivable in the accounts receivable master file is included on the aged trial balance twice.
3. A shipment made in the subsequent period is recorded as a current period sale.

4. The allowance for uncollectible accounts is inadequate because of the client's failure to reflect depressed economic conditions in the allowance.
5. Several accounts receivable are in dispute as a result of claims of defective merchandise.
6. The pledging of accounts receivable to the bank for a loan is not disclosed in the financial statements.
7. Goods shipped and included in the current period sales were returned in the subsequent period.
8. Long-term interest-bearing notes receivable from affiliated companies are included in accounts receivable.
9. The accounts receivable trial balance total does not equal the amount in the general ledger.

Required

a. For each misstatement, identify the balance-related audit objective to which it pertains.

b. For each misstatement, list an internal control that should prevent it.

c. For each misstatement, list one test of details of balances audit procedure that the auditor can use to detect it.

16-25 (Objective 16-3) The following are audit procedures in the sales and collection cycle:

1. Examine a sample of shipping documents to determine whether each has a sales invoice number included on it.
2. Examine a sample of noncash credits in the accounts receivable master file to determine if the internal auditor has initialed each, indicating internal verification.
3. Discuss with the sales manager whether any sales allowances have been granted after the balance sheet date that may apply to the current period.
4. Add the columns on the aged trial balance and compare the total with the general ledger.
5. Observe whether the controller makes an independent comparison of the total in the general ledger with the trial balance of accounts receivable.
6. Compare the date on a sample of shipping documents throughout the year with related duplicate sales invoices and the accounts receivable master file.
7. Examine a sample of customer orders and see if each has a credit authorization.
8. Compare the date on a sample of shipping documents a few days before and after the balance sheet date with related sales journal transactions.
9. Compute the ratio of allowance for uncollectible accounts divided by accounts receivable and compare with previous years.

Required

a. For each procedure, identify the applicable type of audit evidence.

b. For each procedure, identify which of the following it is:
    (1) Test of control
    (2) Substantive test of transactions
    (3) Analytical procedure
    (4) Test of details of balances

c. For those procedures you identified as a test of control or substantive test of transactions, what transaction-related audit objective or objectives are being satisfied?

d. For those procedures you identified as a test of details of balances, what balance-related audit objective or objectives are being satisfied?

16-26 (Objective 16-3) Abou El Yousr Foodstuffs sells products to small grocery stores. Prenumbered shipping documents are required by the company to be issued for each sale. The shipping clerk writes the date on the shipping document whenever there is a shipment or pickup. The final shipment made in the fiscal year ending August 31, 2011, was recorded on document 2167. Shipments are billed in the order the billing clerk receives the shipping documents. For late August and early September, shipping documents are billed on sales invoices as follows:

Shipping Document No.	Sales Invoice No.
2163	5437
2164	5431
2165	5432
2166	5435
2167	5436
2168	5433
2169	5434
2170	5438
2171	5440
2172	5439

The August and September sales journals have the following information included:

SALES JOURNAL—AUGUST 2011

Day of Month	Sales Invoice No.	Amount of Sale (US$)
30	5431	726.11
30	5434	4,214.30
31	5432	419.83
31	5433	1,620.22
31	5435	47.74

SALES JOURNAL—SEPTEMBER 2011

Day of Month	Sales Invoice No.	Amount of Sale (US$)
1	5437	2,541.31
1	5436	106.39
1	5438	852.06
2	5440	1,250.50
2	5439	646.58

Required

a. What are the accounting standards requirements for a correct sales cutoff?

b. Which sales invoices, if any, are recorded in the wrong accounting period? Prepare an adjusting entry to correct the financial statements for the year ending August 31, 2011. Assume that the company uses a periodic inventory system (i.e. inventory and cost of sales do not need to be adjusted).

c. Assume that the shipping clerk accidentally wrote August 2011 on shipping documents 2168 through 2172. Explain how that will affect the correctness of the financial statements. How will you, as an auditor, discover that error?

d. Describe, in general terms, the audit procedures you would follow in making sure that cutoff for sales is accurate at the balance sheet date.

e. Identify internal controls that will reduce the likelihood of cutoff misstatements. How would you test each control?

16-27 (Objectives 16-2, 16-3) The Radio & Electronic Company sells electronics equipment, and has grown rapidly in the last year by adding new customers. The audit partner has asked you to evaluate the allowance for doubtful accounts at December 31, 2011. Comparative information on sales and accounts receivable is included below:

	Year Ended Dec 31, 2010	Year Ended Dec 31, 2011
Sales	US$12,169,876	US$10,452,513
Accounts Receivable	1,440,381	1,030,933
Allowance for doubtful accounts	90,000	75,000
Bad debt charge-offs	114,849	103,471
Accounts Receivable:		
0–30 days	US$897,035	US$695,041
30–60 days	254,269	160,989
60–90 days	171,846	105,997
Over 90 days	117,231	68,906
TOTAL	US$ 1,440,381	US$ 1,030,933

Required

a. Identify what tests of controls and substantive tests of transactions you recommend be performed before conducting your analysis of the allowance for doubtful accounts.

b. Perform analytical procedures to evaluate whether the allowance is fairly stated at December 31, 2011. Assume tolerable misstatement for the allowance account is US$15,000.

16-28 (Objective 16-4) In the confirmation of accounts receivable for the Reliable Service Company, 85 positive and no negative confirmations were mailed to customers. This represents 35% of the dollar balance of the total accounts receivable. Second requests were sent for all nonresponses, but there were still ten customers who did not respond. The decision was made to perform alternative procedures on the ten unanswered confirmation requests. An assistant is requested to conduct the alternative procedures and report to the senior auditor after he has completed his tests on two accounts. He prepared the following information for the audit files:

1. Confirmation request no. 9
   Customer name—Obaida Milling Co.
   Balance—US$3,621 at December 31, 2010
      Subsequent cash receipts per the
         accounts receivable master file:

      January 15, 2011—US$1,837
      January 29, 2011—US$1,263
      February 6, 2011—US$1,429

2. Confirmation request no. 26
   Customer name—ATP Repair Service
   Balance—US$2,500 at December 31, 2010
      Subsequent cash receipts per the
         accounts receivable master file   February 9, 2011—US$500
      Sales invoices per the accounts receivable
         master file (I examined the duplicate invoice)   September 1, 2010—US$4,200

Required

a. If you are called on to evaluate the adequacy of the sample size, the type of confirmation used, and the percent of accounts confirmed, what additional information will you need?

b. Discuss the need to send second requests and perform alternative procedures for nonresponses.

c. Evaluate the adequacy of the alternative procedures used for verifying the two nonresponses.

16-29 (Objective 16-4) You have been assigned to the confirmation of aged accounts receivable for the Blank Paper Company audit. You have tested the aged trial balance and selected the accounts for confirming. Before the confirmation requests are mailed, the controller asks to look at the accounts you intend to confirm to determine whether he will permit you to send them.

He reviews the list and informs you that he does not want you to confirm six of the accounts on your list. Two of them are credit balances, one is a zero balance, two of the other three have a fairly small balance, and the remaining balance is highly material. The reason he gives is that he feels the confirmations will upset these customers because "they are kind of hard to get along with." He does not want the credit balances confirmed because it may encourage the customer to ask for a refund.

In addition, the controller asks you to send an additional 20 confirmations to customers he has listed for you. He does this as a means of credit collection for "those stupid idiots who won't know the difference between an auditor and a credit collection agency."

a. Is it acceptable for the controller to review the list of accounts you intend to confirm? Discuss.   **Required**

b. Discuss the appropriateness of sending the 20 additional confirmations to the customers.

c. Assuming that the auditor complies with all the controller's requests, what is the effect on the auditor's opinion?

CASES

16-30 (Objectives 16-1, 16-2, 16-3) Data Company operates in the information technology field to serve the banking and the services sectors. The company is preparing statistics to be distributed to its customers through an information network. Currently 70 employees work in the company. The draft accounts of the company indicate that the revenues amounted to US$750,000 and net profit amounted to US$33,340 for the year ended December 31, 2010.

Sixty-seven percent of the company's stocks are owned by members of the board of directors, and 33 percent by an Indian company working in the field of information technology which invested in Data Company in 2011. As part of the business deal the Indian company designated a non-executive director from outside the company. The following notes were acquired during the initial audit of the company for the year ended December 31, 2010 and are left for you for a decision.

1. *The Revenues:*
   - The revenues are collected by yearly subscription for using the information network of Data Company Subscriptions and can be collected in advance at the beginning of the year, or on a monthly basis.
   - The current revenues recognition policy:
     - 65% of the revenues are realized in January.
     - 35% of the revenues are realized equally over 11 months.
   - The board of directors justified the use of this policy using the argument that most of the costs of providing their customers with the network are incurred at the beginning of the year. The costs of the programs and collecting the data are incurred before offering the product to the market. The board of directors indicated that most of the marketing and administrative costs are incurred during the stage of customer recruitment and not in the after sales stage.

2. *Intangible Assets:*
   - The draft accounts indicated that there is an intangible asset of US$216,670 representing the patent for developing the company's programs.
   - The company is capitalizing the development costs to be depreciated over three years if the project starts to earn profits.
   - Without that asset the balance sheet will give negative net assets.

3. *Loans:*

As part of the business agreement with the Indian company, it was agreed that:

- The quick ratio or cash cover should not be less than two times.
- The profits should be at least three times interest coverage ratio.
- The board of directors informed you that the contracts terms are not followed and it is not expected to be followed in the next 12 months.

Required   For each of the above notes:

a. Comment on the issues that should be taken into consideration.

b. Determine the appropriate audit guidance.

16-31 (Objectives 16-1, 16-3, 16-4, 16-5) You are auditing the sales and collection cycle for Zoro Electronics, a small electronics manufacturer, who deals with a variety of computer makers. The company is respected in its industry for its creativity and rapid growth, but their accounting office is perpetually neglected, and the sales department frequently makes errors in billing clients. In previous years, your auditing firm has found quite a few misstatements in billings, cash receipts, and accounts receivable. Like many companies, the largest assets are accounts receivable, inventory, and fixed assets.

Zoro Electronics has several large loans payable to local banks, and the two banks have told management that they are reluctant to extend more credit, especially considering that a bigger and well known electronics manufacturer is moving into the area. In previous slow years Zoro Electronics covered deficits with capital it had saved, but its recent expansion has diminished its capital reserves substantially.

In previous years, your response from clients of Zoro Electronics to confirmation requests has been frustrating at best. The response rate has been extremely low, and those who did reply did not know the purpose of the confirmation or their correct outstanding balance. You have had the same experience in confirming receivables with other, similar organizations.

You conclude that control over cash is excellent and the likelihood of fraud is extremely small. You are less confident about unintentional errors in billing, recording sales, cash receipts, accounts receivable, and bad debts.

Required   a. Identify the major factors affecting client business risk and acceptable audit risk for this audit.

b. What inherent risks are you concerned about?

c. In this audit of the sale and collection cycle, which types of tests are you likely to emphasize?

d. For each of the following, explain whether you plan to emphasize the tests and give reasons:
   (1) Tests of controls
   (2) Confirmations
   (3) Substantive tests of transactions
   (4) Analytical procedures
   (5) Tests of details of balances

ACL PROBLEM

16-32 (Objective 16-3) This problem requires the use of ACL software, which is included in MyAccountingLab. Information about installing and using ACL and solving this problem can be found in the Appendix, pages 855–859. You should read all of the reference material preceding the instructions for 'Quick Sort' before locating the appropriate command to answer questions a–f. For this problem use the Metaphor_Trans_All file in ACL Demo, which is a file of outstanding sales invoices (each row represents an invoice transaction).

The suggested command or other source of information needed to solve the problem requirement is included at the end of each question.

Required

a. Determine the total number of invoices (read the bottom of the Metaphor Trans All file screen) and total unpaid invoices outstanding (NEWBAL) for comparison to the general ledger. (Total Field)

b. How many of the invoices included a finance charge (FINCHG) and what was the total amount of the finance charges? (Filter, Count Records, and Total Field)

c. Determine and print accounts receivable outstanding from each customer and total the amount for comparison to part a (Note: remove the filter from step b first). (Summarize and Total Field) Which customer number has the largest balance due?

d. What is the largest and smallest account balance outstanding? (Quick Sort)

e. For the account with the largest balance, prepare and print an aging of the account from the transaction file using the statement date labeled 'STMTTDT.' Use the aging date as of 30/4/2003 and 'NEWBAL' as the subtotal field. (Filter and Age)

f. To better decide the customers to select for confirmation you decide to stratify customer balances into two intervals after excluding all balances less than US$5,000. How many balances are greater than US$5,000? Print the output. (Filter and Stratify)

MYLAB ACTIVITY

Visit MyAccountingLab and complete the following activity:

→ Integrated Case Application: Pinnacle Manufacturing: Part VI

CHAPTER 17

AUDIT SAMPLING FOR TESTS OF DETAILS OF BALANCES

Both Statistical And Nonstatistical Sampling Are Acceptable Under Auditing Standards, But Whichever Is Used, It Must Be Done Right

Bob Lake was the manager on the audit of Images, Inc., a specialty retailer that had shops throughout the Midwest of the United States. Images appealed to upscale working women and offered its own credit card. Images' accounting was done centrally. Transactions were captured online and sales and accounts receivable files were maintained on a database.

Bob Lake's firm encouraged the use of statistical sampling in its practice and provided a training program for the development of a statistical coordinator for each office. The coordinator in Bob's office was Barbara Ennis. Bob believed that sales transactions and accounts receivable confirmation tests should be done using statistical sampling and asked Barbara to help design and oversee the statistical aspects of this testing.

Barbara developed a program for the design of confirmation audit procedures as part of doing tests of details of balances for accounts receivable. Her work included determining sample sizes. She left the program with Bob to carry out and said that she would be available to help evaluate the results after the tests were performed.

When all the confirmation replies were received or alternative procedures were completed several weeks later, Bob called Barbara to do the statistical evaluation. Much to his dismay, he found out that Barbara had left the firm, and worse, there was no statistically trained person to take her place. Bob was under a lot of pressure to get the job completed and decided to make the statistical calculations himself. Based on his calculations, he concluded that the potential misstatement was large, but not material, so Bob concluded the objectives of the confirmation tests had been met.

The next year Images, Inc.'s earnings declined sharply, partially because of large write-offs of accounts receivable. The stock price dropped sharply and a class action suit was filed, naming Bob's firm among the defendants. An outside expert was brought in to review the audit documentation. The expert redid all of Bob's work and found errors in the statistical calculations. The expert calculated that the misstatement in accounts receivable, based on the auditor's sample, was significantly more than a material amount. Bob's firm settled the suit for US$3.5 million.

In Chapter 16, we moved into phase III of the audit process by examining analytical procedures and tests of details of balances for accounts receivable. We will now continue with phase III by determining sample size and items to select from the population for the audit of accounts receivable. Although the concepts in this chapter deal with accounts receivable, they apply to the audit of many other account balances.

As the story about the audit of Images, Inc., demonstrates, auditors must correctly use sampling to avoid making incorrect conclusions about a population. While both statistical and nonstatistical audit sampling methods are used extensively for tests of details of balances, auditors must decide which method to use, depending on their preference, experience, and knowledge about statistical sampling. This chapter should help you make correct inferences about populations using either statistical or nonstatistical methods.

Before starting the study of this chapter, we suggest you refer to Figure 13-9 on page 449 to be sure you understand where we are in the audit process. At this stage, all items in phases I and II will have been completed before auditors determine sample size and items to select from the population. Also, the auditor will have completed substantive analytical procedures and designed audit procedures for tests of details of balances, as covered in Chapter 16 (part of phase III). The auditor cannot perform the audit procedures for tests of details of balances until first deciding sample size and items to select from the population.

Relevant International Standards on Auditing	
ISA 200	Overall Objectives of the Independent Auditor and the Conduct of an Audit in Accordance with International Standards on Auditing
ISA 230	Audit Documentation
ISA 300	Planning an Audit of Financial Statements
ISA 320	Materiality in Planning and Performing an Audit
ISA 450	Evaluation of Misstatements Identified during the Audit
ISA 500	Audit Evidence
ISA 510	Initial Audit Engagements—Opening Balances
ISA 530	Audit Sampling

COMPARISONS OF AUDIT SAMPLING FOR TESTS OF DETAILS OF BALANCES AND FOR TESTS OF CONTROLS AND SUBSTANTIVE TESTS OF TRANSACTIONS

OBJECTIVE 17-1

Differentiate audit sampling for tests of details of balances and for tests of controls and substantive tests of transactions.

Most of the sampling concepts for tests of controls and substantive tests of transactions, which were discussed in Chapter 15, apply equally to sampling for tests of details of balances. In both cases, an auditor wants to make inferences about the entire population based on a sample. Both sampling and nonsampling risks are therefore important for tests of controls, substantive tests of transactions, and tests of details of balances. To address sampling risk, auditors can use either nonstatistical or statistical methods for all three types of tests.

The main differences among tests of controls, substantive tests of transactions, and tests of details of balances are in what the auditor wants to measure.

Type of Test	What it Measures
Tests of controls	• The operating effectiveness of internal controls
Substantive tests of transactions	• The effectiveness of controls
	• The monetary correctness of transactions in the accounting system
Tests of details of balances	• Whether the dollar amounts of account balances are materially misstated

Auditors perform tests of controls and substantive tests of transactions:

- To determine whether the exception rate in the population is sufficiently low
- To reduce assessed control risk and thereby reduce tests of details of balances

Unlike for tests of controls and substantive tests of transactions, auditors rarely use rate of occurrence tests in tests of details of balances. Instead, auditors use sampling methods that provide results in *dollar* terms. There are three primary types of sampling methods used for calculating dollar misstatements in account balances addressed in the this chapter: nonstatistical sampling, monetary unit sampling, and variables sampling.

NONSTATISTICAL SAMPLING

There are 14 steps required in audit sampling for tests of details of balances. These steps parallel the 14 steps used for sampling for tests of controls and substantive tests of transactions, although the objectives differ. As an auditor, you need to understand how audit sampling for tests of details of balances both resembles and differs from audit sampling for tests of controls and substantive tests of transactions. Let's take a closer look:

OBJECTIVE 17-2

Apply nonstatistical sampling to tests of details of balances.

Steps—Audit Sampling for Tests of Details of Balances	Steps—Audit Sampling for Tests of Controls and Substantive Tests of Transactions (see page 521)
Plan the Sample	*Plan the Sample*
1. State the objectives of the audit test.	1. State the objectives of the audit test.
2. Decide whether audit sampling applies.	2. Decide whether audit sampling applies.
3. Define a misstatement.	3. Define attributes and exception conditions.
4. Define the population.	4. Define the population.
5. Define the sampling unit.	5. Define the sampling unit.
6. Specify tolerable misstatement.	6. Specify the tolerable exception rate.
7. Specify acceptable risk of incorrect acceptance.	7. Specify acceptable risk of assessing control risk too low.
8. Estimate misstatements in the population.	8. Estimate the population exception rate.
9. Determine the initial sample size.	9. Determine the initial sample size.
Select the Sample and Perform the Audit Procedures	*Select the Sample and Perform the Audit Procedures*
10. Select the sample.	10. Select the sample.
11. Perform the audit procedures.	11. Perform the audit procedures.

Steps—Audit Sampling for Tests of Details of Balances	Steps—Audit Sampling for Tests of Controls and Substantive Tests of Transactions (see page 521)
Evaluate the Results	*Evaluate the Results*
12. Generalize from the sample to the population.	12. Generalize from the sample to the population.
13. Analyze the misstatements.	13. Analyze the exceptions.
14. Decide the acceptability of the population.	14. Decide the acceptability of the population.

State the Objectives of the Audit Test

Auditors sample for tests of details of balances to determine whether the account balance being audited is fairly stated. The population of 40 accounts receivable in Table 17-1, totaling US$207,295, illustrates the application of nonstatistical sampling. An auditor will do tests of details of balances to determine whether the balance of US$207,295 is materially misstated. Typically, tolerable misstatement defines a material misstatement.

Decide Whether Audit Sampling Applies

As stated in Chapter 15, audit sampling applies whenever the auditor plans to reach conclusions about a population based on a sample. Although auditors commonly sample in many accounts, in some situations sampling does not apply. For the population in Table 17-1, the auditor may decide to audit only items over US$5,000 and ignore all others because the total of the smaller items is immaterial. Similarly, if the auditor is verifying fixed asset additions and finds many small additions and one extremely large purchase of a building, the auditor may decide to ignore the small items entirely. In either case, the auditor has not sampled.

Define a Misstatement

Because audit sampling for tests of details of balances measures monetary misstatements, a misstatement exists whenever a sample item is misstated. In auditing accounts receivable, any client misstatement in a customer balance included in the auditor's sample is a misstatement.

Define the Population

In tests of details of balances, the population is defined as the items making up the *recorded dollar population*. The recorded population of accounts receivable in Table 17-1 consists of 40 accounts totaling US$207,295. Most accounting populations that auditors sample will, of course, include far more items totaling a much larger dollar amount. The auditor will evaluate whether the recorded population is overstated or understated.

Stratified sampling

A method of sampling in which all the elements in the total population are divided into two or more subpopulations that are independently tested and statistically measured.

Stratified Sampling   For many populations, auditors separate the population into two or more subpopulations before applying audit sampling. This is called **stratified sampling**, where each subpopulation is a called a stratum. Stratification enables the auditor to emphasize certain population items and deemphasize others. In most audit sampling situations, including confirming accounts receivable, auditors want to emphasize the larger recorded dollar values, so they define each stratum on the basis of the size of recorded dollar values.

TABLE 17-1	Illustrative Accounts Receivable Population		
Population Item	Recorded Amount	Population Item (*cont.*)	Recorded Amount (*cont.*)
1	US$1,410	21	US$4,865
2	9,130	22	770
3	660	23	2,305
4	3,355	24	2,665
5	5,725	25	1,000
6	8,210	26	6,225
7	580	27	3,675
8	44,110	28	6,250
9	825	29	1,890
10	1,155	30	27,705
11	2,270	31	935
12	50	32	5,595
13	5,785	33	930
14	940	34	4,045
15	1,820	35	9,480
16	3,380	36	360
17	530	37	1,145
18	955	38	6,400
19	4,490	39	100
20	17,140	40	8,435
			US$207,295

By examining the population in Table 17-1, you can see that there are different ways to stratify the population. Assume that the auditor decided to stratify as follows:

Stratum	Stratum Criteria	No. in Population	Dollars in Population
1	>US$15,000	3	US$ 88,955
2	US$5,000–US$15,000	10	71,235
3	<US$5,000	27	47,105
		40	US$207,295

There are many alternative ways to stratify this population. One example is to have four strata (make stratum 3 items between US$2,000 and US$5,000, and add a fourth stratum for items less than US$2,000).

Define the Sampling Unit

For nonstatistical audit sampling in tests of details of balances, the sampling unit is almost always the items making up the account balance. For example, for the accounts receivable in Table 17-1 the sampling unit will be the customer number. Auditors can use the items making up the recorded population as the sampling unit for testing all audit objectives except completeness. If auditors are concerned about the completeness objective they should select the sample from a different source, such as customers or vendors with zero balances. Accordingly, the sampling unit for a completeness test will be customers with zero balances.

Specify Tolerable Misstatement

Auditors use tolerable misstatement, as discussed in Chapter 9, for determining sample size and evaluating results in nonstatistical sampling. The auditor starts with a preliminary judgment about materiality and uses that total in deciding tolerable misstatement for each account. The required sample size increases as the auditor's tolerable misstatement decreases for the account balance or class of transactions.

Specify Acceptable Risk of Incorrect Acceptance

For all statistical and nonstatistical sampling applications, auditors risk making incorrect quantitative conclusions about the population. This is always true unless the auditor tests 100 percent of the population.

Acceptable risk of incorrect acceptance (ARIA) is the amount of risk an auditor is willing to take of accepting a balance as correct when the true misstatement in the balance exceeds tolerable misstatement. ARIA measures the auditor's desired assurance for an account balance. For greater assurance in auditing a balance, auditors will set ARIA lower. (Note that ARIA is the equivalent term to ARACR (acceptable risk of assessing control risk too low) for tests of controls and substantive tests of transactions.) Like for ARACR, ARIA can be set quantitatively (such as 5 percent or 10 percent), or qualitatively (such as low, medium, or high).

There is an inverse relationship between ARIA and required sample size. If, for example, an auditor decides to reduce ARIA from 10 percent to 5 percent, the required sample size will increase. Stated differently, if the auditor is less willing to take risk, a larger sample size is needed.

An important factor affecting the auditor's decision about ARIA is assessed control risk in the audit risk model. When internal controls are effective, control risk can be reduced, permitting the auditor to increase ARIA. This, in turn, reduces the sample size required for the test of details of the related account balance.

You need to understand how ARACR and ARIA interact to affect evidence accumulation. If the auditor concludes that internal controls are likely to be effective, preliminary control risk can be reduced. A lower control risk requires a lower ARACR in testing the controls, which requires a larger sample size. If controls are found to be effective, control risk can remain low, which permits the auditor to increase ARIA (through use of the audit risk model), thereby requiring a smaller sample size in the related substantive tests of details of balances. Figure 17-1 shows the effect of ARACR and ARIA on substantive testing when controls are not considered effective and when they are considered effective.

In addition to control risk, ARIA is directly affected by acceptable audit risk and inversely affected by other substantive tests already performed (or planned) for the account balance. If auditors reduce acceptable audit risk, they should also reduce ARIA. If analytical procedures indicate that the account balance is likely to be fairly stated, ARIA can be increased. In other words, analytical procedures are evidence supporting the account balance, meaning auditors require smaller sample sizes in tests of details of balances to achieve the desired acceptable audit risk. The same conclusion is appropriate for the relationship among substantive tests of transactions, ARIA, and sample size for tests of details of balances. The various relationships affecting ARIA are summarized in Table 17-2.

Estimate Misstatements in the Population

The auditor typically makes this estimate based on prior experience with the client and by assessing inherent risk, considering the results of tests of controls, substantive tests of transactions, and analytical procedures already performed. The planned sample size increases as the amount of misstatements expected in the population approaches tolerable misstatement.

Acceptable risk of incorrect acceptance (ARIA)

The risk that the auditor is willing to take of accepting a balance as correct when the true misstatement in the balance is equal to or greater than tolerable misstatement.

| FIGURE 17-1 | Effect of ARACR and ARIA on Substantive Testing |

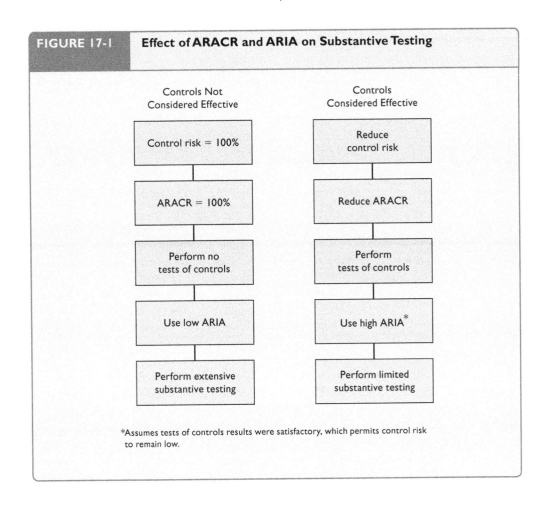

Controls Not Considered Effective

Control risk = 100%

ARACR = 100%

Perform no tests of controls

Use low ARIA

Perform extensive substantive testing

Controls Considered Effective

Reduce control risk

Reduce ARACR

Perform tests of controls

Use high ARIA*

Perform limited substantive testing

*Assumes tests of controls results were satisfactory, which permits control risk to remain low.

| TABLE 17-2 | Relationship Among Factors Affecting ARIA, Effect on ARIA, and Required Sample Size for Audit Sampling |

Factor Affecting ARIA	Example	Effect on ARIA	Effect on Sample Size
Effectiveness of internal controls (control risk)	Internal controls are effective (reduced control risk).	Increase	Decrease
Substantive tests of transactions	No exceptions were found in substantive tests of transactions.	Increase	Decrease
Acceptable audit risk	Likelihood of bankruptcy is low (increased acceptable audit risk).	Increase	Decrease
Analytical procedures	Analytical procedures are performed with no indications of likely misstatements.	Increase	Decrease

Determine the Initial Sample Size

When using nonstatistical sampling, auditors determine the initial sample size by considering the factors we've discussed so far. Table 17-3 summarizes these factors, including the effect of changing each factor on sample size. It shouldn't be surprising that considering all of these factors requires considerable judgment. To help auditors make the sample size decision, they often follow guidelines provided by their firm or some other source. Figure 17-2 presents a grid for combining these factors and a formula for computing sample size based on the AICPA *Audit Sampling Guide*.

TABLE 17-3	Factors Influencing Sample Sizes for Tests of Details of Balances	
Factor	**Conditions Leading to Smaller Sample Size**	**Conditions Leading to Larger Sample Size**
Control risk (ARACR)—Affects acceptable risk of incorrect acceptance	Low control risk	High control risk
Results of other substantive procedures related to the same assertion (including analytical procedures and other relevant substantive tests)—Affect acceptable risk of incorrect acceptance	Satisfactory results in other related substantive procedures	Unsatisfactory results in other related substantive procedures
Acceptable audit risk—Affects acceptable risk of incorrect acceptance	High acceptable audit risk	Low acceptable audit risk
Tolerable misstatement for a specific account	Larger tolerable misstatement	Smaller tolerable misstatement
Inherent risk—Affects estimated misstatements in the population	Low inherent risk	High inherent risk
Expected size and frequency of misstatements— Affect estimated misstatements in the population	Smaller misstatements or lower frequency	Larger misstatements or higher frequency
Dollar amount of population	Smaller account balance	Larger account balance
Number of items in the population	Almost no effect on sample size unless population is very small	Almost no effect on sample size unless population is very small

Assume an auditor applied this formula to the population in Table 17-1 and that tolerable misstatement is US\$15,000. The auditor decided to eliminate from the recorded population the three items making up the first stratum because they exceed tolerable misstatement. These three individually material accounts will be tested separately. The remaining population to be sampled is US\$118,340, which is the combined amount of stratum 2 and 3. Further, assume that the combined assessed inherent and control risk is moderate and that there is a moderate risk that substantive tests of transactions and substantive analytical procedures will not detect a material misstatement. Based on the grid, the required assurance factor is 1.6, and the computed sample size will be 13 [(US\$118,340/US\$15,000) × 1.6 = 12.6].

When auditors use stratified sampling, they must allocate sample size among the strata, typically allocating a higher portion of the sample items to larger population items. In the example from Table 17-1, the auditor must test all items in stratum 1, which is not audit sampling. They decided to allocate the sample size of 13 to seven from stratum 2 and six from stratum 3.

FIGURE 17-2	Formula for Computing Nonstatistical Tests of Details of Balances—Sample Size Based on AICPA Audit Sampling Formula

$$\frac{\text{Population's recorded amount*}}{\text{Tolerable misstatement}} \times \text{Assurance factor} = \text{Sample size}$$

Select the appropriate assurance factor as follows:

Assessed Inherent and Control Risk	Risk That Other Substantive Procedures Will Fail to Detect a Material Misstatement			
	Maximum	Slightly Below Maximum	Moderate	Low
Maximum	3.0	2.7	2.3	2.0
Slightly below maximum	2.7	2.4	2.0	1.6
Moderate	2.3	2.1	1.6	1.2
Low	2.0	1.6	1.2	1.0

*Individual items exceeding tolerable misstatement are tested individually and subtracted from the population for this calculation.

Select the Sample

For nonstatistical sampling, auditing standards permit the auditor to use any of the selection methods discussed in Chapter 15. The auditor will make the decision after considering the advantages and disadvantages of each method, including cost considerations.

For stratified sampling, the auditor selects samples independently from each stratum. In our example from Table 17-1, the auditor will select seven sample items from the 10 population items in stratum 2 and six of the 27 items in stratum 3.

Perform the Audit Procedures

To perform the audit procedures, the auditor applies the appropriate audit procedures to each item in the sample to determine whether it contains a misstatement. In the confirmation of accounts receivable, auditors mail the sample of positive confirmations and determine the amount of misstatement in each account confirmed. For nonresponses, they use alternative procedures to determine the misstatements.

Referring to our example from Table 17-1 again, assume an auditor sends first and second requests for confirmations and performs alternative procedures. Also assume the auditor reaches the following conclusions about the sample after reconciling all timing differences:

| | | Dollars Audited | | |
| | | | | |
Stratum	Sample Size	Recorded Value (sample)	Audited Value (Actual Value of audited items)	Client Misstatement
1	3	US$ 88,955	US$ 91,695	US$ (2,740)
2	7	43,995	43,024	971
3	6	13,105	10,947	2,158
Total	16	US$146,055	US$145,666	US$ 389

Generalize from the Sample to the Population and Decide the Acceptability of the Population

The auditor must generalize from the sample to the population by (1) projecting misstatements from the sample results to the population and (2) considering sampling error and sampling risk (ARIA). In our example, will the auditor conclude that accounts receivable is overstated by US$389? No, the auditor is interested in the *population* results, not those of the sample. It is therefore necessary to project from the sample to the population to estimate the population misstatement.

The first step is to calculate a **point estimate**. The point estimate can be calculated in different ways, but a common approach is to assume that misstatements in the unaudited population are proportional to the misstatements in the sample. That calculation must be done for each stratum and then totaled, rather than combining the total misstatements in the sample. In our example, the point estimate of the misstatement is calculated by using a weighted-average method, as shown below.

Point estimate

A method of projecting from the sample to the population to estimate the population misstatement, commonly by assuming that misstatements in the unaudited population are proportional to the misstatements found in the sample.

Stratum	Client Misstatement ÷ Recorded Value of the Sample	×	Recorded Book Value for the Stratum	=	Point Estimate of Misstatement
1	US$ (2,740)/US$88,955		US$ 88,955		US$(2,740)
2	971/43,995		71,235		1,572
3	2,158/13,105		47,105		7,757
Total					US$ 6,589

The point estimate of the misstatement in the population is US$6,589, indicating an overstatement. The point estimate, by itself, is not an adequate measure of the population misstatement, however, because of sampling error. In other words, because the estimate is based on a sample, it will be close to the true population misstatement, but it is unlikely to be exactly the same. Whenever the point estimate (US$6,589 in the example) is less than tolerable misstatement (US$15,000 in the example), the auditor must consider the possibility that the true population misstatement is greater than the amount of misstatement that is tolerable in the circumstances. This must be done for both statistical and nonstatistical samples.

An auditor using nonstatistical sampling cannot formally measure sampling error and therefore must subjectively consider the possibility that the true population misstatement exceeds a tolerable amount. Auditors do this by considering:

1. The difference between the point estimate and tolerable misstatement (this is called calculated sampling error)
2. The extent to which items in the population have been audited 100 percent
3. Whether misstatements tend to be offsetting or in only one direction
4. The amounts of individual misstatements
5. The sample size

In our example, suppose that tolerable misstatement is US$40,000. In that case, the auditor may conclude it is unlikely, given the point estimate of US$6,589, that the true population misstatement exceeds the tolerable amount (calculated sampling error is US$33,411).

Suppose that tolerable misstatement is US$15,000 (as it was in the example), only US$8,411 greater than the point estimate. In that case, the auditor will consider other factors. If the larger items in the population were audited 100 percent (as was done here), any unidentified misstatements will be restricted to smaller items. If the misstatements tend to be offsetting and are relatively small in size, the auditor may conclude that the true population misstatement is likely to be less than the tolerable amount. Also, the larger the sample size, the more confident the auditor can be that the point estimate is close to the true population value. In this example, when sample size is considered large, auditors will be more willing to accept that the true population misstatement is less than tolerable misstatement. However, if one or more of these other conditions differs, auditors may judge the chance of a misstatement in excess of the tolerable amount to be high and the recorded population unacceptable.

Even if the amount of likely misstatement is not considered material, the auditor must wait to make a final evaluation until the entire audit is completed. The estimated total misstatement and estimated sampling error in accounts receivable must be combined with estimates of misstatements in all other parts of the audit to evaluate the effect of all misstatements on the financial statements as a whole.

Analyze the Misstatements

It is essential for auditors to evaluate the nature and cause of each misstatement found in tests of details of balances. For example, suppose that when the auditor confirmed accounts receivable, all misstatements resulted from the client's failure to record returned goods. The auditor will determine why that type of misstatement occurred so often, the implications of the misstatements on other audit areas, the potential impact on the financial statements, and its effect on company operations. The same approach is followed for all misstatements.

The auditor must do misstatement analysis to decide whether any modification of the audit risk model is needed. In the preceding paragraph, if the auditor concluded that the failure to record the returns resulted from a breakdown of internal controls, it might be necessary to reassess control risk. That in turn will probably cause the auditor to reduce ARIA, which will increase planned sample size. As we discussed in Chapter 9, revisions of the audit risk model must be done with extreme care because the model is intended primarily for planning, not evaluating results.

Action When a Population is Rejected

When the auditor concludes that the misstatement in a population may be larger than tolerable misstatement after considering sampling error, the population is not considered acceptable. At that point, an auditor has several possible courses of action.

Take No Action Until Tests of Other Audit Areas are Completed Ultimately, the auditor must evaluate whether the financial statements taken as a whole are materially misstated. If offsetting misstatements are found in other parts of the audit, such as in inventory, the auditor may conclude that the estimated misstatements in accounts receivable are acceptable. Of course, before the audit is finalized, the auditor must evaluate whether a misstatement in one account may make the financial statements misleading even if there are offsetting misstatements.

Perform Expanded Audit Tests in Specific Areas If an analysis of the misstatements indicates that most of the misstatements are of a specific type, it may be desirable to restrict the additional audit effort to the problem area. For example, if an analysis of the misstatements in confirmations indicates that most of the misstatements result from failure to record sales returns, the auditor can make an extended search of returned goods to make sure that they have been recorded. However, care must be taken to evaluate the cause of all misstatements in the sample before a conclusion is reached about the proper emphasis in the expanded tests. Problems may exist in more than one area.

When auditors analyze a problem area and correct it by adjusting the client's records, the sample items that led to isolating the problem area can then be shown as 'correct.' The point estimate can now be recalculated without the misstatements that have been 'corrected.' (This is only true when the error can be isolated to a specific area. Errors must generally be projected to the population being sampled, even if the client adjusts for the error.) With the new facts in hand, the auditor will also have to reconsider sampling error and the acceptability of the population.

Increase the Sample Size When the auditor increases the sample size, sampling error is reduced if the rate of misstatements in the expanded sample, their dollar amounts, and their direction are similar to those in the original sample. Therefore, increasing the sample size may satisfy the auditor's tolerable misstatement requirements.

Increasing the sample size enough to satisfy the auditor's tolerable misstatement standards is often costly, especially when the difference between tolerable misstatement and projected misstatement is small. Moreover, an increased sample size does not guarantee a satisfactory result. If the number, amount, and direction of the misstatements in the extended sample are proportionately greater or more variable than in the original sample, the results are still likely to be unacceptable.

For tests such as accounts receivable confirmation and inventory observation, it is often difficult to increase the sample size because of the practical problem of 'reopening' those procedures once the initial work is done. By the time the auditor discovers that the sample was not large enough, several weeks have usually passed.

Despite these difficulties, sometimes the auditor must increase the sample size after the original testing is completed.

Adjust the Account Balance When the auditor concludes that an account balance is materially misstated, the client may be willing to adjust the book value based on the sample results. In the preceding example, assume the client is willing to reduce book value by the amount of the point estimate (US$6,589) to adjust for the estimate of the misstatement. The auditor's estimate of the misstatement is now zero, but it is still necessary to consider sampling error. Again, assuming a tolerable misstatement of US$15,000, the auditor must now assess whether sampling error exceeds US$15,000, not the US$8,411 originally considered. If the auditor believes sampling error is US$15,000 or less, accounts receivable is acceptable after the adjustment. If the auditor believes it is more than US$15,000, adjusting the account balance is not a practical option.

Request the Client to Correct the Population In some cases, the client's records are so inadequate that a correction of the entire population is required before the audit can be completed. For example, in accounts receivable, the client may be asked to correct the accounts receivable records and prepare the accounts receivable listing again if the auditor concludes that it has significant misstatements. When the client changes the valuation of some items in the population, the results must be audited again.

Refuse to Give an Unmodified Opinion If the auditor believes that the recorded amount in an account is not fairly stated, it is necessary to follow at least one of the preceding alternatives or to qualify the audit report in an appropriate manner. If the auditor believes that there is a reasonable chance that the financial statements are materially misstated, it would be a serious breach of auditing standards to issue an unmodified opinion.

MONETARY UNIT SAMPLING

OBJECTIVE 17-3

Apply monetary unit sampling.

Monetary unit sampling (MUS)

A statistical sampling method that provides upper and lower misstatement bounds expressed in monetary amounts; also referred to as dollar unit sampling, cumulative monetary amount sampling, and sampling with probability proportional to size.

Monetary unit sampling (MUS) is now the most commonly used statistical method of sampling for tests of details of balances because it has the statistical simplicity of attributes sampling yet provides a statistical result expressed in dollars (or another appropriate currency). MUS is also called dollar unit sampling, cumulative monetary amount sampling, and sampling with probability proportional to size.

Differences Between MUS and Nonstatistical Sampling

MUS is similar to using nonstatistical sampling. All 14 of the steps must also be performed for MUS, although some are done differently. Understanding those differences is the key to understanding MUS. Let's examine these differences in detail.

The Definition of the Sampling Unit is an Individual Dollar A critical feature of MUS is the definition of the sampling unit as an individual dollar (or other currency) in an account balance. The name of the statistical method, monetary unit sampling, results from this distinctive feature. For example, in the population in Table 17-1 on page 577, the sampling unit is 1 dollar and the population size is 207,295 dollars, not the 40 physical units discussed earlier. (A physical unit is an accounts receivable customer balance, an inventory item in an inventory listing, and other such identifiable units in a listing.)

By focusing on the individual dollar as the sampling unit, MUS automatically emphasizes physical units with larger recorded balances. Because the sample is selected on the basis of individual dollars, an account with a large balance has a greater chance of being included than an account with a small balance. For example, in accounts receivable confirmation, an account with a US$5,000 balance has a ten times greater probability of selection than one with a US$500 balance, as it contains ten times as many dollar units. As a result, stratified sampling is unnecessary with MUS. Stratification occurs automatically.

The Population Size is the Recorded Dollar Population For example, the population of accounts receivable in Table 17-1 consists of 207,295 dollars, which is the population size, not the 40 accounts receivable balances. This is the recorded dollar amount of accounts receivable.

Because of the method of sample selection in MUS, which is discussed later, it is not possible to evaluate the likelihood of unrecorded items in the population. Assume, for example, that MUS is used to evaluate whether inventory is fairly stated. MUS cannot be used to evaluate whether certain inventory items exist but have not been counted. If the completeness objective is important in the audit test, and it usually is, that objective must be satisfied separately from the MUS tests.

Preliminary Judgment of Materiality is Used for Each Account Instead of Tolerable Misstatement Another unique aspect of MUS is the use of the preliminary judgment about materiality, as discussed in Chapter 9, to directly determine the tolerable misstatement amount for the audit of each account. Other sampling techniques require the auditor to determine tolerable misstatement for each account by allocating the preliminary judgment about materiality. This is not required when MUS is used. For example, assume that an auditor decides that the preliminary judgment about materiality should be US$60,000 for the financial statements as a whole. That materiality amount of US$60,000 will be used as tolerable misstatement in all applications of MUS—inventory, accounts receivable, accounts payable, and so forth.

Sample Size is Determined Using a Statistical Formula This process is examined in detail after we have discussed the 14 sampling steps for MUS.

A Formal Decision Rule is Used for Deciding the Acceptability of the Population The decision rule used for MUS is similar to that used for nonstatistical sampling, but it is sufficiently different to merit discussion. The decision rule is illustrated on page 592 after the calculation of the misstatement bounds is shown.

Sample Selection is Done Using PPS Monetary unit samples are samples selected with **probability proportional to size sample selection (PPS)**. PPS samples can be obtained by using computer software, random number tables, or systematic sampling techniques. Table 17-4 provides an illustration of an accounts receivable population, including cumulative totals that will be used to demonstrate selecting a sample.

Probability proportional to size sample selection (PPS)

Sample selection of individual dollars in a population by the use of random or systematic sample selection.

TABLE 17-4	Accounts Receivable Population	
Population Item (Physical Unit)	Recorded Amount	Cumulative Total (Dollar Unit)
1	US$ 357	US$ 357
2	1,281	1,638
3	60	1,698
4	573	2,271
5	691	2,962
6	143	3,105
7	1,425	4,530
8	278	4,808
9	942	5,750
10	826	6,576
11	404	6,980
12	396	7,376

Assume that the auditor wants to select a PPS sample of four accounts from the population in Table 17-4. Because the sampling unit is defined as an individual dollar, the population size is 7,376, and four random numbers are needed. Assume that the auditor uses a computer program to generate the following random numbers from between 1 and 7,376: 6,586, 1,756, 850, and 6,499.

Auditors have no way to audit these dollars directly so they must associate the individual dollars with physical units, in this case customer balances. The population physical unit items that contain these random dollars are determined by reference to the cumulative total column. Looking again at Table 17-4, they are items 11 (containing dollars 6,577 through 6,980), 4 (dollars 1,699 through 2,271), 2 (dollars 358 through 1,638), and 10 (dollars 5,751 through 6,576). These four accounts will be audited because the cumulative total associated with these accounts includes the random dollars selected, and the result for each physical unit will be used to make statistical inferences.

The statistical methods used to evaluate monetary unit samples permit the inclusion of a physical unit in the sample more than once. In the previous example, if the random numbers had been 6,586, 1,756, 850, and 6,599, the sample items would have been 11, 4, 2, and 11. Item 11 would be audited once but treated as two sample items statistically, and the sample total would be four items because four monetary units were involved. If audit tests determine that item 11 included an error, it would count as two errors in the statistical evaluation.

One problem using PPS selection is that population items with a zero recorded balance have no chance of being selected with PPS sample selection, even though they may be misstated. Similarly, small balances that are significantly understated have little chance of being included in the sample. This problem can be overcome by doing specific audit tests for zero- and small-balance items, assuming that they are of concern.

Another problem with PPS is its inability to include negative balances, such as credit balances in accounts receivable, in the PPS (monetary unit) sample. It is possible to ignore negative balances for PPS selection and test those amounts by some other means. An alternative is to treat them as positive balances and add them to the total number of monetary units being tested. However, this complicates the evaluation process.

The Auditor Generalizes from the Sample to the Population Using MUS Techniques Regardless of the sampling method selected, the auditor must generalize from the sample to the population by (1) projecting misstatements from the sample results to the population and (2) determining the related sampling error. There are four aspects in doing so using MUS:

1. Attributes sampling tables are used to calculate the results. Tables, such as the one on page 526, can be used, replacing ARACR with ARIA.
2. The attributes results must be converted to dollars. MUS estimates the dollar misstatement in the population, not the percent of items in the population that are misstated. Therefore, auditors can estimate the rate of population dollars that contain a misstatement as a way of estimating the total dollar misstatement.
3. The auditor must make an assumption about the percentage of misstatement for each population item that is misstated. This assumption enables the auditor to use the attributes sampling tables to estimate dollar misstatements.
4. The statistical results when MUS is used are called **misstatement bounds**. These misstatement bounds are estimates of the likely maximum overstatement (upper misstatement bound) and likely maximum understatement (lower misstatement bound) at a given ARIA. Auditors calculate both an upper misstatement bound and a lower misstatement bound.

Misstatement bounds

An estimate of the largest likely overstatements and understatements in a population at a given ARIA, using monetary unit sampling.

This final step, generalizing from the sample to the population, is essential. Generalization is different when the auditor finds no misstatements in the sample compared to when there are misstatements. We will examine generalizing under these two situations next.

Generalizing from the Sample to the Population When No Misstatements are Found Using MUS

Suppose that the auditor is confirming a population of accounts receivable for monetary correctness. The population totals US$1,200,000, and a sample of 100 confirmations is obtained. Upon audit, no misstatements are uncovered in the sample. The auditor wants to determine the maximum amount of overstatement and understatement amounts that could exist in the population even when the sample contains no misstatements. These are called the upper misstatement bound and the lower misstatement bound, respectively. Assuming an ARIA of 5 percent, and using the attributes sampling table on page 526, both the upper and lower bounds are determined by locating the intersection of the sample size (100) and the actual number of misstatements (0) in the same manner as for attributes sampling. The CUER of 3 percent on the table represents both the upper and lower bound, *expressed as a percent*. Because the sample misstatement rate was 0 percent, the 3 percent represents an estimate of sampling error.

Based on the sample results and the misstatement bounds from the table, the auditor can conclude with a 5 percent sampling risk that no more than 3 percent of the dollar units in the population are misstated. To convert this percent into dollars, the auditor must make an assumption about the average percent of misstatement for population dollars that contain a misstatement. This assumption significantly affects the misstatement bounds. To illustrate this, two sets of example assumptions are examined:

Assumption 1 Overstatement amounts equal 100 percent; understatement amounts equal 100 percent; misstatement bounds at a 5 percent ARIA are:

Upper misstatement bound $=$ US$1,200,000 $\times$ 3% $\times$ 100% $=$ US$36,000
Lower misstatement bound $=$ US$1,200,000 $\times$ 3% $\times$ 100% $=$ US$36,000

The assumption is that, on average, those population items that are misstated are misstated by the full dollar amount of the recorded value. Because the misstatement bound is 3 percent, the dollar value of the misstatement is not likely to exceed US$36,000 (3 percent of the total recorded dollar units in the population). If all the amounts are overstated, there is an overstatement of US$36,000. If they are all understated, there is an understatement of US$36,000.

The assumption of 100 percent misstatements is extremely conservative, especially for overstatements. Assume that the actual population exception rate is 3 percent. The following two conditions both have to exist before the US$36,000 correctly reflects the true overstatement amount:

1. All amounts have to be overstatements. Offsetting amounts would have reduced the amount of the overstatement.
2. All population items misstated have to be 100 percent misstated. There cannot, for example, be a misstatement such as a receivable balance of US$226 recorded as US$262. This would be only a 13.7 percent misstatement ($262 - 226 = 36$ overstatement; $36/262 = 13.7\%$).

In the calculation of the overstatement and understatement misstatement bounds of US$36,000, the auditor did not calculate a point estimate and sampling error (called precision amount in MUS) in the manner discussed earlier in the chapter. This is because the tables used include both a point estimate and a precision amount to derive the upper exception rate. Even though the point estimate and precision amount are not calculated for MUS, they are implicit in the determination of misstatement bounds and can be determined from the tables. In this illustration, the point estimate is zero and the statistical precision is US$36,000.

Assumption 2 Overstatement amounts equal 10 percent; understatement amounts equal 10 percent; misstatement bounds at a 5 percent ARIA are:

$$\text{Upper misstatement bound} = \text{US\$1,200,000} \times 3\% \times 10\% = \text{US\$3,600}$$
$$\text{Lower misstatement bound} = \text{US\$1,200,000} \times 3\% \times 10\% = \text{US\$3,600}$$

The assumption is that, on average, those items that are misstated are misstated by no more than 10 percent. If all items were misstated in one direction, the misstatement bounds will be + US$3,600 and − US$3,600. The change in assumption from 100 percent to 10 percent misstatements significantly affects the misstatement bounds. The effect is in direct proportion to the magnitude of the change.

Appropriate Percent of Misstatement Assumption   The appropriate assumption for the overall percent of misstatement in those population items containing a misstatement is an auditor's decision. The auditor must set these percentages based on professional judgment in the circumstances. In the absence of convincing information to the contrary, most auditors believe that it is desirable to assume a 100 percent amount for both overstatements and understatements unless there are misstatements in the sample results. This approach is considered highly conservative, but it is easier to justify than any other assumption. In fact, the reason upper and lower limits are called misstatement bounds when MUS is used, rather than maximum likely misstatement or the commonly used statistical term *confidence limit*, is because of widespread use of that conservative assumption. Unless stated otherwise, the 100 percent misstatement assumption is used in this chapter and problem materials.

Generalizing When Misstatements are Found

So far, we have assumed the samples contain no misstatements. What happens, however, if misstatements are found? We will use the example from the preceding section but assume there are five misstatements instead of none. The misstatements are shown in Table 17-5.

The four aspects of generalizing from the sample to the population we discussed earlier still apply, but their use is modified as follows:

1. *Overstatement and understatement amounts are dealt with separately and then combined.* First, initial upper and lower misstatement bounds are calculated separately for overstatement and understatement amounts. Next, a point estimate of overstatements and understatements is calculated. The point estimate of understatements is used to reduce the initial upper misstatement bound, and the point estimate of overstatements is used to reduce the initial lower misstatement bound. The method and rationale for these calculations will be illustrated by using the four overstatement and one understatement amounts in Table 17-5.

TABLE 17-5	Misstatements Found			
Customer No.	Recorded Accounts Receivable Amount	Audited Accounts Receivable Amount	Misstatement	Misstatement ÷ Recorded Amount
2073	US$ 6,200	US$ 6,100	US$ 100	.016
5111	12,910	12,000	910	.07
5206	4,322	4,450	(128)	(.03)
7642	23,000	22,995	5	.0002
9816	8,947	2,947	6,000	.671

2. *A different misstatement assumption is made for each misstatement, including zero misstatements.* When there were no misstatements in the sample, an assumption was required as to the average percent of misstatement for the population items misstated. The misstatement bounds were calculated showing several different assumptions. Now that misstatements have been found, auditors can use available sample information in determining the misstatement bounds. The misstatement assumption is still required, but it can be modified based on this actual misstatement data.

   Where misstatements are found, a 100 percent assumption for all misstatements is not only exceptionally conservative, it is inconsistent with the sample results. A common assumption in practice, and the one followed in this book, is that the actual sample misstatements are representative of the population misstatements. This assumption requires the auditor to calculate the percent that each sample item is misstated (misstatement ÷ recorded amount) and apply that percent to the population. The calculation of the percent for each misstatement is shown in the last column in Table 17-5. As we will explain shortly, a misstatement assumption is still needed for the zero misstatement portion of the computed results. For this example, a 100 percent misstatement assumption is used for the zero misstatement portion for both overstatement and understatement misstatement bounds.

3. *The auditor must deal with layers of the computed upper exception rate (CUER) from the attributes sampling table.* Auditors do this because different misstatement assumptions exist for each misstatement. Layers are calculated by first determining the CUER from the table for each misstatement and then calculating each layer. Table 17-6 shows the layers in the attributes sampling table for the example at hand. (The layers were determined by reading across the table for a sample size of 100, from the 0 through 4 exception columns.)

4. *Misstatement assumptions must be associated with each layer.* The most common method of associating misstatement assumptions with layers is to conservatively associate the largest dollar misstatement percents with the largest layers. Table 17-7 shows this association. For example, the largest misstatement was .671 for customer 9816. That misstatement is associated with the layer factor of .017, the largest layer where misstatements were found. The portion of the upper precision limit related to the zero misstatement layer has a misstatement assumption of 100 percent, which is still conservative. Table 17-7 shows the calculation of misstatement bounds before consideration of offsetting amounts. The upper misstatement bound was calculated as if there were no understatement amounts, and the lower misstatement bound was calculated as if there were no overstatement amounts.

Most MUS users believe that this approach is overly conservative when there are offsetting amounts. If an understatement amount is found, it is logical and reasonable that the bound for overstatement amounts should be lower than it would be had no

TABLE 17-6	Percent Misstatement Bounds	
Number of Misstatements	Upper Precision Limit from Table	Increase in Precision Limit Resulting from Each Misstatement (Layers)
0	.03	.03
1	.047	.017
2	.062	.015
3	.076	.014
4	.090	.014

| TABLE 17-7 | Illustration of Calculating Initial Upper and Lower Misstatement Bounds | | | |

Number of Misstatements	Upper Precision Limit Portion*	Recorded Value	Unit Misstatement Assumption	Misstatement Bound Portion (Columns 2 × 3 × 4)
Overstatements				
0	.030	US$1,200,000	1.0	US$36,000
1	.017	1,200,000	.671	13,688
2	.015	1,200,000	.07	1,260
3	.014	1,200,000	.016	269
4	.014	1,200,000	.0002	3
Upper precision limit	.090			
Initial misstatement bound				US$51,220
Understatements				
0	.030	US$1,200,000	1.0	US$36,000
1	.017	1,200,000	.03	612
Lower precision limit	.047			
Initial misstatement bound				US$36,612

*ARIA of 5%. Sample size of 100.

understatement amounts been found, and vice versa. The adjustment of bounds for offsetting amounts is made as follows:

1. A point estimate of misstatements is made for both overstatement and understatement amounts.
2. Each bound is reduced by the opposite point estimate.

The point estimate for overstatements is calculated by multiplying the average overstatement amount in the dollar units audited times the recorded value. The same approach is used for calculating the point estimate for understatements. Our example shows one understatement amount of 3 cents per dollar unit in a sample of 100. The understatement point estimate is therefore US$360 (.03/100 × US$1,200,000). Similarly, the overstatement point estimate is US$9,086 [(.671 + .07 + .016 + .0002)/100 × US$1,200,000].

Table 17-8 shows the adjustment of the bounds that follow from this procedure:

| TABLE 17-8 | Illustration of Calculating Adjusted Misstatement Bounds | | | | | |

Number of Misstatements	Unit Misstatement Assumption	Sample Size	Recorded Population	Point Estimate	Bounds
Initial overstatement bound					US$51,220
Understatement amount					
1	.03	100	US$1,200,000	US$ 360	(360)
Adjusted overstatement bound					US$50,860
Initial understatement bound					US$36,612
Overstatement amounts					
1	.671				
2	.07				
3	.016				
4	.0002				
Sum	.7572	100	US$1,200,000	US$9,086	(9,086)
Adjusted understatement bound					US$27,526

- The initial upper bound of US$51,220 is reduced by the estimated most likely understatement amount of US$360 to an adjusted bound of US$50,860.
- The initial lower bound of US$36,612 is reduced by the estimated most likely overstatement amount of US$9,086 to an adjusted bound of US$27,526.

Given the methodology and assumptions followed, the auditor concludes that there is a 5 percent risk that accounts receivable is overstated by more than US$50,860, or understated by more than US$27,526.

It should be noted that if the misstatement assumptions are changed, the misstatement bounds will also change. The method used to adjust the bounds for offsetting amounts is only one of several in use. The method illustrated here is taken from Leslie, Teitlebaum, and Anderson.[17]

Table 17-9 shows the seven steps followed in the calculation of the adjusted misstatement bounds for MUS when there are offsetting amounts. The calculation of the adjusted upper misstatement bound for the four overstatement amounts in Table 17-5 is used to illustrate.

Decide the Acceptability of the Population Using MUS

After the misstatement bounds are calculated, the auditor must decide whether the population is acceptable. To do that, a *decision rule* is needed. The decision rule for MUS is as follows: If *both* the lower misstatement bound (LMB) and upper misstatement bound (UMB) fall between the understatement and overstatement tolerable misstatement amounts, *accept* the conclusion that the book value is not misstated by a material amount. Otherwise, conclude that the book value is misstated by a material amount.

This decision rule is illustrated in Figure 17-3. The auditor should conclude that both the LMB and UMB for situations 1 and 2 fall completely within both the understatement and overstatement tolerable misstatement limits. Therefore, the auditor concludes that the population is not misstated by a material amount. For situations 3, 4, and 5,

TABLE 17-9	Summary of Steps to Calculate Adjusted Misstatement Bounds
Steps to Calculate Adjusted Misstatement Bounds	**Calculation for Overstatements in Tables 17-5, 17-7, and 17-8**
1. Determine misstatement for each sample item, keeping overstatements and understatements separate.	Table 17-5; four overstatements
2. Calculate misstatement per dollar unit in each sample item (misstatement/recorded amount).	Table 17-5; .016, .07, .0002, .671
3. Layer misstatements per dollar unit from highest to lowest, including the percent misstatement assumption for sample items not misstated.	Table 17-7; 1.0, .671, .07, .016, .0002
4. Determine upper precision limit from attributes sampling table and calculate the percent misstatement bound for each misstatement (layer).	Table 17-7; Total of 9.0% for four misstatements; calculate five layers
5. Calculate initial upper and lower misstatement bounds for each layer and total.	Table 17-7; Total of US$51,220
6. Calculate point estimate for overstatements and understatements.	Table 17-8; US$360 for understatements
7. Calculate adjusted upper and lower misstatement bounds.	Table 17-8; US$50,860 adjusted overstatement

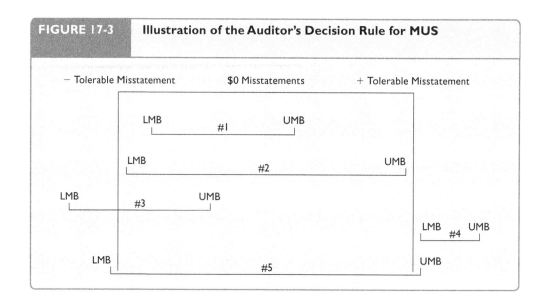

FIGURE 17-3   Illustration of the Auditor's Decision Rule for MUS

either LMB or UMB, or both, are outside tolerable misstatements. Therefore, the population book value will be rejected.

Assume that the auditor in our example had set a tolerable misstatement amount for accounts receivable of US$40,000 (overstatement or understatement). As previously shown, the auditor selected a sample of 100 items, found five misstatements, and calculated the lower bound to be US$27,526 and the upper bound to be US$50,860. Application of the decision rule leads the auditor to the conclusion that the population should not be accepted because the upper misstatement bound is more than the tolerable misstatement of US$40,000.

Action When a Population is Rejected

When one or both of the misstatement bounds lie outside the tolerable misstatement limits and the population is not considered acceptable, the auditor has several options. These are the same as the ones already discussed for nonstatistical sampling on pages 583–584.

Determining Sample Size Using MUS

Our overview of MUS included the step for determining sample size, but we have waited until now to discuss the method for making that calculation, because you first needed to understand average misstatement assumptions. The method used to determine sample size for MUS is similar to that used for physical unit attributes sampling, using the attributes sampling tables. By this point, you have studied the five things necessary for calculating sample size using MUS.

Materiality The preliminary judgment about materiality is normally the basis for the tolerable misstatement amount used. If misstatements in non-MUS tests are expected, tolerable misstatement will be materiality less those amounts. Tolerable misstatement may be different for overstatements or understatements. For this example, tolerable misstatement for both overstatements and understatements is US$100,000.

Assumption of the Average Percent of Misstatement for Population Items That Contain a Misstatement Again, there may be a separate assumption for the upper and lower bounds. This is also an auditor judgment. It should be based on the auditor's knowledge of the client and past experience, and if less than 100 percent is used, the assumption must be clearly defensible. For this example, 50 percent is used for overstatements and 100 percent for understatements.

Acceptable Risk of Incorrect Acceptance ARIA is an auditor judgment and is often reached with the aid of the audit risk model. It is 5 percent for this example.

Recorded Population Value The dollar value of the population is taken from the client's records. For this example, it is US$5 million.

Estimate of the Population Exception Rate Normally, the estimate of the population exception rate for MUS is zero, as it is most appropriate to use MUS when no misstatements, or only a few, are expected. When misstatements are expected, the total dollar amount of expected population misstatements is estimated and then expressed as a percent of the population recorded value. In this example, a US$20,000 overstatement amount is expected. This is equivalent to a .4 percent exception rate. To be conservative, a .5 percent expected exception rate is used.

These assumptions are summarized as follows:

Tolerable misstatement (same for upper and lower)	US$100,000
Average percent of misstatement assumption, overstatements	50%
Average percent of misstatement assumption, understatements	100%
ARIA	5%
Accounts receivable—recorded value	US$5 million
Estimated misstatement in accounts receivable	US$20,000

The sample size is calculated as follows:

	Upper Bound	Lower Bound
Tolerable misstatement	100,000	100,000
Average percent of misstatement assumption	÷ .50	÷ 1.00
	200,000	100,000
Recorded population value	÷ 5,000,000	÷ 5,000,000
Tolerable exception rate	4%	2%
Estimated population exception rate (EPER)	.5%	0
Sample size from the attributes table (page 524)		
5% ARACR, 4% and 2% TER, and .5% and 0% EPER	117	149

Because only one sample is taken for both overstatements and understatements, the *larger* of the two computed sample sizes is used, in this case 149 items. In auditing the sample, if auditors find any understatement amounts, the lower bound will exceed the tolerable limit because the sample size is based on no expected misstatements. Conversely, several overstatement amounts might be found before the tolerable limit for the upper bound is exceeded. When concerned about finding an unexpected misstatement that would cause the population to be rejected, the auditor can guard against it by arbitrarily increasing sample size above the amount determined by the tables. In this illustration, the auditor might use a sample size of 200 instead of 149.

Relationship of the Audit Risk Model to Sample Size for MUS The audit risk model for planning was introduced in Chapter 9 and covered in subsequent chapters as:

$$PDR = \frac{AAR}{IR \times CR}$$

(See pages 288–290 for a description of the terms.)

Chapter 16 discussed how the auditor reduces detection risk to the planned level by performing substantive tests of transactions, substantive analytical procedures, and tests of details of balances. MUS is used in performing tests of details of balances. Therefore, auditors need to understand the relationship of the three independent factors in the audit risk model, plus analytical procedures and substantive tests of transactions to sample size for tests of details of balances.

Table 17-2 on page 579 shows that four of these five factors (control risk, substantive tests of transactions, acceptable audit risk, and substantive analytical procedures) affect ARIA. ARIA in turn determines the planned sample size. The other factor, inherent risk, affects the estimated population exception rate directly.

Audit Uses of Monetary Unit Sampling

MUS appeals to auditors for at least four reasons:

1. MUS automatically increases the likelihood of selecting high dollar items from the population being audited. Auditors make a practice of concentrating on these items because they generally represent the greatest risk of material misstatements. Stratified sampling can also be used for this purpose, but MUS is often easier to apply.

2. MUS often reduces the cost of doing the audit testing because several sample items are tested at once. For example, if one large item makes up 10 percent of the total recorded dollar value of the population and the sample size is 100, the PPS sample selection method is likely to result in approximately 10 percent of the sample items from that one large population item. Naturally, that item needs to be audited only once, but it counts as a sample of ten. If the item is misstated, it is also counted as ten misstatements. Larger population items may be eliminated from the sampled population by auditing them 100 percent and evaluating them separately, if the auditor so desires.

3. MUS is easy to apply. Monetary unit samples can be evaluated by the application of simple tables. It is easy to teach and to supervise the use of MUS techniques. Firms that utilize MUS extensively use computer programs or special tables that streamline sample size determination and evaluation even further than shown in this chapter.

4. MUS provides a statistical conclusion rather than a nonstatistical one.

There are two main disadvantages of MUS.

1. The total misstatement bounds resulting when misstatements are found may be too high to be useful to the auditor. This is because these evaluation methods are inherently conservative when misstatements are found and often produce bounds far in excess of materiality. To overcome this problem, large samples may be required.

2. It may be cumbersome to select PPS samples from large populations without computer assistance.

For all these reasons, auditors commonly use MUS when zero or few misstatements are expected, a dollar result is desired, and the population data are maintained on computer files.

VARIABLES SAMPLING

OBJECTIVE 17-4

Describe variables sampling.

Variables sampling

Sampling techniques for tests of details of balances that use the statistical inference process.

Variables sampling, like MUS, is a statistical method that auditors use. Variables sampling and nonstatistical sampling for tests of details of balances have the same objective—to measure the misstatement in an account balance. As with nonstatistical sampling, when auditors determine that the misstatement amount exceeds the tolerable amount, they reject the population and take additional actions.

Several sampling techniques make up the general class of methods called variables sampling: difference estimation, ratio estimation, and mean-per-unit estimation. These are discussed later.

Differences Between Variables and Nonstatistical Sampling

The use of variables methods shares many similarities with nonstatistical sampling. All 14 steps we discussed for nonstatistical sampling must be performed for variables methods, and most are identical. Some of the differences between variables and nonstatistical sampling are examined after we discuss sampling distributions.

Sampling Distributions

To understand why and how auditors use variables sampling methods in auditing, it is useful to understand sampling distributions and how they affect auditors' statistical conclusions. The auditor does not know the mean value (average) of misstatements in the population, the distribution of the misstatement amounts, or the audited values. These population characteristics must be *estimated* from samples, which, of course, is the purpose of the audit test.

Assume that an auditor, as an experiment, took thousands of repeated samples of equal size from a population of accounting data having a mean value of X. For each sample, the auditor calculates the mean value of the items in the sample as follows:

$$\bar{x} = \frac{\Sigma x_j}{n}$$

where:

$\bar{x}$ = mean value of the sample items
x_j = value of each individual sample item
n = sample size

After calculating ($\bar{x}$) for each sample, the auditor plots them into a frequency distribution. As long as the sample size is sufficient, the frequency distribution of the sample means will appear much like that shown in Figure 17-4.

A distribution of the sample means such as this is normal and has all the characteristics of the normal curve: (1) the curve is symmetrical, and (2) the sample means fall within known portions of the sampling distribution around the average or mean of those means, measured by the distance along the horizontal axis in terms of standard deviations.

Furthermore, the mean of the sample means (the midpoint of the sampling distribution) is equal to the population mean, and the standard deviation of the sampling distribution is equal to SD/√n, where SD is the population standard deviation and n is the sample size.

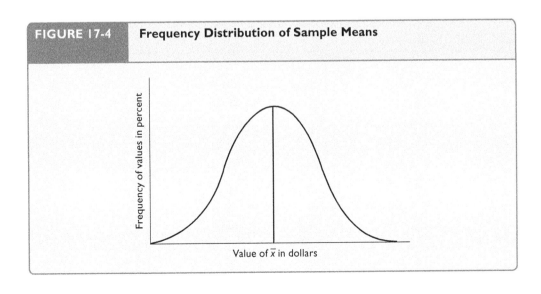

| FIGURE 17-4 | **Frequency Distribution of Sample Means** |

Frequency of values in percent

Value of $\bar{x}$ in dollars

TABLE 17-10	Calculated Sampling Distribution from a Population with a Known Mean and Standard Deviation		
(1) Number of Standard Errors of the Mean (Confidence Coefficient)	(2) Value [(1) × US$1.50]	(3) Range Around $\bar{x}$ [US$40 ÷ (2)]	(4) Percent of Sample Means Included in Range
1	US$1.50	US$38.50 – US$41.50	68.2
2	US$3.00	US$37.00 – US$43.00	95.4
3	US$4.50	US$35.50 – US$44.50	99.7
		(taken from table for normal curve)	

To illustrate, assume a population with a mean of US$40 and a standard deviation of US$15 ($\bar{X} = \$40$ and SD $= \$15$), from which we elected to take many random samples of 100 items each. The standard deviation of our sampling distribution is US$1.50 (SD$/\sqrt{n} = 15\sqrt{100} = 1.50$) The reference to 'standard deviation' of the population and to 'standard deviation' of the sampling distribution is often confusing. To avoid confusion, remember that the standard deviation of the distribution of the sample means is often called the standard error of the mean (SE). With this information, auditors can make the tabulation of the sampling distribution, as shown in Table 17-10 above.

To summarize, three things shape the results of the experiment of taking a large number of samples from a known population:

1. The mean value of all the sample means is equal to the population mean ($\bar{X}$). A corollary is that the sample mean value ($\bar{x}$) with the highest frequency of occurrence is also equal to the population mean.
2. The shape of the frequency distribution of the sample means is that of a normal distribution (curve), as long as the sample size is sufficiently large, *regardless of the distribution of the population*, as illustrated in Figure 17-5.
3. The percentage of sample means between any two values of the sampling distribution is measurable. The percentage can be calculated by determining the number of standard errors between any two values and determining the percentage of sample means represented from a table for normal curves.

Statistical Inference

Naturally, when samples are taken from a population in an actual audit situation, the auditor does not know the population's characteristics and, ordinarily, only one sample

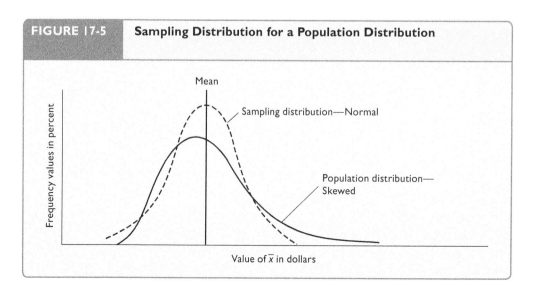

FIGURE 17-5	Sampling Distribution for a Population Distribution

Mean

Sampling distribution—Normal

Population distribution—Skewed

Frequency values in percent

Value of $\bar{x}$ in dollars

is taken from the population. But the *knowledge of sampling distributions* enables auditors to draw statistical conclusions, or **statistical inferences**, about the population. For example, assume that the auditor takes a sample from a population and calculates ($\bar{x}$) as US\$46 and SE at US\$9. (We'll explain how SE is calculated later.) We can now calculate a confidence interval of the population mean using the logic gained from the study of sampling distributions. It is as follows:

$$CI_{\bar{x}} = \hat{\bar{X}} \pm Z \cdot SE$$

where:

$CI_{\bar{x}}$ = confidence interval for the population mean

$\hat{\bar{X}}$ = point estimate of the population mean

Z = confidence coefficient $\begin{cases} 1 = 68.2\% \text{ confidence level} \\ 2 = 95.4\% \text{ confidence level} \\ 3 = 99.7\% \text{ confidence level} \end{cases}$

$Z \cdot SE$ = precision interval

For the example:

$CI_{\bar{x}} = \$46 \pm 1(\$9) = \$46 \pm \$9$ at a 68.2% confidence level

$CI_{\bar{x}} = \$46 \pm 2(\$9) = \$46 \pm \$18$ at a 95.4% confidence level

$CI_{\bar{x}} = \$46 \pm 3(\$9) = \$46 \pm \$27$ at a 99.7% confidence level

The results can also be stated in terms of confidence limits ($CI_{\bar{x}}$). The upper confidence limit (UCL$_{\bar{x}}$) is $\hat{\bar{X}} + Z \cdot \leq SE$ (\$46 + \$18 = \$64 at a 95 percent confidence level) and a lower confidence limit (LCL$_{\bar{x}}$) is $\hat{\bar{X}} - Z \cdot \leq SE$ (\$46 − \$18 = \$28 at a 95 percent confidence level). Graphically, the results are as follows:

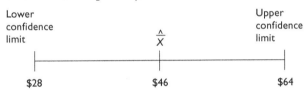

Auditors can state the conclusions drawn from a confidence interval using statistical inference in different ways. However, they must take care to avoid incorrect conclusions, remembering that the true population value is always unknown. There is always a possibility that the sample is not sufficiently representative of the population to provide a sample mean and/or standard deviation reasonably close to those of the population. The auditor can say, however, that the procedure used to obtain the sample and compute the confidence interval will provide an interval that will contain the true population mean value a given percent of the time. In short, the auditor knows the reliability of the statistical inference process that is used to draw conclusions.

Variables Methods

Auditors use the preceding statistical inference process for all the variables sampling methods. Each method is distinguished by what is being measured. Let's examine the three variables methods individually.

Difference Estimation Auditors use **difference estimation** to measure the estimated total misstatement amount in a population when both a recorded value and an audited value exist for each item in the sample, which is almost always the case in audits. For example, an auditor might confirm a sample of accounts receivable and determine the difference (misstatement) between the client's recorded amount and the amount the auditor considers correct for each selected account. The auditor makes an

Statistical inferences

Statistical conclusions that the auditor draws from sample results based on knowledge of sampling distributions.

Difference estimation

A method of variables sampling in which the auditor estimates the population misstatement by multiplying the average misstatement in the sample by the total number of population items and also calculates sampling risk.

estimate of the population misstatement based on the number of misstatements in the sample, average misstatement size, individual misstatements in the sample, and sample size. The result is stated as a point estimate of the population misstatement plus or minus a computed precision interval at a stated confidence level. Referring back to the discussion of sampling distributions, assume the auditor confirmed a random sample of 100 from a population of 1,000 accounts receivable and concluded that the confidence limits of the mean of the misstatement for accounts receivable were between US$28 and US$64 at a 95 percent confidence level. The estimate of the total population misstatement can also be easily calculated as being between US$28,000 and US$64,000 at a 95 percent confidence level (1,000 × US$28 and 1,000 × US$64). If the auditor's tolerable misstatement is US$100,000, the population is clearly acceptable. If tolerable misstatement is US$40,000, the population is not acceptable. An extended illustration using difference estimation is shown on pages 600–606.

Difference estimation frequently results in smaller sample sizes than any other method, and it is relatively easy to use. For that reason, difference estimation is often the preferred variables method.

Ratio estimation

A method of variables sampling in which the auditor estimates the population misstatement by multiplying the portion of sample dollars misstated by the total recorded population book value and also calculates sampling risk.

Ratio Estimation **Ratio estimation** is similar to difference estimation except the auditor calculates the ratio between the misstatements and their recorded value and projects this to the population to estimate the total population misstatement. For example, assume that an auditor finds misstatements totaling US$12,000 in a sample with a recorded value of US$208,000. The misstatement ratio is .06 (US$12,000/US$208,000). If the total recorded value of the population is US$1,040,000 the projected misstatement in the population is US$62,000 (US$1,040,000 × .06). The auditor can then calculate confidence limits of the total misstatement for ratio estimation with a calculation similar to the one shown for difference estimation. Ratio estimation can result in sample sizes even smaller than difference estimation if the size of the misstatements in the population is proportionate to the recorded value of the population items. If the size of the individual misstatements is independent of the recorded value, difference estimation results in smaller sample sizes. Most auditors prefer difference estimation because it is somewhat simpler to calculate confidence intervals.

Mean-per-unit estimation

A method of variables sampling in which the auditor estimates the audited value of a population by multiplying the average audited value of the sample by the population size and also calculates sampling risk.

Mean-Per-Unit Estimation In **mean-per-unit estimation**, the auditor focuses on the audited value rather than the misstatement amount of each item in the sample. Except for the definition of what is being measured, the mean-per-unit estimate is calculated in exactly the same manner as the difference estimate. The point estimate of the audited value equals the average audited value of items in the sample times the population size. The computed precision interval is calculated on the basis of the audited value of the sample items rather than the misstatements. When auditors have computed the upper and lower confidence limits, they decide the acceptability of the population by comparing these amounts with the recorded book value. For example, assume the auditor takes a sample of 100 items from an inventory listing containing 3,000 items and a recorded value US$265,000. If the mean value of the items sampled is US$85, the estimated value of the inventory is US$255,000 (US$85 × 3000). If the recorded value of US$265,000 is within the upper confidence limit, the auditor would accept the population balance. Mean-per-unit-estimation is rarely used in practice because sample sizes are typically much larger than for the two previous methods.

Stratified Statistical Methods

As we discussed earlier in this chapter, stratified sampling is a method of sampling in which all the elements in the total population are divided into two or more subpopulations. Each subpopulation is then independently tested. The calculations are made for each stratum and then combined into one overall population estimate for a confidence interval of the entire population. The results are measured statistically. Stratification is applicable to difference, ratio, and mean-per-unit estimation, but is most commonly used with mean-per-unit estimation.

Stratifying a population is not unique to statistical sampling, of course. Auditors have traditionally emphasized certain types of items when they are testing a population using nonstatistical sampling. For example, in confirming accounts receivable, auditors customarily place more emphasis on large accounts than on small ones. In statistical stratified sampling, however, the approach is more objective and better defined than for nonstatistical stratification methods.

Sampling Risks

We have discussed ARIA for nonstatistical sampling. For variables sampling, auditors use ARIA as well as acceptable risk of incorrect rejection (ARIR). It is important to understand the distinctions between and uses of the two risks.

ARIA   After auditors perform an audit test and calculate statistical results, they must conclude either that the population is or is not materially misstated. ARIA is the statistical risk that the auditor has accepted a population that is, in fact, materially misstated. ARIA is a serious concern to auditors because of the potential legal implications of concluding that an account balance is fairly stated when it is misstated by a material amount.

An account balance can be either overstated or understated, but not both; therefore, ARIA is a one-tailed statistical test. The confidence coefficients for ARIA are therefore different from the confidence level. (Confidence level $= 1 - 2 \times$ ARIA. So, if ARIA equals 10 percent, the confidence level is 80 percent.) The confidence coefficients for various ARIAs are shown in Table 17-11 together with confidence coefficients for the confidence level and ARIR.

ARIR   **Acceptable risk of incorrect rejection (ARIR)** is the statistical risk that the auditor has concluded that a population is materially misstated when it is not. ARIR affects auditors' actions only when they conclude that a population is not fairly stated. When auditors find a balance not fairly stated, they typically increase the sample size or perform other tests. An increased sample size will usually lead the auditor to conclude that the balance is fairly stated if the account is, in fact, not materially misstated. While ARIA is always important, ARIR is important only when there is a high cost to increasing the sample size or performing other tests. Confidence coefficients for ARIR are also shown in Table 17-11.

Acceptable risk of incorrect rejection (ARIR)

The risk that the auditor is willing to take of rejecting a balance as incorrect when it is not misstated by a material amount.

TABLE 17-11	Confidence Coefficient for Confidence Levels, ARIAs, and ARIRs		
Confidence Level (%)	**ARIA (%)**	**ARIR (%)**	**Confidence Coefficient**
99	.5	1	2.58
95	2.5	5	1.96
90	5	10	1.64
80	10	20	1.28
75	12.5	25	1.15
70	15	30	1.04
60	20	40	.84
50	25	50	.67
40	30	60	.52
30	35	70	.39
20	40	80	.25
10	45	90	.13
0	50	100	.0

TABLE 17-12	ARIA and ARIR	
	Actual State of the Population	
Actual Audit Decision	**Materially Misstated**	**Not Materially Misstated**
Conclude that the population is materially misstated	Correct conclusion—no risk	Incorrect conclusion—risk is ARIR
Conclude that the population is not materially misstated	Incorrect conclusion—risk is ARIA	Correct conclusion—no risk

As you examine the summary of ARIA and ARIR in Table 17-12 above, you might conclude that auditors should attempt to minimize ARIA and ARIR. To accomplish that, auditors have to increase the sample size, thus minimizing the risks. However, the cost of that approach makes having reasonable ARIA and ARIR a more desirable goal.

ILLUSTRATION USING DIFFERENCE ESTIMATION

OBJECTIVE 17-5

Use difference estimation in tests of details of balances.

As we've discussed, several types of variables sampling techniques may be applicable to auditing in different circumstances. To illustrate the concepts and methodology of variables sampling, we have selected difference estimation using hypothesis testing because of its relative simplicity. When this method is considered reliable in a given set of circumstances, most auditors prefer it to other variables sampling methods.

For difference estimation, the same 14 steps as nonstatistical sampling are used in determining whether the account balance in the audit of accounts receivable is correctly stated. The following example is based on the use of positive confirmations in the audit of Aliaa Lumber Company. Accounts receivable consists of 4,000 accounts listed on the aged trial balance with a recorded value of US$600,000. Internal controls are considered somewhat weak, and a large number of small misstatements in recorded amounts are expected in the audit. Total assets are US$2,500,000, and net earnings before taxes are US$400,000. Acceptable audit risk is reasonably high because of the limited users of the statements and the good financial health of Aliaa Lumber. Analytical procedures results indicated no significant problems. Assume that all confirmations were returned or that effective alternative procedures were carried out. Hence, the sample size is the number of positive confirmations mailed.

Plan the Sample and Calculate the Sample Size Using Difference Estimation

State the Objectives of the Audit Test The objective of the audit test is to determine whether accounts receivable before consideration of the allowance for uncollectible accounts is materially misstated.

Decide Whether Audit Sampling Applies Audit sampling applies in the confirmation of the accounts receivable because of the large number of accounts receivable.

Define Misstatement Conditions The misstatement condition is a client misstatement determined by the confirmation of each account or alternative procedure.

Define the Population The population size is determined by count, as it was for attributes sampling. An accurate count is much more important in variables sampling because population size directly affects sample size and the computed precision limits. The population size for Aliaa Lumber's accounts receivable is 4,000.

Define the Sampling Unit The sampling unit is an account on the list of accounts receivable.

Specify Tolerable Misstatement The amount of misstatement the auditor is willing to accept is a materiality question. The auditor decides to accept a tolerable misstatement of US$21,000 in the audit of Aliaa Lumber's accounts receivable.

Specify Acceptable Risk The auditor specifies two risks:

1. *Acceptable risk of incorrect acceptance (ARIA).* It is the risk of accepting accounts receivable as correct if it is actually misstated by more than US$21,000. ARIA is affected by acceptable audit risk, results of tests of controls and substantive tests of transactions, analytical procedures, and the relative significance of accounts receivable in the financial statements. For the Aliaa Lumber audit, assume an ARIA of 10 percent.
2. *Acceptable risk of incorrect rejection (ARIR).* It is the risk of rejecting accounts receivable as incorrect if it is not actually misstated by a material amount. ARIR is affected by the additional cost of resampling. Because it is fairly costly to confirm receivables a second time, assume an ARIR of 25 percent. (For audit tests for which it is not costly to increase the sample size, a much higher ARIR is common.)

After auditors specify the tolerable misstatement and ARIA, they can state a hypothesis. The auditor's hypothesis for the audit of accounts receivable for Aliaa Lumber is: accounts receivable is not misstated by more than US$21,000 at an ARIA of 10 percent.

Estimate Misstatements in the Population This estimate has two parts:

1. *Estimate an expected point estimate.* Auditors need an advance estimate of the population point estimate for difference estimation, much as they need an estimated population exception rate for attributes sampling. The advance estimate is US$1,500 (overstatement) for Aliaa Lumber, based on the previous year's audit tests.
2. *Make an advance population standard deviation estimate—variability of the population.* To determine the initial sample size, auditors need an advance estimate of the variation in the misstatements in the population as measured by the population standard deviation. (The calculation of the standard deviation is explained later, when audit results are evaluated.) For Aliaa Lumber, it is estimated to be US$20 based on the previous year's audit tests.

Calculate the Initial Sample Size The initial sample size for Aliaa Lumber can now be calculated using the following formula:

$$n = \left[\frac{SD^*(Z_A + Z_R)N}{TM - E^*} \right]^2$$

where:

n = initial sample size

SD^* = advance estimate of the standard deviation

Z_A = confidence coefficient for ARIA (see Table 17-11)

Z_R = confidence coefficient for ARIR (see Table 17-11)

N = population size

TM = tolerable misstatement for the population (materiality)

E^* = estimated point estimate of the population misstatement

Applied to Aliaa Lumber, this equation yields:

$$n = \left[\frac{20(1.28 + 1.15)4,000}{21,000 - 1,500} \right]^2 = (9.97)^2 = 100$$

Select the Sample and Perform the Procedures

Select the Sample Because a random sample (other than PPS) is required, the auditor must use one of the probabilistic sample selection methods discussed in Chapter 15 to select the 100 sample items for confirmation. In this case the auditor used a computer generated random sample.

Perform the Audit Procedures The auditor must use care in confirming the accounts receivable and performing alternative procedures explained in Chapter 16. For confirmations, a misstatement is the *difference* between the confirmation response and the client's balance after the reconciliation of all timing differences and customer errors. For example, if a customer returns a confirmation and states the correct balance is US$887.12, and the balance in the client's records is US$997.12, the difference of US$110 is an overstatement amount if the auditor concludes that the client's records are incorrect. For nonresponses, the misstatements discovered by alternative procedures are treated identically to those discovered through confirmation. At the end of this step, the auditor determines a misstatement value for each item in the sample, many of which are likely to be zero. The misstatements for Aliaa Lumber are shown in Table 17-13.

Evaluate the Results

Generalize from the Sample to the Population In concept, nonstatistical and difference estimation accomplish the same thing—generalizing from the sample to the population. While both methods measure the likely population misstatement based on the results of the sample, difference estimation uses statistical measurement to compute confidence limits. The following four steps describe the calculation of the confidence limits for Aliaa Lumber Company. (The calculations are illustrated in Table 17-13, steps 3 through 6.)

1. *Compute the point estimate of the total misstatement.* The point estimate is a direct extrapolation from the misstatements in the sample to the misstatements in the population. The calculation of the point estimate for Aliaa Lumber is shown in Table 17-13, step 3.

   It is unlikely that the actual, but unknown, misstatement is *exactly* the same as the point estimate. Instead, it is more realistic to estimate the misstatement in terms of a confidence interval determined by the point estimate plus and minus a computed precision interval. The calculation of the confidence interval is an essential part of difference estimation.

2. *Compute an estimate of the population standard deviation.* The population standard deviation is a statistical measure of the variability in the values of the individual items in the population. If there is a large amount of variation in the values of population items, the standard deviation will be larger than when the variation is small. For example, in the confirmation of accounts receivable, misstatements of US$2, US$275, and US$812 have far more variation than the set US$4, US$14, and US$26. Obviously, the standard deviation is smaller in the second set.

   The standard deviation has a significant effect on the computed precision interval. As one might expect, the auditor's ability to predict total misstatements is better when there is a small amount of variation in the individual sample items.

   The auditor can compute a reasonable estimate of the value of the population standard deviation by using the standard statistical formula shown in

TABLE 17-13	Calculation of Confidence Limits	
Step	**Statistical Formula**	**Illustration for Aliaa Lumber**
1. Take a random sample of size n.	n = sample size	100 accounts receivable are selected randomly from the aged trial balance containing 4,000 accounts.
2. Determine the value of each misstatement in the sample.		75 accounts are confirmed by customers, and 25 accounts are verified by alternative procedures. After reconciling timing differences and customer errors, the following 12 items were determined to be client errors (understatements) stated in dollars:

1.	US$12.75	7.	(.87)
2.	(69.46)	8.	24.32
3.	85.28	9.	36.59
4.	100.00	10.	(102.16)
5.	(27.30)	11.	54.71
6.	41.06	12.	71.56
		Sum =	US$226.48

Step	**Statistical Formula**	**Illustration for Aliaa Lumber**
3. Compute the point estimate of the total misstatement.	$$\bar{e} = \frac{\sum e_j}{n}$$ $$\hat{E} = N\bar{e} \text{ or } N\frac{\sum e_j}{n}$$ where: $\bar{e}$ = average misstatement in the sample $\sum$ = summation e_j = an individual misstatement in the sample n = sample size $\hat{E}$ = point estimate of the total misstatement N = population size	$$\bar{e} = \frac{US\$226.48}{100} = US\$2.26$$ $\hat{E} = 4{,}000\,(US\$2.26) = US\$9{,}040$ or $$\hat{E} = 4{,}000\left(\frac{US\$226.48}{100}\right) = US\$9{,}040$$ (rounded to nearest dollar)
4. Compute the population standard deviation of the misstatements from the sample.	$$SD = \sqrt{\frac{\sum (e_j)^2 - n(\bar{e})^2}{n-1}}$$ where: SD = standard deviation e_j = an individual misstatement in the sample n = sample size $\bar{e}$ = average misstatement in sample	(see table below)

	e_j	$(e_j)^2$
1.	US$ 13	169
2.	(69)	4,761
3.	85	7,225
4.	100	10,000
5.	(27)	729
6.	41	1,681
7.	(1)	1
8.	24	576
9.	37	1,369
10.	(102)	10,404
11.	55	3,025
12.	72	5,184
	US$228	US$45,124

$$SD = \sqrt{\frac{US\$45{,}124 - 100(US\$2.26)^2}{99}}$$

$$SD = US\$21.2$$

(Table 17-13 continued on next page)

TABLE 17-13	Calculation of Confidence Limits *(Cont.)*	
Step	**Statistical Formula**	**Illustration for Aliaa Lumber**
5. Compute the precision interval for the estimate of the total population misstatement at the desired confidence level.	$$CPI = NZ_A \frac{SD}{\sqrt{n}} \sqrt{\frac{N-n}{N}}$$ Where: CPI = computed precision interval N = population size Z_A = confidence coefficient for ARIA (see Table 17-11) SD = population standard deviation n = sample size $$\sqrt{\frac{N-n}{N}} = \text{finite correction factor}$$	$$CPI = 4,000 \cdot 1.28 \cdot \frac{US\$21.2}{\sqrt{100}} \sqrt{\frac{4,000 - 100}{4,000}}$$ $$= 4,000 \cdot 1.28 \cdot \frac{US\$21.2}{10} \cdot .99$$ $$= 4,000 \cdot 1.28 \cdot US\$2.12 \cdot .99$$ $$= US\$10,800 \text{ (rounded)}$$
6. Compute the confidence limits at the CL desired.	$$UCL = \hat{E} + CPI$$ $$LCL = \hat{E} - CPI$$ Where: UCL = computed upper confidence limit LCL = computed lower confidence limit $\hat{E}$ = point estimate of the total misstatement CPI = computed precision interval at desired CL	$$UCL = US\$9,040 + US\$10,800 = US\$19,840$$ $$LCL = US\$9,040 - US\$10,800 = US\$(1,760)$$

Table 17-13, step 4. The standard deviation estimate is determined from the auditor's sample results and is not affected by professional judgment.

3. *Compute the precision interval.* The precision interval is calculated by a statistical formula. The results are a dollar measure of the inability to predict the true population misstatement because the test is based on a sample rather than on the entire population. For the computed precision interval to have any meaning, it must be associated with ARIA. The formula to calculate the precision interval is shown in Table 17-13, step 5.

An examination of the formula in step 5 of Table 17-13 indicates that the effect of changing each factor while the other factors remain constant is as follows:

Type of Change	Effect on the Computed Precision Interval
Increase ARIA	Decrease
Increase the point estimate of the misstatements	Increase
Increase the standard deviation	Increase
Increase the sample size	Decrease

4. *Compute the confidence limits.* Auditors calculate the confidence limits, which define the confidence interval, by combining the point estimate of the total misstatements and the computed precision interval at the desired confidence level (point estimate ± computed precision interval). The formula to calculate the confidence limits is shown in Table 17-13, step 6.

The lower and upper confidence limits for Aliaa Lumber are (US$1,760) and US$19,840, respectively. There is a 10 percent statistical risk that the population is understated by more than US$1,760, and the same risk that it is overstated by more than US$19,840. (Remember, an ARIA of 10 percent is equivalent to a confidence level of 80 percent.)

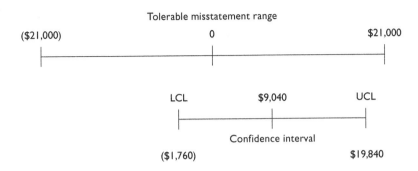

Analyze the Misstatements There are no differences in analyzing misstatements for nonstatistical and statistical methods. The auditor must evaluate misstatements to determine the cause of each misstatement and decide whether modification of the audit risk model is needed.

Decide the Acceptability of the Population To decide whether a population is acceptable, when auditors use a statistical method, they rely on a decision rule, as follows: If the two-sided confidence interval for the misstatements is completely within the plus and minus tolerable misstatements, accept the hypothesis that the book value is not misstated by a material amount. Otherwise, accept the hypothesis that the book value is misstated by a material amount.

This decision rule is illustrated in Figure 17-6. The auditor should conclude that both the LCL and UCL for situations 1 and 2 fall completely within both the understatement and overstatement tolerable misstatement limits. Therefore, auditors can accept the conclusion that the population is not misstated by a material amount. For situations 3, 4, and 5, either LCL or UCL, or both, are outside tolerable misstatements. Therefore, the population book value will be rejected for these situations.

Application of the decision rule to Aliaa Lumber leads the auditor to the conclusion that the population should be accepted, because both confidence limits are within the tolerable misstatement range.

In accepting the population in this way, the auditor is taking a 10 percent chance of being wrong—that is, that the population is, in fact, misstated by a material amount. However, based on the auditor's planning judgments, this level of risk is appropriate.

Analysis Given that the actual standard deviation (21.2) was larger than the advanced estimate (20), and the actual point estimate (US$9,040) was larger than the advanced estimate (US$1,500), it may seem surprising that the population was accepted. However,

FIGURE 17-6	Illustration of the Auditor's Decision Rule for Difference Estimation

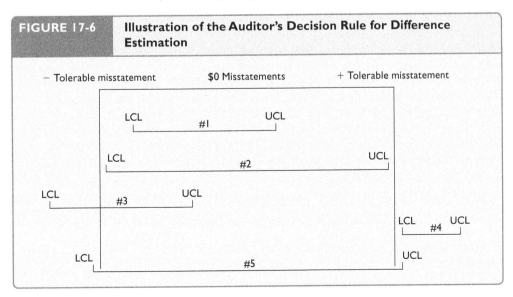

the use of a reasonably small ARIR caused the sample size to be larger than if ARIR had been 100 percent. If ARIR had been 100 percent, which is common when the additional audit cost to increase the sample size is small, the required sample size would have been only 28:

$$\left[\frac{20(1.28 + 0)\ 4,000}{21,000 - 1,500} \right]^2 = 28$$

Assuming a sample size of 28 and the same actual point estimate and standard deviation, the upper confidence limit would have been US$29,559, and therefore, the population book value would have been rejected. Auditors can use ARIR to reduce the likelihood of needing to increase the sample size if the standard deviation or point estimate is larger than was expected.

Action When a Hypothesis is Rejected

When one or both of the confidence limits lie outside the tolerable misstatement range, the population is not considered acceptable. The courses of action for the auditor are the same as those we discussed for nonstatistical sampling, except that a better estimate of the population misstatement has been made.

For example, in the Aliaa Lumber case, if the confidence level had been US$9,040 ± US$15,800 and the client had been willing to reduce the book value by US$9,040, the results would be 0 ± US$15,800. The new computed lower confidence limit would be an understatement of US$15,800, and the upper confidence limit a US$15,800 overstatement, which are both acceptable given the tolerable misstatement of US$21,000. The minimum adjustment that the auditor could make and still have the population acceptable is US$3,840 [(US$9,040 + US$15,800) − US$21,000].

However, the client may be unwilling to adjust the balance on the basis of a sample. Furthermore, if the computed precision interval exceeds tolerable misstatement, no adjustment to the books will satisfy the auditor. This would have been the case in the previous example if tolerable misstatement had been only US$15,000.

SUMMARY

This chapter discussed nonstatistical and statistical audit sampling methods for tests of details of balances. In sampling for tests of balances, the auditor determines whether the dollar amount of an account balance is materially misstated. We then discussed the 14 steps in nonstatistical sampling for tests of balances. When performing nonstatistical audit sampling, the auditor uses judgment in generalizing from the sample to the population to determine whether it is acceptable. Monetary unit sampling is the most common statistical method for tests of balances. This method defines the sampling unit as individual dollars in the recorded account balance, and as a result, larger accounts are more likely to be included in the sample. Variables statistical sampling methods include difference estimation, ratio estimation, and mean-per-unit estimation. These methods compare audited sample values to recorded values to develop an estimate of the misstatement in the account value. Use of variables sampling was illustrated using difference estimation.

ESSENTIAL TERMS

Acceptable risk of incorrect acceptance (ARIA)   p. 578

Acceptable risk of incorrect rejection (ARIR)   p. 599

Difference estimation   p. 597

Mean-per-unit estimation   p. 598

Misstatement bounds   p. 586

REVIEW QUESTIONS

17-1 (Objective 17-1) What major difference between (a) tests of controls and substantive tests of transactions and (b) tests of details of balances makes attributes sampling inappropriate for tests of details of balances?

17-2 (Objective 17-2) Define stratified sampling and explain its importance in auditing. How can an auditor obtain a stratified sample of 30 items from each of three strata in the confirmation of accounts receivable?

17-3 (Objective 17-2) Distinguish between the point estimate of the total misstatements and the true value of the misstatements in the population. How can each be determined?

17-4 (Objective 17-2) Evaluate the following statement made by an auditor: "On every aspect of the audit where it is possible, I calculate the point estimate of the misstatements and evaluate whether the amount is material. If it is, I investigate the cause and continue to test the population until I determine whether there is a serious problem. The use of statistical sampling in this manner is a valuable audit tool."

17-5 (Objective 17-3) Define monetary unit sampling and explain its importance in auditing. How does it combine the features of attributes and variables sampling?

17-6 (Objectives 17-1, 17-2, 17-3, 17-4) Define what is meant by sampling risk. Does sampling risk apply to nonstatistical sampling, MUS, attributes sampling, and variables sampling? Explain.

17-7 (Objectives 17-1, 17-2) What are the major differences in the 14 steps used in nonstatistical sampling for tests of details of balances versus for tests of controls and substantive tests of transactions?

17-8 (Objective 17-3) The 2,620 inventory items described in Question 17-14 are listed on 44 inventory pages with 60 lines per page. There is a total for each page. The client's data are not in machine-readable form. Describe how a monetary unit sample can be selected in this situation.

17-9 (Objective 17-3) Explain how the auditor determines tolerable misstatement for MUS.

17-10 (Objective 17-2) Explain what is meant by acceptable risk of incorrect acceptance. What are the major audit factors affecting ARIA?

17-11 (Objective 17-4) Evaluate the following statement made by an auditor: "I took a random sample and derived a 90 percent confidence interval of US$800,000 to US$900,000. That means that the true population value will be between US$800,000 and US$900,000, 90 percent of the time."

17-12 (Objective 17-2) What is the relationship between ARIA and ARACR?

17-13 (Objective 17-3) What is meant by the 'percent of misstatement assumption' for MUS in those population items that are misstated? Why is it common to use a 100% misstatement assumption when it is almost certain to be highly conservative?

17-14 (Objective 17-3) An auditor is determining the appropriate sample size for testing inventory valuation using MUS. The population has 2,620 inventory items valued at US$12,625,000. The tolerable misstatement for both understatements and overstatements is US$500,000 at a 10% ARIA. No misstatements are expected in the population. Calculate the preliminary sample size using a 100% average misstatement assumption.

17-15 (Objective 17-5) Assume that a sample of 100 units was obtained in sampling the inventory in Question 17-14. Assume further that the following three misstatements were found:

Misstatement	Recorded Value	Audited Value
1	US$ 897.16	US$ 609.16
2	47.02	0
3	1,621.68	1,522.68

Calculate adjusted misstatement bounds for the population. Draw audit conclusions based on the results.

17-16 (Objective 17-3) Why is it difficult to determine the appropriate sample size for MUS? How should the auditor determine the proper sample size?

17-17 (Objective 17-5) What is meant by a decision rule using difference estimation? State the decision rule.

17-18 (Objective 17-2) What alternative courses of action are appropriate when a population is rejected using nonstatistical sampling for tests of details of balances? When should each option be followed?

17-19 (Objective 17-4) Define what is meant by the population standard deviation and explain its importance in variables sampling. What is the relationship between the population standard deviation and the required sample size?

17-20 (Objective 17-5) In using difference estimation, an auditor took a random sample of 100 inventory items from a large population to test for proper pricing. Several of the inventory items were misstated, but the combined net amount of the sample misstatement was not material. In addition, a review of the individual misstatements indicated that no misstatement was by itself material. As a result, the auditor did not investigate the misstatements or make a statistical evaluation. Explain why this practice is improper.

17-21 (Objectives 17-3, 17-4) Distinguish among difference estimation, ratio estimation, mean-per-unit estimation, and stratified mean-per-unit estimation. Give one example in which each can be used. When is MUS preferable to any of these?

17-22 (Objective 17-4) An essential step in difference estimation is the comparison of each computed confidence limit with tolerable misstatement. Why is this step so important, and what should the auditor do if one of the confidence limits is larger than the tolerable misstatement?

17-23 (Objective 17-4) Explain why difference estimation is commonly used by auditors.

17-24 (Objectives 17-3, 17-4) Give an example of the use of attributes sampling, MUS, and variables sampling in the form of an audit conclusion.

MULTIPLE CHOICE QUESTIONS FROM CPA EXAMINATIONS

17-25 (Objective 17-2) The following questions refer to the use of stratified sampling in auditing. For each one, select the best response.

a. Mr. Kasam decides to use stratified sampling. The reason for using stratified sampling rather than unrestricted random sampling is to
  (1) reduce as much as possible the degree of variability in the overall population.
  (2) give every element in the population an equal chance of being included in the sample.
  (3) allow the person selecting the sample to use personal judgment in deciding which elements should be included in the sample.
  (4) allow the auditor to emphasize larger items from the population.

b. In an audit of financial statements, a CPA will generally find stratified sampling techniques to be most applicable to
  (1) recomputing net wage and salary payments to employees.
  (2) tracing hours worked from the payroll summary back to the individual time cards.
  (3) confirming accounts receivable for residential customers at a large electric utility.
  (4) reviewing supporting documentation for additions to plant and equipment.

c. From prior experience, a CPA is aware that the accounts receivable trial balance contains a few unusually large balances. In using statistical sampling, the CPA's best course of action is to
  (1) eliminate any unusually large balances that appear in the sample.
  (2) continue to draw new samples until no unusually large balances appear in the sample.
  (3) stratify the accounts receivable population so that the unusually large balances are reviewed separately.
  (4) increase the sample size to lessen the effect of the unusually large balances.

17-26 (Objectives 17-1, 17-2) The following apply to audit sampling. For each one, select the best response.

a. A number of factors influence the sample size for a substantive test of details of an account balance. All other things being equal, which of the following would lead to a larger sample size?
  (1) Greater reliance on internal control.
  (2) Greater reliance on analytical procedures.
  (3) Smaller expected frequency of errors.
  (4) Smaller measure of tolerable misstatement.

b. An auditor uses audit sampling to perform tests of controls in the acquisition and payment cycle. Those tests indicate that the related controls are operating effectively. The auditor plans to use audit sampling to perform tests of details of balances for accounts payable. The auditor's acceptable risk of incorrect acceptance (ARIA) for the tests of details of balances for accounts payable will most likely be
  (1) the same as the ARACR for tests of controls.
  (2) greater than the ARACR for tests of controls.
  (3) less than the ARACR for tests of controls.
  (4) totally independent from the ARACR used for tests of controls.

c. Which of the following sample planning factors will influence the sample size for a test of details of balances for a specific account?

	Expected Amount of Misstatements	Measure of Tolerable Misstatement
1	No	No
2	Yes	Yes
3	No	Yes
4	Yes	No

DISCUSSION QUESTIONS AND PROBLEMS

17-27 (Objective 17-3) Below is the total monthly sales population for Jafar's Custom Candles. Cumulative amounts have been included to help you complete the problem. The population is somewhat smaller than is ordinarily the case for statistical sampling, but an entire population is useful to show how to select PPS samples.

a. Select a random PPS sample of 10 items, using computer software.

Required

b. Select a sample of 10 items using systematical PPS sampling using the same concepts discussed in Chapter 15 for systematic sampling. Use a starting point of 1857. Identify the physical units associated with the sample dollars. (*Hint:* The interval is 78,493 ÷ 10.)

c. Which sample items will always be included in the systematic PPS sample regardless of the starting point? Will that also be true of random PPS sampling?

d. Which method is preferable in terms of ease of selection in this case?

e. Why will an auditor use MUS?

Population Item	Recorded Amount	Cumulative Amount	Population Item (cont.)	Recorded Amount (cont.)	Cumulative Amount (cont.)
1	US$ 2,493	US$ 2,493	21	US$ 973	US$39,682
2	1,209	3,702	22	1,552	41,234
3	930	4,632	23	2,345	43,579
4	3,027	7,659	24	879	44,458
5	506	8,165	25	5,675	50,133
6	380	8,545	26	589	50,722
7	782	9,327	27	1,234	51,956
8	1,304	10,631	28	1,008	52,964
9	2,604	13,235	29	2,130	55,094
10	5,455	18,690	30	792	55,886
11	2,300	20,990	31	1,354	57,240
12	903	21,893	32	4,197	61,437
13	850	22,743	33	842	62,279
14	1,203	23,946	34	512	62,791
15	3,120	27,066	35	5,768	68,559
16	4,760	31,826	36	1,254	69,813
17	403	32,229	37	2,348	72,161
18	3,349	35,578	38	3,092	75,253
19	2,101	37,679	39	1,843	77,096
20	1,030	38,709	40	1,397	78,493

17-28 (Objective 17-2) You are planning to use nonstatistical sampling to evaluate the results of accounts receivable confirmation for the Meridian Company. You have already performed tests of controls for sales, sales returns and allowances, and cash receipts, and they are considered excellent. Because of the quality of the controls, you decide to use an acceptable risk of incorrect acceptance of 10%. There are 3,000 accounts receivable with a gross value of US$6,900,000. The accounts are similar in size and will be treated as a single stratum. An overstatement or understatement of more than US$150,000 is considered material.

Required

a. Calculate the required sample size. Assume your firm uses the following nonstatistical formula to determine sample size:

Sample size = (Book value of population / Tolerable misstatement) × Assurance factor
An assurance factor of 2 is used for a 10% ARIA.

b. Assume that instead of good results, poor results were obtained for tests of controls and substantive tests of transactions for sales, sales returns and allowances, and cash receipts. How will this affect your required sample size? How will you use this information in your sample size determination?

c. Regardless of your answer to part a, assume you decide to select a sample of 100 accounts for testing. Indicate how you will select the accounts for testing using systematic selection.

d. Assume a total book value of US$230,000 for the 100 accounts selected for testing. You uncover three overstatements totaling US$1,500 in the sample. Evaluate whether the population is fairly stated.

17-29 (Objective 17-3) In the audit of El Montassar Farm Products for the year ended September 30, the auditor set a tolerable misstatement of US$50,000 at an ARIA of 10%. A PPS sample of 100 was selected from an accounts receivable population that had a recorded balance of US$1,975,000. The following table shows the differences uncovered in the confirmation process:

Accounts Receivable per Records	Accounts Receivable per Confirmation	Follow-up Comments by Auditor
1. US$2,728.00	US$ 2,498.00	Pricing error on two invoices.
2. US$5,125.00	-0-	Customer mailed check 9/27; company received check 10/3.
3. US$3,890.00	US$ 1,190.00	Merchandise returned 9/30 and counted in inventory; credit was issued 10/6.
4. US$ 791.00	US$ 815.00	Footing error on an invoice.
5. US$ 548.00	US$ 1,037.00	Goods were shipped 9/28; customer received goods 10/6.
6. US$3,115.00	US$ 3,190.00	Pricing error on a credit memorandum.
7. US$1,540.00	-0-	Goods were shipped on 9/29; customer received goods 10/3; sale recorded 9/30.

Required

a. Calculate the upper and lower misstatement bounds on the basis of the client misstatements in the sample.

b. Is the population acceptable as stated? If not, what options are available to the auditor at this point? Which option should the auditor select? Explain.

17-30 (Objectives 17-2, 17-3, 17-4, 17-5) An audit partner is developing an office training program to familiarize her professional staff with audit sampling decision models applicable to the audit of dollar-value balances. She wishes to demonstrate the relationship of sample sizes to population size and estimated population exception rate and the auditor's specifications as to tolerable misstatement and ARIA. The partner prepared the following table to show comparative population characteristics and audit specifications of the two populations:

	Characteristics of Population 1 Relative to Population 2		Audit Specifications as to a Sample from Population 1 Relative to a Sample from Population 2	
	Size	Estimated Population Exception Rate	Tolerable Misstatement	ARIA
Case 1	Equal	Equal	Equal	Lower
Case 2	Smaller	Smaller	Equal	Higher
Case 3	Larger	Equal	Equal	Lower
Case 4	Equal	Larger	Larger	Equal
Case 5	Larger	Equal	Smaller	Higher

Required

In items (1) through (5) you are to indicate for the specific case from the table the required sample size to be selected from population 1 relative to the sample from population 2.

1. In case 1, the required sample size from population 1 is _____.
2. In case 2, the required sample size from population 1 is _____.
3. In case 3, the required sample size from population 1 is _____.
4. In case 4, the required sample size from population 1 is _____.
5. In case 5, the required sample size from population 1 is _____.

Your answer choice should be selected from the following responses:

a. Larger than the required sample size from population 2.

b. Equal to the required sample size from population 2.

c. Smaller than the required sample size from population 2.

d. Indeterminate relative to the required sample size from population 2.[18]

17-31 (Objective 17-5) In auditing the valuation of inventory, the auditor, Abbas Saleh, decided to use difference estimation. He decided to select an unrestricted random sample of 80 inventory items from a population of 1,840 that had a book value of US$175,820. Saleh decided in advance that he was willing to accept a maximum misstatement in the population of US$6,000 at an ARIA of 5 percent. There were eight misstatements in the sample, which were as follows:

	Audit Value	Book Value	Sample Misstatements
	US$ 812.50	US$ 740.50	US$(72.00)
	12.50	78.20	65.70
	10.00	51.10	11.10
	25.40	61.50	36.10
	600.10	651.90	51.80
	.12	0	(.12)
	51.06	81.06	30.00
	83.11	104.22	21.11
Total	US$1,594.79	US$1,768.48	US$173.69

Required

a. Calculate the point estimate, the computer precision interval, the confidence interval, and the confidence limits for the populations. Label each calculation. Use a computer for this purpose (instructor's option).

b. Should Saleh accept the book value of the population? Explain.

c. What options are available to him at this point?

17-32 (Objective 17-5) Hussein Bahari, CPA, is verifying the accuracy of outstanding accounts payable for Saudi Hardware, a large, single-location retail hardware store. There are 650 vendors listed on the outstanding accounts payable list. He has eliminated from the population 40 vendors that have large ending balances and will audit them separately. There are now 610 vendors.

He plans to do one of three tests for each item in the sample: examine a vendor's statement in the client's hands, obtain a confirmation when no statement is on hand, or extensively search for invoices when neither of the first two is obtained. There is no accounts payable master file available, and a large number of misstatements are expected. Hussein has obtained facts or made audit judgments as follows:

ARIR	20%	ARIA	10%
Tolerable misstatement	US$ 45,000	Expected misstatement	US$20,000
Recorded book value	US$600,000	Estimated standard deviation	US$ 280

Required

a. Under what circumstances is it desirable to use difference estimation in the situation described? Under what circumstances is it undesirable?

b. Calculate the required sample size for the audit tests of accounts payable using difference estimation, assuming that ARIR is ignored.

c. Assume that the auditor selects exactly the sample size calculated in part b. The point estimate calculated from the sample results is US$21,000 and the estimated population standard deviation is 267. Is the population fairly stated as defined by the decision rule? Explain what causes the result to be acceptable or unacceptable.

d. Calculate the required sample size for the audit tests of accounts payable, assuming that the ARIR is considered.

e. Explain the reason for the large increase of the sample size resulting from including ARIR in determining sample size.

f. Hussein Bahari calculates the required sample size using the formula without consideration of ARIR. After the sample size is determined, he increases the sample size by 25%. Hussein believes that this does the same thing as using ARIR without having to bother to make the calculation. Is this approach appropriate? Evaluate the desirability of the approach.

CASES

17-33 (Objective 17-5) You are doing the audit of Mahsa Tire and Parts, a wholesale auto parts company. You have decided to use monetary unit sampling (MUS) for the audit of accounts receivable and inventory. The following are the recorded balances:

Accounts receivable	US$12,000,000
Inventory	23,000,000

You have already made the following judgments:

Materiality for planning purposes	US$800,000
Acceptable audit risk	5%
Inherent risk:	
Accounts receivable	80%
Inventory	100%
Assessed control risk:	
Accounts receivable	50%
Inventory	80%

Analytical procedures have been planned for inventory, but not for accounts receivable. The analytical procedures for inventory are expected to have a 60% chance of detecting a material misstatement should one exist.

You have concluded that it will be difficult to alter sample size for accounts receivable confirmation once confirmations are sent and replies are received. However, inventory tests can be reopened without great difficulty.

After discussions with the client, you believe that the accounts are in about the same condition this year as they were last year. Last year no misstatements were found in confirmation of accounts receivable. Inventory tests revealed an overstatement amount of about 1%.

For parts a–c, make any assumptions necessary in deciding the factors affecting sample size. If no table is available for the ARIA chosen, estimate sample size judgmentally.

a. Plan the sample size for the confirmation of accounts receivable using MUS.   **Required**

b. Plan the sample size for the test of pricing of inventories using MUS.

c. Plan the combined sample size for both the confirmation of accounts receivable and the price tests of inventory using MUS.

d. Using an electronic spreadsheet, generate a list of random dollars in generation order and in ascending order for the sample of accounts receivable items determined in part a.

17-34 (Objectives 17-2, 17-3) You have just completed the accounts receivable confirmation process in the audit of Qena Paper Company, a paper supplier to retail shops and commercial users. Following are the data related to this process:

Accounts receivable recorded balance	US$2,760,000
Number of accounts	7,320
A nonstatistical sample was taken as follows:	
All accounts over US$10,000 (23 accounts)	US$465,000
77 accounts under US$10,000	US$81,500
Tolerable misstatement for the confirmation test	US$100,000
Inherent and control risk are both high	
No relevant analytical procedures were performed	

The following are the results of the confirmation procedures:

	Recorded Value	Audited Value
Items over US$10,000	US$465,000	US$432,000
Items under US$10,000	81,500	77,150
Individual misstatements for items under US$10,000:		
Item 12	5,120	4,820
Item 19	485	385
Item 33	1,250	250
Item 35	3,975	3,875
Item 51	1,850	1,825
Item 59	4,200	3,780
Item 74	2,405	0

a. Evaluate the results of the nonstatistical sample. Consider both the direct implications   **Required**
of the misstatements found and the effect of using a sample.

b. Assume that the sample was a PPS sample. Evaluate the results using monetary unit sampling.

c. Do the preceding analyses using an electronic spreadsheet.

4

APPLICATION OF THE AUDIT PROCESS TO OTHER CYCLES

Part 4 builds on the concepts presented in Chapters 6 through 17 and illustrates how auditing may differ for each cycle. Each of the following chapters deals with a specific transaction cycle or part of a transaction cycle in much the same manner as Chapters 14 through 17 cover the sales and collection cycle.

Each chapter in Part 4 demonstrates the relationship of internal controls, tests of controls, substantive tests of transactions, and analytical procedures to the related balance sheet and income statement accounts in the cycle and to tests of details of balances. The following chapters will discuss the remaining cycles including the acquisition and payment, payroll, inventory and warehousing, and capital acquisition and repayment cycles. The operations, characteristics, and accounts related to each cycle are presented. Also, the application of the audit procedures and evidence to each cycle showing differences in terms of tests of controls and substantive tests.

CHAPTER 18

AUDIT OF THE ACQUISITION AND PAYMENT CYCLE: TESTS OF CONTROLS, SUBSTANTIVE TESTS OF TRANSACTIONS, AND ACCOUNTS PAYABLE

LEARNING OBJECTIVES

After studying this chapter, you should be able to

18-1 Identify the accounts and the classes of transactions in the acquisition and payment cycle.

18-2 Describe the business functions and the related documents and records in the acquisition and payment cycle.

18-3 Understand internal control, and design and perform tests of controls and substantive tests of transactions for the acquisition and payment cycle.

18-4 Describe the methodology for designing tests of details of balances for accounts payable using the audit risk model.

18-5 Design and perform analytical procedures for accounts payable.

18-6 Design and perform tests of details of balances for accounts payable, including out-of-period liability tests.

18-7 Distinguish the reliability of vendors' invoices, vendors' statements, and confirmations of accounts payable as audit evidence.

False Purchases Camouflage Overstated Profits

Comptronix Corporation, a U.S. electronics company, announced that senior members of its management team overstated profits, and there would be material adjustments to the prior years' audited financial statements. Central to the fraud was the use of fictitious accounts payable purchases for large equipment items to overstate fixed assets and hide fictitious sales.

The senior executives circumvented Comptronix's existing internal controls by bypassing the purchasing and receiving departments so that no one at Comptronix could discover the scheme. Comptronix employees usually created a fairly extensive paper trail for equipment purchases. Company internal controls over acquisition and cash disbursement transactions typically required a purchase order, receiving report, and vendor invoice before payment could be authorized by the chief operating officer or the controller/treasurer, who were both participants in the fraud. As a result, the executives were able to bypass controls over cash disbursements and authorize payment for nonexistent purchases without creating any documents for the fictitious transactions.

The company also created fictitious sales and related receivables. The company issued checks to pay for the false purchase transactions. The checks were then redeposited into the company's account and recorded as collections on the fictitious receivables. As a result, it appeared that the fictitious sales were collected, and that payments were made to support the false fixed asset purchases.

The fraud scheme grossly exaggerated the company's performance by reporting profits when the company was actually incurring losses. On the day that the public announcement of the fraud was made, Comptronix's common stock price declined abruptly by 72 percent. The SEC ultimately charged the executives with violating the antifraud provisions of the Securities Act of 1933 and the Securities Exchange Act of 1934. The SEC permanently barred the executives from serving as officers or directors of any public company, ordered them to repay bonuses and trading losses avoided, and imposed civil monetary penalties against them.

Source: *Accounting and Auditing Enforcement Release No. 543,* Commerce Clearing House, Inc., Chicago, U.S.

We'll now discuss the acquisition and payment cycle. The acquisition of goods and services includes the acquisition of such things as raw materials, equipment, supplies, utilities, repairs and maintenance, and research and development. In the first part of the chapter, we'll examine assessing control risk and designing tests of controls and substantive tests of transactions for the classes of transactions in the acquisition and payment cycle. Then, we'll cover performing tests of details of balances for accounts payable.

As with the sales and collection cycle, auditors need to understand the business functions, and documents and records in a company before they can assess control risk and design tests of controls and substantive tests of transactions. We first examine two related topics:

1. The acquisition and payment cycle classes of transactions and account balances in a typical company
2. Typical documents and records used in the acquisition and payment cycle

Relevant International Standards on Auditing	
ISA 200	Overall Objectives of the Independent Auditor and the Conduct of an Audit in Accordance with International Standards on Auditing
ISA 230	Audit Documentation
ISA 265	Communicating Deficiencies in Internal Control to Those Charged with Governance and Management
ISA 300	Planning an Audit of Financial Statements
ISA 320	Materiality in Planning and Performing an Audit
ISA 450	Evaluation of Misstatements Identified during the Audit
ISA 500	Audit Evidence
ISA 505	External Confirmations
ISA 520	Analytical Procedures
ISA 530	Audit Sampling

ACCOUNTS AND CLASSES OF TRANSACTIONS IN THE ACQUISITION AND PAYMENT CYCLE

OBJECTIVE 18-1

Identify the accounts and the classes of transactions in the acquisition and payment cycle.

Acquisition and payment cycle

The transaction cycle that includes the acquisition of and payment for goods and services from suppliers outside the organization.

The objective in the audit of the **acquisition and payment cycle** is to evaluate whether the accounts affected by the acquisitions of goods and services and the cash disbursements for those acquisitions are fairly presented in accordance with IFRS or local accounting standards. Figure 18-1 shows the way accounting information flows through the various accounts in the acquisition and payment cycle.

There are three classes of transactions included in the cycle:

1. Acquisitions of goods and services
2. Cash disbursements
3. Purchase returns and allowances, and purchase discounts

Ten typical accounts involved in the acquisition and payment cycle are shown by T accounts in Figure 18-1. For simplicity, we show only the control accounts for the three major categories of expenses used by most companies. For each control account, examples of the subsidiary expense accounts are also given. Note the large number of accounts affected by this cycle. It is therefore not surprising that auditing the acquisition and payment cycle often takes more time than any other cycle.

FIGURE 18-1	Accounts in the Acquisition and Payment Cycle

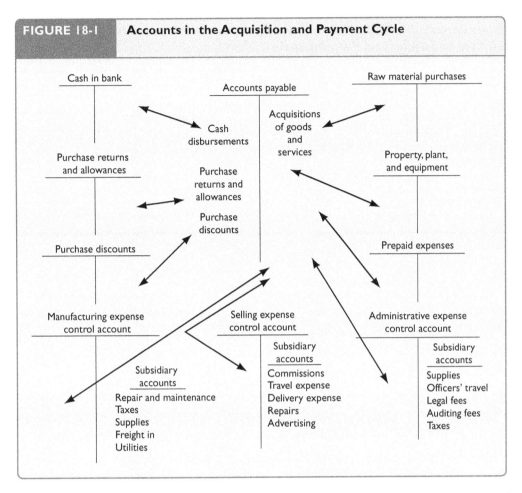

Figure 18-1 shows that every transaction is either debited or credited to accounts payable. Because many companies make acquisitions directly by check or through petty cash, the figure is an oversimplification. We assume that acquisitions made for cash are processed in the same manner as those made by accounts payable.

BUSINESS FUNCTIONS IN THE CYCLE AND RELATED DOCUMENTS AND RECORDS

The acquisition and payment cycle involves the decisions and processes necessary for obtaining the goods and services for operating a business. The cycle typically begins with the initiation of a purchase requisition by an authorized employee who needs the goods or services, and it ends with payment on accounts payable. In the following discussion, the example of a small manufacturing company that makes tangible products for sale to third parties is used, but the principles covered here also apply to service companies, government entities, and other types of organizations.

The third column of Table 18-1 list four business functions that occur in every business in recording the two classes of transactions in the acquisition and payment cycle. The first three functions are for recording the acquisition of goods and services on account, and the fourth function is for recording cash disbursements for payments to vendors. For simplicity, our illustration does not show processing purchase returns and allowances and purchase discounts which are not significant for most companies.

Next, we examine in more detail each of the four business functions, paying particular attention to the typical documents and records used. These are listed in the fourth column of Table 18-1.

> **OBJECTIVE 18-2**
>
> Describe the business functions and the related documents and records in the acquisition and payment cycle.

TABLE 18-1	Classes of Transactions, Accounts, Business Functions, and Related Documents and Records for the Acquisition and Payment Cycle		
Classes of Transactions	**Accounts**	**Business Functions**	**Documents and Records**
Acquisitions	Inventory	Processing purchase orders	Purchase requisition Purchase order
	Prepaid expenses Leasehold improvements Accounts payable	Receiving goods and services	Receiving report
	Manufacturing expenses Selling expenses Administrative expenses	Recognizing the liability	Vendor's invoice Debit memo Voucher Acquisitions transaction file Acquisitions journal or listing Accounts payable master file Accounts payable trial balance Vendor's statement
Cash disbursements	Cash in bank (from cash disbursements) Accounts payable Purchase discounts	Processing and recording cash disbursements	Check Cash disbursements transaction file Cash disbursements journal or listing

Processing Purchase Orders

The request for goods or services by the client's personnel is the starting point for the cycle. The exact form of the request and the required approval depend on the nature of the goods and services and company policy. Common documents include:

Purchase requisition

Request by an authorized employee to the purchasing department to place an order for inventory and other items used by an entity.

Purchase Requisition A **purchase requisition** is used to request goods and services by an authorized employee. This may take the form of a request for such acquisitions as materials by a foreman or the storeroom supervisor, outside repairs by office or factory personnel, or insurance by the vice president in charge of property and equipment. Companies often rely on pre-specified reorder points used by the computer to initiate inventory purchase requisitions automatically.

Purchase order

A document prepared by the purchasing department indicating the description, quantity, and related information for goods and services that the company intends to purchase.

Purchase Order A **purchase order** is a document used to order goods and services from vendors. It includes the description, quantity, and related information for goods and services the company intends to purchase and is often used to indicate authorization of the acquisition. Companies often submit purchase orders electronically to vendors who have made arrangements for electronic data interchange (EDI).

Receiving Goods and Services

Receiving report

A document prepared by the receiving department at the time tangible goods are received, indicating the description of the goods, the quantity received, the date received, and other relevant data; it is part of the documentation necessary for payment to be made.

The receipt by the company of goods or services from the vendor is a critical point in the cycle because it is when most companies first recognize the acquisition and related liability on their records. When goods are received, adequate control requires examination for description, quantity, timely arrival, and condition. A **receiving report** is a paper or electronic document prepared at the time goods are received. It includes a description of the goods, the quantity received, the date received, and other relevant data.

Recognizing the Liability

The proper recognition of the liability for the receipt of goods and services requires *prompt and accurate* recording. The initial recording affects the financial statements and the actual cash disbursement; therefore, companies must take care to include all acquisition transactions, only acquisitions that occurred, and at the correct amounts. Common documents and records include the following.

Vendor's Invoice A **vendor's invoice** is a document received from the vendor and shows the amount owed for an acquisition. It indicates the description and quantity of goods and services received, price (including freight), cash discount terms, date of the billing, and total amount. The vendor's invoice is important because it indicates the amount recorded in the acquisition transaction file. For companies using EDI, the vendor's invoice is transmitted electronically, which affects how the auditor evaluates evidence.

Debit Memo A **debit memo** is also a document received from the vendor and indicates a reduction in the amount owed to a vendor because of returned goods or an allowance granted. It often takes the same form as a vendor's invoice, but it supports reductions in accounts payable rather than increases.

Voucher A **voucher** is commonly used by organizations to establish a formal means of recording and controlling acquisitions, primarily by enabling each acquisition transaction to be sequentially numbered. Vouchers include a cover sheet or folder for containing documents and a package of relevant documents such as the purchase order, copy of the packing slip, receiving report, and vendor's invoice. After payment, a copy of the check is added to the voucher package.

Acquisitions Transaction File This is a computer-generated file that includes all acquisition transactions processed by the accounting system for a period, such as a day, week, or month. It contains all information entered into the system and includes information for each transaction, such as vendor name, date, amount, account classification or classifications, and description and quantity of goods and services purchased. The file can also include purchase returns and allowances or there can be a separate file for those transactions. Depending on the company's needs, the information in the acquisitions transaction file is used for a variety of records, listings, or reports, such as an acquisitions journal, accounts payable master file, and transactions for a certain account balance or division.

Acquisitions Journal or Listing This listing or report is generated from the acquisitions transaction file and typically includes the vendor name, date, amount, and account classification or classifications for each transaction, such as repair and maintenance, inventory, or utilities. It also identifies whether the acquisition was for cash or accounts payable. The journal or listing can cover any time period, typically a month. The journal or listing includes totals of every account number included for the time period. The same transactions included in the journal or listing are also posted simultaneously to the general ledger and, if they are on account, to the accounts payable master file.

Accounts Payable Master File An **accounts payable master file** records acquisitions, cash disbursements, and acquisition returns and allowances transactions for each vendor. The master file is updated from the acquisition, returns and allowances, and cash disbursement computer transaction files. The total of the individual account balances in the master file equals the total balance of accounts payable in the general ledger. A printout of the accounts payable master file shows, by vendor, the beginning balance in accounts payable, each acquisition, acquisition return and allowance, cash disbursement, and the ending balance. Many companies do not maintain an accounts payable master file by vendor. These companies pay on the basis of individual vendor's invoices. Therefore, the total of unpaid vendors' invoices in the master file equals total accounts payable.

Accounts Payable Trial Balance An **accounts payable trial balance** listing includes the amount owed to each vendor or for each invoice or voucher at a point in time. It is prepared directly from the accounts payable master file.

Vendor's Statement A **vendor's statement** is a document prepared monthly by the vendor and indicates the beginning balance, acquisitions, returns and allowances,

---

Vendor's invoice

A document that specifies the details of an acquisition transaction and amount of money owed to the vendor for an acquisition.

Debit memo

A document indicating a reduction in the amount owed to a vendor because of returned goods or an allowance granted.

Voucher

A document used to establish a formal means of recording and controlling acquisitions, primarily by enabling each acquisition transaction to be sequentially numbered.

Accounts payable master file

A computer file for maintaining a record for each vendor of individual acquisitions, cash disbursements, acquisition returns and allowances, and vendor balances.

Accounts payable trial balance

A listing of the amount owed to each vendor at a point in time; prepared directly from the accounts payable master file.

Vendor's statement

A statement prepared monthly by the vendor, which indicates the customer's beginning balance, acquisitions, returns and allowance, payments, and ending balance.

payments to the vendor, and ending balance. These balances and activities are the vendor's representations of the transactions for the period, not the client's. Except for disputed amounts and timing differences, the client's accounts payable master file should be the same as the vendor's statement.

Processing and Recording Cash Disbursements

The payment for goods and services represents a significant activity for all entities. This activity directly reduces balances in liability accounts, particularly accounts payable. Documents associated with the disbursement process that auditors examine include:

Check This document is commonly used to pay for the acquisition when payment is due. Most companies use computer-prepared checks based on information included in the acquisition transactions file at the time goods and services are received. Checks are typically prepared in a multi-copy format, with the original going to the payee, one copy filed with the vendor's invoice and other supporting documents, and another filed numerically. In most cases, individual checks are recorded in a cash disbursements transaction file.

After a check is signed by an authorized person, it is an asset. Therefore, signed checks should be mailed by the signer or a person under the signer's control. When cashed by the vendor and cleared by the client's bank, it is called a cancelled check. At that point it is no longer an asset, but now is a document. In some EDI arrangements, the company submits payments to the vendor electronically through an electronic funds transfer (EFT) between the company's bank and the vendor's bank.

Cash Disbursements Transaction File This is a computer-generated file that includes all cash disbursements transactions processed by the accounting system for a period, such as a day, week, or month. It includes the same type of information discussed for the acquisitions transaction file.

Cash Disbursements Journal or Listing This is a listing or report generated from the cash disbursements transaction file that includes all transactions for any time period. The same transactions, including all relevant information, are included in the accounts payable master file and general ledger.

METHODOLOGY FOR DESIGNING TESTS OF CONTROLS AND SUBSTANTIVE TESTS OF TRANSACTIONS

OBJECTIVE 18-3

Understand internal control, and design and perform tests of controls and substantive tests of transactions for the acquisition and payment cycle.

In a typical audit, the most time-consuming accounts to verify by substantive tests of details of balances are accounts receivable, inventory, fixed assets, accounts payable, and expense accounts. Notice that four of these five are directly related to the acquisition and payment cycle. If the auditor can reduce tests of details of the account balances by using tests of controls and substantive tests of transactions to verify the effectiveness of internal controls for acquisitions and cash disbursements, the net time saved can be dramatic. In well-conducted audits, tests of controls and substantive tests of transactions for the acquisition and payment cycle receive a considerable amount of attention, especially when the client has effective internal controls.

Tests of controls and substantive tests of transactions for the acquisition and payment cycle are divided into two broad areas:

1. Tests of acquisitions, which concern three of the four business functions discussed earlier in this chapter: processing purchase orders, receiving goods and services, and recognizing the liability

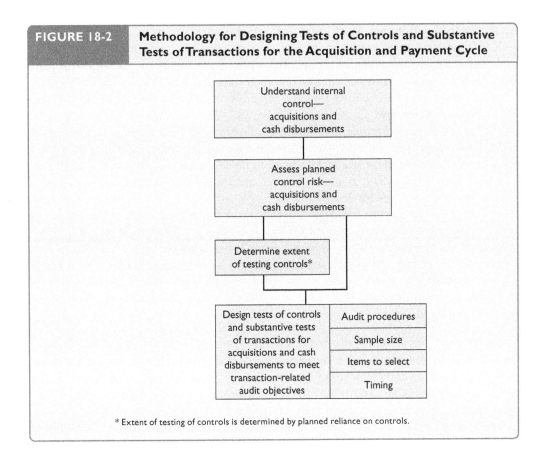

FIGURE 18-2   **Methodology for Designing Tests of Controls and Substantive Tests of Transactions for the Acquisition and Payment Cycle**

* Extent of testing of controls is determined by planned reliance on controls.

2. Tests of payments, which concern the fourth function, processing and recording cash disbursements

Figure 18-2 illustrates the methodology for designing tests of controls and substantive tests of transactions for the acquisition and payment cycle. It is the same methodology used in earlier chapters. Next, let's examine each part of Figure 18-2, starting with understanding internal control.

Understand Internal Control

The auditor gains an understanding of internal control for the acquisition and payment cycle as part of performing risk assessment procedures by studying the client's flowcharts, reviewing internal control questionnaires, and performing walkthrough tests for acquisition and cash disbursement transactions. The procedures for understanding internal control in the acquisition and payment cycle are similar to the procedures performed in other transaction cycles, as discussed in earlier chapters.

Assess Planned Control Risk

Next, the key internal controls for each of the business functions described earlier in this chapter are examined. These are authorization of purchases, separation of the custody of the received goods from other functions, timely recording and independent review of transactions, and authorization of payments to vendors.

Authorization of Purchases Proper authorization for acquisitions ensures that the goods and services acquired are for authorized company purposes, and it avoids the acquisition of excessive or unnecessary items. Most companies require different levels of authorization for different types of acquisitions or dollar amounts. For example, acquisitions of fixed assets in excess of a specified dollar limit require approval by the board of directors; items acquired relatively infrequently, such as insurance policies and long-term service contracts, are approved by certain officers; supplies and services costing less than a designated amount are approved by supervisors and department heads; and some types of raw materials and supplies are reordered automatically when they fall below a predetermined level, often by direct communication with vendors' computers.

After the purchase requisition for an acquisition has been approved, a purchase order to acquire the goods or services must be initiated. A purchase order is issued to a vendor for a specified item at a certain price to be delivered at or by a designated time. The purchase order, usually made in writing and constituting a legal document, is an offer to buy the goods or services.

Companies commonly establish purchasing departments to ensure an adequate quality of goods and services at a minimum price. For good internal control, the purchasing department should be separate from those who authorize the acquisition or receive the goods. All purchase orders should be prenumbered to permit easier accounting for all outstanding purchases orders and should include sufficient columns and spaces to minimize the likelihood of unintentional omissions on the form when goods are ordered.

Separation of Asset Custody from Other Functions Most companies have the receiving department initiate a receiving report as evidence of the receipt and examination of goods. One copy is normally sent to the raw materials storeroom and another to the accounts payable department for their information needs. To prevent theft and misuse, the goods should be *physically controlled* from the time of their receipt until their use or disposal. The personnel in the receiving department should be independent of the storeroom personnel and the accounting department. Finally, the accounting records should transfer responsibility for the goods each time they are moved, from receiving to storage, from storage to manufacturing, etc.

Timely Recording and Independent Review of Transactions In some companies, the recording of the liability for acquisitions is made on the basis of the receipt of goods and services. In others, recording is deferred until the vendor's invoice is received. In either case, the accounts payable department typically has responsibility for verifying the appropriateness of acquisitions. This is done by comparing the details on the purchase order, the receiving report, and the vendor's invoice to determine that the descriptions, prices, quantities, terms, and freight on the vendor's invoice are correct. Typically, the accounts payable department also verifies extensions, footings, and account distributions. In some cases, computer software matches documents and verifies invoice accuracy automatically. The accounts payable department should also account for all receiving reports to assure that the completeness objective is satisfied.

An important control in the accounts payable and information technology departments is the requirement that personnel who record acquisitions do not have access to cash, marketable securities, and other assets.

Authorization of Payments The most important controls over cash disbursements include:

- The signing of checks by an individual with proper authority
- Separation of responsibilities for signing checks and performing the accounts payable function
- Careful examination of supporting documents by the check signer at the time the check is signed

The checks should be prenumbered to make it easier to account for all checks and printed on special paper that makes it difficult to alter the payee or amount. Companies should take care to provide physical control over blank, voided, and signed checks. They should also have a method of canceling supporting documents to prevent their reuse as support for another check at a later time. A common method is to write the check number on the supporting documents.

Suppose, for example, a CPA found that few purchasing transactions were not authorized and the amounts associated with them were not material, but that all documents related to purchasing including purchase requisitions and orders were prepared, and purchases, purchase returns, and discounts were properly recorded in appropriate journals, listings, and master files. In addition, the auditor's assessment was that adequate segregation of duties and responsibilities were maintained through the separation of duties for preparing purchases documents, authorization and approving transactions, and for taking custody of merchandise received. These control elements would allow the auditor to assess control risk within a range of 0.2–0.5 resulting in performing few tests of controls for these activities and transactions for the current year's audit.

Determine Extent of Testing of Controls

After auditors identify key internal controls and deficiencies, they assess control risk. When auditors intend to rely on controls and therefore estimate that a preliminary control risk assessment is below maximum, the auditor performs tests of controls to obtain evidence that controls are operating effectively. As the operating effectiveness of controls improves and is supported by additional tests of controls, the auditor is able to reduce substantive testing.

For example, deficiencies associated with examination of payables internal control procedures for a service company might be as follows:

1. There was no list of approved purchasers, showing the nature of purchases, contracting procedures, purchase credit limits, methods, and payment period.
2. The company does not maintain a copy of checks issued to suppliers but relies on an internal memo prepared by the accounts department.
3. No representation memo or identity documents were received from suppliers who receive checks.
4. The accounts department does not stamp supplier invoices with 'paid' to ensure that such invoices are not paid twice.

Design Tests of Controls and Substantive Tests of Transactions for Acquisitions

Table 18-2 summarizes key internal controls, common tests of controls, and common substantive tests of transactions for each transaction-related audit objective. We assume the existence of a separate acquisitions journal or listing for recording all acquisitions.

As you examine Table 18-2, you should:

- Relate each of the internal controls to transaction-related audit objectives
- Relate tests of controls to internal controls
- Relate substantive tests of transactions to transaction-related audit objectives after considering controls and deficiencies in the system

The audit evidence for an audit engagement will vary with the internal controls and other circumstances. Significant audit efficiencies can be achieved on many audits when controls are operating effectively.

Four of the seven transaction-related audit objectives for acquisitions deserve special attention and are therefore examined more closely. The correctness of many asset, liability, and expense accounts depends on the correct recording of transactions in the acquisitions journal, especially related to these four objectives.

TABLE 18-2   Summary of Transaction-Related Audit Objectives, Key Controls, Tests of Controls, and Substantive Tests of Transactions for Acquisitions

Transaction-Related Audit Objectives	Key Internal Controls	Common Tests of Controls	Common Substantive Tests of Transactions
Recorded acquisitions are for goods and services received, consistent with client (occurrence).	Purchase requisition, purchase order, receiving report, and vendor's invoice are attached to the voucher.* Acquisitions are approved at the proper level. Computer accepts entry of purchases only from authorized vendors in the vendor master file. Documents are cancelled to prevent their reuse. Vendors' invoices, receiving reports, purchase orders, and purchase requisitions are internally verified.*	Examine documents in voucher package for existence. Examine indication of approval. Attempt to input transactions with valid and invalid vendors. Examine indication of cancellation. Examine indication of internal verification.	Review the acquisitions journal, general ledger, and accounts payable master file for large or unusual amounts.† Examine underlying documents for reasonableness and authenticity (vendors' invoices, receiving reports, purchase orders, and purchase requisitions).* Examine vendor master file for unusual vendors. Trace inventory acquisitions to inventory master file. Examine fixed assets acquired.
Existing acquisition transactions are recorded (completeness).	Purchase orders are prenumbered and accounted for. Receiving reports are prenumbered and accounted for.* Vouchers are prenumbered and accounted for.	Account for a sequence of purchase orders. Account for a sequence of receiving reports. Account for a sequence of vouchers.	Trace from a file of receiving reports to the acquisitions journal.* Trace from a file of vendors' invoices to the acquisitions journal.
Recorded acquisition transactions are accurate (accuracy).	Calculations and amounts are internally verified. Batch totals are compared with computer summary reports. Acquisitions are approved for prices and discounts.	Examine indication of internal verification. Examine file of batch totals for initials of data control clerk; compare totals to summary reports. Examine indication of approval.	Compare recorded transactions in the acquisitions journal with the vendor's invoice, receiving report, and other supporting documentation.* Recompute the clerical accuracy on the vendor's invoice, including discounts and freight.
Acquisition transactions are correctly included in the accounts payable and inventory master files and are correctly summarized (posting and summarization).	Accounts payable master file contents are internally verified. Accounts payable master file or trial balance totals are compared with general ledger balances.	Examine indication of internal verification. Examine initials on general ledger accounts indicating comparison.	Test clerical accuracy by footing the journals and tracing postings to general ledger and accounts payable and inventory master files.
Acquisition transactions are correctly classified (classification).	An adequate chart of accounts is used. Account classifications are internally verified.	Examine procedures manual and chart of accounts. Examine indication of internal verification.	Compare classification with chart of accounts by referring to vendors' invoices.
Acquisition transactions are recorded on the correct dates (timing).	Procedures require recording transactions as soon as possible after the goods and services have been received. Dates are internally verified.	Examine procedures manual and observe whether unrecorded vendors' invoices exist. Examine indication of internal verification.	Compare dates of receiving reports and vendors' invoices with dates in the acquisitions journal.*
Acquisitions transactions pertain to the company (rights).	Proper approval by appropriate management for the acquisition. Acquisitions relate to the company's activities.	Examine purchase order for proper approval. Examine purchase request to identify needs of the company.	Examine documents supporting acquisitions.

*Receiving reports are used only for tangible goods and are therefore not used for services, such as utilities and repairs and maintenance. Often, vendors' invoices are the only documentation available.

†This analytical procedure can also apply to other objectives, including completeness, accuracy, and timing.

1. Recorded Acquisitions are for Goods and Services Received, Consistent with the Best Interests of the Client (Occurrence) If the auditor is satisfied that the controls are adequate for this objective, tests for improper transactions and recorded transactions that did not occur can be greatly reduced. Adequate controls prevent the unintentional recording of acquisitions that did not occur, especially recording duplicate acquisitions. Adequate controls are also likely to prevent the client from including as a business expense or asset fraudulent transactions or those that primarily benefit management or other employees rather than the entity being audited. In some instances, improper transactions are obvious, such as the acquisition of unauthorized personal items by employees. In other instances, the appropriateness of a transaction is more difficult to evaluate, such as the payment of officers' memberships to country clubs or expense-paid vacations to foreign countries for management and their families.

2. Existing Acquisitions are Recorded (Completeness) Failure to record the acquisition of goods and services received understates accounts payable and may result in an overstatement of net income and owners' equity. Therefore, auditors consider this an essential objective for acquisitions. It may be difficult in some audits to perform tests of details of balances to determine whether unrecorded transactions exist, so the auditor must rely on controls and substantive tests of transactions for this purpose.

3. Acquisitions are Accurately Recorded (Accuracy) The extent of tests of details of many balance sheet and expense accounts depends on the auditor's evaluation of the effectiveness of the internal controls over the accuracy of recorded acquisition transactions. For example, if the auditor believes that the fixed asset transactions are correctly recorded in the acquisitions journal, it is acceptable to vouch fewer current period acquisitions during tests of details of balances than if the controls are inadequate.

When a client uses perpetual inventory records, tests of details of inventory can also be significantly reduced if the auditor believes the perpetual records are accurate. The controls over acquisitions included in the perpetual records are normally tested as a part of the tests of controls and substantive tests of transactions for acquisitions.

4. Acquisitions are Correctly Classified (Classification) Tests of details of certain individual accounts can be reduced if the auditor believes that internal controls are adequate to provide reasonable assurance of correct classification in the acquisitions journal. Although all accounts are affected to some degree by effective controls over classification, the two areas most affected are current period acquisitions of fixed assets, and all expense accounts, such as repairs and maintenance, utilities, and advertising.

It is relatively time-consuming for auditors to perform inspection tests of current period fixed asset acquisitions and expense accounts for accuracy and classification. Therefore, time-savings can be significant when controls are effective.

Design Tests of Controls and Substantive Tests of Transactions For Cash Disbursements

Table 18-3 for cash disbursements uses the same format as Table 18-2 for acquisitions. We assume for these controls and audit procedures that separate cash disbursements and acquisitions journals exist. Our comments about the methodology and process for developing audit procedures for acquisitions apply equally to cash disbursements.

Auditors typically perform the acquisitions and cash disbursements tests at the same time. For a transaction selected for examination from the acquisitions journal, the vendor's invoice, receiving report, and other acquisition documentation are examined at the same time as the related cancelled check. Thus, the verification is done efficiently without reducing the effectiveness of the tests.

TABLE 18-3	Summary of Transaction-Related Audit Objectives, Key Controls, Tests of Controls, and Substantive Tests of Transactions for Cash Disbursements

Transaction-Related Audit Objectives	Key Internal Controls	Common Tests of Controls	Common Substantive Tests of Transactions
Recorded cash disbursements are for goods and services actually received (occurrence).	There is adequate segregation of duties between accounts payable and custody of signed checks. Supporting documentation is examined before signing of checks by an authorized person. Approval of payment on supporting documents is given at the time checks are signed.	Discuss with personnel and observe activities. Discuss with personnel and observe activities. Examine indication of approval.	Review the cash disbursements journal, general ledger, and accounts payable master file for large or unusual amounts.* Trace the cancelled check to the related acquisitions journal entry and examine for payee name and amount. Examine cancelled check for authorized signature, proper endorsement, and cancellation by the bank. Examine supporting documents as part of the tests of acquisitions.
Existing cash disbursement transactions are recorded (completeness).	Checks are prenumbered and accounted for. The bank reconciliation is prepared monthly by an employee independent of recording cash disbursements or custody of assets.	Account for a sequence of checks. Examine bank reconciliations and observe their preparation.	Reconcile recorded cash disbursements with the cash disbursements on the bank statement (proof of cash disbursements).
Recorded cash disbursement transactions are accurate (accuracy).	Calculations and amounts are internally verified. The bank reconciliation is prepared monthly by an independent person.	Examine indication of internal verification. Examine bank reconciliations and observe their preparation.	Compare cancelled checks with the related acquisitions journal and cash disbursements journal entries. Recompute cash discounts. Prepare a proof of cash disbursements.
Cash disbursement transactions are correctly included in the accounts payable master file and are correctly summarized (posting and summarization).	Accounts payable master file contents are internally verified. Accounts payable master file or trial balance totals are compared with general ledger balances.	Examine indication of internal verification. Examine initials on general ledger accounts indicating comparison.	Test clerical accuracy by footing journals and tracing postings to general ledger and accounts payable master file.
Cash disbursement transactions are correctly classified (classification).	An adequate chart of accounts is used. Account classifications are internally verified.	Examine procedures manual and chart of accounts. Examine indication of internal verification.	Compare classification with chart of accounts by referring to vendors' invoices and acquisitions journal.
Cash disbursement transactions are recorded on the correct dates (timing).	Procedures require recording of transactions as soon as possible after the check has been signed. Dates are internally verified.	Examine procedures manual and observe whether unrecorded checks exist. Examine indication of internal verification.	Compare dates on cancelled checks with the cash disbursements journal. Compare dates on cancelled checks with the bank cancellation date.
Cash disbursement transactions are payments of actual obligations (obligations).	Proper approval before payments are made. Payments relate to acquisitions actually received.	Examine cash disbursement documents for proper approval. Examine cash disbursements documentation.	Examine documents supporting acquisitions.

*This analytical procedure can also apply to other objectives, including completeness, accuracy, and timing.

Attributes Sampling For Tests of Controls and Substantive Tests of Transactions

Because of the importance of tests of controls and substantive tests of transactions for acquisitions and cash disbursements, the use of attributes sampling is common. The approach is similar to that used for the tests of controls and substantive tests of transactions for sales discussed in the Statistical Audit Sampling section of Chapter 15.

There are three important differences in acquisitions and payments compared to other cycles.

1. As discussed in the beginning of the chapter, there are a larger number of accounts involved in this cycle, including both income statement and balance sheet accounts. The effect is an increased potential for classification misstatements, some of which are likely to affect income. An example is a misclassification between repair and maintenance expenses and fixed assets. As a result, auditors often reduce the tolerable exception rate, especially for the classification attribute.
2. It is more common in this cycle for transactions to require significant judgment, such as for leases and construction costs. These judgment requirements result in an increased likelihood of misstatements. As a result, auditors often reduce the tolerable exception rate for the accuracy attribute.
3. The dollar amounts of individual transactions in the cycle cover a wide range. As a result, auditors commonly segregate large and unusual items and test them on a 100 percent basis.

METHODOLOGY FOR DESIGNING TESTS OF DETAILS OF BALANCES FOR ACCOUNTS PAYABLE

Because all acquisition and payment cycle transactions typically flow through accounts payable, this account is critical to any audit of the acquisition and payment cycle. Accounts payable are *unpaid obligations* for goods and services received in the ordinary course of business. Accounts payable includes obligations for the acquisition of raw materials, equipment, utilities, repairs, and many other types of goods and services that were received before the end of the year. Most accounts payable can also be identified by the existence of vendors' invoices for the obligation.

> **OBJECTIVE 18-4**
>
> Describe the methodology for designing tests of details of balances for accounts payable using the audit risk model.

Accounts payable should be distinguished from accrued liabilities and interest-bearing obligations. A liability is an account payable only if the total amount of the obligation is *known and owed at the balance sheet date*. If the obligation includes the payment of interest, it should be recorded as a note payable, contract payable, mortgage payable, or bond payable.

Figure 18-3 summarizes the methodology for designing tests of details for accounts payable. This methodology is the same as that used for accounts receivable in Chapter 16 (see Figure 16-1).

If tests of controls and related substantive tests of transactions show that controls are operating effectively, and if analytical procedures results are satisfactory, the auditor is likely to reduce tests of details of balances for accounts payable. However, because accounts payable tend to be material for most companies, auditors almost always perform some tests of details of balances.

Identify Client Business Risks Affecting Accounts Payable (Phase I)

The recent focus by many companies on improving their supply-chain management activities has led to numerous changes in the design of systems used to initiate and

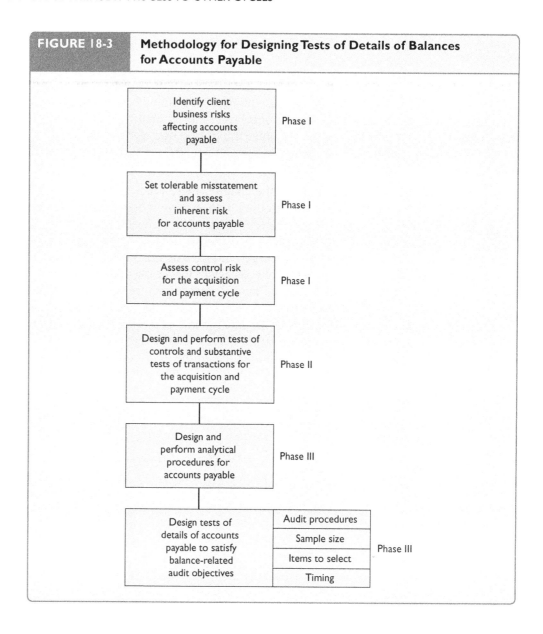

FIGURE 18-3   Methodology for Designing Tests of Details of Balances for Accounts Payable

record acquisition and payment activities. Efforts to streamline the purchasing of goods and services, including greater emphasis on just-in-time inventory purchasing, increased sharing of information with suppliers, and the use of technology and e-commerce to transact business, are changing all aspects of the acquisition and payment cycle for many companies. These arrangements and systems can be complex.

Significant client business risks may arise from these changes. For example, suppliers may have greater access to accounts payable records, allowing them to continually monitor the status of payable balances and to perform detailed reconciliations of transactions. Access by external parties, such as suppliers, to accounting records threatens the likelihood of misstatement if that access is not properly controlled. Also, increased focus on improving the logistics of physically moving inventory throughout a company's distribution chain may increase the difficulty of establishing effective cutoff of accounts payable balances at year-end. The auditor needs to understand the nature of changes to these systems to identify whether client business risks and related management controls affect the likelihood of material misstatements in accounts payable.

Set Tolerable Misstatement and Assess Inherent Risk (Phase I)

Like accounts receivable, a large number of transactions can affect accounts payable. The balance is often large and made up of a large number of vendor balances and it is relatively expensive to audit the account. For these reasons, auditors typically set tolerable misstatement for accounts payable relatively high. For the same reasons, auditors often assess inherent risk as medium or high. They are especially concerned about the completeness and cutoff balance-related audit objectives because of the potential for understatements in the account balance.

Assess Control Risk and Design and Perform Tests of Controls and Substantive Tests of Transactions (Phases I and II)

As shown in Figure 18-3, after auditors set tolerable misstatement and inherent risk for accounts payable, they assess control risk based on an understanding of internal control. The auditor's ultimate substantive tests depend on the relative effectiveness of internal controls related to accounts payable. Therefore, auditors must have a thorough understanding of how these controls relate to accounts payable.

The effects of the client's internal controls on accounts payable tests can be illustrated by two examples:

1. Assume that the client has highly effective internal controls over recording and paying for acquisitions. The receipt of goods is promptly documented by prenumbered receiving reports; prenumbered vouchers are promptly and efficiently prepared and recorded in the acquisition transactions file and the accounts payable master file. Cash disbursements are made promptly when due and immediately recorded in the cash disbursements transactions file and the accounts payable master file. Individual accounts payable balances in the master file are reconciled monthly with vendors' statements, and the computer automatically reconciles the master file total to the general ledger. Under these circumstances, the verification of accounts payable should require little audit effort once the auditor concludes that internal controls are operating effectively.
2. Assume that receiving reports are not used, the client defers recording acquisitions until cash disbursements are made, and because of a weak cash position, bills are often paid several months after their due date. When an auditor faces such a situation, there is a high likelihood of an understatement of accounts payable; therefore, extensive tests of details of accounts payable are necessary to determine whether accounts payable is correctly stated on the balance sheet date.

We discussed the most important controls over accounts payable and the related tests of controls and substantive tests of transactions earlier in this chapter. In addition to those controls, each month an independent person or computer program should reconcile vendors' statements with recorded liabilities and the accounts payable master file with the general ledger. After assessing control risk, the auditor designs and performs tests of controls and substantive tests of transactions for acquisitions and cash disbursements.

Design and Perform Analytical Procedures (Phase III)

The use of analytical procedures is as important in the acquisition and payment cycle as it is in every other cycle, especially for uncovering misstatements in accounts payable. Table 18-4 illustrates analytical procedures for the balance sheet and income statement accounts in the acquisition and payment cycle that are useful for uncovering areas in which additional investigation is desirable.

OBJECTIVE 18-5

Design and perform analytical procedures for accounts payable.

TABLE 18-4	Analytical Procedures for the Acquisition and Payment Cycle	
Analytical Procedure		**Possible Misstatement**
Compare acquisition-related expense account balances with prior years.		Misstatement of accounts payable and expenses.
Review list of accounts payable for unusual, nonvendor, and interest-bearing payables.		Classification misstatement for nontrade liabilities.
Compare individual accounts payable with previous years.		Unrecorded or nonexistent accounts, or misstatements.
Calculate ratios, such as purchases divided by accounts payable, and accounts payable divided by current liabilities.		Unrecorded or nonexistent accounts, or misstatements.

Auditors should compare current year expense totals with prior years to uncover misstatements of accounts payable as well as in the expense accounts. Because of double-entry accounting, a misstatement of an expense account usually also results in an equal misstatement of account payable. Therefore, comparing current expenses such as rent, utilities, and other regularly scheduled bills with prior years is an effective procedure for analyzing accounts payable when expenses from year to year are expected to be relatively stable.

Design and Perform Tests of Details of Accounts Payable Balance (Phase III)

OBJECTIVE 18-6

Design and perform tests of details of balances for accounts payable, including out-of-period liability tests.

The overall objective in the audit of accounts payable is to determine whether the accounts payable balance is fairly stated and properly disclosed. Seven of the eight balance-related audit objectives discussed in Chapter 6 are applicable to accounts payable: existence, completeness, accuracy, classification, cutoff, detail tie-in, and rights and obligations. Realizable value is not applicable to liabilities.

There is an important difference in emphasis in the audit of liabilities and assets. When auditors verify assets, they emphasize overstatements through verification by confirmation, physical examination, and examination of supporting documents. Auditors should not ignore the possibility of assets being understated but should be more concerned about overstatements. The opposite approach is taken in verifying liability balances: that is, the main focus is on understated or omitted liabilities.

The difference in emphasis in auditing assets and liabilities results directly from the *legal liability of auditors*. If equity investors, creditors, and other users determine subsequent to the issuance of the audited financial statements that owners' equity was materially overstated, a lawsuit against the auditing firm is fairly likely. Because an overstatement of owners' equity can arise either from an overstatement of assets or an understatement of liabilities, it is natural for auditors to emphasize those two types of misstatements. The probability of a successful lawsuit against an auditor for failing to discover an understatement of owners' equity is far less likely.

We will use the same balance-related audit objectives from Chapter 16 that we applied to verifying accounts receivable, as they also apply to liabilities, with three minor modifications:

1. The realizable value objective is not applicable to liabilities. Realizable value applies only to assets.
2. The rights aspect of the rights and obligations objective is not applicable to liabilities. For assets, the auditor is concerned with the client's rights to the use and disposal of the assets. For liabilities, the auditor is concerned with the client's obligations for the payment of the liability. If the client has no obligation to pay a liability, it should not be included as a liability.

3. For liabilities, there is emphasis on the search for understatements rather than for overstatements, as we just discussed.

Table 18-5 includes the balance-related audit objectives and common tests of details of balances procedures for accounts payable. The auditor's actual audit procedures vary considerably depending on the nature of the entity, the materiality of accounts payable, the nature and effectiveness of internal controls, and inherent risk. As auditors perform test of details of balances for accounts payable and other liability accounts they may also gather evidence about the four presentation and disclosure objectives, especially when performing completeness objective tests. Other procedures related to presentation and disclosure objectives are done as part of procedures to complete the audit, which we will discuss in Chapter 24.

Out-of-Period Liability Tests Because of the emphasis on understatements in liability accounts, *out-of-period liability tests* are important for accounts payable. The extent of tests to uncover unrecorded accounts payable, often called the *search for unrecorded accounts payable*, depends heavily on assessed control risk and the materiality of the potential balance in the account. The same audit procedures used to uncover unrecorded payables are applicable to the accuracy objective. The following are typical audit procedures:

Examine Underlying Documentation for Subsequent Cash Disbursements Auditors examine supporting documentation for cash disbursements subsequent to the balance sheet date to determine whether a cash disbursement was

TABLE 18-5	Balance-Related Audit Objectives and Tests of Details of Balances for Accounts Payable	
Balance-Related Audit Objective	**Common Tests of Details of Balances Procedures**	**Comments**
Accounts payable in the accounts payable list agree with related master file, and the total is correctly added and agrees with the general ledger (detail tie-in).	Re-add or use the computer to total the accounts payable list. Trace the total to the general ledger. Trace individual vendors' invoices to master file for names and amounts.	All pages need not ordinarily be footed if footing manually. Unless controls are weak, tracing to master file should be limited.
Accounts payable in the accounts payable list exist (existence).	Trace from accounts payable list to vendors' invoices and statements. Confirm accounts payable, emphasizing large and unusual amounts.	Ordinarily receives little attention because the primary concern is with understatements.
Existing accounts payable are included in the accounts payable list (completeness).	Perform out-of-period liability tests (see discussion).	These are essential audit tests for accounts payable.
Accounts payable in the accounts payable list are accurate (accuracy).	Perform same procedures as those used for existence objective and out-of-period liability tests.	Ordinarily, the emphasis in these procedures for accuracy is understatement rather than omission.
Accounts payable in the accounts payable list are correctly classified (classification).	Review the list and master file for related parties, notes or other interest-bearing liabilities, long-term payables, and debit balances.	Knowledge of the client's business is essential for these tests.
Transactions in the acquisition and payment cycle are recorded in the proper period (cutoff).	Perform out-of-period liability tests (see discussion). Perform detailed tests as part of physical observation of inventory (see discussion). Test for inventory in transit (see discussion).	These are essential audit tests for accounts payable. These are called *cutoff tests*.
The company has an obligation to pay the liabilities included in accounts payable (obligations).	Examine vendors' statements and confirm accounts payable.	Normally not a concern in the audit of accounts payable because all accounts payable are obligations.

OVERRIDE OF INTERNAL CONTROL PROCEDURES

The Egyptian Attorney General is investigating a case where, on October 15, 2001, the Suez Canal Company for Containers (SCCO) received royalties for the use of container warehouses from Port Said Authority under a build, operate and transfer (BOT) scheme. The SCCO contracted with the Port Said Authority for the authority to build the first infrastructure for the Rasief project, which had a total length of 1,200 meters and cost US$70 million. The SCCO was responsible for building the container warehouse on the Rasief infrastructure and paying US$3,000 as rent for each square meter and US$3.7 for each container. On September 28, 2006, an Italian company, Trivi, offered to build the second phase of construction of the Port Said Rasief infrastructure at a cost of US$87.5 million with the help of the National Bank of Egypt. The management of Port Said Authority colluded with the chairman of the Suez Canal Company for Containers and the authority gave his company the right to build the second phase of the infrastructure in return for waiving the US$3,000 rent per square meter for a 17-year period and amended the period for managing the container warehouse from 35 years to 49 years. The Attorney General's investigations indicated that there was a total loss to the Government of Egypt of more than US$489 million incurred by waiving the rent for 17 years and the related annual increases over the period of the contract.

Sources: *El Masry El Youm*, May 5, 2011; *Al-Ahram Newspaper*, April 27, 2011; and *Al-akbar*, April 25, 2011.

for a current period liability. If it is a current period liability, the auditor should trace it to the accounts payable trial balance to make sure it is included. The receiving report indicates the date inventory was received and is therefore an especially useful document. Similarly, the vendor's invoice usually indicates the date services were provided. Auditors often examine documentation for cash disbursements made in the subsequent period for several weeks after the balance sheet date, especially when the client does not pay bills on a timely basis.

Examine Underlying Documentation for Bills Not Paid Several Weeks After the Year-End Auditors carry out this procedure in the same manner as the preceding one and for the same purpose. This procedure differs in that it is done for unpaid obligations near the end of the audit field work rather than for obligations that have already been paid.

For example, in an audit with a March 31 year-end, assume the auditor examines the supporting documentation for checks paid through June 28. Bills that are still unpaid on June 28 should be examined to determine whether they are obligations at March 31.

Trace Receiving Reports Issued Before Year-End to Related Vendors' Invoices All merchandise received before the year-end of the accounting period should be included as accounts payable. By tracing receiving reports issued up to year-end to vendors' invoices and making sure that they are included in accounts payable, the auditor is testing for unrecorded obligations.

Trace Vendors' Statements That Show a Balance Due to the Accounts Payable Trial Balance If the client maintains a file of vendors' statements, auditors can trace any statement that has a balance due at the balance sheet date to the listing to make sure it is included as an account payable.

Send Confirmations to Vendors with Which the Client Does Business Although the use of confirmations for accounts payable is less common than for accounts receivable, auditors use them occasionally to test for vendors omitted from the accounts payable list, omitted transactions, and misstated account balances. Sending confirmations to active vendors for which a balance has not been included in the accounts payable list is a useful means of searching for omitted amounts. This type of confirmation is commonly called zero balance confirmation. Additional discussion of confirmation of accounts payable is deferred until the end of this chapter.

Cutoff Tests Accounts payable **cutoff tests** are done to determine whether transactions recorded a few days before and after the balance sheet date are included in the correct period. The five out-of-period liability audit tests we just discussed are all cutoff tests for acquisitions, but they emphasize understatements. For the first three procedures, it is also appropriate to examine supporting documentation as a test of overstatement of accounts payable. For example, the third procedure tests for understatements (unrecorded accounts payable) by tracing receiving reports issued before year-end to related vendors' invoices. To test for overstatement cutoff amounts, the auditor should trace receiving reports issued *after* year-end to related invoices to make sure that they are not recorded as accounts payable (unless they are inventory in transit, which is discussed shortly).

We've already discussed most cutoff tests in the preceding section, but we will focus on two aspects here: the relationship of cutoff to physical observation of inventory and the determination of the amount of inventory in transit.

Relationship of Cutoff to Physical Observation of Inventory In determining that the accounts payable cutoff is correct, *it is essential that the cutoff tests be coordinated with the physical observation of inventory*. For example, assume that an inventory acquisition for US$400,000 is received late in the afternoon of December 31, after the physical inventory is completed. If the acquisition is included in accounts payable and purchases but excluded from inventory, the result is an understatement of net earnings of US$400,000. Conversely, if the acquisition is excluded from both inventory and accounts payable, there is a misstatement in the balance sheet, but the income statement is correct. The only way the auditor will know which type of misstatement has occurred is to coordinate cutoff tests with the observation of inventory.

The cutoff information for acquisitions should be obtained *during the physical observation* of inventory. At that time, the auditor should review the procedures in the receiving department to determine that all inventory received was counted, and the auditor should record in the audit documentation the last receiving report number of inventory included in the physical count. During the year-end field work, the auditor should then test the accounting records for cutoff. The auditor should trace the previously documented receiving report numbers to the accounts payable records to verify that they are correctly included or excluded. For example, assume that the last receiving report number representing inventory included in the physical count was 3167. The auditor should record this document number and subsequently trace it and several preceding numbers to their related vendors' invoices and to the accounts payable list or the accounts payable master file to determine that they are all included. Similarly, accounts payable for acquisitions recorded on receiving reports with numbers larger than 3167 should be excluded from accounts payable.

When the client's physical inventory takes place before the last day of the year, the auditor must still perform an accounts payable cutoff at the time of the physical count in the manner described in the preceding paragraph. In addition, the auditor must verify whether all acquisitions that took place between the physical count and the end of the year were added to the physical inventory and accounts payable. For example, if the client takes the physical count on December 27 for a December 31 year-end, the cutoff information is taken as of December 27. During the year-end field work, the auditor must first test to determine whether the cutoff was accurate as of December 27. After determining that the December 27 cutoff is accurate, the auditor must test whether all inventory received subsequent to the physical count, but on or before the balance sheet date, was added to inventory and accounts payable by the client.

Cutoff tests

Tests to determine whether transactions recorded a few days before and after the balance sheet date are included in the correct period.

FOB destination

Shipping contract in which title to the goods passes to the buyer when the goods are received.

FOB origin

Shipping contract in which title to the goods passes to the buyer at the time that the goods are shipped.

OBJECTIVE 18-7

Distinguish the reliability of vendors' invoices, vendors' statements, and confirmations of accounts payable as audit evidence.

Inventory in Transit   In accounts payable, auditors must distinguish between acquisitions of inventory that are on an **FOB destination** basis and those that are made **FOB origin**. For FOB destination, title passes to the buyer when the inventory is received, so only inventory received on or before the balance sheet date should be included in inventory and accounts payable at year-end. When an acquisition is FOB origin, the company must record the inventory and related accounts payable in the current period if shipment occurred on or before the balance sheet date.

Auditors can determine whether inventory has been acquired FOB destination or origin by examining vendors' invoices. Auditors should examine invoices for merchandise received shortly after year-end to determine whether they were on an FOB origin basis. For those that were, and when the shipment dates were on or before the balance sheet date, the inventory and related accounts payable must be recorded in the current period if the amounts are material.

Reliability of Evidence

Auditors need to understand the relative reliability of the three primary types of evidence ordinarily used for verifying accounts payable: vendors' invoices, vendors' statements, and confirmations.

Distinction Between Vendors' Invoices and Vendors' Statements

Auditors should distinguish between vendors' invoices and vendors' statements in verifying the amount due to a vendor. Auditors get highly reliable *evidence about individual transactions* when they examine vendors' invoices and related supporting documents, such as receiving reports and purchase orders. A vendor's statement is not as desirable as invoices for verifying individual transactions because a statement includes only the total amount of the transaction. The units acquired, price, freight, and other data are not included.

Which of these two documents is better for verifying the correct balance in accounts payable? *The vendor's statement is superior for verifying accounts payable* because it includes the ending balance. The auditor can compare existing vendors' invoices with the client's list and still not uncover missing ones, which is the primary concern in accounts payable.

Which of these two documents is better for testing acquisitions in tests of controls and substantive tests of transactions? *The vendor's invoice is superior for verifying transactions* because the auditor is verifying individual transactions and the invoice shows the details of the acquisitions.

Difference Between Vendors' Statements and Confirmations

The most important distinction between a vendor's statement and a confirmation of accounts payable is the source of the information. A vendor's statement has been prepared by the vendor (an independent third party) but is in the hands of the client at the time the auditor examines it. This provides the client with an opportunity to alter a vendor's statement or to withhold certain statements from the auditor.

A response to a confirmation request for accounts payable is normally an itemized statement sent directly to the auditing firm by the vendor. It provides the same information as a vendor's statement but is more reliable. In addition, confirmations of accounts payable often include a request for information about notes and acceptances payable as well as consigned inventory owned by the vendor but stored on the client's premises. An illustration of a typical accounts payable confirmation request is given in Figure 18-4.

Due to the availability of vendors' statements and vendors' invoices, which are both relatively reliable evidence because they originate from a third party, confirmation of accounts payable is less common than confirmation of accounts receivable. If the client has adequate internal controls and vendors' statements are available for examination, confirmations are normally not sent. However, when the client's internal controls are

FIGURE 18-4	Example of Accounts Payable Confirmation Request

Account No:................
Account Type: DEBIT/CREDIT

Messers / ....

In connection with the examination of our accounts by our auditor Sabah & Saad Co. please confirm the correctness of the following balance being indicated by our records as of December 31, 2011. If we do not receive any reply within a period of 15 days, we will take the non-reply decision as confirming the accuracy of such balance.

BALANCE   **CURRENCY**
.................DEBIT/CREDIT   ....
.................DEBIT/CREDIT   ....

Please sign this statement and return it to our auditors:

Ahmed Sabah
Sabah & Saad Co.

If there are any discrepancies, please furnish details in your reply.

Thank you for your assistance,

Very truly yours
Financial Manager

Name of the Client/Supplier: ....

Account No: ....
Account Type: DEBIT/CREDIT

To Ahmed Sabah
Sabah & Saad Co.

Dear Sir
We confirm that after examining our account balance related to Arabian Hardware Co. in our books as at December 31, 2011 that the above balance is (**correct/incorrect**) and the difference is due to

1. ....
2. ....
3. ....

Very truly yours

Name   : ....
Position   : ....
Signature   : ....
Company stamp: ....

Date: / /

deficient, when statements are not available, or when the auditor questions the client's integrity, it is desirable to send confirmation requests to vendors. Because of the emphasis on understatements of liability accounts, the accounts confirmed should include large, active, and zero balance accounts, and a representative sample of all others.

In most instances when auditors confirm accounts payable, they do it shortly after the balance sheet date. However, if assessed control risk is low, it may be possible to confirm accounts payable at an interim date as a test of the effectiveness of internal controls. Then, if the confirmations indicate that the internal controls are ineffective, it is possible to design other audit procedures to test accounts payable at year-end.

When auditors examine vendors' statements or receive confirmations, there must be a reconciliation of the statement or confirmation with the accounts payable list. Differences are often caused by inventory in transit, checks mailed by the client but not received by the vendor at the statement date, and delays in processing accounting records. The reconciliation is of the same general nature as that discussed in Chapter 16 for accounts receivable. The documents typically used to reconcile the balances on the accounts payable list with the confirmations or vendors' statements include receiving reports, vendors' invoices, and cancelled checks.

Sample Size

Our discussion of tests of details of the accounts payable balance has focused heavily on the typical audit procedures performed, the documents and records examined, and the timing of the tests. The auditor must also consider sample sizes in the audit of accounts payable.

Sample sizes for accounts payable tests vary considerably, depending on such factors as the materiality of accounts payable, the number of accounts outstanding, assessed control risk, and the results of the prior year. When a client's internal controls are deficient, which is not uncommon for accounts payable, almost all population items must be verified. In other situations, minimal testing may suffice.

Statistical sampling is less commonly used for the audit of accounts payable than for accounts receivable. Defining the population and determining the population size is more difficult for accounts payable. Because the emphasis is on omitted accounts payable, auditors must try to ensure that the population includes all potential payables.

SUMMARY

Figure 18-5 summarizes how the four types of audit procedures are used to obtain audit assurance for transactions and accounts in the acquisition and payment cycle. After using procedures to obtain an understanding of internal control and tests of controls, auditors

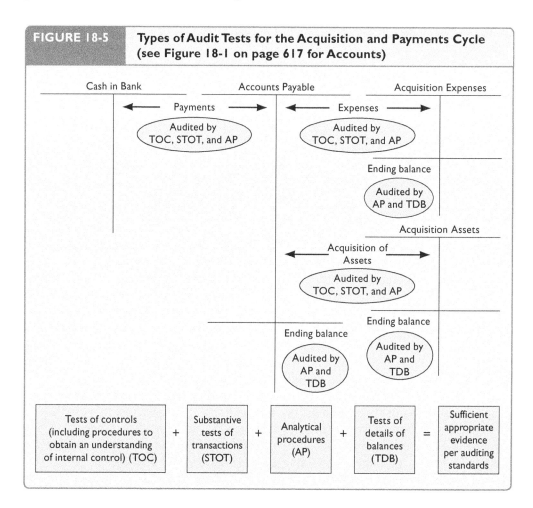

FIGURE 18-5   Types of Audit Tests for the Acquisition and Payments Cycle (see Figure 18-1 on page 617 for Accounts)

can evaluate whether controls over transactions in the cycle are operating effectively. When control risk is assessed as low the auditor can reduce substantive testing of ending balances in the related accounts. On the other hand, a higher assessed control risk results in the need for more substantive testing in related accounts. In this chapter, the ending balance we focused on was accounts payable.

By combining all types of audit tests shown in Figure 18-5, the auditor can obtain a higher overall assurance for transactions and accounts in the acquisition and payment cycle than the assurance obtained from any one test. The auditor can increase the assurance obtained from any one of the tests, and thereby increase the overall assurance for the cycle.

ESSENTIAL TERMS

Accounts payable master file   p. 619

Accounts payable trial balance   p. 619

Acquisition and payment cycle   p. 616

Cutoff tests   p. 633

Debit memo   p. 619

FOB destination   p. 634

FOB origin   p. 634

Purchase order   p. 618

Purchase requisition   p. 618

Receiving report   p. 618

Vendor's invoice   p. 619

Vendor's statement   p. 619

Voucher   p. 619

REVIEW QUESTIONS

18-1 (Objective 18-1) List five asset accounts, three liability accounts, and five expense accounts included in the acquisition and payment cycle for a typical manufacturing company.

18-2 (Objective 18-3) List one possible internal control for each of the seven transaction-related audit objectives for cash disbursements. For each control, list a test of control to test its effectiveness.

18-3 (Objective 18-3) List one possible control for each of the seven transaction-related audit objectives for acquisitions. For each control, list a test of control to test its effectiveness.

18-4 (Objective 18-3) Evaluate the following statement by an auditor concerning tests of acquisitions and cash disbursements: "In selecting the acquisitions and cash disbursements sample for testing, the best approach is to select a random month and test every transaction for the period. Using this approach enables me to thoroughly understand internal control because I have examined everything that happened during the period. As a part of the monthly test, I also test the beginning and ending bank reconciliations and prepare a proof of cash for the month. At the completion of these tests I feel I can evaluate the effectiveness of internal control."

18-5 (Objective 18-3) What is the importance of cash discounts to the client and how can the auditor verify whether they are being taken in accordance with company policy?

18-6 (Objective 18-3) What are the similarities and differences in the objectives of the following two procedures? (1) Select a random sample of receiving reports and trace them to related vendors' invoices and acquisitions journal entries, comparing the vendor's name, type of material and quantity acquired, and total amount of the acquisition. (2) Select a random sample of acquisitions journal entries and trace them to related vendors' invoices and receiving reports, comparing the vendor's name, type of material and quantity acquired, and total amount of the acquisition.

18-7 (Objectives 18-2, 18-3) If an audit client does not have prenumbered checks, what type of misstatement has a greater chance of occurring? Under the circumstances, what audit procedure can the auditor use to compensate for the deficiency?

18-8 (Objective 18-2) What is meant by a voucher? Explain how its use can improve an organization's internal controls.

18-9 (Objective 18-2) Explain why most auditors consider the receipt of goods and services the most important point in the acquisition and payment cycle.

18-10 (Objectives 18-3, 18-6) Explain the relationship between tests of the acquisition and payment cycle and tests of inventory. Give specific examples of how these two types of tests affect each other.

18-11 (Objectives 18-3, 18-4) Explain the relationship between tests of the acquisition and payment cycle and tests of accounts payable. Give specific examples of how these two types of tests affect each other.

18-12 (Objective 18-6) The auditor examines all unrecorded invoices on hand as of February 28, 2012, the last day of field work. Which of the following misstatements is most likely to be uncovered by this procedure? Explain.

   a. Accounts payable are overstated at December 31, 2011.

   b. Accounts payable are understated at December 31, 2011.

   c. Operating expenses are overstated for the 12 months ended December 31, 2011.

   d. Operating expenses are overstated for the two months ended February 28, 2012.[19]

18-13 (Objective 18-7) Explain why it is common for auditors to send confirmation requests to vendors with 'zero balances' on the client's accounts payable listing but uncommon to follow the same approach in verifying accounts receivable.

18-14 (Objectives 18-2, 18-7) Distinguish between a vendor's invoice and a vendor's statement. Which document should ideally be used as evidence in auditing acquisition transactions and which for verifying accounts payable balances? Why?

18-15 (Objective 18-7) It is less common to confirm accounts payable at an interim date than accounts receivable. Explain why.

18-16 (Objective 18-6) In testing the cutoff of accounts payable at the balance sheet date, explain why it is important that auditors coordinate their tests with the physical observation of inventory. What can the auditor do during the physical inventory to enhance the likelihood of an accurate cutoff?

18-17 (Objective 18-6) Distinguish between Free On Board (FOB) destination and FOB origin. What procedures should the auditor follow concerning acquisitions of inventory on an FOB origin basis near year-end?

MULTIPLE CHOICE QUESTIONS FROM CPA EXAMINATIONS

18-18 (Objective 18-3) The following questions concern internal controls in the acquisition and payment cycle. Choose the best response.

   a. A client erroneously recorded a large purchase twice. Which of the following internal control measures would be most likely to detect this error in a timely and efficient manner?

     (1) Footing the purchases journal.

     (2) Reconciling vendors' monthly statements with subsidiary payable ledger accounts.

(3) Tracing totals from the purchases journal to the ledger accounts.

(4) Sending written quarterly confirmations to all vendors.

b. Nermeen, the purchasing agent of Red Sea Hardware Wholesalers, has a relative who owns a retail hardware store. Nermeen arranged for hardware to be delivered by manufacturers to the retail store on a certificate of deposits (COD) basis, thereby enabling her relative to buy at Red Sea Hardware's wholesale prices. Nermeen was probably able to accomplish this because of Red Sea Hardware's poor internal control over

(1) purchase requisitions.

(2) purchase orders.

(3) cash receipts.

(4) perpetual inventory records.

c. Which of the following is an internal control that will prevent paid cash disbursement documents from being presented for payment a second time?

(1) The date on cash disbursement documents must be within a few days of the date that the document is presented for payment.

(2) The official signing the check compares the check with the documents and should deface the documents.

(3) Unsigned checks are prepared by individuals who are responsible for signing checks.

(4) Cash disbursement documents are approved by at least two responsible management officials.

18-19 (Objectives 18-6, 18-7) The following questions concern accumulating evidence in the acquisition and payment cycle. Choose the best response.

a. In auditing accounts payable, an auditor's procedures most likely will focus primarily on management's assertion of

(1) existence.

(2) realizable value.

(3) completeness.

(4) valuation and allocation.

b. Which of the following audit procedures is best for identifying unrecorded trade accounts payable?

(1) Examining unusual relationships between monthly accounts payable balances and recorded cash payments.

(2) Reconciling vendors' statements to the file of receiving reports to identify items received just prior to the balance sheet date.

(3) Reviewing cash disbursements recorded subsequent to the balance sheet date to determine whether the related payables apply to the prior period.

(4) Investigating payables recorded just prior to and just subsequent to the balance sheet date to determine whether they are supported by receiving reports.

c. When using confirmations to provide evidence about the completeness assertion for accounts payable, the appropriate population most likely is

(1) vendors with whom the entity has previously done business.

(2) amounts recorded in the accounts payable subsidiary ledger.

(3) payees of checks drawn in the month after year-end.

(4) invoices filed in the entity's open invoice file.

DISCUSSION QUESTIONS AND PROBLEMS

18-20 (Objective 18-3) Questions 1 through 8 are typically found in questionnaires used by auditors to obtain an understanding of internal control in the acquisition and payment cycle. In using the questionnaire for a client, a 'yes' response to a question indicates a possible internal control, whereas a 'no' indicates a potential deficiency.

1. Is the purchasing function performed by personnel who are independent of the receiving and shipping functions and the payables and disbursing functions?

2. Are all vendors' invoices routed directly to accounting from the mailroom?
3. Are all receiving reports prenumbered and the numerical sequence checked by a person independent of check preparation?
4. Are all extensions, footings, discounts, and freight terms on vendors' invoices checked for accuracy?
5. Does a responsible employee review and approve the invoice account distribution before the transaction is entered in the computer?
6. Are checks automatically posted in the cash disbursements journal as they are prepared?
7. Are all supporting documents properly cancelled at the time the checks are signed?
8. Is the custody of checks after signature and before mailing handled by an employee independent of all payable, disbursing, cash, and general ledger functions?

Required
a. For each of the preceding questions, state the transaction-related audit objective(s) being fulfilled if the control is in effect.
b. For each internal control, list a test of control to test its effectiveness.
c. For each of the preceding questions, identify the nature of the potential financial misstatement(s) if the control is not in effect.
d. For each of the potential misstatements in part c, list a substantive audit procedure that can be used to determine whether a material misstatement exists.

18-21 (Objective 18-3) Following are some of the tests of controls and substantive tests of transactions procedures commonly performed in the acquisition and payment cycle. Each is to be done on a sample basis.

1. Trace transactions recorded in the acquisitions journal to supporting documentation, comparing the vendor's name, total dollar amounts, and authorization for acquisition.
2. Examine documents in support of acquisition transactions to make sure that each transaction has an approved vendor's invoice, receiving report, and purchase order included.
3. Foot the cash disbursements journal, trace postings of the total to the general ledger, and trace postings of individual cash disbursements to the accounts payable master file.
4. Account for a numerical sequence of checks in the cash disbursements journal and examine all voided or spoiled checks for proper cancellation.
5. Prepare a proof of cash disbursements for an interim month.
6. Account for a sequence of receiving reports and trace selected ones to related vendors' invoices and acquisitions journal entries.
7. Review supporting documents for clerical accuracy, correctness of account distribution, and reasonableness of expenditure in relation to the nature of the client's operations.
8. Compare dates on cancelled checks with dates on the cash disbursements journal and the bank cancellation date.

Required
a. State whether each procedure above is primarily a test of control or substantive test of transactions.
b. State the purpose(s) of each procedure.

18-22 (Objective 18-3) Silverline, Inc. is a small manufacturer of women's casual-wear jewelry, including bracelets, necklaces, earrings, and other moderately priced accessory items. Most of its products are made from silver, various low-cost stones, beads, and other decorative jewelry pieces. Silverline is not involved in the manufacturing of high-end jewelry items.

Personnel responsible for purchasing raw material jewelry items for Silverline would like to place orders directly with suppliers who offer their products for sale through internet websites. Most suppliers provide pictures of all jewelry components on their websites, along with pricing and other sales-term information. Customers who have valid business licenses are able to purchase the products at wholesale, rather than retail prices. Customers can place orders online and pay for those goods immediately by using a valid credit card. Purchases made by credit card are shipped by the suppliers after the credit approval is received from the credit card agency, which usually occurs the same day. Customers can also place orders online with payment being later made by check. However, in that event, purchases are not shipped until the check is received and cashed by the supplier. Some of the suppliers allow a 30-day full-payment refund policy, whereas other suppliers accept returns but only grant credit toward future purchases from that supplier.

Required

a. Identify advantages for Silverline if management allows purchasing personnel to order goods online through supplier websites.

b. Identify potential risks associated with Silverline purchase of jewelry pieces through supplier internet websites.

c. Describe advantages of allowing purchasing agents to purchase products online using a Silverline credit card.

d. Describe advantages of allowing purchasing agents to purchase products online with payment made only by check.

e. What internal controls can be implemented to ensure that
   (1) purchasing agents do not use Silverline credit cards to purchase nonjewelry items for their own purposes, if Silverline allows purchasing agents to purchase jewelry using Silverline credit cards?
   (2) purchasing agents do not order jewelry items from the suppliers and ship those items to addresses other than Silverline addresses?
   (3) Silverline does not end up with unused credits with jewelry suppliers as a result of returning unacceptable jewelry items to suppliers who only grant credit toward future purchases?

18-23 (Objectives 18-5, 18-6, 18-7) The following auditing procedures were performed in the audit of accounts payable:

1. For liabilities that are payable in a foreign currency, determine the exchange rate and check calculations.
2. Discuss with the bookkeeper whether any amounts included on the accounts payable list are due to related parties, debit balances, or notes payable.
3. Obtain vendors' statements from the controller and reconcile them to the listing of accounts payable.
4. Obtain vendors' statements directly from vendors and reconcile them to the listing of accounts payable.
5. Examine supporting documents for cash disbursements several days before and after year-end.
6. Examine the acquisitions and cash disbursements journals for the last few days of the current period and first few days of the succeeding period, looking for large or unusual transactions.
7. Trace from the general ledger trial balance and supporting documentation to determine whether accounts payable, related parties, and other related assets and liabilities are properly included on the financial statements.
8. Obtain a list of accounts payable. Re-add and compare with the general ledger.

Required

a. For each procedure, identify the type of audit evidence used.

b. For each procedure, use the matrix on page 642 to identify which balance-related audit objective(s) were satisfied. (Procedure 1 is completed as an illustration.)

c. Evaluate the need to have certain objectives satisfied by more than one audit procedure.

Audit Procedure	Balance-Related Audit Objective						
	Detail tie-in	Existence	Completeness	Accuracy	Classification	Cutoff	Obligations
1				X			
2							
3							
4							
5							
6							
7							
8							

18-24 (Objectives 18-3, 18-6) The following misstatements are included in the accounting records of National Manufacturing Company.

1. The accounts payable clerk prepares a monthly check to Story Supply Company for the amount of an invoice owed and submits the unsigned check to the treasurer for payment along with related supporting documents that have already been approved. When she receives the signed check from the treasurer, she records it as a debit to accounts payable and deposits the check in a personal bank account for a company named Story Company. A few days later, she records the invoice in the acquisitions journal again, resubmits the documents and a new check to the treasurer, and sends the check to the vendor after it has been signed.

2. The amount of a check in the cash disbursements journal is recorded as US$4,612.87 instead of US$6,412.87.

3. The accounts payable clerk intentionally excluded from the cash disbursements journal seven large checks written and mailed on December 26 to prevent cash in the bank from having a negative balance on the general ledger. They were recorded on January 2 of the subsequent year.

4. Each month, a fraudulent receiving report is submitted to accounting by an employee in the receiving department. A few days later, he sends National an invoice for the quantity of goods ordered from a small company he owns and operates in the evening. A check is prepared, and the amount is paid when the receiving report and the vendor's invoice are matched by the accounts payable clerk.

5. Telephone expense (account 2112) was unintentionally charged to repairs and maintenance (account 2121).

6. Acquisitions of raw materials are often not recorded until several weeks after the goods are received because receiving personnel fail to forward receiving reports to accounting. When pressure from a vendor's credit department is put on National's accounting department, it searches for the receiving report, records the transactions in the acquisitions journal, and pays the bill.

Required

a. For each misstatement, identify the transaction-related audit objective(s) that was not met.

b. For each misstatement, state a control that should have prevented it from occurring on a continuing basis.

c. For each misstatement, state a substantive audit procedure that could uncover it.

18-25 (Objectives 18-3, 18-4) In testing cash disbursements for the Abou El Khair Company, you obtained an understanding of internal control. The controls are reasonably good, and no unusual audit problems arose in previous years.

Although there are not many individuals in the accounting department, there is a reasonable separation of duties in the organization. There is a separate purchasing agent who is responsible for ordering goods and a separate receiving department that counts the goods when they are received and prepares receiving reports. There is a separation of duties between recording acquisitions and cash disbursements, and all information is recorded in the two journals independently. The controller reviews all supporting documents before signing the checks, and he immediately mails the checks to the vendors. Check copies are used for subsequent recording.

All aspects of internal control seem satisfactory to you, and you perform minimum tests of 25 transactions as a means of assessing control risk. In your tests, you discover the following exceptions:

1. Two items in the acquisitions journal were misclassified.
2. Three invoices were not initialed by the controller, but there were no dollar misstatements evident in the transactions.
3. Five receiving reports were recorded in the acquisitions journal at least two weeks later than their date on the receiving report.
4. One invoice was paid twice. The second payment was supported by a duplicate copy of the invoice. Both copies of the invoice were marked 'paid.'
5. One check amount in the cash disbursements journal was for US$100 less than the amount stated on the vendor's invoice.
6. One voided check was missing.
7. Two receiving reports for vendors' invoices were missing from the transaction packets. One vendor's invoice had an extension error, and the invoice was initialed that the amount had been checked.

Required

a. Identify whether each of 1 through 7 is a control test deviation, a monetary misstatement, or both.

b. For each exception, identify which transaction-related audit objective(s) was not met.

c. What is the audit importance of each of these exceptions?

d. What follow-up procedures would you use to determine more about the nature of each exception?

e. How would each of these exceptions affect the rest of your audit? Be specific.

f. Identify internal controls that should have prevented each misstatement.

18-26 (Objective 18-6) The physical inventory for Ayad Manufacturing was taken on December 30, 2011, rather than December 31, because the client had to operate the plant for a special order on the last day of the year. At the time of the client's physical count, you observed that acquisitions represented by receiving report number 2631 and all preceding ones were included in the physical count, whereas inventory represented by succeeding numbers was excluded. On the evening of December 31, you stopped by the plant and noted that inventory represented by receiving report numbers 2632 through 2634 was received subsequent to the physical count but before the end of the year. You later noted that the final inventory on the financial statements contained only those items included in the physical count. In testing accounts payable at December 31, 2011, you obtain a schedule from the client to aid you in testing the adequacy of the cutoff. The following schedule includes the information that you have not yet resolved:

| | | **INFORMATION ON THE VENDOR'S INVOICE** | | | |
Receiving Report Number	Amount of Vendor's Invoice	Amount Presently Included in or Excluded from Accounts Payable*	Invoice Date	Shipping Date	FOB Origin or Destination
2631	US$4,256.40	Included	Dec 30, 2011	Dec 30, 2011	Origin
2632	6,320.54	Excluded	Dec 26, 2011	Dec 15, 2011	Destination
2633	3,761.22	Included	Dec 31, 2011	Dec 26, 2011	Origin
2634	7,832.18	Excluded	Dec 16, 2011	Dec 27, 2011	Destination
2635	6,847.77	Included	Dec 28, 2011	Dec 31, 2011	Origin
2636	6,373.58	Excluded	Jan 1, 2012	Dec 31, 2011	Destination
2637	5,878.36	Excluded	Jan 5, 2012	Dec 26, 2011	Origin
2638	3,355.05	Excluded	Dec 31, 2011	Jan 3, 2012	Origin

*All entries to record inventory acquisitions are recorded by the client as a debit to purchases and a credit to accounts payable.

Required

a. Explain the relationship between inventory and accounts payable cutoff.

b. For each of the receiving reports, state the misstatement in inventory or accounts payable, if any exists, and prepare an adjusting entry to correct the financial statements, if a misstatement exists.

c. Which of the misstatements in part b are most important? Explain.

CASE

18-27 (Objectives 18-2, 18-3, 18-4, 18-6) The following tests of controls and substantive tests of transactions audit procedures for acquisitions and cash disbursements are to be used in the audit of Arabian Publishing Company. You concluded that internal control appears effective and a reduced assessed control risk is likely to be cost beneficial. Arabian CFO's active involvement in the business, good separation of duties, and a competent controller and other employees are factors affecting your opinion.

Arabian Publishing Company—Part I
(See below for Part II and Case 19-23 on page 669 for Part III)

Tests of Controls and Substantive Tests of Transactions Audit Procedures for Acquisitions and Cash Disbursements

1. Foot and cross-foot the acquisitions and cash disbursements journals for two months and trace totals to postings in the general ledger.
2. Scan the acquisitions and cash disbursements journals for all months and investigate any unusual entries.
3. Reconcile cash disbursements per books to cash disbursements per bank statement for one month.
4. Examine evidence that the bank reconciliation is prepared by the controller.
5. Inquire and observe whether the accounts payable master file balances are periodically reconciled to vendors' statements by the controller.
6. Examine the log book as evidence that the numerical sequence of checks is accounted for by someone independent of the preparation function.
7. Inquire and observe that checks are mailed by the Arabian CFO or someone under his supervision after he signs.
8. Examine initials indicating that the controller balances the accounts payable master file to the general ledger monthly.
9. Select a sample of entries in the cash disbursements journal, and
   a. obtain related cancelled checks and compare with entry for payee, date, and amount and examine signature endorsement.

    b. obtain vendors' invoices, receiving reports, and purchase orders, and

      (1) determine that supporting documents are attached to vendors' invoices.

      (2) determine that documents agree with the cash disbursements journal.

      (3) compare vendors' names, amounts, and dates with entries.

      (4) determine whether a discount was taken when appropriate.

      (5) examine vendors' invoices for initials indicating an independent review of chart of account codings.

      (6) examine reasonableness of cash disbursements and account codings.

      (7) review invoices for approval of acquisitions by the Arabian CFO.

      (8) review purchase orders and/or purchase requisitions for proper approval.

      (9) verify prices and recalculate footings and extensions on invoices.

     (10) compare quantities and descriptions on purchase orders, receiving reports, and vendors' invoices to the extent applicable.

     (11) examine vendors' invoices and receiving reports to determine that the check numbers are included and the documents are marked 'paid' at the time of check signing.

    c. trace postings to the accounts payable master file for name, amount, and date.

10. Select a sample of receiving reports issued during the year and trace to vendors' invoices and entries in the acquisitions journal.

    a. Compare type of merchandise, name of vendor, date received, quantities, and amounts.

    b. If the transaction is indicated in the acquisitions journal as paid, trace the check number to the entry in the cash disbursements journal. If unpaid, investigate reasons.

    c. Trace transactions to accounts payable master file, comparing name, amount, and date.

Required

Prepare all parts of a sampling data sheet (such as the one in Figure 15-2) through the planned sample size for the preceding audit program, assuming that a line item in the cash disbursements journal is used for the sampling unit. Use either nonstatistical or attributes sampling. For all procedures for which the line item in the cash disbursements journal is not an appropriate sampling unit, assume that audit procedures were performed on a non-sampling basis. For all tests of controls, use a tolerable exception rate of 5%, and for all substantive tests of transactions, use a rate of 6%. Use an ARACR of 10%, which is considered medium. Plan for an estimated population exception rate of 1% for tests of controls and 0% for substantive tests of transactions.

Prepare the data sheet using the computer (instructor option—also applies to Part II).

Part II

Assume a sample size of 50 for all procedures, regardless of your answers in Part I. For other procedures, assume that an adequate sample size for the circumstance was selected. The only exceptions in your audit tests for all tests of controls and substantive tests of transactions audit procedures are as follows:

1. Procedure 2—Two large transactions were identified as being unusual. Investigation determined that they were authorized acquisitions of fixed assets. They were both correctly recorded.

2. Procedure 9b (1)—A purchase order was not attached to a vendor's invoice. The purchase order was found in a separate file and determined to be approved and appropriate.

3. Procedure 9b (5)—Six vendors' invoices were not initialed as being internally verified. Three actual misclassifications existed. The controller explained that he often did not review codings because of the competence of the accounting clerk doing the coding and was surprised at the mistakes.

Required
a. Complete the sampling data sheet from Part I using either nonstatistical or attributes sampling.

b. Explain the effect of the exceptions on tests of details of accounts payable. Which balance-related audit objectives are affected, and how do those objectives, in turn, affect the audit of accounts payable?

c. Given your tests of controls and substantive tests of transactions results, write an audit program for tests of details of balances for accounts payable. Assume:
   (1) The client provided a list of accounts payable, prepared from the master file.
   (2) Acceptable audit risk for accounts payable is high.
   (3) Inherent risk for accounts payable is low.
   (4) Analytical procedure results were excellent.

COMPLETING THE TESTS IN THE ACQUISITION AND PAYMENT CYCLE: VERIFICATION OF SELECTED ACCOUNTS

LEARNING OBJECTIVES

After studying this chapter, you should be able to

19-1 Recognize the many accounts in the acquisition and payment cycle.

19-2 Design and perform audit tests of property, plant, and equipment and related accounts.

19-3 Design and perform audit tests of prepaid expenses.

19-4 Design and perform audit tests of accrued liabilities.

19-5 Design and perform audit tests of income and expense accounts.

Incorrect Classifications Hide A Greater Net Loss

TV Communications Network, a wireless cable television company, materially understated losses in its financial statements by improperly recording US$2.5 million of expenses as a direct decrease in stockholders' equity. The misstatement took the company from an actual net loss of US$4.7 million to a reported loss of only US$2.2 million.

According to the investigation by the SEC, the expenses charged to equity were from disbursements for the development and distribution of brochures promoting the company's business prospects. The payments should have been expensed and reflected in the income statement as advertising expenses.

The internal controls associated with the advertising expenses were clearly inadequate. TVCN typically did not have invoices or other documentation available when payments were made by the company's president, who controlled the bank account. Because of the lack of adequate documentation, when the financial statements were prepared, TVCN employees responsible for recording the expenses did not have sufficient information to properly classify the disbursements. The SEC found that even when documentation was available, the accounts where the transactions were recorded conflicted with the supporting documentation.

Unfortunately, the TVCN's auditor relied on inquiry of the company president as the primary evidence about the nature of the advertising payments. In his substantive testing of transactions exceeding US$10,000, the auditor relied on the company controller to identify all transactions meeting the criteria for review. Needless to say, the controller did not present all transactions meeting the US$10,000 scope. As you might expect, the oversight supervisory authority brought charges against the auditor for failing to comply with auditing standards.

Source: *Accounting and Auditing Enforcement Release No. 534*, Commerce Clearing House, Inc., Chicago, U.S.

In Chapter 18, we noted that transactions in the acquisition and payment cycle affect several asset accounts: supplies, property, plant and equipment, and prepaid expenses accounts, to name a few. Payments made for services also affect many expense accounts. To continue our discussion of the acquisition and payment cycle, this chapter examines audit issues related to other accounts commonly found in the acquisition and payment cycles of most businesses.

The above story about improper audit procedures highlights the importance of understanding the nature of acquisition and payment cycle transactions. Because transactions in this cycle affect numerous accounts in both the balance sheet and the income statement, incorrectly classified transactions may significantly affect reported results. Auditors must understand the nature of transactions flowing through the acquisition and payment cycle so that they can effectively assess the risk of material misstatement and perform further audit procedures to evaluate the accounts in the cycle.

Relevant International Standards on Auditing	
ISA 200	Overall Objectives of the Independent Auditor and the Conduct of an Audit in Accordance with International Standards on Auditing
ISA 230	Audit Documentation
ISA 260	Communication with Those Charged with Governance
ISA 320	Materiality in Planning and Performing an Audit
ISA 450	Evaluation of Misstatements Identified during the Audit
ISA 500	Audit Evidence
ISA 505	External Confirmations
ISA 540	Auditing Accounting Estimates, Including Fair Value Accounting Estimates, and Related Disclosures

TYPES OF OTHER ACCOUNTS IN THE ACQUISITION AND PAYMENT CYCLE

OBJECTIVE 19-1

Recognize the many accounts in the acquisition and payment cycle.

Table 19-1 highlights many of the typical accounts associated with transactions in the acquisition and payment cycle. The types of assets, expenses, and liabilities will differ for many companies, especially those in industries other than retail, wholesale, and manufacturing.

The methodology associated with auditing these accounts is similar to the audits of other accounts discussed in earlier chapters. The methodology is the same as Figure 18-3 in Chapter 18 for accounts payable, except for the name of the account being audited.

TABLE 19-1	Accounts Typically Associated with Acquisition and Payment Cycle Transactions		
Assets	**Expenses**	**Liabilities**	
Cash	Cost of goods sold	Accounts payable	
Inventory	Rent expense	Rent payable	
Supplies	Property taxes	Accrued professional fees	
Property, plant, and equipment	Income tax expense	Accrued property taxes	
Patents, trademarks, and copyrights	Insurance expense	Other accrued expenses	
Prepaid rent	Professional fees	Income taxes payable	
Prepaid taxes	Retirement benefits		
Prepaid insurance	Utilities		

In this chapter, the issues for some of the other key accounts in the acquisition and payment cycle are examined, namely the audit of:

- Property, plant, and equipment
- Prepaid expenses
- Other liabilities
- Income and expense accounts

AUDIT OF PROPERTY, PLANT, AND EQUIPMENT

Property, plant, and equipment are assets that have expected lives of more than one year, are used in the business, and are not acquired for resale. The intent to use the assets as part of the operation of the client's business and their expected lives of more than one year are the significant characteristics that distinguish these assets from inventory, prepaid expenses, and investments. Table 19-2 shows examples of some of the typical classifications of property, plant, and equipment accounts. The acquisition of property, plant, and equipment occurs through the acquisition and payment cycle.

OBJECTIVE 19-2

Design and perform audit tests of property, plant, and equipment and related accounts.

Because the audits of property, plant, and equipment accounts are similar, one example (manufacturing equipment) is used to illustrate an approach to auditing all three types of accounts. Significant differences in the verification of other types of accounts are discussed as they arise.

Overview of Equipment-Related Accounts

The accounts commonly used for manufacturing equipment are illustrated in Figure 19-1. Notice that the debits to manufacturing equipment arise from the acquisition and payment cycle. Because the source of debits in the asset account is the acquisitions journal, the accounting system has normally already been tested for recording current period additions to manufacturing equipment as part of the tests of the acquisition and payment cycle (which we studied in the last chapter). However, because equipment additions are infrequent, often for large amounts, and subject to special controls, such as board of directors' approval, the auditor may decide not to rely heavily on these tests as evidence supporting fixed asset additions.

The primary accounting record for manufacturing equipment and other property, plant, and equipment accounts is generally a **fixed asset master file**. The master file includes a detailed record for each piece of equipment and other types of property owned. Each record in the file includes a description of the asset, date of acquisition, original cost, current year depreciation, and accumulated depreciation for the property.

Fixed asset master file

A computer file containing records for each piece of equipment and other types of property owned; the primary accounting record for manufacturing equipment and other property, plant, and equipment accounts.

The totals for all records in the master file equal the general ledger balances for the related accounts: manufacturing equipment, depreciation expense, and accumulated depreciation. The master file also contains information about property acquired and disposed of during the year.

TABLE 19-2	Classifications of Property, Plant, and Equipment Accounts
Land and land improvements	
Buildings and building improvements	
Manufacturing equipment	
Furniture and fixtures	
Autos and trucks	
Leasehold improvements	
Construction-in-process for property, plant, and equipment	

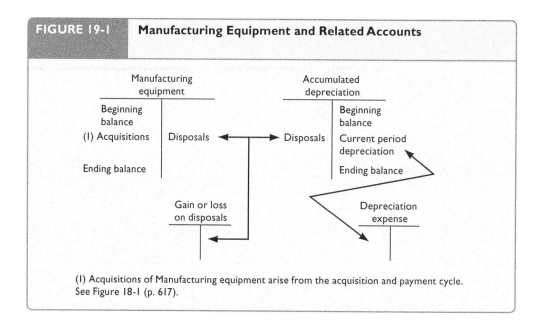

FIGURE 19-1   Manufacturing Equipment and Related Accounts

(1) Acquisitions of Manufacturing equipment arise from the acquisition and payment cycle. See Figure 18-1 (p. 617).

Auditors verify manufacturing equipment differently from current asset accounts for three reasons:

1. There are usually fewer current period acquisitions of manufacturing equipment.
2. The amount of any given acquisition is often material.
3. The equipment is likely to be kept and maintained in the accounting records for several years.

Because of these differences, the auditing of manufacturing equipment emphasizes the verification of current period acquisitions rather than the balance in the account carried forward from the preceding year. In addition, the expected life of assets over one year requires depreciation expense and accumulated depreciation accounts, as shown in Figure 19-1, which are verified as part of the audit of the assets. Finally, equipment may be sold or disposed of, triggering a gain or loss entry that the auditor may need to verify.

Although the approach to verifying manufacturing equipment differs from that used for current assets, several other asset accounts are verified in much the same manner. These include patents, copyrights, catalog costs, and all property, plant, and equipment accounts.

In the audit of manufacturing equipment and related accounts, it is helpful to separate the tests into the following categories:

- Perform analytical procedures
- Verify current year acquisitions
- Verify current year disposals
- Verify the ending balance in the asset account
- Verify depreciation expense
- Verify the ending balance in accumulated depreciation

Next, let's examine the use of these categories of tests in the audit of manufacturing equipment, depreciation expense, accumulated depreciation, and gain or loss on disposal accounts.

Perform Analytical Procedures

As in all audit areas, the type of analytical procedures depends on the nature of the client's operations. Table 19-3 illustrates analytical procedures often performed for manufacturing equipment.

TABLE 19-3	Analytical Procedures for Manufacturing Equipment
Analytical Procedure	**Possible Misstatement**
Compare depreciation expense divided by gross manufacturing equipment cost with previous years.	Misstatement in depreciation expense and accumulated depreciation.
Compare accumulated depreciation divided by gross manufacturing equipment cost with previous years.	Misstatement in accumulated depreciation.
Compare monthly or annual repairs and maintenance, supplies expense, small tools expense, and similar accounts with previous years.	Expensing amounts that should be capitalized.
Compare gross manufacturing cost divided by some measure of production with previous years.	Idle equipment or equipment that was disposed of but not written off.

As you can see, most of the typical analytical procedures assess the likelihood of material misstatements in depreciation expense and accumulated depreciation. Later in the chapter, the substantive tests auditors often focus on for these accounts are discussed.

Verify Current Year Acquisitions

Companies must correctly record current year additions because the assets have long-term effects on the financial statements. The failure to capitalize a fixed asset, or the recording of an acquisition at the incorrect amount, affects the balance sheet until the company disposes of the asset. The income statement is affected until the asset is fully depreciated.

Because of the importance of current period acquisitions in the audit of manufacturing equipment, auditors use seven of the eight balance-related audit objectives as a frame of reference for tests of details of balances: existence, completeness, accuracy, classification, cutoff, detail tie-in, and rights and obligations. (Realizable value is discussed in connection with verifying ending balances.) The balance-related audit objectives and common audit tests are shown in Table 19-4. Existence, completeness, accuracy, and classification are usually the major objectives for this part of the audit.

As in all other audit areas, the actual audit tests and sample size depend heavily on tolerable misstatement, inherent risk, and assessed control risk. Tolerable misstatement is important for verifying current year additions because these transactions vary from immaterial amounts in some years to a large number of significant acquisitions in others.

The starting point for the verification of current year acquisitions is normally a schedule obtained from the client of all acquisitions recorded in the general ledger property, plant, and equipment accounts during the year. The client obtains this information from the property master file. A typical schedule lists each addition separately and includes the date of the acquisition, vendor, description, notation of whether it is new or used, life of the asset for depreciation purposes, depreciation method, and cost.

As you study Table 19-4, notice that the most common audit test to verify additions is to examine vendors' invoices. Additional testing, beyond that which is done as part of the tests of controls and substantive tests of transactions, is often necessary because of the complexity of many equipment transactions and the materiality of the amounts. It is normal for auditors to verify large and unusual transactions for the entire year as well as a representative sample of typical additions. The extent of testing depends on the auditor's assessed control risk for acquisitions and the materiality of the additions.

TABLE 19-4	Balance-Related Audit Objectives and Tests of Details of Balances for Manufacturing Equipment Additions	
Balance-Related Audit Objective	**Common Tests of Details of Balances Procedures**	**Comments**
Current year acquisitions in the acquisitions schedule agree with related master file amounts, and the total agrees with the general ledger (detail tie-in).	Foot the acquisitions schedule. Trace the individual acquisitions to the master file for amounts and descriptions. Trace the total to the general ledger.	Footing the acquisitions schedule and tracing individual acquisitions should be limited unless controls are weak. All increases in the general ledger balance for the year should reconcile to the schedule.
Current year acquisitions as listed exist (existence).	Examine vendors' invoices and receiving reports. Physically examine assets.	It is uncommon to physically examine assets acquired unless controls are weak or amounts are material.
Existing acquisitions are recorded (completeness).	Examine vendors' invoices of closely related accounts such as repairs and maintenance to uncover items that should be manufacturing equipment. Review lease and rental agreements.	This objective is one of the most important for manufacturing equipment.
Current year acquisitions as listed are accurate (accuracy).	Examine vendors' invoices.	Extent depends on inherent risk and effectiveness of internal controls.
Current year acquisitions as listed are correctly classified (classification).	Examine vendors' invoices in manufacturing equipment account to uncover items that should be classified as office equipment, part of the buildings, or repairs. Examine vendors' invoices of closely related accounts such as repairs to uncover items that should be manufacturing equipment. Examine rent and lease expense for capitalizable leases.	The objective is closely related to tests for completeness. It is done in conjunction with that objective and tests for accuracy.
Current year acquisitions are recorded in the correct period (cutoff).	Review transactions near the balance sheet date for correct period.	Usually done as part of accounts payable cutoff tests.
The client has rights to current year acquisitions (rights).	Examine vendors' invoices.	Ordinarily no problem for equipment. Property deeds, abstracts, and tax bills are frequently examined for land or major buildings.

In testing acquisitions, the auditor must understand IFRS, GAAP or local accounting standards to make certain the client follows accounting standards' requirements. For example, the auditor needs to be alert for the possibility of the client's failure to include material transportation and installation costs as part of the asset's acquisition cost and the failure to properly record the trade-in of existing equipment. The auditor also needs to know the client's capitalization policies to determine whether acquisitions are treated consistently with those of the preceding year. For example, if the client's policy is to automatically expense acquisitions that are less than a certain amount, such as US$1,000, the auditor should verify that the policy is followed in the current year.

Auditors should also verify recorded transactions for correct classification. In some cases, amounts recorded as manufacturing equipment should be classified as office equipment or as a part of the building. It is also possible the client has incorrectly capitalized repairs, rents, or similar expenses. Poor internal controls over document preparation, as illustrated by the chapter-opening story about TVCN, can result in significant misclassifications of disbursement transactions.

Clients commonly include transactions that should be recorded as assets in repairs and maintenance expense, lease expense, supplies, small tools, and similar accounts.

The misstatement may result from a lack of understanding of the accounting standards or from clients' desires to avoid income taxes. If auditors conclude this type of material misstatement is likely, they may need to vouch larger amounts debited to the expense accounts. It is a common practice to do so as part of the audit of the property, plant, and equipment accounts.

Verify Current Year Disposals

Transactions involving the disposal of manufacturing equipment are often misstated when company internal controls lack a formal method to inform management of the sale, trade-in, abandonment, or theft of recorded machinery and equipment. If the client fails to record disposals, the original cost of the manufacturing equipment account will be overstated indefinitely, and net book value will be overstated until the asset is fully depreciated. Formal methods of tracking disposals and provisions for proper authorization of the sale or other disposal of manufacturing equipment help reduce the risk of misstatement. There should also be adequate internal verification of recorded disposals to make sure that assets are correctly removed from the accounting records.

The auditor's main objectives in the verification of the sale, trade-in, or abandonment of manufacturing equipment are to gather sufficient evidence that all disposals are recorded and at the correct amounts. The starting point for verifying disposals is the client's schedule of recorded disposals. The schedule typically includes the date when the asset was disposed of, name of the person or firm acquiring the asset, selling price, original cost, acquisition date, and accumulated depreciation.

Detail tie-in tests of the recorded disposals schedule are necessary, including footing the schedule, tracing the totals on the schedule to the recorded disposals in the general ledger, and tracing the cost and accumulated depreciation of the disposals to the property master file.

Because the failure to record disposals of manufacturing equipment no longer used in the business can significantly affect the financial statements, *the search for unrecorded disposals is essential*. The nature and adequacy of the controls over disposals affect the extent of the search. The following procedures are often used for verifying disposals:

- Review whether newly acquired assets replace existing assets
- Analyze gains and losses on the disposal of assets and miscellaneous income for receipts from the disposal of assets
- Review plant modifications and changes in product line, property taxes, or insurance coverage for indications of deletions of equipment
- Make inquiries of management and production personnel about the possibility of the disposal of assets

When an asset is sold or disposed of without having been traded in for a replacement asset, the *accuracy* of the transaction can be verified by examining the related sales invoice and property master file. The auditor should compare the cost and accumulated depreciation in the master file with the recorded entry in the general journal and recompute the gain or loss on the disposal of the asset for comparison with the accounting records. When *trade-in of an asset for a replacement* occurs, the auditor should be sure that the new asset is capitalized and the replaced asset correctly eliminated from the records, considering the book value of the asset traded in and the additional cost of the new asset.

Verify Ending Balance of Asset Account

Two of the auditor's objectives when auditing manufacturing equipment include determining that:

1. All recorded equipment physically exists on the balance sheet date (existence)
2. All equipment owned is recorded (completeness)

When designing audit tests to meet these objectives, auditors first consider the nature of internal controls over manufacturing equipment. Ideally, auditors are able to conclude that controls are sufficiently strong to allow them to rely on balances carried forward from the prior year. Important controls include the use of a master file for individual fixed assets, adequate physical controls over assets that are easily movable (such as computers, tools, and vehicles), assignment of identification numbers to each plant asset, and a periodic physical count of fixed assets and their reconciliation by accounting personnel. A formal method of informing the accounting department of all disposals of fixed assets is also an important control over the balance of assets carried forward into the current year.

Typically, the first audit step concerns the detail tie-in objective: manufacturing equipment, as listed in the master file, agrees with the general ledger. Examining a printout of the master file that totals to the general ledger balance is ordinarily sufficient. The auditor may choose to use audit software to foot an electronic version of the master file or manually test-foot a few pages.

After assessing control risk for the existence objective, the auditor decides whether it is necessary to verify the existence of individual items of manufacturing equipment included in the master file. If there is a high likelihood of material missing fixed assets still included in the master file, the auditor can select a sample from the master file and examine the actual assets. In rare cases, the auditor may decide it is necessary for the client to take a complete physical inventory of fixed assets to make sure they all exist. If a physical inventory is taken, the auditor normally observes the count.

The auditor normally does not need to test the accuracy or classification of fixed assets recorded in prior periods because, presumably, they were verified in previous audits at the time they were acquired. But the auditor should be aware that companies may occasionally have manufacturing equipment on hand that is no longer used in operations. If the amounts are material, the auditor should evaluate whether they should be written down to net realizable value (realizable value objective) or at least classified separately as 'nonoperating equipment.'

In addition to performing procedures to obtain evidence related to balance-related audit objectives for fixed assets, auditors also perform audit procedures related to the three presentation and disclosure objectives for fixed assets. A major consideration

---

SEVEN CHARGED IN BANK FRAUD CASE

Seven people have been charged with defrauding the Dubai Islamic Bank (DIB) out of US$501 million (AED 1.84 billion), documents at the Public Prosecutor's office say. The charges involve the largest sum yet in the Emirate's wide-reaching corruption investigations that began last spring. They follow similar charges for fraud allegedly committed on the property developers Sama Dubai and Mizin.

The prosecution's bill of indictment dated December 25 names seven suspects in the case, two of whom have fled the country, according to Zawya Dow Jones. It said the defendants defrauded DIB by creating fake companies and getting the bank to lend money to projects. Among those charged in the DIB case are a Turkish businessman and two Britons. Also charged are two of DIB's former senior executives, both Pakistanis. A Pakistani businessman with U.S. citizenship is also being sought by the authorities. One of the British executives, who was director of a luxury property development company in Dubai, was also charged with criminal complicity.

The bank said it had set aside provisions for a loss of (approximately) US$135 million (AED 496 million) to cover its exposure to CCH International, a company allegedly connected to several of the defendants. "DIB believes that the current provisions, together with collaterals foreclosed and being pursued, are adequate to cover its exposure to CCH, even in the current economic downturn," the bank said.

Last year, the bank foreclosed on The Plantation, a proposed US$3.5 billion equestrian development in Dubailand that received funds from CCH. In September, the bank seized land allocated to The Plantation in a move that was then contested by the developer.

DIB said it was continuing to chase other assets related to the deal.

Source: M. Morris, 'Seven charged in bank fraud case,' *Arabian Business.com*, March 10, 2009 (www.arabianbusiness.com/seven-charged-in-bank-fraud-case-79273.html).

in verifying disclosures related to fixed assets is the possibility of *legal encumbrances.* Auditors may use several methods to determine whether manufacturing equipment is encumbered, including:

- Read the terms of loan and credit agreements
- Mail loan confirmation requests to banks and other lending institutions
- Have discussions with the client or send letters to legal counsel

The *proper presentation and disclosure* of manufacturing equipment in the financial statements must be evaluated carefully to make sure that accounting standards are followed. Manufacturing equipment should include the gross cost and should ordinarily be separated from other fixed assets. Leased property should also be disclosed separately, and all liens on property must be included in the footnotes. Auditors must perform sufficient tests to verify that all three presentation and disclosure objectives are met.

Verify Depreciation Expense

Depreciation expense is one of the few expense accounts not verified as part of tests of controls and substantive tests of transactions. The recorded amounts are determined by *internal allocations* rather than by exchange transactions with outside parties. When depreciation expense is material, more tests of details of depreciation expense are required than for an account that has already been verified through tests of controls and substantive tests of transactions.

The most important balance-related audit objective for depreciation expense is accuracy. Auditors focus on determining whether the client followed a *consistent depreciation policy* from period to period, and the client's *calculations are correct.*

In determining the former, auditors must weigh four considerations:

1. The useful life of current period acquisitions
2. The method of depreciation
3. The estimated salvage value
4. The policy of depreciating assets in the year of acquisition and disposition

The client's policies can be determined by discussions with appropriate personnel and comparing their responses with information in the auditor's permanent files. In deciding on the reasonableness of the useful lives assigned to newly acquired assets, the auditor must consider the physical life of the asset, the expected life (taking into account obsolescence or the company's normal policy of upgrading equipment), and established company policies on trading in equipment.

Occasionally, changing circumstances may necessitate a company to reevaluate the useful life of an asset. When this occurs, the reevaluation should involve a change in accounting estimate rather than a change in accounting principle. The effect of this on depreciation must be evaluated.

A useful method of auditing depreciation is an analytical procedures test of reasonableness made by multiplying undepreciated fixed assets by the depreciation rate for the year. In making these calculations, the auditor must make adjustments for current year additions and disposals, assets with different lengths of life, and assets with different methods of depreciation. Many auditing firms maintain an electronic spreadsheet in their permanent file that includes a breakdown of the fixed assets by method of depreciation and length of life. If the software calculations are reasonably close to the client's totals and if assessed control risk for depreciation expense is low, tests of details for depreciation can be eliminated.

When an overall reasonableness test cannot be accomplished, more detailed tests are usually needed. To do this, auditors recompute depreciation expense for selected assets to determine whether the client is following a proper and consistent depreciation policy. To be relevant, the detailed calculations should be tied in to the total depreciation calculations by footing the depreciation expense on the property master file and reconciling the total with the general ledger. Because accounting standards require footnote disclosures related to fixed asset depreciation, including disclosure of depreciation methods and related useful lives by asset class, auditors perform procedures to obtain evidence that the three presentation and disclosure-related audit objectives for depreciation are satisfied. For example, auditors compare information obtained through audit tests of the depreciation expense accounts to information disclosed in footnotes to ensure the information presented is consistent with the actual method and assumptions used to calculate and record depreciation.

Verify Ending Balance in Accumulated Depreciation

The debits to accumulated depreciation are normally tested as a part of the audit of disposals of assets, while the credits are verified as a part of depreciation expense. If the auditor traces selected transactions to the accumulated depreciation records in the property master file as a part of these tests, then little additional testing should be required for the ending balance in accumulated depreciation.

Two objectives are usually emphasized in the audit of the ending balance in accumulated depreciation:

1. Accumulated depreciation as stated in the property master file agrees with the general ledger. This objective can be satisfied by test-footing the accumulated depreciation in the property master file and tracing the total to the general ledger.
2. Accumulated depreciation in the master file is accurate.

In some cases, the life of manufacturing equipment may be significantly reduced because of reductions in customer demands for products, unexpected physical deterioration, a modification in operations, or other changes. Because of these possibilities, auditors must evaluate the adequacy of the allowances for accumulated depreciation each year to make sure that the net book value does not exceed the realizable value of the assets.

AUDIT OF PREPAID EXPENSES

OBJECTIVE 19-3

Design and perform audit tests of prepaid expenses.

Prepaid expenses, deferred charges, and intangibles are assets that vary in life from several months to several years. These include:

- Prepaid rent
- Organization costs
- Prepaid taxes
- Patents
- Prepaid insurance
- Trademarks
- Deferred charges
- Copyrights

In some cases, these accounts are highly material. However, in a typical audit, the company does not have many of the accounts listed or they are immaterial.

Analytical procedures are often sufficient for prepaid expenses, deferred charges, and intangibles. In certain audits, some of these assets can be significant. In this section, we examine some of the typical internal controls and related audit tests commonly associated with prepaid expenses. In the following discussion, an example of the audit of prepaid insurance is used as an account representative of this group because:

1. Prepaid insurance is found in most audits—virtually every company has some type of insurance.
2. Problems commonly encountered in the audit of prepaid insurance are typical of this class of accounts.
3. The auditor's responsibility for the review of insurance coverage is an additional consideration not found in the other accounts in this category.

Overview of Prepaid Insurance

Figure 19-2 illustrates the accounts typically used for prepaid insurance and the relationship between prepaid insurance and the acquisition and payment cycle through the debits to the prepaid insurance account. Because the source of the debits in the asset account is the acquisitions journal, the payments of insurance premiums have already been partially tested by means of the tests of controls and substantive tests of acquisition and cash disbursement transactions.

Internal Controls

Internal controls for prepaid insurance and insurance expense can be conveniently divided into three categories: controls over the acquisition and recording of insurance, controls over the insurance register, and controls over the charge-off of insurance expense.

An **insurance register** is a record of insurance policies in force and the expiration date of each policy. Auditors use insurance registers to identify policies in force related to prepaid insurance accounts. Payment terms and amounts for the policies in force are contained in the register. Because the terms and amounts provide the basis for determining prepaid insurance amounts, the auditor independently verifies these terms and amounts to the underlying insurance policies or contracts.

Insurance register
A record of insurance policies in force and the expiration date of each policy.

Companies often have a standard monthly journal entry to reclassify prepaid insurance as insurance expense. If a significant entry is required to adjust the balance in prepaid insurance at the end of the year, it indicates a potential misstatement in the recording of the acquisition of insurance throughout the year or in the calculation of the year-end balance in prepaid insurance.

Audit Tests

Throughout the audit of prepaid insurance and insurance expense, the auditor should keep in mind that the amount in insurance expense is a residual. The residual is based on the beginning balance in prepaid insurance, the payment of premiums during the year, and the ending balance.

The only tests of the balance in the expense account that are ordinarily necessary include analytical procedures and a test to be sure that all charges to insurance expense arose from credits to prepaid insurance. Because the payments of premiums are tested as part of the tests of controls and substantive tests of transactions and analytical procedures, the emphasis in the tests of details of balances is on prepaid insurance.

In the audit of prepaid insurance, the auditor obtains a schedule from the client or prepares one that includes details about specific policies in force. For example, the

---

FIGURE 19-2   Prepaid Insurance and Related Accounts

Prepaid insurance		Insurance expense
Beginning balance	Current period insurance expense	
(1) Acquisitions (insurance premiums)		
Ending balance		

(1) Acquisitions of insurance premiums arise from the acquisition and payment cycle. This can be observed by examining Figure 18-1 (p. 617).

schedule often includes information about each insurance policy in force, policy number, insurance coverage for each policy, premium amount, premium period, insurance expense for the year, and prepaid insurance at the end of the year.

The beginning and ending balances in prepaid insurance are frequently *immaterial* and often there are few transactions debited and credited to the balance during the year, most of which are small and simple to understand. Therefore, the auditor can generally spend little time verifying the balance or the transactions. If the auditor decides not to verify the balance in detail, analytical procedures become increasingly important to identify potentially significant misstatements. Auditors commonly perform the following analytical procedures for prepaid insurance and insurance expense:

- Compare total prepaid insurance and insurance expense with previous years.
- Compute the ratio of prepaid insurance to insurance expense and compare it with previous years.
- Compare the individual insurance policy coverage on the schedule of insurance obtained from the client with the preceding year's schedule as a test of the elimination of certain policies or a change in insurance coverage.
- Compare the computed prepaid insurance balance for the current year on a policy-by-policy basis with that of the preceding year as a test of an error in calculation.
- Review the *insurance coverage* listed on the prepaid insurance schedule with an appropriate client official or insurance broker for adequacy of coverage. The auditor cannot be an expert on insurance matters, but the auditor's understanding of accounting and the valuation of assets is necessary to make sure that a company is not underinsured.

For many audits, *no additional* substantive procedures are needed unless assessed control risk is high or the tests indicate a high likelihood of a significant misstatement. The remaining audit procedures, which are examined next, should be performed only when there is a special reason for doing so. Our discussion of these tests uses the balance-related audit objectives for performing tests of details of asset balances. (Realizable value is not applicable.)

Insurance Policies in the Prepaid Insurance Schedule Exist and Existing Policies are Listed (Existence and Completeness) Tests for existence and omissions of insurance policies in force can be performed on the client's prepaid insurance schedule in one of two ways:

1. Examine a sample of insurance invoices and policies in force for comparison to the schedule.
2. Obtain a confirmation of insurance information from the company's insurance agent. Auditors typically prefer to send a confirmation to the client's insurance agent, because this approach is usually less time-consuming than vouching tests and it provides 100 percent verification.

The Client Has Rights to All Insurance Policies in the Prepaid Insurance Schedule (Rights) The party who will receive the benefit if an insurance claim is filed has the rights. Ordinarily, the recipient named in the policy is the client, but when there are mortgages or other liens, the insurance claim may be payable to a creditor. The review of insurance policies for claimants other than the client is an excellent test of unrecorded liabilities and pledged assets.

Prepaid Amounts on the Schedule are Accurate and the Total is Correctly Added and Agrees with the General Ledger (Accuracy and Detail Tie-in) Audit tests to verify the accuracy of prepaid insurance involve verifying the amount of the insurance premium, the length of the policy period, and the allocation of the premium to unexpired insurance. The amount of the premium for a given policy and its time period can be verified at the same time by examining the premium invoice or the confirmation from an insurance agent. After these two have been verified, the client's calculations of unexpired insurance can be tested by recalculation. The schedule of prepaid insurance can then be footed and the totals traced to the general ledger to complete the detail tie-in tests.

The Insurance Expense Related to Prepaid Insurance is Correctly Classified (Classification) The correct classification of debits to different insurance expense accounts should be reviewed as a test of the income statement. In some cases, the appropriate expense account is obvious because of the type of insurance, such as a policy insuring a piece of equipment. In other cases, allocations are necessary. For example, fire insurance on a building may require allocation to several accounts, including manufacturing overhead. Charging the correct accounts and consistency with previous years are the major considerations in evaluating classification.

Insurance Transactions are Recorded in the Correct Period (Cutoff) Cutoff for acquisitions of insurance is normally not a significant problem because of the small number of policies and the immateriality of the amount. If auditors check cutoff of insurance acquisitions, they do so as part of accounts payable cutoff tests.

AUDIT OF ACCRUED LIABILITIES

A third major category of accounts in the acquisition and payment cycle is **accrued liabilities**, which are the estimated unpaid obligations for services or benefits that have been received before the balance sheet date. Many accrued liabilities represent future obligations for unpaid services resulting from the passage of time but are not payable at the balance sheet date. For example, the benefits of property rental accrue throughout the year. Therefore, at the balance sheet date, a certain portion of the total rent cost that has not been paid should be accrued. Other similar liabilities include:

- Accrued payroll
- Accrued payroll taxes
- Accrued officers' bonuses
- Accrued commissions
- Accrued professional fees
- Accrued rent
- Accrued interest

> **OBJECTIVE 19-4**
>
> Design and perform audit tests of accrued liabilities.

> **Accrued liabilities**
>
> Estimated unpaid obligations for services or benefits that have been received prior to the balance sheet date; common accrued liabilities include accrued commissions, accrued income taxes, accrued payroll, and accrued rent.

A second type of accrual involves estimates where the amount of the obligation due is uncertain, such as the obligation for corporate income taxes when there is a reasonable likelihood that the amount reported on the tax return will be changed after the tax authority audits the return. Accrued warranty costs and accrued pension costs are similar accruals.

The verification of accrued expenses varies depending on the nature of the accrual and the circumstances of the client. For most audits, accruals take little audit time. In other instances, certain accounts, such as accrued income taxes, warranty costs, and pension costs, are often material and require considerable audit effort. The following discussion of the audit of accrued property taxes is used as an example of the audit of an accrued liability account.

Auditing Accrued Property Taxes

Figure 19-3 illustrates the accounts typically used by companies for accrued property taxes, showing the relationship between accrued property taxes and the acquisition and payment cycle through the debits to the liability account. Because the source of the debits is the cash disbursements journal, the payments of property taxes should have already been partially tested by the tests of the acquisition and payment cycle transactions.

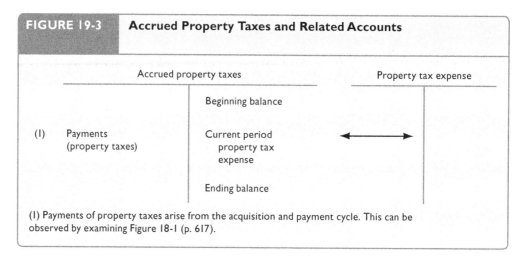

As with insurance expense, the balance in property tax expense is a residual amount that results from the beginning and ending balances in accrued property taxes and the payments of property taxes. Therefore, the emphasis in the tests should be on the ending property tax liability and payments. When auditors verify accrued property taxes, all eight balance-related audit objectives except realizable value are relevant. Two are especially significant:

1. Existing properties for which accrual of taxes is appropriate are on the accrual schedule. The failure to include properties for which taxes should be accrued will understate the property tax liability (completeness). A material misstatement can occur, for example, if taxes on property were not paid before the balance sheet date and not included as accrued property taxes.
2. Accrued property taxes are accurately recorded. The auditor's concern is the consistent treatment of the accrual from year to year (accuracy).

The auditor uses two primary tests for the inclusion of all accruals. Auditors verify the accruals at the same time as the audit of current year property tax payments. In most audits, there are few property tax payments, but each payment is often material, and therefore it is common to verify each one. Auditors also compare the accruals with those of previous years.

The auditor often begins by obtaining a schedule of property tax payments from the client and comparing each payment with the preceding year's schedule to determine whether all payments have been included in the client-prepared schedule. The fixed asset audit schedules also must be examined for major additions and disposals of assets that may affect the property taxes accrual.

After auditors are satisfied that all taxable property has been included in the client-prepared schedule, they evaluate the reasonableness of property taxes on each property used by the client to estimate the accrual. In some instances, the total has already been set by the taxing authority and sent to the client so it is possible to verify the amount by comparing the amount on the schedule with the tax bill. In other cases, the preceding year's total payments must be adjusted for the expected increase in property tax rates.

The auditor can verify the accrued property tax by recalculating the portion of the total tax applicable to the current year for each piece of property. The most important consideration is to use the same portion of each tax payment for the accrual that was used in the preceding year, unless there are justifiable conditions for a change. After the accrual and property tax expense for each piece of property have been recalculated, the totals should be added and compared with the general ledger. In many cases, property taxes are charged to more than one expense account. In that case, the auditor should test for correct classification by evaluating whether the correct amount was charged to each account.

AUDIT OF INCOME AND EXPENSE ACCOUNTS

The auditor must be satisfied that each of the income and expense totals included in the income statement, as well as net earnings, are not materially misstated. The auditor needs to be aware that most users of financial statements rely more heavily on the income statement than on the balance sheet for making decisions. Equity investors, long-term creditors, and short-term creditors are more interested in the ability of a firm to generate profit than in the historical cost or book value of the individual assets.

OBJECTIVE 19-5

Design and perform audit tests of income and expense accounts.

The following two concepts in the audit of income and expense accounts are essential when considering the purposes of the income statement:

1. The matching of periodic income and expense is necessary for a correct determination of operating results.
2. The consistent application of accounting principles for different periods is necessary for comparability.

Both of these concepts must be applied to the recording of individual transactions and to the combining of accounts in the general ledger for statement presentation.

Approach to Auditing Income and Expense Accounts

The audit of income and expense accounts is directly related to the balance sheet and is not a separate part of the audit process. A misstatement of an income statement account almost always equally affects a balance sheet account, and vice versa. As we have discussed in preceding chapters, the audit of income and expense accounts is intertwined with the other parts of the audit. We provide a brief description of these tests here as a review of material covered in earlier chapters. This review shows the interrelated nature of different parts of the audit with income and expense account testing. The parts of the audit directly affecting these accounts are:

- Analytical procedures
- Tests of controls and substantive tests of transactions
- Tests of details of account balances

Our emphasis here is on income and expense accounts directly related to the acquisition and payment cycle, but the same concepts apply to the income statement accounts in all other cycles.

Analytical Procedures

Chapter 8 addressed analytical procedures. Subsequent chapters refer back to those procedures as part of specific audit areas. Analytical procedures should be thought of as part of the test of the fairness of the presentation of both balance sheet and income statement accounts. Table 19-5 shows a few analytical procedures and the possible misstatements they may uncover in the audit of income and expense accounts.

Tests of Controls and Substantive Tests of Transactions

Both tests of controls and substantive tests of transactions have the effect of simultaneously verifying balance sheet and income statement accounts. For example, assume an auditor concludes that internal controls are adequate to provide reasonable assurance that transactions in the acquisitions journal occurred, are accurately recorded, correctly classified, and recorded in a timely manner. By doing so, the auditor obtains evidence about the correctness of individual balance sheet accounts, such as accounts payable and fixed assets, and income statement accounts, such as advertising and repairs. Conversely, inadequate controls and misstatements discovered through tests of

TABLE 19-5	Analytical Procedures for Income and Expense Accounts
Analytical Procedure	**Possible Misstatement**
Compare individual expenses with previous years.	Overstatement or understatement of a balance in an expense account.
Compare individual asset and liability balances with previous years.	Overstatement or understatement of a balance sheet account that will also affect an income statement account (for example, a misstatement of inventory affects cost of goods sold).
Compare individual expenses with budgets.	Misstatement of expenses and related balance sheet accounts.
Compare gross margin percentage with previous years.	Misstatement of cost of goods sold and inventory.
Compare inventory turnover ratio with previous years.	Misstatement of cost of goods sold and inventory.
Compare prepaid insurance expense with previous years.	Misstatement of insurance expense and prepaid insurance.
Compare commission expense divided by sales with previous years.	Misstatement of commission expense and accrued commissions.
Compare individual manufacturing expenses divided by total manufacturing expenses with previous years.	Misstatement of individual manufacturing expenses and related balance sheet accounts.

controls and substantive tests of transactions indicate the likelihood of misstatements in both the income statement and the balance sheet.

The most important means of verifying many of the income statement accounts in each transaction cycle are understanding internal control and the related tests of controls and substantive tests of transactions. For example, if the auditor concludes after adequate tests that control risk can be appropriately assessed as low for transactions in the acquisition and payment cycle, the only additional verification of related income statement accounts, such as utilities, advertising, and purchases, will occur through the performance of analytical procedures and cutoff tests. However, certain income and expense accounts are not verified at all by tests of controls and substantive tests of transactions, and others must be tested more extensively by other substantive testing. These are discussed next.

Tests of Details of Account Balances—Expense Analysis

Auditors must analyze the amounts included in certain income statement accounts even though the previously mentioned tests have been performed. Next, we examine the meaning and methodology of analysis of accounts before moving on to a discussion of when expense account analysis is appropriate.

Expense account analysis

The examination of underlying documentation of individual transactions and amounts making up the total of an expense account.

Expense account analysis involves auditor examination of underlying documentation of individual transactions and amounts making up the detail of the total of an expense account. The documents are the same type as those used for examining transactions as part of tests of acquisition transactions, including invoices, receiving reports, purchase orders, and contracts. Figure 19-4 illustrates a typical audit schedule showing expense analysis for legal expenses.

Although the focus of expense account analysis is on transactions, these tests differ from tests of controls and substantive tests of transactions. The tests of controls and substantive tests of transactions are meant to assess control risk. As such, they are tests of classes of transactions, such as acquisitions, and therefore include many different accounts. In the analysis of expense and other income statement accounts, the auditor verifies transactions in specific accounts to determine whether the transactions are appropriate for the client, properly classified, and accurately recorded.

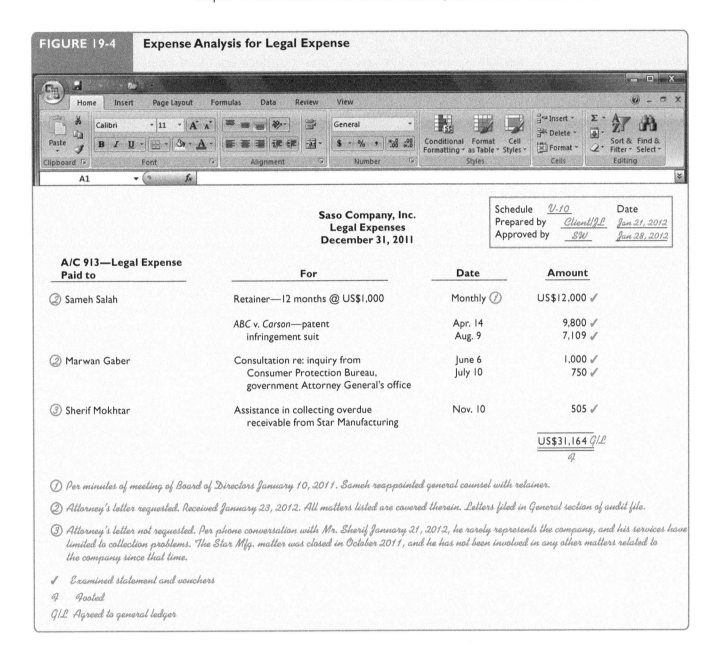

FIGURE 19-4 | **Expense Analysis for Legal Expense**

Saso Company, Inc.
Legal Expenses
December 31, 2011

Schedule *U-10*   Date
Prepared by *Client/JL* *Jan 21, 2012*
Approved by *SW* *Jan 28, 2012*

A/C 913—Legal Expense

Paid to	For	Date	Amount
② Sameh Salah	Retainer—12 months @ US$1,000	Monthly ①	US$12,000 ✓
	ABC v. *Carson*—patent infringement suit	Apr. 14 Aug. 9	9,800 ✓ 7,109 ✓
② Marwan Gaber	Consultation re: inquiry from Consumer Protection Bureau, government Attorney General's office	June 6 July 10	1,000 ✓ 750 ✓
③ Sherif Mokhtar	Assistance in collecting overdue receivable from Star Manufacturing	Nov. 10	505 ✓
			US$31,164 *G/L* *F*

① *Per minutes of meeting of Board of Directors January 10, 2011. Sameh reappointed general counsel with retainer.*

② *Attorney's letter requested. Received January 23, 2012. All matters listed are covered therein. Letters filed in General section of audit file.*

③ *Attorney's letter not requested. Per phone conversation with Mr. Sherif January 21, 2012, he rarely represents the company, and his services have limited to collection problems. The Star Mfg. matter was closed in October 2011, and he has not been involved in any other matters related to the company since that time.*

✓ *Examined statement and vouchers*
F Footed
G/L Agreed to general ledger

Assuming satisfactory results are found in tests of controls and substantive tests of transactions, auditors normally restrict expense analysis to those accounts with a relatively high likelihood of material misstatement. As examples, auditors often analyze:

- Repairs and maintenance expense accounts to determine whether they erroneously include property, plant, and equipment transactions
- Rent and lease expenses to determine the need to capitalize leases
- Legal expense to determine whether there are potential contingent liabilities, disputes, illegal acts, or other legal issues that may affect the financial statements

Utilities, travel expense, and advertising accounts are rarely analyzed unless analytical procedures indicate high potential for material misstatement.

Auditors often analyze expense account transactions as part of the verification of a related asset. It is common, for example, for auditors to analyze repairs and maintenance as part of verifying fixed assets, and insurance expense as part of testing prepaid insurance.

Tests of Details of Account Balances—Allocation

Allocation

The division of certain expenses, such as depreciation and manufacturing overhead, among several expense accounts.

Several expense accounts result from the **allocation** of accounting data rather than discrete transactions. Such expenses include depreciation, depletion, and the amortization of copyrights and catalog costs. The allocation of manufacturing overhead between inventory and cost of goods sold is an example of a different type of allocation that affects expenses.

Allocations are important because they determine whether an expenditure is an asset or a current period expense. If the client fails to follow accounting standards or fails to calculate the allocation correctly, the financial statements can be materially misstated. The allocation of expenses such as depreciation of fixed assets and amortization of copyrights is required because the life of the asset is greater than one year. The original cost of the asset is verified at the time of acquisition, but the charge-off takes place over several years.

Other types of allocations directly affecting the financial statements arise because the life of a short-lived asset does not expire on the balance sheet date. These may include prepaid rent and insurance. Finally, accounting standards require the allocation of costs between current period manufacturing expenses and inventory as a means of reflecting all costs of making a product.

In auditing the allocation of expenditures such as prepaid insurance and manufacturing overhead, the two most important considerations are adherence to accounting standards and consistency with the preceding period. The two most important audit procedures for auditing allocations are tests for overall reasonableness using analytical procedures and recalculation of the client's results.

Auditors commonly perform these tests as part of the audit of the related asset or liability accounts. This may include verifying depreciation expense as part of the audit of property, plant, and equipment, testing amortization of patents as part of verifying new patents or the disposal of existing ones, and verifying allocations between inventory and cost of goods sold as part of the audit of inventory.

SUMMARY

This chapter concludes our discussion of accounts and transactions in the acquisition and payment cycle. To adequately audit the numerous accounts associated with this cycle, auditors need an understanding of key accounts, classes of transactions, business functions, documents, and records related to acquisition and payment cycle transactions. Many of these accounts, such as accounts payable, property, plant, and equipment, depreciation expense, and prepaid expenses, have unique characteristics that affect how the auditor gathers sufficient appropriate evidence about related account balances. And, finally, interrelationships between different audit tests in the acquisition and payment cycle can provide a basis for the auditor's verification of many financial statement accounts.

ESSENTIAL TERMS

Accrued liabilities   p. 659

Allocation   p. 664

Expense account analysis   p. 662

Fixed asset master file   p. 649

Insurance register   p. 657

19-1 (Objective 19-2) Explain the relationship between substantive tests of transactions for the acquisition and payment cycle and tests of details of balances for the verification of property, plant, and equipment. Which aspects of property, plant, and equipment are directly affected by the tests of controls and substantive tests of transactions and which are not?

19-2 (Objective 19-2) Explain why the emphasis in auditing property, plant, and equipment is on the current period acquisitions and disposals rather than on the balances in the account carried forward from the preceding year. Under what circumstances will the emphasis be on the balances carried forward?

19-3 (Objective 19-2) What is the relationship between the audit of property, plant, and equipment accounts and the audit of repair and maintenance accounts? Explain how the auditor organizes the audit to take this relationship into consideration.

19-4 (Objective 19-2) List and briefly state the purpose of all audit procedures that might reasonably be applied by an auditor to determine that all property, plant, and equipment retirements have been recorded in the accounting system.

19-5 (Objective 19-2) In auditing depreciation expense, what major considerations should the auditor keep in mind? Explain how each can be verified.

19-6 (Objective 19-3) Explain the relationship between substantive tests of transactions for the acquisition and payment cycle and tests of details of balances for the verification of prepaid insurance.

19-7 (Objective 19-3) Explain why the audit of prepaid insurance should ordinarily take a relatively small amount of audit time if the client's assessed control risk for acquisitions is low.

19-8 (Objective 19-3) Distinguish between the evaluation of the adequacy of insurance coverage and the verification of prepaid insurance. Explain which is more important in a typical audit.

19-9 (Objective 19-3) What are the major differences between the audit of prepaid expenses and other asset accounts such as accounts receivable or property, plant, and equipment?

19-10 (Objective 19-4) Explain the relationship between accrued rent and substantive tests of transactions for the acquisition and payment cycle. Which aspects of accrued rent are not verified as part of the substantive tests of transactions?

19-11 (Objective 19-4) In verifying accounts payable, it is common to restrict the audit sample to a small portion of the population items, whereas in auditing accrued property taxes, it is common to verify all transactions for the year. Explain the reason for the difference.

19-12 (Objective 19-4) Which documents will be used to verify accrued property taxes and the related expense accounts?

19-13 (Objective 19-5) List three expense accounts that are tested as part of the acquisition and payment cycle or the payroll and personnel cycle. List three expense accounts that are not directly verified as part of the cycle.

19-14 (Objective 19-5) What is meant by the analysis of expense accounts? Explain how expense account analysis relates to the tests of controls and substantive tests of transactions that the auditor has already completed for the acquisition and payment cycle.

19-15 (Objectives 19-2, 19-5) How will the approach for verifying repair expense differ from that used to audit depreciation expense? Why will the approach be different?

MULTIPLE CHOICE QUESTIONS FROM CPA EXAMINATIONS

19-16 (Objective 19-2) The following questions concern internal controls in the acquisition and payment cycle. Choose the best response.

a. Which of the following controls most likely will justify a reduced assessed level of control risk concerning plant and equipment acquisitions?
   (1) Periodic physical inspection of plant and equipment by the internal audit staff.
   (2) Comparison of current-year plant and equipment account balances with prior year balances.
   (3) Review of prenumbered purchase orders to detect unrecorded trade-ins.
   (4) Approval of periodic depreciation entries by a supervisor independent of the accounting department.

b. Which of the following is not an internal control deficiency related to factory equipment?
   (1) Checks issued in payment of acquisitions of equipment are *not* signed by the controller.
   (2) All acquisitions of factory equipment are required to be made by the department in need of the equipment.
   (3) Factory equipment replacements are generally made when estimated useful lives, as indicated in depreciation schedules, have expired.
   (4) Proceeds from sales of fully depreciated equipment are credited to other income.

c. With respect to an internal control measure that will ensure accountability for fixed asset retirements, management should implement controls that include
   (1) continuous analysis of miscellaneous revenue to locate any cash proceeds from sale of plant assets.
   (2) periodic inquiry of plant executives by internal auditors as to whether any plant assets have been retired.
   (3) continuous use of serially numbered retirement work orders.
   (4) periodic observation of plant assets by the internal auditors.

19-17 (Objectives 19-2, 19-5) The following questions concern analytical procedures in the acquisition and payment cycle. Choose the best response.

a. Which of the following comparisons will be most useful to an auditor in auditing an entity's income and expense accounts?
   (1) Prior year accounts payable to current year accounts payable.
   (2) Prior year payroll expense to budgeted current year payroll expense.
   (3) Current year revenue to budgeted current year revenue.
   (4) Current year warranty expense to current year contingent liabilities.

b. The controller of Darwish Manufacturing, Inc. wants to use analytical procedures to identify the possible existence of idle equipment or the possibility that equipment has been disposed of without having been written off. Which of the following ratios will best accomplish this objective?
   (1) Depreciation expense/book value of manufacturing equipment.
   (2) Accumulated depreciation/book value of manufacturing equipment.
   (3) Repairs and maintenance cost/direct labor costs.
   (4) Gross manufacturing equipment cost/units produced.

c. Which of the following analytical procedures should be applied to the income statement?
   (1) Select sales and expense items and trace amounts to related supporting documents.
   (2) Ascertain that the net income amount in the statement of cash flows agrees with the net income amount in the income statement.
   (3) Obtain from the proper client representatives the beginning and ending inventory amounts that were used to determine costs of sales.
   (4) Compare the actual revenues and expenses with the corresponding figures of the previous year and investigate significant differences.

19-18 (Objective 19-2) The following questions concern the audit of asset accounts in the acquisition and payment cycle. Choose the best response.

a. In testing for unrecorded retirements of equipment, an auditor most likely will
   (1) select items of equipment from the accounting records and then locate them during the plant tour.
   (2) compare depreciation journal entries with similar prior year entries in search of fully depreciated equipment.
   (3) inspect items of equipment observed during the plant tour and then trace them to the equipment master file.
   (4) scan the general journal for unusual equipment additions and excessive debits to repairs and maintenance expense.

b. Analysis of which account is *least* likely to reveal evidence related to unrecorded retirement of equipment?
   (1) Accumulated depreciation.
   (2) Insurance expense.
   (3) Property, plant, and equipment.
   (4) Purchase returns and allowances.

c. In connection with the audit of the prepaid insurance account, which of the following procedures is usually not performed by the auditor?
   (1) Recompute the portion of the premium that expired during the year.
   (2) Prepare excerpts of the insurance policies for audit documentation.
   (3) Confirm premium rates with an independent insurance broker.
   (4) Examine support for premium payments.

19-19 (Objectives 19-2, 19-4, 19-5) The following questions concern the audit of liabilities or income and expense accounts. Choose the best response.

a. Which of the following audit procedures is least likely to detect an unrecorded liability?
   (1) Analysis and recomputation of interest expense.
   (2) Analysis and recomputation of depreciation expense.
   (3) Mailing of standard bank confirmation forms.
   (4) Reading of the minutes of meetings of the board of directors.

b. Which of the following *best* describes the independent auditor's approach to obtaining satisfaction concerning depreciation expense in the income statement?
   (1) Verify the mathematical accuracy of the amounts charged to income as a result of depreciation expense.
   (2) Determine the method for computing depreciation expense and ascertain that it is in accordance with accounting standards.
   (3) Reconcile the amount of depreciation expense to those amounts credited to accumulated depreciation accounts.
   (4) Establish the basis for depreciable assets and verify the depreciation expense.

c. Before expressing an opinion concerning the audit of income and expenses, the auditor will *best* proceed with the audit of the income statement by
   (1) applying a rigid measurement standard designed to test for understatement of net income.
   (2) analyzing the beginning and ending balance sheet inventory amounts.
   (3) making net income comparisons to published industry trends and ratios.
   (4) auditing income statement accounts concurrently with the related balance sheet accounts.

DISCUSSION QUESTIONS AND PROBLEMS

19-20 (Objective 19-2) For each of the following misstatements in property, plant, and equipment accounts, state an internal control that the client can implement to prevent the misstatement from occurring and a substantive audit procedure that the auditor can use to discover the misstatement:

1. The asset lives used to depreciate equipment are less than reasonable, expected useful lives.

2. Capitalizable assets are routinely expensed as repairs and maintenance, perishable tools, or supplies expense.
3. Acquisitions of property are recorded at incorrect amounts.
4. A loan against existing equipment is not recorded in the accounting records. The cash receipts from the loan never reached the company because they were used for the down payment on a piece of equipment now being used as an operating asset. The equipment is also not recorded in the records.
5. Computer equipment that is abandoned or traded for replacement equipment is not removed from the accounting records.
6. Depreciation expense for manufacturing operations is charged to administrative expenses.
7. Tools necessary for the maintenance of equipment are stolen by company employees for their personal use.

19-21 (Objectives 19-1, 19-2, 19-3, 19-5) The following audit procedures were planned by Karim Abdel Gaber, CPA, in the audit of the acquisition and payment cycle for Sunny Products, Inc.:

1. Review the acquisitions journal for large and unusual transactions.
2. Send letters to several vendors, including a few for which the recorded accounts payable balance is zero, requesting them to inform us of their balance due from Sunny. Ask the controller to sign the letter.
3. Examine a sample of receiving report numbers and determine whether each one has an initial indicating that it was recorded as an account payable.
4. Select a sample of equipment listed on fixed asset master files and inspect the asset to determine that it exists and to determine its condition.
5. Refoot the acquisitions journal for one month and trace all totals to the general ledger.
6. Calculate the ratio of equipment repairs and maintenance to total equipment and compare with previous years.
7. Obtain from the client a written statement that all mortgages payable have been included in the current period financial statements and have been accurately recorded and that the collateral for each is included in the footnotes.
8. Select a sample of cancelled checks and trace each one to the cash disbursements journal, comparing the name, date, and amount.
9. For 20 nontangible acquisitions, select a sample of line items from the acquisitions journal and trace each to related vendors' invoices. Examine whether each transaction appears to be a legitimate expenditure for the client and that each was approved and recorded at the correct amount and date in the journal and charged to the correct account per the chart of accounts.
10. Examine invoices and related shipping documents included in the client's unpaid invoice file at the audit report date to determine whether they were recorded in the appropriate accounting period and at the correct amounts.
11. Recalculate the portion of insurance premiums on the client's prepaid insurance schedule that is applicable to future periods.
12. When the check signer's assistant writes 'paid' on supporting documents, watch whether she does it after the documents are reviewed and the checks are signed.

Required

a. For each procedure, identify the type of evidence being used.

b. For each procedure, identify whether it is an analytical procedure, a test of control, a substantive test of transactions, or a test of details of balances.

c. For each test of control or substantive test of transactions, identify the transaction-related audit objective(s) being met.

d. For each test of details of balances, identify the balance-related audit objective(s) being met.

19-22 (Objective 19-2) The following types of internal controls are commonly used by organizations for property, plant, and equipment:

1. A fixed asset master file is maintained with a separate record for each fixed asset.

2. Written policies exist and are known by accounting personnel to differentiate between capitalizable additions, freight, installation costs, replacements, and maintenance expenditures.

3. Depreciation charges for individual assets are calculated for each asset; recorded in a fixed asset master file that includes cost, depreciation, and accumulated depreciation for each asset; and verified periodically by an independent clerk.

4. Acquisitions of fixed assets in excess of US$20,000 are approved by the board of directors.

5. When practical, equipment is labeled with metal tags and is inventoried on a systematic basis.

a. State the purpose of each of the internal controls just listed. Your answer should be in the form of the type of misstatement that is likely to be reduced because of the control. **Required**

b. For each internal control, list one test of control the auditor can use to test for its existence.

c. List one substantive procedure for testing whether the control is actually preventing misstatements in property, plant, and equipment.

CASES

Arabian Publishing Company—Part III (See Case 18-27 for Parts I and II)

19-23 (Objectives 19-1, 19-2, 19-5) Examine the tests of controls and substantive tests of transactions results, including the sampling application in Case 18-27 (pp. 644–646), for Arabian Publishing Company. Assume that you have already reached several conclusions.

1. Your tests of details of balances for accounts payable are completed, and you found no exceptions.

2. Acceptable audit risk for property, plant, and equipment and all expenses is high.

3. Inherent risk for property, plant, and equipment is high because in the current year, the client has acquired a material amount of new and used printing equipment and has traded in older equipment. Some of the new equipment was ineffective and returned; an allowance was received on others. Inherent risk for expense accounts is low.

4. New computer equipment and some printing equipment are being leased. The client has never leased equipment before.

5. Analytical procedures for property, plant, and equipment are inconclusive because of the large increases in acquisition and disposal activity.

6. Analytical procedures show that repairs, maintenance, and small tools expenses have increased materially, both in absolute terms and as a percentage of sales. Two other expenses have also materially increased, and one has materially decreased.

7. In examining the sample for tests of controls and substantive tests of transactions, you observe that no sample items included any property, plant, and equipment or lease transactions.

a. Explain the relationship between the tests of controls and substantive tests of transactions results in Case 18-27 and the audit of property, plant, and equipment and leases. **Required**

b. How will the tests of controls and substantive tests of transactions results and your conclusions (1 through 7) affect your planned tests of details for property, plant, and equipment and leases? State your conclusions for each balance-related audit objective. Do not write an audit program.

c. Explain the relationship between the tests of controls and substantive tests of transactions results in Case 18-27 and the audit of expenses.

d. How will the tests of controls and substantive tests of transactions results and your conclusions (1 through 7) affect your planned tests of details of balances for expenses? Do not write an audit program.

19-24 (Objective 19-2) You are doing the audit of the Zarrouk Corporation for the year ended December 31, 2011. The following schedule for the property, plant, and equipment and related allowance for depreciation accounts has been prepared by the client. You have compared the opening balances with your prior year's audit documentation.

**Zarrouk Corporation Analysis of Property, Plant, and Equipment
and Related Allowance for Depreciation Accounts
Year Ended December 31, 2011**

Description	Final Dec 31, 2010	Additions	Retirements	Per Books Dec 31, 2011
Assets				
Land	US$ 225,000	US$ 50,000		US$ 275,000
Buildings	1,200,000	175,000		1,375,000
Machinery and equipment	3,850,000	404,000	260,000	3,994,000
	US$5,275,000	US$629,000	US$260,000	US$5,644,000
Allowance for Depreciation				
Building	US$ 600,000	US$ 51,500		US$ 651,500
Machinery and equipment	1,732,500	392,200		2,124,700
	US$2,332,500	US$443,700		US$2,776,200

The following information is found during your audit:

1. All equipment is depreciated on the straight-line basis (no salvage value taken into consideration) based on the following estimated lives: buildings, 25 years; all other items, ten years. The corporation's policy is to take one-half year's depreciation on all asset acquisitions and disposals during the year.

2. On April 1, the corporation entered into a ten-year lease contract for a die-casting machine with annual rentals of US$50,000, payable in advance every April 1. The lease is cancelable by either party (60 days' written notice is required), and there is no option to renew the lease or buy the equipment at the end of the lease. The estimated useful life of the machine is ten years with no salvage value. The corporation recorded the die-casting machine in the machinery and equipment account at US$404,000, the present value at the date of the lease, and US$20,200, applicable to the machine, has been included in depreciation expense for the year.

3. The corporation completed the construction of a wing on the plant building on June 30. The useful life of the building was not extended by this addition. The lowest construction bid received was US$175,000, the amount recorded in the buildings account. Company personnel were used to construct the addition at a cost of US$160,000 (materials, US$75,000; labor, US$55,000; and overhead, US$30,000).

4. On August 18, US$50,000 was paid for paving and fencing a portion of land owned by the corporation and used as a parking lot for employees. The expenditure was charged to the land account.

5. The amount shown in the machinery and equipment asset retirement column represents cash received on September 5, upon disposal of a machine acquired in July 2007 for US$480,000. The bookkeeper recorded depreciation expense of US$35,000 on this machine in 2009.

6. Sfaxcity donated land and building appraised at US$100,000 and US$400,000, respectively, to the Zarrouk Corporation for a plant. On September 1, the corporation began operating the plant. Because no costs were involved, the bookkeeper made no entry for the foregoing transaction.

Required

a. In addition to inquiry of the client, explain how you would have found each of these six items during the audit.

b. Prepare the adjusting journal entries with supporting computations that you would suggest at December 31, 2011, to adjust the accounts for the preceding transactions. Disregard income tax implications.[20]

CHAPTER 20

AUDIT OF THE PAYROLL AND PERSONNEL CYCLE

The Staff Auditor Must Never 'Simply Follow Orders'

Sherif Osman graduated with a Masters of Accountancy degree from a major university before joining the audit staff of an auditing firm. During his first 'busy season,' he worked on the audit of SyscoME, Inc., a software development company. His immediate supervisor on the SyscoME audit was Kamel Mokhtar. Kamel had been with the firm three years longer than Sherif and worked on the SyscoME audit the previous year. He supervised Sherif's work on capitalized software development costs.

To prepare, Sherif read IFRS No. 7 and had a good understanding of the accounting rules for the capitalization of such costs. He understood, for example, that costs cannot be capitalized until technological feasibility has been established, either through detail program design or product design and the completion of a working model, confirmed by testing.

Kamel drafted an audit program for capitalized software development costs. He told Sherif to verify the payroll costs that were a significant part of the development cost and to talk to Ismail Sallam, SyscoME's controller, about whether the projects with capitalized costs had reached the technological feasibility stage. Sherif tested the payroll costs and found no misstatements. He also made inquiries of Ismail and was told that the appropriate stage was reached. Sherif documented Ismail's representation in the audit files and went on to the next area assigned to him.

Later, Sherif began to have second thoughts. Because management's representations are a weak form of audit evidence, he doubted whether Ismail Sallam was the most knowledgeable person about the technical status of software projects. To resolve his concerns and to verify Ismail's representations, he decided to talk to the responsible software engineers about one of the projects. He intended to clear this with Kamel, but he was at another client's office that morning, so he proceeded on his own initiative. The engineer he talked to on the first project told him that he was almost finished with a working model but had not tested it yet. He decided to inquire about another project and discovered the same thing. Sherif documented these findings on an audit schedule and planned to discuss the situation with Kamel as soon as he returned to the job. When Sherif told Kamel of his findings and showed him the schedule, Kamel told him the following:

"Listen, Sherif, I told you to just talk to Ismail. You shouldn't do procedures that you're not instructed to do. I want you to destroy this schedule and don't record the wasted time. We're under a lot of time pressure and we can't bill SyscoME for procedures that aren't necessary. There's nothing wrong with the capitalized software development costs. The fact that they have working products that they're selling indicates technological feasibility was reached."

Sherif was extremely distressed with this reaction from Kamel but followed his instructions. The following autumn, the local supervisory board conducted an investigation of SyscoME and found, among other things, that the company had overstated capitalized software development costs. The supervisory board brought an action against both the management of SyscoME and its auditors.

LEARNING OBJECTIVES

After studying this chapter, you should be able to

20-1 Identify the accounts and transactions in the payroll and personnel cycle.

20-2 Describe the business functions and the related documents and records in the payroll and personnel cycle.

20-3 Understand internal control and design and perform tests of controls and substantive tests of transactions for the payroll and personnel cycle.

20-4 Design and perform analytical procedures for the payroll and personnel cycle.

20-5 Design and perform tests of details of balances for accounts in the payroll and personnel cycle.

Payroll and personnel cycle

The transaction cycle that begins with the hiring of personnel, includes obtaining and accounting for services from the employees, and ends with payment to the employees for the services performed and to the government and other institutions for withheld and accrued payroll taxes and benefits.

The **payroll and personnel cycle** involves the employment and payment of all employees. Labor is an important consideration in the valuation of inventory in manufacturing, construction, and other industries. As the story involving Sherif Osman and the audit of SyscoME, Inc. demonstrates, improper valuation and allocation of labor can result in a material misstatement of net income. Payroll is also an area in which company resources can be wasted because of inefficiency or stolen through fraud.

As with the sales and collection, and acquisition and payment cycles, the audit of the payroll and personnel cycle includes obtaining an understanding of internal control, assessing control risk, tests of controls and substantive tests of transactions, analytical procedures, and tests of details of balances. In a typical audit, the main differences between the payroll and personnel cycle and other cycles include:

- *There is only one class of transactions for payroll.* Most cycles include at least two classes of transactions. For example, the sales and collection cycle includes both sales and cash receipts transactions, and often includes sales returns and charge-off of uncollectible accounts. Payroll has only one class because the receipt of services from employees and the payment for those services through payroll usually occur within a short time period.
- *Transactions are generally far more significant than related balance sheet accounts.* Payroll-related accounts such as accrued payroll and withheld taxes are usually small compared to the total amount of transactions for the year.
- *Internal controls over payroll are effective for almost all companies, even small ones.* Harsh government penalties encourage effective controls for withholding and paying payroll taxes. Also, employee morale problems can occur if employees are not paid or are underpaid.

Because of these three characteristics, auditors typically emphasize tests of controls, substantive tests of transactions, and analytical procedures in the audit of payroll. Tests of details of balances take only a few minutes for most payroll-related accounts. Before we discuss the tests in the cycle, let's review the transactions and account balances, as well as the documents and records used in the payroll and personnel cycle for a typical company.

Relevant International Standards on Auditing	
ISA 200	Overall Objectives of the Independent Auditor and the Conduct of an Audit in Accordance with International Standards on Auditing
ISA 230	Audit Documentation
ISA 265	Communicating Deficiencies in Internal Control to Those Charged with Governance and Management
ISA 300	Planning an Audit of Financial Statements
ISA 320	Materiality in Planning and Performing an Audit
ISA 450	Evaluation of Misstatements Identified during the Audit
ISA 500	Audit Evidence
ISA 520	Analytical Procedures
ISA 580	Written Representations

ACCOUNTS AND TRANSACTIONS IN THE PAYROLL AND PERSONNEL CYCLE

OBJECTIVE 20-1

Identify the accounts and transactions in the payroll and personnel cycle.

The overall objective in the audit of the payroll and personnel cycle is, of course, to evaluate whether the account balances affected by the cycle are fairly stated in accordance with applicable accounting standards.

Typical accounts in the payroll and personnel cycle are shown in Figure 20-1. T accounts are used to illustrate the way in which accounting information flows through

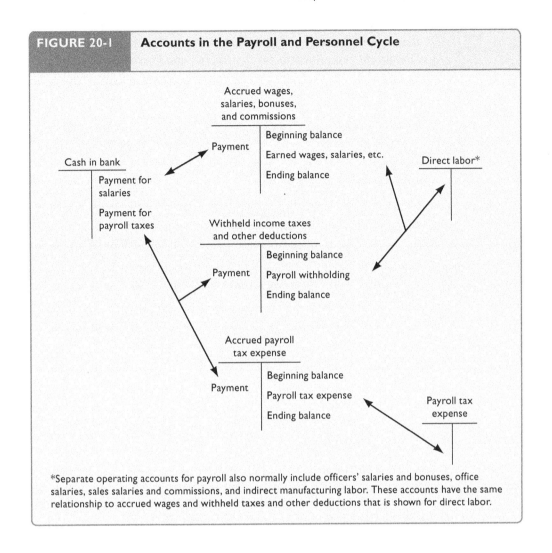

FIGURE 20-1   Accounts in the Payroll and Personnel Cycle

*Separate operating accounts for payroll also normally include officers' salaries and bonuses, office salaries, sales salaries and commissions, and indirect manufacturing labor. These accounts have the same relationship to accrued wages and withheld taxes and other deductions that is shown for direct labor.

the various accounts in the payroll and personnel cycle. In most systems, the accrued wages and salaries account is used only at the end of an accounting period. Throughout the period, expenses are charged when the employees are actually paid rather than when the labor costs are incurred. Accruals for labor are recorded by adjusting entries at the end of the period for any earned but unpaid labor costs.

BUSINESS FUNCTIONS IN THE CYCLE AND RELATED DOCUMENTS AND RECORDS

The payroll and personnel cycle begins with hiring employees and ends with paying them for the services they performed and the government and other institutions for withheld and accrued payroll taxes and benefits. In between, the cycle involves obtaining services from employees consistent with company objectives, and properly accounting for the services.

The third column in Table 20-1 identifies the four business functions in a typical payroll and personnel cycle and illustrates the relationships among the business functions, classes of transactions, accounts, and documents and records. Auditors must understand the business functions and documents and records before they can assess control risk and design tests of controls and substantive tests of transactions.

> **OBJECTIVE 20-2**
>
> Describe the business functions and the related documents and records in the payroll and personnel cycle.

TABLE 20-1	Classes of Transactions, Accounts, Business Functions, and Related Documents and Records for the Payroll and Personnel Cycle			
Class of Transactions	Accounts	Business Functions	Documents and Records
Payroll	Payroll cash All payroll expense accounts All payroll withholding accounts All payroll accrual accounts	Personnel and employment	Personnel records Deduction authorization form Rate authorization form
		Timekeeping and payroll preparation	Time card Job time ticket Payroll transaction file Payroll journal or listing Payroll master file
		Payment of payroll	Payroll check Payroll bank account reconciliation
		Preparation of payroll tax returns and payment of taxes	Payroll tax returns forms

Personnel and Employment

The human resources department provides an independent source for interviewing and hiring qualified personnel. The department is also an independent source of records for the internal verification of wage information, including additions and deletions from the payroll and changes in wages and deductions.

Personnel records

Records that include such data as the date of employment, personnel investigations, rates of pay, authorized deductions, performance evaluations, and termination of employment.

Personnel Records **Personnel records** include such data as the date of employment, personnel investigations, rates of pay, authorized deductions, performance evaluations, and terminations of employment. Figure 20-2 shows an example of an employee payroll sheet.

Deduction Authorization Form This form is used to authorize payroll deductions.

Rate Authorization Form This form is used to authorize the rate of pay. The source of the information is a labor contract, authorization by management, or in the case of officers, authorization from the board of directors.

Timekeeping and Payroll Preparation

Timekeeping and payroll preparation are important in the audit of payroll because they directly affect payroll expense for each period. Adequate controls are necessary to prevent misstatements in the following four activities:

- Prepare time cards by employees
- Summarize and calculate gross pay, deductions, and net pay
- Prepare payroll checks
- Prepare payroll records

Time card

A document indicating the time that the employee started and stopped working each day and the number of hours worked.

Time Card The **time card** is a document indicating the time the hourly employee started and stopped working each day and the number of hours the employee worked.

FIGURE 20-2	Employee Payroll Sheet

Salary for: 11/ 2010 **Employee Code: 65568**

	US $		US $
Total Basic	5750.00	**Gross Salary**	**5750.00**
Incentive	0.00	Social Security	33.72
Work Days	0.00	Health Insurance	0.00
Overtime	0.00	Exempted Special Raises	1787.15
Job Bonus	0.00	**Sub Total**	**3929.13**
Other Allowance	0.00	Personal Limit	57.79
Living Allowance	0.00	Family Limit	72.24
Desert Allowance	0.00	**Taxable Income**	**3799.10**
Transportation Allowance	0.00	First 15000.00 10.00%	21.67
Previous Raise	0.00	Second 20000.00 15.00%	43.34
Deductions Before	0.00	And 20.00% for the remainder	658.68
Gross Salary	**5750.00**	**Total Tax**	**723.69**
Social Security	33.72		
Total Tax	723.70		
Phone Bill	0.00		US $
Other Deductions	2037.17	Social Salary	138.70
Lunch Subsidy	0.00	Social Allowance	130.03
Net Salary	**2955.41**	26.00% Co. share on Basic	36.06
Bank Accounts	**US $**	11.00% Co. share Allow	31.21
	2955.41	1% Other Co. share on Basic	1.39
		Total Company Share	**68.66**
Prepared by: John Salib		14.00% Emp. Share on Basic	19.42
		11.00% Emp. Share on Allow	14.30
Reviewed by: Mohamed Tawila		**Total Employee Share**	**33.72**
		Quarterly Amount	0.00
Approved by: Yasmine Salah		**Total Social**	**102.38**

Time cards may be in paper or electronic form, and they may be prepared automatically by time clocks or identification card readers. Time cards are usually submitted weekly.

Salaried or exempt employees usually do not complete time cards, but may be required to complete time reports to be compensated for overtime, vacation, or sick days.

Job Time Ticket The job time ticket is a form indicating which jobs an employee worked on during a given time period. This form is used only when an employee works on different jobs or in different departments. Job time tickets are often done electronically by a time and expense reporting system.

Payroll Transaction File This computer-generated file includes all payroll transactions processed by the accounting system for a period, such as a day, week, or month. The file contains all information entered into the system and information for each transaction, such as employee name and identification number, date, gross and net pay, various withholding amounts, and account classification or classifications.

GHOSTS ON THE PAYROLL

Melvin Turner was extremely ill and needed expensive medicines to treat his condition. He was responsible for recording payroll hours and preparing payroll records at the not-for-profit organization where he was employed. A separate employee was responsible for adding and deleting employees to the payroll system. However, Turner circumvented this control by looking over her shoulder to steal her user ID and password, allowing him to add fictitious employees to the payroll.

After adding the 'ghost' employees to the payroll, Turner entered wage and other relevant information and arranged for direct deposit of the fictitious employees' pay to his own bank account. He also created fictitious documentation for the ghost employees' work, as well as file copies of the paychecks.

The fraud was detected by the organization's external auditor, who noted that the file copies of the fictitious checks were white, but the file copies of legitimate checks were green. Several additional clues indicated the presence of the fraud:

- Multiple direct deposits were made to the same bank account but under different employees' names.
- None of the fake employees had a personnel file or amounts withheld.
- Employee numbers for the ghost employees were higher than those of other employees.

Confronted with the evidence, Turner pleaded guilty to the charges. Under a plea bargain agreement, he was ordered to make restitution and was sentenced to 15 years of probation.

Source: Joseph T. Wells, 'Keep Ghosts Off the Payroll,' *Journal of Accountancy* (December 2002), pp. 77–82.

The information on the payroll transaction file is used for a variety of records, listings, and reports, such as the payroll journal, payroll master file, and payroll bank reconciliation.

Payroll Journal or Listing This report is generated from the payroll transaction file and typically includes the employee name, date, gross and net payroll amounts, withholding amounts, and account classification or classifications for each transaction. The same transactions included in the journal or listing are also posted simultaneously to the general ledger and to the payroll master file.

Payroll master file

A computer file for recording each payroll transaction for each employee and maintaining total employee wages paid and related data for the year to date.

Payroll Master File The **payroll master file** is a computer file used for recording payroll transactions for each employee and maintaining total employee wages paid for the year to date. The record for each employee includes gross pay for each payroll period, deductions from gross pay, net pay, check number, and date. This master file is updated from payroll transaction files. The total of the individual employee earnings in the master file equals the total balance of gross payroll in various general ledger accounts. Figure 20-3 shows a monthly salary report sorted by department for the period December 2010.

Payment of Payroll

The signing and distribution of payroll must be carefully controlled to prevent theft. To increase control, payroll checks are generally processed separately from other disbursements.

Payroll Check A payroll check is written to an employee in exchange for services performed. The amount of the check is the gross pay less taxes and other deductions withheld including amount deducted for social security. The check is prepared as part of the payroll preparation function, but an authorized signature makes the check an asset. After a payroll check is cashed by an employee, the cancelled check is returned to the company from the bank. Payroll checks are often deposited directly into employees' individual bank accounts.

FIGURE 20-3	**Monthly Salary Report Sorted by Department for the Period December 2010**								
ID	Employee name	Position Title	Basic salary / Social Insurance	Overtime / Health Insurance	Job bonus / Phone bill	Desert allowance / Pers. Adv	Transp. allowance / Other deduct	Other allowance / Salary taxes	Gross salary	Net salary
15	Mostafa Sarhan	Accountant (Collections)	1,258.09 / 33.78	0.00 / 0.00	0.00 / 83.90	0.00 / 0.00	0.00 / 404.33	0.00 / 97.08	1,258.09	530.91
19	Ahmed Ibrahim	Country Financial Controller	6,019.46 / 33.78	0.00 / 0.00	0.00 / 0.00	0.00 / 0.00	0.00 / 2,061.00	0.00 / 723.57	6,019.46	2,931.65
22	Mamdouh Samer	Senior Banking Clerk	767.89 / 33.78	0.00 / 0.00	0.00 / 0.00	0.00 / 0.00	0.00 / 0.00	0.00 / 40.41	767.89	625.90
28	Sami Sedky	Accountant (Collections)	969.25 / 33.78	41.30 / 0.00	0.00 / 53.04	0.00 / 0.00	0.00 / 18.00	0.00 / 94.33	1,010.55	811.40
29	Alaa Radwan	Accountant (Treasury)	600.00 / 33.78	250.57 / 0.00	0.00 / 11.88	0.00 / 0.00	0.00 / 0.00	0.00 / 77.61	850.57	727.30
34	Shaker Adel	Portfolio Financial Manager	3,180.00 / 33.78	0.00 / 0.00	0.00 / 111.08	0.00 / 0.00	0.00 / 54.00	0.00 / 323.74	3,180.00	2,327.41
49	Mohy Sayed	Admin Clerk	550.42 / 33.78	0.00 / 0.00	0.00 / 0.00	0.00 / 0.00	0.00 / 0.00	0.00 / 0.00	550.42	442.16
100	Abdel Rahman Shawky	Credit Controller	3,058.52 / 33.78	0.00 / 0.00	0.00 / 15.52	0.00 / 0.00	0.00 / 180.00	0.00 / 350.02	3,058.52	2,270.68

Payroll Bank Account Reconciliation An independent bank reconciliation is important for all cash accounts, including payroll, for finding errors and fraud. An **imprest payroll account** is a separate payroll account in which a small balance is maintained. The exact amount of each net payroll is transferred by check or electronic funds transfer from the general account to the imprest account immediately before distribution of the payroll. The imprest account limits the client's exposure to payroll fraud, allows the delegation of payroll check-signing duties, and separates routine payroll expenditures from other expenditures. It also simplifies reconciliation of the payroll bank account.

Imprest payroll account

A bank account to which the exact amount of payroll for the pay period is transferred by check or wire transfer from the employer's general cash account.

Preparation of Payroll Tax Returns and Payment of Taxes

Government tax laws require the timely preparation and mailing of payroll tax returns. Most computerized payroll systems prepare payroll tax returns using information on the payroll transaction and master files. To prevent misstatements and potential liability for taxes and penalties, a competent individual must independently verify the output.

Payroll Tax Returns These are forms submitted to tax authorities in most of the Arab countries to show payment of withheld taxes and the employer's tax. The form used is prepared from information on the payroll master file and is usually computer generated. Government withholding and social security payments are due monthly or quarterly, depending on the requirements of the tax and social security laws in various Arab countries, in addition to the amount of withholding.

METHODOLOGY FOR DESIGNING TESTS OF CONTROLS AND SUBSTANTIVE TESTS OF TRANSACTIONS

OBJECTIVE 20-3

Understand internal control and design and perform tests of controls and substantive tests of transactions for the payroll and personnel cycle.

The methodology for designing tests of controls and substantive tests of transactions for the payroll and personnel cycle is the same as that used for both the sales and collection cycle and in the acquisition and payment cycle: understand internal control, assess planned control risk, determine the extent of testing of controls, and design tests of controls and substantive tests of transactions to meet transaction-related audit objectives.

Internal control for payroll is normally highly structured and well controlled to manage cash disbursed, to minimize employee complaints and dissatisfaction, and to minimize payroll fraud. Payroll checks and all related journals and payroll records are usually processed by computer. Because of relatively common payroll concerns from company to company, high-quality computer systems are available.

It is usually not difficult for companies to establish good control in the payroll and personnel cycle. For factory and office employees, there are usually a large number of relatively homogeneous, small-amount transactions. For executives, there are usually fewer payroll transactions, but they are ordinarily consistent in timing and amount. Consequently, auditors seldom expect to find exceptions in testing payroll transactions. Occasionally, control test deviations occur, but most monetary misstatements are corrected by internal verification controls or in response to employee complaints. Even when there are misstatements, they are rarely material.

Tests of controls and substantive tests of transactions procedures are the *most important* means of verifying account balances in the payroll and personnel cycle. These tests are emphasized because of the lack of independent third-party evidence, such as confirmation, for verifying accrued wages, withheld income taxes, accrued payroll taxes, and other balance sheet accounts. Furthermore, in most audits, the amounts in the balance sheet accounts are small and can be verified with relative ease if the auditor is confident that payroll transactions are correctly entered into the computer and payroll tax returns are correctly prepared.

Even though tests of controls and substantive tests of transactions are the most important parts of testing payroll, tests in this area are usually not extensive. Many audits have a minimal risk of material misstatements, even though payroll is often a significant part of total expenses. There are three reasons for this:

1. Employees are likely to complain to management if they are underpaid.
2. All payroll transactions are typically uniform and uncomplicated.
3. Payroll transactions are subject to audit by governments for income tax withholding, and social security.

Understand Internal Control—Payroll and Personnel Cycle

Following the same approach used in Chapter 14 for tests of sales and cash receipts transactions, the internal controls, tests of controls, and substantive tests of transactions for each transaction-related audit objective are summarized in Table 20-2. Again, you should recognize the following:

- Internal controls vary from company to company; therefore, the auditor must identify the controls, significant deficiencies, and material weaknesses for each organization.
- Controls the auditor intends to use for reducing assessed control risk must be tested with tests of controls.
- Substantive tests of transactions vary depending on the assessed control risk and the other considerations of the audit, such as the effect of payroll on inventory.

TABLE 20-2	Summary of Transaction-Related Audit Objectives, Key Controls, Tests of Controls, and Substantive Tests of Transactions for Payroll		
Transaction-Related Audit Objectives	**Key Internal Controls**	**Common Test of Controls**	**Common Substantive Tests of Transactions**
Recorded payroll payments are for work actually performed by existing employees (occurrence).	Time cards are approved by supervisor. Time clock is used to record time. Adequate personnel files are maintained. Employment is authorized. There is separation of duties among personnel, timekeeping, and payroll disbursements. Only employees existing in the computer data files are accepted when they are entered. Check is authorized before issuance.	Examine the cards for indication of approvals. Examine time cards. Review personnel policies. Examine personnel files. Review organization chart, discuss with employees, and observe duties being performed. Examine printouts of transactions rejected by the computer as having non-existent employee numbers. Examine payroll records for indication of approval.	Review the payroll journal, general ledger, and payroll earnings records for large or unusual amounts.* Compare cancelled checks with payroll journal for name, amount, and date. Examine cancelled checks for proper endorsement. Compare cancelled checks with personnel records.†
Existing payroll transactions are recorded (completeness).	Payroll checks are prenumbered and accounted for. Bank accounts are independently reconciled.	Account for a sequence of payroll checks. Discuss with employees and observe reconciliation.	Reconcile the disbursements in the payroll journal with the disbursements on the payroll bank statement. Prove the bank reconciliation.
Recorded payroll transactions are for the amount of time actually worked and are at the proper pay rates; withholdings are correctly calculated (accuracy).	Calculations and amounts are internally verified. Batch totals are compared with computer summary reports. Wage rate, salary, or commission rate is properly authorized. Withholdings, including amounts for insurance and payroll savings, are properly authorized.	Examine indication of internal verification. Examine file of batch totals for initials of data control clerk; compare totals to summary reports. Examine payroll records for indication of authorization. Examine authorizations in personnel file.	Recompute hours worked from time cards. Compare pay rates with union contract, approval by board of directors, or other source. Recompute gross pay. Check withholdings by referring to tax tables and authorization forms in personnel file. Recompute net pay. Compare cancelled check with payroll journal for amount.†
Payroll transactions are correctly included in the payroll master file and are correctly summarized (posting and summarization).	Payroll master file contents are internally verified. Payroll master file totals are compared with general ledger totals.	Examine indication of internal verification. Examine initialed summary total reports indicating that comparisons have been made.	Test clerical accuracy by footing the payroll journal and tracing postings to the general ledger and the payroll master file.
Payroll transactions are correctly classified (classification).	An adequate chart of accounts is used. Account classifications are internally verified.	Review chart of accounts. Examine indication of internal verification.	Compare classification with chart of accounts or procedures manual. Review time card for employee department and job ticket for job assignment and trace through to labor distribution.
Payroll transactions are recorded on the correct dates (timing).	Procedures require recording transactions as soon as possible after the payroll is paid. Dates are internally verified.	Examine procedures manual and observe when recording takes place. Examine indication of internal verification.	Compare date of recorded check in the payroll journal with date on cancelled check and time card. Compare date on check with date the check cleared the bank.†
Payroll transactions pertain to the company (obligations).	Proper approval for payroll transactions. Payroll transctions are for actual employees.	Examine payroll transactions for proper approval. Examine payroll documents.	Examine payroll transactions for supporting documents.

*This analytical procedure can also apply to other objectives, including completeness, accuracy, and timing.
†If check is direct deposited, other procedures are used to verify existence, accuracy, and timing of payment.

- Tests are not actually performed in the order given in Table 20-2. The tests of controls and substantive tests of transactions are combined when appropriate and are performed in as convenient a manner as possible, using an appropriate audit program.

The purposes of many internal controls and the nature of the tests of controls and substantive tests of transactions are apparent for most tests from their descriptions in Table 20-2. Next, the key controls for the payroll and personnel cycle for assessing control risk are discussed.

Adequate Separation of Duties Separation of duties is important in the payroll and personnel cycle, especially to prevent overpayments and payments to nonexistent employees. The payroll function should be kept independent of the human resources department, which controls key payroll activities, such as adding and deleting employees. Payroll processing should also be separate from the custody of signed payroll checks.

Proper Authorization As already noted, only the human resources department should be authorized to add and delete employees from the payroll or change pay rates and deductions. The number of hours worked by each employee, especially overtime, should be authorized by the employee's supervisor. Approval may be noted on all time cards or done on an exception basis only for overtime hours.

Adequate Documents and Records The appropriate documents and records depend on the nature of the payroll system. Time cards or records are necessary for hourly employees but not for salaried employees. For employees compensated based on piece rate or other incentive systems, different records are required. For many companies, time records must be adequate to accumulate payroll costs by job or assignment. Prenumbered documents for recording time are less of a concern for payroll because the completeness objective is normally not a concern.

Physical Control Over Assets and Records Access to unsigned payroll checks should be restricted. Checks should be signed by a responsible employee, and payroll should be distributed by someone independent of the payroll and timekeeping functions. Any unclaimed checks should be returned for redeposit. If checks are signed by a signature machine, access to the machine should be restricted.

Independent Checks on Performance Payroll computations should be independently verified, including comparison of batch totals to summary reports. A member of management or other responsible employee should review the payroll output for any obvious misstatements or unusual amounts. When manufacturing labor affects

CORRUPTION AND UNETHICAL BEHAVIOR OF AN OFFICIAL	During his official working hours, one of the officials in the supplies department of a manufacturing company contacted some of the company's suppliers and got special price offers for the products sold by these suppliers. He suggested that the suppliers execute some transactions with companies owned by his friends as well as some customers of his company. The official presented these business opportunities in return for a commission, all of	which was done without management's permission. Not only was the official doing unauthorized work in company time, but the suppliers then started to raise their product prices, as they found that there was an increased demand for their products due to the new customers introduced by the official. The manufacturing company therefore experienced increased financial burdens as a result of the official's illegal behavior.

inventory valuation or when it is necessary to accumulate costs by job, adequate controls are necessary to verify the proper assignment of costs.

Payroll Tax Forms and Payments

Payroll taxes and other withholdings are important in many companies, both because the amounts are often material and because the potential liability for failure to timely file tax forms can be severe.

Preparation of Payroll Tax Forms As a part of understanding internal control, the auditor should review the preparation of at least one of each type of payroll tax form that the client is responsible for filing. The potential for liability for unpaid taxes, penalty, and interest arises if the client fails to prepare the tax forms correctly. The payroll tax forms in the Arab countries are for such taxes as corporate tax, payroll tax, sales tax, stamp tax, income withholding, and other miscellaneous taxes.

A detailed reconciliation of the information on the tax forms and the payroll records may be necessary when the auditor believes the tax returns may be incorrectly prepared. Indications of potential misstatements in the returns include the payment of penalties and interest in the past for improper payments, new personnel in the payroll department who are responsible for the preparation of the returns, the lack of internal verification of the information, and cash flow problems for the client.

Timely Payment of the Payroll Taxes Withheld and Other Withholdings It is desirable to test whether the client has fulfilled its legal obligation in submitting payments for all payroll withholdings as a part of the payroll tests even though the payments are usually made from general cash disbursements.

Auditors must first determine the client's requirements for submitting the payments, which can be determined by referencing such sources as tax laws, union contracts, and agreements with employees. Once auditors know the requirements, they can easily determine whether the client has made timely payments at correct amounts by comparing the subsequent cash disbursement with the payroll records.

The following extracts relate to the results of the audit of the payroll cycle of an industrial company:

1. The company does not maintain an organization chart showing the level of authority and employees working in each department or division, a matter which prevented us from ensuring that employees are actually performing their jobs in the company according to their contracts.

2. The company does not follow the requirement of corporate governance as it does not have a remuneration committee composed of non-executive board members responsible for proposing the remuneration of the board's members.

3. The comparison between the total amount of wages and salaries of the administrative department and total revenues shows that such salaries represent 50% of total revenues. Such percentage exceeds the percentage used by similar companies operating in the same industry.

4. The company recorded accrued maintenance expenses for US$300,000 even though we discovered from the supporting documents that the actual amount of maintenance expense is equal to US$270,000. This is a difference of US$30,000.

5. The management did not deduct taxes withheld at source related to its transactions with advertising and promotion companies. The company incurred those advertising expenses which were reconciled with the dues of the company.

Inventory and Fraudulent Payroll Considerations

Auditors often extend their payroll audit procedures if payroll significantly affects the valuation of inventory, or when the auditor is concerned about the possibility of material fraudulent payroll transactions, such as nonexistent employees or fraudulent hours.

Relationship Between Payroll and Inventory Valuation When payroll is a significant portion of inventory, which is common for manufacturing and construction companies, the improper account classification of payroll can materially affect asset valuation for accounts such as work in process, finished goods, or construction in process. For example, the overhead charged to inventory at the balance sheet date can be overstated if the salaries of administrative personnel are inadvertently or intentionally charged to indirect manufacturing overhead. Similarly, the valuation of inventory is affected if the direct labor cost of individual employees is incorrectly charged to the wrong job or process. When jobs are billed on a cost-plus basis, revenue and the valuation of inventory are both affected by charging labor to incorrect jobs.

When labor is a material part of inventory valuation, auditors should emphasize testing internal controls over proper classification of payroll transactions. Consistency from period to period is essential for classification and can be tested by tracing job tickets or other evidence of an employee having worked on a job or process to the accounting records that affect inventory valuation. For example, if employees must account for all of their time each week by assigning it to individual jobs, a useful test is to trace the recorded hours of several employees to the related job-cost records to make sure each has been correctly recorded. It may also be desirable to trace from the job-cost records to time cards as a test for nonexistent payroll charges being included in inventory.

Tests for Nonexistent Employees Issuing payroll checks to individuals who do not work for the company (nonexistent employees) often results from the continuance of an employee's check after employment was terminated. Usually, the person committing this type of embezzlement is a payroll clerk, foreman, fellow employee, or perhaps the former employee. Under some systems, a foreman can clock in daily for an employee and approve the time card at the end of the time period. If the foreman also distributes paychecks or if payroll is deposited directly into employees' accounts, considerable opportunity exists for embezzlement.

To detect embezzlement, auditors may compare the names on cancelled checks with time cards and other records for authorized signatures and reasonableness of the endorsements. It is also common to scan endorsements on cancelled checks for unusual or recurring second endorsements as an indication of a possible fraudulent check. Examining checks that are recorded as voided is also desirable to make sure that they have not been fraudulently used.

SALARIES AND WAGES PAID FOR NONEXISTENT EMPLOYEES

A company specializing in the maintenance and cleaning of a housing compound composed of 109 villas has a maintenance contract with the management of the compound for a five-year period starting 2010. The agreement requires the company to provide maintenance and cleaning services in return for the compound management charging the residents a percentage of the costs incurred by the maintenance company on gardens maintenance, electricity and water repairs, maintaining the roads to ensure they are safe, etc.

The auditor took a sample of the salaries and wages related to services provided to the compound for examination. He found that the company had charged the compound management with salaries and wages for some employees who had not been working there at any time during the month of December 2011. The auditor uncovered these fictitious salaries and wages when he compared payroll sheets signed by the company's employees with attendance and leave sheets and the daily job orders prepared by the appropriate departments in the company relating to the cleaning and maintenance services.

Moreover, in the follow-up reports prepared by the appropriate department the auditor could not find the names of those employees. The total amount of these salaries and wages amounted to US$103,000 incorrectly charged to the compound accounts as costs of maintenance and cleaning for the compound.

To test for nonexistent employees, auditors can trace selected transactions recorded in the payroll journal to the human resources department to determine whether the employees were actually employed during the payroll period. The endorsement on the cancelled check written out to an employee can be compared with the authorized signature on the employee's withholding authorization forms.

A procedure that tests for proper handling of terminated employees is to select several files from the personnel records for employees who were terminated in the current year to determine whether each received termination pay consistent with company policy. Continuing payments to terminated employees can be tested by examining payroll records in the subsequent period to verify that the employee is no longer being paid. Naturally, this procedure is not effective if the human resources department is not informed of terminations.

In some cases, the auditor may request a surprise payroll payoff. This is a procedure in which all employees must pick up and sign their check or direct deposit payroll record in the presence of a supervisor and the auditor. Any checks that have not been claimed must be subject to an extensive investigation to determine whether an unclaimed check is fraudulent. Surprise payoff is often expensive but it may be the only likely means of detecting an embezzlement.

Tests for Fraudulent Hours Fraudulent hours occur when an employee reports more time than was actually worked. Because of the lack of available evidence, it is usually difficult for an auditor to discover fraudulent hours. One procedure is to reconcile the total hours paid according to the payroll records with an independent record of the hours worked, such as those often maintained by production control. Similarly, it may be possible to observe an employee clocking in more than one time card under a buddy approach. However, it is ordinarily easier for the client to prevent this type of embezzlement by adequate controls than for the auditor to detect it.

METHODOLOGY FOR DESIGNING TESTS OF DETAILS OF BALANCES

During the first two phases of the audit, auditors assess control risk and perform tests of controls and substantive tests of transactions. After completing these tests and assessing the likelihood of misstatement in financial statement accounts in the payroll and personnel cycle, the auditor follows the methodology for designing tests of details of balances.

The methodology for deciding the appropriate tests of details of balances for payroll liability accounts is the same as that followed in Chapter 16 for accounts receivable and Chapters 18 and 19 for acquisition and payment balance sheet accounts. See Figure 16-1 in Chapter 16 for the accounts receivable methodology.

Identify Client Business Risks Affecting Payroll (Phase I)

Significant client business risks affecting payroll are unlikely for most companies. However, client business risk may exist for complex compensation arrangements, including bonus and stock option plans and other deferred compensation arrangements. For example, many technology and other companies provide extensive stock options as part of their compensation packages for key employees that significantly impact compensation expense and shareholders' equity. Examples of other risks include events such as renegotiation of union contracts and discrimination claims. The auditor should understand the likelihood of these events and determine their potential effects on the financial statements, including footnote disclosures.

Set Tolerable Misstatement and Assess Inherent Risk (Phase I)

Most companies have a large number of transactions involving payroll, often with large total amounts. However, balance sheet accounts are normally insignificant, except for labor charged to inventory.

Aside from the potential for fraud, inherent risk is typically low for all balance-related audit objectives. There is inherent risk of payroll fraud because most transactions involve cash. Therefore, auditors often consider the occurrence transaction-related objective important. Also, for manufacturing companies with significant labor charged to inventory, the potential exists for misclassification between payroll expense and inventory or among categories of inventory. As a part of gaining an understanding of the client, the auditor may identify complex payroll-related issues, such as stock-based compensation plans, that may increase inherent risks related to the accounting and disclosure of those arrangements.

Assess Control Risk and Perform Related Tests (Phases I and II)

Earlier in this chapter, we discussed assessing control risk and the related tests of controls and substantive tests of transactions. Refer to Table 20-2 for a review of these topics.

Perform Analytical Procedures (Phase III)

> **OBJECTIVE 20-4**
>
> Design and perform analytical procedures for the payroll and personnel cycle.

The use of analytical procedures is as important in the payroll and personnel cycle as it is in every other cycle. Table 20-3 illustrates analytical procedures for the balance sheet and income statement accounts in the payroll and personnel cycle. Most of the relationships in the first column are predictable and are therefore useful for identifying areas in which additional investigation is desirable.

Design and Perform Tests of Details of Balances For Liability and Expense Accounts (Phase III)

> **OBJECTIVE 20-5**
>
> Design and perform tests of details of balances for accounts in the payroll and personnel cycle.

The verification of the liability accounts associated with payroll, often termed **accrued payroll expenses**, is ordinarily straightforward if internal controls are operating effectively. When the auditor is satisfied that payroll transactions are being correctly recorded in the payroll journal and the related payroll tax forms are being accurately

> **Accrued payroll expenses**
>
> The liability accounts associated with payroll; these include accounts for accrued salaries and wages, accrued commissions, accrued bonuses, accrued benefits, and accrued payroll taxes.

TABLE 20-3	Analytical Procedures for the Payroll and Personnel Cycle
Analytical Procedure	**Possible Misstatement**
Compare payroll expense account balance with previous years (adjusted for pay rate increases and increases in volume).	Misstatement of payroll expense accounts
Compare direct labor as a percentage of sales with previous years.	Misstatement of direct labor and inventory
Compare commission expense as a percentage of sales with previous years.	Misstatement of commission expense and commission liability
Compare payroll tax expense as a percentage of salaries and wages with previous years (adjusted for changes in the tax rates).	Misstatement of payroll tax expense and payroll tax liability
Compare accrued payroll tax accounts with previous years.	Misstatement of accrued payroll taxes and payroll tax expense

prepared and taxes promptly paid, the tests of details of balances should not be time-consuming.

The two major balance-related audit objectives in testing payroll liabilities are:

1. Accruals in the trial balance are stated at the correct amounts (accuracy).
2. Transactions in the payroll and personnel cycle are recorded in the proper period (cutoff).

The primary concern in both objectives is to make sure that there are no understated or omitted accruals. Next, we examine the major liability accounts in the payroll and personnel cycle.

Amounts Withheld from Employees' Pay Payroll taxes withheld but not yet paid to the government can be tested by comparing the balance with the payroll journal, the payroll tax form prepared in the subsequent period, and the subsequent period cash disbursements. Other withheld items such as retirement savings, union dues, savings bonds, and insurance can be verified in the same manner. If internal controls are operating effectively, cutoff and accuracy can easily be tested at the same time by these procedures.

Accrued Salaries and Wages The accrual for salaries and wages arises whenever employees are not paid for the last few days or hours of earned wages until the subsequent period. Salaried personnel usually receive all of their pay except overtime on the last day of the month, but often, several days of wages for hourly employees are unpaid at the end of the year.

The correct cutoff and accuracy of accrued salaries and wages depend on company policy, which should be followed consistently from year to year. Some companies calculate the exact hours of pay that were earned in the current period and paid in the subsequent period, whereas others compute an approximate proportion. For example, if the subsequent payroll results from three days of employment during the current year and two days of employment during the subsequent year, the use of 60 percent of the subsequent period's gross pay as the accrual is an example of an approximation.

After the auditor has determined the company's policy for accruing wages and knows that it is consistent with that of previous years, the appropriate audit procedure to test for cutoff and accuracy is to recalculate the client's accrual. The most likely misstatement of any significance in the balance is the failure to include the proper number of days of earned but unpaid wages.

Accrued Commissions The same concepts used in verifying accrued salaries and wages are applicable to accrued commissions, but the accrual is often more difficult to verify because companies often have several different types of agreements with salespeople and other commission employees. For example, some salespeople might be paid a commission every month and earn no salary, whereas others will get a monthly salary plus a commission paid quarterly. In verifying accrued commissions, it is necessary first to determine the nature of the commission agreement and then test the calculations based on the agreement. The auditor should compare the method of accruing commissions with that of previous years for purposes of consistency.

Accrued Bonuses In many companies, the year-end unpaid bonuses to officers and employees are such a major item that the failure to record them will result in a material misstatement. The verification of the recorded accrual can usually be accomplished by comparing it with the amount authorized in the board minutes.

Accrued Vacation Pay, Sick Pay, or Other Benefits The consistent accrual of these liabilities relative to those of the preceding year is the most important consideration in evaluating the fairness of the amounts. The company policy for recording the liability must first be determined, and then the recorded amounts must be recalculated.

Accrued Payroll Taxes Payroll taxes can be verified by examining tax forms prepared in the subsequent period to determine the amount that should have been recorded as a liability at the balance sheet date.

Tests of Details of Balances for Expense Accounts Several accounts on the income statement are affected by payroll transactions. The most important are officers' salaries and bonuses, office salaries, sales salaries and commissions, and direct manufacturing labor. Often, costs may be broken down further by division, product, or branch. Fringe benefits such as medical insurance may also be included in the expenses.

Auditors should need to do relatively little additional testing of the income statement accounts in most audits beyond analytical procedures, tests of controls, substantive tests of transactions, and related tests of liability accounts already discussed. Extensive additional testing should be necessary only when auditors uncover significant deficiencies or material weaknesses in internal control, significant misstatements in the liability tests, or major unexplained variances in the analytical procedures. Nevertheless, some income statement accounts are often tested in the payroll and personnel cycle. These include officers' compensation, commissions, payroll tax expense, total payroll, and contract labor.

Officers' Compensation It is common to verify whether the total compensation of officers is the amount authorized by the board of directors, because their salaries and bonuses must be included in monthly, quarterly, or annual tax returns depending on the requirements of the tax laws in different Arab countries. Verification of officers' compensation is also warranted because some individuals may be in a position to pay themselves more than the authorized amount. The usual audit test is to obtain the authorized salary of each officer from the minutes of the board of directors' meetings and compare it with the related earnings record.

Commissions Auditors can verify commission expense with relative ease if the commission rate is the same for each type of sale and the necessary sales information is available in the accounting records. The total commission expense can be verified by multiplying the commission rate for each type of sale by the amount of sales in that category. If the desired information is not available, it may be necessary to test the annual or monthly commission payments for selected salespeople and trace those to the total commission payments.

Payroll Tax Expense Payroll tax expense for the year can be tested by first reconciling the total payroll on each payroll tax form with the total payroll for the entire year. Total payroll taxes can then be recomputed by multiplying the appropriate rate by the taxable payroll. The calculation is often time-consuming because the tax is usually applicable on only a portion of the payroll and the rate may change partway through the year if the taxpayer's financial statements are not on a calendar-year basis. On most audits, the calculation is costly and is not necessary unless analytical procedures indicate a problem that cannot be resolved through other procedures. When necessary, the test is ordinarily done in conjunction with tests of payroll tax accruals.

Total Payroll A closely related test to the one for payroll taxes is the reconciliation of total payroll expense in the general ledger with the payroll tax returns. The objectives of the test are to determine whether payroll transactions were charged to a non-payroll account or not recorded in the payroll journal at all. Because the payroll tax records and the payroll are both usually prepared directly from the payroll master file, the misstatements, if any, are likely to be in both records. Tests of controls and substantive tests of transactions are a better means of uncovering these two types of misstatements in most audits.

Contract Labor To reduce payroll costs, many organizations contract with outside organizations (e.g. IT companies) to provide staffing. The individuals providing the services are employed by the outside organization. The fees paid to the outside organization are tested by comparing the amounts with the signed contract arrangement between the company and the outside services firm.

Presentation and Disclosure Objectives Required disclosures for payroll and personnel cycle transactions and balances are not extensive. However, some complex transactions, such as stock options and other executive officer compensation plans may require footnote disclosure. Auditors may combine audit procedures related to the three presentation and disclosure objectives with tests of details of balances for liability and expense accounts. Other procedures related to presentation and disclosure objectives are further discussed in Chapter 24.

SUMMARY

This chapter described the audit of the payroll and personnel cycle. Figure 20-4 illustrates the major accounts in the payroll and personnel cycle and the types of audit tests used to audit these accounts. Tests of controls and substantive tests of transactions are emphasized because of the significance of transactions and the high quality of internal controls in most companies. Tests of details of balances are normally limited to analytical procedures and verification of accrued liabilities related to payroll.

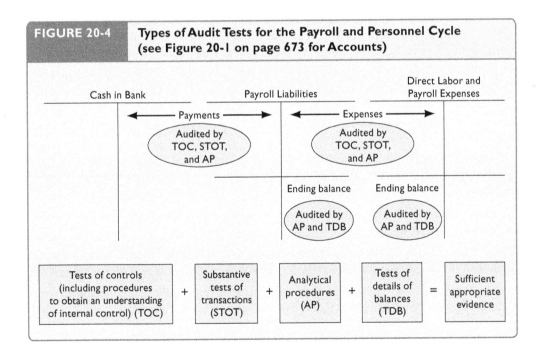

FIGURE 20-4   Types of Audit Tests for the Payroll and Personnel Cycle (see Figure 20-1 on page 673 for Accounts)

ESSENTIAL TERMS

Accrued payroll expenses   p. 684
Imprest payroll account   p. 677
Payroll and personnel cycle   p. 672
Payroll master file   p. 676
Personnel records   p. 674
Time card   p. 674

REVIEW QUESTIONS

20-1 (Objective 20-1) Identify five general ledger accounts that are likely to be affected by the payroll and personnel cycle in most audits.

20-2 (Objectives 20-1, 20-3) Explain the relationship between the payroll and personnel cycle and inventory valuation.

20-3 (Objective 20-3) List five tests of controls that can be performed for the payroll and personnel cycle and state the purpose of each control tested.

20-4 (Objective 20-3) Explain why the percentage of total audit time in the cycle devoted to performing tests of controls and substantive tests of transactions is usually far greater for the payroll and personnel cycle than for the sales and collection cycle.

20-5 (Objectives 20-2, 20-3) Evaluate the following comment by an auditor: "My job is to determine whether the payroll records are fairly stated in accordance with accounting standards, not to find out whether they are following proper hiring and termination procedures. When I conduct an audit of payroll, I keep out of the human resources department and stick to the time cards, journals, and payroll checks. I don't care whom they hire and whom they fire, as long as they properly pay the ones they have."

20-6 (Objective 20-3) Distinguish between the following payroll audit procedures and state the purpose of each: (1) trace a random sample of prenumbered time cards to the related payroll checks in the payroll register and compare the hours worked with the hours paid, and (2) trace a random sample of payroll checks from the payroll register to the related time cards and compare the hours worked with the hours paid. Which of these two procedures is typically more important in the audit of payroll? Why?

20-7 (Objective 20-5) In auditing payroll withholding and payroll tax expense, explain why emphasis should normally be on evaluating the adequacy of the payroll tax return preparation procedures rather than the payroll tax liability. If the preparation procedures are inadequate, explain the effect this will have on the remainder of the audit.

20-8 (Objective 20-4) List several analytical procedures for the payroll and personnel cycle and explain the type of misstatement that might be indicated when there is a significant difference in the comparison of the current year with previous years' results for each of the tests.

20-9 (Objective 20-3) Explain the circumstances under which an auditor should perform audit tests primarily designed to uncover fraud in the payroll and personnel cycle. List three audit procedures that are primarily for the detection of fraud and state the type of fraud the procedure is meant to uncover.

20-10 (Objective 20-2) Distinguish between a payroll master file and a payroll tax return. Explain the purpose of each.

20-11 (Objectives 20-2, 20-3) List the supporting documents and records the auditor will examine in a typical payroll audit in which the primary objective is to detect fraud.

20-12 (Objective 20-3) List five types of authorizations in the payroll and personnel cycle and state the type of misstatement that is likely to occur when each authorization is lacking.

20-13 (Objective 20-5) Explain why it is common to verify total officers' compensation even when the tests of controls and substantive tests of transactions results in payroll are excellent. What audit procedures can be used to verify officers' compensation?

20-14 (Objective 20-2) Explain what is meant by an imprest payroll account. What is its purpose as a control over payroll?

20-15 (Objective 20-3) List several audit procedures that the auditor can use to determine whether payroll transactions are recorded at the proper amounts.

20-16 (Objective 20-3) Explain how audit sampling can be used to test the payroll and personnel cycle.

MULTIPLE CHOICE QUESTIONS FROM CPA EXAMINATIONS

20-17 (Objective 20-3) The following questions concern internal controls in the payroll and personnel cycle. Choose the best response.

a. A factory foreman at Khartoum Corporation discharged an hourly worker but did not notify the payroll department. The foreman then forged the worker's signature on time cards and work tickets and, when giving out the checks, diverted the payroll checks drawn from the discharged worker to his own use. The most effective procedure for preventing this activity is to
   (1) require written authorization for all employees added to or removed from the payroll.
   (2) have a paymaster who has no other payroll responsibility distribute the payroll checks.
   (3) have someone other than persons who prepare or distribute the payroll obtain custody of unclaimed payroll checks.
   (4) from time to time, rotate persons distributing the payroll.

b. The auditor reviews Golden's payroll procedures. An example of an internal control deficiency is to assign to a department supervisor the responsibility for
   (1) distributing payroll checks to subordinate employees.
   (2) reviewing and approving time reports for subordinates.
   (3) interviewing applicants for subordinate positions before hiring is done by the personnel department.
   (4) initiating requests for salary adjustments for subordinate employees.

c. The purpose of segregating the duties of hiring personnel and distributing payroll checks is to separate the
   (1) human resource function from the controllership function.
   (2) administrative controls from the internal accounting controls.
   (3) authorization of transactions from the custody of related assets.
   (4) operational responsibility from the record-keeping responsibility.

20-18 (Objective 20-3) The following questions concern audit testing of the payroll and personnel cycle. Choose the best response.

a. When control risk is assessed as low for assertions related to payroll, substantive tests of payroll balances most likely would be limited to applying analytical procedures and
   (1) observing the distribution of payroll checks.
   (2) footing and crossfooting the payroll register.
   (3) inspecting payroll tax returns.
   (4) recalculating payroll accruals.

b. A common audit procedure in the audit of payroll transactions involves tracing selected items from the payroll journal to employee time cards that have been approved by supervisory personnel. This procedure is designed to provide evidence in support of the audit proposition that
   (1) only proper employees worked and their pay was correctly computed.
   (2) jobs on which employees worked were charged with the appropriate labor cost.
   (3) internal controls over payroll disbursements are operating effectively.
   (4) all employees worked the number of hours for which their pay was computed.

c. In performing tests concerning the granting of stock options, an auditor should
   (1) confirm the transaction with the commercial registrar.
   (2) verify the existence of option holders in the entity's payroll records or stock ledgers.
   (3) determine that sufficient treasury stock is available to cover any new stock issued.
   (4) trace the authorization for the transaction to a vote of the board of directors.

DISCUSSION QUESTIONS AND PROBLEMS

20-19 (Objectives 20-2, 20-3) Items 1 through 9 are selected questions typically found in internal control questionnaires used by auditors to obtain an understanding of internal control in the payroll and personnel cycle. In using the questionnaire for a client, a 'yes' response to a question indicates a possible internal control, whereas a 'no' indicates a potential deficiency.

1. Does an appropriate official authorize initial rates of pay and any subsequent changes in rates?
2. Are written notices required documenting reasons for termination?
3. Are formal records such as time cards used for keeping time?
4. Is approval by a department head or foreman required for all time cards before they are submitted for payment?
5. Does anyone verify pay rates, overtime hours, and computations of gross payroll before payroll checks are prepared?
6. Does an adequate means exist for identifying jobs or products, such as work orders, job numbers, or some similar identification provided to employees to ensure proper coding of time records?
7. Are employees paid by checks prepared by persons independent of timekeeping?
8. Are employees required to show identification to receive paychecks?
9. Is a continuing record maintained of all unclaimed wages?

Required

a. For each of the questions, state the transaction-related audit objective(s) being fulfilled if the control is in effect.
b. For each control, list a test of control to test its effectiveness.
c. For each of the questions, identify the nature of the potential financial misstatement(s) if the control is not in effect.
d. For each of the potential misstatements in part c, list a substantive audit procedure for determining whether a material misstatement exists.

20-20 (Objectives 20-2, 20-3) Following are some of the tests of controls and substantive tests of transactions procedures often performed in the payroll and personnel cycle. (Each procedure is to be done on a sample basis.)

1. Reconcile the monthly payroll total for direct manufacturing labor with the labor cost distribution.
2. Examine the time card for the approval of a foreman.
3. Recompute hours on the time card and compare the total with the total hours for which the employee has been paid.
4. Compare the employee name, date, check number, and amounts on cancelled checks with the payroll journal.
5. Trace the hours from the employee time cards to job tickets to make sure that the total reconciles and trace each job ticket to the job-cost record.
6. Account for a sequence of payroll checks in the payroll journal.
7. Select employees from the personnel file who have been terminated, and determine whether their termination pay was in accordance with the union contract. As part of this procedure, examine two subsequent periods to determine whether the terminated employees are still being paid.

Required

a. Identify whether each of the procedures is primarily a test of control or a substantive test of transactions.
b. Identify the transaction-related audit objective(s) of each of the procedures.

20-21 (Objectives 20-2, 20-3) The following misstatements are included in the accounting records of Al Yasmine Manufacturing Company:

1. Hana Khaled and Hossam Fawzi take turns 'punching in' for each other every few days. The absent employee comes in at noon and tells his foreman that he had car

trouble or some other problem. The foreman does not know that the employee is getting paid for the time.

2. The foreman submits a fraudulent time card for a former employee each week and delivers the related payroll check to the employee's house on the way home from work. They split the amount of the paycheck.

3. Employees often overlook recording their hours worked on job-cost tickets as required by the system. Many of the client's contracts are on a cost-plus basis.

4. Direct labor was unintentionally charged to job 620 instead of job 602 by the payroll clerk when he key-entered the labor distribution sheets. Job 602 was completed and the costs were expensed in the current year, whereas job 620 was included in work-in-process.

5. The payroll clerk prepares a check to the same nonexistent person every week when he key-enters payroll transactions in the computer system, which also records the amount in the payroll journal. He submits it along with all other payroll checks for signature. When the checks are returned to him for distribution, he takes the check and deposits it in a special bank account bearing that person's name.

6. In withholding payroll taxes from employees, the computer operator deducts US$0.50 extra income taxes from several employees each week and credits the amount to his own employee earnings record.

7. The payroll clerk manually prepares payroll checks but often forgets to record one or two checks in the computer-prepared payroll journal.

a. For each misstatement, state a control that should have prevented it from occurring on a continuing basis.

Required

b. For each misstatement, state a substantive audit procedure that could uncover it.

20-22 (Objectives 20-3, 20-4, 20-5) The following audit procedures are typical of those found in auditing the payroll and personnel cycle:

1. Scan journals for all periods for unusual transactions to determine whether they are recorded correctly.

2. Examine evidence of double-checking payroll wage rates and calculations by an independent person.

3. Obtain a schedule of all payroll liabilities and trace to the general ledger.

4. Select a sample of 20 cancelled payroll checks and account for the numerical sequence.

5. Foot and cross-foot the payroll journal for two periods and trace totals to the general ledger.

6. For payroll liabilities, examine subsequent cash disbursements and supporting documents such as payroll tax returns, depository receipts, and tax receipts.

7. Select a sample of 20 cancelled payroll checks and trace to payroll journal entries for name, date, and amounts.

8. Compute direct labor, indirect labor, and commissions as a percentage of net sales and compare with prior years.

9. Examine owner approval of rates of pay and withholdings.

10. Compute payroll tax expense as a percentage of total wages, salaries, and commissions.

11. Discuss with management any payroll liabilities recorded in the prior year that are not provided for in the current period.

12. Select a sample of 40 entries in the payroll journal and trace each to an approved time card.

a. Select the type of test for each audit procedure from the following:

Required

 (1) Test of control
 (2) Substantive test of transactions
 (3) Analytical procedure
 (4) Test of details of balances

b. For each test of control or substantive test of transactions, identify the applicable transaction-related audit objective(s).

c. For each test of details of balances, identify the applicable balance-related audit objective(s).

20-23 (Objectives 20-3, 20-5) The following are steps in the methodology for designing tests of controls, substantive tests of transactions, and tests of details of balances for the payroll and personnel cycle:

1. Design tests of details of balances for the payroll and personnel cycle.
2. Evaluate risk and materiality for payroll expense and liability accounts.
3. Evaluate whether control risk can be assessed as low for payroll.
4. Design and perform payroll- and personnel-related analytical procedures.
5. Identify controls and deficiencies in internal control for the payroll and personnel cycle.
6. Obtain an understanding of the payroll and personnel cycle internal controls.
7. Evaluate tests of controls and substantive tests of transactions results.
8. Design payroll and personnel cycle tests of controls and substantive tests of transactions.
9. Assess inherent risk for payroll-related accounts.

Required

a. Identify (1) those steps that are tests of controls or substantive tests of transactions and (2) those that are tests of details of balances.

b. Put steps that are tests of controls and substantive tests of transactions in the order of their performance in most audits.

c. Put the tests of details of balances in their proper order.

20-24 (Objective 20-3) You are assessing internal control in the audit of the payroll and personnel cycle for Karim Products Company, a manufacturing company specializing in assembling computer parts. Karim employs approximately 200 hourly and 30 salaried employees in three locations. Each location has one foreman who is responsible for overseeing operations. The owner of the company lives in Tripoli and is not actively involved in the business. The two key executives are the vice president of sales and the controller, and both have been employed by the company for more than 15 years.

New hourly employees are hired by the foremen at each location on an as needed basis. Each foreman recommends the wage rate for each new employee as well as wage rate increases. The effectiveness of employees varies considerably and their wages are adjusted accordingly. All wage rates are approved by the controller.

Since each hourly employee works independently, Karim has a highly flexible work schedule policy, as long as they start after 7:00 a.m. and are finished by 6:00 p.m. Each foreman has a supply of prenumbered time cards that they distribute to employees on Sunday morning. Because some employees do not start until later in the day several time cards are kept in a box by the time clock for their use. Hourly employees use time clocks to record when they start and stop working. Each Thursday, after the employees complete their work for the week, the foremen account for the time cards they distributed, approve them, and send them by an overnight courier to the main office in Sert.

The payroll clerk receives the time cards on Saturday and enters the information using payroll software that prepares the checks and the related payroll records. The checks are ready for the controller to sign Sunday morning. She compares each check to the payroll transactions list sent by the payroll department and returns the checks using the same courier to each location. The foremen pick up the checks and distribute each check to the appropriate employee. If an employee is not present at the end of the day the foreman mails it to the employee's address.

Except for the foremen, all salaried employees work in the Sert office. The vice president of sales or the controller hires all salaried employees, depending on their responsibilities, and determines their salaries and salary adjustments. The owner determines the salary of the vice president of sales and the controller. The payroll clerk also processes the payroll transactions for salaried employees using the same payroll software that is used for hourly employees, but all salaried employees use direct deposit so no check is prepared.

The payroll software has access controls that are set by the controller. She is the only person who has access to the salary and wage rate module of the software. She updates the software for new wage rates and salaries and changes of existing ones. The accounting clerk has access to all other payroll modules. The controller's assistant has been taught to reconcile bank accounts and does the reconciliation monthly.

a. Identify the internal control deficiencies in the Karim Products Company's payroll system.

b. For each deficiency, state the type of misstatement that is likely to result. Be as specific as possible in describing the nature of the misstatement. If the potential misstatement involves fraud, identify who is most likely to perpetuate the fraud.

Required

CHAPTER 21

AUDIT OF THE INVENTORY AND WAREHOUSING CYCLE

Phantom Inventory

Mickey Monus was the local hero in Youngstown, Ohio in the U.S. He acquired a local drugstore, and within ten years, added 299 more stores to form the national deep-discount retail chain, Phar-Mor, Inc. The company was viewed as the rising star by some retail experts and was considered to be the next Wal-Mart. Even Sam Walton announced that the only company he feared in the expansion of Wal-Mart was Phar-Mor.

Phar-Mor sold a variety of household products and prescription drugs at substantially lower prices than other discount stores. Monus described the company's strategy as 'power buying,' whereby Phar-Mor loaded up on products when suppliers were selling at rock-bottom prices and passed those savings to cost-conscious customers through deeply discounted prices.

Actually, Phar-Mor's prices were so low that the company was selling goods for less than their cost, causing the company to lose money. However, Monus continued to argue internally that through Phar-Mor's power buying, it would get so large that it could sell its way out of trouble. Unwilling to allow these shortfalls to damage Phar-Mor's appearance of success, Monus and his team began to engage in creative accounting so that Phar-Mor never reported these losses in its financial statements.

Management dumped the losses into 'bucket accounts,' only to reallocate those amounts to the company's hundreds of stores in the form of phantom increases in inventory costs. Monus' team issued fake invoices for merchandise purchases, made fraudulent journal entries to increase inventory and decrease cost of goods sold, and overcounted and double-counted inventory items.

Unfortunately, the auditors never uncovered the fraud. They allegedly observed inventory in only four stores out of 300, and they informed Phar-Mor management months in advance about the stores they would visit. Phar-Mor executives fully stocked the four selected stores but allocated the false inventory increases to the other 296 stores.

The fraud was ultimately uncovered when a travel agent received a Phar-Mor check signed by Monus paying for expenses that were unrelated to Phar-Mor. The agent showed the check to her landlord, who happened to be a Phar-Mor investor, and he contacted David Shapiro, Phar-Mor's CEO. Subsequent investigation of the invalid expenditure eventually led to the discovery of the inventory fraud.

Monus was eventually convicted and went to jail for five years. The CFO, who did not profit personally, was sentenced to 33 months in prison. The audit failure cost the audit firm over US$300 million in civil judgments.

Sources: Adapted from Beasley, Buckless, Glover, and Prawitt, *Auditing Cases: An Interactive Learning Approach*, 4th edition (Prentice-Hall, 2009) pp. 119–131; and Joseph T. Wells, 'Ghost Goods: How to Spot Phantom Inventory,' *Journal of Accountancy* (June 2001), pp. 33–36.

LEARNING OBJECTIVES

After studying this chapter, you should be able to

21-1 Describe the business functions and the related documents and records in the inventory and warehousing cycle.

21-2 Explain the five parts of the audit of the inventory and warehousing cycle.

21-3 Design and perform audit tests of cost accounting.

21-4 Apply analytical procedures to the accounts in the inventory and warehousing cycle.

21-5 Design and perform physical observation audit tests for inventory.

21-6 Design and perform audit tests of pricing and compilation for inventory.

21-7 Integrate the various parts of the audit of the inventory and warehousing cycle.

The **inventory and warehousing cycle** is unique because of its close relationships to other transaction cycles. For a manufacturing company, raw material enters the inventory and warehousing cycle from the acquisition and payment cycle, while direct labor enters it from the payroll and personnel cycle. The inventory and warehousing cycle ends with the sale of goods in the sales and collection cycle.

The audit of inventory, especially tests of the year-end inventory balance, is often the most complex and time-consuming part of the audit. As the audit of Phar-Mor demonstrates, finding misstatements in inventory accounts can be challenging. Factors affecting the complexity of the audit of inventory include:

- Inventory is often the largest account on the balance sheet.
- Inventory is often in different locations, making physical control and counting difficult.
- Diverse inventory items such as jewels, chemicals, and electronic parts are often difficult for auditors to observe and value.
- Inventory valuation is also difficult when estimation of inventory obsolescence is necessary and when manufacturing costs must be allocated to inventory.
- There are several acceptable inventory valuation methods and some organizations may prefer to use different valuation methods for different parts of the inventory, which is acceptable under accounting standards.

Relevant International Standards on Auditing	
ISA 200	Overall Objectives of the Independent Auditor and the Conduct of an Audit in Accordance with International Standards on Auditing
ISA 220	Quality Control for an Audit of Financial Statements
ISA 230	Audit Documentation
ISA 265	Communicating Deficiencies in Internal Control to Those Charged with Governance and Management
ISA 300	Planning an Audit of Financial Statements
ISA 320	Materiality in Planning and Performing an Audit
ISA 450	Evaluation of Misstatements Identified during the Audit
ISA 500	Audit Evidence
ISA 520	Analytical Procedures

BUSINESS FUNCTIONS IN THE CYCLE AND RELATED DOCUMENTS AND RECORDS

OBJECTIVE 21-1

Describe the business functions and the related documents and records in the inventory and warehousing cycle.

Inventory takes many different forms, depending on the nature of the business. For retail or wholesale businesses, the largest account in the financial statements is often merchandise inventory available for sale. To study the inventory and warehousing cycle, we will use an example of a manufacturing company, whose inventory may include raw materials, purchased parts and supplies for use in production, goods in the process of being manufactured, and finished goods available for sale. Still, most of the principles discussed apply to other types of businesses as well.

Figure 21-1 shows the physical flow of goods and the flow of costs in the inventory and warehousing cycle for a manufacturing company. Examine the debits to the raw materials, direct labor, and manufacturing overhead T accounts to see how the inventory and warehousing cycle ties in to the acquisition and payment cycle and the payroll and personnel cycle. The direct tie-in to the sales and collection cycle occurs at the point where finished goods are relieved (credited) and a charge is made to cost of goods sold.

FIGURE 21-1	Flow of Inventory and Costs

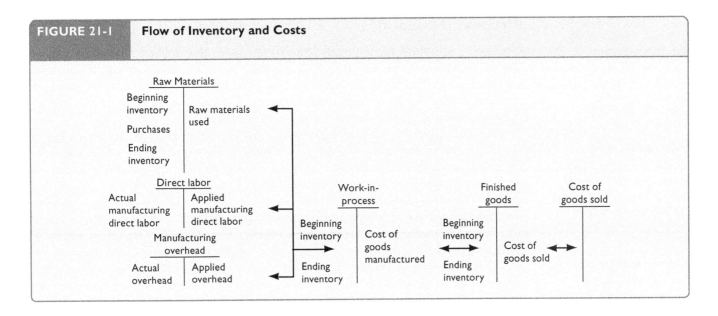

The inventory and warehousing cycle can be thought of as comprising two separate but closely related systems, one involving the *physical flow of goods* and the other the related costs. Six functions make up the inventory and warehousing cycle. Each of these is discussed next.

Process Purchase Orders

The inventory and warehousing cycle begins with the acquisition of raw materials for production. Adequate controls over purchasing must be maintained whether inventory purchases are for raw materials for a manufacturer or finished goods for a retailer. Purchase requisitions are forms used to request the purchasing department to order inventory. These requisitions may be initiated by stockroom personnel as raw materials are needed, by automated computer software when raw materials reach a predetermined level, by orders placed for the materials required to produce a customer order, or by orders initiated on the basis of a periodic raw materials count.

Receive Raw Materials

Receipt of the ordered materials, which is also part of the acquisition and payment cycle, involves the inspection of material received for quantity and quality. The receiving department prepares a receiving report that becomes a part of the documentation before payment is made. After inspection, the material is sent to the storeroom and copies of the receiving documents, or electronic notifications of the receipt of goods, are typically sent to purchasing, the storeroom, and accounts payable. Control and accountability are necessary for all transfers.

Store Raw Materials

Once received, materials are normally stored in a stockroom. When another department needs materials for production, personnel submit a properly approved materials requisition, work order, or similar document or electronic notice that indicates the type and quantity of materials needed. This requisition document is used to update the perpetual inventory master files and record transfers from raw materials to work-in-process accounts. These updates occur automatically in organizations with integrated inventory management and accounting software systems.

Process the Goods

Job cost system

System of cost accounting in which costs are accumulated by individual jobs when material is used and labor costs are incurred.

Process cost system

System of cost accounting in which costs are accumulated for a process, with unit costs for each process assigned to the products passing through the process.

Cost accounting records

The accounting records concerned with the manufacture and processing of the goods and storing finished goods.

Processing inventory varies greatly from company to company. Companies determine the finished goods items and quantities they will produce based on specific orders from customers, sales forecasts, predetermined finished goods inventory levels, and economical production runs. A separate production control department is often responsible for determining the type and quantities to produce.

An adequate cost accounting system is an important part of the processing of goods function for all manufacturing companies. The system shows the relative profitability of the products for management planning and control and values inventories for preparing financial statements. Two types of cost systems exist: job cost systems and process cost systems, but there are many variations and combinations of these systems. In a **job cost system**, costs are accumulated by individual jobs when material is issued and labor costs incurred. In a **process cost system**, they are accumulated by processes, with unit costs for each process assigned to the products passing through the process.

Cost accounting records consist of master files, worksheets, and reports that accumulate material, labor, and overhead costs by job or process as those costs are incurred. When jobs or products are completed, the related costs are transferred from work-in-process to finished goods based on production department reports.

Store Finished Goods

When finished goods are completed, they are placed in the stockroom to await shipment. In companies with good internal controls, finished goods are kept under physical control in a separate, limited-access area. The control of finished goods is often considered part of the sales and collection cycle.

Ship Finished Goods

Shipping completed goods is part of the sales and collection cycle. The actual shipment of goods to customers in exchange for cash or other assets, such as accounts receivable, creates the exchange of assets necessary for meeting revenue recognition criteria. For most sales transactions, the actual shipment becomes the trigger for recognizing the related accounts receivable and sales in the accounting system. Thus, shipments of finished goods must be authorized by a properly approved shipping document.

Perpetual Inventory Master Files

Perpetual inventory master file

A continuously updated computerized record of inventory items purchased, used, sold, and on hand for merchandise, raw materials, and finished goods.

We have not yet discussed one type of record used for inventory: a **perpetual inventory master file**. Separate perpetual records are normally kept for raw materials and finished goods. Most companies do not use perpetuals for work-in-process.

Perpetual inventory master files typically include information about the units of inventory acquired, sold, and on hand. In well-designed computerized systems, they also include information about unit costs.

For acquisitions of raw materials, the perpetual inventory master file is updated automatically when acquisitions of inventory are processed as part of recording acquisitions. For example, when the number of units and unit cost for each raw material acquisition are entered in the computer system, this information is used to update perpetual inventory master files along with the acquisitions journal and accounts payable master file.

Transfers of raw material from the storeroom must be separately entered into the computer to update the perpetual records. Typically, only the units transferred need to be entered because the computer determines the unit costs from the master file.

Finished goods perpetual inventory master files include the same type of information as raw materials perpetuals but are considerably more complex if costs are

FIGURE 21-2	Functions in the Inventory and Warehousing Cycle

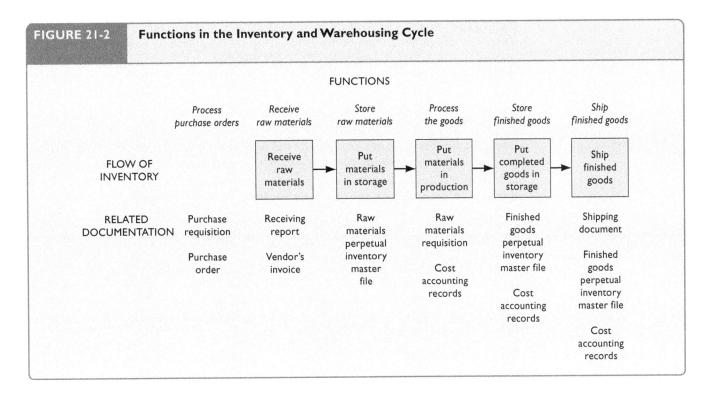

FUNCTIONS

	Process purchase orders	Receive raw materials	Store raw materials	Process the goods	Store finished goods	Ship finished goods
FLOW OF INVENTORY		Receive raw materials	→ Put materials in storage	→ Put materials in production	→ Put completed goods in storage	→ Ship finished goods
RELATED DOCUMENTATION	Purchase requisition Purchase order	Receiving report Vendor's invoice	Raw materials perpetual inventory master file	Raw materials requisition Cost accounting records	Finished goods perpetual inventory master file Cost accounting records	Shipping document Finished goods perpetual inventory master file Cost accounting records

included along with units. Finished goods costs include raw materials, direct labor, and manufacturing overhead, which often requires allocations and detailed record keeping. When finished goods perpetuals include unit costs, the cost accounting records must be integrated into the computer system.

Figure 21-2 summarizes the business functions and the physical flow of inventory from the purchase of raw materials to the shipment of finished goods. It also includes the most common documents used to support the functions and physical flows.

PARTS OF THE AUDIT OF INVENTORY

OBJECTIVE 21-2

Explain the five parts of the audit of the inventory and warehousing cycle.

Now that you are familiar with the business functions and the related documents and records in the inventory and warehousing cycle, we turn our attention to the audit of the cycle. The overall objective in the audit of the inventory and warehousing cycle is to provide assurance that the financial statements fairly account for raw materials, work-in-process, finished goods inventory, and cost of goods sold.

The audit of the inventory and warehousing cycle can be divided into five activities within the cycle:

1. Acquire and record raw materials, labor, and overhead
2. Internally transfer assets and costs
3. Ship goods and record revenue and costs
4. Physically observe inventory
5. Price and compile inventory

Acquire and Record Raw Materials, Labor, and Overhead

This part of the audit includes the first three functions in Figure 21-2. These include processing purchase orders, receiving raw materials, and storing raw materials.

The auditor obtains an understanding of internal controls over these three functions and then performs tests of controls and substantive tests of transactions in both the acquisition and payment cycle and the payroll and personnel cycle. These tests should satisfy auditors that controls affecting the acquisitions of raw materials and manufacturing costs are operating effectively and that acquisition transactions are correctly stated.

Internally Transfer Assets and Costs

Internal transfers of inventory include the fourth and fifth functions in Figure 21-2: process the goods and store finished goods. Clients account for these activities in the cost accounting records, which are independent of other cycles and are tested as part of the audit of the inventory and warehousing cycle.

Ship Goods and Record Revenue and Costs

Recording shipments and related costs is the last function shown in Figure 21-2. Because it is part of the sales and collection cycle, auditors obtain an understanding and test internal controls over recording shipments as a part of auditing that cycle, including procedures to verify the accuracy of the credits to inventory recorded in perpetual inventory master files.

Physically Observe Inventory

Auditors must observe the client taking a physical inventory count to determine whether recorded inventory actually exists at the balance sheet date and is correctly counted by the client. Physical examination is an essential type of evidence used to verify the existence and count of inventory.

Price and Compile Inventory

Inventory compilation tests

Audit procedures used to verify whether physical counts of inventory are correctly summarized, inventory quantities and prices are correctly extended, and extended inventory is correctly footed.

Costs used to value inventory must be tested to determine whether the client has correctly followed an inventory method that is both in accordance with accounting standards and consistent with previous years. Audit procedures used to verify these costs are called price tests. In addition, the auditor must perform **inventory compilation tests**, which are tests to verify whether the physical counts were correctly summarized, the inventory quantities and prices were correctly extended, and the extended inventory correctly footed to equal the general ledger inventory balance.

Figure 21-3 summarizes the five parts of the audit of the inventory and warehousing cycle. Because of the interrelationships of the inventory and warehousing cycle with other cycles, some parts of the audit of inventory are most efficiently tested with the audit tests of other cycles. As noted in Figure 21-3, auditors test the acquisition and recording of raw materials, labor, and overhead as part of the audit of the acquisition and payment and payroll and personnel cycles. Also, they test shipment of goods and recording of revenue and related costs in the audit of the sales and collection cycle. Because we have already discussed obtaining an understanding of internal controls, tests of controls and substantive tests of transactions for these other cycles in earlier chapters, they are not repeated here (the first and third box in Figure 21-3).

The physical observation of inventory and the pricing and compilation of the inventory are audited using analytical procedures and tests of details of balances (the last two boxes in Figure 21-3). For tests of details of balances the auditor must consider business and inherent risks, set tolerable misstatement for inventory, and evaluate the results of the tests of controls and substantive tests of transactions for the transactions and activities in the first three boxes in Figure 21-3.

FIGURE 21-3	Audit of Inventory

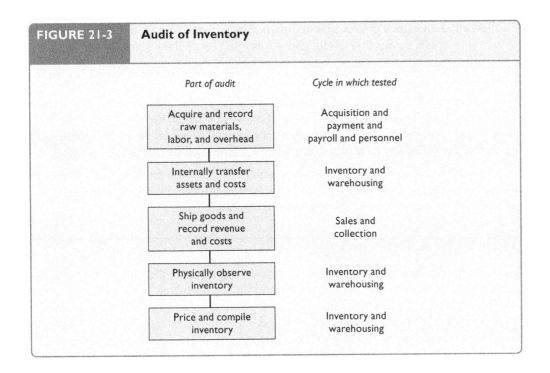

Part of audit	Cycle in which tested
Acquire and record raw materials, labor, and overhead	Acquisition and payment and payroll and personnel
Internally transfer assets and costs	Inventory and warehousing
Ship goods and record revenue and costs	Sales and collection
Physically observe inventory	Inventory and warehousing
Price and compile inventory	Inventory and warehousing

AUDIT OF COST ACCOUNTING

Our discussion of the audit of cost accounting begins with the internal transfer of assets from raw materials to work-in-process to finished goods inventory. We also focus on systems and controls related to the transfer of inventory costs, which are accounted for in the cost accounting records.

Cost accounting systems and controls of different companies vary more than most other audit areas because of the wide variety of items of inventory and the level of sophistication desired by management. For example, a company that manufactures farm machines may have completely different cost records and internal controls than a steel fabricating shop that makes and installs custom-made metal cabinets.

Cost Accounting Controls

Cost accounting controls are those related to processes affecting physical inventory and the tracking of related costs from the time raw materials are requisitioned to the completion of the manufactured product and its transfer to storage. It is convenient to divide these controls into two broad categories:

1. Physical controls over raw materials, work-in-process, and finished goods inventory
2. Controls over the related costs

Almost all companies need physical controls over their assets to prevent loss from misuse and theft. To protect assets, most companies physically segregate and restrict access to storage areas for raw material, work-in-process, and finished goods to control the movement of inventory. In some instances, managers assign custody of inventory to specific individuals who are responsible for protecting the inventory. Clients may use approved prenumbered documents for authorizing movement of inventory to protect the assets from improper use. Copies of these documents should be sent directly to accounting by the persons issuing them, bypassing people with custodial responsibilities. An example of an effective document of this type is an approved materials requisition for obtaining raw materials from the storeroom.

OBJECTIVE 21-3

Design and perform audit tests of cost accounting.

Cost accounting controls

Controls over physical inventory and the related costs from the point at which raw materials are requisitioned to the point at which the manufactured product is completed and transferred to storage.

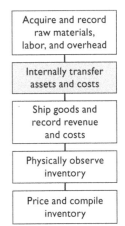

Perpetual inventory master files maintained by persons who do not have custody of or access to assets are another useful cost accounting control for a number of reasons:

- They provide a record of inventory on hand, which is used to initiate production or acquisition of additional materials or goods.
- They provide a record of the use of raw materials and the sale of finished goods, which can be reviewed for obsolete or slow-moving items.
- They provide a record to pinpoint responsibility when there are differences between physical counts and the amounts shown on the perpetual listings.

Also, adequate internal controls that integrate production and accounting records to provide accurate costs for all products are important to aid management in pricing finished goods, controlling costs, and costing inventory.

Tests of Cost Accounting

The concepts in auditing inventory cost accounting are no different from those discussed for other transaction cycles: understand internal controls in the cost accounting system, assess planned control risk, determine extent of testing controls, and design tests of controls and substantive tests of transactions to meet transaction-related audit objectives. The auditor is concerned with four aspects of cost accounting:

1. Physical controls over inventory
2. Documents and records for transferring inventory
3. Perpetual inventory master files
4. Unit cost records

Physical Controls Auditor tests of physical controls over raw materials, work-in-process, and finished goods are limited to observation and inquiry. Auditors can examine the raw materials storage area to determine whether the inventory is protected from theft and misuse by locks or other security measures, including an inventory custodian. They can ask inventory custodians to explain their duties related to their oversight of inventory monitored by them. If auditors conclude that the physical controls are so inadequate that inventory will be difficult to accurately count, they should expand observation of physical inventory tests to make sure that an adequate count is carried out.

Documents and Records for Transferring Inventory The auditor's primary concerns in verifying the transfer of inventory from one location to another are that recorded transfers exist, all actual transfers are recorded, and the quantity, description, and date of all recorded transfers are accurate. Products labeled with standardized bar codes that can be scanned by laser bar-code readers and other technologies make it easier for clients to track the movement of goods through production.

When auditing inventory transfers, auditors first need to understand the client's internal controls for recording transfers before they can perform relevant tests. After they understand the internal controls, they can easily perform tests of controls or substantive tests of transactions by examining documents and records to test the occurrence and accuracy objectives for the transfer of goods from the raw material storeroom to the manufacturing assembly line. For example, auditors may account for a sequence of raw material requisitions, examine the requisitions for proper approval, and compare the quantity, description, and date with the information recorded in the raw material perpetual inventory master files to verify that related controls operated effectively and that amounts are correctly recorded. Similarly, the auditor may compare completed production records with perpetual inventory master files to be sure that all manufactured goods were physically delivered to the finished goods storeroom.

Perpetual Inventory Master Files The reliability of perpetual inventory master files affects the *timing* and *extent* of the auditor's physical examination of inventory. When perpetual inventory master files are accurate, auditors can test the physical inventory before the balance sheet date. An interim physical inventory can result in significant cost savings for both the client and the auditor, and it enables the audit to be completed earlier. The auditor may also reduce tests of physical inventory counts when the client has reliable perpetual inventory records and assessed control risk related to physical observation of inventory is low.

Auditors test perpetual inventory master files by examining documentation that supports additions and reductions of inventory amounts in the master files. For example, as part of the tests of the perpetual records, auditors may examine documents supporting inventory activities including the addition of acquired raw material inventory, the reduction of raw material inventory for use in production, the increase in finished goods inventory when goods have been manufactured, and the decrease when finished goods are sold. Usually, it is relatively easy to test the accuracy of the perpetual inventory master files after the auditor determines the adequacy of the design and implementation of inventory internal controls and the related level of assessed control risk. Auditors test the perpetual records for acquisitions of raw materials in the acquisition and payment cycle, while reductions in finished goods for sale are tested in the sales and collection cycle.

For many companies, traditional documents exist only in electronic form and the perpetual inventory system is integrated with other accounting cycles. As a result, the auditor can test computer controls to support a reduction in control risk, which reduces substantive testing and can result in audit efficiencies.

Unit Cost Records Accurate cost data for raw materials, direct labor, and manufacturing overhead is essential for fairly stated raw materials, work-in-process, and finished goods inventories. To maintain accurate cost data, clients must integrate their cost accounting records with production and other accounting records.

When testing inventory cost records, the auditor must first obtain an understanding of internal control in the cost accounting system. This understanding can be time-consuming because the flow of costs is integrated with accounting records in three other cycles: acquisition and payment, payroll and personnel, and sales and collection.

After auditors understand internal controls affecting cost accounting records, the approach to internal verification of cost accounting records involves the same concepts that were discussed in the verification of acquisition, payroll, and sales transactions. Auditors usually test cost accounting records as a part of the acquisition, payroll, and sales tests to avoid testing the records more than once and to increase audit efficiency. When testing acquisition transactions, auditors should trace the units and unit costs of raw materials to additions recorded in the perpetual inventory master files and the total cost to cost accounting records. Similarly, when clients maintain payroll cost data for different jobs, auditors should trace from the payroll summary directly to job cost records when they audit payroll.

Determining the reasonableness of manufacturing overhead costs assigned to work-in-process is challenging for auditors because management must make assumptions that affect overhead allocations that can significantly affect the unit costs of inventory and therefore the fairness of inventory valuation. In evaluating these overhead cost allocations, the auditor must consider the reasonableness of the allocation method, assuming the method complies with accounting standards, and whether it is consistently applied.

Management typically allocates overhead using total direct labor dollars as the basis for allocation. In this case, the overhead rate should approximate total actual manufacturing overhead divided by total actual direct labor dollars. Because auditors test total manufacturing overhead as part of the tests of the acquisition and payment cycle and test direct labor as part of the payroll and personnel cycle, determining the reasonableness of the rate is not difficult. However, if, for example, manufacturing overhead is applied on the basis of machine hours, the auditor must verify the reasonableness of the machine hours by separate tests of the client's machine records.

Because internal controls over cost accounting records vary significantly among companies, specific tests of controls are not discussed here. Auditors should design appropriate tests based on their understanding of the cost accounting records and the extent to which they will be relied on to reduce substantive tests.

ANALYTICAL PROCEDURES

OBJECTIVE 21-4

Apply analytical procedures to the accounts in the inventory and warehousing cycle.

Analytical procedures are important in auditing inventory and warehousing, as they are in all other cycles. Table 21-1 shows several common analytical procedures and possible misstatements that may be indicated when fluctuations occur. We've discussed several of those analytical procedures, such as gross margin percentage, in relation to other cycles.

In addition to performing analytical procedures that examine the relationship of inventory account balances with other financial statement accounts (as shown in Figure 21-1), auditors often use nonfinancial information to assess the reasonableness of inventory-related balances. For example, auditors may need knowledge about the size and weight of inventory products, their methods of storage (stacks, tanks, etc.), and the capacity of storage facilities (available square footage) to determine whether recorded inventory is consistent with available inventory storage. After performing the appropriate tests of the cost accounting records and analytical procedures, auditors have a basis for designing and performing tests of details of the ending inventory balance.

PHYSICAL OBSERVATION OF INVENTORY

OBJECTIVE 21-5

Design and perform physical observation audit tests for inventory.

Because inventory varies significantly for different companies, obtaining an understanding of the client's industry and business is more important for both physical inventory observation and inventory pricing and compilation than for most audit areas. Examples of key considerations that auditors should consider include the

TABLE 21-1	Analytical Procedures for the Inventory and Warehousing Cycle
Analytical Procedure	**Possible Misstatement**
Compare gross margin percentage with that of previous years.	Overstatement or understatement of inventory and cost of goods sold.
Compare inventory turnover (cost of goods sold divided by average inventory) with that of previous years.	Obsolete inventory, which affects inventory and cost of goods sold. Overstatement or understatement of inventory.
Compare unit costs of inventory with those of previous years.	Overstatement or understatement of unit costs, which affect inventory and cost of goods sold.
Compare extended inventory value with that of previous years.	Misstatements in compilation, unit costs, or extensions, which affect inventory and cost of goods sold.
Compare current year manufacturing costs with those of previous years (variable costs should be adjusted for changes in volume).	Misstatements of unit costs of inventory, especially direct labor and manufacturing overhead, which affect inventory and cost of goods sold.

inventory valuation method selected by management, the potential for inventory obsolescence, and the risk that consignment inventory might be intermingled with owned inventory.

Auditors often first familiarize themselves with the client's inventory by conducting a tour of the client's inventory facilities, including receiving, storage, production, planning, and record-keeping areas. The tour should be led by a supervisor who can answer questions about production, especially about any changes in internal controls and other processes since last year. Table 21-2 shows an example of procedures to be followed by the auditor for a physical inventory count.

While gaining an understanding of the effect of the client's business and industry on inventory, auditors assess client business risk to determine if those risks increase the likelihood of material misstatements in inventory. Examples of common sources of business risk for inventory include short product cycles, potential obsolescence, use of just-in-time inventory, reliance on a few key suppliers, and use of sophisticated inventory management technology.

After assessing client business risk, the auditor decides tolerable misstatement and assesses inherent risk for inventory, which is typically highly material for manufacturing, wholesale, and retail companies. Auditors often assess a high inherent risk for companies with significant inventory, depending on the circumstances. Auditors often have a greater concern for misstatements when inventory is stored in multiple locations, the costing method is complex, and the potential for inventory obsolescence is great.

When assessing control risk, the auditor is primarily concerned with internal controls over perpetual records, physical controls, inventory counts, and inventory compilation and pricing. The nature and extent of these controls varies widely from company to company.

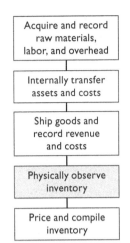

Inventory Observation Requirements

Auditing standards *require* auditors to satisfy themselves about the effectiveness of the client's methods of counting inventory and the reliance they can place on the client's representations about the quantities and physical condition of the inventories. To meet the requirement, auditors must:

- Be present at the time the client counts their inventory for determining year-end balances
- Observe the client's counting procedures
- Make inquiries of client personnel about their counting procedures
- Make their own independent tests of the physical count

| COLLUSION BETWEEN A STOREKEEPER AND A BUYER | When the external auditor of a manufacturing company in Kuwait was carrying out his normal examination of the company's books and records, he received inside information that the storekeeper had colluded with the buyer from one of the company's customers to deliver goods in excess of the quantities requested in return for a cash payment. To conceal the fraud, the storekeeper did not record the additional quantities on the dispatch and delivery documents nor on the store's bin cards. Because there was no system for continuous inventory count or monthly confirmation between the recorded inventory balances, the bin cards, and the warehouse's subsidiary ledger, this fraud was not detected until the external auditor asked to | perform a count of inventory at a time when the storekeeper was absent on sick leave. When the differences between the documents and records were discovered and after he had questioned the assistant storekeeper, the external auditor reported the discrepancies in the company's warehouses to the company's audit department. |

The managing director instructed a representative of the audit department to monitor the merchandise being loaded onto the customer's trucks. After the loads had been checked, the additional items were discovered and the embezzlement became clear. The value of the stolen goods amounted to more than US$800,000. The employee was referred for investigation.

TABLE 21-2	Audit Program—Stocktake Attendance

OBJECTIVE To obtain and record sufficient audit evidence to enable us to form an opinion that closing stock is not materially misstated.

Location	Beirut	Date December 31, 2011
Nature of stocks	Spare parts	
Count method (e.g. counting, weighing, measuring)	Counting	

	WP ref	Comments/results	Initials
A. BEFORE THE COUNT			
1. Obtain the client's stocktaking instructions and assess whether they are adequate. Inform the client of any deficiencies.			
2. Determine the nature and approximate monetary value of the stock to be counted. Note any high value or key stock lines that should be counted on a 100% basis. Consider also any items that were high value in the previous year.			
3. Determine the sample size for test counts.			
4. Where stocks are stored in bulk and cannot be measured accurately, assess the effectiveness of methods used by attending with suitably experienced staff.			
B. DURING THE COUNT			
1. Tour the stockholding areas to ascertain the nature, location, and size of the stocks to be counted.			
2. Note whether the client's staff are following the stocktaking instructions. If not, consider whether we need to extend our test counts.			
3. Ensure that all stock is included in the counting and that all areas are systematically cleared.			
4. Ensure that any defective, obsolete, and slow-moving items are identified and recorded as such on the stock sheets.			
5. Ensure that any items that do not belong to the client are excluded from the count.			
6. Ensure that all differences disclosed by double counts are investigated and resolved.			
7. Record the following text counts in sufficient detail to enable the items selected to be traced to the final stock summary: a. High value and key items (to test for both overstatement and understatement) b. A sample selected from the physical stock items (understatement test) c. A sample selected from the client's count records (overstatement test)			
8. Review procedures for dealing with internal and external movement of goods during the stocktake.			
9. Record purchases/stock and sales/stock cutoff information (e.g. serial numbers of inventory items and dispatch notes).			
10. Examine the serial numbering or other control of count records and note the details.			
11. Where work-in-process is being examined, ensure that adequate information is recorded relating to the degree of completion.			
12. Ensure against subsequent alteration of the stocktaking records by photocopying the stock sheets and recording the numbers of sheets used. (Consult with manager to establish extent of copies to be retained.)			
13. Note below any additional tests that are considered necessary.			
14. The results and conclusions of all work are fully recorded in the working papers and cross-referenced to this program.			

An essential point in the auditing standards is the distinction between who observes the physical inventory count and who is responsible for taking the count. The client is responsible for setting up the procedures for taking an accurate physical inventory and actually making and recording the counts. The auditor is responsible for evaluating and observing the client's procedures, including doing test counts of the inventory and drawing conclusions about the adequacy of the physical inventory.

An auditor's physical examination of inventory is not required if inventory is housed in a public warehouse or overseen by outside custodians. In those situations, auditors verify inventory by confirmation with the custodian. However, if inventory stored with outside custodians represents a significant portion of current assets or total assets, the auditor should apply additional procedures, such as investigating the custodian's inventory procedures, obtaining an independent accountant's report on the custodian's control procedures over the custody of goods, or observing the physical count of the goods held by the custodian, if practical.

Controls Over Physical Count

Regardless of the inventory record-keeping method, the client must make a periodic physical count of inventory, but not necessarily every year. The physical count may be performed at or near the balance sheet date, at an interim date, or on a cycle basis throughout the year. The latter two approaches are appropriate only if there are adequate controls over the preparation and maintenance of the perpetual inventory master files.

Adequate controls over the client's physical count of inventory include proper client instructions for the physical count, supervision by responsible company personnel, independent internal verification of the counts by other client personnel, independent reconciliations of the physical counts with perpetual inventory master files, and adequate client control over count sheets or tags used to record inventory counts.

Auditors need to understand the client's physical inventory count controls before the count of inventory begins. While this understanding is necessary to evaluate the effectiveness of the client's procedures, it also enables the auditor to make constructive suggestions beforehand.

Figure 21-4 represents remarks identified by a local auditing firm resulting from the audit of a tourism complex.

Audit Decisions

The auditor's decisions in the physical observation of inventory are similar to those made for other audit areas. They include selecting audit procedures, deciding the timing of the procedures, determining sample size, and selecting items for testing. The last three decisions are discussed next, followed by a discussion of the appropriate audit procedures.

Timing The auditor decides whether the physical count can be taken before year-end primarily on the basis of the accuracy of the perpetual inventory master files. When a client does an interim physical count, which the auditor will agree to only when internal controls are effective, the auditor observes the inventory count at that time, and also tests transactions recorded in the perpetual inventory records from the date of the count to year-end. When the perpetual records are accurate and related controls operate effectively, it may be unnecessary for the client to count all the inventory at year-end. Instead, the auditor can compare the perpetuals with the actual inventory on a sample basis at convenient times throughout the year, as long as controls over additions and reductions to the perpetual records are tested and found to operate effectively. When there are no perpetuals and the inventory is material, the client must take a complete physical inventory near the end of the accounting period.

FIGURE 21-4	Deficiencies in Inventory Controls and Physical Examination

1. We discovered during supervising the annual physical count of warehouses at the end of 2011 that there were no bin cards available for inventory items on which the name of the item and its code are recorded, a matter which makes it difficult to perform requirements for product counting.
   - We recommend having bin cards for each product item showing all the required data to facilitate the physical count process and achieve internal control on warehouses.

2. We discovered during the audit of the inventory item cards that there are item codes that relate to more than one item. This indicates the lack of internal control over the addition and withdrawal procedures in the warehouses such as:

Item Code	Item Name	Warehouse	Items in same code
3-24/10	Walkers	Maintenance in the main branch	Walkers 60 cm
			Walkers 90 cm
6/24/1	Mosses brush cable 14	Maintenance in El Shorouq branch	Mosses brush cable 14
			Mosses brush cable 18

   - We recommend a review of inventory codes and having a single code for each inventory item.

3. We discovered some variances between the product items included in the computerized perpetual inventory master file and the actual physical count reports, such as:

Warehouse	Item Code	Quantities according to the Computer	Quantities according to actual physical count statements	Average Price per unit US$
Bar c	220008	11	5	31.25
Bar d	222003	2	1	457.43

4. We discovered that the purchasing department did not obtain more than one price offer for some purchases, noting that a percentage of those purchases is bought using one price offer, examples include: purchases made during April for chicken, meat, and other poultry from Allied Brothers (supplier) for US$115,000.
   - We recommend compliance with purchasing procedures by obtaining more than one price offer and choosing the best offer in terms of quality and price through assigning technical members according to the type of purchases.

Sample Size The number of inventory items auditors should count is difficult to specify because auditors concentrate on observing the client's procedures rather than on selecting items for testing. For convenience, sample size in physical observation may be considered in terms of the total number of hours spent rather than the number of inventory items counted. The key determinants of the amount of time needed to test inventory are the adequacy of internal controls over the physical counts, accuracy of the perpetual inventory master files, total dollar amount and type of inventory, number of different significant inventory locations, nature and extent of misstatements discovered in previous years, and other inherent risks.

In some situations, inventory is so material that it requires dozens of auditors to observe the physical count. In other situations, one auditor can complete the observation in a short time. Audit planning for inventory count testing and coordination with client personnel is critical. Poor planning may lead to audit difficulties. For example, it is impossible to observe client personnel counting inventory after they have completed their counts and it is difficult to expand sample sizes or reperform tests after the physical inventory has been taken.

<table>
<tr><td>

THE CRAZY EDDIE, INC. FRAUD

</td><td>

By 1970, Crazy Eddie, Inc., a consumer electronics retail company in the U.S., had 43 consumer sales outlets, sales of US$350 million, reported net income before taxes of US$21 million, and a market value of more than US$500 million. Consumer electronics is a highly cyclical and competitive industry, with significant client business risk. Crazy Eddie seemed to be bucking industry trends by growing as other electronics retailers were struggling, but it was an illusion. By the end of 1989, the company had filed for bankruptcy, closed all stores, and liquidated all assets at a huge loss to investors.

Investigation by regulatory authorities found extensive financial fraud, the most important being a US$65 million overstatement of inventory. Extensive lawsuits were filed against many parties, including the CEO, who was found guilty of fraud and sent to prison.

</td><td>

Naturally, the question arose as to why the auditors failed to uncover the fraud in their annual audit. In their defense, the auditors cited the difficulty of uncovering the well-conceived fraud. The parties involved in or who knew of the fraud included the acting controller, the director of internal auditing, and the director of accounts payable. One example of fraud was the shipment of inventory from store to store immediately before the auditor arrived to count the inventory. Another was the destruction of documentation to conceal inventory shortages at various locations. The auditor argued that it is almost impossible to uncover fraud when there is extensive collusion. The suit against the CPA firm and other defendants was settled out of court.

Source: Adapted from Joseph T. Wells, 'Crazy Eddie and the US$120 Million Ripoff,' *Journal of Accountancy* (October 2000), pp. 93–95.

</td></tr>
</table>

Selection of Items When auditors observe the client counting inventory, they should be careful to:

- Observe the counting of the most significant items and a representative sample of typical inventory items
- Inquire about items that are likely to be obsolete or damaged
- Discuss with management the reasons for excluding any material items

Physical Observation Tests

The most important part of the observation of inventory is determining whether the physical count is being taken in accordance with the client's instructions. To do this effectively, it is essential that the auditor be present while the physical count is taking place.

When the client's employees are not following the inventory instructions, the auditor must either contact the supervisor to correct the problem or modify the physical observation procedures. For example, if the procedures require one team to count the inventory and a second team to recount it as a test of accuracy, the auditor should inform management if both teams are observed counting together.

Table 21-3 lists common tests of details of balances audit procedures for physical inventory observation. Detail tie-in is the only balance-related audit objective not included. That balance-related objective is discussed under compilation of inventory. In the discussion that follows, we assume that the client counts inventory on the balance sheet date and records the inventory counts on prenumbered tags. When they record inventory counts in a different way, audit procedures will vary. In addition to

<table>
<tr><td>

IMPROPER PHYSICAL CONTROLS OVER LOADING MATERIALS FOR SHIPMENT

</td><td>

Fraud was discovered in a multinational paper manufacturing company when a shipment was examined upon arrival in Oman and found to contain cement bags rather than paper materials. The investigation revealed that the cement bags were added to the shipment when the trucks were being loaded at the warehouse of a subsidiary. There had been inadequate supervision of the loading by internal auditors and

</td><td>

by a representative from the inventory control department, which resulted in the cement bags being added to compensate for the weight of the missing paper and to balance the weight of the containers when shipped through El Sokhna Port to Oman.

</td></tr>
</table>

TABLE 21-3	Balance-Related Audit Objectives and Tests of Details of Balances for Physical Inventory Observation	
Balance-Related Audit Objective	**Common Inventory Observation Procedures**	**Comments**
Inventory as recorded on tags exists (existence).	Select a random sample of tag numbers and identify the tag with that number attached to the actual inventory. Observe whether movement of inventory takes place during the count.	The purpose is to uncover the inclusion of nonexistent items as inventory.
Existing inventory is counted and tagged, and tags are accounted for to make sure none are missing (completeness).	Examine inventory to make sure it is tagged. Observe whether movement of inventory takes place during the count. Inquire as to inventory in other locations. Account for all used and unused tags to make sure none are lost or intentionally omitted. Record the tag numbers for those used and unused for subsequent follow-up.	Special concern should be directed to omission of large sections of inventory. This test should be done at the completion of the physical count. This test should be done at the completion of the physical count.
Inventory is counted accurately (accuracy).	Recount client's counts to make sure the recorded counts are accurate on the tags (also check descriptions and unit of count, such as dozen or gross). Compare physical counts with perpetual inventory master file. Record client's counts for subsequent testing.	Recording client counts in the audit files on inventory count sheets is done for two reasons: to obtain documentation that an adequate physical examination was made, and to test for the possibility that the client might change the recorded counts after the auditor leaves the premises.
Inventory is classified correctly on the tags (classification).	Examine inventory descriptions on the tags and compare with the actual inventory for raw material, work-in-process, and finished goods. Evaluate whether the percent of completion recorded on the tags for work-in-process is reasonable.	These tests will be done as a part of the first procedure in the accuracy objective.
Information is obtained to make sure sales and inventory purchases are recorded in the proper period (cutoff).	Record in the audit files for subsequent follow-up the last shipping document number used at year-end. Make sure the inventory for the above item was excluded from the physical count. Review shipping area for inventory set aside for shipment but not counted. Record in the audit files for subsequent follow-up the last receiving report number used at year-end. Make sure the inventory for the above item was included in the physical count. Review receiving area for inventory that should be included in the physical count.	Obtaining proper cutoff information for sales and acquisitions is an essential part of inventory observation. The appropriate tests during the field work were discussed for sales in Chapter 16 and for acquisitions in Chapter 18.
Obsolete and unusable inventory items are excluded or noted (realizable value).	Test for obsolete inventory by inquiry of factory employees and management and alertness for items that are damaged, rust- or dust-covered, or located in inappropriate places.	
The client has rights to inventory recorded on tags (rights).	Inquire about consignment or customer inventory included on client's premises. Be alert for inventory that is set aside or specially marked.	

the detailed procedures in Table 21-3, the auditor should also inspect all physical areas where inventory is warehoused to make sure that all inventory has been counted and properly tagged. Boxes or other containers holding inventory should also be opened during test counts to be certain inventory is physically present. As part of their analytical procedures performed after the client has completed the inventory counts, the auditors may compare high-dollar-value inventory to counts in the previous year and inventory master files as a test of reasonableness.

AUDIT OF PRICING AND COMPILATION

Auditors must verify that the physical counts or perpetual record quantities are correctly priced and compiled. **Inventory price tests** include all the tests of the client's unit prices to determine whether they are correct. Inventory compilation tests include testing the client's summarization of the inventory counts, recalculating price times quantity, footing the inventory summary, and tracing the totals to the general ledger.

Pricing and Compilation Controls

Adequate internal controls surrounding the tracking of unit costs that are integrated with production and other accounting records provides assurance that clients use reasonable costs for valuing ending inventory. **Standard cost records** that indicate variances in material, labor, and overhead costs are helpful to evaluate the reasonableness of production records if management has procedures in place to keep the standards updated for changes in production processes and costs. Management should also have someone independent of the department responsible for determining the costs review them for reasonableness.

To prevent including or overstating the value of obsolete inventory, clients should have a formal review and reporting of obsolete, slow-moving, damaged, and overstated inventory items. The review should be done by a knowledgeable employee who reviews perpetual inventory master files for inventory turnover and holds discussions with engineering or production personnel.

Clients need inventory compilation internal controls to ensure that the physical counts are correctly summarized, priced at the same amount as the unit records, correctly extended and totaled, and included in the perpetual inventory master file and related general ledger inventory accounts at the proper amount. The most important internal control for accurate unit costs, extensions, and footings is internal verification by a competent, independent person, who relies on adequate documents and records that were used for taking the physical count. If the physical inventory counts are recorded by the client on prenumbered tags and carefully reviewed before the personnel who counted the inventory are released from the physical examination of inventory, there should be little risk of misstatement in summarizing inventory count tags.

Pricing and Compilation Procedures

Table 21-4 lists the audit objectives and related tests for inventory pricing and compilation, except for the cutoff objective. As we've already discussed, physical observation is a major source of cutoff information for sales and purchases. Tests of the accounting records for cutoff are done as a part of sales (sales and collection cycle) and acquisitions (acquisition and payment cycle).

Auditors can apply the objectives using information obtained from the client as a frame of reference, including each inventory item's description, quantity, unit price, and extended value. We assume the information reflected in the inventory perpetual listing is recorded in inventory item description order, with raw material, work-in-process, and finished goods listed separately. The listing totals should equal the general ledger balance.

Valuation of Inventory

In performing inventory valuation tests (often called price tests), the auditor has three concerns. First, the method must be in accordance with accounting standards. Second, the application of the method must be consistent from year to year. Third, inventory cost versus market value (net realizable value) must be considered. Because the method

OBJECTIVE 21-6

Design and perform audit tests of pricing and compilation for inventory.

Inventory price tests

Audit procedures used to verify the costs used to value physical inventory.

Standard cost records

Records that indicate variances between projected material, labor, and overhead costs and the actual costs.

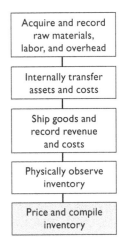

TABLE 21-4	Balance-Related Audit Objectives and Tests of Details of Balances for Inventory Pricing and Compilation	
Balance-Related Audit Objective	**Common Inventory Pricing and Compilation Procedures**	**Comments**
Inventory in the inventory listing schedule agrees with the physical inventory counts, the extensions are correct, and the total is correctly added and agrees with the general ledger (detail tie-in).	Foot the inventory listing schedules for raw materials, work-in-process, and finished goods. Trace the totals to the general ledger. Extend the quantity times the price on selected items.	Unless controls are deficient, extending and footing tests should be limited.
Inventory items in the inventory listing schedule exist (existence).	Trace inventory listed in the schedule to inventory tags and auditor's recorded counts for existence and description. Account for unused tag numbers shown in the auditor's documentation to make sure no tags have been added.	The next five objectives are affected by the results of the physical inventory observation. The tag numbers and counts verified as a part of physical inventory observation are traced to the inventory listing schedule as a part of these tests.
Existing inventory items are included in the inventory listing schedule (completeness).	Trace from inventory tags to the inventory listing schedules and make sure inventory on tags is included. Account for tag numbers to make sure none have been deleted.	
Inventory items in the inventory listing schedule are accurate (accuracy).	Trace inventory listed in the schedule to inventory tags and auditor's recorded counts for quantity and description. Perform price tests of inventory. For a discussion of price tests, see text material on pages 711–714.	
Inventory items in the inventory listing schedule are correctly classified (classification).	Verify the classification into raw materials, work-in-process, and finished goods by comparing the descriptions on inventory tags and auditor's recorded test counts with the inventory listing schedule.	
Inventory items in the inventory listing are stated at realizable value (realizable value).	Perform tests of lower of cost or market, selling price, and obsolescence.	
The client has rights to inventory items in the inventory listing schedule (rights).	Trace inventory tags identified as nonowned during the physical observation to the inventory listing schedule to make sure these have not been included. Review contracts with suppliers and customers and inquire of management for the possibility of the inclusion of consigned or other nonowned inventory, or the exclusion of owned inventory.	

of verifying the pricing of inventory depends on whether inventory items are acquired or manufactured, these two categories are discussed separately.

Pricing Purchased Inventory The primary types of inventory included in this category are raw materials, purchased parts, and supplies. As a first step in verifying the valuation of purchased inventory, the auditor must determine whether the client uses LIFO, FIFO, weighted average, or some other valuation method. Auditors must also determine which costs should be included in the valuation of an item of inventory. For example, the auditor must find out whether freight, storage, discounts, and other costs are included and the auditor must compare the findings with the preceding year to make sure that the costs are determined consistently.

In selecting specific inventory items for pricing, auditors should focus on larger dollar amounts and on products that are known to have wide fluctuations in price. They should also test a representative sample of all types of inventory and departments. Stratified variables or monetary unit sampling is commonly used for these tests.

The auditor should list the inventory items to be verified for pricing and request the client to locate the appropriate vendors' invoices. The auditor must examine sufficient invoices to account for the entire quantity of inventory for the item being tested, especially for the FIFO valuation method. Assume that the client values an inventory item at US$12.00 per unit for 1,000 units, using FIFO. When the auditor examines the most recent invoices for acquisitions of that inventory item, she finds that the most recent acquisition of the inventory item in the year being audited was for 700 units at US$12.00 per unit, and the immediately preceding acquisition was for 600 units at US$11.30 per unit. Using correct FIFO valuation techniques, the inventory items should be included at US$11,790 (700 units at US$12 and 300 at US$11.30). The client's calculations overstates inventory by US$210.00 (US$12,000 – US$11,790). Assuming the client makes this same error on many inventory items, the misstatement amount can be material.

When the client has perpetual inventory master files that include unit costs of acquisitions, it is usually much faster to test the pricing by tracing the unit costs to the perpetuals rather than to vendors' invoices. Naturally, when perpetual inventory records are used to verify unit costs, auditors must test the unit costs recorded in the perpetual records to vendors' invoices as a part of the tests of the acquisition and payment cycle transactions.

Pricing Manufactured Inventory In pricing work-in-process and finished goods, the auditor must consider the cost of raw materials, direct labor, and manufacturing overhead. The need to verify each of these makes the audit of work-in-process and finished goods inventory more complex than the audit of purchased inventory. Nevertheless, several considerations that apply to the audit of purchased inventory still apply, such as selecting the items to be tested, testing for whether cost or market value is lower, and evaluating the possibility of obsolescence.

In pricing raw materials in manufactured products, auditors must consider both the unit cost of the raw materials and the number of units required to manufacture a unit of output. The unit cost can be verified in the same manner as that used for other purchased inventory, by examining vendors' invoices or perpetual inventory master files. Auditors must examine engineering specifications, inspect the finished product, or find a similar method to determine the number of units it takes to manufacture a product.

Similarly, while testing direct labor, auditors must verify the hourly costs of direct labor and the number of hours it takes to manufacture a unit of output. Hourly labor costs can be verified by examining labor payroll or union contracts. Auditors can determine the number of hours needed to manufacture the product from engineering specifications or similar sources.

The proper manufacturing overhead in work-in-process and finished goods depends on the approach the client uses to allocate manufacturing overhead. Auditors must evaluate the method being used for consistency and reasonableness and recompute the costs to determine whether the overhead is correct. For example, if the rate is based on direct labor dollars, the auditor can divide the total manufacturing overhead by the total direct labor dollars to determine the actual overhead rate. This rate can then be compared with the overhead rate used by the client to determine unit costs. Testing of pricing for work-in-process and finished goods is often done in conjunction with tests of standard costs. When auditors have tested standard costs with satisfactory results, they can limit testing of the unit costs of ending inventory to tracing the price used to value ending inventory to the standard cost records.

When the client has standard costs records, an efficient and useful method of determining valuation is to review and analyze variances. Small variances in material, labor, and manufacturing overhead are evidence of reliable cost records.

Cost or Market   In pricing inventory, auditors must consider whether net realizable value is lower than historical cost. For purchased finished goods and raw materials, auditors can test for net realizable value by examining vendor invoices of the subsequent period or recent invoices if no purchases of an inventory item were made after year-end. All manufacturing costs must be considered in evaluating realizable value for work-in-process and finished goods for manufactured inventory. Auditors must consider the sales value of inventory items and the possible effect of rapid fluctuation of prices to determine net realizable value.

INTEGRATION OF THE TESTS

OBJECTIVE 21-7

Integrate the various parts of the audit of the inventory and warehousing cycle.

Figure 21-5 and the discussions that follow summarize and illustrate the audit of the inventory and warehousing cycle as a series of integrated tests.

Tests of the Acquisition and Payment Cycle   When auditors verify inventory acquisitions as part of the tests of the acquisition and payment cycle, they are also obtaining evidence about the accuracy of raw materials acquired and all manufacturing overhead costs incurred except labor. These acquisition costs either flow directly into cost of goods sold or become the largest part of the ending inventory of raw material, work-in-process, and finished goods. In audits where clients have perpetual inventory master files, auditors commonly test these as a part of tests of controls and substantive tests of transactions procedures performed in the acquisition and payment cycle. Similarly, if manufacturing costs are assigned to individual jobs or processes, they are usually tested as a part of the same cycle.

Tests of the Payroll and Personnel Cycle   When auditors verify labor costs, the same conditions apply as for acquisitions. In most cases, the cost accounting records for direct and indirect labor costs can be tested as part of the audit of the payroll and personnel cycle.

Tests of the Sales and Collection Cycle   The relationship between the sales and collection cycle and the inventory and warehousing cycle is not as interwoven as the two cycles we just discussed. Nonetheless, most of the audit testing in the storage of finished goods, as well as the shipment and recording of sales, takes place when the sales and collection cycle is tested. When the client uses standard cost records, auditors may be able to test the standard cost of goods sold at the same time that sales tests are performed.

Tests of Cost Accounting   Tests of cost accounting records are meant to verify the controls affecting inventory that auditors did not verify as part of testing in the preceding three cycles. Auditors test the physical controls, transfers of raw material costs to work-in-process, transfers of costs of completed goods to finished goods, perpetual inventory master files, and unit cost records.

Physical Inventory, Pricing, and Compilation   Physical inventory, pricing, and compilation are each equally important in the audit of inventory because a misstatement in any one activity results in misstated inventory and cost of goods sold. In most audits, cost of goods sold is a residual of beginning inventory plus acquisitions of raw materials, direct labor, and other manufacturing costs minus ending inventory. Because

FIGURE 21-5 | **Interrelationship of Various Audit Tests**

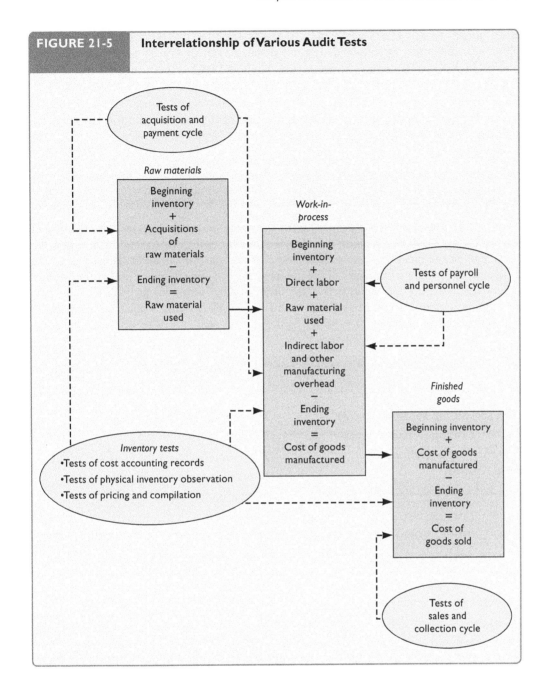

cost of goods sold is a residual and often one of the largest accounts on the income statement, the importance of auditing ending inventory becomes obvious.

In testing physical inventory, auditors may rely heavily on the perpetual inventory master files if they have been tested as a part of one or more of the cycles we've discussed and are considered reliable. When that is the case, auditors can observe and test the physical count at a time other than year-end and rely on the perpetuals to keep adequate records of the quantities.

When testing the unit costs, auditors may also rely, to some degree, on the tests of the cost records made during the substantive tests of transactions. Standard cost records are also useful for comparison with the actual unit costs. When standard costs are used to represent historical cost, they must be tested for reliability.

Finally, as auditors test controls and perform substantive tests related to inventory transactions and balances, they also integrate tests related to balance-related audit objectives with tests performed to satisfy the four presentation and disclosure objectives. Accounting standards require disclosure of inventory valuation methods and other relevant inventory information, such as LIFO reserve information, in the footnotes. The auditor should obtain an understanding of client controls related to inventory disclosures and perform tests of those controls and other substantive tests to obtain sufficient appropriate evidence for each of the four presentation and disclosure objectives.

SUMMARY

In this chapter, we discussed the audit of the inventory and warehousing cycle. Because of the difficulties associated with establishing the existence and valuation of inventories, the cycle is often the most time-consuming and complex part of the audit. This cycle is also unique because many of the tests of the inputs to the cycle are tested as part of the audit of other cycles. Tests performed as part of the inventory and warehousing cycle focus on cost accounting records, physical observation, and tests of the pricing and compilation of the ending inventory balance.

ESSENTIAL TERMS

Cost accounting controls   p. 701

Cost accounting records   p. 698

Inventory and warehousing cycle   p. 696

Inventory compilation tests   p. 700

Inventory price tests   p. 711

Job cost system   p. 698

Perpetual inventory master file   p. 698

Process cost system   p. 698

Standard cost records   p. 711

REVIEW QUESTIONS

21-1 (Objective 21-1) Give the reasons why inventory is often the most difficult and time-consuming part of many audits.

21-2 (Objectives 21-1, 21-7) Explain the relationship between the acquisition and payment cycle and the inventory and warehousing cycle in the audit of a manufacturing company. List several audit procedures in the acquisition and payment cycle that support your explanation.

21-3 (Objectives 21-1, 21-3) State what is meant by cost accounting records and explain their importance in the conduct of an audit.

21-4 (Objective 21-3) Many auditors assert that certain audit tests can be significantly reduced for clients with adequate perpetual records that include both unit and cost data. What are the most important tests of the perpetual records that the auditor must make before reducing assessed control risk? Assuming the perpetuals are determined to be accurate, which tests can be reduced?

21-5 (Objective 21-5) Before the physical examination, the auditor obtains a copy of the client's inventory instructions and reviews them with the controller. In obtaining an understanding of inventory procedures for a small manufacturing company, these deficiencies are identified: Shipping operations will not be completely halted during the physical examination, and there will be no independent verification of the original inventory count by a second counting team. Evaluate the importance of each of these deficiencies and state its effect on the auditor's observation of inventory.

21-6 (Objective 21-5) At the completion of an inventory observation, the controller requested the auditor to give him a copy of all recorded test counts to facilitate the correction of all discrepancies between the client's and the auditor's counts. Should the auditor comply with the request? Why?

21-7 (Objective 21-5) What major audit procedures are involved in testing for the ownership of inventory during the observation of the physical counts and as a part of subsequent valuation tests?

21-8 (Objectives 21-4, 21-5, 21-6) In the verification of the amount of the inventory, one of the auditor's concerns is that slow-moving and obsolete items be identified. List the auditing procedures that can be used to determine whether slow-moving or obsolete items have been included in inventory.

21-9 (Objective 21-5) During the taking of physical inventory, the controller intentionally withheld several inventory tags from the employees responsible for the physical count. After the auditor left the client's premises at the completion of the inventory observation, the controller recorded nonexistent inventory on the tags and thereby significantly overstated earnings. How could the auditor have uncovered the misstatement, assuming that there are no perpetual records?

21-10 (Objective 21-5) Explain why a proper cutoff of purchases and sales is heavily dependent on the physical inventory observation. What information should be obtained during the physical count to make sure that cutoff is accurate?

21-11 (Objective 21-6) Define what is meant by compilation tests. List several examples of audit procedures to verify compilation.

21-12 (Objective 21-4) List the major analytical procedures for testing the overall reasonableness of inventory. For each test, explain the type of misstatement that could be identified.

21-13 (Objective 21-6) Included in the December 31, 2011, inventory of the Salmania Supply Company are 2,600 deluxe ring binders for the amount of US$5,902. An examination of the most recent acquisitions of binders showed the following costs: January 26, 2012, 2,300 at US$2.42 each; December 6, 2011, 1,900 at US$2.28 each; November 26, 2011, 2,400 at US$2.07 each. What is the misstatement in valuation of the December 31, 2011, inventory for deluxe ring binders, assuming FIFO inventory valuation? What would your answer be if the January 26, 2012, acquisition was for 2,300 binders at US$2.12 each?

21-14 (Objectives 21-6, 21-7) The Riyad Manufacturing Company applied manufacturing overhead to inventory at December 31, 2011, on the basis of US$3.47 per direct labor hour. Explain how you will evaluate the reasonableness of total direct labor hours and manufacturing overhead in the ending inventory of finished goods.

21-15 (Objective 21-7) Each employee for the Halab Manufacturing Co., a firm using a job-cost inventory costing method, must reconcile his or her total hours worked with the hours worked on individual jobs using a job timesheet at the time weekly payroll time cards are prepared. The job timesheet is then stapled to the time card. Explain how you could test the direct labor dollars included in inventory as a part of the payroll and personnel tests.

21-16 (Objective 21-5) Assuming that the auditor properly documents receiving report numbers as a part of the physical inventory observation procedures, explain how the proper cutoff of purchases, including tests for the possibility of raw materials in transit, should be verified later in the audit.

MULTIPLE CHOICE QUESTIONS FROM CPA EXAMINATIONS

21-17 (Objective 21-1) The following questions concern internal controls in the inventory and warehousing cycle. Choose the best response.

a. In a company with materials and supplies that include a great number of items, a fundamental deficiency in control requirements will be indicated if
(1) the cycle basis for physical inventory taking was to be used.
(2) minor supply items were to be expensed when acquired.
(3) a perpetual inventory master file is not maintained for items of small value.
(4) the storekeeping function were to be combined with production and record keeping.

b. For control purposes, the quantities of materials ordered may be omitted from the copy of the purchase order that is
(1) returned to the requisitioner.
(2) forwarded to the receiving department.
(3) forwarded to the accounting department.
(4) retained in the purchasing department's files.

c. Which of the following procedures will best detect the theft of valuable items from an inventory that consists of hundreds of different items selling for US$1 to US$10 and a few items selling for hundreds of dollars?
(1) Maintain a perpetual inventory master file of only the more valuable items with frequent periodic verification of the validity of the perpetuals.
(2) Have an independent auditing firm prepare an internal control report on the effectiveness of the administrative and accounting controls over inventory.
(3) Have separate warehouse space for the more valuable items with sequentially numbered tags.
(4) Require an authorized officer's signature on all requisitions for the more valuable terms.

21-18 (Objectives 21-1, 21-3) The following questions concern testing the client's internal controls for inventory and warehousing. Choose the best response.

a. When an auditor tests a client's cost accounting records, the auditor's tests are primarily designed to determine that
(1) costs have been correctly assigned to finished goods, work-in-process, and cost of goods sold.
(2) quantities on hand have been computed based on acceptable cost accounting techniques that reasonably approximate actual quantities on hand.
(3) physical inventories are in substantial agreement with book inventories.
(4) the internal controls are in accordance with accounting standards and are functioning as planned.

b. The accuracy of perpetual inventory master files may be established, in part, by comparing perpetual inventory records with
(1) purchase requisitions.　　(3) purchase orders.
(2) receiving reports.　　(4) vendor payments.

c. When evaluating inventory controls with respect to segregation of duties, an auditor will be least likely to
(1) make inquiries.　　(3) observe procedures.
(2) inspect documents.　　(4) consider policy and procedure manuals.

21-19 (Objectives 21-1, 21-4, 21-5, 21-6) The following questions deal with tests of details of balances and analytical procedures for inventory. Choose the best response.

a. An auditor will be most likely to learn of slow-moving inventory through
(1) inquiry of sales personnel.
(2) inquiry of store personnel.

    (3) physical observation of inventory.

    (4) review of perpetual inventory master files.

b. An inventory turnover analysis is useful to the auditor because it may detect

    (1) inadequacies in inventory pricing.

    (2) methods of avoiding cyclical holding costs.

    (3) the existence of obsolete merchandise.

    (4) the optimum automatic reorder points.

c. An auditor auditing inventory may appropriately apply attributes sampling to estimate the

    (1) average price of inventory items.

    (2) percentage of slow-moving inventory items.

    (3) dollar value of inventory.

    (4) physical quantity of inventory items.

DISCUSSION QUESTIONS AND PROBLEMS

21-20 (Objectives 21-1, 21-3, 21-5, 21-6, 21-7) Items 1 through 8 are selected questions typically found in questionnaires used by auditors to obtain an understanding of internal control in the inventory and warehousing cycle. In using the questionnaire for a client, a 'yes' response to a question indicates a possible internal control, whereas a 'no' indicates a potential deficiency.

1. Is a detailed perpetual inventory master file maintained for raw materials inventory?

2. Does the receiving department prepare prenumbered receiving reports and account for the numbers periodically for all inventory received, showing the description and quantity of materials?

3. Is all inventory stored under the control of an inventory custodian in areas where access is limited?

4. Are all shipments to customers authorized by prenumbered shipping documents?

5. Are physical inventory counts made by someone other than storekeepers and those responsible for maintaining the perpetual inventory master file?

6. Are standard cost records used for raw materials, direct labor, and manufacturing overhead?

7. Is there a stated policy with specific criteria for writing off obsolete or slow-moving goods?

8. Is the clerical accuracy of the final inventory compilation checked by a person independent of those responsible for preparing it?

Required

a. For each of the preceding questions, state the purpose of the internal control.

b. For each internal control, list a test of control to test its effectiveness.

c. For each of the preceding questions, identify the nature of the potential financial misstatement(s) if the control is not in effect.

d. For each of the potential misstatements in part c, list a substantive audit procedure to determine whether a material misstatement exists.

21-21 (Objective 21-1, 21-3, 21-5, 21-6, 21-7) The Radio Corporation has the following internal controls related to inventory:

1. The inventory purchasing system only allows purchases from pre-approved vendors.

2. The perpetual inventory system tracks the average number of days each inventory product number has been in the warehouse.

3. Only authorized inventory warehousing personnel are allowed in inventory storage areas.

4. All inventory products are stored in warehousing areas that are segregated from other storage areas used to house equipment and supplies.

5. On a weekly basis, inventory accounting personnel take samples of inventory products selected from the perpetual inventory system and verify that the inventory is on-hand in the warehouse and that the quantities in the listing are correct.

6. On a weekly basis, inventory accounting personnel select inventory items on hand in the warehouse and verify that the item is included in the perpetual inventory listing at the correct amount.

7. The perpetual inventory system subtotals the quantity of inventory in the system and interfaces with the general ledger system on a daily basis to ensure quantities agree.

8. The perpetual inventory system will not accept inventory additions without the recording on a valid receiving report.

9. All inventory held on consignment at Radio Corporation is stored in a separate area of the warehouse.

For each of the internal controls:

Required

a. Identify the related transaction-related audit objective(s) affected by the control.

b. Describe risks the control is designed to mitigate.

c. Design a test of control to determine if the control is operating effectively.

21-22 (Objectives 21-1, 21-5, 21-6) The following misstatements are included in the inventory and related records of Dubai Manufacturing Company:

1. An inventory item was priced at US$12 each instead of at the correct cost of US$12 per dozen.

2. In taking the physical inventory, the last shipments for the day were excluded from inventory and were not included as a sale until the subsequent year.

3. The clerk in charge of the perpetual inventory master file altered the quantity on an inventory tag to cover up the shortage of inventory caused by its theft during the year.

4. After the auditor left the premises, several inventory tags were lost and were not included in the final inventory summary.

5. When raw material acquisitions were recorded, the improper unit price was included in the perpetual inventory master file. Therefore, the inventory valuation was misstated because the physical inventory was priced by referring to the perpetual records.

6. During the physical count, several obsolete inventory items were included.

7. Because of a significant increase in volume during the current year and excellent control over manufacturing overhead costs, the manufacturing overhead rate applied to inventory was far greater than actual cost.

Required

a. For each misstatement, state an internal control that should have prevented it from occurring.

b. For each misstatement, state a substantive audit procedure that can be used to uncover it.

21-23 (Objectives 21-1, 21-3, 21-5, 21-6) Following are audit procedures commonly performed in the inventory and warehousing cycle for a manufacturing company:

1. Read the client's physical inventory instructions and observe whether they are being followed by those responsible for counting the inventory.

2. Account for a sequence of inventory tags and trace each tag to the physical inventory to make sure it actually exists.

3. Compare the client's count of physical inventory at an interim date with the perpetual inventory master file.

4. Trace the auditor's test counts recorded in the audit files to the final inventory compilation and compare the tag number, description, and quantity.

5. Compare the unit price on the final inventory summary with vendors' invoices.

6. Account for a sequence of raw material requisitions and examine each requisition for an authorized approval.

7. Trace the recorded additions on the finished goods perpetual inventory master file to the records for completed production.

a. Identify whether each of the procedures is primarily a test of control or a substantive test.

b. State the purpose(s) of each of the procedures.

21-24 (Objective 21-5) You encountered the following situations during the December 31, 2011, physical inventory of Bata Shoe Distributor Company:

a. Badar stores a large portion of its shoe merchandise in ten warehouses throughout the Kingdom of Saudi Arabia. This ensures swift delivery service to its chain of stores. You are assigned alone to the Riyadh warehouse to observe the physical inventory process. During the inventory count, several express trucks pulled in for loading. Although infrequent, express shipments must be attended to immediately. As a result, the employees who were counting the inventory stopped to assist in loading the express trucks. What should you do?

b. (1) In one storeroom of 10,000 items, you have test-counted about 200 items of high value and a few items of low value. You found no misstatements. You also note that the employees are diligently following the inventory instructions. Do you think you have tested enough items? Explain.

(2) What would you do if you test-counted 150 items and found a substantial number of counting errors?

c. In observing an inventory of liquid shoe polish, you note that one lot is five years old. From inspection of some bottles in an open box, you find that the liquid has solidified in most of the bottles. What action should you take?

d. During your observation of the inventory count in the main warehouse, you found that most of the prenumbered tags that had been incorrectly filled out are being destroyed and thrown away. What is the significance of this procedure and what action should you take?

21-25 (Objectives 21-5, 21-6) Often, an important aspect of the audit of financial statements is observation of the taking of physical inventory.

a. What are the general objectives or purposes of an auditor's observation of the taking of the physical inventory? (Do not discuss the procedures or techniques involved in making the observation.)

b. For what purposes does the auditor make and record test counts of inventory quantities during observation of the taking of the physical inventory? Discuss.

c. A number of companies employ outside service companies that specialize in counting, pricing, extending, and footing inventories. These service companies usually furnish a certificate attesting to the value of the inventory. Assuming that the service company took the inventory on the balance sheet date:

(1) How much reliance, if any, can the auditor place on the inventory certificate of outside specialists? Discuss.

(2) What effect, if any, will the inventory certificate of outside specialists have upon the type of report the auditor will render? Discuss.

(3) What reference, if any, will the auditor make to the certificate of outside specialists in the audit report?[21]

21-26 (Objective 21-4) You are performing the analytical procedures for the audit of the inventory and warehousing cycle for the Abdullah Printers Company, a wholesale distributor of computer printers and other peripheral hardware. Your data is shown in the following chart (dollar amounts are in thousands):

	2011	2010	2009
Revenue	US$76,476	US$68,222	US$56,741
Cost of goods sold	36,686	33,125	27,804
Beginning inventory	5,977	5,252	4,173
Ending inventory	7,125	5,977	5,252

The gross margin and inventory turnover industry averages are as follows:

	2011	2010	2009
Gross Margin %	49%	49%	48%
Inventory Turnover	5.7	5.8	5.9

Required

a. Calculate the following ratios, using an electronic spreadsheet program (instructor's option):
(1) Gross margin as a percentage of sales
(2) Inventory turnover

b. What does the gross margin tell the auditor as an analytical tool? List several possible reasons for the changes in this ratio.

c. What does the inventory turnover tell the auditor as an analytical tool? List several possible reasons for the changes in this ratio.

d. What should the auditor do to determine the actual cause of the changes?

e. Assume you had already set a certain amount of planning materiality based on acceptable findings in the preliminary analytical procedures. Based on the results calculated in part a compared to the industry averages would you increase substantive testing, decrease substantive testing, or leave substantive testing as originally planned?

21-27 (Objective 21-5) In an annual audit at December 31, 2011, you find the following transactions near the closing date:

1. Merchandise costing US$1,822 was received on January 3, 2012 and the related acquisition invoice recorded January 5. The invoice showed the shipment was made on December 29, 2011, FOB destination.

2. Merchandise costing US$625 was received on December 28, 2011, and the invoice was not recorded. You located it in the hands of the purchasing agent; it was marked 'on consignment.'

3. A packing case containing products costing US$816 was standing in the shipping room when the physical inventory was taken. It was not included in the inventory because it was marked 'Hold for shipping instructions.' Your investigation revealed that the customer's order was dated December 18, 2011, but that the case was shipped and the customer billed on January 10, 2012. The product was a stock item of your client.

4. Merchandise received on January 6, 2012, costing US$720 was entered in the acquisitions journal on January 7, 2012. The invoice showed shipment was made FOB supplier's warehouse on December 31, 2011. Because it was not on hand December 31, it was not included in inventory.

5. A special machine, fabricated to order for a customer, was finished and in the shipping room on December 31, 2011. The customer was billed on that date and the machine excluded from inventory, although it was shipped on January 4, 2012.

Assume that each of the amounts is material.

Required

a. State whether the merchandise should be included in the client's inventory.

b. Give your reason for your decision on each item.[22]

21-28 (Objective 21-5) You have been assigned the inventory observation procedure for Gaza Grocery Market chain. There are multiple stores being counted on the night of December 31, 2011, and you and eight other members of your team are performing simultaneous observations at different unannounced locations. In accordance with auditing standards, you have arrived on that night with the assignment of:

1. making independent tests of the physical count
2. making inquiries of client personnel about counting procedures
3. observing the client counting procedures

When you arrive you quickly locate the manager overseeing the count and request from him a count sheet that is being used by one of the client's ten counters. The count manager is at the front of the store with a portable computer and portable printer. The counters are using electronic instruments to input the counts, which are then uploaded into the computer as the count progresses. Count procedures indicate that each section will be counted twice by different counters; for multiple small items all items are to be removed from the shelf and placed back on the shelf when counting; once the section is counted the section is marked with a tag and the count is brought to the front to upload into the computer. You request a section of the store that has already been counted and are provided with a printout, as shown below.

Task 1—Making independent tests of the physical count. Your first task is to recount the items found by the counter. Also, you have been asked by your manager to select several items from the shelf and test that count to the sheet provided by the client. You select five to count floor to sheet and five to count sheet to floor. Your findings are as follows:

Aisle	Row	Section	Item	Price	Qty. per Records	Client Count	Auditor Count, Sheet to Floor	Auditor Count, Floor to Sheet
10	4	134	Canned string beans	1.25	40	40		
10	4	134	Canned corn	1.35	32	32	32	
10	4	134	Canned peas	1.15	66	67		67
10	4	134	Canned cut beans	1.25	80	80	79	
10	4	134	Canned whole beans	1.25	51	50		50
10	4	134	Canned tomatoes	1.00	48	46	46	
10	4	134	Canned diced tomatoes—zesty	1.10	52	52		60
10	4	134	Canned diced tomatoes—regular	1.10	41	40	41	
10	4	134	Canned stewed tomatoes	1.30	46	45		45
10	4	134	Canned tomato sauce	0.99	40	40		
10	4	134	Canned tomato sauce—spicy	0.89	42	42		44
10	4	134	Canned tomato paste	0.89	71	70	82	
10	4	134	Canned tomato paste—spicy	0.89	80	80		

Task 2—Making inquiries of personnel about counting procedures. After you recount several items, you approach several of the counters and discuss procedures with them. All the counters seem to have the proper understanding of the count procedures as it has been explained to you by the Count Manager.

Task 3—Observing the client's counting procedures. Once you observe the count procedures, you notice that several counters are working together to count the same items at the same time. Also, some counters don't appear to be moving small items from the shelf to count the items behind the front items.

Required

a. Why are the inventory observation locations unannounced?

b. Which procedure in Task 1 tests for existence and which for completeness? What is the audit purpose for testing both of these assertions? Which is typically more important in an audit of the inventory cycle?

c. What is the appropriate follow-up action for the counts observed in the chart above?

d. Is there any necessary follow up on Task 2? How many people would you talk to before you are satisfied?

e. What could be the results of the issues found during Task 3? Which is more important, that the physical counts are absolutely correct, or that the count is being conducted in accordance with the client's procedures? Why? How would you follow up?

CASE

21-29 (Objective 21-6) You are assigned to the December 31, 2011, audit of Al Ammon Automobiles, Inc. The company designs and manufactures automobile structures and engine components. You observed the physical inventory at December 31 and are satisfied that it was properly taken. As part of the inventory price testing, you have requested vendor invoices for all of the selected samples.

Sample Selected for Testing:

MATERIALS COST PER CLIENT RECORDS FOR FINISHED GOODS:

Sample No.	Description	Quantity	Valuation per Books
1	Struts	4,000 units	US$145,000
2	Tires	4,000 units	100,000
3	Fasteners	10,000 units	21,400
4	Molded bumpers	1,000 units	210,000

Below are the vendor invoices related to the samples selected for testing. Your client was not sure which invoices to provide, so they provided all invoices from October through December 2011 for the appropriate vendors.

VENDOR INVOICES:

Vendor Name	Invoice No.	Invoice Date	Description of Items
Mourad Struts	1023	Oct 1, 2011	Struts; 3,000 units; US$35.00 per unit
Talal Tires	45873342-a	Nov 15, 2011	Tires; 4,000 units; US$25.00 per unit
Fasteners To Go	45-111508	Nov 15, 2011	Fasteners, 4,000 units; US$2.00 per unit
Mourad Struts	1032	Dec 20, 2011	Struts; 2,000 units; US$40.00 per unit
Fasteners To Go	45-113008	Nov 30, 2011	Fasteners; 4,000 units; US$2.10 per unit
Bumpers R Us	2309	Dec 21, 2011	Molded bumpers; 500 units; US$200.00 per unit
Fasteners To Go	45-121508	Dec 15, 2011	Fasteners; 4,000 units; US$2.50 per unit
Fasteners To Go	45-123108	Dec 31, 2011	Fasteners; 4,000 units; US$2.60 per unit
Bumpers R Us	2315	Dec 31, 2011	Molded bumpers; 500 units; US$210.00 per unit

Al Ammon Automobiles uses a periodic inventory system and values its inventory at the lower of FIFO cost or market.

Required

a. What is the audit assertion and the audit purpose of inventory price testing?

b. What is your assessment of the valuation of the materials as provided by the client? Prepare an audit schedule to summarize your findings. Use the computer to prepare the schedule (instructor's option).

c. Assume tolerable misstatement for this testing is US$30,000. How would you proceed from this point with respect to audit testing?

MYLAB ACTIVITY

 Visit MyAccountingLab and complete the following activity:

→ **Internet Problem 21-1:** Using Inventory Count Specialists.

AUDIT OF THE CAPITAL ACQUISITION AND REPAYMENT CYCLE

LEARNING OBJECTIVES

After studying this chapter, you should be able to

22-1 Identify the accounts and the unique characteristics of the capital acquisition and repayment cycle.

22-2 Design and perform audit tests of notes payable and related accounts and transactions.

22-3 Identify the primary concerns in the audit of owners' equity transactions.

22-4 Design and perform tests of controls, substantive tests of transactions, and tests of details of balances for capital stock and retained earnings.

A Dishonest Client Will Get The Best Of The Auditor Almost Every Time

Able Construction Company entered into long-term construction contracts, recognizing income using the percentage of completion method of accounting. To finance its operations, Able borrowed funds from the bank and agreed to comply with restrictive loan covenants dependent on reported income from the long-term contracts. The percentage of completion method of accounting requires, among other things, an agreement with well-defined, enforceable terms, a reliable method of estimating costs to complete the contracts, and recognition of losses at the time they become known. As part of the audit of Able, its auditors read the contracts for all projects in progress, tested costs incurred to date, and assessed the ultimate profitability of the contracts, including discussing them with management. A significant part of verifying income under percentage of completion is auditing costs incurred.

In the current year, management's records and schedules of projects indicate that all projects will result in a profit. For each project, there is a separate schedule showing estimated total revenue from the project, costs incurred in the current period, costs incurred to date, estimated total costs, percentage of completion, and profit recognized in the current period. The auditor discussed each project with management, performed audit tests to support the schedule, and concluded that the revenue, expenses, and profit were reasonably stated. Reported income allowed Able to meet several of the restrictive covenants in its loan agreement with the bank.

In fact, Able had incurred a significant loss on one of its major projects. Able engaged a subcontractor to do reconstructive work not anticipated in the original contract bid. In awarding the subcontract, Able entered into an agreement with the subcontractor that the work would not be paid for until after its audit was completed in an effort to defer recording losses associated with the additional work. Management hid the subcontractor's invoices from the auditors as they were received. During the next year, management recognized this loss but doctored the invoices so that it appeared the 'unexpected' additional cost was incurred during that year, and that the previous year's statements were correct and that all loan covenants with the bank were satisfied.

The fraudulent misstatement was discovered several years later when Able went bankrupt and the audit firm was sued by the bank for performing inadequate audits. The firm was ultimately found not responsible, but only after spending extensive time and large amounts of money defending its audit.

Capital acquisition and repayment cycle

The transaction cycle that involves the acquisition of capital resources in the form of interest-bearing debt and owners' equity, and the repayment of the capital.

The final transaction cycle we discuss is the **capital acquisition and repayment cycle**, which concerns the acquisition of capital resources through interest-bearing debt and owners' equity and the repayment of the capital. This cycle also includes the payment of interest and dividends.

Four characteristics of the capital acquisition and repayment cycle influence the audit of these accounts:

1. *Relatively few transactions affect the account balances, but each transaction is often highly material.* For example, bonds are infrequently issued by companies, but the amount of a bond issue is normally large. Their size makes it common for auditors, as a part of verifying the balance sheet accounts, to verify each transaction taking place in the cycle for the entire year. Audit schedules for most accounts in the cycle include the beginning balance of every account, every transaction that occurred during the year, and the ending balance.

2. *The exclusion or misstatement of a single transaction can be material.* As a result, the auditor's primary emphasis in auditing these accounts is often on the completeness and accuracy balance-related audit objectives.

3. *A legal relationship exists between the client entity and the holder of the stock, bond, or similar ownership document.* As the chapter-opening case of Able Construction Company demonstrates, the auditor must determine whether the client has met the requirements of debt or equity agreements. In the audit of the transactions and amounts in the cycle, the auditor must take great care to make sure the significant legal requirements affecting the financial statements have been met and adequately presented and disclosed in the statements.

4. *A direct relationship exists between the interest and dividends accounts and debt and equity.* In the audit of interest-bearing debt, auditors should simultaneously verify the related interest expense and interest payable. This is also true for owners' equity, dividends declared, and dividends payable.

Auditors often learn about capital acquisition transactions while gaining an understanding of the client's business and industry performed as part of the auditor's risk assessment procedures. Also, when public companies issue additional debt and equity securities during the year, the supervisory or oversight capital market boards require auditor consideration of financial information included in the client's new securities offering prospectus. In doing so, auditors frequently identify business risk issues for capital acquisition activities that should be considered in the design of audit procedures for transactions, account balances, and disclosures in the capital acquisition and repayment cycle.

Relevant International Standards on Auditing	
ISA 200	Overall Objectives of the Independent Auditor and the Conduct of an Audit in Accordance with International Standards on Auditing
ISA 230	Audit Documentation
ISA 265	Communicating Deficiencies in Internal Control to Those Charged with Governance and Management
ISA 300	Planning an Audit of Financial Statements
ISA 315	Identifying and Assessing the Risks of Material Misstatement through Understanding the Entity and Its Environment
ISA 450	Evaluation of Misstatements Identified during the Audit
ISA 500	Audit Evidence
ISA 505	External Confirmations

ACCOUNTS IN THE CYCLE

The accounts in a company's capital acquisition and repayment cycle depend on the type of business the company operates and how its operations are financed. All corporations have capital stock and retained earnings, but some may also have preferred stock, additional paid-in capital, and treasury stock. As with other cycles, cash is an important account in the cycle because both the acquisition and repayment of capital affect the cash account. The unique characteristics of the capital acquisition and repayment cycle affect how auditors verify the accounts in the cycle. This cycle often includes these accounts:

- Notes payable
- Contracts payable
- Mortgages payable
- Bonds payable
- Interest expense
- Accrued interest
- Appropriations of retained earnings
- Treasury stock
- Dividends declared

- Cash in the bank
- Capital stock—common
- Capital stock—preferred
- Paid-in capital in excess of par
- Donated capital
- Retained earnings
- Dividends payable
- Proprietorship—capital account
- Partnership—capital account

OBJECTIVE 22-1

Identify the accounts and the unique characteristics of the capital acquisition and repayment cycle.

The methodology for designing tests of details of balances for accounts in the capital acquisition and repayment cycle is the same as that followed for other accounts (see Figure 16-1). The only difference is the name of the account being audited. In determining the tests of details of balances for notes payable, the auditor considers business risk, tolerable misstatement, inherent risk, control risk, the results of tests of controls and substantive tests of transactions, and the results of analytical procedures.

Auditors often set tolerable misstatement at a low level because it is usually possible to completely audit the account balance and transactions affecting the notes payable account balance. Typically, they also set inherent risk at a low level because the correct account value is usually easy to determine. Auditors are normally most concerned about the completeness objective for notes payable account balances and the completeness objective for notes payable disclosures, such as collateral and covenant restrictions for notes payable. Because the cycle usually contains few transactions, control risk and the results of substantive tests of transactions are normally less important for designing tests of details of balances for accounts such as notes payable.

To best understand the audit procedures for many of the accounts in the capital acquisition and repayment cycle, representative accounts that are significant parts of the cycle for a typical business are included in this chapter. The following sections discuss (1) the audit of notes payable and related interest expense to illustrate interest-bearing capital, and (2) the audit of common stock, paid-in capital in excess of par, dividends, and retained earnings to illustrate equity accounts.

Note payable

A legal obligation to a creditor, which may be unsecured or secured by assets.

NOTES PAYABLE

A **note payable** is a legal obligation to a creditor, which may be unsecured or secured by assets, and bears interest. Typically, a note is issued for a period somewhere between one month and one year, but longer term notes exist. Notes are issued for different purposes, and the property pledged as collateral includes a wide variety of assets, such as securities, accounts receivable, inventory, and fixed assets. The principal and interest payments on the notes must be made in accordance with the terms of the loan agreement. For short-term loans, a principal and interest payment is usually required only when the loan becomes due. For loans over 90 days, the note usually calls for monthly or quarterly interest payments.

OBJECTIVE 22-2

Design and perform audit tests of notes payable and related accounts and transactions.

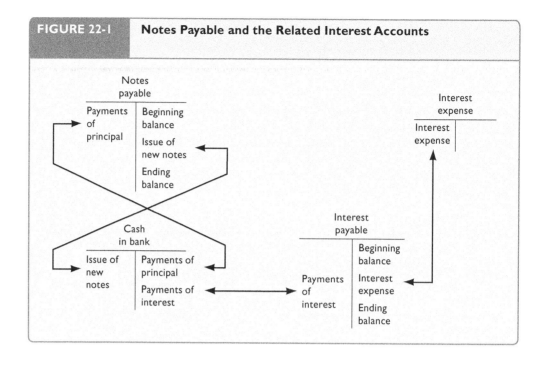

FIGURE 22-1   Notes Payable and the Related Interest Accounts

Figure 22-1 shows the accounts used for notes payable and related interest. Auditors commonly include tests of principal and interest payments as a part of the audit of the acquisition and payment cycle, because the payments are recorded in the cash disbursements journal. But in many cases, because of their relative infrequency, no capital transactions are included in the auditor's sample for tests of controls and substantive tests of transactions. Therefore, it is also normal to test these transactions as a part of the capital acquisition and repayment cycle.

The objectives of the audit of notes payable are to determine whether:

- Internal controls over notes payable are adequate.
- Transactions for principal and interest involving notes payable are properly authorized and recorded in accordance with the seven transaction-related audit objectives.
- The liability for notes payable and the related interest expense and accrued liability are properly stated as defined by seven of the eight balance-related audit objectives. (Realizable value is not applicable to liability accounts.)

Internal Controls

There are four important controls over notes payable:

1. *Proper authorization for the issue of new notes.* Responsibility for the issuance of new notes should be vested in the board of directors or high-level management personnel. Generally, two signatures of properly authorized officials are required for all loan agreements, which usually stipulate the amount of the loan, the interest rate, the repayment terms, and the assets pledged.

2. *Adequate controls over the repayment of principal and interest.* The periodic payments of interest and principal should be subject to the controls in the acquisition and payment cycle. At the time the note was issued, the accounting department should have received a copy of the note, much like it receives vendors' invoices and receiving reports. The accounts payable department should automatically issue checks or electronic fund transfers for the notes when they become due, again in the same manner in which it prepares payments for acquisitions of goods and services. A copy of the note provides the supporting documentation for payment.

3. *Proper documents and records.* These include subsidiary records and control over blank and paid notes by an authorized person. Paid notes should be cancelled and retained under the custody of an authorized official.

4. *Periodic independent verification.* Periodically, the detailed note records should be reconciled with the general ledger and compared with the note holders' records by an employee who is not responsible for maintaining the detailed records. At the same time, an independent person should recompute the interest expense on notes to test the accuracy of the record keeping.

Tests of Controls and Substantive Tests of Transactions

Tests of notes payable transactions involve the issue of notes and the repayment of principal and interest. These audit tests are a part of tests of controls and substantive tests of transactions for cash receipts (see the appropriate section(s) in Chapter 14) and cash disbursements (see the appropriate section(s) in Chapter 18). Additional tests of controls and substantive tests of transactions are often done as a part of tests of details of balances because of the materiality of individual transactions.

Tests of controls for notes payable and related interest should emphasize testing the four internal controls we just discussed. In addition, auditors should verify the accurate recording of receipts from note proceeds and payments of principal and interest.

Analytical Procedures

Analytical procedures are essential for notes payable because tests of details for interest expense and accrued interest can often be eliminated when results are favorable. Table 22-1 illustrates typical analytical procedures for notes payable and related interest accounts.

The auditor's independent prediction of interest expense, using average notes payable outstanding and average interest rates, helps the auditor evaluate the reasonableness of interest expense and also tests for omitted notes payable. Turn to page 260 in Chapter 8 and review Figure 8-8 for an illustration of an auditor's schedule where such an analytical procedure has been performed. If actual interest expense is materially larger than the auditor's estimate, one possible cause is recorded interest payments on unrecorded notes payable.

Tests of Details of Balances

The normal starting point for the audit of notes payable is a schedule of notes payable and accrued interest, which the auditor obtains from the client. Figure 22-2 illustrates a typical schedule, including detailed information of all transactions that took place during the entire year for principal and interest, the beginning and ending balances for

TABLE 22-1	Analytical Procedures for Notes Payable
Analytical Procedure	**Possible Misstatement**
Recalculate approximate interest expense on the basis of average interest rates and overall monthly notes payable.	Misstatement of interest expense and accrued interest or omission of an outstanding note payable
Compare individual notes outstanding with those of the prior year.	Omission or misstatement of a note payable
Compare total balance in notes payable, interest expense, and accrued interest with prior year balances.	Misstatement of interest expense and accrued interest or notes payable

FIGURE 22-2   **Schedule of Notes Payable and Accrued Interest**

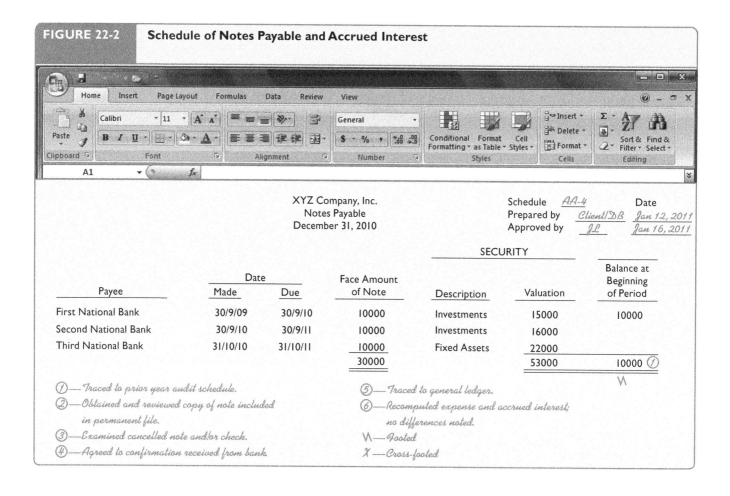

notes and interest payable, and descriptive information about the notes, such as the due date, the interest rate, and the assets pledged as collateral.

When there are numerous transactions involving notes during the year, it may be impractical for auditors to obtain such a schedule. In those situations, auditors are likely to request the client to prepare a schedule of only those notes with unpaid balances at the end of the year, showing a description of each note, its ending

---

LIABILITY TO PAY LIABILITIES

The internal audit department of Rasheed Manufacturing Company prepared its interim internal audit report as at September 30, 2011, which included the following:

1. The company's current liabilities exceeded its current assets by more than US$7,654,685 and the company faces the risk that it will default on the payment of both its interest due and installments associated with long-term loans.

2. The company's extraordinary general meeting approved the increase of the company's authorized and issued capital which was reflected in the balance sheet even though the increases of US$50 million and US$20 million had not yet been recorded in the company's share register.

3. There is a liability on the inter-company current account with the holding company amounting to US$1.5 million. This is a matter which requires a management decision as to whether the liability should be paid.

4. There were a large number of outstanding checks on the bank reconciliation amounting to US$23.5 million. The reasons for the non-payment of these should be investigated.

5. Accrued interest related to mortgage loans as at September 30, 2011 amounting to US$1.25 million has not been recorded.

All the above misstatements uncovered by internal auditors show the importance of having strong controls over the recording of the various liabilities.

FIGURE 22-2   Schedule of Notes Payable and Accrued Interest (Cont.)

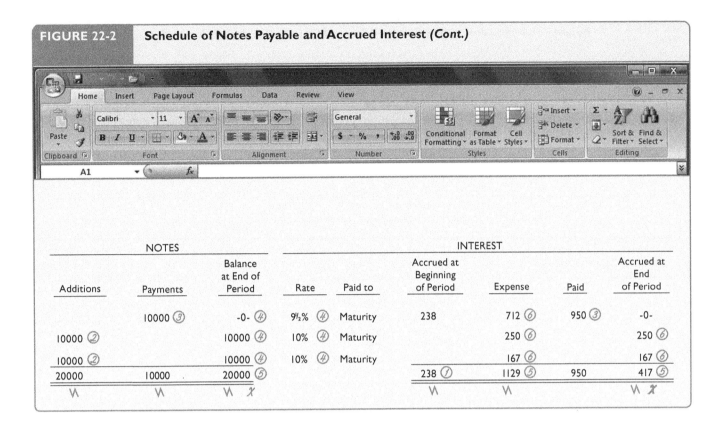

balance, and the interest payable at the end of the year, including the collateral and interest rate.

Table 22-2 summarizes the applicable balance-related audit objectives and common audit procedures as they apply to the schedule of notes payable. Again, the amount of testing depends heavily on the materiality of notes payable and the effectiveness of internal controls.

The two most important balance-related audit objectives in notes payable are:

1. Existing notes payable are included (completeness).
2. Notes payable in the schedule are accurately recorded (accuracy).

These objectives are vital because a misstatement can be material if even one note is omitted or incorrect. Table 22-2 shows common procedures to test for the completeness objective for notes payable. When internal controls over notes payable are deficient, auditors may need to perform extended procedures to test for omitted notes payable. For example, the auditor might send confirmations to creditors that have held notes from the client in the past but are not currently included in the notes payable schedule. The auditor might also analyze interest expense for payments to creditors that are not included in the notes payable schedule, and review the minutes of the board of directors' meetings for authorized but unrecorded notes.

In addition to balance-related objectives, the three presentation and disclosure-related objectives are important for notes payable because accounting standards require that the footnotes adequately describe the terms of notes payable outstanding and the assets pledged as collateral for the loans. If the loans require significant restrictions on the activities of the company, such as compensating balance provisions or restrictions on the payment of dividends, these must also be disclosed in the footnotes. As auditors perform tests of details of balances for balance-related audit objectives, the evidence obtained helps satisfy the notes payable presentation and disclosure objectives.

TABLE 22-2	Balance-Related Audit Objectives and Tests of Details of Balances for Notes Payable and Interest	
Balance-Related Audit Objective	**Common Tests of Details of Balances Procedures**	**Comments**
Notes payable in the notes payable schedule agree with the client's notes payable register or master file, and the total is correctly added and agrees with the general ledger (detail tie-in).	Foot the notes payable list for notes payable and accrued interest. Trace the totals to the general ledger. Trace the individual notes payable to the master file.	These are often done on a 100 percent basis because of the small population size.
Notes payable in the schedule exist (existence).	Confirm notes payable. Examine duplicate copies of notes for authorization. Examine corporate minutes for loan approval.	The existence objective is not as important as completeness or accuracy.
Existing notes payable are included in the notes payable schedule (completeness).	Examine notes paid after year-end to determine whether they were liabilities at the balance sheet date. Obtain a standard bank confirmation that includes specific reference to the existence of notes payable from all banks with which the client does business. (Bank confirmations are discussed more fully in Chapter 23.) Review the bank reconciliation for new notes credited directly to the bank account by the bank. (Bank reconciliations are also discussed more fully in Chapter 23.)	This objective is important for uncovering both errors and fraud. These three procedures are done on most audits. Additional procedures to search for omitted liabilities may be necessary if internal controls are weak.
Notes payable and accrued interest on the schedule are accurate (accuracy).	Examine duplicate copies of notes for principal and interest rates. Confirm notes payable, interest rates, and last date for which interest has been paid with holders of notes. Recalculate accrued interest.	In some cases, it may be necessary to calculate, using present-value techniques, the imputed interest rates or the principal amount of the note. An example is when equipment is acquired for a note.
Notes payable in the schedule are correctly classified (classification).	Examine due dates on duplicate copies of notes to determine whether all or part of the notes are a non-current liability. Review notes to determine whether any are related party notes or accounts payable.	
Notes payable are included in the proper period (cutoff).	Examine duplicate copies of notes to determine whether notes were dated on or before the balance sheet date.	Notes should be included as current period liabilities when dated on or before the balance sheet date.
The company has an obligation to pay the notes payable (obligations).	Examine notes to determine whether the company has obligations for payment.	

OWNERS' EQUITY

OBJECTIVE 22-3

Identify the primary concerns in the audit of owners' equity transactions.

There is an important difference in the audit of owners' equity between a **publicly held corporation** and a **closely held corporation**. In most closely held corporations, which typically have few shareholders (sometimes they are family members in many of the Arab countries), occasional, if any, transactions occur during the year for capital stock accounts. The only transactions entered in the owners' equity section are likely to be the change in owners' equity for the annual earnings or loss and the declaration of dividends, if any. Closely held corporations rarely pay dividends, and auditors spend little time verifying owners' equity, even though they must test the corporate records.

For publicly held corporations, however, the verification of owners' equity is more complex because of the larger numbers of shareholders and frequent changes in the individuals holding the stock. The rest of this chapter deals with tests for verifying the major owners' equity accounts in a publicly held corporation, including:

- Capital and common stock
- Paid-in capital in excess of par
- Retained earnings and related dividends

Figure 22-3 provides an overview of the specific owners' equity accounts discussed. The objective for each is to determine whether:

- Internal controls over capital stock and related dividends are adequate
- Owners' equity transactions are correctly recorded, as defined by the seven transaction-related audit objectives
- Owners' equity balances are properly recorded, as defined by the eight balance-related audit objectives, and properly presented and disclosed, as defined by the three presentation and disclosure-related audit objectives for owners' equity accounts

Other accounts in owners' equity are verified in much the same way as these.

Internal Controls

Several internal controls are important for owners' equity activities. We discuss several of these in the following sections.

Proper Authorization of Transactions Because each owners' equity transaction is typically material, many of these transactions must be approved by the board of directors. The following types of owners' equity transactions usually require specific authorization:

- *Issuance of Capital Stock.* The authorization includes the type of equity to issue (such as preferred or common stock), number of shares to issue, par value of the stock, privileged condition for any stock other than common, and date of the issue.

Publicly held corporation

Corporation with stock that is publicly traded; typically, there are many shareholders and frequent changes in the ownership of the stock.

Closely held corporation

Corporation with stock that is not publicly traded; typically, there are only a few shareholders and few, if any, capital stock account transactions during the year.

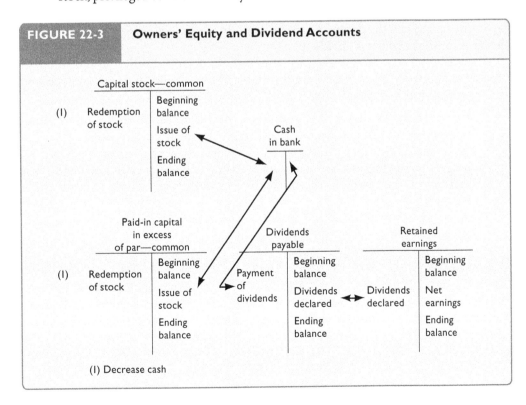

FIGURE 22-3   Owners' Equity and Dividend Accounts

- *Repurchase of Capital Stock.* The repurchase of common or preferred shares, the timing of the repurchase, and the amount to pay for the shares should all be approved by the board of directors.
- *Declaration of Dividends.* The board of directors must authorize the form of the dividends (such as cash or stock), the amount of the dividend per share, and the record and payment dates of the dividends.

Proper Record Keeping and Segregation of Duties When a company maintains its own records of stock transactions and outstanding stock, the internal controls must be adequate to ensure that:

- Actual owners of the stock are recognized in the corporate records
- The correct amount of dividends is paid to the stockholders owning the stock as of the dividend record date
- The potential for misappropriation of assets is minimized

The proper assignment of personnel, adequate record-keeping procedures, and independent internal verification of information in the records are useful controls for these purposes. The client should also have well-defined policies for preparing stock certificates and for recording capital stock transactions.

When issuing and recording capital stock, the client must comply with both the government laws governing corporations and the requirements in the corporate charter or articles of association. The par value of the stock and the number of shares the company is authorized to issue all affect issuance and recording of capital stock.

As a control over capital stock, most companies maintain stock certificate books and a shareholders' capital stock master file. A **capital stock certificate record** records the issuance and repurchase of capital stock for the life of the corporation. The record for a capital stock transaction includes the certificate number, the number of shares issued, the name of the person to whom it was issued, and the issue date. When shares are repurchased, the capital stock certificate book should include the cancelled certificates and the date of their cancellation.

A **shareholders' capital stock master file** is the record of the outstanding shares at any given time. The master file acts as a check on the accuracy of the capital stock certificate record and the common stock balance in the general ledger. It is also used as the basis for the payment of dividends.

The disbursement of cash for the payment of dividends should be controlled in much the same manner as the preparation and payment of payroll, which we described in Chapter 20. Internal controls affecting dividend payments may include:

- Dividend checks are prepared from the capital stock certificate record by someone who is not responsible for maintaining the capital stock records.
- After the checks are prepared, there is independent verification of the stockholders' names and the amounts of the checks and a reconciliation of the total amount of the dividend checks with the total dividends authorized in the minutes.
- A separate *imprest dividend account* is used to prevent the payment of a larger amount of dividends than was authorized.

Independent Registrar and Stock Transfer Agent Any company with stock listed on a securities exchange is required to engage an **independent registrar** as a control to prevent the improper issue of stock certificates. The responsibility of an independent registrar is to make sure that stock is issued by a corporation in accordance with the capital stock provisions in the corporate charter and the authorization of the board of directors. When there is a change in the ownership of the stock, the registrar is responsible for signing all newly issued stock certificates and making sure that old certificates are received and cancelled before a replacement certificate is issued.

Capital stock certificate record

A record of the issuance and repurchase of capital stock for the life of the corporation.

Shareholders' capital stock master file

A record of the issuance and repurchase of capital stock for the life of a corporation.

Independent registrar

Outside person engaged by a corporation to make sure that its stock is issued in accordance with capital stock provisions in the corporate charter and authorizations by the board of directors.

Most large corporations also employ the services of a **stock transfer agent** to maintain the stockholder records, including those documenting transfers of stock ownership. The employment of a transfer agent helps strengthen control over the stock records by putting the records in the hands of an independent organization and helps reduce the cost of record keeping by using a specialist. Many companies also have the transfer agent disburse cash dividends to shareholders, further improving internal control.

Stock transfer agent

Outside person engaged by a corporation to maintain the stockholder records and often to disburse cash dividends.

AUDIT OF CAPITAL STOCK AND PAID-IN CAPITAL

Auditors have four main concerns in auditing capital stock and paid-in capital in excess of par:

1. Existing capital stock transactions are recorded (completeness transaction-related objective).
2. Recorded capital stock transactions occurred and are accurately recorded (occurrence and accuracy transaction-related objectives).
3. Capital stock is accurately recorded (accuracy balance-related objective).
4. Capital stock is properly presented and disclosed (all three presentation and disclosure objectives).

OBJECTIVE 22-4

Design and perform tests of controls, substantive tests of transactions, and tests of details of balances for capital stock and retained earnings.

The first two concerns involve tests of controls and substantive tests of transactions, and the last two involve tests of details of balances and related disclosures.

Existing Capital Stock Transactions are Recorded This objective is easily satisfied when a registrar or transfer agent is used. The auditor can confirm with them whether any capital stock transactions occurred and the accuracy of existing transactions and then determine if all of those transactions have been recorded. To uncover issuances and repurchases of capital stock, auditors also review the minutes of the board of directors' meetings, especially near the balance sheet date, and examine client-held stock record books.

Recorded Capital Stock Transactions Occurred and are Accurately Recorded Extensive auditing is required for transactions involving issuance of capital stock such as the issuance of new capital stock for cash, the merger with another company through an exchange of stock, donated shares, and the purchase of treasury shares. Regardless of the controls, it is normal practice for auditors to verify all capital stock transactions because of their materiality and permanence in the records. The occurrence transaction-related objective can ordinarily be tested by examining the minutes of the board of directors' meetings for proper authorization.

Auditors can readily verify accurate recording of capital stock transactions for cash by confirming the amount with the transfer agent and tracing the amount of the recorded capital stock transactions to cash receipts. (In the case of treasury stock, the amounts are traced to the cash disbursements journal.) In addition, the auditor must verify whether the correct amounts were credited to capital stock and paid-in capital in excess of par by referring to the corporate charter to determine the par or stated value of the capital stock.

Auditing capital stock transactions such as stock dividends, acquisition of property for stock, mergers, or similar noncash transfers is challenging because considerable technical expertise is required and there is often judgment involved to determine proper valuations. For example, in the audit of a major merger transaction, the auditor must often do considerable research to determine the appropriate accounting treatment and proper valuation of the transaction, after considering all the facts in the merger.

Capital Stock is Accurately Recorded Auditors verify the ending balance in the capital stock account by first determining the number of shares outstanding at the balance sheet date. A confirmation from the transfer agent is the simplest way to obtain this information. When no transfer agent exists, the auditor must rely on examining the stock records and accounting for all shares outstanding in the stock certificate records, examining all cancelled certificates, and accounting for blank certificates.

After the auditor is satisfied that the number of shares outstanding is correct, the recorded par value in the capital account can be verified by multiplying the number of shares by the par value of the stock. The ending balance in the capital in excess of par account is a residual amount. It is audited by verifying the amount of recorded transactions during the year and adding them to or subtracting them from the beginning balance in the account.

A major consideration when auditing the accuracy balance-related objective for capital stock is verifying whether the number of shares used in the calculation of earnings per share is accurate. It is easy to determine the correct number of shares to use in the calculation when there is only one class of stock and a small number of capital stock transactions. The problem becomes much more complex when there are convertible securities, stock options, or stock warrants outstanding.

Capital Stock is Properly Presented and Disclosed The most important sources of information for determining whether all three presentation and disclosure-related objectives for capital stock activities are satisfied are the corporate charter, the minutes of board of directors' meetings, and the auditor's analysis of capital stock transactions. The auditor should determine that each class of stock has a proper description, including the number of shares issued and outstanding and any special rights of an individual class. Auditors should also verify the proper presentation and disclosure of stock options, stock warrants, and convertible securities by examining legal documents or other evidence of the provisions of these agreements.

Audit of Dividends

The emphasis in the audit of dividends is on dividend transactions rather than on the ending balance. The exception is when there are dividends payable.

All seven transaction-related audit objectives are relevant for dividends. But typically, dividends are audited on a 100 percent basis. The most important objectives, including those concerning dividends payable, are:

1. Recorded dividends occurred (occurrence).
2. Existing dividends are recorded (completeness).
3. Dividends are accurately recorded (accuracy).

4. Dividends are paid to stockholders that exist (occurrence).
5. Dividends payable are recorded (completeness).
6. Dividends payable are accurately recorded (accuracy).
7. Dividends payable are real and actual obligations (obligations).

Auditors can verify the occurrence of recorded dividends by examining the minutes of board of directors' meetings for authorization of the amount of the dividend per share and the dividend date. When doing so, the auditor should be alert to the possibility of unrecorded dividends declared, particularly shortly before the balance sheet date. A closely related audit procedure is to review the audit permanent file to determine whether restrictions exist on the payment of dividends in bond indenture agreements or preferred stock provisions.

The accuracy of a dividend declaration can be audited by recalculating the amount on the basis of the dividend per share times the number of shares outstanding. If the client uses a transfer agent to disburse dividends, the total can be traced to a cash disbursement entry to the agent and also confirmed.

When a client keeps its own dividend records and pays the dividends itself, the auditor can verify the total amount of the dividend by recalculation and reference to cash disbursed. In addition, auditors must verify whether the payment was made to the stockholders who owned the stock as of the dividend record date. They can test this by selecting a sample of recorded dividend payments and tracing the payee's name on the cancelled check to the dividend records. At the same time, auditors can verify the amount and the authenticity of the dividend check.

Tests of dividends payable should be done in conjunction with declared dividends. Any unpaid dividend should be included as a liability.

Audit of Retained Earnings

For most companies, the only transactions involving retained earnings are net earnings for the year and dividends declared. Other changes in retained earnings may include corrections of prior-period earnings, prior-period adjustments charged or credited directly to retained earnings, and the setting up or elimination of appropriations of retained earnings.

To begin the audit of retained earnings, auditors first analyze retained earnings for the entire year. The audit schedule showing the analysis, which is usually a part of the permanent file, includes a description of every transaction affecting the account.

To accomplish the audit of the credit to retained earnings for net income for the year (or the debit for a loss) auditors simply trace the entry in retained earnings to the net earnings figure on the income statement. This procedure must, of course, take place fairly late in the audit after all adjusting entries affecting net earnings have been completed.

In auditing debits and credits to retained earnings, other than net earnings and dividends, auditors must determine whether the transactions should have been included. For example, prior-period adjustments can be included in retained earnings only if they satisfy the requirements of accounting standards.

After the auditor is satisfied that the recorded transactions were correctly classified as retained earnings transactions, the next step is to decide whether they were accurately recorded. The audit evidence necessary to determine accuracy depends on the nature of the transactions. For example, if an appropriation of retained earnings is required for a bond sinking fund, auditors can determine the correct amount of the appropriation by examining the bond indenture agreement.

Auditors must also evaluate whether any transactions should have been included but were not. For example, if the client declared a stock dividend, the market value of the securities issued should be capitalized by a debit to retained earnings and a credit to capital stock. Similarly, if the financial statements include appropriations of retained earnings, the auditor should evaluate whether it is still necessary to have the appropriation as of the balance sheet date.

Accounting standards require presentation and disclosure of information related to retained earnings. The auditor's primary concern in determining whether presentation and disclosure objectives for retained earnings are satisfied primarily relates to disclosure of any restrictions on the payment of dividends. Often, agreements with bankers, stockholders, and other creditors prohibit or limit the amount of dividends the client can pay. These restrictions must be disclosed in the footnotes to the financial statements.

SUMMARY

This chapter discussed the audit of the capital acquisition and repayment cycle, which includes the primary sources of financing for most businesses. The cycle often involves few transactions, but the individual transactions are often material, which influences the design and performance of tests in the cycle. The approach to auditing this cycle was illustrated for notes payable, related interest expense and accrued interest, and for owners' equity and related accounts. Detailed audit procedures were provided for performing tests of transactions and test of balances to meet both transaction- and balance-related audit objectives for the above accounts.

ESSENTIAL TERMS

Capital acquisition and repayment cycle   p. 726

Capital stock certificate record   p. 734

Closely held corporation   p. 732

Independent registrar   p. 734

Note payable   p. 727

Publicly held corporation   p. 732

Shareholders' capital stock master file   p. 734

Stock transfer agent   p. 735

REVIEW QUESTIONS

22-1 (Objective 22-1) List four examples of interest-bearing liability accounts commonly found in balance sheets. What characteristics do these liabilities have in common? How do they differ?

22-2 (Objectives 22-1, 22-2) Why are liability accounts included in the capital acquisition and repayment cycle audited differently from accounts payable?

22-3 (Objective 22-2) It is common practice to audit the balance in notes payable in conjunction with the audit of interest expense and interest payable. Explain the advantages of this approach.

22-4 (Objective 22-2) Which internal controls should the auditor be most concerned about in the audit of notes payable? Explain the importance of each.

22-5 (Objective 22-2) Which analytical procedures are most important in verifying notes payable? Which types of misstatements can the auditor uncover by the use of these tests?

22-6 (Objective 22-2) Why is it more important to search for unrecorded notes payable than for unrecorded notes receivable? Suggest audit procedures that the auditor can use to uncover unrecorded notes payable.

22-7 (Objective 22-2) What is the primary purpose of analyzing interest expense? Given this purpose, what primary considerations should the auditor keep in mind when doing the analysis?

22-8 (Objective 22-2) Distinguish between (a) tests of controls and substantive tests of transactions and (b) tests of details of balances for liability accounts in the capital acquisition and repayment cycle.

22-9 (Objective 22-2) List two types of restrictions long-term creditors often put on companies when granting them a loan. How can the auditor find out about these restrictions?

22-10 (Objective 22-3) What are the primary objectives in the audit of owners' equity accounts?

22-11 (Objectives 22-3, 22-4) Evaluate the following statement: "The corporate charter and the bylaws of a company are legal documents; therefore, they should not be examined by the auditors. If the auditor wants information about these documents, an attorney should be consulted."

22-12 (Objective 22-3) What are the major internal controls over owners' equity?

22-13 (Objective 22-3) How does the audit of owners' equity for a closely held corporation differ from that for a publicly held corporation? In what respects are there no significant differences?

22-14 (Objective 22-3) Describe the duties of a stock registrar and a transfer agent. How does the use of their services affect the client's internal controls?

22-15 (Objective 22-4) What kinds of information can be confirmed with a transfer agent?

22-16 (Objective 22-4) Evaluate the following statement: "The most important audit procedure to verify dividends for the year is a comparison of a random sample of cancelled dividend checks with a dividend list that has been prepared by management as of the dividend record date."

22-17 (Objective 22-4) If a transfer agent disburses dividends for a client, explain how the audit of dividends declared and paid is affected. What audit procedures are necessary to verify dividends paid when a transfer agent is used?

22-18 (Objective 22-4) What should be the major emphasis in auditing the retained earnings account? Explain your answer.

22-19 (Objectives 22-3, 22-4) Explain the relationship between the audit of owners' equity and the calculations of earnings per share. What are the main auditing considerations in verifying the earnings per share figure?

MULTIPLE CHOICE QUESTIONS FROM CPA EXAMINATIONS

22-20 (Objective 22-2) The following multiple choice questions concern interest-bearing liabilities. Choose the best response.
  a. The audit program for long-term debt should include steps that require the
     (1) verification of the existence of the bondholders.
     (2) examination of any bond trust indenture.
     (3) inspection of the accounts payable master file.
     (4) investigation of credits to the bond interest income account.
  b. During the year under audit, a company has completed a private placement of a substantial amount of bonds. Which of the following is the *most* important step in the auditor's program for the audit of bonds payable?
     (1) Recomputing the annual interest cost and the effective yield.
     (2) Confirming the amount issued with the bond trustee.

(3) Tracing the cash received from the issue to the accounting records.

(4) Examining the bond records maintained by the transfer agent.

c. Several years ago, Mahmoudia Company, Inc., secured a conventional real estate mortgage loan. Which of the following audit procedures will be *least* likely to be performed by an auditor auditing the mortgage balance?

(1) Examine the current year's cancelled checks.

(2) Inspect public records of lien balances.

(3) Review the mortgage amortization schedule.

(4) Recompute mortgage interest expense.

22-21 (Objectives 22-2, 22-3, 22-4) The following questions concern the audit of accounts in the capital acquisition and repayment cycle. Choose the best response.

a. During an audit of a publicly held company, the auditor should obtain written confirmation regarding debenture transactions from the

(1) debenture holders.

(2) client's attorney.

(3) internal auditors.

(4) trustee.

b. An audit program for the audit of the retained earnings account should include a step that requires verification of

(1) market value used to charge retained earnings to account for a 2-for-1 stock split.

(2) approval of the adjustment to the beginning balance as a result of a write-down of an account receivable.

(3) authorization for both cash and stock dividends.

(4) gain or loss resulting from disposition of treasury shares.

c. When *no* independent stock transfer agents are employed and the corporation issues its own stocks and maintains stock records, cancelled stock certificates should

(1) be defaced to prevent reissuance and attached to their corresponding stubs.

(2) *not* be defaced, but be segregated from other stock certificates and retained in a cancelled certificates file.

(3) be destroyed to prevent fraudulent reissuance.

(4) be defaced and sent to the appropriate government authority.

DISCUSSION QUESTIONS AND PROBLEMS

22-22 (Objective 22-2) Items 1 through 6 are questions typically found in a standard internal control questionnaire used by auditors to obtain an understanding of internal control for notes payable. In using the questionnaire for a client, a 'yes' response indicates a possible internal control, whereas a 'no' indicates a potential deficiency.

1. Are liabilities for notes payable incurred only after written authorization by a proper company official?

2. Is a notes payable master file maintained?

3. Is a periodic reconciliation made of the notes payable master file with the actual notes outstanding by an individual who does not maintain the master file?

4. Is the individual who maintains the notes payable master file someone other than the person who approves the issue of new notes or handles cash?

5. Are paid notes cancelled and retained in the company files?

6. Are interest expense and accrued interest recomputed periodically by an individual who does not record interest transactions?

Required

a. For each of the preceding questions, state the purpose of the control.

b. For each of the preceding questions, identify the type of financial statement misstatement that can occur if the control were not in effect.

c. For each of the potential misstatements in part b, list an audit procedure that can be used to determine whether a material misstatement exists.

22-23 (Objective 22-2) The following are frequently performed audit procedures for the verification of bonds payable issued in previous years:

1. Obtain a copy of the bond indenture agreement and review its important provisions.
2. Determine that each of the bond indenture provisions has been met.
3. Analyze the general ledger account for bonds payable, interest expense, and unamortized bond discount or premium.
4. Test the client's calculations of interest expense, unamortized bond discount or premium, accrued interest, and bonds payable.
5. Obtain a confirmation from the bondholder.

a. State the purpose of each of the five audit procedures listed.

Required

b. List the provisions for which the auditor should be alert in examining the bond indenture agreement.
c. For each provision listed in part b, explain how the auditor can determine whether its terms have been met.
d. Explain how the auditor should verify the unamortized bond discount or premium.
e. List the information that should be requested in the confirmation of bonds payable with the bondholder.

22-24 (Objective 22-2) The following covenants are extracted from the indenture of a bond issue. The indenture provides that failure to comply with its terms in any respect automatically makes the loan immediately due (the regular date is 20 years hence). List any audit steps or reporting requirements you think should be taken or recognized in connection with each one of the following:

a. The debtor company shall endeavor to maintain a working capital ratio of 2 to 1 at all times, and in any fiscal year following a failure to maintain said ratio, the company shall restrict compensation of officers to US$100,000 per individual. Officers for this purpose shall include chairman of the board of directors, president, all vice presidents, secretary, and treasurer.
b. The debtor company shall keep all property that is security for this debt insured against loss by fire to the extent of 100% of its actual value. Policies of insurance comprising this protection shall be filed with the trustee.
c. The debtor company shall pay all taxes legally assessed against property that is security for this debt within the time provided by law for payment without penalty and shall deposit receipted tax bills or equally acceptable evidence of payment of same with the trustee.
d. A sinking fund shall be deposited with the trustee by semiannual payments of US$300,000, from which the trustee shall, in his discretion, purchase bonds of this issue.[23]

22-25 (Objective 22-2) The ending general ledger balance of US$186,000 in notes payable for the Ali Manufacturing Company is made up of 20 notes to eight different payees. The notes vary in duration anywhere from 30 days to two years, and in amounts from US$1,000 to US$10,000. In some cases, the notes were issued for cash loans; in other cases, the notes were issued directly to vendors for the acquisition of inventory or equipment. The use of relatively short-term financing is necessary because all existing properties are pledged for mortgages. Nevertheless, there is still a serious cash shortage.

Record-keeping procedures for notes payable are not good, considering the large number of loan transactions. There is no notes payable master file or independent verification of ending balances; however, the notes payable records are maintained by a secretary who does not have access to cash.

The audit has been done by the same auditing firm for several years. In the current year, the following procedures were performed to verify notes payable:

1. Obtain a list of notes payable from the client, foot the notes payable balances on the list, and trace the total to the general ledger.
2. Examine duplicate copies of notes for all outstanding notes included on the listing. Compare the name of the lender, amount, and due date on the duplicate copy with the list.

3. Obtain a confirmation from lenders for all listed notes payable. The confirmation should include the due date of the loan, the amount, and interest payable at the balance sheet date.

4. Recompute accrued interest on the list for all notes. The information for determining the correct accrued interest is to be obtained from the duplicate copy of the note. Foot the accrued interest amounts and trace the balance to the general ledger.

Required

a. What should be the emphasis in the verification of notes payable in this situation? Explain.

b. State the purpose of each of the four audit procedures listed.

c. Evaluate whether each of the four audit procedures was necessary. Evaluate the sample size for each procedure.

d. List other audit procedures that should be performed in the audit of notes payable in these circumstances.

22-26 (Objective 22-2) The Lebanese Company is a medium-sized industrial client that has been audited by your audit firm for several years. The only interest-bearing debt owed by Lebanese Company is US$200,000 in long-term notes payable held by the bank. The notes were issued three years previously and will mature in six more years. Lebanese Company is highly profitable, has no pressing needs for additional financing, and has excellent internal controls over the recording of loan transactions and related interest costs.

Required

a. Describe the auditing procedures that you think will be necessary for notes payable and related interest accounts in these circumstances.

b. How will your answer differ if Lebanese Company were unprofitable, had a need for additional financing, and had weak internal controls?

22-27 (Objectives 22-3, 22-4) The following audit procedures are commonly performed by auditors in the verification of owners' equity:

1. Review the articles of association or incorporation and bylaws for provisions about owners' equity.
2. Analyze all owners' equity accounts for the year and document the nature of any recorded change in each account.
3. Account for all certificate numbers in the capital stock book for all shares outstanding.
4. Examine the stock certificate book for any stock that was cancelled.
5. Review the minutes of the board of directors' meetings for the year for approvals related to owners' equity.
6. Recompute earnings per share.
7. Review debt provisions and senior securities with respect to liquidation preferences, dividends in arrears, and restrictions on the payment of dividends or the issue of stock.

Required

a. State the purpose of each of these seven audit procedures.

b. List the type of misstatements the auditors can uncover by the use of each audit procedure.

22-28 (Objective 22-4) You are an auditor engaged in the audit of the financial statements of West Bank Corporation for the year ended December 31, 2010. An audit firm has not audited West Bank before.

The stockholders' equity section of West Bank Corporation's balance sheet at December 31, 2010, follows:

Stockholders' Equity	
Capital stock 25,000 shares of US$10 par value authorized; 15,000 shares issued and outstanding	US$150,000
Capital contributed in excess of par value of capital stock	85,258
Retained earnings	40,152
Total stockholders' equity	US$275,410

West Bank Corporation was founded in 2000. The corporation has ten stockholders and serves as its own registrar and transfer agent. There are no capital stock subscription contracts in effect.

a. Prepare the detailed audit program for the audit of the three accounts comprising the stockholder's equity section of West Bank Corporation's balance sheet. (Do not include in the audit program the verification of the results of the current year's operations.) **Required**

b. After every other figure on the balance sheet has been audited, it might appear that the retained earnings figure is a balancing figure and requires no further verification. Why does the auditor verify retained earnings as is done with the other figures on the balance sheet? Discuss.[24]

22-29 (Objective 22-3) E-Antiques Inc. is an internet-based market maker for buyers and sellers of antique furniture and jewelry. The company allows sellers of antique items to list descriptions of those items on the E-Antiques website. Interested buyers review the website for antique items and then enter into negotiations directly with the seller for purchase. E-Antiques receives a commission on each transaction.

The company, founded in 2007, initially obtained capital through equity funding provided by the founders and through loan proceeds from financial institutions. In early 2010, E-Antiques became a publicly held company when it began selling shares on a national stock exchange. Although the company had never generated profits, the stock offering generated large proceeds based on favorable expectations for the company, and the stock quickly increased to above US$100 per share.

Management used the proceeds to pay off loans to financial institutions and to reacquire shares issued to the company founders. Proceeds were also used to fund purchases of hardware and software used to support the online market. The balance of unused proceeds is currently held in the company's bank accounts.

a. Before performing analytical procedures related to the capital acquisition and repayment cycle accounts, consider how the process of becoming publicly held will affect accounts at E-Antiques Inc. Describe whether each of the following balances would have increased, decreased, or experienced no change between 2009 and 2010 because of the public offering: **Required**

(1) Cash
(2) Accounts receivable
(3) Property, plant, and equipment
(4) Accounts payable
(5) Long-term debt
(6) Common stock
(7) Additional paid-in capital
(8) Retained earnings
(9) Treasury stock
(10) Dividends
(11) Revenues

b. During 2010, the stock price for E-Antiques plummeted to around US$19 per share. No new shares were issued during 2010. Describe the impact of this drop in stock price on the following accounts for the year ended December 31, 2010:
(1) Common stock
(2) Additional paid-in capital
(3) Retained earnings

c. How does the decline in stock price affect your assessment of client business risk and acceptable audit risk?

CASE

22-30 Objective(s) Your office was selected to audit El Anwar Company. The company trades in household electrical equipment and lighting fixtures of all kinds. Company information is:

- The authorized capital amounted to US$100 million
- The issued capital amounted to US$20 million
- The paid capital amounted to US$15 million

The company owns a number of branches in Ajman, Abou Dabi, Tanta, and Sharjaa and merchandise is distributed to those branches from the company's main warehouses in Dubai where the acquisition process is done centrally.

Required

a. Explain the meaning of the different types of capital and explain how the capital will be audited, verified, and disclosed in the financial statements.

b. As the manager responsible for the audit of El Anwar Company state the procedures necessary to audit the balances of purchases and liabilities at the end of the year.

c. El Anwar Company acquired a long-term loan of US$5 million on January 1, 2010, to fund the building of new branches. As of December 31, 2011 the company has a current account with the lender bank with a balance of US$500,000.

   The following are the conditions of the loan:

   - The loan is to be repaid in ten semiannual installments starting January 2011.
   - The interest is calculated on the basis of 4% higher over the price of the treasury bills plus one thousand percentage on the highest credit balance.

   Explain how to present the loan and the current account balance in the balance sheet for El Anwar Company as of December 31, 2011, writing the notes to the financial statements.

d. Explain how to verify the loan, the current account, and the most important audit evidence you acquired.

MYLAB ACTIVITY

Visit MyAccountingLab and complete the following activity:

→ Internet Problem 22-1: Stock Exchange Requirements.

AUDIT OF CASH BALANCES

Society Expects A Lot From Auditors

From 2003 through 2007, Sameh Abou El Fadl, the controller of Manama Manufacturing Company, paid himself an extra US$2 million in 'bonuses.' He did this by transferring funds from the general account, writing checks to himself from the payroll account, destroying the checks when they were received from the bank, and making entries directly into the company's computer files to disguise the cash theft. Sameh was able to do this because he had almost complete control of the company's accounting process by ensuring that the accountant responsible for bank transactions colluded with him in this fraud.

Although Sherif, the audit partner in Sherif & Co., found a strong control environment at Manama and a good budgeting and reporting system, he assessed control risk at maximum because there was limited segregation of duties. Accordingly, Sherif used a 'substantive' approach to the audit, applying tests of details of balances and analytical procedures to the year-end financial statements. However, he did no tests of controls or substantive tests of transactions due to his close relationship with the owners of the company, which is often found in various audit situations in some Arab countries.

LEARNING OBJECTIVES

After studying this chapter, you should be able to

23-1 Show the relationship of cash in the bank to the various transaction cycles.

23-2 Identify the major types of cash accounts maintained by business entities.

23-3 Design and perform audit tests of the general cash account.

23-4 Recognize when to extend audit tests of the general cash account to test further for material fraud.

23-5 Design and perform audit tests of the imprest payroll bank account.

23-6 Design and perform audit tests of imprest petty cash.

After the deception was discovered—and because Sameh had lost all of the US$2 million and Manama had no fidelity bond insurance—the company sued Sherif & Co. for the stolen funds, claiming breach of contract. Sherif's defense was that he had done the audit in accordance with auditing standards.

The trial revolved around the testimony of two expert witnesses. The witness for the company argued that even though the auditors took a substantive approach to the audit, they should have seen that Sameh had the opportunity to commit the embezzlement through his collusion with the accountant, and should have been more thorough in their audit and found the fraud.

The expert for the defense argued that a substantive audit approach is allowed by auditing standards when control risk is assessed at maximum. Sameh, with the help of the accountant, manipulated the records so carefully that the substantive procedures of the various payroll accounts did not indicate that the theft had occurred. Because no 'red flags' were evident that would have caused the auditors to extend their tests, the audit was clearly satisfactory.

The auditors, Sherif & Co., were found guilty by the court and were required to pay approximately US$2.3 million in damages. As the audit firm was insured against malpractice, the insurance company assumed the compensation paid in return for an increase in future premiums and other costs. The judge indicated that he didn't really understand the technical nature of the arguments made by the expert witnesses, but it was apparent to him that the people who did the audit were extremely bright and competent. Accordingly, the judge believed that the auditors certainly had the ability to find the cash theft and the fact that they didn't meant that they failed to meet their audit performance obligations. The main reasons for this was their close relationship with the owners of the company and their trust and reliance on the ethical rules embedded in the company's system.

Cash is the only account included in every cycle except inventory and warehousing. It makes sense to study this audit area last because the evidence accumulated for cash balances depends heavily on the results of the tests in other cycles. For example, if the auditors' understanding of internal control and tests of controls and substantive tests of transactions in the acquisition and payment cycle cause them to believe that it is appropriate to reduce assessed control risk to low, they can reduce detailed tests of the ending balance in cash. If, however, auditors conclude that assessed control risk should be higher, extensive year-end testing may be necessary.

Cash is important to auditors primarily because of the potential for fraud, as illustrated by the case of Manama Manufacturing, but clients can also make honest mistakes. This chapter highlights the linkage of cash in the bank to transaction cycles and describes substantive tests of the cash balance.

Relevant International Standards on Auditing	
ISA 200	Overall Objectives of the Independent Auditor and the Conduct of an Audit in Accordance with International Standards on Auditing
ISA 240	The Auditor's Responsibilities Relating to Fraud in an Audit of Financial Statements
ISA 315	Identifying and Assessing the Risks of Material Misstatement through Understanding the Entity and its Environment
ISA 450	Evaluation of Misstatements Identified during the Audit
ISA 500	Audit Evidence
ISA 505	External Confirmations
ISA 520	Analytical Procedures

CASH IN THE BANK AND TRANSACTION CYCLES

OBJECTIVE 23-1

Show the relationship of cash in the bank to the various transaction cycles.

A brief discussion of the relationship between cash in the bank and the other transaction cycles serves a dual function:

1. It shows the importance of audit tests of various transaction cycles on the audit of cash.
2. It aids in further understanding the integration of the different transaction cycles.

Figure 23-1 illustrates the relationships of the various transaction cycles, the focal point being the general cash account ('Cash in bank'). By examining Figure 23-1, it is apparent why the general cash account is considered significant in almost all audits, even when the ending balance is immaterial. The amount of cash *flowing* into and out of the cash account is often larger than that for any other account in the financial statements. Furthermore, the susceptibility of cash to embezzlement is greater than for other types of assets because most other assets must be converted to cash to make them usable.

In the audit of cash, auditors must distinguish between verifying the client's reconciliation of the balance on the bank statement to the balance in the general ledger, and verifying whether recorded cash in the general ledger correctly reflects all cash transactions that took place during the year. It is relatively easy to verify the client's reconciliation of the balance in the bank account to the general ledger, but a significant part of the total audit of a company involves verifying whether cash transactions are correctly recorded. For example, each of the following misstatements ultimately results in the

FIGURE 23-1   **Relationships of Cash in the Bank and Transaction Cycles**

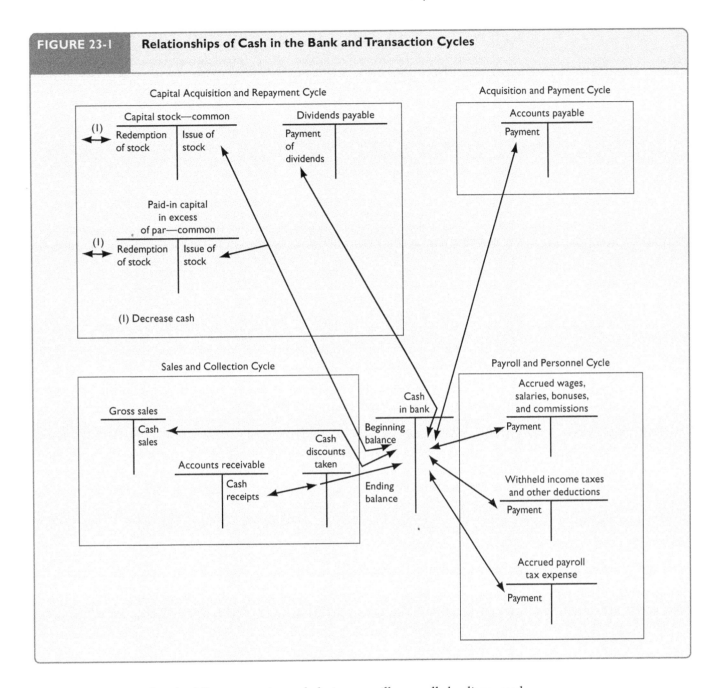

improper payment of or the failure to receive cash, but none will normally be discovered as a part of the audit of the bank reconciliation:

- Failure to bill a customer
- An embezzlement of cash by intercepting cash receipts from customers before they are recorded, with the account charged off as a bad debt
- Duplicate payment of a vendor's invoice
- Improper payments of officers' personal expenditures
- Payment for raw materials that were not received
- Payment to an employee for more hours than he or she worked
- Payment of interest to a related party for an amount in excess of the going rate

If these misstatements are to be uncovered in the audit, their discovery must occur through tests of controls and substantive tests of transactions, which we discussed in preceding chapters. The first two misstatements can be discovered as part of the audit of the sales and collection cycle (Chapter 14), the next three in the audit

<table>
<tr><td>

SALES REPRESENTATIVE STOLE CASH COLLECTED FROM CLIENT

</td><td>

During comparison between bank deposits on the bank statement and what is recorded in the company's subsidiary ledger by an internal auditor, he discovered that one of the sales representatives received the customers' checks for the payment of their debts to the company as well as the bank deposit documents for the cash collections from customers. The representative deposited the customers' checks in the bank without notifying the accountant responsible for recording them in the company's subsidiary ledger and waited until the amounts from future sales transactions were collected from the customers during the following period. He recorded the cash deposit in the bank equal to the amount that was not

</td><td>

recorded before. Following the same pattern, he continued stealing cash collected relating to later sales transactions. Then the representative colluded with some workers to prove that some cash receipts vouchers were missing which were held by other representatives who had left the company. These typical cash thefts are found in various fraud cases related to embezzlement of cash collected from clients. Employees use different techniques to cover their theft and it is the auditor who needs to understand the controls implemented by the company to prevent and detect these types of thefts. He should perform sufficient tests to detect these types of fraud whenever they exist.

</td></tr>
</table>

of the acquisition and payment cycle (Chapter 18), and the last two in the tests of the payroll and personnel cycle (Chapter 20) and the capital acquisition and repayment cycle (Chapter 22), respectively.

Entirely different types of misstatements are normally discovered as a part of the tests of the bank reconciliation. These include:

- Failure to include a check that has not cleared the bank on the outstanding check list, even though it has been recorded in the cash disbursements journal
- Cash received by the client subsequent to the balance sheet date but recorded as cash receipts in the current year
- Deposits recorded as cash receipts near the end of the year, deposited in the bank in the same month, and included in the bank reconciliation as a deposit in transit
- Payments on notes payable debited directly to the bank balance by the bank but not entered in the client's records

TYPES OF CASH ACCOUNTS

OBJECTIVE 23-2

Identify the major types of cash accounts maintained by business entities.

Before dealing with audit tests of the client's bank reconciliation, it is helpful to discuss the types of cash accounts commonly used by most companies, because the auditing approach to each varies. Auditors are likely to learn about the various types of cash balances when they obtain an understanding of the client's business. The following are the major types of cash accounts.

General Cash Account

General cash account

The primary bank account for most organizations; virtually all cash receipts and disbursements flow through this account at some time.

The **general cash account** is the focal point of cash for most organizations because virtually all cash receipts and disbursements flow through this account. For example, the disbursements for the acquisition and payment cycle are normally paid from this account, while the receipts of cash in the sales and collection cycle are deposited in the account.

Imprest Accounts

As discussed in Chapter 20, many companies establish a separate imprest payroll account to improve internal control over payroll disbursements. A fixed balance, such as US$5,000, is maintained in the imprest payroll bank account. Immediately before each pay period, one check or electronic transfer is drawn on the general cash account to deposit the total amount of the net payroll into the payroll account. After all payroll checks have cleared the imprest payroll account, the bank account should have a US$5,000 balance. The only deposits into the account are for the weekly and semi-monthly payroll, and the only disbursements are paychecks to employees.

A somewhat different type of imprest account consists of one bank account for receipts and a separate one for disbursements. There may be several of these in a company for different divisions. All receipts are deposited in the imprest account, and the total is transferred to the general account periodically. The disbursement account is set up on an *imprest basis*, but in a different manner than an imprest payroll account. A fixed balance is maintained in the imprest account, and the authorized personnel use these funds for disbursements at their own discretion as long as the payments are consistent with company policy. When the cash balance has been depleted, a reimbursement is made to the imprest disbursement account from the general account after the expenditures have been approved, usually through an online transfer. The use of such an imprest bank account improves controls over receipts and disbursements.

Branch Bank Account

For a company operating in multiple locations, it is often desirable to have a separate bank balance at each location. **Branch bank accounts** are useful for building banking relations in local communities and permitting the centralization of operations at the branch level.

In some companies, the deposits and disbursements for each branch are made to a separate bank account (see Figure 23-2), and the excess cash is periodically transferred electronically to the main office general bank account. The branch account in this instance is much like a general account, but at the branch level.

Imprest Petty Cash Fund

An **imprest petty cash fund** is not a bank account, but it is sufficiently similar to cash in the bank to merit inclusion. A petty cash account is often something as simple as a preset amount of cash set aside in a strong box for incidental expenses. It is used for small cash acquisitions that can be paid more conveniently and quickly by cash than by check, or for the convenience of employees in cashing personal or payroll checks. An imprest cash account is set up on the same basis as an imprest branch bank account, but the expenditures are normally for much smaller amounts. Typical expenses include minor office supplies, stamps, and small contributions to local charities. A petty cash account usually does not exceed a few hundred dollars and is often reimbursed only once or twice each month.

Cash Equivalents

Companies often invest excess cash accumulated during certain parts of the operating cycle that will be needed in the reasonably near future in short-term, highly liquid **cash equivalents**. These may include time deposits, certificates of deposit, and money market funds. Cash equivalents, which can be highly material, are included in the financial statements as a part of the cash account only if they are short-term investments that are readily convertible to known amounts of cash, and there is insignificant risk of a change of value from interest rate changes. Marketable securities and longer-term interest-bearing investments are not cash equivalents.

Figure 23-3 shows the relationship of general cash to the other cash accounts. All cash either originates from or is deposited in general cash. For the remainder of this chapter, the focus is on auditing three types of accounts: the general cash account, imprest payroll bank account, and imprest petty cash. The other accounts are similar enough to these that we need not discuss them separately.

Branch bank accounts

Separate bank accounts maintained at local banks by branches of a company.

Imprest petty cash fund

A fund of cash maintained within the company for small cash acquisitions or to cash employees' checks; the fund's fixed balance is comparatively small and is periodically reimbursed.

Cash equivalents

Excess cash invested in short-term, highly liquid investments such as time deposits, certificates of deposit, and money market funds.

FIGURE 23-2	An Example of a Checking Account Statement

Regional Bank

Checking Account Statement
Page 1 of 1

Kamel Sayed

Statement date	Account No.
November 8, 2011	00005-123-456-7

Date	Description	Ref.	Withdrawals	Deposits	Balance
Oct 8, 2011	Previous balance				0.55
Oct 14, 2011	Payroll Deposit—Hotels			694.81	695.36
Oct 14, 2011	Web Bill Payment—MasterCard	9685	200.00		495.36
Oct 16, 2011	ATM Withdrawal—Interac	3990	21.25		474.11
Oct 16, 2011	Fees—Interac		1.50		472.61
Oct 20, 2011	Interac Purchase—Electronics	1975	2.99		469.62
Oct 21, 2011	Web Bill Payment—Amex	3314	300.00		169.62
Oct 22, 2011	ATM Withdrawal—First Bank	0064	100.00		69.62
Oct 23, 2011	Interac Purchase—Supermarket	1559	29.08		40.54
Oct 24, 2011	Interac Refund—Electronics	1975		2.99	43.53
Oct 27, 2011	Telephone Bill Payment—Visa	2475	6.77		36.76
Oct 28, 2011	Payroll Deposit—Hotel			694.81	731.57
Oct 30, 2011	Web Funds Transfer—from Savings	2620		50.00	781.57
Nov 3, 2011	Pre-Auth. Payment—Insurance		33.55		748.02
Nov 3, 2011	Check No. 409		100.00		648.02
Nov 6, 2011	Mortgage Payment		710.49		−62.47
Nov 7, 2011	Fees—Overdraft		5.00		−67.47
Nov 8, 2011	Fees—Monthly		5.00		−72.47
	Total		1,515.63	1,442.61	

FIGURE 23-3	Relationship of General Cash to Other Cash Accounts

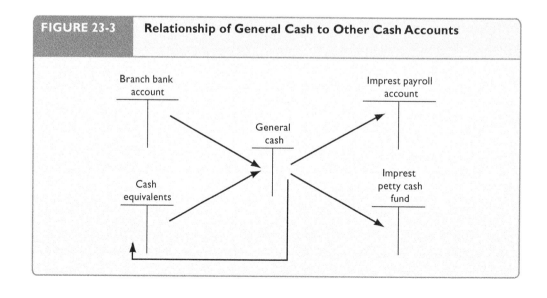

AUDIT OF THE GENERAL CASH ACCOUNT

The trial balance of Arabian Hardware Co. (see Figure 6-5, page 171) includes only one cash account. Notice, however, that all cycles, except inventory and warehousing, affect cash in the bank.

In testing the year-end balance in the general cash account, the auditor must accumulate sufficient appropriate evidence to evaluate whether cash, as stated on the balance sheet, is fairly stated and properly disclosed in accordance with five of the eight balance-related audit objectives used for all tests of details of balances (existence, completeness, accuracy, cutoff, and detail tie-in). Rights to general cash, its classification on the balance sheet, and the realizable value of cash are not applicable.

The methodology for auditing year-end cash is essentially the same as that for all other balance sheet accounts and is discussed in detail.

OBJECTIVE 23-3

Design and perform audit tests of the general cash account.

Identify Client Business Risks Affecting Cash (Phase I)

Most companies are unlikely to have significant client business risks affecting cash balances. However, client business risk may arise from inappropriate cash management policies or handling of funds held in trust for others.

Client business risk is more likely to arise from cash equivalents and other types of investments. Several financial services firms have suffered large trading losses from the activities of individual traders that were hidden by misstating investment and cash balances. For example, trading scandals occurred at both Société Générale, the French bank, and UBS AG, the Swiss bank. They incurred losses of US$7.2 billion in 2008 and US$2.3 billion in 2011, respectively. The auditor should understand the risks from the client's investment policies and strategies, as well as management controls that mitigate these risks.

Set Tolerable Misstatement and Assess Inherent Risk (Phase I)

The cash balance is immaterial in most audits, but cash transactions affecting the balance are almost always extremely material. Therefore, the potential often exists for material misstatement of cash.

Because cash is more susceptible to theft than other assets, there is high inherent risk for the existence, completeness, and accuracy objectives. These objectives are usually the focus in auditing cash balances. Typically, inherent risk is low for all other objectives.

Assess Control Risk (Phase I)

Internal controls over year-end cash balances in the general account can be divided into two categories:

1. *Controls over the transaction cycles* affecting the recording of cash receipts and disbursements
2. *Independent bank reconciliations*

In preceding chapters, we discussed controls affecting the recording of cash transactions, which are essential in assessing control risk for cash. For example, in the acquisition and payment cycle (Chapter 18), major controls include adequate segregation of duties between the check signing and accounts payable functions, signing of checks only by a properly authorized person, use of prenumbered checks printed on special paper, careful review of supporting documentation by the check signer before checks are signed, and adequate internal verification. If controls affecting cash-related transactions are operating effectively, control risk is reduced as are the audit tests for the year-end bank reconciliation.

A monthly **bank reconciliation** of the general bank account on a timely basis by someone independent of the handling or recording of cash receipts and disbursements

Bank reconciliation

The monthly reconciliation, usually prepared by client personnel, of the differences between the cash balance recorded in the general ledger and the amount in the bank account.

is an essential control over the ending cash balance. If a business defers preparing bank reconciliations for long periods, the value of the control is reduced and may affect the auditor's assessment of control risk for cash. The reconciliation ensures that the accounting records reflect the same cash balance as the actual amount of cash in the bank after considering reconciling items. More important, the *independent* reconciliation provides an opportunity for an internal verification of cash receipts and disbursements transactions. If the bank statements are received unopened by the reconciler, and physical control is maintained over the statements until the reconciliations are complete, the cancelled checks, duplicate deposit slips, and other documents included in the statement can be examined without concern for the possibility of alterations, deletions, or additions. A careful bank reconciliation by competent client personnel includes the following actions:

- Compare cancelled checks with the cash disbursements records for date, payee, and amount
- Examine cancelled checks for signature, endorsement, and cancellation
- Compare deposits in the bank with recorded cash receipts for date, customer, and amount
- Account for the numerical sequence of checks, and investigate missing ones
- Reconcile all items causing a difference between the book and bank balance and verify their appropriateness for the client's business
- Reconcile total debits on the bank statement with the totals in the cash disbursements records
- Reconcile total credits on the bank statement with the totals in the cash receipts records
- Review month-end interbank transfers for appropriateness and proper recording
- Follow up on outstanding checks and stop-payment notices

Most accounting software packages incorporate bank reconciliation as a part of end-of-month procedures. Even though the software reduces the clerical efforts in performing the bank reconciliations, the preparer still needs to do most of the procedures listed above. The bank reconciliation control is enhanced when a qualified employee reviews the monthly reconciliation as soon as possible after its completion.

Design and Perform Tests of Controls and Substantive Tests of Transactions (Phase II)

Because the cash balance is affected by all other cycles except inventory and warehousing, an extremely large number of transactions affect cash. In several earlier chapters, we discussed in detail the appropriate tests of controls and substantive tests of transactions for the audit of each cycle. For example, controls over cash receipts were studied in Chapter 14. Cash transactions are audited through these transaction cycle tests.

Design and Perform Analytical Procedures (Phase III)

In many audits, the year-end bank reconciliation is extensively audited. Using analytical procedures to test the reasonableness of the cash balance is therefore less important than it is for most other audit areas.

Auditors commonly compare the ending balance on the bank reconciliation, deposits in transit, outstanding checks, and other reconciling items with the prior year reconciliation. Similarly, auditors normally compare the ending balance in cash with previous months' balances. These analytical procedures may uncover misstatements in cash.

Design Tests of Details of Cash Balance (Phase III)

The starting point for the verification of the balance in the general bank account is to obtain a bank reconciliation from the client for inclusion in the auditor's documentation.

Figure 23-4 shows a bank reconciliation after the client has made adjustments to the account balance. Notice that the bottom figure in the audit schedule is the adjusted balance in the general ledger, which is the balance that should appear on the financial statements. The auditor must determine that the client has made adjustments such as those at the bottom of Figure 23-4, if they are material.

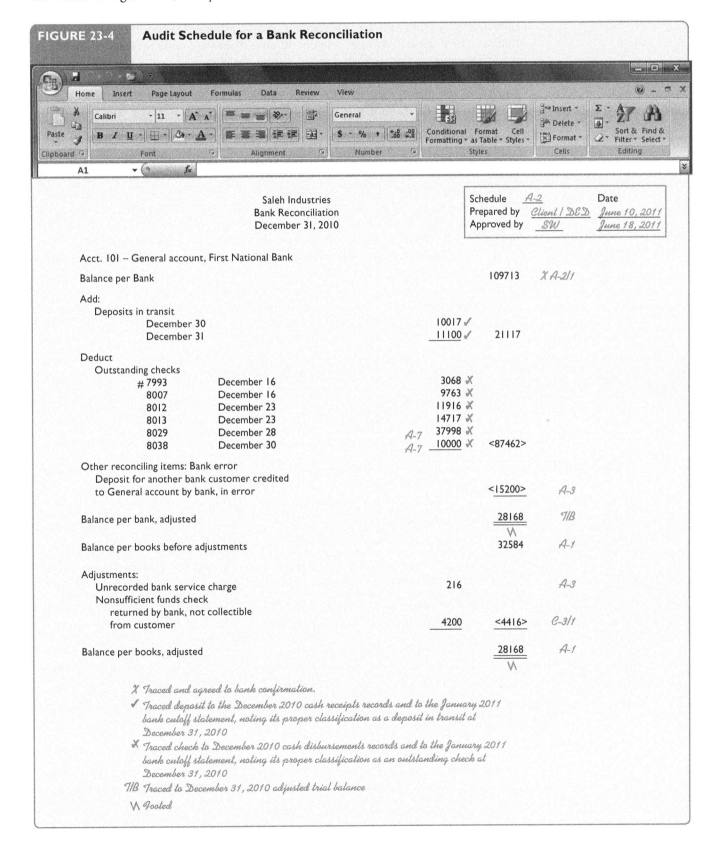

FIGURE 23-4   Audit Schedule for a Bank Reconciliation

Saleh Industries
Bank Reconciliation
December 31, 2010

Schedule   *A-2*   Date
Prepared by   *Client / DED*   *June 10, 2011*
Approved by   *SW*   *June 18, 2011*

Acct. 101 – General account, First National Bank

Balance per Bank		109713	*X A-2/1*
Add:			
Deposits in transit			
December 30	10017 ✓		
December 31	11100 ✓	21117	
Deduct			
Outstanding checks			
# 7993	December 16	3068 X	
8007	December 16	9763 X	
8012	December 23	11916 X	
8013	December 23	14717 X	
8029	December 28	*A-7*	37998 X	
8038	December 30	*A-7*	10000 X	<87462>
Other reconciling items: Bank error			
Deposit for another bank customer credited to General account by bank, in error		<15200>	*A-3*
Balance per bank, adjusted		28168	*T/B*
		ᴧ	
Balance per books before adjustments		32584	*A-1*
Adjustments:			
Unrecorded bank service charge		216	*A-3*
Nonsufficient funds check returned by bank, not collectible from customer		4200	<4416>	*C-3/1*
Balance per books, adjusted		28168	*A-1*
		ᴧ	

X *Traced and agreed to bank confirmation.*

✓ *Traced deposit to the December 2010 cash receipts records and to the January 2011 bank cutoff statement, noting its proper classification as a deposit in transit at December 31, 2010*

X *Traced check to December 2010 cash disbursements records and to the January 2011 bank cutoff statement, noting its proper classification as an outstanding check at December 31, 2010*

T/B *Traced to December 31, 2010 adjusted trial balance*

ᴧ *Footed*

To audit cash in the bank, the auditor verifies whether the bank reconciliation received from the client is correct. The balance-related audit objectives and common tests of details of balances in the audit of the cash account are shown in Table 23-1. The most important objectives are existence, completeness, and accuracy. Therefore, they receive the greatest attention. In addition to these balance-related objectives, the auditor also performs tests related to the three presentation and disclosure objectives, such as review of minutes and loan agreements to determine if there are restrictions on cash that must be disclosed. As in all other audit areas, the actual audit procedures depend on materiality and the risks in cash that the auditor has identified in other parts of the audit.

The following three procedures merit additional discussion because of their importance and complexity: receipt of a bank confirmation, receipt of a cutoff bank statement, and tests of the bank reconciliation.

Receipt of a Bank Confirmation Even though not required by auditing standards, auditors usually obtain a direct receipt of a confirmation from every bank or other financial institution with which the client does business, except when there is an unusually large number of inactive accounts. If the bank does not respond to a confirmation request, the auditor should send a second request or ask the client to communicate with the bank to ask them to complete and return the confirmation to the auditor. Figure 23-5 illustrates a completed standard confirmation for bank accounts.

The importance of **bank confirmations** in the audit extends beyond the verification of the actual cash balance. Typically, the bank confirms loan information and bank balances on the same form, such as the three outstanding loans in Figure 23-5. Information on liabilities to the bank for notes, mortgages, or other debt typically includes the

Bank confirmation

A form through which the bank responds to the auditor about bank balance and loan information provided on the confirmation.

TABLE 23-1	Balance-Related Audit Objectives and Tests of Details of Balances for General Cash in the Bank	
Balance-Related Audit Objective	**Common Tests of Details of Balances Procedures**	**Comments**
Cash in the bank as stated on the reconciliation foots correctly and agrees with the general ledger (detail tie-in).	Foot the outstanding check list and deposits in transit. Prove the bank reconciliation as to additions and subtractions, including all reconciling items. Trace the book balance on the reconciliation to the general ledger.	These tests are done entirely on the bank reconciliation, with no reference to documents or other records except the general ledger.
Cash in the bank as stated on the reconciliation exists (existence). Existing cash in the bank is recorded (completeness). Cash in the bank as stated on the reconciliation is accurate (accuracy).	(See extended discussion for each of these) Receipt and tests of a bank confirmation. Receipt and tests of a cutoff bank statement. Tests of the bank reconciliation. Extended tests of the bank reconciliation. Proof of cash. Tests for kiting.	These are the three most important objectives for cash in the bank. The procedures are combined because of their close interdependence. The last three procedures should be done only when there are internal control deficiencies.
Cash receipts and cash disbursements transactions are recorded in the proper period (cutoff).	*Cash receipts:* Count the cash on hand on the last day of the year and subsequently trace to deposits in transit and the cash receipts journal. Trace deposits in transit to subsequent period bank statement (cutoff bank statement). *Cash disbursements:* Record the last check number used on the last day of the year and subsequently trace to the outstanding checks and the cash disbursements journal. Trace outstanding checks to subsequent period bank statement.	When cash receipts received after year-end are included in the journal, a better cash position than actually exists is shown. It is called 'holding open' the cash receipts journal. Holding open the cash disbursements journal reduces accounts payable and usually overstates the current ratio. The first procedure listed for receipts and disbursements cutoff tests requires the auditor's presence on the client's premises at the end of the last day of the year.

amount and date of the loan, the loan due date, interest rate, and the existence of collateral. Auditors should also obtain confirmation from banks about their clients' lines of credit, compensating balance requirements, or contingent liabilities for guaranteeing the loans of others.

Banks are *not responsible* for searching their records for bank balances or loans beyond those included on the form by the audit firm's client. A statement near the bottom of the form obligates banks to inform the audit firm of any loans not included on the confirmation *about which the bank has knowledge*. The effect of this limited responsibility is to require auditors to satisfy themselves about the completeness objective for unrecorded bank balances and loans from the bank in another manner.

After auditors receive the completed bank confirmation, the balance in the bank account confirmed by the bank should be traced to the amount stated on the bank reconciliation. Similarly, all other information on the reconciliation should be traced to the relevant audit schedules. If the bank confirmation does not agree with the audit schedules, auditors must investigate the difference.

Receipt of a Cutoff Bank Statement A **cutoff bank statement** is a partial-period bank statement and the related cancelled checks, duplicate deposit slips, and other documents included in bank statements, mailed by the bank directly to the auditing firm's office. The purpose of the cutoff bank statement is to verify the reconciling items on the client's year-end bank reconciliation with evidence that is not accessible to the client. To fulfill this purpose, the auditor requests the client to have the bank send the statement for seven to ten days subsequent to the balance sheet date directly to the auditor. Figure 23-5 shows an example of a letter sent to confirm account balance information with financial institutions.

Many auditors verify the subsequent period bank statement if a cutoff statement is not received directly from the bank. The purpose is to test whether the client's employees have omitted, added, or altered any of the documents accompanying the statement. Obviously, this tests for intentional misstatements. The auditor performs the following verification in the month subsequent to the balance sheet date:

- Foot the lists of all cancelled checks, debit memos, deposits, and credit memos
- Verify that the bank statement balances when the footed totals are used
- Review the items included in the footings to make sure that they were cancelled by the bank in the proper period and do not include any erasures or alterations

Tests of the Bank Reconciliation A well-prepared independent bank reconciliation is an essential internal control over cash. Auditors test the bank reconciliation to determine whether client personnel have carefully prepared the bank reconciliation

> **Cutoff bank statement**
>
> A partial-period bank statement and the related cancelled checks, duplicate deposit slips, and other documents included in bank statements, mailed by the bank directly to the auditor; the auditor uses it to verify reconciling items on the client's year-end bank reconciliation.

ELECTRONIC CONFIRMATIONS OF BANK BALANCES

As illustrated by the Parmalat fraud (see page 759), one of the shortcomings of the confirmation process is the inability to authenticate the confirmation respondent. Although not currently required by auditing standards, auditors generally confirm bank balances because they are considered a highly reliable source of evidence about cash in the bank. However, obtaining bank confirmations can be a time-consuming process. Organizations may not respond to confirmation requests, and it may take several weeks to receive confirmation responses through the mail. Automated confirmations using a third-party intermediary can address many of these shortcomings and improve confirmation efficiency and effectiveness.

Authentication checks are performed on all parties to the confirmation process (audit firm, client, and financial institution). A secure value-added network with digital signatures and encryption technology are used to allow the client to authorize the confirmation requests and the auditor to communicate directly with the confirming parties.

Sources: Adapted from George Aldhizer and James Cashell, 'Automating the Confirmation Process: How to Enhance Audit Effectiveness and Efficiency,' *The CPA Journal* (April 2006) p. 6–10; and AICPA Practice Alert 2003-1 (June 2007) (http://www.aicpa.org/download/secps/pralert_03_01.pdf).

FIGURE 23-5	Example of Letter to Confirm Account Balance Information with Financial Institutions

		Salah Industries Bank Confirmation December 31, 2010	Schedule _____ Date Prepared by _____ Jan 10, 2011 Approved by _____ Jan 18, 2011

		Salah Industries
		Customer Name
Financial Institution's Name and Address	National Bank	We have provided to our accountants the following information as of the close of business on December 31, 2010, regarding our deposit and loan balances. Please confirm the accuracy of the information, noting any exceptions to the information provided. If the balances have been left blank, please complete this form by furnishing the balance in the appropriate space below.* Although we do not request nor expect you to conduct a comprehensive, detailed search of your records, if during the process of completing this confirmation additional information about other deposit and loan accounts we may have with you comes to your attention, please include such information below. Please use the enclosed envelope to return the form directly to our accountants.

1. At the close of business on the date listed above, our records indicated the following deposit balance(s):

Account Name	Account Number	Interest Rate	Balance*
General account	19751-974	None	109,713.11 A-2

2. We were directly liable to the financial institution for loans at the close of business on the date listed above as follows:

Account No. / Description	Balance*	Date Due	Interest Rate	Date Through which Interest is Paid	Description of Collateral
N/A	50,000.00	January 9, 2011	10%	N/A	General
N/A	90,000.00	January 9, 2011	10%	N/A	Security
N/A	60,000.00	January 23, 2011	11%	N/A	Agreement

Samir
(Customer's Authorized Signature)

January 3, 2011
(Date)

This information presented above by the customer is in agreement with our records. Although we have not conducted a comprehensive, detailed search of our records, no other deposits or loan accounts have come to our attention.

Soliman Khateeb
(Financial Institution Authorized Signature)

January 8, 2011
(Date)

Vice President
(Title)

Exceptions and/or Comments
None

Please return this form directly to our accountants:	Sherif & Co. CPA Manama, Bahrain

*Ordinarily, balances are intentionally left blank if they are not available at the time the form is prepared

and to verify whether the client's recorded bank balance is the same amount as the actual cash in the bank except for deposits in transit, outstanding checks, and other reconciling items. Figure 23-6 gives some examples of misstatements associated with the audit of cash balances by a local auditing firm with international affiliation.

FIGURE 23-6	Examples of Misstatements of Cash Balances

1. Cash at banks as of December 31, 2010, amounted to US$6,043,102 compared with US$3,335,703 in 2009. The financial department did not utilize cash balances by making deposits to benefit from the available cash balances. We recommend studying methods for utilizing cash balances in current accounts at banks.
2. The balance of cash on consignments as of December 31, 2010, amounted to US$42,000, and we were not notified of the physical count report signed by the physical count committee at that date. We recommend sending us the treasury physical count report signed by the physical count committee.
3. There is no register for the collaterals showing the values, total value, the type of collaterals, the procedures taken over these collaterals, and the date of valuing the collaterals. We recommend that the company should prepare a register for the collaterals.
4. There are a number of small outstanding balances in the bank confirmations which were not recorded in the company's bank subsidiary ledger. We recommend adjusting the balance with these outstanding cheques.
5. We did not receive confirmation for cash in bank balances as at December 31, 2010, amounting to US$14,785,706. This consists of deposits at banks of US$11,516,331 and current accounts at banks of US$3,269,375 and we relied on bank statements in checking the accuracy of those balances.
6. We found that the company did not comply with the accounting standards requirements related to the valuation of foreign currency cash balances using current exchange rate. We recommend management to apply the prevailing current exchange rate.

In verifying the reconciliation, the auditor uses information in the cutoff bank statement to verify the appropriateness of reconciling items. The auditor's verification of the reconciliation involves several procedures:

- Verify that the client's bank reconciliation is mathematically accurate.
- Trace the balance on the bank confirmation and/or the beginning balance on the cutoff statement to the balance per bank on the bank reconciliation to ensure they are the same.
- Trace checks written and recorded before year-end and included with the cutoff bank statement to the list of outstanding checks on the bank reconciliation and to the cash disbursements journal in the period or periods prior to the balance sheet date. All checks that cleared the bank after the balance sheet date and were included in the cash disbursements journal should also be included on the outstanding check list. If a check was included in the cash disbursements journal, it should be included as an outstanding check if it did not clear before the balance sheet date. Similarly, if a check cleared the bank before the balance sheet date, it should not be on the bank reconciliation.
- Investigate all significant checks included on the outstanding check list that have not cleared the bank on the cutoff statement. The first step in the investigation should be to trace the amount of any items not clearing to the cash disbursements journal. The reason for the check not being cashed should be discussed with the client, and if the auditor is concerned about the possibility of fraud, the vendor's accounts payable balance should be confirmed to determine whether the vendor has recognized the receipt of the cash in its records. In addition, the cancelled check should be examined before the last day of the audit if it becomes available.
- Trace deposits in transit to the cutoff bank statement. All cash receipts not deposited in the bank at the end of the year should be traced to the cutoff bank statement to make sure that they were deposited shortly after the beginning of the new year.
- Account for other reconciling items on the bank statement and bank reconciliation. These include such items as bank service charges, bank errors and corrections, and unrecorded transactions debited or credited directly to the bank account by the bank. These reconciling items should be investigated to be sure that they have been treated properly by the client.

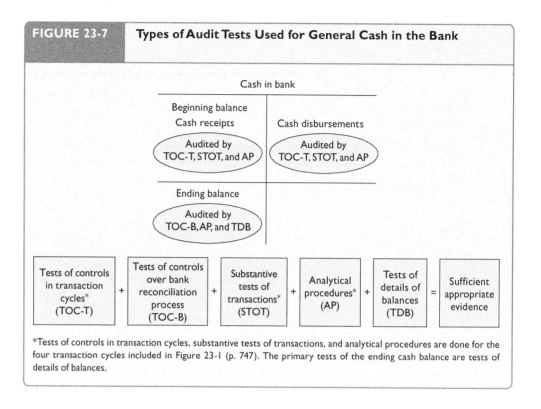

FIGURE 23-7   Types of Audit Tests Used for General Cash in the Bank

*Tests of controls in transaction cycles, substantive tests of transactions, and analytical procedures are done for the four transaction cycles included in Figure 23-1 (p. 747). The primary tests of the ending cash balance are tests of details of balances.

Figure 23-7 illustrates how the types of audit tests are used to audit the general cash account. Observe in the figure that tests of controls, substantive tests of transactions, and analytical procedures are done for each transaction cycle involving the cash account.

FRAUD-ORIENTED PROCEDURES

OBJECTIVE 23-4

Recognize when to extend audit tests of the general cash account to test further for material fraud.

A major consideration in the audit of the general cash balance is the possibility of fraud. The auditor must extend the procedures in the audit of year-end cash to determine the possibility of a material fraud when there are inadequate internal controls, especially the improper segregation of duties between the handling of cash and the recording of cash transactions in the accounting records and the lack of an independently prepared monthly bank reconciliation.

In designing procedures for uncovering fraud, auditors should carefully consider the nature of the deficiencies in internal control, the type of fraud that is likely to result from the deficiencies, the potential materiality of the fraud, and the audit procedures that are most effective in uncovering the fraud.

When auditors are specifically testing for fraud, they should keep in mind that audit procedures other than tests of details of cash balances can also be useful. Procedures that may uncover fraud in the cash receipts area include:

- Confirmation of accounts receivable
- Tests performed to detect lapping
- Review of the general ledger entries in the cash account for unusual items
- Comparison of customer orders to sales and subsequent cash receipts
- Examination of approvals and supporting documentation for bad debts and sales returns and allowances

Similar tests can be used for testing for the possibility of fraudulent cash disbursements.

Even with reasonably elaborate fraud-oriented procedures, it is extremely difficult to detect thefts of cash, as well as fraudulent financial reporting involving cash, especially omitted transactions and account balances. If, for example, a company has illegal offshore cash accounts and makes deposits to those accounts from unrecorded sales, it is unlikely that an auditor will uncover the fraud. Nevertheless, auditors are responsible for making a reasonable effort to detect fraud when they have reason to believe it may exist. The following procedures for uncovering fraud are directly related to year-end cash balances, extended tests of the bank reconciliation, proof of cash, and tests of interbank transfers.

Extended Tests of the Bank Reconciliation

When the auditor believes that the year-end bank reconciliation may be intentionally misstated, it is appropriate to perform extended tests of the year-end bank reconciliation. The extended procedures verify whether all transactions included in the journals for the last month of the year were correctly included in or excluded from the bank reconciliation and verify whether all items in the bank reconciliation were correctly included. Let's assume that there are material internal control weaknesses and the client's year-end is December 31. Using a common approach, auditors:

1. Start with the bank reconciliation for November and compare all reconciling items with cancelled checks and other documents in the December bank statement.
2. Compare all remaining cancelled checks and deposit slips in the December bank statement with the December cash disbursements and receipts journals.
3. Trace all uncleared items in the November bank reconciliation and the December cash disbursements and receipts journals to the client's December 31 bank reconciliation to make sure they are included.
4. Verify that all reconciling items in the December 31 bank reconciliation represent items from the November bank reconciliation and December's journals that have not yet cleared the bank.

In addition to these four tests, the auditor must carry out procedures subsequent to the end of the year with the use of the bank cutoff statement. These tests are the same as previously discussed.

FAKE BANK CONFIRMATION HIDES MASSIVE FRAUD

The SEC charged Italian dairy and food conglomerate Parmalat Finanziaria S.p.A with one of the largest and most brazen financial frauds in history. Parmalat was Italy's eighth largest company and a global consumer brand that sought to be the 'Coca-Cola of milk.' The assets in Parmalat's 2002 financial statements were overstated by at least €3.95 billion (approximately US$4.9 billion). Investigators claim that over the period 1990 to 2003, Parmalat inflated revenues through fictitious sales to help justify loans from global banks. Two outside auditors allegedly came up with the audacious creation of a bogus milk producer in Singapore that provided 300,000 tons of milk powder to a Cuban importer through a Cayman Islands subsidiary. Parmalat claimed that the Cayman Islands subsidiary held €3.95 billion in cash in a New York bank, but the account did not exist. A forged bank confirmation was sent to the subsidiary's auditors to support the fraudulent cash balance.

Sources: Adapted from Peter Gumbel, 'How It All Went So Sour,' Time (December 13, 2004) (http://www.time.com/time/magazine/article/0,9171,785318,00.html); and Securities and Exchange Commission Accounting and Auditing Enforcement Release No. 2065, July 28, 2004 (http://www.sec.gov/litigation/litreleases/lr18803.htm).

Proof of Cash

Auditors sometimes prepare a proof of cash when the client has material internal control weaknesses in cash. The auditor uses a proof of cash to determine whether the following were done:

- All recorded cash receipts were deposited
- All deposits in the bank were recorded in the accounting records
- All recorded cash disbursements were paid by the bank
- All amounts that were paid by the bank were recorded

Proof of cash

A four-column audit schedule prepared by the auditor to reconcile the bank's record of the client's beginning balance, cash deposits, cleared checks, and ending balance for the period with the client's records.

A **proof of cash** includes the following four reconciliation tasks:

1. Reconcile the balance on the bank statement with the general ledger balance at the beginning of the proof-of-cash period.
2. Reconcile cash receipts deposited per the bank with receipts recorded in the cash receipts journal for a given period.
3. Reconcile cancelled checks clearing the bank with those recorded in the cash disbursements journal for a given period.
4. Reconcile the balance on the bank statement with the general ledger balance at the end of the proof-of-cash period.

A proof of cash of this nature is commonly called a four-column proof of cash that contains one column for each of the four types of information listed above. A proof of cash can be performed for one or more interim months, the entire year, or the last month of the year. The concern in an interim-month proof of cash, as shown in Figure 23-8, is not with the ending cash balance. Rather, the auditor's focus is on reconciling the amounts recorded in the books with the amounts included in the bank statement.

When doing a proof of cash, the auditor is combining substantive tests of transactions and tests of details of balances. A proof of cash receipts (see Figure 23-9 showing a cash receipt voucher) is a test of recorded transactions, whereas a bank reconciliation is a test of the balance in cash at a point in time. A proof of cash is an excellent method of comparing recorded cash receipts and disbursements with the bank account and with the bank reconciliation. However, the proof of cash disbursements is not effective for discovering checks written for an improper amount, fraudulent checks, or other misstatements in which the dollar amount appearing on the cash disbursements records is incorrect. Similarly, a proof of cash receipts is not useful for uncovering the theft of cash receipts or the recording and deposit of an improper amount of cash.

Tests of Interbank Transfers

Kiting

The transfer of money from one bank to another and improperly recording the transfer so that the amount is recorded as an asset in both accounts; this practice is used by embezzlers to cover a theft of cash.

Embezzlers occasionally cover a theft of cash by a practice known as **kiting**: transferring money from one bank to another and incorrectly recording the transaction. Near the balance sheet date, a check is drawn on one bank account and immediately deposited in a second account for credit before the end of the accounting period. In making this transfer, the embezzler is careful to make sure that the check is deposited at a late enough date so that it does not clear the first bank until after the end of the period. If the interbank transfer is not recorded until after the balance sheet date, the amount of the transfer is recorded as an asset in both banks. Although there are other ways to commit this fraud, each involves increasing the bank balance to cover a shortage by the use of interbank transfers.

To test for kiting, as well as for unintentional errors in recording interbank transfers, auditors can list all interbank transfers made a few days before and after the balance sheet date and trace each to the accounting records for proper recording. Figure 23-10 shows an interbank transfer schedule with four interbank transfers

FIGURE 23-8   Interim Proof of Cash

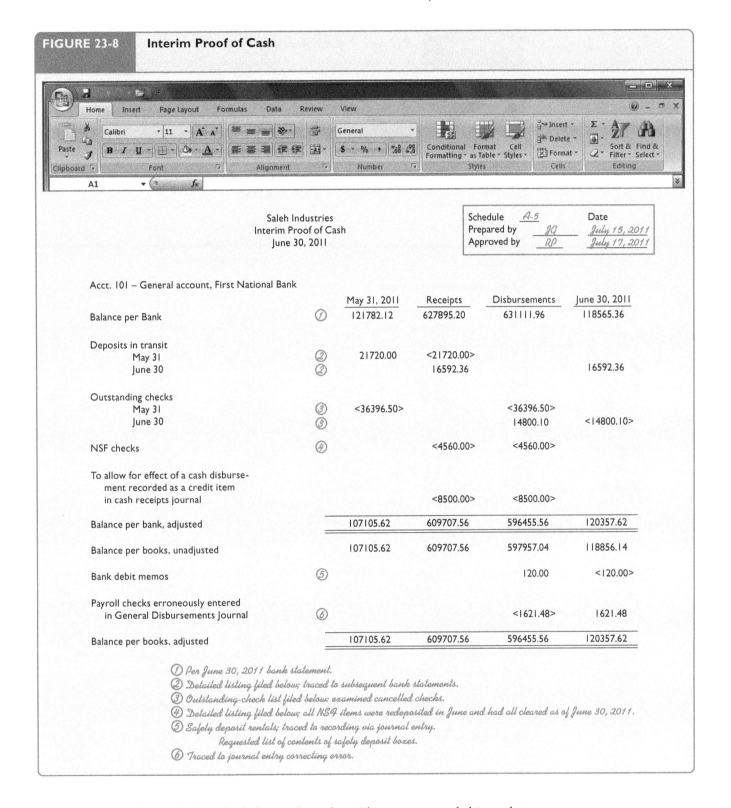

Saleh Industries
Interim Proof of Cash
June 30, 2011

			Schedule	A-5	Date	
			Prepared by	JG	July 15, 2011	
			Approved by	RP	July 17, 2011	

Acct. 101 – General account, First National Bank

		May 31, 2011	Receipts	Disbursements	June 30, 2011
Balance per Bank	①	121782.12	627895.20	631111.96	118565.36
Deposits in transit					
May 31	②	21720.00	<21720.00>		
June 30	②		16592.36		16592.36
Outstanding checks					
May 31	③	<36396.50>		<36396.50>	
June 30	③			14800.10	<14800.10>
NSF checks	④		<4560.00>	<4560.00>	
To allow for effect of a cash disburse-ment recorded as a credit item in cash receipts journal			<8500.00>	<8500.00>	
Balance per bank, adjusted		107105.62	609707.56	596455.56	120357.62
Balance per books, unadjusted		107105.62	609707.56	597957.04	118856.14
Bank debit memos	⑤			120.00	<120.00>
Payroll checks erroneously entered in General Disbursements Journal	⑥			<1621.48>	1621.48
Balance per books, adjusted		107105.62	609707.56	596455.56	120357.62

① Per June 30, 2011 bank statement.
② Detailed listing filed below; traced to subsequent bank statements.
③ Outstanding-check list filed below; examined cancelled checks.
④ Detailed listing filed below; all NSF items were redeposited in June and had all cleared as of June 30, 2011.
⑤ Safety deposit rentals; traced to recording via journal entry.
    Requested list of contents of safety deposit boxes.
⑥ Traced to journal entry correcting error.

made shortly before and after the balance sheet date. There are several things that should be audited on the interbank transfer schedule.

- *The accuracy of the information on the interbank transfer schedule should be verified.* The auditor should compare the disbursement and receipt information on the schedule to the cash disbursements and cash receipts records to make sure that it is accurate. Similarly, the dates on the schedule for transfers that were received and disbursed should be compared with the bank statement. Finally,

FIGURE 23-9	Example of Cash Receipt

Salem Industrial Co., Kuwait

Cash Receipt

Developer X

Receipt date:	July 13, 2011
Receipt Number:	87
Customer Number:	1

Description: Escrow Deposit

Item	Description	Qty	Unit Desc.	Unit Price	Amount
Check	Check Deposit			US$0.00	US$5,000.00
				Total Charges:	US$5,000.00

Item	Description	Amount
Check	18933	US$5,000.00
	Total Charges:	US$5,000.00

cash disbursements and receipts records should be examined to make sure that all transfers a few days before and after the balance sheet date have been included on the schedule. (The tick mark explanations on the schedule in Figure 23-10 indicate that these steps have been taken.)

- *The interbank transfers must be recorded in both the receiving and disbursing banks.* If, for example, there was a US$10,000 transfer from Bank A to Bank B but only the disbursement was recorded, this is evidence of an attempt to conceal a cash theft.
- *The date of the recording of the disbursements and receipts for each transfer must be in the same fiscal year.* In Figure 23-10, the dates in the two 'date recorded in books' columns [(4) and (7)] are in the same period for each transfer; therefore, they are correct. If a cash receipt was recorded in the current fiscal year and the disbursement in the subsequent fiscal year, it may be an attempt to cover a cash shortage.
- *Disbursements on the interbank transfer schedule should be correctly included in or excluded from year-end bank reconciliations as outstanding checks.* In Figure 23-10, the December 31, 2011 bank reconciliation for the general cash account should include outstanding checks for the second and third transfers but not the other two. [Compare the dates in columns (4) and (5).] Understatement of outstanding checks on the bank reconciliation indicates the possibility of kiting.
- *Receipts on the interbank transfer schedule should be correctly included in or excluded from year-end bank reconciliations as deposits in transit.* In Figure 23-10, the December 31, 2011 bank reconciliations for the savings and payroll accounts should indicate a deposit in transit for the third transfer but not for the other three. (Compare the dates for each transfer in the last two columns.) Overstating deposits in transit on the bank reconciliation indicates the possibility of kiting.

FIGURE 23-10	Interbank Transfer Schedule

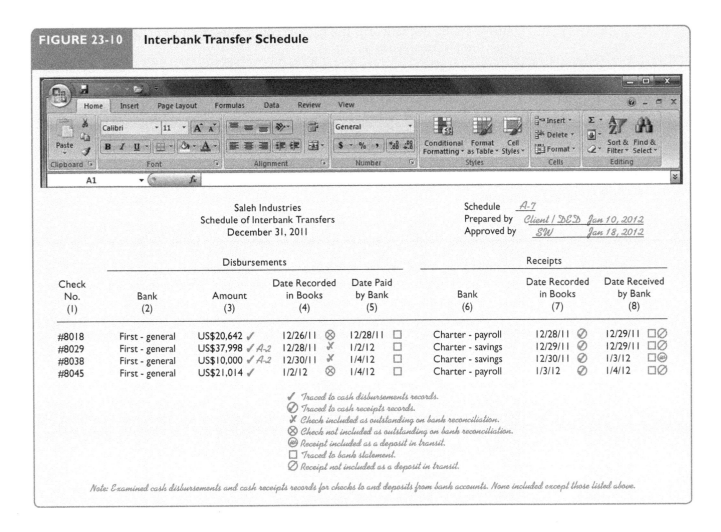

Even though audit tests of interbank transfers are usually fraud oriented, they are often performed on audits in which there are numerous bank transfers, regardless of internal controls. In addition to the possibility of kiting, inaccurate handling of transfers can result in a misclassification between cash and accounts payable. The materiality of transfers and the relative ease of performing the tests make many auditors believe they should always be performed.

AUDIT OF THE IMPREST PAYROLL BANK ACCOUNT

Tests of the payroll bank reconciliation should take only a few minutes if there is an imprest payroll account and an independent reconciliation of the bank account, such as that described for the general account. Typically, the only reconciling items are outstanding checks. For most audits, the great majority of those clear shortly after the checks are issued. In testing the payroll bank account balances, auditors must obtain the bank reconciliation, a bank confirmation, and a cutoff bank statement. The reconciliation procedures are performed in the same manner as those described for general cash except that tests of the outstanding checks are normally limited to a reasonableness test. Naturally, extended procedures are necessary if the

OBJECTIVE 23-5

Design and perform audit tests of the imprest payroll bank account.

controls are inadequate or if the bank account does not reconcile with the general ledger imprest cash balance.

AUDIT OF IMPREST PETTY CASH

Petty cash is a unique account. Although it is often immaterial in amount, many auditors verify petty cash primarily because of the potential for embezzlement and the client's expectation that auditors will examine the account, even when the amount is immaterial.

Internal Controls Over Petty Cash

The most important internal control for petty cash is the use of an imprest fund that is the responsibility of *one individual*. In addition, petty cash funds should not be mingled with other receipts, and the fund should be kept separate from all other activities. There should also be limits on the amount of any expenditure from petty cash, as well as on the total amount of the fund. The types of expenditures that can be made from petty cash transactions should be well defined by company policy.

When a disbursement is made from petty cash, adequate internal controls require a responsible official's approval on a prenumbered petty cash form. The total of the actual cash and checks in the fund, plus the total unreimbursed petty cash forms that represent expenditures, should equal the total amount of the petty cash fund stated in the general ledger. Periodic surprise counts and a reconciliation of the petty cash fund should be made by an internal auditor or other responsible official.

Audit Tests For Petty Cash

The emphasis in verifying petty cash should be on testing controls over petty cash transactions rather than the ending balance in the account. Even if the amount of the petty cash fund is small, the potential exists for numerous improper transactions if the fund is frequently reimbursed.

In testing petty cash, auditors should first determine the client's procedures for handling the fund by discussing internal controls with the custodian and examining the documentation for a few transactions. When control risk is assessed as low and few reimbursement payments occur during the year, it is common for auditors not to test any further, for reasons of immateriality. When auditors do test petty cash, the two most common procedures are to count the petty cash balance and to carry out detailed tests of one or two reimbursement transactions. The primary procedures should include:

- Foot the petty cash vouchers supporting the amount of the reimbursement
- Account for a sequence of petty cash vouchers
- Examine the petty cash vouchers for authorization and cancellation
- Examine the attached documentation, which often includes cash register tapes, invoices, and receipts, for reasonableness

Petty cash tests can be performed at any time during the year, but as a matter of convenience, they are typically done on an interim date. If the balance in the petty cash fund is considered material, which is rarely the case, it should be counted at the end of the year. Unreimbursed expenditures should be examined as a part of the count to determine whether the amount of unrecorded expenses is material.

SUMMARY

In this chapter, we have seen that transactions in most cycles affect the cash account. Because of the relationship between transactions in several cycles and the ending cash account balance, the auditor typically waits to audit the ending cash balance until the results of tests of controls and substantive tests of transactions for all cycles are completed and analyzed. Tests of the cash balance normally include tests of the bank reconciliations of key cash accounts, such as the general cash account, imprest payroll account, and imprest petty cash fund. If auditors assess a high likelihood of fraud in cash, they may perform additional tests such as extended bank reconciliation procedures, a proof of cash, or tests of interbank transfers.

ESSENTIAL TERMS

Bank confirmation   p. 754

Bank reconciliation   p. 751

Branch bank accounts   p. 749

Cash equivalents   p. 749

Cutoff bank statement   p. 755

General cash account   p. 748

Imprest petty cash fund   p. 749

Kiting   p. 760

Proof of cash   p. 760

REVIEW QUESTIONS

23-1 (Objectives 23-1, 23-2) Explain the relationships among the initial assessed control risk, tests of controls and substantive tests of transactions for cash receipts, and the tests of details of cash balances.

23-2 (Objectives 23-1, 23-2) Explain the relationships among the initial assessed control risk, tests of controls and substantive tests of transactions for cash disbursements, and the tests of details of cash balances. Give one example in which the conclusions reached about internal controls in cash disbursements will affect the tests of cash balances.

23-3 (Objective 23-3) Why is the monthly reconciliation of bank accounts by an independent person an important internal control over cash balances? Which individuals will generally not be considered independent for this responsibility?

23-4 (Objective 23-3) Evaluate the effectiveness and state the shortcomings of the preparation of a bank reconciliation by the controller in the manner described in the following statement: "When I reconcile the bank account, the first thing I do is to sort the checks in numerical order and find which numbers are missing. Next I determine the amount of the uncleared checks by referring to the cash disbursements journal. If the bank account reconciles at that point, I am all finished with the reconciliation. If it does not, I search for deposits in transit, checks from the beginning outstanding check list that still have not cleared, other reconciling items, and bank errors until it reconciles. In most instances, I can do the reconciliation in 20 minutes."

23-5 (Objective 23-3) How do bank confirmations differ from positive confirmations of accounts receivable? Distinguish between them in terms of the nature of the information confirmed, the sample size, and the appropriate action when the confirmation is not returned after the second request. Explain the rationale for the differences between these two types of confirmations.

23-6 (Objective 23-3) Evaluate the necessity of following the practice described by an auditor: "In confirming bank accounts, I insist upon a response from every bank the client has done business with in the past two years, even though the account may be closed at the balance sheet date."

23-7 (Objective 23-3) Describe what is meant by a cutoff bank statement and state its purpose.

23-8 (Objective 23-3) Why are auditors usually less concerned about the client's cash receipts cutoff than the cutoff for sales? Explain the procedure involved in testing for the cutoff for cash receipts.

23-9 (Objective 23-2) What is meant by an imprest bank account for a branch operation? Explain the purpose of using this type of bank account.

23-10 (Objective 23-4) Explain the purpose of a four-column proof of cash. List two types of misstatements it is meant to uncover.

23-11 (Objective 23-3) When the auditor fails to obtain a cutoff bank statement, it is common to verify the entire statement for the month subsequent to the balance sheet date. How is this done and what is its purpose?

23-12 (Objective 23-4) Distinguish between lapping and kiting. Describe audit procedures that can be used to uncover each.

23-13 (Objective 23-5) Assume that a client with excellent internal controls uses an imprest payroll bank account. Explain why the verification of the payroll bank reconciliation ordinarily takes less time than the tests of the general bank account, even if the number of checks exceeds those written on the general account.

23-14 (Objective 23-6) Distinguish between the verification of petty cash reimbursements and the verification of the balance in the fund. Explain how each is done. Which is more important?

23-15 (Objectives 23-3, 23-4) Why is there a greater emphasis on the detection of fraud in tests of details of cash balances than for other balance sheet accounts? Give two specific examples that demonstrate how this emphasis affects the auditor's evidence accumulation in auditing year-end cash.

23-16 (Objective 23-3) Explain why, in verifying bank reconciliations, most auditors emphasize the possibility of a nonexistent deposit in transit being included in the reconciliation and an outstanding check being omitted rather than the omission of a deposit in transit and the inclusion of a nonexistent outstanding check.

23-17 (Objective 23-3) How will a company's bank reconciliation reflect an electronic deposit of cash received by the bank from credit card agencies making payments on behalf of customers purchasing products from the company's online website, but not recorded in the company's records?

MULTIPLE CHOICE QUESTIONS FROM CPA EXAMINATIONS

23-18 (Objectives 23-3, 23-4) The following questions deal with auditing year-end cash. Choose the best response.

   a. An auditor obtains a January 10 cutoff bank statement for a client directly from the bank. Few of the outstanding checks listed on the client's December 31 bank reconciliation cleared during the cutoff period. A probable cause for this is that the client
      (1) is engaged in kiting.
      (2) is engaged in lapping.
      (3) transmitted the checks to the payees after year-end.
      (4) has overstated its year-end bank balance.

b. The auditor should ordinarily mail confirmation requests to all banks with which the client has conducted any business during the year, regardless of the year-end balance, because
(1) this procedure will detect kiting activities that would otherwise not be detected.
(2) the confirmation form also seeks information about indebtedness to the bank.
(3) the mailing of confirmation forms to all such banks is required by auditing standards.
(4) this procedure relieves the auditor of any responsibility with respect to nondetection of forged checks.

c. The usefulness of the bank confirmation request may be limited because the bank employee who completes the form may
(1) be unaware of all the financial relationships that the bank has with the client.
(2) not believe the bank is obligated to verify confidential information to a third party.
(3) sign and return the form without inspecting the accuracy of the client's bank reconciliation.
(4) not have access to the client's bank statement.

23-19 (Objective 23-4) The following questions deal with discovering fraud in auditing year-end cash. Choose the best response.

a. Which of the following is one of the better auditing techniques to detect kiting?
(1) Review composition of authenticated deposit slips.
(2) Review subsequent bank statements and cancelled checks received directly from the banks.
(3) Prepare year-end bank reconciliations.
(4) Prepare a schedule of bank transfers from the client's books.

b. The cashier of Al Riyad Company covered a shortage in his cash working fund with cash obtained on December 31 from a local bank by cashing an unrecorded check drawn on the company's Jeddah bank. The auditor would discover this manipulation by
(1) counting the cash working fund at the close of business on December 31.
(2) preparing independent bank reconciliations as of December 31.
(3) investigating items returned with the bank cutoff statements.
(4) confirming the December 31 bank balances.

c. A cash shortage may be concealed by transporting funds from one location to another or by converting negotiable assets to cash. Because of this, which of the following is vital?
(1) Simultaneous bank confirmations.
(2) Simultaneous bank reconciliations.
(3) Simultaneous four-column proofs of cash.
(4) Simultaneous surprise cash counts.

DISCUSSION QUESTIONS AND PROBLEMS

23-20 (Objectives 23-3, 23-4) The following are misstatements that might be found in the client's year-end cash balance (assume that the balance sheet date is June 30):

1. A check was omitted from the outstanding check list on the June 30 bank reconciliation. It cleared the bank July 7.
2. A check was omitted from the outstanding check list on the bank reconciliation. It cleared the bank September 6.
3. Cash receipts collected on accounts receivable from July 1 to July 5 were included as June 29 and 30 cash receipts.

4. A bank transfer recorded in the accounting records on July 1 was included as a deposit in transit on June 30.
5. The outstanding checks on the June 30 bank reconciliation were underfooted by US$2,000.
6. A loan from the bank on June 26 was credited directly to the client's bank account. The loan was not entered as of June 30.
7. A check that was dated June 26 and disbursed in June was not recorded in the cash disbursements journal, but it was included as an outstanding check on June 30.

Required

a. Assuming that each of these misstatements was intentional (fraud), state the most likely motivation of the person responsible.

b. What control can be instituted for each fraud to reduce the likelihood of occurrence?

c. List an audit procedure that can be used to discover each fraud.

23-21 (Objectives 23-3, 23-4) The following audit procedures are concerned with tests of details of general cash balances:

1. Obtain a bank confirmation from each bank with which the client does business.
2. Compare the balance on the bank reconciliation obtained from the client with the bank confirmation.
3. Compare the checks returned along with the cutoff bank statement with the list of outstanding checks on the bank reconciliation.
4. List the check number, payee, and amount of all material checks not returned with the cutoff bank statement.
5. Review minutes of the board of directors' meetings, loan agreements, and bank confirmation for interest-bearing deposits, restrictions on the withdrawal of cash, and compensating balance agreements.
6. Prepare a four-column proof of cash.
7. Compare the bank cancellation date with the date on the cancelled check for checks dated on or shortly before the balance sheet date.
8. Trace deposits in transit on the bank reconciliation to the cutoff bank statement and the current year cash receipts journal.

Required   Explain the objective of each.

23-22 (Objective 23-3) In connection with an audit you are given the following worksheet:

Bank Reconciliation, December 31, 2011

Balance per ledger December 31, 2011		US$27,253.85
Add:		
Cash receipts received on the last day of December and charged to 'cash in bank' on books but not deposited		3,715.27
Debit memo for customer's check returned unpaid (check is on hand but no entry has been made on the books)		450.00
Debit memo for bank service charge for December		35.00
		US$31,454.12
Deduct:		
Checks drawn but not paid by bank (see detailed list below)	US$3,295.15	
Credit memo for proceeds of a note receivable that had been left at the bank for collection but which has not been recorded as collected	1,200.00	
Checks for an account payable entered on books as US$297.50 but drawn and paid by bank as US$694.50	397.00	(4,892.15)
Computed balance		26,561.97
Unlocated difference		416.44
Balance per bank (checked to confirmation)		US$26,978.41

Checks Drawn but Not Paid by Bank

No.	Amount
573	US$267.27
724	39.92
903	454.67
907	291.80
911	648.29
913	737.52
914	529.10
916	36.00
917	117.26
	US$3,295.15

Required

a. Prepare a corrected reconciliation.

b. Prepare journal entries for items that should be adjusted prior to closing the books.[25]

23-23 (Objective 23-4) You are doing the first-year audit of Yacht Sporting Club and have been assigned responsibility for doing a four-column proof of cash for the month of October 2011. You obtain the following information:

1. Balance per books	September 30	US$ 10,725
	October 31	5,836
2. Balance per bank	September 30	6,915
	October 31	8,276
3. Outstanding checks	September 30	1,811
	October 31	2,615
4. Cash receipts for October	per bank	28,792
	per books	20,271
5. Deposits in transit	September 30	5,621
	October 31	996

6. Interest on a bank loan for the month of October, charged by the bank but not recorded, was US$596.

7. Proceeds on a note of the Khater Company were collected by the bank on October 28 but were not entered on the books:

Principal	US$ 2,900
Interest	396
	US$ 3,296

8. On October 26, a US$1,144 check of the Billings Company was charged to Yacht Sporting Club's account by the bank in error.

9. Dishonored checks are not recorded on the books unless they permanently fail to clear the bank. The bank treats them as disbursements when they are dishonored and deposits when they are redeposited. Checks totaling US$1,335 were dishonored in October; US$600 was redeposited in October and US$735 in November.

Required

a. Prepare a four-column proof of cash for the month ended October 31. It should show both adjusted and unadjusted cash.

b. Prepare all adjusting entries.

CASE

23-24 Objective(s) Your company is responsible for the audit of Skin Fitness Company which offers the product packaging services for health care companies. Most of the Skin Fitness Company's clients are large sized companies but recently they have expanded to include small and medium sized companies. Products are delivered to Skin Fitness

Company and on receipt details of the shipment are entered in the company's computerized system by clerks in the warehouse. The system is updated when the packaging process is completed and the shipment of the packages to customers is recorded. After confirming the shipments, the sales invoices are printed from the system in the accounts office.

Mariam, who is an accountant in the company, checks and authorizes all of the sales invoices before sending them to the clients. At the end of each week the system prepares a list of the completed shipments and those not yet sent. Mariam is also responsible for entering the transactions in the client accounts (the sales ledger) and sending the monthly statements to the clients. At the end of each month she lists the clients whose debts are overdue. There are no other procedures to monitor the debtors.

Because of the expansion of the business, the company moved to new headquarters at the end of August 2010 having obtained a loan, repayable over ten years in monthly installments. The draft accounts for the fiscal year ended at September 30, 2010, showed a severe deterioration in the company's cash liquidity despite the increased profits. The initial analytical examination referred to the increase in uncollected finished work and the creditors by percentages higher than the percentage of the increase in the inventory turnover.

Required

a. Identify the factors leading to the cash flow problems of Skin Fitness Company then suggest policies and procedures that could be applied to improve the company's cash flow.

b. Identify the audit procedures that could be performed to ensure collecting the value of the finished work not yet collected and the creditors balances.

PART

5

COMPLETING THE AUDIT

Part 5 includes only one chapter and covers the fourth and final phase of an audit: completing the audit. Even when auditors perform the other phases of an audit well, if they do a poor job carrying out the completion phase, the quality of the audit will be low. When auditors perform the planning phase (phase I) and the two testing phases (phases II and III) well, the completion phase is typically relatively easy.

CHAPTER 24

COMPLETING THE AUDIT

Good Review Requires More Than Looking At Audit Files

Marwan Abdel Dayem, an audit senior of Dayem, Sohail & Co., assigned staff assistant Atef Mazen to the audit of accounts payable for El Khateeb Industries, a large equipment manufacturer. Accounts payable is a major liability account for a manufacturing company, and testing accounts payable cutoff is an important audit area. Testing primarily involves reviewing the liability recorded by the client by examining subsequent payments to suppliers and other creditors to ensure that they were correctly recorded.

Marwan observed that Atef was spending a lot of time on the phone, apparently on personal matters. Shortly before the audit was completed, Atef announced that he was leaving the firm. Despite Atef's distractions due to his personal affairs, he completed the audit work he was assigned within the budgeted time.

Because of Marwan's concern about Atef's work habits, he decided to review the audit files with extreme care. Every schedule he reviewed was properly prepared, with tick marks entered and explained by Atef, indicating that he had made an extensive examination of underlying data and documents and had found the client's balance to be adequate as stated. Specifically, there were no payments subsequent to year-end for inventory purchases received during the audit period that had not been accrued by the company.

When Marwan finished the audit, he notified Salwa Refaie, the engagement audit manager, that the files were ready for her review. She had considerable knowledge about equipment manufacturers and also about El Khateeb Industries. Salwa reviewed all of the audit files, including analytical procedures performed during the audit. After calculating additional analytical procedures during her review, she contacted Marwan and told him accounts payable did not seem reasonable to her. She asked him to do some additional checking. Marwan went back and looked at all the documents that Atef had indicated in the audit files that he had inspected. It was quickly apparent that Atef had either not looked at the documents or did not know what he was doing when he inspected them. There were almost US$5 million of purchases applicable to the December 31, 2010, audit period that had not been included as liabilities. Salwa's review probably saved Dayem, Sohail & Co. significant embarrassment or worse.

Summary of the
Audit Process

```
┌─────────────────────┐
│      PHASE I        │
│   Plan and design   │
│  an audit approach  │
└─────────────────────┘
           │
┌─────────────────────┐
│      PHASE II       │
│   Perform tests of  │
│      controls and   │
│   substantive tests │
│   of transactions   │
└─────────────────────┘
           │
┌─────────────────────┐
│     PHASE III       │
│  Perform analytical │
│     procedures and  │
│   tests of details  │
│      of balances    │
└─────────────────────┘
           │
┌─────────────────────┐
│      PHASE IV       │
│    Complete the     │
│   audit and issue   │
│   an audit report   │
└─────────────────────┘
```

Starting with Chapter 6, the first three phases of the audit process were studied, as outlined by the flow chart in the margin. Attention is now given to the fourth and final phase which is shaded in the figure: completing the audit. As the chapter-opening case illustrates, the final phase of the audit demands careful and thoughtful review of the audit by an experienced and knowledgeable person. In addition to reviewing the results, several other aspects of completing the audit are critical to the success of an audit. In this chapter, the seven parts of completing the audit outlined by the flow chart in the margin on page 775 are covered.

Relevant International Standards on Auditing	
ISA 230	Audit Documentation
ISA 250	Consideration of Laws and Regulations in an Audit of Financial Statements
ISA 260	Communication with Those Charged with Governance
ISA 320	Materiality in Planning and Performing an Audit
ISA 450	Evaluation of Misstatements Identified during the Audit
ISA 540	Auditing Accounting Estimates, Including Fair Value Accounting Estimates, and Related Disclosures
ISA 550	Related Parties
ISA 560	Subsequent Events
ISA 570	Going Concern
ISA 580	Written Representations
ISA 700	Forming an Opinion and Reporting on Financial Statements
ISA 720	The Auditor's Responsibilities Relating to Other Information in Documents Containing Audited Financial Statements

PERFORM ADDITIONAL TESTS FOR PRESENTATION AND DISCLOSURE

OBJECTIVE 24-1

Design and perform audit tests related to presentation and disclosure audit objectives.

Chapter 6 described the need to perform procedures to satisfy the three categories of audit objectives: transaction-related objectives, balance-related objectives, and presentation and disclosure-related objectives. Our discussion of the first three phases of the audit explained how auditors design and perform audit tests to obtain sufficient appropriate evidence to support each of these categories of audit objectives. Our illustrations of transaction cycle testing emphasized performing audit tests to support the seven transaction-related and the eight balance-related audit objectives. We've discussed how those procedures also provide evidence about the three presentation and disclosure objectives, which are summarized in the first column of Table 24-1.

As part of phase IV of the audit, auditors evaluate evidence they obtained during the first three phases of the audit to determine whether they should perform additional procedures for presentation and disclosure-related objectives. Auditors approach obtaining evidence for presentation and disclosure objectives consistently with how they approach obtaining evidence for transaction-related and balance-related objectives.

- Perform procedures to obtain an understanding of controls related to presentation and disclosure objectives as a part of risk assessment procedures.
- Conduct tests of controls related to disclosures when the initial assessment of control risk is below maximum.
- Perform substantive procedures to obtain assurance that all audit objectives are achieved for information and amounts presented and disclosed in the financial statements.

TABLE 24-1	Presentation and Disclosure Audit Objectives
Audit Objectives	**Examples of Substantive Procedures**
Completeness (including occurrence)—All disclosures that should have been included in the financial statements have been included.	Use a disclosure checklist to determine if the financial statements include all disclosures required by accounting standards including disclosure that accounts receivable are pledged as collateral.
Classification and understandability—Financial information is appropriately presented and described and disclosures are clearly expressed.	Review financial statements to determine if assets are properly classified between current and non-current categories. Read the footnotes for clarity.
Accuracy and valuation—Financial and other information are disclosed fairly and at appropriate amounts.	Reconcile amounts included in the long-term debt footnotes to information examined and supported in the auditor's long-term debt audit working papers.

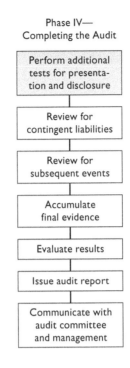

Phase IV—
Completing the Audit

Perform additional tests for presentation and disclosure

Review for contingent liabilities

Review for subsequent events

Accumulate final evidence

Evaluate results

Issue audit report

Communicate with audit committee and management

The second column of Table 24-1 includes examples of substantive procedures related to the presentation and disclosure objectives.

Often, procedures for presentation and disclosure-related objectives are integrated with the auditor's tests for transaction-related and balance-related objectives. For example, as part of the audit of accounts receivable, auditors evaluate the need to separate notes receivable and amounts due from affiliates and trade accounts due from customers. They must also determine that current and noncurrent receivables are classified separately and any factoring or discounting of notes receivable is disclosed.

While much of the information presented and disclosed in the financial statements is audited as part of the auditor's testing in earlier phases of the audit, in phase IV auditors evaluate evidence obtained during the first three phases of the audit to assess whether additional evidence is needed for the presentation and disclosure objectives. In phase IV, auditors also evaluate whether the overall presentation of the financial statements and related footnotes complies with relevant accounting standards. This includes an evaluation of whether individual financial statements reflect the appropriate classification and description of accounts consistent with requirements and that the information is presented in proper form and with the proper terminology required by accounting standards.

One of the auditor's primary concerns related to presentation and disclosure-related objectives is determining whether management has disclosed all required information (completeness objective for presentation and disclosure). To assess risks that the completeness objective for presentation and disclosure is not satisfied, auditors consider information obtained during the first three phases of audit testing to determine if they are aware of facts and circumstances that should be disclosed.

Due to the unique nature of disclosures related to contingent liabilities and subsequent events, auditors often assess the risks as high that all required information may not be completely disclosed in the footnotes. Audit tests performed in earlier audit phases often do not provide sufficient evidence about contingent liabilities and subsequent events. Therefore, auditors design and perform procedures in every audit to review for contingent liabilities and subsequent events as part of their phase IV testing. These procedures are discussed next.

REVIEW FOR CONTINGENT LIABILITIES AND COMMITMENTS

A **contingent liability** is a potential future obligation to an outside party for an unknown amount resulting from activities that have already taken place. Material contingent liabilities must be disclosed in the footnotes. Three conditions are required for a contingent liability to exist:

OBJECTIVE 24-2

Conduct a review for contingent liabilities and commitments.

TABLE 24-2	Likelihood of Occurrence and Financial Statement Treatment

Likelihood of Occurrence of Event	Financial Statement Treatment
Remote (slight chance)	No disclosure is necessary.
Reasonably possible (more than remote, but less than probable)	Footnote disclosure is necessary.
Probable (likely to occur)	• If the amount can be reasonably estimated, financial statement accounts are adjusted. • If the amount cannot be reasonably estimated, note disclosure is necessary.

Contingent liability

A potential future obligation to an outside party for an unknown amount resulting from activities that have already taken place.

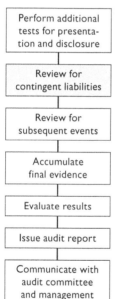

Phase IV—
Completing the Audit

1. There is a potential future payment to an outside party or the impairment of an asset that resulted from an existing condition
2. There is uncertainty about the amount of the future payment or impairment
3. The outcome will be resolved by some future event or events

For example, a lawsuit that has been filed but not yet resolved meets all three conditions.

The uncertainty of the future payment can vary from extremely likely to highly unlikely. It is up to the auditor to exercise his professional judgment when deciding whether to assess the level or degree of uncertainty. This professional judgment is also exercised when deciding to evaluate whether the client has applied the appropriate treatment. Table 24-2 shows a summary of the three levels of likelihood of occurrence and the appropriate financial statement treatment for each likelihood.

Contingency footnotes should describe the nature of the contingency to the extent it is known and the opinion of legal counsel or management as to the expected outcome. Figure 24-1 is an illustration of a footnote for pending litigation and company guarantees of debt.

Auditors are especially concerned about certain contingent liabilities:

• Pending litigation for patent infringement, product liability, or other actions
• Income tax disputes
• Product warranties
• Notes receivable discounted
• Guarantees of obligations of others
• Unused balances of outstanding letters of credit

Auditing standards make it clear that management, not the auditor, is responsible for identifying and deciding the appropriate accounting treatment for contingent liabilities. In many audits, it is impractical for auditors to uncover contingencies without management's cooperation.

FIGURE 24-1	Contingent Liability Footnote

There are various suits and claims pending against the company and its consolidated subsidiaries. It is the opinion of the company's management, based on current available information, that the ultimate liability, if any, resulting from such suits and claims will not materially affect the consolidated financial position or results of operations of the company and its consolidated subsidiaries.

The company has agreed to guarantee the repayment of approximately US$14,000,000 loaned by a bank to several affiliated corporations in which the company owns a minority interest.

The auditor's primary objectives in verifying contingent liabilities are:

- Evaluate the accounting treatment of known contingent liabilities to determine whether management has properly classified the contingency (classification presentation and disclosure objective).
- Identify, as for as possible, any contingencies not already identified by management (completeness presentation and disclosure objective).

Closely related to contingent liabilities are **commitments**. They include such things as agreements to purchase raw materials or to lease facilities at a certain price and to sell merchandise at a fixed price, as well as bonus plans, profit-sharing and pension plans, and royalty agreements. The most important characteristic of a commitment is the *agreement to commit the firm to a set of fixed conditions* in the future, regardless of what happens to profits or the economy as a whole. Presumably the entity agrees to commitments to better its own interests, but they may turn out to be less or more advantageous than originally anticipated. Companies ordinarily describe all commitments either in a separate footnote or combine them with a footnote related to contingencies.

Commitments

Agreements that the entity will hold to a fixed set of conditions, such as the purchase or sale of merchandise at a stated price, at a future date, regardless of what happens to profits or to the economy as a whole.

Audit Procedures for Finding Contingencies

Many of these potential obligations are verified as an integral part of various segments of the audit rather than as a separate activity near the end of the audit. For example, auditors test for unused balances in outstanding letters of credit as a part of confirming bank balances and loans from banks. Similarly, auditors consider the possibility of income tax disputes as a part of analyzing income tax expense, reviewing the general correspondence file, and examining revenue agent reports. Even if contingencies are verified separately, auditors commonly perform the tests well before the last few days of completing the audit to ensure their proper verification. Tests of contingent liabilities near the end of the audit are more of a review than an initial search.

The first step in the audit of contingencies is to *determine whether any contingencies exist* (occurrence presentation and disclosure objective). As you know from studying other audit areas, it is more difficult to discover unrecorded transactions or events than to verify recorded information. Once the auditor knows that contingencies exist, evaluating their materiality and the footnote disclosures can ordinarily be satisfactorily resolved.

The following are some audit procedures commonly used to search for contingent liabilities, but not all are applicable to every audit:

- Inquire of management (orally and in writing) about the possibility of unrecorded contingencies. In these inquiries, the auditor must be specific in describing the different kinds of contingencies that may require disclosure as reminders to management of contingencies they overlooked or do not fully understand. If management overlooked a contingency or does not fully comprehend accounting disclosure requirements, the inquiry can be helpful to identify required disclosures. At the completion of the audit, auditors typically ask management to make a written statement as a part of the letter of representation (discussed later in this chapter) that it is aware of no undisclosed contingent liabilities. Naturally, inquiries of management are not useful in uncovering the intentional failure to disclose contingencies.
- Review current and previous years' tax position reports for income tax settlements. The reports may indicate areas or years in which there are unsettled disagreements. If a review has been in progress for a long time, there is an increased likelihood of a tax dispute.
- Review the minutes of directors' and stockholders' meetings for indications of lawsuits or other contingencies.

- Analyze legal expense for the period under audit and review invoices and statements from legal counsel for indications of contingent liabilities, especially lawsuits and pending tax assessments.
- Obtain a letter from each major attorney performing legal services for the client as to the status of pending litigation or other contingent liabilities. This procedure is examined in more depth shortly.
- Review audit documentation for any information that may indicate a potential contingency. For example, bank confirmations may indicate notes receivable discounted or guarantees of loans.
- Examine letters of credit in force as of the balance sheet date and obtain a confirmation of the used and unused balances.

Evaluation of Known Contingent Liabilities

If auditors conclude that there are contingent liabilities, they must evaluate the significance of the potential liability and the nature of the disclosure needed in the financial statements to obtain evidence about the completeness (including occurrence) presentation and disclosure objective. In some instances, the potential liability is sufficiently well known to be included in the statements as an actual liability. In other instances, disclosure may be unnecessary if the contingency is highly remote or immaterial. Auditing firms often obtain a separate evaluation of the potential liability from its own legal counsel, especially highly material ones, rather than relying on management or management's attorneys. For those contingencies that require disclosure, the auditor also reviews the draft footnote to ensure that the disclosed information is understandable and fairly states the conditions of the contingency.

Audit Procedures for Finding Commitments

The search for unknown commitments is usually performed as a part of the audit of each audit area. For example, in verifying sales transactions, the auditor should be alert for sales commitments. Similarly, commitments for the purchase of raw materials or equipment can be identified as a part of the audit of each of these accounts. The auditor should also be aware of the possibility of commitments when reading minutes, contracts, and correspondence files.

Inquiry of Client's Attorneys

OBJECTIVE 24-3

Obtain and evaluate letters from the client's attorneys.

Inquiry of the client's attorneys

A letter from the client requesting that legal counsel inform the auditor of pending litigation or any other information involving legal counsel that is relevant to financial statement disclosure.

Inquiry of the client's attorneys is a major procedure auditors rely on for evaluating known litigation or other claims against the client and identifying additional ones. The auditor relies on the attorney's expertise and knowledge of the client's legal affairs to provide a professional opinion about the expected outcome of existing lawsuits and the likely amount of the liability, including court costs. The attorney is also likely to know of pending litigation and claims that management may have overlooked.

Many auditing firms analyze legal expense for the entire year and have the client send a standard inquiry letter to every attorney the client has been involved with in the current or preceding year, plus any attorney the firm occasionally engages. In some cases, this involves a large number of attorneys, including some who deal in aspects of law that are far removed from potential lawsuits.

The standard inquiry to the client's attorney, prepared on the client's letterhead and signed by one of the company's officials, should include the following:

- *A list including (1) pending threatened litigation and (2) asserted or unasserted claims or assessments with which the attorney has had significant involvement.* This list is typically prepared by management, but management may request that the attorney prepare the list.

- *A request that the attorney furnish information or comment about the progress of each item listed.* The desired information includes the legal action the client intends to take, the likelihood of an unfavorable outcome, and an estimate of the amount or range of the potential loss.
- *A request of the law firm to identify any unlisted pending or threatened legal actions or a statement that the client's list is complete.*
- *A statement informing the attorney of the attorney's responsibility to inform management of legal matters requiring disclosure in the financial statements and to respond directly to the auditor.* If the attorney chooses to limit a response, reasons for doing so are to be included in the letter.

Figure 24-2 provides an example of a typical standard letter sent to the attorney for return directly to the auditor's office. Notice the first paragraph requests that the attorney communicate about contingencies up to approximately *the date of the auditor's report.*

Attorneys in recent years have become reluctant to provide certain information to auditors because of their own exposure to legal liability for providing incorrect or confidential information. To learn more about attorneys' concerns, read the boxed feature 'The Legal View.' The nature of the refusals by attorneys to provide auditors with complete information about contingent liabilities falls into two categories:

1. The attorneys refuse to respond due to a lack of knowledge about matters involving contingent liabilities.
2. The attorneys refuse to disclose information that they consider confidential.

FIGURE 24-2	An Example of an Attorney Letter for XYZ Company

Adel Hamoda & Co. Attorneys in law

March 1, 2011

Our auditors, Salma & Salwa Co., CPAs, are conducting an audit of our financial statements for the fiscal year ended December 31, 2010. In connection with their audit, we have prepared and furnished to them a description and evaluation of certain contingencies, including those attached, involving matters with respect to which you have been engaged and to which you have devoted substantive attention on behalf of the company in the form of legal consultation or representation. For the purpose of your response to this letter, we believe that as to each contingency an amount in excess of US$5,000 would be material, and in total, US$50,000. However, determination of materiality with respect to the overall financial statements cannot be made until our auditors complete their audit. Your response should include matters that existed at December 31, 2010, and during the period from that date to the date of the completion of their audit, which is anticipated to be on or about March 15, 2011. Please provide to our auditors the following information:

1. Such explanation, if any, that you consider necessary to supplement the listed judgments rendered or settlements made involving the company from the beginning of this fiscal year through the date of your reply.
2. Such explanation, if any, that you consider necessary to supplement the listing of pending or threatened litigation, including an explanation of those matters as to which your views may differ from those stated and an identification of the omission of any pending or threatened litigation, claim, and assessment or a statement that the list of such matters is complete.
3. Such explanation, if any, that you consider necessary to supplement the attached information concerning unasserted claims and assessments, including an explanation of those matters as to which your views may differ from those stated.

We understand that whenever, in the course of performing legal services for us with respect to a matter recognized to involve an unasserted possible claim or assessment that may call for financial statement disclosure, you have formed a professional conclusion that we should disclose or consider disclosure concerning such possible claim or assessment, as a matter of professional responsibility to us, you will so advise us and will consult with us concerning the question of such disclosure. Please specifically confirm to our auditors that our understanding is correct. Please specifically identify the nature of and reasons for any limitations in your response.

XYZ Company

THE LEGAL VIEW

The lawyer is the expert on litigation, yet differences in lawyers' and auditors' responsibilities with respect to common clients have resulted in contentious difficulties. Although auditors are responsible for determining there is 'adequate disclosure' under relevant accounting standards ... lawyers are responsible for 'winning the case.' Because information provided by lawyers may affect a case adversely, these responsibilities may conflict.

Many lawyers believe that, despite a client's request that they provide the auditor with information, they should be less than candid in letters to auditors because of concern their replies may

- Impair the client–lawyer confidentiality privilege
- Disclose a client confidence or secret
- Prejudice the client's defense of a claim
- Constitute an admission by the client

The authoritative guidance for lawyers ... warns lawyers they must be careful in communications with auditors as the public interest is to protect the confidentiality of larger client communications.

Lawyers normally should refrain from expressing judgments on outcome—either likelihood or amount of loss. The net effect is auditors generally can obtain relatively complete responses on the existence of litigation and the dates when the underlying cause occurred.,. but less complete responses on the likelihood of an unfavorable outcome and the amount of potential loss.

In addition to an implicit hesitancy to provide evidential matter on likelihood and amount of loss, the American Bar Association (ABA) statement gives lawyers definitions of *probable* and *remote* as follows:

- *Remote.* The ABA says an unfavorable outcome is remote if the prospects for the client not succeeding in its defense are judged to be extremely doubtful and the prospects of success by the claimant are judged to be slight.
- *Probable.* The ABA says an unfavorable outcome for the client is probable if the claimant's prospects of not succeeding are judged to be extremely doubtful and the client's prospects for success in its defense are judged to be slight.

Source: Excerpted from an article by Bruce K. Behn and Kurt Pany, 'Limitations of Lawyers' Letters,' *Journal of Accountancy* (February 1995), pp. 62–63.

Unasserted claim

A potential legal claim against a client where the condition for a claim exists but no claim has been filed.

For example, the attorney might be aware of a violation of a patent agreement that could result in a significant loss to the client if it were known (**unasserted claim**). Such an instance falls under the second category. The inclusion of the information in a footnote could actually cause the lawsuit and therefore be damaging to the client.

If an attorney refuses to provide the auditor with information about material existing lawsuits (asserted claims) or unasserted claims, *auditors must modify their audit report to reflect the lack of available evidence* (a scope limitation, which requires a qualified or disclaimer of opinion). This requirement in the auditing standards has the effect of requiring management to give its attorneys permission to provide contingent liability information to auditors and to encourage attorneys to cooperate with auditors in obtaining information about contingencies.

In the U.S., explicit regulations exist to ensure that attorneys working for public companies report any violations of federal securities laws committed by the company. If the legal officer or CEO fails to appropriately respond, the attorney must report violations to the company's audit committee. Responding to these requirements, the American Bar Association subsequently amended its attorney–client confidentiality rules to permit attorneys to breach confidentiality if a client is committing a crime or fraud.

In Arab countries, no similar regulations or guidelines exist to require attorneys to provide all needed information. Management of companies put pressure on their legal consultants to ensure auditors receive all requested information about possible lawsuits.

REVIEW FOR SUBSEQUENT EVENTS

OBJECTIVE 24-4

Conduct a post-balance-sheet review for subsequent events.

The third part of completing the audit included in the sidebar is the review for subsequent events. The auditor must review transactions and events that occurred after the balance sheet date to determine whether any of these transactions or events affect the fair presentation or disclosure of the current period statements. The auditing procedures

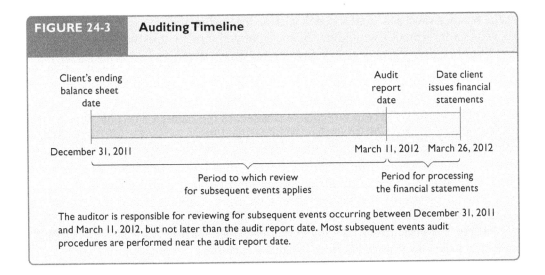

FIGURE 24-3 | **Auditing Timeline**

The auditor is responsible for reviewing for subsequent events occurring between December 31, 2011 and March 11, 2012, but not later than the audit report date. Most subsequent events audit procedures are performed near the audit report date.

required by auditing standards to verify these transactions and events are commonly called the **review for subsequent events** or *post-balance-sheet review*.

The auditor's responsibility for reviewing subsequent events is normally limited to the period beginning with the balance sheet date and ending with the date of the auditor's report. Because the date of the auditor's report corresponds to the completion of the important auditing procedures in the client's office, the subsequent events review should be completed near the end of the audit. Figure 24-3 shows the period covered by a subsequent events review and the timing of that review.

Types of Subsequent Events

Two types of **subsequent events** require consideration by management and evaluation by the auditor: those that have a direct effect on the financial statements and require adjustment of the current year's financial statement amounts and those that have no direct effect on the financial statement amounts but for which disclosure is required.

Those That Have a Direct Effect on the Financial Statements and Require Adjustment Some events that occur after the balance sheet date provide additional information to management that helps them determine the fair presentation of account balances as of the balance sheet date. Information about those events helps auditors in verifying the balances. For example, if the auditor is having difficulty determining the correct valuation of inventory because of obsolescence, the sale of raw material inventory as scrap in the subsequent period will indicate the correct value of the inventory as of the balance sheet date.

Subsequent period events, such as the following, require an adjustment of account balances in the current year's financial statements if the amounts are material:

- Declaration of bankruptcy by a customer with an outstanding accounts receivable balance because of the customer's deteriorating financial condition
- Settlement of litigation at an amount different from the amount recorded on the books
- Disposal of equipment not being used in operations at a price below the current book value
- Sale of investments at a price below recorded cost

When subsequent events are used to evaluate the amounts included in the year-end financial statements, auditors must distinguish between conditions that existed

---

Review for subsequent events

The auditing procedures performed by auditors to identify and evaluate subsequent events; also known as a *post-balance-sheet review*.

Subsequent events

Transactions and other pertinent events that occurred after the balance sheet date that affect the fair presentation or disclosure of the statements being audited.

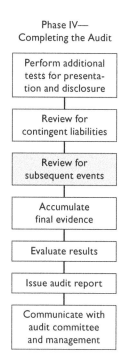

at the balance sheet date and those that came into being after the end of the year. The subsequent information should not be incorporated directly into the statements if the conditions causing the change in valuation took place after year-end.

Those That Do Not Have a Direct Effect on the Financial Statements but for Which Disclosure is Required Subsequent events of this type provide evidence of conditions that did not exist at the date of the balance sheet being reported on but are so significant that they require disclosure even though they do not require account adjustment. Ordinarily, these events can be adequately disclosed by the use of footnotes, but occasionally, one may be so significant as to require disclosure in *supplemental financial statements* that include the effect of the event as if it had occurred on the balance sheet date. An example is an extremely material merger.

Events or transactions occurring in the subsequent period that may require disclosure rather than an adjustment in the financial statements include:

- A decline in the market value of securities held for temporary investment or resale
- The issuance of bonds or equity securities
- A decline in the market value of inventory as a consequence of government action barring further sale of a product
- The uninsured loss of inventories as a result of fire
- A merger or an acquisition

However, auditors for publicly held companies as well as family owned give great attention to subsequent events and apply both criteria associated with the occurrence of subsequent events by recommending to management of various clients the adjustment and/or disclosure of those events in the current period financial statements.

Audit Tests

There are two categories of audit procedures for the subsequent events review:

1. Procedures normally integrated as a part of the verification of year-end account balances
2. Procedures performed specifically for the purpose of discovering events or transactions that must be recognized as subsequent events

The first category includes cutoff and valuation tests done as a part of the tests of details of balances. For example, auditors examine subsequent period sales and acquisition transactions to determine whether the cutoff is accurate. Auditors also test the collectability of accounts receivable by reviewing subsequent period cash receipts to evaluate the valuation of the allowance for uncollectible accounts. Procedures for cutoff and valuation have been discussed sufficiently in preceding chapters and are not repeated here.

The second category of tests are performed specifically to obtain information to incorporate into the current year's account balances or footnotes as tests of the completeness presentation and disclosure objective. These tests include the following:

Review Records Prepared Subsequent to the Balance Sheet Date Auditors should review journals and ledgers to determine the existence and nature of significant transactions related to the current year. If journals are not kept up-to-date, auditors should review documents that will be used to prepare the journals. Auditing standards recommend that company auditors inquire about and examine statements issued during the subsequent events review period, such as relevant internal audit reports, and monthly financial positions.

Review Internal Statements Prepared Subsequent to the Balance Sheet Date In the review auditors should emphasize changes in the business compared to results for the same period in the year under audit and changes after year-end. They should pay careful attention to major changes in the business or environment in which the client is operating. Auditors should discuss the interim statements with management to determine whether they are prepared on the same basis as the current period statements, and also inquire about significant changes in the operating results.

Examine Minutes Issued Subsequent to the Balance Sheet Date Auditors must examine the minutes of stockholders' and directors' meetings subsequent to the balance sheet date for subsequent events affecting the current period financial statements.

Correspond with Attorneys As discussed earlier in the chapter, auditors correspond with attorneys as a part of the search for contingent liabilities. Auditors normally request the attorney to date and mail the letter as of the expected completion date of field work to fulfill the auditors' responsibility for subsequent events.

Inquire of Management Inquiries vary from client to client, but normally include significant changes in the assets or capital structure of the company after the balance sheet date, the current status of items that were not completely resolved at the balance sheet date, and unusual adjustments made subsequent to the balance sheet date.

Inquiries of management about subsequent events must be done with appropriate client personnel to obtain meaningful answers. For example, it is not useful for the auditor to discuss tax or union matters with an accounts receivable supervisor. Depending on the information desired, auditors usually make inquiries of the controller, vice presidents, and the president.

Obtain a Letter of Representation The letter of representation written by the client's management to the auditor formalizes statements made by management about different matters throughout the audit, including discussions about subsequent events. This letter is mandatory and includes other relevant matters. This letter is discussed in the following section.

Dual Dating

Occasionally, the auditor determines that a subsequent event that affects the current period financial statements occurred after the field work was completed but *before the audit report was issued*. The source of such information is typically management or the media. For example, what if an audit client acquired another company after the auditor's last day of field work? Using the dates in Figure 24-3, assume the acquisition occurred on March 23, when the last day of field work was March 11. In that situation, auditing standards require the auditor to extend audit tests for the newly discovered subsequent event to make sure that it is correctly disclosed. The auditor has two equally acceptable options for expanding subsequent events tests:

1. Expand all subsequent events tests to the new date
2. Restrict the subsequent events review to matters related to the new subsequent event

For the first option, auditors simply change the audit report date to the new date. For the second option, the auditor issues a **dual-dated audit report**, meaning that the audit report includes two dates: the first date for the completion of field work, except for the specific exception, and the second date, which is always later, for the exception. In the example, assume the auditor returned to the client's premises to perform audit tests pertaining only to the acquisition and completes those tests on March 31. The audit report will be dual-dated as follows: March 11, 2011, except for note 17, as to which the date is March 31, 2011.

Dual-dated audit report

The use of one audit report date for normal subsequent events and a later date for one or more subsequent events that come to the auditor's attention after the field work has been completed.

FINAL EVIDENCE ACCUMULATION

OBJECTIVE 24-5

Design and perform the final steps in the evidence-accumulation segment of the audit.

Phase IV—
Completing the Audit

- Perform additional tests for presentation and disclosure
- Review for contingent liabilities
- Review for subsequent events
- Accumulate final evidence
- Evaluate results
- Issue audit report
- Communicate with audit committee and management

In addition to the review for subsequent events, the auditor has several final evidence accumulation responsibilities that apply to all cycles. Five types of final evidence accumulation are discussed in this section: perform final analytical procedures, evaluate the going-concern assumption, obtain a management representation letter, consider information accompanying the basic financial statements, and read other information in the annual report. Each of these is done late in the audit.

Perform Final Analytical Procedures

Auditing standards require auditors to perform analytical procedures during the completion of the audit. They are useful as a final review for material misstatements or financial problems not noted during other testing and to help the auditor take a final objective look at the financial statements. It is common for a partner to do the analytical procedures during the final review of audit documentation and financial statements. Typically, a partner has a good understanding of the client and its business because of ongoing relationships. This knowledge combined with effective analytical procedures help the partner identify possible oversights in an audit. The opening story in the audit of El Khateeb Industries illustrates this point.

When performing analytical procedures during the final review stage, the partner generally reads the financial statements, including footnotes, and considers:

1. The adequacy of evidence gathered about unusual or unexpected account balances or relationships identified during planning or while conducting the audit.
2. Unusual or unexpected account balances or relationships that were not previously identified.
3. Past experience with similar clients in the same industry. The partner would perform comparisons identifying accounts balances with unusual variances giving rise to possible further investigations.
4. Contacting management for more explanation about transactions, accounts balances or changes in accounting policies.

Results from final analytical procedures may indicate that additional audit evidence is necessary.

Evaluate Going-Concern Assumption

ISA 560 and ISA 570 require the auditor to evaluate whether there is a substantial doubt about a client's ability to continue as a going concern for at least one year beyond the balance sheet date. Auditors make that assessment initially as a part of planning but may revise it after obtaining new information. For example, an initial assessment of going concern may need revision if the auditor discovers during the audit that the company has defaulted on a loan, lost its primary customer, or decided to dispose of substantial assets to pay off loans. Auditors use analytical procedures, discussions with management about potential financial difficulties, and their knowledge of the client's business gained throughout the audit to assess the likelihood of financial failure within the next year.

A final assessment of the entity's going concern status is desirable after all evidence has been accumulated and proposed audit adjustments have been incorporated into the financial statements. When auditors have reservations about the going-concern assumption, they must evaluate management's plans to avoid bankruptcy and the feasibility of achieving these plans. Making the final decision whether to issue a report with a going-concern emphasis of a matter paragraph can be time-consuming and difficult. (For more discussion of going-concern emphasis of matter paragraphs, refer to the types of audit reports in Chapter 3.)

Obtain Management Representation Letter

Auditing standards require the auditor to obtain a **letter of representation** documenting management's most important oral representations made during the audit. The letter is prepared on the client's letterhead, addressed to the auditing firm, and signed by high-level corporate officials, usually the president or chief executive officer and chief financial officer. While the letter implies that it has originated with the client, it is common practice for the auditor to prepare the letter and request the client to type it on the company's letterhead and sign it. Refusal by a client to prepare and sign the letter requires a qualified opinion or disclaimer of opinion. The letter should be dated no earlier than the date of the auditor's report to make sure that there are adequate representations about subsequent events.

The three purposes of the client letter of representation are:

1. *To impress upon management its responsibility for the assertions in the financial statements.* It is easy for management to forget that they are responsible, not the auditor, for the fair presentation of financial statements, especially in smaller companies that lack personnel with expertise in accounting.
2. *To remind management of potential misstatements or omissions in the financial statements.* For example, if the letter of representation includes a reference to pledged assets and contingent liabilities, honest management may be reminded of its unintentional failure to disclose the information adequately, which helps satisfy the completeness presentation and disclosure objective. To fulfill this objective, the letter of representation should be sufficiently detailed to act as a reminder to management.
3. *To document the responses from management to inquiries about various aspects of the audit.* This provides written documentation of client representations in the event of disagreement or a lawsuit between the auditor and client. Because it is more formal than oral communication, a letter of representation also helps reduce misunderstandings between management and the auditor.

Matters that should be included in the letter of representation are:

1. *Financial statements*
   * Management's acknowledgment of its responsibility for the fair presentation of the financial statements
   * Management's belief that the financial statements are fairly presented in conformity with IFRS, GAAP, or local accounting standards
2. *Completeness of information*
   * Availability of all financial records and related data
   * Completeness and availability of all minutes of meetings of stockholders, directors, and committees of directors
3. *Recognition, measurement, and disclosure*
   * Management's belief that the effects of any uncorrected financial statement misstatements are immaterial to the financial statements
   * Information concerning fraud involving (a) management, (b) employees who have significant roles in internal control, or (c) others where the fraud could have a material effect on the financial statements
   * Information concerning related party transactions and amounts receivable from or payable to related parties
   * Unasserted claims or assessments such as contingent liabilities and commitments that the entity's lawyer has advised are probable of assertion and must be disclosed in the financial statements
4. *Subsequent events*
   * Bankruptcy of a major customer with an outstanding account receivable at the balance sheet date
   * A merger or acquisition after the balance sheet date

Letter of representation

A written communication from the client to the auditor formalizing statements that the client has made about matters pertinent to the audit.

In the U.S., there are more regulations to be observed by auditors for listed companies. PCAOB Standard 5 requires the auditor to obtain written representations from management about its responsibility for internal control over financial reporting and management's conclusion about the effectiveness of internal control over financial reporting as of the end of the fiscal period. Auditors of public companies may obtain a combined representation letter for both the audit of the financial statements and the audit of internal control.

The above requirements are not yet applicable to any Arab countries. Auditors in Arab countries are required to form an opinion only on the financial statements without any separate reports about the internal controls.

A client representation letter is a written statement from a nonindependent source and therefore *cannot be regarded as reliable evidence*. However, the letter does provide documentation that management has been asked certain questions to make sure that management understands its responsibilities and to protect the auditor if management files claims against the auditor.

In some audits, the auditor may find other evidence that contradicts statements in the letter of representation. In such cases, the auditor should investigate the circumstances and consider whether representations in the letter are reliable.

Consider Information Accompanying the Basic Financial Statements

Clients often include additional information beyond the basic financial statements in materials prepared for management or outside users. Figure 24-4 illustrates the basic financial statements and additional information.

Auditing standards intentionally refrain from defining or restricting supplementary information to enable companies to individualize the information to meet the needs of statement users. However, several types of information are commonly included in the additional information section, such as detailed comparative statements supporting the totals on the primary financial statements for accounts such as cost of goods sold and operating expenses.

Auditors must clearly distinguish their audit and reporting responsibility for the primary financial statements and for additional information. Usually, the auditor has

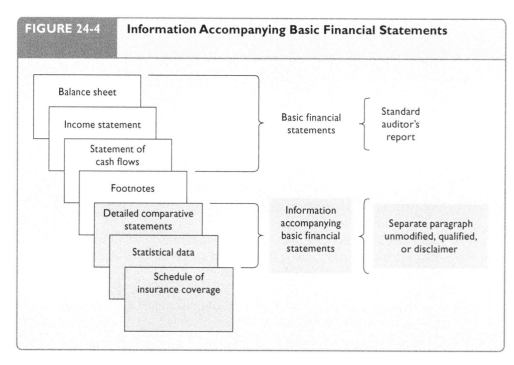

FIGURE 24-4   Information Accompanying Basic Financial Statements

not performed a sufficiently detailed audit to justify an opinion on the additional information, but in some instances, the auditor may be confident that the information is fairly presented. The profession's reporting standards require the auditor to make a clear statement about the degree of responsibility taken for the additional information. Two types of opinions are allowed: a positive opinion indicating a high level of assurance or a disclaimer indicating no assurance.

When the auditor issues an opinion on additional information accompanying the financial statements, materiality is the same as that used in forming an opinion on the basic financial statements. As a result, the additional procedures required are less extensive than if the auditor were issuing an opinion on the information taken by itself, such as in a report on specified elements or accounts. Additional wording is added to the auditor's standard report when expressing an opinion on the additional information, such as this example:

> *Our audit was conducted for the purpose of forming an opinion on the basic financial statements taken as a whole. The accompanying information on pages x through y is presented for purposes of additional analysis and is not a required part of the basic financial statements. Such information has been subjected to the auditing procedures applied in the audit of the basic financial statements and, in our opinion, is fairly stated in all material respects in relation to the basic financial statements taken as a whole.*

If the auditor decides that sufficient evidence has *not* been accumulated for the additional data to justify an unmodified opinion, the paragraph will be modified to indicate that the auditor disclaims an opinion on the additional information.

Read Other Information in the Annual Report

Auditing standards as well as local laws in various Arab countries require the auditor to read **other information included in annual reports** pertaining directly to the financial statements. For example, assume that the board of directors' report in the annual report refers to an increase in earnings per share from US$2.60 to US$2.93. The auditor is required to compare that information with the financial statements to make sure it corresponds. Other examples are the board of directors' report and explanations of company activities included in annual reports. It usually takes auditors only a few minutes to make sure that the nonfinancial statement information is consistent with the statements. If auditors conclude that a material inconsistency exists, they should request the client to change the information. If the client refuses, which would be unusual, the auditor should include an emphasis of a matter paragraph in the audit report or withdraw from the engagement.

Other information included in annual reports

Information that is not a part of the financial statements but is published with them; auditors must read this information for inconsistencies with the financial statements.

EVALUATE RESULTS

After performing all audit procedures in each audit area, including the review for contingencies and subsequent events and accumulating final evidence, the auditor must integrate the results into *one overall conclusion* about the financial statements. Ultimately, the auditor must decide whether sufficient appropriate audit evidence has been accumulated to warrant the conclusion that the financial statements are stated in accordance with IFRS, GAAP or local accounting standards applied on a basis consistent with those of the preceding year. The five main aspects of evaluating the results are discussed next.

OBJECTIVE 24-6

Integrate the audit evidence gathered and evaluate the overall audit results.

Sufficient Appropriate Evidence

To make a final evaluation as to whether sufficient appropriate evidence has been accumulated, the auditor reviews the audit documentation for the entire audit to determine whether all material classes of transactions, accounts, and disclosures have been adequately tested, considering all circumstances of the audit. An important part of the review is to make sure that all parts of the audit program have been accurately completed and documented, and that all audit objectives have been met. The auditor must decide whether the audit program is adequate, considering problem areas identified as the audit progressed. For example, if misstatements were discovered during tests of sales, the initial plans for tests of details of accounts receivable may have been insufficient.

As an aid in deciding whether the audit evidence is adequate, auditors often use a **completing the audit checklist** which is a reminder of items that may have been overlooked. Figure 24-5 illustrates part of a completing the audit checklist.

If auditors conclude that sufficient evidence has not been obtained to decide whether the financial statements are fairly presented, they have two choices: accumulate additional evidence or issue either a qualified opinion or a disclaimer of opinion.

Evidence Supports Auditor's Opinion

An essential part of evaluating whether the financial statements are fairly stated involves the auditor's review of their summary of misstatements found in the audit. When any one misstatement is material, auditors should propose that the client correct the financial statements. It may be difficult to determine the appropriate amount of adjustment because the exact amount of the misstatement may be unknown if it involves an estimate or includes sampling error. Nevertheless, the auditor must decide on the required adjustment. (In some audits there may be more than one material misstatement.)

In addition to individually material misstatements, there are often several immaterial misstatements that the client did not adjust. Auditors must combine

Completing the audit checklist

A reminder to the auditor of aspects of the audit that may have been overlooked.

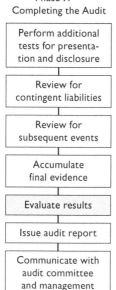

Phase IV—
Completing the Audit

Perform additional tests for presentation and disclosure

Review for contingent liabilities

Review for subsequent events

Accumulate final evidence

Evaluate results

Issue audit report

Communicate with audit committee and management

FIGURE 24-5	Completing the Audit Checklist		

		Yes	No
1. Examination of prior year's audit documentation			
a. Were last year's audit files examined for areas of emphasis in the current year audit?		_____	_____
b. Was the permanent file reviewed for items that affect the current year?		_____	_____
2. Reliability of financial statements			
a. Was a comparison made between account balances and information in footnote for accuracy?		_____	_____
b. Do the footnotes include disclosure of all accounting policies adopted by the company in preparing the financial statements?		_____	_____
c. Does the auditor's report reflect all the results of the audit lists and examination?		_____	_____
3. Internal control			
a. Has internal control been adequately understood?		_____	_____
b. Is the scope of the audit adequate in light of the assessed control risk?		_____	_____
c. Have all significant deficiencies and material weaknesses been reported in writing to those charged with governance?		_____	_____
4. General documents			
a. Were all current year minutes and resolutions reviewed, abstracted, and followed up?		_____	_____
b. Has the permanent file been updated?		_____	_____
c. Have all major contracts and agreements been reviewed and abstracted, copied, or downloaded to ascertain that the client complies with all existing legal requirements?		_____	_____

individually immaterial misstatements to evaluate whether the combined amount is material. They can keep a record of these misstatements and combine them in different ways, but many auditors use an **unadjusted misstatement audit schedule** or *summary of possible misstatements*. An example of an unadjusted misstatement worksheet is given in Figure 24-6.

The schedule in Figure 24-6 includes both known misstatements that the client has decided not to adjust and projected misstatements, including sampling error, and total possible misstatements for several financial statement categories. The bottom left portion of the audit schedule, under the heading 'Conclusions,' includes a comparison of possible overstatements and understatements to materiality. A summary of this audit schedule is often included with management's representation that the uncorrected misstatements are immaterial.

Unadjusted misstatement audit schedule

A summary of immaterial misstatements not adjusted at the time they were found, used to help the auditor assess whether the combined amount is material; also known as a *summary of possible misstatements*.

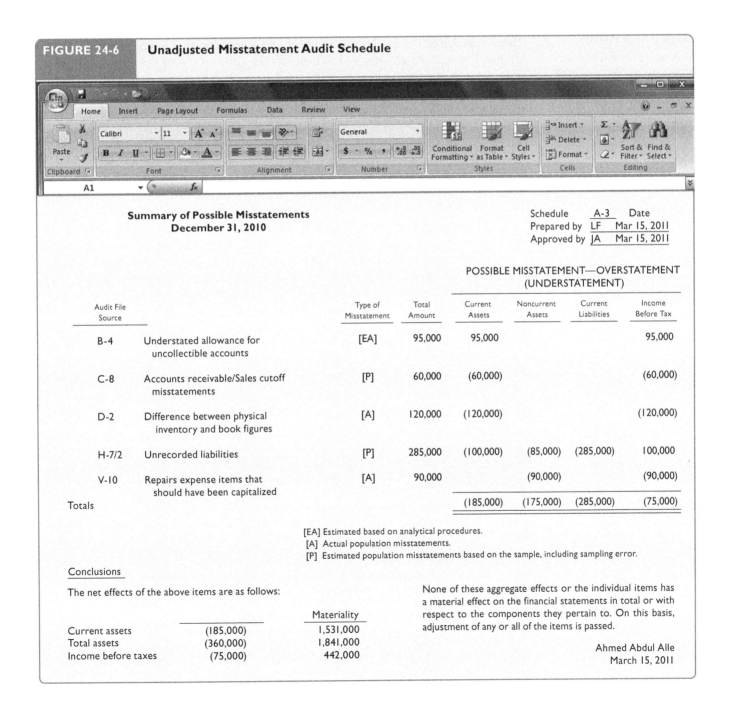

FIGURE 24-6   **Unadjusted Misstatement Audit Schedule**

Summary of Possible Misstatements
December 31, 2010

Schedule   A-3   Date
Prepared by   LF   Mar 15, 2011
Approved by   JA   Mar 15, 2011

POSSIBLE MISSTATEMENT—OVERSTATEMENT (UNDERSTATEMENT)

Audit File Source		Type of Misstatement	Total Amount	Current Assets	Noncurrent Assets	Current Liabilities	Income Before Tax
B-4	Understated allowance for uncollectible accounts	[EA]	95,000	95,000			95,000
C-8	Accounts receivable/Sales cutoff misstatements	[P]	60,000	(60,000)			(60,000)
D-2	Difference between physical inventory and book figures	[A]	120,000	(120,000)			(120,000)
H-7/2	Unrecorded liabilities	[P]	285,000	(100,000)	(85,000)	(285,000)	100,000
V-10	Repairs expense items that should have been capitalized	[A]	90,000		(90,000)		(90,000)
Totals				(185,000)	(175,000)	(285,000)	(75,000)

[EA] Estimated based on analytical procedures.
[A]   Actual population misstatements.
[P]   Estimated population misstatements based on the sample, including sampling error.

Conclusions

The net effects of the above items are as follows:

		Materiality
Current assets	(185,000)	1,531,000
Total assets	(360,000)	1,841,000
Income before taxes	(75,000)	442,000

None of these aggregate effects or the individual items has a material effect on the financial statements in total or with respect to the components they pertain to. On this basis, adjustment of any or all of the items is passed.

Ahmed Abdul Alle
March 15, 2011

If auditors believe that there is sufficient evidence but they conclude that the financial statements are not fairly presented, they again have two choices: The statements must be revised to the auditor's satisfaction or either a qualified or an adverse opinion must be issued. Notice that the options here are different from those in the case of insufficient evidence.

Financial Statement Disclosures

Before completing the audit, auditors must make a final evaluation of whether the disclosures in the financial statements satisfy all presentation and disclosure objectives. As we discussed at the beginning of this chapter, auditors must design and perform audit procedures to obtain evidence that the three presentation and disclosure objectives are satisfied.

Financial statement disclosure checklist

A questionnaire that reminds the auditor of disclosure problems commonly encountered in audits and that facilitates final review of the entire audit by an independent partner.

As part of the final review for financial statement disclosures, many auditing firms require the completion of a **financial statement disclosure checklist** for every audit. These questionnaires are designed to remind the auditor of common disclosure problems in financial statements and to facilitate the final review of the entire audit by an independent partner. Figure 24-7 illustrates a partial financial statement disclosure checklist. Naturally, a checklist is not sufficient to replace the auditor's knowledge of the proper application of the relevant accounting standards for the circumstances of the audit.

Audit Documentation Review

There are three reasons why an experienced member of the audit firm must thoroughly review audit documentation at the completion of the audit:

1. *To evaluate the performance of inexperienced personnel.* A considerable portion of most audits is performed by audit personnel with fewer than four or five years of experience. These people may have sufficient technical training to conduct an adequate audit, but their lack of experience affects their ability to make sound professional judgments in complex situations.
2. *To make sure that the audit meets the auditing firm's standard of performance.* Within any auditing firm, the quality of staff performance varies considerably, but careful review by top-level personnel in the firm helps to maintain a uniform quality of auditing.
3. *To counteract the bias that often enters into the auditor's judgment.* Auditors must attempt to remain objective throughout the audit, but they may lose proper perspective on a long audit when complex problems need to be solved.

FIGURE 24-7 **Financial Statement Disclosure Checklist: Property, Plant, and Equipment**

1. Are the following disclosures included in the financial statements or notes:
   a. Balances of major classes of depreciable assets (land, building, equipment, and so forth) at the balance sheet date?
   b. Allowances for depreciation, by class or in total, at the balance sheet date?
   c. General description of depreciation methods for major classes of depreciable assets?
   d. Total amount of depreciation charged to expense for each income statement presented?
   e. Basis of evaluation of depreciable assets?
2. Are carrying amounts of property mortgaged and encumbered by indebtedness disclosed?
3. Are details of sale and leaseback transactions during the period disclosed?
4. Is the carrying amount of property not a part of operating plant—for example, idle or held for investment or sale-segregated?
5. Has consideration been given to disclosure of fully depreciated capital assets still in use and capital assets not presently in use?

UNRECORDED ADJUSTMENTS PROVE COSTLY TO AUDIT FIRM	

In the U.S., in March 2002, the SEC announced it had completed its investigation of the accounting practices at Waste Management, Inc. and had filed suits against the company and several of its top executives charging them with perpetrating a massive financial statement fraud lasting more than five years. The SEC alleged that management manipulated the company's financial results using a multitude of improper accounting practices to meet predetermined earnings targets.

As part of the investigation, the SEC noted that Waste Management's auditors, Arthur Andersen, had identified the company's improper accounting practices and quantified much of the impact of those practices on the company's financial statements. According to SEC filings, Andersen annually presented company management with Proposed Adjusting Journal Entries (PAJEs) to correct errors that understated expenses and overstated earnings in the company's financial statements. Management consistently refused to make the adjustments called for by the PAJEs, and, instead, entered into an agreement with Andersen to write off the accumulated errors over periods of up to ten years. However, as time progressed, management never complied with the terms of this secret agreement.

The SEC eventually settled charges with Andersen and four of its partners related to the 1992 through 1996 audited financial statements. Andersen agreed to pay a penalty of US$7 million, the largest ever assessed against an accounting firm at the time. Commenting on the SEC's actions, Richard Walker, SEC Director of Enforcement, noted:

"Arthur Andersen and its partners failed to stand up to company management and thereby betrayed their ultimate allegiance to Waste Management's shareholders and the investing public. Given the positions held by these partners and the duration and gravity of the misconduct, the firm itself must be held responsible for the false and misleading audit reports."

Source: Beasley, Buckless, Glover, and Prawitt, *Auditing Cases: An Interactive Learning Approach*, 4th Edition, pp. 103–110, Prentice Hall.

Except for a final independent review, which is discussed shortly, the **review of audit documentation** should be conducted by someone who is knowledgeable about the client and the circumstances in the audit. Therefore, the auditor's immediate supervisor normally conducts the initial review of audit files prepared by another auditor. For example, the least experienced auditor's work is ordinarily reviewed by the audit senior. The senior's immediate superior, who is normally a supervisor or manager, reviews the senior's work and also reviews, less thoroughly, the schedules of the inexperienced auditor. Finally, the partner assigned to the audit must ultimately review all audit documentation, but the partner reviews those prepared by the supervisor or manager more thoroughly than the others. While performing the review, each reviewer has discussions with the auditor responsible for preparing the audit documentation to learn how significant audit issues were resolved. Except for the final independent review, most audit documentation review is done as each segment of the audit is completed.

Review of audit documentation

A review of the completed audit files by another member of the audit firm to ensure quality and counteract bias.

Independent Review

At the completion of larger audits, it is common to have the financial statements and the entire set of audit files reviewed by a completely independent reviewer who has not participated in the audit, but is a member of the audit firm doing the audit. An **independent review** is required by the Big Four and many auditing firms with international experience, including the review of interim financial information and the audit of internal controls. This reviewer often takes an adversarial position to make sure the conduct of the audit was adequate. The audit team must be able to justify the evidence it has accumulated and the conclusions it reached on the basis of the circumstances of the audit.

Independent review

A review of the financial statements and the entire set of audit files by a completely independent reviewer to whom the audit team must justify the evidence accumulated and the conclusions reached.

Summary of Evidence Evaluation

Figure 24-8 summarizes evaluating whether there is sufficient appropriate evidence and whether the evidence supports the opinion on the financial statements. It shows that the auditor evaluates the sufficiency and appropriateness of the evidence by first evaluating achieved audit risk, by account and by cycle, and then making the same

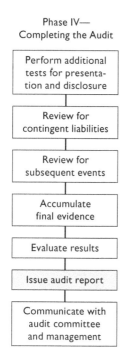

Phase IV—
Completing the Audit

Perform additional
tests for presenta-
tion and disclosure

Review for
contingent liabilities

Review for
subsequent events

Accumulate
final evidence

Evaluate results

Issue audit report

Communicate with
audit committee
and management

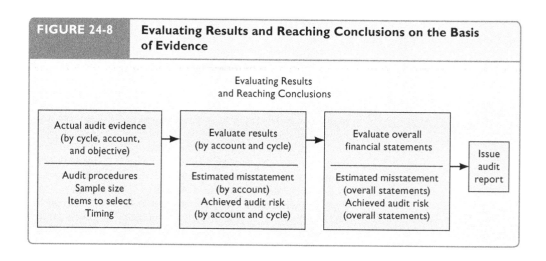

FIGURE 24-8   Evaluating Results and Reaching Conclusions on the Basis of Evidence

evaluation for the overall financial statements. The auditor also evaluates whether the evidence supports the audit opinion by first estimating misstatements in each account and then for the overall financial statements. In practice, the evaluation of achieved audit risk and estimated misstatement are made at the same time. On the basis of these evaluations, the audit report is issued for the financial statements.

ISSUE THE AUDIT REPORT

The auditor should wait to decide the appropriate audit report to issue until all evidence has been accumulated and evaluated, including all steps of completing the audit discussed so far. Because the audit report is the only thing that most users see in the audit process, and the consequences of issuing an inappropriate report can be severe, it is critical that the report be correct.

In most audits, the auditor issues an unmodified report with standard wording. Firms usually have an electronic template of this report and need to change only the name of the client, title of the financial statements, and date.

When an auditing firm decides that a standard unmodified report is inappropriate, there will almost certainly be extensive discussions among technical partners in the auditing firm and often with client personnel. Most auditing firms have comprehensive audit reporting manuals to assist them in selecting the appropriate wording of the report they decide to issue.

COMMUNICATE WITH THE AUDIT COMMITTEE AND MANAGEMENT

OBJECTIVE 24-7

Communicate effectively with the audit committee and management.

After the audit is completed, several potential communications from the auditor may be sent to the audit committee or others charged with governance, including communication of detected fraud and illegal acts, internal control deficiencies, other communications with the audit committee, and management letters. The first three of these communications are required by auditing standards to make certain that those charged with governance, which is often the audit committee and senior management, are informed of audit findings and auditor recommendations. The fourth item, management letters, is often communicated to operating management.

Communicate Fraud and Illegal Acts

Auditing standards require the auditor to communicate all fraud and illegal acts to the audit committee or similarly designated group, regardless of materiality. The purpose is to assist the audit committee in performing its supervisory role for reliable financial statements.

Communicate Internal Control Deficiencies

As discussed in Chapter 10, the auditor must also communicate in writing significant internal control deficiencies and material weaknesses in the design or operation of internal control to those charged with governance. In larger companies, this communication is made to the audit committee and in smaller companies it may be made to the owners or senior management.

Other Communications with Audit Committee

Auditing standards require the auditor to communicate certain additional information obtained during the audit to those charged with governance, which is generally the audit committee. The purpose of this required communication is to keep the audit committee, or others charged with governance, informed about significant and relevant information for the oversight of the financial reporting process and to provide an opportunity for the audit committee to communicate important matters to the auditor. Thus, the auditing standard requirements are designed to encourage two-way communications between the auditor and those charged with governance. There are four principal purposes of this required communication:

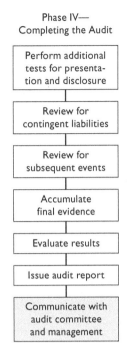

Phase IV—
Completing the Audit

Perform additional tests for presentation and disclosure

Review for contingent liabilities

Review for subsequent events

Accumulate final evidence

Evaluate results

Issue audit report

Communicate with audit committee and management

1. *To communicate auditor responsibilities in the audit of financial statements.* This communication includes discussion by the auditor that the audit of financial statements is designed to obtain reasonable, rather than absolute, assurance about material misstatements in the financial statements.

2. *To provide an overview of the scope and timing of the audit.* The purpose of this required communication is to provide a high-level overview, such as the auditor's approach to addressing significant risks and consideration of internal control, and timing of the audit. Details of the nature and timing of audit procedures is not appropriate to avoid compromising the effectiveness and predictability of the audit.

3. *To provide those charged with governance with significant findings arising during the audit.* These communications might include discussion of material, corrected misstatements detected during the audit, the auditor's view of qualitative aspects of significant accounting practices and estimates, and significant difficulties encountered during the audit, including disagreements with management, among other matters.

4. *To obtain from those charged with governance information relevant to the audit.* The audit committee or others charged with governance, such as the full board of directors, may share strategic decisions that may affect the nature and timing of the auditor's procedures.

Communications about significant findings arising during the audit are normally made in writing. Communications about other matters may be made orally or in writing, with all oral communications documented in the audit files. Communications should be timely to allow those charged with governance to take appropriate actions. Generally, communications about the auditor's responsibilities and the audit scope and timing occur early in an audit, while communications about significant findings usually occur throughout the entire engagement period.

In the U.S. the Sarbanes–Oxley Act of 2002 includes additional communication requirements for auditors of public companies. For example, auditors must communicate all alternative treatments of financial information within generally accepted accounting principles that have been discussed with management, ramifications of the alternative disclosures and treatments, and the treatment preferred by the auditor. As the audit is completed, the auditor should determine that the audit committee is informed about the initial selection of and changes in significant accounting policies or their application during the current audit period, as well as the reasons for any changes. The auditor should also communicate information about methods used to account for any significant unusual transactions and the effect of significant accounting policies in controversial or emerging areas.

Similar but less detailed requirements exist in many Arab countries. Auditors are required to provide members of audit committees with information about the internal controls, major adjustments to financial statements, changes in accounting policies, and material misstatements. These should be detailed in the auditor's management letter.

Management Letters

A management letter is intended to inform client personnel of the auditor's recommendations for improving any part of the client's business. Most recommendations focus on suggestions for more efficient operations. The combination of the auditor's experience in various businesses and a thorough understanding gained in conducting the audit places the auditor in a unique position to provide assistance to management.

Many auditing firms write a management letter for every audit to demonstrate to management that the firm adds value to the business beyond the audit service provided. Their intent is to encourage a better relationship with management and to suggest additional tax and permitted management services that the auditing firm can provide.

A management letter differs from a letter reporting significant deficiencies in internal control. The latter is required when there are significant deficiencies or material weaknesses in internal control, and must follow a prescribed format and be sent in accordance with the requirements of auditing standards in the U.S. under the Sarbanes–Oxley Act. A management letter is optional and is intended to help the client operate its business more effectively.

Each management letter should be developed to meet the style and preferences of the auditing firm and the needs of the client. Some auditors combine the management letter with the letter about significant deficiencies and material weaknesses. On smaller audits, it is common for the auditor to communicate operational suggestions orally rather than by a management letter.

In the Arab world, the structure of the audit firm, the sufficiency of resources, and the number of audit clients determine the pattern of issuing management letters to various clients. In big audit firms, auditors assist management in modifying their company's financial statements on an interim basis with the aim to reduce the cost and effort of the audit. A big audit firm prepares a short management letter in relation to deficiencies in internal control over financial reporting and presents it to those charged with governance, including the board of directors and the audit committee. On the other hand, medium and small size audit firms tend to prepare a detailed management letter to be presented to management, highlighting material misstatements and deficiencies in the clients' internal control systems. Partners in smaller firms aim to show the quality of the services provided to their clients compared with the Big Four audit firms. Severe competition among audit firms forces many medium and small size audit firms to prepare management letters to show that they are providing high quality audit and assurance services.

SUBSEQUENT DISCOVERY OF FACTS

After the auditor issues the audit report and completes all communications with management and the audit committee, the audit is finished. Usually, the next major contact between the auditor and client occurs when the planning process of the next year's audit begins.

Although it rarely happens, auditors sometimes learn *after the audited financial statements have been issued* that the financial statements are materially misstated. Examples are the inclusion of material nonexistent sales, the failure to write off obsolete inventory, or the omission of an essential footnote.

When this **subsequent discovery of facts** occurs, the auditor has an obligation to make certain that users who are relying on the financial statements are informed about the misstatements. (If the auditor had known about the misstatements before the audit report was issued, the auditor would have insisted that management correct the misstatements or, alternatively, a different audit report would have been issued.) It does not matter whether the failure to discover the misstatement was the fault of the auditor or the client. In either case, the auditor's responsibility remains the same. Although subsequent discovery of facts is not part of completing the audit, it is included in this chapter because it is easier to understand in this context.

If the auditor discovers that the statements are misleading after they have been issued, the most desirable action is to request that the client issue an immediate revision of the financial statements that includes an explanation of the reasons for the revision. If a subsequent period's financial statements are completed before the revised statements would be issued, it is acceptable to disclose the misstatements in the subsequent period's statements. When pertinent, the client should inform the appropriate oversight capital market supervisory board and other regulatory bodies of the misstated financial statements. The auditor is responsible to make certain that the client has taken the appropriate steps to inform users of the misstated statements.

If the client refuses to disclose the misstated statements, the auditor must inform the board of directors. The auditor must also notify regulatory bodies having jurisdiction over the client that the statements are no longer fairly stated and also, when practical, each person who relies on the financial statements. If the stock is publicly held, it is acceptable to request the appropriate capital market oversight supervisory board and the stock exchange to notify stockholders.

The subsequent discovery of facts requiring the recall or reissuance of financial statements *arises only from business events that existed before the date of the auditor's report.* For example, a revision of the financial statements is *not required* if an account receivable is believed to be collectible after an adequate review of the facts at the date of the audit report, but the customer subsequently files bankruptcy. If the customer had filed for bankruptcy before the audit report date, however, there is a subsequent discovery of facts.

The auditor's responsibility for subsequent events review ends on the date of the completion of the field work. Auditors have no responsibility to search for subsequent facts, but if they discover that issued financial statements are incorrectly stated, they must take action to correct them. In most cases, subsequent discovery of facts occurs when auditors discover a material misstatement in issued financial statements during the subsequent year's audit, or when the client reports a misstatement to the auditor.

Figure 24-9 illustrates the periods covered by the review for subsequent events, processing the financial statements, and subsequent discovery of facts after the audit report date. As you review the figure, note that auditors have no responsibility to review subsequent events after the audit report date. If auditors discover subsequent facts after the audit report date (March 11, 2012), but before the financial statements are issued (March 26, 2012), they will require that the financial statements be revised before they are issued. Auditors will also follow one of the two options discussed in the 'Dual Dating' section.

OBJECTIVE 24-8

Identify the auditor's responsibilities when facts affecting the audit report are discovered after its issuance.

Subsequent discovery of facts

Auditor discovery that the financial statements are materially misstated *after* they have been issued.

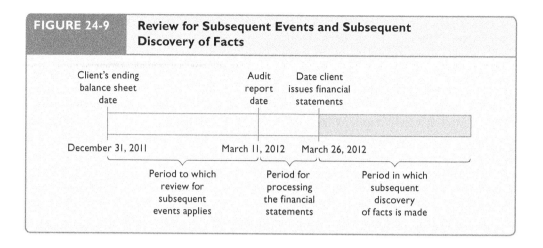

FIGURE 24-9   **Review for Subsequent Events and Subsequent Discovery of Facts**

SUMMARY

The completion phase of the audit is critical to ensuring a quality audit. In this phase, auditors perform additional tests for presentation and disclosure, including reviewing for contingencies and subsequent events. Auditors also review the sufficiency of the audit evidence and the decisions reached to determine whether they support the audit opinion. Auditors then communicate with the audit committee and management about important audit findings and other matters. In the Arab countries, auditors, whether in Big Four or medium/ small size audit firms, perform the above tasks related to completing the audit. The efficiency and effectiveness of the review of contingent liabilities, commitment, subsequent events, and assessment of final audit results depends on the competence and experience of the auditors in those firms and the continued professional education provided to senior as well as trainee auditors in relation to accounting and auditing standards.

ESSENTIAL TERMS

Commitments   p. 777

Completing the audit checklist   p. 788

Contingent liability   p. 775

Dual-dated audit report   p. 783

Financial statement disclosure checklist   p. 790

Independent review   p. 791

Inquiry of the client's attorneys   p. 778

Letter of representation   p. 785

Other information included in annual reports   p. 787

Review for subsequent events   p. 781

Review of audit documentation   p. 791

Subsequent discovery of facts   p. 795

Subsequent events   p. 781

Unadjusted misstatement audit schedule   p. 789

Unasserted claim   p. 780

REVIEW QUESTIONS

24-1 (Objective 24-1) Identify and describe the three presentation and disclosure audit objectives.

24-2 (Objective 24-1) Describe the purpose of a financial statement disclosure checklist and explain how it helps the auditor determine if there is sufficient appropriate evidence for each of the presentation and disclosure objectives.

24-3 (Objective 24-2) Distinguish between a contingent liability and an actual liability and give three examples of each.

24-4 (Objective 24-2) In the audit of Al Amal Company, you are concerned about the possibility of contingent liabilities resulting from income tax disputes. Discuss the procedures you could use for an extensive investigation in this area.

24-5 (Objective 24-2) Explain why an auditor is interested in a client's future commitments to purchase raw materials at a fixed price.

24-6 (Objective 24-3) Explain why the analysis of legal expense is an essential part of every audit.

24-7 (Objectives 24-2, 24-3) During the audit of the Masratah Manufacturing Company, Ibrahim El Gabaly, CPA, has become aware of four lawsuits against the client through discussions with the client, reading corporate minutes, and reviewing correspondence files. How should El Gabaly determine the materiality of the lawsuits and the proper disclosure in the financial statements?

24-8 (Objective 24-3) Distinguish between an asserted and an unasserted claim. Explain why a client's attorney may not reveal an unasserted claim.

24-9 (Objective 24-3) Describe the action that an auditor should take if an attorney refuses to provide information that is within the attorney's jurisdiction and may directly affect the fair presentation of the financial statements.

24-10 (Objective 24-4) Distinguish between the two general types of subsequent events and explain how they differ. Give two examples of each type.

24-11 (Objectives 24-3, 24-4) In obtaining letters from attorneys, Nermeen Fouad's aim is to receive the letters as early as possible after the balance sheet date. This provides her with a signed letter from every attorney in time to properly investigate any exceptions. It also eliminates the problem of a lot of unresolved loose ends near the end of the audit. Evaluate Nermeen's approach.

24-12 (Objective 24-4) What major considerations should the auditor take into account in determining how extensive the review of subsequent events should be?

24-13 (Objective 24-4) Identify five audit procedures normally done as a part of the review for subsequent events.

24-14 (Objectives 24-4, 24-8) Distinguish between subsequent events occurring between the balance sheet date and the date of the auditor's report, and subsequent discovery of facts existing at the date of the auditor's report. Give two examples of each and explain the appropriate action by the auditor in each instance.

24-15 (Objective 24-5) Samar Salah, an auditor, believes that the final summarization is the easiest part of the audit if careful planning is followed throughout the audit. She makes sure that each segment of the audit is completed before she goes on to the next. When the last segment of the audit is completed, she is finished with the audit. She believes this may cause each part of the audit to take a little longer, but she makes up for it by not having to do the final summarization. Evaluate Samar's approach.

24-16 (Objectives 24-1, 24-5, 24-6) Compare and contrast the accumulation of audit evidence and the evaluation of the adequacy of the disclosures in the financial statements. Give two examples in which adequate disclosure could depend heavily on the accumulation of evidence and two others in which audit evidence does not normally significantly affect the adequacy of the disclosure.

24-17 (Objectives 24-5, 24-7) Distinguish between a client letter of representation and a management letter and state the primary purpose of each. List some items that might be included in each letter.

24-18 (Objective 24-5) Explain what is meant by information accompanying basic financial statements. Provide two examples of such information. What levels of assurance may the auditor offer for this information?

24-19 (Objective 24-5) What is meant by reading other financial information in annual reports? Give an example of the type of information the auditor is examining.

24-20 (Objective 24-6) Distinguish between regular audit documentation review and independent review and state the purpose of each. Give two examples of potential findings in each of these two types of review.

24-21 (Objective 24-7) Describe matters that the auditor must communicate to audit committees.

MULTIPLE CHOICE QUESTIONS FROM CPA EXAMINATIONS

24-22 (Objective 24-2) The following questions deal with contingent liabilities. Choose the best response.

a. The audit step most likely to reveal the existence of contingent liabilities is
   (1) a review of vouchers paid during the month following the year-end.
   (2) an inquiry directed to legal counsel.
   (3) accounts payable confirmations.
   (4) mortgage-note confirmation.

b. When obtaining evidence regarding litigation against a client, an auditor will be *least* interested in determining
   (1) the period in which the underlying cause of the litigation occurred.
   (2) the probability of an unfavorable outcome.
   (3) an estimate of when the matter will be resolved.
   (4) an estimate of the potential loss.

c. When a contingency is resolved subsequent to the issuance of audited financial statements, which correctly contained disclosure of the contingency in the footnotes based on information available at the date of issuance, the auditor should
   (1) take no action regarding the event.
   (2) insist that the client issue revised financial statements.
   (3) inform the audit committee that the report cannot be relied on.
   (4) inform the appropriate authorities that the report cannot be relied on.

24-23 (Objective 24-5) The following questions concern letters of representation. Choose the best response.

a. A principal purpose of a letter of representation from management is to
   (1) serve as an introduction to company personnel and an authorization to examine the records.
   (2) discharge the auditor from legal liability for the audit.
   (3) confirm in writing management's approval of limitations on the scope of the audit.
   (4) remind management of its primary responsibility for financial statements.

b. The date of the management representation letter should coincide with the
   (1) balance sheet date.
   (2) date of the auditor's report.
   (3) date of the latest subsequent event referred to in the notes to the financial statements.
   (4) date of the engagement agreement.

c. Management's refusal to furnish a written representation on a matter that the auditor considers essential constitutes
   (1) prima facie evidence that the financial statements are not presented fairly.
   (2) a violation of the Code of Corporate Governance in Saudi Arabia.
   (3) an uncertainty sufficient to preclude an unmodified opinion.
   (4) a scope limitation sufficient to preclude an unmodified opinion.

24-24 (Objective 24-4) The following questions deal with review of subsequent events. Choose the best response.

a. Subsequent events for reporting purposes are defined as events that occur subsequent to the
   (1) balance sheet date.
   (2) date of the auditor's report.
   (3) balance sheet date but before the date of the auditor's report.
   (4) date of the auditor's report and concern contingencies that are not reflected in the financial statements.

b. An example of an event occurring in the period of the auditor's field work subsequent to the end of the year being audited that normally will not require disclosure in the financial statements or auditor's report is
   (1) serious damage to the company's plant from a widespread flood.
   (2) issuance of a widely advertised capital stock issue with restrictive covenants.
   (3) settlement of a large liability for considerably less than the amount recorded.
   (4) decreased sales volume resulting from a general business recession.

c. Merihan has audited the financial statements of Saso Corporation for the year ended December 31, 2010. Merihan's field work was completed on February 27, 2011; Merihan's auditor's report was dated February 28, 2011, and was received by the management of Saso on March 5, 2011. On April 4, 2011, the management of Saso asked that Merihan approve inclusion of this report in their annual report to stockholders, which will include unaudited financial statements for the first quarter ended March 31, 2011. Merihan approved the inclusion of the auditor's report in the annual report to stockholders. Under the circumstances, Merihan is responsible for inquiring as to subsequent events occurring through

   (1) February 27, 2011.   (3) March 31, 2011.
   (2) February 28, 2011.   (4) April 4, 2011.

24-25 (Objective 24-5) The following questions concern information accompanying basic financial statements. Choose the best response.

a. Which of the following best describes the auditor's reporting responsibility concerning information accompanying the basic financial statements in an auditor-submitted document?
   (1) The auditor has no reporting responsibility concerning information accompanying the basic financial statements.
   (2) The auditor should report on the information accompanying the basic financial statements only if the auditor participated in its preparation.
   (3) The auditor should report on the information accompanying the basic financial statements only if the auditor did not participate in its preparation.
   (4) The auditor should report on all the information included in the document.

b. Omar, an auditor, has been requested by a client, Alfa Corp., to prepare information in addition to the basic financial statements for this year's audit. Which of the following is the best reason for Alfa's requesting the additional information?
   (1) To provide an opinion about the supplemental information when certain items are not in accordance with IFRS or local accounting standards.
   (2) To provide Alfa's creditors a greater degree of assurance as to the financial soundness of the company.
   (3) To provide Alfa's management with information to supplement and analyze the basic financial statements.
   (4) To provide the documentation required by the appropriate capital market oversight supervisory board in anticipation of a public offering of Alfa's stock.

c. Omar, CPA, has been requested by a client, Rainco Corp., to prepare additional information accompanying the basic financial statements for this year's audit. In issuing the additional information, Omar must be certain to
   (1) issue a standard short-form report on the same audit.
   (2) include a description of the scope of the audit in more detail than the description in the usual short-form report.

    (3) state the source of any statistical data and that such data have not been subjected to the same auditing procedures as the basic financial statements.

    (4) maintain a clear-cut distinction between management's representations and the auditor's representations.

DISCUSSION QUESTIONS AND PROBLEMS

24-26 (Objective 24-2) In an audit of the Marco Corporation in Lebanon as of December 31, 2011, the following situations exist. No entries have been made in the accounting records in relation to these items.

1. During the year 2011, the Marco Corporation was named as a defendant in a suit for damages by the Darling Company for breach of contract. An adverse decision to the Marco Corporation was rendered and the Darling Company was awarded US$4 million damages. At the time of the audit, the case was under appeal to a higher court.

2. On December 23, 2011, the Marco Corporation declared a common stock dividend of 1,000 shares with a par value of US$1 million of its common stock, payable February 2, 2012, to the common stockholders on record December 30, 2011.

3. The Marco Corporation has guaranteed the payment of interest on the ten-year, first mortgage bonds of the Top Company, an affiliate. Outstanding bonds of the Newart Company amount to US$5.5 million with interest payable at 5% per annum, due June 1 and December 1 of each year. The bonds were issued by the Top Company on December 1, 2009, and all interest payments have been met by that company with the exception of the payment due December 1, 2011. The Marco Corporation states that it will pay the defaulted interest to the bondholders on January 15, 2012.

Required

  a. Define contingent liability.

  b. Describe the audit procedures you would use to learn about each of the situations listed.

  c. Describe the nature of the adjusting entries or disclosure, if any, you would make for each of these situations.[26]

24-27 (Objectives 24-4, 24-8) The field work for the June 30, 2011, audit of Salam Brewing Company was finished August 19, 2011, and the completed financial statements, accompanied by the signed audit reports, were mailed September 6, 2011. In each of the highly material independent events (a through i), state the appropriate action (1 through 4) for the situation and justify your response. The alternative actions are as follows:

1. Adjust the June 30, 2011, financial statements.
2. Disclose the information in a footnote in the June 30, 2011, financial statements.
3. Request the client to recall the June 30, 2011, statements for revision.
4. No action is required.

The events are as follows:

  a. On December 14, 2011, the auditor discovered that a debtor of Salam Brewing went bankrupt on July 15, 2011, due to declining financial health. The sale had taken place January 15, 2011.

  b. On December 14, 2011, the auditor discovered that a debtor of Salam Brewing went bankrupt on October 2, 2011. The sale had taken place April 15, 2011, but the amount appeared collectible at June 30, 2011, and August 19, 2011.

  c. On August 15, 2011, the auditor discovered that a debtor of Salam Brewing went bankrupt on August 1, 2011. The most recent sale had taken place April 2, 2008, and no cash receipts had been received since that date.

  d. On August 6, 2011, the auditor discovered that a debtor of Salam Brewing went bankrupt on July 30, 2011. The cause of the bankruptcy was an unexpected loss of a major lawsuit on July 15, 2011, resulting from a product deficiency suit by a different customer.

e. On August 6, 2011, the auditor discovered that a debtor of Salam Brewing went bankrupt on July 30, 2011, for a sale that took place July 3, 2011. The cause of the bankruptcy was a major uninsured fire on July 20, 2011.

f. On July 20, 2011, Salam Brewing settled a lawsuit out of court that had originated in 2008 and is currently listed as a contingent liability.

g. On September 14, 2011, Salam Brewing lost a court case that had originated in 2010 for an amount equal to the lawsuit. The June 30, 2011, footnotes state that in the opinion of legal counsel there will be a favorable settlement.

h. On July 20, 2011, a lawsuit was filed against Salam Brewing for a patent infringement action that allegedly took place in early 2011. In the opinion of legal counsel, there is a danger of a significant loss to the client.

i. On May 31, 2011, the auditor discovered an uninsured lawsuit against Salam Brewing that had originated on February 28, 2011.

24-28 (Objective 24-7) In a letter to the audit committee of the Summer Wholesale Company, Salah Ismail, the auditor, informed them of material weaknesses in the control of inventory. In a separate letter to senior management, he elaborated on how the material weaknesses could result in a significant misstatement of inventory by the failure to recognize the existence of obsolete items. In addition, Ismail made specific recommendations in the management letter on how to improve internal control and save clerical time by installing a computer system for the company's perpetual records. Management accepted the recommendations and installed the system under Ismail's direction. For several months, the system worked beautifully, but unforeseen problems developed when a master file was erased. The cost of reproducing and processing the inventory records to correct the error was significant, and management decided to scrap the entire project. The company sued Ismail for failure to use adequate professional judgment in making the recommendations.

a. What is Ismail's legal and professional responsibility in the issuance of management letters? *Required*

b. Discuss the major considerations that will determine whether he is liable in this situation.

24-29 (Objective 24-5) Amira Nadin, an auditor, has prepared a letter of representation for the president and controller to sign. It contains references to the following items:

1. Inventory is fairly stated at the lower of cost or market and includes no obsolete items.
2. All actual and contingent liabilities are properly included in the financial statements.
3. All subsequent events of relevance to the financial statements have been disclosed.

a. Why is it desirable to have a letter of representation from the client concerning these matters when the evidence accumulated during the course of the audit is meant to verify the same information? *Required*

b. To what extent is the letter of representation useful as audit evidence? Explain.

c. List several other types of information commonly included in a letter of representation.

24-30 (Objective 24-4) The following unrelated events occurred after the balance sheet date but before the audit report was prepared:

1. The granting of a retroactive pay increase
2. Declaration of a stock dividend
3. Sale of a fixed asset at a substantial profit
4. Determination by the government of additional income tax due for a prior year
5. Filing of a lawsuit by the government against the company.

a. Explain how each of the items might have come to the auditor's attention. *Required*

b. Discuss the auditor's responsibility to recognize each of these in connection with the report.[27]

	FIGURE 25-4	**An Example of a Review Report**

	To The Chairman and the Board of Directors of Habiba Investment Company
Introduction	We have reviewed the accompanying financial statements of Habiba Investment Company as represented in the balance sheet as of March 31, 2011, and the related statements of income, changes in shareholders' equity, and cash flows for the period then ended, and a summary of significant accounting policies and other explanatory notes. Management is responsible for the preparation and fair presentation of this interim financial information in accordance with the International Financial Reporting Standards. Our responsibility is to express a conclusion on this interim financial information based on our review.
Scope of Limited Review	We conducted our review in accordance with the International Standards on Review Engagements No. 2410, Review of Interim Financial Information Performed by the Independent Auditor of the Entity. A review of these interim financial statements consists of making inquiries, primarily of persons responsible for financial and accounting matters, and applying analytical and other review procedures. A review is substantially less in scope than an audit conducted in accordance with the International Standards on Auditing and consequently does not enable us to obtain assurance that we were aware of all significant matters that might be identified in an audit. Accordingly we do not express an audit opinion on these financial statements.
Conclusion	Based on our review, nothing has come to our attention that causes us to believe that the accompanying interim financial statements do not present fairly, in all material respects, the financial position of the company as of March 31, 2011, its results of operations and cash flows for the period then ended in accordance with the International Financial Reporting Standards.
	Horwath, Abou Shakra
	Lebanon, June 15, 2011

2. The second paragraph states that a review consists primarily of inquiries and analytical procedures, is substantially less in scope than an audit, and no opinion is expressed.

3. The third paragraph expresses limited assurance *in the form of a negative assurance* that 'we are not aware of any material modifications that should be made to the financial statements.'

The date of the review report should be the date of completion of the auditor's inquiry and analytical procedures. Each page of the financial statements reviewed should include the reference 'See auditor's review report.' The auditor should read any other information included with the interim financial information and should consider whether any such information is materially inconsistent with the interim financial information. For example, in the accompanying information management may present alternative measures of earnings that give a more realistic picture of the financial performance than the interim financial information. Such alternative measures may not be clearly defined or reconciled with the interim.

Failure to Follow IFRS or local accounting standards If a client has failed to follow IFRS or local accounting standards in a review engagement, the auditor should report this violation of the standard to the appropriate level of management and those charged with governance and should consider the possibility that the report may need to be modified. (IFRS or local accounting standards is the same for all historical financial statements, including reviews.) The report should disclose the effects of the departure as determined by management or the auditor's review procedures. Even if the effects have not been determined, the disclosure must appear in the report in a *separate paragraph*. The following provides an example of suggested wording:

As disclosed in note X to the financial statements, IFRS require that land be stated at cost. Management has informed us that the company has stated its land at appraised value and that, if IFRS had been followed, the land account and stockholders' equity would have been decreased by US$500,000.

We were not able to determine the basis used for pricing issued inventory items for production and sales in violation of the company stated accounting policy "issued inventory items are priced in accordance with the average cost method."

We discovered that the company does not maintain a register of fixed asset, a matter which prevented us from verifying the accuracy of the depreciation expense and accumulated depreciation for the financial year ending December 31, 2010...

In performing the review service, the auditor should comply with the ethical requirements relevant to the audit of the annual financial statements of the company. These ethical requirements govern the auditor's professional responsibilities in the following areas: independence, integrity, objectivity, professional competence and due care, confidentiality, professional behavior, and technical standards. The auditor should implement quality control procedures that are applicable to the service engagement. Finally, the auditor should exercise his professional judgment when planning and performing the review, recognizing at the same time that circumstances may exist that cause the interim financial information to require material adjustment in accordance with the applicable financial reporting framework.

Compilation Services

Compilation service

A nonaudit engagement in which the accountant undertakes to present, in the form of financial statements, information that is the representation of management, without undertaking to express any assurance on the statements.

A **compilation service** engagement is defined in ISRS 4410, Engagements to Compile Financial Statements, as one in which accountants prepare financial statements and present them to a client or third party without providing any *assurance about those statements*. Many auditing firms prepare monthly, quarterly, or annual financial statements for their clients. These statements are usually for internal use by management, although they may also be provided to external users. The accountant who is engaged to perform a compilation service is not required to be independent. The financial statements can be issued without additional disclosures such as footnotes. Engagements to provide limited assistance to a client in preparing financial statements such as selecting the appropriate accounting policies do not constitute an engagement to compile financial information. In all circumstances, management must continue to assume complete responsibility for the completeness and accuracy of financial statements.

When accountants submit financial statements and expect them to be used by a third party, they are required to, at least, issue a compilation report that accompanies the statements. It is not permissible for the accountant to prepare and present financial statements to a client that plans to provide them to external users without, at a minimum, having satisfied the requirements for a compilation engagement, including the issuance of a compilation report. When the accountant does not expect the financial statements to be used by a third party, he does not have to issue a compilation report, as long as he documents in the engagement letter with the client an understanding regarding the services to be performed and a restriction that the financial statements are for management's use only.

Requirements for Compilation

Compilation does not absolve accountants of responsibility, as they are always responsible for exercising due care in performing all duties. In a compilation engagement, an accountant must accomplish the following:

- Establish an understanding with the client about the type and limitations of the services to be provided and a description of the report, if a report is to be issued.
- Possess knowledge about the accounting principles and practices of the client's industry.

- Know the client, including the nature of its business transactions, accounting records, and content of its financial statements (the knowledge can be less than that for a review).
- Make inquiries to determine whether the client's information is satisfactory.
- Read the compiled financial statements and be alert for any obvious omissions or errors in arithmetic and IFRS or local accounting standards including non-disclosure of any significant matters of which the accountant has become aware.

Accountants do not have to make other inquiries or perform other procedures to verify information provided by client personnel. But if they become aware that the statements are not fairly presented, they should obtain additional information. If the client refuses to provide the information, the accountant should withdraw from the compilation engagement.

Form of Report Appendix 2 to ISRS 4410, Engagements to Compile Financial Statements, presents two forms of compilation reports: a standard report to compile financial statements and another compilation report with an additional paragraph that draws attention to a departure from the applicable financial reporting framework. Figures 25-5 and 25-6 show the two forms of compilation reports under ISRS 4410. It is worth noting that in the U.S. there are three types of compilation reports. The use of each depends on whether management elects to include all the required disclosures with the financial statements and whether the accountant is independent.

1. *Compilation with full disclosure.* A compilation of this type requires disclosures in accordance with GAAP, the same as for audited financial statements or reviews.
2. *Compilation that omits substantially all disclosures.* Management may elect not to present the statement of cash flows. This type of compilation is acceptable *if the report indicates the lack of disclosures* and the absence of disclosures *is not*, to the CPA's knowledge, *undertaken with the intent to mislead users.* Typically, this type of statement is used primarily for management purposes.
3. *Compilation without independence.* A CPA firm can issue a compilation report with full or omitted disclosures even if it is not independent of the client, as defined by the *Code of Professional Conduct.* When the accountant lacks independence, the last paragraph of the report must state: 'We are not independent with respect to Sawalah Company.'

For all three types of compilation reports, the following elements are also required:

- The date of the accountant's report is the date of completion of the compilation.
- Each page of the financial statements compiled by the accountant should state 'See accountant's compilation report.'
- If the client fails to follow GAAP, the auditor must include the same modifications in the compilation report that are used in a review report.

FIGURE 25-5   **Compilation Report with Full Disclosure**

Compilation Report to Management of XYZ

On the basis of information provided by management we have compiled, in accordance with the International Standard on Related Services applicable to compilation engagements, the balance sheet of XYZ Company as of December 31, 2010, and the related statements of income and cash flows for the year ended. Management is responsible for these financial statements. We have not audited or reviewed these financial statements and accordingly express no assurance thereon.

Samir Ibrahim & Co.
Accountants & Consultants

Abu Dhabi, Feb 15, 2011

FIGURE 25-6	Compilation Report with a Departure from the Applicable Financial Reporting Framework

Compilation Report to Management of XYZ

On the basis of information provided by management we have compiled, in accordance with the International Standard on Related Services applicable to compilation engagements, the balance sheet of XYZ Company as of December 31, 2010 and the related statements of income and cash flows for the year ended. Management is responsible for these financial statements. We have not audited or reviewed these financial statements and accordingly express no assurance thereon.

Management has elected to omit substantially all of the disclosures and the statements of cash flows required by International Financial Reporting Standards. If the omitted disclosures were included in the financial statements, they might influence the user's conclusions about the company's financial position, results of operations, and cash flows. Accordingly, these financial statements are not designed for those who are not informed about such matters.

Soliman & Co.
Accountants & Consultants

Kuwait, 21 Feb 2011

REVIEW OF INTERIM FINANCIAL INFORMATION FOR PUBLIC COMPANIES

OBJECTIVE 25-2

Describe special engagements to review interim financial information for publicly held companies.

Public company interim review

Reviews of interim, unaudited financial information performed to help public companies meet their reporting responsibilities to regulatory agencies.

All oversight financial supervisory boards in Arab countries require that quarterly financial statements be reviewed by the company's external auditor prior to the company's submission of such statements to them for review. At a minimum, auditing firms must perform review procedures of the footnote information.

Like reviews under ISRE 2410, a **public company interim review** includes five requirements for review service engagements. The auditor must: (1) obtain knowledge of the accounting principles of the client's industry, (2) obtain knowledge of the client, (3) make inquiries of management, (4) perform analytical procedures, and (5) obtain a letter of representation.

Also like ISRE 2410 reviews, reviews for public companies do not provide a basis for expressing positive opinion level assurance. Ordinarily, auditors perform no tests of the accounting records, independent confirmations, or physical examinations. However, the two types of reviews differ in several areas. Below are the key differences:

- Because an annual audit is also performed for the public company client, the auditor must obtain sufficient information about the client's internal control for both annual and interim financial information.
- Similarly, because the client is audited annually, the auditor's knowledge of the results of these audit procedures is used in considering the scope and results of the inquiries and analytical procedures for the review.
- Under ISRE 2410, the auditor makes inquiries about actions of directors' and stockholders' meetings; for a public company, the auditor reads the minutes of those meetings.
- The auditor must also obtain evidence that the interim financial information agrees or reconciles with the accounting records for a public company interim review. For example, the auditor might compare the interim financial information to the general ledger.

If the auditor determines the interim statements violate IFRS or local accounting standards, the report should be modified. The language of the modification is similar to that used in a review under ISRE 2410, except that the auditor should state the effect of the departure, if the amount can be determined.

ASSURANCE ENGAGEMENTS

Chapter 1 described assurance services as independent professional services that improve the quality of information for decision makers. Individuals who are responsible for making business decisions seek assurance services to help improve the reliability and relevance of the information on which they base their decisions. The International Standard on Assurance Engagements 3000, Assurance Engagements Other Than Audits or Reviews of Historical Financial Information, uses the terms 'reasonable assurance engagement' and 'limited assurance engagement' to distinguish between the two types of **assurance engagements** the practitioner is allowed to perform.

The difference between 'reasonable assurance' and 'limited assurance' depends on the nature of conclusions made by the practitioner. The objective of a reasonable assurance engagement is to reduce the assurance engagement risk to an acceptably low level to serve as a basis for a positive conclusion by the practitioner. On the other hand, the objective of a limited assurance engagement is to reduce the assurance engagement risk to a level that is acceptable in the circumstances of the engagement, but where that risk is greater than for a reasonable assurance engagement, it forms the basis of a negative conclusion by the practitioner.

Auditors have increasingly been asked to perform a variety of audit-like, or reasonable assurance, services for different purposes. In a reasonable assurance engagement, practitioners report on the reliability of information or an assertion made by another party. An example is when a bank requests an auditor to report in writing whether an audit client has adhered to all requirements of a loan agreement.

> **OBJECTIVE 25-3**
>
> Describe assurance engagements other than audit or reviews of historical financial information.

> **Assurance engagement**
>
> A service in which the audit firm issues a report about the reliability of subject matter or of an assertion that is the responsibility of another party.

Assurance Standards

When carrying out a reasonable assurance engagement the practitioner should adopt the following procedures to ensure that sufficient appropriate evidence is obtained:

a. Understand the reason for the engagement together with an understanding of the client's internal control
b. Assess the risks that could result in information being materially misstated
c. Devise tests and other procedures to determine whether any of the risks identified have occurred. Carry out any further procedures including inspection, confirmation, or analytical review that are deemed to be necessary
d. Evaluate the sufficiency and appropriateness of the evidence gathered

The most notable differences between the assurance standards and International Standards on Auditing are in the nature of the engagement to be performed by the auditor or the practitioner. ISAE 3000 requires practitioners to have adequate knowledge of the subject matter. For example, if a practitioner is to assure to a company's compliance with environmental protection laws, he or she should have a thorough knowledge of those laws and the methods used by the company to assure compliance. The practitioner must evaluate the subject matter against suitable criteria. The practitioner should plan and perform an engagement with an attitude of professional skepticism while recognizing that there may be circumstances that cause the subject matter information to be materially misstated.

On the other hand, limited assurance services may include assignments where the auditor is expected to provide a negative opinion.

Types of Assurance Engagements

The ISAE gives only broad definitions of the different types of assurance engagements. Assurance services are only defined in conceptual terms because new services are likely to arise.

The AICPA and the Canadian Institute of Chartered Accountants (CICA) have jointly developed assurance services related to e-commerce and information technology. These groups of services are known as *WebTrust* and *SysTrust*. In addition, the AICPA has developed specific standards in the following areas:

- Prospective financial statements
- Pro forma financial information
- Reports on internal control over financial reporting for private companies
- Compliance with laws and regulations
- Agreed-upon procedures engagements
- Management's discussion and analysis

Standards are necessary for these types of engagements because accountants and auditors already perform these services in sufficiently large numbers and need more specific guidance than the general assurance standards provide. However, the absence of specific standards for a type of service does not imply that it is inappropriate to provide such a service.

In the Arab world, these type of assurance engagements are mainly provided in Kuwait, Egypt, Jordan, Saudi Arabia, and the Gulf countries. Audit firms provide their services for agreed-upon procedures for specific accounts in the financial statements, due diligence, reviews, examination of prospective financial statements, and special assessment of the efficiency and effectiveness of internal control over financial reporting. Auditors in those countries may be required by government bodies or investigating authorities to test whether a business is complying with laws and regulations governing the company's activity.

ISAE 3000 states that the assurance report should be in writing and should contain a clear expression of the practitioner's conclusion about the subject matter information. Assurance reports are tailored to the specific engagement circumstances, using a short- or long-form style of reporting. However, the following basic elements should be included:

a. A title, stating that the report is an independent assurance report.
b. Details of the person or party to which the report is addressed.
c. An identification and detailed description of the subject matter information showing the qualitative or quantitative characteristics of the subject matter.
d. Identification of the criteria against which the subject matter was evaluated or measured to help users understand the basis for the practitioner's conclusion.
e. A statement confirming that the engagement was performed in accordance with International Standards on Assurance Engagements (ISAE).
f. A summary of the work undertaken by the practitioner and his conclusion.

Levels of Service

The assurance standards may include the following levels of engagements and related forms of conclusions:

1. Examinations
2. Reviews
3. Agreed-upon procedures

Examination

An assurance engagement that results in a positive opinion as to whether or not the assertions under examination conform with the applicable criteria.

In addition, compilation engagements are defined for prospective financial statements.

An **examination** results in a *positive* conclusion. In this type of report, the auditor makes a direct statement about whether the presentation of the assertions, taken as a whole, conforms to the applicable criteria. Figure 25-7 shows an examination report written under the general guidance of the assurance standards. This is for an

FIGURE 25-7	Examination Report for Assurance Service

To Management
Arab African Securities, Inc.

We have examined the accompanying statements for investment performance statistics of the Arab African Securities Model Portfolio for the year ended December 31, 2010. Arab African Securities' management is responsible for the statement of investment performance statistics. Our responsibility is to express an opinion based on our examination.

Our examination was conducted in accordance with International Standards on Assurance Engagements 3000 and accordingly included examining, on a test basis, evidence supporting Arab African Securities Model Portfolio's statement for investment performance statistics, and performing such other procedures as we considered necessary in the circumstances. We believe that our examination provides a reasonable basis for our opinion.

In our opinion, the schedule referred to above presents, in all material respects, the investment performance statistics of Arab African Securities Model Portfolio for the year ended December 31, 2010, based on the actual results that would have been obtained if the buy–sell recommendations for the portfolio were followed as described in the buy–sell recommendations set forth in Note 1.

engagement to determine that the rate of return on a hypothetical portfolio, based on a brokerage firm's buy–sell recommendations, is correct as represented in the firm's promotional materials. A report on an examination is unrestricted as to distribution by the client after it is issued. This means that a client can distribute the information widely, including to prospective investors, and for sales and marketing purposes.

In a **review**, the auditor provides a *negative assurance* conclusion. For a negative assurance report, the auditor's report states whether any information came to his attention to indicate that the assertions are not presented in all material respects in conformity with the applicable criteria. A review report is also unrestricted in its distribution.

In an **agreed-upon procedures engagement**, all procedures the auditor will perform are agreed upon by the auditor, the responsible party making the assertions, and the specific persons who are the intended users of the auditor's report. The degree of assurance included in such a report varies with the specific procedures agreed to and performed. Accordingly, such reports are limited in their distribution to only the involved parties, who know the procedures the auditor will perform and the level of assurance resulting from them. The report should include a statement of what procedures management and the auditor agreed to and what the auditor found in performing the procedures.

Figure 25-8 summarizes the reporting levels for assurance engagements. Next we discuss four common types of engagements for which detailed AICPA standards have been issued: *WebTrust* services, *SysTrust* services, prospective financial statements, and agreed-upon procedures.

Review

An assurance engagement that results in a negative opinion as to the auditor's awareness of any information indicating that the assertions are not presented in conformity with the applicable criteria.

Agreed-upon procedures engagement

An engagement in which the procedures to be performed are agreed upon by the auditor, the responsible party making the assertions, and the intended users of the auditor's report; the auditor's report is presented in the form of a negative assurance.

FIGURE 25-8	Types of Engagements and Related Reports

Type of Engagement	Amount of Evidence	Level of Assurance	Form of Conclusion	Distribution
Examination	Extensive	High	Positive	General
Review	Significant	Moderate	Negative	General
Agreed-upon procedures	Varying	Varying	Findings	Limited

WEBTRUST SERVICES

OBJECTIVE 25-4

Understand the nature of *WebTrust* assurance services.

WebTrust

An assurance service designed to provide reasonable assurance that a company's website complies with *Trust Services* principles and criteria for business-to-consumer electronic commerce.

In a **WebTrust** engagement, a client engages an auditor to provide reasonable assurance that a company's website complies with certain *Trust Services* principles and criteria for one or more aspects of e-commerce activities. A site that meets the *Trust Services* principles is eligible to display the *WebTrust* electronic seal on its transaction or order page, which is intended to give users of the site assurance about the site's credibility. At least once every 12 months, the CPA firm updates its testing of the e-commerce aspects to ensure that the client's site continues to comply with the *Trust Services* principles and criteria. The audit firm also updates its report. If the site does not comply, the seal can be revoked.

The *WebTrust* service is a specific service developed under the broader *Trust Services* principles and criteria jointly issued by the AICPA and CICA. When performing *WebTrust* assurance services, the CPA firm assesses whether the company's website complies with the five *Trust Services* principles, which are shown in Table 25-1. These *Trust Services* principles represent broad statements of objectives. To provide more specific guidance, there are related *Trust Services* criteria for each of the five principles. A company must conform to these criteria to obtain and maintain its *WebTrust* seal.

SYSTRUST SERVICES

OBJECTIVE 25-5

Understand the nature of *SysTrust* assurance services.

SysTrust

An assurance service designed to provide reasonable assurance that a company's computer system complies with *Trust Services* principles and criteria.

As more organizations become dependent on information technology, the security, availability, and accuracy of computer systems are critical. An unreliable system can trigger a chain of business events that negatively affect the company, its customers, suppliers, and other business partners. The **SysTrust** service provides assurance to management, the board of directors, or third parties about the reliability of information systems used to generate real-time information.

In a *SysTrust* engagement, the *SysTrust* licensed CPA evaluates a company's computer system using *Trust Services* principles and criteria and determines whether controls over the system exist. The CPA then does tests to determine whether those controls were operating effectively during a specified period. If the system meets the requirements of the *Trust Services* principles and criteria, an examination-level unmodified assurance report is issued under AICPA attestation standards. The report may address a single *Trust Services* principle or any combination of *Trust Services* principles.

TABLE 25-1	Five *Trust Services* Principles
Principle	The entity discloses and maintains compliance with its
Security	security practices, ensuring that the system is protected against unauthorized access (both physical and logical).
Availability	availability practices, ensuring that the system is available for operation and use as committed or agreed.
Processing Integrity	processing integrity, ensuring that system processing is complete, accurate, timely, and authorized.
Online Privacy	online privacy practices, ensuring that personal information obtained as a result of e-commerce is collected, used, disclosed, and retained as committed or agreed.
Confidentiality	confidentiality practices, ensuring that information designated as confidential is protected as committed or agreed.

An organization may request a *SysTrust* engagement for a system that is in the pre-implementation phase. For this type of engagement, the CPA reports on the suitability of the design of controls, and the report covers a point in time rather than a period of time.

PROSPECTIVE FINANCIAL STATEMENTS

As implied by the term, **prospective financial statements** refer to predicted or expected financial statements in some future period (income statement) or at some future date (balance sheet). An example is management's predictions of the income statement and balance sheet one year in the future.

Most auditors believe there are significant opportunities and potential risks for them to provide credibility to prospective financial information. It is widely accepted that users want reliable prospective information to aid their decision making. If auditors can improve the reliability of the information, information risk may be reduced in the same way it is in audits of historical financial statements. The risks arise because the actual results obtained in the future may differ significantly from the results predicted in the prospective financial statements. Regulators, users, and others may criticize and even sue auditors, even if the prospective statements were fairly stated, given the information available when they were prepared.

Prospective financial statements

Financial statements that deal with expected future data rather than with historical data.

Forecasts and Projections

ISAE 3400, The Examination of Prospective Financial Information, requires that auditors should research evidence to prove that management's best estimate assumptions, on which the prospective financial information is based, are not unreasonable. In the case of hypothetical assumptions, auditors should ensure that such assumptions are consistent with the purpose of the information. The standard describes "Prospective Financial Information" as financial information based on assumptions about events that may occur in the future and possible actions by an entity. Such information is highly subjective in nature and an auditor should exercise his professional judgment in its preparation. Prospective financial information can be in the form of a forecast, a projection, or a combination of both in the case where management prepares a one-year forecast plus a five-year projection. ISAE 3400 defines two types of prospective financial statements:

1. **Forecasts** are prospective financial statements that present an entity's *expected* financial position, results of operations, and cash flows, to the *best* of the responsible party's knowledge and belief. Banks commonly require this information as a part of loan applications or when management prepares such information and presents it to shareholders, regulatory bodies, and other interested parties.

2. **Projections** are prospective financial statements that present an entity's financial position, results of operations, and cash flows, to the best of the responsible party's knowledge and belief, given one or more *hypothetical assumptions*. For example, projected financial statements might assume the company is able to increase the price of its primary product by 10 percent with no reduction in units sold or when an entity is in a start-up phase or is considering a major change in the nature of operations.

Forecasts

Prospective financial statements that present an entity's expected financial position, results of operations, and cash flows for future periods, to the best of the responsible party's knowledge and belief.

Projections

Prospective financial statements that present an entity's financial position and results of operations and cash flows for future periods, to the best of the responsible party's knowledge and belief, given one or more hypothetical assumptions.

There is considerable literature available to management to help them prepare both forecasts and projections. This literature, along with guidance for auditors, is presented in both the ISAE 3400 and the AICPA *Guide for Prospective Financial Statements*, which includes criteria against which such an engagement can be compared.

Use of Prospective Financial Statements

Prospective financial statements are prepared for one of two audiences:

1. *General* use statements are prepared for use by any third party, such as the inclusion of a financial forecast in a prospectus for the sale of vehicles trading company's bonds.
2. *Limited* use statements are prepared solely for third parties with whom the responsible party is dealing directly, such as the inclusion of a financial projection in a bank loan application document.

Forecasts can be provided for both general and limited use. However, projections are restricted to the latter, because limited users are in a better position to understand the prospective statements and related assumptions than other parties. For example, a potential venture capital investor can ask the responsible party about hypothetical assumptions in a projection, whereas a removed user, such as a reader of a company prospectus, can not. Because general users may have difficulty interpreting hypothetical assumptions without obtaining additional information, the standards prohibit their general use. There is an exception to this rule: a projection may be issued as a supplement to a forecast for general use.

Examination of Prospective Financial Statements

ISAE 3400 clearly states that auditors are not assuring to the accuracy of the prospective financial statements. Instead, they examine the underlying assumptions and the preparation and presentation of the forecast or projection. ISAE 3400 indicates that the auditor should provide only a moderate level of assurance when reporting on the reasonableness of management's assumptions. However, when, in the auditor's judgment, an appropriate level of satisfaction has been obtained, the auditor may express positive assurance regarding the assumptions. For examinations of forecasts and projections, there are four elements:

1. Evaluating the preparation of the prospective financial statements
2. Evaluating the support underlying the assumptions
3. Evaluating the presentation of the prospective financial statements for conformity with the applicable presentation guidelines
4. Issuing an examination report

These elements are based on accumulating evidence about the completeness and reasonableness of the underlying assumptions, as disclosed in the prospective financial statements. The auditor should not accept an engagement when the assumptions are clearly unrealistic or when the auditor believes that the prospective financial information will be inappropriate for its intended use. To make the evaluation, the auditor needs to become familiar with the client's business and industry, consider the internal control over the system used to generate the results, the qualifications and expertise of those persons preparing prospective information, identify the significant matters on which the client's future results are expected to depend ('key factor'), and determine that appropriate assumptions have been included with respect to these key factors.

Figure 25-9 illustrates a report on an examination of a forecast with an unmodified opinion. As the figure shows, the auditor's report on an examination of prospective financial statements is similar to the standard audit report for audited financial statements except for wording differences due to the unique labeling of the prospective financial statements and the inclusion of statements by the auditor about these three key distinctions:

1. A statement that the prospective results may not be achieved.
2. A statement that the auditor assumes no responsibility to update the report for events and circumstances occurring after the date of the report.
3. The date of the examination report (because the report is a forecast, the date of the forecasted balance sheet is after the report date).

FIGURE 25-9	Example of Examination of a Forecast with Unmodified Opinion

Independent Auditor's Report

We have examined the accompanying forecasted balance sheet, statements of income, statement of changes in owners' equity, and cash flows of Allstar, Inc., as of December 31, 2010, and for the year then ending. Allstar's management is responsible for the forecast. Our responsibility is to express an opinion based on our examination.

Our examination was conducted in accordance with International Standards on Assurance Engagements and, accordingly, included such procedures as we considered necessary to evaluate both the assumptions used by management and the preparation and presentation of the forecast. We believe that our examination provides a reasonable basis for our opinion.

In our opinion, the accompanying forecast is presented in conformity with International Standards on Assurance Engagements, and the underlying assumptions provide a reasonable basis for management's forecast. However, there will usually be differences between the forecasted and actual results, because events and circumstances frequently do not occur as expected, and those differences may be material. We have no responsibility to update this report for events and circumstances occurring after the date of this report.

If the auditor believes that one or more significant assumptions do not provide a reasonable basis for the prospective financial information, he or she should either express an adverse opinion on the prospective financial information in the report or withdraw from the engagement. Moreover, if the auditor believes that the presentation and disclosure of the prospective financial information is not adequate, he or she should express a qualified or adverse opinion on the prospective financial information, or withdraw from the engagement as appropriate.

AGREED-UPON PROCEDURES ENGAGEMENTS

OBJECTIVE 25-7

Describe agreed-upon procedures engagements.

When the auditor and management or a third-party user agree that the audit will be limited to certain specific audit procedures, it is referred to as an agreed-upon procedures engagement. Many auditors refer to these as procedures and findings engagements because the resulting reports emphasize the specific audit procedures performed and the findings of those completed procedures.

Agreed-upon procedures engagements appeal to auditors because management, or a third-party user, specifies the procedures they want done. An example would be when an auditing firm is asked to issue an opinion to an oversight supervisory board that a listed company complied with capital market law.

ISRS 4400, Engagements to Perform Agreed-Upon Procedures Regarding Financial Information, is the primary professional standard which discusses agreed-upon procedures engagements. The standard indicates that an engagement to perform agreed-upon procedures includes the performance of certain procedures by auditors regarding individual items of financial data (e.g. accounts payable, accounts receivable, purchases from related parties, and sales and profits of a segment of an entity), a financial statement (e.g. a balance sheet), or even a complete set of financial statements. As the auditor provides only a report of the factual findings of agreed-upon procedures, no assurance is expressed. Users themselves are responsible for assessing the procedures and findings reported by the auditor and drawing their own conclusions. The report of the auditor on agreed-upon procedures is restricted only to those parties who agreed that the procedures be performed.

In an agreed-upon procedures engagement an auditor might calculate the internal rate of return, beta risk for measuring volatility, and other relevant information of

FIGURE 25-10	A Report of Factual Findings in Connection with Accounts Payable

To the Management of ABC

We have performed the procedures agreed with you and enumerated below with respect to the accounts payable of ABC Company as at June 30, 2011, set forth in the accompanying schedules. Our engagement was undertaken in accordance with the International Standard on Related Services applicable to agreed-upon procedures engagements. The procedures were performed solely to assist you in evaluating the validity of the accounts payable and are summarized as follows:

1. We obtained and checked the addition of the trial balance of accounts payable as at June 30, 2011, prepared by ABC Company, and we compared the total to the balances in the related general ledger account.
2. We compared the list of major suppliers and the amounts owing at June 30, 2011, to the related names and amounts in the trial balance.
3. We obtained suppliers' statements or requested suppliers to confirm balances owing at June 30, 2011.
4. We compared such statements or confirmations to the amounts referred to in item 2. For amounts which did not agree, we obtained reconciliations from ABC Company. For reconciliations obtained, we identified and listed outstanding invoices, credit notes and outstanding checks, each of which was greater than US$10,000. We located and examined such invoices and credit notes subsequently received and checks subsequently paid and we ascertained that they should in fact have been listed as outstanding on the reconciliations.

We report our findings below:

a. With respect to item 1 we found the addition to be correct and the total amount to be in agreement.
b. With respect to item 2 we found the amounts compared to be in agreement.
c. With respect to item 3 we found there were suppliers' statements for all such suppliers.
d. With respect to item 4 we found the amounts agreed, or with respect to amounts which did not agree, we found ABC Company had prepared reconciliations and that the credit notes, invoices and outstanding checks over US$10,000 were appropriately listed as reconciling items with the following exceptions:

   • There were variances amounting to US$23,000 between the amount recorded for three suppliers and accounts payable subsidiary ledger and the total of supporting documents for those suppliers.
   • There were some delays in recording invoices for suppliers accounts amounted to US$15,000.
   • No confirmations were sent to a number of suppliers accounts balances amounting to US$8,000.

Because the above procedures do not constitute either an audit or a review made in accordance with International Standards on Auditing or International Standards on Review Engagements, we do not express any assurance on the accounts payable as of June 30, 2011.

Had we performed additional procedures or had we performed an audit or review of the financial statements in accordance with International Standards on Auditing or International Standards on Review Engagements, other matters might have come to our attention that would have been reported to you.

Our report is solely for the purpose set forth in the first paragraph of this report and for your information and is not to be used for any other purpose or to be distributed to any other parties. This report relates only to the accounts and items specified above and does not extend to any financial statements of ABC Company, taken as a whole.

Ghassan & Sohil & Co.

Date: July 15, 2011
Address:

interest to investors for a mutual fund. Also, an auditor might do agreed-upon procedures to assess the collectability of receivables, impairment of assets, and the value of obsolete inventory. Independence is not a requirement for agreed-upon procedures engagements. Also, the auditor should document matters which are used to prepare the report of factual findings, and evidence that the engagement was carried out in accordance with ISRS 4400. (Figure 25-10 shows an example of a report of factual findings in connection with accounts payable.)

OTHER AUDITS OR LIMITED ASSURANCE ENGAGEMENTS

Now that we have discussed compilation and review services for nonpublic companies, as well as reviews of interim financial information for public companies, we will examine other types of audit and assurance services that fall within the auditing standards but are not audits of historical financial statements in accordance with GAAP, IFRS, or local accounting standards. Some of these services include: audits of financial statements prepared on other comprehensive bases of accounting (OCBOA); audits of specified elements, accounts, or items; and debt compliance letters.

OBJECTIVE 25-8

Describe other audit and limited assurance engagements related to historical financial statements.

Other Comprehensive Basis of Accounting

Auditors often audit statements prepared on a basis other than GAAP, IFRS, or local accounting standards. Auditing standards apply to these audit engagements, but the reporting requirements differ somewhat from those described in Chapter 3. Bases other than GAAP or IFRS for which reports may be issued include:

- *Cash or modified cash basis.* With cash basis accounting, only cash receipts and disbursements are recorded. Under the modified cash basis of accounting, the cash basis is followed except for certain items, such as fixed assets and depreciation. Physicians, auditors, and attorneys often follow this accounting method.
- *Basis used to comply with the requirements of a regulatory agency.* Common examples include the uniform system of accounts required of railroads, utilities, and some insurance companies.
- *Income tax basis.* The same measurement rules used for filing tax returns are often used for financial statement preparation, even though this is not in accordance with GAAP, IFRS or local accounting standards. Many small businesses use this method.
- *A definite set of criteria having substantial support.* An example is the price-level basis of accounting. The method of accounting must be applied to all material items in the financial statements.

Auditors usually do these audits in the same way as when clients follow GAAP, IFRS, or local accounting standards. Naturally, the auditor must fully understand the accounting basis that the client is required to follow.

When clients follow a comprehensive basis other than GAAP, IFRS, or local accounting standards, the auditor must make sure the statements clearly indicate that they are prepared using a basis other than GAAP, IFRS, or local accounting standards. If the statements imply that GAAP, IFRS, or local accounting standards are followed, the reporting requirements covered in Chapter 3 apply. Consequently, terms such as *balance sheet* and *statement of operations* must be avoided by the client. Instead, a title such as 'statement of assets and liabilities arising from cash transactions' is appropriate for a cash basis statement. Figure 25-11 is an example of a report prepared on a partnership following the income tax basis of accounting.

Specified Elements, Accounts, or Items

Auditors are often asked to audit and issue reports on specific aspects of financial statements. A common example is a report on the audit of sales of a retail store in a shopping center to be used as a basis for rental payments. Other common examples include reports on royalties, profit participation, and provision for income taxes.

Auditing firms typically do audits for specified elements, accounts, or items. This type of audit is much like an ordinary audit of financial statements except it is applied to

FIGURE 25-11	Example of an Auditor's Report for Income Tax Basis of Accounting

Independent Auditor's Report

We have audited the accompanying statements of assets, liabilities, and capital-income tax basis of Triangle Partnership as of December 31, 2010 and 2009, and the related statements of revenue and expenses–income tax basis and changes in partners' capital accounts–income tax basis for the years then ended. These financial statements are the responsibility of the Partnership's management. Our responsibility is to express an opinion on these financial statements based on our audits.

We conduct our audits in accordance with International Standards on Auditing. Those standards require that we plan and perform the audit to obtain reasonable assurance about whether the financial statements are free of material misstatement. An audit includes examining, on a test basis, evidence supporting the amounts and disclosures in the financial statements. An audit also includes assessing the accounting principles used and significant estimates made by management, as well as evaluating the overall financial statement presentation. We believe that our audits provide a reasonable basis for our opinion.

As described in Note X, these financial statements were prepared on the basis of accounting that the Partnership uses for income tax purposes, which is a comprehensive basis of accounting other than International Financial Reporting Standards.

In our opinion, the financial statements referred to above present fairly, in all material respects, the assets, liabilities, and capital of Triangle Partnership as of December 31, 2010 and 2009, and its revenue and expenses and changes in partners' capital accounts for the years then ended, on the basis of accounting described in Note X.

less than the full financial statements. There is one main difference in audits of specified elements, accounts, or items and audits of complete financial statements—materiality is defined in terms of the elements, accounts, or items being audited rather than for the overall statements. The effect is to ordinarily require more evidence than if the item being verified is just one of many parts of the statements. For example, if the sales account is being reported on separately, a smaller misstatement is more likely to be considered material than it is when sales are one of many accounts in a full financial statement audit.

Auditors must extend their audit efforts to include other elements, accounts, or items that are interrelated with those that are being audited. For example, in expressing an opinion on sales, the auditor must also consider the effect of accounts receivable on sales.

Debt Compliance Letters and Similar Reports

Clients occasionally enter into loan agreements that require them to provide the lender with a report from an auditor about the existence or nonexistence of some condition. For example, a bank may require a company to maintain a certain dollar amount of working capital at a specified date and to obtain an audit report that states whether the company complied with the stated working capital requirements.

Auditors may issue reports on debt compliance and similar engagements as separate reports or, by adding a paragraph after the opinion paragraph, as part of a report that expresses their opinion on the financial statements. In either case, the auditor must observe the following matters in such engagements:

- Auditors must be qualified to evaluate whether the client has met the provisions in the engagement. In the audit of a debt compliance agreement, auditors are normally qualified to evaluate whether principal and interest payments were made when due, whether the proper limitations were maintained on dividends, working capital, and debt ratios, and whether the accounting records were adequate for conducting an ordinary audit. However, auditors are not qualified to determine whether the client has properly restricted its business activities to the requirements of an agreement or if it has title to pledged property. These are legal questions and the code of ethics for professional accountants prohibits the auditor from practicing as an attorney in such circumstances.

Independent Auditor's Report

We have audited, in accordance with International Standards on Auditing, the balance sheet of El Sabah Company as of December 31, 2010, and the related statements of income, changes in owners' equity, and cash flows for the year then ended, and have issued our report thereon dated February 16, 2011.

In connection with our audit, nothing came to our attention that caused us to believe that the company failed to comply with the terms, covenants, provisions, or conditions of sections XX to XX, inclusive, of the Indenture dated July 21, 2008, with Kuwait International Bank insofar as they related to accounting matters. However, our audit was not directed primarily toward obtaining knowledge of such noncompliance.

This report is intended solely for the information and use of the boards of directors and management of El Sabah Company and Kuwait International Bank and should not be used for any other purpose.

- The auditor should provide a debt compliance letter only for a client for whom the auditor has done an audit of the overall financial statements. A debt compliance letter on a matter such as the existence of a current ratio of 2.5 or better would be difficult to accomplish without having conducted a complete financial statement audit.
- The auditor's opinion is a *negative assurance*, stating that nothing came to the auditor's attention that would lead the auditor to believe there was noncompliance.

Figure 25-12 provides an example of a separate report on debt compliance. Note that the final paragraph restricts distribution of the report to the directly affected parties.

SUMMARY

This chapter described many of the other services offered by an audit firm. The types of services offered continue to grow and expand as society demands assurance on new and different types of information. Depending on the nature of the service, the guidance for performing the service may come from auditing standards, accounting and review services standards, or assurance standards. Table 25-2 provides a summary and examples of the primary categories of services discussed in this chapter.

TABLE 25-2   **Primary Categories of Other Assurance Services Engagements**

Type of Engagement	Example	Source of Authoritative Support
Audits of historical financial statements prepared in accordance with IFRS or local accounting standards	Audit of General Mills' financial statements	Auditing standards
Assurance engagements under the assurance standards	Assurance of General Mills' e-commerce system availability	Attestation (assurance) standards and *Trust Services* availability principles and criteria
Reviews or compilations of historical financial statements prepared in accordance with IFRS or local accounting standards	Review of Gadallah's Shoe Store's quarterly financial statements	Accounting and review services standards for nonpublic companies; auditing standards for public companies
Audits or limited assurance engagements other than audits, reviews, or compilations of historical financial statements prepared in accordance with IFRS or local accounting standards	Audit of Gadallah's Shoe Store's ending balance in inventory	Auditing standards

ESSENTIAL TERMS

Agreed-upon procedures engagement   p. 817

Assurance engagement   p. 815

Compilation service   p. 812

Examination   p. 816

Forecasts   p. 819

Projections   p. 819

Prospective financial statements   p. 819

Public company interim review   p. 814

Review   p. 817

Review service   p. 807

SysTrust   p. 818

WebTrust   p. 818

REVIEW QUESTIONS

25-1 (Objective 25-1) What is meant by the term *level of assurance*? How does the level of assurance differ for an audit of historical financial statements, a review, and a compilation?

25-2 (Objective 25-1) What is negative assurance? Why is it used in a review engagement report?

25-3 (Objective 25-1) Distinguish between compilation and review of financial statements. What is the level of assurance for each?

25-4 (Objective 25-1) Distinguish the two and three forms of compilation reports that an accountant can provide to clients under both international as well as U.S. compilation standards.

25-5 (Objective 25-1) List five things that are required of an accountant for a compilation.

25-6 (Objective 25-1) What steps should accountants take if during a compilation engagement they become aware that the financial statements are misleading?

25-7 (Objective 25-1) What procedures should the auditor use to obtain the information necessary to give the level of assurance required of reviews of financial statements?

25-8 (Objective 25-1) What should auditors do if during a review of financial statements they discover that International Financial Reporting Standards are not being followed?

25-9 (Objectives 25-1, 25-2) What are the differences between the review reports for a private company under ISRE 2410 and for the interim financial statements of a public company?

25-10 (Objective 25-2) Explain why a review of interim financial statements for a public company may provide a greater level of assurance than a review under ISRE 2410.

25-11 (Objective 25-4) List the five *Trust Services* principles and explain whether a *WebTrust* licensed auditor can report on an entity's compliance with those principles individually or in combination.

25-12 (Objective 25-5) Describe the purpose of a *SysTrust* assurance services engagement.

25-13 (Objective 25-6) Explain what is meant by prospective financial statements and distinguish between forecasts and projections. What four things are involved in an examination of prospective financial statements?

25-14 (Objective 25-8) What is the purpose of an engagement for specified elements, accounts, or items? List the four special requirements for reports on specified elements, accounts, or items. State the reporting requirements for statements prepared on a basis other than GAAP, IFRS, or local accounting standards.

25-15 (Objective 25-8) The Absco Corporation has requested that Sawsan Mohab, CPA, provide a report to the Union Bank as to the existence or nonexistence of certain loan conditions. The conditions to be reported on are the working capital ratio, dividends paid on preferred stock, aging of accounts receivable, and competence of management. This is Sawsan's first experience with Absco. Should Sawsan accept this engagement? Substantiate your answer.

MULTIPLE CHOICE QUESTIONS FROM CPA EXAMINATIONS

25-16 (Objective 25-1) The following are miscellaneous questions about compilation and review services. Choose the best response.

a. It is acceptable for an auditor to be associated with financial statements when not independent with respect to the client and still issue a substantially unmodified report for which of the following:

(1) Audits of companies following IFRS or local accounting standards.

(2) Audits of companies on a comprehensive basis of accounting other than GAAP, IFRS, or local accounting standards.

(3) Review of financial statements following IFRS or local accounting standards.

(4) Compilation of financial statements following IFRS or local accounting standards.

b. An auditor is performing review services for a small, closely held manufacturing company. As a part of the follow-up of a significant decrease in the gross margin for the current year, the auditor discovers that there are no supporting documents for US$40,000 of disbursements. The chief financial officer assures her that the disbursements are proper. What should the auditor do?

(1) Include the unsupported disbursements without further work in the statements on the grounds that she is not doing an audit.

(2) Modify the review opinion or withdraw from the engagement unless the unsupported disbursements are satisfactorily explained.

(3) Exclude the unsupported disbursements from the statements.

(4) Obtain a written representation from the chief financial officer that the disbursements are proper and should be included in the current financial statements.

c. Which of the following best describes the responsibility of the accountant in performing compilation services for a company?

(1) The accountant has to satisfy only himself or herself that the financial statements were prepared in conformity with IFRS or local accounting standards.

(2) The accountant must understand the client's business and accounting methods and read the financial statements for reasonableness.

(3) The accountant should obtain an understanding of internal control and perform tests of controls.

(4) The accountant is relieved of any responsibility to third parties.

d. In performing a compilation of financial statements of a nonpublic entity, the accountant decides that modification of the standard report is not adequate to indicate deficiencies in the financial statements taken as a whole, and the client is not willing to correct the deficiencies. The accountant should therefore

(1) perform a review of the financial statements.

(2) issue a special report.

(3) express an adverse audit opinion.

(4) withdraw from the engagement.

25-17 (Objectives 25-3, 25-6) The following questions concern assurance engagements and reports issued by auditors, other than those on historical financial statements. Choose the best response.

a. Which of the following professional services is considered an assurance engagement?
   (1) A management consulting engagement to provide IT advice to a client.
   (2) An income tax engagement to prepare tax returns.
   (3) An engagement to report on compliance with statutory requirements.
   (4) A compilation of financial statements from a client's accounting records.

b. Which of the following statements concerning prospective financial statements is correct?
   (1) Only a financial forecast is normally appropriate for limited use.
   (2) Any type of prospective financial statement is normally appropriate for limited use.
   (3) Only a financial projection is normally appropriate for general use.
   (4) Any type of prospective financial statement is normally appropriate for general use.

c. An auditor is reporting on cash basis financial statements. These statements are best referred to in the opinion of the auditor by which of the following descriptions?
   (1) Cash receipts and disbursements and the assets and liabilities arising from cash transactions.
   (2) Financial position and results of operations arising from cash transactions.
   (3) Balance sheet and income statements resulting from cash transactions.
   (4) Cash balance sheet and the source and application of funds.

DISCUSSION QUESTIONS AND PROBLEMS

25-18 (Objective 25-1) Evaluate the following comments about compiled financial statements: "When accountants associate their name with compiled financial statements, their only responsibility is to the client and that is limited to the proper summarization and presentation on the financial statements of information provided by the client. The opinion clearly states that the auditor has not conducted an audit and does not express an opinion on this fair presentation. If users rely on compiled financial statements, they do so at their own risk and should never be able to hold the accountant responsible for inadequate performance. Users should interpret the financial statements as if they had been prepared by management."

25-19 (Objective 25-1) The following items represent a series of unrelated procedures that an accountant may consider performing in an engagement to review or compile the financial statements of a nonpublic entity. Procedures may apply to only one, both, or neither type of engagement.

1. The accountant should establish an understanding with the entity regarding the nature and limitations of the services to be performed.
2. The accountant should make inquiries concerning actions taken at the board of directors' meetings.
3. The accountant should obtain a level of knowledge of the accounting principles and practices of the entity's industry.
4. The accountant should obtain an understanding of the entity's internal control.
5. The accountant should perform a physical examination of inventory.
6. The accountant should perform analytical procedures designed to identify relationships that appear to be unusual.
7. The accountant should send a letter of inquiry to the entity's attorney to corroborate the information furnished by management concerning litigation.
8. The accountant should obtain a management representation letter from the entity.
9. The accountant should make inquiries about events subsequent to the date of the financial statements that have a material effect on the financial statements.

Required

a. Indicate which procedures are required to be performed on a review engagement.

b. Indicate which procedures are required to be performed on a compilation engagement.[28]

25-20 (Objective 25-1) You are doing a review service and related tax work engagement for Red Sea Construction Company. You have made extensive inquiries of management about their financial statements and have concluded that management has an excellent understanding of its business and is honest, but lacking in knowledge of technical accounting issues. In doing the review you determine the following:

1. Repairs and maintenance expense has increased significantly compared to the preceding year. The president states that this seems to have been a year with a lot of repairs, in part because their equipment is getting older.

2. Property tax expense is the same as last year even though Red Sea purchased a new building, including the land. The president states that there are no real estate taxes on the new building and land until next year.

3. Based on your knowledge of the construction industry you know that the pipes Red Sea uses in construction have had a decrease in selling price to construction companies near the end of the current year. The president states that even though they have a large pipe inventory it will all be used in the next year or two, so the current price doesn't matter because they won't need to buy any.

4. Accounts receivable has increased almost 25% compared to the previous year, but the allowance for uncollectible accounts has stayed the same. The president states that even though receivables have increased, they still expect uncollectible accounts to be less than the stated allowance.

5. In discussions with the president you determine that there is a material uninsured lawsuit against the company from a former customer. The president believes it is a trivial lawsuit and will not permit a footnote about it for fear that it will result in similar lawsuits from other customers.

Required

a. Beyond inquiries and analytical procedures, what are the auditor's responsibilities in performing review service engagements?

b. Describe what you should do in each of the preceding situations, assuming each one is material.

25-21 (Objectives 25-4, 25-5) Each of the following represents different client requests for engagements related to *WebTrust* and *SysTrust* assurance services.

a. Ware Hospital Systems, Inc. is in the process of developing a new patient records system. Management has approached a licensed *SysTrust* auditor to perform a *SysTrust* engagement on its new system. Specifically, management wants the auditor to examine the system's processing integrity using the *Trust Services* processing integrity principle and criteria. The examination will be scheduled prior to the new system's implementation.

b. MoonBay.com's management requested that their auditor perform a *WebTrust* assurance service on their assertion about MoonBay.com e-commerce policies' compliance with the five *Trust Services* principles and criteria. Although the auditor is not a registered *WebTrust* provider, the audit firm is a member of the local professional association.

c. The board of directors of Seven Hardware Company has requested that their auditor perform a *SysTrust* assurance services engagement on its information technology system. The board has requested that the auditor, who is a licensed *SysTrust* provider, report solely on the company's IT availability policies and controls using the *Trust Services* availability principle and criteria.

d. Management of Microtech Technology, Inc. requested that its auditors perform a *WebTrust* assurance services engagement on its e-commerce security policies. The audit firm performed the *WebTrust* services as of April 30, 2010, and has not updated its work. Management wants its *WebTrust* seal to stay posted on its website through to May 31, 2011.

Required   Consider each request separately. Describe whether the requested assurance service can be performed.

25-22 (Objective 25-8) You have been requested by the management of Gabril & Co. to issue a debt compliance letter as a part of the audit of Sauadi Fruit Farms, Inc. Gabril & Co. is a supplier of irrigation equipment. Much of the equipment, including that supplied to Sauadi, is sold on a secured contract basis. Sauadi Fruit Farms is an audit client of yours, but Gabril is not. In addition to the present equipment, Gabril informs you they are evaluating whether they should sell another US$500,000 of equipment to Sauadi Fruit Farms. You have been requested to send Gabril a debt compliance letter concerning the following matters:

1. The current ratio has exceeded 2.0 in each quarter of the unaudited statements prepared by management and in the annual audited statements.
2. Total owners' equity is more than US$800,000.
3. The company has not violated any of the legal requirements of Gulf fruit-growing regulations.
4. Management is competent and has made reasonable business decisions in the past three years.
5. Management owns an option to buy additional fruit land adjacent to the company's present property.

Required   a. Define the purpose of a debt compliance letter.

b. Why is it necessary to conduct an audit of a company before it is acceptable to issue a debt compliance letter?

c. For which of the five requested items is it acceptable for an audit firm to issue a debt compliance letter? Give reasons for your answer.

MYLAB ACTIVITY

Visit MyAccountingLab and complete the following activity:

→ Internet Problem 25-1: Accounting and Review Services Committee.

CHAPTER 26

INTERNAL AND OPERATIONAL AUDITING

Good Auditing Often Results In Improved Cash Flows

Ashraf Allam is an experienced internal audit staff member with Financial Consultancies for Marketable Securities (FCMS). FCMS has been growing rapidly, adding customers and agents daily. The company provides various types of financial consultancy, in particular valuation studies. To address the growing volume of receivables, FCMS implemented a new state-of-the-art computerized information system.

Ashraf was assigned to test the accuracy of the aging of the accounts receivable system and the adequacy of the allowance for doubtful accounts. He took an initial sample of 50 invoices selected at random from a population of 500 outstanding bills. He used the sample to project an aging and develop an estimate of the required allowance for doubtful accounts. His tests indicated the allowance could be understated by as much as US\$5 million. Ashraf was worried because he knew that the current economic conditions in the Arab countries were not stable and were affecting many businesses. He also knew that due to the customs and culture in the Arab environment, customers may promise to pay their debts and businesses are patient in requesting the payment of the debts at due dates.

Ashraf informed Ibrahim Abdel Aziz, the head of internal audit, of the situation. Ibrahim informed the chief financial officer (CFO) that as long as the tests indicated there could be a material misstatement, FCMS must expand the sample until it was clear whether the allowance was materially misstated.

Ashraf's second sample increased the total sample to 100 outstanding bills, with essentially the same results. However, at Ibrahim's request, he analyzed the items from both a management standpoint and an accounting standpoint. When Ibrahim and Ashraf met with the CFO to discuss the updated information, Ibrahim pointed out that the real problem was not the allowance but that receivables were out of control, and FCMS faced a significant loss in cash flows if management didn't act quickly. The CFO quickly agreed and responded by instructing two accountants to analyze the aging of all 500 consultancy bills and to institute a large-scale collection effort. Not only did the analysis and collection efforts improve cash flows, they also showed that Ashraf's estimate was right on target.

LEARNING OBJECTIVES

After studying this chapter, you should be able to

26-1 Explain the role of internal auditors in financial auditing.

26-2 Explain the relationship between internal auditing and external auditing.

26-3 Distinguish operational auditing from financial auditing.

26-4 Provide an overview of operational audits.

26-5 Plan and perform an operational audit.

The last chapter discussed types of assurance services that external auditors provide. This chapter examines the activities of internal auditors, who perform a significant amount of financial auditing similar to that done by external auditing firms. As Ashraf Allam of Financial Consultancies demonstrates in the introductory story, internal auditors can have a significant impact on a company's operational efficiency and effectiveness, as well as on earnings and cash flow.

Relevant International Standards on Auditing	
ISA 260	Communication with Those Charged with Governance
ISA 315	Identifying and Assessing the Risks of Material Misstatement through Understanding the Entity and Its Environment
ISA 610	Using the Work of Internal Auditors

The concepts and methodologies studied in the preceding 25 chapters of this book apply to external and governmental audits. This chapter examines the role of internal auditors in financial auditing, and then looks at operational auditing.

INTERNAL FINANCIAL AUDITING

OBJECTIVE 26-1

Explain the role of internal auditors in financial auditing.

As discussed in Chapter 1, companies employ their own internal auditors to do both financial and operational auditing. During the past two decades, the role of internal auditors has expanded dramatically, primarily because of the increased size and complexity of many corporations. Because internal auditors spend all of their time within one company, they have much greater knowledge about the company's operations and internal controls than external auditors. That kind of knowledge can be critical to effective corporate governance. All the codes of corporate governance in the majority of the Arab countries as well as stock markets now require their registrants to have an internal audit function.

The Institute of Internal Auditors professional practices framework provides the following definition of internal auditing:

> Internal auditing is an independent, objective assurance and consulting activity designed to add value and improve an organization's operations. It helps an organization accomplish its objectives by bringing a systematic, disciplined approach to evaluate and improve the effectiveness of risk management, control, and governance processes.

This definition reflects the changing role of internal auditors. They are expected to provide value to the organization through improved operational effectiveness, while also performing traditional responsibilities, such as:

- Reviewing the reliability and integrity of information
- Ensuring compliance with policies and regulations
- Safeguarding assets

The objectives of internal auditors are considerably broader than the objectives of external auditors, providing flexibility for internal auditors to meet their company's needs. At one company, internal auditors may focus exclusively on documenting and testing controls. At another company, internal auditors may serve primarily as consultants, focusing on recommendations that improve organizational performance. Not only may internal auditors focus on different areas, but the extent of internal auditing may vary from one company to another. Internal audit reports are not standardized because the reporting needs vary for each company and the reports are not relied on by external users.

Institute of Internal Auditors

Professional guidance for internal auditors is provided by the **Institute of Internal Auditors (IIA)**, an organization that establishes ethical and practice standards, provides education, and encourages professionalism for its approximately 160,000 worldwide members. The IIA has played a major role in the increasing influence of internal auditing. For example, the IIA has established a highly regarded certification program resulting in the designation of certified internal auditor (CIA) for those who meet specific testing and experience requirements.

The IIA professional practice framework includes a code of ethics and IIA **International Standards for the Professional Practice of Internal Auditing** (known as the Red Book). All IIA members and CIAs agree to follow the institute's *Code of Ethics*, which requires compliance with the standards. Figure 26-1 outlines the IIA *Code of Ethics*, which is based on the ethical principles of integrity, objectivity, confidentiality, and competency.

As shown in Figure 26-2, the International Standards for the Professional Practice of Internal Auditing are divided into attribute standards for internal auditors and audit departments, and performance standards for the conduct and reporting of internal audit activities.

The IIA created specific standards within each category. For example, Attribute Standard 1100 on Independence and Objectivity, includes individual standards to

Institute of Internal Auditors (IIA)

Organization for internal auditors that establishes ethical and practice standards, provides education, and encourages professionalism for its members.

International Standards for the Professional Practice of Internal Auditing

Guidelines issued by the Institute of Internal Auditors covering the attributes and performance of internal auditors.

FIGURE 26-1	Institute of Internal Auditors Ethical Principles and Code of Ethics

ETHICAL PRINCIPLES

Integrity	The integrity of internal auditors establishes trust and thus provides the basis for reliance on their judgment.
Objectivity	Internal auditors exhibit the highest level of professional objectivity in gathering, evaluating, and communicating information about the activity or process being examined. Internal auditors make a balanced assessment of all the relevant circumstances and are not unduly influenced by their own interests or by others in forming judgments.
Confidentiality	Internal auditors respect the value and ownership of information they receive and do not disclose information without appropriate authority unless there is a legal or professional obligation to do so.
Competency	Internal auditors apply the knowledge, skills, and experience needed in the performance of internal auditing services.

RULES OF CONDUCT

1. Integrity	Internal auditors:
	1.1. Shall perform their work with honesty, diligence, and responsibility.
	1.2. Shall observe the law and make disclosures expected by the law and the profession.
	1.3. Shall not knowingly be a party to any illegal activity or engage in acts that are discreditable to the profession of internal auditing or to the organization.
	1.4. Shall respect and contribute to the legitimate and ethical objectives of the organization.
2. Objectivity	Internal auditors:
	2.1. Shall not participate in any activity or relationship that may impair or be presumed to impair their unbiased assessment. This participation includes those activities or relationships that may be in conflict with the interests of the organization.
	2.2. Shall not accept anything that may impair or be presumed to impair their professional judgment.
	2.3. Shall disclose all material facts known to them that, if not disclosed, may distort the reporting of activities under review.
3. Confidentiality	Internal auditors:
	3.1. Shall be prudent in the use and protection of information acquired in the course of their duties.
	3.2. Shall not use information for any personal gain or in any manner that would be contrary to the law or detrimental to the legitimate and ethical objectives of the organization.
4. Competency	Internal auditors:
	4.1. Shall engage only in those services for which they have the necessary knowledge, skills, and experience.
	4.2. Shall perform internal auditing services in accordance with the International Standards for the Professional Practice of Internal Auditing.
	4.3. Shall continually improve their proficiency and the effectiveness and quality of their services.

FIGURE 26-2	International Standards for the Professional Practice of Internal Auditing

ATTRIBUTE STANDARDS

1000 Purpose, Authority, and Responsibility. The purpose, authority, and responsibility of the internal audit activity must be formally defined in an independent audit charter, consistent with the Definition of Internal Auditing, the Code of Ethics, and the *Standards*. The chief audit executive must periodically review the internal audit charter and present it to senior management and the board for approval.

1100 Independence and Objectivity. The internal audit activity must be independent, and internal auditors must be objective in performing their work.

1200 Proficiency and Due Professional Care. Engagements must be performed with proficiency and due professional care.

1300 Quality Assurance and Improvement Program. The chief audit executive must develop and maintain a quality assurance and improvement program that covers all aspects of the internal audit activity.

PERFORMANCE STANDARDS

2000 Managing the Internal Audit Activity. The chief audit executive must effectively manage the internal audit activity to ensure it adds value to the organization.

2100 Nature of Work. The internal audit activity must evaluate and contribute to the improvement of risk management, control, and governance processes using a systematic and disciplined approach.

2200 Engagement Planning. Internal auditors must develop and document a plan for each engagement including the engagement's objectives, scope, timing, and resource allocations.

2300 Performing the Engagement. Internal auditors must identify, analyze, evaluate, and document sufficient information to achieve the engagement's objectives.

2400 Communicating Results. Internal auditors must communicate the engagement results.

2500 Monitoring Progress. The chief audit executive must establish and maintain a system to monitor the disposition of results communicated to management.

2600 Management's Acceptance of Risks. When the chief audit executive believes that senior management has accepted a level of residual risk that may be unacceptable to the organization, the chief audit executive must discuss the matter with senior management. If the decision regarding residual risk is not resolved, the chief audit executive must report the matter to the board for resolution.

Statements on Internal Auditing Standards (SIASs)

Statements issued by the Internal Auditing Standards Board of the IIA to provide authoritative interpretations of the IIA Practice Standards.

address organizational independence (1110), individual objectivity (1120), and impairments to independence and objectivity (1130).

In addition, the IIA developed specific implementation standards for assurance and consulting engagements. For example, Implementation Standard 1110.A1 provides guidance for applying Attribute Standard 1110 on organizational independence for assurance engagements, stating that the internal audit activity should be free from interference in determining the scope of internal auditing, performing work, and communicating results.

You may want to compare these standards to the AICPA generally accepted auditing standards as well as International Standards on Auditing as explained in Chapter 2 (Tables 2-3 and 2-4), to note similarities and differences. **Statements on Internal Auditing Standards (SIASs)** are issued by the Internal Auditing Standards Board to provide authoritative interpretations of the standards.

Figure 26-3 shows an example of an internal audit checklist.

Relationship of Internal and External Auditors

OBJECTIVE 26-2

Explain the relationship between internal auditing and external auditing.

The responsibilities and conduct of audits by internal and external auditors differ in one important way. Internal auditors are responsible to management and the board, while external auditors are responsible to financial statement users who rely on the auditor to add credibility to financial statements. Nevertheless, internal and external auditors share many similarities:

- Both must be competent as auditors and remain objective in performing their work and reporting their results.
- Both follow a similar methodology in performing their audits, including planning and performing tests of controls and substantive tests.
- Both consider risk and materiality in deciding the extent of their tests and evaluating results. However, their decisions about materiality and risks may differ because external users may have different needs than management or the board.

FIGURE 26-3	Internal Audit Checklist—Surprise Visit

Cash Receipts and Deposits:

Objective: To verify whether proper cash controls are in place to safeguard cash until being deposited and that cash is deposited within 24 hours from the time of receipt.

Methodology:

- Review a sample of cash receipts and ensure that cash collections are being handed in and deposited daily.
- Perform a stock count on the cash receipt vouchers stock.
- Identify cash receipts vouchers serial numbers gaps and ensure that missing vouchers are cancelled and maintained in a separate file sequentially with all cancelled copies.
- Discussion with the finance manager and accounting staff and review of any documentary evidence.

3.1	Are cash receipts being safeguarded in a secure location while in the premises of the company?					
3.2	Are cash receipts deposited in the bank account the next working day?					
3.3	Is the person posting the cash receipts different from the one receiving the cash?					
3.4	Are cash receipt books (used and unused) maintained in a secure location? And are finance dept books checked to ensure that all receipts were entered in the system and that those not entered were cancelled and all copies were maintained on file sequentially?					
3.5	Are there adequate records maintained to track receipt vouchers books (new & used)?					
3.6	Is a periodic physical count performed on the cash receipts stock by an independent employee from the finance dept?					
3.7	Does an individual (i.e. finance manager) reconcile the deposited amount to the general ledger on a daily basis? Observe or obtain any reconciliation documentation.					
3.8	Are all checks received in the legal name of the company? (Endorsed checks should not be accepted.)					

On the other hand, there are a number of differences between the role of the internal auditors and the external auditors.

- Internal auditors are employees of the company who report to the chief operating officer, the board of directors, and the audit committees, a matter which minimizes the independence status. It has been reported that a large number of internal audit managers resigned from their positions because of restrictions imposed on their ability to carry out their duties. This is especially true in situations where the audit committee does not exist or its role is not effective. Whereas external auditors are appointed by the shareholders at the annual general meeting and only shareholders have the right to reappoint or replace the auditors.
- Internal auditors perform both a financial audit as well as an operational audit as they examine the reliability of recorded transactions on a daily basis. They provide recommendations to management on how to improve the efficiency and effectiveness of the company's systems and operations, including internal controls and accounting systems. An external auditor's main responsibility is to form an opinion about the reliability of information in the company's financial statements.
- Internal auditors select a large number of transactions for examination while the external auditors rely heavily on sampling techniques in performing their audit.

External auditors rely on internal auditors when using the audit risk model to assess control risk. If internal auditors are effective, the external auditors can significantly reduce control risk and thereby reduce substantive testing. As a result, external auditors may reduce their fees substantially when the client has a highly regarded internal audit function. External auditors typically consider internal auditors effective if they are:

- Independent of the operating units being evaluated
- Competent and well trained
- Have performed relevant audit tests of the internal controls and financial statements

Auditing standards also permit the external auditor to use the internal auditor for direct assistance on the audit. By relying on the internal audit staff for performing some of the audit testing, external auditors may be able to complete the audit in less time and at a lower fee especially if they can study the internal audit report (see Figure 26-4). When internal auditors provide direct assistance, the external auditor should assess their competence and objectivity, and supervise and evaluate their work.

Management letters presented to clients in many Arab countries often include remarks associated with the nonexistence of an internal audit department to audit all transactions and payments. The recommendations of the auditors would be that an internal audit department directly reporting to the non-executive chairman as well

FIGURE 26-4	Internal Audit Report of CBC Industrial Co.		
Comment of internal audit	**Recommendation**	**Management Action Plan**	**Due date**
1. Credit Sales • Customers exceeding their credit ceilings by US$17,000 were not approved by the company sales manager in accordance with the credit policy. • 78 of 1400 (5.6%) customers' and distributors' payment terms on the customer master file exceeded the approved payment terms specified in the credit policy (all distributors' payment terms were changed from 7 to 20 credit days). • Customers' credit ceilings were not updated on a quarterly basis in accordance with the credit policy. As a result, many customers' credit ceilings were not properly stated.	• The company should strictly adhere to its credit policy. Exceptions should be approved by the company chief operation officer. • Postdated checks should not be accepted for due invoices.	- The credit policy has been amended, and approved by the CFO. - Due to the recent crisis we had several cases of overdue payments which has been heavily affected by the crisis, accordingly we had to show some flexibility without risking losing money. - Customers' credit ceilings have been updated except for some customers due to the current circumstances, but it has been amended in June 2011.	Done

2. Insurance
1. The company did not have adequate insurance coverage to cover the following:
  • Fixed assets items were overinsured by US$27 million. As a result, the company paid roughly US$46,000 in extra insurance premiums
  • Inventory
  • Cash in the safe
2. Three employees' job descriptions were incorrectly stated on the fidelity insurance policy. Specifically, job descriptions for three clearance employees were incorrectly stated as cashiers on the insurance policy.
3. The cashier deposited cash amounts exceeding US$85,000 without having an armed individual accompany him to the bank as clearly stated in the insurance policy.
	• To reduce the risk of loss, company assets must be covered with adequate insurance at all times. Any sudden increase in asset values must be associated with an amendment to the insurance policy.
	• Employees' job descriptions should be correctly stated on the policy.
	• The company should strictly adhere to the provisions of the policy when depositing large cash amounts.
		- Insurance coverage was for the two premises regardless of which machineries and inventories were in each one of them.
		- In Aug 2010, when we prepared the policy values we took into account the additions of the assets which we believed that they would be operating with in two months' time.
		- We will amend the covered amounts in the new policy which will be concluded within two weeks.
		- Cash in safe is now covered in a separate policy.
		- Job descriptions for the three employees has been amended.
		- Starting from May 2011, if the amount exceeds US$85,000, we ask the bank to transfer the money in an armored vehicle.
			Done
			
			Aug 15, 2011
			
			Done

as the board of directors should be established. In situations where an internal audit department exists, comments about the department often include the fact that the department does not directly report to the non-executive chairman, that no appropriate plans or audit programs exist, and that no interim reports are prepared for presentation to those charged with governance. To remedy these deficiencies, it is often recommended that members of the board of directors receive more training in corporate governance to make the company more efficient and effective. Internal auditors must also possess the qualifications and experience needed to undertake the required audit tasks.

OPERATIONAL AUDITING

Beyond financial auditing activities, internal auditors, government auditors, and external auditors also do **operational auditing**, which deals with the efficiency and effectiveness of an organization. Other auditors use the terms *management auditing* or *performance auditing* instead of *operational auditing* to refer to these activities, while others do not distinguish among the terms *performance auditing*, *management auditing*, and *operational auditing* and use them interchangeably.

We prefer to use *operational auditing* broadly, as long as the purpose of the test is to determine the effectiveness or efficiency of any part of an organization. Testing the effectiveness of internal controls by an internal auditor may therefore be considered part of operational auditing—if the purpose is to help an organization operate its business more effectively or efficiently. Similarly, determining whether a company has adequately trained assembly line personnel may also be operational auditing, if the purpose is to determine whether the company is effectively and efficiently producing products.

Operational auditing
The review of an organization for efficiency and effectiveness. The terms management auditing, performance auditing, and operational auditing are synonymous terms.

Differences Between Operational and Financial Auditing

The three major differences between operational and financial auditing are the purpose of the audit, distribution of the report, and inclusion of nonfinancial areas in operational auditing.

Purpose of the Audit This is the most important difference. Financial auditing emphasizes whether historical information was correctly recorded, while operational auditing emphasizes effectiveness and efficiency. Financial auditing is oriented to the past, while operational auditing focuses on improving future performance. An operational auditor, for example, may evaluate whether a type of new material is being purchased at the lowest cost to save money on future raw material purchases.

Distribution of the Reports Financial auditing reports are typically distributed to external users of financial statements, such as stockholders and bankers, while operational audit reports are intended primarily for management. The widespread distribution of financial auditing reports requires a well-defined structure and wording, as shown in Figure 3-1. The limited distribution of operational reports and the diverse nature of audits for efficiency and effectiveness allow operational audit reports to vary considerably from audit to audit. Figure 26-4 shows an example of an internal audit report for CBC Industrial Co.

Inclusion of Nonfinancial Areas Financial audits are limited to matters that directly affect the fairness of financial statement presentation, while operational audits cover any aspect of efficiency and effectiveness in an organization. For example, an operational audit might address the effectiveness of an advertising program or efficiency of factory employees.

OBJECTIVE 26-3
Distinguish operational auditing from financial auditing.

OBJECTIVE 26-4

Provide an overview of operational audits.

Effectiveness

The degree to which the organization's objectives are accomplished.

Efficiency

The degree to which costs are reduced without reducing effectiveness.

Effectiveness Versus Efficiency

Before an operational audit can be performed, auditors must define specific criteria for measuring effectiveness and efficiency. In general, **effectiveness** refers to meeting objectives, such as producing parts without defects. Efficiency refers to determining the resources used to achieve those objectives, such as determining whether parts are produced at minimum cost.

Effectiveness In an operational audit for effectiveness, an auditor, for example, might need to assess whether corporate management has met its assigned objective of achieving elevator safety in a factory. To determine the company's effectiveness measures, the auditor must establish specific criteria for elevator safety. For example, is the company's objective to inspect all elevators in the factory at least once a year? Is the objective to ensure that no fatalities occurred as a result of elevator breakdowns, or that no breakdowns occurred?

Efficiency Like effectiveness, there must be defined criteria for what is meant by doing things more efficiently before operational auditing can be meaningful. It is often easier to set efficiency than effectiveness criteria if **efficiency** is defined as reducing cost without reducing effectiveness. For example, if two different production processes manufacture a product of identical quality, the process with the lower cost is considered more efficient. Operational auditing commonly uncovers several types of typical inefficiencies, including:

Types of Inefficiency	*Example*
• Acquisition of goods and services is excessively costly.	• Bids for purchases of materials are not required.
• Raw materials are not available for production when needed.	• An entire assembly line must be shut down because necessary materials were not ordered.
• There is duplication of effort by employees.	• Identical production records are kept by both the accounting and production departments because they are unaware of each other's activities.
• Work is done that serves no purpose.	• Copies of vendors' invoices and receiving reports are sent to the production department where they are filed without ever being used.
• There are too many employees.	• The office work could be done effectively with one less administrative assistant.

Relationship Between Operational Auditing and Internal Controls

Management establishes internal controls to help meet its goals. As we discussed in Chapter 10, three concerns are vital to establishing good internal controls:

1. Reliability of financial reporting
2. Efficiency and effectiveness of operations
3. Compliance with applicable laws and regulations

Obviously, the second of these three client concerns directly relates to operational auditing, but the other two also affect efficiency and effectiveness. For example, management needs reliable cost accounting information to decide which products to continue producing and the billing price of products. Similarly, failure to comply with a law, such as the Sarbanes–Oxley Act in the U.S. or the Companies Acts in any of the Arab countries, can result in a large fine to the company.

Two things distinguish internal control evaluation and testing for financial and operational auditing: purpose and scope.

Purpose The purpose of operational auditing of internal control is to evaluate efficiency and effectiveness and to make recommendations to management. In contrast, internal control evaluation for financial auditing has a primary purpose: to determine the extent of substantive audit testing required.

For both financial and operational auditing, the auditors may evaluate the control procedures in the same way, but for different purposes. An operational auditor might test whether internal verification procedures for duplicate sales invoices are effective to ensure that the company does not offend customers, but also to collect all receivables. A financial auditor often does the same internal control tests, but the primary purpose is to reduce confirmation of accounts receivable or other substantive tests. (A secondary purpose of many financial audits is also to make operational recommendations to management.)

Scope The scope of operational auditing concerns any control affecting efficiency or effectiveness, while the scope of internal control evaluation for financial audits is restricted to the effectiveness of internal control over financial reporting and its effect on the fair presentation of financial statements. For example, an operational audit can focus on policies and procedures established in the marketing department to determine the effectiveness of catalogs in marketing products.

Types of Operational Audits

Operational audits fall into three broad categories: functional, organizational, and special assignments. In each case, part of the audit is likely to concern evaluating internal controls for efficiency and effectiveness.

Functional Audits Functions are a means of categorizing the activities of a business, such as the billing function or production function. Functions may be categorized and subdivided many different ways. For example, the accounting function may be subdivided into cash disbursement, cash receipt, and payroll disbursement functions. The payroll function may be subdivided into hiring, timekeeping, and payroll disbursement functions. A **functional audit** deals with one or more functions in an organization, concerning, for example, the efficiency and effectiveness of the payroll function for a division or for the company as a whole.

A functional audit has the advantage of permitting specialization by auditors. Certain auditors within an internal audit staff can develop considerable expertise in an area, such as production engineering. They can be more efficient and effective by spending all their time auditing in that area. A disadvantage of functional auditing is the failure to evaluate interrelated functions. For example, the production engineering function interacts with manufacturing and other functions in an organization.

Organizational Audits An operational audit of an organization deals with an entire organizational unit, such as a department, branch, or subsidiary. An **organizational audit** emphasizes how efficiently and effectively functions interact. The plan of organization and the methods to coordinate activities are important in this type of audit.

Special Assignments In operational auditing, **special assignments** arise at the request of management for a wide variety of audits, such as determining the cause of an ineffective IT system, investigating the possibility of fraud in a division, and making recommendations for reducing the cost of a manufactured product.

Functional audit

An operational audit that deals with one or more specific functions within an organization, such as the payroll function or the production engineering function.

Organizational audit

An operational audit that deals with an entire organizational unit, such as a department, branch, or subsidiary, to determine how efficiently and effectively functions interact.

Special assignments

Management requests for an operational audit for a specific purpose, such as investigating the possibility of fraud in a division or making recommendations for reducing the cost of a manufactured product.

Who Performs Operational Audits

Operational audits are usually performed by one of three groups: internal auditors, government auditors, or auditing firms.

Internal Auditors Internal auditors are in such a unique position to perform operational audits that some people use the terms *internal auditing* and *operational auditing* interchangeably. It is, however, inappropriate to conclude that all operational auditing is done by internal auditors or that internal auditors do only operational auditing. Many internal audit departments do both operational and financial auditing, often simultaneously. Because they spend all their time working for the company they are auditing, internal auditors have an advantage in doing operational audits. They can develop considerable knowledge about the company and its business, which is essential to effective operational auditing.

To maximize their effectiveness for both financial and operational auditing, the internal audit department should report to the board of directors or president. Internal auditors should also have access to and ongoing communications with the audit committee of the board of directors. This organizational structure helps internal auditors remain independent. If internal auditors report to the controller, it is difficult for them to do independent evaluations and make recommendations to senior management about inefficiencies in the controller's operations.

Government Auditors Different government auditors perform operational auditing, often as a part of doing financial audits. The most widely recognized government auditor group in the U.S. is the United States Government Accountability Office (GAO), and Audit Bureaus in many Arab countries which are concerned with financial and operational audits.

Examples of performance audits performed by government auditors include the following:

Economy and efficiency audit

A government audit to determine whether an entity is acquiring, protecting, and using its resources economically and efficiently; the causes of any inefficiencies or uneconomical practices; and whether the entity has complied with laws and regulations concerning matters of economy and efficiency.

* *Economy and efficiency audits.* The purpose of an **economy and efficiency audit** is to determine:

  1. Whether the entity is acquiring, protecting, and using its resources economically and efficiently
  2. The causes of inefficiencies or uneconomical practices
  3. Whether the entity has complied with laws and regulations concerning matters of economy and efficiency

Program audit

A government audit to determine the extent to which the desired results or benefits established by the legislature or other authorizing body are being achieved; the effectiveness of organizations, programs, activities, or functions; and whether the entity has complied with laws and regulations applicable to the program.

* *Program audits.* The purpose of a **program audit** is to determine:

  1. The extent to which the desired results or benefits established by the legislature or other authorizing body are being achieved
  2. The effectiveness of organizations, programs, activities, or functions
  3. Whether the entity has complied with laws and regulations applicable to the program

The first two objectives of each of these types of performance audits are clearly operational in nature, while the final objective concerns compliance.

FALSIFICATION OF THE BALANCE SHEETS OF GOVERNMENT AGENCIES

The General Accounting Office in the Kingdom of Saudi Arabia classified 50 percent of accounting offices (12 in total) to be within the list of under observation institutions. This was due to their involvement in falsification of the ending balances of some governmental agencies' budgets, which is considered as manipulation of public funds.

As a result those offices may be vulnerable to write-off and would then be included on a black list. The General Accounting Office indicated that if evidence is provided for the indictment of these 12 accounting offices, this will result in submitting the names of officials to the appropriate professional accounting association to take the necessary action.

Source: *Okaz*, September 25, 2011

To illustrate specific operational activities of governmental audit, the following three examples are taken from an article in the publication *Internal Auditor*:

- A separate hospital with its own administrative staff occupied three buildings on the grounds of another state hospital. Our audit showed that the limited workload of the administrative activities of this separate hospital and its proximity to the offices of the main hospital would permit consolidation of the administrative functions of the two hospitals at a saving of US$145,000 a year.
- A local school district exercised control over 29 individual facilities. Our audit showed that the unused classroom facilities amounted to about 28 percent or the equivalent of eight schools and that enrollment was continuing to decline. We recommended consolidating and closing of individual facilities to the extent possible. Such action would not only reduce costs but also provide greater flexibility in class sizes and course offerings.
- The outstanding accounts receivable at a teaching hospital increased from US$7 million to US$11 million during a two-year period. An audit showed that this serious situation was caused, in part, by a lack of aggressive follow-up action, insufficient supervision, and insufficient staff to keep up with an increasing workload.[29]

Auditing Firms When an auditing firm does an audit of historical financial statements, part of the audit often consists of identifying operational problems and making recommendations that may benefit the audit client. The recommendations can be made orally, but they are typically included in a management letter.

The background knowledge about a client's business, which an external auditor must obtain while doing an audit, often provides useful information for giving operational recommendations. For example, suppose that the auditor determined that inventory turnover for a client slowed considerably during the current year. The auditor should determine the cause of the reduction to evaluate the possibility of obsolete inventory that would misstate the financial statements. In determining the cause of the reduced inventory turnover, the auditor may identify operational causes, such as ineffective inventory acquisition policies, that can be brought to the attention of management. An auditor who has a broad business background and experience with similar businesses is more likely to be effective at providing clients with relevant operational recommendations than a person who lacks those qualities.

Clients commonly engage an auditing firm to do operational auditing for one or more specific parts of its business. For example, a company can ask the auditing firm to evaluate the efficiency and effectiveness of its computer systems. Usually, management engages the auditing firm for these audits only when the company does not have an

---

CORRUPTION BETWEEN GOVERNMENT OFFICIALS AND BUSINESSMEN

The former Minister of Tourism in Egypt approved the sale of more than 35 million square meters of land to two prominent businessmen for a price of US$1 per square meter in 2008 even though a special committee was formed to value the land and determined the fair value of the land to be US$3 a square meter. The question is where was the Central Audit Organization when the sale was made and why was the Attorney General not informed of the corruption by the head of this organization? A second question is where were the government auditors when the matter was presented to Giza Criminal Court? After several hearings, the court sentenced the former Minister of Tourism and the two businessmen to five years imprisonment. All three are jointly required to pay more than EGP 293,700 million (US$49 million). Also, the court found that the businessmen had not started the projects for which the land was sold to them and that their aim was just to acquire the land for future price appreciation.

Source: *El-Ahram*, June 2, 2011

internal audit staff or if the internal audit staff lacks expertise in a certain area. In some cases, management or the board of directors outsources the entire internal audit function to an auditing firm or co-sources select internal audit activities, such as IT operational auditing activities, to be done jointly by an auditing firm and certain members of the company's internal audit staff. In most cases, the auditing firm's management consulting staff performs these services. Note that auditing firms cannot provide these services to their publicly traded company audit clients.

Independence and Competence of Operational Auditors

The two most important qualities for an operational auditor are *independence* and *competence*. The auditor should report to the appropriate level of management to ensure that investigation and recommendations are made without bias. Independence is seldom a problem for external auditors because they are not employed by the company being audited. The independence of internal auditors is enhanced by having the internal audit department report to the board of directors or president. Similarly, government auditors should report to a level above the operating departments. The Audit Bureau, for example, reports directly to parliament as a means of enhancing independence.

The responsibilities of operational auditors can also affect their independence. The auditor should not be responsible for operating functions in a company or for correcting deficiencies when ineffective or inefficient operations are found. For example, it would negatively affect auditors' independence when they audit an IT system for acquisitions if they designed the system or are responsible for correcting deficiencies they found during the audit.

While it is acceptable for auditors to recommend changes in operations, operating personnel must have the authority to accept or reject those recommendations. If auditors had the authority to require implementation of their recommendations, their independence would be reduced.

Competence is, of course, necessary to determine the cause of operational problems and to make appropriate recommendations. When operational auditing deals with wide-ranging operating problems, however, competence can be a major obstacle. For example, imagine the difficulties of finding qualified internal auditors who can evaluate both the effectiveness of an advertising program and the efficiency of a production assembly process. The internal audit staff doing that type of operational auditing will presumably have to include some personnel with backgrounds in marketing and others in production.

Criteria for Evaluating Efficiency and Effectiveness

OBJECTIVE 26-5

Plan and perform an operational audit.

A major challenge of operational auditing is in selecting specific criteria for evaluating whether efficiency and effectiveness have occurred. In auditing historical financial statements, accounting standards provide the broad criteria for evaluating fair presentation, and audit objectives facilitate more specific criteria in deciding whether accounting standards have been followed. In operational auditing, there are no well-defined criteria.

To establish criteria for operational auditing, auditors could define the objectives as determining whether some aspect of the entity could be made more effective or efficient, and recommending improvements. This approach may be adequate for experienced and well-trained auditors, but it provides little guidance for most auditors.

Specific Criteria   More specific criteria are usually desirable before starting an operational audit. For example, suppose that you are doing an operational audit of the equipment layout in plants for a company. Here are some specific criteria, stated as questions, that might be used to evaluate plant layouts:

- Were all plant layouts approved by home office engineering at the time of original design?
- Has home office engineering done a reevaluation study of the plant layout in the past five years?
- Is each piece of equipment operating at 60 percent of capacity or more for at least three months each year?
- Does the layout facilitate the movement of new materials to the production floor?
- Does the layout facilitate the production of finished goods?
- Does the layout facilitate the movement of finished goods to distribution centers?
- Does the plant layout effectively use existing equipment?
- Is the safety of employees endangered by the plant layout?

Sources of Criteria To develop specific evaluation criteria, the operational auditor can use several sources, including:

- *Historical performance.* Criteria can be based on actual results from prior periods. By using these criteria, auditors can determine whether things have become 'better' or 'worse' in comparison. The advantage of this approach is that the criteria are easy to derive. However, they may not provide much insight into how well or poor the results are compared to what they could be.
- *Benchmarking.* Entities within or outside the client's organization may be sufficiently similar to the client's organization to use their operating results as criteria. Auditors should use care in selecting organizations to use as benchmarks. It makes little sense to benchmark with dissimilar organizations or those that perform at a substandard level. For internal comparable entities, the data are often readily available to use as criteria. Outside organizations are often willing to make their operating information available. Also, benchmarking data are often available through industry groups and governmental regulatory bodies.
- *Engineered standards.* It may be possible in some engagements to develop criteria based on engineered standards. For example, auditors can use time and motion studies to determine efficient production output rates. These criteria are often time-consuming and costly to develop because they require considerable expertise, but in some cases it may be worth the cost. Standards can be developed by industry groups for use by all their members, thereby spreading the cost.
- *Discussion and agreement.* Sometimes objective criteria are difficult or costly to obtain, and are best developed through discussion and agreement. The parties involved should include management of the entity to be audited, the operational auditor, and the entity or persons to whom the findings will be reported.

Phases in Operational Auditing

The three phases in an operational audit are planning, evidence accumulation and evaluation, and reporting and follow-up.

Planning Planning for operational audits is similar to planning for audits of historical financial statements that we've discussed in earlier chapters. Like auditors of financial statements, the operational auditor must determine the scope of the engagement and communicate it to the organizational unit. It is also necessary to:

- Staff the engagement properly
- Obtain background information about the organizational unit
- Understand internal control
- Decide on the appropriate evidence to accumulate

The major difference between planning an operational audit and a financial audit is the diversity created by the breadth of operational audits, which often makes it difficult to decide on specific objectives. Auditors select objectives based on the criteria developed for the engagement, depending on the specific circumstances at hand. For example, the objectives for an operational audit of the effectiveness of internal controls over petty cash will be dramatically different from those of an operational audit of the efficiency of a research and development department. Yet, these diverse objectives might be part of a single operational audit.

The breadth of operational audits often makes staffing more complicated than in a financial audit. Not only are the areas diverse, such as production control and advertizing, but the objectives within those areas often require special technical skills. For example, the auditor may need an engineering background to evaluate performance on a major construction project.

Finally, unlike financial audits, operational audits require auditors to spend more time with the interested parties agreeing on the terms of the engagement and the criteria for evaluation. Regardless of the source of the criteria for evaluation, it is essential that representatives of the entity to be audited, the operational auditor, and the entity or persons to whom the findings will be reported are clear and in agreement on the objectives and criteria involved.

Evidence Accumulation and Evaluation The eight types of evidence introduced in Chapter 7 and discussed throughout this book are equally applicable to operational auditing. Because internal controls and operating procedures are a critical part of operational auditing, it is common to use inspection, client inquiry, analytical procedures, and observation extensively. Confirmation, reperformance, and recalculation are used less extensively for most operational audits than for financial audits because the existence and accuracy objectives are not relevant for most operational audits.

To illustrate evidence accumulation in operational auditing, reconsider the example of the company evaluating the safety of elevators in a factory. Assume the parties agree that the objective is to determine whether a competent inspector makes an annual inspection of each elevator in the factory. To satisfy the completeness objective, auditors might examine blueprints of buildings and elevator locations and trace them to the company's list to ensure that all elevators are included in the population. Additional tests on newly constructed buildings will be appropriate to assess the timeliness with which the central listing is updated.

Assuming auditors determine that the company's list is complete, they can select a sample of elevator locations and collect evidence as to the timing and frequency of inspections. The auditor may want to consider inherent risk by doing greater sampling of older elevators or elevators with previous safety defects. The auditor may also want to examine evidence of the elevator inspectors' competence by reviewing resumes, training programs, competency examinations, and performance reports. It is also likely that the auditor will want to reperform the inspection procedures for a sample of elevators to obtain evidence of inconsistencies in reported and actual conditions.

Just like financial auditors, operational auditors must accumulate sufficient appropriate evidence to provide a basis for a conclusion about the objectives being tested. For an audit of elevator safety, the auditor must accumulate sufficient evidence about elevator safety inspections. After the evidence is accumulated, the auditor must decide whether it is reasonable to conclude that an inspection is made annually of each elevator in the factory by a competent inspector.

Reporting and Follow-Up Two major differences in operational and financial auditing reports affect operational auditing reports:

1. In operational audits, the report is usually sent only to management, with a copy to the unit being audited. The lack of third-party users reduces the need for standardized wording in operational auditing reports.
2. The diversity of operational audits requires a tailoring of each report to address the scope of the audit, findings, and recommendations.

Operational auditors often take a significant amount of time to clearly communicate audit findings and recommendations. On performance audits, when reports are being prepared following specific requirements, specified content must be included, but considerable freedom is permitted in the form of the report. Follow-up is common in operational auditing when auditors make recommendations to management to determine whether the recommended changes were made, and if not, why not.

Examples of Operational Audit Findings

Each issue of the *Internal Auditor*, a bimonthly publication of the IIA, includes several internal operational audit findings submitted by practicing internal auditors. Most of the findings deal with efficiency rather than effectiveness. Readers of the journal are more likely to find efficiency findings more interesting than those related to effectiveness. An operational audit resulting in savings of US$68,000 will probably engage readers more than a report on improved accuracy of financial reporting. The following examples from the *Internal Auditor* include examples related to effectiveness and to efficiency:

Use the Right Tool A company leased 25 heavy-duty trucks for use by service employees who installed and repaired about 20,000 vending machines in a large metropolitan area. All of the trucks were equipped with hydraulic lift-gates for loading and unloading vending machines.

The internal auditor found that only a few of the trucks were actually delivering and picking up vending machines. Most of the trucks were used for service calls, which consisted of on-the-scene repair of coin boxes or other simple adjustments not requiring the hydraulic lift-gates. The auditor recommended most of the heavy-duty trucks be phased out and replaced by conventional light vans. Management agreed and the savings in lease rates and operating expenses were estimated at US$25,000 a year.

Computer Programs Save Manual Labor A company offering profit-sharing plans requires an annual audit of such profit-sharing plans. Internal auditors tested the profit-sharing plans, but also performed an operational review, which provided a number of valuable recommendations to management.

The IT auditors on the audit team developed several computer-assisted audit programs to test control over enrollment in and termination from the company's profit-sharing plan. The computer assistance saved manual labor and detected several employees who were not eligible for the plan, such as employees with less than the required one year of service and terminated employees still on the plan. The computer portion of the audit program also detected conflicting data between the payroll and profit-sharing plan master files.

When shown the results of the audit, management corrected all of the problems and instituted additional controls to prevent the problems in the future. And the additional controls were ... well, guess. Yep, they wanted the IT auditors to leave their computer programs in the machine. The profit-sharing plan manager uses the programs periodically as a control to detect enrollment errors.[30]

SUMMARY

This chapter discussed the financial auditing activities of internal auditors and the effect of internal auditors on external audits. Increasingly, internal auditors and government auditors, as well as auditing firms, are also asked to perform operational audits of the efficiency or effectiveness of a company or government unit. In these engagements, the appropriate criteria for evaluating efficiency or effectiveness is essential.

ESSENTIAL TERMS

Economy and efficiency audit   p. 840

Effectiveness   p. 838

Efficiency   p. 838

Functional audit   p. 839

Institute of Internal Auditors (IIA)   p. 833

International Standards for the Professional Practice of Internal Auditing   p. 833

Operational auditing   p. 837

Organizational audit   p. 839

Program audit   p. 840

Special assignments   p. 839

Statements on Internal Auditing Standards (SIASs)   p. 834

REVIEW QUESTIONS

26-1 (Objectives 26-1, 26-2) Explain the role of internal auditors for financial auditing. How is it similar to and different from the role of external auditors?

26-2 (Objectives 26-1) What is the nature of the two categories of standards in the IIA International Standards for the Professional Practice of Internal Auditing?

26-3 (Objective 26-1, 26-2) Explain the difference between the independence of internal auditors and external auditors in the audit of historical financial statements. How can internal auditors best achieve independence?

26-4 (Objective 26-2) Explain how financial auditing is similar to and different from internal audit.

26-5 (Objective 26-3) Describe what is meant by an operational audit.

26-6 (Objective 26-3) Identify the three major differences between financial and operational auditing.

26-7 (Objective 26-4) Distinguish between efficiency and effectiveness in operational audits. State one example of an operational audit explaining efficiency and another explaining effectiveness.

26-8 (Objective 26-4) Distinguish among the following types of operational audits: functional, organizational, and special assignment. State an example of each for a not-for-profit hospital.

26-9 (Objective 26-4) Explain why many people think of internal auditors as the primary group responsible for conducting operational audits.

26-10 (Objective 26-4) Explain the role of government auditors in operational auditing. How is this similar to and different from the role of internal auditors?

26-11 (Objective 26-4) Under what circumstances are external auditors likely to be involved in operational auditing? Give one example of operational auditing by an auditing firm.

26-12 (Objective 26-5) Explain what is meant by the criteria for evaluating efficiency and effectiveness. Provide five possible specific criteria for evaluating effectiveness of an IT system for payroll.

26-13 (Objective 26-5) Identify the three phases of an operational audit.

26-14 (Objective 26-5) Explain how planning for operational auditing is similar to and different from financial auditing.

26-15 (Objective 26-5) What are the major differences between reporting for operational and financial auditing?

MULTIPLE CHOICE QUESTIONS FROM CPA, IIA, AND CMA EXAMINATIONS

26-16 (Objectives 26-1, 26-2, 26-4) The following questions deal with independence of auditors. Choose the best response.

a. The operational auditor's independence is most likely to be compromised when the internal audit department is responsible directly to the
   (1) vice president of finance.
   (2) president.
   (3) controller.
   (4) executive vice president.
   (5) audit committee of the board of directors.

b. The independence of the internal audit department will most likely be assured if it reports to the
   (1) president.
   (2) controller.
   (3) treasurer.
   (4) audit committee of the board of directors.
   (5) vice president of finance.

c. Which of the following may compromise the independence of an internal auditor?
   (1) Reviewing IT systems before implementation.
   (2) Performing an audit where the auditor recently had operating responsibilities.
   (3) Failing to review the audit report with the auditee prior to distribution.
   (4) Following up on corrective action in response to audit findings.

26-17 (Objectives 26-3, 26-4, 26-5) The following questions deal with operational auditing. Choose the best response.

a. Which of the following best describes the operational audit?
   (1) It requires constant review by internal auditors of the administrative controls as they relate to the operations of the company.
   (2) It concentrates on implementing financial and accounting controls in a newly organized company.
   (3) It attempts and is designed to verify the fair presentation of a company's results of operations.
   (4) It concentrates on seeking aspects of operations in which waste would be reduced by the introduction of controls.

b. The evaluation of audit field work of an operating unit should answer the following questions:
   (1) What are the reasons for the results?
   (2) How can performance be improved?
   (3) What results are being achieved?

   What is the chronological order in which these questions should be answered?
   (1) 3—1—2
   (2) 1—3—2
   (3) 3—2—1
   (4) 1—2—3
   (5) 2—3—1

c. The purpose of governmental effectiveness or program auditing is to determine if the desired results of a program are being achieved. The first step in conducting such an audit is to
(1) evaluate the system used to measure results.
(2) determine the time frame to be audited.
(3) collect quantifiable data on the program's success or failure.
(4) identify the legislative intent of the program being audited.

26-18 (Objectives 26-1, 26-4, 26-5) The following questions deal with internal auditing departments and their responsibilities. Choose the best response.

a. Which of the following is generally considered to be a major reason for establishing an internal auditing function?
(1) To relieve overburdened management of the responsibility for establishing effective systems of internal control.
(2) To ensure that operating activities comply with the policies, plans, and procedures established by management.
(3) To safeguard resources entrusted to the organization.
(4) To ensure the accuracy, reliability, and timeliness of financial and operating data used in management's decision making.
(5) To assist members of the organization in the measurement and evaluation of the effectiveness of established systems of internal control.

b. Which of the following is generally considered to be the primary purpose of an internal auditor's evaluation of the adequacy of internal control?
(1) To determine whether the established internal controls are functioning as intended by management.
(2) To determine the extent of reliance the internal auditor can place on the established internal controls in the process of evaluating the financial statements prepared by the organization.
(3) To determine whether all risks and exposures of the enterprise have been reduced or eliminated by the established internal controls.
(4) To determine whether the established internal controls provide reasonable assurance that the objectives and goals of the organization will be met in an efficient and economical manner.

c. With regard to corrective action on audit results, which of the following is not the internal auditor's responsibility?
(1) Soliciting auditees' suggestions for corrective actions.
(2) Recommending possible alternative corrective actions.
(3) Directing the corrective actions.
(4) Determining that the corrective actions are responsive to the audit results.
(5) Evaluating new policy statements to determine whether they address the unsatisfactory conditions disclosed in the audit results.

CASES

26-19 (Objectives 26-1, 26-2, 26-4, 26-5) Wave Corporation has an internal audit department operating out of the corporate headquarters. Various types of audit assignments are performed by the department for the eight divisions of the company. The following findings resulted from recent audits of one of Wave Corporation's divisions:

1. One of the departments in the division appeared to have an excessive turnover rate. Upon investigation, the personnel department seemed to be unable to find enough workers with the specified skills for this department. Some workers are trained on the job. The departmental supervisor is held accountable for labor efficiency variances but does not have qualified staff or sufficient time to train the workers properly. The supervisor holds individual workers responsible for meeting predetermined

standards from the day they report to work. This has resulted in a rapid turnover of workers who are trainable but not yet able to meet standards.

2. The internal audit department recently participated in a computer feasibility study for this division. It advised and concurred on the purchase and installation of a specific computer system. Although the system is up and operating, the results are less than desirable. The software and hardware meet the specifications of the feasibility study, but there are several functions unique to this division that the system has been unable to accomplish. Linking of files has been a problem. For example, several vendors have been paid for materials not meeting company specifications. A revision of the existing software is probably not possible, and a permanent solution probably requires replacing the existing computer system with a new one.

3. One of the products manufactured by this division was recently redesigned to eliminate a potential safety defect. This defect was discovered after several users were injured. At present, there are no pending lawsuits because none of the injured parties has identified a defect in the product as a cause of the injury. There is insufficient information to determine whether the defect was a contributing factor.

The director of internal auditing and assistant controller is in charge of the internal audit department and reports to the controller in corporate headquarters. Copies of internal audit reports are sent routinely to Wave's board of directors.

a. Explain the additional steps in terms of field work, preparation of recommendations, and operating management review that ordinarily should be taken by Wave Corporation's internal auditors as a consequence of the audit findings in the first situation (excessive turnover).   **Required**

b. Discuss whether there are any objectivity problems with Wave Corporation's internal audit department as revealed by the audit findings. Include in your discussion any recommendations to eliminate or reduce an objectivity problem, if one exists.

c. The internal audit department is part of the corporate controllership function, and copies of the internal audit reports are sent to the board of directors.
   (1) Evaluate the appropriateness of the location of the internal audit department within Wave's organizational structure.
   (2) Discuss who within Wave should receive the reports of the internal audit department.[31]

26-20 (Objectives 26-4, 26-5) Superior Co. manufactures automobile parts for sale to the major Kuwaiti automakers. Superior's internal audit staff is to review the internal controls over machinery and equipment and make recommendations for improvements when appropriate. The internal auditors obtained the following information during the assignment:

1. Requests for purchase of machinery and equipment are normally initiated by the supervisor in need of the asset. The supervisor discusses the proposed acquisition with the plant manager. A purchase requisition is submitted to the purchasing department when the plant manager is satisfied that the request is reasonable and that there is a remaining balance in the plant's share of the total corporate budget for capital acquisitions.

2. Upon receiving a purchase requisition for machinery or equipment, the purchasing department manager looks through the records for an appropriate supplier. A formal purchase order is then completed and mailed. When the machine or equipment is received, it is immediately sent to the user department for installation. This allows the economic benefits from the acquisition to be realized at the earliest possible date.

3. The property, plant, and equipment ledger control accounts are supported by lapse schedules organized by year of acquisition. These lapse schedules are used to compute depreciation as a unit for all assets of a given type that are acquired in the same year. Standard rates, depreciation methods, and salvage values are used for each major type of fixed assets. These rates, methods, and salvage values were set ten years ago during the company's initial year of operation.

4. When machinery or equipment is retired, the plant manager notifies the accounting department so that the appropriate entries can be made in the accounting records.

5. There has been no reconciliation since the company began operations between the accounting records and the machinery and equipment on hand.

Required

Identify the internal control deficiencies and recommend improvements that the internal audit staff of Superior Co. should include in its report regarding the internal controls over fixed assets. Use the following format in preparing your answer:[32]

Deficiencies	Recommendations
1.	1.

26-21 (Objectives 26-4, 26-5) Amar's Apartments has been leasing apartments for 20 years and is owned by Amar Omar. The company has had the same staff for the past five years—one leasing office employee, one property manager, and one maintenance person. The company has approached your public accounting firm because the owner believes that there are some inefficiencies with the front office personnel, and worse, he suspects that the leasing office employee may have been embezzling money over the course of her employment. Amar has asked your firm to:

1. Evaluate cash receipts for missing items.
2. Evaluate the internal controls of the leasing office and recommend changes.

As the senior assigned to this operational audit, you know that there are three phases to operational audits: planning, accumulating evidence, and reporting and follow up.

Planning

The planning phase requires you, the senior, to asses the situation and decide on the test work necessary to address the two objectives.

Required

a. For your planning phase concerning objective 1, what information would you collect and what tests would you perform to accomplish the two criteria set forth by the owner, Amar?

b. For the tests related to objective 1, your manager has suggested a staff of eight auditors to perform the procedures. Do you feel this would appropriately staff the engagement?

c. For your planning phase concerning objective 2, what information would you collect and what tests would you perform to accomplish the two criteria set forth by the owner, Amar?

Accumulating Evidence

After discussions with management you find there are 50 units with an average rent of US$600 per month and the complex has a vacancy rate of 10%. Per discussions with the client, all payments are brought to the leasing office manager, who inputs the payments into the computer and deposits them to the bank. The leasing office manager is also responsible for reporting to the owner, Amar. The property manager handles all complaints and requests from tenants and coordinates with the maintenance person for all repairs as necessary. The owner has little involvement in this property as he has multiple other properties to manage.

Among the possible tests you suggested, the manager on the audit has decided to do a test of details to compare the daily cash receipts with the amount recorded in the general ledger as follows:

Month	Rent per General Ledger	Rent per Cash Receipts
January	US$24,385	US$24,385
February	24,876	24,876
March	25,980	25,980
April	25,998	25,998
May	26,453	26,453
June	26,111	26,111
July	24,567	24,567
August	25,654	25,654
September	26,543	26,543
October	23,112	23,112
November	22,111	22,111
December	22,653	22,653

Required

d. What assertion does the accumulated evidence address? What does the accumulated evidence tell you?

e. Assume that Amar is positive that the leasing office employee is stealing tenant rent payments as he has evidence of at least one occasion on which this has happened. How would you alter the test work to further address the issue of misappropriated cash? What assertion does this address? Prepare an audit schedule to summarize your findings. Use the computer to prepare the schedule (instructor's option).

Reporting and Follow Up

Ultimately you find that the leasing office employee was physically altering the payees on the rent checks to her own name and depositing those checks into her own bank account. The leasing office employee would then enter the leasing office software and delete the invoice and accounts receivable for that tenant so it would appear that nothing was missing. The employee was caught when she missed a day of work and a tenant came in with a payment and was told she owed for the prior month, when in fact the employee had stolen her check from the prior month but had forgotten to delete the invoice out of the system.

Required

f. How would you present your findings to the owner?

g. What suggestions would you make to prevent this from happening in the future?

MYLAB ACTIVITY

Visit MyAccountingLab and complete the following activity:

→ Internet Problem 26-1: University Internal Audit Departments.

ENDNOTES

1. 2010 Handbook of International Quality Control, Auditing, Review, Other Assurance, and Related Services Pronouncements, *International Federation of Accountants.*
2. Statute of the UAE Accountant & Auditors Association, http://www.aaa4uae.com/pdf/mainlaw_english.pdf
3. Federal Law of the United Arab Emirates No.22 of 1995 Regarding Organization of the Auditing.
4. Accounting and Auditing Organisation for Islamic Financial Institutions website, http://www.aaoifi.com/aaoifi/TheOrganization/Objectives/tabid/64/language/en-US/Default.aspx
5. AICPA adapted.
6. Based on the EFSA's External Auditors Supervisory Oversight Board, minutes of meetings, May 6, 2010.
7. AICPA adapted.
8. AICPA adapted.
9. AICPA adapted.
10. Adapted from PCAOB, AS 5, para 65.
11. Kaizensox Consulting, Corporate Frauds and Risks Mitigation in the Middle East–4th Annual Anti Fraud Conference, organized by Indiaforensic, Mumbai, June 11, 2010.
12. AICPA adapted.
13. AICPA adapted.
14. AICPA adapted.
15. AICPA adapted.
16. Detail tie-in is included as the first objective here, compared with being objective 6 in Chapter 6, because tests for detail tie-in are normally done first.
17. D. A. Leslie, A. D. Teitlebaum, and R. J. Anderson, Dollar Unit Sampling: A Practical Guide for Auditors, Toronto, (Copp, Clark and Pitman, 1979).
18. AICPA adapted.
19. AICPA adapted.
20. AICPA adapted.
21. AICPA adapted.
22. AICPA adapted.
23. AICPA adapted.
24. AICPA adapted.
25. AICPA adapted.
26. AICPA adapted.
27. AICPA adapted.
28. AICPA adapted.
29. From *Round Table*, © 1982 by The Institute of Internal Auditors, Inc., 249 Maitland Avenue, Altamonte Springs, Fla, U.S. 32701. Reprinted with permission.
30. From *Round Table*, © 1982 by The Institute of Internal Auditors, Inc., 249 Maitland Avenue, Altamonte Springs, Fla U.S. 32701. Reprinted with permission.
31. CMA adapted.
32. CMA adapted.

We are grateful to the following for permission to reproduce copyright material:

Figures

Figure 2.1 from 'Structure of IAASB standards', published by the International Federation of Accountants (IFAC); Figure 3.11 adapted from 'Audit Report with a Qualified Opinion: Departure from the Financial Reporting Framework, ISA 706 emphasis of matters paragraphs and other matters paragraphs in the independent auditor's report', IAASB, published by the International Federation of Accountants (IFAC) in 2010; Figure 3.13 adapted from Audit Report with an Adverse Opinion: Departure from the financial reporting framework, ISA 705 modifications to the opinion in the independent auditor's report, IAASB, published by the International Federation of Accountants (IFAC) in 2010; Figure 3.14 adapted from 'Audit report with a disclaimer of audit opinion: scope limitation, ISA 705 modifications to the opinion in the independent auditor's report', IAASB, published by the International Federation of Accountants (IFAC) in 2010; Figure 3.28 adapted from 'Audit Report with other Matter Paragraph for material inconsistency (proposed) ISA 706 Emphasis of Matter Paragraphs and other Mater Paragraphs in the Independent Auditor's Report', IAASB, published by the International Federation of Accountants (IFAC) in 2010; and Figure 3.29 adapted from 'Auditor's Report on Summary Financial Statements with modifications' from *ISA 810 Engagements to Report on Summary Financial Statements*, IAASB, published by the International Federation of Accountants (IFAC) in 2010 and used with permission of IFAC; Figure 5.2 from 'XI (Inspiring Star the future is here)' by Nuqul Group Jordan. Reproduced by permission of Nuqul Group, Amman, Jordan; Figure 10.8 adapted from "Section 404 Compliance in the Annual Report", *Journal of Accountancy*, pp.43–48 (Michael Ramos), October 2004, copyright © 2004, American Institute of CPAs. All rights reserved. Used with permission; Figure 11.2 from 'The 2007 Oversight System Report on Corporate Fraud', Oversight Systems, Inc., 2007. Reproduced with permission; Figure 11.4 from *Nuqul Group Corporate Integrity Hotline Brochure*, www.nuqulgroup.com. Reproduced by permission of Nuqul Group, Amman, Jordan; Figure 11.7 from *2008 Report to the Nation on Occupational Fraud and Abuse*, copyright © Association of Certified Fraud Examiners, 2008; Figure 25.2 from 'Analytical Procedures the Auditor May Consider When Performing a Review of Interim Financial Information' Appendix 2 of IFAC Standard *Review of Interim Financial information performed by the independent auditor of the Entity*, published by the International Federation of Accountants (IFAC) in 2010; and Figure 25.4 from 'Example of a Management Letter of Representation in Standard letter of representation', published by the International Federation of Accountants (IFAC) in 2010 and used with permission of IFAC.

Tables

Table 1.1 adapted from *AICPA Special Committee on Assurance Services*, copyright © American Institute of CPAs. All rights reserved. Used with permission; Table 2.1 adapted from "Revenue and Other Data for the Largest CPA Firms in the United States", *Accounting Today*, 2007, www.accounting-today.com. Reproduced with permission of SourceMedia; Table 2.3 from IFSB, http://www.ifsb.org/published.php, accessed 3 July 2012. Reproduced by permission of Islamic Financial Services Board; Table 2.4 from *International Standards on Auditing*, http://www.ifac.org/auditing-assurance/clarity-center/clarified-standards, published by the International Federation of Accountants (IFAC) and used with permission of IFAC; Table 5.1 from *Elements of the Code of Ethics for Professional Accountants*, IESBA, revision, published by the International Federation of Accountants (IFAC) in 2010; Table 5.2 from 'Fundamental Principles' in *Code of Ethics for Professional Accountants*, IESBA, revision, section 100.5, published by the International Federation of Accountants (IFAC) in 2010; and Table 5.3 adapted from 'Types of Threats' in *Code of Ethics for Professional Accountants*, IESBA, revision, Section 100.12, published by the International Federation of Accountants (IFAC) in 2010 and used

Text

ACL INSTALLATION AND INSTRUCTIONS

ACL is generalized audit software used by auditors to extract and analyze data on a client's computerized systems. Generalized audit software is discussed on pages 414–415 of the text.

The ACL Problems included in selected chapters (Chapters 7, 8, 11, 12, 14, and 16) are intended to provide you with an introduction to ACL. An in-depth study of its use is beyond the scope of most first auditing courses. The guidance provided in this Appendix is intended only to help you solve the problems in the text.

Software Installation

The software should be installed on your personal computer. For any other installation, see your instructor.

1. Insert the CD in the CD holder on your computer.
2. On the opening screen, select 'Install' and select the 'ACL 9 Educational Edition.' Proceed through the prompts to completion.
   - You must accept the license agreement to complete the installation
   - Select complete setup
   - Exit after the installation is complete

Opening ACL

An icon to open the ACL Education Edition should be on your desktop after installation. If it does not appear, then go to Windows Start and select 'Programs' to then locate the ACL Desktop Education Edition link. Select the 'ACL Desktop Education Edition' to launch the software.

Finding Companies, Tables, and Using Commands

The main screen *Welcome to ACL* should appear when you open ACL. Look at that screen now.

On that screen, you will see a header 'ACL Projects.' Click on the link for 'Open an existing project.' You will then see a list of four projects. The ACL assignments in the text use only two of these projects: ACL_Demo and Sample_Project. Both of these projects have several files, which ACL calls tables. You will first click on a project to identify the tables, which will appear in the left side of your screen window once you click on the project folder. (*Note:* When you open ACL again, any projects you have accessed will appear under 'Recent Projects' and can be accessed using those links.)

Note: From now on, when you see italics it means you should use your computer to follow an instruction. The arrow sign (→) indicates an additional action to be taken.

Click Sample_Project to open the tables under Sample_Project → Click the plus sign next to the yellow tables folder → Click the plus sign next to the yellow accounts payable subfolder.

Observe that there are now two blue lined boxes under the accounts payable subfolder. Each of those represents a table.

Double-click AP_Trans and observe that a typical ACL table labeled AP_Trans for accounts payable transactions opens. On the bottom row of that screen, the number of records in the table is listed (102). The table includes columns with titles and data in each column. That is the information that auditors verify using various commands.

Click the top of the Invoice Amount column on the table (make sure the column is now all dark) → Go to the Windows drop-down options at the top of the screen and select 'Analyze' (on the Menu bar) → Under 'Analyze,' select 'Total Fields' (on the drop-down list).

The amount shown on the screen should be 278,641.33. You just used an ACL command (Total Fields) to calculate the total of the invoice amounts in the table. That sure beats using an adding machine or reentering the data in Excel. (*Note:* Commands can be accessed through the Menu bar or using the icons at the top of the screen. In this text we use the Menu bar.)

Click the small x below the large X at the top right hand side of your screen to close that window and return to the AP_Trans table.

→ *Click the small x below the large X to close the AP_Trans table. This will return you to the 'Welcome to ACL' screen; 'Sample Project' will be open on the left side of the screen.*

→ *Click the large X to exit ACL.*

You will use the remainder of this material to help you answer the assigned questions in the text. The first three functions (Quick Sort, Filters, and Computed Fields) are not considered ACL commands. The remaining functions included here are all ACL commands. You will use these commands in ACL homework problems that are included in selected chapters. The descriptions below provide a brief overview of the functions that will be used to complete those problems. Within each ACL homework problem in the text, you will see the commands needed to answer the problem listed within parentheses in that problem.

Quick Sort   Used to sort data in any field, either from lowest to highest or vice versa.
1. *Click on the column heading of the field you want to sort.*
2. *Right click using your mouse to find the → Quick Sort Ascending or Quick Sort Descending (you can right click Quick Sort Off to undo the sort).*

Filters   Used to ask questions of data in a table without adding a new field.
1. *Click the Edit View Filter button [icon] in an open table to enter the Edit View Filter window.*
2. *Use the Expression box to build an expression.*
3. The Expression box is where you build filters using the available fields in the current table, as well as the operators (=, < >, AND, etc.). There are three components to a filter: (1) field, (2) operator, and (3) a numeric value, character value, or date.
4. *In the Available Fields portion of the window, double-click the name of the field for which you are building a filter. Notice that the field name is inserted in the Expression box.*
5. *Use the operator buttons (=, +, <, >, etc.) and the numeric keypad on the keyboard to build the filter. Note:* If you are performing a recalculation to determine if the original calculation already in the data table is correct, use < > as the operator with no spaces between the less than and greater than signs.

6. *Enter an appropriate string or value after the operator. Use the following guidelines:*
   - **Numeric values**—enter as a number with no commas or dollar signs. For example, to enter US$1,000, type 1000.
   - **Character values**—enclose with one or two quotations. For example, to enter department D10, type "D10" or 'D10.' Use the same case as is used in the data field.
   - **Dates**—click on the Date button located just below the mathematical operators to open the Date Selector box. Click the drop-down arrow to enter the monthly calendar box. Select the date, then click OK.

7. For more complex filters, use the AND, OR, or NOT operators and repeat the preceding process for each portion of the filter. **After selecting an AND, OR, or NOT, it is necessary to repeat all three components** [(1) field, (2) operator, and (3) a numeric value, character value, or date] **of the filter.**

8. An example of an expression to select all invoices from transaction type IV with invoice dates equal to or before 31/12/2007 is as follows:

$$TXN\_TYPE = \text{"IV"} \text{ AND } INVDATE <= \text{`20071231`}$$

9. *Click OK to complete the filter.*
10. *If you want to change the filter, click* ▣ *again to return to the Edit View Filter window. Make changes in the filter and click OK.*
11. You can also apply additional commands to a filtered table until you remove the filter.
12. *Click the Remove Filter button* ▣ *after you have completed all additional tests on the filtered table to return to the unfiltered table.*

Computed Fields Used to ask questions of data in a table by adding a new field. The new field is derived from calculations using other fields in the table.

1. *Click Edit → Table Layout to open the Layout Options window.*
2. *Select the 'Edit Fields/Expressions' tab folder on the top row of the Layout window.*
3. *Click the Add a New Expression button* ▣, *which is the third button down on the left side of the window under the 'Edit Fields/Expressions' tab. (You may need to expand the window to see the* ▣.)
4. *Add a name for the computed field in the Name box that describes the new column. Also add a column title in the Alternative Column Title box, which will appear in the Table after you complete the new field.*
5. *Click the Expression button* ▣, *which is located to the right of the Name box to open the Expression box.*
6. *Build an expression in the Expression box in the same way as for filters.*
7. *After building the expression, click OK to return to the original tables window.*
8. *Click the Accept Entry button* ▣ *on the top left of the screen to save the new computed field.*
9. The new field can be added to the table view by completing the following steps:
   - Close the Edit Fields/Expressions window if it is still open.
   - *Return to the data table which contains all the data for the file you are examining. Place the cursor in the column heading to the right of where you want the new computed field to appear in the table view.*
   - *Right click and then Click Add Columns from the drop-down menu.*
   - *Double-click on the name of the new computed field you just created.*
   - *Click OK. The new computed field now appears in the table view.*

Age Command Used to accumulate data in a table by age, usually for accounts receivable.

1. *Click Analyze → Age to open the Age window.*
2. *Use the Age On drop-down arrow to select the date field you want to run the Age command on.*
3. *In the Subtotal Fields portion of the command dialog, click on the name of the numeric field you want to list for each aging interval.*
4. *Enter a date in the Cutoff Date box using the calendar. This date is used to calculate the aging. It is typically the client's year-end date.*
5. *Click OK to run the Age command.*

Classify Command Used to count and aggregate the number and percentage of records for each value of a character field and to subtotal the numeric fields for the field.

1. *Click any cell in the column for the document number or any other character field you want summarized (do not click the column heading).*
2. *Click Analyze → Classify, then select the field you want to classify on. Next click on the quantity field in the Subtotal Field that you want summarized.*
3. *Click OK.*

Count Command Used to count records in a table that you have filtered. (For a table that has not been filtered, the record count is indicated at the bottom of the open table.) After a filter is applied to a table, observe that there is now a ?/ in the lower left corner that replaces the original count.

1. *Click Analyze → Count Records.*
2. *Click OK. The new count replaces ?/ in the lower left corner.*

Duplicates Command Used to detect duplicates in the sequence of numbers in a table, usually document numbers.

1. *Click on the column heading for the document numbers you want to test for duplicates.*
2. *Click Analyze → Look for Duplicates.*
3. *The result is a list of duplicates if any exist. When prompted click on OK and type any output file name such as 'Duplicates' (you can change the radio button from 'file' to 'screen' under the output tab if you want to see the output on your screen and not save it to a file).*

Gaps Command Used to detect gaps in the sequence of numbers in a table, usually document numbers.

1. *Click on the column heading for the document numbers you want to test for gaps.*
2. *Click Analyze → Look for Gaps. The result is a table of gaps if any exist.*

Statistics Command Used to identify characteristics in client data files to better understand the data being audited.

1. *Click Analyze → Statistical → Statistics to open the Statistics window.*
2. *Select the numeric or date field(s) you want to generate statistics on by clicking on the line(s) containing the field name(s). Use the Shift or Control key to select more than one field.*
3. *Click OK to run the command.*

Stratify Command Used to accumulate stratification of numeric information in a field.

1. Select the field on which you intend to stratify. Use Quick Sort to identify large and small population items you want to exclude from the stratification.
2. *Click Analyze → Stratify to open the Stratify window.*
3. *Use the Stratify On drop-down arrow to choose the name of the field you want to stratify.*
4. *Enter the minimum and maximum values in the minimum and maximum boxes with no dollars or commas.*
5. *Click OK to run the Stratify command.*

Summarize Command Used to count records and accumulate numeric amounts for a character or date field.

1. *Click Analyze → Summarize to open the Summarize window.*
2. *In the Summarize On portion of the window, click on the field you want to summarize on.* For example, in the AP_Trans table in Sample_Project, if you want the total amount of all invoices for each vendor, you would summarize on vendor number. Once you click on the desired field, click 'OK.'
3. *In the Subtotal Fields portion of the window, click on the name of the numeric field you want to accumulate for each summary category* (for example, invoice amount).
4. *When prompted, click OK and type any name for the file you are summarizing such as 'Customers.'*
5. *Click OK for a new table.*

Total Command Used to total one or more data fields for a table.

1. *Click on the column heading for the column you want to total.*
2. *Click Analyze → Total Fields to obtain a total.*

GLOSSARY

Absence of causal connection | عدم وجود علاقة السببية
An auditor's legal defense under which the auditor contends that the damages claimed by the client were not brought about by any act of the auditor.

Acceptable audit risk | خطر المراجعة /التدقيق المقبول
A measure of how willing the auditor is to accept that the financial statements may be materially misstated after the audit is completed and an unmodified audit opinion has been issued; see also audit assurance.

Acceptable risk of assessing control risk too low (ARACR) | الخطر المقبول لتقييم خطر الرقابة فى مستوى منخفض
The risk that the auditor is willing to take of accepting a control as effective or a rate of monetary misstatements as tolerable when the true population exception rate is greater than the tolerable exception rate.

Acceptable risk of incorrect acceptance (ARIA) | الخطر المقبول للاعتقاد الخاطئ بصحة المعلومات
The risk that the auditor is willing to take of accepting a balance as correct when the true misstatement in the balance is equal to or greater than tolerable misstatement.

Acceptable risk of incorrect rejection (ARIR) | الخطر المقبول للرفض غير الصحيح للمعلومات
The risk that the auditor is willing to take of rejecting a balance as incorrect when it is not misstated by a material amount.

Accounting | المحاسبة
The recording, classifying, and summarizing of economic events in a logical manner for the purpose of providing financial information for decision making.

Accounting records | مستندات المحاسبة
The records of initial entries and other supporting documents such as invoices, cheques, fund transfers, contracts, minutes of meetings, reconciliations, and disclosures.

Accounts payable master file | أستاذ مساعد حسابات دائنة
A computer file for maintaining a record for each vendor of individual acquisitions, cash disbursements, acquisition returns and allowances, and vendor balances.

Accounts payable trial balance | ميزان مراجعة فرعي للحسابات الدائنة
A listing of the amount owed to each vendor at a point in time; prepared directly from the accounts payable master file.

Accounts receivable balance-related audit objectives | أهداف مراجعة ارصدة الحسابات المدينة
The eight specific audit objectives used by the auditor to decide the appropriate audit evidence for accounts receivable.

Accrued liabilities | الخصوم أو الالتزامات المستحقة
Estimated unpaid obligations for services or benefits that have been received prior to the balance sheet date; common accrued liabilities include accrued commissions, accrued income taxes, accrued payroll, and accrued rent.

Accrued payroll expenses | مصاريف المرتبات المستحقة
The liability accounts associated with payroll; these include accounts for accrued salaries and wages, accrued commissions, accrued bonuses, accrued benefits, and accrued payroll taxes.

Acquisition and payment cycle | دورة الشراء والسداد
The transaction cycle that includes the acquisition of and payment for goods and services from suppliers outside the organization.

Adverse opinion | الرأي المعارض
A report issued when the auditor believes the financial statements are so materially misstated or misleading as a whole that they do not present fairly the entity's financial position or the results of its operations and cash flows in conformity with IFRS.

Aged trial balance | ميزان المراجعة تحليل أعمار الديون
A listing of the balances in the accounts receivable master file at the balance sheet date broken down according to the amount of time passed between the date of sale and the balance sheet date.

Agreed-upon procedures engagement | الإجراءات المتفق عليها
An engagement in which the procedures to be performed are agreed upon by the auditor, the responsible party making the assertions, and the intended users of the auditor's report; the auditor's report is presented in the form of a negative assurance.

AICPA | الجمعية الأمريكية للمحاسبين القانونيين
American Institute of Certified Public Accountants, a voluntary organization of CPAs that sets professional requirements, conducts research, and publishes materials relevant to accounting, auditing, management consulting services, and taxes.

Allocation | التخصيص
The division of certain expenses, such as depreciation and manufacturing overhead, among several expense accounts.

Allocation of the preliminary judgment about materiality | توزيع التقدير المبدئى للأهمية النسبية
The process of assigning to each balance sheet account the misstatement amount considered to be material for that account based on the auditor's preliminary judgment.

Alternative audit procedures | إجراءات المراجعة البديلة
The follow-up of a positive confirmation not returned by the debtor with the use of documentation evidence to determine whether the recorded receivable exists.

Analytical (Audit) procedures | إجراءات المراجعة التحليلية
Use of comparisons and relationships to assess whether account balances or other data appear reasonable.

Analytical procedures | إجراءات الفحص التحليلى
Use of comparisons and relationships to assess whether account balances or other data appear reasonable.

Annual report | التقرير السنوي
The document prepared by the management of the company on an annual basis, to be presented to shareholders at the annual general meeting and includes the auditor's report, the audited financial statements, and board of directors' or chairman's report.

Application controls | وسائل رقابة التطبيقات الآلية
Controls related to a specific use of IT, such as the inputting, processing, and outputing of sales or cash receipts.

Application service providers (ASPs) | مقدمى خدمة تطبيقات آلية
A third-party entity that manages and supplies software applications or software-related services to customers through the internet.

Appropriateness of evidence | مدى مناسبة الادلة
A measure of the quality of evidence; appropriate evidence is relevant and reliable in meeting audit objectives for classes of transactions, account balances, and related disclosures.

Assessment inquiry | الاستفسار بغرض التقييم
Inquiry to corroborate or contradict prior information obtained.

Assessment of control risk | تقييم خطر الرقابة
A measure of the auditor's expectation that internal controls will neither prevent material misstatements from occurring nor detect and correct them if they have occurred; control risk is assessed for each transaction-related audit objective in a cycle or class of transactions.

Assurance engagement | اختبارات التأكد
A service in which the audit firm issues a report about the reliability of subject matter or of an assertion that is the responsibility of another party.

Assurance service | خدمات التأكد
An independent professional service that improves the quality of information for decision makers.

Attestation service | خدمات التحقيق
A type of assurance service in which the CPA firm issues a report about the reliability of an assertion that is the responsibility of another party.

Attribute | الخاصية
The characteristic being tested for in the population.

Attributes sampling | خصائص المعاينة معاينة الخصائص
A statistical, probabilistic method of sample evaluation that results in an estimate of the proportion of items in a population containing a characteristic or attribute of interest.

Audit assurance | تأكيدات المراجعة /التدقيق
A complement to acceptable audit risk; an acceptable audit risk of 2 percent is the same as audit assurance of 98 percent; also called overall assurance and level of assurance.

Audit committee | لجنة المراجعة /التدقيق
Selected members of a client's board of directors whose responsibilities include helping auditors to remain independent of management.

Audit documentation | مستندات المراجعة /التدقيق
The principal record of auditing procedures applied, evidence obtained, and conclusions reached by the auditor in the engagement.

Audit evidence | ادلة المراجعة
Any information used by the auditor to determine whether the information being audited is stated in accordance with established criteria.

Audit failure | فشل المراجعة أو التدقيق
A situation in which the auditor issues an incorrect audit opinion as the result of an underlying failure to comply with the requirements of auditing standards.

Audit file | ملف المراجعة /التدقيق
One or more folders or any other storage media whether in physical or electronic form, containing all records forming the audit documentation for a specific engagement.

Audit firm | مكتب المراجعة /التدقيق.
A sole practitioner, partnership, or corporation of professional accountants; an entity that controls such parties, through ownership, management, or other means; and an entity controlled by such parties, through ownership, management, or other means.

Audit of historical financial statements | تدقيق/مراجعة القوائم المالية التاريخية
A form of attestation service in which the auditor issues a written report stating whether the financial statements are in material conformity with accounting standards.

Audit plan | خطة المراجعة /التدقيق
A detailed direction on how to perform the audit, including the nature, timing, and extent of audit procedures to be undertaken by the auditor and his subordinates.

Audit procedure | أجراء المراجعة /التدقيق
Specific acts performed by the auditor in gathering evidence to determine if specific assertions are being met; or detailed instruction for the collection of a type of audit evidence.

Audit program | برنامج المراجعة /التدقيق
List of audit procedures for an audit area or an entire audit; the audit program always includes audit procedures and may also include sample sizes, items to select, and timing of the tests.

Audit program | برنامج المراجعة /التدقيق
The audit procedures resulting from the auditor's decisions about the appropriate audit procedures for each audit objective, class of transaction, and account balances organized in the format in which they will be performed.

Audit report | تقرير مراقب الحسابات
The communication of audit findings to users.

Audit risk | مخاطر المراجعة أو التدقيق
The risk that the auditor will conclude after conducting an adequate audit that the financial statements are fairly stated and an unqualified opinion can therefore be issued when, in fact, they are materially misstated.

Audit risk model | نموذج خطر المراجعة /التدقيق
A formal model reflecting the relationships between acceptable audit risk (AAR), inherent risk (IR), control risk (CR), and planned detection risk (PDR); PDR = AAR/(IR × CR).

Audit sampling | عينة المراجعة
Testing less than 100 percent of a population for the purpose of making inferences about that population.

Audit strategy | استراتيجية المراجعة /التدقيق
Overall approach to the audit that considers the nature of the client, risk of significant misstatements, and other factors such as the number of client locations and past effectiveness of client controls.

Auditing | المراجعة او التدقيق
The accumulation and evaluation of evidence about information to determine and report on the degree of correspondence between the information and established criteria.

Auditing around the computer | المراجعة/التدقيق حول الحاسب
Auditing without relying on and testing automated controls embedded in computer application programs, which is acceptable when the auditor has access to readable source documents that can be reconciled to detailed listings of output or when sufficient nonautomated controls exist.

Auditing through the computer | المراجعة /التدقيق عبرالحاسب
Auditing by testing automated internal controls and account balances electronically, generally because strong general controls exist.

Automated controls | وسائل الرقابة الآلية الداخلية
Application controls done by the computer.

Balance-related audit objectives | أهداف مراجعة الأرصدة
Eight audit objectives that must be met before the auditor can conclude that any given account balance is fairly stated; the general balance-related audit objectives are existence, completeness, accuracy, classification, cutoff, detail tie-in, realizable value, and rights and obligations.

Bank confirmation | مصادقة البنك
A form through which the bank responds to the auditor about bank balance and loan information provided on the confirmation.

Bank reconciliation | مذكرة تسوية البنك
The monthly reconciliation, usually prepared by client personnel, of the differences between the cash balance recorded in the general ledger and the amount in the bank account.

Blank or blind confirmation form | المصادقات العمياء (بدون أية بيانات)
A letter, addressed to the debtor, requesting the recipient to fill in the amount of the accounts receivable balance; it is considered a positive confirmation.

Block sample selection | اتيار العينة باستخدام المجموعات
A nonprobabilistic method of sample selection in which items are selected in measured sequences.

Board of directors | مجلس الأدارة
Persons elected by the entity's shareholders to manage, direct, and monitor the affairs of the company.

Branch bank accounts | حسابات البنك بالفرع
Separate bank accounts maintained at local banks by branches of a company.

Budgets | الموازنات
Written records of the client's expectations for the period; a comparison of budgets with actual results may indicate whether or not misstatements are likely.

Business failure | فشل الشركة
The situation when a business is unable to repay its lenders or meet the expectations of its investors because of economic or business conditions.

Business functions for the sales and collection cycle | الدورة التجارية لعمليات البيع والتحصيل النقدى
The key activities that an organization must complete to execute and record business transactions for sales, cash receipts, sales returns and allowances, write-off of uncollectible accounts, and bad debt expense.

Capital acquisition and repayment cycle | دورة الحصول على رأس المال والمدفو عات الخاصة به
The transaction cycle that involves the acquisition of capital resources in the form of interest-bearing debt and owners' equity, and the repayment of the capital.

Capital stock certificate record | سجل أسهم رأس المال
A record of the issuance and repurchase of capital stock for the life of the corporation.

Cash equivalents | أشباه النقود أو ما يعادل النقدية
Excess cash invested in short-term, highly liquid investments such as time deposits, certificates of deposit, and money market funds.

Certified public accountant | المحاسب المعتمد القانوني
A person who has met the country's regulatory requirements, including passing the Uniform CPA Examination, and has thus been certified; a CPA may have as his or her primary responsibility the performance of the audit function on published historical financial statements of commercial and noncommercial financial entities.

Chart of accounts | دليل الحسابات
A listing of all the entity's accounts, which classifies transactions into individual balance sheet and income statement accounts.

Classes of transactions in the sales and collection cycle | أنواع العمليات الخاصة بدورة البيع والتحصيل
The categories of transactions for the sales and collection cycle in a typical company: sales, cash receipts, sales returns and allowances, write-off of uncollectible accounts, and bad debt expense.

Client business risk | خطر أعمال العميل
The risk that the client will fail to achieve its objectives related to (1) reliability of financial reporting, (2) effectiveness and efficiency of operations, and (3) compliance with laws and regulations.

Close family | الأقارب
Any parent, child, or sibling who is not a dependent. (See immediate family.)

Closely held corporation | الشركات المغلقة
Corporation with stock that is not publicly traded; typically, there are only a few shareholders and few, if any, capital stock account transactions during the year.

Collusion | تواطؤ
A cooperative effort among employees to steal assets or misstate records.

Commitments | التعهدات
Agreements that the entity will hold to a fixed set of conditions, such as the purchase or sale of merchandise at a stated price, at a future date, regardless of what happens to profits or to the economy as a whole.

Comparative financial statements | القوائم المالية المقارنة
Comparative information including amounts and other disclosures related to the prior period and used for comparison with the financial statements of the current period.

Compensating control | الرقابة التعويضية
A control elsewhere in the system that offsets the absence of a key control.

Compilation service | خدمات التجميع
A nonaudit engagement in which the accountant undertakes to present, in the form of financial statements, information that is the representation of management, without undertaking to express any assurance on the statements.

Completing the audit checklist | إعداد قائمة تحقيق أعمال المراجعة
A reminder to the auditor of aspects of the audit that may have been overlooked.

Compliance audit | مراجعة الالتزام
(1) A review of an organization's financial records performed to determine whether the organization is following specific procedures, rules, or regulations set by some higher authority; (2) an audit performed to determine whether an entity that recieves financial assistance from the federal government has complied with specific laws and regulations.

Computed upper exception rate (CUER) | معدل الاستثناء المحتسب للمستوى الأعلى
The upper limit of the probable population exception rate; the highest exception rate in the population at a given ARACR.

Confirmation | المصادقات
The auditor's receipt of a written or oral response from an independent third party verifying the accuracy of information requested.

Contingent fee | الأتعاب المشروطة
A fee calculated on a predetermined basis relating to the outcome of a transaction or the result of the services performed by the firm. A fee that is established by a court or other public authority is not a contingent fee.

Contingent liability | الالتزامات العرضية
A potential future obligation to an outside party for an unknown amount resulting from activities that have already taken place.

Contributory negligence | الإهمال المؤثر
An auditor's legal defense under which the auditor claims that the client failed to perform certain obligations and that it is the client's failure to perform those obligations that brought about the claimed damages.

Control activities | مقومات أو أنشطة الرقابة
Policies and procedures, in addition to those included in the other four components of internal control, that help ensure that necessary actions are taken to address risks in the achievement of the entity's objectives; they typically include the following five specific control activities: (1) adequate separation of duties, (2) proper authorization of transactions and activities, (3) adequate documents and records, (4) physical control over assets and records, and (5) independent checks on performance.

Control deficiency | عنصر أو نقطة ضعف في نظم الرقابة
A deficiency in the design or operation of controls that does not permit company personnel to prevent or detect misstatements on a timely basis.

Control environment | بيئة الرقابة
The actions, policies, and procedures that reflect the overall attitudes of top management, directors, and owners of an entity about internal control and its importance to the entity.

Control risk | خطر الرقابة
A measure of the auditor's assessment of the likelihood that misstatements exceeding a tolerable amount in a segment will not be prevented or detected by the client's internal controls.

Control risk matrix | مصفوفة خطر الرقابة
A methodology used to help the auditor assess control risk by matching key internal controls and internal control deficiencies with transaction-related audit objectives.

Corporate minutes | محاضر الشركات أو المنشآت
The official record of the meetings of a corporation's board of directors and stockholders, in which corporate issues, such as the declaration of dividends and the approval of contracts, are documented.

Corresponding figures | أرقام العام الماضي
Comparative information including amounts and other disclosures related to prior period and used as an integral part of the current period financial statements, and are intended to be read only in relation to the amounts and disclosures relating to the current period.

Cost accounting controls | الرقابة على محاسبة التكاليف
Controls over physical inventory and the related costs from the point at which raw materials are requisitioned to the point at which the manufactured product is completed and transferred to storage.

Cost accounting records | مستندات محاسبة التكاليف
The accounting records concerned with the manufacture and processing of the goods and storing finished goods.

Criminal liability for accountants | المسئولية الجنائية للمحاسبين
Defrauding a person through knowing involvement with false financial statements.

Current files | الملف الجاري
All audit files applicable to the year under audit.

Cutoff bank statement | كشف حساب القطع
A partial-period bank statement and the related cancelled checks, duplicate deposit slips, and other documents included in bank statements, mailed by the bank directly to the auditor; the auditor uses it to verify reconciling items on the client's year-end bank reconciliation.

Cutoff misstatements | الأخطاء المرتبطة باختبارات القطع
Misstatements that take place as a result of current period transactions being recorded in a subsequent period, or subsequent period transactions being recorded in the current period.

Cutoff tests | اختبارات القطع
Tests to determine whether transactions recorded a few days before and after the balance sheet date are included in the correct period.

Cycle approach | أساس تبويب حسابات المراجعة
A method of dividing an audit by keeping closely related types of transactions and account balances in the same segment.

Database management systems | نظم إدارة قواعد البيانات
Hardware and software systems that allow clients to establish and maintain databases shared by multiple applications.

Debit memo | إشعار مدين
A document indicating a reduction in the amount owed to a vendor because of returned goods or an allowance granted.

Difference estimation | تقديرات الاختلافات
A method of variables sampling in which the auditor estimates the population misstatement by multiplying the average misstatement in the sample by the total number of population items and also calculates sampling risk.

Digital signatures | التوقيع الالكترونى
Electronic certificates that are used to authenticate the validity of individuals and companies conducting business electronically.

Direct financial interest | المصالح المالية المباشرة
The ownership of stock or other equity shares by members or their immediate family.

Direct projection estimate of misstatement | التقدير المباشر للتحريف
Estimate of likely misstatement in a population based on a sample, excluding sampling risk, and calculated as net misstatements in the sample, divided by the total sampled, multiplied by the total recorded population value.

Directed sample selection | اختيار العينة الموجه
A nonprobabilistic method of sample selection in which each item in the sample is selected based on some judgmental criteria established by the auditor.

Disclaimer of opinion | الأمتناع عن أبداء الرأي
A report issued when the auditor is not able to become satisfied that the overall financial statements are fairly presented or the auditor is not independent.

Dual-dated audit report | تقرير المراجع ذو التاريخين
The use of one audit report date for normal subsequent events and a later date for one or more subsequent events that come to the auditor's attention after the field work has been completed.

Earnings management | إدارة الأرباح
Deliberate actions taken by management to meet earnings objectives.

Economy and efficiency audit | مراجعة الكفاءة واقتصاديات التشغيل
A government audit to determine whether an entity is acquiring, protecting, and using its resources economically and efficiently; the causes of any inefficiencies or uneconomical practices; and whether the entity has complied with laws and regulations concerning matters of economy and efficiency.

Effectiveness | الفعالية
The degree to which the organization's objectives are accomplished.

Efficiency | الكفاءة
The degree to which costs are reduced without reducing effectiveness.

Embedded audit module approach | طريقة المراجعة /التدقيق بإدخال مثال عملى بالنظام
A method of auditing transactions processed by IT whereby the auditor embeds a module in the client's application software to identify transactions with characteristics that are of interest to the auditor; the auditor is then able to analyze these transactions on a real-time, continuous basis as client transactions are processed.

Emphasis of a matter paragraph |
An unmodified report in which the financial statements are fairly presented, but the auditor believes it is important, or is required, to refer to a matter other than those presented or disclosed in the financial statements that, in the auditor's judgment, is relevant to users' understanding of the audit, the auditor's responsibilities or the auditor's report.

Encryption techniques | طرق التشفير
Computer programs that change a standard message into one that is coded, then decoded by the recipient using a decryption program.

Engagement letter | خطاب التكليف
An agreement between the CPA firm and the client as to the terms of the engagement for the conduct of the audit and related services.

Engagement partner | الشريك المسئول
The partner or any other person in the CPA firm who would responsible to complete the engagement and certify the financial statements.

Engagement risk | خطر قبول المهمة
The risk that the auditor or audit firm will suffer harm because of a client relationship, even though the audit report rendered for the client was correct.

Entity-level controls | الرقابة على مستوى الوحدة
Controls that have a pervasive effect on the entity's system of internal control; also referred to as company-level controls.

Error | الخطأ
An unintentional misstatement of the financial statements.

Estimated population exception rate (EPER) | معدل الاستثناء لتقديرات المجتمع
Exception rate the auditor expects to find in the population before testing begins.

Ethical dilemma | المأزق الاخلاقى
A situation in which a decision must be made about the appropriate behavior.

Ethics | الأخلاق
An integrated structure of code of professional conduct and set of best practices established from moral duties and responsibilities which show how a professional should behave in given circumstances.

Evidence mix | مجموعة أو مزيج الأدلة
The combination of the types of tests to obtain sufficient appropriate evidence for a cycle; there are likely to be variations in the mix from cycle to cycle depending on the circumstances of the audit.

Examination | الفحص
An assurance engagement that results in a positive opinion as to whether or not the assertions under examination conform with the applicable criteria.

Exception rate | معدل الاستثناء
The percent of items in a population that include exceptions in prescribed controls or monetary correctness.

Expense account analysis | تحليل حساب المصروفات
The examination of underlying documentation of individual transactions and amounts making up the total of an expense account.

External document | المستند الخارجى
A document, such as a vendor's invoice, that has been used by an outside party to the transaction being documented and that the client now has or can easily obtain.

Financial interest | المصالح المالية
An interest in an equity or other security, debenture, loan, or other debt instrument of an entity, including rights and obligations to acquire such an interest and derivatives directly related to such interest.

Financial statement audit | مراجعة القوائم المالية
An audit conducted to determine whether the overall financial statements of an entity are stated in accordance with specified criteria (usually U.S., international accounting standards or local accounting standards).

Financial statement disclosure checklist | قائمة استقصاء الخاصة بالقوائم المالية
A questionnaire that reminds the auditor of disclosure problems commonly encountered in audits and that facilitates final review of the entire audit by an independent partner.

Firewall | برامج الحماية (الجدار الناري)
A system of hardware and software that monitors and controls the flow of e-commerce communications by channeling all network connections through a control gateway.

Fixed asset master file | استاذ مساعد أصول ثابتة
A computer file containing records for each piece of equipment and other types of property owned; the primary accounting record for manufacturing equipment and other property, plant, and equipment accounts.

Flowchart | خريطة تدفق
A diagrammatic representation of the client's documents and records and the sequence in which they are processed.

FOB destination | التسليم محل المشترى
Shipping contract in which title to the goods passes to the buyer when the goods are received.

FOB origin | التسليم محل البائع
Shipping contract in which title to the goods passes to the buyer at the time that the goods are shipped.

Forecasts | توقعات
Prospective financial statements that present an entity's expected financial position, results of operations, and cash flows for future periods, to the best of the responsible party's knowledge and belief.

Forensic auditor | محلل ومكتشف الغش
The process of investigating cases of fraud in the company's financial statements, accounting books, and records and any other documents used in the company's operations and white-collar crime.

Foreseeable users | المستخدمين المرتقبين
An unlimited class of users that the auditor should have reasonably been able to foresee as being likely users of financial statements.

Foreseen users | المستخدمين المحددين
Members of a limited class of users whom the auditor is aware will rely on the financial statements.

Fraud | الغش
An intentional misstatement of the financial statements.

Fraud risk factors | عناصر خطر الغش
Entity factors that increase the risk of fraud.

Fraud triangle | مثلث الغش
The three conditions of fraud: incentives/pressures, opportunities, and attitudes/rationalization.

Fraudulent financial reporting | التلاعب بالقوائم المالية
Intentional misstatements or omissions of amounts or disclosures in financial statements to deceive users.

Functional audit | مراجعة الأنشطة او الأنظمة
An operational audit that deals with one or more specific functions within an organization, such as the payroll function or the production engineering function.

Further audit procedures | إجراءات المراجعة /التدقيق الإضافية
Combination of tests of controls, substantive tests of transactions, analytical procedures, and tests of details of balances performed in response to risks of material misstatement identified by the auditor's risk assessment procedures.

General authorization | الترخيص العام
Companywide policies for the approval of all transactions within stated limits.

General cash account | حساب البنك العام
The primary bank account for most organizations; virtually all cash receipts and disbursements flow through this account at some time.

General controls | وسائل الرقابة العامة
Controls that relate to all parts of the IT function.

Generalized audit software (GAS) | برامج المراجعة /التدقيق العامة
Computer programs used by auditors that provide data retrieval, data manipulation, and reporting capabilities specifically oriented to the needs of auditors.

Generally accepted auditing standards (GAAS) | معايير المراجعة /التدقيق المتعارف عليها
Ten auditing standards, developed by the AICPA, consisting of general standards, standards of field work, and standards of reporting, along with interpretations; often called auditing standards.

Going concern | فرض ألأستمرارية
The assumption under which a business is established and reflects the financial viability of the business enterprise.

Government accountability office auditor | جهاز المحاسبات الحكومى
An auditor working for the U.S. Government Accountability Office (GAO) or the equivalent in each of the Arab world countries; the GAO reports to and is responsible solely to congress or parliament.

Haphazard sample selection | اختيار العينات غير المنتظم
A nonprobabilistic method of sample selection in which items are chosen without regard to their size, source, or other distinguishing characteristics.

Hardware controls | وسائل الرقابة على الحاسب
Controls built into the computer equipment by the manufacturer to detect and report equipment failure.

Illegal acts | مخالفة القوانين
Violations of laws or government regulations other than fraud.

Immediate family | الأقارب الأقرباء
A spouse or dependent.

Imprest payroll account | الحساب البنكى الخاص بالمرتبات
A bank account to which the exact amount of payroll for the pay period is transferred by check or wire transfer from the employer's general cash account.

Imprest petty cash fund | العهدة المالية
A fund of cash maintained within the company for small cash acquisitions or to cash employees' checks; the fund's fixed balance is comparatively small and is periodically reimbursed.

Income smoothing | تحقيق توازن الإيرادات
Form of earnings management in which revenues and expenses are shifted between periods to reduce fluctuations in earnings.

Independence in appearance | الاستقلال الظاهرى
The auditor's ability to maintain an unbiased viewpoint in the eyes of others.

Independence of mind | الاستقلال الذهنى
The auditor's ability to take an unbiased viewpoint in the performance of professional services.

Independent auditors | المراجع المستقل
Certified public accountants or accounting firms that perform audits of commercial and non-commercial financial entities.

Independent checks | الفحص المستقل
Internal control activities designed for the continuous internal verification of other controls.

Independent registrar | المسجل المستقل
Outside person engaged by a corporation to make sure that its stock is issued in accordance with capital stock provisions in the corporate charter and authorizations by the board of directors.

Independent review | الفحص المستقل
A review of the financial statements and the entire set of audit files by a completely independent reviewer to whom the audit team must justify the evidence accumulated and the conclusions reached.

Indirect financial interest | المصالح المالية غير المباشرة
A financial interest beneficially owned through a collective investment vehicle, estate, trust, or other intermediary over which the individual or entity has no control or ability to influence investment decisions. A close, but not direct, ownership relationship between the auditor and the client; an example is the ownership of stock by a member's grandparent.

Information and communication | البيانات والاتصالات
The set of manual and/or computerized procedures that initiates, records, processes, and reports an entity's transactions and maintains accountability for the related assets.

Information asymmetry | تفاوت المعلومات
The concept that the manager generally has more information about the true financial position, results of operations, and cash flow of the company than the absentee owner.

Information risk | خطر المعلومات
The risk that information upon which a business decision is made is inaccurate.

Informational inquiry | الاستفسار بغرض الحصول على معلومات
Inquiry to obtain information about facts and details the auditor does not have.

Inherent risk | الخطر الكامن
A measure of the auditor's assessment of the likelihood that there are material misstatements in a segment before considering the effectiveness of internal control.

Initial audit planning | التخطيط المبدئي أو الأولى للمراجعة
Involves deciding whether to accept or continue doing the audit for the client, identifying the client's reasons for the audit, obtaining an engagement letter, and developing an audit strategy.

Initial sample size | حجم العينة الأولى
Sample size determined by professional judgment (nonstatistical sampling) or by statistical tables (attributes sampling).

Input controls | وسائل الرقابة على المدخلات
Controls designed by an organization to ensure that the information to be processed by the computer is authorized, accurate, and complete.

Inquiry | الاستفسار
The obtaining of written or oral information from the client in response to specific questions during the audit.

Inquiry of the client's attorneys | الاستفسار من محامى العميل
A letter from the client requesting that legal counsel inform the auditor of pending litigation or any other information involving legal counsel that is relevant to financial statement disclosure.

Inspection | الفحص المستندي
The auditor's examination of the client's documents and records to substantiate the information that is or should be included in the financial statements.

Inspection of records and documents | الفحص المستندي والدفتري
Examination of internal and external documents and records whether they are in paper form, electronic form, or other media.

Institute of Internal Auditors (IIA) | جمعية المراجعين الداخليين
Organization for internal auditors that establishes ethical and practice standards, provides education, and encourages professionalism for its members.

Insurance register | دفتر أو سجل التأمينات
A record of insurance policies in force and the expiration date of each policy.

Internal audit function | وظيفة المراجعة الداخلية
An evaluation activity performed by qualified and experienced internal auditors who are responsible to examine, assess, and monitor the effectiveness of the internal control to prevent and detect fraud and tests daily transactions of the company.

Internal auditors | المراجع الداخلى
Auditors employed by a company to audit and report directly to the company's board of directors and management.

Internal control | الرقابة الداخلية
A process designed to provide reasonable assurance regarding the achievement of management's objectives in the following categories: (1) reliability of financial reporting, (2) effectiveness and efficiency of operations, and (3) compliance with applicable laws and regulations.

Internal control over financial reporting |
الرقابة الداخلية عن التقارير المالية
An engagement in which the auditor reports on the effectiveness of internal control over financial reporting; such reports are required for public companies under Section 404 of the Sarbanes–Oxley Act in the U.S.

Internal control questionnaire |
قائمة استقصاء أو استبيان الرقابة الداخلية
A series of questions about the controls in each audit area used as a means of indicating to the auditor aspects of internal control that may be inadequate.

Internal document | المستند الداخلى
A document, such as an employee time report, that is prepared and used within the client's organization.

International Standards for the Professional Practice of Internal Auditing | المعايير الدولية للأداء المهني للمراجعة الداخلية
Guidelines issued by the Institute of Internal Auditors covering the attributes and performance of internal auditors.

International Standards on Auditing (ISAs) | معايير المراجعة /التدقيق الدولية
Statements issued by the International Auditing and Assurance Standards Board of the International Federation of Accountants to promote international acceptance of auditing standards.

Interrogative inquiry | الاستفسار بغرض التحقيق
Inquiry used to determine if the interviewee is being deceptive or purposefully omitting disclosure of key knowledge of facts, events, or circumstances.

Inventory and warehousing cycle | دورة المخازن والمخزون
The transaction cycle that involves the physical flow of goods through the organization, as well as related costs.

Inventory compilation tests | اختبارات شاملة للمخزون
Audit procedures used to verify whether physical counts of inventory are correctly summarized, inventory quantities and prices are correctly extended, and extended inventory is correctly footed.

Inventory price tests | اختبارات تسعير المخزون
Audit procedures used to verify the costs used to value physical inventory.

Invoice confirmation | مصادقات خاصة بالفواتير
A type of positive confirmation in which an individual invoice is confirmed, rather than the customer's entire accounts receivable balance.

Islamic accounting | المحاسبة الإسلامية
An accounting process which provides appropriate information (not necessarily limited to financial data) to stakeholders of an entity which will enable them to ensure that it is continuously operating within the boundaries of Shari'a and delivering on its socioeconomic objectives.

Job cost system | نظم تكاليف الأوامر
System of cost accounting in which costs are accumulated by individual jobs when material is used and labor costs are incurred.

Key audit partner | الشركاء الرئيسيين للمراجعة /التدقيق
The engagement partner, the individual responsible for the engagement quality control review, and other audit partners, if any, on the engagement team who make key decisions or judgments on significant matters with respect to the audit of the financial statements on which the firm will express an opinion. Depending upon the circumstances and the role of the individuals on the audit, 'other audit partners' may include, for example, audit partners responsible for significant subsidiaries or divisions.

Key controls | عناصر أو أساليب الرقابة الأساسية
Controls that are expected to have the greatest effect on meeting the audit objectives.

Kiting | تحويلات غير قانونية
The transfer of money from one bank to another and improperly recording the transfer so that the amount is recorded as an asset in both accounts; this practice is used by embezzlers to cover a theft of cash.

Known misstatements | التحريف المعلوم
Specific misstatements in a class of transactions or account balance identified during the audit.

Lack of duty to perform | عدم وجود واجب تعاقدي
An auditor's legal defense under which the auditor claims that no contract existed with the client; therefore, no duty existed to perform the disputed service.

Lapping of accounts receivable | ترحيل حسابات مدينة
The postponement of entries for the collection of receivables to conceal an existing cash shortage.

Lead schedule | المستند المؤيد
An audit schedule that contains the detailed accounts from the general ledger making up a line item total in the working trial balance.

Legal liability | المسئولية القانونية
The professional's obligation under the law to provide a reasonable level of care while performing work for those served.

Letter of representation | خطاب التمثيل
A written communication from the client to the auditor formalizing statements that the client has made about matters pertinent to the audit.

Likely misstatements | التحريف المتوقع
Misstatements that arise from either differences between management's and the auditor's judgment about estimates of account balances or from projections of misstatements based on the auditor's test of a sample from a population.

Local area networks (LANs) | الشبكات المحلية
Networks that connect computer equipment, data files, software, and peripheral equipment within a local area, such as a single building or a small cluster of buildings, for intracompany use.

Management assertions | تأكيدات الإدارة
Implied or expressed representations by management about classes of transactions, related account balances, and presentation and disclosures in the financial statements.

Management letter | تقرير المراجعة/التدقيق التفصيلى
An optional letter written by the auditor to a client's management containing the auditor's recommendations for improving any aspect of the client's business.

Manual controls | وسائل الرقابة اليدوية
Application controls done by people.

Material misstatement | التحريف الهام
A misstatement in the financial statements, knowledge of which would affect a decision of a reasonable user of the statements.

Material weakness | نقاط الضعف الهامة
A significant deficiency in internal control that, by itself, or in combination with other significant deficiencies, results in a reasonable possibility that a material misstatement of the financial statements will not be prevented or detected.

Materiality | الأهمية النسبية
The magnitude of an omission or misstatement of accounting information that, in the light of surrounding circumstances, makes it probable that the judgment of a reasonable person relying on the information would have been changed or influenced by the omission or misstatement.

Mean-per-unit estimation | تقدير المتوسط للوحدة
A method of variables sampling in which the auditor estimates the audited value of a population by multiplying the average audited value of the sample by the population size and also calculates sampling risk.

Misappropriation of assets | سرقة الأصول
A fraud involving the theft of an entity's assets.

Misstatement bounds | حدود المخالفات
An estimate of the largest likely overstatements and understatements in a population at a given ARIA, using monetary unit sampling.

Misstatement of fact | تحريف الحقائق
Information contained in documents related to audited financial statements that is not related to matters appearing in the audited financial statements, and is incorrectly measured, presented, or disclosed.

Monetary unit sampling (MUS) | اخذ عينات وحدة نقدية
A statistical sampling method that provides upper and lower misstatement bounds expressed in monetary amounts; also referred to as dollar unit sampling, cumulative monetary amount sampling, and sampling with probability proportional to size.

Monitoring | الرقابة اللاحقة
Management's ongoing and periodic assessment of the quality of internal control performance to determine that controls are operating as intended and are modified when needed.

Narrative | الشرح الوصفي
A written description of a client's internal controls, including the origin, processing, and disposition of documents and records, and the relevant control procedures.

Negative confirmation | المصادقات السلبية
A letter, addressed to the debtor, requesting a response only if the recipient disagrees with the amount of the stated account balance.

Non-negligent performance | عدم وجود إهمال في الأداء
An auditor's legal defense under which the auditor claims that the audit was performed in accordance with auditing standards.

Nonprobabilistic sample selection | اختيار العينة غير الاحصائي
A method of sample selection in which the auditor uses professional judgment to select items from the population.

Nonsampling risk | الخطر غير الناتج عن المعاينة
The risk that the auditor fails to identify existing exceptions in the sample; nonsampling risk (nonsampling error) is caused by failure to recognize exceptions and by inappropriate or ineffective audit procedures.

Nonstatistical sampling | اختيار العينة بأسلوب غير احصائي
The auditor's use of professional judgment to select sample items, estimate the population values, and estimate sampling risk.

Note payable | أوراق دفع
A legal obligation to a creditor, which may be unsecured or secured by assets.

Observation | الملاحظة
The use of the senses to assess client activities.

Occurrence rate | معدل الحدوث
See Exception rate.

Operational audit | مراجعة العمليات
A review of any part of an organization's operating procedures and methods for the purpose of evaluating efficiency and effectiveness.

Operational auditing | مراجعة الأداء أو عمليات التشغيل
The review of an organization for efficiency and effectiveness. The terms management auditing, performance auditing, and operational auditing are synonymous terms.

Organizational audit | مراجعة الوحدات التنظيمية
An operational audit that deals with an entire organizational unit, such as a department, branch, or subsidiary, to determine how efficiently and effectively functions interact.

Other information | المعلومات الأخرى
Information that could be financial or non-financial (other than the client's financial statements and the auditor's report thereon) which is required to be included with the audited financial statements and the auditor's report either by law, regulation, or custom.

Other information included in annual reports | المعلومات الأخرى بالتقرير السنوي
Information that is not a part of the financial statements but is published with them; auditors must read this information for inconsistencies with the financial statements.

Other matter paragraph | فقرة أيضاحية أضافية
An unmodified report in which the financial statements are fairly presented, but the auditor believes it is important, or is required, to refer to a matter other than those presented or disclosed in the financial statements that, in the auditor's judgment, is relevant to users' understanding of the audit, the auditor's responsibilities, or the auditor's report.

Output controls | وسائل الرقابة على المخرجات
Controls designed to ensure that computer-generated data are valid, accurate, complete, and distributed only to authorized people.

Overall audit strategy | الأستراتيجية العامة للمراجعة /للتدقيق
The auditor's general plan for the proposed performance of the audit. The plan identifies the scope, timing, staffing, and direction of the audit and is the first step to prepare a detailed audit plan to ensure a quality audit.

Parallel simulation testing | اختبارات المحاكاة المتوازية
An audit testing approach that involves the auditor's use of audit software, either purchased or programmed by the auditor, to replicate some part of a client's application system.

Parallel testing | الاختبارات المتوازية
A company's computer testing approach that involves operating the old and new systems simultaneously.

Partner | الشريك
Any individual with authority to bind the firm with respect to the performance of a professional services engagement.

Payroll and personnel cycle | دورة المرتبات و الأجور
The transaction cycle that begins with the hiring of personnel, includes obtaining and accounting for services from the employees, and ends with payment to the employees for the services performed and to the government and other institutions for withheld and accrued payroll taxes and benefits.

Payroll master file | استاذ مساعد الأجور
A computer file for recording each payroll transaction for each employee and maintaining total employee wages paid and related data for the year to date.

Peer review | تقييم أداء المراجع
The review by CPAs of a CPA firm's compliance with its quality control system.

Permanent files | الملف الدائم
Auditors' files that contain data of a historical or continuing nature pertinent to the current audit such as copies of articles of incorporation (or association), bylaws, bond indentures, and contracts.

Perpetual inventory master file | أستاذ مساعد المخزون باستخدام الجرد
A continuously updated computerized record of inventory items purchased, used, sold, and on hand for merchandise, raw materials, and finished goods.

Personnel records | ملفات العاملين
Records that include such data as the date of employment, personnel investigations, rates of pay, authorized deductions, performance evaluations, and termination of employment.

Persuasiveness of evidence | مدى معقولية الأدلة
The degree to which the auditor is convinced that the evidence supports the audit opinion; the two determinants of persuasiveness are the appropriateness and sufficiency of the evidence.

Pervasive | مخالفة جسيمة
A misstatement or misstatements contained in the audited financial statements that are considered highly material in its effects on users' decisions concerning such statements.

Phases of the audit process | مراحل تنفيذ أعمال المراجعة
The four aspects of a complete audit: (1) plan and design an audit approach, (2) perform tests of controls and substantive tests of transactions, (3) perform analytical procedures and tests of details of balances, and (4) complete the audit and issue an audit report.

Phases of the audit process | مراحل عملية المراجعة /التدقيق
The four aspects of a complete audit: (1) plan and design an audit approach, (2) perform tests of controls and substantive tests of transactions, (3) perform analytical procedures and tests of details of balances, and (4) complete the audit and issue an audit report.

Physical examination | الجرد الفعلى
The auditor's inspection or count of a tangible asset.

Pilot testing | الاختبار المبدئى
A company's computer testing approach that involves implementing a new system in just one part of the organization, while maintaining the old system at other locations.

Planned detection risk | خطر الاكتشاف المخطط
A measure of the risk that audit evidence for a segment will fail to detect misstatements exceeding a tolerable amount, should such misstatements exist; PDR = AAR/ (IR × CR).

Point estimate | تقدير النقطة
A method of projecting from the sample to the population to estimate the population misstatement, commonly by assuming that misstatements in the unaudited population are proportional to the misstatements found in the sample.

Positive confirmation | المصادقات الايجابية
A letter, addressed to the debtor, requesting that the recipient indicate directly on the letter whether the stated account balance is correct or incorrect and, if incorrect, by what amount.

Preliminary judgment of materiality | التقدير الاولى للأهمية النسبية
The maximum amount by which the auditor believes that the statements could be misstated and still not affect the decisions of reasonable users; used in audit planning.

Premature revenue recognition | الاعتراف بالإيراد قبل تحققه
Recognition of revenue before IFRS or local accounting standards' requirements for recording revenue have been met.

Presentation and disclosure-related audit objectives | أهداف العرض والإفصاح فى المراجعة
Three audit objectives that must be met before the auditor can conclude that presentation and disclosures are fairly stated; the three presentation and disclosure-related audit objectives are completeness, valuation and accuracy, and classification and understandability.

Probabilistic sample selection | اختيار العينة الاحتمالى
A method of selecting a sample such that each population item has a known probability of being included in the sample and the sample is selected by a random process.

Probability proportional to size sample selection (PPS) | المعاينة على أساس الاحتمالات النسبية للحجم
Sample selection of individual dollars in a population by the use of random or systematic sample selection.

Procedures to obtain an understanding | إجراءات للحصول على تفهم
Procedures used by the auditor to gather evidence about the design and implementation of specific controls.

Procedures to obtain an understanding of internal control | إجراءات تفهم نظم الرقابة الداخلية
Procedures used by the auditor to gather evidence about the design and implementation of specific controls.

Process cost system | نظم تكاليف المراحل
System of cost accounting in which costs are accumulated for a process, with unit costs for each process assigned to the products passing through the process.

Processing controls | وسائل الرقابة على التشغيل
Controls designed to ensure that data input into the system are accurately and completely processed.

Professional accountant | المحاسب المهنى
An individual who is a member of an IFAC member body.

Professional accountant in business | المحاسب المهني فى السوق
A professional accountant employed or engaged in an executive or non-executive capacity in such areas as commerce, industry, service, the public sector, education, the not-for-profit sector, regulatory bodies or professional bodies, or a professional accountant contracted by such entities.

Professional services | الخدمات المهنية
Services requiring accountancy or related skills performed by a professional accountant, including accounting, auditing, taxation, management consulting, and financial management services.

Professional skepticism | الشك المهني

An attitude of the auditor that neither assumes management is dishonest nor assumes unquestioned honesty.

Professionalism | المهنية

The conduct, aims, or qualities that characterize or mark a profession or professional person.

Program audit | برنامج المراجعة

A government audit to determine the extent to which the desired results or benefits established by the legislature or other authorizing body are being achieved; the effectiveness of organizations, programs, activities, or functions; and whether the entity has complied with laws and regulations applicable to the program.

Projections | تنبؤات

Prospective financial statements that present an entity's financial position and results of operations and cash flows for future periods, to the best of the responsible party's knowledge and belief, given one or more hypothetical assumptions.

Proof of cash | التحقق من النقدية

A four-column audit schedule prepared by the auditor to reconcile the bank's record of the client's beginning balance, cash deposits, cleared checks, and ending balance for the period with the client's records.

Proof of cash receipts | التحقق من صحة المتحصلات النقدية

An audit procedure to test whether all recorded cash receipts have been deposited in the bank account by reconciling the total cash receipts recorded in the cash receipts journal for a given period with the actual deposits made to the bank.

Prospective financial statements | القوائم المالية المستقبلية

Financial statements that deal with expected future data rather than with historical data.

Prudent person concept | مفهوم الشخص الحذر

The legal concept that a person has a duty to exercise reasonable care and diligence in the performance of obligations to another.

Public Company Accounting Oversight Board (PCAOB) | الهيئة الحكومية للإشراف على مراجعة شركات مسجلة بالبورصات الأمريكية

Board created by the Sarbanes–Oxley Act to oversee auditors of public companies, including establishing auditing and quality control standards and performing inspections of registered accounting CPA firms.

Public company interim review | الفحص الدوري للشركات المسجلة بالبورصة

Reviews of interim, unaudited financial information performed to help public companies meet their reporting responsibilities to regulatory agencies.

Public interest entity | شركات ذات النفع العام

A listed entity, and an entity defined by regulation or legislation as a public interest entity or for which the audit is required by regulation or legislation to be conducted in compliance with the same independence requirements that apply to the audit of listed entities.

Publicly held corporation | شركات الاكتتاب العام

Corporation with stock that is publicly traded; typically, there are many shareholders and frequent changes in the ownership of the stock.

Purchase order | أمر شراء

A document prepared by the purchasing department indicating the description, quantity, and related information for goods and services that the company intends to purchase.

Purchase requisition | طلب شراء

Request by an authorized employee to the purchasing department to place an order for inventory and other items used by an entity.

Qualified opinion | الرأي المتحفظ

A report issued when the auditor believes that the overall financial statements are fairly stated but that either the scope of the audit was limited or the financial data indicated a failure to follow IFRS.

Quality control | رقابة الجودة

Methods used by a CPA firm to ensure that the firm meets its professional responsibilities to clients and others.

Random number table | جداول الأرقام العشوائية

A listing of independent random digits conveniently arranged in tabular form to facilitate the selection of random numbers with multiple digits.

Random sample | العينة العشوائية

A sample in which every possible combination of elements in the population has an equal chance of constituting the sample.

Ratio estimation | تقديرات باستخدام النسب

A method of variables sampling in which the auditor estimates the population misstatement by multiplying the portion of sample dollars misstated by the total recorded population book value and also calculates sampling risk.

Realizable value of accounts receivable | القيمة المتوقع تحصيلها من الحسابات المدينة

The amount of the outstanding balances in accounts receivable that will ultimately be collected.

Reasonable assurance | التأكد المناسب

The concept that audit function is not a guarantee for complete accuracy of the financial statements after being audited as the auditor performs his audit on a test basis and provides a high but not an absolute level of assurance.

Recalculation | المراجعة أو التدقيق الحسابي

The rechecking of a sample of the computations made by the client, including mathematical accuracy of individual transactions and amounts and the adding of journals and subsidiary records.

Receiving report | تقرير استلام

A document prepared by the receiving department at the time tangible goods are received, indicating the description of the goods, the quantity received, the date received, and other relevant data; it is part of the documentation necessary for payment to be made.

Related party | الأطراف ذوي العلاقة

Affiliated company, principal owner of the client company, or any other party with which the client deals, where one of the parties can directly or indirectly influence the management or operating policies of the other.

Related party transaction | معاملات الأطراف ذوي العلاقة

Any transaction between the client and a related party.

Relevance of evidence | مدى مناسبة الأدلة

The relationship between the audit evidence and the objective or assertion for the controls, transactions, account balances, and disclosures being tested.

Relevant assertions | التأكيدات المناسبة

Assertions that have a meaningful bearing on whether an account is fairly stated and used to assess the risk of material misstatement and the design and performance of audit procedures.

Reliability of evidence | مدى مصداقية الأدلة
The extent to which evidence is believable or worthy of trust; evidence is reliable when it is obtained (1) from an independent provider, (2) from a client with effective internal controls, (3) from the auditor's direct knowledge, (4) from qualified providers such as law firms and banks, (5) from objective sources, and (6) in a timely manner.

Reperformance | التدقيق أو المراجعة المكررة
The auditor's independent tests of client accounting procedures or controls that were originally done as part of the entity's accounting and internal control system.

Representative sample | العينة الممثلة للمجتمع
A sample with characteristics the same as those of the population.

Review | فحص محدود او دوري
An assurance engagement that results in a negative opinion as to the auditor's awareness of any information indicating that the assertions are not presented in conformity with the applicable criteria.

Review engagement | خدمات الفحص المحدود
An assurance engagement that enables an auditor to state whether, on the basis of procedures which do not provide all the evidence that would be required in an audit, anything has come to the auditor's attention that causes the auditor to believe that the financial statements are not prepared, in all material respects, in accordance with an applicable financial reporting framework.

Review for subsequent events | فحص الأحداث اللاحقة
The auditing procedures performed by auditors to identify and evaluate subsequent events; also known as a post-balance-sheet review.

Review of audit documentation | فحص مستندات المراجعة /التدقيق
A review of the completed audit files by another member of the audit firm to ensure quality and counteract bias.

Review of historical financial statements | الفحص المحدود للقوائم المالية التاريخية
A form of attestation in which a CPA firm issues a written report that provides less assurance than an audit as to whether the financial statements are in material conformity with generally accepted accounting principles, International Financial Reporting Standards or local standards.

Review service | خدمات الفحص المحدود او الدوري
A review of unaudited financial statements designed to provide limited assurance that no material modifications need be made to the statements in order for them to be in conformity with IFRS or, if applicable, with another comprehensive basis of accounting.

Revised judgment about materiality | التقدير المعدل للأهمية النسبية
A change in the auditor's preliminary judgment made when the auditor determines that the preliminary judgment was too large or too small.

Risk | الخطر
The acceptance by auditors that there is some level of uncertainty in performing the audit function.

Risk assessment | تقييم الخطر
Management's identification and analysis of risks relevant to the preparation of financial statements in accordance with generally accepted accounting principles.

Risk of material misstatement | الخطر المرتبط بتحريف هام
The combination of inherent risk and control risk (IR × CR).

Sales and collection cycle | دورة البيع والتحصيل
Involves the decisions and processes necessary for the transfer of the ownership of goods and services to customers after they are made available for sale; it begins with a request by a customer and ends with the conversion of material or service into an account receivable, and ultimately into cash.

Sample exception rate (SER) | معدل الاستثناء للعينة
Number of exceptions in the sample divided by the sample size.

Sampling distribution | توزيع العينة
A frequency distribution of the results of all possible samples of a specified size that could be obtained from a population containing some specific parameters.

Sampling error | خطأ العينة
Errors that result because the auditor has sampled only a portion of the population.

Sampling risk | خطر المعاينة
Risk of reaching an incorrect conclusion inherent in tests of less than the entire population because the sample is not representative of the population; sampling risk may be reduced by using an increased sample size and an appropriate method of selecting sample items from the population.

Sarbanes–Oxley Act | قانون ساربنس اوكسلى
A U.S. federal securities law passed in 2002 that provides for additional regulation of public companies and their auditors; the Act established the Public Company Accounting Oversight Board and also requires auditors to audit the effectiveness of internal control over financial reporting.

Scope limitation | قيود علي عمل المراقب /المدقق
A situation where the auditor is unable to obtain sufficient competent evidence that may prevent the auditor from expressing an unmodified opinion.

Securities Act of 1933 | قانون البورصة أو السوق المالية لعام١٩٩٣
A U.S. federal statute dealing with companies that register and sell securities to the public; under the statute, third parties who are original purchasers of securities may recover damages from the auditor if the financial statements are misstated, unless the auditor proves that the audit was adequate or that the third party's loss was caused by factors other than misleading financial statements.

Securities and Exchange Commission (SEC) | هيئة سوق المال الامريكية
A U.S federal agency that oversees the orderly conduct of the securities markets; the SEC assists in providing investors in public corporations with reliable information upon which to make investment decisions.

Securities Exchange Act of 1934 | قانون البورصة أو السوق المالية لعام١٩٣٤
A U.S. federal statute dealing with companies that trade securities on national and over-the-counter exchanges; auditors are involved because the annual reporting requirements include audited financial statements.

Separation of duties | الفصل بين الواجبات)الوظائف(المتعارضة
Separation of the following activities in an organization: (1) custody of assets from accounting, (2) authorization from custody of assets,

(3) operational responsibility from record keeping, and (4) IT duties from outside users of IT.

Service center | مركز تقديم الخدمة
An organization that provides IT services for companies on an outsourcing basis.

Shareholders' capital stock master file | أستاذ مساعد رأس المال
A record of the issuance and repurchase of capital stock for the life of a corporation.

Significant deficiency | الضعف المؤثر
One or more control deficiencies exist that are less severe than a material weakness, but important enough to merit attention by those responsible for oversight of the company's financial reporting.

Significant risks | الخطر المؤثر
Risks the auditor believes require special audit consideration; the auditor is required to test the operating effectiveness of controls that mitigate these risks in the current year audit, if control risk is to be assessed below the maximum.

Special assignments | التكليف الخاص
Management requests for an operational audit for a specific purpose, such as investigating the possibility of fraud in a division or making recommendations for reducing the cost of a manufactured product.

Specific authorization |
Case-by-case approval of transactions not covered by company-wide policies.

Standard cost records | مستندات التكاليف المعيارية
Records that indicate variances between projected material, labor, and overhead costs and the actual costs.

Standard unmodified audit report | الرأي غير المتحفظ
The report a CPA issues when all auditing conditions have been met, no significant misstatements have been discovered and left uncorrected, and it is the auditor's opinion that the financial statements are fairly stated in accordance with IFRS.

Statements on Auditing Standards (SASs) |
معايير المراجعة/التدقيق الأمريكية
Pronouncements issued by the AICPA to interpret generally accepted auditing standards.

Statements on Internal Auditing Standards (SIASs) |
معايير المراجعة الداخلية
Statements issued by the Internal Auditing Standards Board of the IIA to provide authoritative interpretations of the IIA Practice Standards.

Statistical inferences | الاستنتاج الاحصائى
Statistical conclusions that the auditor draws from sample results based on knowledge of sampling distributions.

Statistical sampling | المعاينة الإحصائية
The use of mathematical measurement techniques to calculate formal statistical results and quantify sampling risk.

Stock transfer agent | مسئول الحفظ للأسهم
Outside person engaged by a corporation to maintain the stockholder records and often to disburse cash dividends.

Stratified sampling | المعاينة الطبقية
A method of sampling in which all the elements in the total population are divided into two or more subpopulations that are independently tested and statistically measured.

Subsequent discovery of facts | الاكتشاف اللاحق لبعض الحقائق
Auditor discovery that the financial statements are materially misstated after they have been issued.

Subsequent events | الأحداث اللاحقة
Transactions and other pertinent events that occurred after the balance sheet date that affect the fair presentation or disclosure of the statements being audited.

Substantive tests | الاختبارات التفصيلية أو اختبارات التأكد
Audit procedures designed to test for dollar (monetary) misstatements of financial statement balances.

Substantive tests of transactions | الاختبارات الأساسية للمعاملات
Audit procedures testing for monetary misstatements to determine whether the six transaction-related audit objectives have been satisfied for each class of transactions.

Substantive tests of transactions | اختبارات تفاصيل المعاملات
Audit procedures testing for monetary misstatements to determine whether the seven transaction-related audit objectives have been satisfied for each class of transaction.

Sufficiency of evidence | مدى كفاية الأدلة
The quantity of evidence; proper sample size.

Summary financial statements | القوائم المالية المختصرة
A summary of the original historical financial statements which contains less detail than such statements, while still providing sufficient information to users to enable them to make their investment decisions.

Supporting schedules | المستندات المؤيدة
Detailed schedules prepared by the client or the auditor in support of specific amounts on the financial statements.

Systematic sample selection | اختيار العينة بأسلوب متماثل
A probabilistic method of sampling in which the auditor calculates an interval (the population size divided by the number of sample items desired) and selects the items for the sample based on the size of the interval and a randomly selected starting point between zero and the length of the interval.

SysTrust | *SysTrust*
An assurance service designed to provide reasonable assurance that a company's computer system complies with Trust Services principles and criteria.

Tax inspector | مأمور الضرائب
Auditors who work for a tax authority and conduct examinations of taxpayers' returns.

Test data approach | طريقة البيانات الاختبارية
A method of auditing an IT system that uses the auditor's test data to determine whether the client's computer program correctly processes valid and invalid transactions.

Tests of controls | اختبارات نظم الرقابة
Audit procedures to test the effectiveness of controls in support of a reduced assessed control risk.

Tests of details of balances | اختبارات تفاصيل الأرصدة
Audit procedures testing for monetary misstatements to determine whether the eight balance-related audit objectives have been satisfied for each significant account balance.

Those charged with governance | المسئولين عن الحوكمة
The person(s) with responsibility for overseeing the strategic direction of the entity and its obligations related to the

accountability of the entity, including overseeing the financial reporting and disclosure process.

Tick marks | علامة المراجعة أو التدقيق
Symbols used on an audit schedule that provide additional information or details of audit procedures performed.

Time card | كارت الوقت
A document indicating the time that the employee started and stopped working each day and the number of hours worked.

Timing difference | اختلاف فى المواعيد
A reported difference in a confirmation from a debtor that is determined to be a timing difference between the client's and debtor's records and therefore not a misstatement.

Tolerable exception rate (TER) | معدل الاستثناء المحتمل
The exception rate that the auditor will permit in the population and still be willing to conclude the control is operating effectively and/or the amount of monetary misstatements in the transactions established during planning is acceptable.

Tolerable misstatement |
التحريف المسموح به أو أقصى تحريف يصل به المدقق في البند محل المراجعة (على مستوى الحساب أو الرصيد)
The materiality allocated to any given account balance; used in audit planning.

Transaction-related audit objectives | أهداف مراجعة المعاملات
Seven audit objectives that must be met before the auditor can conclude that the total for any given class of transactions is fairly stated; the general transaction-related audit objectives are occurrence, completeness, posting and summarization, accuracy, classification, timing, and rights and obligations.

Types of tests | أنواع الاختبارات
The five categories of audit tests auditors use to determine whether financial statements are fairly stated: risk assessment procedures, tests of controls, substantive tests of transactions, analytical procedures, and tests of details of balances.

Ultramares doctrine | مفهوم التراميرز
A common-law approach to third-party liability, established in 1931 in the case of Ultramares Corporation v. Touche, in which ordinary negligence is insufficient for liability to third parties because of the lack of privity of contract between the third party and the auditor, unless the third party is a primary beneficiary.

Unadjusted misstatement audit schedule | كشف المخالفات غير المعدلة
A summary of immaterial misstatements not adjusted at the time they were found, used to help the auditor assess whether the combined amount is material; also known as a summary of possible misstatements.

Unasserted claim | الالتزامات غير مؤكدة (العرضية)
A potential legal claim against a client where the condition for a claim exists but no claim has been filed.

Unmodified audit report with emphasis of a matter or other matter | الرأي غير المتحفظ بإيضاحات
An unmodified report in which the financial statements are fairly presented, but the auditor believes it is important, or is required, to provide additional information for a matter appropriately presented or disclosed in the financial statements that, in the auditor's judgment, is of such importance that it is fundamental to users' understanding of the financial statements.

Unusual fluctuations | التغيرات غير العادية
Significant unexpected differences indicated by analytical procedures between the current year's unaudited financial data and other data used in comparisons.

Variables sampling | معاينة المتغيرات
Sampling techniques for tests of details of balances that use the statistical inference process.

Vendor's invoice | فاتورة المورد
A document that specifies the details of an acquisition transaction and amount of money owed to the vendor for an acquisition.

Vendor's statement | كشف حساب المورد
A statement prepared monthly by the vendor, which indicates the customer's beginning balance, acquisitions, returns and allowance payments, and ending balance.

Voucher | قسيمة
A document used to establish a formal means of recording and controlling acquisitions, primarily by enabling each acquisition transaction to be sequentially numbered.

Vouching | مراجعة مستندية
The use of documentation to support recorded transactions or amounts.

Walkthrough | التتبع
The tracing of selected transactions through the accounting system to determine that controls are in place.

WebTrust | *WebTrust*
An assurance service designed to provide reasonable assurance that a company's website complies with Trust Services principles and criteria for business-to-consumer electronic commerce.

Wide area networks (WANs) | الشبكات الممتدة جغرافياً
Networks that connect computer equipment, databases, software, and peripheral equipment that reside in many geographic locations, such as client offices located around the world.

Working trial balance | ميزان المراجعة
A listing of the general ledger accounts and their year-end balances.

INDEX